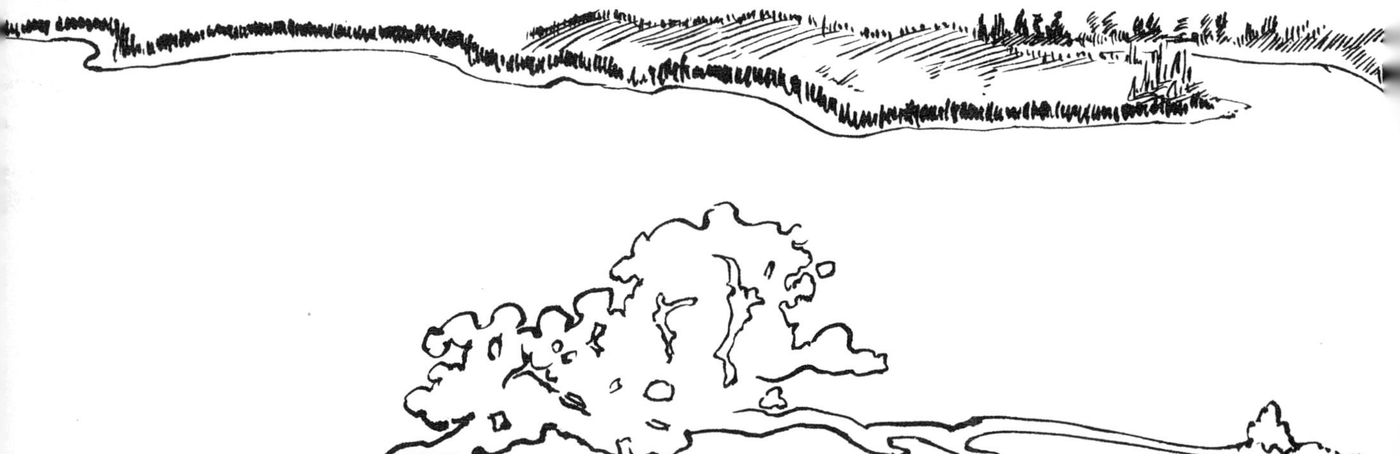

MAN'S PLACE IN NATURE

McGRAW-HILL BOOK COMPANY
New York San Francisco St. Louis
Düsseldorf Johannesburg Kuala Lumpur
London Mexico Montreal
New Delhi Panama Rio de Janeiro
Singapore Sydney Toronto

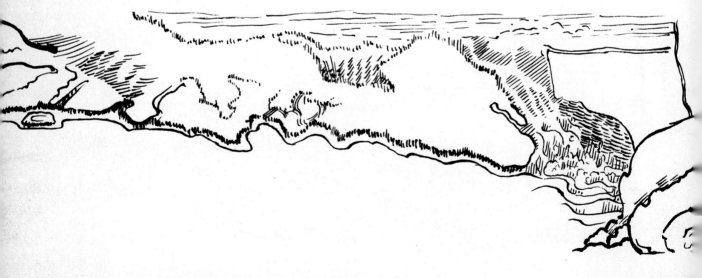

MAN'S PLACE IN NATURE

C. F. HOCKETT

GOLDWIN SMITH PROFESSOR OF LINGUISTICS AND ANTHROPOLOGY
CORNELL UNIVERSITY

This book was set in Baskerville by York Graphic Services, Inc. The editors were Ronald D. Kissack and Marge Eakins Woodhurst, and the production supervisor was Michael A. Ungersma. Cover and drawings were done by Sue Sellers; cartography by Sue Sellers and Brent Ryan; graphs and charts were done by Judith L. McCarty; and the photo editor was William Rosenthal.

The printer was The Murray Printing Company; the binder, Rand McNally & Company.

MAN'S PLACE IN NATURE

Library of Congress Cataloging in Publication Data

Hockett, Charles Francis.
    Man's place in nature.

    Includes bibliographical references.
    1. Anthropology. I. Title.
GN31.H6   301.2   72-7424
ISBN 0-07-029120-9

1234567890   MURM   79876543

for
J Milton Cowan
with unending gratitude

CONTENTS

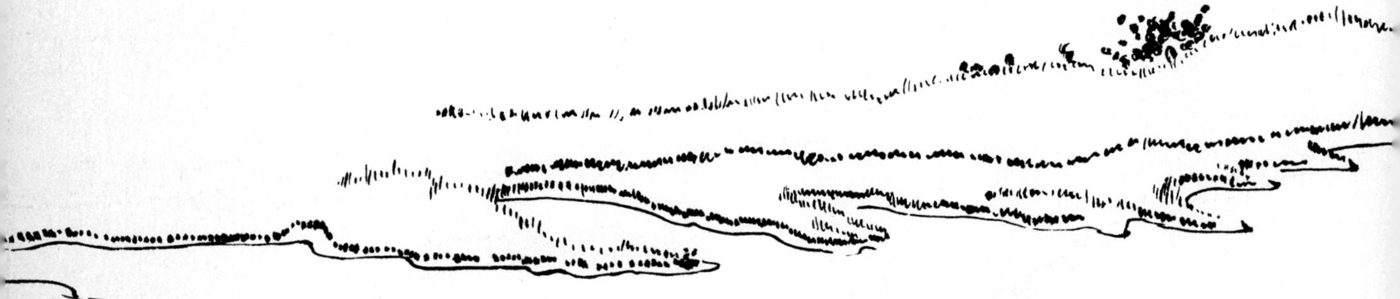

1

×

PRELUDE

The question of questions for mankind—the problem which underlies all others, and is more deeply interesting than any other—is the ascertainment of the place which Man occupies in nature and of his relations to the universe of things. Whence our race has come; what are the limits of our power over nature, and of nature's power over us; to what goal we are tending; are the problems which present themselves anew and with undiminished interest to every man born into the world.

So wrote Thomas Henry Huxley a century ago, in a work whose title was drawn from this very passage: *Man's Place in Nature.* The book now before you bears the same title because it is about the same thing.

It would be a breach of propriety to use Huxley's title unless one were prepared to accept its implications. To speak of man's place in nature is to assert that we human beings are in and part of the natural order. Any study or discussion of nature that ignores man's presence is necessarily incomplete. Likewise, any discussion of human affairs that pretends man is not part of nature and subject to all the "laws of nature" (whatever they may be) is founded on fantasy.

To clarify this, let us turn to Shakespeare, who gives a poetic answer to Huxley's question of questions (Jaques in *As You Like It* II.7):

> All the world's a stage,
> And all the men and women merely players.

This is metaphor, but helpful if we remember two points. The first is that there are no spectators for the human drama, except insofar as we are our own audience. The second is that we must think of the stage, at first bare and empty, giving rise through torment and travail both to the props and to the actors.

We are part of Earth, and our history is part of its history.

That is our theme. The story of man is that of his emergence in the physical universe of which he is still, and must necessarily ever remain, a part, and of his gradual discovery and acceptance of this as the ironclad constraint within which he must pursue his joys, suffer his sorrows, and define his ideals.

Not everyone accepts this view. Some disagree through lack of understanding, or from wishful thinking, or from no thinking at all. Some hold alternative views from deeply meditated conviction. It is interesting to note that those whose opinions have resulted from the most careful thinking are just those ready to modify them when new evidence comes to their attention. However, there need be no quarreling about such matters. I state my orientation so that you will know from the outset what it is and can make proper allowances. I want to show you, as best I can, the seductively beautiful panorama of the universe and of ourselves within it that this orientation affords. As individuals we occupy little space and endure for at most a few decades. We have no alternative but to devote the bulk of our attention to immediate practical issues. But occasionally we must look up from our routine daily tasks, and when we do it is surprising how far we can see: for hundreds of millions of light years into the starry skies, and for thousands of millions of years into the past (the future remains always more obscure). This may not make us either happier or sadder, but we then return to everyday matters refreshed, because we understand a little better who and what we are.

There are two dangers to be avoided. They are mirror twins, threatening from either side; the more we struggle to avoid the one, the more we are apt to succumb to the other. One is the ease with which typical human characteristics can be erroneously ascribed to other parts of nature. The other is the cynical denial of the reality of those same characteristics in ourselves because they do not recur elsewhere. It can be no part of our plan either to anthropomorphize nature or to dehumanize man. It is obvious that people are different from monkeys, cats, snakes, algae, atoms, and galaxies. Investigation properly seeks not to deny the differences, and neither to exaggerate nor to belittle them, but to learn exactly what they are and how they have come about.

Anthropology is the branch of science in which such issues are investigated, the branch of science devoted to the determination of man's place in nature.

What the differences are and *how they have come about:* these two phrases define the scope of our inquiry, and their order defines its arrangement.

Part One treats of man and his ways in the "ethnographic present": that is, in that thin slab of worldwide human history about which we can gather information through direct observation or written records.[1] For perspective we shall occasionally have to leave that domain, for a look at animals other than man or for a tentative guess about historical origins, but the principal focus is as stated.

Human beings obviously live in many different ways. How much variety is there? What are the norms (if any) and what are the attested extremes? Under what conditions do differences of culture lead to tolerance and enrichment, and in what circumstances do they yield hatred and conflict? What is the "common denominator" of humanness, shared by all human groups but not with animals of any other species? These are the sorts of questions to which we shall address ourselves in Part One. We can expect few definitive answers, but can hope for suggestive ones.

The Intermezzo is a succinct codification of the *mechanisms of change* of relevance for life in general, human life, and human history.

Part Two is narrative. Since man is part of Earth, we start with the origin of Earth, treat of the beginnings of life, and follow the lines of continuity and change that

---

[1] *Ethnography* is one phase of anthropology: to wit, the systematic study of human community life. The term "ethnographic present" was coined three decades ago (Chapple and Coon 1940; see the References), but with a meaning different from that we give it above. Our usage will conform to our definition.

led from the earliest living forms to the earliest members of our own species. Much of this we do very quickly. Then, in more detail, we trace man's wanderings, adventures, and achievements from his earliest appearance up to the present.

In order not to interrupt the flow of the exposition, notes and references are given at the end of the book, beginning on page 673, instead of at the ends of chapters. For the same reason, if a technical or semitechnical term used in passing is one that may be already known to many readers, we do not pause for a definition; however, most terms of this sort are entered in the Glossarial Index, with either a definition or a reference to the passage in which the definition will be found. The following types of supplementary information are also, for the most part, relegated to the Index: (1) the provenience and dates of birth and death of a person named in the text; (2) the location, by latitude and longitude, of a place (e.g., of an archaeological site); (3) the formal taxonomic designation of a plant or animal.

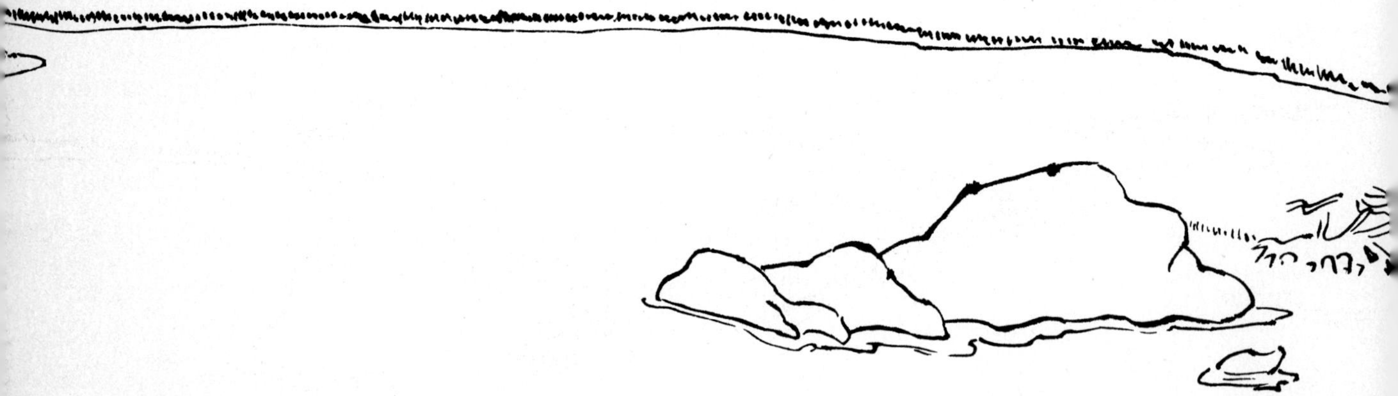

PART ONE

✖

VARIATIONS ON HUMAN THEMES

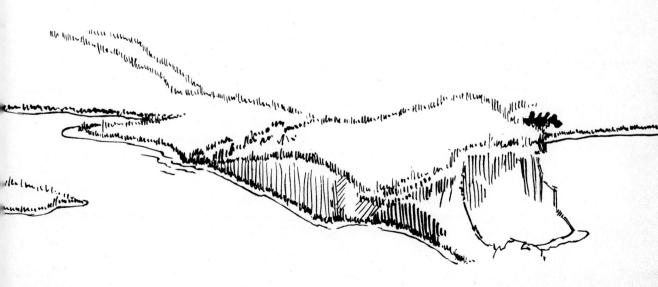

2

×

WILD RICE, STURGEON, AND POWER PACKS: THE CLASSICAL MENOMINI

If we want to find the answers to the questions set forth in the Prelude, we dare not view the world exclusively through the distorting lenses Western society has placed before our eyes. Our first step, then, is to examine the ways of life of a community just as human as our own and yet strikingly different. There are literally millions of human groups to which we could turn for this purpose provided our information about them were adequate. For example, in India alone, only a small part of the inhabited world, there are today at least 500,000 villages, no two identical. My choice for this chapter is governed by available data, and beyond that by my own taste and sympathies.

Picture yourself sitting in one of a group of canoes, on a day in A.D. 1634, paddling southwards along the northwestern shore of Lake Michigan. You are in the exploring party of the Sieur Jean Nicolet, sent by Samuel de Champlain to find the headquarters of the Winnebago Indians and intercede with them on behalf of your allies the Hurons. The outposts of French culture lie many weeks' journey behind you, by canoe and portage, at Québec on the lower St. Lawrence. This is uncharted wilderness. The only members of your party who may have been here before are an Indian guide or so. You know that you have entered the mouth of a long, narrow bay, but the peninsula that forms its other shore lies below the horizon to the east. You call it *une grande baie;* later this will become simply *Grande Baie,* ultimately to be twisted by speakers of English into *Green Bay.* Your destination lies ahead at its southernmost tip.

The coast you are skirting is damp and sandy, with scattered dunes and here and there the mouth of a small river. Beyond the beaches and dunes you see the edge of the forest, but rarely far into it because the land does not rise much. Farther north the woods consisted mainly of conifers (pines, spruces, firs, cedars, tamarack), but now there is an increased intermingling of hardwoods: birches, beeches, basswood, oaks, poplars, elms, maples, ash, hickory. Your guides tell you the forest is crisscrossed by small streams and studded with pools and ponds, the haunt of coot and hern and of all manner of birds, beasts, and fish. You have spent your nights camped ashore at places you hoped would be safe. The smoke of your campfires has mingled with the wild incense of the damp night woods; you have heard the cries of forest denizens and the startling screech of a distant sliver-cat (crossed branches scraping together in the wind), and have endured attacks by wood ticks, black flies, and endless swarms of mosquitoes.

Now ahead, you see another river mouth, and near it a village: scattered rectangular huts made of felled saplings; various smaller structures of sticks covered with bark sheets, reed mats, or animal skins; a few mangy dogs; and scantily clad Indians. Perhaps your party stops, but only briefly, because you must press ahead on your mission. You do learn that these people are the *Folles Avoines,* the 'wild rice [eaters]'.[1]

Thus did the ethnographic present dawn unobtrusively on the people who now call themselves the *omēʔnomenēwak.*[2] In English this word has been standardized with the spelling *Menomini* as the name of the people and of their language, and with the spelling *Menominee* as the name of a river, probably but not certainly that at whose mouth the encounter took place.

For the Menomini in their summer village on the shores of *kɛʔcekam,* the 'great lake' (Lake Michigan), the first encounter with Europeans was unscheduled and startling, but not completely unheralded. Rumors of light-skinned strangely dressed men far away towards the rising sun had been reaching them for half a generation or more through intervening tribes, together with a few objects of European manufacture such as beads. Another third of a century was to pass before the next attested direct contact with the French: Nicolas Perrot, a fur trader, visited them about 1667; in 1669 some Jesuit missionaries arrived, destined to stay only for a decade and a half. The tribal leaders who conferred with Perrot and received the missionaries had been young children when Nicolet's party passed by; the leaders of Nicolet's time were toothless old men or dead. It is not surprising that the legends of first contact written down two and a half centuries later blend together episodes of various early encounters, embellish them from later knowledge of European ways, and spice the mix from fancy for the sake of a good story. They tell us something of the orientation of the Menomini at the time the tales were recorded (1880–1930), but are of little historical value.

Unfortunately, no systematic ethnographic studies were made until the very recent period just mentioned. Yet it is with the Menomini of what we shall dub the "classical period," the first half of the seventeenth century, that we shall deal here, as accurately as the surviving evidence permits.

BACKGROUND

Most of the history of the Menomini before the classical period blends indiscernibly into the poorly attested story of man in the New World (pp. 427–433).

We do know that the Menomini are among the descendants of people who were living around 1000 B.C. in the eastern Great Lakes country: on the southern shore

[1]Literally 'wild oats'. The plant now called "wild rice" in English resembles the cultivated rice of the Orient more than it does European oats, but the French did not yet know rice very well.

[2]The form is plural; the singular lacks the final *-ak.* For those who are curious, rough instructions for the pronunciation of Menomini words are given on p. 674.

of Georgian Bay, as far south as Lake Ontario, and as far north as Lake Nipissing and the Mattawa River (neither date nor location is exact). These people spoke the language we now call "Proto Algonquian" (p. 301). By A.D. 500–1000 the descendants of the Proto Algonquians had expanded and split into a multiplicity of tribes and tribelets occupying much of the northeastern quadrant of the continent, with a tongue stretching south along the Atlantic coast and with outliers deep into the arctic. In the northernmost parts of what thus became Algonquian country, the Algonquians may have been the first human inhabitants; at least, no archaeological evidence of predecessors has yet been found.[3] Elsewhere they doubtless pushed other tribes aside, or destroyed them, or in part absorbed them.

But before long they were themselves being attacked or put to flight by a new wave of migrants from the south: the Iroquoians. These people were agriculturalists, as well as hunters-and-gatherers, and were hungry for land on which to raise maize, beans, and squash. The early Algonquians did not till the soil; those who did in recorded times had acquired the habit from the Iroquoians or, along the Atlantic coast, from southern neighbors who were neither Algonquian nor Iroquoian. The New World agricultural complex reached the lower Mississippi Valley about 1000 B.C. (p. 488), where climatic conditions favored it. Successful farming increases the food supply, which multiplies the population, which yields population pressure; surplus people move away if there is any place to go. The Iroquoians began, probably in the lower Mississippi Valley, as unsuccessful nonagricultural competitors; forced out, they moved north and east in successive small waves; the spreading agricultural complex had caught up with them before first European contact.

The Iroquoians were also warlike. Inexorably they drove a wedge through Ohio and Pennsylvania, into southern Michigan, southwestern Ontario, New York, and southeastern Quebec. Maize, beans, and squash require a growing season of at least 100 frost-free days. This establishes an irregular boundary through the Northeastern Woodlands, north of which agricultural efforts of this type are fruitless. The Iroquoians had not reached the boundary everywhere when matters were rendered more complicated by the arrival of settlers from across the Atlantic, but they were close to it, and their raids, reputation, and influence stretched beyond. A few Iroquoian groups made peace with the Algonquians—for instance, the Hurons, whom we have seen (p. 8) as allies of the French. The price the peacemakers paid was high: they became, like the Algonquians and in due time the French, fair prey for the main body of Iroquoians, who had remarkably increased their power by banding together to form a league centered in western New York.

Every indication is that the Menomini arrived in their classical home either before the depredations of the invading Iroquoians began or else early in the Iroquoian period. They had surely been there for a century or so before Nicolet's voyage, comfortably adjusted to a strip of lake shore that included the mouths of the Menominee River and various lesser streams and to an indefinite but sizable stretch of forest to the west. They arrived from the north or south, not across Lake Michigan, because the Great Lakes are too broad to invite a direct crossing in bark or dugout

[3] The ice of the most recent glacial advance (the Late Würm: p. 413) was reluctant to recede from the northeastern quadrant of North America. As late as 8000–7000 B.C. it still covered much of what is now Great Lakes country, and it may have lingered in Labrador even later.

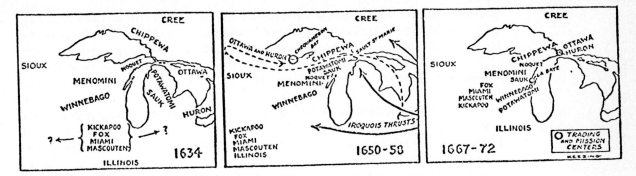

FIGURE 2-1. THE MENOMINI AND THEIR NEIGHBORS. The three maps show tribal distributions at successive points during the seventeenth century. Of the tribes named, these were of Algonquian speech: Menomini, Cree, Chippewa (= Ojibwa), Ottawa, Potawatomi, Kickapoo, Fox, Miami, Mascouten, Sauk, Illinois (for "Noquet" see the text). The Winnebago and Sioux spoke Siouan languages; the Huron were Iroquoian. (From Keesing 1939, with the permission of the American Philosophical Society.)

canoes. The Winnebago (p. 8), of Siouan speech and Great Plains linguistic and cultural affinities, were their neighbors from the start, living farther south near the lake which takes its modern name from them.

Because the Great Lakes are too broad for canoe crossings, and because the focal points first of Iroquoian agitation and later of European infiltration all lay to the east, the Green Bay region of Wisconsin was a protected spot. The surviving Winnebago and Menomini are still there, though not quite where they used to be. Like twigs caught in an eddy in a rushing stream, the two tribes have been swirled round and round, as Indian communities nearer the ends of the lake have repeatedly been replaced, dislodged, destroyed, or swept westwards. Thus, except for the Winnebago, the Menomini had no permanent neighbors. The earliest records mention a people farther north called the "Noquet," who then vanish without trace so that what they were is anybody's guess. My guess is that they were not neighbors at all, just additional local groups of Menomini. For the rest, see Figure 2-1. All this motion, in many directions but with a long-term trend towards the west, was instigated by the Iroquoians; the additional impetus supplied by the French, British, and Dutch was at first hardly noticeable.

✖ In the classical period the Menomini numbered at most two or three thousand, even if we include the Noquet (see above). In the summer they lived in small villages, not much more than a hundred to a village, all located by rivers and most of them at the river mouths on the shore of the bay. They fished, chiefly for sturgeon. They planted small patches of several varieties of maize, along with beans and squash. They gathered edible berries and roots.

THE YEAR

When it began to grow cold in the autumn, they migrated upstream into the forest, establishing winter camps where the trees and the low hills afforded more protection from the weather than is available along the shore. Wisconsin winters are cold (*Wisconsin* is from some Algonquian language—not Menomini—and means 'where it is cold'), and the prevailing northwest winds can be bitter, depositing copious quantities of snow that preclude all travel except by snowshoe, a device well known to all the North American aborigines who had use for it. Yet protection from the elements was only one reason for the annual migration. The winter camps were smaller and more numerous than the summer villages, scattered more thinly over a larger territory. Such distribution was appropriate for the major winter economic activity, hunting.

When the ice on the streams broke up in the springtime, they returned by canoe and portage to the summer villages.

Another late winter or early spring activity was sugar-making. The sugar maple (Menomini *sōpomāhtek*) is ready to tap nowadays approximately in April, and the current Menomini word for April is *sūpomāhkwan-kēso͡ʔ* 'sugar-making month', but they claim that the seasons have changed and that this used to be done earlier, in late February or in March. In any case, this took them from their winter camps unless the camps were near the maples, for sugar-making was a collective ceremonial activity and an occasion for fun as well as work.

Similarly, they were drawn from their summer villages in mid September to gather in numbers at the small lakes where the wild rice was almost ready to harvest: their current name for September is *pawāhān-kēso͡ʔ*, in which *pawāhān* designates the special paddle used in this harvest (p. 19).

Thus the four major punctuations in the seasonal cycle were the fall migration upstream, the late-winter sugar-making, the spring migration downstream, and the September rice-gathering. Hunting was at its peak during the winter, but never completely stopped. Fishing reached its maximum in summer, but from their winter camps they fished the streams and small lakes, especially for suckers, often cutting a hole in the ice to do so: a month name vaguely equivalent to February is *namēpen-kēso͡ʔ* 'sucker [or carp] month'. Wild plant foods were gathered as they were in season, as suggested by two more month names, *atēhemen-kēso͡ʔ* 'strawberry month', about our June, and *mēn-kēso͡ʔ* 'blueberry month', our late July or August. Apart from foodstuffs, the barks of several trees, including the cedar, were gathered for making mats: *pahkuan-kēso͡ʔ* 'bark-peeling month' was approximately equivalent to May. Reeds of several kinds were gathered from shallow waters in June and July, for mats and baskets, but this has left no trace in the surviving names of months. (We are not certain that month-naming was an aboriginal habit, but even if it was not the names chosen as the custom was introduced carry relevant information.)

KNOWLEDGE OF ENVIRONMENT

More sporadic than these seasonally scheduled activities were certain matters that took a few Menomini away from their regular stamping grounds.

Here one thinks first of war; but, although the Menomini were involved in many a conflict in later times, during the classical period they seem to have gotten along fairly peaceably not only with the Winnebago (with whom they never broke) but also with all their changing neighbors to the north except the Sauk.

Another factor was the need for certain raw materials not to be found at home. Pipestone (catlinite) was available only from sites to the west controlled by the Santee Dakota, but it is known that expeditions of Menomini were permitted access. We do not know where they got their salt (if any) and their tobacco before both became available through European traders. There is no evidence that they raised their own tobacco. Some American Indian groups undertook occasional journeys of several hundred miles in search of salt—the only reason, in late aboriginal times, that Indians ever visited what is now West Virginia, which otherwise remained uninhabited. The Menomini probably did not go that far from home, but it is possible they went elsewhere. Both tobacco and salt may, of course, have been obtained by trade even before Europeans came along. In any case, it is clear that the Menomini were aware in a general way of the geography of a region considerably larger than their own homeland.

Yet, not only for their food but also for their clothing, shelter, tools, weapons, utensils, toys, and all other accoutrements, the Menomini were almost wholly dependent on the raw materials supplied by their immediate environment and on the techniques for manipulating those raw materials that were inherited from their forebears. In a sense this assertion is empty, since it holds for any human (or other animal) community, and for the human species as a whole—one never gets something from nothing; you can't just *make* something, but must always make something *from* something. But it can direct our attention to what the Menomini environment afforded that they were able to use.

Despite the bit of Iroquois-type agriculture, they were essentially hunters, fishers, and gatherers. For this way of life, the environment was bountiful as long as other people didn't interfere too much.[4] Hunting and fishing supplied not only food but also furs, hides, and sinew and bone. Gathering yielded not only food but also wood and bark (for houses, bows, arrows, implement handles, drying racks, canoes, paddles, clubs), vegetable dyes, reeds for mats, fibers for cordage, medicine for various ailments, twigs and fallen logs for fires. The inorganic environment supplied water for drinking and cooking and running streams for travel, clay for pottery, and various kinds of stones for knives, arrowheads, adzes, axes, pipes, and so on. It was all there, demanding only skill and hard work, which the Menomini supplied in abundant measure.

✖ Subject to interruption by special events (such as the seasonal migrations), the daily cycle followed the same basic plan throughout the year. The first period of each day began at dawn, the next at dusk, and the last at bedtime. THE DAY

At dawn the women rose, fetched water, built or rebuilt the fire, and prepared breakfast while the men were getting up. Breakfast was the first of two regular meals per day. The men and boys ate first; then the women ate as the men and boys were off to the hunting or fishing grounds. Whether they went to hunt or to fish depended, as we have seen, largely on the season. The men of a single settlement did not necessarily all go together, particularly in the summer when local groups were larger; and sometimes some would stay home for one or another reason. The women worked at home and nearby, tending the crops, processing food, gathering bark and reeds,

---

[4] Bloomfield's manuscript Menomini-English lexicon (see the notes and references for this chapter, p. 674), based on texts collected for other purposes and hence incomplete, includes 37 names of mammals indigenous to the region, 53 bird names, 15 names of fish, and 20 names of other vertebrates and of invertebrates other than insects. Smith (1923) identifies about 275 native plant species, of which over 200 were used in some way by the Menomini, 40 of them as food.

collecting edible roots and berries, working on clothing, weaving mats, and caring for infants and young children.

Hunting or fishing parties normally returned just before twilight, except that hunts often lasted several days so that the return might be at any time. Twilight was the signal for the other regular meal. The ensuing period, until bedtime, was for relaxation, recreation, story-telling (important for the education of the young), and ceremonies of various sorts; from some of these the women were excluded so that they had to seek their own entertainment. In the summer, the evening was the time for a young unmarried man to go courting, serenading his sweetheart on a reed fife and sometimes, if the signs were favorable, sneaking into her dwelling and spending the night with her.

Some days were different—like our old-fashioned Sundays, though with no such regular periodicity.[5] Everyone stayed home, to receive visitors from other local groups and to conduct day-long ceremonials, partly for pleasure, partly to maintain proper relations with the Higher Powers of the world or to reestablish such relations when something had happened to threaten them. In our society there used to be "blue laws" prohibiting, among other frivolous things, Sunday ball games. In contrast, very rough team sports something like hockey or shinney, played with clubs and a heavy wooden ball, were a Menomini ceremonial highlight, much favored by certain of the Higher Powers. Women played their own games, and were present at those played by men only as spectators and to supply food and the like as it was needed.

Equilibrium throughout the world—what we might justly call ecological balance, though of course conceptualized differently—was important. Long experience had taught them that the balance is delicate and easily disrupted. Doing things the right way demanded alertness and skill. Inadvertent mistakes were bound to occur, and departures from normal expectations were the indication that they had. A serious deviation, such as the failure of a hunt or an illness that resisted routine therapy, required diagnosis by experts, and could lead to a special ceremonial day of the kind we have outlined.

HOUSING ✗

THE WINTER HOUSE

The first order of business after each autumn upstream migration was to build winter houses or to rebuild and refurbish ones left over from the preceding winter. This was women's work.

The typical winter house (Figure 2-2) was the variety called in English a "wigwam"; this word is from the Ojibwa generic term for 'house', which is in turn cognate with the Menomini term *wēkewam*.[6] To build one, you begin with about sixteen saplings, each 18 feet long and perhaps $1\frac{1}{2}$ inches in diameter at the larger end. Four of these are set in the ground at the corners of a rectangle 5 or 6 feet from front to back and 10 or 12 feet from side to side. The two in front are bent towards each other and lashed; similarly the two behind. The other poles are then set into the ground

[5] Our seven-day week seems like a fixed part of the order of nature, but of course it is not (see pp. 139–140).

[6] Ojibwa is another Algonquian language, descended from the Proto Algonquian mentioned on p. 9.

FIGURE 2-2. THE WINTER HOUSE ("WIGWAM"). This and the other photographs in the present chapter were taken between 1900 and 1920, and thus show various postcontact items: e.g., the jacket hanging in the foreground. (From Skinner 1921.)

along an oval perimeter, and arched transversely over the original frame. All are lashed together. A mat is placed in the center of the floor, to mark where the fireplace will be. The door, in the center of the long front side, typically faces south, to minimize the inroads of wind, rain, and snow. The frame is then covered by double mats of cattail reeds, in horizontal strips winding around the house from one doorpost to the other. The successive tiers overlap, so that precipitation will be shed. A smoke hole is left at the top, directly over the mat that marks the fireplace. A weighted mat is hung in the doorway. The mats are lashed into place. A rush mat is fastened to one side of the smoke hole, to be drawn over it in case of rain or snow. The lashings and tyings are done with cord made of basswood fiber. However, there is nothing absolutely fixed about the materials. Sometimes the house covering is sheets of cedar or birch bark instead of reed mats, and there are other fibers besides basswood.

Inside the lodge, around the side from doorpost to doorpost, a platform is built by driving stakes into the ground at intervals, 18 or 20 inches from the wall, then laying poles across these, then a grill of smaller sticks, and boughs of balsam or other evergreens; bedding of bearskins or other animal skins goes on top of the boughs (blankets were used as early as they became available). The inner walls may be lined with reed mats woven and colored to give pleasant designs.

Implements and packages are stored under the platform or hung from the walls. A shallow pit may be dug in the center of the floor for the fire; the advantage is that it reduces the danger that sparks will reach the flammable structural materials of the house, but sometimes the fire was laid directly on the ground. Stones are set in position to support cooking vessels, and a wooden frame may be erected so that a kettle can be suspended from it. The stones also moderate the flow of heat, since they absorb it when the fire is high and radiate it when the fire is allowed to die down. Metal cooking utensils (like blankets and some other trade items of European origin) were adopted just as soon as they became available, with no nonsense about sticking to the old ways for the sake of tradition. Earlier, vessels had been made of crude earthenware, or of slow-burning types of wood or bark, or the stomach of a recently killed large animal was cleaned out and used for boiling.

OTHER STRUCTURES

The winter lodge was not the only architectural design; in fact, Menomini has more than twenty words for different types of structures, differing in materials and in intended use. The crudest, resorted to in case of necessity, were made by digging into a soft hillside and covering the opening with a screen of brush, or by erecting a lean-to of poles and brush against a rocky cliff.

Near each winter lodge a small structure of the same design but barely large enough for a single person was also built. This was not an "outhouse" in our sense,[7] but for a girl or woman during menstruation, who must be kept from even the most casual contact with men, lest they be thereby unfitted for their economic tasks. She must therefore not enter the main house, or touch any of the ordinary tools or utensils of the family, but prepare her own food with separate equipment. If a visitor asked after a female member of a family, the answer *akuaceh pōtawεw* 'outdoors she-builds-her-fire' signaled this state of affairs.

Other smaller structures served various other purposes. Some of these were erected as the occasions for them arose and abandoned or disassembled when the need was over. One type was the sweat lodge, in which one took a scented steam bath for cleanliness and medicinal purposes. It was regularly placed at the edge of a stream, from which the ice would be cleared away if necessary, so that after an hour or so of sweating the bather could plunge briefly into the frigid water.

THE SUMMER HOUSE

The spring return to the summer villages also required the building of new houses or the repairing of old ones. We do not know whether this was done by women, men, or both.

A summer house was rectangular rather than oval in floor plan, and had a gabled roof rather than a dome-shaped top; it was built with a framework of poles kept straight rather than being bent, covered with sheets of bark that were sometimes as large as 3 feet by 6 (Figure 2-3). The summer houses were larger than the winter lodges: 12 or 15 feet one way, 18 or 20 the other. The construction was essentially rainproof. It allowed enough leakage of air to be cool during the hot summer, but therefore was not much protection if for some reason one had to stay in it during the winter.

[7]For such functions the Menomini, like the earliest European frontiersmen and settlers in eastern North America, merely retired to a suitable spot in the brush. Cattails served as diapers for infants.

FIGURE 2-3. SUMMER HOUSE. The residence of Sōmen Jim in the early part of the twentieth century. (From Skinner 1921.)

Some summer houses may have been longer than the maximum dimension we have given, with a door at each end: two (related) families would live in it, each using its own door. In more recent times larger structures were built for ceremonial gatherings (Figure 2-4). Smaller auxiliary buildings clustered around a summer house as around a winter lodge.

Much summertime household activity was carried on outdoors; the house afforded refuge from inclement weather and a place to sleep. The fire, needed not for warmth but only for cooking and as a source of light at night, was usually outdoors. Even in the winter many activities, including cooking, were conducted outdoors more often than we would expect, conditioned as we are by our effete central heating systems.

✖ Menomini habits of dress and bodily adornment changed so rapidly under European influence that the details for the classical period are no longer recoverable. But two general points can be made.   **CLOTHING**

(1)   The first is that, like the other Indians of the Northeastern Woodlands, they often wore very little, even in cold weather. An animal skin (later a blanket) might be draped loosely over the shoulders when venturing out of the winter lodge, a man or child wearing nothing else above the waist.[8] The summer minimum was a belt

[8]While such light winter clothing demands fortitude, it is possible that the Indians of the Northeastern Woodlands were heir to some special physiological adaptation to the cold (see p. 432).

(a)

(b)

FIGURE 2-4. A MODERN CEREMONIAL "LONG HOUSE." (a): the skeleton, in part like that of a wigwam. (b): the completed structure (covering of skins or possibly of canvas), surrounded by tents. (From Skinner 1921.)

and breechclout, supplemented (probably) by some sort of breast covering for women, but often discarded altogether by children and even by men. The breechclout was a strip of some flexible material, passed between the legs and tucked over the belt in front and in back. The belt also supported a pouch, used for carrying things.

However, men did not undertake overnight winter hunts thus lightly clad, and there must have been various other occasions on which more elaborate clothing was donned.

(2)   This brings us to the second general point: the more elaborate clothing must have resembled our own in basic outline, since ours is an adaptation to textiles of a pattern of tailored skin clothing widespread in the arctic, subarctic, and more northerly temperate zones of both the Old World and the New in the last few thousand

years. Versions are attested for other Northeastern Woodlands peoples, if not for the Menomini of the classical period. Such clothing divides the body up into zones, for each of which a special garment is cut and sewn; contrast the draped saris and sarongs of the tropics.

The separate garments are typically a cap, a shirt, leggings, and shoes, the shirt and leggings overlapping the foundation of belt and breechclout. Small animals such as otters and raccoons supply excellent fur for caps, while larger ones like deer or moose furnish better skins for the other parts, especially if they are tanned and perhaps dyed.

A single legging covers a single leg from ankle to crotch, like a long stocking with no foot part. Western trousers came into existence when separate garments for the two legs were widened and sewn together at the top; this origin is reflected by our continuing habit of speaking of a *pair* of trousers (or pants).

Deerskin shoes of a number of styles were worn by the Indians; the bottoms were soft, for they were protection more against the cold than against rough ground. One feels these ought really to be called "moccasins"; but this is just the Algonquian word (Menomini *mahkε̄sen*) for any kind of footwear, even the sort of heavy leather-and-rubber boots an Indian may nowadays buy in a store. The Indian shoes were fastened with shoestrings, much as are ours; tie strings were also used to fasten the front of the shirt and to tie each legging around the leg. The strings were usually thin strips of hide. Buttons and buttonholes are of Old World warm-climate origin, and in Europe were added to the tailored-skin-clothing tradition, or its textile variant, only in the fourteenth century.

We know nothing of the classical Menomini fashions of coiffure or of bodily adornment or scarification. American Indian males tend to have very light beards; shaving was presumably no problem. We do know they sometimes coated all or part of their bodies with animal grease. Whatever their overt explanation, this would combat the cold and would afford some protection against mosquitoes and other insects. Yet certain bugs, especially lice, must have been a continual source of annoyance, as they have been for primates from time immemorial and still are for a large portion of our species. Menomini *enāʔnεw,* literally 'he places him thus', is a euphemism for 'he looks for lice on the other's head', reflecting a pattern of mutual aid that dates back tens of millions of years to the earliest tree-dwelling primates whose forelimbs were capable of such use.

GETTING FOOD

× Gathering

The gathering of most wild plant foods involved nothing more than picking, cutting, or digging, and a container to put the crop into for the trip back to camp.

Wild rice was more complicated. Its collection typically required a team of three, in a canoe (bark, usually birch, or dugout): a man to pole it through the muddy waters, and two women to knock the grains off the tops of the plants into the canoe. The man used a long pole with a fork at the far end, which afforded leverage as it pressed against the roots of the rice plants; an unforked pole would simply sink into the muddy bottom of the lake. The women used paddles, and then paused to thresh the rice with their feet or hands in order to remove the spiny beards. This was dangerous, for the spines are sharp and may penetrate the skin; also, they fly through the air and if one enters the eye it almost always destroys the sight (a hazard reflected by the Menomini word *pōhkeʔkow* 'he or she has one eye' or 'one-eyed person'[9]). Ashore, the rice had to be winnowed, by shaking it on flat trays so that the chaff rose to the top and could be skimmed or blown off. Only then was it ready for cooking, or for packing home to be cooked later. Like oriental rice, it expands greatly when boiled.

The wild rice still grows where it used to grow and is still gathered in much the same way. Many readers of this book may have eaten it, for it can be purchased at supermarkets in the United States and Canada—for a stiff price, so that it now counts as a gourmet food, not as the staple it was for the Menomini.

FISHING

Some fishing was done with hook and line, but sturgeon, the chief summertime fish, were usually speared, from rocks along the shores of the rivers or from canoes. Nets and snares of several types were also used. In winter, a hole was cut through the ice and covered by a small hut of boughs, so that the fisherman could look down into the water without interference from the bright light reflecting from clouds and snow. A lure was lowered on a cord, and when a fish swam into range it was stabbed and pulled out.

FOOD PREPARATION

Meat and fish were dried in the sun; meat could be roasted on a spit over a fire; and meat, fish, and maize may have been baked in hot ashes. The commonest cooking procedure, however, was boiling, to yield soups and stews in great variety and of all degrees of thickness.

Modern tradition holds that the commonest seasoning was maple sap or syrup, rather than salt.

HUNTING

Hunting was done with bows and arrows, snares, spears, knives, clubs, and one additional device to be mentioned in a moment. The bows were about three feet long, straight rather than curved when not strung, made often of a single piece of hickory or ash but perhaps sometimes of two pieces of wood glued together lengthwise and wrapped at intervals with buckskin or sinew. Other favorite woods were white oak, elm, and hemlock. Arrowheads were of flint, quartz, or antler; copper points turn up after the classical period, but were used only in war. The shafts were of wood, and feathered. Quivers were made of the skins of various small animals.

Anyone—man, woman, child—could quite unceremoniously dispatch a rabbit, squirrel, or bird that was so unfortunate as to wander within reach. The quest for

[9]Nowadays also an 'ace' (playing card).

(a)   (b)

FIGURE 2-5. A POWER PACK AND ITS CONTENTS. The bag is of basswood bark twine. The side shown in (a) has woven designs representing the Underground Panther; the reverse, in (b), displays women and eagles. The contents include smaller pouches, and dolls related to various Higher Powers. (From Skinner 1913, with the permission of the American Museum of Natural History.)

larger game was more serious and called for careful preparation. The weapons we have mentioned were not enough. The hunting party must include someone who was heir to the proper powers and who owned, as embodiment of and channel for those powers, a *pēhcekonāh*. The ethnographers render this word as 'sacred pack' or 'medicine bundle', but I think both translations carry unsuitable connotations, and prefer 'power pack'. Menomini power packs were of a number of kinds (no two, indeed, were identical), but most were for war or for hunting, and the latter concern us here.

Examine a power pack in a museum (Figure 2-5). The outer covering, carefully folded and tied, may be an animal skin or a woven bag. When this is opened there are one or several small packages of soft white doeskin or other fine material. These, in turn, hold such objects as the teeth or claws of some animal, dried berries or roots, a bit of moss, a pebble or so, a shell.

Our puzzlement deserves, as comment, a paraphrase of a remark offered early in this century by a canny Menomini: suppose someone who had never seen a radio came upon one and peered into it. He would be confronted by a meaningless jumble of bits of wire, glass, and plastic. The radio is worthless except to one who knows how to use it, which means, among other things, that he knows it must be hooked up properly to a source of electrical power.

A power pack, as a mere collection of objects, is equally useless. But its owner also owns certain songs and stories that only he has the right to sing and recite, and these activate the ingredients of the pack. He may have assembled the pack himself, following instructions received during his puberty dream (p. 30) from the Higher Power who at that time befriended him and gave him the songs and stories. Or he may have inherited or purchased the pack and the necessary accompaniments from someone else. In this case, they may not be fully effective until the new owner has successfully sought the proper dreams as endorsement of his ownership.

A group hunt proceeded as follows. Leaving home, the hunters sought a "clean place" in the woods. There the power pack was carefully opened. The men performed a dance, and smudged their weapons in incense taken from the pack. When they set out from this point, the influence of the pack had already spread through the forest and stupefied the game, guaranteeing success provided the hunters observed all ancillary taboos and requirements.[10]

An overriding requirement was that animals might not be killed merely for pleasure, only for economic need. When in search of animals of a particular species, the unseen leaders of that species must be placated during the ceremonies, or they would not allow any of their kind to be taken.

The bear was particularly difficult. It might not be killed without special rituals, and before the fatal blow was struck apologies had to be directed to the specific animal. After the kill the bear's bones were carefully collected so that they would not become food for dogs, and the skull was hung in a tree. Some sort of special treatment of bears is widespread throughout the north, in Europe and Asia as well as in America (ethnologists class this as a "circumpolar" trait, like the tailored skin clothing mentioned on page 18). No one will scoff who has seen a bear in action. One reflection of this well founded bear-respect is that people may come to speak of the animal with some euphemism instead of his "right" name: the Russian word for 'bear' is literally 'honey-eater', and the commonest Menomini word was *awēhsɛh*, literally 'little what's-his-name'.

PEOPLE ✗ The primary unit of Menomini social organization was the family, consisting of a woman, her children, and her husband. After the classical period, wars at times resulted in a short supply of adult males; at such times some men had more than one wife. We do not know to what extent this had been true earlier.

We also do not know where a newly married couple lived—whether preferentially with the husband's people, with the wife's, or separate from both. Nor do we have any evidence as to whom a man could marry, except that a favored match was of a pair who were the children of a brother and a sister (*cross cousins*). The evidence for this is kinship terms. 'My mother's brother' and 'my father's sister (or) mother's brother's wife' are respectively *nesēh* and *nesēkih;* diminutives of these two words, *nesēnɛh* and *nesēkihsɛh,* are respectively 'my father-in-law' and 'my mother-in-law'. The first three of these kinship terms have special vocative forms used in directly addressing

---

[10]The use of a war pack was similar. A raiding party found a staging area near the enemy camp; the owner of the pack stayed there with it as the others performed their before-dawn raid and then returned, with scalps, evidence of having counted coup, and their wounded.

the individual concerned: 'O my maternal uncle!' and so on. The fourth does not, in keeping with the fact that it was highly improper for a man to speak to his mother-in-law or even to refer to her in her presence.

A favored pattern for marital matching, such as the "cross-cousin marriage" we have just described, can never be an absolute rule. There has to be leeway, because the accidents of birth and death can otherwise leave some individuals with no suitable mate. Among the Menomini, as in tribal societies generally, *everybody* gets married, whatever the difficulties.

CLANS AND PHRATRIES

Above the level of the family, and apart from the local grouping by villages and winter camps, was a system of *clans,* some of them linked in pairs, and all falling into a set of seven larger and looser groupings that we may call *phratries.* A child's clan and phratry were those of his father. If a man's father's sister married into a clan different from that of the father, then her daughter would also belong to that different clan; thus favored cross-cousin marriage may have meant that ordinarily one did not marry within one's clan.

Clans and phratries were named after animals or other natural objects. For example, one phratry had as its three clans those called *sekāc-okēmāw* 'unwilling chief' (also the name of the whole phratry), *mɛhkēnāh* 'snapping turtle', and *kitēmīw* 'porcupine'. One clan was called *tekōw* 'wave'.

Before one jumps to the conclusion that these labels indicate mystical ties between the members of the clan and the animals or other objects called by the same words, one should remember our current habit of naming athletic teams: the St. Louis *Cardinals,* the Baltimore *Orioles,* the Detroit *Tigers,* and so on. In fact, however, although the word "mystical" may be wrong, in the view of the Menomini there were such ties, not necessarily between (say) the people of the Porcupine clan and living porcupines, but indirectly via the semihuman protoporcupine of the early days of the world, and accounts were passed down from generation to generation telling of the episodes of antiquity that had brought about the associations.

The clan and phratry system served to orient individuals and families vis-à-vis others, to help them keep track of their special responsibilities and privileges in the fabric of Menomini society and to remind them of their place in the precariously balanced ecology of the whole world. In recent times each clan has had a sort of chief, and the chieftainship of the whole tribe has been hereditary in the Unwilling Chief clan; but this degree of formalization is intrusive (pp. 147–148). In the old days there were no "chiefs" as we mean that term. Rather, certain individuals were the trusted leaders for some activities, other individuals for others.

DESIGNATIONS FOR INDIVIDUALS

Individuals addressed or referred to other individuals by name, kinship term, or special epithet.

NAMES. Some personal names were words used for nothing else, like our *William* or *Jane.* Some were words that also had clear everyday meanings: *kemēwan* 'it's raining' or a man's name 'Rain'; *kohkēkāpowet* '(one who) stands turned', also a woman's name.

Perhaps the majority were distorted or unusual forms of everyday words, or forms derived from everyday words for the special use. Men's names of this sort can be rendered, by way of example, as 'Rough Face', 'Big Wind', 'Farm', 'Young Eagle', 'Bad Eagle', 'Earth Stander', 'Blocks My Way', 'Keeps Going Fast'; *oskas* 'Claw' began as the name of a famous nineteenth-century leader, then became in turn the English name of a city in Wisconsin and of a brand of overalls (*Oshkosh*). The comparable women's names often included an element meaning 'woman', or one referring to clouds or to the flow of water: 'Eagle Woman', 'Sky Woman', 'Cut Cloud Woman', 'Low Cloud Woman', 'Shines Hot Woman', 'Flows Fast', 'Flows Forever'.

The giving of names was important, as we shall see (p. 29).

KINSHIP TERMS.   These always included an element designating the person relative to whom the individual was being referred to: thus *nekī⁷s* 'my son', but *kekī⁷s* 'your son' and *okī⁷san* 'his, her son'; to say simply 'a son' required a circumlocution, 'one who is a son' or 'one who has a father'.

All systems of kinship terminology class some relatives together under a single designation, but the exact way in which this is done varies from one community to another (pp. 191–201). Of course, the fact that a Menomini would refer to two or more people as, say, *netāh* 'my father's brother' by no means meant that he was forced to treat them alike in all other ways, any more than one of us is forced to treat all his uncles alike.

However, in certain situations protocol simplified matters by prescribing certain formal manifestations of relative status. Generally, the young owed respect to the old, and the old owed protection to the young. In this context, a number of kinship terms were used as a matter of politeness when addressing a stranger whose relation to oneself, if any, was not known: 'grandfather', 'grandmother', 'grandchild', 'older brother', 'younger sibling', a few others. The choice of term of address made by the first person to speak in such an encounter could set the tone, perhaps smooth the way. The extended use of kinship terms reached even references to certain Higher Powers: in ritual speech one said *kemēhsomēhsāhtekonawak* 'our grandfathers the trees' and *kōhkomēhsahkamekonaw* 'our grandmother earth'. Words indistinguishable from kinship terms in their grammatical behavior carried the meanings 'my enemy', 'my sweetheart, lover', 'my fellow participant in a ceremony', and 'my totem' (that is, the ancestral animal or object associated with my clan).

SPECIAL EPITHETS.   If relations between a man and his mother-in-law were strained and indirect, certain other relationships were marked by a prescribed and formalized freedom from ordinary constraints. Those involved played nasty tricks on each other, and addressed each other with coarse epithets, pseudo kinship terms often made up on the spot: 'my fellow penis man', 'my fellow testicled one', 'my fellow dog'. Such deeds and words were the occasion for great laughter among onlookers, and the victim could not take offense.

THE TENOR OF INTERPERSONAL RELATIONSHIPS

Certain shared experiences could establish a tie between two men of a sort whereby neither could properly refuse any request from the other, even if compliance entailed impoverishment and hardship; there are cases on record in which it did. Only general constraint, and the basic reciprocality of the tie, kept matters even in the long run. There is some evidence that in the classical period this sort of tie was primarily or exclusively between members of the same clan.

In general, any household was expected to extend a helping hand when it was needed. Orphaned children were adopted, perhaps whenever possible by the father's brother (*netāh* 'my father's brother' also means 'my stepfather') or the mother's sister (*nenīh,* also 'my stepmother'). More casually, a passing stranger, if his intentions were obviously peaceful, was regularly invited in and fed, with formulas that seem cold to us but that were not. The host would say "Come in if you wish, but if you prefer not to that is all right"; if the stranger entered the lodge he would sit across the fireplace from the host, who would then say "This is what we have to eat; eat if you wish, or refrain if you prefer." Phrases of this sort were as stereotyped as is a casual "How do you do" among us, but behind the stereotypy lurked a cardinal emphasis among the Menomini on the right of every individual to make his own decisions in all that concerned him.

The same emphasis was found in many other contexts. Any object or skill that was viewed by the Menomini as "property" was the property of an *individual*—person, animal, or Higher Power—never of any sort of collectivity. Among other Algonquian tribes some power packs belonged to a clan or club; among the Menomini they were all private property. Even an infant had his own things, and his parents could not dispose of them without some sort of sign of the infant's approval. An unmarried girl's "virtue" was her own possession; she could yield to a suitor, or to several suitors in succession, as she pleased, with no fear of the wagging of venomous tongues or that such behavior would interfere with her finding a suitable husband. What did not belong to some specific owner did not belong to any owner at all—it was not property.

The sharing and exchanging of commodities under such conditions entails established patterns of quid pro quo. In their later dealings with Europeans the understandings were rarely mutual, and the Menomini (like other North American Indians) would often want to take something back because what they had received in exchange had turned out to be brummagem. This it was that gave rise to the scurrilous and undeserved epithet "Indian giver." Among themselves, on the other hand, transactions usually went smoothly. The commodity given in exchange for something might be a song or a story rather than a physical object, or might be just the right to use the song, story, or artifact for a certain period of time, rather than a permanent transfer.

However, when a girl became a wife, she was bestowing the right of sexual access exclusively on her husband, for life or until some subsequent arrangement was explicitly worked out to the satisfaction of all. The husband did not have the privilege of transferring this commodity to anyone else, but neither did the wife. If she transgressed, her husband could with impunity cut off her nose or her ear.

DECISIONS, PROBLEMS, AND SOLUTIONS

Long experience had taught the Menomini that things do not always work out according to expectation and agreement. Steps were taken to render important decisions binding, and there were procedures for righting things when they had gone awry.

This was the context in which tobacco put in its appearance. Smoking was not an everyday vice, but a method of ceremonial solemnization of transactions. Various Higher Powers were fond of tobacco. An offering might be made to a friendly Power in exchange for the privilege of being successful in a hunt, or to an inimical Power to ward off molestation.

When families or local groups found themselves at odds, a conciliatory council would be held to resolve the dispute, and the first step at such a council was to pass around the pipe.

Occasionally there was a murder. To forestall the possibility of a destructive feud, a council would be held. Representatives of the murderer's family or clan offered the pipe to the delegates from the victim's group. If it was refused, things looked bad. If it was refused four times the situation was desperate and talk would be useless; the council was over. Discussion, when it took place, might lead to the conclusion that the murderer had been fully or partly justified, in which case the most needed to put things right was a transfer of goods or services. If, on the other hand, the judgment was that the murder was without provocation, the murderer was forthwith surrendered to and executed by the kin of the victim. The episode was then closed, and the survivors, though with no great rejoicing, could go about their ordinary affairs.

Character

In addition to the strong emphasis Menomini culture put on the autonomy of the individual, a premium was placed on emotional equanimity in the face of the unavoidable small annoyances and large agonies of life.

Our standard portrayal in fiction of the strong, silent, stoic Indian, enduring torture without a murmur, is not a caricature, for this was in fact the ideal—without implying that the Indians were masochists or sadists, for they neither sought nor inflicted pain for pain's sake. What can't be cured must be endured. We have seen how the Menomini endured the cold in ways in which we could not; this was one manifestation. When there was little or no food, they went hungry and occupied themselves with other things. A woman in childbirth was not to cry out, and rarely did. When pain was inflicted on the young for training purposes (p. 30), there were avenues of escape for one who could stand no more. He who chose such an alternative was not scorned as a weakling, since that would have violated the principle of self-determination; but he knew that by his withdrawal he was subjecting himself to certain handicaps, and might later have to seek further ordeals to overcome them.

VARIABILITY. A description of norms, such as the foregoing, gives no indication of the living variety of personality types that clustered about the norms.

The Menomini were not all cut to a single pattern, differing from one another only as to sex and age. In innate ability (insofar as that can be measured), the range was doubtless what would be found by scooping up at random an equivalent number of people from the streets of any modern city: ordinary folks, with few geniuses and few morons. Likewise, some were wise, others foolish; some generous, others self-centered; some were bores, others lively and with broad interests.

In recent times (probably also earlier) the Menomini have themselves acknowledged that some of their number were expert and convincing public speakers, while others were unusually maladroit, apt to stutter and stammer and to get mixed up in their syntax. In the classical period probably most of them were strictly monolingual, but a few may have been like the dignified old woman Leonard Bloomfield met in 1920, who in addition to her own language was fluent in Potawatomi and Ojibwa and could manage, when necessary, in Winnebago and in English. The proper analog in our society would be a lively and intelligent grandmother, keenly interested in the problems of those about her, who had received her education at Radcliffe or Vassar followed by lengthy sojourns in Europe.

THE WORLD

× The Menomini had not our Western habit of spinning out consistent verbal pictures of the world; hence we introduce a measure of unreality when we draw together the threads of evidence and do it for them. Except for this factor, the following seems accurate.

The Tiers and Their Inhabitants

The surface of the earth, where we live, is the middle one of nine parallel tiers. We can invade the edge of the next layer up by climbing a tree or ascending a hill, and can penetrate a bit into the next one down by digging a hole or entering a cave, but for the most part we are confined, in this life, to our own familiar stratum.

Before a person's conception and birth, his animating force resided elsewhere; it is not clear where. During life a person consists of a *metε̄ˀcyak* 'soul, spirit' (*netε̄ˀcyak* 'my soul') animating the body (*nēyaw* 'my body, person, self'). The same is true of a game animal or bird. It is the body that dies; the soul takes a long trail to a place of happiness far in the west. To commit suicide is *nεˀtaw wēyaw* 'he kills his (own) body'; similarly, murder, or the slaughter of an animal without authorization, is an invasion of property rights, since a soul is thus deprived of its most precious possession.

In the highest tier of the world dwells *mε̄c-awε̄tok* 'great spirit', identified with the sun; the bare word *awε̄tok,* without the modifier *mε̄c* 'big', names any spirit or animal or any human being with unusual powers. In the next tier downwards live the Thunderers, each of which has a name; their activities can often be seen and heard. Somehow associated with them is the morning star. In the next tier live the golden eagles and the white swan; in the tier just above our own live birds of many species, headed by the bald eagles and by hawks, kites, and swallows.

In the lowest tier lives the Great White Bear; next upwards the Great Underground Panther, represented on the surface of the earth by the panther and the lynx; next the White Deer; and just beneath the earth, occasionally seen lurking in a cave or scurrying along close to the ground, the Horned Hairy Serpent.

The tiers are flat and extend indefinitely in all directions; our own has the structure of a large island floating on an endless sea. The Menomini live here; so, at some distance, do other groups of men; so do animals and fish. Certain other entities reside in our tier, far enough away or so furtive that they are rarely seen: various hobgoblins, cannibals, and giants in the icy north; a malevolent living skeleton that can kill with its eyes and that haunts the forests after nightfall. Certain large boulders are, or are the haunts of, spirits; when one's path takes one by such a boulder it is wise to offer a bit of tobacco.

ATTITUDES

Among the varied inhabitants of the nine tiers there are many subtle connections, some of them obvious to all, some known only to one or another expert, some revealed as yet to no one.

The scheme of the world is well fixed, but our knowledge of it is not—new and potentially helpful discoveries can be sought, and experience can show that older views were in error or incomplete. One's convictions about the scheme of things are conservative, for that is the course of wisdom, but not inflexible and not intolerant. One listens respectfully to someone expounding an alternative interpretation, and recognizes that it may be part of the truth. Any theory endorsed by a successful practical demonstration will find its adherents, who do not necessarily thereupon abandon earlier, seemingly conflicting, views.

Thus, in the late seventeenth century a Jesuit priest persuaded a group of Menomini to let him put his crucifix atop a pole which had been planted near the mouth of a river to induce the sturgeon to enter the river, in place of the object (not identified in the account) that the Menomini had placed on it. The next morning the sturgeon appeared in abundance. The Indians were therefore eager to learn more. The Jesuit thought he was making converts; the Menomini felt that they were adding a valuable new technique to their repertory.

This attitude explains why a number of movements of the sort Europeans call "religious" have been successful among the Menomini in the centuries since the classical period. The first of these, dating possibly from before the first European contact, was the *metēwen* or 'Mystic Rite', at one time widespread among the Algonquian tribes of the Northeastern Woodlands; its teachings are very close to the classical Menomini views of the world and of man's place in it. Several "secret societies" and "professions" (the ethnographers use both terms) have come in, or have developed indigenously, each involving a set of special skills, rites, objects, and powers. Catholic Christianity made temporary inroads in the late seventeenth century, then returned with more permanent success early in the nineteenth. A hundred years after that, the Native American Church (the proper name for the so-called Peyote Cult) spread from the Southwest and gained some adherents. But, of course, many other things have changed radically in the last three centuries. For the classical period I think it would not be valid to denote any special segment of the Menomini way of life as their "religion" (chapter 10).

TALES

The scheme of the world is well fixed, but it was not always so. Knowledge of the earlier formative stage is transmitted via the stories told in the long winter evenings around the fire.

The Menomini distinguish two kinds of tales, and often mention at the beginning of a story which kind it is. They may say "this is only an *ācemwan*," using the generic term for 'tale'. Or they will say the story is an *ātɛʔnōhkakan* (plural *ātɛʔnōhkakanan*), the kind that concerns us here. One story of this sort could be very long, with many episodes, and would be told part by part on a succession of evenings. These stories deal

with a far-off time when the world as we know it was in process of formation. The spirit animals enter in human or semi-human form, and the powers of the sky still dwell on earth. These stories are considered as true; they are told to inform and instruct; they often explain the origin of things, especially of plants and animals, and of customs. Even the lovable ineptitudes of *mɛʔnapos* ['Big Rabbit', the "Culture Hero," the unromanticized and often ribald prototype of Longfellow's Hiawatha] indicate by contrast the correct human way of obtaining food and the like.[11]

We can read these stories now, in English or (at the cost of many hours' labor to achieve a reading knowledge of the language the Menomini themselves never wrote) in written transcriptions of the oral originals. But we can barely understand them. We can only vaguely imagine their impact when heard in the cracked voice of a wise old man, as we sit half asleep by the fire, surrounded on all sides by the very world he is telling us about and wondering what adventure the morrow may bring to ratify his age-old truths.

BIRTH AND CHILDHOOD

At the onset of labor, a woman retired to the menstrual hut (p. 16), since the blood attendant on childbirth was contaminating just as was that of menstruation. The infant was bound on a cradleboard, later carried on the mother's back (or perhaps on that of an aunt or older sister) when she needed to cart the child around and yet have her hands free for her household and food-gathering tasks. Holes were pierced in the infant's shoes so that if some spirit tried to coax it whence it had come it would refuse on the grounds that its shoes were too poor for such a long journey. A boy child's penis was pinched, that his passion when he grew up might be moderate.

A child was his own person from the beginning, and within wide limits was allowed to behave as he pleased. He began speaking within a few weeks, but at first in a special dialect that was unintelligible to most adults, although a few specialists were sometimes able to understand bits of it. The child was given a name by an expert in such matters, who was paid for his services; the expert got the name from a Higher Power, sometimes in a dream but sometimes without going to that trouble. It was important that the name be right. If it was not, the child's soul showed this by causing the body to get sick. The parents and the experts then had to try again.

PUBERTY

Despite the wide range of freedom of choice, children of both sexes were taught to fast when still quite young, as preparation for the puberty ordeal. These preliminary

[11] Bloomfield 1928, p. XII. Reprinted with the permission of the American Ethnological Society.

fasts were brief trial runs, not expected to culminate in any converse with unseen powers. They interrupted the regular daily routine of the young years, when the children accompanied the adult women at their tasks and learned skills through informal apprenticeship.

In the winter, the children heard over and over again the recitals of *ātɛˀnōhkakanan* (p. 29), as well as the personal accounts of the experiences of others, and thus slowly acquired a sense of orientation in the world beyond their immediate view.

Boys knew that their adult responsibility would be hunting, and played at hunting long before they were old enough to accompany parties of grown men. The first game killed by a boy, even if only a tiny squirrel or a baby bird, was made the featured food at a feast, as a solemn collective endorsement of his acceptance of his future role.

THE PUBERTY FAST.   The first and greatest crisis in a boy's life, the event which changed him from a child into an adult, was his fast at puberty. He was sent alone into the forest, where he blackened his face with a charred stick and refrained from all food and water day after day. Eventually he had a significant dream.

Some dreamed events are just the workings of imagination, but some are real, and the dreamer can tell the difference. He was visited by a spirit animal, one of the Higher Powers of the heavens—or, sometimes, most unfortunately, by one of the inimical spirits of the nether layers. A dream of the latter kind could be rejected, unless it recurred, in which case one eventually had to accept it.

In a favorable dream, the dreamer was befriended by a spirit, who might take him on a journey to one or another far part of the world, show him useful things, teach him some songs, and give him various charms, sometimes for a power pack but sometimes of a more ordinary sort. When the dreamer awoke he had to go through the woods and find the waking-life objects corresponding to the dream objects he had received.

The difficulty in being forced to accept the favors of a less friendly spirit was that the accompanying powers were more dangerous. The recipient (unless he himself chose to become malevolent, as few did) had to be more careful to guarantee that his acts be beneficial rather than detrimental.

The dream fast did not always work. Sometimes the searcher could take no more hardship, and broke his vigil without having dreamed. He might then try again later.

The importance of the puberty dream was that it told the boy—henceforth a young man—who and what he was and what his role in life could be. Of course, in any case he would be a hunter, a fisherman, sometimes a warrior, surely a husband and father. But would he be an organizer of hunts, sharing his special powers with others, or merely a follower? Would he become a trusted expert in diagnosing troubles among people or between people and Higher Powers? If so, what kind? Would he become in time a teller of *ātɛˀnōhkakanan*, a singer of special songs, a healer of the sick? The fullest puberty dream did not determine these matters completely, but the thinnest one indicated the proper general direction for the young man's subsequent striving. Thereafter he turned to the proper experts for waking-time guidance, as well as seeking further aid through dreams, with or without a preparatory fast.

We know little of the puberty fast and dreaming of girls, through no fault of the Menomini but because our reports were assembled by male ethnographers at a time when our own culture was strongly male-oriented. We know that some girls fasted, but not that all did; we do not know how such a fast was timed relative to the girl's first experience of "making her fire outdoors" (p. 16), which by regulation lasted ten days and was the first major climax of her life. The dream guidance received by a girl had to do with activities and skills appropriate for Menomini women. But these included the healing of the sick and some sorts of diagnosis of social difficulties, not just economic and child-raising tasks.

MARRIAGE AND MATURITY

Marriage could be the outcome of the summer courting of a girl by a young man (p. 14). More often, a young man's wife was chosen for him by his parents, who approached the prospective bride's family. If their suit was successful, they gave them presents and the bride went with the groom to his house. A year later, the wife's parents were supposed to give gifts to the groom's family of a value at least equal to that of the gifts they had accepted in agreeing to the marriage.

We have already described the ordinary activities of adult life. The expected routines, of course, might be cut off at any time by illness and death, accident and death, war and death, just as among us today. The survivors regrouped as best they could; children were adopted if necessary; widows and widowers remarried when a suitable new mate could be found.

OLD AGE AND DEATH

An elderly man or woman was valued for his or her skills, if any, even if feebleness prohibited participation in vigorous activities. Some had no such skills, having lost whatever special powers they might formerly have possessed. Such "useless old men" were tolerated, and according to tales a role was sometimes found for them: something new and unfamiliar—in one story brandy, when first introduced by traders—was tested on them to see if it was safe.

Death was a change from one status to another.

The death of an infant or child was dealt with simply.

For an adult, the soul was disoriented by the shock of dying just as it had been by the trauma of birth, and needed help. The corpse was dressed in its best clothes and its face was painted. A wake was held until sunset of the day of the death. The body was removed from the house through a hole made in the rear, so that the soul would not tag along to the grave, but sometimes it did anyway. At the graveside the body was laid on the ground, and a feast was held at which the participants could leave no orts. The chief mourner placed offerings, including tobacco, by the corpse, which was then lowered into the shallow grave. The next of kin stepped over the grave and ran home by circuitous routes, again so that the soul would not follow.

For if things went wrong the soul might linger, unhappy and causing unhappiness. But if everything went right, and the soul was cheered on its way by appropriate gifts and charms, it would proceed up the long, long road towards the setting sun, lonely on the journey but serene in its knowledge of the peace and contentment that lay at its end.

3

×

ANOTHER PART OF THE FOREST: BABOONS

Our second step is to take a look at ways of life that are not human at all—not variations on a *human* theme.

Why should we do this? The reason is that if we confine our attention to human beings we are likely to be overimpressed by the differences from one community to another and miss the crucial similarities. We can zero in on the human common denominator only if we also achieve some grasp of what is not—or, at least, not exclusively—human.

Baboons are primates,[1] as we are, but the relationship is fairly remote. A rough computation suggests that any two human beings in the world today are related not more distantly than as 150,000th cousins. A baboon and a human being are related no *less* distantly than as 5,000,000th cousins. Baboons are Old World monkeys. Men are hominoids, a group that includes also all the apes. The latest common ancestors of hominoids and Old World monkeys lived not more recently than 50,000,000 years ago, perhaps even earlier. Thus the lines of descent leading respectively to baboons and to men have been separate for a very long time.

Even so, we shall find some similarities.

Where baboons and men (or any other pair of ultimately related species) are alike, the reason can be either of these two: (1) the shared feature was characteristic of the common ancestor and has been retained by both lines of descent ever since (*common heritage*); (2) the two lineages have faced similar vicissitudes of existence and have adapted to them in similar ways (*parallelism*).

These two factors cannot be wholly sorted out, but we do know of one partial parallelism. The early primates lived in the trees. During the Miocene, a geological epoch that began about 28,000,000 years ago and lasted for some sixteen million years, climatic changes induced successive contractions and expansions of Earth's forest cover. Some Old World primates managed to retreat when the trees did, and still live in them today. Others were caught in dwindling isolated groves, and faced the alternatives of extinction or of adaptation to a largely or wholly terrestrial existence. Some of the hominoids who survived this expulsion from the trees were

---

[1]We shall learn more of what this means later (chapter 5).

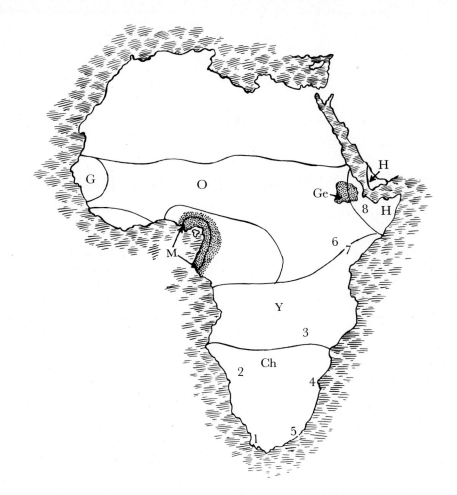

FIGURE 3-1. DISTRIBUTION OF BABOONS. G = guinea baboon; O = olive baboon; Y = yellow baboon; Ch = chacma baboon; H = hamadryas baboon; M = mandrill and drill (enclaves partly within the territory of other baboons, plus the island of Fernando Po); Ge = gelada baboon. The numerals show the locations of field studies. Specifically mentioned in this chapter are 1, the Cape Peninsula; 6, Nairobi Park, Kenya; and (in passing) 8, within the area of the hamadryas baboons. (Data from DeVore and Hall 1965 and from Napier and Napier 1967.)

our own ancestors. Some of the monkeys who lived through the same predicament in another part of the forest were the ancestors of today's baboons.

The parallelism ends with that. The two groups met the challenge with different inherited equipment, and their ultimate patterns of life on the ground were, as we shall see, correspondingly different.

✕ Baboons belong to the genus *Papio*. There is disagreement among the experts as to just how inclusive this genus should be, but the distribution of all the animals anyone has wanted to class as baboons is shown in Figure 3-1. Their territory is

**BABOONS
AND THEIR
ENVIRONMENTS**

FIGURE 3-2. OLIVE BABOONS. [From Irven DeVore (ed.), *Primate behavior: Field studies of monkeys and apes,* Holt, New York, 1965. Courtesy of Irven DeVore.]

extensive and varied, ranging from dense forest through meadowlike savanna to dry, hilly, rocky country with no trees at all. The animals vary too, and perhaps constitute two or more species, though surely the chacma baboons of South Africa and the olive baboons of Kenya are only local variants of a single species. Field studies have been conducted in open territory rather than in forest, at points marked on the map.

Adult male chacmas and olives (Figure 3-2) average about 75 pounds. The body, exclusive of the tail, may be more than a yard in length, and the tail, sprouting almost vertically from the rump when the animal is on all fours, adds another two feet or more. The adult females are much smaller than the adult males, averaging about 30 pounds. The pelage is somewhat coarse, thinnest and shortest about face, ears, hands, and feet, thickest and longest on the neck and shoulders of adult males.

A baboon can quickly cover a short stretch of ground by bipedal *running*, but the only *walking* gait is quadrupedal, weight resting on the digits rather than on the palms and soles; the trunk is horizontal and the arms and legs give the impression of all being equally long. When the animal sits on its haunches, with knees bent, the arms look longer than the legs.

The tail is not prehensile, nor are the feet of adults. The hands are, and are used for grooming, for clinging and climbing, for bringing food to the mouth, for lifting small stones in search of edible grubs and worms, but rarely for carrying and never for throwing things. Hand carrying is virtually precluded, when the animal is on the ground, by the quadrupedal gait. In no use of the hands is there any clear sign of a favoring of one over the other: one-handed operations are performed sometimes with the right, sometimes with the left (cf. p. 416).

The period of gestation ranges from 154 to 183 days. The infants are black at birth, but turn lighter (brown, olive-brown, yellowish, reddish) during maturation. For about a month after birth the infant clings to and climbs about the fur on the mother's ventral surface, feeding at will. During this phase the marked opposability of the infant's big toes is important; with further growth the prehensility of the rear extremities is reduced. After a month the infant begins to venture onto the mother's back, and soon rides there most of the time; a bit later it makes short trips away from her. Weaning begins at six months and is complete in another six. The eruption of deciduous and permanent teeth is timed to accord with this. Both upper and lower canines grow long and protruding (typical for Old World monkeys), especially in males, and if the animal lives long enough he may outlast his teeth, which slowly erode through usage and decay.

Females mature more quickly than males. Menarche can come at three and a half, whereas male puberty is not reached until closer to five and the male does not achieve his full growth until seven or eight. This helps to account for the fact that in the typical community there are about twice as many adult females as adult males.

The menstrual cycle averages thirty-five days. To start the cycle, the region around the vagina, clearly visible below the tail and between the legs when the animal is in typical quadrupedal stance, begins to swell, and in some types of baboons to develop a startling coloration. The swelling reaches a maximum after ten or twelve days, stays constant for about eight, and then diminishes for about sixteen. The maximum swelling marks the optimum time for conception, and serves to attract males (p. 42).

Once a male baboon reaches puberty, his potential sexual appetite is uninterrupted. But it is aroused almost exclusively by those females that show sexual swelling (females may be receptive only then).

One chacma baboon in captivity survived to the ripe old age of forty-five. In their natural habitat they do not live to die of old age (p. 44); it is unlikely that one in a million lasts as long as twenty years.

✳ By "dwelling pattern" we mean the way animals group together, and how they move around relative to one another and to the terrain in which they live (p. 45). Baboons live in groups called "troops" by the specialists; for the sake of uniform terminology we shall call them "bands." The average size of a band of chacmas or olives is between thirty and fifty, but the distribution curve is flat: two observed bands had fewer than ten members each, and one had more than 180. The density of population in a region is a function of the richness of the food supply and other

THE DWELLING PATTERN AND DAILY CYCLE

such factors, but band size shows no great correlation with this. Where there are fewer baboons, there are fewer bands.

There is some tendency for very large bands to split. No corresponding inclination has been observed for undersized bands to merge. It is apparently most unusual for a single animal to switch bands, but we shall later describe one of the two observed instances (p. 42).

NIGHT

The emancipation of baboons from the trees is not complete, except that some bands, living in treeless regions, make do with rocky cliffs as the best available substitute. The night is passed in sleeping, high in the trees (or in shallow caves and on ledges on the cliffsides), reasonably safe from marauders (Figure 3-3). As dusk approaches, a band returns from wherever it has been during the day to a familiar arboreal sleeping place, often the one occupied the preceding night, and all members find spots to spend the hours of darkness. They build no nests, but avail themselves of natural crotches and corners. All is secure well before darkness falls, and the animals do not venture down again until after dawn. Baboons share two age-old fears with all primates, and a third with all except a few nocturnal types: they are afraid of snakes, of falling, and of the dark.

DAY

During the day a band has little to fear from small or middle-sized enemies (except snakes), but the largest adult male is no match for a lion. In lion country, baboons stay closer to the trees all day, ready to seek refuge. They do this even when nearby open country tempts them with a more abundant food supply than is to be found near the trees. Because of these sensible safety measures, a healthy baboon rarely becomes lion food. The currently observable pattern of interaction between baboons and lions has apparently been operative for a very long time, since it appears to have become a matter of mutual understanding. If a lion approaches, the baboons do not race pell-mell for safety, but move negligently to the trees and up into them. The lion does not make a frenzied charge, but pads up and then away in blasé fashion, playing his part in a *pro forma* ritual, knowing perfectly well he is not going to have baboon for brunch. The lions persist because, as we shall see, there *are* circumstances in which a baboon gets caught.

Baboon breakfast begins as soon as the band has descended from the trees in the morning and has reached something edible. The typical pattern, subject to change because of unusually rich or sparse food, is a quiet period at one spot in the morning, another somewhere else at noon, and a third back near the sleeping trees in the evening. Between these pauses the animals are on the march or making shorter stops. Stops are also made at watering places. Individuals and small subgroups leave off feeding from time to time during the rests, to conduct other activities, but the search for and consumption of food is the major collective enterprise of the daylight hours.

Foraging really is a collective enterprise, because the band (unless it is unusually large) wanders about as a unit. How far it travels depends on the density of food.

(a)

(b)

FIGURE 3-3. Baboon sleeping sites. [From Irven DeVore (ed.), *Primate behavior: Field studies of monkeys and apes,* Holt, New York, 1965. (a) courtesy of Irven DeVore; (b) courtesy of K. R. L. Hall.]

If there are ample sources near the sleeping site, the band may pass the whole day within a hundred feet or so of that site. If food is sparse, and there are either scattered trees or no lions, it may travel as much as 10 or 15 miles, though this is rare. The average total distance covered is perhaps 5 or 6 miles, the farthest point from headquarters reached on the path being well less than half that.

Baboons consume all the animal food they can find and catch: worms, grubs, insects; scorpions (sting and all), small lizards and nonvenomous snakes;[2] near the seacoast, various shellfish; eggs and fledglings; occasionally a young and helpless fellow mammal such as a baby gazelle. They are, to be sure, predominantly vegetarian, but only because plant food is so much more abundant. They eat plants and plant parts in enormous variety. Our observers report that it is almost easier to itemize the plants they bypass than to list the ones they use.

Over a period of weeks or months a band may range entirely within an area of a few square miles, centering roughly on a single sleeping site; or, within an area of the same size, it may use in unpredictable sequence several different familiar sleeping sites. The animals become uncomfortable if forced too far from some home base, but there is no defense of a fixed boundary. In the long run, any single band probably performs a gradual random migration, occasionally finding a new sleeping site and occasionally no longer returning to an old one. But the rate is too slow for this to have been securely observed.

SOCIAL STRUCTURE

Only an adult male baboon is large enough to be a match for enemies (other than a lion or an armed human being). A female, juvenile, or infant, venturing on a lone mission, would quickly disappear. No such asocial enterprises are undertaken. The most striking aspect of the adaptation of baboons to daytime surface life is their intricate pattern of social behavior. A baboon community is a highly structured band, in which members of different ages, sizes, and sexes have different responsibilities.

The fully grown adult males—one to half a dozen per band—are in charge. Sometimes they deal roughly with weaker band members, and generally they preempt the best food and the most desirable females, but they pay for their privileges by maintaining order in the group and by protecting all from external danger. Usually their mere presence is enough to ward off enemies, for there is as much interspecies understanding between the baboons and smaller predators as there is with lions. A hyena, a wild dog, or a jackal may stalk a small baboon who seems to be alone, but a whiff or glimpse of the rest of the band nearby, or a glance or, at most, a threatening approach by a full-sized male, will turn him away. Actual combat is exceedingly rare. Everything is done with symbols.

Sometimes, while eating, the members of a band are interspersed among the members of a band of ungulates who are potential prey for the same predators. The baboons and ungulates largely ignore each other. But the association is useful for both. The grazers have the better noses; the baboons have the better vision and perhaps the better hearing. If a member of either species detects the approach of an enemy, his danger signal is acted on by the members of both species. Moving to the defense, a large male baboon may in effect protect the ungulates as well as his own kind.

[2]This does not belie their fear of snakes. For neither baboons nor humans does fear unfailingly enforce flight.

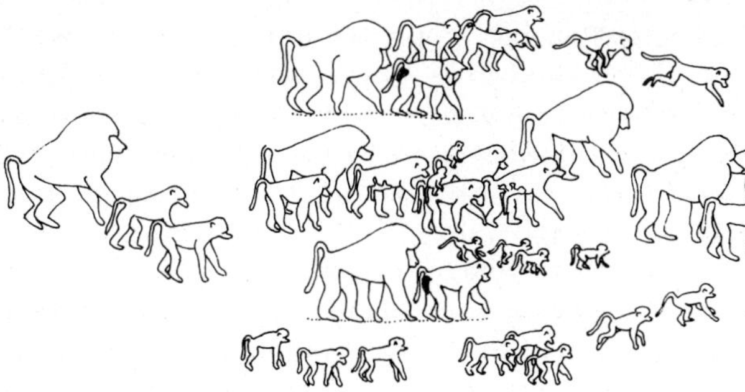

FIGURE 3-4. THE LINE OF MARCH. The females shown with dark hindquarters are in oestrus and are with their consorts. (After Hall and DeVore 1965.)

Sometimes, also, especially at a watering place in the dry season, two or more baboon bands come together and partly intermingle. They are a bit wary of each other: the adult males tend to collect near the line of contact or interpenetration. But they usually leave each other alone. When the two bands separate there has been no interchange of membership. From this and other evidence it is clear that all members of a band (except infants) recognize almost all the other members of the same band as *individuals*.

When a band is moving on the ground, as from one feeding place to another, it follows a fixed order of march which sets forth the social structure of the group in a clear spatial array (Figure 3-4). The less dominant adult males and the juveniles form an elongated ring at the perimeter, like the sentinels posted around a human military encampment. The dominant males are in the middle, the foci of clusters composed otherwise of mothers ridden by new infants, older infants walking for themselves, and mature females with no young. Thus the weakest members of the band are closest to the strongest. Some of the childless mature females are in oestrus; these usually walk close by the males who are their temporary consorts. A younger or smaller male may proceed ahead of the main body, or move parallel to its line of march on one side, at a separation of as much as half a mile. If in front, he is seemingly scouting out the route, but he frequently glances back and is probably taking his cues from the dominant males—sometimes the main body veers off at an angle and the scout has to skedaddle to get in front again. If outside trouble is encountered, the big males immediately move towards it. Their standard location at the center is no mark of cowardice, but strategic, since they are there approximately equidistant from all the boundaries where difficulties may develop.

THE SCHEDULING OF OTHER ACTIVITIES

× Sleeping at night, eating and fixed-order marching during the day, form a framework into which all other baboon activities must be fitted.

Elimination poses no problem. Whilst in the trees, baboons behave like arboreal monkeys, relieving themselves as the need arises and letting gravity take over. This can be inferred from the early-morning location of excrement; the animals easily avoid it as they climb down, and it is soon disposed of by dung beetles. During the day, the band covers a large area so that no special measures need be taken. Urination is completely uninhibited. If the band is on the move, defecation requires only a momentary halt for the individual, too brief to disrupt the order of march.

Other activities are conducted during the daytime rests, for though eating and drinking are the main reasons for the pauses they do not completely fill them. During a pause the spatial pattern of the march blurs or disappears. They sit by ones, twos, or fews, and feed. The older infants and younger juveniles congregate in small groups and play, often seeking out the friends with whom they have played before. There are minor squabbles, sometimes stopped by older band members if they threaten to become serious. Pregnant females at term drop their young. Pairs, occasionally trios, indulge in grooming. Adult males and oestrous females pair off and copulate. It is unlikely that any of these things ordinarily happen at night in the trees. Any of them may go on during any daytime pause. There is, however, some tendency for grooming to concentrate in the three principal rest periods (early morning, noon, and evening), and for copulation to be most frequent in the morning.

Grooming is done with hands and mouth, the hands pushing furrows through the hair of the groomed animal and either a hand or the mouth removing foreign objects; these are often swallowed. Everybody grooms everybody, but not with equal frequency or intensity. Among adults, females are groomers oftener than males are, and the grooming of a female usually continues for longer at a time. The most frequent pairing is two adult females. A mother with an infant is especially attractive to other females, and the infant may then get some of the attention too. Indeed, for the first two or three months an infant gets interested attention from everyone, though systematic grooming is mainly the mother's responsibility. The next commonest arrangement is the grooming of an adult female, especially one in oestrus, by an adult male. Older infants sometimes groom their mothers, but mainly they and the younger juveniles pair off, blending grooming with play.

ROLES BY SEX AND AGE ✖   INFANCY

From the fourth through the twelfth month of life, while the young baboon is still mostly riding on his mother's back and is still being suckled (with decreasing frequency), he moves around more and more on his own during pauses. At first he stays close to his mother and feeds in parallel with her; possibly he is learning what and how to eat and what to avoid. He explores the environment by picking up sticks or stones, sometimes carrying one for a while in hand or mouth. He may approach any band member with a touch, a slap, or an attempt to groom. Even the adult males tolerate this. Soon, however, such approaches are made mainly to his approximate age mates. Startled or threatened, he runs to his mother for protection, and she may run to offer it.

By the end of the year the pattern is changing. Adult females other than the mother become hostile to the older infant; if they threaten or attack him his squeals bring the mother or an adult male to his aid. Before long the mother, too, though not becoming actively hostile, ceases to be receptive, refusing to suckle him and increasingly disinclined to carry him (perhaps he is simply getting too heavy). By at latest fifteen months he is completely weaned, is walking on his own when the band is on the march, is seeking companionship mainly from age mates, and is running for safety not to the mother but to the handiest adult male.

THE JUVENILE STAGE

These changes constitute the transition from infant to juvenile. There is no discernible difference between the treatment of male and of female infants, and as juveniles the two sexes participate in age-mate play groups on equal footing. The juvenile group coheres during the march, and its members tend to stay together while feeding.

It seems likely that the play groupings involve, and help to develop, specific friendships and animosities that sometimes survive as the young grow up: a baboon can sustain a friendship or nurse a grudge for a long time. This is not certain, but is suggested by the ways in which adults treat each other: acts of friendship and of animosity do not seem always to be the result of immediate circumstances.

EARLY MATURITY

A female leaves her play group at or shortly after menarche, and a male leaves at about the same age. The former moves into a grooming cluster of adult females, ready now to accept her full share of adult responsibilities.

The male, on the other hand, on the verge of puberty but still too small to be able to do anything about it, enters into a phase of his life that must be as tough to take as is the comparable phase in the life of the average middle-class male human being in Western culture. With their increasing size, and other changes, the maturing males become unacceptable to the younger members of juvenile play groups. Their play participation becomes too rough and dangerous, and full-grown males may have to intervene to prevent injury. But the adult males themselves will not accept the subadult males as companions, and will not allow them access to the mature females. The subadult males become the young punks, treated with disdain and dislike and developing plenty of hostility of their own. Only to a limited extent do they associate even with one another. Their lives are as lonely as a baboon's life can be. It may be this that leads them on occasion to move so far away from the rest of the band when it is on the march, where they play the collectively useful role of scouts (p. 39).

ADULT FEMALES

The duty of adult females is to become pregnant, bear infants, and care for them. The oestral cycle is interrupted by pregnancy and its resumption may be delayed by lactation, so that, with no sexual swelling, the female during this interval is not a target for copulation. The privileged status of a mother with an infant (p. 40) disappears as the infant moves from her charge to join a peer play group. Beyond this, little is yet known about the social relationships of adult females with one another.

Adult Males

We have seen something of the behavior of mature males vis-à-vis juveniles, infants, and subadult males; let us now see how they deal with one another.

It is reported that among the hamadryas baboons of Ethiopia (Figure 3-1, p. 33) a band includes just one full-grown male, so that there are no such dealings. But among the chacmas and olives there are usually several per band. There is considerable flexibility in the resulting social arrangements. In some bands, for some intervals, one of the adult males is clearly the most powerful. That he is not invariably the undisputed leader results from the incidence of special friendships and cooperation. Two smaller mature males may form a sort of cabal: neither could individually overrule the wishes of the biggest male, but jointly they can.

Our observers report an interesting case of a change of pattern, which is also the only case observed in detail of an outsider joining a band. The band, numbering about forty, was watched in Nairobi Park, Kenya; we designate the males by the names given them by the observers. The oldest was Gam; Curly and Humbert were younger; Lip and Rink smaller. Gam, despite worn-down canines, could lick or outface Curly in a direct confrontation; Curly was similarly dominant over Humbert; and Humbert over Gam. But Curly and Humbert enlisted each other's aid, and, as a pair, were the leaders. One morning Humbert was missing. At about the same time, Lone, a subordinate male of a neighboring band, vanished. The disappearances were unrelated and, as we shall see (p. 44), totally unmysterious. Surprisingly, Lone did not vanish without trace, but turned up later hovering around the edges of the band from which Humbert had disappeared, behaving much like a subadult male. Slowly he worked his way closer to the core (also the pattern for the subadult who is finally getting big enough), and presently a new dominance arrangement had emerged: Gam and Lone as duarchs, with Curly displaced down towards Lip and Rink.

The only unusual feature of this episode is the arrival of the outsider. Given the inexorability of aging and the inevitability of death, readjustments necessarily occur from time to time. An aging leader does not inevitably struggle to thwart the efforts of ambitious younger animals to displace him. To the contrary: an occasional elderly and nearly toothless male was observed who, to all appearances, had been happy to relinquish his responsibilities to younger aspirants and spend the rest of his days in quiet contemplation.

Within a band there is a good deal of quarreling, pestering, threatening, and other manifestations of hostility, including occasional combat. Except perhaps when food is very scarce, the only obvious occasion for a direct conflict of interest is when two adult males both want access to the same female. But most fighting is not in this context. It goes on usually when there are *not* any immediate vital issues. Thus it serves to establish, to reinforce, and occasionally to restructure the dominance hierarchy so that when a real contretemps arises the order of priorities is already clear and the difficulty can be handled without fresh friction and delay.

SEXUAL BEHAVIOR

× Only the fully mature males participate in sexual activity. Of them, the one or two most dominant preempt the females as they reach the peak of their oestrous cycles.

A dominant male and such a female will form a consort pair and keep close company for a few days, during which the female is not usually available to any other male. The subordinate mature males have to settle for the females who have not yet reached the oestral maximum or have passed beyond it. Conception is most likely close to the peak of the cycle. Thus, although all adult males may copulate with all the mature females, the probability is that most infants are sired by the most dominant. This is perhaps of survival importance for the band and for the species.

Although band members recognize one another as individuals (p. 70), there is no way in which a baboon father could identify his own children, and it is unlikely that half siblings (offspring of the same mother) are aware of their relationship. It is quite possible that a female continues to recognize and to be recognized by her own child as long as both live. This is a necessary condition for the avoidance of intercourse between mother and son. We do not know that it is avoided, but it may be. Until recently, such matters were not investigated for nonhuman primates because it was blithely assumed that only human beings have incest prohibitions. Now we are not so sure.

The copulatory position, as apparently for all monkeys (not for apes: p. 68) is exclusively that of the dorsal approach and mounting. A female invites a male by "presenting": crouching with rump towards the male, lifting the tail, and glancing over the shoulder to see if the male is approaching. If the male approaches, he sometimes just grooms or sniffs instead of mounting; mounting does not invariably lead to intromission; intromission does not always lead to ejaculation. A single mounting lasts from ten to twenty seconds. Males mount, and females are mounted, as often as twenty or thirty times per day. The copulation of a particular pair normally takes the form of a series of mountings at intervals during the day, but the spacing shows regional variation. In the Cape groups, about two minutes intervened between the successive mountings of a series, probably with only the last of the series ending with ejaculation; in Nairobi Park, the intervals were thirty minutes or longer, but almost every mounting achieved ejaculation.

✘ Our observers attempted to note, tabulate, and describe the various recurrent actions that seemed to be specialized for communication. One list includes fourteen vocal signals, thirty-two signals consisting of some sort of body motion, and sixteen different ways in which one animal touches another. Most of these are used in most bands. Two points merit mention.

COMMUNICATION

(1) Many signals resemble actions performed "for real," except for some modification or truncation. For example, a threat gesture of a male baboon consists of opening the mouth wide and tilting the head back so that the long and dangerous canines are in full view (note the male in the background in Figure 3-2, p. 34). This is something like the motion involved in an actual attack with the teeth. A real attack follows the gesture only rarely. The gesture differs somewhat from the best position preparatory for a real attack: the eyebrows are raised, exposing the whites of the eyes against the dark surrounding hair and helping to make the gesture unambiguous to him against whom it is directed. The real attack would be more sneaky.

Again, as a sign of submissiveness to another male, a male often uses a bodily gesture and posture like the female's act of presenting to invite sexual attention. The male thus addressed sometimes acknowledges the message and reaffirms his dominance by briefly mounting the submissive male. This makes the pattern of dominance of one adult male over another somewhat resemble that of adult males over females.

(2)   We think of monkeys as chattering as noisily as we ourselves do. One of the most surprising things about baboons is the extent to which they conduct their complex affairs in silence. To be sure, there are vocal signals, but they are used rarely. A rest period of several hours, with feeding, moving about, play, copulation, and all sorts of other activities, may be marked by no vocal sound at all.

The noisiest primates (except for ourselves) are those that live in trees. They cannot see one another, which makes visual signaling less useful, and their lofty positions afford safety against ground predators who may be attracted by the racket. In the savannas where the baboons live, both of these factors are exactly reversed.

ILLNESS AND DEATH   ✗ The welfare of the individual baboon rests totally on his participation in the collective behavior of the band. As long as he or she stays with the community there is protection against serious harm, though a less dominant animal sometimes has to put up with considerable abuse.

But there is one situation in which no baboon except a very young infant can count on help from others. Monkeys are fine hosts for all the bacterial and invertebrate parasites that thrive on man. A baboon that gets sick, or receives a crippling injury, has to fend for himself. The band will not wait when it is time to move, and will not slow its pace. An infant is lost if too weak to cling to the mother.

As regards sickness, this behavior is beneficial for the band, which is thus removed from a possible source of infection. Moreover, the mechanism constantly weeds out the congenitally weak, thus guarding the gene pool against deterioration.

In most of this, baboons resemble other monkeys and apes.

When sick or injured, the average monkey or ape seeks a protected spot, preferably a cave or a hollow where there is a trickle of moisture and where predators cannot easily follow, and sweats it out. If he dies, he dies. If he recovers, he tries to rejoin his fellows.

Baboons may sometimes do this, but what has been most often observed is a handicapped animal trying to drag himself along with the moving band and falling ever farther behind. That is what the lions, hyenas, jackals, and wild dogs are waiting for. A really powerful adult male may occasionally survive the ordeal; the rare transfer of a male from one band to another may begin with a separation of this sort. Eventually, however, this is the way of death for all baboons. The animal isolated out of the trees one day is gone by the morning of the next.

4

✕

WHY DO ORGANISMS BEHAVE AS THEY DO?

Our description of baboons in the preceding chapter will help us be realistic, and our characterization of the Menomini in chapter 2 will keep us from too narrow a conception of what it means to be human, as we begin now to consider the following two of our fundamental questions (p. 3, here slightly rephrased): How are human beings like other animals? How are they different?

In this chapter and the next two we deal with the first question; the point is to avoid claiming as an exclusive human prerogative anything that in fact is not. In the ensuing two chapters (7 and 8) we take up the second question, thus beginning to zero in on man's uniqueness.

✕ The terminology we are about to introduce is only one of many that could be used; for our purposes it has certain advantages (p. 47 below).

SCHEDULING

The Dwelling Pattern

At any one instant an animal is in a *place*. As time passes, some animals (*sessile* ones, all aquatic) stay in the same place, whereas all others (*motile* animals) move around within some region. The size of the region, relative to that of the animal, depends on the kind of animal, but is rarely great: many a housefly, for example, spends its entire life within the confines of a single room.

The total area covered by the peregrinations of a motile animal is only part of the story. One must consider also the amount of time spent at each spot. The golden plover of Alaska, a migratory bird, winters in Hawaii, so that twice a year it covers a long distance. But most of its life is spent at one or the other terminus of the migratory route, where it moves around over only a small area.

If we watch an animal briefly, its movements are apt to seem random. To some extent they are. The motions of no material body allow absolutely precise prediction, and organisms are more capricious in this respect than are inert hunks of matter. The flight of a bird is harder to predict than that of a hurled stone. But animal movements are not completely random. There is patterning, discernible if one watches long and carefully enough.

Consider a pair of robins who have mated and nested in the springtime. The nest is the base of operations. They spend most of their time there, because they sleep in or near the nest and the female broods her eggs there. The male leaves the nest, at certain times each day, in search of food, some of which he may take back to the female, though she occasionally leaves the eggs to forage for herself. These flights rarely carry the bird more than a hundred feet or so from the nest. Before mating and nesting the pattern was different, and when the eggs have hatched it will change, but for an interval of a week or two each day's activities and motions follow roughly the same plan. This plan, appropriate for the brooding season, is one of a series of plans that succeed one another to form the yearly cycle. Also, for any one bird, it is one of a series that together forms the typical life cycle, one version for the male, a partly different one for the female.

The total plan of location and peregrination of any one animal constitutes what we shall call the *dwelling pattern* of that animal.

The Rest of Scheduling

A dwelling pattern can be thought of as a more or less complicated underlying *schedule* for the actual locations and peregrinations of the animal. But the schedule consists of more than just the dwelling pattern. It includes the relative timing of everything the animal does—not only how and when it moves from place to place (this is the dwelling-pattern part) but also what activity it carries on at any one place or while in motion. The robin's schedule moves him from the nest at dawn; when he lights on the ground the schedule provides for him to look and listen for worms and to grab them in his beak and pull them out of the earth when they are found.

Any animal's schedule supplies leeway and alternatives. An overly rigid schedule would preclude survival. The robin's schedule does not specify whether a particular foraging flight is to be to the north or the east; windage and inbuilt randomness settle that. If the robin finds no worm at a particular spot, he hops along and tries another. Scheduling is loose, probabilistic, and contingent.

Distinctive and Nondistinctive

An animal's scheduling determines, in a general way, the nature and timing of its encounters with inanimate things, with organisms of other species, and with other animals of its own species. From the animal's point of view, its scheduling constitutes a set of *expectations* about its actions, their ordering, their probable results, and appropriate responses to outside stimuli. Of course the unexpected, even the catastrophic, sometimes happens—no scheduling can provide for all contingencies.

By virtue of an animal's expectations many physical differences are ignored. An animal obviously cannot respond to differences which its sensory apparatus is incapable of detecting, but that merely sets an outer limit. A robin's senses are surely such that it can tell the difference between a worm here and a worm there. But for the foraging robin, a worm here and a worm there are both worms; a worm in the ground and a cherry in a tree are both food.

Borrowing a term from linguistics, we shall describe such customarily ignored differences as *nondistinctive*. Other differences (*distinctive* ones for the particular animal in its setting of the moment) are heeded. This female brooding on this nest and that female on that nest are not interchangeable. This one is mine, and if instead I fly to that one she will chase me away. Thus, in the perception of any one animal, scheduling *structures the world* in a particular way.

This superimposed structuring is related to the actual physical structure of the world, but is not the same thing, and clearly it differs for different kinds of animals. Among human beings (and perhaps more than we usually realize among animals of certain other species) it also differs more or less from one community to another.[1]

The Utility of the Scheduling Terminology

Scheduling affords a convenient way of organizing one's information about a particular animal or animal community. The reader will recognize that it was so used in our characterizations of the Menomini and of baboons. The scheduling framework forces one to try to locate each kind of behavior in place, time, and circumstance. Thus it brings matters together that belong together (and, incidentally, reveals gaps in one's information).

As a frame of reference, scheduling helps us avoid teleological pseudoexplanations of events. When we ask a fellow human being why he did something, the answer is often "because I wanted to" (or more complicated words to that effect). There is no denying that some of the actions of organisms are goal-directed. The "wanting to" is nevertheless not an explanation; it is simply another bit of scheduled behavior (pp. 83–85).

However, we do want to think of scheduling as explanatory rather than merely as a descriptive convenience. We want to assert that an animal behaves in a certain way in such-and-such circumstances *because* it is scheduled to.

For us to use the term in this way it is necessary that an animal's schedule be a physical reality. It resides partly in the animal: in its genes, its central nervous system (if any) and accumulated experience, and the rest of its structure; and partly in the environment: in the natural cyclicities of day and night, of the seasons, and of other organisms, and in such constants as the gravity field.

Used thus, though the scheduling terminology enables one to set down the known facts even when one does not know the exact lines of causality that have brought them about, at the same time it forcibly reminds one that there *are* real physical causes and hints at what they may be.

For example, consider the regional differences in the timing of copulation among baboons (p. 43). We say the baboons of a particular region are scheduled to copulate with a certain spacing and rhythm. This asserts that the phenomenon is not a whimsical fact in an arbitrarily disjointed universe, but causally related to other matters. Are genetic differences responsible for the regional differences? Or do different

[1]We use the term "community," here and later, to denote any cluster of organisms of a single species that live together. This is an extension of its sense in anthropology. Ecologists use the same word to denote all the organisms of *all* species that live in a particular region and affect one another's lives.

baboon communities pass down different customs? Or partly each? That is not yet known, and the scheduling terminology reminds us of our ignorance.

We need not dwell on the environmental constants that play a part in scheduling. Any organism too large to be borne by air currents will fall if dropped from a height. That is a regularity of scheduling, but hardly a *biological* fact: a stone will fall too, and an organism falls because it is made of matter, not because it is alive.

We do need to treat in more detail of those scheduling mechanisms that are uniquely biological and either universal or widespread. There are two: *genetics* and *tradition*.

GENETICS ✖ In a general way, we know that an important part of the scheduling of any organism—animal or other—is supplied by genetic material.

All organisms are composed of structural units called *cells*. Most organisms begin as single cells. Some (for example, bacteria and amoebae) remain unicellular. In others, the original cell grows and divides and redivides until there are many: a newborn human infant consists of about 26,000,000,000,000 cells. In most organisms, most cells include a *nucleus*, and it is in this that the genetic material is to be found.[2]

Every organism begins its life with a specific allotment of genes inherited from its parent or parents. These supply neither the necessary energy nor the required matter for growth, metabolism, and behavior; they simply *direct* the utilization of energy and the shipping-around and chemical conversion of matter. Any physical structure that performs this sort of function may be described as carrying *information* (chapter 6).

Gene Structure and Action

We know a little of how genes act. A gene is a molecule of ribonucleic acid (RNA) or of deoxyribonucleic acid (DNA), or (more often) a segment of such a molecule. It is composed of a string of parts called nucleotides. There are five chemically distinct nucleotides: four of them occur in RNA, a different four in DNA. The specificity of a gene is the linear sequence in which nucleotides of the different types are arranged in the string—just as the specificity of a written word is the linear sequence of its letters, so that "EVIL", "VILE", "LIVE", "VEIL", and "LEVI" are all different even though just the same letters appear in them. There are some constraints on possible arrangements, but the strings are sufficiently long that an exceedingly large number of chemically distinct genes are theoretically possible, a number far larger than the number of elementary particles in the observable universe.

[2]Exceptions, for the record: Viruses, though composed of genetic material, are not cellular (but many biologists prefer to say they are not alive, hence not organisms). Some plants can be grown from (multi-cellular) root or stem cuttings. Bacterial cells and those of blue-green algae have genetic material but no nuclei. Some plants and some protozoa, all with nuclei, have also genetic material ("plasmagenes") outside the nuclei; maybe other organisms do too, not yet recognized by investigators. In some multicellular organisms certain types of cells lose their nuclei, and genes, upon maturity: e.g., the red blood cells of mammals.

Part of the information carried by any gene is about its own structure. When the environing conditions are right, as they are periodically, every gene directs the synthesis of a replica of itself. The process is complicated, and occasionally "noisy": that is, something happens so that the replication is not exact. Any such change is a (*gene*) *mutation*. There are also mutations that affect not the structure of an individual gene but its location and orientation relative to others.

Otherwise, the specificity of a gene shows up in the way it controls nearby chemical reactions. Complicated protein molecules called *enzymes* are synthesized in cell nuclei under the direction of the genes; these pass out of the nucleus and in their turn govern other chemical reactions, so that the organism metabolizes, grows, and behaves in a particular way.

Genes and Environment

However, the action of a specific gene depends on its environment, including other genes. Likewise, the action of the total allotment of genetic material in any one cell depends on its changing environment in that cell.

The career of an organism is thus the result of the interplay between the regulating action of the genetic material and the totality of the organism's environment, including all the other organisms of the same species in whose company the organism may find itself.

That the action of the genetic material depends on its milieu is made clear in the growth of any multicellular organism. As the organism grows, most of the cells inherit exactly the genetic material of the original single cell. Yet they come to be organized into a variety of tissues with remarkably diverse structures and functions.

That the career of a whole organism is only monitored by its genes, not absolutely determined thereby, is also abundantly clear. One example will serve. The deciduous perennial woody shrub that we call a "hydrangea" and grow because its flowers are large and pretty bears sometimes blue blossoms and sometimes pink ones. It would be difficult, if not impossible, to breed selectively for one or the other color, because it depends in the first instance not on the genes but on whether the soil is acid or alkaline.

Above the level of the single organism is the *population*: a more or less localized group of organisms of a single species whose pattern of reproduction passes down its own genes from generation to generation, the exchange of genes with other populations being relatively rare. A grove of maple trees is a population if it is far enough removed from other maple trees to prevent the arrival of much wind-blown pollen from elsewhere. The Menomini only occasionally intermarried with other tribes, and hence constituted a population. Each baboon band is a separate population, the necessary conditions for exchange of genes arising seldom (p. 42). Whether the members of a population interact other than in reproduction, and, if so, how, depends on the species. The genes of a whole population constitute its *gene pool*. Like the career of a single organism, the history of a population can be viewed as the result of the interplay between its gene pool and the population's total environment.

Since any organism inherits its genes from its parent or parents, offspring are always fairly much like their parents, and the members of any single population of a species tend to resemble one another.

On the other hand, an offspring is rarely *exactly* like a parent. One reason is that in most species there is an inbuilt randomness as to just which of a parent's genes are passed on to any one offspring; thus (as everyone knows) two brown-eyed human parents, if their own genes are the proper assortment, may have both brown-eyed and blue-eyed children. A second reason is mutations (p. 49), which may take place at any time. The result is that perhaps no two organisms in the world are *absolutely* identical genetically (one-egg twins may be an exception).

Viewing a population at any one time, we know, then, that genetics is one of the mechanisms responsible both for similarity and for diversity. If our concern is with what happens to the population as time passes (as it will be especially in chapter 23), we see, in the same way, that genetics is a mechanism both of *continuity* and of *change.*

DEGREES OF PERSISTENCE

Some genetic effects are more persistent than others, in the sense that they manifest themselves in virtually any environment in which the organism can survive at all.

A human example will serve. The Sherpas have lived for a very long time high in the Himalayas. Human beings face various problems at high altitudes: especially, the air is thin and its oxygen content lower than nearer to sea level. The Sherpas apparently carry a genetic adaptation to low air pressure and oxygen content. The oxygen is used more efficiently inside the separate cells of the body than it is by us lowland-dwellers. Recently some Sherpas have moved down from the higher mountains to settle in and near Darjeeling. Investigators are not yet certain, but they think that Sherpa children conceived and born at the lower altitudes retain this intracellular efficiency of oxygen-utilization. In other words, the genetic effect is "locked in": it does not require to be released by environmental factors that pertain only at extreme altitudes.

In contrast, consider the genetic adaptation of various groups of Quechuas to the heights of the Andes. Quechua children conceived and born in the mountains develop large chests and capacious lungs. Quechua genes provide for this (as European genes typically do not), but do not force it. Among highland Quechua families that have settled along the coastal plains, the children do not show the hypertrophy.

GENES AND BEHAVIOR

It is patent that genes play a role in the scheduling of behavior. Baboon genes make baboons; human genes make humans; baboons do not (and cannot) behave like humans, nor vice versa.

How about such a subtle intraspecies difference as that in the spacing and rhythm of copulation among baboon bands in different parts of Africa? We do not ask here whether this *is* primarily genetic, only whether in principle it *could* be, and the answer is clearly affirmative.

Let us illustrate first with a case in which the role of the genetic factor is partly known. We turn from baboons to certain of our remote hominoid cousins (p. 57): the orangutans of Sumatra and Borneo. Orangutans build complicated nests in the trees, sometimes several per day. An infant orang, taken away from its mother very shortly after birth and raised away from its kind, starts building nests at a certain age. If such an infant is isolated in the wild, his nests are soon pretty satisfactory. If he is in a cage, with no proper raw materials, the results aren't very good, but he persists in going through the motions as best he can anyway. Clearly, then, orangutan genes carry something of importance for nest-building. So much is forced on us, however abysmal our ignorance of the biochemical details.

That does not mean, of course, that orang nest-building is *solely* genetic. To make that inference we should have to have gathered evidence of another sort. Thus (as a pure guess), it might be that the young become effective nest-builders much more quickly under the guidance of their elders than in isolation. Or (another guess) there may be local variations and short-term changes in style of nest-building, largely or wholly not genetic, superimposed on the genetic substrate.

Returning to baboons, note that to test the balance of genetic and nongenetic components in their copulatory practices we might try to switch some infants between bands whose practices are different. It is not at all clear that this could be managed. Baboons past infancy show such high specificity of response to other members of their own bands that an intrusive infant might just be destroyed or ejected. But suppose it could be done. Then the sexual comportment of the adopted baboon, when it had matured, would bear testimony to the relative importance of its genes, inherited from its ancestral band, and of its upbringing in the bosom of its adoptive band.

✗ Without genes there would be neither continuity nor change in the life of any population of organisms, for the simple reason that there would be no organisms. Genes are the basic stuff of life. Thus, the genetic mechanism of continuity and change is just exactly as widespread as life itself.

But it is not the only such mechanism. There is a second, perhaps not universal but shared at least by a very large number of animal species: *tradition*. To characterize this adequately we must work up to it in steps.

LEARNING

No animal can behave in a way forbidden by its genes or precluded by the structure whose development its genes have directed. A human being cannot digest cellulose like a cow or wave his tail like a dog. But the genes always leave some leeway, and any animal—perhaps any organism—may come to manifest regularities of behavior that are not even indirectly the result of gene action. We say in such a case that the animal has acquired the behavioral pattern by *learning*.

The genes help set limits as to what an animal *can* learn; what it *does* learn depends

TRADITION

on its environment. A mynah bird has the genetically bestowed capacity to pick up, and then to repeat at intervals, any of a wide variety of sound patterns, including those of animal calls and of short phrases in a human language. But, of course, a particular mynah bird does not utter what sounds to us like *Good morning!* unless it has been exposed to that particular acoustic pattern under the right circumstances.

By what sort of experience does an animal learn? Let us watch an experiment. Investigators put a hungry earthworm at the bottom end of a simple maze shaped like a T, and place a bit of favorite earthworm food at the end of one of the two arms. If the worm turns the right way when it reaches the crossbar, it gets the food; if it turns the wrong way it goes hungry. In the earliest trials, the worm's turns, if not random, at least show no correlation with the location of the food. After enough successive runs, it turns towards the food more often than the other way.

The paradigm here is *trial and error*, in which a particular behavioral pattern is *reinforced* by success, or is *weakened* by failure. The presence of human investigators is obviously not necessary. Any animal, driven by such recurrent factors as hunger, runs "mazes" supplied by its environment. The details vary from species to species and, for a single animal, from one period of life to another. An earthworm learns a T maze very slowly. At the opposite extreme, certain animals, at certain points in their lives, can acquire certain learned habits in a *single* successful trial.

INFORMATION AND ITS STORAGE

Our next step is a slight detour whose relevance will appear shortly.

We said on page 48 that genes can be described as carrying information. Information is simply recurrent or enduring *specificity*—the opposite or absence of randomness. If two physical systems have the same specificity of structure, they will manifest the same specificities of behavior. Within somewhat shaky limits, we can also infer, from the fact that two physical systems behave in similar ways, that they are similar in structure. In any case, if an organism does the same thing more than once, the specificity of the recurrent behavior forces us to infer an enduring specificity of structure—in the organism, in its environment, or partly in each.

Any stable or meta-stable spatial array of matter is stored information. The converse is also true: it is impossible to store information except by coding it into some sort of stable spatial array. Genes fully meet this requirement. At a larger size-level, any *hard* thing meets it. All the hard or tough and relatively durable parts of an organism are thus stored information of one sort or another. For example, the skeleton of a vertebrate develops under the guidance of the genes, but it is then the skeleton that "remembers" the general shape of the whole animal. If the animal breaks a bone, information has been lost: the bone may not heal properly.[3]

[3]The value of old bones and teeth to the palaeontologist is that they still contain much of the information they carried for their original owners; and it is just because of the striking durability of this type of information storage that bones and teeth are more likely to survive than are an animal's softer parts.

The Storage of Learned Behavior

Whether a particular behavioral pattern be innate or learned, information about it has to be stored somewhere within the animal. The innate patterns are coded in the genes. Where are acquired patterns laid down?

Remember that we are speaking of *specificities* of behavior. A prizefighter develops strong arm muscles. So does a concert pianist. The bodily change is brought about by either kind of training, and is essential for both activities, but is specific to neither. The prizefighter cannot, merely by virtue of his training for boxing, play the piano; nor the other way around. Furthermore, if something happens to a concert pianist's arms and hands so that he can no longer use them, there is a sense in which he still "knows how" to play. That know-how cannot reside in the deteriorated or missing muscles.

We think next of the central nervous system, especially of the brain. Within limits, that is the right answer. But three points must be noted:

(1) Some animals have no brains, and not even any specialized nervous tissue; yet they learn (p. 84).

(2) A nervous system functions to *transmit* information from one part of an animal's body to another, and to *process* the information in such a way that the actions of different parts of the body are coordinated. A circulatory system does some of this too (distributing chemical messages in the form of hormones), but the nervous system is the great specialist in information-transmission and -processing. Its function in information-storage is an addition to that.

(3) Some of the information stored in a nervous system is laid down by gene action. Only the capacity not so used is available for the recording of learned behavior patterns.

We know something of how nerves transmit information. We know little or nothing as to how they store it. Most hypotheses about this have been disproved. Recently, various experiments have converged towards the proposal that the basic unit of memory in a nervous system is the same as the basic genetic unit: a coded molecule of nucleic acid. Even if this is true, it does not mean that such a memory unit is a gene. Genes have the special property that they are passed (by replication) from one generation to the next intact except for occasional mutations. Coded nucleic acids in nervous tissue are not replicated and passed on any more than is the strength of a muscle acquired by exercise. Whatever is learned by parents vanishes with them; if their offspring acquire the same habits they have been learned afresh. That is what is meant by the *noninheritability of acquired characteristics*.

Brains

Human beings are primates; primates are mammals; mammals are vertebrates. Not all animals have brains, but all vertebrates do. The brains of mammals differ from those of other vertebrates, except birds, in the large size of the *cerebral hemispheres*. These consist of white tissue, the corpus striatum, with an outer layer of gray matter, the pallium or *cerebral cortex*. In birds the inner white matter is enlarged; in mammals it is the cortex that shows increased thickness and area. Among primates (and for a scattering of other mammals) the area is further increased by *convolutions*, a wrinkling and folding of the surface.

It seems almost beyond doubt that the cortex is a specialized organ of information-storage. It also seems that it is especially adapted for the storage of *learned* patterns, relatively little of the information in it being laid down by direct order of the genes. Finally, it appears that in a general way a larger cortex has room for more information than a smaller one. However, this last point is borne out only when we compare the cortexes of different species. For a single species, variations of brain or cortex mass from one individual to another seem to have, within very wide limits, no bearing on the individual's learning capacity. Thus, the difference between (for example) chimpanzee and human brains is not *just* that the latter are larger. There must be more subtle differences too.

Brains are metabolically expensive. At birth, the average human brain accounts for over 12% of the total body mass; at maturity, this has been reduced to 2%, but the brain still requires about 10% of the total blood supply. The brain-body mass ratios of other mammals are mostly much smaller, but the metabolic cost is nevertheless notable.

How does such a costly organ earn its keep?—especially since, at birth, the cortex is largely empty of any useful information?

For many animals, the initially unused capacity would be of no value at all. The newly hatched fish, amphibian, or reptile is on its own. Unless it has inherited, through the genes, the right responses to environment, or can acquire suitable ones very quickly without any guidance from more mature members of its species, it dies. There is little leeway for learning. But the newborn mammal goes through a period during which it is nourished by its mother and protected, by her or others, from serious environmental harm. There is more leisure for the learning of appropriate adult ways, and therefore a greater capacity can be not merely tolerable but actively advantageous.

Adults as Maze-Builders

We are close to tradition, but a few steps must still be taken before we reach it.

Suppose an individual animal devises, through trial-and-error learning, a better way of doing something members of his species need to do. This can have no relevance for his community or his species unless there is some mechanism by which the new pattern can be passed on to others. Genes won't do this. Although what an animal does determines whether or not some of his genes are passed on, it has no effect on the detailed structure of the genetic material: recall the noninheritability of acquired characteristics (p. 53).

What is required, then, is a state of affairs of the following sort. The genetically scheduled early behavior of the infant must be to some extent random, varied, and imprecise. Those about the infant must be scheduled to behave vis-à-vis the infant in such ways that certain patterns of activity on his part are rewarded and hence reinforced, whereas others are punished and in time extinguished. Furthermore, the distribution of approval and discouragement by those about the infant must correlate with the extent to which his actions, on a particular occasion, resemble or deviate from the programmed patterns of adult behavior in comparable circumstances. Each of these factors is necessary. If the infant's behavior is already stereotyped, he cannot learn. If those about him do not perform their conditioning roles correctly, the infant will learn the wrong things.

Every mammalian mother heeds the foregoing precepts of child care insofar as the infants of her species require supplementation through learning of what their genes have supplied. A mother house cat noses her brood back towards their nest if they are wandering too far, and cuffs them gently with a paw when they misbehave. Among the more gregarious mammals, additional members of the community in time take part in infant training.

Maternal Effects, Teaching, and Tradition

Finally we must ask: when the infant is suitably flexible, and when the comportment of its mentors is right, what is it that schedules the relevant performance of the mentors? Is it primarily their genes or their own training?

When the genes are predominantly responsible, then the pattern acquired by the infant is in a sense genetic, though due to the genes of some other individual—usually the mother—rather than to its own. Clearcut cases of this are known as "maternal effects."

But when the conditioning behavior of the mentors was itself acquired largely by training from earlier mentors, whose conditioning behavior was likewise largely the result of training, and so on back indefinitely, then we call the conditioning behavior *teaching*, and call the mechanism *tradition* (or *culture*).[4]

THE INTERPLAY OF GENETICS AND TRADITION

× Tradition, then, is the biological mechanism of continuity and change that has appeared, as an addition to the genetic mechanism, among some birds and many mammals, especially among primates. We are probably right in believing that it reaches its acme in man, but we should be wrong to assume that it is exclusively human.

From the point of view of genetics, tradition is part of the environment. From the point of view of tradition, genetics is part of the environment. In the frame of reference of scheduling, genetics and tradition—wherever the latter as well as the former is operative—are simply two mechanisms of continuity and change, functioning vis-à-vis that which is environmental for both in governing behavior.

[4]The latter term is preferred by anthropologists when speaking of human beings. I shall use both, but mainly the former, since the word *culture* has acquired an embarrassingly ambiguous diversity of meanings in anthropological usage. For example, one common habit of anthropologists (when off their guard) is to *contrast* the "cultural" and the "biological." This is inevitably misleading. All aspects of the behavior of organisms are biological, by definition. The mechanism we have described in the text, be it called "tradition" or "cultural transmission" or something else, is just as biological as is the genetic mechanism.

Tradition plays a part in the scheduling of the behavior of any species that possesses the mechanism. Among migratory waterfowl, for example, in the opinion of many ornithologists, knowledge of the flightpath is passed down via tradition. Fledglings do not know it. They learn it on their first round-trip migration, during which they are guided by the older birds that have made the migration before. If a fledgling tarries too far behind the flock, he can reach the proper terminus only by sheer luck.

Note that in this case the teaching behavior of the older birds is no special activity: they teach the migratory route merely by flying it, and the young learn it by flying along. In other cases, perhaps especially among primates, some adult behavior is *specialized* for teaching, not achieving any other goal at the same time.

In species for which tradition is strong and genetics leaves ample flexibility, tradition can bring about an adaptation of a community's ways of life to changed environmental circumstances much more rapidly than can genetics. The effect of a favorable mutation, or of a fortunate recombination of genes, can spread through a population only at a rate determined by the length of the interval between generations. The spread of a new fashion by teaching and learning is not constrained to that periodicity. It is true that, for the most part, the young learn from the old, but this is not inevitable: among human beings, at least, an old man or woman may learn something from a child. Obviously this potentiality of more rapid accommodation to changing environmental demands bestows great survival value both on tradition and on the genes that yield the structures that make tradition possible.

Within limits, tradition can even overrule genetics. Today a girl's eyes may appear blue either because of or despite her genes, since she may be concealing brown irises under tinted contact lenses. And the mechanism of tradition allows the "inheritance of acquired characteristics" that the nature of the genetic mechanism precludes (p. 53). Several thousand years of circumcision have not altered Jewish genes: males are still born with foreskins. Yet for several thousand years the adult Jewish male has had none!

5

✗

WHY DO PRIMATES BEHAVE AS THEY DO?

PRIME MATES

Lost in the bush, I thought I saw a lemur,
But not for sure; perhaps it was a loris.
His eyes were large, his skin was trichophorous,
His shinbones short, but quite a lengthy femur.
We stood and stared and shared a sudden tremor
As knowledge of our cousinhood dawned for us.
How, in the end, would evolution score us,
The talking biped and the furry dreamer?

But then I found that I had been mistaken:
Not lemur, loris, but—aye! I eye aye-aye!
All empathy gone, I left the beast forsaken
To go my way, not even saying bye-bye.
And yet my faith forevermore was shaken,
And I'll remember till the day I die-die.

We human beings are organisms; we are animals; more specifically, we are primates. So are the lemur, loris, and aye-aye mentioned in the above bit of anthropomorphic fluff. There are two great groups of primates: the *prosimians* (including the three types just named) and the *anthropoids*. The latter fall in turn into three sets: New World monkeys, Old World monkeys (including baboons), and hominoids (including men). The full formal classification is presented for handy reference in Box 5-1, and the current geographical distribution of major groups, except man, is shown in Figures 5-2, 5-3, and 5-4.

Evolutionary biologists tell us the cousinhood of primates is closer than the relationship of any current primate to any nonprimate. Shared features may therefore be the result of common heritage rather than of parallelism (p. 32). We must recognize and acknowledge those characteristics that human beings have in common with one or more other primate species. They may be vitally important in making us what we are, but they cannot be claimed as uniquely human.

We first describe certain gross structural and behavioral respects in which most primates differ from most other mammals. Then we discuss *sociality* and its sources; and then certain aspects of primate learning and tradition, especially *play*.

In comparing brains we have to allow for body size. Other factors being equal, larger animals have larger brains than smaller ones, but the increase is not proportionate: that is, the larger animals have a lower brain-body mass ratio.

BOX 5-1. Classification of the modern Primates and of fossil Hominoidea.

A dagger (†) marks groups known only through fossils.

order	PRIMATES
suborder	PROSIMII (prosimians)
infraorder	LEMURIFORMES
superfamily	Tupaioidea
family	Tupaiidae (tree shrews)
subfamily	Tupaiinae: *Tupaia, Anathana, Dendrogale, Tana, Urogale*
subfam.	Ptilocercinae: *Ptilocercus*
superfam.	Lemuroidea
fam.	Lemuridae (lemurs)
subfam.	Lemurinae: *Hapalemur, Lemur, Lepilemur*
subfam.	Cheirogaleinae: *Cheirogaleus, Microcebus, Phaner*
fam.	Indridae (indris, wooly lemurs): *Lichanotus, Propithecus, Indri*
superfam.	Daubentonioidea
fam.	Daubentoniidae: *Daubentonia* (aye-aye)
infraorder	LORISIFORMES
fam.	Lorisidae
subfam.	Lorisinae (lorises): *Loris, Nycticebus, Arctocebus, Perodicticus*
subfam.	Galaginae (bush babies, galagos): *Galago, Euoticus*
infraorder	TARSIIFORMES
fam.	Tarsiidae: *Tarsius* (tarsiers)
suborder	ANTHROPOIDEA
superfam.	Ceboidea (New World monkeys)
fam.	Cebidae
subfam.	Aotinae: *Aotes, Callicebus*
subfam.	Pitheciinae: *Cacajao, Pithecia, Chiropotes*
subfam.	Alouattinae: *Alouatta* (howlers)
subfam.	Cebinae (capuchins, titis): *Cebus, Saimiri*
subfam.	Atelinae (spiders, woolies): *Ateles, Brachyteles, Lagothrix*
subfam.	Callimiconinae: *Callimico*
fam.	Callithricidae: *Callithrix, Leontocebus*
superfam.	Cercopithecoidea (Old World monkeys)
fam.	Cercopithecidae
subfam.	Cercopithecinae: *Macaca* (macaques), *Cynopithecus, Cercocebus, Papio* (most baboons), *Comopithecus, Mandrillus, Theropithecus, Cercopithecus, Allenopithecus, Erythrocebus*
subfam.	Colobinae: *Presbytis, Pygathrix, Rhinopithecus, Simias, Nasalis, Colobus*
superfam.	Hominoidea (apes and men)
fam.	†Oreopithecidae: †*Apidium*, †*Parapithecus*, †*Oreopithecus*
fam.	Pongidae (apes)
subfam.	Hylobatinae: †*Pliopithecus*, *Hylobates* (gibbons), *Symphalangus* (siamangs)
subfam.	†Dryopithecinae: †*Dryopithecus*, †*Gigantopithecus*
subfam.	Ponginae: *Pongo* (orangutans), *Pan* (chimpanzees), *Gorilla* (gorillas)
fam.	Hominidae: †*Ramapithecus*, †*Australopithecus*, *Homo* (including †*H. erectus* and *H. sapiens*)

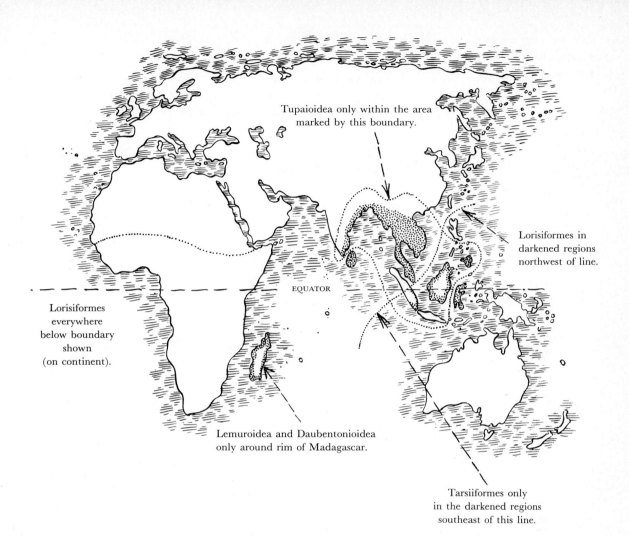

Tupaioidea only within the area
marked by this boundary.

Lorisiformes in
darkened regions
northwest of line.

Lorisiformes
everywhere
below boundary
shown
(on continent).

EQUATOR

Lemuroidea and Daubentonioidea
only around rim of Madagascar.

Tarsiiformes only
in the darkened regions
southeast of this line.

FIGURE 5-2. Present-day distribution of the Prosimii.

Comparing primates with all other mammals, one finds that for any given body size the ratio of brain mass to total body mass is about twice as much for the former as for the latter.

There is also a difference in this respect between anthropoids and prosimians. The smallest anthropoid brain is that of the marmoset, a South American monkey. The marmoset is about the size of the tarsier or the African bush baby (both prosimians), but its brain is three times as big. The enlargement affects various parts, but chiefly the cerebral cortex (p. 53).

For monkeys lumped together, the percentage of body mass accounted for by the brain is about 1.6. For chimpanzees the figure is 0.7%, and for gorillas only 0.24%, but these apes are large, the gorilla exceedingly so.

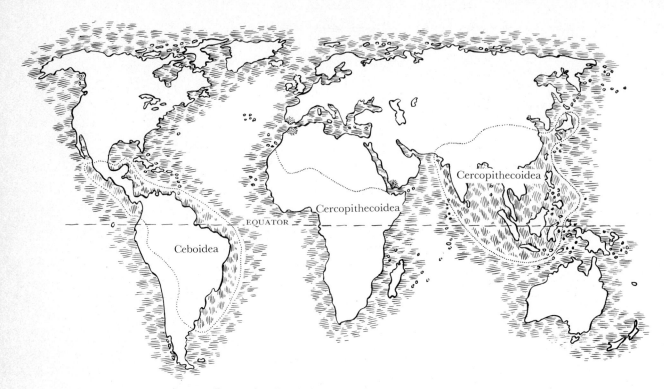

FIGURE 5-3. Present-day distribution of monkeys (Anthropoidea other than Hominoidea). Note the two small regions marked by shading, in northwest Africa (and Gibraltar) and in southwestern Arabia.

Even in the least manlike of the primates, the prosimian tree shrews, the cortex is convoluted (p. 54). It is clear that primates as a group have a major investment in brains. Our inferences from this fact could be sharper if we understood better than we do how brains work, but we can at least safely infer that primates have a relatively large capacity for the storage of learned behavior patterns (p. 53).

LIFE SPAN

The life span of an animal is how long it is apt to live, if not destroyed by accident or disease, until it simply wears out (Table 5-5). Among mammals, there is some correlation of life span with body mass, larger species generally living longer. But primates—and apparently also Chiroptera (bats)—are exceptions, with longer spans than mammals of the same size of other orders. Rats and mice live three or four years. The mouse lemur, the smallest of the prosimians and the smallest primate (adult mass typically less than $2\frac{1}{2}$ ounces), has been kept in captivity for eight or more years, still going strong.

EARLY LIFE STAGES

The greater life span of a primate begins with stretched-out early phases of the life cycle. The points we are about to make seem also to fit with the high metabolic

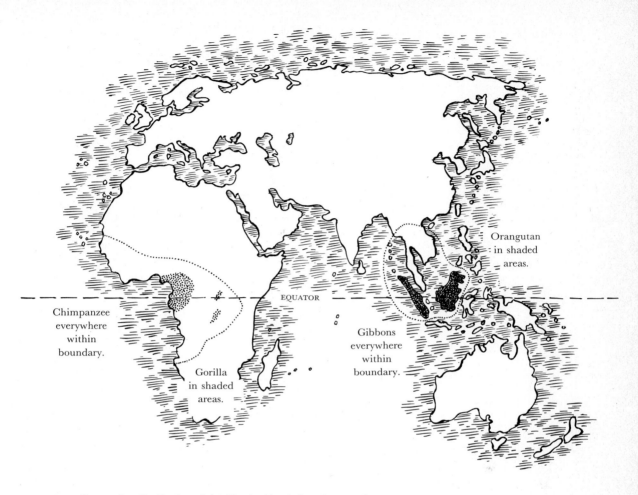

Orangutan
in shaded
areas.

EQUATOR

Chimpanzee
everywhere
within
boundary.

Gibbons
everywhere
within
boundary.

Gorilla
in shaded
areas.

FIGURE 5-4. Present-day distribution of the Hominoidea (other than man).

cost of brain tissue and with the recovery of that cost through early learning of behavior patterns needed for survival.

GESTATION.   For placental mammals[1] in general the length of the period of gestation increases with body size and with either higher latitude or higher altitude of habitat. Making full allowance for these factors, we find that primate gestation periods are longer than those of nonprimates. Small rodents (mice and rats) and small insectivores (shrews) average a bit over twenty days in the uterus. The primates in this size range are the tree shrews and the mouse lemur. The period of gestation of the former is in excess of forty days, of the latter sixty to seventy days.

LITTER SIZE AND BIRTHRATE.   The primate embryo and fetus gets more concentrated biochemical attention from its mother than do most other unborn mammals. Multiple

[1] The few egg-laying mammals are of course irrelevant for this comparison. We also leave out of account the marsupials (pouched mammals: kangaroos and such), since to provide for their sharply different reproductive economy would introduce unnecessary complications.

TABLE 5-5. Some life-span estimates.

y-axis (years): 150, 100, 90, 80, 70, 60, 50, 40, 30, 20, 10, 9, 8, 7, 6, 5, 4, 3, 2, 1 years

Mammals:
man, *Homo sapiens*
fin whale, *Balaenoptera physalus*
Indian elephant, *Elephas maximus*
African elephant, *Loxodonta africanus*
hippopotamus, *Hippopotamus amphibius*
orangutan, *Pongo pygmaeus*
horse, *Equus caballus*
chimpanzee, *Pan troglodytes*
polar bear, *Ursus arctos*
hamadryas baboon, *Papio hamadryas*
ox, *Bos taurus*
cat, *Felis catus*
fruit bat, *Eidolon helvum*
dog, *Canis familiaris*
wild boar, *Sus scrofa*
goat, *Capra hircus*
gray squirrel, *Sciurus carolinensis*
guinea pig, *Cavia porcellus*
golden hamster, *Mesocricetus auratus*
mouse, *Mus musculus*
rat, *Rattus norvegicus*
American mole, *Scalopus aquaticus*

Birds:
raven, *Corvus corax*
pigeon, *Columbia livia*
canary, *Serinus canarius*
American robin, *Turdus migratorius*
emerald-throated hummingbird

Reptiles:
box tortoise, *Terrapene carolina*
alligator, *Alligator mississippiensis*
copperhead, *Agkistrodon contortrix*
water turtle, *Chrysemys scripta*
garter snake, *Thamnophis syrtalis*

An arrowhead at the end of the line means that the estimate is known to be low. (Data taken, with permission, from Altman and Dittmer, eds., 1972.)

births are standard for all but the largest nonprimate mammals; some of the insectivores of Madagascar produce litters of eighteen or twenty. Among primates, the mouse lemur and some of his prosimian kin, and certain New World monkeys, run to twins. Otherwise, the standard is one infant per birth. Only one human birth of approximately each eighty is multiple, and only one of each $80^2 = 6400$ is of triplets or more.

In almost all primate species there is less than one birth per female per year: the infant gets more concentrated attention after birth as well as before.

MAMMARY APPARATUS. Mammals that produce multiple litters tend to have many mammary glands. The standard equipment for all primate females is a single pair of glands on the chest ("pectoral" mammae). On the other hand, primate mammary glands, like those of the mammals man has subjected to domestication, are permanent (once maturation has developed them); in other mammals they appear in season but are otherwise scarcely apparent except under microscopic examination.

WEANING. After birth, a primate goes through a relatively longer period of infant dependency than do the young of other placental mammals. This postnatal dependency does not come to a sudden end, but weaning means it is tapering off. After that, the young of some mammalian species part company with the mother very quickly. Mice are weaned in two or three weeks, rats in about a month, house cats in four or five weeks, and dogs in seven to ten weeks. Each must fend for itself as soon as weaning is complete. Among primates, weaning takes place after a minimum of about five months, for certain of the lemurs; the maximum is five or six years, in certain human communities—but here weaning is slow, the child consuming all sorts of other foods long before his terminal taste of maternal milk. In the primate situation, after weaning, the break between offspring and parents is gradual. The total period of infant dependency is estimated as lasting a year only for certain nocturnal prosimians. For human beings it may continue, in a sense, for fifteen years or more.

PREHENSILE APPENDAGES

For many mammals the limbs serve only as organs of locomotion, and it is the mouth that is used for manipulating small pieces of the environment. The use of the forelimbs for manipulation is not exclusive to primates—a rodent or a catlike carnivore may hold something to the mouth in the forepaws—but seems to be carried farther by them than by others.

In man this is obvious: we use our hands in countless ways, and would not be human—would not have become human—without them. But all primates catch food in their hands and bring it to the mouth. The aye-aye of Madagascar makes a nest at night; so do all apes except gibbons. The twigs and leaves they use are gathered by hand, carried in hand or mouth. Monkeys and apes pick up loose objects and hold them in front of the eyes and nose for examination. Infant nonhuman primates cling to their mother's fur with hands and feet; many prosimians and all anthropoids use prehensile appendages, instead of or in addition to the mouth, in infant care and in grooming.

Most primate species today live in trees, and it is assumed (p. 32) that formerly all did. The special characteristics of primate appendages match their double function as organs of arboreal locomotion and of manipulation.

Thus, a rodent climbs a tree trunk with clawholds, either ascending or descending head first. Except for a few prosimians, primates have not claws but nails. A primate climbs with handholds and footholds, ascending a tree head first and descending stern first.

Again: mammals whose main organ of manipulation is the mouth have a patch of hair-free moist skin, the rhinarium, on and around their noses. This serves to render the detection of odors more accurate, but also it is a region of high touch-sensitivity near the mouth, guiding the latter's manipulative actions. Prosimians have a rhinarium; anthropoids do not. But primate finger tips and toe tips, close to the nails, are precise touch-detectors, and the palms of the hands and soles of the feet (other than our own feet) are pretty accurate too.

The dual function of primate extremities appears in the range of *grips* used. In a *power grip* the emphasis is on muscular strength and touch-sensitivity plays a minor role: the digits are curled around an object and pressure is applied between them and the palm (or sole), while the thumb (or big toe) either idles or presses in at an angle [Figure 5-6(b)]. Arboreal locomotion demands a power grip: the mass of the whole animal is being propelled. At the other extreme are various *precision grips* that exploit touch-sensitivity [Figure 5-6(a)]. These are carried farthest by those primates that have readily opposable thumbs or big toes. Figure 5-6 (c) and (d) show human variants.

The characteristic primate association of locomotion and manipulation appears also when the tail is prehensile. All primates, except hominoids and a few Old World monkeys, have tails, but they are prehensile only for certain New World monkeys (the spiders, woolies, and howlers: Box 5-1). These have excellent use for a "fifth limb." In the rainy season the ground below their trees is covered with water, so that there is no way of getting from one tree to another by descending to the ground. For swinging through the treetops an additional prehensile extremity is a boon. The monkey uses the tail also for manipulation, curling it strongly for a power grip, delicately for a precision grip. There is a hairless region near the tip of the tail, with which the monkey senses what is touched quite well indeed (nonprehensile primate tails lack this). Perhaps the tail is not involved in infant care or in grooming, but that it plays a part in interindividual transactions is attested by Figure 5-7.

POSTURE AND PHYSIOGNOMY

A human being sits, stands, walks, and runs with his trunk approximately vertical. We think of nonprimate mammals as mostly keeping their trunks near the horizontal—though there are well known exceptions, such as a kangaroo, or a squirrel running up or down a tree trunk.

In this respect nonhuman primates are somewhat more like us than might at first appear. The most thoroughly arboreal types, to be sure, may swing from branch to branch with their trunks passing through every imaginable orientation. Others tend

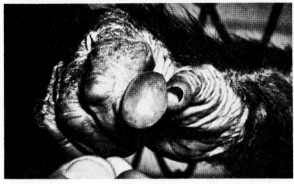

(a)

(b)

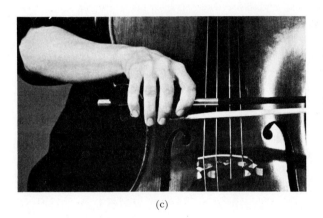

(c)

(d)

FIGURE 5-6. PRIMATE GRIPS. (a) shows the precision grip of right hand of a young chimpanzee. The thumb is short; the other fingers have to be curled back to form one arm of the pincers. (b) shows the power grip of the right hand of a prosimian, the slender loris (*Loris tardigradus*), grasping a tree limb. The second finger is foreshortened in this species, and so does not show. (c) and (d) show remarkable human variants. The cellist's right-hand position, holding the bow, is a derivative of the precision grip. His left-hand position, on the fingerboard, is a derivative of the power grip. Yet bowing requires power, and fingering requires enormous precision as well as rapid change from one position to another. (Chimpanzee and loris from J. R. and P. H. Napier, *A handbook of living Primates,* Academic Press, New York, 1967, courtesy of J. R. and P. H. Napier. Cellist's hands courtesy of William Rosenthal.)

to keep the trunk nearly vertical during a leap, and for all primates the posture of alert relaxation is one or another form of haunch sitting, resembling our own. The moving monkey does not look like a miniature furry human being; the sitting monkey sometimes does.

FIGURE 5-7. PRIMATE PHYSICAL CONTACT FOR SOCIAL SECURITY. A pair of South American monkeys (*Callicebus moloch*), male on right. (Courtesy of the San Diego Zoo.)

The resemblance is increased because the monkey twists its face into various expressions. Anthropoids have mobile facial muscles; those of prosimians are less flexible, and those of nonprimate mammals not at all so. Monkeys and apes use facial gesture communicatively; as we do. Figure 5-8 shows a series of typical chimpanzee facial expressions. We can't know just what emotional states these different expressions signal, but the *diversity* is apparent, and plays a part in the way chimpanzees deal with one another.

SEXUALITY

Sexual maturity comes late for primates, as compared with other mammals, in keeping with their stretched-out life cycle (p. 60).

The commonest rule for placental mammals—many smaller species are exceptions—is for the cycle of ovulation to match the yearly climatic cycle, with one ovulation, or one brief period of ovulation, per year. The male cycle matches that

FIGURE 5-8. Some chimpanzee facial expressions. (After Kohts 1935, cited in Campbell 1966.)

of the female: his testicles descend and his sexual appetite develops only at the appropriate time.

Some of the prosimians of Madagascar have a single annual breeding season, but most primates do not. Even among the tree shrews, in some respects the least typical of all the primates, the female has many ovulations per year and the male has a permanent scrotum. The other prosimians, and the New World monkeys, have no regular breeding season, the females ovulating more than once per year but perhaps with no clear periodicity. Only for Old World monkeys and the hominoids has ovulation taken on the fairly regular frequency and timing by virtue of which we in Western culture have come to call it "menstruation" (from Latin *menstruālis* 'monthly').

SEXUAL INTEREST AND BEHAVIOR. Although it is difficult to judge such matters, it would seem that for most mammals copulation is not a source of great enjoyment, just the relief of a seasonal tension.

For primates the situation is different, the nearer to man the more radically so. Sexual interest on the part of both sexes is virtually uninterrupted once maturation has turned it on. It has ups and downs, but rarely dips to zero and rarely reaches the feverish heights characteristic of the once-a-year mammals during their rutting season.

But if the primate sex drive is more nearly continuous, it is also more diffuse, and has been blended in varying measure with a drive that in origin had nothing to do with sex: the drive to groom and be groomed. Primate grooming behavior often has sexual overtones, and most primate sexual behavior has groominglike aspects. The act of copulation tends to be preceded, sometimes followed, by a period of sex play, in which the participants make use of all the prehensile appendages and touch-sensitive surfaces they have—mouth, hands, feet, perhaps tail. And there are episodes of sex play which do not culminate in coitus. We know these in our particular variant of human culture as the necking and petting of adolescents, but the basic pattern is pandemic among primates.

The only difficulty with this dilution of sexuality is that impregnation may not always take place at the physiologically appropriate time. In most other mammals the male is the unquestioned initiator of sexual encounters, the female reasonably passive. But among primates the male may not, without help, reach the proper peak of passion at the appropriate moment. Lacking a season of rest and recuperation, he may be exhausted, unable to achieve erection or insufficiently supplied with semen. Or, given the blending of sex and grooming, he may be more interested in pawing than in procreating.

By way of compensation, primate females have developed various means of enticement. As with all mammalian females, their odor changes with their periodicity, attracting males at the proper time. In many monkeys (e.g., baboons: p. 35) the female has a patch of "sexual skin" on her rump, which turns one or another bright color when her internal physiology is optimally adjusted for the reception of the male. Human females, lacking this genetic gift, have from time immemorial resorted to various supplementary means of adornment. Females in all primate species assume postures, or perform motions, that serve to invite the male's attention.

Of course, there are great variations, not only from species to species but also from community to community and from one individual to another. Thus, in an earlier and less cleanly period of our Western society, well behaved women used perfume, not to enhance their attractiveness (as they themselves often supposed), but to mask their sexual odor and thus moderate the behavior of the men about them. Such special cases do not invalidate our by-and-large characterization of the primates as over against other mammals.

Copulatory positions. For most mammals the copulatory position is dorsal: the female's back is to the male, who is described as "mounting" her. The porcupine and the hamster (both rodents) and the two-toed sloth (one of the South American edentates) are known or reputed to use only a ventral position, in which the male and the female are face to face, the latter reclining on her back.

Many prosimians and monkeys, perhaps all of them, use only the dorsal position. But hominoids are persistent experimenters. All species of hominoids have been observed to use the dorsal approach and the ventral approach, each in as many variants as their respective anatomies and ingenuities permit.

What is more, all species of hominoids (apparently not monkeys or prosimians) indulge in the various sorts of sexual activities classed in recent Western society as "perversions": the use of bodily projections other than the penis, of bodily openings other than the vagina, male homosexuality, female homosexuality, mutual masturbation, autoeroticism.

It is not being anthropomorphic to propose that the participants in these partly sexual, partly grooming, and partly acrobatic encounters are having fun. I think the truth lies the other way around. *Primates enjoy physical proximity and bodily contact.* That is an important formative factor in primate character, as we shall see below (p. 73). Our own pleasure in such matters (except insofar as it is inhibited by one or another sort of cultural overlay) is a general hominoid trait, to some extent a general primate one, not distinctively human.

SOCIALITY × In comparison with most other mammals, most primates are unusually sociable. To say this means three interrelated things.

Gregariousness

In the first place, most primate species tend to be gregarious rather than eremitic.

The most solitary of mammals are those for whom, except during the breeding season, the approach of another adult of the same species is the signal for threat, combat, or withdrawal. The dwelling pattern (p. 45) is such that encounters of the sort are rare. Each animal moves about in the vicinity of some home base. The perimeter of the animal's territory is not defined, except by increasing distance from home base and by the increasing chance of encountering another member of the same species if the latter happens to be wandering equally far, in just the right direction, from his own headquarters.[2]

In contrast, gregarious animals live most of the time in clusters of a handful, dozens, or even hundreds. The whole cluster typically has a region within which its members move around, largely in parallel, though (depending on the species) sometimes more compactly and sometimes more diffusely, and sometimes broken up into subclusters of one or another sort. A member of a particular cluster usually recognizes the difference between another member of the same cluster and an "alien" of the same species. The approach of an alien may be the signal for threat, combat, or withdrawal, just as with loners, though not invariably so. The approach of another member of the same cluster typically does not trigger such a reaction—at least, the style and outcome of the encounter are different. Intermingling of clusters is unusual, but with some species (e.g., baboons: p. 39) sometimes two whose territories are adjacent may come quite close together, as at a watering place, and then move apart again with little noticeable interaction. The clustering may show seasonal variations (e.g., that of the Menomini: p. 11). In the long run, there are inevitably changes: a larger cluster may subdivide; undersized groups occasionally merge; individuals very rarely switch allegiance.

Degree of gregariousness correlates with the typical size of a cluster and the average distance between its members. A herd of grazing animals is sometimes very large (hundreds or thousands), and on occasion its members are crowded into a very small space. A gregarious animal is accustomed to the nearby presence not merely of others of its kind, but of specific familiar individuals. Isolated, he soon shows signs of discomfort: this is a circumstance for which his scheduling does not provide. On the other hand, there is a limit beyond which no animal can tolerate crowding, even if basic physiological functions are provided for. In laboratory tests of this, the animals in time refuse to eat or breed, and die.

Nonhuman primate clusters vary considerably in size, depending on species and on such circumstances as the richness of the food supply. A few prosimians are either regularly solitary or can live for a long time alone when necessary. Otherwise, the size range is from a few to a few dozen, rarely over a hundred. Thus, primates are not as gregarious as some herd animals.

SOCIAL STRUCTURE

But there is another factor in sociality: the degree of complexity of the internal organization of the cluster.

---

[2]This relation of an individual (or of a cluster, as in the next paragraph) to the region in which it lives may be called *nucleated territoriality*. Certain species, particularly human beings in some cultures and some birds at certain points in their life cycles, show *perimeter-marked territoriality:* the animal establishes certain landmarks and defends the perimeter of his region against intruders. Nucleated territoriality is much commoner.

Differences of sex and age are always relevant. The simplest social structuring would be a type in which one animal's scheduled reactions to another depended only on the sex and age of each and on whether they are allies or aliens. Probably no vertebrate manifests this nadir of simplicity. At least there is some variability of reaction depending on what each animal happens to be doing at the time of the encounter.

The peak of complexity would be a situation in which no member of a large cluster treated any two other members in the same way in identical settings. This extreme is also never attained—not even by humans.

Consider a successful politician. He may know thousands of people by name (calling different people by different names is treating them differently). Yet in campaigning he puts all the strangers he meets into one or another of a small set of categories and treats all those of a single category in the same way, kissing the babies, giving a warm handshake to the men, flirting with the unattractive women and maintaining his reserve with the attractive ones.

INNER CIRCLE AND BEYOND. Broadly speaking, the politician's behavior is like that of any mammal except the rabidly nongregarious ones. Any member of a mammalian cluster deals with some of his fellows as individuals, treating no two of them exactly alike, while he lumps others together into categories and behaves the same way towards all those in a category.

The members of the former set we shall call the particular animal's *inner circle*. The exact arrangement changes with time and age. The infant's inner circle may include at first only the mother. Even the infant's siblings from the same birth may be treated alike, the categorical distinction between sibling and nonsibling age mate being maintained by the greater proximity of the former. For a juvenile or an adult, if the cluster is small then the inner circle may be coterminous with it. If the cluster is larger, then beyond the inner circle there is a fuzzy mass of "others" of various sorts—males, females, old ones, young ones, big ones, little ones—with whom relations are stereotyped, yet whose collective presence in the background is registered as fitting and proper.

The fact that A is in the inner circle of B does not imply that the reverse is true, nor does it necessarily connote friendship or intimacy. For example, in a cluster with a single dominant adult male (a common situation), all members know his identity and treat him with respect, but few are buddy-buddy with him, and he may not acknowledge the individuality of some who perforce acknowledge his. In modern technological human society this asymmetry is carried to an extreme. A television star, or any other "public figure," is known to millions he will never meet. He does not lump them together and treat them all alike; he is quite helpless to do anything but lump them together and treat them all *at once,* as a mass rather than as discrete though indefinitely replicated individuals.

SOCIAL CLASSES. For a single animal the reality of social structure is of the sort we have described: an inner circle, and beyond it, if the cluster is large enough, vaguely familiar characters dealt with collectively or categorically. But social structure is more than what it is for any *one* member of a cluster.

The "social view" through the eyes of two different animals, say juvenile males

A and B, can be quite similar even if the identities of the members of the two inner circles are different. What C is to A, individual D is to B; for A, B and D are in the background, while for B, A and C are. If we set out to describe the structure of the whole cluster by peering in turn through the eyes of each member, we would find ourselves saying much the same thing over and over again as we turned from one juvenile male to another—and then, suddenly, we would find ourselves describing quite a different scene as we switched to a juvenile female, or to an infant male, or to the unique dominant male if there is one.

The members of a cluster, at any one moment, thus belong to a number of different *social classes*.

A particular social class may of necessity have only a single member (for example, the dominant adult male), or it may have many. If two animals belong to the same social class, their social view is much the same, though they may not know each other and though the specific individuals with which the two interact are in part different: your mother is not my mother, though each of us has a mother. Two members of a single social class have approximately the same scheduling. Their scheduling thus structures the world for them (p. 47) in approximately the same way. The part of this superimposed structuring of the world that has to do with their perception of and dealings with other animals of the same species is just their "social view," as we have been calling it here.

TYPES OF SOCIAL STRUCTURE. Now we can very simply define *social structure* as the structure of an animal cluster in terms of social classes. And *social behavior* is the scheduled interindividual transactions on which social structure rests and which it helps to perpetuate.

There are two extremes of social structure for which we need labels. In one, the members of a sizable cluster (dozens) fall entirely into very small subclusters (one to half a dozen); the inner circle of each member of a subcluster includes normally only the other members of the same subcluster; relations between members of different subclusters are minimal, though rarely inimical. Such a cluster is a *congeries*.

At the opposite extreme is a situation in which at least one member of a cluster is in the inner circles of all members (except infants). Such a cluster is a *band*.

For situations between these two extremes we can resort to description instead of additional terms. Our general label, for congeries or band or anything between, is *community* (p. 43, including fn. 1).

Even those prosimians who tend to be solitary could be described as living in congeries in which inner circles are small. Other prosimians, and many monkeys, live in congeries with larger subgroups. Other monkeys and all apes live in communities which approach or attain the status of bands, and life in bands was the classical human pattern, modified only in relatively recent times.

The difference between a prosimian congeries with very small inner circles and the pattern of the truly solitary mammal is that the latter usually reacts hostilely to others of his kind, whereas the member of the congeries, though often alone, normally tolerates company and sometimes actively seeks it. Few nonprimate mammals achieve enduring band structure. Yet it is not quite exclusive to primates: wolves show something similar (p. 472).

Consider now two members of an animal community, each of a particular social class and each occupying a particular niche in—or beyond—the inner circle of the other. No matter what the social structure of the whole community may be, the scheduled transactions between our two selected animals may be more stereotyped or less so.

To say that they are stereotyped means that the way in which the behavior of one affects that of the other depends on little more than the "social identity" of the former for the latter—on what spot the first occupies in the social view of the second. The scheduled transactions are the less stereotyped, or the more variable (and the less predictable!), the more they depend also on where the animals are and on what each is doing at the time.

In any animal community, transactions are most stereotyped between aliens and least so when each animal is within the inner circle of the other. In the latter situation one finds striking differences in degree of stereotypy from one species to another, and it is here that the difference between other mammals and primates (even setting humans aside) is greatest. Primates who know each other simply do *more different things* together.

THE WELLSPRINGS OF SOCIALITY

Sociality and community-formation pay off in that they afford a higher level of safety for the average member of the community and thus promote the chances of survival of the community as a whole. If there is no very active cooperation in such enterprises as finding food, sociality nevertheless reduces the chance that one member of the community will destroy another. Also, the principle of "safety in numbers" is real, even for the loosest congeries. A few members at its geographical fringes may be seized, but the rest are warned and can try to avoid the predator, whose appetite is in any case not big enough for it to want to consume all the animals in the group.

Social grouping is only one of several patterns that can serve to perpetuate a species in the face of environmental hazards. Another pattern is for individuals to be so large and powerful that potential predators have little chance. A third is for them to produce so many young that a few survive to reproduce even if most succumb. The primate way is the first of these three, and we like it because it is our own: in our terms, it shows a desirable ethical balance between mutual aid and emphasis on individual "rights." We must acknowledge, however, that the pattern is the *source* of our ethical attitudes. There is no objective sense in which we can claim that the primate pattern is "better" than the others.

The primary source of mammalian sociality is the nutritional tie between mother and offspring. That is shared by all. Even among loners the newborn stay with their mother for a while, before they are abandoned or dispatched to go their lonesome (but not lonely) ways.

To this, the primates add at least two factors.

One is the extended period of infant care implied by the long life span and large cortex. The primate moves from the literal bosom of his mother to the figurative bosom of his community, where he may experience some rude shocks but which nonetheless cuddles and coddles him much as his mother did. It takes a (relatively) long time for him to learn all the tricks of his trade so that he is ready to accept adult responsibilities. The large cortex makes a long learning period necessary; it also makes a lot of learning possible. Among the things that must be learned are all the subtle social distinctions appropriate for the particular community. A less efficient brain would not supply adequate storage room for the necessary information. This is true regardless of what percentage of the information is laid down by the genes, as some of it surely is, rather than by learning.

Perhaps more important is the special diffused and diluted sexuality of primates. Driving seasonal sexuality would not serve to build communities and hold them together; aggregates of animals whose sex drive is of that sort have arisen through some other factor. Continuous or more frequent sexual interest on the part of males might lead them to maintain retinues of females, to be available as the need arose. Some primates do this, but it does not seem important or widespread. Rather, it is the uninterruptedness or high frequency of sexual interest on the part of both sexes, together with the amalgam of sex and grooming, that is responsible. Primates *have fun* together. When not actually in bodily contact, they behave in one another's presence in ways that serve as symbols for the various sorts of direct contact and that impart some of the same pleasurable sensations.

✖ Learning and tradition take on a special form among primates because of the various ingredients of primate character we have described.

LEARNING, TRADITION, AND PLAY

Learning requires the reinforcement of some behavioral patterns and the weakening of others, by virtue of consequences that are sometimes, though perhaps not inevitably, describable as "rewards" and "punishments." Especially among primates, a reward can be merely the suspension of an expected punishment, and vice versa; and under some conditions either can be symbolic rather than corporeal.

Two extreme types of primate learning situation seem especially worthy of mention:

(1)   If the young animal is rewarded when he performs, with sufficient accuracy, some action he has just observed, and if this happens in diverse circumstances, he is being rewarded not only for the specific actions but also for *imitating*. He is acquiring a general technique of great value for the subsequent learning of specific behavior patterns. He is *learning-to-learn*. Some animals may have a genetically determined tendency to imitate, but even if this is so the habit of imitating still requires firming up by events of the sort we have outlined. It is significant that we refer to imitation as "aping," but also important that human beings are much apter apers than apes are.

It is after a primate has learned-to-learn that he may be observed learning certain specific acts, through imitation, despite the absence of any obvious reward. It is as though the reward part of the paradigm had been built directly into the animal by his learning-to-learn. Imitation has become its own reward.

(2)   Some primates learn some things well, with suitable rewards and punishments, despite the absence of any model. A human male, for example, does not have to

learn how to be a proper male from other males. There are instances of boys raised entirely by women who nevertheless become thoroughly masculine men (as their particular culture judges such things). The women cannot demonstrate masculinity, but they know how a man should behave. They reward the boy when he behaves that way, and frown their disapproval when he does not. This has been called *learning by complementarity.*

PLAY

The most pervasively important special factor in primate learning and tradition is *play.*

A high-school student, bored by what his teacher is saying and looking longingly out the window at a friend practicing football, would not easily be convinced that he and his friend are both engaged in variations on the basic theme of mammalian play. But it is so.

All mammals play—while they are young. Primates stay young longer than other mammals do, and so play more. St. Paul said (1 Corinthians 13:11): "When I was a child, I spake as a child, I understood as a child, I thought as a child: but when I became a man, I put away childish things." Most mammals do this. The primates, especially man, tend not to heed the admonition—which is doubtless why St. Paul was impelled to give it. Instead, they continue in a certain amount of play as long as they live.

The best approach is through an example.

Dogs sometimes get into vicious fights, resulting in injury or death. The fighting involves complicated maneuvers and a close watch on the motions of the antagonist. The two circle each other warily, and each tries to dash in and grab the other with his jaws, without himself being grabbed. Other things being equal, a big powerful dog is a better fighter than a small weak one. But one of the other things that is not always equal is experience: *other* other things being equal, the experienced fighter is the better one.

Now let us watch some puppies. One thing they do is pair off and go through a ceremony that looks very much like fighting—except that neither gets hurt. The jaws grab and hold, but do not squeeze. We say that the puppies are *playing* at fighting.

DEGREES OF SERIOSITY. The difference between playing and the real thing is, then, that the former is in some sense less serious. But seriosity is a matter of degree, and intermediate degrees are also observable.

For example, a fight between full-grown dogs is not always carried through to the bitter end. One of them, convinced by how things are going that he cannot win, will withdraw and run away (and live to fight another day), or will back off and perform a doggy gesture interpreted by the other as an admission of defeat. The game is played by understood rules. Normally the victor quits when the vanquished does. This is especially apt to be the case if the purpose of the fight is clear and consists of access to something both want but only one can have. If the participants are males quarreling over the favors of a female, the victor in the truncated combat moves on towards his goal, whilst the vanquished, by conceding, has saved enough energy to wait for another streetcar.[3]

PLAY AS LEARNING. Puppy play-fighting is excellent training for adult fighting; it perhaps serves also to prevent adult fighting from being always as deadly as it might otherwise be. In a world in which adult combat of one sort or another is of importance (not only fights within the species but those with prey or predator), the training takes on survival value, and there tends to be selection for animals which, while young, find immediate reward in the play activity in the form of some sort of enjoyment. This enjoyment is what we call *fun*.

Play at fighting is not the only kind. About some things, of course—for example, eating and sleeping—young mammals show just as much seriosity as do adults. About many others—locomotion, manipulation, grooming, fighting, copulation, infant care—the young adopt a let's-pretend-and-have-fun attitude until they have grown the equipment and developed the skills necessary for the fully adult ways of doing things.

Play is fun, and not marked by seriosity; but, especially among primates, it is extremely important for survival. If the maturing primate has not yet learned how to do a certain thing by playing at it, he does not do it well or may not be able to do it at all when he really needs to. This has been tested in laboratories and zoos. For example, an infant male rhesus monkey (Box 5-1, p. 58) was deprived of any chance to toss and tumble with his age mates, though allowed to watch such behavior as well as to observe the conduct of adults. When he reached maturity he would try to mount a female, but with clumsy motions and from the wrong angle—much to the amused disgust of the female if she was experienced in such matters (Figure 5-9). The same holds for almost every other item in the complex behavioral repertory of primate communities.

PLAY AND INNOVATION. The English word "play" has several areas of meaning in everyday usage. In one, it contrasts with "work" or with "real." In another, it contrasts with "precision of fit," as when we say that the steering wheel of a car has too much play in it and needs tightening. It is no idle play on words to assert that overtones of both these everyday meanings are appropriate when we use the term in our technical sense.

Thus, infant mock-ups of adult reactions are imprecise and more variable than the adult models, because the infant has not yet learned exactly where are the boundaries between actions that count in adult life as distinctively different (p. 47). This means that the context for play must be one in which ineptitudes of performance, within wide limits, will not lead to disaster.

For man and the primates most like him, where play does not come to a sudden end with maturity, some variability may continue, and then becomes especially important. The exact traditional way of doing something is guaranteed to be a good way as long as conditions do not change. If conditions do change, as is in the long

[3]Usually combats of this sort settle, not which male will approach the female, but which male the female will approach. When she indicates her choice the fight stops.

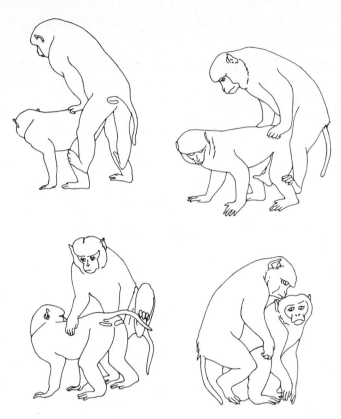

FIGURE 5-9. THE IMPORTANCE OF PLAY. These are rhesus monkeys (*Macaca mulatta*). The female is experienced. The male in the upper two drawings grew up under normal conditions; that in the lower two was experimentally deprived of opportunities for youthful play and does not know how to copulate. (From W. A. Mason, "The effects of social restriction on the behavior of rhesus monkeys: 1. Free social behavior," *Journal of Comparative and Physiological Psychology,* 53.582–589, 1960. Copyright 1960 by the American Psychological Association, and reproduced by permission.)

run inevitable, the variability affords a means of possible adaptation: a new means may be found to an old end, without waiting for the slow and often unsuccessful workings of genetic selection. That is what we mean when we say that necessity is the mother of invention. But for the most manlike primates the old saw has cut the truth in half. Suppose conditions are not changing much. The traditional way is then a good way, but not necessarily the only one that will work. Variability may yield an equally satisfactory alternative, which spreads, like a fad or fashion, in competition with the older way; or it may lead to a better way which in time completely displaces the inherited one. Since experimentation is prolonged play, and play is fun, we may supply the other half of the truth by asserting that, while necessity is the mother of invention, fun is the father.

The possible creative yield of variability involves a concomitant risk. Every innovative act is, in a sense, an error, though most errors are not innovative and many are dangerous. The risk explains why most primate communities, including most human societies, living under conditions that afford only a thin margin for survival, have been of a conservative bent—even though much more innovative than other animals. Our crops need rain. My people have always evoked the rain by the ritual I am about to perform. You tell me my ritual will have no effect on whether it rains or not. Perhaps that is true where you come from. Perhaps it is even true here. But think how terrible it would be if you are wrong! My people would starve, and the responsibility would be mine. This human episode clothes with words what nonhuman primates must do wordlessly; otherwise there is little difference.

On the whole, though, what must be stressed about the extension of mammalian play from childhood into maturity among some of the primates, especially among ourselves, is not the conservatism we have just described but the maintenance of some flexibility throughout life, making possible radical—if often painful—readjustments should circumstances call for them loudly enough. The hoary cantrip "you can't change human nature," insofar as it has any ascertainable meaning, is false. There is no better paradigm of this than the legend of St. Paul himself (Acts 9:1–9). At the time of his conversion he had long since abandoned childish ways. Yet in a single day he changed from the most fanatic opponent of Christianity into its most dedicated adherent. The Christian doctrine that it is never too late to repent achieves its power by being so thoroughly in accord with this particular feature of the human version of primate character.

6

✖

INFORMATION, COMMUNICATION, AND HOMEOSTASIS

The notion of "information" has come up at a number of points in the last two chapters. We shall be able to avoid various metaphysical pitfalls in the discussion of human affairs, later in this book, by giving explicit attention here and now to information and certain allied matters.

Think of any ongoing organic entity: a single cell, a multicellular organism, a community. Three commodities must flow, in, through, out, and from one part to another: matter, energy, and information.

The ties among the three are intimate. We have seen (p. 52) that stored information necessarily takes the form of a stable spatial array of matter and, further, that any stable spatial array of matter is stored information. Again, no information can be *transmitted* without the degradation of some energy. However, the activity instigated by a signal bears no simple quantitative relation to the amount of energy in the signal. When the shotgun is loaded a pressure of an ounce or so on the trigger unleashes power enough to kill a man. If it is not loaded, the same manipulation yields a faint click. Thus, organisms can at times achieve large ends with small means, while at other times their most violent struggles are to no avail.

The transmission and storage of information, and the recovery of stored information, always involve triggering rather than direct energy flow. Thus genes supply neither energy nor matter, but merely direct their action (p. 42). The energy in the light that strikes the retina governs the production of quite different energy by chemical transformations within the nervous tissue, some of which goes to waste but some of which passes along the optic process to the brain (light strikes a dead eye too, but a dead eye does not see). When a drunk staggers out of a saloon under his own power because the barkeep has threatened to throw him out bodily otherwise, the energy in the barkeep's threat is not that expended by the drunk.

Within an organism, information must be shipped around or the parts of the organism do not coordinate. In a carnivorous animal it does no good for the nose to smell or the eyes to see potential prey if the organs of locomotion then move in the wrong direction or the jaws fail to seize the food. It is also essential that certain kinds of information be stored. For example, without appropriate built-in frames of reference, the animal cannot distinguish between food and nonfood.

✖ Information-processing is as important for the well-being of a community as for that of an individual organism. Its failure in the individual is an illness, often fatal. If it breaks down in a community, the community falls apart.

But where are the nervous system, the circulatory and endocrine systems, of a community?

As a matter of fact, certain invertebrates (coelenterates and bryozoans) do form communities called *colonies* in which the members are connected by a shared nerve net, so that information passes from one to another the same way it moves within a single member. Among other invertebrates (insects) there is a sort of communal analog of an endocrine system: one insect emits chemicals akin to hormones, called "pheromones," which pass through the air and enter the bodies of others, where they facilitate or inhibit various responses.

But among vertebrates the first of these arrangements is impossible and the second, though it may exist, plays only a limited role in the coordination of community life. In general, if information is to be passed from one vertebrate to another, the sender must code it into bodily behavior which either has a direct trigger effect on the receiver or leaves traces that do. The former is *direct transmission* and is, of course, how human (spoken) language works. An instance of the latter is one in which the sender's actions leave a trail or spoor that the receiver detects before it fades beyond recognition; this is *delayed transmission* or *(external) storage,* and is how human writing systems work. In addition, if information is to flow the receiver must be equipped (through genetics, learning, or both) with the proper circuitry for interpreting the observed actions, or the observed results of the actions, of the sender.

All behavior which, potentially or actually, transmits information from one animal to another is *communicative.*

Therefore virtually all animal behavior is at least potentially communicative. If an act of one animal fails to convey information because there is no other animal around at the proper moment, that means only that in the particular instance no communication was effected. Communicative behavior is not some special segment of behavior, but simply *all* behavior as viewed from a particular angle.

SPECIALIZATION

It nevertheless remains true that some actions seem "more communicative" or "more exclusively communicative" than others. Let us try to make this distinction in a more precise way.

A communicative act is necessarily an act: that is, it involves physical motion and the expenditure of energy. The communicative consequences of the act are "trigger" effects, as already described. But the act necessarily also has direct energetic consequences. When these are biologically *unimportant,* we say that the act is communicatively *specialized.*

For example, suppose a monkey or a prosimian detects the recent presence at a particular spot of another member of the same species, because he smells the urine or other bodily discharge that the other has deposited at the spot. If the urine was passed merely because of pressure in the bladder, then the transmission of information is only incidental. But it is known that many species of primates, like some other mammals, deposit urine in the absence of any immediate urinary necessity, thus staking claims on specific objects or areas. A monkey freshly introduced into a zoo cage will go quickly to its four corners and befoul them. Some prosimians even have special glands used for such *scent marking*. The act of scent marking has no direct energetic consequences of biological importance; only the communicative consequences count.

Again: if one monkey grabs at an insect and another sees him do it, the first is doing something whose direct energetic consequences are biologically important: if he catches the insect he has something to eat. The act is therefore not communicatively specialized, even though the other monkey's comportment may be influenced by his observation of it. But now suppose that a monkey or ape finds a good source of food, and that as he begins to eat he utters a particular call, one he is scheduled to produce in these circumstances and not in others. The direct energetic consequences of the call are only that the sound waves spread through the air and damp out. These consequences are of no biological importance. But other monkeys or apes, hearing the cry, are triggered into approaching and getting a share of the food. The uttering of the cry is communicatively specialized.

What counts here is not whether the animal is *trying* to collect his colleagues—maybe he is, but that would be hard to judge by observation and he cannot tell us if we ask. It does not even matter that the trigger consequences of the call *are* biologically important for the community. What makes the call communicatively specialized is only that the direct energetic consequences are biologically trivial.

MEANING

Some signals achieve their communicative effects by "standing for" something other than themselves. When a speaker of English utters, say, the word "erysipelas," the effect on his hearers turns on an associative tie between the sound of that word and a particular thing or situation, or particular kind of thing or situation, in their experience. We say that, for them, the signal has a *meaning*.

Many animal signals have meanings, but that is not necessary in order for them to function in communication. A broader approach is necessary, as follows.

ALTERATION OF BEHAVIORAL PROBABILITIES

First we stand with a receiver and watch a sender. An action by A, observed by B, at least tells B what A is doing at the moment—namely, performing a particular action rather than some other. That is new information for B. The action may surprise B, or he may have expected it, but in the nature of things he could never have anticipated it in all detail. The particular act also tells B something of what he should expect next from A, though here, also, B can operate only in terms of relative probabilities. So information is always transmitted, whether or not A's act has a meaning in the sense we have defined, and regardless of its degree of communicative specialization.

Thus, when one monkey sees another grab at an insect, he knows that the other monkey has done this rather than something else he might have been expected to do. If the grab is successful, the observing monkey now can know that the observed monkey's next act is more apt to be that of putting the insect in his mouth than that of throwing it away, and he can revise his own plans accordingly if any revision is called for.

Now we focus our attention on a receiving animal. At any given instant, the receiver is at a certain point in his schedule (p. 46). The schedule, we remember, is not ironclad. With the fullest possible general information, the most we could do would be to assign numbers to each act in the receiver's entire behavioral repertory, each the measure of the relative probability that that act will be the next one he performs. The transmitter now does something, which means that he sends some signal to the receiver. *If the receiver's probabilities for subsequent action are in any way altered* by this signal, then information has been transmitted. But that is almost invariably the case for every act of every animal, provided there are other animals about, regardless of goal-directedness, of degree of communicative specialization, and of the presence or absence of meanings.

QUANTIFYING INFORMATION

⌘ Under ideal conditions, the amount of information carried by an incoming signal can be quantified. The technical details are not important, but the principle is.

Suppose I ask you to tell me about something, under conditions such that you are constrained to respond in one or the other of just two ways: say, by a bald *yes* or a bald *no.* Your answer then conveys less information to me than it would if you were free to choose your reply from a set of four, or ten, or a hundred alternatives. On the other hand, if I could know in advance that your reply was going to be a certain one, then the reply would give me no information at all.

Thus, the number of alternative acts in a repertory from which, on a given occasion, a particular one is performed is one factor controlling how much information is received. This has to be determined from the advance information and expectations of the receiver. The other factor is the relative probability (as estimated by a particular receiver) that the incoming signal will be one or another of those in the transmitter's repertory. A more nearly even distribution of probabilities yields more information than a less even distribution.

Note that therefore the same signal from the same transmitter can convey different amounts of information to different receivers. We find this surprising only if we make the mistake of thinking of information as like energy. But there is no "law of conservation of information," comparable to the basic physical law of conservation of energy.[1] Thus, think of telling a joke to an audience some of whom have heard it before and some of whom have not.

[1]Information is tied directly to *entropy:* the greater the entropy, the less the information. The entropy of a physical system is the degree to which the spatial distribution of the energy in the system approaches completely even distribution. An iron bar hot at one end and cold at the other has lower entropy than it will have when the heat has spread evenly through its length. Entropy is not "conservative": in fact, the second law of thermodynamics is that, in the long run, in any physical system, entropy tends to increase, approaching a maximum for the particular system.

Drawing by C.E.M.; © 1961 by The New Yorker Magazine, Inc.

FIGURE 6-1. Code noise.

NOISE ✖ Sometimes you fail to understand what someone else says because you cannot hear it clearly enough. Sometimes you hear perfectly well, but still misunderstand—or think you have understood but find later that you have not.

Anything that interferes with the accurate transmission of information is *noise*. There are two sorts.

Channel noise is extraneous stuff that reaches the receiver together with the signal, rendering it difficult to sort the signal out and identify it. It is hard to talk in a boiler factory, and would be difficult to communicate with an olfactory code in a perfume factory. Mutations during the replication of genes are due to channel noise.

Code noise results from discrepancies between the codes used by a transmitter and a receiver, or those used by different receivers. If you tell a new joke to two people and only one of them laughs, code noise is responsible. For another example, see Figure 6-1.

Communicative systems combat the effects of channel noise by being *redundant*: the signals of a repertory tend to be sharply distinct from one another, so that if a particular transmitted signal is distorted when it reaches the receiver it is still not easily confused with any of the others. For an example, consider a writing system such as that of English. With twenty-six letters there are $26^2 = 676$ theoretically possible two-letter words, $26^3 = 17,576$ theoretically possible three-letter words, and so on. But we use only a small portion of these combinations. If we see an unused one, we know it is a misprint (due to channel noise) and can usually figure out which actual word was intended by the transmitter. The high genetic stability of species is a pretty good sign that the genetic code has this same sort of redundancy.

Code noise is combatted by recalibration. Any complex system of communicative behavior acquired mainly by learning (for example, any human language) requires constant recalibration from one member of the community to another; yet discrepancies always remain and misunderstandings can always arise.

✘ From what has now been said about communication in general, and from what was said in chapter 5 about primates, we see immediately that primate communication (even leaving ourselves aside) is richer and fuller than is the communicative behavior of most other animals. We need only recall (p. 72) that primates do more *different things* together. Their scheduling structures their world in such a way that a larger number of behavioral and perceptual differences count as distinctive.

When arboreal primates, instead of scattering to the four winds, stay together in the trees by hearing and heeding one another's calls, communication is at work. When a gibbon finds food and utters a certain call as he eats it, communication is at work. When a monkey or a prosimian at the edge of a congeries screams as he is attacked by a predator, communication is at work. Grooming is communication as well as grooming; sex is communication as well as sex; so also fighting, play, and learning. Any way in which one animal's scheduling is contingent on what other animals do is a communicative convention. When a threatening, warning, or enticing gesture, grimace, or call does what otherwise might have to be done by direct bodily contact, we have communication of the special sort in which signals have meanings (p. 80): a food call means food; a warning call means danger; a threat means attack; a look of love means love.

PRIMATE COMMUNICATION

✘ Twenty-three hundred years ago, when Aristotle was trying to systematize Greek knowledge of the world, he listed several different kinds of "causes" of an event. One type was the "final cause" or "purpose": a stone falls *because* its proper place is down rather than up; a flower turns to face the sun *because* it needs the sunlight; and so on.

We have since learned that such teleological "explanations" are futile, not only for stones and atoms but also in the realm of organic behavior and even in that of human affairs. There is no way in which a later event can be causally responsible for an earlier one.

That does not deny the existence of purposive or goal-directed behavior. What is denied is that the purpose *explains* the behavior. Instead, the purpose must itself be explained (p. 47).

Our reason for bringing the matter up in this chapter is that the explanation of goal-directed behavior seems to lie in certain special kinds of information-processing, characteristic of certain physical structures. Purposive behavior is manifested by many

FEEDBACK AND PURPOSIVE BEHAVIOR

organisms (perhaps by all), by many communities of organisms (perhaps by all), and by certain mechanical devices built by human beings. All of these are marked by certain key structural arrangements. As far as is currently known, purposive behavior may not be manifested anywhere else in the universe.

MECHANICAL EXAMPLE

Consider a system consisting of a house, a furnace, and a thermostat. When it is running, the furnace supplies heat to the house, some of which leaks away if it is colder outdoors than inside. The thermostat samples the energy supplied by the furnace, constantly measuring the temperature in its immediate vicinity. If that temperature rises above a certain threshold, the thermostat sends a signal and turns the furnace off. If it falls below a certain threshold, the thermostat turns the furnace on. The thermostat controls the furnace, and is in turn controlled by *feedback* from the furnace via the air in the house.

The energy that runs this system comes from the fuel burned in the furnace. There is also a little in the form of electricity, carrying instructions from the thermostat to the off-on switch of the furnace, but one could allow the furnace to operate a generator so that this energy, too, would be supplied by the fuel. Most of the energy goes to heating the house. Only a small fraction is consumed by the feedback mechanism.

Obviously there is no teleology in this system in the sense of a later state of affairs being the cause of an earlier one. There could not be! The system works as it must work in terms of its physical structure. But its physical structure is such that its operation tends to maintain a steady state: a departure from the state is sensed and action is taken to restore it. Any device, organic or hardware, whose structure is such that it behaves in this way is a *servomechanism* or *homeostatic mechanism*.

ORGANIC EXAMPLE

Now consider the behavior of a paramecium, a single-celled but very complicated animal. A paramecium has a long, slipper-shaped body, with a stiff cover through which project hundreds of tiny cilia. The cilia wave in a coordinated fashion to propel the animal through the water. The animal has definite front and rear ends, and the motion is generally forward. If food is encountered, it is taken in through the mouth, located near the middle of the right-hand side. If an obstacle is encountered, the cilia reverse their direction of beating and back the animal up; then it makes a slight turn and moves forward again. If further obstacles are encountered it does the same repeatedly until a free path is found.

The behavioral repertory is small: motion forwards or backwards, eating or not eating. The control and sequencing of these types of behavior can only be based on a sensing of what lies ahead. Two devices for this sensing are known. There is a constant flow of the liquid medium from the region in front of the animal towards its mouth, generated by special motions of the cilia ahead of the mouth; and when the animal comes to an obstacle the front cilia touch it.

The rest of the control requires internal circuitry not yet identified. It is clear, though, that the paramecium manifests goal-directed behavior: it *hunts* for food. There must be an off-on switch for eating. There must be at least one more switch, with two settings: in one setting there is forward motion, while in the other there is backward motion and a turn. These switches are operated directly or indirectly by feedback from the environment, but in such a way that the paramecium is more apt to find food than it would be by purely random motion or by sitting still. Most of the energy supplied by the food is used to maintain general metabolism, growth, and, eventually, reproduction by fission. Only part of it is required to operate the various feedback mechanisms.

The Homeostatic Theory

It has suited our needs to describe the paramecium, in the first instance, in such a way as to make it seem almost as simple as the house-heating system. That underscores the parallelism, showing us that there is no more teleology in the behavior of the paramecium than there is in that of the house-heating system: in each case, behavior results from structure.

Actually, the paramecium is a great deal more complicated. The house-heating system can change its mode of behavior only by wearing out. The paramecium can change by learning. Although only a single cell, so that it cannot have any specialized nerve tissue in the sense in which many multicellular animals do, it can accommodate, within limits, to changed circumstances, which means that it contains the wherewithal for the storage of acquired habits.

The *homeostatic theory* proposes, in the first instance, that the internal structural changes that accompany learning (in a paramecium or in a human being) take the form of modifications of circuitry that produce new servomechanisms, interlocking with those already present.

The theory proposes, second, that *all* goal-directed behavior, in any organism and in any community of organisms, rests on the workings of servomechanisms. Without feedback there is no goal-directed behavior. With it there is.

Enough is known in certain instances to render the homeostatic theory highly plausible. Thus, the various bodily mechanisms that work together in maintaining the fairly constant body temperature of a warm-blooded animal (a mammal or a bird) seem to be hooked together in the right way to function by feedback. The same holds for the diverse structures that control the blood-sugar level, for those that keep an animal upright, for those that time the emptying of the bladder, and for numerous others. In situations involving artifacts as well as organisms, it is obvious that a violinist plays with his ears as much as with his fingers, and airplane pilots are unhappy when navigational aids too completely prevent their piloting "by the seat of the pants."

Of course, no one at present can trace, say, the circuits by virtue of which a young man feels the itch to write a sonnet for his beloved. The homeostatic theory, like any scientific theory, is only a hypothesis (p. 654). We accept it because it is the only proposal so far available that tells us what to look for in the more complicated and obscure cases of seemingly goal-directed behavior. Instead of supplying emotionally satisfying pseudoexplanations and thus forestalling inquiry, it highlights our ignorance.

7

×

MAN THE TINKERER:
HARDWARE AND HUMANNESS

Man is like all organisms in that his growth, metabolism, and behavior are monitored by genes, like most or all of his fellow animals in that he can learn, and like some of them in that he has tradition (chapter 4). He is like other primates in his stretched-out life cycle, his sexuality, his sociality, his continuation of play into maturity, and the other respects set forth in chapter 5; most of these he carries farther than do the other primates.

Man is unlike any other organism in his brain, which even on the primate scale is enormous and which doubtless differs from other brains in more subtle ways that are equally or more important (p. 416). He is also unique in at least two crucial behavioral respects: his manipulation of the environment with tools, and his power of speech. Surely both are tied in with his unusual brain (as well as with each other), though we do not know exactly how.[1]

In this chapter we take up the first of these two behavioral uniquenesses; in chapter 8 we discuss the second.

TOOLS ⊠ Any man-made object is an *artifact*. A thoroughgoing classification of artifacts would be too cumbersome for our needs, but we do require to recognize certain basic distinctions.

I have before me a specimen of one of the (seemingly) simplest of present-day artifacts: a pencil. A pencil is a *tool*: that is, an artifact used to change the state or condition of some target object. In contrast, a water pitcher is a utensil, an anvil or a table is a working surface, and other artifacts are of diverse other sorts.

A pencil is a *direct* tool, in the sense that when it is being used no other apparatus intervenes between user and target. Compare an arrow, propelled by a bow rather

[1]Of course there are other human anatomical-physiological uniquenesses: hairlessness, a thoroughly opposable thumb, a small mouth, upright posture and a striding bipedal gait, and more. We do not belittle these, but merely postpone our treatment of them to a more convenient place (in Part Two: chapters 25–27).

than by the user's arm, or a hammer when the force of its blow is to be transmitted to the target object through a chisel.

A direct tool is typically a single solid object with no moving parts. Every direct tool has a *handle* and a *head*. The former is the part grasped by the user, usually in his hand or hands. The latter is the part applied to the target. My pencil, in fact, has two heads with opposite functions: one is usable for putting certain kinds of marks onto certain kinds of surfaces; the other, properly applied, will remove the same sorts of marks—or at least smear them around and cover them with particles of dirt so that they are no longer legible.

KINDS OF DIRECT TOOLS

Direct tools can be classed (among other ways) in terms of the shape of the head and the manner in which it is applied to the target. Such a classification is shown in Table 7-1. A pencil used to draw or write is a tool of type 13; one used to erase is of type 10. A further criterion, not incorporated into the table, is the relative hardness or toughness of tool head and target object. Any contact of head and object changes both, but typically one more than the other. A pencil point scratched on paper results principally in a detachment of particles of the graphite which then adhere to the

TABLE 7-1. A functional classification of direct tools.

A direct tool is a single solid piece, used by a human operator on some target object. The part held by the operator is the *handle;* the part that acts on the target is the *head.*

PART OF TOOL APPLIED TO TARGET:	MANNER OF APPLICATION:			
	THROWING	SWINGING	PRESSURE Normal to target	Tangent to target
FACE	1 *to pelt*	4 *to hammer*	7 *to squeeze*	10 *to abrade*
EDGE	2 *to swipe*	5 *to chop*	8 *to crease*	11 parallel to edge: *to slice*
				12 perpendicular to edge: *to scrape*
POINT	3 *to spear*	6 *to poke*	9 *to pierce*	13 *to scratch*

EXAMPLES: 1: throwing a stone at. 2: throwing a discus so that its edge cuts into. 3: hurling a harpoon or spear at. 4: swinging a stone against. 5: as a butcher swings a cleaver. 6: as an ice pick against ice. 7: pressing a stone against. 8: (rare) pressing a blade against. 9: pressing a needle into or through. 10: sliding a stone along, pressing. 11: as cutting bread or sawing wood. 12: as scraping toast, or in using a plane on wood. 13: as with a nail against wood.

paper; a nail scratched on soft wood results mainly in a removal of particles from the surface of the wood.

The thirteen kinds of direct-tool action shown in the table are in part matched by possible actions of some part of the human (or other animal) body on a target object. Thus, a fist or the palm of a hand makes the kind of head called a "face" in the table, to mock direct-tool action of types 4, 7, and 10. The incisors, or a fingernail, supply an edge; a fingertip is a blunt point, and an elongated canine tooth (of the sort our ancestors once had but we have now lost) is a sharp one. But since the body has no detachable parts—unless we so class excrement—tool actions of types 1, 2, and 3 are impossible without artifacts.

Primary and Derivative Tools

You could not make a pencil with your bare hands. Most tools today can be made only with the help of other tools.

There are exceptions. If you are strolling through a meadow and want to try to flush a gopher, you can pick up a stray piece of dead wood, break off any unwanted projections, and poke it down the gopher hole. If the gopher emerges and you want to disable and capture it, you can grab a pebble and throw it with no reshaping at all.

The stick and the pebble are *primary* tools: bits of the environment appropriated and manipulated with at most such reshaping as can be effected by the direct application of parts of the body. An artifact (such as a pencil) that is not primary is *derivative,* meaning that it was produced with the aid of other artifacts.

Human and Nonhuman Tools

Man is not the only animal that produces artifacts: witness beehives, anthills, the houses and dams of beavers, the nests of birds and of some nonhuman primates.

Man is also not the only animal that uses tools. Some birds hold thorns in their beaks and use them as implements. Chimpanzees, probably our nearest nonhuman kin in the world today, have recently been observed manifesting three kinds of tool behavior:

(1)   In season, chimps eat termites. Termites live in hills, and if they are to be eaten they must first be extracted from their homes. A hungry chimpanzee breaks off a long, thin twig from a plant, strips it of leaves and buds, and carries it—as far as a couple of hundred feet—to a termite hill. There he inserts it down through one of the openings, holds it for a few minutes, and then withdraws it. The termites that have clung to it are scooped off in the mouth (Figure 7-2). When the chimp's hunger has been satisfied, he discards the stick; next time he prepares another.

(2)   A thirsty chimp takes a large leaf, crushes it, and dips it into a pocket of a tree branch or fallen tree trunk in which rain water has collected. When the improvised sponge has absorbed water, the animal conveys it to his mouth and sucks it (Figure 7-3). He may use the same sponge several times before discarding it.

(3)   Female chimpanzees sometimes use the broad leaves of tropical plants as toilet paper, or to clean themselves or their infants.

FIGURE 7-2. Chimpanzee termiting. (Courtesy of Baron Hugo van Lawick, National Geographic Society.)

In the light of such evidence, it may seem that man's use of tools differs from the similar behavior of other animals only in degree. Even if we compare the technologically most primitive human community with the most extensively tool-using nonhuman animal, the difference of degree is vast. However, there does seem to be one important difference in kind. All the nonhuman examples we have given are of primary tools. Only human beings, as far as we know, make and use derivative tools.

THE FOUR HISTORIES OF AN ARTIFACT

Let us look at my pencil a bit more closely.

It is 7.5 inches long, with a hexagonal cross section. Its diameter from edge to edge is 0.312 inch, from face to face 0.25 inch; its mass is 0.32 ounce. It is a composite

FIGURE 7-3. Chimpanzee using leaf-sponge to drink. (Courtesy of Baron Hugo van Lawick, National Geographic Society.)

of a number of different materials. Mostly it consists of two pieces of wood, probably cedar, each with a semicircular groove running its length, glued together so that the grooves form a hollow cylinder whose diameter is about 0.13 inch. This cylinder holds a rod of "lead": actually, a substance made by mixing graphite (a mineral: carbon in tiny hexagonal crystals), clay (any of several minerals: hydrous aluminum silicates), and water; extruding the mix in long spaghettilike strings; and then baking. The outer surface of the wood is coated with varnish, a substance of varied vegetable and mineral derivation, and on this an inscription appears in ink or paint of a different color. At one end there is a sleeve of aluminum, holding in place a short cylindrical bulb of a vulcanized mixture of caoutchouc, vegetable oils, sulfur, and fine pumice (particles of volcanic glass).

The History of Matter

My pencil is a tiny episode in the history of matter (for that matter, so am I—and so are you). All the matter that now constitutes the pencil was in the primordial cloud that condensed long ago to form the Solar System, and all of it was in the particular piece of that cloud that coagulated to form Earth (chapter 24). Bits of it have migrated in complicated crisscrossing paths during the last five thousand million years—round and round among the hydrosphere, the atmosphere, the crust, into living organisms and then out again. Just recently, guided by human action, these migrations have brought it together into its current configuration. The configuration is new; the matter is old.

The configuration—for *this* particular matter—is temporary, for it will vanish as the pencil is sharpened and used and resharpened, as the eraser is worn down, as the stub is finally too short to grasp and is tossed in the waste basket, thence to find its way to a trash fire or a refuse heap. The loss of the configuration, however, will not destroy the matter, which will go on to subsequent adventures, on and on for thousands of millions of years yet to come.

The History of Energy

My pencil is a tiny episode in the history of the energy transformations of our planet. To make it, materials had to be extracted from vegetable and mineral sources in many parts of the world, entailing the human expenditure of energy. The materials had to be brought together; their transportation degraded more energy. Then they had to be trimmed and shaped and processed and assembled—more energy. Then the final product had to travel to me.

A rough measure of the total energy degraded at human behest in the manufacture and delivery of the pencil is what I had to pay for it: about 4 cents. That is not much, but multiply it by the number of pencils produced in the world (in the United States alone, during the 1960s about 1,500,000,000 per year) and you get quite a tidy sum, hence a sizable number of ergs. Nor are we quite done. When I sharpen the pencil I expend energy. It will even require a little to throw the stub away when I don't want it any more.

Now, energy never vanishes, but we humans can use it only in certain forms, and as we use it it becomes unavailable. Entropy increases. The net long-term effect of human action is to raise the temperature of the environment. There are only a few sources of high-grade energy available for human exploitation. It is a good bet that every bit of the energy rendered unusable in getting my pencil made and into my hands was the product of the chief of these: chlorophyll-monitored photosynthesis (the others are wind power, water power, and nuclear power, and I suppose some of the machines in the pencil factory may have been run by electricity from a hydroelectric plant). There is a maximum rate at which photosynthesis can supply high-grade energy. If we use it up faster than it is produced we are going downhill. Maybe some day we shall have to get along with fewer pencils.

The History of Know-How

My pencil is a wee episode in the history of human technological know-how. As I use it up, the configuration of the participating matter by virtue of which it is a pencil will, in a sense, live on, because there are other pencils and because, although pencils do not reproduce on their own, human activity reproduces them. The *pattern* for a pencil exists in the pencil itself (as stored information: p. 52); it also exists in multiple copies in human brains and records.

As time goes by the pattern may change. It has in the past. Pencils did not have attached erasers until the late 1850s. A hundred or so years before that, the graphite for pencils was not mixed with clay. Two hundred years before that, a pencil was a stick of raw graphite wrapped in twine. Six centuries ago there were no pencils; one wrote and drew with other tools (sticks of charcoal or chalk, styluses, pens, brushes).

The Descent of Tools

We have discussed our humble pencil respectively in terms of the migrations of *matter,* of the transformations of *energy,* and of the transmission of *information.* These are three interrelated aspects of human history, because they are three interrelated aspects of the history of the universe. But there is one more perspective to be considered.

My pencil is a tiny episode in the *descent of tools.*

Every human being has two parents, at least two and at most four grandparents, at least two and at most eight great grandparents, at least two and at most 2^n ancestors of the nth ascending generation. For large enough n, these ancestors were not yet human. If we turn this around and trace the line of development from prehuman animals to ourselves (as we shall in Part Two), we are tracing what Darwin called the "descent of man."

An artifact has parents too: not the people who made it nor the patterns followed; not the raw materials processed in its manufacture; not the energy degraded in producing it; but the *other artifacts* used in making it. There exist in the world today, at various scattered places, a sizable number of man-made implements, utensils, vehicles, and pieces of specialized machinery that in historical fact played a direct part in manufacturing my pencil and in getting it to me. Just as the physiological parents of any organism are older than their offspring, so the parents of my pencil all came into existence before my pencil did. Each of them had its own parents, the grandparents of the pencil. In principle, the line of artifactual ancestry could be traced back indefinitely into the past. When we turn this around and trace it forward from the beginnings of human or prehuman technology to the present, we are tracing the descent of tools.

Of course, neither of these ancestries could be sorted out in all detail. The evidence of details tends very quickly to disappear. The lack of full information does not deny either the reality or the relevance of artifactual ancestry, any more than my ignorance of the identity of my physiological ancestors of a thousand years ago implies that I didn't have any. It means simply that we have to speak in more general terms— which is all we want to do anyway.

The analogy breaks down in one respect. The ancestry of a human being, or of any other organism in the world today, traces unbroken all the way back to the beginnings of life itself—there is no such thing as the "spontaneous generation" of new organisms. But throughout human history there has been a continuous trickle of new primary tools, supplementing the supply of derivative artifacts already on hand.

It is nevertheless clear that the new artifacts a human community can produce at a given time depend not only on its accumulated know-how and the available raw materials, but also on what artifacts are already on hand. That brings us to our next major point.

✗ A human community has, at any one moment, something that scarcely needs to be mentioned for a nonhuman animal community: it has a *technological base*. This consists of

(1) the accumulated know-how in the brains and records of the community;
(2) all the artifacts already in existence;
(3) the available *and recognized* material resources of the environment;
(4) the available *and recognized* sources of usable energy in the environment.

The matter of recognition is obviously important. Consider a group of people living by a waterfall. Their perception of it may be of various sorts. Perhaps it is a beautiful thing to watch; perhaps it is the dwelling of a benevolent or a malevolent spirit; perhaps they wash their clothes in the pool at its base. But it is not a source of usable energy, not part of category 4 of their technological base, unless they know how to build a waterwheel or in some other fashion arrange for the falling water to perform work they want done. Everything else, all the existing artifacts and all the features of the environment, must be judged in terms of know-how.

The Importance of Inherited Artifacts

The importance of the artifacts already at hand (as an ingredient of the technological base) is impressed on us when we are forced by circumstances to do a familiar thing without the usual implements: say, to change a tire without a jack, or to open beer cans at a picnic when we have left the beer-can opener at home.

It can be further underscored by playing, in imagination, the game of "start over from scratch." Daniel Defoe played this game in his novel *Robinson Crusoe* (first published in England in 1719). Defoe's motives were apparently moral and political, but the book caught on for a different reason, and in the ensuing centuries the game became an enormously popular theme in romantic fiction. Europe was exploring and expanding, and technology was developing apace. The rest of the world seemed very large, very mysterious—and, to the haughty ethnocentric European, very primitive. It was fun for the stay-at-home to read of what a clever and stubborn fellow European could accomplish with nothing to work with but unspoiled nature and his own inner resources. The reader could take vicarious pleasure and pride in the protagonist's successes, yet escape the attendant hard work and suffering by sitting comfortably by a warm fire as he read. Novels in the *Crusoe* genre were technological fiction, almost science fiction; only in the twentieth century has the myth arisen that they were written mainly for children.

Actually, though, none of these stories plays the game quite fairly. The castaway has at least the ragged clothes on his back (nakedness was too demeaning), and a few oddments in his pockets. In Jules Verne's *L'Ile mystérieuse* (*The Mysterious Island*, 1874), a handful of characters—carefully chosen by the author to have complementary abilities—are dumped onto an uncharted South Pacific island by a disintegrating balloon. They start humbly, but by no means with nothing. One of them wears spectacles, which have survived the wreck; they use one of its lenses to concentrate the sun's rays and get a fire started. Another, *mirabile dictu,* finds three grains of wheat in the lining of his coat, and in a year they are eating honest French bread.

A better player of the start-over-from-scratch game, if the rules are to be strictly enforced, would be a capable adult classical Menomini. If somehow isolated from his fellows and left with no artifacts whatsoever in a familiar environment in summer (we have to grant him the advantage of a favorable season), he would probably have been able to survive the following winter. Surely he could not have reconstructed all the material wealth of ongoing Menomini culture. He would not have known how to do certain things, and he would have known in principle how certain things are done and yet not have been able to do them. For in every human community, no matter how simple, the total stock of abilities-to-do-things is distributed among different people (that is simply an aspect of social structure, and explains why Verne selected his cast of characters so carefully): there is some duplication, but no one person is master of all the arts and crafts, and only cooperation makes it possible to bring each bit of know-how to bear as it is needed. Our marooned Menomini would have made a few primary tools, used them to produce a handful of simple derivative artifacts, and then employed all those to obtain a bare minimum of food, clothing, and shelter.

But that is all the rules of the game require. Today virtually no one raised in Western society could do it. We have become so interdependent in terms of specializations of know-how, and so dependent on highly derivative artifacts for our most elementary needs, that, deprived of them, we would die. Somewhere along the line—in fact, at several successive cruxes in the evolution of human technology—we have passed points of no return.

THE BIOSPHERE AND THE NOOSPHERE

× The last aspect of human tool-use that we shall discuss here has to do with its impact on our planet. What we shall say has little bearing on the content of our next chapters, but will come to the fore again during Part Two.

The Biosphere

The set of all organisms alive at a given moment, plus all the matter that has been moved around or chemically changed through the action of organisms, is the *biosphere.*

The *active* segment of the biosphere consists of the living organisms themselves. Their collective total mass has been estimated at 11,000,000,000,000 tons, which sounds like a lot but which is only 0.00000017% of the total mass of Earth (Table 7-4).

The *inactive* segment, produced by the metabolism and behavior of organisms, is much more extensive. Atmospheric oxygen, the layer of ozone in the ionosphere, and some portion of the iron in the crust and hydrosphere, are part of it, since their present location is due directly or indirectly to photosynthesis by green plants. Coral reefs, chalk cliffs and beds, and many other limestones are also part of it. So are some portions of various other types of rock; so is coal, and probably petroleum and natural gas. Nitrate deposits, such as those of Chile, are the result of the action of nitrogen-fixing bacteria or of certain blue-green algae. Calcareous shells of marine microorganisms accumulate at the bottom of the sea at a current rate (at least in parts of the Pacific) of 0.25 inch per year. Some 30% of the sea bottom is covered with ooze from just one type of protozoon (the genus *Globigerina*). Soils, which cover much of the land surface in a blanket of varying depth, are mixtures of tiny particles broken from bedrock by the mechanical action of water, ice, and wind, of bits of decaying organic material collectively called "humus," of moisture, and of living organisms.

When we find a recognizable piece of the body of a past organism, we call it a *fossil*. When we think of living organisms as producers of the inactive biosphere—as agents in the physical and chemical evolution of Earth—we may call their action *fossilization*.

The Noosphere

Man lives in the biosphere and is part of it. Within it, and as part of it, his hand and brain have been acting to produce another sort of shell: the *noosphere*.

The biosphere is ancient: it has been evolving for at least three thousand million years. The noosphere is new. Even 50,000 years ago it scarcely existed. But it has grown prodigiously. In the last decade we have stretched it out in thin tendrils to touch Moon, Mars, and Venus.

TABLE 7-4. Masses and densities.

Earthly Masses (in grams)	
Earth	5,983,000,000,000,000,000,000,000,000
Hydrosphere	1,250,000,000,000,000,000,000,000
Atmosphere	5,200,000,000,000,000,000,000
Active biosphere (all living matter)	10,000,000,000,000,000,000
All living human beings	145,000,000,000,000

Densities (in grams per cubic centimeter, making that of water = 1)	
Observable universe, average	0.000 000 000 000 000 000 000 000 007
Air in stratosphere	0.000 09
Room air	0.001 2
Cork	0.24
Butter	0.87
Ice	0.917
Water	1.00
Typical land mammal, average	1.07
Crust of Earth, average	2.5
Whole earth, average	5.5
Inner core of Earth	12
Densest stellar interior	100,000

Other organisms act on and modify their environments through their metabolism and by the direct application of movable parts of their bodies. We do that too, but we also alter the environment, on a scale vastly greater than that achieved by any other species, through the manipulation of tools. It is the massive consequences of this use of tools that justify the term "noosphere"; we are not just being anthropocentric when we fail to supply a comparable term for the segment of the biosphere that derives solely from the action of song sparrows, or from that of elm trees, or the like.

As we already know, the word "artifact" refers to any material object shaped by human action (p. 86). More generally, the process by which human action changes the material structure of the world may be called *artifaction*. A scar on Earth's crust where a mineral outcropping has been removed, or a field of wheat where once there was virgin forest, may not be what we would ordinarily call an artifact, but each is the result of artifaction and thus a feature of the noosphere.

Like the biosphere, the noosphere has two parts, one active and one inactive.

As matter of any sort migrates into a human community it becomes part of the active noosphere, and retains that status as long as it continues to play a role in the life of the community: anything from the intimate role of being inhaled or eaten to the relatively remote and static function of roads, walls, dikes, and dams.

Eventually, all the matter that migrates into a human community flows out again, in one or another form: as waste products of metabolism, as cadavers, as the smoke and ashes of campfires or the fumes and liquid discharge from chemical plants, as broken or worn-out artifacts. We pointed out in passing in chapter 2 (p. 13) that you can't just *make* something, but must always make something *from* something. In the same way, when you are done with something you can't just make it disappear. All the discarded matter from human life forms the inactive segment of the noosphere. It is still part of the noosphere because it has been moved around and processed by human action. Thus, the noosphere includes, at any moment, not only all the matter participating in human community life but also all the cesspools, graveyards, garbage dumps, slag heaps, and trash piles of the world.

There are now two points to be made. One has to do with our knowledge of the past, the other with our prospects for the future.

Biosphere and Noosphere as Historical Evidence

The current structure of the biosphere and noosphere is our evidence—and by definition the only evidence we have—for their past history. The current structure of the biosphere is our only evidence for the history of life; the current structure of the noosphere is our only evidence for human history as a segment of the history of life.

Thus, biologists of various sorts observe how organisms function today, and infer that matters must have been more or less similar in the past. They observe the active biosphere. Palaeontologists (and geologists) supplement this by analyzing the structure of the inactive biosphere, especially though not exclusively the recognizable pieces of earlier organisms that we call fossils.

In the same way, anthropologists and others observe how people and their things behave in present-day human communities, and infer that matters must have been more or less similar in the past. What they observe is the active noosphere. Documentary historians infer earlier events (relatively recent ones) from a special segment of the active noosphere called collectively "written records." The cesspools, graveyards, garbage dumps, slag heaps, and trash piles are the happy hunting grounds of the archaeologists.

THE NOOSPHERE AS HUMAN ENVIRONMENT

By virtue of the action of certain bacteria and other agents, some of the matter of the inactive noosphere is eventually recycled. But the process of recovery for fresh use is either very slow or else costly in energy degradation. Hence the mass of the inactive noosphere is constantly increasing.

There is an axiom in biology that we may call the "junk principle." It holds for any cell, for any organism, for any community of organisms; that is, for any biological entity of any size or complexity, up to and including a species with worldwide distribution. *No biological entity can live in a medium of its own wastes.* The reason is simple: the accumulated wastes interfere with access to fresh raw materials.

Because of this, artifaction has a twofold nature. It is creative in that it builds the kind of world human beings want to live in. It is destructive in that it threatens a kind of world in which we may not be able to live at all. The problem of balance between the creativity and the destructiveness of human action, the problem of balance in human ecology, is today beginning to confront us on a global scale. If we had no other reason for wanting to study man's place in nature, this fact would afford an eminently practical one.

8

✗

MAN THE CHATTERER: THE TONGUE IS A FIRE

—a world of iniquity: so is the tongue among our members, that it defileth the whole body, and setteth on fire the course of nature; and it is set on fire of hell. For every kind of beasts, and of birds, and of serpents, and of things in the sea, is tamed, and hath been tamed of mankind: But the tongue can no man tame; it is an unruly evil, full of deadly poison. Therewith bless we God, even the Father; and therewith curse we men, which are made after the similitude of God. Out of the same mouth proceedeth blessing and cursing.

James 3:6–11

St. James's remarks may strike us as overly humorless or metaphorical, but they are not too strong. We are what we are because of tools and language, and without the latter our use of the former would be feeble. The development of language in our ancestry—and, as far as we know, nowhere else in the universe—sowed the seeds of a revolution in the history of Earth whose consequences cannot yet be known; they may in time prove as far-reaching as those of the emergence of life itself.

An understanding of language is therefore essential for any understanding of man's place in nature.

Understanding is not the same as mere familiarity. Language is familiar enough: we all know what speaking and listening are because we all speak and listen. That means that we do not have to begin our characterization of language with a display of specimens, as one would have to begin a description of some exotic insect or mineral that most people had never seen. However, we shall find that some of our everyday notions about language are not entirely in accord with the results of objective investigation.

We begin with three general points.

(1) Whatever else language may be, it is communicative; hence our earlier assertions about communication (chapter 6) all apply. Language is not the only instrument of human communication, just the most subtle and powerful. We supplement speech by body motions, by facial gestures, and by variations of register, volume, and quality of voice that are not part of language even though they use the same

channel (vocal-auditory). The pedigree of these ancillary devices is probably more ancient than that of language itself, though doubtless the emergence of language reworked them in many ways: they are now cultural (i.e., traditional: p. 55) rather than genetic, to a greater extent than we usually realize, and vary from one human community to another. We also have communicative systems derived from language in one way or another. All this is charted in condensed form in Box 8-1.

BOX 8-1. Modes of human communication.

1. ARTIFACTLESS MODES, via acts carried on and perceived without any specialized nonbodily apparatus, though involving universal physical media (e.g., the air, for sound waves)
   1.1. INTIMATE MODES, involving touch, taste, smell: a large element of sexual activity; nursing; kissing; nose-rubbing; hand-pressing; shin-kicking under a table; playful spanking; changes in bodily odors and reactions thereto; etc.
   1.2. PRIMARILY VISUAL:
      1.21. NONGESTURAL: rubbing one's forehead; scratching one's nose; temple throbbing; eyelid position and flicker; facial color change; etc. With no clear line of demarcation, these merge into
      1.22. GESTURAL: The "come here" beckoning (different in Mexico and the United States); the frown of disapproval; thumbing the nose; shrugging the shoulders; affirmative nods and negative shakes of the head (meanings reversed among the Eskimos); the motions of any single dance tradition; etc.
   1.3. PRIMARILY AUDITORY:
      1.31. NONVOCAL: sneezing; coughing; nose-blowing; crepitation; stomach-growling; belching; the sound of footsteps; hand-clapping; choking; kinds of noisiness of breathing because of asthma or infective obstructions; etc. These merge only into 1.321 below.
      1.32. VOCAL:
         1.321. NONLINGUISTIC: true emotional cries and true imitations of animal sounds (if any: not words like *ouch, meow, ding-dong*); laughing; giggling; weeping; wordless singing and humming; whistling; variations of voice quality and the like during speech; etc. These do *not* seem to merge with the next:
         1.3221. LANGUAGE proper.
         1.3222. Artifactless modes which are delinguistic (derived from a specific language, and often confused with language): sung words; whispering; whistle talk among the Mazateco Indians or in the Canary Islands; a few others.
2. ARTIFACTED MODES, involving specialized manufactured equipment: trail marks; smoke signals; drum signals; strings on fingers as reminders; the plastic arts; many elements of sports and games; transfer of coins, currency, instruments of credit; picture-"writing" and true writing; instrumental music; special notations for music, chemistry, mathematics, knitting, etc.; telegraphy, telephony, radio; etc. To these we may add activities in which only the receiver (or observer) uses special apparatus: radar; diagnosis with stethoscope, catheter, and the like.

We may also classify all these other than language into those that are PRELINGUISTIC, in the sense that their pedigree is older than that of language, and those that are POSTLINGUISTIC, in that language was used to establish them. In the latter, the role of language may be

1. ENABLING: conventions are established by talking things over (e.g., the agreement reached between Paul Revere and his colleague);
2. MODEL: the conventions of a postlinguistic system are derived in some way from those of language or of a language: writing, mathematics; at second remove, telegraphy;
3. PIGGYBACK: the meanings of signals in the postlinguistic system are things in language; this holds for most usages in writing systems, where a letter stands for a sound or a character for a word.

It should be noted that one entry in Box 8-1 is writing systems. In our highly literate Western society we inherit a strong tendency to confuse language and writing and to speak of the former in terms actually appropriate only for the latter. Of course writing is important, and in the proper context we shall describe how it arose and how it works (pp. 571–581). But writing is *not* a manifestation of language on a par with speech. Historically, it is a derivative from language, and a relatively recent one at that. In this chapter we deal only with language itself.

(2)   No other species has a language; our own species has not one language but many—four or five thousand, by the only sort of rough count that is possible. Although there is no shock for us in this well known fact, it does require explanation. Why doesn't everybody speak the same language?

For that matter, why don't all human communities practice the same marital customs, subscribe to the same religion, operate from the same technological base, have eyes and skin of the same color and hair of the same texture? I don't mean to answer one question with another. The point is that the answers to all such questions lie in the *fact of change* and in the specificities of history.

The language of any community changes as time goes by; so do the rest of its lifeways, some rapidly, some slowly. If a community splits into daughter communities out of touch with one another (something that has happened repeatedly for tens of thousands of years), the subsequent changes in each are in time relatively independent of those in the others; hence, instead of mere change, one has *divergence*.

That is the answer in a nutshell, and all the answer we shall get in this chapter. The more detailed consideration of mechanisms of change (in language and in other compartments of human life) belongs later (chapter 23).

(3)   What kind of "system" is a language? A naïve beginner at learning a foreign language sometimes looks eagerly into the textbooks hoping to find some simple key, some short list of elementary principles from which, once he has mastered them, everything else will follow easily and "logically," much as such an elaborate system as Euclidean geometry grows from a small set of axioms or postulates. Even some specialists have flirted with notions of this sort.

It is indeed the case that the speakers of a language use the same set of elementary signaling units (the same "sound system," as we shall shortly call it) no matter what they are talking about. Moreover, in each language there are a few other phenomena that appear almost every time a speaker opens his mouth. One of these in English is that it is hard to say anything without heeding the difference between singular and plural (*the boy runs* : *the boys run*). In other languages other features have this pervasive character.

Beyond that, though—and it doesn't carry us far—the naïve expectation is false.

You could practice French until you were blue in the face, and still be at a loss the first time you entered a French bakery unless you had just happened to learn the usages appropriate for *that specific setting*. Or, suppose you have not yet learned that the singular of the English word *insignia* is *insigne,* or that the English word for the upper shell of a turtle is *carapace.* How could you possibly *infer* these specific facts from anything else about English? The facts are independent: you either know them or you don't.

Acquiring a language thus demands thousands of unrelated individual acts of learning. In every language there are certain semantic domains within which the vocabulary and usages form a system with a neatly patterned core, though with frayed edges; in another connection we shall present an example (pp. 192–197). But, as a whole, every language sprawls as formless as an amoeba.

✖ Various observations of infant chimpanzees, normal human children, and human children afflicted with one or another peripheral deficiency (such as deafness or blindness) validate the following two assertions:

GENETICS AND TRADITION IN LANGUAGE

(1) The acquisition of language by an infant organism requires both human genes (and the bodily structures those genes yield) and nurture in the bosom of an ongoing human social group. Neither of these suffices without the other.

(2) In humans, the drive to be in touch with one's fellows, through language or, if necessary, some surrogate system, is genetic, and so strong that enormous obstacles can be overcome. (As evidence we need merely mention Helen Keller.)

In the normal course of events, a child begins to acquire language by the age of eighteen to twenty-four months. This can be prevented only by environmental insults so drastic that the child has little chance of surviving at all. The essential wherewithal for acquiring language is "locked into" the genes (p. 50). The appearance of language is as inevitable as menarche or the sprouting of axillary hair. In fact, the former shows less variability from one part of the human world to another than do the latter. Moreover, the earliest steps in the child's acquisition of language are much alike for children everywhere, no matter what language is spoken by surrounding adults (p. 116). This suggests that all the thousands of languages in the world today are, and for a long time have been, erected on a single groundplan.[1] This inference is amply supported by the studies of individual languages all over the world that have accumulated during the last century or so.

Of course, almost from the earliest stages the child's language behavior moves in the direction of the particular language to which he is exposed. That it can and does do this must be in part due to genetics. But the detailed adjustments are brought about by the same mechanisms that account for changes of language habit throughout adult life; we shall say more of them below. The details are wholly a matter of tradition (cultural transmission), different from one community to another. There is something genetic about language (among human beings) versus no language (all other species), and doubtless also about the degree of skill with which individuals master and use their language, but there is nothing genetic about Chinese versus Puyallup, Eskimo versus English. If an infant is raised from a tender age in a speech

[1]This does not imply that the groundplan is wholly in the genes. Neither the universality nor the stability of a phenomenon is *in itself* adequate evidence that it is purely genetic—or that it is purely traditional.

community other than that of his parents, he comes to speak the language of the adopting community, showing no traces of that of his parents. His genes impede this only if they have produced a structure—say, a harelip or cleft palate, or a brain defect—that would equally interfere with his acquisition of *any* language.

SOUND SYSTEMS ✖ Any speaker of any language, at any age past infancy, speaks and understands in terms of a set of habits of articulation and hearing that constitute the *sound system* of his language.

Thus, in speaking, one aims one's motions of articulation at a series of articulatory targets. For example, if one is about to utter the English word *bit,* the first set of targets at which one aims—all three at the same time—are (1) a momentary closure of the lips; (2) a closure of the connection between the upper part of the pharynx and the rear end of the nasal passage; and (3) a pressure of lung air through the tightened vocal cords that sets them into vibration. If, instead, one is about to utter *pit,* then the initial set of targets includes the first two of the three just described, but, instead of the third, (4) a relaxation of the vocal cords so that air from the lungs passes between them unimpeded.

A speaker's aimings at articulatory targets are highly skilled acts, acquired by thousands of hours of practice and normally maintained in superb control throughout life by continued use. The structural arrangement necessary for homeostasis (p. 85) is clearly present: the speaker monitors his production of speech via two kinds of feedback, feeling the motions of his organs of speech and hearing the sound that the motions produce. Yet typically his aim is rather careless, and the resulting actual articulation sloppy. Speakers can get away with sloppy performance because *listening* is also done with enormous skill.

In listening to the speech of others, we sometimes miss what is said because it has been articulated muddily or because there is too much irrelevant sound from other sources reaching our ears along with the speech signal. In an extreme case—such as when we hear someone mumbling in his sleep, or lean close to the lips of a dying man to catch his last words—we sometimes try to puzzle out what was said by trial and error: we ourselves articulate various things, until we find something the meaning of which suits the context and the acoustic shape of which matches the distorted signal we heard from the other person.

Even in routine circumstances, listening is done through a good deal of irrelevant noise, and it is likely that we understand (when we do) through the same mechanisms: (1) reliance on context, both of the situation in which the speaking takes place and of what has already been said, and (2) trial-and-error articulatory matching, by which we discover the articulatory targets at which we ourselves would aim in order to produce a signal acoustically like the one we have heard. All this goes on very fast, and for the most part the activity is confined to our central nervous systems, without any muscular motions visible to others.

To be sure, there are circumstances in which no such trial and error is needed, the actual acoustic shape of what we have heard being unambiguous. There are extreme cases in which it doesn't matter just what someone has said: he has called our attention or has issued an emergency warning, and as long as he has produced a sufficiently loud signal, that is enough. But such cases are rare. Listening is a remarkable ability. Note how easy we find it, at a cocktail party in a crowded room, to focus on any of several different ongoing conversations, "tuning in" on that one and treating all the others as noise to be filtered out.

Finiteness and Discreteness

The *elementary signaling units* of a language are such articulatory targets as momentary lip closure, vibration of vocal cords, and so on, as described for English above.

In the languages of the world the total number of such units is always not only finite but fairly small. Counted in one consistent way, the number ranges from a low of about eight to a high of perhaps sixteen. Alternatively, we can count the number of distinctively different simultaneous bundles of units (often called "phonemes": like English *p* in *pit* versus *b* in *bit*): the range is from slightly under a dozen to perhaps six dozen.

The elementary signaling units are, in any one language, *discretely different* from one another. There is no such thing in a language as an "indefinitely small difference of sound." In English we have words *pit* and *bit,* differing only at the beginning. If a speaker produces something acoustically intermediate between these two, we interpret it as the one or the other; or, if we can't, we register what we have heard as ambiguous between just these two possibilities, and, if it is important, ask the speaker which one he said. There is no way in which we can interpret what we have heard as some third word, different from both of the two listed.

Range of Variability

Sound systems vary more widely from language to language than does any other aspect of language.

For example, in the articulatory region in which English has just the two phonemes (target-bundles) *p* and *b,* some languages have three, or four, or even five; but some have just one, and a few have none at all! When the number is the same, the details are often different. Chinese and French are like English in having just two phonemes in the region of English *p* and *b.* But the Chinese *p* and *b* are not like the English pair and neither of these pairs is like the French; in fact, Chinese *b* is much like French *p* (Figure 8-2).

Despite all this, the range of sound systems in the world's languages is not so great as one might guess. There seem to be certain loose bounds. Although the reasons for them are not fully understood, any experienced specialist can easily design, on paper, a "sound system" he knows could not be that of any real language.

More striking is the discrepancy between human articulatory motions and non-human animal cries. A parrot or mynah bird (p. 52) can be trained to mock very closely the acoustic contours of a human word or phrase, but the apparatus the bird uses for this is nothing like our own. Primates, especially apes, have body parts more similar to ours, though by no means identical (and the differences may be important:

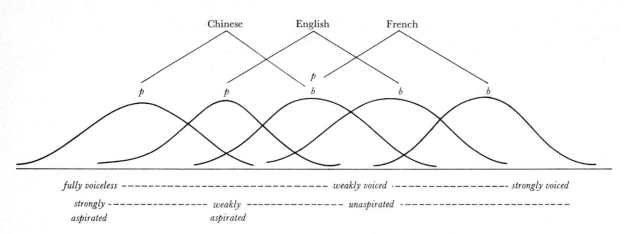

FIGURE 8-2. Contrasting lip consonants in three languages. "Aspirated" means released with a puff of breath; "unaspirated" means released without the puff. The phonetic scale runs from strongly aspirated and fully voiceless (no vibration of the vocal cords) to unaspirated and strongly voiced. The curves show the statistical distributions of actual "shots" at the articulatory targets in the three languages; the peaks of the curves are the "bullseyes" and define the functioning and contrasting units.

p. 414). In any case, in their communicative calls they never use the special motions that produce the characteristic "vowel sounds" and "consonant sounds" of all human language.

LINGUISTIC FORMS ✖ Of course there is more to a language than its sound system.

It is true that some of the ways in which we have fun with language—tongue twisters and the like—turn partly on the sound system. This element in language is real, and in view of the general importance of primate play probably always has been. But language would never have evolved merely as a toy.

The major biological function of talking is to *redistribute information* among the members of a community. The kind of talking with which we do this may be called *consultative prose*. It is different from, usually duller than, some other kinds of talking, but it is the germ from which all other kinds derive. It is consultative prose that gets information shared and gets joint plans made. It is in this use of language that the usages of different members of a community are recalibrated, so that they do not fray out in a dozen different directions and render mutual understanding difficult or impossible.

Of course, consultation does not invariably work—sometimes it turns into a knock-down and drag-out fight. But the efficiency with which language redistributes information makes possible cooperative behavior of a complexity, and adjustment to changed living circumstances of a rapidity and degree of effectiveness, unknown in the life of any other species. This points towards the other aspects of language.

Certain arrangements of elementary signaling units (in any one language) are associated, sometimes precisely and sometimes very vaguely, with certain things or situations, or kinds of things or situations, in the experience of the speakers of the language. Any such recurrent arrangement of signaling units is a linguistic *form,* and that with which it is associated is the *meaning* of the form (p. 80).[2]

For example, in English the sound we make when we utter the word *salt* or *lemon* is a form; the meanings are (roughly) a certain mineral substance sometimes used on food and a certain kind of fruit. There is no definite upper limit on the size of a form: *he put some salt on the lemon* is a form; so is a whole poem, or a whole novel, or, for that matter, the whole Bible. But large forms are composed of smaller ones, in ways we shall describe later, and most of our attention here will be given to fairly small ones.

The associations between forms and their meanings are mediated by circuits in the brains of the users of the language. We have no neurophysiological information about these circuits—perhaps even the use of the word "circuits" is wrong or overly metaphorical. But we do know that, whatever their physical nature, they are not provided by genes. The infant, or the immigrant to a speech community from somewhere else, has to acquire them by learning. Without the brains, the associations would not exist. That the English word for lemon is *lemon* is not a botanical fact about the fruit; it is a fact about speakers of English. That is what is meant by the assertion, often heard, that the relation of forms to meanings is *arbitrary.*

Note that although we speak loosely of a message (linguistic or otherwise) "carrying" meaning, the meaning is not *in* the message as milk is in a bottle or oil is in a pipeline. Rather, the meaning is *called to the attention of* the receiver by the message. You can tell someone over the telephone what you are having for dinner, but you can't give him a taste. All this underscores the communicative nature of language: remember (p. 78) that the transmission of information involves *triggering* rather than direct energetic action. If a person knows the same language you know, he has the right triggers built into him, and you can pull them by talking to him.

Note also that although the tie between shapes and meanings is mediated by the brain (that is presumably where the triggers are), the meanings themselves are not *in* the brain any more than the sounds are. Thus, if I ask you for the salt, you do not reach into your head for it, but, if you are a good fellow and, like me, a speaker of English, stretch your hand out over the table to where the salt is and pass it.

DUALITY OF PATTERNING

× Utterances convey meanings. Yet any utterance in a particular language consists, without residue, of an arrangement of elementary signaling units which are in themselves completely meaningless.

English *pig* and *pat* are meaningful: each recurs in endless numbers of utterances, contributing its bit to the meaning of the whole utterance. But the *p* at the beginning of *pig* and *pat,* though it also recurs, is not in itself associated with any constant feature of meaning. The role of the elementary signaling units, then, is not to carry meaning

[2]Some forms seem not to have any meanings in this simple sense: for example, we have the word *unicorn* although there are no unicorns. This point will come up later (p. 112).

We say that a form *has* a *shape* (in terms of the sound system of the language) and a *meaning,* or, alternatively, that the form *is* a shape *with* a meaning. Two forms can have the same shape: *tax* and *tacks.* Some investigators use the term "referent" instead of "meaning."

but merely to *keep forms apart.* If I ask you to pass the salt, you do not suppose that I want the sugar or the pepper, because the forms *salt, sugar,* and *pepper* sound different.

To say what we have just said is to say that a language has *duality of patterning.* This term derives from the fact that the sound system of a language has its own patterning, permitting certain arrangements of elementary signaling units and precluding others (in English we can begin an utterance with *tr-,* but not with *rt-*), and that this patterning is very largely independent of the patterning of arrangement of forms in larger forms.

No known system of nonhuman animal communication has duality of patterning. The feature bestows a great advantage, which may not be immediately obvious but is easily illustrated by a nonlanguage example.

In Longfellow's account, Paul Revere and his assistant had to work out a code by which information about one or the other of just two possibilities could be transmitted across the Charles River at night. They needed two signals, and agreed on a single lantern as one, two as the other. But suppose they had needed a code to handle several hundred different possibilities. To number the possibilities and assign *n* lanterns as the signal for the *n*th possibility would have been both inefficient and dangerous: inefficient because Paul's assistant would have had to store several hundred lanterns in the church tower (even if it turned out that he actually used only one); dangerous because distinguishing from a distance between, say, 174 and 175 flickering lanterns is difficult and the probability of error is great.

So suppose Paul and his colleague agree that each signal of the code is to consist of a row of five lights, each of which can be red (R), amber (A), or green (G). This yields 243 signals, but requires only fifteen lanterns to be available, one of each color for each position. The assignment of meanings to signals is arbitrary, but agreed on in advance: for example, RRRRR may mean "the British are coming by water in many small boats," RRRAG "by water in a few large boats," ARAGG "some by water and some by land," and so on. Unless Paul is color-blind, he will have little trouble identifying the signal that is actually transmitted.

This modified and enlarged Paul Revere system is unlike language in several respects, but does have duality of patterning. Each whole signal is a form. The possible colors for lights in the five positions are the elementary signaling units, meaningless in themselves but serving to differentiate any one form from all others.

The major disadvantage of duality of patterning is that the relation of forms to meanings is necessarily arbitrary (p. 105). There is no way in which the form with a particular meaning can be made to resemble its meaning. Accordingly, no language in the world has more than a small scattering of "onomatopoetic" forms, like English *meow* to denote the sound made by a cat or *ding-dong* to denote that of a bell, and even in these there is a considerable arbitrary element. (For example, in German a bell says not *ding-dong* but *bim-bam;* if the form were completely nonarbitrary then it would be the same in all human languages.)

The great advantage of duality of patterning more than compensates for this marginal disadvantage: a small number of elementary signaling units, chosen (or evolved) to be easily and accurately replicable by human action and maximally distinguishable by human senses, can be combined into a very large number of arrangements that can serve as forms. And that is precisely the state of affairs in every human language.

✖ Where do linguistic forms come from? **BORROWING**

Part of the answer, for any one user of language, lies in the fact that people imitate one another. Primates are better imitators than other animals, and human beings are the best of all (p. 73). Thus, a linguistic form may spread from one speaker to another within a single speech community or, under certain circumstances, between speech communities. Anthropologists call the spread of a linguistic form, or of any other feature of traditional behavior, "diffusion." Linguists call the mechanism *borrowing,* though it could also simply be called *learning.* If I borrow a linguistic form from someone else—that is, if I observe and imitate his usage—my language habits are thereby altered. Obviously this mechanism plays a great part in the development of language in the child. But it does not become inoperative at childhood's end. We continue to acquire new linguistic forms by borrowing as long as we live.

Either the shape or the meaning of a form may be modified as the form is borrowed. This is most obvious when a speaker of language A who has some familiarity with language B imports a form from B into his repertory for A. For him, the meaning of the borrowed form depends on the particular context in which he was exposed to it. Moreover, the sound systems of A and B are more or less incongruent; when he utters the form in language A he is apt to aim at articulatory targets appropriate for A, not for B. Thus, we do not pronounce recent imports from French, such as *raison d'être, encore,* or *de Gaulle,* as a Frenchman does, and only the third of these has approximately the same meaning in English as in French. In exchange, the French do not pronounce such borrowings from English as *parking, sport,* or *Kennedy* as we do.

For a child borrowing (that is, learning) forms from the surrounding older people in his own speech community, the discrepancies are eventually less noticeable. If an English-speaking child tells you a *newspaper* is a thing a boy throws onto the front porch and mommy wraps the garbage in it, you assume that in due time he will be exposed to the form in enough different contexts to render its meaning for him closer to its meaning for adults. If a young child's articulation is obscure, you assume that with more practice it will improve.

Yet usage never becomes completely uniform in any community. No two human beings speak *exactly* the same language. Even in a small, tight-knit community, there is variability from speaker to speaker. The usages of people who carry on transactions with one another require constant recalibration (p. 83). Since learning never completely stops and there is no such thing as mastering "the whole language" in some precise sense (p. 100), there is flexibility as well as variability. The variability means that misunderstandings can arise, and they often do. The flexibility means that they can be cleared up, and they often are.

✖ Where do linguistic forms come from? Another part of the answer is that we make **ANALOGY** them up as they are needed. **AND BLENDING**

At any moment in his life beyond early childhood, any human being carries around in his head several tens of thousands of linguistic forms, ready to be uttered if the occasion arises or to be understood if someone else utters them. This stored stock of forms is his *lexicon*.

But if he opens his mouth and speaks, he is not constrained to select merely from these stored forms. Repeatedly, every day of his life, a user of language says something he has *never before said nor heard*! And usually he is understood! The coining of new utterances is par for the course, so routine that usually we find no novelty in the novelty. Mostly we do not even recognize it. There are marginal exceptions, but ordinarily we cannot tell whether what someone says is being read off from his lexicon or is being made up as he goes along.

This *openness* (or "productivity") of language is the feature in which it differs most radically from all other primate communicative systems of which we have any direct knowledge—save only certain human systems (such as writing, or African drum signals) known to be recent derivatives from language.

A system which is not open is *closed*. Gibbons, for example, chatter a good deal, but careful observation reveals that each actually uttered call is one or another of a finite (and relatively small) total repertory of possible calls. A gibbon never produces a *new* call.

Openness in human language is made possible largely because human beings *analogize*. Here are examples.

(1) ANALOGY WITHOUT INNOVATION

I meet you one morning. The situation is much like various earlier situations in which I met someone in the morning. In the earlier situations my speech response was to pull from my lexicon and utter the linguistic form *Good morning!*; and in the earlier situations that response was acceptable, leading to no confusion or tragedy. As the earlier situations were to the earlier responses, so the current situation is to the new response: I say *Good morning!*

In this version analogizing yields no new forms; it is much like what other animals do. A gibbon encounters food. On earlier occasions, encountering food (and at the same time being hungry) has led to his emission of the food call, with no unfortunate results. On the analogy of such earlier occasions, he utters the food call this time too. Apart from the fact that gibbon calls may be genetic (this is not certain) while any human linguistic form is clearly traditional, there is this difference: the situation in which a human being uses a particular linguistic form sometimes shows (to others than the speaker) only a tenuous similarity to the conditions in which he has used or heard it before. It is today a dull commonplace to refer to a woman with a sour disposition as a *lemon*. In the history of the English-speaking world, however, there had to be a first occasion on which someone referred to some woman with this term, and on the first occasion it must have been a striking novelty. Any such widely deviant analogical extension of the meaning of a linguistic form is called *metaphor*.

Yet metaphor is a matter of degree. Every new occurrence of an old form is to some extent metaphorical, because a new situation is never exactly like any earlier one. It may nevertheless be responded to as though it were; the flexibility with which new situations are responded to is part of an animal's scheduling. In the most minimal sense, we have to assert that metaphor occurs also in nonhuman animal communication.

(2)   ANALOGY WITH NONSPEECH INNOVATION

A newly arrived exchange student from India accompanied an American student to a cafeteria for breakfast. Both got tea. The exchange student laboriously opened the tea bag and poured the tea leaves into his cup. The American explained that that was unnecessary—the hot water would suffuse through the paper and get the tea flavor. The new arrival thanked him, and proceeded to drop a paper packet of granulated sugar unopened into his cup.

With or without speech, we seek solutions to new problems on the analogy of known successful solutions to earlier ones.

(3)   ANALOGY WITH INNOVATION IN SPEECH

At a luncheon table papa and a small son take turns asking mama to pass things. We assume that this is the son's first experience with crackers and with cheese—or the first in which there was any appropriate talk about them to which he paid any attention:

> Papa: Please pass the rolls.
> Son: Wanna woll too, Mommy.
> Papa: Please pass the crackers.
> Son: Wanna cwacka too, Mommy.
> Papa: Please pass the cheese.
> Son: Wanna chee too, Mommy.

Papa's utterances and mama's actions serve to define the new linguistic forms for the son. Obviously, if *rolls* refers to several and *roll* to one, and if *crackers* and *cheese* refer each to several, then the way to refer to just one of the latter sorts of things is to use the forms *cracker* and *chee*.[3]

The boy's whole utterances *Wanna cwacka too, Mommy* and *Wanna chee too, Mommy* are innovations: utterances he has never heard nor said before. They are the product of inferences made by him, or by his brain. They are not "logical" inferences, but *analogical* ones; and, in fact, as our example of the tea and sugar bags also shows, it is quite regularly by analogy rather than by "logic" that human beings make inferences. An inference so made may be right or wrong; some sort of empirical test is required to find out. The boy's second inference was wrong, as judged by adult English, and doubtless his parents, after laughing, taught him the accepted grownup usage.

It is the error in the son's second inference (*chee*) that makes the example a good one for us. Innumerable times, however, analogical coinages yield forms already in

---

[3] Spelling is irrelevant here, especially since the boy is too young to know anything of reading and writing. *Rolls, crackers,* and *cheese* all end, in pronunciation, with a *z*-sound, while *roll, cracker,* and *chee* differ by lacking it.

the lexicons of surrounding speakers (like the boy's coinage *cracker*), or new forms that are just those the surrounding speakers might well coin under comparable circumstances.

(4)   CONFLICTING ANALOGIES: BLENDING

Typically, a situation that evokes speech is not *exactly* like any earlier situation. Usually there are crosscutting resemblances to diverse earlier situations. Thus there is typically more than one analogical basis for the selection from lexicon, or for the production by fresh coinage, of a linguistic form appropriate for the new situation.

It is in this connection that human speech differs most drastically from the communicative behavior of other animals. Humans can follow two (or more) analogies at once, yielding a *blend*.

A child, having been exposed in various circumstances to the two utterances *Do it like this* and *Do it this way,* came out with the blend *Do it like this way,* a form which persisted for several months before it was extinguished by the continuing impact of adult models.

Once upon a time, speaking of something my family had done of which I was at once proud and a bit ashamed, I commented by saying *We weren't sure we could avord it.* Here *avord* was the best I could do towards trying to pronounce *afford* and *avoid* at the same time.

We notice blending when it yields something blatantly deviant, as in the two examples given above. But it is at work all the time we speak, yielding new utterances that are routinely understandable and so "natural" (in terms of the language habits of the hearers as well as those of the speaker) that their newness passes unnoticed. Blending, rather than simple analogy, is the real keynote of the openness of human language.

OTHER INNOVATIVE MECHANISMS ✖ It should not be concluded that borrowing on the one hand, blending and analogizing on the other, are the only mechanisms that yield new linguistic forms. There are at least two others, less important than those we have described, and there may be additional ones that have as yet escaped observation.

One of the known additional mechanisms is *short-term forgetting* by a speaker. Someone says *Now, as far as those new classes we're putting in the new rooms over in G building, I think we should put Miss Jones in charge.* The introductory phrase *as far as* calls for a subsequent *are concerned* or the like, but the speaker has lost track of that in the continuing work of speaking, and leaves it out. Someone says *I think that, since they really do seem honest in their intentions, that we ought to let them try.* In formulating the inserted *since*-clause the speaker forgets he has uttered the conjunction *that,* and so utters it again. I have heard both of these (and have seen the second one in print) in situations in which they had to be due to lapses of memory. However, anything one speaker says (even as a slip of the tongue) *may* be picked up and used by others. So there seem to be young speakers of English for whom the modified patterns are standard, not deviant.

The other additional mechanism is *uncorrected mislearning.* This could be regarded as a special case of borrowing, except that the result is an innovation rather than merely the spread to new speakers of an old form. In each of the following pairs of phrases with similar sound and meaning, one is older and the other has come into existence through mishearing of the older one:

$$\textit{Here we go gathering } \begin{cases} \textit{nuts and may} \\ \textit{nuts in may} \end{cases}$$

$$\begin{cases} \textit{cut-and-try} \\ \textit{cut-and-dried} \end{cases} \textit{methods}$$

$$I \begin{cases} \textit{couldn't} \\ \textit{could} \end{cases} \textit{care less}$$

$$\textit{get a new } \begin{cases} \textit{lease} \\ \textit{leash} \end{cases} \textit{on life}$$

$$\textit{that's the way the cookie } \begin{cases} \textit{crumbles} \\ \textit{crumples} \end{cases}$$

$$\textit{he's the } \begin{cases} \textit{spit and image} \\ \textit{spittin' image} \end{cases} \textit{of his father}$$

The first member of the first pair is British; the second is American and may have arisen because the plant *may* is unfamiliar in North America. In the last, *spit and image* is an allusion to Caribbean voodoo, but the interpretation as *spitting image* is now commoner. In the other pairs I am not sure which member is older.

✗ The analogies which are ready to function, singly or by blending, in a speaker's production of new linguistic forms constitute his *grammar.*

GRAMMAR AND LEXICON

Analogies vary widely in their degree of *productivity*: in the probability that a new form will be coined by them if the proper situation presents itself. The kind of book we customarily call a "grammar" concentrates on the analogies that are the most productive and hence the most pervasive (p. 100); there are a lot of them, so that such a book can be bulky, and yet no description ever covers everything in any one person's grammar.

Any user of English past childhood has been exposed to thousands of singular-plural pairs like *boy : boys, girl : girls, room : rooms.* If he subsequently hears and acquires a new singular (e.g., *an intaglio*), he has no trouble forming its plural, if the occasion arises, by adding a *z*-sound at the end; or, borrowing a new plural (say, *plastrons*), it requires no remarkable genius for him to form the singular by dropping the final *z*-sound.

Any user of English past childhood also knows that the plural of *man* is not *mans,* as the prevalent pattern would suggest, but *men.* The plural *men* is "irregular"; this is merely a way of saying that the form actually in use deviates from the prevalent pattern. But the difference in shape and meaning of the pair *man* : *men* is also part of the grammar of English, in the sense that it is *potentially* a basis for the analogical creation of new forms. In fact, certain youthful addicts of science fiction refer to themselves as *fen* (sometimes with the paired feminine form *fenne,* the explanation of which we leave to the reader). Likewise, when Ogden Nash coined *tronastery* to denote a place for storing trunks, he was not exceeding the bounds of English, though probably no one had ever before exploited the particular basis (*monk* : *monastery*).

We see immediately why it would be virtually impossible for any description of the grammar of a language to be truly complete.

We see also why a description of a language (or a characterization of language in general) must recognize its sprawling nature and not oversystematize. In any given context, a speaker exploits only that part of his total stored language habits that is relevant for the particular context. In doing so, he temporarily imposes a certain degree of systematization on that part. In another context, a different segment of his lexicon comes to the fore. The linguist, as grammarian and lexicographer, tries to organize everything into a single coherent presentation. This is a valid enterprise, but we must acknowledge that it is something the ordinary user of a language never does, and we must not unwittingly assume that the language has the same structure in the brain of a user as it has in our comprehensive report.[4]

The lexicon of a speaker supplies the basis for the analogies that *are* the grammar. The grammar yields new linguistic forms, for the most part so routine that they are instantly forgotten; if they recur, they are being coined afresh. However, anything one speaker says *may* be repeated by him or imitated by others, so that it works its way into the lexicon.

LANGUAGE IN ACTION ✗   DISPLACEMENT

Coming back from a tour of inspection, a member of my band says *There are berries beyond that hill.* The rest of us did not know that, and we cannot see or smell them from here. But we can now go gather some if we are hungry or foresighted; or, with more use of language, we can arrange for some of us to go berrying whilst the rest do other things.

This anecdote illustrates *displacement*: communicating about something that is not in evidence at the place and time of the communication. It is such a commonplace for us human beings that it seems hardly to deserve mention, to say nothing of a special label. Yet the phenomenon is rare or nonexistent in the lives of other animals. For example, when a gibbon finds food he utters the food call as he proceeds to eat; he does not go back to the rest of his band and report the discovery.

It is displacement that makes lying possible: there could be no point to a false assertion if its falseness were immediately obvious to one's audience. It is the combination of displacement and openness that makes it possible to say things that may or may not be true (*Maybe there are still some deer left in those woods*), or to describe

---

[4]Compare our warning about the intrusive factor in our systematization of the Menomini conception of the cosmos (p. 27).

things that may or may not exist (*an animal something like an antelope or deer but with a single horn sprouting from the middle of his forehead*). That which can be described can be given a name (*a unicorn*), whether it actually exists or not. Thus language generates fictions.

False or uncertain statements need not be vicious. Combined with play, they yield verbal fun and its various derivatives: jokes and word games, teasing stories, allegory, folklore and literature, philosophy, mathematics. Taken seriously they can yield beliefs that are clung to despite evidence tending to subvert them. But, combined with empirical testing and skepticism, they yield science (p. 652).

SOLILOQUY

A person who can converse with others can also talk with himself.

In general, anything a person can do or experience overtly can be imagined (or remembered) without any overt input or output; this is what we mean by "thinking." I can drive from my home to my office; I can sit quietly at home and trace the route, including its sights, sounds, and smells, in my imagination. I can listen to a phonograph record of Sousa's "Stars and Stripes Forever," or I can play for myself a rather low-fidelity recording of it that I carry inside my head. Any human being can do these things or others like them.

Perhaps other animals think too. Some of them have central nervous systems, and it is hard to believe that they are totally unable to use them the way human beings do, although they cannot report such internal goings-on to us as our fellow humans can. There is good indirect evidence that some nonhuman animals dream, and dreaming is something like thinking.

However, it is only we human beings who can dream, imagine, or think in *language* and its derivatives, or in language and other modalities at the same time; and this is an important difference.

Conversational consultation in a group—as when the scout brings back the report of berries beyond the hill—not only redistributes information (p. 104) but also serves to bring bits of information into new alignments relative to other bits, permitting wiser planning for subsequent action. Various alternative courses can be discussed, their possible consequences considered, and a joint decision be reached. In a general way, whatever benefit a group of humans can achieve by being able to talk things over is also available to the lone human who can talk things over with himself. True, the lone human can only call on the information he has managed to store inside himself or is gathering by direct observation at the moment. But the revealing realignments and improved plans for action can eventuate just as they do for a group. Thus, language bestows on each individual, even when he is alone, some of the collective wisdom and efficiency in information-processing of his community.

EDITING

In our everyday consultative use of language our interest focuses on the information a speaker is giving us. We are not particularly concerned with his choice of words or his manner of delivery. If we don't understand, we ask a question. If we do, we go on to the next point: the information is retained, but the speech itself vanishes, for there was nothing memorable about it. Apart from that, we may, at most, get the vague impression that speaking is sometimes more coherent and sometimes less so. It takes a special effort to focus our attention on a speaker's actual delivery, so as to observe the specific features that mark it as more or less smooth.

When we make that special effort, we discover that talking is *work*. Sometimes, to be sure, a vocal response to some stimulus is as immediate and unpremeditated as a knee jerk. More typically, a speaker has some range of choice as to just what he will say, which means that as he is speaking he must constantly plan ahead.

To illustrate this we start with extreme cases.

When we read a fine poem or a bit of polished prose, or hear an orator deliver a well prepared address—or, for that matter, contemplate a beautiful painting or listen to a beautiful piece of music—the smoothness and perfection of the experience can make us forget the effort expended by the artist in preparing his product for our consumption. But anyone who himself tries a bit of artistic creativity discovers quickly what an enormous amount of time and energy is demanded.

Although artists and other creators go about their tasks in divers ways, a key paradigm is always involved. At any point in the creating process, the creator has in view some general pattern or *plan*, and he proceeds by analogically conditioned trial and error to flesh it out. The plan may be a subordinate part of a larger one; it may in turn generate subordinate projects as steps towards its fulfillment. The plan itself is reached and established by analogically conditioned trial and error. The artist's efforts, of course, are not always successful; some plans are modified or abandoned.

Thus, consider someone attempting to write a Petrarchan sonnet on a particular theme. His plan has two aspects. Formally, there is the prescribed rhythm and rhyme scheme. Semantically, the ultimate product must convey the information (or "elicit the mood") the poet intends. Note, however, that he is in no way bound to compose the first line first, the second line second, and so on. He may start anywhere, and work back and forth and sideways, tinkering and revising as he sees fit, as long as, in the end, the result accords with the plan. In principle, then, we must distinguish between the *order of composition* and the *order of delivery*.

Let us use the term *editing* for the analogically conditioned trial-and-error process of generation we have just described.

Poetry is very different from consultative prose. The latter conveys information and is then forgotten. In poetry, there is supposed to be something memorable about the exact wording—indeed, some people memorize a poem they like, which means that for them it becomes a single lexical unit. That is why the creation of a poem demands a great deal of editing. At the same time, when the poem is finally finished all traces of editing have been removed, so that, as delivered, it represents the acme of smoothness and coherence.

But editing plays a part in our talking whenever we have any choice as to what we are going to say, which means practically all the time. Everyone has had the experience of finding a comment "on the tip of his tongue" but deciding, just in time, to keep it to himself; everyone has had the experience of having to pause and stammer a bit because a needed word has eluded one's memory, or because two or more expressions seem equally apposite and one has to decide which to use.

Editing is less extensive in consultative prose than in literary discourse because there is less time for it and because the plans are humbler. Also, not all of the editing is done covertly. Signs of it turn up in what is actually spoken aloud.

Thus, we may hear a speaker's plan abandoned because in the continuing work of speaking it has been forgotten: examples were given in another connection on page 110.

Or someone says *When I got there to downt- —ya know, to the center of town, I mean on Main Street right, uh, right opposite, ya know, Joe's Diner, or, wull, maybe just before I got there, I* . . .. He is fumbling for an acceptable formulation, and is rejecting some of what he actually utters aloud. He makes various "hesitation" sounds (*uh, ya know, wull*) that hold the stage for him as he hunts for a way to continue, and that also signal the audience that part of what has actually been uttered is to be cancelled out.

The example may seem extreme, but there is much more of this in everyday speech than we usually realize. As hearers, interested in the information, we may sometimes grow impatient, but we are expert at playing the speaker's game with him (we speak the same way ourselves!), and so cancel out what he asks us to and retain only his ultimate "intended" utterance.

In everyday speech, as in poetry, there is in principle a distinction between the order of composition and the order of delivery. What counts communicatively, however, is the latter. It is crucial to note that, if there are no overt signs of editing in what someone says, or if we ignore the signs that are there (as we usually do), then we have no way of recovering the order of composition.

We read a sonnet. We do not have to know the poet's order of composition, the details of his trial-and-error editing, in order to get the impact of the sonnet. Someone says *He was caught by the police.* We cannot know whether the speaker has just coined this on the analogy of *John was punished by his mother, The birds were trapped by the hunter,* and the like; or first thought *The police caught him* and inverted that (by another analogy) before uttering it; or drew the whole sentence from memory where it had been stored as a lexical unit; or something else. As listeners, we are not obliged to make our process of interpretation match the editing sequence the speaker actually used on the particular occasion. We can parse and construe what we have heard in any fashion we find convenient—or not at all—in our efforts to understand it.

CHILD LANGUAGE

✕ When an infant first starts to speak he has a small lexicon but no grammar. His nascent speech behavior does not show openness, but is *closed,* like the modified Paul Revere system we described on page 106, or like the typical nonhuman primate call system. Each utterance he produces is one he has learned as a whole. For a while, his stock of utterances is enlarged only by the borrowing of further whole utterances. A particular utterance from the child may match an adult phrase of several words, but that does not mean that, for the *child,* it has been built by analogy and blending.

Evidence that the child's system has become open is when he says something he could not have heard from others. We are not sure, but it seems likely that the earliest coinage involves a recombination of what, to adults, are a familiar vowel-and-consonant form (roughly, what we call a word or phrase) and a familiar intonation.[5] For example, suppose the child has heard and used *Mama(.)* and *Daddy(.)* with a falling intonation (colorless comment), *Mama?* and *Daddy?* with a rising intonation (querulous, surprised, or attention-calling), and *Bobby(.)* with a falling intonation, but that somehow he has never heard *Bobby?* with a rising intonation. He may nevertheless one day say *Bobby?* in appropriate circumstances. A few such episodes, with the endorsement of favorable adult reactions, serve to render the intonations and the vowel-and-consonant combinations separate for him, as they are for adults, and his system has become open, with grammar as well as lexicon.[6]

PIVOT GRAMMAR

Openness usually appears before the child has completely mastered the sound system of his language. Recent observations suggest that there then ensues a stage lasting several months in which his incipient grammatical system is about the same regardless of what language is spoken by the surrounding adults.

The early open system is one in which many utterances consist (apart from intonation) of two parts. One part is drawn from a relatively small stock of forms we may call *pivots*, the other from a rather larger stock of forms we might call *names* (there is nothing important about either of these labels). The child seems to be able to produce any combination of a pivot and a name that circumstances render appropriate. Illustrating with childish English, we may thus have:

PIVOTS: *allgone, byebye, big, more, pretty, my, see, nightnight, hi;*

NAMES: *boy, sock, boat, fan, milk, plane, shoe, vitamins, hot, Mommy, Daddy,* etc.

Thus, if a friend has just departed or a glass of milk has just been drunk up, appropriate utterances are *allgone boy, allgone milk;* if the child is being taken off to bed and must leave a toy behind he can say *byebye boat;* and so on. In context, these utterances are intelligible to sympathetic adults.

This type of simple open system has been called "pivot grammar." In terms of meaning, the names refer to things, to impressions (*hot*), or to people, while the pivots are comments or observations of some sort on what is named. The order is not fixed: some pivots tend to come first, others second. The pattern, then, is COMMENT followed by TOPIC, or sometimes TOPIC followed by COMMENT. In another language, the shapes of the forms would of course be different, as would some of the meanings (all children have mothers, but not all have toy boats), but the *pattern* would be the same.

[5]Intonation is part of a language, and not to be confused with the communicatively significant but nonlinguistic variations of register, volume, and quality of voice we mentioned on p. 99.

[6]Probably most children develop *receptive* openness earlier than *productive* openness: that is, they respond appropriately to simple new utterances on the analogy of familiar old ones before they make their own first analogical coinages.

We now make two observations.

(1) HUMAN GENERALITY. Every language in the world has one or more sentence patterns involving just the two kinds of constituents found in childish pivot grammar, though the order is predominantly or exclusively topic first in some languages, predominantly or exclusively comment first in others, and though every language has also a plethora of more elaborate patterns.

(2) HOMINOID POTENTIAL. Efforts to teach a nonhuman primate to speak a human language have always failed abysmally. Recently, however, an experiment of a different sort was attempted. Washoe, an infant female chimpanzee, was raised in conditions as much as possible like those to which a human infant is exposed, except that when addressing her, and when communicating with one another in her presence, the experimenters used not language but the American Sign Language for the Deaf. Despite its name this is not a language, because it is not vocal-auditory; it also lacks duality of patterning (p. 105). But otherwise it is very much like language—specifically, very much like English. In particular, it is an open system, in which new messages can be produced by putting pieces of old and familiar ones together into new combinations.

The notion behind the experiment was the realization that many different factors may play a part in preventing a nonhuman primate from learning a language: perhaps the body parts homologous to human speech organs are wrongly shaped, or inadequately innervated; perhaps acoustic input to the ears cannot be processed in the necessary way; perhaps one or more segments of the brain cannot do what the brain of a human child does as he learns to speak. The experiment with Washoe changed some of these factors while leaving others alone: specifically, it replaced the vocal-auditory channel of language by a gestural-visual channel.

In eleven months Washoe had acquired and was freely using thirty-odd gestures, and was putting them together into composite messages just as do human users of the system. Moreover, she was producing composite messages to which she had not been exposed, and these were intelligible to her human mentors. That is, she was successfully coining new messages on the analogy of old ones. Her degree of flexibility had become almost an exact match of that of a human child in the pivot-grammar stage. She may or may not pass beyond that stage, but that is already much more than has traditionally been expected from any nonhuman animal.

We have no evidence that chimpanzees in the wild use any communicative system (vocal, gestural, or other) marked by the degree of openness characteristic of pivot grammar. Perhaps they don't. Yet the experiments with Washoe show that the *potential* is there.[7]

In pivot grammar, thus, we seem to have found a limited variety of openness much older than human language, an inherited kernel on which our cousins the chimpanzees may never have built, but on which all human languages have elaborated and with which each individual human being begins his linguistic life history.

[7] A somewhat different series of experiments with another chimpanzee has yielded similar results; thus it is unlikely that Washoe was, by rare accident, a sporadic chimpanzee genius.

**DIFFERENCES
IN GRAMMAR
AND LEXICON**

✖ Grammar and lexicon differ from language to language just as sound systems do (p. 103), though not so radically. Within grammar and lexicon, patterns at small size-levels show a wider range of variation from one language to another than do those at larger size-levels.

Every language has a kind of linguistic form called *words* (though child speech, before the appearance of openness, does *not* have words). Roughly, a word is a form that can on occasion occur as a whole utterance, but that does not consist wholly—apart from intonation—of smaller forms that can so occur. Thus, English *boy, boys, boyish* are words, but *-s, -ish* are smaller than words, and *good boy* is larger than a word.

Any speaker's lexicon includes many individual words, as well as linguistic forms larger or smaller than words.

By "patterns at small size-levels" we mean the analogies by which new words, or new forms smaller than words, are created, together with the inherited irregular forms (like plural *men*, p. 111) that may offer resistance to such innovations. It is here that languages are most whimsically varied. To be sure, there are also differences in the patterns for building phrases, clauses, and sentences, but they are less extreme. The greatest similarities among languages appear in the way clauses can be joined together into still larger forms, as two are joined with the help of *if* in English *If you don't stop teasing me I'll eat you up,* or with the help of *when* in *When he refused to stop teasing me I ate him up.*

DIFFERENCES IN MEANINGS

Another aspect of the grammatical and lexical differences among languages is in the meanings of the "small change" elements—the commonest, shortest, and handiest linguistic forms. This is not the same as differences as to what can be said, an issue to which we will turn in a moment; it has to do with what it is easier or more difficult to say. A Cree Indian expresses in two quick syllables, *ēskēw,* what must be expressed in English by the long expression *he makes a hole in the ice to hunt for beaver.* Contrariwise, the short English form *sidewalk* would have to be matched by a long Cree expression. The point is simple and obvious: people develop quick and convenient ways of saying the things their ways of life require them to say most often.

Here, as in grammatical patterns, languages differ less at large size-levels than at small. There are complicated meanings that require expression by long forms in any language. Consider *He picked up the pebble between the thumb and forefinger of his left hand and lifted it over his head, pivoting his arm at the shoulder with wrist and elbow straight.* The meaning of this could be expressed in various other ways in English, and can be said in more than one way in any other language. The English sentence achieves its net effect because smaller forms that carry certain meanings are combined together in certain ways. In another language, the smaller forms used would not in general exactly match the smaller forms that appear in the English sentence, but the patterns of combination, also different from those of English, would be such as to produce, for all practical purposes, the same net effect.

I have chosen the example because it involves the English words *arm, hand,* and *finger*. Arms, hands, and fingers are standard equipment in every human society. Simple linguistic forms with the exact meanings of the English words are not. Many languages have a word *X* which means 'upper arm', a word *Y* 'forearm-and-hand', and a word *Z* 'finger-or-toe'. This would not prevent a speaker of such a language from matching the meaning of our English sentence as closely as he needed to. The irrelevant parts of the meanings of *X, Y,* and *Z* would be cancelled out by grammar and context—just as, in English, we are not confused by the sentence because *arms* also means weapons and *hand* also means a seaman or farm laborer.

Focusing our attention on the short and handy linguistic forms of languages, then, we can say that different languages chop up the world of experience in different ways; and that, because most use of language takes place in context and few utterances consist of single words, one of these ways is about as effective as another. In a very general sense, we can propose that anything that can be said in any language can be said in any language.

But to this dictum there are two sorts of exceptions.

(1) One is the obvious fact that if the speakers of a language have never had any contact with something—say, for example, with steam technology—then the language supplies them with no way to talk about it. Here the most important point is that if a community acquires steam technology (or the like), it quickly develops adequate means for talking about it. Every language is flexible enough to allow this. It may be accomplished in part by borrowing forms from another language, in part by altering the meanings of older forms, in part by the analogical creation of new forms. The Fijian word for a steamship is *sitima*, borrowed from English *steamer*. Trains were introduced into Fiji a number of decades after their first contact with steamships; the Fijian word for a train is *sitima-ni-vanua* 'steamship of the land'. We can check any impulse to think of this as quaint by remembering that most of our English legal and military terminology, as well as thousands of nontechnical words (*chair, table*), are of French origin.

(2) The other exception is found in those uses of language which reflect primate play: punning jokes; more seriously, literature, especially poetry. A pun turns on the similarity or identity in sound of forms that have different meanings. There is no reason why two different languages should supply the raw materials for the same puns. A tongue-twister turns, similarly, on the sounds of forms. A literal translation of *Peter Piper picked a peck of pickled peppers* into French (*Pierre le joueur de musette a cueilli une livre de poivrons marinés*) may be intelligible French, but it is not a French tongue-twister.

This factor alone can serve to render poetry and certain kinds of prose untranslatable. More often, the difficulty stems partly from this factor and partly from the first: there are at least subtle differences (if not big ones) in what the speakers of the language have experienced and therefore have found ways to talk about. It is all very well to translate a short linguistic form in one language into a lengthy paraphrase or explanation in another, but then the flavor and the connotations of the short form, so important to poetry, are lost. The very brevity can be crucial.

✗ It would be wrong to pay attention to the differences among languages and ignore the features they all share. There are a few grammatical and lexical points common to all languages.

(1) All languages have intonations as well as ordinary ("vowel-and-consonant") forms (p. 116). It may be that certain features of intonation are universal; we are not yet sure.

(2) Every language supplies the machinery for sentences of the topic-plus-comment or comment-plus-topic sort (p. 116).

(3) Every language supplies forms like *I* and *you,* the meanings of which depend on who is speaking and who is being addressed. Every language supplies a set of forms more or less like English *this, here, now* versus *that, there, then,* the meanings of which depend on where and when the forms occur (*here* can mean 'at my house' when I am at home, 'at my office' when I am at work, and so on).

(4) Every language supplies *proper names* of individuals and of places, and patterns and raw materials for coining forms that are bestowed on individuals or places as proper names.

(5) Every language includes *kinship terms,* like English *father, mother, sister, brother,* though with great differences of coverage (pp. 191–201).

(6) In no language do the special kinds of forms we have listed exhaust the lexicon; in every language *most* of the lexicon consists of forms that are not of any of these special kinds. In every language these remaining forms fall into various types depending on their typical patterns of use (this is where such grammarians' terms as "noun," "verb," "adjective" become useful).

I can discern no compelling biological or physical reason why a communicative system that is in all other respects like language should also have these features; yet it is a fact that every language has them. It may surprise some readers that we can also add one more:

(7) In every human community, language is used for literary, artistic, or poetic purposes as well as for routine consultation.

✗ Let us add up our answers to this question. Those forms not coined by a given generation in a particular speech community are borrowed from other speech communities or inherited from earlier generations. The same holds for each earlier generation.

Thus, just as surely as all living organisms in the world today trace their ancestry back all the way to the beginnings of life itself, so also all the thousands of languages of the ethnographic present trace back, with no break in continuity, to the earliest languagelike behavior of our incipiently human ancestors. To push the question to the extreme and ask where the *first* linguistic forms came from is simply to ask about the beginnings of language, a fascinating topic to which we shall return in due time (chapters 25 and 27).

SUMMARY

✖ Language requires a human brain, but we do *not* know how brains work or what it is about the human brain that makes language possible.

Language requires human genes, but we do *not* know what it is in human genes that builds the necessary features into brains and other structures.

The capacity for language and the drive to acquire language are genetic, but the details of any one language are traditional.

Language uses the vocal-auditory channel and only that (some of its derivatives use other channels).

Every language has a sound system, a lexicon, and a grammar. The function of the sound system is to keep utterances apart; every language has duality of patterning.

The momentary lexicon of any speaker past childhood consists of tens of thousands of linguistic forms, large and small.

The relation between the shape and the meaning of a linguistic form is arbitrary.

Every language has openness: new forms are freely coined on the analogies of old ones. The analogies, inherent in the lexicon, constitute the grammar of the language.

Every language has displacement: people can talk about things that are not present at the place and time of the talking. Hence, also, every language yields fictions and hypotheses.

The principal biological function of language is to redistribute information among the members of a human group. Every occurrence of this use of language also serves to recalibrate the language habits of the members of the group.

People can think in language as they can in other modalities. The process of speaking involves analogically conditioned trial and error (editing), much of it covert.

Sound systems differ from language to language more than do other aspects of language design, but all exploit the same set of humanly possible articulatory motions. In grammar and lexicon, languages differ more at small size-levels than at large ones. Languages differ in the ways they chop up the world for lexical reference, and in the connotations and overtones of forms, but they are all equally adaptable to new communicative demands.

All languages have intonation; all have sentence patterns of the topic-and-comment sort, plus many others that diverge more from one language to another; all have personal pronouns, deictic elements (like *this* and *that*), proper names, kinship terms, and forms that are none of these special kinds. All communities use their language for artistic as well as for practical purposes.

The language of any community changes as time goes by.

9

✖

COUNTERPARTS AND COUNTERPOINTS: COMPARING HUMAN COMMUNITIES

"This 'ere *jam* tastes *fishy*!" (a British sailor at Murmansk in 1918, having received as his share of the loot a jar of caviar).

The first round is over: we have found (chapters 4–6) certain important ways in which human beings are like many or all other organisms, and have discussed (chapters 7 and 8) two crucial respects in which man is unique. We are ready to begin the systematic investigation of human unity and variety.

A seemingly sensible procedure for this investigation is to assemble some sort of master list of human institutions, from athletics through morals to zoological lore, and then to survey them one by one, describing for each the attested range of variation among human communities. Let us call this the "checklist method." In a way, any possible approach is some variant of this one. But unless used with great caution, the checklist method can introduce serious distortions of the facts. The aim of this chapter is to explain why.

The study of man is trickier than that of the rest of nature. One reason is that man's behavior is more complicated and fickle than that of stars, atoms, or nonhuman organisms. A more subtle reason is that, since we ourselves are human, it is harder to be objective. When we look at anything, but most especially when we look at ourselves, we tend to see what we want to see rather than what is there. There is no simple way to overcome this, but it is important to try. An opinion clung to in the face of mounting evidence to the contrary ceases to be a hypothesis and becomes a delusion. Delusions are ugly, and dangerous since in the long run they can militate against survival.

It is quite wrong, though, to suppose that objectivity entails coldness or disinterest. For optimum results the study of man requires, in addition to a striving for objectivity, an ingredient which is of little or no importance in the study of other aspects of the world: *compassion*.

To be compassionate is to try to "feel with" someone else, someone in another culture or in a different niche in one's own: to try to perceive, however dimly, what the world is like for him. The sequel is sometimes the attempt or desire to ameliorate the other person's condition, and that is fine provided it does not degenerate into unintelligent do-goodism (p. 279). But here we are not concerned with this sequel, only with the initial step.

It would be absurd to demand that a physicist feel compassion towards electrons, or an astronomer towards stars. The vaunted sympathy of some people for some nonhuman animals, or even for plants, is largely bogus. But every human society requires that its members be compassionate towards some of their fellow human beings. The pattern is universal, old, and typically human. It is part of human sociality, and important for survival. This is one reason why the student of human behavior must be compassionate. He can claim no grounds for exemption from a moral requirement imposed on everyone else.

The same considerations lead us to an equally important second reason. Among the facts about any human community are the ways in which its members react to one another and to their environment: that is, the ways their scheduling structures the world for them (p. 47). This is equally so for a community of some other species, say of baboons. But the baboons cannot tell an investigator how they feel about things. Human beings can—sometimes. To ignore this information when it is available, to neglect the *inside view* of the lifeways of a human community, would be to leave out matters of vital interest to us as fellow human beings. In the study of human affairs, then, compassion is not just a moral obligation, but also an observational instrument of great power.

The availability of this instrument does not mean that we can ignore the approaches and techniques of general biology and of physics. Compassion is an addition, not a replacement. The *outside view* is also necessary.

For example, consider the classical Menomini theory that the world consists of nine flat tiers, of which our own, the middle one, is a large piece of land floating on an endless sea (p. 27). This was part of their inside view, and helped in one way or another to establish the tenor of their existence. But we also need outside-view information as to the latitude, longitude, climate, and topography of their habitat, for that played a part in their lives and their history whether they knew it or not.

The difference between the outside view and an inside view must not be confused with that between objectivity and subjectivity. To be sure, for a member of a human community that we are examining, his own inside view is subjective. But for us as observers—even of our own culture!—both views demand objectivity. We must be as honest in reporting how members of the culture feel about the world, without distortion in terms of how *we* react, as we strive to be in describing, in physical and general biological terms, what their world is really like.

✕ We know (pp. 102–104) that every language has its own sound system.   **A LANGUAGE**
   Now, suppose someone who has never been exposed to any language but English   **EXAMPLE**
is suddenly set down among speakers of French. What he hears makes no sense to

him. He can listen, at first, only in terms of his English sound system, which is the wrong one. His initial registration of French does not illustrate the outside view: that we should get by analyzing French speech with oscillographs and spectrographs or with the benefit of rigorous training in practical phonetics. Rather, it illustrates the confusion which results when behavior governed by one *inside* view is registered and interpreted from a different *inside* view. If our English-speaking castaway wants to learn French, he dare not continue to filter the sound of French through his English speech habits, and will be helped very little by resort to objective acoustic recordings. French does not sound to those who speak it the way it sounds to a high-fidelity recording system. The speakers of a language hear it as they *want* it to sound, as they know it *should* sound. Our castaway must train himself to share the articulatory-acoustic prejudices of the French.

If that is so, then how can we effect any objective comparison of the sound systems of English and French? In terms of either, the other is whimsically arbitrary.

Here the outside view helps. Speakers of all languages have the same endowment of apparatus for producing and detecting sounds: they all have lips, teeth, tongues, jaws, noses, and pharynxes, and their ears are built in much the same way. The sound system of any language exploits this shared potential. Its speakers are trained to heed some differences of articulatory motion (which are thereby *distinctive* differences: p. 47) and to ignore others; this is a small but vital part of their scheduling. Sound systems can be described in terms of the common potential as frame of reference, and thus, indirectly, those of different languages can be compared.

This simple example is paradigmatic. In principle, the same technique is involved in comparing *any* aspect of the inside views of different human communities. However, we must immediately acknowledge that the task is a great deal harder for most phases of culture than it is for sound systems. We must be prepared for frustrations in later chapters, for we shall encounter practical obstacles that have so far proved insurmountable, and shall often have to speak with great hesitancy and charity.

SELF-VALIDATING AND NON-SELF-VALIDATING FEATURES

✖ For an investigator, all features of an inside view are on a par: he must report them as accurately as he can whether they strike him as sensible or absurd.

In another sense, however, we can distinguish between those features of an inside view which are correct by definition, because they *define* what they apply to, and those that are capable of being empirically true or false.

Of the first category, sound systems again afford an example. Our English-speaking castaway may misinterpret French sounds, but he cannot be wrong about the nature of this or that feature of his own English sound system because his (unspoken) understanding of that system *is* the system.[1] Again, the role of fathers differs from one human culture to another: a classical Chinese view of the nature of social fatherhood cannot be wrong for *Chinese* fatherhood, because the view and the phe-

---

[1] Our reference here is not to what a person will *say* about the sound system of his language, which is quite a different matter, and often in error.

nomenon are the same thing (p. 216). These are only two out of a great many instances in which a feature of an inside view is *self-validating*.

But every inside view has also features of a second sort, features which are not automatically self-validating, so that they may be correct or in error.

The Menomini believed that certain plants and plant parts are edible and that certain others are poisonous. By and large, they were right, not merely relative to Menomini metabolism but with respect to that of all human beings. Their plant lore was the result of numberless generations of empirical exploration and discovery.

The Menomini conceived the world as composed of flat tiers. This view, also, was the result of observation and of whatever sorts of empirical testing they could attempt. The peoples we Westerners used to call by the foolish ethnocentric term "primitives" are not incompetents or ignoramuses. They do the best they can with their heritage and their ingenuity. Therefore their views are to be respected. Respect is not the same thing as acceptance. The world they thought to be flat was exactly the world we believe to be round. On this score one of the two opinions is necessarily wrong, and the bulk of the evidence now available shows that the Menomini opinion was.

THE SOURCES OF THE OUTSIDE VIEW

× The boundary between self-validating features of an inside view and features that are in principle subject to empirical check is a fuzzy one. In order to illustrate both clearly I have taken extreme examples. The fuzziness is an excellent reason for humility in the face of the inside view of some other community.

For instance, how about the undeniable fact that in the West Indies people have died from voodoo curses (p. 269)? The cultures in question have inside-view explanations for this. Are we in Western society wise enough to be sure their explanations are totally wrong? Are we sure we have an empirically correct alternative explanation?

We value, as we should, the way of science. But it is very easy for us to confuse an inherited prejudice of our own culture with a hard result of empirical investigation, and whenever we do this our supposed outside view becomes contaminated and unfit for the use to which we want to put it.

In fact, the outside view must not be casually identified with the results of Western science. The Western contribution is important, taking the form of systematic cross-checks and careful experiment. But these are applied in principle to a collection of hypotheses and theories contributed by every community of which we have any knowledge and, indirectly, by many for which all historical evidence has been lost. The first investigator was the first incipient human whose language made it possible for him to ask a question and try to discover the answer.

Somewhat paradoxically, then, the outside view forms a larger or smaller segment of *every inside view*: namely, the segment which is not self-validating and which has been empirically checked and found reliable. The outside view is thus cross-cultural, rather than intracultural. It grows and changes; it is not complete and never will be. We use what we have of it as best we can, but we do not sneer at inside-view mistakes which have been generated as byproducts of man's varied adventure. We acknowledge that the growing outside view is, in the end, the collective achievement of our whole species.

✗ Human beings throughout history have functioned primarily as members of small communities. But we must not think of those communities as segregated like so many bacteriological cultures in test tubes in a laboratory. Isolation is obviously not the prevalent current pattern, and has pertained only sporadically in the past. Neighboring communities have recurrent dealings of one sort or another, and migrations bring people of differing ways of life together.

Whenever diverse human communities come into contact, there is an inevitable measure of "cross-cultural noise." Trivial examples are abundant. The Cockney sailor's reaction to Russian caviar (p. 122) is one. Another appeared in the late nineteenth century, in the confrontation between the Menomini and a new wave of European immigrants. Menomini has a speech sound *t* (p. 674) which is in general much like our English *t.* But from the inside views the two are different, in this way: one important fact about English *t* (as in *ten* or *pat*) is that it is in distinctive contrast with *d* (as in *den* or *pad*). There is no such contrast in Menomini. Their pronunciation of *apēt* 'as he sits' strikes us sometimes as ending in (English) *t,* sometimes as ending in (English) *d,* though they will be unaware of having produced any such difference. Conversely, when the Menomini, knowing very little English, asked about the identity of the newly arrived Europeans and were told *They're Swedish,* they ignored the to them irrelevant distinction between *t* and *d.* The epithet they then coined in their own language for a person of this new sort was *sayēwenet* 'one who is sweet'.

A single cross-cultural misunderstanding of this kind is insignificant, but in bulk they can have a serious cumulative effect, perhaps more disruptive than that of certain obvious large differences. The same can be observed within the internally mottled fabric of a complex composite society such as our own. Among us it sometimes happens that a couple with diverse backgrounds get married: say, a Jewish boy and a Catholic girl. The difference of religious affiliation is apt to be talked out in advance, leading to an overt agreement as to how it will be handled. The marriage may then founder, not on the rock of religion, but on the scattered shoals of petty annoyances which neither anticipated and which have no discernible connection with religion: he prefers to squeeze the toothpaste tube flat while she likes to roll it up from the end; she wants towels hung up neatly and he likes to toss them rumpled on the rack; she says *greasy* and he *greazy;* she has been trained to drape spare clothes on doorknobs, he to put them into drawers or closets; and so on endlessly. We do not usually think of such trivia as cultural, but of course they are—what else could they be?

What is a doorknob? Webster's *Third New International Dictionary* says "a knob that when turned releases a door latch."[2] As far as it goes—as far as it is intended to go—this definition is unimpeachable. It makes no pretense of telling us how doorknobs can lead to interpersonal tension. In Morris's "idioverse"—in his personal excerpt of our vast, complex culture—a doorknob is part of a door, manipulated to open the

---

[2]Copyright 1971 by G. & C. Merriam Co., publishers of the Merriam-Webster Dictionaries, and quoted by permission.

door or to close it, maybe also sometimes a thing to fidget with. In Maureen's idioverse, of course a doorknob is what you use for opening or closing a door, but it is also something else: it falls into the category of projections from the wall of a room on which one can conveniently hang up a garter or a brassiere until ready to do something else with the garment. Morris's idioverse has this category, but it includes only coathooks, nails, and the like, not doorknobs.

Now, what is a *t*-sound? A treatise on general phonetics is apt to define it as "any voiceless apical stop." Any human being is capable of producing a *t*-sound, thus defined, unless he has literally lost his tongue. A Menomini and a speaker of English can both produce such a sound, and often do. For the Menomini, the articulation falls into a functional category that also includes voiced apical stops (*d*-sounds); for the speaker of English, it falls into a functional category which *contrasts* with the category of voiced apical stops. For Maureen the category of projections-to-hang-clothes-on includes doorknobs; for Morris, projections *contrast* with doorknobs.

The whole recipe for fishy jam thus resides in forgetting the principle of *distinctive contrast* that we mentioned way back in chapter 4, and in ignoring the fact that what is distinctive for one culture (or individual) is not necessarily so for another. Cross-cultural noise is code noise (p. 82).

✖ Now we can turn back to the checklist method (p. 122) and see what cautions must be exercised in its use.

We know something of our own culture, and (from chapter 2) something about the Menomini. The differences between classical Menomini culture and our own do not span the whole spectrum of human variability. Nor can we infer that all human communities of the ethnographic present have shared everything common to these two. Yet the differences are sufficiently striking, and the similarities profound enough, to afford a point d'appui.

Two things would be easy: (1) assembling a checklist of activities carried on in all human communities but also by other animals (e.g., eating, eliminating, procreating); (2) itemizing affairs which are exclusively human but not universal (for example, playing tiddledywinks).

Our quest is harder. We want to squeeze down on lists of the two kinds just mentioned until they converge on the common denominator of the ethnographic present: the set of features shared by all human communities but not with other animals. Instead of starting with a master list, we must proceed in a trial-and-error fashion and *end* with the list.

We already know two items that belong on the ultimate list: language and derivative tools. There must be many more. Earlier investigators have made the attempt we are about to make, and two famous formulations are presented in Boxes 9-1 and 9-2.

The common denominator, whatever it turns out to contain, is the ground bass of the human passacaglia, the theme on which cultures develop their divergent elaborations. All variations harmonize with the theme, but in juxtaposition with one another they can yield a deafening and deadly clash of symbols.

BOX 9-1. Wissler's proposed universal "cultural scheme."

1. SPEECH
   Languages, writing systems, etc.
2. MATERIAL TRAITS
   a. Food habits.   b. Shelter.   c. Transportation and travel.   d. Dress.   e. Utensils, tools, etc.   f. Weapons.   g. Occupations and industries.
3. ART
   Carving, painting, drawing, music, etc.
4. MYTHOLOGY AND SCIENTIFIC KNOWLEDGE
5. RELIGIOUS PRACTICES
   a. Ritualistic forms.   b. Treatment of the sick.   c. Treatment of the dead.
6. FAMILY AND SOCIAL SYSTEMS
   a. The forms of marriage.   b. Methods of reckoning kinship.   c. Inheritance.   d. Social control.   e. Sports and games.
7. PROPERTY
   a. Real and personal.   b. Standards of value and exchange.   c. Trade.
8. GOVERNMENT
   a. Political forms.   b. Judicial and legal procedures.
9. WAR

—from Wissler 1923.

BOX 9-2. Murdock's partial list (alphabetical) of "elements common to all known cultures."

age-grading, athletic sports
bodily adornment
calendar, cleanliness training, community organization, cooking, cooperative labor, cosmology, courtship
dancing, decorative art, divination, division of labor, dream interpretation
education, eschatology, ethics, ethnobotany, etiquette
faith healing, family, feasting, fire making, folklore, food taboos, funeral rites
games, gestures, gift giving, government, greetings
hair styles, hospitality, housing, hygiene
incest taboos, inheritance rules
joking
kingroups, kinship nomenclature
language, law, luck superstitions
magic, marriage, mealtimes, medicine, modesty concerning natural functions, mourning, music, mythology
numerals
obstetrics
penal sanctions, personal names, population policy, postnatal care, pregnancy usages, property rights, propitiation of supernatural beings, puberty customs
religious ritual, residence rules
sexual restrictions, soul concepts, status differentiation, surgery
tool making, trade
visiting
weaning, weather control

—from Murdock 1945

We shall have to deal with fishy jam as we encounter it. But we must try hard not to manufacture it ourselves. Some questions about human lifeways can be asked and answered meaningfully from the outside view. Many, however, demand the inside view, which must then always be *that of the community itself,* never that of the investigator.

That is where we can most easily be led astray, and that is where our warning about the checklist method becomes imperative. A participant in modern Western society, examining another culture, can always (if he wants to or if he is not careful) find something to which to attach any positively charged label familiar to him from the West—labels like "religion," "superstition," "government," "science." But that is to interpret the ways of life of another community from *our* inside view, which is just what we want to avoid. We don't want to force the facts of another culture into the categories of the West; we don't want to squeeze them into some arbitrary set of categories that we invent for the purpose. We want to discover the *other* culture's categories, and report them and their content. That is, we want to deal with any one community by finding out *what are the distinctive contrasts for that community.* The comparison of cultures becomes meaningless unless we can do this.

It is with this orientation that we shall, in the next three chapters, examine three items which practically everyone has assumed are unquestionably part of the human common denominator: religion, property, and government.

10

✠

MAN THE WORSHIPER? RELIGION AND WORLD VIEW

The noun *religion* does not occur in either of our checklists (Boxes 9-1, and 9-2, p. 128), but the corresponding adjective appears in the heading of Wissler's group 5, "religious practices," and in Murdock's term "religious ritual." The use of these phrases, in place of the bare noun, emphasizes the view that, in all cultures, people do not just stand around from time to time thinking and feeling religiously, but *do* something about it. Each list includes also a number of other items that we tend to associate more or less closely with religion.[1] It is clear that both investigators propose religion as a human universal. That has been the consensus of the experts for a century or more.

Whether the consensus is true or false depends, of course, on what we mean by the term "religion." We are not forced to use this word as part of our technical vocabulary in ethnography; perhaps, in fact, it would be preferable if we did not. If we do, then there are two extremes of definition to be avoided as useless. One is a usage so constrained that only some one small group (say, members of the Church of England, as proposed by Parson Thwackum in Fielding's novel *Tom Jones*) could claim to have religion. The other is a usage so broad and diffuse that every human community would have it *by definition.* What we need is an operational criterion for a particular sort of *distinctive contrast,* which can then be discovered in any community for which it is functional and not in one in which it is not.

Our Western society is changing now, but until recently there was for most of us (including those who became ethnographers) a distinctive contrast between the *sacred* and the *secular* (or *profane*), or between the *spiritual* and the *material,* or between the *supernatural* and the *natural.* The first terms of these three pairs are not necessarily synonyms. But rather than entering into abstract subtleties, let us consider an indisputable paradigm.

[1]Thus, from Murdock's list: cosmology, divination, dream interpretation, eschatology, faith healing, folklore, funeral rites and mourning (in Wissler's group 5), luck superstitions, magic, medicine (Wissler's group 5), mythology (Wissler's group 4), propitiation of supernatural beings, puberty customs, and soul concepts. From Wissler we must add scientific knowledge (group 4).

✗ Behold a tiny agricultural village in the midwestern part of the United States in, say, the 1890s. The village is the marketing center for the farming families who dwell scattered through the surrounding countryside; those who live in the village itself include a few storekeepers, a banker, an innkeeper, a saloonkeeper, a schoolteacher, a doctor, assorted hangers-on, and a protestant minister. One of the structures in the village is a church. Thither the farmers and villagers repair each Sunday morning, with their families, unless prevented by illness or by temporarily impassable roads. They sing hymns, pray and recite in unison, and listen to a sermon. They greet one another, exchange gossip, and return home, sometimes chastened, sometimes disturbed, but always with the feeling that they are better off for having done their religious duty. At home, during the week, they take a moment to pray before each meal and before retiring. A few members of the community do not do these things regularly, or perhaps do not do them at all, but everyone agrees—even the delinquents—that they really should. Church attendance swells at Christmas and Easter, and for occasional revival meetings which may bring a delinquent back to the fold. The pastor sometimes visits a family of his parishioners, to check on their spiritual welfare. He is turned to for marriages, after the birth of a child for its christening, and for funerals. In case of prolonged drought he may gather his flock at the church to pray for rain. For all their sincerity, most of them forget their umbrellas.

The events we have sketched form the bulk of the religious activities of the community. Those who participate in them are expected not merely to go through the appropriate motions but also to *feel*, as deeply as possible, the momentary close communion with God. There can be no doubt that many of them do. A sign of this is that in case of serious personal trouble no one waits for the minister's help, but prays directly to God for guidance.

Except for these activities and events, some of them tightly scheduled and others more sporadic, most of the activities in our sample community are *not* religious. In his morning prayer the farmer may say "Give us this day our daily bread"; but "God helps them who help themselves": the farmer relies on his own savvy to get the field plowed, the seed planted, the wheat harvested and threshed; his wife counts on her own know-how as she tends the garden, feeds the chickens, and bakes the bread. Such activities are not antireligious—not "sinful"—but merely *non*religious. Indeed, there is the Biblical passage "Render unto Caesar the things which are Caesar's; and unto God the things that are God's"—an endorsement from the very fount of Christianity of the dichotomy between the sacred and the secular. When it occurs to him, the farmer readily acknowledges that God is the Author of all things, but one does not pester Him with trivia. When, despite all human effort and ingenuity, misfortune befalls, he finds and gives comfort by saying that "it was the Lord's will." Most of the time, however, he neither speaks nor thinks thus. Some aspects of life are religious; others are not.

Despite some marginal blurring, the functional contrast is clear. It is rendered even clearer by interpersonal differences. Women are supposed to be "more religious" than men, except that the minister is supposed to be most religious of all: he is supposed to refrain from certain common practices (drinking, smoking, swearing) on religious grounds, and to disapprove of those activities on the part of others, at least when he is present to observe them. Anyone other than the pastor who occupies himself too much with religion is viewed as an impractical visionary or as a bigot, depending on whether he keeps his strict ideals to himself or tries to impose them on others. Too much religion is as improper as too little.

SHARED FEATURES   ✗ There are many parallels between the ways of life of our prototypical midwestern agricultural community and those of the classical Menomini, but there are also crucial differences. Let us first note the similarities.

Both had faith in things unseen, or dimly seen, or rarely perceived, as well as in the direct evidence of the senses. The farmer believed in God and angels and the Devil; he may have believed in ghosts, at least when walking past a graveyard on a dark night (not as part of his religion); he believed in the capacity of seed to sprout and grow into useful plants (not as part of his religion). The Menomini believed in the Higher Powers, including those with whom he never had direct contact, and in the channeled potency that moved through a power pack or some lesser charm. But, for that matter, I believe that Earth turns on its axis, though I have never seen it doing so and doubt that I ever shall.

Both participated in special ceremonies designed to try to keep everything in proper adjustment. Both entered at times into direct communion with normally unseen powers, or engaged in activities aimed at that. Both were expected to feel, and often did feel, deep emotions of reverence and awe.[2]

Both had some notion of the structure of the world, of how it had begun, and of how it would eventually end. Neither had the habit of organizing these notions into a systematized cosmology—verbal system-building is rare. The world views of both involved various inconsistencies, which normally gave rise to no trouble. It is perfectly possible to believe both that the world is round and that it is flat, as long as no crux arises in which one must base action on both beliefs at the same time.

Both believed in a human soul or spirit distinct from the body, already in existence before birth (though, for both, the doctrine about this remained unelaborated) and surviving the body after death. Both sought special solemnization for the major crises of life: birth and death, for the farmer also marriage, for the Menomini also puberty. Both acknowledged the obvious close kinship of illness and death.

Neither involved any superstition. This term belongs to the vocabulary of fishy jam. I label your beliefs superstitious only if I do not share them and am arrogantly sure that they are silly and that my own are well founded.

COMMON DENOMINATOR

The parallels we have just listed verge on the human common denominator of the ethnographic present.

[2]Deep and special emotions, at any rate. We have no way of being sure that the English words *reverence* and *awe* are appropriate for an inside view other than our own.

Every ongoing culture supplies its members with a reasonably coherent *world view,* and every world view involves extrapolation beyond the immediately observable. Nonhuman animals have world views too, in the sense that their scheduling structures the world for them in specific ways. The characteristically human feature of human world views is a product of language: a person can believe in things he has never seen and may never see, because he has been told about them by others in whom he has confidence (*There are berries beyond that hill; The lab tests show some Enterococci in your bladder; The Third Thunderer himself told me to carry a beaver claw in my pouch; Christ died for our sins*). The man who claims to believe nothing except on the evidence of his own senses is lying, for if it were true he could not even talk.

Few world views, if any, are completely consistent. Few are talked about in a systematizing way.

People in all cultures on occasion feel (or are expected to feel) deep emotions. In all cultures there are more or less tightly scheduled ceremonies. Birth and death are major crises in all societies; for these, and for any others defined by the particular society, there are established rituals.

Acceptance of the soul-body distinction is nearly universal, though not quite: a few communities seem to have no interest in such matters, and some very tiny segments of Western society reject the notion altogether.

✖ The major difference between our midwestern rural group and the classical Menomini is that the latter seem to have had no shred of the *contrast* between natural and supernatural, or of that between the religious and the nonreligious. **DIFFERENCES**

The farmer's ghosts, if he believed in them, formed a nonreligious part of the supernatural; his religion entailed natural things (sending the minister's family a jar of his wife's preserves) as well as supernatural ones (God, divine intervention). When the farmer went to church he participated in a religious ceremony; when he went to a grange meeting or a political gathering he participated in a ceremony that was not religious except perhaps for an opening prayer.

A quick review of the ways of life we have described for the Menomini will show that *everything* was natural, *everything* was secular—or, as we can say with equal logical validity, *everything* was supernatural, *everything* was sacred. Our difficulty in grasping this stems from our necessary use of English words in talking about it. The English words have the connotation of contrast built into them from the long dualistic tradition of the West. We have to make a special effort at compassion in order to grasp even fleetingly the feeling of the unity of the world and of life that was the birthright of every Menomini.

In their lack of a distinctive contrast between the religious and the nonreligious, the Menomini seem to have conformed to the prevalent pattern in the ethnographic present. On this score the Menomini were typical, whereas the dichotomy found in many segments of Western society is unusual.

Let us be clear about what we are asserting.

When we say that every human society supplies its members with some reasonably consistent world view, the generalization is like the one we made in chapter 8 to the effect that every language has a sound system. A sound system is part of the design of any language; it is a system *within* which there are certain distinctive contrasts, different from one language to another. A world view is part of the design of any human culture; it is a system *within* which there are functioning contrasts which may be similar or dissimilar as we pass from one human community to another.

Then, when we say that most human cultures in the ethnographic present have had no special segregated religious institution, we are asserting only that in most world views the distinctive contrast between religion and nonreligion plays no part. It remains true (and important) that many of the *ingredients* are present which, in a society such as our own, are segregated and polarized to yield the contrast.

We can also say—in fact, we are obliged to say—that the Menomini had no supernatural and no science. To deny them science does not mean that they did not have a great deal of very accurate knowledge of the world in which they lived—of course they did. It means only that the Menomini world view involved no *contrast* between objective or empirical information and that obtained by what we would think of as other means (e.g., direct revelation). This contrast, also, seems to be relatively rare and recent in the world. For a Menomini, what he learned from a Higher Power during his puberty dream was in every way on a par with what he learned as a child following his mother around on her chores or as a young man shown or told things by older people of broader experience.

However, the Menomini world view seems to have resembled what we now think of as the scientific ideal (rarely attained) in one way: it tended to be undogmatic.[3] Any belief could be modified by a suitable new experience. There was the important difference that a Menomini's crucial belief-modifying experience was often highly personal, whereas modern scientific experiences ("experiments") are expected to be public and replicable.

A DIFFERENT BASIC WORLD-VIEW CONTRAST ✘ The existence in our Western culture of distinctive contrasts not functional in certain other world views should alert us to the possibility that other communities may have deep-seated contrasts missing in ours. Were there such contrasts among the classical Menomini? The record is too tattered to be sure, but one possibility is worth presenting.

The clue is an all-pervading feature of the Menomini language. Menomini nouns form their plurals in two different ways:

SINGULAR	PLURAL	ENDING
manētōw 'a game animal'	*manētōwak*	*-ak*
wēkewam 'a house'	*wēkewaman*	*-an*

We can speak of nouns of the "k-class" and of those of the "n-class." The difference of plural-formation is the handiest clue to the class to which a noun belongs, but

---

[3]Here we find a difference between the Menomini and our midwestern farmers. The farmers would have viewed many Menomini customs as superstitious (p. 132). The Menomini would not have reciprocated.

the ramifications go farther. When a noun is subject of a verb, the verb must show the class to which the noun belongs. The same is true when a noun is object of a verb. And when one refers to something with a pronoun, the form of the pronoun depends on the class of a noun that might have been used: *ayom* 'this k-class thing' but *yōm* 'this n-class thing'.

The system thus dichotomizes the world, and is reflected in almost everything a Menomini utters aloud or thinks to himself. The system is old, tracing back at least to Proto Algonquian (p. 10) and probably even earlier.

What concerns us is the kinds of meanings carried by nouns of the two classes. No simple single statement will cover all cases—that is never possible for any phenomenon of this sort in any language, because the way things are in a language at a given moment is always the consequence of all sorts of tiny historical accidents as well as of consistent analogizing trends (p. 139). Formal as well as semantic factors play a part. If a longer noun is derived from a shorter k-class noun, the derived one also belongs to the k-class, whatever its meaning: thus 'doll' is k-class because it is derived from the k-class noun 'man'. With ample allowance for known and unknown factors of this sort, we can still make some statistically valid generalizations.

The first is that nouns naming people, animals, or Higher Powers belong to the k-class. Some nouns naming appurtenances or characteristics of such entities also belong to the k-class. This may explain, at least historically, why such words as 'stone' and 'high bluff along a river' are k-class: we noted earlier (p. 28) that a large boulder is often a spirit or the home of one. If an n-class noun is used also to refer to a person, animal, or spirit, it becomes k-class in that usage: 'twins' is a k-class plural of the n-class noun 'navel', and an n-class noun becomes k-class as a personal name (p. 23).

The second is that any reference by a speaker to himself or to the addressee is of the k-class type. That is, the ascription to anything of the power of speech or of understanding speech renders the thing k-class at least for the nonce. The word for 'skull' is n-class, but there is a myth in which one of the characters is a rolling skull which speaks and is spoken to, and in that context the verb forms and the pronouns all make k-class reference.

There are also some specific facts to be noted. The word for 'soul, spirit' is k-class; the word for 'body' is n-class (p. 27). The word *awētok,* which we defined on page 27 as denoting any spirit or animal or any human being with unusual powers, is k-class, and its meaning may actually be a bit broader: namely, any entity capable of participating in communication. Remember also that Menomini children were believed to begin talking soon after birth, though at first in a special dialect that most grown-ups could not understand (p. 29). Game animals can understand speech: one had to address apologies to a bear before killing it (p. 22). Ritual song and the ceremonial use of a power pack were a type of higher-order communication that transcended ordinary talking.

The hypothesis towards which these facts perhaps point is this: The classical Menomini world view was marked by a fundamental distinctive contrast between entities that *can participate in communication* and those that cannot. In keeping with their flexibility about details (p. 28), the boundary was not razor sharp, but the contrast was nonetheless functional.

This contrast is one we can grasp, though it plays no great part in our own views. It is most certainly *not* to be equated with any of the fundamental contrasts of the Western world view; that would be like ignoring the differences between the Menomini sound system and that of English (and thus calling a Swede 'one who is sweet'). But it may have played as pervasive a part in Menomini life as the supernatural-natural contrast has at times played in our own.

Inferring an alien world view from the available evidence can be very difficult. I like to think my inference about the Menomini is right, but I cannot really vouch for it. It may rely too much on language evidence. Any attempt at a similar inference from the meanings of the nouns assigned to the two genders of French (masculine *le bateau* 'the boat', feminine *la table* 'the table') would quite properly be met with hoots of derision. World views, then, are not a topic on which any investigator should speak with too strident a voice.

CHANGING WORLD-VIEW THEMES ✖ It is worthy of note that in one human culture after another in the ethnographic present we find a certain array of thematic material playing parts in the world view: life, death, crises, human relations, human versus nonhuman, the perceived environment and what may lie beyond the horizon. This is like the fact that the sound systems of all the world's languages exploit much the same range of articulatory-acoustic potential. The systematizations into interlocking sets of contrasting categories differ widely; the materials systematized differ much less.

But they differ some. Various less weighty elements get caught up into the mix, coming to play important roles for those who hold a particular world view though they may strike outsiders as unintelligible or as absurd. Why is black the color of mourning in the West? In China, white is; in some cultures there is no association at all between mourning and a color. Why is east the principal compass direction in China, while for us north is? Why did the Menomini cosmos consist of nine layers, rather than of ten or eight or some other number?

The answers to such questions can be found only in the specificities of history. The world view of any community changes as time goes by, influenced constantly by the exigencies and unexpectednesses of community existence. Talking about things plays a part in the change, but only a part. If our hypothesis about the Menomini is indeed correct, one nevertheless must not suppose either that the grammatical pattern of k-class and n-class nouns was *the* cause of the world-view theme or the other way around. Causality comes in tiny momentary pieces. In some specific life setting, a noun shifts its type because of its meaning, which fits the world view in a certain way, and the shift becomes fixed; in another specific setting, a noun shifts its meaning slightly because of its type; over a long period of time a rough correlation emerges.

Note that no specialized caste of philosophers is required. The shapers of world views are for the most part ordinary people, who (in the long run) influence the speculations of philosophers much more than the other way around.

Thus, wherever the evidence affords us a bit of historical perspective, we can discern both cumulative trends and sporadic alterations in evolving world views just as we can in any other aspect of life. We shall illustrate this now by a discussion of *numbers* and *numerals,* first (as necessary background) in general terms and then with specific attention to the recurrent world-view theme of *favored numbers.*

Numbers and Numerals

A number, like a color or a size, exists in the universe whether or not human beings (or any other intelligent entities the universe may have spawned) communicate about it. A number is a property of some set of things. An oxygen atom has six electrons in its valence shell. This was so when our galaxy was being born and will be so when its last star is dying. Our knowledge of the fact is a matter of discovery, not of invention.

Just when two sets of things have the same number, the sets can be put into what mathematicians call "one-to-one correspondence." You form pairs, each consisting of one thing from each set, and the two sets are exhausted at the same time. Establishing one-to-one correspondences is not an exclusively human practice. If a monkey or ape puts the tips of the fingers of his two hands together, like a prissy old man, he is establishing a one-to-one correspondence between the fingers of one hand and those of the other. Similarly, human beings can establish certain one-to-one correspondences, or can attempt to do so, without "counting." Think of Og's wife, thousands or tens of thousands of years ago, ladling out stew until each of those present has a portion and then stopping.

But how can one attempt to put two sets of things into one-to-one correspondence if they are separated in space or time? For example, how can one attempt this between a flock of sheep before a storm and the same flock after the storm? The solution to this problem was a human *invention* (not a discovery), and is called *counting.*

The whole process involves two steps. Let the two sets of things be *A* and *B*. First, you establish a one-to-one correspondence between *A* and some inexpensive, easily portable set that you construct especially for the purpose. This intervening, purely instrumental set is then transported (outside the body, like any other artifact, or inside the brain, like any other piece of remembered information) to the scene of *B*, where you try to establish a one-to-one correspondence between the intervening set and *B*. Thus, indirectly—and assuming no deterioration of the instrumental set between the first step and the second—you can find out whether *A* and *B* have the same number or one is larger than the other.

A crucial feature in this is that one must learn to ignore everything about the objects of a set except just those properties that identify a thing as belonging to the set (the *distinctive* properties for the particular purpose). To count the sheep on a hillside you must ignore differences among the sheep but heed those between sheep and rocks, trees, dogs, or people, and those between a sheep on the hillside and a sheep somewhere else. However, you must pay enough attention to the differences between one and another object of the set to be sure you do not count the same object more than once.

The objects or things or patterns of behavior that you use in counting are *numerals.* A numeral is not a number but a symbol that means a number. Numbers belong to physics; numerals are features of human behavior and belong to physics only in the sense that all human behavior is part of the behavior of the physical universe.

Counting by human beings is probably very old. We can imagine Og's wife taking a sharp-edged pebble and a stick, surveying the dinner guests and cutting a notch in the stick for each, then going to the pot and ladling out one serving per notch. A notched stick was then a numeral. For optimum efficiency, numerals need to be cheaply replicable, efficiently portable, and made of material that one will not be tempted to put to some other use (since that would destory the record). Where sticks and stones are plentiful a notched stick is pretty good. Even better is some set of body parts: fingers and toes or, conceivably, teeth, except that teeth are not out in view and are more easily lost than fingers and toes. Counting by turning fingers down (or up) in some conventional order, and by remembering which was the last one turned, is the next to the most efficient of all techniques ever devised, and is surely exceedingly ancient.

But for a speaking animal, spoken numerals are the most efficient of all. Over and over again, all over the world, we find significant similarities between the word for 'five' and that for 'thumb', 'little finger' (showing that the habit of enumeration can start at either edge of the hand), or 'hand'; or between 'ten' and 'both hands'; and so on. Larger numerals are everywhere expressed using multiples of five, or of ten, or of twenty (fingers and toes together: 'one man' for twenty, 'one man and one hand' for twenty-five, and so on). Nowhere, except in the recent innovative usages of mathematicians for certain special purposes, are they systematically expressed as multiples of three or seven or twelve or the like. The evidence is decisive. It points, though, to many scattered inventions and reinventions of word counting under the influence of finger counting, not to some single early culture hero.

In the ethnographic present, how high the members of a community can count in words depends only on how high they need to count. The Bororo (in the Mato Grosso of South America) have a word for 'one', a word for 'two', and a cumbersome phrase for 'three'; beyond this they have little need except for vague terms like 'few' and 'many'. Our English-speaking ancestors of a millennium ago could count conveniently only up to 999,999; *million, milliard, billion,* and so on are later inventions. When a community confronts a need for numerals larger than those already at hand, there may be a brief period of difficulty, but finding a way never takes long. This fact deserves registration in our forthcoming checklist of human universals (Table 12-1, p. 154); yet it is merely a specific case of the free coinage of new forms afforded by the nature of human language.

FAVORED NUMBERS

If you buy a matched set of teacups in the United States you get six or twelve of them. In Japan you get five or ten. In such matters, the English-speaking world runs to dozens and half dozens, Japan to dizaines and half dizaines. Different human cultures, then, may highlight different numbers in comparable contexts, just as they may pluralize nouns in different ways (or not at all).

Some instances of this have deeper implications than does our initial example.

Thirteen, as we all know, is widely disfavored in the West as inherently unlucky. On the other hand, many cultures strongly *favor* certain numbers.

A favored number n works like this: unless there is some persuasive empirical reason for viewing or grasping something in sets of some other number, one tends to view or grasp it in sets of n. Suppose $n = 4$ (this was so among many North American Indian communities). You don't falsify obvious facts to favor the number. But instead of saying that you have five digits per hand you can say that you have four fingers—and a thumb. You class north, south, east, and west together as *the* cardinal directions and keep up and down separate, instead of lumping all six together (as did, for example, the Zuni). Instead of describing a hero as "brave, bold, and manly," you can characterize him as "brave, bold, manly, and upright." A real man may have three sons or five or none, but a character in a myth will have the ideal number. Ceremonially prescribed gifts can be in sets of four. Ceremonies can have four parts, or last four days, or involve four chief participants. Heaven can have four tiers (as among the Menomini), or four sets of four, rather than eleven or twenty.

Fourness can thus be underscored in many ways without any truly violent distortion of immediate reality, and, indeed, without anyone being particularly aware of it. Numeral words function as numerals in practical counting contexts, but they also occur in displaced speech and speculative discourse (p. 112), and can have a feedback impact on that segment of an inside view which is self-validating (p. 124).

One and two don't count. There are so many singletons and pairs in life that these numbers are favored everywhere—or nowhere; take your pick. From one or another community we find evidence for the stronger or weaker favoring (or disfavoring) of most of the integers from three up to thirteen. Special numbers larger than that are chosen because they factor into smaller special numbers. For example, in early Rome there was a ceremony in which a certain act was performed twenty-seven times. Twenty-seven is the product of three threes, and three was the favored number.

Nonhuman animals don't have favored numbers, nor do all human communities. The phenomenon is clearly a possible, but not inevitable, ingredient of human culture. Where we find it, we can be sure that it arose over a long period of time by steps most of which were unnoticeably small. A little favoring, perhaps empirically based, in one context can lead analogically to a favoring in another context, and so on. No culture ever acquired its favored number as a big sudden gift from some erratic genius.

The historical details are largely lost to us, but we know a little of the history of number-favoring in the West, where the favored numbers have long been seven and three.

The prominence of seven was given a boost by the Babylonian observation that there are just that many heavenly bodies (visible to the naked eye) that wander around against the backdrop of fixed stars: Sun, Moon, Mercury, Venus, Mars, Jupiter, and Saturn. We do not suppose this was the *origin* of sevenness, because, had the Babylonians favored six or eight at the time, accommodation would have been easy (give Sun a special status to emphasize six, or invent an invisible addition to make eight). But with a little emphasis on seven already there, combined astronomy, astrology, and mythology gave it added impetus.

Part of our heritage from this is the seven-day week. In Western calendrical matters seven forced three out because the environmentally given lunar month in fact has twenty-eight days, and seven and twenty-eight yield no three, only a four (i.e., weeks per month). However, there are traces, as in early Rome, of a temporarily countervailing calendrical emphasis on three, dividing the month into month-thirds instead of into weeks and thus suppressing the seven.

Threeness is attested also in ancient Greece, and in the Hebraic tradition at the time of Jesus. It is still with us, manifested in all sorts of subtle ways as well as in more obvious ones. The child in our culture learns very quickly that three is the appropriate number for blind mice, little pigs, bears, little mittened kittens, and billy goats gruff; soon he realizes also that there are just three kinds of people (men, women, and children); in school he learns of our tripartite government (legislative, executive, and judicial). Many threenesses he registers out of awareness. For example, national flags, which are Western in origin, are usually divided into several contrasting "fields," and the commonest number of fields is three; also, a flag uses several colors, and three is the commonest number of colors.

In discourse, three beats four all hollow. I mean, for example, that we are happy to describe someone with as many as three adjectives ("mean, ugly, and furtive") but uncomfortable if we must add a fourth. We have an abundance of two-part catchphrases ("life and limb," "black and blue") and many three-part ones ("faith, hope, and charity," "life, liberty, and the pursuit of happiness," "liberté, égalité, fraternité"), but few longer than that. The statistics of composite book titles works out the same way. In such matters two is common but colorless, four is clumsy, awkward, ungainly, and stilted, while three is round, firm, and fully packed. There is a cadence to *A, B, and C* that is fitting and proper, just as iambic pentameter is ideal for serious English poetry. The favoring of iambic pentameter is no accident, for its basic meter, despite the name, is not a five but a sedate three:

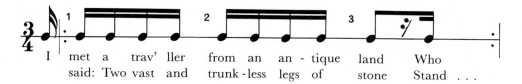

At first consideration, all the foregoing may seem to have nothing to do with world views. To show that it indeed does, all we need mention is the enormously prominent manifestation of threeness in the Holy Trinity of Christianity. The relevance of the diversified trivial threenesses of which we have given a small sample is this: a few emotionally charged manifestations of a favored number, or of any other such potential world-view theme, do not suffice to maintain it; they can be swept away, like slang, by a new fad. The founding fathers of the church would have had a very hard time in putting across this particular theme of Christianity had threeness not already been manifested subtly in many different life contexts among their intended proselytes.

11

✖

MAN THE OWNER? PROPERTY

The term *property* heads Wissler's group 7 (Box 9-1). Murdock (Box 9-2) lists property rights, along with gift-giving, hospitality, inheritance rules, trade, and various others the reader might be inclined to add under the same rubric.

In the preceding chapter we discovered that the contrast between religion and nonreligion is not part of the human common core because it is not universal. Here we shall learn that property is not part of the common denominator, despite its universality, because it is not *exclusively* human (p. 127): nonhuman animals have property too. What is typically human about human property can therefore only be some special twist added in all human communities to the shared animal substrate.

✖ From the outside view, property-oriented behavior involves owners, things owned, and relations among owners. The terminology of ownership has no relevance except for situations in which there is a distinction between nonproperty and property, or between one owner's property and that of another, or both.

FUNDAMENTAL TERMS

If a kind of thing is property for a particular community, then it is a *commodity*.

If all members of an animal community, or all communities of a species, need a certain thing, and if that thing is available in abundance, then the thing is not a commodity. Air has never been a commodity for land animals. For modern industrial man, with increasing atmospheric pollution, it is perhaps becoming one; if we establish a settlement on Moon or Mars, where air will have to be imported or manufactured, it will be one.

If all members of an animal community need something which is not in abundant supply, but there is nothing that can be done about the shortage, then the thing is not a commodity. Suppose a group of herbivores wander into a region where the diet, though ample, is deficient in some crucial mineral. They need it so badly that those who do not get enough may die. But they are quite helpless.

If no one in an animal community wants a particular thing, then it is not a commodity, no matter how abundant or rare it may be.

The commodities for a community, then, are the things which some of the members of the community need or want, which they can on occasion get by expending appropriate effort, but which are not always available just when they are wanted. The unavailability can be due to competition from other communities (of the same species or of another), to competition within the community, or to the physico-geographical environment.

In any viable community of any species of animal there must be understandings about commodities, shared by all members and passed down from generation to generation through the genes, by tradition, or both. By "understandings" we mean scheduled ways of resolving conflicts of interest when they arise. The pattern may be simply that when (for example) there is not enough food for all the stronger take it and the weaker get whomped if they try for any. But among such highly social animals as primates matters are rarely that simple. Baboons do not share food in the sense of collecting it and passing it around, but they share access to feeding grounds. While a dominant adult male may shoo off another adult who ventures to feed too close by, he will not only tolerate inroads by prejuvenile young but protect them. Moreover, most issues are settled symbolically, through gestures of threat and submission and the like, rather than by out-and-out combat.

The baboons show us not only the reality of nonhuman animal property but also the great generality of property *rights*. And we see where such rights come from. There are no rights in the inorganic world; they are not inexorable consequences of the laws of physics. They are matters of social convention, established by evolutionary trial and error in any species whose communities have them, and subject to change or veto without notice by the vicissitudes of history. Baboons ascribe certain rights to infants. If a predator or a more powerful baboon deprives an infant of his rights, this imposes no strain on the fabric of the universe, due then to recoil in the form of retribution. The infant's band may protect or punish; but that is all.

From the outside view the same is true of human rights, although innumerable inside views propose the contrary. "We hold these truths to be self-evident, that all men are created equal, that they are endowed by their Creator with certain unalienable Rights, that among these are Life, Liberty and the pursuit of Happiness": such rhetoric can have a splendid impact on human conduct, but it does not alter the workings of physical law.

PREHUMAN COMMODITIES ✘ Let us list the things that were probably treated as property by our forebears before they began to use tools very much or to learn to talk. The present-day behavior of other primates and of other mammals can serve as a clue:

(1)   Each animal owns his own body and its parts. One does not ordinarily think of one's hand or foot as a commodity. But an extremity can be lost, by accident or in combat, and then its importance is pretty obvious to the loser and to others.

(2)   Each animal owns the space he occupies at the moment and an indefinitely bounded shell of the surrounding space. The shell can be invaded, by invitation, for certain purposes such as sex or grooming. Otherwise, encroachment is a threat and is responded to by flight or counterthreat.

(3)   Each animal owns the food he collects.

(4)   Each animal owns the nesting material he gathers, and the nest he builds with it as long as he wants to use it.

(5)   Each animal has the right to dispose of bodily wastes (which might be described as "negative commodities"), provided it is done in a way that does not invade the rights of others.

(6)   Each animal has the right to groom and to be groomed by certain others; an infant has the right to be suckled and coddled by its mother and the right to protection from others; each adult male has, in season, the right of access to one or another female (the baboons show that the details may be very complicated: p. 43); conversely, each adult female has the right to the attentions of a male and some choice as to which male it will be.

(7)   The band as a whole owns its headquarters, and an indefinitely bounded range centering thereon (nucleated territoriality: p. 69 fn. 2).

The foregoing may be incomplete. It sounds funny because nonhuman animal behavior is not usually discussed in terms of property and rights. The reader can translate into some other terminology if he wishes. Our reason for the unusual turn of phrase is only to help us bridge the gap from prehuman to human.

✖ The development of tool-carrying, -use, and -manufacture added many items to the category of commodities: the tools themselves, and all the artifacts made with them, in gradually increasing quantity and variety. In due time it also significantly added to the bulk of "negative commodities" that something must be done about: worn-out artifacts that clutter one's way, and useless or even noxious byproducts. Let us recall the junk principle (p. 97). It has played a part from the very beginning in stimulating the movements of human individuals and the wanderings of human groups.

HUMAN FACTORS

The development of language eventually yielded, for some groups of human beings, certain kinds of "incorporeal property" (e.g., a song, or the right to sing it; or a personal name, which in some inside views is the same type of property as is a body part). Mainly, however, the effect of language was to make it possible to argue and theorize about property—something our prehuman ancestors were not equipped to do.

We said at the beginning of this chapter that if there is anything typically human about human property it must be some special twist added in all human communities to the shared animal substrate. It should now be clear that any such twist must rest on tools and talking. Let us therefore consider how people talk about property, and let us begin with the Menomini.

MENOMINI PROPERTY TALK

In Menomini, as in English, a *thing* can be defined as that named by a noun that does not denote a person or a place. One of the ways in which Menomini nouns are inflected is to show *allocation*. The bare (uninflected) noun *manōmɛh* means 'wild rice plant'; compare the allocated forms *nemānōmenɛm* 'my rice plant', *kemānōmenɛm* 'thy rice plant', *omānōmenɛm* 'his, her rice plant'. The noun has a plural: *manōmenan*:

one can say *nemānōmenɛman* 'my rice plants' and the like. Also, one can pluralize the entity to which the object is allocated: *nemānōmenɛmenawan* 'our (but not your) rice plants'; *omānōmenɛmowāw* 'their rice plant' and so on.

So far, Menomini would seem to differ from English only in the details of the grammatical machinery used. It seems, and is, trivial that we have to use several words ('my rice plant') to do what they do with one. But we now reach a significant difference.

Some Menomini nouns occur *only* in allocated forms. Thus one has *nesēt* 'my foot' (*nesētan* 'my feet'), *kesēt* 'thy foot', *osēt* 'his, her foot', and *mesēt* 'someone's foot', but no form distinct from all of these to mean simply 'a foot'.

Nineteenth-century travelers and missionaries were prone to put a prejudicial interpretation on such phenomena. They proposed that such usages reflect an inherent inability of the "primitive mentality" to handle abstractions. Inferences of this sort stem from insufficient knowledge of the language and from European chutzpa; they are unadulterated claptrap. In fact, the Menomini use *mesēt,* the form which allocates the foot to an unspecified human possessor, also for the unit of length we call a *foot* in English, and this usage is no more confusing to them than is, for us, our use of the word *hand* in several different senses (p. 119). And *osēt*, which in its structure means 'his, her foot', is also regularly used for an animal foot that has been detached so that its relation to the rest of the animal is no longer relevant. Furthermore, the latter form can be inflected for allocation all over again if there is reason to do so: I can say *netōsetɛman* 'my its feet' of the pigs' feet I have purchased for dinner.

But if we proceed with caution we can obtain from the Menomini data, if not a conclusion, at least a hypothesis.

A Menomini noun which does not occur in unallocated form is "dependent." There are two classes of dependent nouns. One consists mainly of kinship terms (pp. 191–201). The other comprises for the most part names of parts of the body, human or animal: 'my hand', 'my back', 'his [a fish's] gills', 'his fin', and so on. 'Body, person' and 'soul' (p. 27) are also dependent nouns of this second class. So are words meaning 'scab, scar', 'tears', and a few others like that, and the names of a number of intimate articles such as 'necklace, scarf', 'bag, pocket', 'warclub'. The general word for 'house' (p. 14) is an independent noun, *wēkewam.* Inflected for allocation, this yields *netōwēke-wam* 'my house' in the sense of modern legal ownership; 'my dwelling' is a related dependent noun, *nēk.* Kept apart in the same way are 'my blanket' in the sense of ownership and in the sense of the one habitually worn.

We see that Menomini distinguishes with reasonable sharpness between two differ- ent patterns for expressing possession. One consists of the allocational inflection of an independent noun (one which also occurs freely in unallocated form). Let us call this "loose possession." The other consists in the use of a dependent noun; this we will call "intimate possession." The latter refers to kin, to people (or sometimes animals or spirits) with which one has kinship-like relations, to body parts, to articles which are worn or carried on the person, and to things with which one has some other sort of especially close tie (e.g., 'my home'). We cannot be sure that a meaning of the type just described will be conveyed by a dependent noun, but we can be virtually certain that a dependent noun will have this sort of meaning.

The crucial point is that Menomini intimate possession relates chiefly to things that were commodities for our prehuman ancestors: person, body parts, home base, and kin (or access to them in certain connections). The exceptions are artifacts of a highly personal sort which as a category are of great antiquity though some of the specific items (e.g., eyeglasses) are modern.

OTHER EVIDENCE

If this situation were unique to the Menomini we would hardly be justified in describing it here. But it is not. Dependent and independent nouns are common to all the Algonquian languages. Many other families of languages in aboriginal America, and some elsewhere, have similar machinery. The contrast between loose and intimate possession is even more widespread, maintained by diverse grammatical machinery but always with kin or body parts or both in the intimate class.

I discern no trace of the contrast in English (though it may be there, concealed, like the purloined letter, by its obviousness); in French it is quite clear. Speaking of a loose possession, one says, for example, *Je veux laver ma voiture* 'I want to wash my car', with the possessive form *ma* 'my'; of a body part one says *Je veux me laver les mains* 'I want to wash the hands for myself', with a reflexive verb and with the definite article *les* in place of the possessive.

✖ From the facts that the loose-intimate contrast is very widespread and that it is very stubborn (maintaining itself even when linguistic change completely reworks the machinery for its expression) we infer that it is also very old. This brings us to our hypothesis about human property.

A PROPERTY HYPOTHESIS

Early in human history, as our ancestors became tool-users and talkers, ways of speaking came to reflect, and thus to render firm and to help transmit, a contrast inherited from prehuman times that we could characterize as that between "self" and "environment."

The self and its parts and prerogatives formed the category of intimate possessions: just the things that had been commodities before our humanization (p. 142), together with those artifacts that were most closely associated with the person because they were worn or carried and because they were very important. For example, a club is an extension of the hand and arm and equally crucial for survival.

At the same time, a subsidiary distinction developed within the "environment" pole of the underlying contrast: on the one hand, those things that have been appropriated for the nonce, places occupied temporarily, objects used and then discarded; on the other, the same things when not appropriated and things that were never appropriated. This contrast is that between loose possessions and things that are not possessions at all.

In fine, then, these two binary contrasts gave early man *three* distinct sets of things: intimate possessions, loose possessions, and nonpossessions.

This state of affairs is not exactly a feature of the human common denominator, in the sense of something shared by all human communities everywhere. Rather, our hypothesis proposes it as the historically shared *base line* on which different cultural lineages have rung their varied changes. Individual items have repeatedly switched from one category to another, depending on the changing nature and richness of the environment, on developing technology, and on human imagination. Communities have devised new sorts of things owned (names, songs, ceremonies, souls) and new kinds of owners (gods, groups, corporations, governments).

In the total sweep of human history, at least in the last ten thousand years or so, the main trend seems to have been an expansion of the second category at the expense of the third and the first. The invasion of the third category by the second increases the quantity and variety of commodities; the encroachment of the second into the first depersonalizes property relations.

When cultures with sharply different property practices come into direct contact the resulting fishy jam is often flavored with potassium cyanide.

The nastiest examples of this stem from the fact that hunters-gatherers tend not to regard land as property, while, for obvious reasons, tillers of the soil do. This difference was the source of all sorts of troubles between the nonagricultural Menomini and the agricultural European settlers in Wisconsin in the nineteenth century. The presumably benevolent government in Washington was of little help, since at the time it was unable to think except in agriculturally oriented terms: farming and servicing farmers were the only conceivable ways of civilized life, the cornerstone of all justice and morality. With its left hand, European civilization forced the Menomini onto a piece of land too small for successful hunting and gathering but virtually worthless for agriculture, and established a boundary around it—an invisible line that cut irrationally through streams, clearings, and even individual trees, that was no barrier to breezes, birds, or game, but which the Menomini were not supposed to cross. With its right hand, it tried to compensate them for their loss (and to salve "civilized" conscience) by making them into farmers!

As for the depersonalization of property relations: we know all too well (because we live in the looming shadow of its consequences) that for the last few thousand years in certain parts of the world some human beings, even as they owned property of the intimate sort, have themselves, together with their intimate possessions, been *owned* as property of the loose kind. Agriculture has played a central part in this, too. Nonagricultural peoples are capable on occasion of treating strangers with unspeakable cruelty, but reports of anything among them resembling systematic slavery are rare and unreliable. However, the telling of this sad tale belongs later.

In our Western tradition the word "property" has tended more and more to refer only to the loose kind, as though there were no other. Remembering this change of meaning, we see the significance of the fact that, where the idealistic American Declaration of Independence, from which we quoted earlier (p. 142), speaks of "Life, Liberty and the *pursuit of Happiness*," all three terms referring to highly personal things, the more practical Constitution speaks instead—and only belatedly, in the fifth article of the Bill of Rights—of "life, liberty, or *property*."

12

✖

MAN THE POLITICIAN?
GOVERNMENT AND DECISION-MAKING

The term *government* is Wissler's heading for his group 8 (Box 9-1, p. 128); Murdock's alphabetical list (Box 9-2, p. 128) includes this term and such related items as community organization, family, law, penal sanctions, and status differentiation.

In 1675–1676 there was a bloody hassle in New England between the English settlers and the Indians, since known as "King Philip's War." The hero of humanity memorialized by this epithet was Metacomet, a sachem of the Wampanoag tribelet. The settlers called him Philip because they could not pronounce his real name. They bestowed the title "king" on him because they did not know what a sachem was and assumed that, since the Indians were obviously human beings like themselves, they must live within a political system more or less like their own.

Thus does cross-cultural noise arise in the realm of the social and political.

It arises, of course, on both sides of any cultural interface. I don't imagine "King Philip's" people understood the English settlers any better than they were understood by them. The settlers thought a sachem was something like a king; the Indians doubtless supposed a king was something like a sachem. However, the settlers belonged to a literate tradition that kept written records, and the Wampanoag did not. That is why it is easier to find examples of misunderstandings in the one direction than in the other, and why we Europeans seem almost always to be the misunderstanders. We can guess only in the most general way about the confusions that must have arisen in pre-European times between Algonquians and Iroquoians, or between the Menomini and their allies the Winnebago, or in thousands of other cross-cultural transactions all over the world at which no record-keepers were present.

Political organization is not an exclusively Western phenomenon. But the contrast between the political and the nonpolitical, like that between the religious and the nonreligious, has been foisted willy-nilly on many non-Western peoples, sometimes despite the most honorable of intentions, during the period of the expansion of Europe—in form and substance by colonial administrators, in falsifying interpretation by travelers, missionaries, and ethnographers. Our Western political institutions have passed through various phases that still live in our collective memory, so that we can conceive of monarchy, of oligarchy, of democracy, even of a situation in which the government pursues a largely hands-off policy and allows citizens to manage their own affairs with little interference or assistance. But if we try to imagine living with no government at all—with no *state*—all we can conjure up is anarchism of the Bakunin type, which rests firmly on our traditional contrast between the political and the nonpolitical in the very fact that it preaches the elimination of the state on moral grounds.

The fact is that through most of human history most people have lived in conditions which would have rendered anarchism as meaningless as any other political doctrine. The fundamental error of Europeans dealing with (most) non-European communities has been not that of misinterpreting their political institutions, but that of assuming they had any.

When the British in North America realized that a New England sachem was not a king, they took to rendering the Indian term as 'chief'; but they still put the wrong interpretation on it. The Ojibwa term *okimā*, the Menomini cognate *okēmāw,* are regularly translated as 'chief'. A much more appropriate translation would be 'Big Man in Tribe'—on the analogy of the college student usage of a decade ago, "Big Man on Campus." An *okimā* among the Ojibwa was anyone in whom the members of the community had confidence, anyone to whom they would turn for counsel and leadership. As we said of the Menomini (p. 23), so also among the Ojibwa there were different leaders for different sorts of activity—war leaders, hunting leaders, ceremonial leaders, clan leaders. Some men were leaders in several connections, others only in one. When the Canadian government insisted that the Ojibwa of any one band must surely have a single paramount "chief," the Ojibwa perforce acquiesced, but they refused to call the government's selection an *okimā* and accorded him no respect other than what he had already earned. Instead, they coined the term *okimākkān,* which can be rendered as 'fake chief'.

Take away the limited recent contrast between the religious and the nonreligious; what is left, shared by all, is a world view (p. 133) that permits of highly diverse internal structuring from one culture to another. Similarly, lift off all the Western-based philosophical speculations of our political theorists and "political scientists" from Aristotle to the present; the contrast between the political and the nonpolitical vanishes, but something important is left, shared by all: the scheduled processes of collective *decision-making*.

All animals with nervous systems, and perhaps some organisms without, make decisions. So does any animal community that deserves to be called a band rather than a congeries (p. 71). The problem, then, here as in the case of property, is to see if there is some uniquely human factor common to all human decision-making.

The prehuman background needs no fresh discussion. Our treatment of it in connection with property (pp. 141–143) will serve. By the definition of "commodity," any disagreement among the members of a primate band or between such a band and outsiders is about commodities. Collective decision-making is the means of resolving disagreements, or in some cases (as among baboons: p. 42) of forestalling them. The process among nonhuman primates reflects social structure, and shows that at any one moment some members of a band are leaders, others followers. Decisions are made occasionally through open combat, more often via the manipulation of symbols. It is obvious what becoming human adds: more sources of conflict of interest, and language as a subtle and flexible instrument with which to try to resolve them.

CONSULTATION

✖ Let us examine more closely the consultative use of language (p. 104).

In our culture, a committee with more than six members can get nothing done unless it works through subcommittees. Two people can confer on a problem and reach a solution or recommendation if their interests are not too sharply in conflict. They do it with informal "consultative prose," used in normal conversational interchange. Interruptions, though sometimes annoying, are par for the course. Three can do this; so can four, or five, or—with a little trouble—six. In a social gathering of more than six people, two or more conversations take place simultaneously, the participants occasionally regrouping. If seven or more have something of collective import to work out, so that division into smaller groups is precluded, the consultation becomes formal. Whoever is speaking talks in a more deliberate and elevated style, and is at least metaphorically on the stage, while the rest are audience. The switch from one speaker to another is sluggish and the proceedings may require the control of a moderator or chairman. At its peak, this has led to such codifications as Robert's Rules of Order.

The only part of this which is unique to Western society is Robert's Rules. The rest seems to be a generally human matter. Even the number six, as the boundary between possible informality and one or another sort of formality, is apparently universal. Furthermore, two other factors make for formality whenever they appear in any community: the presence of participants who do not know one another very well, and the seriousness or solemnity of what is being discussed. The hallmark of all formal consultation is a reduction of the rate at which relevant information is transmitted. We see the extreme in a present-day international conference, where endless hours are devoted to agreeing on protocol and it sometimes seems that the conferees will never get around to the topics of substance they have presumably gathered together to discuss.

✖ Now, what does a numerically small, technologically simple community have to consult about, and who does the consulting?

Routine matters call for no collective decisions, because (by definition) there are generally understood scheduled ways of handling them. Since most human beings are inveterate chatterers they may be conversed about at great length, but that is not the same thing. In this connection we should note that the great majority of the daily tasks people perform in any society call for no special consultation, and are not done because of fear of punishment or hope of reward but merely through inertia. In a society presumably governed by codified laws (pp. 567–571), the average individual is mostly as unaware of his conformity to the laws as M. Jourdain (in Molière's *Bourgeois Gentilhomme*) was that he had been talking prose all his life. It is well that this is so. If we had to talk out or think out everything we do before doing it, our species would have vanished before it really got started.

Consultation, then, is about the unexpected, the unscheduled, the unusual, or, given human foresight, is sometimes devoted to laying joint plans against such unpredictable happenings. Consultations may be contingently scheduled, in the sense that the (unscheduled and unpredictable) occurrence or threat of an emergency will be the occasion for one. The outcome of the consultation is then often a *change* of scheduling, though this is not invariably so and when it is the alteration is often proposed as merely temporary. The *purpose* of consultation is almost always a plan of action by which those involved can return as soon as possible to the status quo. Collective decision-making is a homeostatic device, like a thermostat (p. 84): a registered or anticipated deviation from the norm triggers a counteracting adjustment that tends to restore the norm. Of course, the *result* of collective decision-making does not always accord with the aim.

As a simple example, suppose a Menomini couple have a son who is approaching marriageable age. While this situation is neither unexpected nor in itself a departure from a norm, steps must be taken, because were he to remain unmarried the deviation would be serious. If the young man's mother has a brother who has a daughter of the right age, and if there are no other males for whom she would be the most suitable bride, the solution may be easy. Otherwise negotiation may be required. Many people can have a stake in the decision, and there can be numerous conflicts of interest. It is unlikely that all involved will come together to settle things in a formal conclave. There will be a series of consultations involving pairs or trios of people, some of them perhaps formal for reasons other than the number of participants (p. 149), with requests, offers, objections, counteroffers, and compromises, until a generally acceptable plan has been worked out. The arrangement that everyone now knows will be satisfactory may be firmed up by a formal visitation (p. 31) that is not really a consultation even if it overtly conforms to the pattern of one, but only an acknowledgment that the necessary consultation has taken place.

We saw in chapter 2 something of the ritualized procedure by which the Menomini strove to restore equilibrium after a murder. We mentioned in passing the organization for a hunt and that for a war raid (p. 22). We noted that parents were likely to consult a specialist in seeking the right name for a new child, or a better name if the first one did not work. We ignored certain relatively simple consultations that must have taken place to maintain the yearly and daily schedules: everyone knows we will soon be going to gather the wild rice (or the maple sap, or the blueberries), but do we leave today, tomorrow, or the next day? Such trivial decisions also have to be made, but ethnographers have rarely noted them and reported about them, presumably because they are either too obvious or too subtle.

CONFORMITY AND INITIATIVE

× Some kinds of group enterprises require advance consultation and arrangements to which all will adhere for the duration. When the chips are down, each participant must know what his duties are. Detailed decisions will have to be made so quickly that there will be no time to talk them over. Some one person must be chosen to make the major ones, and the others must agree to do as he bids, even at great personal sacrifice, for the sake of the group as a whole.

Here one thinks first of military expeditions against other communities. There are surely other contexts calling for the same pattern (for example, hunts for large and dangerous game, and certain kinds of complicated ceremonies), but war is an important one. Good battle plans are as crucial for success as are good weapons or individual skill in wielding them. If every soldier in an army makes his own decisions, the army loses the battle. If no soldier does anything on his own initiative but simply obeys all orders exactly, the army loses the battle. Success requires a delicate balance between submission to central authority and individual initiative. Other things being equal, the community whose members can achieve this balance wins; those that cannot, lose. This has been a factor in human history for many thousands of years.

✂ Group enterprises demand leaders, and important group decisions need the counsel of experts. One becomes an expert via innate ability reinforced by apprenticeship, experience, and (for many communities, including the Menomini) aid from Higher Powers or their analog. The accidents of birth may help: in many communities the child of an expert is expected to become one, and is afforded more opportunities for the kind of training an expert needs. But this does not always work even where it is the anticipated thing. In any case, it is the success of an expert that endorses his standing in the community. Living a longer time means more accumulated experience on which to draw; hence it is only to be expected that the "Big Men in Tribe" will be adult, even elderly. A nonhuman primate is unlikely to retain his status as leader past his prime, because physical strength is important for his dominance. Without language, his greater stock of accumulated expertise counts for nothing because there is no way in which his band can make use of it. But a human being may still be honored and consulted when he is too decrepit to move anything but his lips.

The pattern of leadership in a "simple" community, however it may shift with the passage of time, accords with the more general pattern of social structure (p. 70), in which differences of sex and age are always relevant. Women readers of this book will have detected something in chapter 2 that men readers may have missed (though if they did they should hang their heads in shame): among the Menomini, the men seem to have had most of the fun. Actually, this impression may be false; we get it by interpreting Menomini ways in terms of our own inside view instead of striving to understand theirs. Our current unsettled distribution of responsibilities and privileges between the sexes is most unusual, and very recent even in our own culture. The Menomini way was a trivial variant of the distribution attested for all hunting-and-gathering societies known in the ethnographic present and unquestionably the standard for our whole species throughout most of its history, since it stems from two simple facts: (1) animals move around and plants don't; (2) among mammals, including humans, the females bear and suckle the young. The first fact means that hunting demands greater motility than gathering; the second fact means that women cannot move around as freely as can men. It is therefore biologically efficient in a nonagricultural community for the women to do most of the gathering and the men most of the hunting; this also makes the men the first line of defense against predators and enemies.

LEADERS AND SPECIALISTS

The assortment of other activities varies from culture to culture, but always fits somehow into this basis. In particular, children may become leaders among children, and women may become leaders in women's and children's affairs, but the leaders of the whole community are almost always adult males, and often enough it is only the adult males of the community who participate in formal consultations. Whether or not this is to our liking, we have no right to assume that the women (or the children) in such arrangements find them oppressive or that the men find them liberating.

The function of consultation in human decision-making and the inevitability of formality and sluggishness when more than a handful of participants are involved open the path to a new source of prestige: leadership in the very process of formal consultation.

To keep a conference moving, to be sure that all the relevant facts are brought out, that all viewpoints are expressed, that decisions really meet with majority approval, demands a very special skill. In many societies the ability to do this is one of the most important requirements for a leader, who may sometimes go to great lengths (for little obvious personal reward) to maintain harmony, and may himself rarely express an opinion on the issues under discussion. Yet a decision finally reached is typically "his," in the senses that it is ascribed to him by the community and that he accepts it and does what he can to carry it out.

RESOLUTION OF
CONFLICTS
OF INTEREST

✖ How are conflicts of interest resolved through consultation? A wants x; B wants y; and A and B think it is impossible for both to get what they want. In nonhuman animal groups, if A is stronger or otherwise dominant B gets a beating or, knowing that persistence will earn him one, gives up. Of course this can happen with humans too. But consultation may lead to a different outcome.

Invariably, the topic of discussion is not just x and y but also many other things considered desirable by one or both. The verbal interchange may show that it is, after all, possible for both to get what they want. Or it may turn out that if one or both will modify their aims slightly they become compatible. It can even happen that A persuades B that he doesn't really want y after all—he had mistaken y for something else.

The least characteristically human of all resolutions (though it happens constantly) is for one participant to get his way through the threat of force. This, too, is persuasion, but of an extreme kind. A convinces B that however much he wants y, if he tries to achieve it he runs the risk of losing something he values even more: his life, his bodily integrity, or some part of his intimate possessions (p. 145). This outcome is human in that it is accomplished with words, but what is accomplished is just what nonhuman animals manage without language; thus it is no more a part of the human common denominator than is eating.

When two members or factions of a single community get into an argument which is moving towards violence or towards the threat of it, others in the community often step in. The interests of A and B are not the only ones involved. There is also the peace and harmony of the whole community and of its other members. Here is another role for the moderator, the expert in the management of consultations. But if A and

B belong to different communities or are themselves communities, there is no nonpartisan moderator, and the outcome can be a duel, murder, or all-out war. This last is uniquely human. Other animals fight, but they do not wage war.

✖ The rough characterization of human decision-making given above applies, in a general way, to all human beings living in what we may call *tribal society*. Most of our species through most of human history have lived in societies of this type. Thus, as in the case of property, we have outlined here not the human common denominator of the ethnographic present but the historical base line from which all special developments have evolved.

There have been any number of such special developments *within* the basic pattern, generating so great a diversity that different tribal societies can find one another's decision-making procedures mutually incomprehensible.

In a few cases, however, there came about special developments *beyond* the basic pattern, slowly giving rise to *civil society,* the sort of social order in which we now live. Civil society differs in key ways from tribal society. Nowhere is it as much as ten thousand years old, and as recently as two hundred years ago it had still barely touched many human communities, but its spread has been relentless. Like the depersonalization of property relations (p. 146), its origin and spread are tied up intimately with those of agriculture.

The seeds of civil society (as we shall see later in greater detail: chapter 33) are the use or threat of force in resolving conflicts of interest, and the role of moderator (who can also threaten force). In civil societies communities become *states.* A community or a group of communities constitutes a state if and only if it contains within itself a special institution, not coterminous with the whole society, called a *government.* The government, in the name of the state, holds the sole prerogatives of moderating internal conflicts (at least major ones) and of controlling negotiations with outsiders, especially other states. The government is a patterned arrangement of people and things which are replaced as time goes by while the arrangement itself persists. Not everyone in the state is in the government, but all acknowledge its existence and its power and prerogatives—sometimes gratefully, sometimes with sorrow and anger. The machinery of the state (that is, the government) by definition recognizes no power of veto by any higher authority except, in some cases, the gods, and this is not much of an exception when the will of the gods must be expressed through official channels. The machinery can be captured by one or another interest group, and can pass from one such group to another, but is self-perpetuating: it can be nibbled at by rebellion, but can rarely be destroyed except through conquest by a more powerful state.

In a civil society the decision-making process becomes impersonal, just as do property relations. The elements of primate play and of lack of seriosity (p. 74), which can leaven and enliven negotiations in tribal society, are suppressed. The person present in the flesh to steer a consultation or arbitrate a dispute serves not as a prestigious and experienced individual (though he may be both) but as an agent of the impersonal government; his counsel derives not from personal wisdom but from law and legal precedent.

Any tribal society, or any small cohesive segment of a civil society, must contend sometimes with antisocial individuals, who refuse to play the game by the accepted rules and more or less seriously disrupt the tenor of community existence. A small percentage of such people is actually socially useful, in that it serves to keep the run-of-the-mill members of the community on their toes. When the rate of antisocial acts becomes too high, public indignation mounts and drastic action is taken. When it falls low, vigilance relaxes and a few people whose tendencies have been held in check through fear of reprisal start misbehaving.

In civil society an entirely new contrast develops: some people are *criminals,* guilty of acts against the state or against the social order the government is pledged to maintain. To be sure, some criminals are antisocial, and many antisocial individuals are criminals. But that the correlation is far from perfect can be demonstrated merely by listing a few of the famous criminals of our Western tradition: Martin Luther King, Jr., Robert E. Lee, John Brown, George Washington, Socrates, Oedipus the King, and Jesus of Nazareth.

POLITICAL AND NONPOLITICAL ✖ No government can control *everything* done by the people of the state; even if it wants to, the goal is physically and biologically impossible (for the nearest known approximation, see p. 562).

TABLE 12-1. Substantive findings about human universals through chapter 12.

SHARED WITH SOME NONHUMAN ANIMALS	PART OF HUMAN HISTORICAL BASE LINE	UNIVERSAL IN ETHNOGRAPHIC PRESENT	
✖	✖	✖	(common characteristics of all vertebrates, all mammals, all primates, etc.; see chapters 4–6)
	✖	✖	derived tools (see chapter 7)
	✖	✖	language (see chapter 8)
✖	✖	✖	a world view
	✖	✖	world view involving belief in things not directly observed nor directly observable
	✖?	✖?	curiosity about one's nature
	✖	✖	ritual
?	✖	widespread	rituals for crises in life cycle (birth, death, etc.)
✖	✖	✖	social structure and sociality
✖	✖	✖	leadership
✖	✖	widespread	male dominance
✖	✖	✖	intimate property versus nonproperty
	✖	✖	loose property
	✖		males as chief hunters, females as chief gatherers
✖	✖	✖	collective decision-making
	✖	✖	consultation (with language) in collective decision-making
	✖	✖	informal versus formal consultation
?	✖	✖	moderator as type of leader
	widespread	widespread	war

Other items will be added in subsequent chapters. We know that the following do *not* belong on the list: government, the state, national boundaries, impersonal and legalized property relations, religion, science.

Thus it is just in these circumstances—in the special context of civil society, new and rare against the total sweep of human history—that we find the distinctive contrast between the political and the nonpolitical. In tribal society there is no such contrast. In civil society, the political is everything that concerns the government, and the nonpolitical is everything else. Items can switch category, and the boundary can be now sharp, now blurred; but the contrast itself, once firmly established, becomes so deeply engrained in our collective inside view that it seems as natural and permanent as the stars in their courses.

✖ As specified in chapter 9, a major aim of chapters 10, 11, and 12 has been to **SUMMARY** underscore the importance of characterizing each human society from its own inside view. We have seen how failures to do this lead to false generalizations about the human common denominator.

But we have also had some findings of substance. They are summarized in Table 12-1. Note especially the headings of the three columns on the left, which spell out the "human common denominator" somewhat more explicitly.

13

✕

THE CATEGORIES OF WE:
HUMAN CLUSTERING AND CLUMPING

"But this *is* Me!" said Bear, very much surprised.
"What sort of Me?"
"Pooh Bear."[1]

The most germinal difference between humans and other animals is that humans have language. No matter what aspect of human life we are investigating, if we are concerned with the inside view it is helpful to see how those involved talk about it. This is the approach we shall use here, as we look further into human twists and turns on primate social structure.

Every language supplies its speakers with a form equivalent to English *I* (p. 120). The pronoun *I* means the person who utters it, except that in direct quotation it denotes the entity to which the words are ascribed. Setting quotation aside, if we know who has said *I* we know what that occurrence of the form denotes. If we cannot see the speaker and do not recognize his voice, or if, in a crowd, we cannot tell which person has spoken, our situation is like that of Rabbit in Milne's Pooh story, and like him we may ask for clarification.

I is convenient, but dull. Gesture can and often does convey the same information. In the American Sign Language for the Deaf, the system taught to the baby chimp Washoe (p. 117), the information is conveyed by pointing to one's own chest. Washoe does this in exactly the right circumstances and with complete freedom. It could be argued that there is nothing uniquely human about the first person singular pronoun except the fact that it is a linguistic form. Whatever else the signals may mean, when a lion roars he is saying 'I', when a gorilla drums on his chest he is saying 'I', when an infant cries he is saying 'I'.

We is a different matter, as exciting as *I* is dull. In terms of meaning the traditional label for this pronoun, "first person plural," is a misnomer. In languages in which nouns have plurals, the plural form refers to several of whatever the singular names

[1]From *Winnie-the-Pooh*, by A. A. Milne. Copyright, 1926, by E. P. Dutton & Co., Inc. Renewal, 1954, by A. A. Milne. Reprinted by permission of the publishers.

one of: *a hand, some hands.* But *we* denotes a plurality of speakers only in ritualized chant or song where in fact a number of people utter the same words at the same time. Ordinarily it is just a single person who says *we,* and what he denotes is *some group of which he is a member and for which he is at the moment the spokesman.*

But that is utterly revealing! Primates are what they are as individuals because of their patterns of participation in society, so that social structure and personality, while not to be identified, are linked together more intimately than the two sides of a single coin. If we hear someone call himself *me* we have learned nothing about him. If we observe the occasions on which he says *we,* and can determine what groupings he denotes by that word in various contexts, we have learned a lot. On the one hand, we know now how his society is structured for him. On the other, we have discovered "what sort of Me" he is. The *we* reveals the inside view of the social order, and the *we* reveals the *me.*

Many languages have two or more forms partly equivalent to English *we.* A very common distinction turns up in Algonquian. If a Menomini, speaking to you, says *nena³* 'we', he is denoting a group to which he belongs but you do not; if he says *kena³* 'we', he is naming one to which you and he both belong. The first is a *we-not-you,* the second a *we-not-they.* Any occurrence of either makes a dichotomous distinction. The same factors play a part in the still more complicated set of forms in Fijian, shown in Box 13-1. In English and the other languages of Europe, whether an uttered *we* is meant as one kind or as the other has to be inferred from context.

But Washoe invented the distinction for herself. In imitation of English, the American Sign Language for the Deaf has only a single 'we': one points to one's own chest twice. Washoe sometimes does this, usually meaning 'we-excluding-you'; for 'we-including-you', which she has more occasion to use, she points first to her interlocutor (the sign for 'you') and then to herself. Some of the earlier missionaries among the Algonquians were less perceptive than Washoe, much to the amusement of their flocks. In preaching, the missionary would say 'we are all sinners'—but inadvertently use the 'we-excluding-you' form, thus exempting the Indians from the indictment.

BOX 13-1. Fijian personal pronouns.

The forms of immediate concern are those enclosed in the small box; the others will be mentioned later (pp. 187 and 189).

Fijian has not one or two but six different personal nonsingular pronouns, three exclusive (that is, excluding the addressee or addressees) and three inclusive. The rest of the differentiations turn on the size of the plurality:

	FIRST PERSON		SECOND PERSON	THIRD PERSON
ONE	*au*		*ko*	*koya*
	EXCLUSIVE	INCLUSIVE		
TWO ONLY	*keirau*	*daru*	*(ko)drau*	*rau*
A FEW	*keitou*	*(da)tou*	*(ko)dou*	*ratou*
MANY	*keimami*	*da*	*(ko)nii*	*ra*

Some occurrences of a *we*-form denote a haphazard temporary grouping. On a plane, I can say "I wonder when they're going to feed us" to a total stranger; at the end of the trip the passengers disperse and I never see him again. This sort of usage is not devoid of social significance, because there are, or have been, societies in which those caught up in such a casual collection would be hesitant to refer to it as *we*. Our major interest, however, focuses on more permanent groupings, the concentric social circles in which an individual lives and moves and has his being and to every one of which he will on occasion refer with a *we*-form.

DWELLING PATTERNS ✖ So much for our clue to inside views of human social structure. The outside-view approach that complements it is that of the dwelling pattern (p. 45) or, more broadly, of human ecology: the spatial clustering and clumping of human beings into communities, the sessile or motile nature of the clumps, the patterns and routes by which matter and energy flow into, through, and out of communities, and the patterns of replacement of worn-out parts (mainly by reproduction, sometimes by recruitment).

There are important respects in which a single organism, a colony (p. 343), and an animal community (nonhuman or human) are similar. Some overenthusiastic students of human behavior have wanted to underscore the similarities by flatly asserting that "society is an organism"; but that puts an unnecessary metaphorical overload into the already taut term "organism." We can point up the pertinent parallels minus misleading metaphor.

A motile aquatic organism wanders around in its niche, taking in food as it comes to it and leaving its waste behind. This is one way to try to live, and there are many biological units that follow the same plan. A baboon band does. So does many a human band of hunters-and-gatherers. So does a herd of herbivores (bison, caribou, reindeer), and one form of animal husbandry leads to symbiotic units that live in this way (p. 462).

A sessile aquatic organism stays in one place, but reaches out somehow to draw food in and expels its wastes at an angle and with a force that gets them out of the way. This is another pattern for living, and this pattern, too, is followed by diverse biological units. A band (or congeries) of treetop monkeys reaches out for insects, fruit, leaves, buds, and the like, and drops its waste matter to the ground below. A stable agricultural village lives at some source of fresh water; it sends members out, like detachable tentacles, to till the surrounding fields and bring in the food; it gets its water from upstream, and discards its wastes downstream. A stable fishing village functions similarly.

When the parts of a biological unit cooperate mainly by metabolizing in parallel, we call the unit a "colony" or a "congeries." To the extent to which the parts cooperate actively, each supplying something the other parts need, we call the unit a "multicellular organism" or, if the parts are themselves organisms, a "band."

Now it is a fact about many primates that their groupings tend strongly to be of the band type. But at an even higher size-level of organization, a level at which the parts are themselves bands and the whole biological unit is some grouping bigger than a band, we can find both colonylike and organismlike arrangements. A set of tiny fishing villages may huddle together, each of band size, each functioning independently of and not in competition with the others in most ways, but all cooperating when necessary against outsiders. This is colonylike. Or a village or town may include one subgroup that raises crops, another that fishes, and others that produce no food but concentrate on making things the farmers and fishers need or on regulating the flow of commodities, people, and information. This is organismlike. Such a town may even support a class of people who make little or no contribution: this is parasitism.

The preceding discussion is not metaphorical. We have not been indulging in vague and doubtfully helpful comparisons. Rather, we have been classing biological units of various sizes and degrees of complexity, not according to size or degree of complexity but according to the general contours of their ways of handling the problem of continued existence. A single paramecium in a brackish puddle is a biological unit; an urban aggregate of ten million human beings is a biological unit. Neither can maintain itself except through a constant appropriate flow of matter and the corresponding degradation of energy. If an excess of inadequate or inappropriate matter is imported, if internal distribution is faulty, if wastes are not effectively collected and expelled, the unit is poisoned and, unless the difficulties are corrected, will die. This holds with blind impartiality for paramecia and for cities.

BAND AND FAMILY

✖ The family is a social group characterized by common residence, economic cooperation, and reproduction. It includes adults of both sexes, at least two of whom maintain a socially approved sexual relationship, and one or more children, own or adopted, of the sexually cohabiting adults.[2]

The author of this characterization was intending to speak only of our own species, but we do not have to heed the restriction. The baboon groupings we described in chapter 3 are families. Common residence means living together; the baboons do that. Economic cooperation means mutually beneficial agreements about commodities; the baboons have those. The adult males cohabit with the mature females by a complicated but clearly socially approved arrangement of priorities, and are thus the physiological fathers of the infants. Exact paternity is unknown and unknowable; the baboons couldn't care less. The adult males behave towards infants in a manner we human beings want to describe as paternal.

We did not use the term "family" in describing baboons because there was no need for this word in addition to the term "band." The two labels would have denoted the same grouping. It is a reasonable guess that this was the situation also for our remote prehuman ancestors.

If so, then something special happened in our ancestry: the typical band came to include *more* than one family, thus introducing a distinctive contrast between the two types of organization. The multifamily band is undeniably part of the human historical base line (p. 146). If it can no longer be described as universal, that is because in civil society things have happened to render the term "band" inapplicable; the family is still with us.

[2] From *Social Structure* (p. 1), by George Peter Murdock. Copyright, 1949, by The Macmillan Company. Quoted by permission of The Macmillan Company.

The factors that led to the development of the band-family contrast are unknown. In what follows (in this chapter and the next few) we focus mainly on tribal society, as the historical background from which civil societies have emerged, but also offer a few remarks on transitional stages between the former and the latter.

BAND, VILLAGE, AND CITY ✕ A human band is a group of people who live and work together enough of the time that everyone in the group knows everyone else as an individual. Except for infants, every member is in the inner circle (p. 70) of every other member.

Among the classical Menomini the people of a single summer village probably constituted a band in this sense. The smaller groups in the scattered winter camps did not, for in cases of such seasonal variation we shall reserve the term for the largest grouping that fits the definition.

BAND AND TRIBE

It is immediately clear that even in tribal society the band is often not the largest group to which an individual will refer as *we*. There were at least two Menomini villages in the classical period, possibly ten or twelve. They were tied together by a common language, a common tradition, the repeated exchange of personnel (especially for marriage), and, negatively but importantly, by the obvious fact that other neighbors, such as the Winnebago and the Ojibwa, were *not* Menomini.

It is to such more inclusive *we*-groups that we refer with the word "tribe." Ideally, we should call a set of bands a tribe only when the band members themselves draw the bounds for us, telling us who belongs and who does not. But most of the observations on which we must rely were made only as conditions were being upset by the expansion of Europe, which, along and beyond the spreading frontier, pressed many a band into strange new alignments. It is clear that the degree of cohesion of bands with other bands shows great variety and that it can change radically with the passage of time. Through most of human history the band has been much more vivid and durable than any sort of superband alliance.

BAND SIZE AND DISPERSION

Band size and dispersion are controlled by ecological and social factors. Ecologically, what counts is the degree of bountifulness of the environment relative to the technological base (p. 93), especially the technology of food-getting.

Bands of hunters-and-gatherers (with little or no fishing and no agriculture) consist on the average of about fifty people, and a seasonal breakup into smaller groups is common. The average is lower where there is less food, higher where there is more. Roughly, the average is lower in high latitudes and higher in low latitudes, though special local conditions can upset this correlation.

The lower limit is also affected by two other factors: the basically sociable nature of primates, and the requirement that a band include enough people to take care of the whole variety of activities necessary for collective survival.

The first factor alone is enough to explain why expulsion from his band is the worst punishment that can be meted out to anyone in tribal society. In some environments an able adult can survive alone for a long time, but he has nothing to live for. Having no *we,* he is no longer any sort of *me.* The exile inevitably seeks to join some other band or to gain readmission to his own. (In more populous societies, ostracization works just as effectively: there is nothing as lonely as being surrounded by total strangers or by people who treat you as one.)

The variety of things to be done in even the technologically most primitive bands of hunters-and-gatherers should not be underestimated—remembering that primate nature is such that the necessities include fun as well as food. It may be that all the adult males can do all the things any adult male is expected to do, but some of them are better at one task, some at another. Besides, one or another may be temporarily incapacitated, so that his responsibilities must be shouldered for the nonce by someone else. Just enough expertise to go around when everyone is in good shape does not suffice. There must be a safety margin beyond that. Nor are men and women interchangeable—nor adults and children. The band requires not only a certain minimum number of members but also a distribution by sex and age that does not depart too radically from balance. If a band becomes unviably small, its surviving members may seek to recruit replacements from friendly neighboring bands (perhaps most often by marriage or adoption), or even to merge with another band.

Similarly, if a band becomes too large it may split. The natural lines of cleavage are in terms of family affiliation. Given six or eight families, two or three (hardly just one, unless it is unusually large) may move off. The fissioning can be amicable and regretted, everyone recognizing that it is a matter of economic necessity, and the intention may at first be only a temporary separation. Or it can be in response to internal rivalries.

What makes a band too big? The commonest factor is ecological: an unusual increase in population, an unusual diminution in the bounty of the environment, or both, so that support must be sought over a region larger than can be exploited from a single headquarters. Sometimes a compromise can be found, like that of the classical Menomini who lived in smaller more scattered groups when necessary and in larger less scattered ones when possible. In other cases no such compromise is available.

But something else can happen. Environmental or technological changes can increase the quantity of food and other necessities obtainable in a small region, so that bands converge on the favored area or individually grow larger.

This can come about among peoples who remain essentially hunters-and-gatherers, but the effect is likely to be temporary. About 1675, the Indians of the North American Great Plains began to domesticate the feral horses that were descended from animals that had escaped from the Spanish settlers of Mexico.[3] The Plains were full of bison, and the use of horses made it possible for the Indians to become expert bison hunters. The Indian population increased. The bison population diminished, for they were being slaughtered more rapidly than they could reproduce. By 1850 this fine new

[3]The Indians' first horses, and the skill of riding, may have been obtained directly from the Spanish. There is dispute on this point.

way of life—the one we still celebrate in story and movies—had again become impossible. It would have disappeared even if the European frontier that was edging westwards through the Plains at about that time had not put an end to it.

A better basis is good fishing. Fish can wander over vast territories, eating and growing, in a watery niche that human beings cannot directly exploit, and can then migrate to or through some bottleneck where waiting humans can capture them. We saw that the Menomini summer villages were founded on sturgeon. On a much bigger scale, the Indian tribes of the North American Northwest Coast relied on salmon, and many of their local groups were quite large.

The best basis, though, is effective agriculture. Arable land can supply from 10 to 100 times as many calories per acre per year through the cultivation of high-yield crops as it can through hunting and gathering or even animal husbandry. In fact, it has been estimated that without agricultural methods the world today could support a total population of only about 30,000,000, less than one one-hundredth the number of individuals who currently make up our species. And the nature of farming cuts down on wandering. At most, a short move may be needed every few years as fields are overtilled, become unproductive, and need a rest.

VILLAGES

Whatever be the basis for the increase in size of bands, if they grow too large they cease to be bands for a social rather than an ecological reason: there are so many people living close together that the average member of the group can no longer know all the others as individuals. The boundaries of the inner circles of the members of the community cease to be coterminous with the boundary of the whole community. Each individual treats all those beyond his own inner circle in terms of categories (p. 70).

It has been suggested that a stable aggregate, periodic or permanent, too large to be a band, but lacking the structure characteristic of a city (see below), be called a "village."[4] Villages in this technical sense average 250 to 300 people, as compared with the average of 50 for bands. Those dependent on agriculture combined with a little animal husbandry are larger, averaging about 450 and sometimes reaching 1000.

A small village, examined closely, often turns out to be little more than a number of bands settled very close together. Each lives in its own neighborhood, with the same kind of internal structure an isolated band would have. The boundary lines between neighborhoods are known to the residents, though they may not be obvious to a stranger. With such proximity there must be agreements among the bands about many things. Yet interband relations may take much the same form they have for the spatially separated bands of a single tribe, since the latter arrangement, too, demands a measure of mutual understanding.

As villages get larger, more and more collective decisions have to be made. The regulation of affairs calls for increasing centralization of authority, and band structure

[4]The Menomini aggregates we called "summer villages" (p. 11) were not villages in this technical sense.

can be weakened or even disappear altogether. The inner circle of the typical villager now includes his immediate family, his nearest neighbors, a random scattering of relatives and acquaintances in other parts of the village, and the village big shots. In the band-based village, everyone falls into one or another of a set of pairwise disjunct groups (the bands); the smallest *we*-group larger than the family is the same group for any two members of the same band. In the centralized bandless village, the smallest *we*'s larger than families are overlapping sets of people, not apt to be identical for any two individuals.

AGRICULTURAL DWELLING PATTERNS. Agriculture-based villages are the largest type; the upper limit to the size of agricultural villages is again set by ecological and technological considerations.

In the United States and Canada today (except in the Old South), we think of farm families as living in isolated farmhouses amidst their fields and pastures, far from any neighbors, and gathering on occasion at some central hamlet for fellowship and commodity-exchange. We described this, in another connection, in chapter 10 (p. 131). With the advent of automobiles, good roads, and mechanized farming techniques this rural dwelling pattern has been rapidly disappearing, but it prevailed for a hundred years or more and is to be found also in northern Europe, Argentina, and parts of the world where it has been carried by English-speaking settlers.

Yet it is unusual. Most tillers of the soil, since the beginnings of agriculture, have been peasants. They live clustered in villages, walk out to their fields each morning, and trudge back each night. If a village is to have a certain population, a certain minimum amount of land must be tilled. Limits on the amount of land available can be set by agriculturally useless terrain and by competition with other villages. A limit is also set by how far a villager can commute each day and still have enough time and energy to break up the soil, plant, cultivate, harvest, and carry the fruits of the labor back to the village.

The typical agricultural village can support more people than are directly involved in food production. The possible ratio of nonfarmers to farmers depends in part on soil fertility, but much more on technology. For example, in the 1920s, farm land in China and in North America (the United States and southern Canada) was equally productive per acre, but the technological difference was such that it took 100 times as many man-hours per acre in China as in North America to obtain the same yield. A much higher percentage of Americans could therefore be nonfarmers.

VILLAGE AND CITY

Although the typical agricultural village can support more people than are directly involved in food production, here, again, there is a limit. If a localized community includes more people than can be fed from its own territory, and yet is stable, then it must be the case that some food is imported from elsewhere. This state of affairs can come about and be maintained in various ways; in any case, we call the local concentration of people not a village but a *city*.

Usually we think of a city as large. If we want to insist on that, then not every settled cluster of people can be classed as village or city. When farming families live scattered amidst their fields, they are served by a central hamlet that is too small for us to be comfortable calling it a city but which is not a village because the people who supply it with food do not live in it. Similarly, somewhere within a group of peasant villages one usually finds a market town whose inhabitants produce little of their own food. These and other special types seem, however, in the main to be byproducts of the basic sequence of band-village-city.

14

✕

THE CATEGORIES OF WE:
THE FAMILY AND ITS EXTENSIONS

Human beings, like other social animals, are held together by proximity and familiarity. They also form groupings of various sorts on the basis of child care and sex, which in an ultimate evolutionary sense seem to have been the sources of primate sociality (p. 72).

MATERNITY

Among mammals physiological maternity is obvious. For human beings, the "social mother" of a child, at birth, is invariably the physiological mother. The normal expectation in all communities of the ethnographic present is that this relationship will continue as long as mother and child both survive, the details of maternal care and of filial duty changing as the child grows up and the mother grows old. In all societies alternative arrangements are available, especially via adoption. These are uniformly viewed as emergency measures, resorted to when special circumstances require.

The death of the mother when her child is young is one such circumstance. However, surprisingly often in tribal societies a child is adopted not because he has been orphaned but because the adopting family is childless. The balance of children and adults is as important to a family as it is to a band (p. 161). A childless couple will go to extraordinary lengths of bickering and bargaining to take over a child from kinfolk who have more children than they "need."

PATERNITY

Physiological paternity is not obvious. There are some human communities whose members deny any knowledge of it. The role of the male in procreation was surely not known to our prehuman ancestors. Its discovery must have taken place at least once, perhaps many times, during human history. Whatever be the historical details, it seems unlikely that knowledge of physiological paternity played any noteworthy part in the development of the universal human band-family contrast (p. 159).

In almost all known human communities, the "social father" of a child is a mature male who maintains, or is expected to maintain, a regular relation of sexual activity and of economic cooperation with the mother, and who is therefore the mother's husband. If no such adult male, living or dead, is identifiable, then the child is fatherless.

Father-child relations show much greater variability in detail from one society to another than do mother-child relations. For example, in many communities the mother's brother is assigned some of the responsibilities towards the child which in our Western society we consider the father's "natural" prerogative. In tribal societies, emergency arrangements for transferring the father's duties to someone else probably have to be evoked more often than do such measures for reassigning the mother's role. It is true that mothers run the very serious dangers of childbirth, but otherwise, among hunters-and-gatherers, the women and children lead a somewhat more sedentary and safer life than do the adult males, whilst the latter run the active dangers of hunting and war and constitute the first line of defense against marauders. Also, women are physiologically more durable than men. Widows are commoner than widowers.

The Family

The human family, then, rests on the prolonged period of human infant helplessness, on *social maternity* (which is usually the same as physiological maternity), and on *social paternity* (which statistically tends to be, but often is not, the same as physiological paternity).

Marriage

Marriage is a society's way of getting together a male and a female to be the social father and social mother of children. This definition is cross-cultural and does not depend on inside views.

The family is universal; marriage is not quite, since in a very few societies children have no social father. Even where they do, we find great diversity. Some of it is hinted at in Box 14-1, wherein is presented and defined the standard terminology for kinds

BOX 14-1. Kinds of marriage.

TERM	DEFINITION	COMMENTS
monogamy	one husband, one wife	statistically prevalent in all societies; preferred norm in many
polygamy:		
polygyny	one husband, several wives	permitted in most societies; preferred norm in many
polyandry	several husbands, one wife	rare as a norm, but attested
group marriage	several husbands, several wives	nowhere the norm

of marriage. The box is only a bare outline. It would be pointless merely to list all the communities in the world under four headings to correlate with the four types of marriage defined in the box. In examining any one society, for realism we have to distinguish at least among the following: (1) the type of marital arrangement that is statistically prevalent; (2) the type preferred when attainable, whether statistically prevalent or not (and who holds the preference, since different subgroups may prefer different things); (3) the type or types that are considered less desirable but are tolerated for a minority or are resorted to in emergency circumstances; in a civil society also (4) the types that are legally proscribed but in fact occur.

Sex

It is obvious that human marriage and family have something to do with sex and its regulation. The formally codified laws of our Western society (at least in the United States) posit that no form of sexual activity is permissible except heterosexual relations between monogamous marital partners. For the child, the bachelor, the spinster, the widow, the widower, sex has no legal existence. The evidence for this is the variety of things prohibited by and punishable under the law.

The existence of the laws also attests to the actual occurrence of all kinds of activities that are prohibited, since the government of a civil society is unlikely to establish a legal barrier against something that nobody has any inclination to do anyway (p. 568). But human beings are hominoids, and are going to behave in such matters as hominoids do (p. 68). In no human society, civil or tribal, are sexual activities *in fact* confined wholly to marital partners. Most societies recognize and approve (or tolerate) sexual outlets other than marriage, and regulate them only in such a way as to prevent the destruction of the vitally necessary institutions of marriage and family.

Marriage and family, then, involve sex but do not rest wholly on it nor wholly control it. Marriage is the human way of establishing families; family is the human way of recruiting and training replacement personnel for the community.

✖ Suppose we consider marital and family arrangements in a "typical" band of hunters-gatherers. This is what all our ancestors were for a very long time, and some such peoples have survived into the ethnographic present and have been studied. Our example, however, will be a fictitious composite, designed to show a reference norm that may rarely have been exactly attained, and to illustrate some of the factors that can lead to departures from and changes of norms.

A PROTOTYPE: THE EAGLES

We shall call our band the Eagles. Friendly or neutral neighboring bands include the Cypresses, the Downrivers, and the Herons, all of which speak dialects the Eagles can understand with little difficulty.

There are thirty-one Eagles. There will be thirty-two when Nada's baby is born (if it lives), unless feeble old Tani dies first. Tani is the oldest of seven married men, each with one wife. There are four adolescent boys and three nubile girls who should be getting married in the next year or so. The other ten Eagles are children and infants. Of the seven families, the smallest is a still childless couple, the largest includes four children.

At the time we are talking about, the environment is kind. The whole band can get enough to eat by exploiting a range accessible from a single headquarters. The women and children gather plant foods in the vicinity of the camp. The men go out in groups of from two to five in search of game. The plant foods are distributed only within the separate families. The meat killed by the men is shared by all, but is distributed through the heads of families rather than directly to individuals. Other sorts of economic cooperation are largely within families, and if an individual gets into trouble he turns first to others in his own family for help. There are crosscutting friendships; there are occasional enterprises which demand cooperation between more people than belong to any one family; there are individuals who are turned to by all because they are the experts at certain necessary things. Yet family membership is exceedingly important.[1]

The situation we have described is in ecological and social equilibrium. The marriages are monogamous not for some deep philosophical or moral reason (though the Eagles may have one or another sort of theory about it) but because the numbers of males and females are approximately equal, because a man needs only one wife in order to obtain a satisfactory share of plant food, companionship, and sex, because a woman needs only one husband to get enough flesh food, companionship, and sex, and because one mother and one father are enough for a child. The monogamous arrangement within the band is economically efficient and emotionally satisfying.

Now let us consider some of the kinds of events that can throw things out of balance, and the kinds of adjustments that can be made.

SPORADIC POLYGYNY ✕ Old Tani dies. His widow and her children thus become an incomplete family. Without a husband and father they no longer have standard access to the things and services that would be provided by or through him. The easiest way to handle this is for the widow to get a new husband. One of the four adolescent men may marry her. But customs as to who should marry whom may discourage or prohibit that. An alternative is for one of the men who already has a wife to "adopt" not only the orphans but also the widow, so that she becomes a second wife to him. This step entails certain adjustments in interpersonal relations and attitudes, but so would any other handling of the crisis. The economic burden imposed on the husband of two wives is not doubled. Meat is in any case apportioned in terms of the sizes of family groups, and the husband now has more women and children gathering plant foods of which he can claim a share.

Developments of this sort are the commonest source of sporadic polygyny in essentially monogamous tribal communities, and almost all tribal societies allow polygyny under such emergency circumstances even if otherwise it is prohibited.

---

[1]The assertions in this paragraph are not hypothetical, but apply without modification to almost all bands of hunters-gatherers known in the ethnographic present. Otherwise (for instance, as to the number of members) our characterization of the Eagles can at most qualify as realistic.

Peoples experienced in polygyny know what sorts of tensions it can produce and are wise in the ways of minimizing them. If Tani's widow is adopted as a second wife, she and her children do not move into the hut occupied by her new husband's first wife, but stay in their own, and the husband divides his time between them. The families of the Eagles' camp have at best little privacy, but this continued maintenance of separate households keeps the two wives out of each other's hair as much as the housing arrangements permit. Separate houses for the wives and their children, or separate compartments in a compound, is the standard practice in all human communities in which polygyny has been successful.[2]

LEVIRATE, SORORATE, AND SORORAL POLYGYNY

Another way of minimizing friction is for marital arrangements to be made among people who are already close. If Tani has a brother, he may be the most logical one to be Tani's successor. Some communities have instituted this as standard: it is called the *levirate*. Or Tani's widow may have a married sister whose husband will take her on. Whenever the wives of a single husband are by preference sisters (and whatever the circumstances, those we have described or others), the practice is called *sororal polygyny*.

We have posited that Tani is old and feeble, but even so he might outlive his wife. If his wife dies, the contretemps is of a different sort. The economic and social responsibilities of men and those of women in tribal societies are so different that a widower with children is no simple mirror image of a widow with children. Tani needs his children; he cannot just step aside and let greedy relatives seize them. But he cannot be a mother as well as a father.

This is *not* the situation that yields polyandry. Some communities have no patterned way of handling it, so that the widower has to find a new wife as best he can. But some communities have the *sororate*: the family from which Tani obtained his original wife is under obligation to supply him with a replacement—a younger sister, or some other kinswoman whose relationship to the first wife fits the rules of the particular group.

OTHER FACTORS IN SPORADIC POLYGYNY

Sporadic polygyny in essentially monogamous tribal societies does not always conform to the lines of causality we described above.

Sometimes a "Big Man in Tribe" (p. 148) has two or three wives though this means that some of the other men have to wait longer to get any wife at all. The increased variety of sexual companionship and amount of economic assistance may be one of the emoluments of successful leadership. To understand this, we need to recognize that hunters-gatherers live sometimes in marginal environments where eking out a living is chancy. The successful leader is the one who finds sources of food and who

---

[2]The nineteenth-century American Mormons did not know this, and their polygyny was accordingly a dismal failure. It is said that some twentieth-century Mormons maintain a much more successful polygyny because they have learned to heed the principle of separation and privacy.

accepts the blame when the food supply is inadequate. He works very hard, may not eat quite as well as do his followers, and needs all the practical help his wives can give him.

RESIDENCE AND BRIDE PRICE

✕ We noted that the Eagles included four unmarried men and three unmarried women of marriageable age. If three of the men marry the three girls (assuming for the moment that that is allowable) the fourth man is left out in the cold. Perhaps he has an older brother who is already married, and perhaps arrangements can be made for him to share his brother's wife. But polyandry is very rare. In most known tribal societies the arrangement just suggested, if tolerated, would be not a marriage but a temporary expedient agreed to by the older brother and his wife out of love for the boy and concern for his welfare. Such friendly accommodations are not uncommon. We make a terrible mistake if we neglect love as a motive for human action, or if we assume that what is done through love can be viable only if it is guided by our publicly proclaimed Western principles of sexual morality.

It is more likely that the fourth young man will eventually have to seek a wife outside his own band. The Eagles have fewer eligible females than males. If the Cypresses (let us say) have one eligible female in excess, then the Eagles' problem and the Cypresses' problem can be solved at the same time.

Where will the couple then live? The principal possibilities are displayed in Box 14-2. There may be no firm precedent, the couple taking up residence with his band or hers as is more convenient (*bilocal* residence). The young man may have to earn his bride by throwing his lot in permanently with the Cypresses (*matrilocal* residence), or by a specified period of service to them before he can take her back to his own band (*matri-patrilocal* residence). Or compensation to the bride's family or band may

BOX 14-2. Residence practices.

TERM	DESCRIPTION	OCCURRENCE
patrilocal	emphasizes groom's close kin ties more than those of bride	very common
matrilocal	emphasizes bride's close kin ties more than those of groom	fairly common
avunculocal	bride and groom settle with or near a maternal uncle of the groom, who is often the bride's father	rare
matri-patrilocal	matrilocal for a specified period, then patrilocal	fairly common
bilocal	patrilocal or matrilocal (or patrilocal or avunculocal) depending on specific circumstances	fairly common
neolocal	loosens kin ties of both bride and groom	rare

Patrilocal and matrilocal are now sometimes also called respectively "virilocal" and "uxorilocal." Recognition that the difference between patrilocal and matrilocal is one of degree obviates the need for a number of additional terms proposed by some specialists.

take some other form, so that she comes immediately to live with the Eagles (*patrilocal residence*). The other patterns listed in the box are less common among hunters-gatherers, though not unknown.[3]

Whatever the arrangement, our young Eagle will probably have to *earn* his Cypress bride. It is interesting to note that, the world over, transfers of goods and services in connection with a marriage tend to balance out as a net payment to the bride's people rather than as one to the groom's. Women are people, not chattels, and their interests and preferences are often given the most careful consideration. Yet it is the men who make the decisions. If the male head of a family consents to the marriage of one of his girls, he is giving up not only her own economic services but also (if her marriage means that she will leave his household) the children she will bear. He wants something in fair exchange.

What could be fairer or simpler than for the price of a bride given to be one taken? In technologically simple bands where population is small and worldly goods meager, an arrangement of this sort is often standard. So, after formal consultation between the leaders of the Eagles and Cypresses, perhaps our young Eagle is permitted to take a Cypress bride, the understanding being that the next time a Cypress needs a wife the Eagles will supply one. Since everyone knows which adolescents are about to reach marriageable age, the agreement may even specify the exact individuals, who are thereby betrothed.

✘ In the foregoing we assumed that three of the four young unmarried Eagles could take as their wives the three unmarried Eagle women. In many bands, however, one or all of these pairings would be impossible.

Any individual in any human society belongs to some group of kin or ostensible kin within which he cannot marry. Such a group is *exogamous*. Marriage within an exogamous group is by definition incestuous. Sometimes certain premarital or extramarital sex relations are allowed within the group, provided the pair involved are not too closely related, but sometimes this also is prohibited. The one absolutely universal bar is against mother-son incest; as we have seen (p. 43) this may be more widespread and much older than our own species. Taboos against relations between father and daughter, brother and sister, and half brother and half sister are very common, but even the first of these three is not universal. Beyond these cases, the variations are great. In some societies cross cousins (p. 22) are allowed to marry but parallel cousins are not (a parallel cousin is the child of your father's brother or of your mother's sister). Elsewhere this is exactly reversed. In the United States, some states forbid the marriage of first cousins; others do not.

EXOGAMY, ENDOGAMY, AND PREFERRED MARRIAGES

---

[3]There are also all sorts of special twists and turns—looked at from the inside, probably no two communities have absolutely identical residence practices. Investigators have coined additional terms in order to cover these; I think it is better to keep the technical terms relatively general and cover finer details, when necessary, by description.

Incest

In tribal society incestuous marriages just don't happen, unless living circumstances have become so terrible that all normal expectations have been discarded and survivors are resorting to desperation measures.

The classic examples of brother-sister marriage always given in anthropology textbooks are not of this emergency kind, but of a second sort: in the royal families of the pre-European Incas (Peru), of pre-European Hawaii, and of certain periods in ancient Egypt, the ruler came to be so unspeakably holy that no one could be his successor except a son born to him by his full sister. What was thus not merely permitted but demanded of the ruler was taboo to everyone else (of course, the king was free otherwise to bestow his ennobling sexual attentions on practically any woman that caught his fancy).

In populous civil societies, where local communities are large enough that everyone does not know everyone else's business, we find a third sort of example, since hidden minorities can get away with practices that the majority abhor or that are prohibited by law. Two decades ago an investigator who must here remain nameless became curious about such matters, and with little trouble unearthed, within a single state of the United States, *twenty* brother-sister pairs, each living together as husband and wife and calmly participating in the standard round of middle-class suburban activities, going to church, sending their children to school, joining the P.-T.A., playing bridge—overtly in every way indistinguishable from their nonincestuous neighbors. One of these couples were the son and daughter of an earlier brother-sister mating of the same concealed kind.

Band Exogamy

Among the Eagles, perhaps a brother and sister who developed an irresistible yen for each other could run off and try to present themselves as proper man and wife to some distant band; but I think this topsy-turvy romantic notion is more apt to occur to a modern student of tribal society than to any real tribesman. If we are modeling our hypothetical Eagles on the best known human bands, then it is quite possible that *none* of the four unmarried youths can marry *any* of the three unmarried girls, not because of their degree of consanguinity but because they belong to the same band. *Band exogamy* is widespread.

Endogamy

A further possibility is that the Eagles, the Cypresses, the Downrivers, and the Herons, each band exogamous, form together an *endogamous* group, in that a young man of any of the four bands is expected if possible to find his wife in one of the other three, rather than in some more distant and alien community. Customs of endogamy are not quite so widespread as are those of exogamy, and are generally looser, but there are known cases in which they are strict.[4]

---

[4]No matter how strict an endogamous rule is supposed to be, in practice it never completely halts the flow of genes across the group boundary. Only geographical isolation has ever done that.

Preferred Marriages

A few people here and there, as we have seen, have been forced or permitted by circumstances to marry unusually close kinsmen. In a similar way, habitual endogamy has never prevented a minority of very "distant" marriages: at the end of the Second World War, American servicemen brought wives home from all over the world; an occasional Menomini married a Winnebago, Ojibwa, or Potawatomi; once, when the ancient Romans ran short of women, they captured as many as they could from the Sabines. However, the commonest arrangement is for men to seek their wives in the "middle distance."

It is as though our species had learned from thousands of years of experience that a marriage is most apt to be successful if the couple are neither totally accustomed to each other in advance nor so different in background that every necessary understanding has to be worked out from scratch after the marriage. This compromise is most easily managed if there is some established pattern, adhered to when possible. A Menomini youth by preference married a cross cousin (p. 22). If he had several, other factors came into play; if he had none, the preferred pattern had to be set aside.

Preferential cross-cousin marriage is widespread, but there are also other practices. For example, among some Arab groups a man's best marriage is with his father's brother's daughter.

✶ Returning to endogamy, let us note that if it is to be strict the endogamous group must be large. The reason stems from the balance of male and female births. In a sufficiently big population the balance tends to remain even. But this is true only because, for every woman somewhere who bears more daughters than sons, there is one somewhere else who bears more sons than daughters. If a group is so small that only a half dozen or so women are of childbearing age at any one time, the ratio can get out of kilter, disrupting both marital customs and patterns of economic cooperation. Thus, a group no larger than the Eagles would not be likely to remain endogamous for long.

DEMOGRAPHIC BALANCE AND MARITAL PATTERNS

The balance of the sexes is related to marriage practices in some other ways.

Only two kinds of marriage are compatible with even numbers of marriageable males and females: group marriage and monogamy. The former is not attested as the norm for any human community. The latter, supplemented by sporadic polygyny of the sorts we have already described, is very common.

Neither polygyny nor polyandry can be common unless one or both of two conditions are met: (1) the balance is disturbed so that there are more marriageable adults of one sex than of the other, or (2) some people of one sex don't get married at all.

Polygyny

One way to disturb the balance in the face of essentially equal numbers of male and female births is for women to marry at a younger age than men (cf. p. 35). In many parts of sub-Saharan Africa the economy is such that the closely cooperating family group needs more adult women than adult men. A man needs several wives;

a woman needs cowives if she is not to be brutally overworked. Polygyny is the norm; the age differential between husbands and wives makes it feasible.

Polygyny has become standard or preferred also in some populous civil societies in which, if there is any discernible excess of women over men, the polygyny is in part the cause of the excess rather than merely its effect. There are economic classes, and in fact, if not in law, polygyny is the prerogative of the upper strata. For every man who has more than one wife there are one or more who have no wives at all. The wifeless man is at best underprivileged, at worst a serf or slave. In the earlier civil societies of the Old World, as reflected, for example, in the Old Testament or in *The Arabian Nights' Entertainments,* a petty king or a "merchant prince" maintained a harem, in part a variety of polygenous marriage but in part a sort of private brothel. Most men had only one wife each. The excess males were withdrawn from the marital market by being expended as soldiers, by becoming holy men bound by vows of celibacy, or by being converted into eunuchs.

POLYANDRY

Systematic polyandry is rare. Where it occurs (mainly in certain groups in India and Tibet) there is in fact an excess of adult males over adult females. As in most other social orders, the men, not the women, are dominant. The economic circumstances are such that the men must go far from home to make a living, staying away weeks or months at a time, so that two or more are rarely at home simultaneously. Whichever one is at home at the appropriate time, or whichever one has most recently performed some established ceremony with the wife, is the social father of the child; it does not matter whether he is the physiological father.

The polyandry serves to keep the population down, since the number of children a woman can bear depends on the lengths of the human periods of gestation and suckling, not on the number of males with whom she copulates. Though other factors are doubtless involved (p. 220), limiting the population is one of the main reasons for the polyandry. That this is so is evidenced further by the rather common practice of female infanticide.[5] Here, then, as in the case of some communities with preferred polygyny, the lack of numerical balance between the sexes is as much an effect as a cause of the marital practice.

DESCENT GROUPS ✘ We now return to our Eagles, and shall assume that they and their three sister bands are each exogamous, that residence is patrilocal, and that a child belongs to the band into which he is born. With these factors fixed, we shall tinker with population and ecology.

For a century, life is bountiful. Each band swells in numbers, and must therefore exploit a larger territory. The bands fission (p. 161). The new bands acquire new names, but the people descended from Eagles continue to call themselves Eagles, and

---

[5]In tribal society generally, infanticide is rare and usually motivated by immediate economic hardship. The main exception is that in the case of multiple births all, or all but one, of the infants may be destroyed through fear.

similarly for the descendants of the original Herons, Downrivers, and Cypresses. Some families regroup in such a way that a single local band may include, for example, both Eagles and Herons. If a man is an Eagle, his sons are Eagles and must find wives who are not; his daughters are Eagles and will be sought as wives by men who are not. Perhaps cross-cousin marriage or some other such pattern comes to be preferred.

CLANS, PHRATRIES, AND LINEAGES

The Eagles, Cypresses, Downrivers, and Herons are now no longer *local* groups (bands); instead, they have become *clans,* specifically *patrilineal* ones (Box 14-3). The clans are exogamous. We cannot speak of a residence rule relative to the clans, since they are not localized, but we can speak of patrilocal residence if a couple is still supposed to settle in a way that maintains the ties of proximity the husband had before he got married. Though dispersed, the clans may retain certain functions other than control of the marriage pattern: perhaps a clan gets together from time to time

BOX 14-3. Descent practices and types of kin-based groups.

DESCENT PRACTICES

A KIN-BASED GROUP IS	IF ONE'S MEMBERSHIP IS DETERMINED BY THAT OF ONE'S
patrilineal	father
matrilineal	mother
bilateral	father and mother

(But in some cases none of these three is the rule. See p. 176, fn. 6.)

TYPES OF KIN-BASED GROUPS

TERM	DEFINITION
clan	the smallest kin-based group larger than the family (or lineage: see below) for which membership is patrilineal or matrilineal, provided that there are at least two such groups and that each member of the community belongs to exactly one of them
lineage	like a clan when members actively trace themselves to a (real and named) common ancestor
phratry	the smallest kin-based group larger than the clan, with the same provisos; it follows that each clan, as well as each individual, belongs to exactly one phratry
moiety	a phratry (or clan, if there are no phratries) when there are exactly two of them
kindred	the kin group where descent is bilateral, consisting of all one's sufficiently close relatives through either parent (clans are pairwise disjunct; kindreds overlap)

For "double descent" see the text, p. 177. All efforts to standardize the large terminology for kin-based groupings have so far failed. In this book we use only the terms listed above, in the sense here assigned them.

---

for ceremonial activities, or perhaps it has a council which meets on occasion to defend a mistreated clansman or to punish one who has transgressed. Clan exogamy may in time go by the board. We still speak of clans as long as clan membership is noted and heeded in some way by the people themselves.

At this point we have reached another uniquely human phenomenon. Only with the memory and foresight imparted by language can animals maintain functioning groups that are not dependent on constant or frequent physical proximity. Nonhuman primates have bands; they cannot have clans.

Only a minor change is required in our posited initial conditions for the events we have described to give rise to *matrilineal* clans instead of to patrilineal ones. In that case residence might have been and remained matrilocal. Or, after marriage a man might take his wife to live in the local group of his mother's brother, to whose clan he belongs (*avunculocal* residence: Box 14-2); this is one way of maintaining male dominance in a matrilineal society.

It does not take much imagination to see how two small clans might form an alliance, or how one clan might grow large and split, either of these giving rise to a *phratry* (Box 14-3). It is also easy to realize that people in tribal society could in time lose track of the actual genealogies of clan members, so that a clan comes to be composed of ostensible rather than altogether of real kin—or, better, so that clan membership itself becomes, from the inside view, a sort of kinship equivalent.

The kinship-like nature of clans is often underscored within a community by a claim (or a pretense—it is not always taken seriously) of descent from some very remote, perhaps fabulous, progenitor or progenetrix; this does not mean that in historical fact all clans start as small groups of close relatives. On the other hand, the members of a clanlike group sometimes do descend from a relatively recent named common ancestor. In this case the group is often called a *lineage* rather than a clan. Sometimes one finds both lineages and clans, with the amount of emphasis on the two in all sorts of balances.[6]

Patrilineal and Matrilineal

Many factors can play a part in determining whether clans (or lineages) will be patrilineal or matrilineal. The chief factor is probably economic. Where closely cooperating groups of males are of paramount importance, as for hunting and fishing, it is more efficient for males not to have to regroup as they grow to manhood. Hence residence tends to be patrilocal, and clans or lineages, if they develop, tend to be patrilineal. Agriculture, as a development from gathering, is typically women's work when it first appears, promoting the habit of keeping girls together as they grow into womanhood, and thus encouraging matrilocality and matrilineality. These generalizations hold up fairly well, but, of course, are not perfect.

[6]Sometimes the important consideration is to be able to trace one's ancestry back to some revered figure, through either male or female connecting links. The lineage is then neither patrilineal nor matrilineal, and is not likely to be exogamous.

Some communities have both patrilineal and matrilineal kin-based groups, a situation called *double descent*. This situation is common in Australia. Each tribesman belongs to one or the other of two patrilineal moieties (Box 14-3) and also to one or another of several matrilineal clans. Both groupings are exogamous. Let the patrilineal groups be A and B; let the matrilineal ones be 1, 2, 3, and 4. An A1 male must thus find a wife who is neither A nor 1, which means from among the B2, B3, or B4 females. The A1 male's father was an A2, an A3, or an A4; his mother was a B1. If he marries a B2 female, his children will be A2.

This is rendered seemingly more complicated because the people who practice double descent do not have labels for our A and B, our 1, 2, 3, and 4. Instead, they name the intersections: "Battlers," let us say, for A1, and so on. Note the dizzying effect if we cast information in this shape: a Battler male must find a wife from among the Runts, the Dandies, or the Curlers; his father was a Warbler, a Grouch, or a Hopper; his mother was a Redspear; if he marries a Runt his children will be Warblers.[7] The system is set forth in full in Table 14-4. In Table 14-5 is presented indirect information about another common Australian scheme. The reader who likes puzzles will enjoy trying to infer the underlying pattern from the information given.

The Australian aborigines take enormous pleasure in the complexities of their systems, gossiping endlessly about them not in abstract logical terms but in terms of the problems faced by specific individuals and how they may be solved. We see here a social manifestation not only of sex, child care, and economics, but also of the human version of primate play, working itself out in communities whose material appurtenances are as simple as any known in the ethnographic present. They have been willing to pay a price for their fun. The population is sparse. The marriage

[7]The names are faked; I am not sure enough of the denotations of the ones actually used by any Australian group.

TABLE 14-4. An Australian marriage pattern.

Husband:	Wife: Battler	Warbler	Grouch	Hopper	Redspear	Runt	Dandy	Curler
Battler	—	—	—	—	—	Warbler	Grouch	Hopper
Warbler	—	—	—	—	Battler	—	Grouch	Hopper
Grouch	—	—	—	—	Battler	Warbler	—	Hopper
Hopper	—	—	—	—	Battler	Warbler	Grouch	—
Redspear	—	Runt	Dandy	Curler	—	—	—	—
Runt	Redspear	—	Dandy	Curler	—	—	—	—
Dandy	Redspear	Runt	—	Curler	—	—	—	—
Curler	Redspear	Runt	Dandy	—	—	—	—	—

Row headings (left) indicate affiliation of husband, column headings (top) that of wife. The entry at the intersection of a row and a column indicates the affiliation of the children; a dash means the marriage is prohibited. The "solution" to the system is given in the text.

rules so greatly restrict who can marry whom that a man often has either to marry an elderly widow or else wait for years for a suitable girl child to grow to marriageable age. The moral is obvious. We must not expect *ever* to find people behaving solely from physiological and economic necessity, nor entirely in accord with the dictates of any system of "logic"—even their own. The fun factor is always latent, and bursts through the surface in the most unimaginably unpredictable contexts.

KINDREDS ✳ We return now to our Eagles as originally described (p. 167), with no clans, no special marriage restrictions except against close incest, no fixed rule of residence. The *we*-groups are family and band. As siblings grow up and start their own families, they remain aware of their siblinghood and their children know their aunts and uncles and grandparents. People who have lived in the same household, or whose parents have lived in the same household, tend to feel somewhat closer to one another than to others. Privileges and obligations of the family kind can, as it were, be inherited.

This can lead to a state of affairs in which the duties and privileges of individuals vis-à-vis others are governed by how closely they are related, through either father or mother. The closest ties are those between parents and children, between siblings, or between husband and wife; the next closest are those between grandparents and grandchildren; then uncle or aunt and nephew or niece; then cousin and cousin. At least, it could work out that way; let us say that it does, and that beyond those degrees of connection one's obligations are only those of normal decency towards members of the same band or of the same tribe.

In this situation, each individual is at the focus of a *kindred* (Box 14-3). Siblings have identical kindreds. Otherwise, kindreds overlap: an individual is at the focus of only one, but he falls within the boundaries of many others. For instance, I am in the kindred that focuses on a cousin on my father's side, and he or she is in mine; I am in the kindred that focuses on a cousin on my mother's side, and he or she is in mine; but these two cousins of mine do not belong to each other's kindreds.

Exogamy is apt to play a part in the definition of kindreds, in the sense that the people I am not permitted to marry all belong to the kindred that focuses on me; but the kindred may be more inclusive than the exogamous group, the remoter connections marked by more tenuous patterns of prescribed behavior.

TABLE 14-5. An Australian puzzle.

IF A MAN IS A	HIS SON'S CHILD IS A	HIS DAUGHTER'S CHILD IS A	IF A WOMAN IS A	HER SON'S CHILD IS A	HER DAUGHTER'S CHILD IS A
Brown	Brown	Jones	Brown	Jones	Brown
Jones	Jones	Brown	Jones	Brown	Jones
Smith	Smith	Williams	Smith	Williams	Smith
Williams	Williams	Smith	Williams	Smith	Williams

N.B.: A child never belongs to the same named kin group as either parent.

For fun we have used common English surnames. Who can marry whom? How is the named kin group of a child determined by the named kin groups of his parents? What is the underlying system of (unnamed) patrilineal and matrilineal groups?

As a type of kin-based group, the kindred is described as *bilateral* because one's kindred depends on the identity of both parents. There are two crucial differences between this type of kin-based group and any sort of clan pattern with patrilineal, matrilineal, or double descent. One is that kindreds overlap, whereas clans are pairwise disjunct. The other is that kindreds typically have fuzzy outer boundaries: that is, as one moves from near to remote kin, duties and privileges do not suddenly disappear but gradually fade.

Our own custom in contemporary (or slightly old-fashioned) Western society can only be interpreted as involving kindreds. Kindred boundaries are fuzzy and show great variation. Some in our society feel very close to second cousins or to great uncles and aunts; some, once separated from their parental households, feel little or nothing for their siblings.

THE HOUSEHOLD

× In most of the twists and turns we have imposed on our hypothetical Eagles, the family has remained the so-called *nuclear family*: husband, wife, and their children. Most *localized family aggregates* or *households* throughout the world in the ethnographic present have consisted merely of a nuclear family. This has been true even in those societies in which other variants are found and in which some other pattern is the ideal.

There are several ways in which a household can differ from the nuclear-family type. In particular, there are two ways in which it can be larger and more complicated. One is via polygamy; the other is via *extension*—that is, by married children living with their parents as they raise their own families, so that the household typically includes more than two generations. The types of enlarged family aggregate to which these practices give rise are tabulated in Box 14-6.

BOX 14-6. Types of household aggregates.

TYPE	DESCRIPTION	OCCURRENCE AS PREFERRED NORM
"kernel" family	woman and children only; brothers for male tasks	very rare
separate nuclear household	husband, wife, children; occasional "emergency" polygyny	common
composite household:		
unextended	normally only two generations per household	
with favored polygyny		common
with polyandry		rare
extended	three or more generations per household	
normally monogamous		common
with favored polygyny		common

In almost all societies, regardless of the preferred norm, most actual family aggregates depart only slightly from the membership of the separate nuclear household.

The Importance of Norms

It makes a great deal of difference whether a composite family aggregate represents a movement away from a preferred norm or towards one.

(1) When old Tani died and his brother "adopted" his widow and her children, that may have been standard operating procedure and may have worked out well for all involved, but just the same it was a way of handling an emergency, and represented a departure from the monogamous norm. The members of the polygynous family, or of the two intersecting nuclear families of which it was composed, managed their interpersonal relations as much as possible on the model established by the norm.

Compare with this a composite group consisting of a man, his two wives, and their children in one of the societies of the Near East or of Africa in which polygyny is the ideal sought by any man who can achieve it. Here the man has only two wives only because he has been unable to obtain more. He is moving, not *away* from an ideal, but *towards* one—even if he never reaches it. Expectations are different; interpersonal relations accordingly take on a different flavor.

The difference is also reflected in such things as the physical arrangements of housing. Among the Eagles, the huts occupied by Tani's widow and by her new husband's other wife are apt to be simply two of the huts of the settlement. In the society where polygyny is preferred, our man with two wives lives in some sort of compound in which there are separate houses for the wives (see also below, p. 183), or else in a large house with separate compartments.

(2) Compare also the following two situations. Either in the United States or in pre-Communist China one can easily find a household composed of a man and his wife, their son and the son's wife, and one or more young children of the latter couple.

This situation can arise in the United States in either of two ways. Sometimes a young couple live for a time with the parents of one or the other because they are economically unprepared to go into housekeeping for themselves, and often they have a child or so during this period so that the household contains three generations. Or, a family may be joined by a widowed grandmother, a widowered grandfather, by both grandparents if they are feeble and impoverished, or (more frequently fifty years ago than now) by an unmarried or widowed sister of the husband or of the wife. Any of these deviations is a departure from our American middle-class ideal, which is that a household should be composed of a nuclear family and no one else. The departures are matters of necessity, and can give rise to serious interpersonal tensions: who is the boss? who is entitled to make what decisions?

Now switch the scene to pre-Communist China, where most family aggregates were no larger or smaller than in the United States but where the preferred arrangement was the large patriarchal household composed of a man, his wife or wives, his married sons and their wives and children, perhaps even a few children of a fourth generation. Here the specific household we have posited is likewise a departure from an ideal, but in exactly the opposite direction. The oldest man is unquestionably the head of the household. His wife is the *lău tàitai,* the 'Old Madame', the unchallenged boss of women's and children's affairs, who may regret she has only one daughter-in-law to lord it over but who does her best within the imposed limitation. The son will become the head of the household only when his father dies; even after that, he will continue to manifest filial piety in the family shrine. His wife begins as an outsider, very gradually accepted into the family. Her acceptance will be truly complete only when she becomes the *lău tàitai.* That will be when the old man's wife dies—unless in his dotage he takes another wife, which he just might do, upsetting everything. To be sure, there are many sources of interpersonal tension in this arrangement, as in the Western one, but the tensions are different in kind because from childhood everyone involved has been trained in a different set of expectations.

The difference can be emphasized by considering our linguistic clue, the use of *we*-forms. The major cleavage in the American family is between the older couple and the younger. A member of either of these pairs will often address the other pair with an exclusive *we*, a *we-not-you* (p. 157). The major cleavage in the Chinese family is between the two adult men and the *lău tàitai* on the one hand, the young wife on the other. Any member of the former group will address the young wife with an exclusive *we*, a *we-not-you.* The young wife has a long, hard row to hoe before she earns acceptance into the group in which any member can address any other with an inclusive *we.* In the American situation there is no drive towards an inclusive *we*; the goal is separation.

DEVIANT PATTERNS

Households can differ from the nuclear-family type without necessarily being larger or more complicated. Here, again, we must distinguish between sporadic exceptions to the norm or ideal of a community, on the one hand, and, on the other, the established custom of a whole community or subcommunity which deviates in some unusual way from what seem to have been the commonest patterns throughout human history.

SPORADIC DEVIATION. For this, we need only consider the American family portrayed in a popular TV series of the 1960s: a widower with three sons, raising them with the help of a bachelor uncle who knows how to cook and keep house. Allowing for dramatic distortion and middle-class bowdlerization, the portrayal was reasonably realistic. Such household groups exist and survive.

SEMISYSTEMATIC DEVIATION. Very different is the situation found today in the ghettos of many American cities and in some depressed rural areas of the South. The situation is characterized by a relatively sessile population of women and children and a relatively motile population of adult males. The women stay put because the exigencies of child care call for that, and they give the children all the love they can. The men move around because they cannot find permanent employment. They cannot find permanent employment because they do not have the training for it and because they are black in a society dominated by whites. They cannot get the training because they are black in a society dominated by whites. As long as a man can stay put, he behaves economically and physiologically as a husband to a woman and as a father to her children. When he has to move he does, and seeks a new liaison in his new location; the woman stays put and accepts a new liaison as the most natural way of obtaining the food and the adult male companionship she and her children need.

The basic links in these households are those between adult women and between women and children. The husband-wife and father-child links are often close, but impermanent. The pattern is one of desperation. The people who live this way are exposed on all sides to other ideals. All of them would much rather have economic stability, and almost all of them would rather have permanent monogamous marriages. In the face of staggering odds, they are doing the best they can to attain a measure of the warmth of family life desired by all human beings.

SYSTEMATIZED DEVIATION. However, the sources of evil in the situation just described are the economic depression and the fact that the actual family pattern deviates so strikingly from the one considered ideal by those involved.

Given adequate food and satisfying symbols of status, in a different setting similar marital and household arrangements can apparently be happy. The true kernel of the family consists only of a woman and her children. Necessary male economic activities can be performed by brothers rather than by husbands. Husbands may then come and go by an approved pattern, or the role of impregnators may be played by visitors who are so sporadic that we cannot call them husbands at all.

The evidence for this is the state of affairs in a small minority of human communities, of which the best attested is that of

the Nayar of Malabar in southwest India. The Nayar were a warrior caste whose men were, when of military age, engaged as full time soldiers. They spent most of this time in barracks or away on wars. The young women often went as house servants in Brahmin households and were often taken as concubines by the Brahmin men. This was considered a great privilege. The men, after their military service was over, returned 'home'; i.e. to the house in which they were born. The girls born there also treated it as a permanent base and finally lived there full-time. Thus, a consanguineal household grew up [one marked by genetic ties rather than by marital ties] . . .. Stable marital relationships were difficult to maintain under these conditions, and the natolocal residence pattern [living where you were born] was the outcome. The mound on which the house was built was known as the *taravad*, and the unit living there came to be known by this name also. The taravad represented a lineage which was itself part of a clan, as the Nayar had not unnaturally developed a matrilineal system of groupings . . ..

The eldest of the warrior brothers of a *taravad*—the one who finished his war service first—would be the head of the group. The *taravad* owned land and livestock and the brothers worked this under the direction of the head. Meanwhile the women of the *taravad* were having children who would eventually take up their places as working males of the unit after their period as warriors.

The impregnation of the women was not a random affair. As we have seen, the girls might well have children by the Brahmin overlords, but also, before they reached puberty, they were 'married' to a man of a lineage with which their natal lineage had a special relationship. This 'marriage' was then dissolved and the woman was free to take as many as twelve 'lovers' or temporary husbands . . . .. The number of lovers may seem rather large, but as many of them at any one time might be away on military duties, the large number gave some reserve strength to the task force. These men had visiting rights with their 'wives', and if one of the men on visiting found another's spear or shield outside the house, then he would go away and try again the next night.[8]

In this exceedingly unusual situation we have households and families, but no marriage, because a child has no social father (p. 166). Those responsibilities of an adult male which we think of as paternal were shouldered by the child's mother's brothers.

Our evidence for the Nayar is not very full, but there is no reason to assume that they were not reasonably content with their pattern of life—as content as stability, security, and well understood expectations can render people. Yet it is worth noting that the Nayar were not an isolated community working out their own way of life with minimal interference from others. They were a segment of a complex civil society, maintained by the Brahmans to whom they were subservient and by the various lower castes who lived in the same territory, performing certain specialized tasks for the benefit of the whole society (or perhaps for the benefit of the Brahmans), and governing their reproductive and sexual affairs in a way suited to their peculiar social niche.

There are instances of standard fatherless households less deviant than the Nayar. In parts of western Africa, a man's wives live in separate houses scattered among the other houses of a compoundlike village. The man visits his wives and their children, but his own headquarters is the house in which his mother and siblings live. The children "belong" to the wife, not to him. Just as he stays in his mother's house, his sons, upon marriage, will stay in the houses in which they were born. The marital tie is more enduring than among the Nayar, and involves more mutual obligations. In some cases (for instance, among the Ashanti) the husband must be

[8]From *Kinship and Marriage* (pp. 100–101), by Robin Fox. Penguin Books Ltd., 1967. Copyright, 1967, by Robin Fox; reprinted with the permission of author and publisher.

TABLE 14-7. More human universals (continued from Table 12-1, p. 154).

SHARED WITH SOME NONHUMAN ANIMALS	PART OF HUMAN HISTORICAL BASE LINE*	UNIVERSAL IN ETHNOGRAPHIC PRESENT	
	✗		multifamily bands (band ≠ family)
	(widespread)		loose groupings of bands into "tribes"
✗	✗	✗	social maternity = physiological maternity
	✗	✗	social paternity tending to equal physiological paternity
?(how defined?)	✗	✗(almost)	marriage
✗	✗	✗	prohibition of mother-son incest
	✗	✗	further incest prohibitions, yielding exogamous groups
✗	✗	✗	at least vague tendencies towards (large) endogamous groups
	✗	✗	functional social groupings (e.g., clans) not dependent on frequent physical proximity

*For some items this means "the eve of the ethnographic present," with no implications about earlier states of affairs.

fed by his wife or one of his wives, though he eats in his own home: at mealtime she dispatches a child to take his already cooked dinner to him.

SUMMARY ✕ The few human universals that have turned up incidentally in this chapter and the preceding one are listed in Table 14-7.

For family and marriage, we in effect gave a summary before proceeding to examples and details (pp. 165–167). We have not covered all known variants, but we have touched on the norms and the extremes. The time and space that must be devoted to unusual arrangements tends to distort our perspective. Of course it is worthy of note that our species has been able to adapt to such a wide variety of familial and marital arrangements. It may only be a personal cultural prejudice that makes me want to underscore something else: I think it is significant that, all over the world and as far back in history as we can penetrate, the simple nuclear household has been far and away the statistically prevalent pattern.

15

THE CATEGORIES OF WE: ADDRESS AND REFERENCE

Systems of personal pronouns include forms like English *you, he, she, they* as well as *I* and various sorts of *we*'s (p. 157). Also, as indicated on page 120, all languages supply their speakers with kinship terms (like *father, mother*) and with personal names (like English *William,* Menomini *oskas* 'Claw'). Many languages, if not all, include various special forms used as *titles*: English *mister, Mrs., miss, sir.* The patterns of usage of forms of these sorts in a human community are one facet of social structure, and afford a clue to the other facets. In this chapter we shall examine this, with special emphasis on personal pronouns of the second and third person and on kinship terminologies.

✖ In my extreme youth I did some unplanned ethnographic field work the results of which will serve well as a point of departure.   **QUAKER PRONOUNS**

I was born in 1916 in the urban Middle West; my parents were both born in 1875 and were raised as Quakers in the rural or small-town Middle West. I had an older brother and two older sisters; sometimes the household included also a grandparent or an aunt. I was not raised in the Quaker church, but the Quaker tradition made itself felt.

Our household pronominal habits were these. In addressing two or more people, whether members of the household or outsiders or partly each, we used the form *you*: "Would you children come upstairs right away now!" In speaking to a single outsider, we used the form *you*: "Hi, Bill! Can you come out and play?" Likewise, when anyone not in our household spoke to one or more of us, we heard the form *you*. But when one of our household spoke to a single other member of the household, the pronoun was *thee*: "Mother, would thee answer the telephone?" "Charles, is this thy toy or Robert's I just stumbled over?"

A consideration of these data will show that, as far as I could judge during my earliest speaking years, every household in the world followed the same practices. I can remember being firmly of this opinion. The shocking revelation came one day when I overheard a neighborhood playmate address his mother as *you*. It took me several days (and, if I remember aright, one bloody nose) to adjust, to realize that

THE CATEGORIES OF WE: ADDRESS AND REFERENCE   **185**

the *thee*-world was very small and special and a bit odd, and that everyone else just said *you* indiscriminately to everyone.

Most readers of this book have never used any pronoun but *you* to anyone (unless they speak some other language as well as English). Assuming that this is the case for you, you may now use me as an informant. What was the difference, you ask me, between *thee* and *you* in the Quaker English of your childhood, assuming that only a single person was being addressed?

The answer is that *thee* connoted family solidarity, warmth, and togetherness, an intimate sharing of interests and goals which ran too deep to be more than momentarily ruffled by the occasional intramural spats. *You,* in contrast, did not imply dislike, disdain, coldness, formality, heightened or diminished respect, nor increased or decreased politeness. It meant "you are not a *thee,*" and "your pronominal usage is therefore different, and I would not want to embarrass either of us by addressing you in a way to which you are not accustomed." The family was a crucial *we*-group (p. 158), the smallest and most tight-knit to which any of us belonged. We said *thee* to those to whom we would have spoken with an inclusive *we*-form if English had had one, and *you* to those for whom an exclusive *we*-form would usually have been appropriate.

BOX 15-1. Two pronominal systems.

(a) Classical Greek

	ONE	EXACTLY TWO	TWO OR MORE
FIRST PERSON	*egṓ*	*nṓ*	*hēmêis*
SECOND PERSON	*sý*	*sphṓ*	*hȳmêis*
THIRD PERSON	—*	*sphêis*	

*One or another demonstrative pronoun was used, most of them distinguishing sex.

(b) Tunica

	ONE	TWO	THREE OR MORE
FIRST PERSON	*ʔíma*	*ʔínima*	
SECOND PERSON: MALE(S) ONLY OR BOTH SEXES	*má*	*wínima*	
FEMALE(S) ONLY	*héma*	*hínima*	
THIRD PERSON: MALE(S) ONLY OR BOTH SEXES	*ʔúwi*	*ʔúnima*	*séma*
FEMALE(S) ONLY	*tíhči*	*sínima*	

✖ Standard English is unusual in supplying only a single second-person pronoun. Most languages of the ethnographic present furnish at least a two-way contrast based on number of addressees: for example, Menomini (glossed by Biblical English equivalents as a matter of convenience) *kenah* 'thou', to a single person and referring only to him, versus *kenua*ˀ 'ye', to several people, or to a single person but referring to some plurality to which he belongs. English had just this contrast half a millennium ago, but has since in general lost it. It is retained in some local British dialects as well as in Biblical usage; it has been reintroduced in a good many nonstandard regional dialects in the form of a distinct plural *youse* (rhymes with *booze*) or *y'all*. Classical Greek, Sanskrit, and the language of the Tunica Indians of the lower Mississippi Valley have a more or less fully maintained three-way number contrast (Box 15-1). Fijian has a four-way contrast (Box 13-1, p. 157).

For social structure, we get more interested when we find distinctions that do not turn wholly on something as simple and obvious as number of addressees. The universally available additional factor is sex, but by far the commonest linguistic pattern is for it to be ignored in pronouns. For this, we do better to consider third-person pronouns along with those of the second person. Chinese *tā* and Menomini *wenah* are like most of the world's third-person singular pronouns: they denote merely any person other than speaker or addressee. We have no pronoun with that meaning. The languages of Europe, including English, are unusual in that they make the sex distinction in third-person pronouns (*he* : *she*) but not in the second person. Some Semitic languages and various others (including Tunica, Box 15-1) make it in both.

Pronouns and Social Classes

In civil and incipiently civil societies the patterns of usage of two or more second-person pronouns often reflect additional factors, and changes of usage can signal changes of social structure.

We can represent many of the possibilities (not all) in a two-dimensional table (Box 15-2, Table a). The row headings have to do with the relative social status of speaker and addressee; the column headings indicate whether the two are familiar with each other ("intimate": each is in the inner circle of the other) or encounter each other only sporadically ("remote": at least one is not personally known to the other). A third factor, not represented in the table, is the degree of formality (p. 149) of the context in which the speaking takes place. For example, perhaps when a man and wife talk in private their relationship is intimate, whereas when they speak to each other in the presence of certain sorts of outsiders they switch to remote usage.

In Table b (Box 15-2) the pigeonholes are filled in with the French second-person pronouns to accord with the standards of usage of a century ago. In that era, an inferior would address a superior as *vous* and be addressed by the latter as *tu* whether the two knew each other personally or not. A son addressed his father, a waiter addressed a patron in a restaurant, as *vous*. The father used *tu* to his son; the patron used *tu* to the waiter and hailed him by saying *Garçon!* 'Boy!' Strangers whose relative social status was not obvious stuck to *vous*. When status was or became known and was equal, they used *vous* unless they struck up a sufficiently close friendship, in which case the switch from *vous* to *tu* could be marked by all the shyness and hesitancy characteristic of romantic Victorian courtship.

There have been changes in the last hundred years. You no longer hail a waiter with *Garçon!*—not if you want service. You say *Monsieur!* 'Sir!' and stick to *vous,* unless, of course, you and he happen to be buddies and he calls you *tu* too. Many a child uses *tu* to his parents, although some are not permitted to, and some of those who do are trained to switch to *vous* in the presence of outsiders, particularly of elderly old-fashioned aunts. The new situation is displayed in Table c (Box 15-2). The forms in parentheses indicate uncertainties of usage or survivals of the older pattern in some circles. If the newer pattern were to become firm, then we should no longer need the rows in our diagram, and could represent the situation as in Table d. This would be like what, as a five-year-old, I thought American usage was with *thee* and *you.*

BOX 15-2. Status factors in pronominal usage.

Table a.   General Framework.

	INTIMATE	REMOTE
INFERIOR TO SUPERIOR		
EQUAL TO EQUAL		
SUPERIOR TO INFERIOR		

Table b.   French Pronominal Usage a Century Ago.

	INTIMATE	REMOTE
INFERIOR TO SUPERIOR	*vous*	*vous*
EQUAL TO EQUAL	*tu*	*vous*
SUPERIOR TO INFERIOR	*tu*	*tu*

Table c.   Current French Pronominal Usage.

	INTIMATE	REMOTE
INFERIOR TO SUPERIOR	*tu (vous)*	*vous*
EQUAL TO EQUAL	*tu*	*vous*
SUPERIOR TO INFERIOR	*tu*	*vous (tu)*

Table d.   Outcome if Tendency Continues.

	INTIMATE	REMOTE
ANYONE TO ANYONE	*tu*	*vous*

Now, what changed in France? Was it just the ranges of meaning of the two pronouns, or was it the social structure? If the latter has changed to level out all differences of status, then the row headings are meaningless. In actuality, there has been *some* change in social structure, a continuation of a trend towards egalitarianism that began with the French revolution or earlier. The drift in pronominal usage not only signals this change but forms part of it, since it is impossible to distinguish between a position in social structure and the *totality* of characteristic behavior that marks it. But the egalitarian ideal is still far from having been reached. Poor people in France may be spoken to with a style of politeness more like that accorded rich people, but they still do not eat as well.

Status, Person, and Number

Although the coinage of new words of some sorts is commonplace (p. 108), the successful introduction of a new personal pronoun is not.[1] When society changes and new pronominal usages are needed, what most often happens is that the old inherited forms are used in additional ways.

I think we can hazard the guess that before the rise of civil society personal pronouns, apart from distinctions of person (speaker versus addressee versus others), made at most differentiations of number and of sex, and more commonly the former than the latter. If so, then it is not surprising that differentiations based on relative social status should often be grafted onto distinctions of number. Recall the "royal *we*" common in medieval Europe. It was almost as though grammatical plural versus singular depended not on number of discrete individuals but on number of units of some sort of "mass of prestige": a king "weighed" enough to balance any number of commoners, and so said *we* of himself (nowadays only newspaper editors have the gall to do this). His subjects had to conform, so they used the second-person plural form in speaking to him (*ye* instead of *thou* in medieval English), sometimes a third-person plural form in speaking about him.

This sort of development was not confined to Europe. The Fijian nonsingular pronouns of the second and third persons (Box 13-1, p. 157) have honorific uses as well as those that turn literally on number. The pattern escapes the simple framework of Table a in Box 15-2, since there are four distinct pronouns for each person instead of two, and in the honorific use the higher the grammatical number the greater the respect. A ranking chief is addressed as *konii* and usually referred to as *ra*; lesser officials merit only the "few" form or the "two" form.

Another common mark of deference when the lowly address the mighty is to pretend the addressee is not being spoken to: one uses third-person forms ("Would His Serene Majesty perchance care for another platter of pickled peacocks' pancreases?"). This alternative underlies the development mentioned in footnote 1.

The chamberlain or noble lord who must demean himself in one of these ways

---

[1]Yet it can happen. Spanish *usted* and *ustedes,* polite second-person singular and plural, are in origin phrases meaning 'your mercy' and 'your mercies'. Some now colorless first- and second-person pronouns of Japanese and other oriental languages descend from phrases expressing abject humility and fawning obeisance.

in the presence of the king is not going to settle for any less kowtowing from his own underlings.[2] So it can work out that *ye* means ambiguously either two or more people of any sort or a single person on a higher rung of the social ladder than oneself, while *thou* means a single person who is one's equal or inferior. It worked out that way, at any rate, in English and in French, culturally linked by the Norman Conquest. It worked out differently in German and Spanish, where the current formal second-person pronouns are old third-person forms.

**THE HISTORY
OF QUAKER
AND GENERAL
ENGLISH USAGE**

✷ English usage had reached the pattern just described in the seventeenth century when the Quaker movement began.

The sixteenth and seventeenth centuries in England were marked by great fuss about the proper sorting-out of the political versus the nonpolitical, the religious versus the nonreligious, and the political versus the religious (chapters 10 and 12). The Quakers were extremists who in effect denied the distinctive contrast between the religious and the nonreligious by insisting that Christ's teachings, supplemented by direct divine guidance (the "inner light," that could come to *anyone,* not only to the members of some privileged clergy who had a direct pipeline to God), should guide one in all things. This doctrine seemed also to deny the distinction between the political and the nonpolitical. The Quakers would not doff their hats, nor bow, nor wear finery, nor take oaths, nor address anyone as *ye* or *you* instead of *thou* and *thee.*[3] Their pattern of pronominal usage was merely part of their general insistence on the equality of all men in the sight of God, to Whom alone deference was due. One could hardly expect the British governmental authorities to stand for that sort of thing. The Quakers, with various other extremists, suffered considerably. Many came to America, which proved for a while to afford only partial refuge.

Meanwhile, however, in the rest of Anglo-American society an increasing democracy worked itself out along different lines. Pronominally, "politeness" was generalized until the old second-person singular was abandoned altogether, at which point there was no longer any choice of pronoun with which to express differences of politeness or of anything else. The Quaker pronominal usage, without itself having changed, could nevertheless no longer count as a protest. It became an oddity, one of the marks of separatism of a tiny queer minority. For a while, Quakers continued to say *thee* to everyone, while non-Quakers said *you* to everyone including Quakers. Eventually, Quakers began to constrain their use of *thee* to other Quakers. This was the state of affairs in the Quaker group into which I was born. By that time most Quakers had abandoned most of the other outer marks of what they were. For example, their clothes had become like everyone else's. A pattern of speech is cheaper to maintain and, because it is drilled into one at a tender age, harder to change than a style

---

[2] The historical sequence was by and large the opposite of this. Lords had treated serfs with haughtiness and demanded servility in return long before the clear emergence of a hierarchy with a king at the top.

[3] A trend totally unrelated to what we discuss in the text was spreading the old accusative forms *you* and *thee* at the expense of the old nominatives *ye* and *thou,* and the old second-person verb endings were dying out. This explains the current general *you are* and American Quaker *thee is.* British Quakers retain *thou art* and the like.

of dress, but many Quakers had by that time also put the old pronoun aside, and since then it has been increasingly disused. The last three stages of this sequence are charted in Box 15-3.

✴ Kinship terms, like personal pronouns, are linguistic forms. If we are to understand how they work in a particular community we must be sure of three things: (1) their identity, (2) their shapes, and (3) their meanings.

KINSHIP TERMINOLOGY

(1) IDENTITY. A kinship term designates an individual by indicating his relationship to a specific other individual. In the technical discussion of kinship the latter is called *ego*. *Ego* in Latin means 'I', but it is just as well to forget that. To be sure, when I say *my father* ego is I, but ego is you when I say *your mother* and ego is Charlie when anyone says *Charlie's aunt*. If Joe and Bill are the only children in a certain family, then I can say *Joe's brother* and Joe can say *my brother* to denote the same person denoted by *Bill*.

These examples illustrate the use of a kinship term for *reference*—like any use of a personal pronoun of the *third* person. Some kinship terms are also used, like a personal pronoun of the *second* person, for *address*: Joe, speaking to his father, can call out *Hey, Dad!* or *Dad, let me wear your jacket tonight*. In English, Joe is much more apt to call his brother Bill *Bill* than *brother*. In some languages (by no means in all) that is exactly reversed, the kinship term being used most of the time and the individual's name only rarely.

Not all terms that denote kin are kinship terms. English *sibling* is not, and *child* is marginal. Kinship terms are in everyone's active everyday vocabulary. *Sibling*, in contrast, is constrained to technical discourse (or to mock-learnèd humor). *Child* is an everyday word, but has marginal status for a reason we shall see shortly.

(2) SHAPE. Whether or not we are interested in pronunciation for its own sake, we have to pay enough attention to it to avoid confusing forms that the users of

BOX 15-3. Three stages in Quaker and non-Quaker pronominal usage.

The addressees are singular throughout. In the earliest stage Quakers are publicly peculiar; in the second they keep their peculiarity to themselves; in the third they are apparently like everyone else.

SPEAKER:		ADDRESSEE: QUAKER	NONQUAKER
QUAKER	stage 1:	*thee*	*thee*
	stage 2:	*thee*	*you*
	stage 3:	*you*	*you*
NONQUAKER	stage 1:	*you*	*you*
	stage 2:	*you*	*you*
	stage 3:	*you*	*you*

the terms keep distinct. Recall that the Menomini missed our English distinction between *sweet* and *Swede* (p. 126). Suppose, now, that in some language the terms for father's brother and for mother's brother are respectively *unk* and *unkh,* the latter with a terminal puff of breath suppressed in the former. We could easily miss this difference, since English does not train us to listen for it. We would then assume that the speakers of the language have a single term for all uncles, and this error would vitiate all our further inferences about their kinship terminology.

(3) MEANING. Suppose we observe that in a certain community one refers to one's father as *X.* We now know *something* of the meaning of *X.* But remember what the meaning of a linguistic form is (p. 105), that the meanings of forms in different languages are rarely exact matches (p. 119), and that one can seldom learn the full meaning of a form through a single observation. So, suppose subsequently we find that one also utters *X* to refer to one's father's brother. Our first impulse is to say "these people call their paternal uncles 'father'." That is wrong. It confuses shape and meaning, and it confuses one language with another. The fact is that *X* has a range of meaning not exactly matched by that of any simple form in English. What we must say is something like this: *X* means 'any son of father's father'.

What we have asserted so far about kinship terms is true because they are linguistic forms. Beyond this, something is true of the kinship terms of every community of the ethnographic present which has been adequately studied: unlike the total lexicon of a language (p. 101), they form a more or less neatly patterned system. That is why we speak of kinship *terminology* rather than merely of kinship *terms.*

AMERICAN KINSHIP TERMINOLOGY   ✖ We start with the familiar, and treat it in considerable detail so that we may deal with other systems more briefly.

American English has exactly fifteen basic kinship terms (forms that cannot be broken down into smaller meaningful parts), of which two are marginal.

The first systematic feature is in the way the terms indicate the *sex* of the kin they denote. Six denote males: *father, son, husband, brother, uncle, nephew.* Six denote females: *mother, daughter, wife, sister, aunt, niece.* Three do not distinguish sex: *parent, child, cousin.*

Parent and *child* are marginal because they are hardly used in address (one does not say *Lend me a dime, parent*); the others all are, though some of them only rarely (p. 197). The two are also marginal in that they duplicate, with ambiguity as to sex, pairs of terms which distinguish sex: *parent* is the same as *father or mother,* and *child* is the same as *son or daughter. Cousin,* though not indicating sex, does not duplicate terms that do, and is thus not marginal (at least, not in this respect). The main kinship use of the two borderline terms is in the plural, where they can circumvent longer phrases and avoid highlighting either of the sex-differentiated terms by putting it first: thus, *parents* instead of either *father and mother* or *mother and father. Child* is marginal in still a third respect, in that we also use it of any sufficiently young person, regardless of kinship, in contrast with *adult.*[4]

---

[4]In passing, it is interesting to note that only nine of these fifteen terms were in our language a millennium ago. Old English had a number of others that have since been lost, in part replaced by and in part driven out by the six we have borrowed from French (*uncle, aunt, nephew, niece, cousin, parent*).

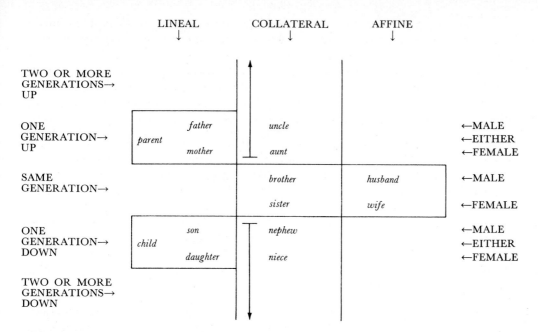

FIGURE 15-4. The core terms of American kinship (except *cousin*).

The second systematic feature has to do with *generation*. Three of the terms refer to kin one generation older (earlier) than one's own: *father, mother, parent*. Two refer to kin of any generation earlier than one's own: *uncle, aunt*. Four refer to kin of one's own generation: *brother, sister, husband, wife*. Three denote kin one generation younger (later) than one's own: *son, daughter, child*. Two refer to kin of any generation later than one's own: *nephew, niece*. This leaves *cousin*, which is vague as to generation.

The third systematic feature is a three-way distinction among *lineal, collateral,* and *affine* kin. (1) Lineal kin are in one's direct line of ancestry or descent: *father, mother, parent, son, daughter, child.* (2) Collateral kin involve a sibling relationship. *Brother* and *sister* name one's own siblings; *uncle* and *aunt* denote any sibling of a direct ancestor; *nephew* and *niece* apply to any direct descendant of one's own sibling; a *cousin* is any direct descendant of an uncle or aunt. In addition, a relative acquired through the marriage of a collateral is, with one exception, treated terminologically like a sibling of the collateral. My uncle's wife, like his sister, is my *aunt*; my niece's husband, like her brother, is my *nephew*; my cousin's spouse or sibling is also my *cousin*. The exception is the spouse of my own sibling: my brother's wife is a kind of a sister, but a special kind with a special name (*sister-in-law*; see below). (3) Affine kin are those to whom one is tied by one's own marriage: *husband* and *wife* are the only terms, and apply only to one's own spouse.

The information given above is enough fully to differentiate the fifteen basic terms. The same information is presented diagrammatically in Figure 15-4, except that the troublesome word *cousin* is left out. In Figure 15-5 it is presented via a genealogical chart.

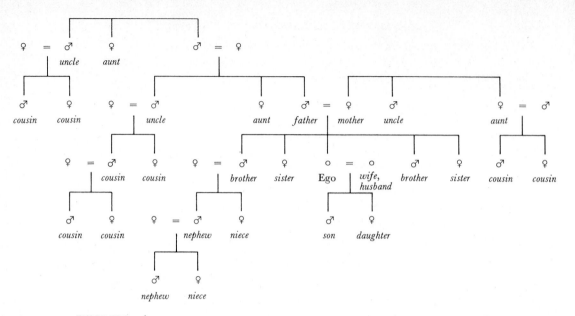

FIGURE 15-5. A GENEALOGICAL CHART SHOWING THE CORE TERMS OF AMERICAN KINSHIP. The equals sign means "married." "♂" is male, "♀" female; not shown for ego and spouse because it doesn't matter which is which.

A fourth feature deserves mention although it does not work independently of the first three. Define one "link" in the chain of connection between kin to be a single parent-child relationship, a single sibling relationship, or a single tie between marital partners. Kin are *primary* if the chain of connection consists of exactly one link: *father, mother, parent, son, daughter, child, brother, sister, husband, wife.* Kin are *secondary* if the chain necessarily involves at least two links: *uncle, aunt, cousin, nephew, niece.*

A fifth feature likewise fails to be independent of the first three. Given vertebrate reproduction, monogamy, and the definitions of the terms as set forth above, it turns out that *my X* can refer only to a single individual (at any one time) if *X* is *father, mother, husband,* or *wife.* But if *X* is any of the other terms then *my X* is in principle ambiguous. Of course, it can work out in a particular family that someone has, say, only one aunt whom he would ever have occasion to talk about, so that he can just say *my aunt* without danger of misunderstanding. But the disambiguition in such a case is achieved by the circumstances, not by the meaning of the kinship term. A term that necessarily denotes only a single individual is *descriptive*; one that is inherently ambiguous is *classificatory.*[5] Terms of both sorts are found in every kinship terminology, but the ratio of the number of the former kind to the number of the latter kind varies.

[5]"Descriptive" is not a very good label. But retention of these terms honors the memory of Lewis Henry Morgan (1818–1881), the founder of anthropological studies of kinship. He used the labels for whole kinship terminologies, which has turned out to be unprofitable; we use them for individual kinship terms, but in senses akin to his.

Converses and Reciprocality

If A refers to B with term *X* and B refers to A with term *Y,* then *X* and *Y* are *converses.* If *X = Y,* the single term is *reciprocal. Cousin* is reciprocal; *brother* is reciprocal between brothers, and *sister* between sisters. Otherwise, we have the following pairs of converses in English:

father, son	*uncle, nephew*
father, daughter	*uncle, niece*
mother, son	*aunt, nephew*
mother, daughter	*aunt, niece*
parent, child	*brother, sister*
	husband, wife

Any converse of any of the fifteen basic terms is itself a basic term. In this sense, the set is "closed."

The Periphery

In another sense it is not: English has an indefinitely large number of additional kinship terms. Some are alternatives for one or another of the basic set. Some make distinctions among kin named in a less precise way by terms of the basic set. Some name kin for which the basic set supplies no term at all. Thus:

(1)   Forms are made with *grand-* plus a basic term: *grandfather, grandmother, grandparent, grandson, granddaughter, grandchild; grandnephew, grandniece. Grand-* means 'one more generation removed' in the direction indicated by the underlying basic term. Thus, a *grandfather* is a parent's father, and so on. The first six *grand-* terms name kin not nameable by basic terms. The last two denote explicitly a male or female grandchild of a sibling, for which the bare terms *nephew* and *niece* can also be used.

(2)   Some of the terms so far considered have by-forms of familiarity or endearment, used especially within a household and perhaps most often by or to children. With a few exceptions, the terms that have such by-forms are those used in address (p. 191) as well as in reference. Alongside *father* there are *papa, pop, pops, dad, daddy,* and the like; alongside *mother* there are *mama, mom, mommy, mum, mummy,* and various others. I know of no such by-forms for *daughter, parent, child, nephew, niece,* for any of the *grand-* terms except *grandfather (grandpop, grandpa, gramps)* and *grandmother (granny, grandma, grandmama),* or for any of the compound terms discussed below. But some of these nursery forms are sometimes used in a loose or extended sense. For example, a child in a household that contains his great grandfather but no grandfather may call him *gramps.*

(3)   Forms are made with the modifier *great,* which means the same thing as *grand-. Great uncle* and *great aunt* are the converses of *grandnephew* and *grandniece.* Otherwise, we have *great grandfather, great grandmother,* and so on, from any *grand-* term, and even from a shorter *great* term, as in *great great grandfather* or *great great great grandfather.* In practice, one soon loses count.

(4)   Some people distinguish cousins by the pattern *first* (*second,* etc.) *cousin,* alone or with a following *once* (*twice,* etc.) *removed.* First cousins are the children of siblings; second cousins are the children of first cousins. My first cousin once removed is either a child of my first cousin or a first cousin of my parent. But usages vary. In any case, these phrases are heard mostly in discussions of genealogy at family get-togethers. Their status is somewhere between that of hard-core kinship terms and that of the technical terms used by ethnographers and sociologists when they stick their noses into other people's affairs.

(5)   Relatively close secondary affines are denoted by *-in-law* added to a basic term: *father-in-law, mother-in-law* and their converses *son-in-law, daughter-in-law,* and the pair *brother-in-law, sister-in-law* which (apart from sex) are their own converses. A form such as *uncle-in-law* is uttered only in jest; usually one resorts to a paraphrase, *my wife's uncle* or whatever. In address, the *-in-law* is left off. Here, again, there are disagreements in usage. I will say *brother-in-law* of my wife's brother or of my sister's husband, but not, as some people will, of my wife's sister's husband. The plural *in-laws* denotes one's affines collectively.

(6)   If a spouse is widowed or divorced and remarries, the terms for the relationships between the new spouse and the children of the former spouse take the prefix *step-*: *stepfather, stepmother, stepparent, stepson, stepdaughter, stepchild.* If the new spouse already has children we get also *stepbrother, stepsister.* Siblings in such a situation who have one physiological parent in common evoke a different modifier: *half brother, half sister.* None of these terms is likely to be used in address. In reference, when family affairs are amicable the prefixes are left off except in describing the relationships to someone who does not know them.

(7)   A confusing feature of American usage is that within a household terms are sometimes used like proper names, in a pattern established with a young child as covert point of reference (unmentioned ego). A man may thus both refer to and address his wife as *Mother* or *Mom,* his wife's mother as *Grandma.* His wife calls him *Daddy* whether she is speaking to the children, to her mother, or to Daddy himself. These usages do not wholly replace the unshifted ones, so there can be ambiguity: when the father of the children says *Mother* it may be uncertain whether he means his wife or his mother-in-law. The fact that the shifted terms have the children as point of reference is an indication of the child-centeredness of the twentieth-century American family (p. 212).

(8)   Finally, it seems to be not at all confusing that some of the terms are used also in generic and metaphorical senses. Anyone who is someone's father is *a father,* so we can have a *Prospective Fathers' Club* or the like. We can speak poetically of our *fathers* (or *forefathers*) rather than of our ancestors. The extension is similar in the *Sons* (or *Daughters*) of the American Revolution. It becomes metaphorical, and in motivation much like the extended use of certain Menomini kinship terms for nonkin (p. 24), when a child says *Uncle Egbert* and *Aunt Hortense* of close friends of his parents. A priest is a *father* even when he treats one like a Dutch *uncle.* Any nun except a *mother* superior, and any member of a sorority except the house*mother,* is a *sister.* "All

men are *brothers.*" Washington was the *father* of his country. "Our *Father,* Who art in heaven." The metaphor is progressively less personal when we say: Ohio is the *mother* of presidents; a filmy precipitate in vinegar is *mother*-of-vinegar; necessity is the *mother* of invention, and fun is the *father* (p. 76).

For address, some of the extended meanings seem almost to have displaced the central ones. We don't address a brother as *brother* or a child as *my son, my daughter, my child*; the former is left to panhandlers or lodge members, the latter to priests.

SUMMARY

Our American English kinship terminology consists of a tightly patterned small core, supplemented by a few stable derivatives, an indefinite number of nursery by-forms, and a set of patterns for creating additional terms when circumstances call for them. The system is solid at the center, frayed towards the edges. That is normal, not only for kinship terminologies but also for the other terminological systems included in the lexicons of the world's languages (p. 101). If in the next century or so something happens to make kinship ties more important in our society, the hard center will expand. If, as at present seems more probable, events continue to de-emphasize this aspect of life, some of the soft edge will dissolve away.

✖ Melanesian Pidgin English is an aberrant dialect of English spoken in parts of New Guinea and nearby islands by people who have no other language in common; nowadays it is learned from infancy in some communities.[6] Suppose a visitor whose language is standard English meets a family in which there are two sons and two daughters. One of the sons refers to the other as *my brother* and to the girls as *my sisters,* and all is well. Then one of the daughters refers to the sons as *my sisters* and to the other girl as *my brother*—and the visitor is thrown into confusion.

SIBLING TERMS

The Melanesian Pidgin English usage is perfectly consistent; it is just not the same as ours. If the terms had funny shapes, instead of sounding like the ordinary English words, our visitor would not be so disturbed. But the fact that the shapes were borrowed from standard English is irrelevant. Their term *brother* means 'sibling of same sex as ego', and their term *sister* means 'sibling of sex opposite to that of ego'.

In either English or Melanesian Pidgin English, *brother* and *sister* constitute what we shall call a *compact set* of sibling terms: exactly one term for any possible sibling

[6]A pidgin form of a language arises when people of diverse language backgrounds are thrown together in circumstances in which they must make themselves understood as best they can for immediate practical purposes and no one cares about learning the language of anyone else in any more "elegant" way. One of the participating languages in the formation of a pidgin is usually dominant over the others, and it is from this one that the pidgin acquires most of its lexicon; the sound system, however, becomes loose, and the grammar is regularized and simplified, resting mainly on features in which the participating languages are superficially similar. When children are born and raised using a pidgin, the pidgin becomes a *creole.*

of any ego. Menomini has three sibling terms meaning respectively 'older brother', 'older sister', and 'younger sibling' (sex irrelevant). These three are a compact set; however, Menomini also has two terms that partly duplicate the three: one used only for the brother of a male and one only for the sister of a female, relative age irrelevant in both cases.

Chinese has a compact set of four: 'older brother', 'younger brother', 'older sister', and 'younger sister'.

The features that play a part in differentiating the sibling terms in the examples we have given (including English) are these: (1) sex of referent (male, female); (2) sex of ego (male, female); (3) relative sex of referent and ego (same, opposite); (4) relative age of referent and ego (older, younger). Almost by definition (p. 191), sibling terms reflect no other features. Note that feature (3) is not independent of (1) and (2).

A system that ignores *all* these features has a single sibling term, 'sibling'. This is attested in the Polynesian outlier community of Kapingamarangi, where, as generally in Polynesian communities, kinship terms are used almost exclusively for reference, personal names occurring in direct address.

A system that heeded all the features would have eight terms:

m's o'r bro	m's o'r sis	w's o'r bro	w's o'r sis
m's y'r bro	m's y'r sis	w's y'r bro	w's y'r sis

However, no known system has this completely elaborated compact set. Attested systems show variety, but within certain constraints. Exceptions to the following are few and scattered, and may be only apparent, due to inaccuracies of reporting; if the exceptions are real, the generalizations at least retain statistical validity:

> Every system supplies at least one compact set.
> No system reflects sex of ego unless it also reflects sex of referent, though this may be in terms of same versus opposite rather than direct.
> No compact set makes more differentiations for female referents than for male ones.
> No system makes more differentiations for younger referents than for older ones.
> Systems with more than four terms consist of a compact set and some leftovers, or even of two compact sets with or without leftovers.

Whenever a system includes more than one compact set, then there is some choice of alternative terms for certain ego-referent pairs; the significance of this will concern us later (p. 202).

Box 15-6 lists a variety of actually attested systems, with the names of some of the communities that use them.

AUNTS AND UNCLES

Extensive trial and error has shown that a useful classification of aunt terms heeds just three points: the term (or terms) for a mother's sister; the term (or terms) for a father's sister; and the term (or terms) for mother. In a compact set, there may be separate terms for each of these three, or two of them may receive the same term and the third another, or all three may be denoted by a single term. The combinatorial possibilities are listed in Table 15-7. Four of them are well attested, and have been assigned the rather cumbersome labels we include in the table.

Uncle terms tend to correlate with aunt terms. In the table, interchange "fa" and "mo" in the headings of the columns and replace "sis" by "bro"; the table thereby becomes one showing the five ways in which uncles (and father) can be handled terminologically. Furthermore if the aunt terms of a terminology are "generational" (line 1) the uncle terms probably are too; and so on.

Some terminologies include enough terms to constitute two compact sets of different types. For example, for males Navajo has terms X, Y, and Z fitting type (5), but also a fourth term, W, that means 'father or father's brother'; W and Z form a compact set of type (2).

First Cousins

Here, also, experience has shown that a useful classification does not have to heed all theoretically possible criteria. We distinguish paternal (father's side) or *agnatic* cousins, listed in the left-hand column below, from maternal or *uterine* cousins, on

BOX 15-6. Sibling terminologies.

COMPACT SETS:					
ONE TERM			sibl		1
TWO TERMS					
by sex of referent		bro	sis		2
by relative sex		same sibl	opp sibl		3
by relative age		o'r sibl	y'r sibl		4
THREE TERMS		o'r bro	o'r sis	y'r sibl	5
		o'r same	y'r same	opp	6
		same	m's sis	w's bro	7
		m's bro	w's sis	opp	8
FOUR TERMS	o'r bro	o'r sis	y'r bro	y'r sis	9
	o'r same	y'r same	m's sis	w's bro	10

ATTESTATIONS:
1. Nukuoro, Kapingamarangi
2. English, French, German
3. Melanesian Pidgin English, Chiricahua and Mescalero Apache
4. Papago
5. (with leftovers) Menomini
6. Fijian
7. Samoan
8. (see below)
9. Chinese, Chipewyan
10. Hawaiian
  2 and 9. Beaver, Hupa
  3 and 9. Navajo
  5 and 8. Ojibwa

the right; and we distinguish parallel cousins (top row) from cross cousins (bottom):

fa's bro's child	mo's sis's child
fa's sis's child	mo's bro's child

With due regard for sex and age (when these are relevant in the system), the terms for cousins may now be the same from one type to another, or different, and may be the same as or different from sibling terms. For example, in southern Chinese communities (speakers of Toishan dialects) sibling terms distinguish sex and relative age, and terms for first cousins do the same; there is a set of terms for parallel agnatic cousins (father's brother's children), a different set for all other first cousins, and neither of these sets is the same as the set of sibling terms. English, also, keeps cousins distinct from siblings, but the same term refers to a cousin of any type.

Table 15-8 displays the commonest types of cousin terminologies; the kinship terminologies characterized by these types are often referred to by the labels at the left.

CRITERIAL FEATURES IN KINSHIP TERMINOLOGIES

✖ We saw earlier (p. 198) that sets of sibling terms reflect, at most, only four criteria, of which one (relative sex) can be regarded as a way of combining two of the others.

Taking whole terminologies, instead of just some identifiable part, we find that *no system in the world* heeds any criteria other than the following (of which only the eighth has not come up in the course of our discussion):

(1) sex of referent (brother : sister);
(2) sex of ego (man's brother : woman's brother);
(3) sex of a key intervening kinsman (father's brother : mother's brother);
(4) relative generation (uncle : brother);
(5) relative age within a generation (older brother : younger brother);
(6) lineal versus collateral (p. 193) (father : uncle);
(7) absence or presence of a marital link (brother : brother-in-law; father's brother : father's sister's husband);
(8) status (living or dead, single or married, or the like) of a key intervening kinsman (son of father's living brother : son of father's deceased brother).

TABLE 15-7. Aunt terms.

		MO	MO'S SIS	FA'S SIS	
(1)	"Generational"	X	X	X	Hawaiian
(2)	"Bifurcate merging"	X	X	Y	Comanche, Kiowa Apache
(3)	(no label)	X	Y	X	(rare or unattested)
(4)	"Lineal"	X	Y	Y	English, Sarci
(5)	"Bifurcate collateral"	X	Y	Z	Hupa, Menomini, ancient Roman, south Chinese

In a single row, if the same letter occurs in more than one column then the same kinship term is used for the kin indicated at the heads of the columns. For example, in English X is *mother* and Y is *aunt,* with the distribution shown in row (4).

Sex and age, birth, marriage, and death are the raw stuff of human life. If a species is going to talk, it is going to have the vocabulary with which to talk about these things. *Any* terminology that makes a reasonable number of distinctions by some of these criteria, supplemented by ordinary paraphrase and discussion, will serve to keep individuals aware of who and what they are, of their ties to others, of their assorted privileges and duties as members of their families and their communities. The most significant thing about kinship terminology is that we have it—all of us, in every community of the ethnographic present and probably for tens of thousands of years into the past. Other animals don't.

✖ What are the sources of the differences of kinship terminology from one community to another? Do different systems have differential impacts on the behavior of their users, or are they simply arbitrarily different but equally satisfactory machinery for dealing with the same problems?

IMPLICATIONS OF KINSHIP TERMINOLOGY

RELATION TO PATTERNS OF DESCENT, RESIDENCE, AND MARRIAGE

For instance: if people live in strongly organized exogamous patrilineal clans, can we expect them to pay more detailed attention to kinsmen who belong to the same

TABLE 15-8. Cousin terms and the classification of kinship terminologies based on them.

	SIBLING	PARALLEL COUSIN		CROSS COUSIN		INSTANCES
		FA'S BRO'S CHILD	MO'S SIS'S CHILD	FA'S SIS'S CHILD	MO'S BRO'S CHILD	
(1) "Hawaiian"	X	X	X	X	X	Hawaiian, Ifugao, Comanche
(2) "Eskimo"	X	Y	Y	Y	Y	Copper Eskimo, Taos, English, French
(3) "Iroquois" (a)	X	X	X	Y	Y	Iroquois, Menomini, Dakota, Nayar
(4) "Iroquois" (b)	X	Y	Y	Z	Z	
(5) "Omaha," "Crow," and "Sudanese" (a)	X	X	X	Y	Z	"Omaha": Omaha, Iatmul, Winnebago; "Crow": Crow, Ashanti; "Sudanese": Dinka, Shilluk
(6) "Omaha," "Crow," and "Sudanese" (b)	X	Y	Y	Z	W	
(7) (no standard label)	X	Y	Z	Z	Z	South Chinese

The difference between (a) and (b) in rows (3) through (6) seems of secondary importance. For instance, Menomini has terms used exclusively for siblings, putting it in 4b, but also some that refer indifferently to siblings or parallel cousins, fitting 4a.

In "Crow," the term for father's sister's son is the same as that for father's brother; the term for father's sister's daughter is the same as that for father's sister; male ego's mother's brother's child is equated with male ego's own child; female ego's mother's brother's child is equated with female ego's nephew or niece.

In "Omaha," the term for mother's brother's son is the same as that for mother's brother; the term for mother's brother's daughter is the same as that for mother's sister; male ego's father's sister's child is equated with male ego's nephew or niece; female ego's father's sister's child is equated with female ego's own child. "Omaha" is thus just the reverse of "Crow" in its handling of cross cousins.

"Sudanese" systems fit line (5) or (6) but do not meet the specifications for either "Crow" or "Omaha."

clan than to those who do not, and to distinguish the former from the latter in their kinship terminology as well as in other ways?

Proposals of this general sort are reasonable, and in a general way are confirmed. Box 15-9 shows the correlations that have been derived from large sample surveys of human communities. The assertions in the box are tendencies only, and none is free from exceptions. But that is what we should expect. Too many specific historical factors enter into each individual case for any such correlations to be either simple or exact.

CORRELATION WITH INTERPERSONAL TRANSACTIONS

Since a kinship term denotes a referent not absolutely but relative to some ego, it points to a *pair* of people—to what later we are going to call a *dyad* (p. 215). Its converse points to the same dyad from the opposite direction.

Consider two Menomini brothers. The older can call the younger 'younger sibling' and be called 'older brother' in return; or the older can call the younger 'man's brother' and receive the same term reciprocally. The former pair of sibling terms reflects the solidarity of grown-ups—or of adolescents who want to think of themselves as mature—for whom sex is important, vis-à-vis children too young for their sex to matter. The older brother calls the younger one 'younger sibling' in a mood or context in which he might also address the younger one with an exclusive *we*-form, meaning

BOX 15-9. Correlation tendencies of cousin and uncle terms with each other and with other features of social organization.

DESCENT PRACTICES (Table 14-3)	COUSIN TERMS (Table 15-8)	AUNT TERMS (Table 15-7)
bilateral	"Hawaiian"	"generational"
	"Eskimo"	"lineal"
weakly matrilineal	"Iroquois"	
strongly matrilineal or patrilineal	"Sudanese"	subtype (a) —— "bifurcate merging"
strongly matrilineal	"Crow"	subtype (b) —— "bifurcate collateral"
strongly patrilineal	"Omaha"	

(Box 14-2) bilocal residence ↔ "generational"
neolocal residence ↔ "lineal"
other residence ↔ distinct terms for kin linked through intervening kinsmen of different sex

(Box 14-6) isolated nuclear families ↔ "lineal"
Band exogamy goes with "bifurcate merging" terminology. But when a set of bands forms an endogamous group, "Hawaiian" cousin terms (hence "generational" uncle terms) are promoted.
Sororal polygyny ↔ "bifurcate merging"
Nonsororal polygyny ↔ "bifurcate collateral"

VARIATIONS ON HUMAN THEMES

'we grown-ups'. The second pair reflects the solidarity of males vis-à-vis females, or, perhaps better, of men as over against women and children. It goes with a use of an inclusive *we*-form by either brother in speaking to the other.

HYPOTHESIS.   In a similar way, whenever in any community a single dyad allows a choice of terms, we assume there must be some difference of connotation which controls and is reflected by the choice.

More generally, we may assume that if a dyad is distinguished from other dyads by having its own pair of kinship terms (mutual converses, or a single term used reciprocally), then there are important ways in which the transactions between the members of the dyad differ from other interpersonal transactions. From our English sibling terms we are entitled to infer that brother-brother transactions differ from brother-sister transactions and that both of these differ from sister-sister transactions. From Chinese sibling terms we can infer that dealings between an older brother and a younger brother are different from those between an older brother and a younger sister, and so on.

Such inferences from kinship terminology require to be checked by observation of other aspects of social life. In general, they are confirmed. Occasionally a specific inference of the sort is wrong. But when we find a distinction maintained only terminologically, we suspect that there were formerly nonspeech behavioral correlates which have fallen into desuetude and that terminological change is lagging behind other kinds of social change.

THE CONVERSE IS FALSE.   We fall into grave error if we reverse the above argument.

The following is a general truth, which holds for kinship terminologies because it holds for all language behavior. If a language regularly *makes* a certain distinction, it can be exceedingly difficult to speak in such a way as to ignore or neutralize it; but if a language regularly *ignores* a certain distinction, it is usually easy to add it when one wants to.

Thus, in English most nouns inflect for singular and plural (*boy* : *boys*). If something is named by such a noun, the implication of one or of more than one cannot be avoided, though it can be circumvented by awkward circumlocution (*That boy or those boys who finishes or finish his or their work before five o'clock will receive a reward*). Chinese nouns, on the other hand, do not inflect for number. To mention a kind of thing with no implication as to number, one merely uses the bare noun. But it is also easy to add as vague or precise a numerical specification as is appropriate in particular circumstances.

For sibling terms the shoe is on the other foot. Chinese terms reflect relative age. One cannot mention a brother without specifying older or younger; one can render the relative age indeterminate only through a cumbersome circumlocution. English sibling terms do not reflect relative age. But when relative age is important, the problem of specifying it is utterly trivial.

It follows that, from the fact that two dyads are not distinguished in formal terminology, we can never infer that the difference between them is ignored by those who use the terminology.

For example, the poverty of our English sibling terms in no way implies that differences of age are unimportant in American families. In fact, American children go through a stage in which relative age (and relative body mass, which tends to correlate) is deeply significant. The bare terms *brother* and *sister* are inadequate. They are therefore supplemented, by slang coined as required in the individual family or by somewhat more stable, but still informal, expressions passed on from the children of one family to those of another: *big brother, kid* (or *little*) *brother, big sister, kid* (or *little*) *sister*. These match the Chinese terms except that the latter are formal and used throughout life, whereas the English informal terms are set aside, or are used only jokingly, once the siblings have all grown up.

16

✖

THE SIDES OF THE COIN:
SOCIAL STRUCTURE AND PERSONALITY

> Primates are what they are as individuals because of their patterns
> of participation in society, so that social structure and personality,
> while not to be identified, are linked together more intimately than
> the two sides of a single coin.

We struck this note early in chapter 13 (p. 157); it will continue to reverberate through this chapter and the next few. In this chapter we consider why the assertion quoted above is true.

Some people make "society" very mysterious: it hovers like an invisible cloud above and beyond any of the individuals who participate in it. I am not sure, but I suspect that this attitude turns up mainly in civil societies, where any one person is vaguely aware of a mass of others whom he does not and cannot know personally, and where the depersonalization of human relations (p. 146) can affect many things.

If we encounter a notion of this sort as an ingredient of an inside view, of course we have to accept it and report it as accurately as we can. From the outside view, however, it is all nonsense.

✖ Recalling the discussion of chapter 5, we note that social structure is in fact nothing more than the distribution of scheduled activities among the members of a community. If everyone behaved in exactly the same way, there would be no social structure. But that is impossible. At the very minimum, there are differences of scheduled behavior dependent on sex and age. Among the primates there are always further differences. If adult male baboon A is dominant over his whole band, while adult male B is dominant over all except A, then A and B occupy different positions in the social structure.

ROLE AND PERSONALITY

An individual's position in social structure is his *role*.

If A gets old and weary and B becomes the leader, B has taken over A's role and A has shifted to a different one. The selection and inauguration of a new president of a country, a corporation, or a college, and the retirement of the incumbent, constitute a shift of the same kind. When a member of a human community dies he leaves a hole in the social structure, a role with no one filling it: that is what rules of inheritance are all about (p. 256). If an understudy steps in then the social structure remains intact. But if the role remains unoccupied for long it may wither away, changing the social structure.

An individual's position in social structure thus correlates with how he behaves. When we see someone of our own community whom we already know, all we have to do is recognize who he is, and we know from previous experience what role he occupies and, within limits, how he is going to comport himself. When we see someone we do not know personally, his appearance, his body motions (especially facial gestures: p. 66), his clothing and adornment and his way of handling whatever intimate possessions he is carrying (p. 144), his tone of voice and what he says, quickly tell us *what* he is socially, if not precisely *who* he is. We have to judge and class people this way, because there is in the end no possible other source of information about them. Everything a person does that is observable is communicative (p. 79), as interpreted by those about him according to the established communicative conventions of his community, and part of what is communicated is social role.

Furthermore, a person judges *himself* (achieves his "self-image," to use psychiatric jargon) on essentially the same basis, since he observes some of his own behavior by feedback and is guided otherwise by the reactions his behavior elicits from others.

An individual's position in social structure correlates with how he behaves. But when we speak of an individual's personality, what can we possibly mean other than just that?

The similarities go further. In discussing social structure it if often convenient to say that an individual occupies not one role but several, each a different aspect or "subrole" of his total role as we defined it earlier. An adult male Menomini could thus have one role as husband, another as father, a third as member of a hunting party, a fourth as member of his clan, and so on; he occupied all these (sub)roles simultaneously, but manifested one or another, in a scheduled way, depending on circumstances. If we carry this out to the end, we find ourselves proposing that an individual has as many different (sub)roles as there are (1) people whom he treats as individuals, (2) distinct categories of people the members of each one of which he treats in terms of the category (p. 70), and (3) distinct groups of people whom he treats as collectivities (as when a war chief harangues his tribe, or a TV comedian goes into his act before a nationwide audience). Now, in the other terminology—that of personality—we would merely say that the total personality of our adult male Menomini had various facets, one evoked in his relations with his wife, another coming to the fore when he joined a hunting party, and the like.

Role versus Personality

Are we to conclude from the foregoing that the terminologies of social structure and of personality are, at bottom, just two different ways of talking about the same thing?

No; that conclusion would be wrong. Our assertion that they are closely related is valid; our warning that they are nevertheless not to be identified is also correct.

The reason why they are not the same is that in any one human society only certain differences of behavior are recognized (by the people themselves) as *distinctive* for social role. Other differences are nondistinctive in that connection, though relevant as manifestations of personality. Whether this is also true of nonhuman primates we cannot say. If it is not, then the partial segregation of social position from personality is part of the exclusively human common core, doubtless dependent in some indirect way on language.

Note some examples. The old medicine man was clumsy; his heir is more skillful; but both count as medicine men. The old king was a good king, concerned for the welfare of his people; the new one is bad, devoting himself to hunting, drinking, and wenching; but both are kings. If we wanted to draw a diagram of the social structure of some community, and were willing to ignore nondistinctive variations of personality, we could represent roles by points and dyadic relationships by connecting lines. But if we wanted to allow for some indication of personality, we should have to represent the roles by small regions. The sizes of the regions and the fuzziness or sharpness of the boundaries would depend on the inside view of the particular community. An individual occupies a certain role as long as his comportment keeps him any where within the region; which part of the region he lingers in, or how he moves around in it, is his personality; only if he pushes completely though the boundary is he abdicating.[1]

ROLES AS CONTROLS

It is probably true in all societies that most individuals find themselves from time to time in contexts in which they must control their behavior very rigidly, social role taking over almost completely, and at other times in situations in which they can relax and follow the whim of the moment within wide limits.

Why do people ever accept limitations on behavior imposed by social role? In general this is a foolish question. The main factor is inertia (p. 149). Primate conservatism (p. 77) plays a part. Sometimes fear of punishment or hope of reward is concrete and immediate.

Some ethnographers have suggested that these factors can intertwine in different ways in different cultures. They propose that there are cultures in which behavior is governed largely by "shame," and others in which the chief constraining factor is "guilt."

In a shame culture (pre-twentieth-century Japan is offered as an instance) one refrains from certain sorts of behavior in public because others would disapprove, and the approbation of one's fellows is deeply important, but in private one can behave as one wishes. In a guilt culture (nineteenth-century U.S.A.) one does not misbehave even in private, because it would impair one's self-image (p. 206) or offend God, from Whom one cannot hide.

---

[1] Another way to describe this is to say that social structure *quantizes* the multidimensional continuum of possible personality types—just exactly as a sound system quantizes the multidimensional continuum of possible articulatory motions.

Like most binary contrasts invented by students of human behavior, this one is probably an oversimplification of the facts for any one person or culture, and it is more likely that both factors are found, in one connection or another, in every community. It seems to me also that guilt is probably best viewed merely as the internalization of shame, just as one's self-image is an internalization, however distorted, of the images one presents to others. I do not understand where else guilt could come from.

Furthermore, how is privacy to be defined? If I am alone in a room and no one can see (or hear) me through the walls, I have privacy. For some purposes it is enough to be out in the open with no one nearby. In some cultures privacy is defined quite differently. People in Japan in general live in closer physical proximity to one another than do most people in the United States. Each Japanese has relatively little space to himself. Each avoids invading the personal space of others by minimizing body motions and by speaking in low tones. The American tourist in Japan, or in certain other crowded parts of the world, is a loudmouth. (Compare also the detailed precision of a miniature Japanese garden with the sprawling landscape viewed from an American middle-class picture window.) In Samoa, houses are built with twelve posts in an oval, supporting the thatched roof, but often with no walls because circulation of air is important. Two of the spaces between posts are doors. One enters or leaves through a door, not through any of the other interstices, although they look just like the doors. Furthermore, though light passes readily through the other interstices, one does not *see* through them. If a crime is committed in a "private" part of the house, a passer-by who cannot observe it through a doorway is not a witness.

Concealment of Personality

The inside-view irrelevance of personality for social role is accentuated on key public occasions in many cultures by devices that screen out individual variations or even conceal personal identity.

Considering the nature of human communication, a screening device must in some way stylize an individual's communicative sounds or motions. So, crucial ceremonial words are sung to a fixed tune, or are pronounced in some prescribed colorless monotone—by the leaders in a Menomini interclan conference (p. 26), by a minister saying "I now pronounce you man and wife," by a robed judge saying "I sentence you to be hanged by the neck until you are dead, and may God have mercy on your soul." Ceremonial dancers often wear masks (for example, katchina dancers among the Hopi Indians of Arizona, or the actors and the chorus in ancient Greek drama): for the nonce they are to be accepted as the characters they represent, not as fellow tribesmen or citizens. The headsman or hangman at an execution wears a hood over his head. This symbolizes his role at the same time that it conceals everything else about him. Policemen in our society wear uniforms that cover everything except face and hands; by some strange alchemy this renders them equally faceless. In the military services it is known that not every enlisted man will respect or admire every officer; the recruit is warned "it is not the man you salute, but the uniform."

Such concealment devices turn up at cruxes where social role counts for everything and individuality for nothing. The cruxes are not invariably grim: a clown wears a mask of greasepaint, and if chorus girls are well trained the audience can hardly tell one from another in the line.

Sometimes some people refuse to conform. The condemned criminal who vows to get even with the judge who pronounced sentence on him is rejecting the rules of the game: it is most antisocial of him to ignore the established symbols of anonymity and to think of individuals as individuals merely because that is what they really are.

STATUS

Social structure affects personality in an obvious way: if one is born into a certain spot in the social order, one is trained from infancy to pass, during one's lifetime, through a certain sequence of roles, for which certain types of comportment are expected and other types are not.

The members of the community have certain attitudes towards one and towards the role one occupies; these attitudes establish, or constitute, the *status* associated with the role. Status may be *ascribed*, *achieved*, or in part each.

The distinction is sometimes taken to depend wholly on whether one is born to one's role or has to work for it, but that is an oversimplification stemming from the Horatio Alger period of our American social history. That way of differentiating between the two would not tell us whether the status acquired by a Menomini by virtue of his puberty dream was ascribed or achieved.

A more general approach, which allows fully for differences of inside views, is this. Ascribed status is that which adheres primarily to a role, and attaches itself to the individual in the role no matter how he has come to occupy it. Achieved status derives from the individual's special way of playing his role or, if his society holds that he has had a choice of roles, from the choice he has made; in either case, achieved status derives from personality, but may then rub off on the role. If a thief hates a policeman merely because he is a policeman, that is part of the policeman's ascribed status (and has nothing to do with accidents of birth). If the thief feels drawn to a particular cop despite his hatred and fear of the fuzz, that is part of the particular policeman's achieved status.

THE IMPACT OF PERSONALITY ON SOCIAL STRUCTURE

One's way of behaving in one subrole is likely to affect one's manner in other subroles. We shall talk more about this later (chapter 17) because it helps to explain, on the one hand, the kinds of emotional troubles people can get into in many societies and, on the other, certain deep-seated differences among human cultures.

Again, suppose a particular person plays a role with a certain style. In time, the members of his community can come to feel that the role ought to be played that way, forgetting the divergent styles of predecessors. Since it is inside-view expectations that *define* the role, such a change in expectations constitutes a change in the role itself.

AMERICAN
MIDDLE-CLASS
SEX ROLES,
1890–1960

✖ There is no more striking example of the interplay of social role and personality than what some American adolescents of high-school and college age have done about maleness versus femaleness in recent decades. We shall present this example in extenso. It has two advantages. First, because it is familiar and immediate, it defines our terms more vividly. Second, it shows that our frame of reference applies to the here and now, not just to peculiar cousins in obscure corners of the world or odd ancestors in the distant past.

You can tell whether a newborn infant is male or female if it is naked, but swaddling conceals sex unless you use, say, pink for girls and blue for boys, as was once a widespread custom in the white American middle class.[2] Physiologists class genetically monitored sexual characteristics as "primary" (differences of genitalia and mammary apparatus) or "secondary" (degree of hairiness, distribution of subcutaneous fatty tissue, voice quality and register after adolescence). A difference of color of infant clothing, established and maintained by tradition rather than genes, is neither of these; we may call it, then, a "tertiary" sexual characteristic.

In secondary characteristics, and even in primary ones, there is a closer intergradation than we middle-class white Americans used to want to admit. Some females are pretty hairy, and some males have remarkably sparse beards; I have heard voices over the telephone that utterly failed to identify the sex of the speakers. This did not suit us. We wanted a clear-cut sexual dimorphism because it would be easier to deal with socially. We did what many societies have done: we polarized sexual differences by an appropriate specification of tertiary characteristics, making all women seemingly more like one another and more clearly different from men than they are physiologically.

The precise fashions involved in this changed over the decades. The ideal belle of the forties had broader shoulders, stronger arms, a thicker (and healthier) waist, a flatter cross section through the midriff, and was taller and longer-legged than her predecessor of the nineties, and probably would have struck the latter's boyfriends as horribly masculine, but her feminine style suited her contemporaries just fine. By the 1940s, girls shaved their legs and, if necessary, their faces; they supplemented breasts too small to conform to the ideal with pneumatic brassieres; they wore long or thick head hair, facial makeup, dresses or skirts and blouses, on occasion high heels. This was the white middle-class female *uniform*. Boys and men wore pants, no makeup, short head hair, occasionally a moustache (beards had been abandoned to a thin scattering of oldsters as a symbol of age and dignity); they wore low heels and walked with a "masculine" stride, and carried things in pockets, a device alien to the female attire. Girls' and women's body motions were supposed to be "naturally" graceful. Boys' body motions were expected to be gawky. Boys and men sweated and sometimes stank. Girls and women merely perspired (fifty years earlier thay had only "glowed"),

[2]It is hard to define the exact bounds for the generalizations of this section. The constraints "white" and "middle class" are intended only as suggestive. But see Cleaver 1968.

It should be noted that in the sweep of human history the twentieth century is altogether weird and unprecedented. The unusual problems our species has faced on a worldwide scale surely have something to do with the developments recounted in the text. Our presentation of the broader scene is deferred to the very end of the book (chapter 41).

and in theory had no body odor, neutralizing it with deodorants or perfume (p. 68).

The code involved differences more subtle than any yet mentioned, some of which were transmitted out of awareness and rarely overtly discussed. Little girls were trained not to knit their brows, because females were supposed to have smooth foreheads; there was no such requirement for American men, nor for either sex in Europe. The feminine way to sit cross-legged was with thighs tight together; the masculine way was to rest the calf of one leg horizontally on the knee of the other. In hand motions, women kept the palms concealed; men often did not. In smoking, a girl held the cigarette between forefinger and middle finger, palm towards mouth, while a boy held the cigarette between thumb and forefinger, palm away from mouth. In picking up a coffee cup, women held at least the fifth finger aloft; men who did this risked being called sissies.

These remarkably narrowly standardized ideal styles of femaleness and maleness conditioned mating behavior. By and large, the "prettiest" girls (those who most closely approached the ideal) married not the "prettiest" boys but those with the best economic prospects. The standards played a part in determining what sort of young woman a businessman would hire as a stenographer or a shopkeeper as a clerk, even if he had no ulterior designs on her. For those who were genetically close to the ideal anyway, the stylization made little trouble. For those who were not—and this was inevitably the majority—life was often disheartening. Young women who couldn't make the grade ran to fat or developed a "librarian's slouch" as unconscious symbols of their dejected withdrawal from the sexual sweepstakes, and became schoolteachers or librarians. Many a young couple got married with false expectations, and were disillusioned when the marks of sexuality on the basis of which they had been attracted to each other came off with the clothing.

As additional background, we must note that although in a historical sense tertiary sexual characteristics are the most evanescent, this does not accord with their relative priority in the growing awareness of the middle-class child born and raised in the era we are talking about. The training given by parents in such matters was only slowly recovering from its mid-Victorian nadir of unreality, and was in full accord with the children's literature of the day, in which the *only* sexual characteristics are tertiary ones. In L. Frank Baum's Oz books, on which many of my generation were raised and which are still kept in print in the face of the disdain of children's librarians, the Scarecrow, made of a suit of clothes stuffed with straw and then magically brought to life, is a male because his clothing is male; the Patchwork Girl, made of clothes stuffed with cotton, is a female because her clothing is female (Figure 16-1). Perhaps the difference of stuffing is symbolic—straw after the farmer's chores in the field, cotton after his wife's domestic tasks. In any case, the personalities and behavior ascribed to these characters are determined by the clothing. Baum's flesh-and-blood heroines are as daintily feminine and his flesh-and-blood heroes as ruggedly, boyishly, or paternally masculine as one could wish, but of course there is never any talk of physiological sex. That is as taboo as mention of urination or defecation. The land of Oz is a fairyland because all these nasty things, like death, are unknown.

Now, by 1950 some other things had been happening in the white American middle class for about half a century. Middle-class parents had been raising their children

FIGURE 16-1. MALE AND FEMALE BAUM CREATED THEM. The Scarecrow and the Patchwork Girl meet for the first time. This is John R. Neill's illustration (originally in color) for L. Frank Baum's *The Patchwork Girl of Oz* (Reilly and Lee 1913), pages 170–171.

to "think for themselves." The first generation of children raised this way were not able to carry it very far, for they quickly learned that although the *reasoning* was to be independent, the *conclusions* reached by it had better agree with the views of their parents. But as these children grew up and themselves became parents, the innovation was carried a bit further. By 1950, adolescents were prepared to take the consequences of disagreeing with their parents' opinions, and parents had become at least slightly more prepared to tolerate such differences. A second trend was that in the 1890s the middle-class household was adult-oriented, children staying mainly in the nursery, while by 1950 the children spread noisily all over the house and parents were lucky if they could retain privacy in their own bedroom. In the 1890s parents performed and children were the audience (still widely so in Britain); by 1950 the children were the performers and the parents the audience. A third trend was that parents were increasingly insistent in telling their children that girls are "just as good" as boys; after all, women had finally gotten the vote in 1920, and during the Second World War had served by the thousands in industry and in noncombatant wings of the armed services. As compared with the 1890s, mama and papa were becoming harder to tell apart: mama might go out and work, and papa often did the dishes and vacuumed the rugs. Finally, adolescents were indulging much more freely (as well as much more openly) in premarital sex relations, and were thus better informed as to what physiological maleness and femaleness are like when the cultural overlay is peeled off.[3]

Between 1950 and 1960, high-school and college students were putting these various things together and discovering frauds: a contradiction between social sexuality and "real" sexuality, a contradiction between verbal protestations of equality and the actual differences of patterns of punishment and reward doled out to males and to females. They took action. They set aside the tertiary sexual differentiators. Girls began to wear slacks or pants, low heels, and little or no makeup. Boys took to long hair. Since beards are physiological, the boys let them grow if they would. By 1960 it was often difficult to tell whether a college student was male or female, unless one got a front view and saw a beard. If there was none the determination remained difficult.

Not all young people took to the new style. Some took it up or rejected it through faddism, the desire to emulate individuals they admired. This is always the case. Imitation of the prestigious can help explain the spread of a fashion, but can hardly account for its origin (cf. p. 290). Even the originators (whoever they were) may well not have been aware of the contributing factors we have outlined, but a factor does not have to be noticed in awareness to be effective.

In the view of many older people, the new thing in 1960 was a contrast between "clean-cut young people" who dressed and behaved essentially in the traditional way and "those dirty hippies" who had made the change and who were doubtless homosexuals, juvenile delinquents, or communists to boot. Yet the new style has been persistent. The "hippies" and their successors (there have been many labels for them) were apparently prepared to accept the censure of initial reactions, partly because their special sex-deemphasizing attire gave them a feeling of solidarity, partly because they believed deeply in what they were saying to the world. The message is loud and clear for any who will heed. It cannot be paraphrased in words without great loss of eloquence, but here is a fuddy-duddy translation: You can take your artificial polarization of female versus male and stick it. It's deceptive and dishonest. When sex *is* important, we know what we are and what our friends are, and the real differences are enough. But why bother otherwise? In class or on the street, just treat each of us as an individual human being.

Sexual differentiation is not the only thing young people have complained and tried to take action about in recent decades. In intersecting groups of varying sizes, they have challenged personal cleanliness, obligatory heterosexuality, racial inequities, the dignity of labor, the arbitrary classification of nicotine and alcohol as legal but of marijuana as illegal, monogamy, any established religion (including atheism), the draft, parliamentary procedure, legal process and the authority of the courts, the habitual use by the government of the "threat of communism" as sufficient basis for its international stance and military actions, the authority of a "science" which has "proof-positive" in the toothpaste ads and builds hydrogen bombs for overkill (p. 659). Most of these things preclude the sort of direct action taken about sexual differentiation, for in that case they were able to say what ought to be done simply

---

[3] Increasing freedom of premarital sex got two special lifts: (1) from the greater availability of automobiles in the late 1930s; (2) directly after the Second World War, from a striking though temporary diminution in the incidence of venereal disease.

by *doing* it. But they are searching for effective techniques with great diligence and ingenuity.

In terms of personality and role, the kids are proclaiming not egalitarian views but the very opposite: no two people are alike and there is no reason why we should force them to be. The "frauds" they find in our social order involve too small a variety of good-status roles, or too narrow a definition of how certain roles must be played, or too automatic an assignment of ascribed status where, in their opinion, status should be achieved. The "American dream" has been of a social order which allows the fullest possible freedom of choice for each individual (p. 652); the overly narrow channeling of types into stereotypes imposed by a dominant middle class is an unwarranted "tyranny of the majority" (in John Stuart Mill's phrase), just as undemocratic as any tyranny of a minority.

Most annoying, the majority has been blind to its tyranny. In an economy of abundance, ten million indulgent parents have accustomed their young children to the notion that you don't usually have to wait very long or work very hard to get what you want; hence kids are schooled to believe in "instant solutions." Confident in the American dream, ten million parents and teachers have said to older children "be yourselves; make up your own minds; your ideas are just as apt to be right as anyone else's"—and then the children, accepting the counsel, forming their own opinions, and trying to put them into effect, have found themselves laughed at, frowned on, or—worst of all—ignored. No treatment could be more cunningly contrived to arouse frustration and anger.

As far as I can see, the current fast rate of apparent social change is unprecedented. The hopeful slogan of twenty years ago are the empty clichés of today. The parents of the rebelling adolescents are disoriented and disillusioned because their own youthful dreams for themselves and their society have not worked out. They cannot think and act as flexibly as can their children, not because they are older (p. 75) but because they have hostages to fortune whose welfare they care about—the very children who are rebelling. They hesitate to abandon their own hard-won views, but cannot honestly be certain the kids are wrong. Besides, in defense of their own self-images, their memories are faulty. So one quinquagenarian parent laments to another:

> I objurgate today's new generation,
> Their lives built out of random quantum zips,
> Like Pot, Watusi, Happenings. The hips
> Prefer frenetic kitsch and wild sensation
> To deep and patient art. Their sole ambition:
> To junk their heritage. It quite escapes
> Me why these psychedelized jackanapes
> Can't face, like Men, the looming threat of fission.
>
> When you and I were young, we knew our place:
> We stopped (I think) whenever told to stop it.
> The grown-ups set (as I recall) the pace;
> Our lot, to heed their will and never rap it,
> To grow up if we could, or die with grace.
> Now *we're* mature! (Or are we just decrepit?)

17

✕

I AND THOU: DYADS AS SOCIAL BUILDING BLOCKS

As promised (p. 202), we turn now to a consideration of certain aspects of social structure in terms of dyads.[1] A dyad is an *I* and a *thou*; or sometimes an *I* and a *ye,* or a *we exclusive* and a *thou,* or a *we exclusive* and a *ye.* Most intimately, it is the I and the non-I of a *we inclusive.* In other words, it is a pair of people or of groups of people who are engaged in some transaction or who are scheduled to engage in transactions from time to time.

The behavior of a dyad reflects the social roles and the personalities of the participants, but also depends on the setting, especially on who else is around, as the following anecdote shows.

Between planes, I sat in the corner of a small airport saloon. Wonder of wonders, the air was not redolent with cheap canned music. Two engineers from a nearby industrial research laboratory were at the bar, animatedly talking ship. No one else was present except the bartender. A woman entered, sat down, and ordered a drink. The engineers did not look up and did not change the substance of their conversation, but their volume dropped about five decibels.

On many occasions the arrival of a new person radically restructures things, disengaging some dyads and engaging others ("Won't you change partners and dance with me?"). In our anecdote this did not happen, but the woman's entry *perturbed* the dyad of engineers in a culturally prescribed way.

REASONS FOR THE DYAD APPROACH

There are several reasons why the approach in terms of dyads and perturbations makes sense.

(1)   It is hard for most of us human beings to focus on more than one interlocutor at a time, so that most active transactions tend to take place between confronting pairs. The presence of others is registered, but marginally and often partly out of awareness, so that they can be viewed as perturbers. For that matter, sometimes a

---

[1] The first phrase in the title of this chapter stems from *Ich und Du* (1923) by M. Buber (1878–1965); English translation by R. G. Smith, 2d ed., Scribner, N.Y. (1958). In this profound poem, Buber builds his view of the cosmos from the contrast between the personal *I-thou* and the impersonal *I-it.*

dyad is alone. In a community where privacy is rare, this can itself be a kind of perturbation.

(2) A second reason is that the various dyads in an ongoing community are by no means independent. The patterns of interaction appropriate for different dyads are different, but all must mesh together in some fashion if the community is to endure.

(3) Finally, we have only a limited capacity to adjust our comportment from one confrontation to another. Our style of interaction with one person is never totally distinct from our way of adjusting to another. In particular, a person thrown by circumstances into a new dyad has no recourse but to try to accommodate to it on the analogies of his successful responses and confirmed expectations in old and familiar dyads, or in the image of dyads of other people which he has observed (compare p. 109).

Anything that can be talked about in terms of roles can also be discussed in terms of dyads. In fact, since a dyad involves a pair of roles, we could define "dyad" first (carefully heeding the difference between personality and social position: p. 207) and then define a role as half a dyad.

But we shall waste no time plowing over old ground with the new terminology. We proceed to take up three interrelated topics for which the modified approach is particularly apposite: in this chapter, dominant dyads in the household; in chapter 18, role conflicts and personal dilemmas; in chapter 19, intimate dyads as models for remote ones.

DOMINANT DYADS ✕

> Mother-in-law broke it: it was a mud pot;
> Daughter-in-law broke it: it was a gold vase.
> *Tamil proverb.*

Everyone knows that in the typical (or perhaps somewhat caricatured) American or British middle-class family of the late Victorian era Father was the dominant figure. He went out and earned the family's living; his wife did or supervised the housework and brought him his pipe and slippers when he came home tired at the end of the day. She exercised immediate control over the children (and servants), but her authority was delegated by Father, who was the court of last resort. Father faced the outside world, was concerned with business and politics; mother could not even vote. Father chose the schooling for the children, approved the careers for his sons and the suitors for his daughters. Major decisions might or might not be prefaced by family consultations, but either way it was Father who made them.

If we recall the typical nineteenth-century Chinese family, as described briefly in chapter 14 (pp. 180–181), we note that Father was the dominant figure there too. He went to work; he did no household chores; his wife's authority over the children was delegated; he made all major family decisions.

Yet we know these two types of families were profoundly different. Apparently the difference did not rest on which family member was dominant, for that was the same in both. To some extent, the difference turned on opposite directions of striving (p. 180) and showed up clearly when the household included more than two generations. But it also reflected which *dyad* was dominant. The dominant dyad in the

Chinese family was father and son. If there was no son, the family was defective or broken. The tie between man and wife was secondary. The dominant dyad in the American family was (and still is) husband and wife. If the wife died the family was broken. The tie between either parent and child was secondary.

This does not say that the Chinese did not love their spouses or that the Americans did not love their children and parents. It is a matter of relative emphasis. Consider a woman in labor, giving birth to a son, but with difficulties such that only one of them can be saved. Our American myth is that any woman in this spot will say, forget me and save the baby. Even if true, this is irrelevant to our point. By and large, the Chinese husband would have ruled, however sorrowfully, in favor of the child, while the American husband, though perhaps terribly torn, would have ruled the other way.[2] The Chinese household with no wife-and-mother, the American family with no children, was an object of pity but hardly of scorn.

Let us say it one more way. In nineteenth-century China, the basic and often difficult social task for a young man was to get a son. Finding a wife was a means to this end; if that did not work, he resorted to adoption or, if he could afford it, took a concubine. In nineteenth-century America, the basic and often difficult social task for a young man was to get a wife. Children were a byproduct—not unwelcome, but an added source of difficulty because before he could get married he had to be in a position to accept and support them.

In Box 17-1 the "logic" of these two systems, and of one other, is compared.

[2]Or we can try the old chestnut about the canoe. A man who can swim is in a canoe with his wife and his aged father who cannot. The canoe capsizes and he can rescue only one. The Chinese was expected to rescue his father, the American his wife.

BOX 17-1. The "logic" of kin connections in traditional China, in the nineteenth-century United States, and in certain parts of India.

Throughout, A is a man, B is a woman, and C is their male child. The assertions put into words what the actual participants would rarely if ever verbalize. We use the terms *husband, wife, father, mother,* and *son* throughout; but the display demonstrates that the kinship terms rendered by these words in fact have sharply different meanings even if, purely in terms of genetic and marital connections, they denote exactly the same kin.

	CHINA	UNITED STATES	INDIA
A says:	C is my son and B is his mother, so B is my wife.	B is my wife and C is her son, so C is my son.	B is my wife and C is her son, so C is my son.
B says:	A is my husband and C is his son, so C is my son.	A is my husband and C is his son, so C is my son.	C is my son and A is his father, so A is my husband.
C says:	A is my father and B is his wife, so B is my mother.	A is my father and B is my mother, so they are husband and wife and I am their son.	B is my mother and A is her husband, so A is my father.

✖ Clearly, which dyad in a household is dominant can make a great difference for everyone. We do not know that a dominant dyad is inevitable; if it is, the strength of the dominance may vary. If there is any at all, then other household ties are built about and subordinated to the dominant one. What are the possibilities?

The nuclear family (p. 179), though not universal, contains all but one of the dyads that need be considered (the exception will be added in a moment). If a man and a woman have enough children of assorted sexes, then, neglecting relative age, there are the following dyads:

	husband : wife	
father : son	father : daughter	
	mother : son	mother : daughter
brother : brother	brother : sister	sister : sister

A few types of households lack some of the above or greatly minimize them: e.g., the Nayar (p. 182), with no husbands, have no fathers. Polygamous or extended households supply more: cowife and cowife, half siblings, grandparent and grandchild, and so on. With one exception, these additional dyads turn out to be more tenuous than those listed above. Where this is not so, the members of the dyad are apt to be related also in some other way: for instance, cowives who are also sisters (p. 236). The exception, which must be added to the first column of the table, is mother's brother and sister's son, which we shall abbreviate to

uncle : nephew

There are now two likely constraints. The first is that at least one member of the dominant dyad be male. The norm in a few cultures may be an exception to this. The second is that at least one member of the dominant dyad be adult. No community norm violates this, though a sporadically unusual household may.

Another way to tabulate the candidates is according to the fundamental nature of the relationship between the members of the dyad:

SEXUAL	FRATERNAL	PARENTAL
husband : wife	brother : brother	father : son
	brother : sister	father : daughter
	sister : sister	mother : son
		mother : daughter
		uncle : nephew

Note also that the dyads listed in the first and second columns are composed of members of the same generation, while those in the third column are composed of members of two successive generations.

We might also think of classing the dyads into those that are "exclusive" and those that are not, where by this we mean that a given person can play a given role in only one dyad of the kind at a time. Thus, a son has only one father. But while a father *may* have only one son, in principle he can have many, so that the father-son dyad is not exclusive. Neither, in principle, are any of the others. The exclusiveness of the husband-wife dyad in our own society is the result of an added feature: monogamy.

✗   HUSBAND-WIFE WITH POLYGYNY (?): THE HAUSA

There is at least one polygynous society in which the husband-wife dyad is suspected of being dominant: the Hausa (northern Nigeria). As in other societies of the same part of Africa, people live in close clusters of dwellings known as compounds. When a man takes a wife, particularly his first, he establishes her in a house in his father's compound, but before long he removes her to a far part of the compound or to a neighboring one, avowedly to circumvent destructive quarrels between her and his mother or other women of his father's household, in which he would have to function as the uncomfortable mediator. Hausa women stay close to home, so that a short move is enough to achieve this. That is fortunate, because the man must live close enough to continue to cooperate with his father in agricultural work.

Here it is clear that the husband-wife tie, even though not exclusive, takes precedence over the mother-son or brother-sister tie (in some neighboring African societies this is not so); but it is not obvious that it dominates the father-son or brother-brother dyad.

MOTHER-SON: SOUTH ASIA

The Tamil proverb quoted on page 216 reflects a state of affairs common in South Asia. The reader may have had to do a double take on it, since we have our own mother-in-law jokes, but ours usually concern a *man* and his *wife's* mother, while the Tamil aphorism is about a *woman* and her *husband's* mother.

As is tiresomely the rule almost everywhere, the men are in charge—of everything that concerns the household's economic ties with the outside world; in this regard a man is associated with and subordinate to his father. Within the household, the oldest woman is the leading figure. The males, particularly her sons, work for her. A male child's closest bonds are to his mother, nor is he expected to "outgrow" this as a boy child is in societies such as our own. With one exception that we shall discuss later (the tie to a *guru:* p. 242), his most intimate and rewarding male companionship is found not with father or uncles but with brothers or with peers outside the family. Perhaps this is natural compensation: his mother differs from him in both age and sex, a brother or chum in neither. When he marries, he brings his bride to live in his mother's household. The bride's position is strictly subordinate (the proverb shows this). It will improve when she has sons of her own, but will reach its acme only when and if she becomes the *māter familiās,* the oldest woman.

COMPARISON WITH THE WEST.   But in these South Asian households the brother-brother tie, and by extension the tie between male friends who are peers but not of the same household, can also be very strong. It is not unusual in parts of India to see a pair of young men walking down the street hand in hand or arm in arm.

In American society this used to be permitted for girls, or for a girl and a boy, but is not permissible for two boys. The reason is not far to seek. The dominant dyad in our society is husband-wife, marked (in principle) by both affection and overt sexuality.[3] Affection and sexuality are thus linked, and when we observe or manifest the former we suspect the latter. In the Indian situation the two are not linked, since the fountainhead of affection is the mother-son dyad, with no overtones of sex, and the latter is constrained (in principle) to a husband-wife relationship in which affection, though certainly not prohibited, is not of the essence. Hence hand-holding and the like by males indicate affection but are no sign of homosexuality. I do not know why comparable public behavior by females in American society is not interpreted as a symptom of homosexuality, but in general it did not used to be so interpreted. Today girls are becoming more like boys in our society (pp. 210–214), and we see less of this public fondling than formerly.

BROTHER-BROTHER AND POLYANDRY

South Asia is culturally too complex for any simple assertion to be valid everywhere. There are communities to which the remarks we have made do not apply at all. There may be some where our comments miss the mark only slightly.

Where the mother-son dyad is dominant, the brother-brother (or peer-peer) dyad is apt to be strong. In some communities in South Asia the relative strength of these two is perhaps reversed, so that the brother-brother dyad is dominant in the household. One suspects this (perhaps wrongly) when an Indian asserts "the friendship between two men is the most sacred of all human relations." There may then be some historical connection between the fairly common mother-son household of South Asia and the scattered polyandrous households (p. 174) in which the cohusbands are invariably either brothers or some other set of intimately allied males. For, surely, the dominant dyad in a household of this latter sort is that of brother and brother (or equivalent), and the tie of their shared wife to her sons is subordinate. The polyandrous family may be an arrangement whereby a close-knit set of male companions can replicate itself.

THE NAYAR

Before leaving South Asia, note that we do not know what dyad was dominant among the Nayar (p. 182). In the South Asian setting, we would suspect brother-brother or mother-son; but perhaps it was brother-sister, sister-sister, or any of the "parental" dyads (p. 218) that involve no father. Perhaps it was mother-daughter, violating the first constraint of page 218.

BROTHER-SISTER OR SISTER-SISTER: THE ASHANTI

We mentioned the Ashanti earlier (p. 183). The household consists in essence of a set of siblings of both sexes and of the children of the women. The men have wives (and children) in other households of the village, whom they visit, but their home

---

[3]Of course we are not here denying the importance of diffuse primate sexuality, blended inextricably with grooming (p. 67), in virtually all the social behavior of human beings in all cultures. It is a matter of varying balances of different ingredients, which we know can differ greatly from one community to another.

is with their sisters. The brother-sister tie is clearly stronger than the husband-wife tie. Because of male importance, the brother-sister tie may be the dominant one.

But future study should heed some other possibilities. The tie between sisters may be stronger than that between brother and sister, since the men have familial involvements away from the household and the women do not (their husbands come to them). Of the parental dyads, mother-child ties would seem to be closer than those between uncle and nephew or niece, which are in turn clearly closer than those between father and child.

BROTHER-SISTER OR BROTHER-BROTHER: THE YAO

Households among the Yao of Nyasaland are to some extent similar. But in each group of siblings who dwell together one brother stays home and keeps his wife and children with him, while the other brothers visit their wives and children in other households as among the Ashanti. The stay-at-home brother is in charge, so that the dominant dyad is either brother-brother or brother-sister.

MOTHER-DAUGHTER (?): THE HOPI

Among the Hopi of the North American Southwest, sisters live fairly close together after marriage, though not in the same house (a "house" in this case is a compartment or apartment in a pueblo). A married man keeps some of his property at his sister's home and takes some of it to his wife's home, but he is somewhat of a stranger in both. Marriage is not very binding. In contrast to the Nayar, there really are husbands, but they wander in and out and are often replaced. So none of the following dyads can be strong: husband-wife, father-child, brother-sister, uncle and nephew or niece. An immature male, with only these weak relationships in his future, is no candidate for membership in the dominant dyad. The house in which he grows up was built by men, but belongs to his mother and will be inherited by his sister. The dominant dyad is apparently mother-daughter.

FATHER-DAUGHTER (?): THE APACHE

Not far from the Hopi (geographically speaking) live various Apache groups. When an Apache woman gets married, she and her female kin build a house near her father's home. The newlyweds live there, and the groom has extensive economic involvements with and duties towards the bride's father. A man needs male economic assistance. He cannot get it from his brothers or grown-up sons, since with matrilocal residence they live too far away. He gets it from his sons-in-law. The dominant dyad here is either father-daughter or else consists of father-in-law and son-in-law—a candidate not on our list (p. 218). In the latter case, the woman is simply the instrument for getting the members of the dyad together.

UNCLE-NEPHEW: THE HAIDA

At the time of an Apache marriage, the father and daughter have been in intimate association for a couple of decades whereas the son-in-law is a newcomer. This surely affects the relative strength of the two dyads (father and daughter, father-in-law and son-in-law).

Suppose, however, that in a situation something like that of the Apache the prospective son-in-law cannot claim his bride until he has served her father for a period of time—like the ambitious young man in the late Victorian era who had to prove his worth to the boss before he could hope to marry the boss's daughter, or like Jacob serving Laban seven years each for Leah and Rachel in Genesis. Suppose, moreover, that the prospective son-in-law is already his prospective father-in-law's nephew—his sister's son (as Jacob was Laban's). That is, let the community be one which favors cross-cousin marriage of this variety. Then the older man and the younger one are already kin before the marriage, and have had time to get to know each other.

This situation, called the *avunculate* (and obviously associated with avunculocal residence: Box 14-2, p. 170), is attested, with minor variations, in a number of societies, and is our reason for having included the uncle-nephew dyad in our list of candidates for dominance.

One example is the Haida, who live on the Queen Charlotte Islands just off the mainland of British Columbia. The habit there was that a boy left his parent's home at about nine or ten and joined the household of his mother's brother. Later he married one of his uncle's daughters if he could. If he had to marry someone else, he nevertheless established postmarital residence close enough to his uncle for economic cooperation to continue. In such a setting, the uncle-nephew dyad could dominate. Whether it ever actually has is not yet known.

REPLACEMENT AND CONTINUITY

✗ Human beings, as Metazoa, eventually die, but many of them first replicate themselves by reproduction. Human households are mortal too, in the long run. But here mortality can be combatted in two ways, not just in one: by replication and by perpetuation.

(1) The American household, as an institution, endures by replication. A child of a household grows up, gets married, and starts his or her own household. The new household is cast more or less in the mold of the old one, but it is not the *same* household any more than a child is the same person as one of his parents. Endurance via replication is in complete accord with domination of the household by the husband-wife dyad. A new marriage necessarily means a new household. Continuity through time is necessarily precluded.

(2) When the household is dominated by a fraternal dyad (p. 218) the situation is somewhat different. Siblings are like husband and wife (in a husband-wife society) in that they belong to the same generation. To be sure, there may be a considerable age span, but where a fraternal dyad is dominant this is not nearly so important as is a difference of generation. Siblings differ from husband and wife in that they have been in the same household from birth, though they come into power only at maturity. Since the husband-wife dyad is subordinate, the fact that spouses must be imported, and that some of the siblings may have to be exported to be spouses elsewhere, is irrelevant. There is more continuity through time. As the dominant

grown-up siblings become old and one by one die off, the next generation of siblings is reaching maturity to take over—in the same household. Sibling sets pass through the household from birth to death in successive waves, so that superimposed on the continuity there is a kind of periodicity. One sees here elements of both replication and perpetuation.

(3) When the household is dominated by a parental dyad (p. 218), there is no standard formula for replication since in principle none should be needed—the household never dies. Parts are replaced; the essential structure is invariant. When the oldest male in a Chinese household joins his ancestors, he retains his prestige and is worshiped in the family shrine; a few of the more remote ancestors come to be worshiped collectively (as a category: p. 70) rather than as individuals; to the new oldest male is delegated all the temporal authority; there are enough infants around that the slight difference in number of mouths to be fed is hardly felt. Individuals have changed roles; roles and dyads are the same as ever.

Of course, in the above we are speaking of ideals, not of statistical norms. The ideals are important because they define the direction of striving for those who have not attained them (p. 224).

The Restoration of Disturbed Equilibrium

Since the husband-wife household is not in any case expected to endure for more than a lifetime, the fact that it can be disrupted in a number of ways is of no vital importance as long as children are cared for until they are old enough to fend for themselves.

In household systems where there is major emphasis on continuity through time, the balance can be disturbed in two ways (other than by sudden catastrophe): too few people, and too many people.

"Too few" is defined in terms of essential roles; "too many" is defined in terms of the economics of food, clothing, and shelter.

Suppose that in a polyandrous household where the cohusbands are brothers the wife has no sons, or only one. The pattern is broken unless some special arrangement can be made—say, one involving cousins. Suppose that in a Chinese household a man has no sons, or that he outlives them all. Either he arranges to adopt one, or the lineage dies.

Suppose now, on the other hand, that in a sister-sister household (if there be such) a woman has more daughters than can be provided for in her household or in any single household. Or imagine that in a Chinese household a man has more sons than his material wealth can provide for as they reach the age of getting wives and children of their own.

The people who live by any one ideal pattern know that things like these can happen, and there are always contingently scheduled ways of trying to handle the emergencies. If nothing else, there are fixed priorities, such as primogeniture, by which a man's oldest son inherits his estate no matter what the consequences for the younger sons, or share-and-share-alike, whereby the estate is perforce divided evenly no matter how small the individual allotments.

Whether the standard emergency procedures work well or ill, inevitably some households become extinct, or send off splinters who must fend for themselves, or fission into smaller households. Such outcomes, escaping the homeostatic controls of the system, are one of the mechanisms by which, in time, one standard household pattern can grow into or be replaced by another. In any sort of society, if over a period of time families spin off an excessively large number of rootless young men and women, something is going to break.

AS THE TWIG IS BENT? ✖ All households have children or are expected to, and one of the responsibilities of any household system is to train the children for effective participation in adult roles. This training is as important an ingredient in human replication as is reproduction, and in the last analysis is why human beings have such institutions as marriage, family, and household.

Box 17-2 will be useful in the following discussion: it displays the reasonable adult expectations of children of various sorts in households of different types.

A child's household contains three kinds of dyads: those in which he already participates; those in which he does not yet but as an adult probably will; and those in which he will never participate. He is also exposed to three kinds of roles: those he can play as a child; those which he may have to play as an adult; and those he will never play. We have not said the same thing twice. For example, the Chinese boy already belongs to a father-son dyad, but can play only the son's role in such a dyad until he grows up and has a son of his own.

The child can begin early to accommodate to a subordinate role in a parental dyad (p. 218), by both observation and imitation. The Chinese boy can observe how his father treats his grandfather, and then treat his father the same way; he can note

BOX 17-2. Reasonable adult-role expectations of young children in households of different types.

IF THE DOMINANT DYAD IS:	THEN WHO CAN EXPECT TO GROW UP TO PLAY:		
	(1) DOMINANT ROLE IN DOMINANT DYAD?	(2) ONLY SUBORDINATE ROLE IN DOMINANT DYAD?	(3) NO ROLE IN DOMINANT DYAD?
husband : wife	boy	girl	———
brother : brother	oldest boy	nonoldest boy	girl
brother : sister	boy	girl	———
sister : sister	oldest girl	nonoldest girl	boy
father : son	boy	———	girl
father : daughter	boy	girl	———
mother : son	girl	boy	———
mother : daughter	girl	———	boy
uncle : nephew	boy	———	girl

We assume here that within a dyad male dominates female and older dominates younger of same sex. There are exceptions, but they seem to be sporadic (deviations within the pattern of a society) rather than systematic.

how his father deals with his (the father's) mother, and then deal with his own mother in a similar fashion.

Information about the proper way of playing the superordinate role in a parental dyad, or certain other roles that require being an adult, can be gathered by observation when one is young but then has to be stored away for future reference. Sometimes a pseudoimitation is permitted, even encouraged. Little American girls play with dolls, rehearsing certain aspects of motherhood long before they can be mothers. Older sisters have been known to "mother" younger brothers in American society—usually much to the younger brothers' disgust.

Often, perhaps always, this training by observation and imitation has to be supplemented by other pedagogical devices: tales that point a moral, proverbs, stories of remote kin or of neighbors who came to grief through misbehavior, maxims, precepts, the invention of spirit entities actually in imitation of, but in the inside view as prototypes for, certain categories of kin. This was part of the function of the *ātɛʔnōhkakanan* recited in winter evenings by the Menomini (p. 29): Big Rabbit, the culture hero, did such-and-such and got away with it because he was endowed with special powers; we are not, and hence cannot afford to behave that way.

One reason for this supplementation is that any real household is apt to deviate from the ideal; it may deviate so much that the child's home contains no living model for certain roles or dyads. How can a Chinese boy observe the proper manifestation of filial piety if he lives with his father and mother and no one else? In a sibling-dominated society, how can a little girl learn how she should treat her brother if there is no maternal uncle around? How can an American boy learn to be a man, and a proper husband, if he is raised by sisters, mothers, and aunts? Well, children *do* learn despite such obstacles, partly through complementarity (p. 74), partly through verbal explication, partly, in due time, through bumbling trial and error. *What* they learn depends much less on the structure of their actual household than on the prototype taken as ideal by the particular community.

DISSONANCE

In some societies the child's home is not really a very good training ground for his eventual adult roles even if it does conform to the society's ideal.

Consider a community that practices the avunculate (p. 222). During his tenderest years a boy develops bonds of affection for and dependence on those around him: his father and mother, his siblings, his father's maternal uncle and intervening kin. None of these ties will be of basic importance when he grows up, since then he will be living with or near his own maternal uncle, perhaps married to his cross cousin. His adult tie to his maternal uncle (and, perhaps, father-in-law) may not necessarily be marked by affection—instead, it may be characterized by considerable tension and hostility—; yet it will be very close and important. There is a *dissonance* between the roles and dyads in his parental home and those of his adult home. The twig is bent one way, then must be forcibly recurved. (His sister's case is somewhat better, provided cross-cousin marriage really works; but often it does not).

TRANSITIONS AND RITES OF PASSAGE. In the tale in Genesis, Jacob's parents decided that none of the local girls was good enough for him, and so packed him off alone to find Uncle Laban and strike up some sort of economic and marital deal. The transition was sudden and sharp.[4] It is not surprising that Jacob got took like a country rube by a city slicker. Where the avunculate is standard, as among the Haida, the blow is often softened. As we saw (p. 222), the boy was sent to live with his uncle long before he was ready for marriage, so that old ties would have time to fade and new ones to grow. Yet in this case the shift of residence is itself a sudden change, a crisis in life history surely as great as that of his subsequent marriage.

Age is a biological universal, so that it is necessarily the case in every society (human or other animal) that one's roles change as one grows older. The ethnographer's term for the consequences is *age grading*. The transition from one age grade to the next can rarely be imperceptibly gradual. Most or all human societies do something overtly about this.

They do one of two things. First: they may underscore and sharpen the switch with some sort of ceremony of initiation, called (by ethnographers) a *rite of passage*. A Menomini's puberty fast (p. 30) was a rite of passage. Before the ceremony the individual belongs to one age-defined group and must behave accordingly, though he learns by observation and hearsay how he will be expected (or permitted) to behave later. After the ceremony, only the new patterns of behavior are acceptable, the old ones being permanently laid aside. Except for the ceremony itself, which is often physically or emotionally painful for the initiate, this formalization seems to ease matters because it reduces uncertainties as to how one must or may behave.

Second: a society may try to soften a transition by spreading it out in time. But what usually happens in this case is that the transition itself becomes an age grade, inserted between the two it links, so that, in the end, there may be two rites of passage instead of one.

EXAMPLES. The Haida followed the second course: they spread out the transition from childhood to adulthood so that it constituted a separate age grade, and marked its termini by not particularly ceremonial ceremonies that could nevertheless be regarded as rites of passage (change of residence at the one end, marriage at the other). We have supposed above that this was useful because of the dissonance between a male child's household setting and the same individual's adult household environment.

This may also be part of the explanation for some of the other societies in which male adolescence is dealt with as a separate age grade.

In a number of New Guinea tribes, boys are segregated at puberty. The Kapauku of western New Guinea simply put those of a single household into a separate room of the house; this hardly counts. In the east, the Gururumba send all the boys of a village to a separate bachelors' house, from which they emerge a few months later for a collective puberty ceremony. The Manus of the Admiralty Islands off the north coast also used to have a bachelors' house, but the adolescent men lived in it for five years or more, entering it one by one as they reached puberty and leaving it

[4]"Sudden" does not mean unexpected or unprepared for, only taking place in an interval of time that is short as compared with the duration of preceding and following states.

one by one as they got married. If this was not a device for resolving some sort of household dissonance, it must at any rate have had a serious impact on typical household structure.

Dissonance and Contamination

Another arrangement that seems to produce household dissonance is husband-wife dominance, at least when coupled with monogamy and with the nuclear family as the household unit. That is what we have in the United States (and, with minor variations, in all of Western society). Nor do we have any formal arrangement for trying to reduce the dissonance. Our nearest approach to a bachelors' house is college, but not all young men go and many young women do.

Here is how the dissonance arises.

A boy in an American nuclear family is child to his parents and brother to his siblings; as an adult, he will become husband to his wife and father to his children. The overlap in dyads is only a secondary one (father-son); the overlap in roles is null. With a few terms changed, the same holds for a girl.

The girl does get a little practice during childhood at certain aspects of motherly behavior (p. 225), but the boy gets virtually none at fatherly conduct and neither is supposed to get any apprenticeship at all for subsequent participation in the dominant husband-wife dyad. The only domestic model the children have for adult relations between people of opposite sex is the dealings they observe between father and mother; but if a brother and sister (to say nothing of two brothers or two sisters) venture to imitate that the consequences are terrible.

In this situation it is only to be expected that the different dyads should gradually contaminate one another.

In one direction, it is not surprising that, in this of all possible household arrangements, the controls should occasionally slip so that a brother and sister end up, in defiance of all overt sanctions, as husband and wife (p. 172). Yet that is rare. Contamination in a different direction has been commoner.

A century ago, in our middle-class tradition, a wife's treatment of her husband, insofar as it resembled her behavior in any other role, mocked her treatment of her father. By the 1920s, with the gradual change in the status of women (p. 210), one could notice that the wife-husband dyad had begun to resemble the mother-son tie. That is, wives had begun to "mother" their husbands just as little girls had been mothering their brothers and their dolls. The expected comportment of adolescent and young adult males was thus rendered more infantile, while that of adolescent and young adult females became more difficult to distinguish from that of matrons (and vice versa).

It was no help that adolescence was being prolonged at the same time by economic factors. Among hunters-gathers, a male of seventeen is fully equipped for marriage. In civil societies this is usually delayed; in the American middle class in the 1920s the male of seventeen had hardly finished high school and was apt still to have college ahead of him. Male adolescence became a sort of limbo (compare the baboons: p. 41). The young man was physiologically ready for mating but not equipped for marriage either economically or in terms of the necessary fund of information about proper husbandhood. Adolescent sexual experimentation increased enormously. "Trial" marriages, ending in divorce, became all but standard; they were a possible way of learning roles that it had been impossible to learn about as children. And scholars innocent of any taint of cross-cultural sophistication wrote learnèd tomes demonstrating that it is inherent in the order of the universe that adolescence, especially that of males, be a period of storm and stress. The highly specific factors responsible for the phenomenon in our society were either overlooked or misinterpreted as human universals.[5]

---

[5]These remarks do not run counter to, but supplement, what we said earlier about recent American revisions of maleness and femaleness (pp. 210–214).

18

✖

PEOPLE IN QUANDARIES

The features of social organization we have been talking about exert a profound influence on the lives of individual human beings. The quality of life for an individual can perhaps differ as radically from one human community to another as does the quality of life for any human being from that of a nonhuman primate. Social structure can effect this large difference even if the material appurtenances of two communities are much the same.

Yet the discussion of the preceding chapter seems somewhat aloof. One reason, at least, is that we were rapidly scanning whole life histories, or skipping abruptly from an individual's childhood to his maturity. No one lives that way. We live our lives from day to day, from hour to hour, from minute to minute. If household patterns really have the pervasive impact we have claimed, it must be manifested not in large vague hunks but in many of our momentary quandaries and choices.

✖ We shall call any member of any dyad an *actor*. Usually, then, an actor is an individual; but since some dyads have as at least one pole a group of people functioning as a unit (p. 215) an actor may also be such a group. At any given moment during a transaction between the members of a dyad, each actor is in a *state*. Each action, of the actor or of his respondent in the dyad, replaces a state by a new state. Sometimes the difference between the earlier state and the later one is trivial; sometimes it is sharp; sometimes it is small but cumulative over a series of successive states. Some action of a perturber (p. 215), or some other event in the environment of the dyad, can also replace a state by a new one. An individual also passes through a succession of states when he is all alone, but for the most part that will concern us less.

Our term "state" is in principle perfectly general: we can regard a whole life history as composed of a very large number of successive states and of actions that lead from one to the next. If you have just exhaled, you are in a state in which you can inhale or not or can inhale more or less deeply. At the extreme, the notion of state is that inane. We thus have no interest in most states of most actors, or in most events that change one state to the next. Most of one's own states are notoriously forgettable.

ACTOR AND STATE

If two successive states differ only trivially, we lump them together and call them a single state.

We are interested in those states that are in some way imbued with drama. Which are these? What makes a state dramatic? Why does a good novelist dwell on certain human contretemps and pass over others in silence?

As to details of content, this depends on the community. But there are also some very general ways in which states can differ from one another, and these have a bearing on which states are zestful, which ones dull, in *any* community.

State Parameters

I shall itemize and describe six *state parameters:* six partly independent ways in which two states can differ. There may be more, but of these six I am sure. They are cross-cultural, applying to all people in all communities and probably to nonhuman animals too. The six are: the degrees of *uncertainty*, of *freedom of choice*, of *urgency*, of *pleasantness*, of *anxiety*, and of *seriosity*.

THE UNCERTAINTY of a state has to do with how accurately the actor can predict from it what the next state will be. The connection is inverse: the greater the uncertainty, the less the predictability of what state will come next (cf. p. 81). Suppose we call the current state S_c, and represent the array of all possible next states as S_1, S_2, . . . , S_n. If the states of this array are all equally probable (as the actor himself sees the matter), then the uncertainty is greater with larger n, less with smaller n. For fixed n, the uncertainty is maximal if the next states are all equally probable, less if they are not; at the extreme, if one of them had probability 1 and all the others probability 0, there would be no uncertainty at all. But that extreme is never attained in actuality.

Our actor is Joe, who has put himself in state S_c by proposing marriage to Jill. The possible next states are that Jill will have said yes, that she will have said no, and that she will have said maybe. If Joe believes these three outcomes are equally probable, the uncertainty of S_c is maximal. If he assigns a probability of 0.99 to a no answer, only 0.01 to yes and maybe together, the uncertainty is very small. In the latter case he will be surprised by yes or maybe, only disappointed by no. In the former case none of the outcomes will surprise him more than either of the others.

FREEDOM OF CHOICE. In the example just given, the transition from state S_c to the next state depends on actions of someone else, not of the actor. The situation is different if the actor can himself take the initiative in changing the current state to the next one. We need merely consider Jill's state after Joe has proposed. She can decide whether to say yes, no, or maybe. What is *chance* for Joe is *choice* for her. This is our next parameter. Joe's state is characterized by low freedom of choice, Jill's corresponding state apparently by high freedom.

But it is more complicated than that. An actor's state may be such that the next move is his, and he may consider a whole packet of possibilities, and yet feel compelled to act in a certain way. Uncertainty and freedom of choice are both inside-view matters. The former depends on the actor's own estimate (in or out of awareness) of the probabilities. The latter depends on the actor's own feeling as to how free he is. In our Western culture that feeling is sometimes verbalized in an almost paradoxical way. Having made a decision and acted on it, a person will say "I thought it over and decided there was really nothing else I *could* do." This announces not low but *high* freedom; that must be so, because the person is claiming credit for having of his own free will chosen an ethically correct course rather than any of various tempting but unethical alternatives.

URGENCY. It makes sense to speak of the urgency of a state when the actor believes—or hopes—that he has some freedom of choice. A state is urgent if it will be replaced by another independently of the actor's action unless he acts quickly. Let the actor be a doctor. In the emergency ward, waiting for him to choose between whole blood and plasma, the patient dies. When it is your move in tennis (that is, the ball is coming towards you over the net) your state is urgent. When it is your move at chess, you can take more time. The less urgent a state is, the more time a group functioning as an actor (p. 215) has for consultation (p. 149), and the more time an individual actor has for the kind of one-man consultation we call "thinking" or "editing" (p. 113).

PLEASANTNESS. It is patent that some states are more pleasant than others. The prototype of unpleasantness is physical pain, and we could say that all animals go to great pains to avoid great pains, though smaller discomforts are sometimes accepted if they seem to lie on the most obvious road to some compensating (that is, pleasant) reward. All this is true in more devious ways for human beings than for other animals, but is not unique to our species. The complex cultural overlays of human communities mean that states characterized by no physical pain may also be unpleasant, and thus avoided when possible; the details vary from one community to another.

ANXIETY is not pain, but the anticipation of possible pain. An actor's state is marked by (high) anxiety if he feels that the most probable succeeding states will lead to one marked by pain or by some other form of unpleasantness. For most of us, most of the time, anxiety is itself unpleasant. A good contrast between high and low anxiety is afforded by how one feels when he has just sat down in a special kind of chair—a dentist's chair versus a barber's chair.

SERIOSITY. A partisan spectator at a collegiate football game may be anxious because he wants his team to win and fears it may lose. A player may be equally anxious, sometimes no more so, for the same reason. But the anxieties of the two are nevertheless somehow different. If this is unconvincing, consider the anxiety of the players in a football game versus that of soldiers in battle. Perhaps the latter anxiety is greater (the stakes are higher), but the difference does not seem to be wholly one of degree. We provide for this difference by establishing seriosity (p. 74) as an additional parameter. The soldier's anxiety is marked by high seriosity. The football partisan's anxiety has low seriosity—unless, forsooth, he has been so foolish as to place a large wager on the outcome of the game.

Psychiatrists sometimes distinguish between "wet" and "dry" anxiety, with reference to the amount of sweating, particularly in the palms of the hands. This may correlate with our sixth parameter, but if so I don't know whether it is wetness or dryness that goes with high seriosity.

GOALS. A *goal* of an actor is a state he wants to reach; if the goal looms close, he is *eager*. Presumably a goal has high pleasantness, or, at least, the actor thinks it will. If an animal is hungry, its goal is a state of satiation; if an animal is sleepy, its goal is to be asleep. If a human being is hungry, his goal is to be eating, unless this is overridden by some larger consideration such as a cause his devotion to which makes him willing to go on a hunger strike.

An actor's degree of purposiveness in any state may be an additional state parameter. But it may be that it is determined by and can be inferred from the six parameters we have described.

MOODS AND EPISODES

In any community, people go through whole long series of successive states—series lasting minutes, hours, or days—in which the parameters change very little or change steadily in specifiable directions. We say (in everyday terms) that the individual is in a particular "mood"; or that the series of states constituted an "episode" in life history.

Certain typical moods or episodes in various cultures, though greatly different in detailed content, are similar in the ways the parameters move or don't move, and some of these are hinted at by such words as "game," "ritual," "adventure," "quandary." I direct the reader's attention to Box 18-1, wherein it is shown that a number of such types of mood or episode can be not merely characterized but cross-culturally *defined* in terms of the parameters.

KINDS OF QUANDARIES

× A person is in a quandary if he doesn't know what to do—unless he doesn't care what he does, in which case we describe him as being not in a quandary but "at loose ends."

Thus a quandary is a state or mood, though not all states are quandaries.

If the actor does not know what to do, he must believe that he has some choice, so freedom of choice cannot be zero. Uncertainty must be mid to high, for otherwise the freedom of choice would mean that the actor would proceed at once to make his decision. Urgency cannot be dire, or there would be no time for the actor to contemplate the possibilities: the state would change despite his inaction, resolving the dilemma or replacing it by a new one.

The values of the other three parameters vary from one quandary to another. An *interesting* quandary, however (p. 230), is one for which at least one parameter has an extreme value. We empathize with the doctor in an emergency ward who must decide quickly between whole blood and plasma, because seriosity is high, anxiety is probably high, and urgency, while allowing a little time for thought, does not allow very much.

Fairly high urgency coupled with low seriosity makes for *excitement.* This characterizes our state if we are not really deeply involved with the doctor and his patient—say, if they are merely characters in a play we are watching, and our involvement is via a temporary and partial willful suspension of disbelief.

Of all potentially interesting quandaries, the ones that concern us here are those that arise in the transactions of some dyad in some community.

A quandary of a single person may in this case be that of (1) a partner in a single dyad, (2) a person who participates in two socially distinct dyads in both of which his partner is the same other person, or (3) a person who is simultaneously in two dyads with different partners. A group can be in a quandary if (4) it forms one pole of a dyad and its members are in disagreement as to how the group's transactions in that dyad should be conducted.

(1)   A Single Dyad

If A and B form a dyad, A's attitude towards B may be marked by one or another degree of affection, submissiveness, or hostility.

Affection means that A seeks through his actions (or by his inaction) to establish states for B which are pleasant, because that will in general establish pleasant states for A too. Submissiveness means A's willingness to let his subsequent states depend on B's actions. Hostility is of two sorts. Suspicious hostility is that in which A's actions, if he takes any, are designed to prevent B from establishing states unpleasant for

BOX 18-1. Properties of some characteristic episodes and moods.

	PREDICTABILITY	FREEDOM OF CHOICE	URGENCY	PLEASANTNESS	ANXIETY	SERIOSITY
in dentist's chair	high	low	mid to high	low	high	mid to high
in barber's chair	high	low	mid to high	mid to high	low	mid to low
meeting a truck in your lane coming over a hill	high	low	high	low	high	high
listening to familiar music	high	low	low	high	low	low
playing chess	mid	high	low	mid to high	variable	low to mid
playing football	mid	mid	mid to high	mid to high	mid to high	mid
watching football	mid	low	low	mid to high	mid to high	low
doctor with emergency patient	mid to high	mid to low	high	?	mid to high	high
doctor with patient with slow disease	mid to high	mid to high	low	?	low to mid	high
participating in armed combat	mid to low	mid to low	mid to high	low	high	high
listening to new music	mid to low	low	low	variable	low	low
Quandary	mid to high	mid to high	mid to low	variable	variable	variable
Boredom	high	high	low	low	low	low
Sleep	high	low	low	high	low	?
Ritual	high	low	variable	high	low	?
Game	mid	mid	variable	high	variable	low
Adventure	mid to low	mid	variable	high to mid	variable	low to mid

A (it does not matter whether or not B is actually trying to do this). Submissiveness without suspicion is trust; submissiveness despite suspicion is resignation. The other sort of hostility is that in which A seeks to establish unpleasant states for B because that will at the same time establish pleasant states for A himself: A finds pleasure in B's discomfiture or suffering. The Germans call this pleasure *Schadenfreude;* it seems to have no convenient English label.

These factors can be mixed in various proportions and can change with time.

CASUAL DYADS. In a casual dyad, say one composed of a store clerk and a customer who have never seen each other before and may never see each other again, there may be no discernible trace of any of the factors. Society establishes polite conventions so that such casual encounters are relatively depersonalized and run smoothly. The states passed through in the encounter tend to have low seriosity. Yet, whether we are the clerk or the customer, we find some such episodes more pleasant than others. The attitudinal ingredients are not wholly neutralized.

DURABLE DYADS. The states passed through by the members of a more durable dyad, especially one composed of members of a single household, tend to have higher average seriosity. Such a dyad differs from a casual one in two ways. First, the attitudinal ingredients are likely to manifest themselves more strongly. Second, smoothness is even more important. In our culture, a man insulted by a strange clerk in a store is not apt to nurse his resentment for long, but a man mistreated by his wife or his boss may sulk for days.

IMPACT OF HOUSEHOLD PATTERNS. An established household pattern does something about both of these problems. First, it trains each individual from childhood (as best it can: see pp. 224–228) as to what attitudes he *should* have towards his partner in any dyad in which he participates or in time will participate. This puts a bias on the choices the individual will tend to make whenever a state presents him with an array (p. 230) of alternatives, and thus reduces his quandaries. Second, it orders the dominances within each dyad, and those among the dyads, so that the mutual attitudes of partners will be as compatible as possible. This does not mean that the attitudes are the same; instead of that, they may differ but complement each other. If Jack Sprat can eat no fat and his wife can eat no lean, they get along just fine.

Thus, an established household pattern schedules not only the *behavior* but also— perhaps even more—the *attitudes* of the people who grow up in it. The traditional Chinese girl child was trained to be submissive to her eventual husband, to feel affection for him if she could, and in any case to suppress any hostility she might develop towards him. The traditional Chinese boy child was trained to be non-submissive towards his wife, and to maximize affection for and minimize hostility towards her within the overriding constraint of his duties towards his father and, in due time, to his son. These orientations are not the same, but they complement each other neatly. In the absence of perturbing factors, each member of such a dyad, raised to manifest and expect these attitudes, should be able to find fulfillment within it without ever being faced by any really serious quandaries.

The nineteenth-century American middle-class girl was raised to "love, honor, and obey" her eventual husband: that is, first of all to feel affection for him, secondly (?) to avoid hostility towards him, and thirdly (?) to be submissive to him. Perhaps the second and third should be interchanged. Her husband had been trained to "love, honor, and cherish" her, which meant, first, to feel affection for her, second, to avoid hostility towards her, and, third, to temper his demands on her submissiveness by the depth of his affection. Here, again, the scheduled attitudes were not identical, but complementary.

There may be an uncle-nephew society in which a young boy is trained to assume the following attitude towards his mother's brother: submissiveness, some measure of affection, and a degree of suspicious hostility which must be kept in check (that is, not be allowed to govern choices of action, lest the consequences be unfortunate). But coupled with this is training for the eventual role of uncle in an uncle-nephew dyad, where the attitude must be nonsubmissiveness, some measure of affection, and perhaps some of each sort of hostility (p. 233); the last must be curbed, but not so drastically as must the nephew's. The uncle can at least tease his nephew; the nephew cannot reciprocate, but must store up any resentment he feels and take it out on his own nephew—unless he can rid himself of it more quickly by teasing a little brother or a dog.

(2) COEXISTENT DYADS

If A and B are partners in two socially distinguished dyads, there can be the complication that relative to one dyad they should behave in one way (and have certain mutual attitudes) while relative to the other their behavior and attitudes should be different.

EPHEMERAL COEXISTENCE. When I was in college I took a course in which my father served briefly as guest lecturer. Thus, for a few days, he and I were both father-son and teacher-student. It turned out that for him the former relationship took precedence, while for me the latter did. I was greatly embarrassed when I held up my hand and he said "Charles, did thee have a question?" (p. 185); he would have been equally embarrassed to say, instead of that, "Mr. Hockett, did you have a question?"

This was an ephemeral coincidence of dyads. There was no clear precedent; each of us had to improvise, and we improvised differently. Such fleeting coincidences are rare enough to present quandaries when they do occur, but common enough to be potentially interesting. Writers of fiction make plots turn on them. A detective discovers that the criminal he is looking for is the man who saved his life when they were in the war together. In burlesque (e.g., Boccaccio's *Decameron*) a man discovers at an assignation that the woman who has agreed to commit adultery with him is his wife in disguise. In melodrama, a man going to a brothel is sent to a room where the prostitute turns out to be his daughter. In heartwarming potboilers, a business man befriends a bright orphan who is then revealed as his long lost son.

Ephemeral coincidences of dyads happen in complex societies, not in tribal societies where local groups are so small that everybody knows everybody else. In both, there are certain kinds of coincidences that are avoided. The average medical doctor in our society will not take a seriously ill member of his own family as a patient. He has been trained to believe that his efficacy as a physician depends on having an attitude towards his patient which is a special mixture of concern and aloofness. For a member of his own family, he can have the concern but not the aloofness. A lawyer is not *permitted* to take a case which would involve him in a protagonistic and an antagonistic relationship with the same person at the same time. (The rule of "conflict of interest" is otherwise stated, but has this consequence.) Some business firms and some colleges have a rule against "nepotism": one may not have a member of one's immediate family as a subordinate, or even as a coworker, for fear the family relationship will interfere with the smooth workings of the business relationship.[1] One firm of Meiji bankers in Japan handled this in a more drastic way: the head of the household was not allowed to marry and had to adopt his most competent employee to be his successor. Within households and kin groups, a rule of exogamy is a device for preventing coincidences of dyads that may involve bad dilemmas, and to some extent a rule of endogamy may have the same effect and purpose.

PLANNED COINCIDENCE.　But there are also situations in which two dyads are expected to coincide, either sporadically or else permanently once they have come together. When this is the case, the dyads are *made* compatible.

Consider small family businesses in Europe and the United States in the nineteenth century. There was no nonsense about nepotism. The proprietor's son was fully expected to follow in his father's footsteps, first getting the necessary training, perhaps "working his way up from the bottom" as part of his apprenticeship, but obviously favored over other employees (whose resentment of the favoritism was usually impotent) and destined ultimately to inherit the business or a share of it.

We know there are societies in which a man is expected to marry a cross cousin if possible. When cross cousins marry they do not cease to be cross cousins. In such a society, cross cousins of opposite sex learn as children to have attitudes towards each other compatible with the expected mutual attitudes of husband and wife. Marriage is then not a contradiction but a deepening or a fulfillment.[2]

And there are communities where sisters may become cowives (p. 218). Where sororal polygyny is preferred because cowives will get along better if they are also sisters, little girls play at cowifery as a little American girl plays at motherhood. There are about as many polygynous societies in which the assumption goes the other way: that is, sisters should be friends and the potential jealousies of cowifery should not be wished on them. Sisters therefore get *that* sort of training as children, and if, contrary to usual custom, an instance of sororal polygyny arises, it works out badly.

(3)　OVERLAPPING DYADS

In our society, if a man is courting two women or a woman is being courted by two men we have an example of the "eternal triangle"—an epithet intimating a

---

[1]The use of *nepotism* for this is interesting. The word is from Latin *nepōs* 'nephew', implying some trace of the avunculate in the history of Western society. Otherwise we would presumably call the improper favoring of a relative something like *filialism,* from Latin *filius* 'son'.

[2]Mother-in-law avoidance, as among the Menomini, serves to obviate dyad or role quandaries; it is not clear just how.

universality not in accord with the facts of history. There are triangles in all societies, but they are of many kinds and no single kind is "eternal."

The essence of this altogether nonmathematical sort of triangularity is that a person is in a quandary arising from conflicting duties or desires in two dyads in which his partners are distinct. There are nonstandard and socially (or legally) disapproved solutions for the dilemma of the girl with two suitors. She can take one as a husband, the other as a paramour, or the three may be able to establish a workable ménage à trois. The legally endorsed expectation in our society is, of course, that she choose one and reject the other or else reject both. This does not eliminate her dilemma, but it makes the alternatives sharper. The difference between a fuzzy quandary and a sharply defined one is like the difference between an open-ended essay question in an examination and a multiple-choice question. At worst, the latter is oppressive because all the alternatives seem wrong; at best, the task is easier because one does not have to flounder in search of possible answers.

Household patterns minimize triangular quandaries in two ways. First, they assign clear priorities of responsibility. In the last analysis, this is the whole meaning of "dominance" when we speak of dominant dyads. Second, they tend to arrange the different dyads in which a single individual may participate in such a way that conflicting obligations or desires are least likely to arise.

PRIORITIES OF RESPONSIBILITY have already been exemplified: the Chinese husband (versus the American one) whose wife is in dangerous labor delivering a son, or who can save only his wife or only his father when both are in deadly peril (p. 217). These are extreme quandaries. If the culture prescribes an unambiguous choice in extreme cases, the cultural guidelines in less serious quandaries are pretty clear.

Suppose, as another example, that a man of an exogamous patrilocal band or of an exogamous patrilineal clan takes a wife. The woman's band membership changes; typically her clan membership does not. But she now has potentially divided loyalties. This situation has been faced by countless women through human history. Men, too, have been confronted by divided loyalties, but more rarely and eftsoons less seriously.[3]

Sometimes the expectations for the woman on this spot are straightforward. In a strong father-son or husband-wife culture, she knows that if troubles arise between her husband and, say, her brother, she must support the former. Even her brother expects that. She is regarded as a traitor if she does not. In some cultures this is exactly reversed: the woman must support her brother. However, this is a type of triangle about which many communities lack precedents. The woman in a crisis situation then faces a fuzzy dilemma instead of a multiple-choice question with the right answer already marked. Any choice is a bad one. These are the communities in which the status of women is lowest of all.

COMPATIBILITY OF ROLES. The other provision made by household patterns is for an individual's most important roles to be in minimally competing dyads. Again, we have already had a possible example (p. 220): in the mother-son communities

---

[3]One wouldn't think so from the fuss they make about it—at least in Western society, where male heroes, martyrs, and saints are much more apt to be remembered or fictionalized than female ones. Women make their difficult choices quietly and suffer the consequences in silence.

of South Asia, a man's boon companion is not likely to demand anything of him—other than time and attention—that his mother wants, or vice versa. To be at the same time a proper son and a loyal chum presents few dilemmas. If the reasoning is correct, then we should also expect that the mother's closest tie, other than to her son or sons, would be to someone of her own generation and sex, provided any such person is available. Because of the residence pattern it would have to be either a sister-in-law of her husband or else just some female age mate in the neighborhood. Whether this is so or not I do not know.

Still following the same logic, we should expect that the closest tie of a traditional Chinese male, other than to his father and sons, would be to someone of his own generation and of the opposite sex—obviously, a wife or concubine. One can find evidence suggesting this, despite the unquestionably sharp subordination of the husband-wife dyad to the father-son dyad. Philosophical speculation arising from the Chinese world view reflects both. We shall see later (p. 244) that Confucius elevated the father-son tie to the status of a universal principle in human relations. The husband-wife tie is reflected in the doctrine of *yáng* and *yīn*, the male principle of creativity, dominance, the heavens, and the female principle of fertility, submissiveness, the earth, which harmoniously complement each other and stand in contrast but yet interpenetrate.

How about our own husband-wife culture?

A hundred years ago the most relaxing antithesis a man could find within the family to his relationship with his wife was his dealings with his son, and when a woman was not preoccupied with her husband or with the care of small children her most intimate companionship was with daughters or, possibly, her own mother. The husband also had opportunities for relaxing ties outside the household, and his need for them was attested by a host of saloons, gymnasiums, lodges, clubs, alumni associations (of noncoeducational academies and colleges), business associations, and political brotherhoods, from which children were barred completely and which were taboo to women except sometimes as entertainers. This fits the pattern. The dominance of the husband-wife dyad puts such an emphasis on the association of sex with affection (p. 220) and with suppression of hostility that if any other dyad is to be marked by strong affection it is best one in which sex is out of the question. This turned the wife to her daughters and the husband to his sons; the husband's outside male ties were a relief from both, yet never totally comfortable because both affection and hostility had to be kept in check. The weakest outside tie of all was the old school tie, because the intimate association of the adolescent with other youths left traces of immature affection of which the adult male was ashamed.

More recently, our American culture has also allowed a man to develop an intimate and rewarding relationship with his daughters. The closeness of many a contemporary father-daughter tie may be a man's reaction to the increasing extent to which the other women in his life (mother, aunts, sisters, wife) tend to "mother" him (p. 227): a daughter, at least, treats one like a man.[4]

---

[4]This change has also helped give rise to the exclusively Western institution of the *dirty old man:* to wit, any male old enough to have a nubile daughter who pretends he can have a "fatherly" interest in any nubile female other than his own daughter.

VARIATIONS ON HUMAN THEMES

(4) Group Dilemmas

Insofar as a group functions as a pole of a dyad, its quandaries are like those of a single individual who does not know what to do in his dealings with someone else. Group consultation to decide on a course of action is much like the problem-oriented thinking of an individual in a comparable situation. For the process of consultation itself, we have all the variable attributes discussed earlier in another connection (p. 149): limits on the size of an informal group, patterns of formal procedure, the role of moderator.

A group quandary can be decomposed into quandaries of participating subgroups or individuals, thus directly or indirectly into quandaries of individuals. (In principle this is always true; in practice, if a group is large a participant can come to feel that he is dealing with "impersonal" forces: p. 205). The quandaries of the participating individuals are then just of the sorts we have already discussed.

For example, consider an American husband and wife who are distressed by the behavior of their adolescent son. When they take the problem up with each other, their son is the *substance* of their transaction, but in this activity they constitute an engaged dyad in which either can be in a quandary about the other (the first type of quandary we talked about) or in a dilemma because of loyalty divided between partner and offspring (the third kind). The substance is different, but they may or may not reach an agreement, may or may not get angry with each other, and so on, just as though the substance were whether the wife should buy an expensive new dress, or whether the husband should try to cut down on his smoking.

✖ Some people are crazy. In our society the truth of this is endorsed by the fact that patients are diagnosed by medical men as suffering from "mental" or "emotional" diseases and are then sometimes confined in special hospitals or wards. In 1950 more American hospital beds were occupied by schizophrenics than by sufferers from all other diseases put together. At that same time, the favorite emotional illness (or the favorite diagnosis) in certain other segments of Western society was manic-depressive psychosis, and in still other parts it was paranoia. These terms have reasonably well defined clinical meanings. The diagnoses are made with care and are based on observed behavioral tendencies of the patients.

In other societies, other types of radical deviation from normal behavior are recognized. The more northerly Ojibwa, the Cree, and some other aboriginal tribes of the North American subarctic were subject to what the Ojibwa called "Windigo possession" (*wīntikō*, Cree *wīhtikōw*, was a rarely seen frightful icy monster, the incarnation of the fury of the subarctic winter). Under a seizure of this sort one might grab a weapon and try to destroy one's closest friends and relatives, sometimes, at least, because of a hunger for human flesh. The Malays and others in peninsular and insular Southeast Asia spoke of "running amok"; the behavior was in part the same.

Physiological Aspects

All of us have at one time or another felt unusually great anger, anxiety, or fear. "Feel" is the right word: whatever be the factors that have led to the state, one's physiology is altered—quivering muscles, increased or erratic pulse, heavy or irregular breathing, modified sweating (p. 231), blurred vision or impaired hearing, sometimes difficulties with sphincter control. Following such leads, physiological chemists have isolated a battery of substances whose injection into the bloodstream will evoke (or suppress) signs and symptoms similar to the clinical manifestations of one or another sort of emotional illness. Many of these have a measurable effect also on nonhuman laboratory animals, such as mice or monkeys. It is clear that there is some physiological common denominator, shared not only by all strains of our species but also by placental mammals in general.

On the other hand, it has also been noted that there is a wide variation of response to such substances, not only from individual to individual but also in a single individual from one time to another (addicts of LSD report bad trips as well as good ones). Moreover, experimenters have induced "neurosis" in rats and guinea pigs without any drugs at all, by forcing them to try to solve unsolvable problems or merely by prolonged overcrowding (p. 69).

Social and Cultural Aspects

Thus, any proposal that insanity is "purely" a matter of major disturbances of body chemistry is misplaced emphasis. Let us remember that any act of learning or of forgetting by any animal involves alterations of internal chemistry, though typically of a subtle and localized sort, not observable through gross physiological tests (p. 53). "Mental" disorders are disorders of learning, of information-processing, of communication, whether brought on by diet, by drugs, by environmental pressures, or by some combination of such factors. Genetics and diet may render some individuals more prone than others to certain kinds of behavioral upsets, but whether the upsets will actually occur, what specific form they will take, and how they will be responded to by the individual's comrades—all these things depend on the cultural setting.

The specific factors that trigger deviant behavior vary from community to community. The "content" of an obsession varies from culture to culture: there really are patients who think they are Napoleon, but not in a community which never heard of Napoleon. Behavior acceptable in one community may be classed as off-limits in another; the person who manifests it in the former community is not insane even if he has such-and-such a "psychosis-inducing" substance in his blood stream, while the one who manifests it in the latter may be treated as crazy even if he does not.

Above all, cross-cultural diagnosis is impossible. There is an instructive though horrible story of a Navajo living in town, away from his fellows, whose unhappiness and queer behavior landed him in a hospital. A diagnosis was made (in standard Western psychiatric terms) and treatment was undertaken, but with no effect. Finally someone with a trace of cross-cultural enlightenment came along and had him released to his own people, whereupon he was sound and healthy.

Sanity and insanity thus require to be defined within each culture, in terms of the inside view of that culture. This does not mean that cross-cultural generalization is impossible, only that it must be made in terms of systems of functional contrasts rather than in terms of the presence or absence of specific items (p. 129).

Etiology

In any community, an individual may incline towards deviant behavior which is unacceptable to his fellows. In any community, that which triggers such inclinations (though doubtless more readily in those with certain genetic constitutions than in others) is quandaries and conflicts of the sorts we have been describing in this chapter, placing such stress on the individual's capacity for adjustment that he breaks and "escapes from reality." Here "reality" must be defined *wholly* in terms of the inside view of the community. The escape may be so slight as to pass unnoticed, or may be so extreme as to be alarming, and between these two there are no sharp boundaries. The individual's state parameters (pp. 230–232) diverge, in some contexts, from what his fellows would consider reasonable. His choices become unpredictable and unreliable. His personality becomes, at worst, incompatible with his assigned roles. If the deviation is extreme and cannot be cured, the individual must be removed or destroyed.

Perhaps no individual is ever insane in his own perception, except insofar as his fellows persuade him that his deviations from what they define as normality are dangerous to himself as well as to others. This sort of social feedback sometimes rescues an incipient deviant from his growing divergence. But often it plays an active part in the etiology of the insanity, by increasing the individual's quandaries and fears.

In any case, note that a *community*, by definition, cannot be insane. It is the community that establishes the norms relative to which deviation is judged. In a complex society sometimes everyone in a family or a village is thought by outsiders to be a bit queer, but that is not the same thing: it is fishy jam.

19

✕

INTIMATE DYADS AS PROTOTYPES

It has been true for a long time in Western society that the teacher-student dyad has resembled a parent-child dyad. A century ago, when male dominance was still unchallenged, the schoolmaster was typically a man, and his discipline over his charges was like that of a father except that it was sometimes more severe.

For the past few decades most of the teachers in our kindergartens and elementary schools have been women. This is either because or why we expect the teacher of small children to be maternal rather than paternal towards them; it is reflected in the fact that, just when a little girl is having the most fun mothering her dolls and her smaller siblings, she is most apt to declare that she wants to be a schoolteacher when she grows up. The proportion of male teachers is greater in high schools, and the males win hands down in colleges and universities. The high-school or college student is old enough to confront "paternal" authority directly, no longer needing the protection of an intervening mother figure. Just so, in an earlier day, the child in a family emerged in time from under the mother's wing to unmediated exposure to father.

We tend to think of all this as part of the order of nature. It is—part of the order of *our* nature, which means our culture. In traditional India, the teacher was a *guru.* Most gurus were male, as were most of their disciples, but this was never absolutely inflexible and today there are many exceptions. Not every student who sought discipleship made it. The really successful guru attracted more would-be disciples than he could accept. Ideally, the guru, together with his circle of adherents, formed a household, with unobtrusive servants to take care of menial tasks and with untutored family members (wives, children) kept out of the way. The disciples were thus free to follow the master around virtually all of his waking hours, serving him in small ways, giving signs of obeisance, accepting his assignments of intellectual tasks, and ever alert to pounce on pearls of wisdom from his lips.

Recent changes in South Asia brought about by interaction with the West have not much affected the ideal. Many a South Asian graduate student coming to an American university has felt rejected because he hoped to become a disciple of some American guru and there just aren't any to be found. Many an American professor has been first flattered, then annoyed and puzzled, finally frantic, because of the frequency with which his graduate students from South Asia call on him at home.[1]

The guru-disciple dyad and our teacher-student dyad have in common that both have to do with the transmission of special skills or doctrines. Otherwise, as we have seen, they are totally different. The explanation lies in the difference of household patterns. The guru-disciple relationship is modeled on the mother-son tie of a mother-son culture. The disciple is dependent on the guru as the son is on the mother; the disciple shares physical intimacy (totally free of any sexual connotation) with the guru as the son does with the mother; the disciple worships the guru—sometimes lying prostrate before him for long periods of time—just as the son worships the mother. The disciple finds a counterbalancing relief from this in his relations with other disciples, just as the son seeks brothers or chums as a counterfoil for his deep and complex tie to his mother.

WHY ARE INTIMATE DYADS PARADIGMATIC?

× Along such lines as those described, the household pattern of every human culture tends to suffuse through the rest of the social order and give it its special flavor. There are two reasons why this should be so.

The Human-History Reason

In the history of our species, participation in small, intimate groups, composed largely or wholly of kin, went on for tens of thousands of years before the appearance anywhere of durable communities of any larger sort. It does not matter, in this connection, that we are unable to trace the origin of the human band-family contrast. What counts is that our sociality is *primate* sociality, not the herd or horde variety characteristic of some of our more remote cousins (p. 69). Millions of years of primate evolution, and hundreds of thousands of years of hominid evolution, have equipped us for efficient and satisfying participation in a relatively small number of intimate but distinct dyads. When circumstances force the appearance of a new sort of dyad, people are going to try to handle it more or less as they have been handling old and familiar dyads. We saw an almost pandemic result of this in chapter 14 (p. 176): members of a clan treat one another as kin even if they know they are not, and if necessary invent a common ancestor to fit. The Menomini greet a stranger by a hopefully appropriate kinship term (p. 24); this is extremely widespread.

Kin dyads are very old, and so is one other: a dyad of mutual aliens (p. 69). We can hardly call the stranger-stranger dyad an intimate one, but it is at least thoroughly familiar; so, when new dyads are arising on the model of old ones, habitual reactions to aliens can play a part. Throughout human (and primate) history, a major ingredient in attitudes towards aliens has been suspicious hostility (p. 233). The alien

[1] Points like the following, often registered out of awareness, hardly reduce the cross-cultural noise. The South Asian affirmative head gesture is rather like the American negative one. A giggle signaling pleasurable amusement in the West indicates embarrassment from status insecurity in South Asia. American housewives manifest a baffling pride at the spotlessness of a room in the house which weirdly combines the disparate functions of bathhouse and latrine. And a Westerner has the nasty habit of carrying around bits of nasal discharge wrapped in a piece of cloth in his pocket.

is human but different; or he is not quite human, yet similar: he always may and often does want something one does not wish to relinquish. Since he is an alien, his actions are unpredictable. Avoidance is the wisest course when possible. When it is not, all sorts of strange and distressing things happen. Surely this is one of the major sources of hostility *within* a society.

THE LIFE-HISTORY REASON

Our second reason may just be the first in different guise. Each individual human being starts his life within a household of some sort, and learns most thoroughly the roles into which he is forced earliest. A newcomer to the child's inner circle is initially responded to either as though he were indistinguishable from some member of that inner circle, or else as an alien. To be sure, with more exposure and with further tutelage the child enlarges his inner circle, makes more subtle distinctions within it, and acquires greater skill at categorizing a stranger before yielding to any impulsive reaction. But any animal deals with a novel situation analogically, on the basis of its partial similarities to old and familiar situations (p. 108). A human being is no exception, despite greater flexibility maintained for a longer time (p. 74).

So, as the child grows to man's estate, he may put aside the overt symbols of childishness, but does not completely outgrow or altogether suppress the attitudes of the child. My father is grown old and feeble and will soon pass to his reward, but I shall put my trust in our Heavenly Father, to Whom I have become as a little child, and He will care for me as a good shepherd watches over his sheep (—when the social order makes this particular mixed metaphor appropriate). Or: and He will protect me as a wise liege lord protects his lieges; so the king, if not a god, at least rules by divine right and is a father to his people.[2]

DIFFERENT MODELS, DIFFERENT RESULTS

These particular analogies make, or have made, fine sense in our Western tradition.[3] They do not make sense in South Asia, where many important deities are goddesses. They would be bizarre in China, where the household point of departure is so different that analogical extrapolations from it are also radically different.

Twenty-four centuries ago Confucius set forth, in the *Treatise on Filial Piety,* the proper etiquette of ruler towards subjects and of subjects towards ruler *exactly* in terms of the classical Chinese father-son dyad. As reason for the prescribed etiquette he said only that when people behave in accordance with its dictates then all is in order

[2]Psychotherapists have labels for a special case of what we are talking about here. A patient often comes to deal with his therapist on the model of his dealings with his (the patient's) father or other intimate kin: this is "transference." If the therapist responds in kind, as he often does, it is "counter-transference."

[3]But not always the same sense. Christians have been referring to their God as "Father" for two thousand years. The force of the metaphor has changed from one stage to another in the social history of the West, and the metaphor has been more useful at some times than at others. With the altered status of American fathers between a century ago and now, the metaphor has become almost hollow. Yet I have not yet heard any young Christian start a prayer with "Hey, Pop!"

and at peace—the sanction of social homeostasis in a society in which normality is defined by the dominance of father-son.

A few maverick sinologists have argued that the father-son pattern was induced in the Chinese household by the Confucian political arrangement rather than vice versa. Now, there is no overriding reason why a person should not sometimes attempt to handle a situation in an intimate dyad on the analogy of his successful handling of some episode in a more remote dyad. But it is clear that by and large the influence passes in the other direction, in traditional Chinese culture as everywhere else. The mavericks are wrong. In fact, Confucius made his recommendations because it seemed to him that rulers were straying from the path of rectitude and needed to be reminded of their duties.

✖ When we dissect the institutions of a society into simpler components, we find that the influence of the household pattern sometimes manifests itself with delay, and that it manifests itself in more than one way.

HOW THE INFLUENCE IS CHANNELED

Delay

Delay is well illustrated by a point made in the last footnote (fn. 3, p. 244): when a contemporary American Christian refers to his God as "Father" this reflects a social status of fathers which is largely passé. However, devout Christian families in our culture cling to the older household pattern more strongly than many others do, illustrating also the phenomenon of feedback. Thus if God is the perfect Father in the loving care and firm guidance He gives us all, then the human father must try hard to be, not a perfect father, which would make him godlike and constitute *lèse-déité,* but the best father he can.

Similarity and Contrast

If a dyad not composed of kin is *like* a dyad of kin (as Chinese ruler-subject was supposed to be like father-son), the influence amounts to imitation. But a nonhousehold dyad may also *differ* from any household dyad and still be the result of household influence. Of this, too, we have had an example: the all-adult-male saloons, lodges, clubs, and the like in which a late-Victorian or early post-Victorian middle-class American husband sought *relief by contrast* from his household involvements (p. 238). These two mechanisms—the comfort of familiarity and the relief of contrast—work together to give the larger structure of any complex society its texture.

✖ One important dyad in modern Western industrial society seems at first to resist the kind of analysis we have been presenting: boss-worker or employer-employee. We can highlight the matter by first describing what this dyad has come to be like in modern industrialized Japan, traditionally a father-son culture though different in a number of ways from that of China.

BOSS-WORKER

In a Japanese factory a foreman is much like a (Japanese-style) father to those who work under him. The workers show him respect and affection; he gives them counsel and affection as well as instructions. Sometimes the workers are far from their homes, and are housed in a factory dormitory. A worker, especially a girl, will seek guidance from her foreman in matters we would say have nothing to do with the factory—guidance she would seek from parents were she home. On a holiday the whole group may go together to public baths or on an outing, maintaining at play the structure of interrelationships in which they stand at work. The shop is a sort of household and the group is a sort of family.

The contrast with our situation could hardly be greater. There seems to be nothing remotely familial about the boss-worker tie in American industry. Sometimes the owner of the only factory in a small town tries to be paternal towards his employees and the town, but however genuine the effort it is viewed with great suspicion by everyone else. We even characterize it with the word *paternalistic,* which differs from *paternal* much as Ojibwa *okimākkān* 'fake chief' differs from *okimā* 'chief' (p. 148). The owner is mixing things that won't mix. The employees know that when the chips are down he will have to base his decisions on profit and loss, not on compassion.

German historical sociologists speak of a contrast between *Gemeinschaft* and *Gesellschaft,* which we may render here as 'community' and 'corporation'. They propose that, in the history of European society, community has slowly given way to corporation as the basis for action. Community, in this sense, is built out of dyads modeled closely on household dyads; corporation is marked by the depersonalization of human relationships in civil society, in which decisions made by those in the position to make them often seem to have nothing to do with the welfare of any participating individual or group. It would then be impersonal "corporate" attitudes that have invaded the employer-employee relationship, driving out, in the end, all vestiges of community spirit.

But why should this have happened in the West and not in Japan? The easy answer is that Japan has not been industrialized long enough yet. Perhaps that is true. Perhaps in the long run industrialization is incompatible with certain types of interpersonal relationships, so that one or the other has to give way. Meanwhile, however, we are confronted with a striking difference which requires a more penetrating explanation.

The clue lies in the difference between a father-son culture and a husband-wife culture, since in the former the household is in principle immortal and in the latter each individual household in time dies (p. 222). In the former, the individual cannot function efficiently—can hardly exist—with no household roots. If he leaves home to work in a factory, the factory must supply a surrogate. In the latter, any individual may have to survive for a few years with no household, after he has left that of his parents and before he establishes his own; in any case, there is no way in which an industry could supply an employee with an adequate surrogate for a household of the husband-wife type.

In addition, the Western boss-worker dyad doubtless inherits some of its characteristics from the master-slave relationship that played so crucial a role in the economy of the West for such a long time. Factory workers and other menials are still occasionally called "wage slaves."

✖ No one should jump to the conclusion that household patterns are the only factor responsible for the differences among human cultures. Trying to trace everything to a single cause is a nineteenth-century European philosophical game that should by now be beneath our dignity. The household pattern is itself influenced by other things. Were that not so, we should find no variation in it from one community to another.

In point of fact, we have already mentioned two apparently germinal differences between traditional Japan and the United States, neither of which can be taken as altogether the consequence of the other. The difference of household pattern is one. The other is the difference in the average physical closeness of people to one another (p. 208), giving rise to differences in the distribution of shame and guilt as motivations for action.

Now consider the contrasting styles in which Japanese and Americans play baseball. In Japan, when the batter is called out, he bows to the umpire and retires to the dugout. An argument, or a cry of "Kill the umpire!" from the stands, is unthinkable. This represents a degree of ritualization in interpersonal transactions in Japan that is difficult for an American to understand.

The ritualization is compatible with the household pattern and with living close together, but may not be the necessary consequence of either or of both together. Some investigators have proposed a third factor, not to be lightly dismissed. The Japanese live on seismically unstable islands where disaster of nonsocial origin can strike at any time. Noting the nature of ritual (Box 18-1, p. 233), we realize that a ritualization of interpersonal behavior—even in baseball—can supply a degree of predictability, thus of security, that compensates for the unpredictability of the physicogeographical environment.

20

THE HANDLING OF ROUTINE CRISES: THANATOPSIS

A *crisis* in the life of a human community is any serious quandary that affects the whole community. The most universal and mundane of all human crises is death, known to be inevitable, and yet infrequent enough in the average face-to-face community to be a shock when it does happen. That renders the social handling of death an excellent example of the social handling of crisis, and we shall use it as such in this chapter.

All physiological and social crises in the life history of an individual are of potential community significance and may be afforded one or another sort of cultural recognition and endorsement (p. 226). Birth and death are special, in that the former adds a member to the community and the latter deletes one.

In a big community, especially a civil society, this is trivial and is heeded, if at all, impersonally in terms of statistics. Thus, the United States has a Bureau of the Census.

In a household, in a band of hunters-gatherers, in any face-to-face subcommunity of a larger society, both events are notable, but death more so than birth. Think of our prototypical Eagles (p. 167). There might be one or two deliveries per year, but as many as half of all those delivered might not survive infancy. Birth is slow and chancy, involving nine months of pregnancy, the trauma of parturition, and then several years of growing before the child has learned to walk and talk and can begin in a small way to do things that need to be done. The embryo, foetus, or infant that does not survive all the hazards of these early stages simply does not count as an addition to the community. Accordingly, abortion, miscarriage, and infant mortality, however saddening, do not count socially as "death." Setting aside such aborted lives, and allowing for wide variation in age at time of (noninfant) death, we note that in a group such as the Eagles five or ten years might sometimes pass with no adult deaths at all.

Kinds of Death

Deaths are sudden or gradual.

Sudden death is a risk in combat, in hunting, in childbirth, and to some extent just in living, since one may be eaten by a tiger, bitten by a venomous snake, tripped at the top of a precipice, or struck by an automobile.

Gradual death is preceded by a period of illness or other incapacitation. Nonhuman primates know nothing (socially) of noninfant illness, since the monkey or ape that gets sick is abandoned to his own devices (p. 44). But human beings have reason to cherish their old and feeble (p. 387), and by transfer often care for the ill or injured who are not elderly[1] (curing, not prostitution, is the oldest profession). Hence human beings know of the connection between illness and death. They know that a sick person is more apt to die than a well person, but also that even an extremely sick person sometimes recovers.

Sleep, Illness, and Death

Like some other mammals (p. 113), human beings dream when they are asleep. Unlike others, a human being can tell about a dream when he wakes up. We know that dreams are fanciful distortions of the experiences and expectations of waking life. But this is rarely an obvious or even a plausible theory to the dreamer or to those to whom he reveals his dream. Furthermore, there is an apparent contradiction between the dreamer's report and the testimony of others. He describes a wild adventure; they have seen him lying asleep all the time. In illness, sleep gives way to trance and delirium, and again there is a discrepancy between the invalid's subjective account and the events witnessed by others.

How can such contradictions be resolved? This must have puzzled our ancestors for a long time. But early in human history they hit on the explanation still given by most communities of the ethnographic present. The explanation strikes us as obvious only because it is so familiar; its invention demanded true genius.

Lo: A person is not just one thing, but two. He is a tangible, visible material body, and also an intangible, invisible animating soul. The body cannot survive long without the soul, but can make out unattended for short periods. During sleep the soul may take off for adventures in the spirit world—a world different from that of waking life, but whose reality is attested precisely by dreams and visions. During illness, inimical powers may try to prevent the soul's return to the body. Illness is the physical manifestation of this unseen battle.

No one human world view would say exactly this and no more. There are endless variations. But all turn on the same basic theme. Any version resolves the dilemma of equally honest conflicting reports. Of course you saw my body lying here while I was off on my adventures, because I left it behind while I—my soul—went forth to seek them.

The step to understanding death is now easy. Slow death is slow in the sense that those in attendance cannot always tell the exact instant of transfiguration. His breathing stopped and I could feel no pulse, but when I came back a few minutes later he stirred and moaned. A person is dead only if he stays dead; otherwise he has only been deathly ill. Obviously, then, death is the manifestation of a definitive

---

[1] Some tribes in exiguous environments have taken to the practice of disposing of the elderly by abandonment or by a coup de grâce when they can no longer carry their share of the burden. Some of the hyperborean tribes of northeastern Siberia did this. The old person might himself ask for the euthanasia: there was little left for him in this world, and a hastened departure to the next was a kindness to those he loved.

separation of soul from body, upon which the empty husk becomes a cadaver. In sudden death, the body has been so badly broken by physical agencies that the soul is forced to flee.

The Soul Doctrine

In this way, our distant forebears evolved the doctrine of a soul that survives the body, a doctrine inherited into almost all subsequent world views and incorporated in due time into most of those recent systems of belief we call religions (chapter 10).

The soul doctrine is not a theory in the scientific sense, not because it is false (it may be true!) but because there is no socially shared way of disproving it: whatever actually happens can be explained without abandoning the doctrine. In contrast, a scientific theory is supposed to contain within itself specification of the conditions under which it must be rejected or modified (pp. 652–659).

The prevalence of the soul doctrine has been a mixed blessing. On the credit side, millions of human beings have been able to face their own death, or to accept that of a loved one, with reasonable serenity because it is, after all, just another transition from one age grade to another. On the debit side, the notion that death is just another transition has promoted human cruelty. If I believe that in killing I merely hasten the victim's arrival in another world, murder is scarcely more than a peccadillo; no line of moral argument, no threat of dire consequences, has ever been able to convince most people to the contrary. Also, if peaceful death is so trivial, then death as a punishment is no penalty unless it is effected by bestial and lingering torture. But if I believe that all any man is or has is his life in this world, I shall be slow to anger and quick to forgive. We must not be surprised that some of the bloodiest pages in all of human history are those written in the last two millennia by the spread of Christianity and of Islam.

The Problems of Death

Because of the soul doctrine, the survivors of a deceased person are typically faced with a fourfold problem. Something must be done about the cadaver, about the soul, about the estate, and about the vacated roles.

THE CADAVER ✘ The corpse of a healthy person killed suddenly is like that of a slaughtered pig or deer, and one thing to do is to eat it.

Cannibalism

Sporadic cannibalism from extreme hunger is known all over the world, and a sacrificial murder to obtain food is only slightly rarer. The eating of the heart or some other portion of a slain enemy is widespread but has a motivation other than hunger: the victor wishes to inherit the courage, or some other attribute, of the vanquished.

Systematic cannibalism is not common, yet is well attested. When Europeans first reached Fiji, in the late eighteenth and early nineteenth centuries, they found the archipelago thickly settled by people organized into small warring kingdoms, and being eaten was the standard fate of prisoners of war. Between 1825 and 1885 a number of travelers and missionaries rejoined the stockpile of the biosphere via this path. The facts of the case are discernible through all the exaggerations and rationalizations of the European accounts. Cannibalism was not a ritual appendage of war between tribes, but one of the *reasons* for war. If provoking a war was for the moment diplomatically inconvenient, a raiding party might go out to the reefs and capture a few women and children of a neighboring tribe who were gathering shellfish, taking both the people and the shellfish home as food. "Long pig" was a gourmet dish for which the Fijians had a hankering: the explanation was as simple as that.

Before we jump to the conclusion that they were unutterably callous and savage, we should consider three things. First: from a demographic point of view, the rate of destruction of Fijians through cannibalism was at its peak trivial as compared to their decimation by diseases imported from Europe. In one five-year period in the late nineteenth century a measles epidemic swept away a full 75 percent of the population. Second, the pot and the kettle: we can well pause to compare the "uncivilized" warfare and cannibalism of the Fijians with the systematic "civilized" xenocide practiced by some modern nations, preeminently (but not exclusively) by Nazi Germany in the 1940s. Third: we would do well to find out about the typically human tender loving care the Fijians bestowed on one another within the household and the village.[2] There is a universal human rule: you do not kill, and certainly do not eat, those you love. If in dire straits you are tempted to kill and eat a friend, you must first become estranged from him.

OTHER DISPOSAL TECHNIQUES

There is another universal human rule: you do not eat a diseased cadaver, human or nonhuman. Therefore, for two reasons, the cadaver of a fellow tribesman who has died a slow death (p. 249) has to be handled in some other way. From the general biological point of view, it is a waste product of metabolism comparable to excreta and will become increasingly unpleasant to be near as saprophytes consume it. In accordance with the junk principle (p. 97), the survivors either move away from it or move it away from themselves.

The former procedure is now rare, but was doubtless standard for many hundreds of thousands of years before the domestication of fire (p. 403) or the development of efficient digging tools. For the latter takes only two forms (other than dumping the corpse into deep water, which is rarely possible): burning and burial. Both demand technological sophistication. A modest cooking fire will roast a corpse but will not reduce it to ashes; for that one must have a carefully designed pyre. A shallow grave or a mere pile of stones covering the corpse will not shut off the outflow of volatile byproducts of decay.

[2] Thank you for waiting. Now we can go ahead to conclude that the Fijians were unutterably callous and savage, but that they were like almost everybody else in this respect, and also like everybody else in that *most* of their behavior was marked by warmth and compassion.

There are enough known variants of these two techniques to fill an Old Curiosity Shop or a wing of an ethnographic museum. Disposal of the remains immediately after death is unusual, even in the tropics where the saprophytes work fast. Embalming, known at least as early as 3000 B.C. (in Egypt), slows down the rate of decay so that disposal can be postponed longer. Many communities, our own among them, dress the body of the deceased up in finery and put it on display. We say this is so friends and relatives can come and pay their "last respects"; other cultures offer different explanations. One Australian tribe used to follow the practice of stopping up the cadaver's bodily orifices and placing the corpse on a platform (downwind from the settlement, I trust), where it was left until it exploded from the internal accumulation of decay gasses. I do not know the inside-view reasoning behind this, but it was surely as convincing for those who adhered to the custom as is, for us, our own reasoning for our own funeral procedures.

RITUALIZATION

People can feel deeply that a certain way of disposing of the cadaver of a deceased person is the only right way, and that any deviation (except, perhaps, towards greater pomp) is a sin against the survivors, against the soul of the deceased, or against the gods. Probably the feeling comes first, the justification for the protocol later as a rationalization. The bereaved are numbed by shock and grief, and often by fear at the reminder of their own mortality. A prescribed routine makes it possible for them to be preoccupied for a while with necessary small tasks, and this wards off whatever rash random acts or thoughts they might otherwise yield to. The function of funereal ritual is the function of all ritual: it sharply reduces unpredictability and thus relieves people of the emotional burden of making decisions.

Thus it comes about that in Western society we bury our great ones with barbaric brouhaha (think of the state funerals for Sir Winston Churchill and for former president Dwight D. Eisenhower), and feel a twinge of conscience if we fail to provide a minimum "decent burial" in potter's field for the most insignificant tramp or pauper. Thus, also, it comes about that the disposal of a cadaver can play a part in power struggles and form a convincing ingredient in works of dramatic art. The *Antigone* of Sophocles turns on Antigone's determination to give her brother Polyneices, fallen in heroic combat, proper burial, flouting the command of her uncle Creon, king of Thebes, that the corpse be left on the battlefield to be gnawed by dogs. The tragedy lies in that each of the two is acting from the purest and most unselfish of motives.

THE SOUL ✂ Ritualization of the disposal of a cadaver stems, we have seen, from the emotional need for fixed protocol in a time of numbness. The rationalization for the ritual, however, arises from the soul doctrine in the version it takes in the particular community—especially from imperfections in that doctrine. Were the "person" identified completely with the soul, and were the severance of soul and body taken to be absolute and irreversible, then the ritual could deal with other things and the body could be disposed of in whatever way was most practical.

This is not the prevailing custom in any known community of the ethnographic present. Somehow, shreds of the personality of the deceased adhere to his cadaver. This must be older than the soul doctrine, and the doctrine, even in the hands of powerful organized religions, has never completely extirpated it. Often enough, no effort to do so is made. Instead, the pre-soul view is given some sort of position alongside the soul doctrine. For example, in the Christian sacrament, it is held by some that the consecration of the bread and wine transforms them literally into the flesh and blood of Christ, so that it is literally by ritual cannibalism that the suppliants receive their purification (compare the eating of the heart of a slain enemy to inherit his courage: p. 250).

CLASS DIFFERENCES

Some men are more powerful or important than others; so, also, are their souls and cadavers. Antigone and Creon quarreled over the corpse of a hero. Neither gave a fig about the nearby corpses of plebeian pages and shield-bearers. A ruler may be so powerful that his soul will survive indefinitely after death while the souls of commoners, if they have any, are thought slowly to fade away. Eventually, perhaps only after thousands of years, the soul of the ruler may wish to revisit this world. Survivors must make this possible or run the risk of vengeance from heaven. So the body of the pharaoh was mummified and placed in a vast, secure tomb surrounded by all the splendor to which he was accustomed, that when he chose to reawaken he would find himself in a fitting environment. Belief in a general "resurrection of the body," held by various segments in the history of the West, is a democratization of this special dogma for the charismatic leader.

CONTINUING OBLIGATIONS

Apart from the impact of the soul doctrine on what survivors do about a cadaver, a funeral often initiates a long series of obligations of some of the survivors towards the departed soul itself. The manifestation of these obligations tends to be shaped by the prevalent household pattern. In traditional China, the rhythms of everyday life were punctuated by periodic visits to the household shrine, where the living members of the household worshiped the deceased ancestors of the male lineage; this was a compulsory manifestation of filial piety. In South Asia, ceremonial obligations to one's mother do not cease upon her death. In the Judeo-Christian tradition you continue (ideally) to honor your father and your mother as long as *you* live: you visit the cemetery once a month or once a year and put flowers on their graves; you pray for their souls or hire specialists to do so in your stead. Fortunately, as the generations pass and more and more deceased ancestors accumulate, the distant ones are permitted to merge together into an honorable blur that can be respected all at once; otherwise we should have so many beads to count in our memorial devotions that there would be no time for anything else.

COMMON SOUL THEMES

The soul doctrine takes enough varied forms to fill another giant wing of that ethnographic museum we mentioned earlier. No two communities hold absolutely identical views, and often enough factions within a community favor conflicting doctrines. Yet a number of themes are widespread.

Perhaps the most familiar to us is the notion of reward or punishment in the afterlife for conduct in this world—including the extreme punishment of extinction or, in other inside views, the extreme punishment of not being allowed to attain total oblivion. In a civil society a belief of this sort can afford an excellent instrument of social control (p. 583).

Another theme is the belief that the soul of a dead person can communicate with the living, at least under certain conditions.

Somewhat more vague is the assumption that a departed soul can watch over a living person and influence his life in one way or another. This is often tied to a fear that the soul even of a dead comrade can become inimical and dangerous, perhaps also that no efforts of the survivors can completely forestall the possibility.

A fourth theme is the theory of reincarnation, held in some communities to be inevitable for all, by others (e.g., the Menomini) to be sporadic, and considered desirable by some, a crashing bore by others.

Honoring the Dead

The soul doctrine and attitudes towards the dead arose together, and yet are separable.

For the past century or so in Western society, there have been individuals who reject the notion that the soul survives the body at death but who cling to the view that there is some sort of nonmaterial entity that animates the living body and is the seat of awareness and will. Usually they call this "mind" rather than "soul"; but the essence of soul-body or mind-matter dualism is retained.

Today there are people who not only reject any theory of a nonmaterial soul or mind but consider such beliefs insidiously dangerous to human welfare. Yet a scholar of this persuasion does not hesitate to dedicate a book to the memory of the master at whose knees he acquired the persuasion! Why should he? A change of intellectual convictions is one thing. An abandonment of the reverence and love we feel for some of our fellows, even after they have died, would be quite another: it would be a rejection of a precious heritage from millions of years of primate sociality and tens of thousands of years of humanness.

THE ESTATE ✖ The estate of the deceased consists, in any community, of everything that was regarded as his property before he died. We have discussed the nature of property (chapter 11); hence we know that the estate will include intimate possessions and may also include loose ones. Also, in general it will include both material commodities and nonmaterial rights of access or use. Among the latter are the prerogatives of occupying certain roles; these we set aside for separate treatment (p. 257).

The property does not all vanish upon its owner's death. It must be redistributed or discarded. Here conflicts of interest can come into active play, and quandaries can be minimized only by carefully established and well understood policies. Every ongoing community has such policies; in every ongoing community they occasionally break down, so that some sort of litigation ensues.

It would be helpful as background if we could know something of estate policies very early in human history, after the development of the three-way contrast among intimate possessions, loose possessions, and nonpossessions (p. 145), but before the invention of the soul. Think of Og, the intrepid hunter, whose sole material possessions are his breechclout and his spear, and who has finally been bested by a quarry too cagey for him. His band will abandon him or throw him away as soon as they are sure he is dead. By him lies his spear, intact, and around his middle his breechclout still clings. I find it plausible to suppose that Og's comrades may identify these items of terribly intimate property so closely with Og himself that they treat them as part of his carcass. On the other hand, a good spear may represent an investment of many hours of skilled craftsmanship, and so may a good breechclout. It is therefore equally plausible that Og's band will recover them, if they can, for someone else to use.

However this may actually have been, when our ancestors grew souls things changed because a property-owner need not vacate all his property rights when he dies. His soul is one of the interested parties in the disposal of the estate, a fact to be considered both by established policies and in litigation.

PROPERTY-DESTRUCTION

The custom of burying or burning some of the intimate possessions of a deceased person along with his cadaver, or of destroying the possessions in some other fashion so that they cannot be reused, is exceedingly common. Funereal destruction of property was characteristic of most of the tribes of western North America in late aboriginal days; it reached a peak on the Northwest Coast in the form of the "funeral potlatch," which may possibly be the germ from which the other potlatch customs of such tribes as the Kwakiutl grew.[3] But we do this ourselves, in Western society. A body is buried (or, infrequently, cremated) in the fine clothes in which it has been displayed for mourning and at the funeral. The heirs can go broke if they invest in an elegant casket and coffin and then fail to recover the outlay from their share of the estate.

The explanation offered for the funereal destruction of property varies widely. Often it strikes an outsider as no explanation at all, just as comforting words that help the bereaved feel they are doing the "right thing." Given the soul doctrine, a deeper explanation sometimes hinted at, if not stated exactly as we are about to state it, is that the objects to be destroyed also have souls—functional equivalents that can survive in the spirit world—to which the soul of the deceased has title but which he cannot obtain unless the physical objects are "killed" in an appropriate way.

This reasoning can lead to almost catastrophic results in some communities when the deceased is a sufficiently powerful figure. Slaves or prisoners may be slaughtered

---

[3]A potlatch was a party to which a great family invited another, and at which the hosts boasted of their wealth by destroying material property or certain symbols thereof. The guests were obliged to return the invitation and destroy even more stuff, or lose status.

to supply his soul with a suitable retinue; a wife may be strangled (Fiji) or burned alive on her husband's funeral pyre (*satī*, South Asia) so that she will not be parted from him.

PROPERTY-INHERITANCE

If there is anything left over when the soul of the departed has been provided for, this residue is distributed according to the customs of the particular community.

In a civil society the government takes its share in the form of death dues, and may legally regulate the disposal of the rest; often the government's claim outranks even that of the deceased's soul.

In a tribal society there are no death dues, but habits may be so firmly fixed that the heirs have little option. For that matter, in many a tribal society the residue is so small that there is nothing to quarrel about—the survivors are much more concerned with who will take over the dead person's duties than with who will inherit his material possessions, and the latter may be determined by the answer to the former.

In either civil or tribal society, the deceased may be allowed more option than the survivors, provided he makes his will clearly known before he dies. Or, believing that he is about to die, a property-owner may distribute things as outright gifts while he is still alive (that is one way to circumvent inheritance taxes).

ADVANCE ARRANGEMENTS

Rules often bestow certain things or prerogatives on an heir at his own birth, or at some subsequent crucial transition, rather than upon someone else's death. Conventions about this are rules of inheritance insofar as they govern the passing-down of property (of one sort or another) from generation to generation.

In any community, a child at birth is given a name. Often this name is later changed, or further names are acquired. Quite generally, the names are viewed as personal property. Sometimes, if a powerful person has or takes a certain name, no one else in the community is allowed to have it; in fact, if the name is a word that also means something else (cf. p. 23), people may be compelled to abandon that word in its everyday meaning and resort to some paraphrase. In traditional Jewish circles, a child should be given the name of a deceased ancestor (partly in the ancestor's honor, partly because the ancestor no longer needs it); but if for some reason this is not done, at least the child must not be given the name of a living relative. In societies with kin-based lineages or clans, lineage or clan affiliation is a birthright, not something inherited upon a predecessor's death. In our society, each individual inherits his surname from his father upon his own birth; a woman then inherits an additional surname from her husband upon marriage.[4]

---

[4]Western surnames in part reflect clan organization in earlier stages in the history of Europe—but not altogether. Iceland retains a practice formerly general among the Germanic tribes: John son of William is 'John William's-son' and Mary daughter of William is 'Mary William's-daughter'; in the next generation the record of William is gone. Some of our surnames were formerly patronymics of this sort.

Impact of Household Pattern

Not unexpectedly, inheritance customs are affected by the household pattern. In traditional China a deceased person who was not the head of a household would leave little property worth fussing about, and when the head of a household died his heir was simply his successor: any disagreement about the former was at the same time an argument about the latter. Among the Hopi (p. 221), houses were built by men, but inherited by women from women.

Heirs within a household or family are almost everywhere more likely than an heir from outside (other than a government). Our American legend of inheriting a fortune from a rich uncle one has never met is based on an event that actually happens only once in a coon's age, yet reflects our general feeling that one would rather leave what one has to distant relatives than to complete strangers.

✖ The members of a family or a community may feel very vividly the hovering presence of the souls of the recently departed, but everyone understands that there are some things a disembodied soul cannot do. A dead mother cannot suckle her infant. A deceased ancestor may offer benediction and spiritual guidance, but he cannot plow a field. The things a person can do and is expected to do while he is alive constitute his roles; those which he can no longer do after he dies are vacated roles. If the vacated roles are a privilege, someone living covets them. If they are necessary to the life of the community, someone still living must assume them.

THE VACATED ROLES

A society always has customs about such things, and we have already had examples: the levirate, the sororate, and sororal polygyny (p. 169); standing provisions for adoption (p. 165); the fact that the child of a specialist—a medicine man, a cobbler, a wainwright—is almost universally trained to follow in parental footsteps (p. 209). More generally, the whole apparatus of kin-based groupings, of lineages and clans and kindreds of all sorts, is a human response to the absolute need of a social animal for community continuity in the face of the inevitable slow turnover of personnel.

It is significant that the transmission of vacated roles to heirs outside the household and family is most frequent exactly in the society in which the household is itself most transitory: our own. The son of a restaurant owner may take over on his father's retirement or death; the son of an attorney may go to law school and join his father's firm; but for each member of our society who does this there are many whose adult roles are completely divorced from those of their parents. Roles of these sorts have become loose property: the heir to a role can sell it, if he so desires, and use the proceeds to enhance the completely different role he has chosen for himself.

21

✖

CRISIS AND CREATIVITY

GENIUS

His eyes see colors other eyes don't see
Between our red and yellow, green and blue;
But when he paints then we can see them too.

His ears hear sounds to which our ears are stone.
But when he orchestrates he pulls them free
And makes them audible to you and me.

Where there's no spire he sees a spire aspiring.
He shapes the earth until the shape has grown
And then his dream is one we make our own.

She felt a kind of twinge we never knew;
She molded it in words with care untiring,
Then kilned it in a drawer for patient firing.

I, too, am deftly pointing. Go! Why linger
Stupidly staring at my upraised finger?

Human behavior is in part automatic response, in part random, and in part goal-directed. Most of our goals derive from the traditional and familiar rather than from the new and strange. The ratio of goal-directed acts to automatic or random responses is much greater for us than for other animals, so that, as seen from outside, human behavior is much less predictable. No other species manifests nearly so wide a variety of conduct and goals from one community to another as we do.

In all communities, people in quandaries make decisions, or else procrastinate until the decision is taken out of their hands. Little quandaries produce little decisions; big quandaries produce big ones. Decisions are conditioned by what people think they want and by what they think they can do about getting it: that is, by their scheduling. The consequence of their action—or inaction—may be what they thought they wanted, or may deviate from it in one or another direction. Either way, the state resulting from the action differs from the state that led to the action, and the difference is distinctive (p. 46) because otherwise there would have been no change of state (p. 229).

From an inside view, it is often anticipated that eventually a state will be reached identical with some earlier one, so that community life proceeds in various sorts of interlocked cycles, such as a diurnal cycle, a seasonal cycle, a life cycle. But from the outside view, which affords a panorama of the restive biosphere of which any community is a part, and often enough in retrospect from an inside view, it is seen that no subsequent state ever exactly replicates an antecedent one. Conditions and expectations are at least a little different, so that scheduling is never quite what it was before.

We know what a crisis is (p. 248): any big and serious quandary in the life of a community. Certain types of crisis are bound to recur from time to time. The members of the community know about these—for example, about death—and through experience have accumulated a set of contingently scheduled ways of trying to handle any crisis of the type when it does arise. This reduces the quandary without necessarily altogether eliminating it. Certain types of crisis, also, have slow onsets, or, as it were, cast their shadows before: people can therefore plan ahead, or take advance action, again reducing the indecision when the critical state is finally reached.

At the extreme, however, a crisis may be so totally unexpected or so drastic that no preparation for it was possible. A crisis of this extreme kind is a *disaster.* Human and prehuman history has never been free from unpredictable disasters of nonhuman origin—earthquake, volcanic eruption, storm, fire, flood, drouth, pestilence, famine; repeatedly they have swept whole communities into extinction, though—so far—the species as a whole survives. If a disaster completely destroys a community there is no quandary because there is no one to be in one. But if it merely tears a community to shreds, then the remnants can sometimes pull themselves together and work out some new plan of existence.

In this chapter we shall first see what survivors have sometimes been able to do in the wake of disaster. This is revealing because it is in that context that the sharpest demands are placed on human ingenuity.

However, that is not all there is to the matter. We shall therefore complete the chapter with a more general treatment of the human "creative impulse."

DISASTER AND RECONSTRUCTION

× In earlier chapters we have spoken at times as though every member of our species lived always within the matrix of a stable, firmly established culture.

This was largely the case through the long period of human history in which our forebears were hunters-gatherers organized into small bands. But in the last six or eight thousand years, in increasingly large parts of the world, it has been otherwise. Individuals have been wrested from their natal environments and forced into menial positions in alien societies. Whole tribes have been captured and scattered into the fabric of the society of their captors, where they and their descendants, if any, have typically been denied most of the privileges the captors were in the habit of according one another. Or conquered peoples have been left where they were, but forced to work for the benefit of their masters rather than for their own.

SLAVES AND FELLAHIN.   The more detailed history of these developments will occupy us in Part Two. Here we need to note certain general points. The ultimate cause was agriculture. Until the very recent rise of mechanized farming, crop-raising demanded backbreaking labor and was demeaning to the human spirit. People avoided it if they could. With rare exceptions, those unable to escape it were either slaves or else free men with what has been called the "fellahin mentality."

From the point of view of those in power, the latter are better than the former. One reason is that it is really quite difficult for almost anyone (obviously there are exceptions) to engage in systematic and prolonged brutalization of any of his fellow human beings. Slaveholders have had to indulge in all sorts of fancy rationalizations. For another, slavery is dangerous. The slave retains, as the fellah does not, the virility to hate what he is forced to do and be. A slaveholding society is a perpetual armed camp, because with embarrassing frequency the slaves can tolerate their lot no longer and prefer to rebel, even at the risk of almost certain death. Fellahin, on the other hand, are kept in check by their own inside view: they assume that their pattern of toil from dawn to dusk is the only decent thing, the key to the kingdom of heaven; their resentment is directed not towards their (often unrecognized) masters but towards scapegoats; if they look to something different and better it is as a reward in the next life for good behavior in this one.

Between slavery and fellahship as we have described them there are endless intergradations, and some of these have had separate labels (e.g., the "serfs" of the European feudal period). However, legalistic definitions and terms are beside the point for our purposes, because they necessarily fail to be valid cross-culturally. Thus, the fact that some people classed legally as "slaves" (*servī*) in ancient Rome were better off than most "free" Romans is unimportant: the *principal* function of slaves in Rome was to do difficult, dull, or dangerous things their masters wanted done but would not or could not do themselves.

THE DIREST DISASTER.   The worst disaster that can overtake an individual is to be forcibly removed from the role of free participant in his familiar natal society to that of menial slave in another. Throughout the history of slavery there have been some who refused to accept this fate. Most of the rebels have simply met with early and nasty deaths. A few have managed to escape and to establish communities of their own, usually in hostile environments because only such places afforded sanctuary.

Episodes of this sort are the most extreme examples of reconstruction in the wake of disaster, and bear the most eloquent testimony of human creativity. It is a pity that our evidence for them is so scant, but in the nature of the case it must be. Nevertheless, we shall describe here, as best we can, one example: the Maroons of Jamaica.

THE SETTING

Off the coast of Venezuela a submarine mountain range stretches north, its higher peaks piercing the surface to form the Lesser Antilles. It then curves to the west, through Puerto Rico and into Santo Domingo, where it splits, a more northerly continuation forming Cuba and approaching the tip of Yucatán, a more southerly

FIGURE 21-1. The Antilles. (Drawing courtesy of Karen Allaben.)

ridge swinging towards Honduras and emerging from the sea, except for scattered shoals, only as Jamaica (see Figures 21-1 and 21-2).

This island is 145 miles long, 51 miles across (north to south) at the widest; the total area is 4411 square miles. The coastal plain is narrow except in the south and southeast. The hinterland is mountainous. Almost half the area is 1000 feet or more above sea level, and in the northeast there are peaks rising to more than 7000 feet. The rest of the highlands is limestone plateau, with a few smooth areas but mainly broken up in an extreme fashion by ridges and potholes. The temperature in the southeastern coastal plain averages 74 to 86°F; in the mountains, 39 to 45°F, cold enough to be very uncomfortable at night if one lacks adequate shelter or clothing. Rainfall is heaviest in May and June and in October and November, and there is no real dry season. The rain is carried off by dozens of short rivers, few of them navigable, and by underground drainage. The hurricanes that are born far out in the Atlantic usually pass Jamaica on one side or the other—but not always.

Because the environment is tropical, biological variety is great; because it is insular, many species and even a few genera are found nowhere else. But this diversity is

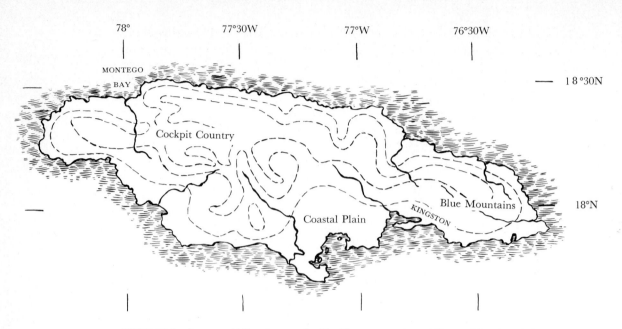

FIGURE 21-2. Jamaica. (After the map in *The Gleaner geography and history of Jamaica*, 1967.)

of plants, invertebrates, fresh-water fishes, amphibians, reptiles, and birds. The only land mammals to reach Jamaica before man arrived were twenty species of bats and a "cony" (genus *Geocapromys,* a rodent with South American affinities).

THE ARRIVAL OF MAN. Man arrived, we do not know just when, from South America, whence he had migrated in stout canoes from island to island along the line of the Lesser and Greater Antilles. There is evidence for a number of successive migratory waves along this route, but possibly only one, and that one relatively recent, made it all the way to Jamaica. In 1494 the first European visitors found it thickly settled by Subtainos (perhaps as many as 60,000 of them), whose language was of the Arawakan family. Other languages of this family were or are spoken in scattered parts of the West Indies and of the Orinoco and Amazon basins of northeastern South America.

THE ARRIVAL OF EUROPEANS. The first European visitors were the party of the first of the conquistadores, the émigré Spaniard (possibly in origin a Spanish Jew) from Genoa, Cristóbal Colón. Columbus, as we now call him, may have been drawn on in part by a thirst for knowledge, but what the Spanish Crown was after was gold and silver, considered then the only respectable form of national wealth. Thanks to a supernova in our part of the Home Galaxy some six to ten thousand million years ago (p. 317), it was possible for an inside view to incorporate this folly. The experts who had accompanied Columbus said there were no such minerals in Jamaica. Just the same, in 1509 Spaniards arrived, settled in, and started to search. By the time they became convinced that Columbus's experts had been right, they had hit on another use for the island: it was an excellent place for raising food to supply the

Spanish invaders of the mainland, whose quest for respectable wealth was working out better. They brought in seed and planted crops; they imported European domestic animals, herding some but turning hogs loose to root for themselves and multiply so that they could be hunted down when needed for pork. They also brought in mice, rats, and assorted Old World microbes, but not on purpose.

It must not be thought that the few thousand Spaniards did all this work of mining and farming themselves. They made the Subtainos do it. The Indians didn't like it, but the Spanish held the power so they had no alternative except to die. That they did, in great numbers, from overwork, starvation, European diseases for which they had no inherited resistance (cf. p. 432), and outright suicide from hopelessness. In a century only a hundred or so of them were left.

THE ARRIVAL OF AFRICANS.   The Spanish would have had to quit long before that except that there was another source of manpower: Africa.

By the sixteenth century slavery *within* sub-Saharan Africa was an old story: petty kingdoms quarreled and fought, and prisoners of war were put to work at unpleasant tasks. A systematic exportation of Africans to be slaves elsewhere had arisen at latest by the tenth century, with Arabs as the traders and chief consumers, though some of these transported Africans got to Europe: a sprinkling of them were working alongside slaves of other origins in the Italian city-states of the thirteenth century, and by 1300 African labor worked the plantations of Cyprus.

The first African slaves in western Europe (unless the Moors in Spain had had some) were imported in 1444 by Portuguese sea captains; they had been acquired in northern Africa in exchange for captive Moors. Thereafter the Portuguese established slave-trading posts on the Guinea Coast. The economy of the Iberian Peninsula had little use for slave labor, and the imported Africans faded away before long into the general peasant population.

In overseas territories of colonial exploitation the story was different. The peasants of the peninsula could not be shipped abroad as farmers and laborers because they were needed at home to raise food. Three Africans were imported into Jamaica by Juan de Esquivel, its first governor. Then, as the Subtainos vanished, slaves from west Africa were brought in to replace them. Either the slaves or the slavers brought along some other west African things, particularly plants and seeds. Many trees that flourish in Jamaica today are of west African origin: among these is the akee (*Blighia sapida*), a tree whose fruit, poisonous when underripe or overripe, is nourishing when properly collected and plays a part in the excellent Jamaican "national dish," codfish and akee.

The slaves came from many different tribes, but a considerable proportion were Ashanti (p. 183) and Yoruba from the Gold Coast, and Ibo and Fanti from Nigeria. They were shuffled in transit. A slave in Jamaica (or, in due time, elsewhere in the New World) typically found himself laboring in the company of fellow slaves of different cultural and linguistic backgrounds, with an overseer whose culture was even more strikingly alien. They had to communicate with their bosses and with one another, at first, in a thin pidginized Portuguese or Spanish (see fn. 6, p. 197), for they had no other language in common. As children were born and raised in the slave population, this was the language they learned, and in which they picked up whatever shreds and tatters of west African tribal lore their mothers could recall. But there was a constant thin trickle of new imports from Africa, to reinforce the fading tradition.

THE BRITISH.   The seventeenth century in Europe was a period of massive struggle between Spain and England, and the conflict extended to the Caribbean. The British seized Jamaica from the Spanish in 1655, and expelled the last of the Spaniards in 1660. Such Africans as stayed on thus had to start replacing their creolized Spanish by some sort of English.

Britain's exploitation was different. For a while the island served as a haven for the privateers who preyed on Spanish shipping. Various tropical crops were coming to be known and wanted in Europe, and the British established plantations in Jamaica to raise them. This meant a need for more slaves. In 1672—just when the first French Jesuits were at their ill-fated work among the Menomini, far away through the wilderness to the north—there were approximately 70 sugar refineries, 60 indigo mills, and 60 cacao mills in Jamaica, working full time to supply the European demand, and all manned, like the plantations, by slaves. In that same year the Royal African Company was founded, with a monopoly on the English slave trade. As Britain opened up more and more areas of the New World, Kingston (on Jamaica's southeast coast) became a major slave market: the Royal African Company brought its wares there for resale to consumers or retailers.

Judging matters in the impersonal economic terms considered relevant in Europe at the time, Jamaica can be said to have reached the zenith of its "prosperity" about 1800. Coffee and sugar had become the major export crops, and 300,000 slaves were working the fields and the mills.

Thereafter matters went downhill. The slave trade was abolished in 1807: no more replacements from Africa. In 1833 slavery was outlawed throughout the British empire, the law to take full effect after a five-year period of "training" for freedom. The cost of labor mounted. In 1846 Parliament abolished a tariff which theretofore had favored England's colonial sugar producers over other sources. The planters were impoverished. They had few jobs to offer their former slaves, nor did the exslaves in general want to take those few. The import of labor from India was authorized a decade or so later, and a railway was built to help get produce to the coast, but neither helped much. Freed of the burden of working themselves into early graves for someone else's profit, the population increased, and reverted largely to a subsistence and local-market economy.

In the mid twentieth century, finally, things got something of a new start from the discovery and exploitation of enormous sources of bauxite (Jamaica has the world's greatest known reserves of this rich source of aluminum) and later, in a smaller way, from a rise of tourism. In 1960 the population stood at 1,609,814, of which three fourths were classed officially as Negroes (that is, individuals of largely sub-Saharan African ancestry), 15% as of mixed descent, a handful as Asian Indians and as Chinese, and 18,000 as Europeans. On 6 August 1962 Jamaica became an independent member of the British Commonwealth.

The Maroons

ORIGINS. The Spaniards' treatment, first of the Subtainos and then of Africans, was not particularly harsh as such things go. They were callous rather than intentionally cruel. They belonged to a hierarchically organized civil society in which everyone assumed that some people are superior to others, and in which those in any station, high or low, were supposed to perform their tasks and accept their lot. The church reinforced this by holding out the promise of heavenly reward for all who behaved themselves, hellish punishment for those who did not, thus generating the fellahin mentality wholesale.

But in all this there was no trace of the notion of *racial* superiority.[1] They made the Subtainos and the Africans work hard not because they despised people with darker skins and different facial contours, but because in their world view that was what peasants were for. The Subtainos disappeared, and the Africans did not, for three reasons: (1) the Africans brought with them an inherited immunity to Old World diseases which ravaged the Subtainos (whose ancestors had not been in the Old World for at least 25,000 years); (2) the Africans had some tradition of submitting to slavery, or of seeming to and resisting it in subtle ways that had some chance of success; and (3) the Subtainos could be replenished only through natural increase within Jamaica, whereas the supply of fresh Africans was seemingly inexhaustible.

From the very beginning, some slaves rebelled and tried to escape. There was no "submarine seaway" to sneak them off the island, comparable to the underground railway established by abolitionists in the years prior to the American War of the Northern Revolution. The Spanish had abandoned the high country, agriculturally unrewarding, as soon as they were convinced it held no valuable ores. The only way to flee was to brave the unknown terrors of the highlands, where the difficulty of pursuit and recapture was matched by the uncertainty of finding food and other bare necessities of life.

Dozens or hundreds of runaways must have failed. A few of the stalwart and lucky—mainly adult males—succeeded, and in due time banded together in hidden and hardly accessible spots. Some Subtainos may have gone along or joined them, including perhaps a scattering of Subtaino women.

When the runaways reached the point of being able to work together, they began raiding the farms and ranches of the lowlands for food and equipment, and liberated

[1] The human populations of sub-Saharan Africa were genetically as diverse as any other set of human populations in an area of comparable size, but they did share shades of skin color much darker than those common in Europe. The Portuguese and Spanish slavers simply lumped them all together in terms of this common characteristic and called them *Negros* 'black ones', a term of no necessary opprobrium at the time.

Snobbishness based on (a false theory of) race is rare in human history. It is attested mainly (1) in northern China before the Manchu dynasty, and (2) among the fair-skinned speakers of Germanic languages in northern Europe, including England and its overseas extensions, in recent centuries. North Europeans were developing certain egalitarian views; by deciding that "Negroes" were not really quite human, they were able to rationalize their treatment of them. The Spanish treated African slaves like human beings of low birth; the English treated them like cattle. British antislavery tracts of the eighteenth and early nineteenth centuries read like publicity tracts from the nuttier branches of the Society for the Prevention of Cruelty to Animals.

more women. One source of food in the hills was the wild hogs that by now roamed over the whole island (p. 263). It may be from this that the runaways acquired their epithet *Maroons,* an anglicization of Spanish *morranos* 'hog-hunters'; but another possible source is *cimarrones* 'wild ones'.

HISTORY.   The Maroons received their biggest single influx of reinforcements in 1655–1660, as the British were taking over and kicking the Spaniards out. The Spanish had to leave; they could not take their slaves with them, and saw no reason to bequeath them to their enemies; so they let them go. Forthwith the freed slaves moved to the highlands and joined the by now well established Maroon settlements.

After that there were three separate ingredients in the island's population: the Spanish-speaking Maroons, concentrated in hidden villages in the Blue Mountains of the northeast and in the Cockpit Country of the northwest; the British buccaneers and planters;[2] and new waves of slaves. (Any surviving Subtaino genes had been swamped beyond detectability.) The new slaves were eventually imported from every imaginable part of sub-Saharan Africa, a few perhaps even from Madagascar, as European slavers found they were approaching the end of the once seemingly inexhaustible supply from the Guinea Coast and were forced to spread their activities further afield. These new slaves, of course, had to accommodate as best they could to the English of their masters. That helped make them alien to the Maroons. Yet the latter eventually abandoned Spanish for English, no doubt mainly through the influence of women carried off in their repeated raids of the lowlands. By 1700 the Maroons numbered at least 2000.

The founding fathers of the Maroons were not idealists seeking to establish a Utopian community to show the rest of the world how to live. They did not even consciously seek to establish a community. Their aims were individual survival and a bit of self-determination. The British quickly abandoned as foolhardy any notion of trying to reconquer and reenslave them. Instead, they sought agreements whereby the Maroons would change from raiding to trading. They granted them "amnesty" (a quaint and arrogant British legal term, absurd in the circumstances), in exchange for a pledge that the Maroons would return, for a fee, any runaway slave who came to them for sanctuary or who fell into their hands whilst seeking a hiding place.

Sometimes the Maroons kept the bargain; occasionally they did not. Sometimes the British adhered to their end of it, sometimes not. The peace was an armed truce between enemies neither of which placed any trust in the good faith of the other—and with excellent reason. Many times, the Maroons helped the British quell slave rebellions that might otherwise have overwhelmed them. Withal, the skirmishes between Maroons and British never wholly stopped, and twice assumed such magnitude that the British classed them as "wars," the first ending in 1738, the second in 1796. The latter closed with a shipment of about 600 Maroons from villages near Montego Bay (on the northwest shore) to Nova Scotia, where some were resettled on land purchased for them and whence others were "repatriated" to Sierra Leone; their descendants still retain their identity.

[2]To which group, as is well known, was born, in 1755, Alexander Hamilton, the most aristocratic of the architects of our American republic.

Back in Jamaica, with the abolition of slavery the distinction between Maroon and non-Maroon African began to fade away, the former becoming more peaceable in the measure in which the British lion's local fangs were blunted. Yet, a century later, the Maroons still thought of themselves as different, and their fellow Jamaicans acknowledged this.

Maroon Lifeways

We can recognize three periods in Maroon history: a formative period, ending in 1660; a classic period, terminating in the mid nineteenth century with the abolition of slavery; and a period of dissolution since then as the reasons for separate identity have slowly diminished.

Economy. In the classic period the Maroons made their living as scratch farmers; as gatherers of edible wild plant parts (such as the fruit of the akee: p. 263); as keepers of a few barnyard animals; as hunters of hogs and whatever other small game was to be found (lizards? birds?); as collectors of shellfish and fish from the streams of the Blue Mountains and occasionally from deserted stretches of seacoast when they felt they could go there with safety (the Cockpit Country is largely drained by underground seepage, and so supports little aquatic life); and as bandits. Sometimes they picked up a bit of cash or credit from the return of runaway slaves, and used it to purchase necessities they could not make for themselves, but for the most part such objects were acquired as booty, and the need for them was the major reason for their raids of the lowlands.

Residence pattern. They lived in scattered villages of a few dozen people each. Larger settlements were precluded for two reasons: first, a certain minimum area had to be exploited to supply each individual with enough food; second, a British attack on a larger settlement would have been more disastrous. Later some of the settlements grew larger. Housing was makeshift, assembled from what local building materials (saplings, sticks, grass) were available, and probably much resembled the slave shacks of the lowlands.

Tools and crafts. As slaves, the precursors of the Maroons had grown accustomed to working with European tools and utensils, and had had little or no opportunity to maintain any tradition of African—or of American Indian—craftsmanship. Doubtless the Maroons of the formative period had made emergency use of all sorts of rigged substitutes, manufactured of local raw materials with whatever knives, hatchets, and hammers they had been able to carry off as they escaped or to "liberate" later. But Spanish and British accoutrements were better, and were obtained whenever possible and preserved with care. In the 1940s a visitor to Accompong, a surviving Maroon village in the Cockpit Country, found heavy water jars which she thought were of Spanish style and suspected of having been in use for three or four centuries. At that time the only identifiable items of African or American Indian stylistic source were (1) hammocks, now known in many parts of the world but of Caribbean Indian origin (the word *hammock* is Arawakan), which one elderly man still knew how to braid, and (2) a few musical instruments, increasingly disused.

One of these instruments was called an *abeng,* made from a ruminant's horn by breaking off the tip and cutting a mouthpiece in the side. In the classic period this instrument was used for long-distance communication. Its sound could be heard a long way off—perhaps 25 miles—and by relaying from village to village a message could be sent almost the length of the island in an hour. Thus it was possible for Maroons everywhere to receive advance warning of threatening moves by the British. For communication to be this flexible, there has to be some fairly complicated code known to all but kept from the enemy. One is immediately reminded of west African drum signals: the west African languages are tonal,[3] and by using tuned drums and imitating on them the tonal and rhythmic contours of spoken sentences (with a few stylized conventions) very subtle distinctions of meaning can be maintained. The code is easy to remember because it derives from the language, and inherits its flexibility from that of language. We have no way of knowing that abeng-signaling stemmed from this source. But it may have done; and, if so, this means that some conventionalized knowledge of at least one west African language was maintained by the transplanted Africans of Jamaica for a very long time.

At the opposite extreme from hammocks and musical instruments, our visitor to Accompong in the 1940s found the Maroons living mostly in tiny frame houses, built by carpenters hired from outside.

In the material appurtenances of life, then, we can infer that the Maroons were utilitarian, taking little time to make an artifact attractive as well as efficient, and attaching no sentiment to old-style things when new and better ones could be obtained. This is not surprising; compare the Menomini acceptance of European trade goods (p. 16). We know nothing of Maroon clothing in the classical period, but doubtless it conformed to the inference we have just made.

AFRICAN SURVIVALS.   In other aspects of life, though, they kept more of Africa in the culture they assembled for themselves, and clung to it so tenaciously that it was still obvious to our ethnographically informed visitor of the 1940s.

The Ashanti of west Africa have a large stock of tales about a trickster spider named *Anansi.* The older folks at Accompong in the 1940s still told these stories (about *Nansi,* the name having been truncated and anglicized). This is representative of the kind of information that could be carried across the Atlantic in the heads of the slaves, without any physical apparatus to remind them of it, and that could then be passed down by word of mouth (p. 264). Other retained Africanisms were of the same sort. A dancing tradition was kept, with music to match; later it was supplemented by British folk dancing and the different sort of music required for that.

WORLD VIEW.   The shock of enslavement and transportation ought to administer a thorough drubbing to one's world view. Yet we have all heard (in a vague and inaccurate way) of "voodoo," a West Indian institution of African origin which it is wrong to interpret as a religion, as magic, or as medical practice, because calling it any of these is forcing it into our own categories (p. 129). The Jamaican variety

---

[3]That is, among the differences of sound that serve to keep forms apart (p. 106) are differences of voice pitch. What in our frame of reference sounds like a single word can be two or three, distinguished by pitch or pitch contour and with totally unrelated meanings.

is called *obeah*. Obeah curses have been known to kill people, and obeah blessings to cure them. Our own theories of the lines of causality involved would differ from the obeah theories, but that does not reawaken the dead victims nor render the cured beneficiaries sick again. In the 1940s obeah was on the wane, but for a long time it had existed alongside the Christianity to which most Maroons sooner or later became formal adherents, despite the fact that the Christian view interpreted obeah as a competing religion and frowned on it.

SOCIAL ORGANIZATION reflected African models at least at low size-levels. At higher size-levels, and in terminology, there were indications of European influence. The loose banding-together of the Maroon villages in the classic period was in response to the menace of the British. The strong influence of the head man of a village over many aspects of community life may be African, or may have arisen in Jamaica in response to local exigencies; the term for him, *colonel,* signals the nature of the most extensive kind of contact the Maroons had with the British for many, many decades.

MARRIAGE AND FAMILY.   Earlier (pp. 183 and 220) we noted that a number of West African tribes have households dominated by the brother-sister or sister-sister dyad. It seems likely that many slaves brought to Jamaica came from tribes in which marriage was polygynous and in which women formed the mainstay for household continuity, while husbands (if not brothers) were peripheral. The conditions of slavery, and the fleeting, fleeing ways of the formative period, affected this only in that there was often a considerable shortage of women. "Conversion" to Christianity, with its emphasis on monogamy, had still by the 1940s had no influence except on the terminology of marital and household affairs.

Girls begin to accept sexual intercourse at an early age, often before menarche. There are certain conventions about place and time; otherwise, families object only if they find the particular man undesirable. If pregnancy develops, and comes satisfactorily to term, the father acknowledges the paternity and accepts a measure of economic responsibility for the mother and for the child. We shall invent a term for this and say that the girl and the man have contracted *alpha-marriage.* The children born by a woman in this way are called her *illegitimates*; this looks like an ordinary English word, but in the speech of the Maroons it has totally different connotations from those of the "same" word in our own usage. A woman may bear children in several different alpha-marriages, but apparently she does not participate in two alpha-marriages at the same time.

Later, a man and a woman may enter into what we shall call *beta-marriage.* In this, they take up residence together and either go through a Christian wedding ceremony with accompanying festivities or make it known that they plan to do so as soon as they can afford to. For the woman, beta-marriage supplants any earlier marital connections and precludes, unless her beta-husband dies, any other beta-marriages. The beta-husband accepts his wife's *illegitimates,* if she has any, and takes on a share of economic responsibility for them, though their alpha-fathers may continue to contribute. Beta-marriage is monogamous for the husband too, but he may continue as the husband in one or more alpha-marriages or may contract new ones if he is economically able to. The man calls his beta-offspring his *yard children.*

This arrangement for sexual, familial, and household affairs is not exactly like any known in west Africa, but points of similarity can be discerned alongside points of difference.

MAROONS AND OTHER RURAL JAMAICANS

Some of the points made in the last few paragraphs seem to apply not only to the Maroons but also to the general rural population of Jamaica.

If a practice is now widespread on the island, we can rarely know whether it was shared from the outset, or spread from Maroons to non-Maroons, or vice versa. In marital arrangements, there is a subtle difference, not in practices but in attitudes. The non-Maroons, exposed more directly and continuously to European influence, are aware that only what we above called beta-marriage constitutes marriage in the British legal and Christian sense, and this sometimes troubles them. Some, achieving adequate economic affluence, abandon the old ways altogether in exchange for British colonial middle-class respectability. There is little sign that the Maroons have yet had any such inclination.

SUMMARY

The sketchy portrayal given above could be rendered more graphic by resorting to the techniques of historical fiction, but that would romanticize the Maroons and go beyond the evidence. I have tried to avoid this. Maroon lifeways may not seem very desirable to us. Certainly they lacked some of the amenities of our current civilization, such as organ transplants and TV commercials. But they were as consistent and coherent as the culture of most human communities of the ethnographic present, and probably as fulfilling.

The remarkable thing is that people should be able to pull themselves together and get the business of life going again after having passed through the most terrible hellfires that have ever burned on our planet. Their success should encourage us as we face our own problems, and for the lesson they deserve a niche in the pantheon and a day in the devotional calendar of every lover of human freedom.

BETTER MOUSETRAPS ✖ When the chips are down, ordinary people show that they can perform the labors of Hercules. If we stopped with that, our characterization would be askew. Like the legendary mill that kept grinding out salt whether or not anyone needed it, human beings insist on trying to manifest their ingenuity even when not spurred on by hunger, cold, loneliness, or fear.

THE TWO FACES OF CREATIVITY

A person tries something new for one of two reasons: because he has to, or because he wants to. The *aims* of innovations are thus of two sorts: on the one hand, getting necessary things done despite difficulties; on the other, having fun.

The major *mechanism* of innovation is the same regardless of aim: analogically conditioned trial and error. We described this in some detail for innovative behavior in language (pp. 107–109), and need not repeat.

The *base line* for an innovation is the innovator's personal excerpt of the total heritage of his community, including that segment of the technological base (p. 93) to which he has access. We would not expect a Menomini of the classical period to start inventing the calculus, nor a Maroon to start composing symphonies. By the same token, a present-day middle-class American is not apt to devise a better power pack (p. 21) or a new sort of obeah figurine (p. 268). The cultural setting not only constrains one's analogical point of departure for innovation but also limits what sorts of innovations it will occur to one to try, in either serious or nonserious contexts.

SOCIAL CONSTRAINTS

Furthermore, the cultural setting bears crucially on which innovations may survive and which ones are killed aborning.

This sometimes has unhappy consequences.

One can hardly deny that individuals differ widely as to degree and kind of ingenuity, and that most large and socially important innovations have been the contribution of a small scattered minority, appropriately revered—when their identities are known—as culture heroes; but this is not altogether a matter of inborn differences of capacity.

There are social settings in which the drive towards originality is stifled or is channeled in directions inappropriate for most of those who show it. The "establishment" is conservative (p. 77); the "establishment" does not want anyone to rock the boat. There is rarely an "establishment" in the sense of some willful group of little men who control everything for their own fell purposes. This false personalization of social structure is as misguided as is the common notion that society has nothing at all to do with people (p. 205). But there are social arrangements in which individuals of limited ability occupy positions from which they can base effective decisions on their jealousy of others of possibly greater brilliancy. These arrangements generate *civil serfdom:* people seek mediocre rewards by performing monotonous chores in a minimally acceptable way, and keep their bright ideas, if any, to themselves because they would lose their sinecures if they didn't.

People can even be trained not to have any bright ideas. I have seen the eager eyes of first-graders ready to pounce on and retain every tiniest scrap of information about the world their teacher can show them, and I have seen some of the same children in the vast wasteland of junior high school, their eyes glazed with boredom and suppressed hostility. The bread-and-circuses which keeps our civil serfs docile is *kitsch:* mass-produced pseudo art, depressants disguised as stimulants; pulp and slick fiction written to formula by hacks, hillbilly music with any genuine folk element carefully obliterated, antiintellectual revivalist religion, calendar art, sensational journalism, and the strident amplifications of these in movies, radio, and television.[4]

[4]Even the kitsch artist has to master his craft, and his ingenuity from time to time breaks through the formulaic constraints. By any standards, then, the best of kitsch is better than the poorest of intendedly "serious" art, so that there is no neat boundary between hack work at one extreme and durable masterpieces at the other.

Something akin to civil serfdom can be found in tribal societies, Wherever found, it is the result of a faulty working-out of a kind of control which is in fact vital for community welfare. Human creativity is potentially so great that it does require to be checked and channeled, lest all mutual understandings be swamped and the community disintegrate.

The Best Constraint

The positive form that has been taken by this necessary group monitoring is *pride of craftsmanship.*

When Pericles of Athens was an old man [runs a possibly apocryphal anecdote] he sat sunning himself in front of his house and watching his grandson play in the dust of the street. He said, "What do you want to do when you grow up?" The grandson said, "I want to clean the streets of Athens." "All right," said Pericles; "but see that you clean them as they have never been cleaned before."

A man takes pride in being able to do well something that it is difficult to do at all, and others usually respect him for the achievement. We applaud the performer who can ride a unicycle on a slack wire, though the stunt has no "practical" payoff except entertainment, because we know most of us could not learn to do it. We give kudos to the pathologist who can examine a biopsy sample and tell the physician what it shows. If no one makes an art of garbage and trash collection, that is because in our society we have not realized that this, too, can be done artfully, and we are the worse off for the spot of blindness.

Pride of craftsmanship is so intimately tied to human sociality that it must be as old as the first pebble tools of our hardly-yet-human ancestors. Manufacturing a stone blade or point is no easy task. If you doubt this, go find a pebbly stream bed and try. The artisan of a million years ago had to know his stones by touch and sight as well as a modern cabinetmaker must know his woods or a modern composer his harmony; he had to apply his blows and pressures with the strength and precision of a modern surgeon. Doing something difficult well means a careful apprenticeship to older masters, so that one acquires all the traditional technique and makes it one's own—not in verbal theory, but in precise coordination of eye and hand. Doing something difficult well also means that the tradition incorporates the fun element as well as serious considerations, so that, in general, a chipped flint or a trimmed wooden spear shaft that is merely sharp or straight or strong enough to do its job does not suffice: in addition, it should be *attractive* to one or more of the senses. The fun factor thus blends into utilitarian considerations (much as primate grooming blended into primate sex; p. 67), to generate the aesthetic component of craftsmanship. The aesthetic component then feeds back into nonserious activities to influence games and sports and to give rise to what we in our culture call the arts: dancing, singing, story-telling, carving, painting, and so on. (How these are categorized depends on the inside view of each culture, but all communities have them.)

Pride of craftsmanship is the best available guarantee that the craftsman's products will be socially valuable. At the same time, it insures that the craftsman will be rewarded for his labor in the best way humanly possible. Finally, it certifies that innovations will stem from true expertise, and thus have the best chance of being improvements over older fashions or customs. Even genius can sputter away like a Fourth-of-July sparkler if undisciplined, whereas if monitored by pride of craftsmanship it can light the world.

AN EXEMPLAR. What we have just said has been said many times, best of all, I think, in Richard Wagner's opera *Die Meistersinger von Nürnberg.*

The setting is sixteenth-century Nürnberg in Bavaria, where all enterprises are organized into crafts with masters and apprentices. One of these, organized the same way though it is an avocation rather than a vocation, is the composing and singing of songs. Wagner divides his perception of his own creative mission between two characters. One is Hans Sachs, the master cobbler and high in the council of the master singers, whose knowledge of and reverence for the artistic tradition from which he cannot escape are matched by a sense of humor and by a benign acceptance of any younger person who can. The other is Walther von Stolzing, a journeyman singer who comes to town and becomes a contender for Sach's daughter's hand. Walther demonstrates disciplined creativity in the song he sings to win her, since it departs sharply from the tradition and yet grows forth from it as naturally as a blossom from a bud, spreading its petals wider at each reprise.

Wagner's opera is a powerful statement of the doctrine of pride of craftsmanship and its compatibility with innovation, because from beginning to end it *exemplifies* the very point it is making.

Of all that, Wagner was quite aware. Today we can detect a further relevant symbolism that he doubtless would have denied. Wagner was a culture hero. Like all real culture heroes, he was thoroughly human. He was a colossal egotist, and his personal life was unsavory. Also, like all real culture heroes, he was in most ways a creature of his specific cultural background. He was rabidly anti-Semitic, and almost equally scornful of any other segment of humanity that did not participate fully in what he took to be the mainstream of European civilization. In his setting, some of these distasteful traits may have been essential as releasers of his creative impulse; without them he might have been a hack turning out kitsch. The opera thus teaches a further lesson: our lives are impoverished indeed if we reject the gifts of clay-footed gods.

UNIVERSALITY

There is abundant evidence of not only the antiquity but also the universality of pride of craftsmanship. Opinions (such as Wagner's) to the effect that true creativity is the special prerogative of some restricted sector of our species, or that it demands "civilization" (meaning, presumably, civil society of the Western type) as its backdrop, are quickly given the lie by the most cursory sort of cross-cultural survey.

From the tribal or incipiently civil societies of the ethnographic present we have amazing textiles from aboriginal Peru, basketry from pre-European California, wood carvings from Africa and Oceania, stone carvings from the Eskimo, fishhooks from northern Eurasia, ceramics from Mexico, Middle America, and various parts of the Old World, and many others.

This limited and partial list is confined to the sorts of things that can be collected and displayed in museums, and to examples that impress us because they conform to our own canons of artistic excellence. Sticking to these same criteria, we must add the most striking example of all: the drawings of thirty to twenty thousand years ago that have survived on the walls of caves in France and Spain for us to admire. Experts have argued that the motivation for these drawings must have been "magical" or "religious." These terms are vague (chapter 10), but here beside the point anyway, because it is patent that, whatever the nature of their inside-view theories, the artists who drew the pictures were working with great skill and care.

If we now allow also for artistry in activities that leave no material traces (dancing, singing, and so on) and for pride of craftsmanship guided by canons of excellence other than our own, we begin to get some glimpse of the true depth and breadth of human creativity.

22

✖

THE COMMON DENOMINATOR OF MAN

How much variety has there been in human lifeways? Under what conditions do differences of culture lead to hatred and conflict, and in what circumstances do they yield tolerance and enrichment? What is the common denominator of humanness, shared by all human communities but not with animals of any other species?

These are the sorts of questions we posed for our inquiry in Part One (p. 3).

What we have discovered of the human common denominator—admittedly only an approximation, with various gaps and uncertainties—is summarized in Table 22-1.

TABLE 22-1. Human universals.

SHARED WITH SOME NONHUMAN ANIMALS	PART OF HUMAN HISTORICAL BASE LINE	UNIVERSAL IN ETHNOGRAPHIC PRESENT	
✖	✖	✖	common characteristics of all Vertebrata, all Mammalia, etc.
✖	✖	✖	primary tools
	✖	✖	derived tools
	✖	✖	clothing (or harness)
✖	✖	✖	grooming (of body and hair)
✖	✖	✖	prepared shelter
?	✖	✖	toilet training
	✖	✖	fire-keeping
	widespread	almost universal	fire-making
	widespread	✖	cooking
	?	✖	scheduled mealtimes
✖	✖	✖	food preferences and prejudices
	✖	✖	language
	?	✖	personal names
	?	✖	kinship terminologies based (at most) on the criteria listed on p. 200
	widespread	✖	counting with number words
	?	widespread	favored numbers
	?	✖	some way of keeping track of the passage of time

For completeness, data assembled in earlier displays of the same kind (pp. 154 and 183) are repeated.

Human diversity is just as important as the common features of humanness, but I know of no way to condense our findings on this into a useful résumé.

However, related to diversity is the matter of correlations: that is, which practices in one connection have proved to be compatible with which practices in other connections? There are two points to be made:

(1) Perhaps the more important is for us to recognize how little we know. Our limited knowledge of correlations is mostly a matter of cross-cultural statistics, achieved by leaving out of account details that (from inside views) may well make crucial differences. Emphasis on the husband-wife dyad has coexisted with monogamy and possibly with polygyny (p. 219). Could it exist conjoined to polyandry? Is emphasis on the father-son dyad in the long run compatible with industrialization (p. 246)? Would civil society be possible without agriculture (p. 153, p. 549)? Because of our own cultural predilections we may have strong opinions on these and other such matters, but we have no valid empirical grounds for certainty.

(2) Almost equally vital is that we not get into a false notion of the "whole culture" of a community, comparable to a common false notion about the kind of system a language is (p. 100). Diverse aspects of a community's life typically have

TABLE 22-1. Human universals (*continued*).

SHARED WITH SOME NONHUMAN ANIMALS	PART OF HUMAN HISTORICAL BASE LINE	UNIVERSAL IN ETHNOGRAPHIC PRESENT	
✕	✕	✕	sociality and social structure
✕	✕	✕	sex and age relevant in social structure
✕	✕	✕	age grading
?	?	widespread	rites of passage
✕	✕	often	physical strength relevant in social structure
rare	✕	✕	accumulated information and other factors relevant in social structure
✕	✕	✕	leadership
✕	✕	widespread	male dominance
	✕		males as chief hunters, females as chief gatherers
✕	✕	✕	collective decision-making
	✕	✕	consultation in collective decision-making (dependent on language and its derivatives)
	✕	✕	informal vs. formal consultation
	✕	✕	moderator as type of leader
	✕	✕	band (or its derivatives) ≠ family
	✕	✕	functional social groupings (i.e., clans) not dependent on constant or frequent physical proximity
	widespread		loose groupings of bands into "tribes"

hidden connections, and some of them are strongly functional; but others are merely like the sporadic pervasiveness of a speech habit (p. 100) or of a favored number (p. 138). There is no evidence that everything in a community's way of life must hang together in a neatly patterned consistent whole. People don't live by logic; they live by analogy. Life in any community is full of tendencies to reshape some matters on the pattern of others, but also full of crosscutting analogies that resist such regularizations. The "whole of a culture" can no more be inferred from a part than the "whole of a language" can.

The list of human universals in Table 22-1 has, for most of us, some surprises, both of inclusion and of omission. Man is not quite what we have thought he is. This brings us to our one valid generalizing recommendation: people (in any culture) should struggle to avoid mistaking their own ways of life for basic laws of nature.

Since most readers of this book, like the writer, were nurtured in Western society, it is important in this connection to emphasize those characteristics of our own culture which are *not* universal despite our sometimes strong conviction that they are—or that they should be. The features we are about to list are not all necessarily exclusively Western, but each is absent in one or more communities about whose ways of life we have reliable information. A recognition of the nonuniversality of these familiar features, of the fact that human beings have been able to live honorable and rewarding

TABLE 22-1. Human universals (*continued*).

SHARED WITH SOME NONHUMAN ANIMALS	PART OF HUMAN HISTORICAL BASE LINE	UNIVERSAL IN ETHNOGRAPHIC PRESENT	
	widespread	widespread	war
✗	✗	✗	intimate property vs. nonproperty
	✗	✗	loose property
	✗(?)	✗	inheritance rules
✗	✗	✗	social maternity = physiological maternity
	usually	usually	social paternity = physiological paternity
?(how defined?)	✗	almost universal	marriage
✗	✗	✗	prohibition of mother-son incest
	✗	✗	further incest prohibitions, yielding exogamous groups
	?	widespread	tertiary sexual characteristics devised and exploited
	?	widespread	a single dominant dyad in the household
	?	widespread	one member of dominant dyad male (if not both)
	probably	✗	one member of dominant dyad adult (if not both)

lives without one or another of them, is a giant step towards the sort of cross-cultural sophistication and tolerance that we so desperately need in today's world. Here is the list:

society as something above and beyond individuals; (at the same time, inconsistently) "the establishment" as the result of the conscious machinations of powerful, and probably evil and selfish, men;

morality and justice as impersonal absolutes; the notion that in any category there is a unique "best," whether or not yet attained;

government and the state; the political versus the nonpolitical; law;

legalized and impersonal property relations; land as property; marked and defended boundaries, including national boundaries; fictitious (legal) entities as owners of property;

religion; philosophy; science;

marriage and social fatherhood; the nuclear family as the ideal household; emphasis on the husband-wife tie (and on romantic love, and on sexual frustration as the fount of all emotional troubles); the sanctity of the home and of motherhood; marriage as the only valid setting for sexual expression;

TABLE 22-1. Human universals (*continued*).

SHARED WITH SOME NONHUMAN ANIMALS	PART OF HUMAN HISTORICAL BASE LINE	UNIVERSAL IN ETHNOGRAPHIC PRESENT	
?	✖	✖	dyad conflicts
		✖	transactions in more remote (and larger) social groupings derived analogically, by similarity or contrast, from those in intimate (small) social groupings
?	✖	✖	personality ≠ social role
	✖	✖	personality and social role influence each other
	?	widespread	masking of personality (or personal identity) on crucial public occasions
	?	✖	ascribed vs. achieved status
probably	✖	✖	the state parameters (pp. 230–232)
✖	✖	✖	quandary
?	✖	✖	boredom
✖	✖	✖	sleep
✖(?)	✖	✖	dreaming
?	✖	✖	ritual
✖	✖	✖	play
?	✖	✖	game
	?	✖	joking
?	?	widespread	adventure
✖	✖	✖	affection

the dignity of labor and (in contradiction) the conviction that people are "naturally" lazy; the importance of individual initiative; the inevitability of change and perhaps of "progress"; the (apparently conflicting) opinion that "you can't change human nature."

Until very recently, the average Westerner assumed that all human societies are, or should be, organized about these principles. When shown that some are not, his first response is either that the people who lack them are "savages" who don't count, or that they are benighted and will in time learn, or should be taught, the ways of civilization. The former goes with our cruelty to non-Westerners, as in slavery; the latter governs our Western variety of do-goodism (p. 123), in which the religious, commercial, or military missionary believes that the only way for people in other societies to achieve honor and happiness is for them to become like us.

Only a small step from this brings us to the attitude of those specialists who look hard in other societies for "primitive forms" of our own institutions, and by hook or crook manage to find them. The full realization that a human community simply *doesn't have to have* (for example) any political organization or behavior, comes very hard. But if we are ever to achieve a useful understanding of our fellow man, that is the sort of realization we must attain. Anything less is pinchbeck.

TABLE 22-1. Human universals (*continued*).

SHARED WITH SOME NONHUMAN ANIMALS	PART OF HUMAN HISTORICAL BASE LINE	UNIVERSAL IN ETHNOGRAPHIC PRESENT	
✗	✗	✗	submissiveness
✗	✗	✗	hostility
	✗	✗	a world view
		rare	systematic talking about world view
	probably	✗	world view involving belief in things not directly observed or observable
	✗	✗	curiosity about one's nature (not every individual, but some in every known society)
	?	✗	doing something positive about death
	✗	✗	knowledge of relationship of sickness and death
	widespread	widespread	cherishing the elderly
	✗	✗	care of the ill or injured
	?	widespread	a soul theory
✗	?	widespread	sporadic cannibalism
	?	widespread	culture heroes
?	✗	✗	creativity
	probably	almost universal	pride of craftsmanship
	✗	✗	creative arts of various sorts, always including literature.

23

✕

INTERMEZZO: OF TIME
AND THE RIVER

Pánta rheî 'All is flux' (Heraclitus of
Ephesus, about 500 B.C.)

Throughout man's career most people have been only dimly aware that conditions and ways of life change. A past radically different from the present has been remote and unreal, touched on by origin myths told as much for pleasure as for instruction. Actual changes have been perceived as short-term cyclical ones (p. 150), and when a deviation has been detected people have usually made homeostatic efforts to return matters to a remembered—or misremembered—norm.

But the conditions and ways of life do change, and so do the organisms that do the living. The discovery of this and the gradual establishment of history as science rather than as wish-fulfilling mythopoiesis were achievements of Western society, with at most minor parallels elsewhere; this is one of the good things the West has to offer the rest of humanity.[1] A true sense of history is an essential ingredient in genuine cross-cultural sophistication and understanding.

Why are cyclicities inexact? What are the mechanisms of change?

Our discussion of these matters is inserted here, between Parts One and Two, because it belongs equally with both. It is connected to Part One because change is a reality for all communities, and because different human communities have been affected by, and have dealt with, changing conditions in different ways. It is relevant for the narrative account of Part Two because we cannot hope to understand how things *have* changed—the concrete facts of history—unless we have a grasp of the mechanisms by which they *do* change.

Students of human conduct sometimes search for the "laws of history." *There are none*—except the basic laws of physics, which, by definition, are never violated by human action or by any other sort of event. Remembering this can save us from all manner of metaphysical and teleological traps. But what we need mainly here is not so much those overarching and inviolate principles, approximations to which are to be found in any good textbook of physical science, as the special derivative guises in which they are manifested in the domain of life and in the narrow sector thereof which is the life of our own species.

From chapter 4 we know that (apart from constant or changing features of the inorganic environment) there are two channels for continuity and change in the organic world: the genetic and the traditional. The former is coterminous with life itself. The latter is widespread, but strong only for primates and strongest of all for human beings, where it is reinforced by language and by tools and other artifacts.

[1]Or it can be, if we learn to write history from the total human point of view instead of with a distorting ethnocentric Western bias.

Language is principally traditional (pp. 101–102), but its unique nature renders it subject to certain sorts of change not to be found in other aspects of tradition, human or otherwise. Hence the scope of the following remarks will be sometimes just one, sometimes several at the same time, of the following: genetics, learning, tradition (as a whole), and language.

VARIATION AND SELECTION

We describe variation and selection first in the context in which they were first recognized by investigators; that of genetics.

Genetic Selection

We recall (chapter 4) that organisms typically live in clusters called "populations."[2] Each individual has a set of genes; the total stock of genes of the population is its gene pool. Because of mutations, and for many species also because of the random sorting and recombining of genes involved in bisexual reproduction, it is unusual for two members of a population to have exactly the same set of genes. Ordinarily, then, the gene pool of the population contains greater variety than is found in any one of its members.

Each individual begins its life with a specific allotment of genes. The career of the individual organism is the result of the interplay between the action of its genes and the totality of environmental factors. From the point of view of selection, only one feature of this career is relevant: the organism either reproduces before it dies or it does not. If it reproduces, then some of its genetic material is passed on to new organisms. If it does not reproduce, its genetic material dies with it.

In a given environment, then, genes and gene combinations that increase the probability of successful reproduction tend to spread to more and more of the individuals of a population, while those that militate against reproduction tend to be confined to fewer and fewer, and in time may disappear altogether. Still other genes may be neutral in their bearing on the chances of successful reproduction; whether their incidence in the gene pool increases or diminishes is characterized as *fortuitous*.

What happens if the environment changes or the population migrates? Some genetic features that were formerly advantageous may now be neutral or disadvantageous, and vice versa. The conditions have changed. One of two things happens. If the change is too sudden or drastic, the population becomes extinct. Or it may manage to hang on long enough for selection to adjust the character of the population to meet the new circumstances. If the latter happens, then we say (after the fact) that the population has *adapted.* If we can discern the genes or the genetically monitored features that made the adaptation possible, we say (after the fact) that they had *survival value.*

We have now stated the essence of genetic selection. The mechanism works through individuals, but its relevant impact is to alter the gene pool, and thus the character, of the population. The individual counts only (1) as a temporary carrier of genes,

[2] In our usage (fn. 1, p. 47) we could equally well say "community," except that "population" sounds better in the context of genetics, "community" better when discussing tradition, social structure, and the like.

or, in some cases, (2) as a nonreproducing member of the population whose behavior is such as to increase the probability that other individuals will reproduce.[3]

Furthermore, the relevant impact is a mass statistical one. A particular individual carrying genes with survival value may be destroyed before it has reproduced; a particular individual carrying "bad" genes may survive to pass them on. By and large, however, "good" genes get passed on more than bad ones, simply because, in genetic matters, this circular and after-the-fact definition of "good" and "bad" is the only one possible.

Genetic selection is a powerful mechanism of change because it continues to work over enormously long periods of time, and because *almost all organisms die without reproducing!* (see Box 23-1).

[3]For example, consider the sterile females of a swarm of bees or a nest of ants, without whose activity the queen would die. This is one of numberless twists and turns in cooperative living that exist because selection has brought them about, and that persist because, as of the moment, the conditions of life to which they are successful adaptations continue to pertain.

BOX 23-1.

THE POWER OF DEATH
ALMOST ALL ORGANISMS DIE WITHOUT REPRODUCING!

The female of the ling (*Molva molva,* a fish related to the cod), produces in a lifetime about 28,000,000 eggs. Each can become an organism if fertilized. On the average, only two of this number are fertilized and survive to reproduce in their turn.

A human (*Homo sapiens*) male in the course of a lifetime may ejaculate as many as 400,000,000,000 sperm—each a potential organism, provided it fertilizes an ovum and the zygote develops. But the most prolific kings of Old Testament legend, calling on the cooperation of hundreds of women, produced only scores of children, and most human males father from none to three or four.

There are many familiar illustrations of how fast a single species would increase if all the progeny of a single parent or pair of parents could survive. The illustrations are rendered dramatic by ignoring all curbing factors, such as that the necessary raw materials and energy would in time be exhausted. Here are three examples:

Starting point	Initial mass	Period in which mass would be doubled	Time it would take for the total mass to equal that of	
			Earth	The observable universe
1 pair of elephants	8.7 tons	50 yr	3500 yr	7350 yr
1 pair of houseflies	0.0175 oz	42 hr	163 days	306 days
1 bacterium	0.00000000001 oz	5 min	11 hr	18 hr

In the same vein: if Adam and Eve and all their progeny, starting in Bishop Ussher's 4004 B.C., had heeded the admonition to be fruitful and multiply only at the lazy rate by which each couple would have four children each thirty-eight years, the total mass of humanity in 1967 would have equaled that of the observable universe.

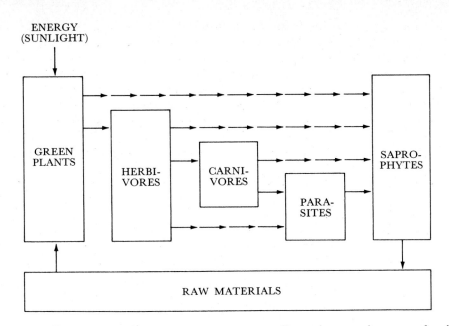

FIGURE 23-2. THE BASIS FOR BALANCE IN AN ECOLOGICAL ZONE. Green plants use the energy of sunlight to synthesize complex organic substances out of the raw materials. Herbivores live by eating green plants. Carnivores live by eating herbivores (some of them also eat green plants, and one another). Parasites of various sorts live on carnivores and herbivores. Saprophytes (mainly bacteria and some fungi) live on the waste matter of other organisms, and on their substance when they die, and return raw materials to the soil, the water, and the air. In this complex process, energy becomes unavailable (entropy increases); the rate at which this happens depends on the exact details, which depend on the number and nature of organisms of particular types. Energy will be "used up" (rendered unavailable) as fast as it is supplied; if at some point in the chain the rate becomes too high, adjustments are inevitable.

SELECTION AND ECOLOGY

Consider a geographical region with fairly sharp boundaries and containing a certain variety of organisms. Such a region is an *ecological zone*; within it, the habitat of organisms of any single type is an ecological *niche*. The zone boundary is a population boundary for any type of organism that lives in the zone. Such boundaries are rarely razor-sharp, but they are definite enough to justify what we say first below, and permeable enough to warrant what we say last.

The life in an ecological zone exists in a rough balance, with certain limits as to how many and how few organisms of any one kind can be tolerated; Figures 23-2 and 23-3 show part of the basis for this. The balance can be tipped by inorganic factors (changes of temperature or of precipitation) or by the immigration or emigration of organisms, or the flow of genes across the boundary, in inappropriate numbers. It is also changed to some extent by any alteration in the gene pool of any included population of one kind of organism, since such a change modifies the environment of all the other organisms in the zone.

The history of life in an ecological zone is thus a series of mutual adjustments, each brought about by selection and each changing the conditions for the further

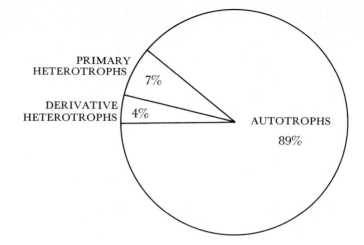

FIGURE 23-3. Ecological balance. In a typical ecological zone the percentages of the total *living mass* of organisms of different kinds are about as shown. Autotrophs are green plants; primary heterotrophs are organisms that live by consuming green plants or their products; derivative heterotrophs are those that live by consuming primary heterotrophs.

The ratios vary around the figures given. Here are figures for (1) a subtropical marine (or littoral) zone, and (2) a temperate damp grassland:

	(1)	(2)
autotrophs	93%	84.6%
primary heterotrophs	4.3%	10.3%
derivative heterotrophs	2.7%	5.1%

(After Keeton 1967.)

workings of selection. Equilibrium is often restored after it has been only slightly disturbed, but sometimes it is not, and the whole life system of the zone goes into a tailspin. Eventually, then, a different balance is established, perhaps only as the zone is reseeded, as it were, from elsewhere.

A single example of disruption and readjustment will do. Many of the ecological zones of the eastern United States were formerly marked by the presence of stands of the American chestnut tree, *Castanea dentata.* This tree supplied food for humans and for various insects, birds, and woodlands mammals, and wood used in great quantity by human carpenters and cabinetmakers. About 1900 a fungus, *Endothia parasitica,* was inadvertently brought to Long Island from the Orient. Fungi, like animals, depend on the products of the metabolism of green plants for their food. In its earlier habitats, *E. parasitica* had achieved a balance with organisms of other species, neither destroying nor being destroyed by them. In the new environment it went wild, thriving particularly on the American chestnut. In less than four decades the tree was virtually wiped out, and the fungus, for lack of food, had also become rare. A scattering of isolated healthy trees showed that, given time, the gene pool of the American chestnut population might have enabled the species to survive the environmental change; but, so far, there is no sign that it will ever be restored to its former abundance. Carpenters and cabinetmakers have had to switch to other woods, and the animals that ate the nuts have had to resort to other foods. The reverberating consequences in individual ecological zones are hardly known, but may in some cases have been extensive.

Our example shows that the boundaries of ecological zones are indeed permeable: we call a boundary a "boundary" only because influences operate across it less frequently than they do within a single zone. There are many ways in which organisms can be carried from one zone to another; human action, the agency in the case of the chestnut blight, is only one. Furthermore, zone boundaries can migrate. Isolation is relative, and always temporary. Change in one region may go on for a considerable time in independence of events elsewhere, but eventually a change anywhere can lead to consequences anywhere else.

Thus it is that the domain of selection, in the final analysis, is not the individual, not the population, not even the ecological zone, but the whole biosphere.

Is Selection a "Law of Nature"?

Selection is not a universal phenomenon in the sense in which, say, the law of gravitation is.[4] As far as we know, it plays no part in the history of galaxies, stars, or planets, and none in the affairs of elementary particles and atoms.

Suppose we have a hundred thousand (or a hundred trillion) absolutely indistinguishable entities of some sort. Each is capable of manifesting either of two kinds of behavior, one of which we will call "continued existence," the other "disappearance." The environmental circumstances are such that 20% of the entities will continue to exist through a particular interval of time, while the remaining 80% will disappear. But since they are absolutely indistinguishable, it can be of absolutely no consequence just which ones survive and which ones vanish. As a concrete example, consider dropping into a quantity of water an amount of table salt 1.25 times the maximum the water can hold in solution. To be sure, highly complicated and specific physicogeometrical facts play a part in determining just which molecules of sodium chloride break into sodium and chlorine ions and which crystals settle to the bottom. But one sodium chloride molecule is like another, one sodium ion is like another, and one chlorine ion is like another.[5] Thus it simply *cannot matter* which 80% of the crystals dissolve and which 20% do not. There is in such a situation no trace of selection.

Selection comes into play only in situations in which, in addition to a clear distinction between continued existence and disappearance, there is some mechanism of *innovation* that yields *diversity*, and some sort of *competition* among the diverse varieties. But this is just to say that *there can be no selection without variation.*

These conditions are met by genes. The process by which life forms are altered through genetic variation and selection is (*organic*) *evolution.*

However, as we shall now see, the conditions are not met *only* by genes.

[4]It is unfortunate that we use the same word "law" in this context and in dealing with certain institutional features of civil societies, because the two meanings in fact are totally unrelated. The source of the confusion is described on p. 517.

[5]To make the case perfect we have to assume identity of all isomers and all isotopes, of both the salt and the water.

SELECTION IN LEARNING AND IN TRADITION

In chapter 4 (pp. 51–55) we outlined the process by which an individual may acquire, through experience, patterns of behavior that are not carried by the genes. Initial trial-and-error efforts towards some goal show a degree of randomness; success reinforces the successful patterns, and failure weakens or extinguishes the unsuccessful ones. We need no paraphrase in the terminology of selection to see that selection operates in learning as it does in genetics except that in learning its domain is the individual.

Since tradition rests on learning, selection also operates here, but in a fashion that once again emphasizes the group rather than the individual. Tradition yields diversity (variation) because the members of a community inherit different sets of genes and different excerpts of the total tradition of their community, and hence come up with differing solutions for the same problems. Given this source of variation, selection then operates at two levels:

(1) The first hurdles a traditional innovation must pass are those of competition with other ways of doing the same thing. It is the interplay of individuals within a community, channeled by its social structure, that in the first instance determines which few innovations survive, which many die aborning. For details in the human case we refer back to Part One, especially chapter 21; below (p. 289) we say a bit more specifically about language.

(2) If a traditional innovation does get established in a community, it may then bear on the community's success or failure in reproduction (consider, for example, a battle between people with firearms and people without). Reproduction does not in itself transmit nongenetic traits, but it is a necessary antecedent—parents cannot pass their skills to offspring if there are no offspring. If a community becomes extinct, both its traditions and its gene pool vanish.

Thus, *relative to reproduction*, changes in tradition, like those in a gene pool, may be either selective or fortuitous (p. 283), and this can change with changing circumstances. Fortuitousness is especially important in the human case. Many trends and episodes in history would be totally incomprehensible if we assumed that all changes in tradition must be selective. For instance, favored numbers (pp. 138–140) cannot be selective, or by now all human communities would favor the same one. Counting often has survival value, but it is wholly immaterial whether a community says *one two three* or *un deux trois* or *yī èr sān* or what have you. What is true of numerals is true of linguistic forms in general: their phonetic shapes do not matter in the slightest as long as their users can keep them apart.

SELECTION AND PURPOSE

Genetic variation and selection are not purposive. There are no feedback circuits, no homeostatic mechanisms by which they could be (pp. 83–85). Organisms cannot plan their breeding to improve their strain; they have no control over mutations; they have no way of foreseeing environmental changes which their descendants may encounter. Perhaps some day this will cease to be so for our own species, but up to now it applies to us as to all other organisms in the world. Genetic variation and selection are as blind as the revolution of the planets about Sun or the crumbling of seashore rock under the impact of pounding waves.

In contrast, purposive or goal-directed behavior can be and actively is involved in learning. Let us speak just of mammals (for convenience of wording, and with no implication that nonmammalian organisms are incapable of learning: p. 85). The "finished" parts of the newborn mammal are chock full of all sorts of interlocking servomechanisms. When the infant mammal is hungry it *seeks* food. The rewards of successful behavior, the rewards that reinforce the circuits for the behavior patterns that led to success, are the fulfillments of purposes. What is more, some of the connections built into the cortex by learning complete the circuitry of new homeostatic mechanisms: a mammal learns *new* purposes.

The development of communicative behavior that links the members of a community together (so that they tend to form a band rather than a congeries: p. 71) implies that a single servomechanism can pass through several individuals; then the collective comportment of a group can be goal-directed. Tradition makes possible the transmission of learned purposes from one individual or group to another. Also, selection in tradition involves goal-directed behavior in that it is in the pursuit of goals that individuals—and, in some cases, cooperating groups of individuals—come up with new things or with possible new ways of doing things. Whether an innovation is accepted by others also depends sometimes (at least in the human case) on an estimate, accurate or inaccurate, of whether it will help one towards some goal.

Despite all the above, the role of purpose in history is very limited.

In the first place, remember that to say the universe contains purpose does not imply that the universe is purposive, any more than to assert that the universe contains telephone poles implies that the universe is a telephone pole. There was no purposive behavior in the universe[6] until Earth spawned life and until genetic variation and selection, operating quite purposelessly, had led to life forms that contain homeostatic mechanisms. In the long run such mechanisms necessarily have survival value—for if an organism's inbuilt purpose is self-destruction, it is not likely to reproduce. Thereafter, the behavior of *individuals* was in part goal-directed. *Collective* purposes appeared only as selection led to certain types of community-formation.

In the second place, not even human history can usefully be characterized as composed of purposes. Of course people plan, individually and in consulting groups. But the consequence of an action is rarely in exact accord with the intent of the actor, and it is the actions and their consequences, not the purposes, that have so far formed the fabric of human history.

✷ We now greatly narrow the domain of our discussion. What we say in this section has no relevance except for our own species, but is of considerable importance for us because of the crucial role of language in making us what we are.

LANGUAGE CHANGE

---

[6]At least not in our immediate neighborhood. Life, or something like it, may have emerged also in the history of various planets of far stars.

The language of every human community changes as time goes by.

Language changes because it is used. The major mechanisms of change are mostly just the major mechanisms of use: borrowing and analogy, as discussed in chapter 8 (but see p. 291 below). The lexicon is altered by borrowings and by analogical or other coinages that catch on and endure. The lexical bases for analogies are thereby modified, which means that the grammar is altered too.

Big changes in a language are slow, and wholly fortuitous relative to the reproductive success or failure of the speakers (p. 288). Big changes are the cumulative results of many little innovations. The latter are adaptive in terms of the immediate context in which they occur, but may then either survive or lose out in competition with other usages. The factors that promote or militate against survival can be itemized:

FACTORS FAVORING SURVIVAL. If a newly coined form is long, complicated, and routine, it merely does its job of transmitting information and is then, like all consultative prose (p. 104), forgotten.

Otherwise, there are two conditions under which an innovation is more likely to survive: (1) it is unobtrusive and follows some familiar pattern, or (2) it fills some need.

(1) If a child or a weary adult says *mans* instead of *men*, it is not apt to spread into general usage. The inherited plural *men*, though irregular, is uttered so frequently that a deviation stands out like a sore thumb. On the other hand, the verb *stride* is fairly rare, and there are probably many people who have never heard its past participle *stridden*. So if someone says *strided*, this regularizing innovation may be picked up. A few centuries ago users of English were accustomed to hearing a good many nouns pluralized in more than one way. Against that backdrop, the innovating regular plurals that have come down to us as *books* and *cows* were unobtrusive, which is why they managed to survive. The earlier plurals, now lost, would currently have become respectively *beech* and *kye*.

(2a) An innovation may fill a need because there is no inherited form with the same meaning. Giving a newborn child a name is an innovation of this sort. When the steamship came to Fiji the Fijians had no word for it, and the borrowing *sitima* afforded them one (p. 119). When tea and algebra reached the English-speaking world, the words *tea* and *algebra* came right along with them. When the first sound films were introduced, people called them *talkies*; it was only somewhat later, when all entertainment films were of the new sort, that the older term *movies* was reinstated and *talkies* fell into disuse.

(2b) The need filled by an innovation may turn on connotations and be that of prestige, real, or imagined. We all tend to imitate the speech, as well as the other mannerisms, of those whom we admire and with whom we should like to identify; we may therefore adopt a new term for something even though we already have an old term with the same denotation.

A version of this accounts for the high rate at which slang becomes obsolete and is replaced by new slang. An ingroup that wants to be exclusive develops various mannerisms to serve as signals of group membership, and some of these are special ways of saying things. If the ingroup is prestigious, those who are not members but would like to be imitate the mannerisms. But as soon as everybody around is freely using a particular catch phrase, that spoils it for its original function and the ingroup has to invent a replacement. Thus it is that in the last decades adolescent middle-class Americans have run through a whole series of special ways of saying 'take one's departure', including *absquatulate, vamoose, scram, beat it, blow, split, cut out*, and many others. Something very similar to this probably accounts for the fact that the technical jargon of such a field as sociology turns over at a rate much greater than that at which significant new findings are made.

OBSOLESCENCE. The lexicon of a single individual changes as some forms are disused and forgotten. I cannot recall the name of the street on which I once lived in Shawnee, Oklahoma; while I lived there the street name was actively in my vocabulary. Sometimes we experience a momentary block on a form we know we have learned, and have to paraphrase (*I want some of those metal things with two projections that you put on the wall near a window to tie the curtain strings around*, because the speaker cannot recall *awning cleat*).

As long as an individual lives, it remains possible that the right concatenation of circumstances will serve to elicit a disused and apparently forgotten form. But for the collective lexicon of a community, a form can be lost beyond all recovery when the last person to have learned it dies.

SOUND CHANGE

We come now to a mechanism of language change that seems to be quite unlike anything in genetics or in nonlanguage aspects of tradition.

Sound change is a continual slow change of habits of pronunciation and hearing, which goes on in every speech community without anyone ever either noticing it or having any control over it. But we can notice its results when we observe that the pronunciations of the "same" forms differ from one dialect of a language to another, and when written records show that a later pronunciation differs from an earlier one. Our modern English word *stone* was pronounced a thousand years ago something like *stawn* or *stahn*; *cow* was pronounced *koo*; *mine* was *meen*; *ear* (on the head) and *ear* (of grain), now identical, were distinct.

The articulatory targets which constitute the elementary signaling units of a language exist only as statistical norms abstracted from actual speech by the central nervous systems of those who use the language. The users control the language so well that they can afford to be careless in their articulation. This, and all manner of accidental factors, play parts in determining the actual articulatory and acoustic shape of specific acts of speech. If there is a drift in some determinate direction of the "shots" (the actual articulatory motions) aimed roughly at a certain target, the target is dragged along in the same direction. The whole set of targets that constitute signaling units may thus slowly migrate.

Since the only function of a sound system is to keep utterances apart (p. 106), there is nothing to impede such a slow migration except the requirement that the system continue to be rich enough to do its job. Most of the time, sound change just moves the targets around a little. But occasionally it happens that two targets move closer together and merge into one. Some forms that earlier sounded different may thus come to sound the same: for example, *ear* and *ear*. Conversely, sometimes a single target splits into two. But this requires special conditions: the *articulatory environments* for the two directions of drift must be different. Thus, English *p* could change in one way in *pin, pick*, another way in *pan, pack*; but not one way in the nouns *pin, pick* and a different way in the verbs *pin, pick*, since that is not a difference of articulatory environment.

When sound change has led to a restructuring of a sound system, the result is *irreversible*. It is clear that what sound change has coalesced, sound change cannot uncoalesce; and the probability is vanishingly small that analogy and borrowing should proceed in such a way as to restore just the situation that had pertained before the restructuring.

Sound change modifies the shapes of linguistic forms in ways on which *the meanings of the forms have no bearing*. If the meanings of two forms whose shapes are becoming more and more similar are such that misunderstandings may result, what happens is that at least one of the forms is replaced in usage by some paraphrase the shape of which is not ambiguous. For example, the English of a millennium ago had two words, one meaning 'permit' and one meaning 'prevent', both of which have now become *let*. But we now use this shape freely only in the first sense. In the second it occurs only in a few fixed phrases, such as *without let or hindrance* in law or *a let ball* at tennis.

The reader may never have heard of *a let ball*. He may instead know the expression *a net ball*. When *let* 'hinder' had dropped out of general use, the inherited phrase *a let ball* for a ball whose trajectory has been interrupted ceased to be quickly intelligible. Since the impediment that stops the flight of a tennis ball is usually the net, some people, in learning the game, may actually have thought they heard *a net ball* when the traditional expression was shouted from the other end of the court. By such episodes, the more obvious newer phrase has come into use alongside the older one.

This does *not* illustrate *l* becoming *n* by sound change. It shows the coining of a *new form*, followed by competition between the new and the old. If the old one eventually dies out, the total event will have constituted the *replacement* of one form by another. *Sound change neither creates new forms nor destroys old ones; it only changes what forms sound like*.

Sound change is a mass phenomenon of communities, detectable only through its results in the long sweep of community history, not in the linguistic life histories of individuals. It is an inevitable byproduct of duality of patterning (pp. 105–107), and thus, we assume, came into operation when the communicative behavior of our ancestors first acquired that feature (p. 414).

SPECIAL PHENOMENA   ✖ The operation of the mechanisms of organic evolution is uninterrupted and world-wide. The changes that they effect depend on the circumstances of time and place. Certain conditions for and certain kinds of change are known to recur; these need to be named and described. The context is primarily genetics. But there are some striking parallels in language, and whenever relevant we also bring tradition as a whole into the picture.

RACIAL DIFFERENTIATION AND SPECIATION

SPECIES.[7] The gene-flow barriers that set populations off one from another are of two sorts, extrinsic and intrinsic. If animals that cannot swim or fly live on two islands a hundred miles apart, they belong to different populations no matter how similar they are. Such a barrier is extrinsic. On the other hand, horses and goats belong to different populations even if they graze the same pasture, because their genetic constitutions are so different that no crossbreeding is possible. This barrier—and only this sort—is intrinsic.

Barriers of either sort serve to delimit populations. Only intrinsic barriers delimit species. In two steps, we can say:

(1) At a given time, all the individuals of a single population belong to the same species.

(2) At a given time, two populations are of the same species just if there is no intrinsic barrier to gene flow between them.

In connection with step (2), note that the route for gene flow does not have to be direct. Suppose one has populations $A, B, \ldots, N$, and suppose that A and N are genetically so different that no crossbreeding is possible. But if genes can migrate from A to N via successive crossbreedings of A and B, B and C, and so on to N, then A and N belong to the same species. In such a case it is even possible for the two extreme forms of the species to coexist as separate populations in a single ecological zone! (see Figure 23-4).

The foregoing definition of species is followed in principle by taxonomists. In practice there are great difficulties. Hence the official taxonomic designations of sets of organisms do not always reflect the facts:

(1) Dogs are formally *Canis familiaris*, and wolves are *C. lupus*. The designations are old, and are retained even though it is now known that dogs and wolves can interbreed and hence belong to the same "real" species.

(2) Horses are *Equus caballus*; asses are *E. asinus*. Put together and left to their own devices, they will copulate and the females will be impregnated. The offspring of a male ass and a female horse is a mule. The offspring of a male horse and a female ass is a hinny. All male mules and hinnies are sterile, and thus dead ends for gene flow. An occasional female is not sterile. So there is, in fact, a bridge for gene flow between horses and asses, albeit an extremely narrow one.

---

[7] We leave out of account here those organisms that reproduce without any sharing of genetic material. I do not know how species are defined for these, but the approach has to be very different—and so are the evolutionary implications.

We also set aside certain developments brought about by human action, such as the experimental production of a type of plant that has both radishes and cabbages in its ancestry. We lose a little generality, because human intervention is just as natural a factor in organic evolution as is anything else. But we don't lose much, since achievements of this sort are terribly recent.

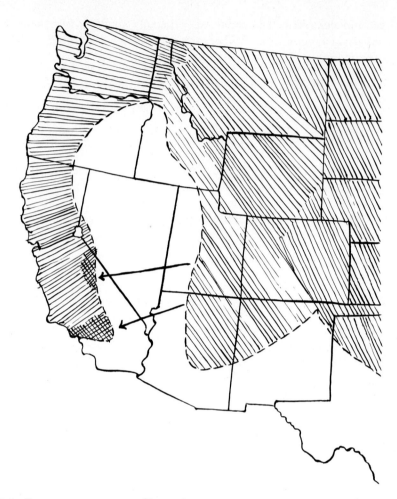

FIGURE 23-4. Distribution in western North America of varieties of the bee *Hoplitis producta*. The changing direction of the hatching is intended to represent the gradual variation of type from one place to another. The arrows show recent migrations from the Great Basin to California, where the distinct varieties, even though of the same species, cannot interbreed. (After Mayr 1963.)

(3)   The case of lions (*Panthera leo*) and tigers (*P. tigris*) is much like that of horses and asses, most of the crosses being sterile; but here it takes a special sort of coddling of the animals in zoos to get them to copulate.

(4)   The American bison (*Bison bison*) and the Asiatic buffalo (*Bubalus bubalis*) have recently been experimentally crossbred, but with even more human trouble than for lions and tigers: insemination may have to be artificial, and the pregnant female's diet has to be handled with great care or the embryo dies and is reabsorbed.

We see that even intrinsic barriers to gene flow are a matter of degree. In terms of evolutionary consequences, the difference between a very narrow bridge for gene flow and no bridge at all can be more trivial than that between a narrow bridge and a broad one.

RACIAL DIFFERENTIATION. The preceding discussion was constrained to organisms and populations coexisting at a given point in time. Now let us observe what may happen as time passes. We take the simplest possible point of departure: a species all of whose members, at the start, belong to a single population.

In course of time, the population can prosper and multiply, spread into more territory, and be split up by all sorts of vicissitudes until it has become many populations.

The different daughter populations live in different ecological zones, facing diverse problems of existence. Variation and selection are thus apt to operate in different ways. Some daughter populations may become extinct. Those which survive may become more and more different in character from one another.

Thus does *racial differentiation* arise. Any genetic differentiation among the populations of a single species is racial differentiation. The degree of differentiation may be slight or great, and can vary as time passes. As long as the extrinsic barriers to gene flow are not too strong, individual genetic traits can spread from one population to another. Differences of environment promote diversity; continued gene flow among the populations tends to retain unity.

Sometimes it works out that the populations fall into sets, the gene pools of those in a single set resembling one another markedly more than do those of populations in different sets. One may then profitably speak of *subspecies* or *races* of the species. But sometimes this does not happen, the amount of difference between neighboring gene pools being uniformly slight. In this case the term "subspecies" or "race" is superfluous and one does better to speak directly in terms of the populations.

If, as far as *intrinsic* barriers go, almost any two populations of a species can directly interbreed, we can describe the species as *tightly connected*. If there are many pairs of populations between which genes can pass only indirectly, then the species is *loosely* connected. The degree of connectedness is another characteristic that can change as time passes—in either direction. An excellent example of a diverse and widespread but very tightly connected species is our own, *Homo sapiens*.

SPECIATION is the splitting of a single species into two or more. Racial differentiation does not inevitably lead to speciation, but it can. Variation and selection are such that extrinsic barriers to gene flow tend to give rise to intrinsic ones. Consider the chain of populations A through N that we described on page 293. Genes can flow between A and N only indirectly. But now suppose that one of the linking populations, say E, becomes extinct, or that mutations change things in such a way that cross-breeding of E with D is no longer possible. Such an event breaks the bridge for gene flow, and thenceforth there are two species.

Except in human laboratories (fn. 7, p. 293), *this is the only way in which speciation comes about.* Furthermore (possibly with a similar proviso), the chances that a broken bridge will ever be rebuilt are virtually zero. Hence speciation is effectively *irreversible*.

Its evolutionary significance derives from that fact. As long as diverse populations retain the possibility of exchanging genes, the adventures of either may have some bearing on the genetic character of the other. Once they have become separate species, their future careers are independent.

Dialect Differentiation and Language Split

Consider, now, a human community of something between a few dozen and a few thousand people, living in such circumstances that it is likely that everyone will converse with almost everyone else at least once or twice in a lifetime. As time goes by, language change is inevitable, but, as long as the kind of contact we have described is not disrupted, the language will change in pretty much the same way for the whole community. After a hundred years, or after ten thousand, the community will still have a single language.

Now suppose that something happens to split the community into smaller communities among which contact is rare and desultory. For convenience we will speak of just two daughter communities. At first, they have the same language. But the conditions for language change are different. An innovation in either daughter community may spread to everyone in that daughter community, but is not so likely to spread to the other. Since change in the two communities is independent, the consequence is divergence. We know something about the rate of divergence under the circumstances we have described, and it seems to be close to constant (in genetics it is not). In a century or less, the two daughter communities have noticeably different dialects, but those dialects are still *mutually intelligible* in the sense that representatives of the two communities can understand each other in a consultation during which each uses the dialect of his own community. If the separation continues, then after something between one and two millennia the divergence is so great that the dialects are no longer mutually intelligible.

They may still, however, be dialects of a single language. The parallel with genetics is obvious. The test which assigns dialects to a single language or to separate languages is exactly like that for assigning populations to species. Consider the chain A through N on page 293, but let the links now be the dialects of human communities and let the pairwise criterion be mutual intelligibility. If A and B are mutually intelligible, B and C likewise, and so on to N, then A and N are dialects of a single language.

Furthermore, language split is exactly analogous to speciation: thus, if the chain between A and N is broken by the disappearance of a crucial intervening dialect, or if such an intervening dialect changes so much that it is no longer mutually intelligible with one of its neighbors, one language has become two. *This is the only way in which language split comes about.*

Finally, language split is like speciation in being irreversible.

In one respect the parallel breaks down. If two human communities speak mutually unintelligible dialects (of the same language or not), direct exchange of information can still be rendered possible if some members of one community learn some of the dialect of the other. Such learning is commonplace all over the world. One result is that forms can be borrowed from one dialect (or language) into another no matter how dissimilar they are. There is nothing like this in genetics.

EXTINCTION

For a population and its gene pool, the term "extinction" is self-explanatory: both become extinct just if all members die without reproducing. The dialect of a human community can become extinct through the death of all community members, or merely if over a period of time all members shift to some other dialect or language.

A language becomes extinct when all its dialects do; a species becomes extinct when all its populations do. An example of a now extinct language is Etruscan, spoken in Italy in Roman times. An example of an extinct species is *Dinornis robustus*, one of the flightless birds (moas) formerly common in New Zealand.

In principle we must distinguish from the foregoing the case in which an earlier species or language does not disappear but merely evolves so radically that we prefer different names for its descendants. The Old English of King Alfred's era is now *dead*, in the sense that no one today can understand it unless he studies it as he would a contemporary foreign language. But it is not extinct, because in a thousand years it became modern English. In organic evolution, biologists use the same word "extinct" in both senses and are forced to distinguish by paraphrase. We shall not follow their lead, but stick to the definition given above. *Dinornis robustus* is extinct. The hominids of some tens and hundreds of thousands of years ago, classed as *Homo erectus*, are no longer with us, but neither are they extinct, because they evolved into our own species, *Homo sapiens*.

LAG

If a population encounters a sudden and drastic change of living conditions, survival is unlikely. If the environmental change is slower or more subtle, the results take a while to work themselves out. Neither extinction nor genetic accommodation is instantaneous; either requires a number of generations.

Meanwhile, during the *lag* time, the external character of the population may be altered. In a single generation, a change of diet, latitude, altitude, temperature, humidity, or environing microorganisms may yield a different body size, shape, or coloration, or modify the pattern of susceptibility to disease, without, for a while, altering the gene pool. Such changes are then not the results of, but additional conditioning factors for, genetic selection.

Thus, if we observe two populations of a species, living in different niches and different in appearance and behavior, we cannot immediately conclude that their gene pools are sharply different. Especially if one population is a newcomer to its current environment, the difference may be due to the lag effect.

PERSISTENCE

Now suppose a population has been living in a particular environment for a long time, so that it is genetically well adapted to the conditions encountered there, and imagine that the zone is invaded by another population of the same species, emigrants from a niche of a different sort. The two populations interbreed, becoming a single population. The invaders have brought an infusion of new genes. But any of the new genes that militate against survival in the environment will tend in time to be eliminated from the joint gene pool, while any indigenous genes particularly useful for survival in that environment will tend to be maintained. Thus, in the long run, the local type will tend to *persist*.

An excellent example is the human populations of the Andes (p. 50). When the Spanish arrived early in the sixteenth century, the indigenous populations had had many thousands of years to adapt to life at extreme elevations. Interbreeding began immediately and has never stopped. But the genes that produce large chests and capacious lungs are still there; infants inheriting European genes that militate against large lungs have not survived to reproduce.

TEMPO EFFECTS

Most evolutionary changes in life forms are very slow compared with the tempo of our everyday activities. But when we examine them on their own time scale we find that some have come about more rapidly than others. Certain concatenations of circumstances apparently allow variation and selection to effect major alterations in relatively brief periods of time.

One relevant factor is the nature of the geographical distribution of a species.

THE SEWALL WRIGHT EFFECT. Imagine a population living in a particular niche, and suppose that its gene pool contains a factor whose manifestations have no bearing on whether an individual will survive to reproduce. The factor's incidence may nevertheless change merely through the workings of chance: which chromosomes are passed on in reduction, which pairs of organisms mate, and so on. Sewall Wright showed statistically that in a small enough population—100 or less—the factor may spread to all members, or may vanish completely, in just a few generations. The larger the population, the greater the number of generations required.

Since living conditions can change, the Sewall Wright effect means that a population may suddenly find itself unusually well equipped or virtually doomed, not by selection but fortuitously (p. 283).

THE HOLMES EFFECT. Now consider a species distributed in small groups over some region. Each group breeds mainly within itself, but with occasional gene leakage from one to another. Genetic adaptation is promoted. The smallness of the groups and their independence makes for the Sewall Wright effect in each. The different groups face more or less similar environmental challenges; some of them adapt in one way, some in another. If a particular group is unsuccessful, its failure does not condemn the whole species to extinction. On the other hand, if a group is successful, the slight leakage of genes can carry the machinery of success to the other groups.

This is the *Holmes effect*; the reason for the name will be given in a moment.

THE TURNER EFFECT. One can go a little farther. Somewhere in the total region occupied by the species is a "focal area," where the organisms have lived longest and have reached the best balanced adjustment to their environment. At the fringes, environmental challenges are sharper and more diverse. Genetic innovations get their start mainly at the focal area, where more variation can be tolerated. They spread to the frontiers, where they meet more severe tests; favorable ones for the particular frontier become then part of the genetic repertory for the whole species. The frontiers are the testing grounds; the focal area is the locus for stabilization and consolidation. This is the *Turner effect*.

GENETICS AND TRADITION. The Sewall Wright effect apparently has to do only with genetics. The Holmes and Turner effects were presented above in genetic terms, but that is not essential. They can be manifested just as well when the mechanism of innovation is tradition and the machinery of spread is cultural diffusion (p. 107). It was in the human cultural context that the two were discovered, by scholars who did not realize the full power and generality of what they were saying:

Oliver Wendell Holmes, Jr., while a member of the United States Supreme Court, was a staunch defender of states' rights on the grounds that the separate states should be free to run independent experiments, the outcomes of which could then be heeded to benefit the whole country.

The historian Frederick Jackson Turner argued that, as long as the United States had a geographical frontier, that was where social innovations met their acid test, while the more sedate longer-settled parts of the country were the locus of consolidation.

ADAPTIVE RADIATIONS

Sometimes it happens that a type of organism (a subspecies, a species, a small group of closely related species) originally confined to some small region spreads out and differentiates, in the course of a relatively brief interval, to yield descendants adapted to a wide variety of ecological niches in a much larger total territory. The same can happen (at least among human beings) with tradition rather than genetics as the essential mechanism. Such a sequence is an *adaptive radiation*.

For example, from about 150,000,000 to about 100,000,000 years ago the placental mammals were few and not greatly differentiated. Then in the course of a mere thirty million years they proliferated and changed to become several thousand species in highly varied niches all over the world.

It is unlikely that any adaptive radiation could be predicted. However, enough of them are attested by the fossil and historical record to describe, in a general way, what happens.

The vicissitudes encountered by the populations of some type of organism in some small but varied region can lead to their development of a combination of properties— we shall call it a *key complex*—that equips them not only for efficient existence in that region but also for more facile adaptation to some of the kinds of living conditions to be found elsewhere. In these initial stages the Holmes and Turner effects surely play a part. The populations that have achieved the key complex have, as it were, crossed an "adaptive threshold"; similar organisms elsewhere have not. As the key complex spreads, partly by gene flow and partly by migrations of its carriers, it enables its carriers to establish toeholds in many different sorts of environments. Further selective changes then adapt the organisms in different environments in different ways.

✗ In this section we discuss, not mechanisms of change, but a way of finding out about the past that the nature of change makes possible.

If a group of species (or of languages) are all descended from a single earlier species (or language), we say they are (*phylogenetically*) *related*. We usually assume that all the species in the world today are ultimately related, and it may also be that all the world's languages are, but there is currently no way of being certain. However, these possibilities mean that what counts is not mere relatedness so much as degrees of closeness of relationship: men and apes are more closely related than are either to monkeys; English and German are more closely related than is either to French.

When the relationship is not too distant, it is possible to compare the diverse descendants and to infer (1) the lines of phylogenetic connection and (2) something of the nature of the common ancestor. In either organic evolution or language history, the procedure for doing this is the *comparative method*, and, by a metaphor, one is said to *reconstruct* the common ancestor. In the case of language, a common ancestor is given a label beginning with the word *Proto*: for example, "Proto Indo-European" (Figure 23-5).[8]

Reconstruction is possible because certain kinds of changes are known to be effectively irreversible. All strategies of historical inference (p. 96) rest on known irreversibilities of one sort or another: for example, a document must be written before it can find its way to a catacomb or attic; an animal must live and die before it can become a fossil; when an organism dies and the flow of carbon through it ceases, whatever carbon-14 is present proceeds to disintegrate at a known fixed rate. Ultimately, all irreversibilities are manifestations of one of the laws of nature, the second law of thermodynamics (fn. 1, p. 81). In the two domains of the comparative method the key irreversibilities are especially powerful. It is the lack of a comparably pervasive irreversibility that prevents the development of any explicit comparative method for aspects of tradition other than language.

In organic evolution the crucial irreversibility is that of speciation (p. 295). Without it, we should be helpless. A proposal that human beings share recent ancestors with oysters or rattlesnakes—or that some of us have the first phylogenetic connection, others the second—would be as worthy of consideration as that our nearest nonhuman kin are apes. Even with the irreversibility of speciation, many inferences are only matters of relative likelihood. For example, as we reconstruct the Stem Hominoids of twelve or fifteen million years ago as the latest common ancestors of men and African apes (pp. 362–368), it seems much more plausible to assume that they did not have language and that our separate lineage acquired it, than to imagine that they had language and that the ancestral African apes lost it. But some of the other features one is tempted to ascribe to the Stem Hominoids are more subject to challenge.

For language, the key irreversibility is not an analog of speciation in organic evolution, even though it is true that language split is irreversible. Rather, it is the irreversibility of the restructurings brought about by sound change (p. 291). Were

---

[8]Evolutionary biologists do not use "Proto" in this way; they have no simple terminological convention for a common ancestor.

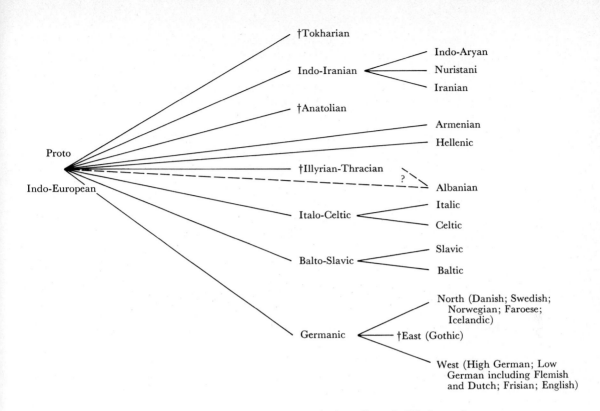

FIGURE 23-5. THE INDO-EUROPEAN LANGUAGE FAMILY. The figure shows lines of affiliation and ancestry, but nothing of the dates. A dagger (†) means that the branch is extinct. The parent language, Proto Indo-European, had its own phylogenetic connections, but we do not know what they were.

it not for this, any historical guess about specific languages would be as plausible as any other. But since sound change does operate, the comparative method in language history has been beautifully elaborated and its results, when it is carefully applied, are marvelously secure. Specialists have been able to reconstruct in considerable detail proto languages for which there are no written records whatever. Figure 23-5 displays the known relationships of English; Figure 23-6 shows those of Menomini.

The comparative method cannot be applied to languages among which the relationships are too distant. The similarities have to be discernible and one has to be able to eliminate those that are due to borrowing. Given enough time, similarities due to common ancestry are concealed beyond recognition by language change. Thus, we can never assert for sure that two languages are *not* related—the relationship may simply be too distant for recovery. If we had only the evidence of the languages as now spoken, the reconstruction of Proto Indo-European could probably not have been achieved. It was made possible because we have written records several thousand years old for some of its branches (though not of the proto language itself).

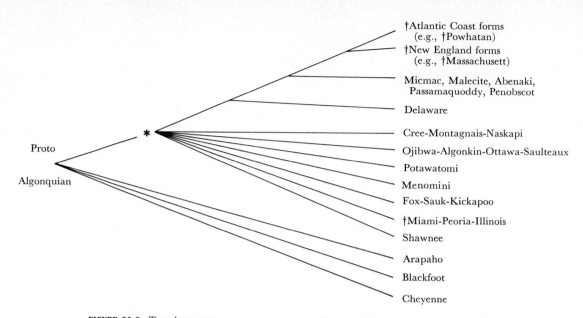

FIGURE 23-6 THE ALGONQUIAN LANGUAGE FAMILY. The asterisk marks the stage mentioned on p. 10 and there, for convenience, called "Proto Algonquian"; in the reconstruction of that stage the three Plains languages (Arapaho, Blackfoot, and Cheyenne) were not taken into account. Further research will doubtless require modification of the picture. A dagger (†) marks branches or groups no longer spoken and known only through (post-Columbian) records, generally unreliable and difficult to interpret.

There does not seem to be quite the same kind of limitation on the depth of application of the comparative method in organic evolution. This may be because of fossil evidence. Written records are for language history what fossils are for evolution, but the analog is inexact. Organisms started leaving some faint fossil traces practically as soon as life began. Speaking leaves none at all, and language was already tens of thousands of years old when writing was invented.

RUNNING CALENDAR

Read each page of this calendar from bottom to top. The time scale is inverse logarithmic, so that each page covers ten times as long a period as the next. Geological Eras, Periods, and Epochs are indicated to the left of the time scale. At the beginning the focus is on major events in the history of Earth; at the end, on key events in human history (terminating about 200 years ago, about A.D. 1800). Towards the end, only a few of the details given in the text are listed; the reader can use them to orient himself as he locates others.

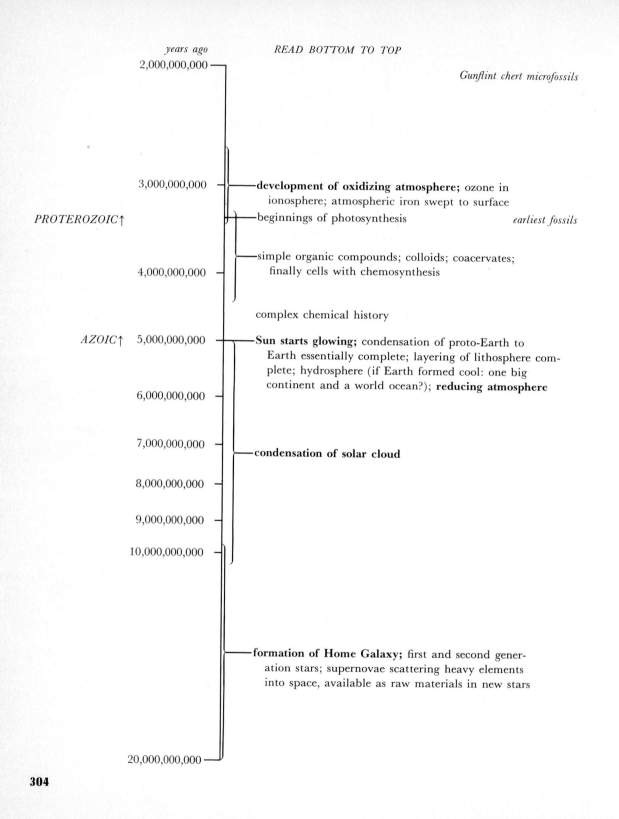

years ago

READ BOTTOM TO TOP

2,000,000,000 —

Gunflint chert microfossils

3,000,000,000 — **development of oxidizing atmosphere;** ozone in
ionosphere; atmospheric iron swept to surface

PROTEROZOIC↑ — beginnings of photosynthesis   *earliest fossils*

— simple organic compounds; colloids; coacervates;
finally cells with chemosynthesis
4,000,000,000 —

complex chemical history

AZOIC↑ 5,000,000,000 — **Sun starts glowing;** condensation of proto-Earth to
Earth essentially complete; layering of lithosphere com-
plete; hydrosphere (if Earth formed cool: one big
continent and a world ocean?); **reducing atmosphere**
6,000,000,000 —

7,000,000,000 — **condensation of solar cloud**

8,000,000,000 —

9,000,000,000 —

10,000,000,000 —

— **formation of Home Galaxy;** first and second generation stars; supernovae scattering heavy elements
into space, available as raw materials in new stars

20,000,000,000 —

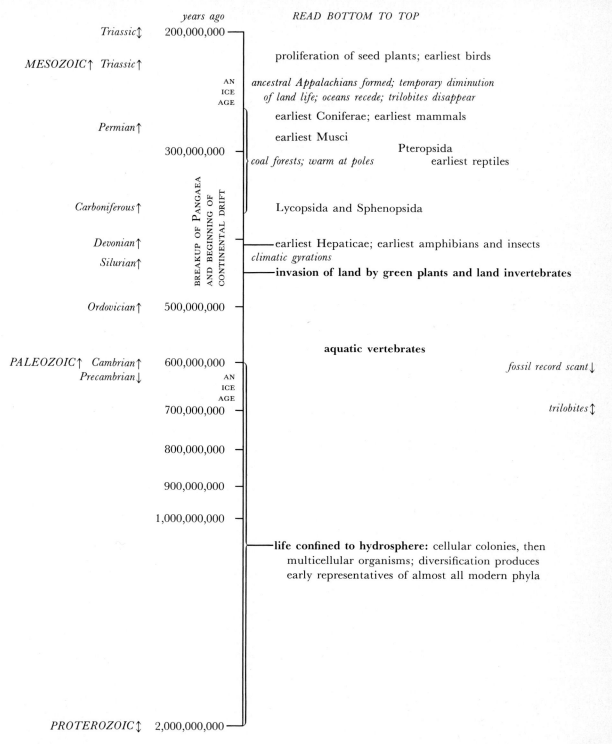

years ago   *READ BOTTOM TO TOP*

Triassic ↕   200,000,000 ——

MESOZOIC ↑ *Triassic* ↑   proliferation of seed plants; earliest birds

AN
ICE   *ancestral Appalachians formed; temporary diminution*
AGE   *of land life; oceans recede; trilobites disappear*

Permian ↑   earliest Coniferae; earliest mammals

earliest Musci

300,000,000   Pteropsida
coal forests; warm at poles   earliest reptiles

BREAKUP OF PANGAEA
AND BEGINNING OF
CONTINENTAL DRIFT

Carboniferous ↑   Lycopsida and Sphenopsida

Devonian ↑   —— earliest Hepaticae; earliest amphibians and insects
Silurian ↑   *climatic gyrations*
                  —— **invasion of land by green plants and land invertebrates**

Ordovician ↑   500,000,000 ——

aquatic vertebrates

PALEOZOIC ↑ *Cambrian* ↑   600,000,000 ——   *fossil record scant* ↓
Precambrian ↓   AN
                                ICE
                                AGE
                  700,000,000 ——   *trilobites* ↕

                  800,000,000 ——

                  900,000,000 ——

                  1,000,000,000 ——

                  —— **life confined to hydrosphere:** cellular colonies, then
                       multicellular organisms; diversification produces
                       early representatives of almost all modern phyla

PROTEROZOIC ↕   2,000,000,000 ——

305

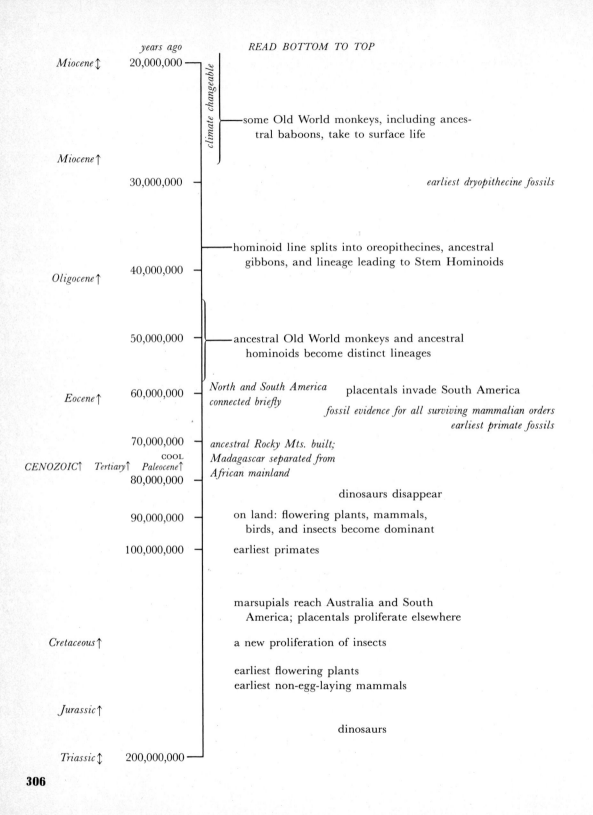

years ago
READ BOTTOM TO TOP

Miocene ↕   20,000,000 —

climate changeable

—some Old World monkeys, including ancestral baboons, take to surface life

Miocene ↑

30,000,000 —

earliest dryopithecine fossils

—hominoid line splits into oreopithecines, ancestral
gibbons, and lineage leading to Stem Hominoids

Oligocene ↑   40,000,000 —

50,000,000 —

—ancestral Old World monkeys and ancestral
hominoids become distinct lineages

North and South America   placentals invade South America
connected briefly
Eocene ↑   60,000,000 —

fossil evidence for all surviving mammalian orders
earliest primate fossils

70,000,000 —

ancestral Rocky Mts. built;
COOL   *Madagascar separated from*
CENOZOIC ↑   Tertiary ↑   Paleocene ↑   *African mainland*
80,000,000 —

dinosaurs disappear

90,000,000 —

on land: flowering plants, mammals,
birds, and insects become dominant

100,000,000 —

earliest primates

marsupials reach Australia and South
America; placentals proliferate elsewhere

Cretaceous ↑

a new proliferation of insects

earliest flowering plants
earliest non-egg-laying mammals

Jurassic ↑

dinosaurs

Triassic ↕   200,000,000 —

306

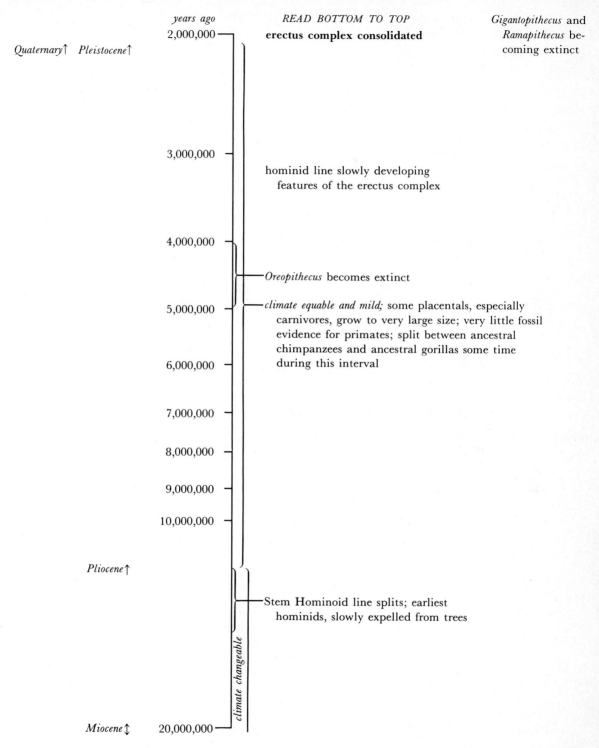

years ago

Quaternary↑ *Pleistocene*↑

2,000,000 —

READ BOTTOM TO TOP

erectus complex consolidated

Gigantopithecus and
Ramapithecus be-
coming extinct

3,000,000

hominid line slowly developing
features of the erectus complex

4,000,000

Oreopithecus becomes extinct

climate equable and mild; some placentals, especially
carnivores, grow to very large size; very little fossil
evidence for primates; split between ancestral
chimpanzees and ancestral gorillas some time
during this interval

5,000,000 —

6,000,000 —

7,000,000 —

8,000,000 —

9,000,000 —

10,000,000 —

Pliocene↑

Stem Hominoid line splits; earliest
hominids, slowly expelled from trees

climate changeable

Miocene↕   20,000,000 —

307

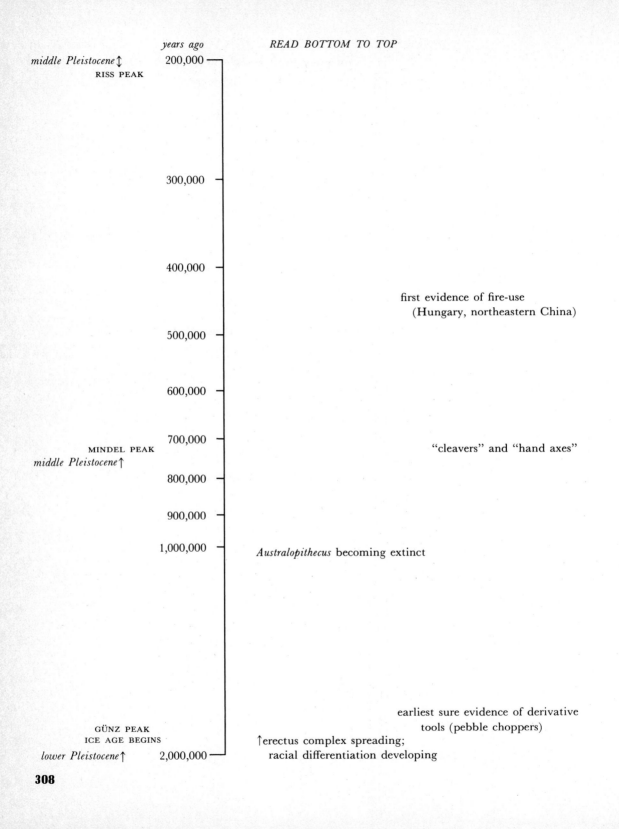

years ago

READ BOTTOM TO TOP

middle Pleistocene ↕   200,000 —
RISS PEAK

300,000 —

400,000 —

first evidence of fire-use
(Hungary, northeastern China)

500,000 —

600,000 —

MINDEL PEAK   700,000 —
middle Pleistocene ↑

"cleavers" and "hand axes"

800,000 —

900,000 —

1,000,000 —

Australopithecus becoming extinct

earliest sure evidence of derivative
tools (pebble choppers)

GÜNZ PEAK
ICE AGE BEGINS
↑erectus complex spreading;
lower Pleistocene ↑   2,000,000 —
racial differentiation developing

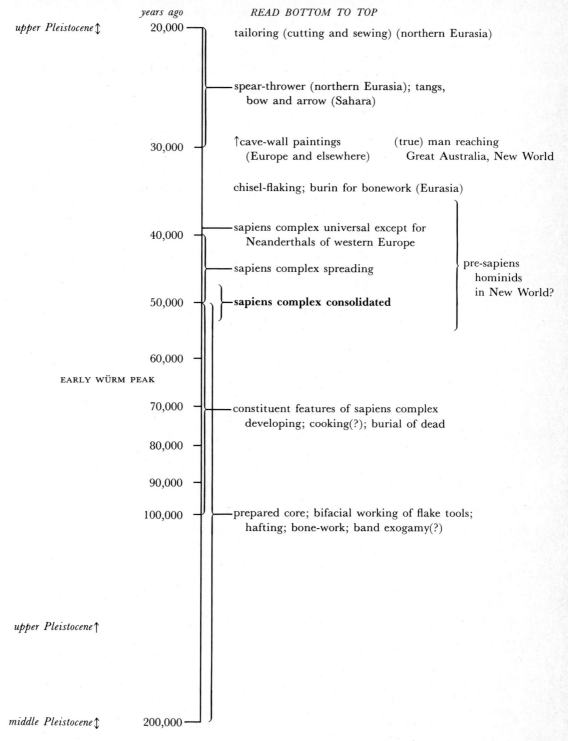

years ago   *READ BOTTOM TO TOP*

upper Pleistocene ↕   20,000 ── tailoring (cutting and sewing) (northern Eurasia)

── spear-thrower (northern Eurasia); tangs,
              bow and arrow (Sahara)

30,000 ── ↑cave-wall paintings   (true) man reaching
           (Europe and elsewhere)   Great Australia, New World

chisel-flaking; burin for bonework (Eurasia)

40,000 ── sapiens complex universal except for
           Neanderthals of western Europe

── sapiens complex spreading   pre-sapiens
                                        hominids

50,000 ── **sapiens complex consolidated**   in New World?

60,000 ──

EARLY WÜRM PEAK

70,000 ── constituent features of sapiens complex
           developing; cooking(?); burial of dead

80,000 ──

90,000 ──

100,000 ── prepared core; bifacial working of flake tools;
           hafting; bone-work; band exogamy(?)

upper Pleistocene ↑

middle Pleistocene ↕   200,000 ──

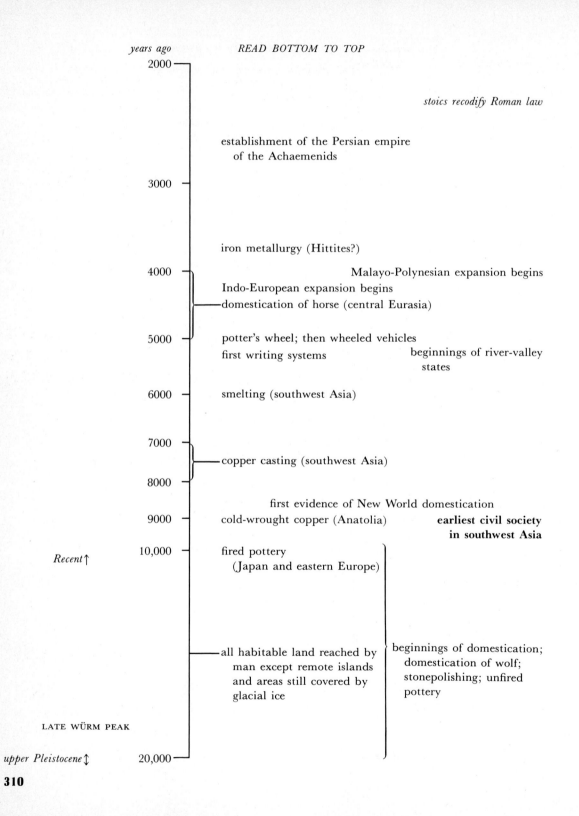

years ago

READ BOTTOM TO TOP

2000 —

stoics recodify Roman law

establishment of the Persian empire
    of the Achaemenids

3000 —

iron metallurgy (Hittites?)

4000 —   Malayo-Polynesian expansion begins
Indo-European expansion begins
domestication of horse (central Eurasia)

5000 —   potter's wheel; then wheeled vehicles
first writing systems   beginnings of river-valley
                                  states

6000 —   smelting (southwest Asia)

7000 —
    copper casting (southwest Asia)
8000 —

          first evidence of New World domestication
9000 — cold-wrought copper (Anatolia)   **earliest civil society**
                                   in southwest Asia

Recent ↑   10,000 — fired pottery
          (Japan and eastern Europe)

all habitable land reached by   beginnings of domestication;
  man except remote islands   domestication of wolf;
  and areas still covered by   stonepolishing; unfired
  glacial ice   pottery

LATE WÜRM PEAK

upper Pleistocene ↕   20,000 —

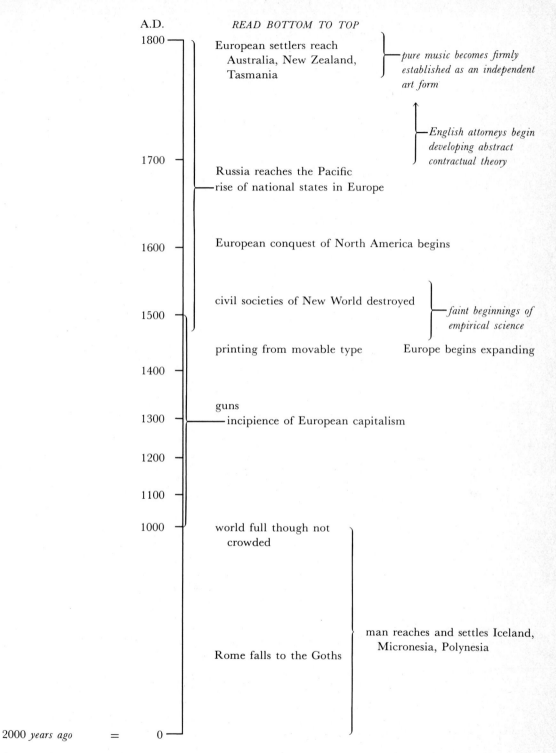

A.D.

READ BOTTOM TO TOP

1800 — European settlers reach
Australia, New Zealand,
Tasmania

*pure music becomes firmly
established as an independent
art form*

*English attorneys begin
developing abstract
contractual theory*

1700 — Russia reaches the Pacific
rise of national states in Europe

1600 — European conquest of North America begins

civil societies of New World destroyed

*faint beginnings of
empirical science*

1500 —

printing from movable type   Europe begins expanding

1400 —

guns
1300 — incipience of European capitalism

1200 —

1100 —

1000 — world full though not
crowded

man reaches and settles Iceland,
Micronesia, Polynesia

Rome falls to the Goths

2000 *years ago*   =   0 —

311

PART TWO

✖

BY HIS BOOTSTRAPS

24

×

THE FIRST FIVE THOUSAND MILLION YEARS

How man differs from the rest of nature and *how the differences have come about* (p. 3): of these intertwined issues, which together define the scope of our inquiry, we emphasized the first in Part One and shall now focus on the second.

Where shall we start? Before we describe what man has done, we want to tell how he came to be. But before man, life was; before life, matter was. Life, including man, was born of Earth and remains part of her. Therefore to capture and characterize man's emergence we must begin the story with the formation of Earth. 5,000,000,000 years is a nice round estimate of the age of Earth—with a margin of error much greater than the brief terminal interval that will still not have been covered at the end of this chapter.

It will be useful to follow the narrative of this and subsequent chapters on our Running Calendar, pages 304 to 311.

EARTH'S BIRTH ✕ Let us recall that Earth is one of nine planets which, together with their satellites (including Moon) and various oddments (asteroids), revolve about Sun; the whole assemblage is the Solar System (Figure 24-1). Sun is one of some 100,000,000,000 stars which, along with clouds of dust and gas, form our Home Galaxy (Figures 24-2 and 24-3). There are plenty of other galaxies: within current observational limits, perhaps as many as there are stars in the Home Galaxy.

Stars differ in mass, size, density, and how much radiation they give off; in all these respects Sun is about average. A star shines because the great pressure and high temperature at its core maintain thermonuclear reactions, whose excess energy excites matter near the surface, yielding radiation.

Stars are not eternal. They are episodes in the history of matter, just as are people and pencils (p. 90), though admittedly they last a little longer (Figure 24-4). A star is born when a rotating cloud of dust and gas, coagulating under the mutual gravitational attraction of its constituent particles, becomes dense enough to start self-sustaining thermonuclear reactions. The critical density is not reached unless the cloud has a mass at least some 17,000 times that of Earth (53 times that of Jupiter, our

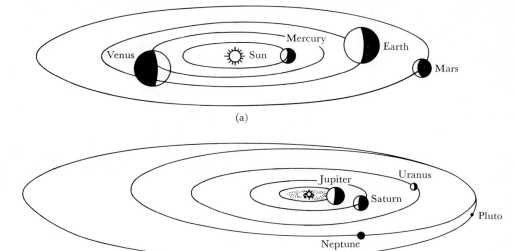

(a)

(b)

	MEAN DISTANCE OF ORBIT FROM SUN (miles)	INCLINATION OF ORBIT FROM PLANE OF ECLIPTIC	PERIOD OF REVOLUTION ABOUT SUN (days)	MASS (Earth = 1)	RADIUS (Earth = 1)	DENSITY (Earth = 1)
Sun			(rotates about axis in 25 days)	332,000	109	0.255
Mercury	35,800,000	7°00′	88	0.055	0.38	0.996
Venus	67,200,000	3°23′	225	0.816	0.95	0.951
Earth	92,956,000	0°00′	365	1	1	1
Moon	(like Earth . . . .)			0.0123	0.27	0.605
Mars	142,000,000	1°51′	687	0.107	0.53	0.717
Asteroids				total 0.002		
Jupiter	484,000,000	1°18′	4,380	317.9	10.9	0.223
Saturn	887,000,000	2°29′	10,600	95.2	9.2	0.123
Uranus	1,780,000,000	0°48′	30,700	14.5	3.7	0.289
Neptune	2,800,000,000	1°48′	59,900	17.4	3.5	0.435
Pluto	3,690,000,000	17°12′	92,900	?	0.46	?

FIGURE 24-1. THE SOLAR SYSTEM. (a) and (b) are perspective views, the former of the inner planets and the latter of the outer. Sun and the orbits are *not* drawn to scale; the planets in each view are drawn to scale relative to the other planets in the same view. The table gives essential data. (From Whipple 1968, with the permission of Harvard University Press.)

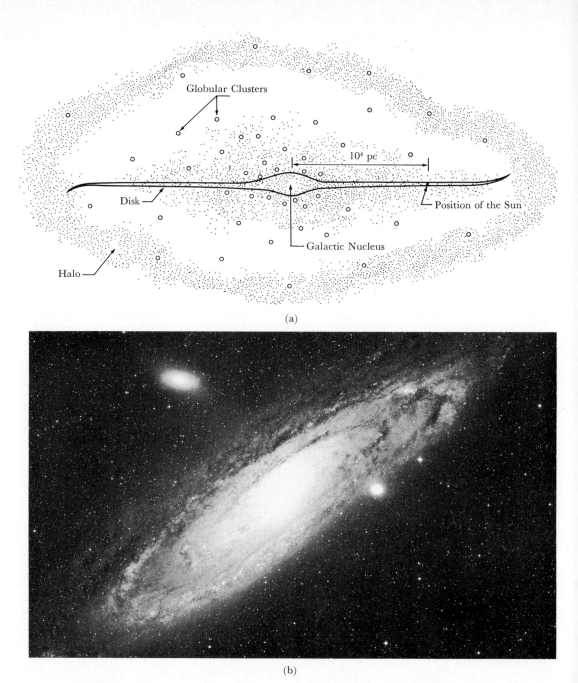

(a)

(b)

FIGURE 24-2. (a) is a schematic edge view of the Home Galaxy, with position of Sun marked. 10^4 pc (parsecs) = 3.3×10^{17} kilometers, say 200,000,000,000,000,000 miles. (b) is the spiral galaxy in Andromeda, which appears from Earth with one face turned slightly towards us. It is believed that a similar view of the Home Galaxy would look much the same. (Schematic drawing after Shklovskii and Sagan 1966. Photograph courtesy of the California Institute of Technology, Mt. Wilson Observatory.)

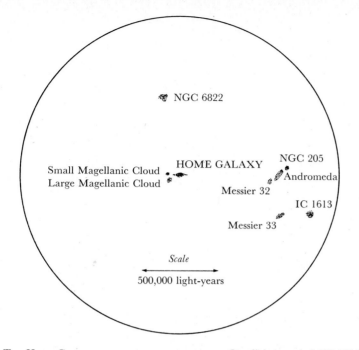

FIGURE 24-3. THE HOME GALAXY AND ITS NEAREST NEIGHBORS. One light-year is 5,875,500,000,000 miles. The galaxies are not all in the same plane, but it is difficult to portray them in a way that gives a sense of depth. (After George Gamow's drawing in his *The Birth and Death of the Sun,* The Viking Press, Inc., 1940.)

largest planet; one twentieth that of Sun). This sets a lower limit to the range of possible stellar masses.

The interiors of stars also are alchemical factories, the reactions building atomic nuclei of heavier elements out of certain lighter ones by fusion, and then producing other of the lighter ones by fission. The transmutational chains all start with hydrogen and many of them end with iron. We don't know where the hydrogen came from to start with, but it still accounts for about 75% of the total mass of the observable universe; helium makes up most of the rest; iron, so far, accounts for only 0.0075%.

Ordinary stars synthesize many of the elements. Only a certain especially massive type can produce the really heavy elements like gold and uranium. From time to time, the balance of forces in a star is disrupted and the star explodes. This is a *nova* or, if the star was of the especially massive type, a *supernova*. The explosion does not inevitably end the star, but much of the matter that it has transmuted is scattered into space, becoming available for a new cycle of condensation and star-formation. There must have been a supernova in our part of the Home Galaxy not long—say, a few thousand million years—before the formation of the Solar System, because otherwise we should have none of the heavy elements which in fact we have.

For a star to have a retinue of planets, small portions of the prestellar cloud must break off and condense separately. We don't know how or how commonly this

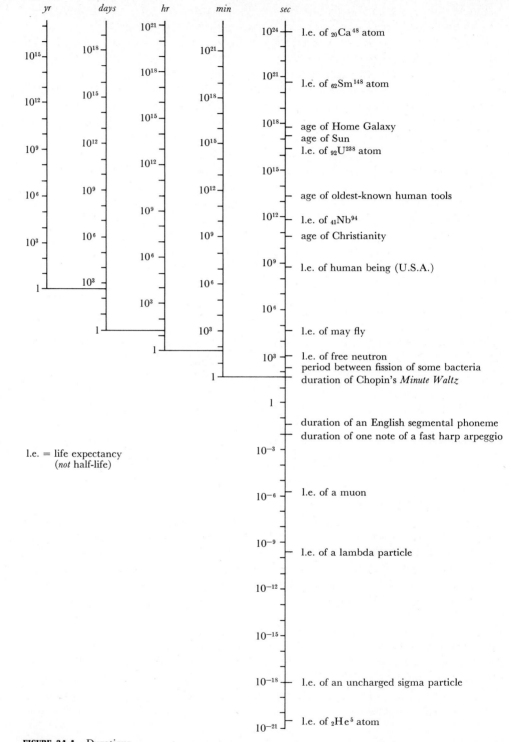

FIGURE 24-4. Durations.

happens, but the Solar System is not unique: Barnard's star, one of our nearest neighbors, has at least one planet, half again the size of Jupiter.

For matter of any density and rigidity, there is a limit to the size of a body that can maintain other than roughly spherical shape. This manifestation of the law of gravitation is *isostasy,* and still today plays a part in the behavior of Earth.[1] The threshold for stable nonspherical shape is many orders of magnitude below that for radiation-free coagulation. After our own primordial cloud had shed some small marginal bits, then as each of the subaggregates became sufficiently dense it assumed approximately spherical shape. The asteroids, true enough, are irregular. But they are small, and may not have formed as part of the original condensation; instead, they may be pieces of a planet formed like the rest, in an orbit between those of Mars and Jupiter, that subsequently broke up.

The present-day angular momentum of the Solar System, represented by the rotation of Sun and by the rotations and revolutions of the planets and satellites, is a residue of the angular momentum of the original cloud. Earth's rotation about its axis had to be faster in early days than now, since tidal forces (the gravitational attraction of other bodies, especially Moon and Sun) are gradually slowing it. At the beginning it was probably about four hours, as compared with today's twenty-four.

There is no reason to assume that the primordial cloud was either markedly warmer or sharply cooler than the range of temperatures at planetary surfaces today (Figure 24-5). The nascent Sun got hot in the way all incipient stars do. Thereafter its radiation, and the tiny bits of matter the radiation drives ahead of it (the "solar wind"), played a part in the development of the orbiting and condensing subaggregates that were to become the planets and their satellites.

Before Sun started shining, the nascent Earth, still a diffuse cloud, had probably several hundred times its present mass. It consisted largely of hydrogen, helium, neon, methane (CH_4), ammonia (NH_3), and cyanides (built on the radical CN), perhaps also some water vapor (H_2O). The relative proportion of different elements was not the same as their relative abundance in the universe as a whole (Table 24-6): thanks to that recent supernova, there was an excess of heavy atoms. However, the disparity was due to become much greater:

In the cloudy pre-Earth, heavier particles tended to precipitate towards the center, displacing the lighter ones so that they concentrated in the outer reaches where Sun's radiation could reach them. Even the heavier of the so-called inert gasses, argon, krypton, and xenon, moved mostly towards the surface, since these, like helium and neon, enter into compounds only with great difficulty. Lighter molecules, ions, and atoms near the surface of the cloud were given additional energy by Sun's radiation, reached the speed of escape from nascent Earth's gravitational field, and thus leaked

---

[1] The tendency towards spherical distribution is in terms of mass, not volume. Mountains are higher than plains (that is, they stretch slightly farther from Earth's center)—and mountains are composed of materials less dense than the rest of the crust. Departures from sphericity can be maintained through the structural strength of crystalline materials in the crust. But when the migrations of matter near the surface yield sufficiently great stresses, the materials fracture and *tectonic* movements readjust the shape towards greater stability. These movements never wholly stop, but the big and sometimes disastrous ones we call earthquakes are infrequent and localized.

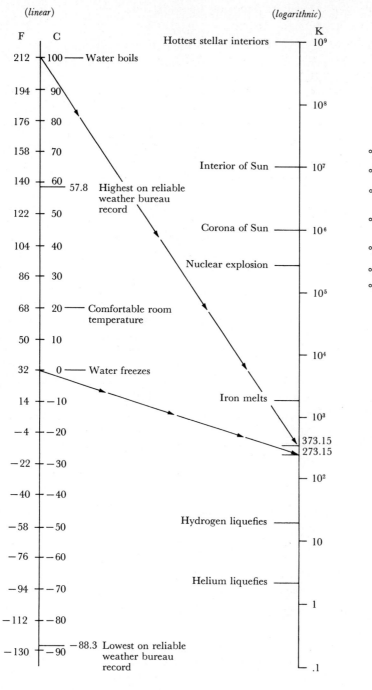

FIGURE 24-5. Temperatures.

      BY HIS BOOTSTRAPS

away. Much the same happened to the small neighboring cloud that was coalescing to form Moon, and to the other inner planets (Mercury, Venus, Mars). It did not happen on the same scale with the outer planets (Jupiter, Saturn, Uranus, Neptune, Pluto) because all but Pluto are—and were—so much more massive, so that the speed of escape is greater, and because they are so much farther from Sun.

At least 99% of the original mass of the terrestrial cloud was lost in this way,

TABLE 24-6. Relative abundance of the elements.

The relative cosmic abundance of the first thirty elements of the periodic table (all the others are rarer), compared with their current relative abundance in Earth as a whole, in the crust, in the hydrosphere, and in the atmosphere (dry—ignoring water vapor). The numbers can be directly compared only within a single column; each integer then represents approximately ten times as much of the element as does the next smaller figure; 0 means either missing or traces.

ELEMENT		COSMIC	TERRESTRIAL	CRUST	HYDROSPHERE	ATMOSPHERE
H	hydrogen	10	8	7	8	0
He	helium	9	0	1	0	1
Li	lithium	2	0	6	2	0
Be	beryllium	1	0	5	0	0
B	boron	1	0	4	3	0
C	carbon	6	7	6	4	3
N	nitrogen	7	4	5	2	6
O	oxygen	7	10	9	9	6
F	fluorine	3	0	6	3	0
Ne	neon	7	1	0	0	2
Na	sodium	4	8	8	7	0
Mg	magnesium	6	9	8	6	0
Al	aluminum	5	9	9	3	0
Si	silicon	6	10	9	3	0
P	phosphorus	4	8	7	2	0
S	sulfur	5	9	6	6	0
Cl	chlorine	4	8	6	7	0
Ar	argon	3	2	2	0	4
K	potassium	5	8	8	5	0
Ca	calcium	4	9	8	4	0
Sc	scandium	1	0	0	0	0
Ti	titanium	3	8	6	0	0
V	vanadium	2	0	5	0	0
Cr	chromium	4	8	5	0	0
Mn	manganese	4	8	6	1	0
Fe	iron	6	10	7	1	0
Co	cobalt	4	9	4	0	0
Ni	nickel	3	9	5	0	0
Cu	copper	2	6	5	1	0
Zn	zinc	2	1	5	1	0

including most of our original allotment of hydrogen and helium, most of our stock of the heavier inert gasses, some of our nitrogen, and probably any molecular oxygen (O_2) there may have been. The hydrogen and oxygen we held on to were locked up at the time in heavier molecules, especially in water and minerals. The inert gasses we kept were trapped in tiny bubbles within solid particles.

EARTH'S INFANCY

× The upshot of these processes of formation was that, when Earth had become dense enough to qualify as a planet rather than a cloud, its structure was something like that of an onion, with concentric layers of different sorts of stuff.

Today that layered structure (Figure 24-7) is as follows:

The innermost layer, of rock and other hard materials, is the *lithosphere.* Wrapped around that is a thin shell of liquid, the *hydrosphere.* But this is discontinuous, since in places the lithosphere rises above the liquid to touch the outermost shell, the *atmosphere,* composed of gasses. (By the "surface" of Earth we ordinarily mean the bottom of the atmosphere, not its outer reaches.)

The lithosphere is itself layered. Its outermost shell is the *crust*: the continents and ocean basins, composed mainly of granite and basalt. Most of our quotas of radioactive isotopes also managed to migrate into the crust during the original condensation, and their remnants are still there. The crust extends to a depth of from 20 to 35 miles, thinner under the ocean than ashore. There it forms an interface with the *mantle,* made of heavier rocks. At 1800 miles there is another boundary, beyond which lies the *core,* mainly of iron, nickel, and cobalt under tremendous pressure. The core reaches to the center of Earth; its radius is about 1520 miles. It is very dense and hot, and its outer reaches may be molten; the center must be solid, because Earth is a magnet and a magnetic field is only a manifestation of matter in the solid (crystalline) state.

The hydrosphere, largely water, is layered wherever deep enough, in that the surface turbulence of ripples, waves, and swells has no effects at depths greater than a few dozen yards, and in that no sunlight penetrates more than 650 feet.

The atmosphere is about 80% nitrogen, and most of the rest is oxygen. Its innermost shell is the *troposphere,* which reaches up to from 3 to 14 miles, thinner at the poles, thicker in the tropics. This is the "weather shell," marked by the same turbulence that characterizes the outer shell of the hydrosphere. Beyond it is the weatherless *stratosphere,* up to some 50 miles, and beyond that the *ionosphere,* which has no definite outer boundary but just gets less and less dense at increased distances. The ionosphere contains oxygen in the form of ozone (O_3), enough to absorb or deflect most of the ultraviolet in Sun's radiation so that it does not reach Earth's surface.

The structure of infant Earth differed from its modern structure in a number of ways. Of course there was no life yet. Three other points must be noted.

(1) The early atmosphere, consisting of the gasses we did not lose during the condensation supplemented by outgassing from the surface, was composed mainly of hydrogen, carbon dioxide (CO_2), and water vapor, with perhaps some methane, ammonia, hydrogen sulfide (H_2S), and doubly ionized iron (Fe^{++})—that is, iron atoms

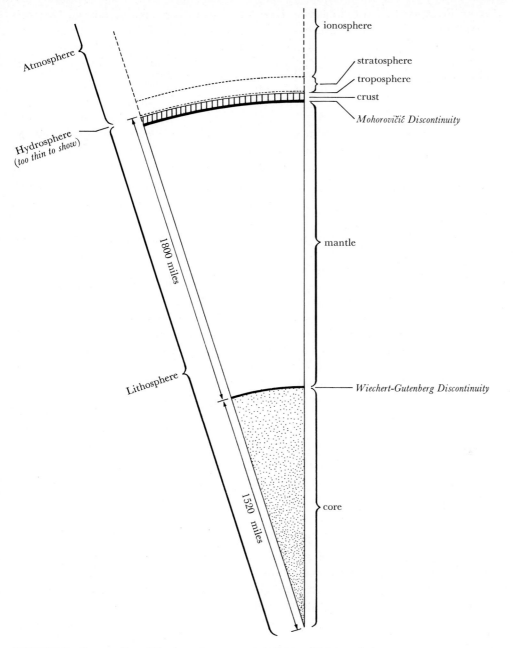

ionosphere

stratosphere

troposphere

crust

Mohorovičič Discontinuity

mantle

Wiechert-Gutenberg Discontinuity

core

Atmosphere

Hydrosphere
(*too thin to show*)

Lithosphere

1800 miles

1520 miles

FIGURE 24-7. Cross-section of Earth to show concentric layers. (Not to scale.)

from whose valence shells both electrons have been stripped. Such iron ions are enormously greedy for free oxygen with which to combine, but at the time there was none available. Thus there also could have been no ionosphere—or, at least, no ozone in it. Therefore the ultraviolet radiation of Sun reached the surface in merciless quantities.

(2)   At the beginning there may not have been any hydrosphere.

The difficulty is that we do not know the temperature at the time of Earth's consolidation. The sources of heat were three: the consolidation itself, Sun's radiation, and the disintegration of radioactive isotopes in the crust. If these factors added up to yield an initial average surface temperature greater than the boiling point of water (212°F if we assume, probably without justification, that the pressure was much the same as now), then our water supply was largely in the atmosphere. By one extreme estimate, it was so much hotter than that at the outset that the crust was molten, and may have taken as much as two thousand million years of cooling before the atmospheric water finally precipitated as rain. On the other hand, Earth may have formed cool, so that the hydrosphere is as old as the rest.

(3)   A third gross difference is in the distribution of thicker and thinner regions of crust.

When the hydrosphere did form, the thicker regions kept their granitic heads above water as continental expanse, while the water covered the thinner regions as ocean. But the original distribution of continent and ocean must have been very different from what it is now. The reconstruction so far achieved goes back only to 500,000,000 years ago, at which time there was apparently a single enormous land mass, dubbed "Pangaea" ('whole-earth') by the geologists. Pangaea may have resulted from an earlier drifting together of smaller masses, or conceivably may have survived with little change from the initial formation; we do not yet know. But after the date given, it broke up and the pieces began to move around in a slow drift that still continues (Figure 24-8).

WATER   �x   If the hydrosphere was not original, its formation was a major revolution in Earth's history. Water has played a threefold role: in the migrations of matter at and near Earth's surface; in heat-flow and temperature control; and in chemical activity.

SURFACE TURBULENCE

When a sizable quantity of matter all moves in the same direction at the same time, the motion is said to be *molar*. Most of the molar motion of Earth—apart from its rotation and revolution—takes place in a thin shell that includes the troposphere, the hydrosphere, and an indefinite amount of the crust, for a total thickness of perhaps 20 miles. This shell of turbulence is older than the biosphere, but the biosphere grew within it and all life, including our own, is part of it. What moves most in the shell of turbulence is water. Air moves faster, but is much less dense; rock is denser but moves much more slowly. When you or your dog runs down the street, two thirds of the momentum is that of moving water.

In addition to tides and ocean currents, water moves a lot because its freezing and boiling points are related so strategically to the range of temperatures at Earth's

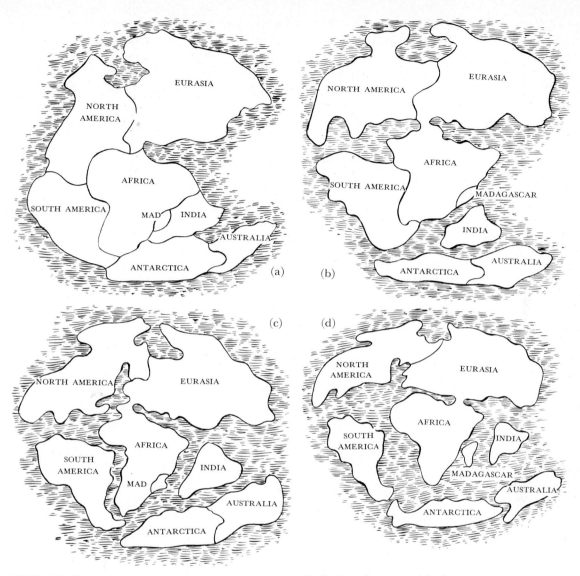

FIGURE 24-8. PANGAEA AND CONTINENTAL DRIFT. (a) shows the distribution of continental land masses as reconstructed for the end of the Permian. (b) shows the redistribution, by drift, by the end of the Triassic; (c) is late Jurassic; (d) is at the end of the Cretaceous. For the dating in years of the geological periods (Permian etc.) see the Running Calendar, pp. 304–311. (After Robert S. Dietz and John C. Holden, "Reconstruction of Pangaea: Breakup and dispersion of continents, Permian to present," *Journal of Geophysical Research,* 75.4939–4956, 1970.)

surface. Water vapor constantly enters the atmosphere by evaporation from the hydrosphere and by sublimation from glaciers. Carried to colder regions by air currents, it condenses and falls back as rain or snow. Much of this precipitation is directly back into the sea, yet each second 15,000,000 tons of it fall on land surface.

Some of this freezes. Some sinks below the surface and seeps along in underground channels. About a third stays on the surface and runs downhill as far as it can, principally back to the sea. Now, water is an effective agent for transporting other substances because, given enough time, it can dissolve almost anything. In its downhill journey on or under the ground, it picks up and carries along solid matter, some of it bodily by mechanical action, most of it in solution. Most of this sediment is deposited elsewhere ashore, as the water evaporates or its flow becomes more sluggish. But solid matter is carried in this way from the land into the oceans at a current rate of 88 tons per second. The sea is salt, and fresh water is fresh, because when water evaporates the things dissolved in it are mostly left behind.

Thus, since the formation of the hydrosphere water has played a major part in resculpturing the face of Earth.

TEMPERATURE

Whatever may have been the case earlier on, once Earth had a hydrosphere its surface temperature was subject to only minor fluctuations. Liquid water can absorb large amounts of heat without boiling, and can lose large amounts without freezing; thus it can both cool off hot substances and warm up cold ones. Moreover, since it travels easily, it can readily carry heat from warmer to colder places. In fact, warm water flows in surface currents, such as the Gulf Stream, from the tropics towards the poles; cold water flows in the other direction in currents near the ocean floor; the arctic and antarctic are therefore warmer and the tropics cooler than they would otherwise be.

It is true that variations of world temperature have been great enough to bring glaciers to within 30 or 40 degrees of latitude from the equator at certain times, and to melt them completely at others. But these effects require a variation of only a few tens of degrees in the average surface temperature. The reasons for even this small amount of fluctuation are not fully understood. The cold spells are *ice ages.* We know of the last three, possibly the only three, through which Earth has passed: the Precambrian, the Permian, and the Quaternary (see the Running Calendar, pp. 304–311). The Quaternary Ice Age began a mere two million years ago; we may still be living in it.

CHEMICAL ACTIVITY

In cosmic perspective, chemistry is a rarity. Chemical behavior is that of matter organized into atoms, and depends in the first instance on their outermost (or "valence") shells of electrons. There is no chemical activity inside stars, because the concentration of energy is too high: atomic nuclei can capture and hold orbital electrons only for fractions of a second. Atoms can last a little longer near stellar surfaces, but only a little. They can endure for eons in interstellar clouds, but there the density and energy-level are so low that the atoms have little chance to form compounds. We have now accounted for *at least* 99% of the matter in a galaxy such as our own, perhaps closer to 99.99%. Where is that last tiny portion? In the only really favorable place for chemical behavior: in planets.

A planet has a *chemical history.* It begins when the preplanetary cloud becomes dense enough for the formation of compounds. It affects, and is affected by, the sorting-out of substances during the condensation. It is kept going by outside sources of energy, especially radiation from the planet's primary (the star it orbits). It ends when the planet is destroyed by an explosion of its primary, or when some state of stable equilibrium is reached.

In our case—Earth's case—the period of condensation witnessed the formation of water and of other simple compounds built from the most abundant elements; and either this period or an early stage during which the crust was molten (if there was any such stage: p. 324) saw the formation of the great variety of inorganic compounds, or *minerals,* of which the rocks of the crust were initially composed.

Matter in the crystalline (solid) state is chemically inactive. Gasses can be chemically active, but flow so readily that they tend quickly to reach a state of equilibrium. Thus, if a planet or satellite consists solely of a lithosphere, as does Moon, nothing much happens, and if it consists only of a lithosphere and an atmosphere, as does Venus, the situation is not much better.

Earth, however, not only kept an atmosphere but at an unknown time acquired a hydrosphere. Our chemical history therewith took a special turn.

There are compounds that form most readily in a mixture of gasses but which are likely to disintegrate again unless they find sanctuary in a less turbulent medium, such as water. There are many compounds that form most readily in the range of temperatures at which water is liquid. The formation of some of these is also greatly promoted if the constituents are in the form of ions in an aqueous solution: the jiggling-around of the ions gives them a chance to come together. But the very same jiggling can pull them apart again. If a delicate molecule is to endure, the amount of random jiggling has to be reduced, either by a lowering of the temperature or through the evaporation of some of the water; at the same time, the molecule must be shielded from high-energy radiation.

It was therefore crucial, as our hydrosphere formed, both that there was enough water to cover a large part of the surface and that there was not enough to cover it all. Had the early oceans rolled unbroken everywhere, before many hundreds of millions of years the result would have been much the same as that of no hydrosphere: an unutterably dull chemical homogeneity.

As it was, winds scraping dry land carried dust particles aloft, to serve as condensation surfaces for water vapor, yielding clouds. The clouds afforded temporary local protection against Sun's radiation, and electrostatic differences between clouds or between cloud and surface produced lightning discharges. Compounds forming in the lower atmosphere under the protection of clouds or at night, perhaps most often with lightning as the source of the necessary energy, could sink into deep water, or migrate under projecting rock ledges, and thus avoid destruction when the clouds dispersed or day broke.

Also, some rain fell on land. Some spots ashore were wetter, some drier; some hotter, some colder; and at any one spot these factors changed with time. Running water dissolved different substances in different places, brought them together in varying proportions, and evaporated more or less completely to yield an endless variety of solutions, colloids, suspensions, and dry residues.

Thus, thanks to our partial hydrosphere, Earth's sphere of turbulence (p. 324) before long achieved, not homogeneity, but a remarkably high degree of chemical and physicochemical *diversity*.

LIFE ✖ Life is part of Earth's chemical history: a chemical chain reaction that began in a small way at some time during Earth's first two thousand million years and then gradually involved more and more of Earth's substance, until, already many hundreds of millions of years ago, the active biosphere was virtually coterminous with the sphere of turbulence and the inactive biosphere was many times that extensive.

The steps and stages in the emergence of life are far from fully understood. We know, in a general way, that three things must have happened: (1) the formation of various relatively simple carbon-based compounds; (2) the synthesis of some of these into macromolecules capable of catalyzing the formation of others more or less like themselves; and (3) the assembling of such materials into packets of just the right sort.

INGREDIENTS

The *elements* in living matter are necessarily just those supplied by the universe, and it is hardly surprising that their proportions in organisms are much the same as their relative abundance at or near Earth's surface (Table 24-9).

At the size-level of simple molecules—say, from a half dozen to a dozen or so constituent atoms—living matter is characterized by a dazzling array of carbon compounds: hydrocarbons (carbon and hydrogen and nothing else), carbohydrates (those two and oxygen), and various types that include also a little nitrogen, sulfur, phosphorus, or the like. Among the latter are *amino acids,* all of which include nitrogen, and *nucleotides,* with a crucial bit of phosphorus. These carbon compounds abound today, but, except for a few of the hydrocarbons, only as products and byproducts of the metabolism of organisms. That affords us no clew as to how young Earth's chemistry could have produced them before there were any organisms, as it must have done.

Recall the possible role of lightning mentioned a few paragraphs back. Today a lightning discharge affects the atmosphere mainly by converting ordinary molecular oxygen (O_2) into ozone (O_3). But Earth's original atmosphere contained no free oxygen, though it contained plenty of that element, as well as hydrogen, carbon, and nitrogen, in simple molecular combinations. Suppose we fill a chamber with a mixture of gasses more or less matching the early atmosphere, and then pass a powerful electric spark through the mixture. Investigators have done this, and have subjected the residues to painstaking analysis. They find minute traces of various simple carbon compounds, including even amino acids.

This shows us, then, one mechanism by which Earth *could* have produced its earliest stocks of the compounds. There are doubtless others, and several may actually have played a part. In one respect the mechanisms were surely all alike: all of them were extremely inefficient, in the sense that the degradation of great amounts of energy yielded only tiny quantities of the new substances.

Thermodynamic efficiency in the synthesis of carbon compounds rests on the presence of suitable catalysts. A catalyst is a substance in the presence of which a particular chemical reaction takes place with less triggering energy than is otherwise required, and hence more rapidly than when there is none of the catalyst about.

A complicated carbon-based molecule is built out of simpler ones by removing an atom or so from each of the simpler ones and sticking the remainders together. This is easy to mock up by hand with a tinkertoy model, and happens readily enough in the presence of appropriate catalysts. Otherwise it is an exceedingly rare event.

But the suitable catalysts for the synthesis of carbon compounds are themselves carbon compounds, in general much more complex than those we have mentioned so far!

Stage two, then, could not have begun until the inefficient mechanisms of stage one had been at work for a very long time. The stocks of simpler carbon compounds had to have become so large, and their distributions so wide, that *some* of them were

TABLE 24-9. Composition of the human body.

For this purpose the human body is reasonably representative of all land mammals, and not too bad for animals in general; the balance in plants and in microorganisms is somewhat different. (After Blum 1968.)

	IN HUMAN BODY:		RELATIVE ORDER OF ABUNDANCE: (1 = most abundant, etc.)	
	PERCENT OF TOTAL MASS	PERCENT OF TOTAL ATOMS	IN HYDROSPHERE	IN CRUST
water	65–70			
other	35–30			
ELEMENTS				
hydrogen	10.2	63.5 ⎫	2	10
oxygen	66.0	25.6 ⎬ 98.2	1	1
carbon	17.5	9.1 ⎭	10	14
nitrogen	2.4	1.06	16	28
calcium	1.6	0.25	7	5
phosphorus	0.9	0.18 ⎬ 99.92	19	11
sodium	0.3	0.07	4	6
potassium	0.4	0.06	8	7
chlorine	0.3	0.05	3	15
sulfur	0.2	0.04	6	13
magnesium	0.05	0.01 ⎭	5	8
iron	0.005	0.006	23	4
zinc	0.002	0.0002	24	23
copper	0.0004	0.00006	25	25
manganese	0.00005	0.00006	26	26
nickel, cobalt, aluminum, titanium, boron, iodine, arsenic, lead, tin, molybdenum, vanadium, silicon, bromine, fluorine	traces	<0.1%		

together in just the right proportions and just the right circumstances for more complex synthesis. Of the circumstances we know only that they must have been unusual.

Once the synthesis began, however, its rate increased exponentially. The first faint traces of catalysts hastened the production of more macromolecules, or the tearing apart of some older types and the reassembly of the constituents into new types. Some of the new macromolecules were also catalysts, yielding more production.

Not all macromolecules, of course, are catalysts. Of those that are, the two most important are *proteins* and *nucleic acids.*

PROTEINS. A protein macromolecule is a chain of amino acids. Only twenty-odd amino acids are at all common (Box 24-10), though a good many others exist. The simplest known proteins nowadays consist of several dozen amino acid links, and some have hundreds of constituents. Since, in principle, any amino acid can occur as any link, the total number of possible chemically distinct proteins is exceedingly large.

Catalyzing proteins play a part in the formation (and the dissolution) of other proteins, and of various other carbon-based substances. None of them catalyze the production of nucleic acids.

The earliest proteins in Earth's chemical history were doubtless very small—say, only a half dozen or so links. But the action of these paved the way for the synthesis of more complicated ones, which then superseded them. In fact, one suspects that there were many successive "generations" of catalyzing macromolecules before the emergence of those which survive today.

NUCLEIC ACIDS. A nucleic acid macromolecule consists of a chain of nucleotides (Box 24-11). We spoke of their variety and function on page 48.

Nucleic acids catalyze the formation of proteins and of other nucleic acids. In addition, some of them, at least, are *autocatalysts*: if the proper raw materials are nearby, the nucleic acid molecule directs their organization into a replica of itself. As far as is known, no protein is an autocatalyst.

STRUCTURAL MACROMOLECULES. Certain relatively simple carbohydrates (p. 328) are *sugars;* macromolecules built by the chaining of sugars are *polysaccharides* (Box 24-12).

Polysaccharides are not catalysts, and their synthesis depends on the action of proteins that are. Once assembled, however, some of them are such that it also takes appropriate protein catalysts to break them apart again. This, plus the fact that they can tangle together into strong threads or membranes, makes them excellent structural and protective materials. Cellulose, the chief structural ingredient in green land plants, and chitin, found in fungi and in the exoskeletons of crustaceans and insects, are both polysaccharides; others are found in other organisms.

Some complicated proteins also make excellent structural materials.

ENERGY MOLECULES. Even in the presence of catalysts it takes some triggering energy either to build a chemical bond or to break one. In some cases it takes more to build the bond than to break it. The excess is stored in the bond itself, and when the bond is broken the excess becomes available to do something else.

BOX 24-10. An album of amino acids.

Most of the amino acids contain the group shown on the right; the empty box stands for the rest of the molecule, different from one amino acid to another.

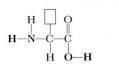

In the following display of several amino acids, the group shown above is represented by "R" and the rest of the structure is given in full. Note that cystine has two R's, and that proline has a modification in which the N is directly hooked into the rest of the molecule, as well as indirectly through a C.

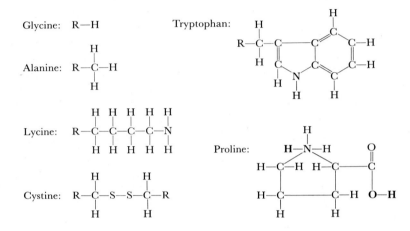

Chaining of amino acids into long protein molecules involves the dropping of the H and OH parts of R printed in boldface above, each such pair yielding a molecule of water. Schematically, with three amino acid molecules shown:

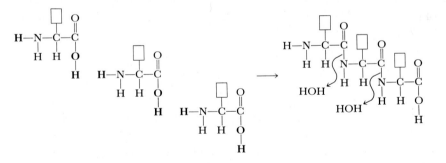

A typical protein molecule consists of a very precise sequence of dozens, hundreds, or even thousands of amino acid ions; for example, ribonuclease (taken from the pancreas of cows for experimentation) has been shown to contain 107 such ions, representing 17 different amino acids, plus 17 NH_3 groups. In the actual molecule the chain is not straight, but twisted around in space, into a helix or other complex arrangement; and stability is increased by hydrogen bonds and other supplementary local ties between parts of the chain brought into proximity by the twisting.

The structure of *adenosine triphosphate* ("ATP") is shown in Figure 24-13. The bonds represented in the figure by wavy lines are of the type we have just described. When the outermost wavy bond is broken, the yield is adenosine diphosphate ("ADP"), a free phosphate, and energy.

There are two reasons for believing that ATP and ADP may have appeared very

BOX 24-11. An album of nucleotides.

Nucleic acids involve five nitrogen bases—two purines and three pyrimidines:

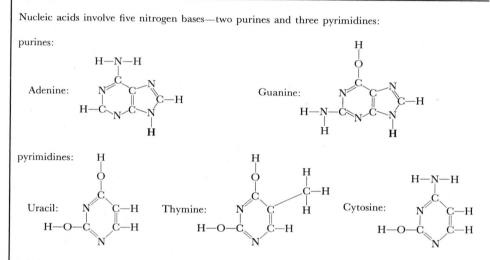

When a purine is hooked into a chain, the H shown in boldface drops. When a pyrimidine is hooked into a chain, the configuration shown at the "southwest" corner, identical for all three, is modified to

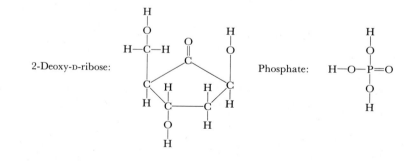

, leaving the N free to form another connection.

In RNA the chaining involves the sugar D-ribose and a phosphate; in DNA, the sugar 2-deoxy-D-ribose and a phosphate. We show the latter:

The combination of a base and a sugar is a nucleoside; the addition to this of the phosphate forms a nucleotide.

BY HIS BOOTSTRAPS

early in Earth's chemical history. One is that the constituents (adenine, the sugar D-ribose, and phosphate) are all simple enough that they could have been synthesized by the inefficient mechanisms of stage one; furthermore, all three turn up also in nucleotides. The other reason is that they are now universal. Every living cell in the biosphere ships energy from one place to another in the form of ATP. It is synthesized

The chaining is then like this (where "R" is the nitrogen base):

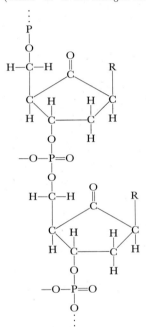

The whole chain is twisted into a double spiral with hydrogen-bond cross-ties. In DNA, the participating nitrogen bases are adenine, guanine, cytosine, and thymine; in RNA, uracil occurs instead of thymine. The H-bond cross-ties in the spiral are established with absolute regularity between adenine and thymine or uracil, and between guanine and cytosine. Each "bridge" between the "back-bones" of the double spiral thus involves just three rings (since the purines each have two, the pyrimidines each one). Here is a schematic drawing of a segment of such a double-spiral macromolecule, with dimensions marked ("Å" = ångström = 10^{-8} cm = 0.000000004 in.):

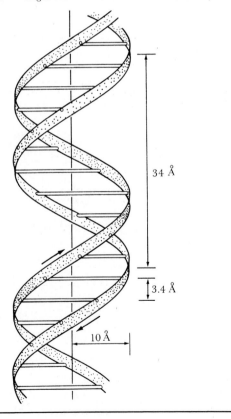

at those points in the cell where the proper catalysts and a source of energy are available, and it is broken down elsewhere to yield the energy for other metabolism, for growth, and for movement.

Many other substances—including proteins—yield usable energy upon their decomposition in the presence of the right catalysts. Almost as widespread today as the ATP process is the oxidation of the sugar glucose into carbon dioxide and water; the only organisms that do not do this are certain bacteria. Substances that can be efficiently converted or decomposed into glucose are therefore useful for storing energy. Other sugars, and fats, are such substances. So are the polysaccharides starch and cellulose, in both of which the constituent links are glucose. For this function starch is better than cellulose because the bonds between the links are much more easily

BOX 24-12. Some sugars and polysaccharides.

Two common simple sugars (or *monosaccharides*) are glucose and fructose. Both are $C_6H_{12}O_6$, but with different structural arrangements:

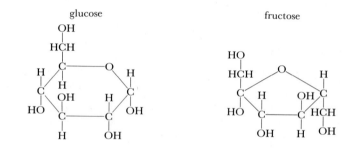

The joining together of simple sugars into larger molecules is called *polymerization*. In terms of the orientation of the structural formulas given above, the joining is "end to end," with an oxygen link and yielding a molecule of water (H_2O) as byproduct:

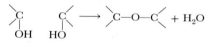

Sucrose, the sugar we get from cane or beets, is a *disaccharide*, involving one molecule each of glucose and fructose:

sucrose

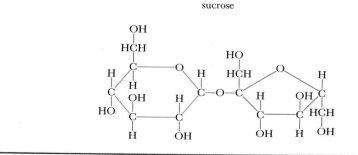

broken; in reverse, this is what renders cellulose better than starch as a structural material.

PACKAGING

You could have a beakerful or an oceanful of the kinds of substances we have just been describing and still not have anything remotely like living matter. The ingredients are necessary but not sufficient. Also crucial are the exact proportions and the precise geometrical arrangement. Furthermore, in any organism both of these are constantly changing, in a patterned way.

All life today is cellular (p. 48). The earliest living forms must have been cells.

Cellulose is a polysaccharide in which all the links are glucose; a single macromolecule of cellulose contains at least 3000 links, often more. Each link is turned 180° from the preceding one, around the axis that joins them:

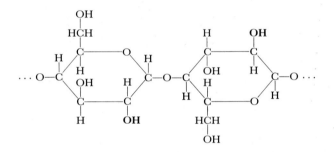

Cellulose macromolecules are linear, with little tendency to twist.

Chitin is not, strictly speaking, a polysaccharide, because it contains some nitrogen. It is like cellulose except that in each participating link the OH group shown in boldface in the above structural formula is replaced by the radical $NHCOCH_3$.

Starch is like cellulose except that the successive links are not turned. This puts the $CHCH_2OH$ part on the same side of the links, so that the whole macromolecule tends to curl or twist:

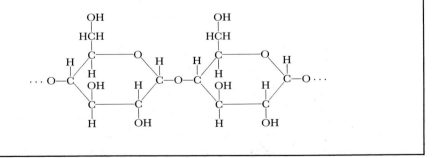

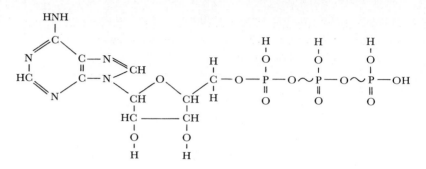

FIGURE 24-13. Adenosine triphosphate (ATP).

If we strip the requirements for cellular makeup to a bare minimum, they would seem to be the following:

(1) A durable protective envelope that keeps the big molecules inside from scattering, but that passes small molecules so that raw materials can enter and waste products be expelled.

(2) Some means (such as ATP) for shipping energy from one place to another.

(3) Proteins that can (a) get energy from some of the raw materials and (b) use others to synthesize structural materials, more proteins, and substances suitable for further processing by nucleic acids.

(4) A quota of nucleic acids capable of autocatalysis and of the catalysis of relevant proteins.

(5) Internal partitioning, via membranes and tubes of structural materials, so that catalysts and raw materials get together in the right places and at the right times.

Beyond this, the whole assembly must be such that all constituents increase in quantity, so that the cell grows, and in time the substances must be so distributed that the cell divides into two, each approximately a replica of the original.

I don't know whether this sounds simple or complicated, but it can't sound as complicated as the reality. Cells are marked by extreme specificity of detailed structure, which means enormous amounts of information (p. 32). If we had all the information, we could build a cell in the laboratory. On the other hand, the earliest cells must have been much simpler than any now in existence.

We don't know how stage three got started. Some of the stage-two production of macromolecules had to come first, but maybe not much.

We do have a few clues from physical chemistry.

COLLOIDS.   Consider a mixture consisting of a liquid *suspending medium* (say, water) and a quantity of some *suspended phase.* In a *suspension,* the latter is in such massive pieces that they will precipitate out unless the mixture is constantly stirred. We assume the suspended phase is not water-soluble, since if it is the big pieces break up and the mixture becomes a *solution.* In a solution the suspended phase is in pieces comparable in size to the individual molecules of the suspending medium, and precipitation is forestalled merely by thermal agitation. Between these extremes is the *colloid*, in which the suspended particles range in diameter roughly from 0.00000004 to 0.00004 inch. The particles in a colloid are too small to precipitate, but large enough to give the mixture some very special properties.

One of these is that if some of the suspending medium is removed the colloidal particles may coagulate into an interconnected mass of filaments. This is the "gel" state; the state we described first is the "sol" state. Both are thoroughly familiar: egg white is a sol-state colloid, but changes to gel state when the egg is boiled, removing some of the water.

Another property is that a complicated colloid may form into *coacervates*: aggregates of the particles, not coagulated because they are held apart by thin membranes, and surrounded by a larger membrane that separates them from the surrounding medium. Though small, a coacervate is large enough to contain hundreds or thousands of the constituent colloidal particles.

Now, some carbon-based macromolecules are large enough that if you mix them with water—and if they don't dissolve—they form a colloid rather than a solution. And if there are enough different kinds of macromolecules in the same colloidal mixture, some of them may collect into coacervates.

INFERENCE. The inference is that events of this sort led to stage three.

Early coacervates were presumably of many different sizes and compositions. Some perhaps contained only proteins, to the exclusion of nucleic acids; others vice versa. Some may have contained incompatible ingredients that triggered one another's dissolution. Some had such fragile protective membranes that they quickly disintegrated. Some grew a bit, through the catalytic action of included macromolecules on raw materials that seeped in, before they fell apart. Some did not fall apart, but pinched through at the middle and divided into smaller ones (a structure as simple as an oil droplet in water will do this if the proper stress is applied). From time to time a small one invaded a larger one, bringing ingredients together in a new combination—usually, but not invariably, with disastrous results for both.

And, during all this, in the temporary partial protection of coacervates, catalyzing macromolecules were slowly synthesizing more complex ones that then, in time, replaced them.

The chance may seem very small that such random events could ever result in just the right proportions and arrangements for life. But the process may have gone on in many different places in Earth's sphere of turbulence, and may have continued for hundreds of millions of years. And, in fact, life did appear.

EARTH'S GREENING AND RUSTING

✖ As soon as some coacervates had become cells, such nonliving ones as were still about were reduced to the status of food—or poison—for the living ones. Before long most of the nonliving ones disappeared. Perhaps all of them did, but it may be that some survived and evolved to become today's viruses.

We don't know where the earliest cells developed. Perhaps it was in microscopic cracks ashore, where neither moisture nor radiation was excessive. If so, then as successive generations of cells became tougher they spread to puddles and ponds, to lakes and rivers, and finally to the open sea, where types of diverse origin came into competition. The ocean may not have been the womb of life, but it was surely the cradle. Land life as we now understand that term lay still far in the future.

Chemosynthesis

We must not think of the hydrosphere at this early stage as "teeming" with life. The process of living requires the degradation of energy, and at the time the sources of usable energy were strictly limited.

Some types of cells were doubtless able to obtain the energy they needed from other types, and there had to be some that could get it directly from relatively simple substances in their environments. The latter process is *chemosynthesis,* still practiced today, in many different forms, by various bacteria.

But chemosynthesis requires some stock of simple carbon compounds, as sources of energy or as building materials or both, and if that stock is replenished only by the metabolism of other organisms then the whole process is circular and will run down. At the time of which we are speaking, the only nonliving sources for the compounds were the terribly inefficient mechanisms of stage one.

Photosynthesis

What happened to boost the level of organic activity was doubtless the most revolutionary event in all the history of the biosphere. Some organisms came, through mutation, to synthesize the substance *chlorophyll,* which converts the energy of sunlight into chemically usable form. This conversion is *photosynthesis.*

The molecular structure of chlorophyll is shown in Figure 24-14. Note the presence of an atom of magnesium, not one of the most abundant elements, yet common enough to form today about one fiftieth of Earth's crust.

Chlorophyll is activated by radiation of wavelengths near 0.00000172 inch and 0.00000272 inch (bluish green and orangish red), but usually—nowadays—there are pigments ("carotenoids") nearby that are activated by neighboring and intervening wavelengths and pass the energy on to the chlorophyll, rendering the process more efficient.

Activation knocks a single electron from a low-energy orbit to a very high-energy state. There are then two distinct processes:

(1)   In one, "cyclic phosphorylation," the electron cascades down through successive energy levels, the released energy being used in various chemical changes in neighboring substances, until it returns to its original low-energy orbit in the chlorophyll molecule.

(2)   In the other, "noncyclic phosphorylation," the electron is captured by a molecule of another substance, initiating a chain of reactions during which free oxygen (O_2) is released and an electron is torn in turn from a molecule of some other pigment, to cascade downwards until it replaces the electron lost from the chlorophyll molecule.

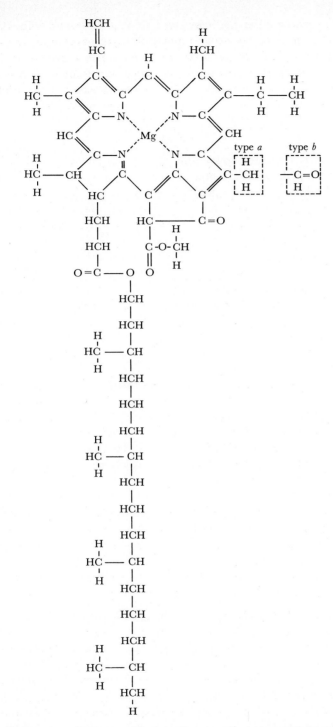

FIGURE 24-14. Chlorophyll. Types *a* and *b*, shown here, are the commonest; two rarer types are not represented. The magnesium (Mg) atom in the "head" has a valence of only two; the bonds holding it to the four neighboring nitrogen (N) atoms "resonate"—that is, shift back and forth extremely fast.

Both of these produce, at one or more steps, ATP, the nature and function of which we described on page 332. The second also yields free oxygen.

When sunlight is divested, by absorption, of the wavelengths that activate chlorophyll, and the rest is reflected, it looks green. The cells that developed chlorophyll, and their descendants that retain it, include certain bacteria, the blue-green algae, some other one-celled organisms, and all the green plants.[2]

Consequences

The immediate result of the appearance of chlorophyll was that the biosphere had access to an incalculably greater source of energy for its activity. Sun shone on Earth no harder than before, but great gobs of radiant energy that had earlier made no contribution were now usable. Before photosynthesis life may have been rare and scattered. After it, the hydrosphere soon became a seething caldron.

Chlorophyll also changed Earth's structure. Noncyclic phosphorylation poured increasing quantities of O_2 into the atmosphere, the first it had held since long before the beginning of life. This swept out the ionized iron (p. 322), which fell to the surface as iron oxides—rust. Some of the oxygen rose high in the sky and was converted by solar radiation into ozone, thus forming the ionospheric shield which has ever since protected the surface from direct exposure to Sun's destructive ultraviolet.

Oxygen in the atmosphere brought to an end the old synthesis of carbon compounds by lightning and other inorganic agencies, but with the new source of fresh energy that did not matter.

Oxygen in the atmosphere, and in solution in the hydrosphere, also made possible the development of new ways of life for organisms that could not directly exploit sunlight for themselves. Animals, for example, live by eating green plants or by eating other animals that do. Green plants convert ADP into ATP in two different ways: by photosynthesis, and by oxidizing glucose (p. 334). Animals do only the latter. Animals get the glucose from what they eat, which means ultimately from green plants, and obtain the oxygen from the surrounding hydrosphere or atmosphere, which also means indirectly from green plants. The parasitism is thus two-pronged. However, animal metabolism yields nitrogenous waste products that plants can use. Moreover, if animal metabolism had not developed soon after the appearance of chlorophyll, atmospheric oxygen might have become so plentiful that the plants would have burned up.

The Timetable

We said earlier (p. 328) that life got started sometime during Earth's first two thousand million years.

We know this from fossils—microscopically small ones whose existence was scarcely suspected as recently as twenty years ago. The oldest date from about 3,200,000,000 years ago. Under careful examination, they seem to show nonnucleated cells somewhat

[2]The glorious riot of color of the autumn woods is the carotenoids, which have been there all summer but which become visible only as the chlorophyll breaks up and disappears (in deciduous plants) with the increasing cold.

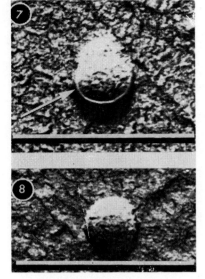

(a)

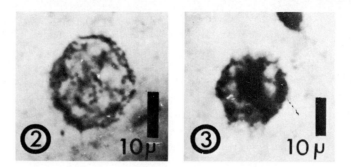

(b)

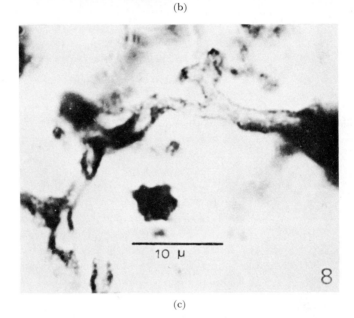

(c)

FIGURE 24-15. THE OLDEST KNOWN FOSSILS. (a) and (b): from the Fig Tree formation of Precambrian rocks, South Africa, age about 3,200,000,000 years. (a) is interpreted as transverse sections of rod-shaped bacteriumlike one-celled organisms. The comparison line is one micron long (about 0.00004 inch). (b) shows algalike spheres, diameters somewhat less than twenty microns. (c): a filamentous (multicellular?) formation from the Gunflint Chert sediments of the Laurentian Shield, Canada, diameter of cross-section about two microns, age about 2,000,000,000 years. [Photomicrographs by Elso S. Barghoorn; reproduced with his permission from *Science* 152.760 Figs. 7, 8 (6 May 1966), 156.508 Figs. 2, 3 (28 April 1967), 147.568 Fig. 8 (5 February 1965).]

like those of modern bacteria and blue-green algae (Figure 24-15). By 2,000,000,000 years ago there are also what appear to be multicellular filaments and traces of spherical bodies that were probably spores. At latest by the later date, then, chlorophyll photosynthesis was in full swing, the atmosphere was being oxygenated, and some many-celled organisms had appeared.

That does not mean that the photosynthetically supported biosphere achieved a stable balance in a hurry. Initially there may have been wild gyrations. Even later, there may have been catastrophic episodes. Earth's magnetic field has something to do with maintaining the ionosphere, and there is evidence that the field has been subject to fluctuations (this may have some bearing on the incidence of ice ages). Moreover, the Solar System does not hold still. In addition to various local motions, all the matter of the Home Galaxy revolves about the galactic axis; the Solar System makes one revolution each 200,000,000 years. We may on occasion have moved through an interstellar cloud that cut down on the amount of incident sunlight. Also, we may have passed within a hundred light-years or so of a supernova—on the average, one happens somewhere in the Home Galaxy each fifty years. If we did, hard radiation came sleeting right through the ionosphere and all other barriers, to strike at tissues and genetic material, destroying some organisms and triggering all sorts of mutations in others. Were the timing of such episodes known to us, we might discover that they played a part in some of the seemingly sudden turnovers in prevalent life forms.

MULTICELLULARITY

✕ As soon as there was life, there began the process of variation and selection that constitutes organic evolution (chapter 23). All subsequent events in the history of the biosphere are to be ascribed to this process.

One very early development (we do not know whether it began before or after chlorophyll) was the clustering of cells into cooperating aggregates.[3] We do not know how such clustering got started, but we can make some plausible conjectures.

Cells increase their numbers by fission. The general plan is that the cell grows and elongates, the genetic material doubles and half migrates to either end, and then the cell pinches through at the middle and divides, each daughter inheriting a full quota of genes (Figure 24-16). When the division is complete, the daughter cells move apart. Cellular aggregation presumably began when a pair of daughter cells were prevented from moving apart but managed to survive anyway.

Any cell, to live, must absorb raw materials and discard wastes. If two cells are to survive stuck together, two extreme arrangements are possible, as diagrammed in Figure 24-17. Suppose their metabolism is identical. Then neither cell must absorb raw materials from the other, and neither must discard harmful wastes into the other (recall the junk principle: p. 97). They metabolize in *parallel*. In the other arrangement, their metabolism differs in such a way that what is discarded by one includes just the raw material needed by the other. One feeds for both; the other secretes for both; they metabolize in *series*.

In larger cooperating aggregates of cells either of these two arrangements may

[3]This was not necessarily the first instance of biological cooperation. Today cells are very complicated, the outer membrane or wall containing not only a quantity of more or less homogeneous "cytoplasm" but also diverse smaller structures or "organelles," each with its own protective membrane: mitochondria, Golgi bodies, lysosomes, ribosomes, chloroplasts, nuclei, and others. It has been seriously proposed that these—or some of them—began, long ago, as separate free-living organisms, and that cells were the results of their random but eventually viable clustering into the larger assemblages (compare our description on p. 337).

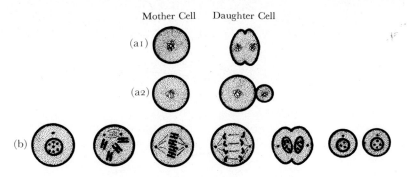

Mother Cell   Daughter Cell

(a1)

(a2)

(b)

FIGURE 24-16. CELL FISSION. (a1) shows it in sketchy outline; (a2) is a bacterial variant, *budding,* in which one daughter cell is much smaller than the other. (b) shows the advanced form known as *mitosis:* the nuclear material, organized into strings called *chromosomes,* is duplicated; half migrates to each half of the cell; then the cell divides. (After Weisz 1967.)

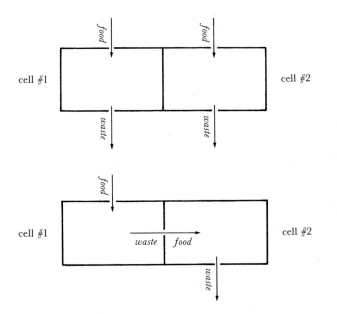

FIGURE 24-17. Metabolism in parallel and in series.

predominate. When the principal plan is metabolism in parallel, the aggregate is a *colony.* When there is extensive metabolism in series, it is a (multicellular) *organism.* The difference is one of degree, with no gap between the extremes.

The earliest aggregates were surely both small and colonial, and it must have been in the modified environment of such aggregates that the mutations took place leading to larger aggregates with increasing metabolism in series. Apparently this happened at least twice, independently (see Figure 24-18), since multicellular green plants and multicellular animals are so different. (For that matter, fungi and slime molds are

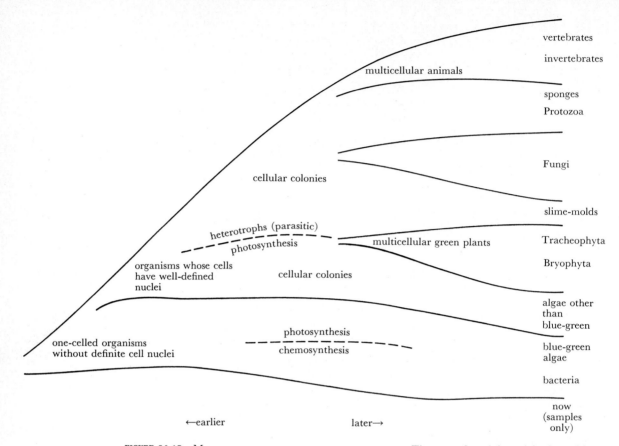

FIGURE 24-18. MAIN LINES OF DIFFERENTIATION OF LIFE FORMS. Time goes from left to right, but with no exact scale. The modern groups named at the right end are only representative. (Adapted from the scheme of R. H. Whittaker, as modified by L. Margulis; see Margulis 1971.)

strikingly different from both.) But simple aggregates still abound: for example, of the bacteria called "cocci," some tend to go around in pairs, some in longer strings, and some in clumps.

The smallest speck that can be seen by the unaided human eye, even against a contrasting background, has a diameter of about 0.004 inch. A few one-celled organisms (certain amoebae) are larger than that, but most are much smaller.[4] This tends to conceal the fact that, even today, one-celled organisms greatly predominate. The best way to emphasize this is to give each cell, rather than each organism or colony, a vote. At any one moment there are perhaps 100,000,000,000,000,000,000,000,000,000 living cells in the biosphere. At least 90% of these, perhaps as high as 99%, opt for solitary life. Multicellularity is rare!

[4]Yet still large enough for great internal complexity. The smallest bacteria are spherical with a diameter of about 0.00004 inch. That is enough volume for as many as a million colloidal particles, thus for at least hundreds of thousands, perhaps millions, of macromolecules.

Furthermore, multicellular life forms are absolutely dependent on this broad base of unicellular organisms. In the economy of the biosphere, organisms with chlorophyll obtain the fresh energy, but bacteria (and some other one-celled organisms) perform many of the chemical conversions that supply multicellular organisms with their immediate needs and that break down waste matter for possible recycling. Bacteria live around us, on us, and in us. Sometimes they make us sick, but we could not exist without them.

Reproduction and Sex

For a unicellular organism, cellular fission is reproduction. For a multicellular aggregate, fission is merely growth: most such aggregates today (not quite all) grow through the successive fissionings of a single original cell, the *zygote*. Before this can happen, the zygote must itself be produced.

Obviously some viable pattern of multicellular reproduction must be as old as multicellularity itself. Today about as simple a pattern as one can find appears among the green algae. A *Volvox* colony consists of from 500 to 50,000 cells embedded on the surface of a sphere of secreted gelatinous material (Figure 24-19). All have flagella pointing outwards. Cytoplasmic strands connect adjacent cells, presumably carrying information, for the flagella act together and the sphere moves as a unit. The cells metabolize largely in parallel. Yet those on one side of the sphere have active light-sensitive spots, and when the sphere moves this side always faces in the direction of the motion. And only a few cells, at the rear, function as zygotes, fissioning to produce new colonies that develop in the gelatinous interior of the old one. Eventually the parent colony falls apart and releases the new ones; the cells of the parent colony then die.

This is a far cry from such a multicellular organism as a tree or a human being, with millions of millions of millions of cells organized into tissues, those into organs, and those into organ systems. But it illustrates the key features of multicellularity: the specializing of some participating cells for reproduction; the relegation of all others to supportive functions of one sort or another; the secretion of substances that form part of the aggregate without being part of any participating cell; and the eventual inevitable death of all cells except those few that live on in the next generation. Almost equally par for the course is for some cells to die long before the whole aggregate does, their substance and arrangement then being crucial for the aggregate: for example, very few of the cells in a vertebrate bone are alive (that is why a broken bone takes so long to knit).

The special reproductive plan involving *sex* must be nearly as ancient as multicellularity, since it is now so widespread.

In this plan, adult organisms produce two different kinds of cells specialized for reproduction, and they are not zygotes but *gametes* (Figure 24-20). In the process that leads to a gamete there occurs a fission not preceded by a doubling of genetic material (the *reduction division*); hence a gamete contains only half the standard quota. Later, through, two gametes, one of each kind, fuse together (*fertilization*); a gamete that finds no partner with which to fuse does not last very long. The resulting single cell, with a full genetic complement, is the zygote.

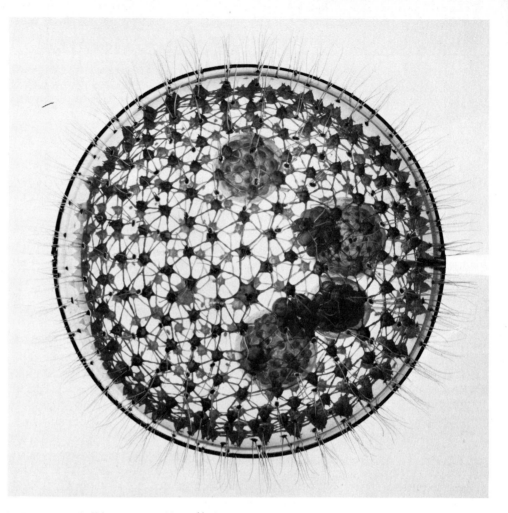

FIGURE 24-19. A *Volvox* colony. About $\frac{1}{25}$ inch in diameter. This is a photograph of a glass model. (Courtesy of The American Museum of Natural History.)

In some current species, including many plants, every adult individual produces gametes of both kinds. In many others, including ourselves and all other vertebrates, the gametes that fuse into a zygote have to come from separate adult organisms, because *males* produce only gametes of one type and *females* only those of the other. The sex (male or female) of the zygote, and of the adult into which it develops, is then genetically determined.

The popularity of sex in the biosphere can be understood in terms of its evolutionary advantage. The mechanism randomizes (within limits) the regroupings of genes from one generation to the next, and thus supplements gene mutation as a source of variation. Some of the new gene combinations may not be viable, but a

BY HIS BOOTSTRAPS

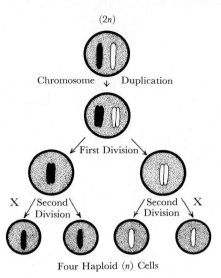

(2n)

Chromosome ↓ Duplication

First Division

X / Second \   / Second \ X
  \ Division   Division /

Four Haploid (n) Cells

FIGURE 24-20. REDUCTION DIVISION. The steps marked "X" are reduction divisions. One or more of the cells in the bottom row ("haploid" cells, each with only half the standard quota of genetic material) are gametes. The diagram does not show the random scattering of chromosomes (and genes) during the first division, that serves, along with mutations, to produce variations in the species. (After Weisz 1967.)

few may yield organisms better equipped than their parents to cope with current environmental challenges.

✖ Since man is the focus in this book, the increasing anthropocentrism in what follows is legitimate. From the outset we have emphasized that not all the features that make us what we are are uniquely human (see, for example, p. 57). Many are shared with a larger or smaller set of nonhuman animal cousins. It is the origins of these that we now trace.

**A SKETCH OF
ANIMAL HISTORY**

Taxonomists assign most multicellular animals to the subkingdom Metazoa, and group the 1,200,000-odd current species of this subkingdom into twenty-three phyla. This is shown in Figure 24-21; the next three figures show more detail for the phylum that includes man; and Box 24-25 summarizes man's official taxonomic position.

Most of the phyla of Figure 24-21 are exclusively marine in habitat, and those that are not include mostly animals that live in fresh water or near the shore. The two major exceptions are the Arthropoda, which include the insects, and the Chordata, which include us. We assume that to start with all Metazoa lived in the water, and also that it was during the watery phase that the phyla differentiated. The latter conclusion is not based on direct fossil evidence, because relevant fossils are extremely rare until the beginning of the Cambrian, about 600,000,000 years ago (see the Running Calendar, p. 305). But when the fossils do appear, they show that almost all of the metazoan phyla of today were already in existence.

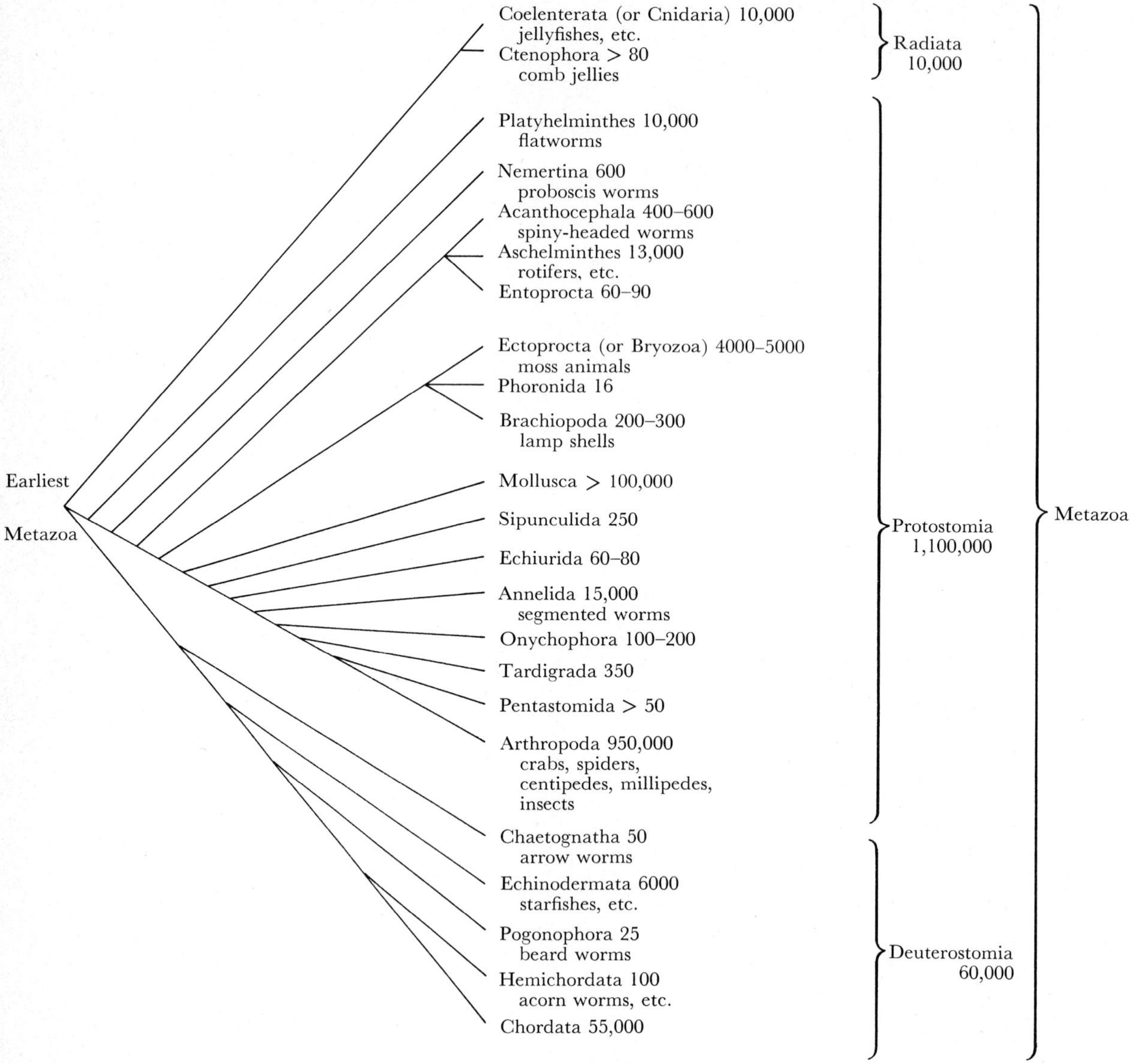

Coelenterata (or Cnidaria) 10,000
  jellyfishes, etc.
Ctenophora > 80
  comb jellies

} Radiata
  10,000

Platyhelminthes 10,000
  flatworms
Nemertina 600
  proboscis worms
Acanthocephala 400–600
  spiny-headed worms
Aschelminthes 13,000
  rotifers, etc.
Entoprocta 60–90

Ectoprocta (or Bryozoa) 4000–5000
  moss animals
Phoronida 16
Brachiopoda 200–300
  lamp shells

Mollusca > 100,000
Sipunculida 250
Echiurida 60–80
Annelida 15,000
  segmented worms
Onychophora 100–200
Tardigrada 350
Pentastomida > 50
Arthropoda 950,000
  crabs, spiders,
  centipedes, millipedes,
  insects

} Protostomia
  1,100,000

Chaetognatha 50
  arrow worms
Echinodermata 6000
  starfishes, etc.
Pogonophora 25
  beard worms
Hemichordata 100
  acorn worms, etc.
Chordata 55,000

} Deuterostomia
  60,000

Earliest Metazoa

} Metazoa

FIGURE 24-21. Metazoa (multicellular animals). The headings in the main column are of *phyla*. The grouping indicated on the right is taxonomic; on the left is given a guess as to the phylogenetic connections. The figures indicate estimates of numbers of species.

In the Water

Our heritage from early aquatic ancestors includes: motility; bilateral symmetry; an alimentary canal with an intake opening (mouth) at the front end and an outflow opening (anus) at the rear; a clustering of specialized sense organs near the mouth;

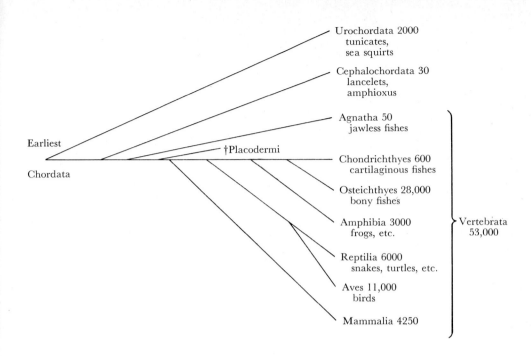

FIGURE 24-22. THE CHORDATA (CHORDATES). The dagger (†) means known only through fossils. The other conventions are as for Figure 24-21.

a central nervous system in the form of a long cord with an enlargement (the brain) at the front end; a circulatory system for internal transport; kidneys; teeth and bones; movable extremities; and lungs.

MOTILITY. The earliest metazoans may have been sessile. At the beginning of adulthood, a sessile aquatic animal anchors itself at an appropriate spot and stays there the rest of its life, feeding on what comes by and expelling its wastes and its gametes (or offspring). The offspring, however, once past the embryonic stage, first become not adults but *larvae,* able to move about in search of a place to settle. It is suspected that motile animals evolved by a process known as *neoteny*: genetic changes modified the developmental timetable, so that the larvae took on certain adult characteristics, especially the ability to reproduce. Thereafter, in time, the sessile phase was abandoned altogether.

BODY SHAPE AND ORGANIZATION. Various body shapes will do for sessile animals. Many show radial symmetry, around a mouth that points upwards; may surface floaters show similar organization about a mouth that points downwards (Figure 24-26). Furthermore, in most such animals there is no separate anus, the mouth serving a double function.

In an aquatic animal that swims about in search of food, such arrangements are inefficient. Much better is a cigar-shaped body with front and rear ends, the mouth

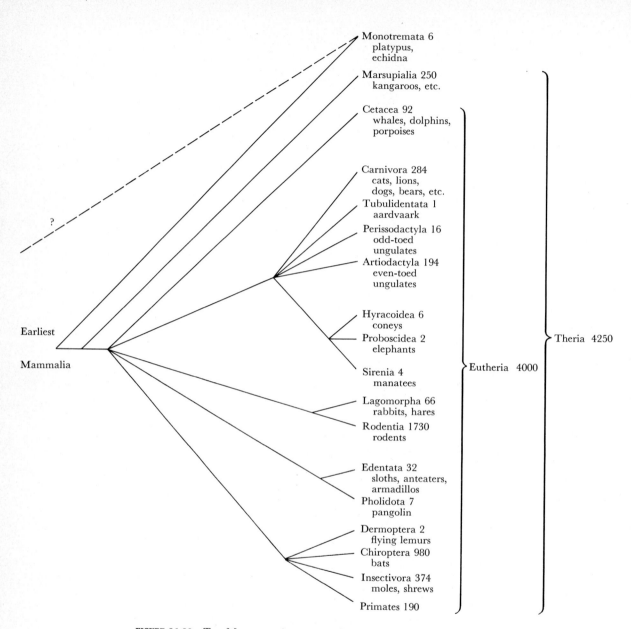

FIGURE 24-23. THE MAMMALIA (MAMMALS). Groups known only through fossils are not shown.

pointing forwards. A separate anus towards the rear is then convenient in terms of the junk principle, since the same movements that carry the animal towards possible food carry it away from its excretions. Gravity operates at right angles to the animal's longitudinal axis, so that the structures of the back and belly may and usually do differ. But there is no such factor differentiating left and right, and the animal may

BY HIS BOOTSTRAPS

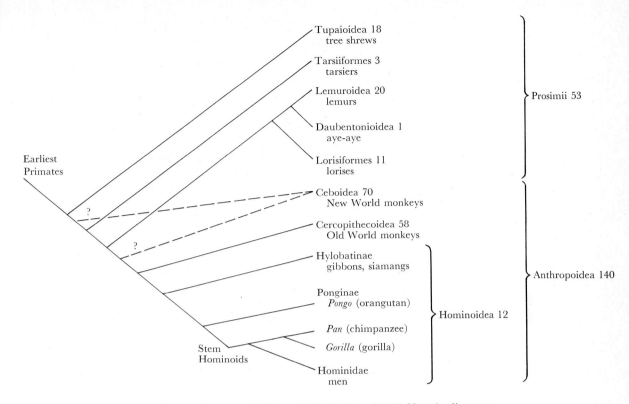

FIGURE 24-24. The Primates. Conventions are as for Figures 24-21, 24-22, and 24-23. Note the discrepancy, towards the bottom, between the formal taxonomy on the right and the likely phylogeny as shown on the left. Also, the position of the New World monkeys is not secure (dotted lines and question marks).

need to turn either way; hence the value of bilateral symmetry. Even the motile larvae of sessile animals tend to show these bodily arrangements (Figure 24-27).

SPECIAL SENSES AND BRAIN. A moving animal needs to be able to detect what lies ahead—be it food or danger—and to test possible food before ingesting it. This led to the clustering of special sense organs at the head end. One was the chemical sense later split, in our own ancestry, into taste and smell. Some photosensitivity is widespread; eyes more or less like our own developed independently, during the watery phase, in several lineages. Hearing is a specialization of touch; it began with vibration detectors stretching along each side of the body (the "lateral line organs"), but the concentration of these in the head (as the inner ears) came about long before our ancestors crawled ashore.

The brain, a lumpy local enlargement of the central nervous system, developed in the head because that was where the specialized sense organs were clustering.

CIRCULATORY SYSTEM. If an aquatic animal is small enough, food and oxygen can be distributed everywhere merely by diffusion. There is a size above which that is impossible, and no aquatic animals larger than that critical size—and no nonaquatic animals of any size—would exist if it had not been for the evolutionary appearance of a circulatory system, which picks up oxygen from gills or lungs, food from appropriate spots in the alimentary canal, carries them to all tissues, and transports wastes to appropriate collecting points for disposal.

KIDNEYS, TEETH, AND BONES. In vertebrates, one of the collecting points for disposal is the kidney, specialized for the separation and discarding of nitrogenous wastes. The kidney operates by filtering, and is dependent on the difference of osmotic pressure on the two sides of a membrane. Comparative physiology leads to the inference that the earliest kidneys worked efficiently only when the animal was immersed in fresh water, and thus, indirectly, to the proposal that the vertebrates evolved in inland waters rather than in the oceans. When, later, they found their way to salt water (and some of them eventually to air), the original kidney had to be supplemented in all sorts of ways.

The earliest vertebrates had no tissues tougher than cartilage. In a backhanded way, the kidney seems to have led to the development of hard parts. Kidneys are fine for nitrogenous wastes but do not work well on metallic salts; hence, among us today, such ills as kidney stones, gallstones, arthritis. The early vertebrates may have been plagued by similar troubles. But a pattern evolved by which the uneliminated

BOX 24-25. Man's complete formal taxonomic status.

Kingdom:	ANIMALIA
Subkingdom:	METAZOA
Section:	DEUTEROSTOMIA
Phylum:	CHORDATA
Subphylum:	VERTEBRATA
Class:	MAMMALIA
Subclass:	THERIA
Infraclass:	EUTHERIA
Cohort:	UNGUICULATA
Order:	PRIMATES
Suborder:	ANTHROPOIDEA
Superfamily:	HOMINOIDEA
Family:	HOMINIDAE
Genus:	*Homo*
Species:	*Homo sapiens.*

Each term on the left names a *category;* each term on the right names a *taxon.* A taxon is a set of actual organisms, living or extinct or some of each.

A genus name is an invariable singular noun; a species name consists of a genus name followed by an invariable adjective. Both are always italicized. Where context makes the genus clear, it is often abbreviated to its first letter: *Equus caballus* and *E. asinus* (horses and asses). Designations of taxa above the genus level are invariant plural nouns; they are never italicized and always capitalized.

In principle, the name of a taxon designates a set of organisms *and that is all.* The connotations of the words used in the designation (when they have connotations) are irrelevant and must be ignored.

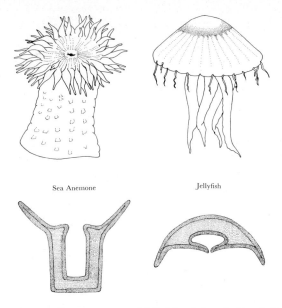

Sea Anemone   Jellyfish

FIGURE 24-26. Radial symmetry. Sea anemones and jellyfishes belong to the phylum Coelenterata (grade or subkingdom Radiata). Characteristic of many of these is a shape called "polyp," represented by the sea anemone, with oral cavity at the top, or another shape called "medusa," as in the jellyfish, with oral cavity at the bottom. Some species go through both shapes during their life cycles. (After Weisz 1967.)

salts migrated to the skin and were laid down in protective armor plates; fossils show a great variety. In due time the individual plates became smaller and some were drawn into the mouth as teeth, anchored to an incipiently bony jaw; then the external armor was largely discarded. This arrangement is retained still by the cartilaginous fishes (Chondrichthyes, Figure 24-22: sharks, skates, rays). In the lineage that led to us, the theretofore cartilaginous skeleton was slowly calcified into true bone.

Teeth made possible a new kind of eating. The toothless predecessors were filter-feeders: bits of food were strained out as water passed through the gills, and then swallowed. Now teeth were used to seize food and force it back towards the throat, and the gills abandoned their alimentary function. Land vertebrates would never have evolved without this, since filter-feeding in air is impossible.

Movable extremities.   A motile aquatic animal propels itself not by waving fins but by sinuous motions of the whole body (Figure 24-28). Fins appeared, among early fishes, as the protective armor was going out of fashion, but they serve for balance and steering, not for propulsion.

There was an early split among the bony fishes (Osteichthyes, Figure 24-22) into those with fleshy lobe-fins and those with flat, membranous fins. Most modern fishes are descended from the latter, all land vertebrates from the former.

Lungs.   The early fishes had both gills and lungs, still retained by a few modern

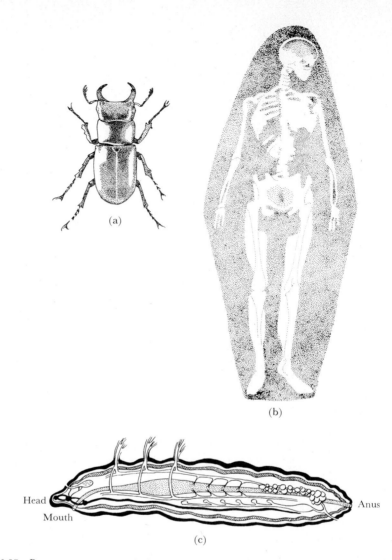

FIGURE 24-27. BILATERAL SYMMETRY. (a) is the exoskeleton of a beetle, (b) the endoskeleton of a human being. (c) is a generalized diagram of an animal designed for motility; the view is a section through the axis of symmetry. (After Weisz 1967.)

species (fresh-water types in Africa, South America, and Australia [5]) though for most the original lungs have become "swimming bladders," masses of light tissue whose location gives buoyancy and helps in balance. The ancestry of the land vertebrates clearly lay through lobe-finned fishes for which the lungs were functional.

[5]Because of continental drift (p. 324), these regions were closer together 450,000,000 years ago than they are now.

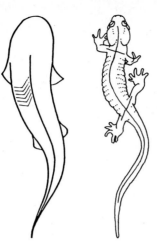

FIGURE 24-28. SWIMMING AND WALKING. The fish (left) curves and recurves its body, pushing the water backwards and itself forwards; the fins merely stabilize. Today's newt (right), like the earliest lungfishes and amphibians, moves its body in the same way, but it is the legs against the ground that propel. Note that left fore and right hind limbs (or fins) advance together, then right fore and left hind. (After Campbell 1966.)

POND, SWAMP, AND STRAND

The lobe-finned lungfishes lived in inland ponds, and spent most of their time in the water. The climate of the time was tempestuous, and sudden recessions of the water level may sometimes have stranded them. Otherwise, if they ventured ashore it was for food. There was plenty to be had, for life's initial invasion of the land was already lost in the mists of the past: plants, diverse microorganisms, and various invertebrates were already ashore, and some of the latter may already have become insects.

The survival advantage of strong fins for the lungfishes was, then, not that they could march bravely out of their ponds to conquer a new world, but rather that, when danger threatened, they could *get back to the water*. Those whose fins were too weak failed, and therefore did not reproduce. Thus, by selection, fins became stronger and eventually evolved into legs equipped with bones, joints, and muscles. Those to which this happened were no longer fishes, but Amphibia.

The Amphibia evolved, or retained, a three-stage life cycle in which the embryo develops into a larva, which then in due time undergoes a major bodily reorganization (*metamorphosis*) into the adult form. (Frogs are Amphibia, and still do this: witness tadpoles.) It was the adults that had genuine legs and showed various other modifications promoting efficiency of life ashore—for example, a reorganization of the ear for the detection of sound transmitted through air. The larvae were still tied to the water. They had no lungs, only gills, and they had to feed on aquatic vegetation. Furthermore, the adults had to return to the water for reproduction, since eggs laid ashore dried out and died.

These factors did not keep the Amphibia from diversifying and spreading; fossils show them all over. For well over fifty million years, starting about 400,000,000 years ago, they were masters of the land, competing only with insects, parasites, and one another. But then some of them took further adaptive steps, and those that did not share the changes mostly lost out.

The crucial new changes were two: internal fertilization and the land egg.

INTERNAL FERTILIZATION. Aquatic animals whose reproduction involves the co-operation of individuals of two sexes in general practice *external fertilization*: the female deposits her eggs and the male his sperm in approximately the same place, and random water currents determine whether any of them pair off to form zygotes.

External fertilization is manifestly impossible in air. The alternative, internal fertilization, is possible in either medium: a pair of individuals, one of each sex, come together in the act of *copulation*, during which sperm from the male enter the body of the female, so that the eggs may be fertilized before they are laid. Male mammals have a special organ for this, the *penis*, and so do many reptiles. But birds manage with no such device, so that its pedigree may not be so ancient as that of internal fertilization itself.

THE LAND EGG had a tough protective shell that prevented premature desiccation, and contained enough foodstuff for the embryo to undergo more development before hatching. Furthermore, with the land egg the larval stage was compressed so that the organism that emerged upon hatching was an essentially complete, though miniature, adult.

By about 340,000,000 years ago some strains had undergone these changes; they were therefore no longer Amphibia, but Reptilia. They may still have spent a lot of time in and near the water, but they were potentially emancipated from it as the Amphibia never were.

Another feature of this emancipation was a new kind of breathing. Adult amphibians (e.g., frogs) breath by swallowing. Reptiles started using abdominal and thoracic muscles, and all their descendants still do, except that turtles, whose ribs are immovable, use only the former.

COLD WEATHER AND WARM BLOOD

The habitats of the lungfishes, the amphibians, and the early reptiles were the swampy forests that stretched over a warm Earth's land surface from pole to pole and that prevailed for a hundred million years; the fossilized remains of the trees are now our *coal*.

A bit less than 300,000,000 years ago the forests began to wane, and in another forty or fifty million years Earth was in the grip of the Permian Ice Age. Worldwide warmth was not restored until a little before 200,000,000 years ago.

The effects on land life of the prolonged cold were profound. The types of plants that had formed the coal forests vanished; seed plants (Spermopsida: Figure 24-29) took their place, first appearing about 260,000,000 years ago. Insects experienced a

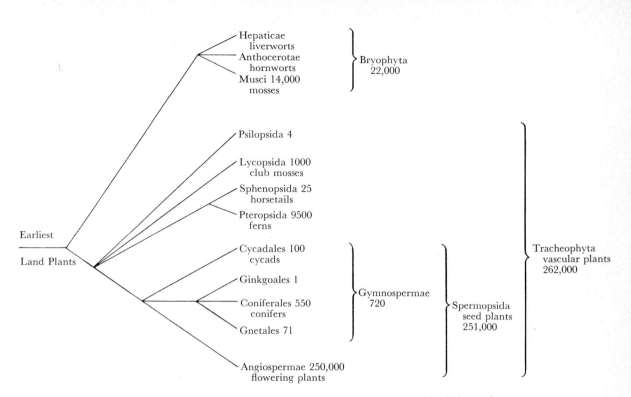

FIGURE 24-29. LAND PLANTS. Conventions as in Figure 24-21: taxonomy on right, probable phylogenetic connections on left.

large loss, and did not begin a new proliferation until about 150,000,000 years ago, when they were perhaps given a boost by the appearance of the earliest flowering plants (Angiospermae, the type of seed plant now dominant). Amphibians were almost extinguished, but not quite. Reptiles suffered, but survived and afterwards went through a remarkable series of adaptive radiations that spread them into thousands of ecological niches, not only on land but in the air and back in the sea.

Also, the Permian Ice Age probably supplied the environmental leverage that selected for warm-bloodedness. At least two different reptilian strains moved independently in this direction: one, before the peak of the Ice Age, evolved ultimately into the mammals; the other, considerably later, gave rise to the birds.

Another selective factor in the case of the premammals was that they were carnivorous. Herbivores can be leisurely in their search for food, and can then relax and consume it. Carnivores have to stalk and chase their prey and sometimes have to fight it. This necessarily means a higher rate of metabolism.

WARM-BLOODEDNESS.[6] The essence of warm-bloodedness is a set of devices for controlling heat flow, by virtue of which the body temperature of the animal remains

[6]Etymologically the term is a misnomer, like *malaria* 'bad air' and *atom* 'indivisible'. As in many such cases, we simply retain the term and ignore the etymology.

approximately the same regardless of wide variations in the temperature of the surroundings. (Of course there are limits—any animal will freeze or cook if the environment gets sufficiently cold or hot.) A cold-blooded animal has no such built-in devices, so that its body temperature is always about the same as that of the ambient.

Warm-bloodedness depends in the first instance on a thermodynamic *inefficiency* of intracellular metabolism. The amount of energy lost as heat is the measure of the inefficiency. But thermodynamic inefficiency is not biological inefficiency if it keeps the animal warm and alive. Besides, there are various biochemical reactions that take place best if the temperature is just right.

Mammalian (or premammalian) devices for *retaining* heat include a coat of hair, a subcutaneous layer of fat, and a roly-poly body shape that minimizes the ratio of surface to volume. Hair was a modification of the protective scales that the ancestors of the mammals had had since they first developed hard parts (p. 353). Mammalian body shapes vary greatly, but none are as skinny as snakes and worms. A subsidiary device for *generating* heat is shivering. The chief device for *discarding* heat is sweating. Amphibians and reptiles neither shiver nor sweat. Of course, these mechanisms did not appear all at once, nor are all of them retained by all modern mammals. But they seem to have been part of the common mammalian heritage.

Body design and digestive economy. Figure 24-30 compares the bodily arrangement of a lizard or alligator (both reptiles) with the prototypical arrangement for mammals. In the latter, the tail becomes a light appendage, and the legs are swung down under the trunk instead of projecting outward from the flanks. The mammalian arrangement makes for efficient rapid motion, appropriate for a carnivore that must pursue its dinner.

Reptiles and amphibians swallow their food whole, and digest it only in the stomach and small intestine. One of the earliest innovations among the premammals was to start using the teeth for chewing, not merely for seizing, and to secrete saliva to begin the digestion in the mouth. The teeth differentiated, yielding slicers and piercers (incisors and canines) at the front, grinders (premolars and molars) along the sides. There were some structural rearrangements in mouth and nose so that the animal could chew and breathe at the same time. These modifications, too, were excellent for an animal whose way of life required a high metabolic rate: the "assembly-line" processing of food was more efficient than the old way, and less frequently interrupted breathing guaranteed a steadier supply of oxygen.

Waking and sleeping. Reptiles show short bursts of energetic activity alternating with long periods of torpor. The hibernation or aestivation of some mammals, a way of surviving seasonally recurrent periods of intense cold or of drastic food shortage, resembles reptilian torpor and may have evolved from it.

The familiar contrast of *waking* and *sleeping* is quite different. Only mammals and birds show it—but they all do, even those mammals that hibernate or aestivate. The alternation between the states is tied not to the annual cycle but to the diurnal one. It seems that warm-bloodedness made possible periods of intense activity lasting much longer than those shown by reptiles, but that this then had to be paid for by a special new sort of daily rest and recuperation.

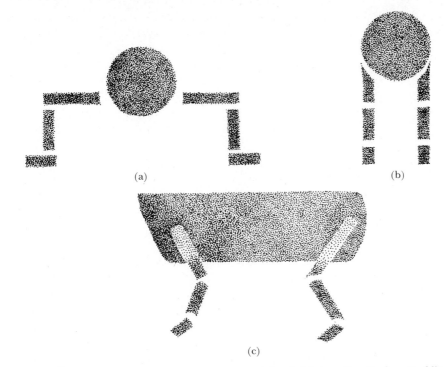

(a)   (b)

(c)

FIGURE 24-30. Reptilian versus mammalian body shape. (a) and (b) show the attachment of limbs to trunk respectively in a reptile (or amphibian) and in a mammal. (c) shows the orientation of mammalian limb joints.

Life with Mother

The evolutionary innovations that turned premammals into mammals were a series of changes in reproduction and infant care.

Lactation. A widespread modern mammalian practice is for a mother to lick and groom her infants and for them to lick and groom her. Mammals need tiny quantities of several complex substances called *vitamins*. One of these, vitamin D, is especially important in early life to assist in the processing of calcium. Vitamin D is synthesized in mammalian skin under the action of sunlight, but in most species it is not absorbed directly but is ingested by licking (cf. p. 388).

Imagine, now, perhaps 200,000,000 years ago, a small, furry, warm-blooded, egg-laying premammal whose offspring lick her after they have hatched. Apart from the vitamin D obtained from the mother's fur, the offspring must fend for themselves. Mutations take place: certain of the sweat glands on the abdomen come to secrete, in season, a fluid that differs from perspiration in that it contains various substances needed for the offspring's nutrition—even calcium, to go with the vitamin D! The new fluid is *milk*; the glands have become *mammary glands* (or *mammae*); and the animals are now *mammals*.

Today lactation is combined with egg-laying only by the duck-billed platypus and the echidna of Tasmania, Australia, and New Guinea.[7] All other mammals show the consequences of the next step.

BIRTH.   If warmth is essential for continued life, how, in a cool climate, is the embryo to be kept warm before the egg hatches? We know that many birds handle this problem by sitting on the eggs. The mammalian solution was evolving about 150,000,000 years ago: the egg came to be retained inside the body of the mother, until it hatched and was expelled at the same time. Females developed a special chamber for this, the *uterus*. The retention of the fertilized egg until it is ready to hatch constitutes *gestation* (or *pregnancy*), and the simultaneous hatching and expulsion is *birth*. The arrangement is not uniquely mammalian, but recurs in some snakes and some fishes.

The mammals that took to this plan were the earliest Theria. Their descendants include the Metatheria (Marsupialia, pouched mammals) and the Eutheria (placental mammals). Fossil marsupials are found on all continents but Africa, but with the subsequent success of the placentals the marsupials came to be confined to South America and Great Australia,[8] which for long periods were cut off from the rest of Earth's land surface; there, free from placental competitors, they underwent extensive adaptive radiations.

A pouch is an abdominal envelope covering the mammary glands, into which the offspring move when they are born and in which they go through an initial period of extrauterine development. The earliest Theria may have had pouches; if so, they were later abandoned by the placentals (and even by some recent marsupials).

THE PLACENTA.   The third great step in our own ancestry, the step that led to the earliest Eutheria, was a gradual increase in the efficiency of the placenta. This is a device that supplies nourishment from the mother to the unborn young as the food stored in the yolk of the egg gives out, and which affords a route for the elimination, through the mother, of waste products of the unborn young's metabolism. The mother quite literally eats, breathes, and eliminates for her unborn young. Something like the placenta is apt to appear in any animal that bears its young, but the marsupials have it at most in primitive form.

In the individual placental mammal, the placenta appears only as it is needed, developing in the uterus along with the embryo. It is "deciduous," meaning that it is discarded (as the "afterbirth") when it has done its job. Since marsupials have little or no placenta, the young have to be born when the yolk gives out; they are scarcely more than embryos, and the period of nourishment and protection in the pouch is crucial. In placentals, the placenta takes over from the pouch. With the switch from yolk to placenta as source of nourishment, the embryo becomes a *fetus*, retained for a further period of intrauterine growth before birth. The young at birth still need

[7]Both of order Monotremata, subclass Prototheria (see Figure 24-23, p. 350). Today's monotremes are very different from all other mammals; some specialists believe they arose independently from a distinct set of reptilian predecessors.

[8]The one exception is the opossum of North America. "Great Australia" is our name for the single earlier land mass that is now Tasmania, Australia, New Guinea, and some neighboring small islands; see p. 423 and Figure 28-1, p. 424.

nourishment from the mother's mammary glands, but in all other ways are much better equipped to fend for themselves than are newborn marsupials.

The Placental Panorama and the Primates

The mammalian developments described above took place in a world dominated by reptiles, some of them of enormous size (dinosaurs). The earliest placental mammals were very small, probably scurrying about to make a living in the lower levels of the vegetation.

But starting about 150,000,000 years ago the dinosaurs were on the wane, and by 75,000,000 years ago they were gone. We do not know what caused their decline and demise. It may have been some cosmic environmental change (p. 342), or perhaps merely the rise of a new sort of dominant land plant (the Angiospermae: p. 357) to which the herbivores among them could not adapt. Since the carnivores lived by eating the herbivores, that would eventually kill them off too.

In any case, as of about 100,000,000 years ago the circumstances had become such that the placental mammals began an adaptive radiation, spreading out in all directions from their earlier sheltered habitats and differentiating to yield, in some thirty million years, the diversity shown in Figure 24-23 (p. 350). Like the reptilian radiation that had followed the Permian Ice Age, this one gave rise not only to varied land types but even to fliers (Chiroptera: bats) and to ocean swimmers (Cetacea: whales).

One of the directions open for migration by the placentals of 100,000,000 years ago was upwards, higher into the trees. Amongst those that moved that way were our own ancestors, the earliest primates. The ensuing tens of millions of years of selection in terms of the exigencies of arboreal life gave the primates their special stamp, much of it retained when, later, some of them again climbed down to the ground.

Since we described the primates in some detail in Part One, we can here bring our all-too-skimpy sketch of man's preprimate ancestry to a close, with this even scantier summarizing

SYNOPSIS

Our oceanic forebears once were sessile,
As are our kin the Echinodermata.
The law of life was Don't move till you've gotta—
Float on the top, or on the bottom nestle.
Their shape was more like mortar than like pestle,
But some, with slight medulla oblongata,
Refused to sit (though still not Vertebrata)
And scattered, partly widdershins, part dessil.

All these, we say, were being *neotenic*:
They kept their youthful figures as they grew.
A few became progressively more sthenic,
Then teethed, then boned, then broke the shore taboo,
Got legs, land eggs, got hair and thermogenic,
Climbed trees, came down—and here are I AND YOU.

25

×

THE EMERGENCE OF MAN: CARRYING AND WALKING

Had they been capable of such thoughts, the earliest primates might have felt, when first established in the trees, that they had found a home in which their children could live happily ever after.

Life is never like that. Trees are living things too, a slowly varying facet of the restive biosphere. A blight that devours certain forms of vegetation, a fungus or a virus, may swerve by mutation into more virulent version, or be vectored by breeze or bugs into virgin territory. A fire, set by lightning or volcano, may devastate a belt of forest, leaving its faunal denizens dead, or displaced and doomed unless they fast find another home. As climate shifts, what was once jungle can imperceptibly become savanna with scattered groves along its rivulets, or treeless veldt, or even desert; in a different interval of time or space all this can be reversed.

As we noted on page 32, it was such climatic gyrations during the Miocene that levered certain Old World monkeys and certain hominoids out of the trees. The monkeys included the ancestors of today's baboons. Among the hominoids were the latest common ancestors of today's chimpanzees, gorillas, and men; we shall call them the *Stem Hominoids*. Figure 25–1 shows them, together with various fossil types and all their living descendants, in an arrangement that gives not only the likely phylogenetic connections but also something of the chronology. Table 25–2 presents relevant information about all the modern hominoids.

THE STEM HOMINOIDS × Here is a characterization of the Stem Hominoids, based on the comparative method (p. 300) supplemented by guesses.

They lived somewhere in forested areas of the Old World tropics.

They were larger than gibbons but smaller than their surviving descendants. Males were larger than females. They were hairy and tailless. They had mobile facial muscles, a flat or receding jaw, a slight "simian shelf" (a bony plate extending horizontally backwards within the curve of the lower jaw, at its base: Figure 25-3), and some thickening of the skull in the semblance of a sagittal crest (Fig. 25-4). The canine teeth tended to be large and interlocking, so that chewing had to be up and down with little lateral motion (Figure 25-5). The tooth pattern, on either side above and

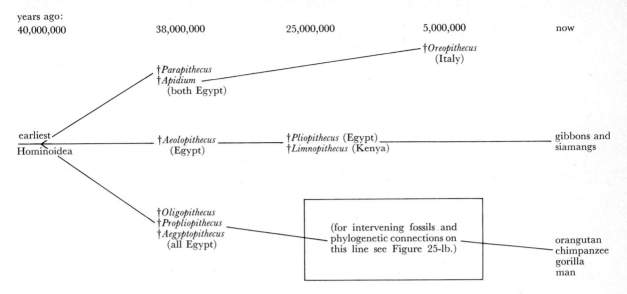

FIGURE 25-1a. THE HOMINOIDEA. Unlike earlier figures of this type, this one includes rough estimates of the dates (at the top). The daggered genus names are all of attested fossil types; the places are where the fossils were found.

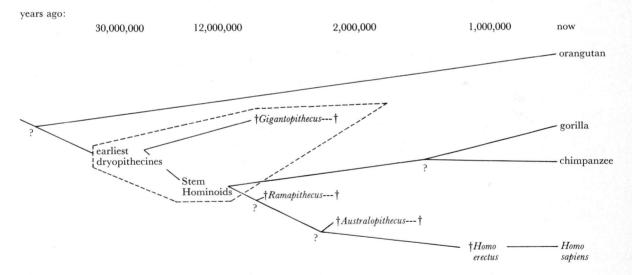

FIGURE 25-1b. THE BIG APES, MAN, AND FOSSILS. (For the small apes and more distant fossil types, see Figure 25-1a.) The dashed line encloses a set of fossils known collectively as "dryopithecines": the earliest were ancestral to us (through the Stem Hominoids), but the later ones mainly were not. The question mark signals indefiniteness of dates. *Ramapithecus* is known from India and Kenya from about two million years ago; *Australopithecus* is attested from south, west, and east Africa, southwest Asia, Java, and China, over a period of a million years, most recently in south Africa.

below, was two incisors, one canine, two premolars, and three molars (Figure 25-6), but sporadically there was an extra molar or premolar. The chromosome count was 48; later, in man's lineage, one pair was lost.

They lived in bands of widely varying size, averaging fifteen to thirty. Many a band included only a single adult male, but there were variations in this too. A band showed nucleated territoriality (p. 69), centering on trees with which they were thoroughly familiar and in which they built their nests, fresh ones each night.

They were expert climbers and spent much of their lives in the trees. They slept in them from dusk to dawn, which in the tropics means nearer to half of each twenty-four–hour period than to the third characteristic of ourselves in recent times. They were active during the day. Some activities, particularly the constant search for food, led them not only among the trees but also to the ground below. They left the trees more easily than their ancestors had, but were not so predominantly terrestrial as are today's baboons.

On the ground, they could lift themselves on their hind legs far enough to raise their heads above shoulder-high brush to look about; and this they did for many

TABLE 25-2. Characteristics of living Hominoidea.

TRAIT	GIBBON *Hylobates*	ORANGUTAN *Pongo*	GORILLA *Gorilla*	CHIMPANZEE *Pan*	MAN *Homo sapiens*
Chromosome number (2n)	44	48	48	48	46
Gestation	about 210 days	233? 275? days	251–289 days	225? 242 days	270–275 days
Deciduous dentition erupts	1–6 mo	4–12 mo	complete early in second year	2½–14½ mo	6–30 mo
Permanent dentition erupts	2½–8 yr	3½–10 yr	complete in eleventh year	3–10 yr	6–19½ yr
Age at sexual maturity	5–8 yr	6–8 yr	6–8 yr	7–11 yr	11–14 yr
Longevity	31 yr 6 mo (captivity)	30 yr 8 mo (captivity)	33 yr 5 mo (captivity)	41–46 yr (captivity)	72 yr (life expectancy)
Adult male height mass	403–635 mm 4300–7928 gm	1364–1370 mm 69 kg (Sumatra)	1685–1725 mm 140–180 kg	770–925 mm 48–49 kg	(great racial variation)
Adult female height mass	408–622 mm 4100–6800 gm	1148–1150 mm 37 kg (Sumatra)	—— 75–110 kg	700–850 mm 40–41 kg	(great racial variation)
Sexual dimorphism	slight	marked, esp. in mass	marked, in mass		slight in mass, greater in proportions
Cranial capacity	82–125 cm³	male 405–540 cm³ female 320–400 cm³	male 340–685 cm³	290–500 cm³	1000–2200 cm³
Mastoid process	absent	usually slight	variable	less than in man	well developed
Foramen magnum		far back on base of skull	far back on base of skull	far back on base of skull	towards middle of base of skull
Sagittal crest	occasional	present in 70% of males	in most adults	occasionally in large adults	absent
Nuchal crest	absent	present	all males, some females	absent	absent; small ridge only
Simian shelf	present	present	present	present	absent

reasons, including curiosity. They could sit with arms free for manipulative motions. They could walk or run on all fours. They could run, but not walk very well, bipedally.

Though omnivorous, they settled for a largely vegetarian diet. Except for the suckling of infants they did not share food.

In feeding and grooming they used mouth and hands. In nest-building they manipulated twigs and branches mainly with the hands, but if raw materials had to be carried any distance through the trees they would often transfer them to the mouth to leave the hands free for locomotion. Infants clung to the hair of their mothers with their hands, perhaps also with feet; mothers (or others) sometimes carried infants in an arm. They turned stones or other objects by hand in search of food. Sometimes they picked up sticks or stones and threw them, at predators or aliens, or playfully at one another (not at prey). The arm was joined to the shoulder in a way that allowed a swing of arm and hand through a larger arc than can be managed by monkeys.

They made, or had the capacity to make, carry, and use crude tools (cf. the chimpanzees: p. 88), and to transmit tool practices through the generations by tradition.

TRAIT	GIBBON *Hylobates*	ORANGUTAN *Pongo*	GORILLA *Gorilla*	CHIMPANZEE *Pan*	MAN *Homo sapiens*
Chin	absent	absent	absent	absent	present
Vertebral column:					
cervical	7	7	7	7	7
thoracic	13	12	13	13 (variable)	12
lumbar	5	4	3–4	4	5
sacral	5	5–6	5–6	5–6	3–5
Canine teeth	long and saberlike slight sexual dimorphism upper diastema*	longer in males upper diastema	long and saberlike slight sexual dimorphism upper diastema	longer in males upper diastema	nonprojecting diastema rare
Upper/lower limb ratio	upper much longer	upper longer	upper longer	upper longer	lower longer
Habitat	arboreal	arboreal	90% terrestrial for adults during day	arboreal 50–75% of daylight hours	terrestrial
Sleeping location	in trees	in trees	usually on ground; sometimes in trees	trees	terrestrial
Locomotion	brachiation; infrequent bipedalism or quadrupedalism on ground	modified brachiation; bipedal or quadrupedal on ground	brachiation in young; adults, brachiation, or quadrupedal on ground	modified brachiation; mainly quadrupedal on ground	bipedal on ground
Bands	1–4 adults with offspring		5–30 in band; average 17; occasional lone adult	highly variable; largest observed group 23 (temporary)	
Tools	none observed	stick-throwing	stick-throwing	see p. 88	

*"Diastema" means a separation between second incisor and canine.

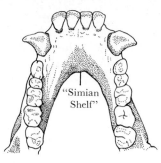

FIGURE 25-3. Simian shelf. The lower dentition of a chimpanzee. (After Clark 1959.)

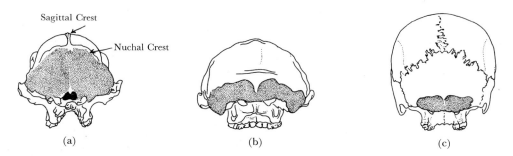

(a) (b) (c)

FIGURE 25-4. Crests. (a) is a posterior view of the skull of a gorilla, (b) of *Homo erectus*, (c) of modern man. Note the progressive reduction in both sagittal crest and nuchal crest. (After Weidenreich 1941 and Campbell 1966.)

In all these uses of the hands there was little if any trace of preference for one hand over the other.

The period of pregnancy was about thirty weeks. Twinning was as rare as it is for us now. The young required and received maternal care for many months. Nursing females held infants to the breast in their arms, though the infant helped by clinging to the mother's fur. The eruption of permanent teeth began at two and one half or three. The onset of ovulation in females was at eight or nine years; general growth stopped for both sexes at nine or ten. The life span was potentially thirty or forty years, but death was largely from accident, disease, or predation, not from old age. Corpses were abandoned, as were members of the band (past infancy) too sick, injured, or feeble to fend for themselves.

The females showed a year-round menstrual cycle instead of a rutting season. Cyclical changes in the region of the female's external genitalia were less striking than for most Old World monkeys. The females may have been sexually receptive much of the time, but the virtually uninterrupted physiological receptivity of human females was a later development in our own lineage. Sexual interest on the part of males was continuous from puberty on. By the time of the Stem Hominoids the intermingling of sex, grooming, and play (p. 67) was old hat. Copulation was effected with any of a wide variety of positions, and "perversions" of all sorts were well known.

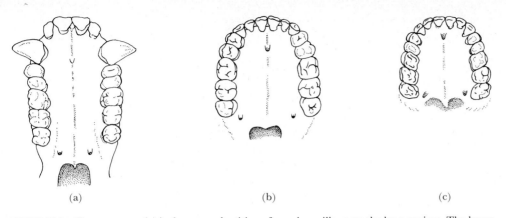

(a)   (b)   (c)

FIGURE 25-5. CANINE TEETH. (a) is the upper dentition of a male gorilla; note the long canines. The lower canines of the great apes are also elongated, as shown for a chimpanzee in Figure 25-3. (b) and (c) are the upper dentition, respectively, of *Australopithecus* and of modern man, drawn to the same scale. The hominid dentition has become smaller since australopithecine times, some two million years ago, but *Australopithecus* already showed reduced canines. (After Clark 1959.)

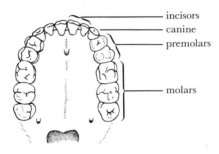

incisors
canine
premolars

molars

FIGURE 25-6. THE HOMINOID TOOTH PATTERN. All hominoids and all contemporary Old World monkeys show the pattern illustrated here with the upper dentition of modern man.

Adult males were sexually interested in nubile females and "paternally" interested in infants, but were not tied in to any sort of permanent family less inclusive than the whole band. Everyone was potentially interested in everyone else for grooming. An animal knew which female was his own mother, and a mother knew her children whatever their ages. Fathers and maternal half siblings were not recognized. Copulation between mother and son may have been avoided; the basis for any other incest prohibition was lacking.

Inbreeding within the band was the rule. Relations with adjacent bands were normally neutral to hostile, rarely friendly, but there was enough contact to provide for some gene exchange.[1]

Within a band, social structure, though different in details, was probably as

[1] These circumstances (small bands, largely independent but with some gene transfer) promoted the Holmes and Turner effects (pp. 298–299). In our lineage from the Stem Hominoids, this arrangement continued for millions of years.

complicated and flexible as for today's baboons, and turned on the same major factors: age, sex, and physical prowess, modified in a variable way by clique-formation and individual cleverness.

Collective enterprises of many sorts required intragroup coordination. This was effected by various forms of communication: patterns of body motion, facial gestures, prodding and manipulating, changes of body odor, and a closed call system of vocal signals (p. 108). Since the Stem Hominoids lived in and near the trees more than savanna baboons do, they were probably noisier (p. 44). The conventions of some of these forms of communication were transmitted in part by tradition, rather than wholly by genes.

The First Hominids

In the late Miocene, as continuous forest cracked and receded, many bands of Stem Hominoids were caught in slowly diminishing isolated groves. If a grove shrank to nothing, the hominoids in it became extinct unless their physique made it possible for them to traverse a bit of open land to another grove. Thus, the survival value of the requisites for safe ground travel was not that the animals could therewith begin a new way of life out of the trees, but that, when necessary, they could get to a place where the traditional arboreal way could be continued.

Sometimes a band forced to emigrate would be a grove's total population. Perhaps more typically, population pressure in a diminishing grove would force bands into competition over its dwindling resources, and the less powerful bands would be displaced. Likewise, a migrating band reaching a new grove would often find it already occupied, again making for competition. In the long run, the trees were held by the more powerful, while the weaker repeatedly had to get along as best they could in the fringes of the forest.

The trees went to the strong, and the chimpanzees and gorillas are their surviving descendants. Our own ancestors, the earliest *hominids,* were the failures, abandoning the trees not because they wanted to but because they were kicked out.

THE IMPACT OF SURFACE LIFE

× As the early hominids were eking out a meager existence in an environment for which they were ill equipped, the Miocene epoch drew slowly to a close. The transition to the Pliocene was marked by some climatic antics, but then things settled down. Temperature and rainfall varied little. The oceans covered various regions that earlier had been, and later again became, low-lying coastal plains or land bridges between continental masses. For ten million years, starting about 12,000,000 years ago, the conditions for land life remained fairly constant. Some land mammals, particularly among the Carnivora, grew to very large size.

Pliocene fossils of primates are virtually unknown. Hominids, our ancestors and kindred types, may have been widely distributed in the Old World, or may have been confined to a small region where there were uniquely protective niches. They were challenged by competing animals, but not by radical changes of vegetation or unexpected rigors of climate. For nearly the whole of the Pliocene they remained small and small-brained, using only the crudest of tools and staying in or near wooded territory, perhaps using the trees much as modern baboons do.

Yet by the beginning of the Pleistocene, about two million years ago, they had changed. This we know directly from fossils (Figure 25-1). A million generations of surface life had given selection ample time to work. Let us try to infer what it did. Remember that these are inferences—we cannot go back in a time machine and watch things happening.

CARRYING

× When the early hominids were expelled from the trees they moved as bands, and took the essential geometry of their nucleated territoriality with them. At any halt, no matter how temporary, some point became for the nonce home base, a focus relative to which the members of the band oriented themselves as they moved about. Headquarters was the safest place to be if for no other reason than the safety of numbers. They also took with them the practice of nest-building (something the ancestral baboons had lacked). Suppose that a band that carries this impulse is forced to pass a night away from the trees. The setting is different, but the impulse is going to manifest itself. Thus, from the beginning, the hominids had the ingrained habit of poking and prying at things.

Among the Stem Hominoids, the earliest moves from one grove to another would have been to a target in sight from the point of departure. But among the hominids movements eventually started with no destination in view. Treeless country holds discomforts and dangers. There may be little available water, for the trees tend to cluster where it is more abundant. And there are fleet four-footed predators, as well as herbivores big enough to be dangerous. One cannot altogether avoid these other animals, since their location often signals the presence of water, or of food fit also for consumption by hominids.

The trick that made survival possible for some bands was *hand carrying.*

The Stem Hominoids had had fine arms and hands, and had used them in a variety of ways. These structures and practices were inherited by the hominids, but had to be blended into a new pattern. In the trees, hands are largely occupied with climbing. On the ground, the conditions for carrying are in no wise improved if the hand must revert to the status of a foot, as it does to this day among the baboons. But if some sort of walking on two legs can be managed, then the hand is freed.

Two sorts of hand carrying on the ground may have been very early: that of crude weapons of defense, and that of scavenged food.

(1) The earliest weapon-carrying could have been a sort of accident. Imagine a hominid sitting on the ground and pounding something (a nut?) with a handy stone. A predator approaches. There are no trees near enough for escape into them. Our hero jumps up and runs away as best he can on two legs, but keeps his grasp on the stone for no better reason than that he does not need the hand for anything else. Cornered, he turns, and either strikes out at the predator with the stone or else throws it. The predator falls, or runs off—and whatever in our hero's genes or life experience or both has contributed to his behavior stands a chance of being passed

on. Ten thousand generations later, his descendant is lugging around a stick or stone even when there is no obvious need for it.[2]

(2)   The first carrying of scavenged food back to headquarters (instead of consuming it on the spot, the typical primate habit) may also have been an accident. A scavenging hominid is eating the remains of a carnivore's kill where he has found it, and is surprised by the carnivore returning for another meal from the same kill. The hominid runs off towards headquarters, still holding a piece of meat in his hand. In time, the practice develops of carrying the spoils off without waiting for the predator to turn up.

BIPEDALISM   ✕ When environmental changes in the Miocene forced some Old World anthropoids to the ground, they were not by preference and inherited nature either bipeds or quadrupeds, but climbers. This meant that *any* pattern of ground walking demanded adjustments. We have no more right to be surprised that our own ancestors favored bipedalism than that the ancestral baboons chose quadrupedalism.

The Stem Hominoids may have experimented with both. Chimps and gorillas move on the ground either with feet only or on all fours. Their bipedal gaits are awkward, and not sustained for long at a time, but have in their favor that they keep the trunk nearly vertical with the head high. Their quadrupedal gait is more efficient, yet shows signs of its relative newness in that the weight of the front part of the body is not rested on the heel and palm of the hand, as it is by terrestrial Carnivora and Rodentia, but on the knuckles (Figure 25-7).

Hominid bipedalism has gone through two stages, *shuffle* and *stride*.

(1)   THE SHUFFLE STAGE

This stage must have lasted through most of the Pliocene. At the outset, shuffle bipedalism was no more efficient than walking on all fours, perhaps less so. We assume it was favored anyway, because it left the hands free for carrying.

The awkwardness of bipedal walking in the shuffle stage stemmed from the proportions of the different parts of the body and the ways the parts were hinged together and muscled. The legs were at least as short as the arms. In the upright posture the feet were flat on the ground (as they still are), but large big toes projected inwards, of little help in the supporting or moving of the body's weight and sometimes a hindrance because they could catch on obstacles. The legs were bent at the knee, and met the trunk at an angle at the hip joints, the trunk held not vertically but sloping forward. These angles at the joints were necessary in order that the center of gravity could be held directly over the point of contact between feet and ground. The sustaining of the body's weight in this posture is hard on the leg muscles because they must be held tense; otherwise the assemblage collapses. Forward motion takes the form of awkward running in which the legs move rapidly to keep up with the

[2]If this use of weapons did not develop very early, then how did our ancestors survive the Pliocene, when many land animals were increasing in size (p. 368), without themselves getting larger?

FIGURE 25-7. QUADRUPEDAL STANCES. The baboon, above, rests his weight on the palms of his hands, as do many quadrupedal mammals. The gorilla, below, uses his knuckles. (After Campbell 1966.)

body, or of a clumsy walk with which the feet are neither raised nor advanced very far.

Animals whose bipedal locomotion is of these sorts, and who cannot resort to quadrupedal locomotion because the hands are otherwise occupied, cannot undertake long pilgrimages. During the shuffle stage our ancestors stuck to the fringes of the forest, or lived in well wooded savanna (terrain where the ground cover is somewhat like that in open savanna but there are more trees, signaling more water and more game). It was in such environments that selection slowly changed their anatomy to make for more efficient walking on two feet.

(2) THE STRIDE STAGE

The changes included these (not necessarily in this order): The toes got smaller and lost most of their earlier prehensility (Figure 25-8). The legs got longer relative to the length of the arms (Figure 25-9). The knees and hip joints straightened, with major modifications in the shapes of the bones, particularly of the pelvis (Figure 25-10).

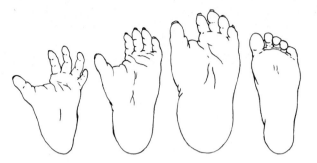

FIGURE 25-8. FEET. From left to right: chimpanzee, lowland gorilla, mountain gorilla, and modern man. (After Campbell 1966 and Morton 1964.)

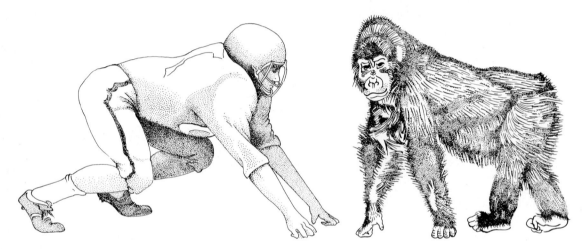

FIGURE 25-9. LIMB PROPORTIONS. The scale is adjusted to make the football linesman on the left and the gorilla on the right look the same size; actually the gorilla is much more massive. Note that the backs slope at about the same angle from the horizontal. But the gorilla's legs are straight, whereas to achieve this position the linesman must bend his legs at knees and ankles. [Linesman drawn from a photograph supplied courtesy of P. J. Butterfield, football coach, Ithaca College; gorilla, also redrawn, by permission of the trustees of the British Museum (Natural History).]

When he is standing upright, a human being's knees "lock": that is, the bones of the calf move directly under the femur (thighbone), the bottom of the latter resting firmly on the top of the former, so that the weight of the body is supported by a column of *bone* and the tension on the muscles is reduced. The trunk is vertical above the extended legs, instead of sloping forward. An ape cannot bend a leg backward at the hip so that the angle it forms with the axis of the trunk is greater than 180°. Human beings can. The spine is not straight, but curves forward behind the abdomen, backwards behind the chest, and forward again at the neck (Figure 25-11). The abdomen protrudes, tending to shift the trunk's center of gravity forward; this is

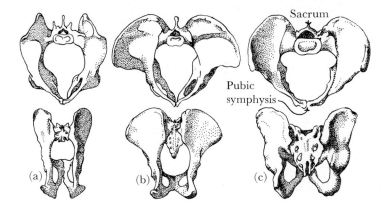

FIGURE 25-10. The pelvis. Top views (above) and rear views (below) of (a) a macaque, (b) a gorilla, and (c) modern man. (After Campbell 1966.)

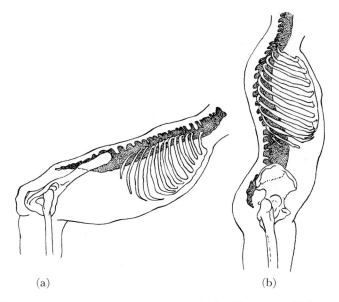

FIGURE 25-11. The joining of the pelvis to the femur. (a) in chimpanzee; (b) in man. Note also the typical curves of the human spine, in contrast to the essentially straight spine of the chimpanzee. (After Campbell 1966.)

compensated for by a startling enlargement of the muscle known as the gluteus maximus, which constitutes most of the substance of the buttock (Figure 25-12). Buttocks are exclusively human. There are variations in their shape and massiveness, but all human racial strains have them and other animals do not.

If an erect ape relaxes the tension on his muscles, he falls forward. The shuffling gait consists of beginning a forward fall and then advancing a leg to check it.

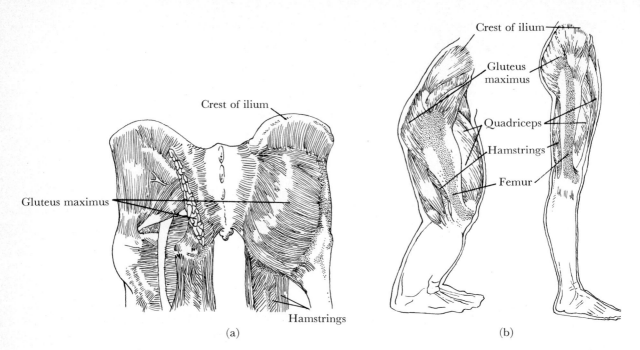

FIGURE 25-12. THE GLUTEUS MAXIMUS AND THE BUTTOCKS. (a) is a rear view of the muscles of the human thigh and hip; the gluteus maximus appears on the right, but is removed on the left to reveal the structures beneath it. (b) compares the leg and hip muscles of gorilla (on left) and man (on right). The gluteus maximus is present in all Primates, but assumes a new shape and size with human upright posture. (After Buettner-Janusch 1966.)

If an erect human relaxes his muscles he falls too, but not necessarily forward. The human stride begins (from upright resting position) with a fall that is *directed* forward by muscular action, and then continues as each leg in turn exerts a positive push against the ground to keep the body's mass moving in the same direction (Figure 25-13). The toes of the trailing foot push the ground as the foot is lifted. The leg is bent at the knee so the foot will clear the ground as it swings. The leg straightens again at the knee (which may but does not always lock) before contact is made. The heel of the advancing foot strikes the ground first, to supply the support as the other leg and foot then go through the same sequence of motions. The pelvis swings in cadence to shift the weight of the trunk from one leg to the other and back. It is in this that the enlarged gluteus maximus comes into action, the motions of the legs being provided for mainly by other muscles. The head bobs up and down and from side to side; the arms swing (even if the hands are carrying things) as part of the machinery of maintaining balance—and the coordination of this swinging retains the age-old quadrupedal pattern of the earliest amphibians, in that the left arm moves forward with the right leg, the right arm with the left leg (Figure 25-14).

The foregoing applies for smooth, level ground. In rough terrain matters are more awkward. The body's mass may have to be lifted or carefully lowered, and the knees may get fewer chances to lock, so that more work must be done with muscles and less with bone. Walking on rough ground is thus less efficient and more tiring.

LONG LEGS. The advantage of a long leg is twofold.

If the thighs are massive, as human thighs are, instead of spindly, as are those of most monkeys and apes, the body's center of gravity is lowered relative to the point at which the supporting extremities are hinged to the trunk. This promotes stability.

The other part of the advantage relates to the fact that in the walking of all animals (not running, in which contact with the ground is periodically lost) the forward swing of a lifted appendage is governed by the law of the pendulum: the duration of the swing depends only on the length of the pendulum (the leg), not on its mass nor on how large an arc it moves through. Any walking animal slows down by moving its legs through smaller arcs, speeds up by enlarging the arcs, in neither case materially altering the rate at which the feet touch the ground. Long legs yield long strides, so that much ground can be covered quickly with minimal expenditure of energy.

HUNTING AND FOOD-SHARING

× Apart from the inherited social nature of the Pliocene hominids, hand carrying and shuffle bipedalism were the twin pillars on which their life rested. These two features supported each other; and they led to, and were reinforced by, a further series of gradual innovations.

The early hominids, like the Stem Hominoids before them, were at least 95% vegetarian in practice (if we may judge from modern chimpanzees and baboons), but omnivorous in principle. What little meat they got, other than insects and grubs, was small birds or mammals taken when wounded or helpless, or the leftovers from the meals of carnivores.

We have seen (p. 369) that the earliest tools to be carried were probably weapons for defense against predators, not for offense. But occasionally the use of such a weapon would kill the predator. Why waste the meat? The change must have been very slow, but eventually weapons of defense became weapons of offense and the hunted became the hunters.[3]

Meat is a highly efficient and compactly packaged food as compared with uncultivated plants (cultivated ones are a different story: p. 162). A small kill does not go far, but a larger one may yield more food than can be consumed by the hunter. Sharing the meat might come about painlessly, in that when the hunter is sated he does not care if others take the leavings. However, food-sharing may also have been promoted by the habit of hauling scavenged food back to headquarters before eating it.

We have assumed above that hunting began as an individual enterprise. It is less dangerous and more efficient if done by a cooperating group. Some hominid bands developed the means for such cooperation, came to be better fed than those that did not, and were thereby better equipped for survival. However, the increased food

[3] This use of large animals may have been long delayed by the problem of getting through the hide to the edible inside (see p. 389).

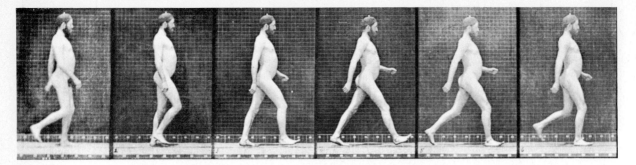

FIGURE 25-13. THE HUMAN STRIDING GAIT. This is one of a number of remarkable photographic studies made by Eadweard Muybridge in the 1880s. (Rephotographed by Sol Mednick from the original, and reproduced here through the courtesy of Miriam F. Mednick.)

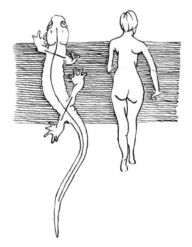

FIGURE 25-14. Fore and hind limb coordination in locomotion.

supply would have gone for nought if band members had engaged in too much serious quarreling over its distribution. The most successful bands were thus those in which social structure became more complicated, with flexible but binding agreements as to who had what responsibility, finer-grained coordination of the actions of band members temporarily engaged in a collective task, and increasing concern of each member for the welfare of the rest. Only bands of this sort were able to survive an occasional enforced migration over open land, by carrying along not only their infants but also their weapons and some accumulation of spare food.

OTHER CHANGES ✗   TOILET TRAINING

The tree-dwelling Stem Hominoids had had no problem with disposal of bodily wastes, nor did their hominid descendants as long as they continued to pass their nights aloft (compare the baboons: p. 36). Once permanently on the ground, how-

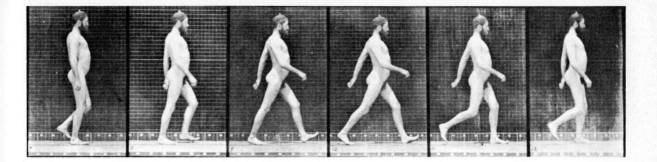

ever, keeping home base clean was important, increasingly so as that slowly became the place to store such things as surplus food. Improved hunting aggravated this because meat yields more offensive fecal matter than does a vegetarian diet.

Four-footed ground-ranging carnivores carry an answer built into their genes: they set aside certain spots in their territories as latrines, or scratch holes in the dirt and bury their dung. Arboreal primates have no such customs. The hominids that came to face the problem did not wait for matters to be settle through slow genetic selection. Instead, they worked out solutions by experimentation and passed them on to their successors by tradition. Rules governing where one may or may not defecate and urinate are part of the dwelling pattern of every human community, and teaching these rules to children looks like one of the oldest features of human culture.

Rest Posture

The anatomical changes that turned shuffle into stride had side effects unrelated to locomotion.

The buttocks, consisting of the large parts of the gluteus maximus muscles (p. 373) with an overlay of subcutaneous fat, give us cushions to sit on. Some apes and monkeys have "ischial callosities": hardened thickened hairless areas of skin in this region, which afford protection while sitting. If our ancestors ever had these, the buttocks took their place.

More Toilet Training

When a nonhuman mammal defecates, the fecal matter drops away and leaves the anal region clean. With the anatomical adjustments for stride bipedalism, the human anus is often squeezed between the inner edges of the buttocks, and during defecation stool may adhere to the flanking skin. Remembering the sanitary behavior of female chimpanzees (p. 88), we may guess that the general human way of handling this is very old. It was an additional early manipulative use of a hand. But it was, and still is, cultural rather than genetic: the child has to be *taught* the approved manner of anal cleansing.

COPULATION

All the hominoids are copulative experimenters (p. 68). Yet, in human communities the world over, despite racial differences in typical body contours and cultural differences as to what is approved, the ventral approach for copulation predominates over the dorsal approach.

We infer that, for the hominids that were moving towards stride bipedalism, the topographical changes in the area of the external reproductive organs affected the attainable variety of copulatory positions. In particular, some females must have had buttocks so large that a dorsal approach was difficult or impossible.

For the adult female, the favoring of the frontal approach changed the relative roles of the adult male and the infant, in that it made for a closer similarity between her reception of an infant (as for suckling) and of a lover. This could help, via behavioral analogy (p. 109), to spread the "tender emotions" of mammalian mother-infant relations to other interpersonal relationships within the band.

THE PRICE OF BIPEDALISM

Give any bright sophomore student of mechanical engineering the specs on mammalian muscle and bone, and he can design a more sensible erect biped than evolution did. The vertebrate skeleton did not evolve (until, as it were, only yesterday) in terms of upright posture, and its adaptation to the demands of that posture is architecturally absurd, particularly in that the entire weight of the trunk, head, and arms rests on two tiny areas of contact, one on each side, between the bottom of the pelvis and the head of the femur—and those areas of contact are sloping, not horizontal! It is a slapdash job, and so we suffer from hernias, "low back pain," slipped discs, and various other species-specific ills.

SEXUAL DIMORPHISM

Most serious of all, the resculpturing of the pelvis for upright posture threatened to narrow the female's birth canal and thus make difficulty in parturition (p. 386). Some compromise was necessary.

Among humans, accordingly, the female pelvis is broader than the male. The arms of both sexes hang down, not vertically but sloping slightly inwards from the shoulders and then outwards from the elbow, to form with the trunk the "carrying angle" (Figure 25-15). This permits the arms to clear the hips during walking. On the average, the angle is greater for females than for males. Finally, the more complicated internal machinery of the female abdomen requires more room than is needed for male apparatus. This is provided in part by the fact that the ratio of leg length to total height is smaller for females than for males.

TEETH, JAW, AND CHIN

Monkeys and apes have sharp, prolonged canine teeth, important for piercing, and aligned sharp-edged incisors crucial for slicing and tearing. A hard-pointed tool (as of stone) is a substitute canine; an edged tool is a substitute for the incisors. When,

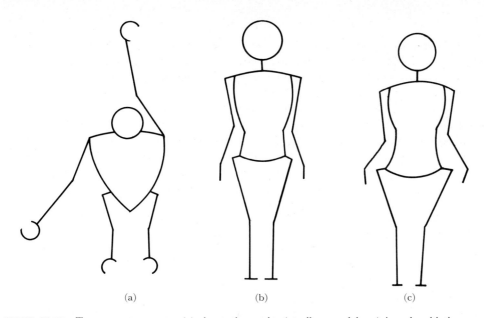

(a)   (b)   (c)

FIGURE 25-15. THE CARRYING ANGLE. (a) shows the angles (at elbow and knee) in a brachiating ape. (b) and (c) show them in man, the striding biped, with the sexual differences, brought about by other factors, between male (b) and female (c). [(a) and (b) from *The Origin of Races,* by Carleton S. Coon, Knopf, New York, 1963, p. 158. Copyright 1962 by Carleton S. Coon; reproduced with the permission of author and publisher.]

and only when, such tools began to be made and used by the hominids did it become possible for the canines to becomes shorter and for the teeth and the whole jaw to become less massive, without loss of efficiency in the manipulation of the environment, and with some gain because the head thereby became lighter.

Such hominid jaws as have survived from about two million years ago already show shortened canines (Figure 25-6). We are therefore able to infer the making and using of appropriate tools even when none are found in association with the fossils.

A less projecting jaw in an erect biped also makes for better visibility when walking, since the ground in front can be viewed without bowing the head to get the jaw out of the line of sight.

Finally, the reduction of teeth and jaw was accompanied by a reshaping of the jawbone to form a chin (Figure 25-16), and by the loss of the simian shelf if our ancestors had any (p. 362).

✖ The increasing complexity of hominid social structure could not have come about without a concomitant increase in the flexibility of communication. In achieving this, the successful hominids eventually exploited the vocal-auditory channel. There are two descernible reasons why this channel should have been favored.

IMPROVED COMMU-NICATION

(1)   Back in the trees, the Stem Hominoids had often had to switch a carried

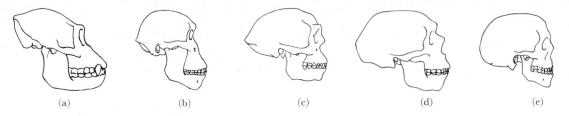

FIGURE 25-16. GROWTH OF THE CHIN. (a) is a modern ape, given for comparison; (b) is *Australopithecus;* (c) is "Pithecanthropus" (probably to be assigned to genus *Homo*); (d) is a Neanderthal; (e) is modern man. [(a) after Clark 1960; (b) through (e) after Buettner-Janusch 1966.]

object from hand to mouth because the hand was needed for locomotion. On the ground, the early hominids increasingly favored bipedal locomotion. As this freed the hands *for* carrying, it freed the mouth *from* that function.

(2) In collective hunting, the actions of the participants must be closely coordinated. Their hands hold weapons and are thus unavailable for any complicated semaphore. Their visual attention must be divided between the motions of the quarry and those of other participants. But their ears are free, and their mouths are not occupied with crucial activities that prevent or impede the production of vocal sounds.

Against the second point, however, we must allow for the need for silence during certain parts of a hunt lest the quarry be alerted, and for the general desirability of not making so much noise that dangerous predators are attracted.

Against both reasons are the facts that no known nonhuman primate vocal-auditory communication exceeds the limits of a closed call system, and that experiments with contemporary monkeys and apes show their vocal-auditory channel to be ill adapted for any vocal-auditory system very much like human language (recall Washoe: p. 117).

What all this means is that selection had quite a job to do. The closed call system inherited from the Stem Hominoids had to be opened up. If they had the limited capacity for the acquisition of an open system that Washoe has shown, it had to be increased; if they did not have it, it had to be developed. And the brain had to change in such a way as to hook up that capacity with the vocal-auditory channel instead of with gestures.

We know the ultimate outcome, but we do not know the timetable. In the discussion that follows I shall phrase what is said in terms of an early concentration of the vocal-auditory channel. That may be wrong. It is possible that the crucial changes we are about to describe took place not in a purely vocal-auditory system but in one which made use of some much more complicated channel, including both sounds and visible body motions. The definitive switch to a concentration on mouth and ear would then have been much later, accompanying the events to be described below in chapter 27 (pp. 413–415).

BLENDING

To see how a closed call system (or call-and-gesture system) might begin to open, let us describe what may occasionally happen among the gibbons, or other apes, today.

Suppose a gibbon finds himself in a situation characterized by both the presence of food and the imminence of danger. The factors, we shall say, are closely balanced. The normal consequence among gibbons is that one or the other factor prevails and just one call is given. This time we imagine our gibbon atypical. Instead of emitting either the food call or the danger call, he utters a cry that has some of the characteristics of each: he produces a *blend* of the two (p. 110).

This is beyond the experience of the other gibbons of his band. Depending on acoustic conditions, some of them may hear the actual cry as the food call, others as the danger call, and others as nonsense. It is unlikely that any hear it as a new signal, conveying two kinds of information at once. The consequences are thus negligible.

But now suppose that the early hominids had a somewhat richer call system (though closed) functioning in a somewhat more complex social order. Then we may also assume that this type of event occasionally happened, and that sooner or later the other members of a band responded appropriately, thus handling an unusually complex situation more efficiently than otherwise. With this reinforcement, the habit of blending two calls to produce a new one would gain ground.

We have to assume that this is what happened, because blending is the only way in which a closed system can move towards openness of the kind characteristic of language.

Let us represent the acoustic contours of one inherited call arbitrarily with the sequence of letters *ABCD* and those of another with *EFGH*. All we mean to indicate is that each call possesses various acoustic properties on which primate ears can focus attention—it does not matter just what they are. Now we recall the *redundancy* that must characterize any feasible communicative system (p. 82): as a particular signal leaves a transmitter it must be sufficiently different from all the other signals in the repertory that, if portions of it do not reach the receiver, the received signal is usually still unambiguous. Thus, if *ABCD* is uttered but noise or distance masks part of it out, so that the receiver hears only *AB*, he can still identify which call it is. Suppose, now, that *ABCD* means 'food here' and *EFGH* means 'danger coming'. Finding both food and danger, the hominid comes out with *ABGH*. If this new call is established, there has been an important change: the two old calls and the new one are all henceforth *composite*. For, in *ABCD*, the part *AB* now means 'food' and the part *CD* means 'no danger'; in *EFGH*, *EF* now means 'no food' and *GH* means 'danger'.

PRELANGUAGE

The most crucial aspect of the foregoing is *not* that there are now a larger number of signals in the repertory.

Suppose that before any successful blending there are exactly 10 calls in the system, and suppose (unrealistically) that each comes to be blended with each of the others. The yield is exactly 100 calls. To be sure, communication is more flexible, and that has survival value; otherwise these things would never have happened. Yet a system of exactly 100 calls is in principle just as closed as is one of just 10.

Much more vital in the long run is that after successful blending some calls are composite.

This means that a receiver must listen more carefully. Detecting only *AB* is inadequate, since the transmitter may have emitted *ABCD, ABGH,* or perhaps any of various other composite calls of which *AB* is a part. Channel noise, poor hearing, and inattention can all lead to disaster if essential information is missed. There is a premium on heeding acoustic detail.

For a transmitter, it means that the habit is arising of analogically building a new composite signal, to fit the specific circumstances, out of meaningful parts of signals already known. There is clear value in being able to do this swiftly, accurately, and intelligibly.

But every member of the band is sometimes a receiver, at other times a transmitter. Moreover, as an animal transmits he continues to function as a receiver, hearing his own call. Thus the two effects, though we have itemized them separately, both apply to all band members.

The lines of development we have described slowly gave rise to a vocal-auditory communicative system very different from a close call system: to an open system that we shall call *prelanguage.*

In a call system, the signals are unitary and indivisible. In prelanguage, the typical call was composite, built from individually meaningful pieces that recurred in other calls, the patterns for putting the pieces together also being familiar from other calls. There was no definite number of possible calls, for a new one could be coined on the analogy of old ones, and could be understood (sometimes) from context and from its partial similarities to various old ones. There was also no definite number of individually meaningful pieces, since a new blending might wrest from some call a piece larger or smaller than any already in use.

All this is enough like language in the ethnographic present that we may henceforth speak, not of "calls," "meaningful pieces," and "patterns for putting pieces together," but of prelinguistic *utterances, forms,* and *grammatical patterns* (chapter 8). The modifier "prelinguistic" is important. Prelanguage was not language. Though much more flexible than any closed call system, for a long time it must have remained feeble indeed as compared with any language in the world today. In particular, it could not exploit the kinds of articulatory motions now used (p. 103), because hominid anatomy was not yet properly shaped for them; and it lacked duality of patterning (p. 105), an absolutely crucial feature of language.[4]

IMPLICATIONS

The evolution of a close call system into prelanguage required an enormous amount of time, just as the other developments on which we have touched came about at

---

[4]No communicative system with just the design features of prelanguage has been observed. Our characterization of it is an interpolation, I believe realistic, based on a comparison of language with the communicative behavior of various contemporary nonhuman animals.

an extremely leisurely pace. It is irrelevant that the production of a single blend is a brief episode. A potentially germinal event could occur repeatedly with no visible effect, or with effect on a band that later became extinct for unrelated reasons, for every one occurrence that had minuscule but durable consequences.

Watching nonhuman animals, and trying to understand their behavior, we sometimes tend to ascribe human motives or capacities to them. Here is an early hominid with a piece of meat in his hand, scurrying back home from a carnivore's kill, though the carnivore is not in evidence. Here is one carrying around a stick or stone, with nothing in view to use it on. Shall we say they are manifesting "memory" and "foresight"? That they are remembering earlier episodes in which the behavior was useful and taking precautions against a possible recurrence? This would put the cart before the horse. Because of their survival value, practices of the sorts we have described gradually *gave rise* to what we now call memory and foresight, but in evolutionary terms those human attributes are more effects than causes.

We have to examine the probable lines of causality in greater detail. We must try to see how, in the long haul, the minuscule but viable consequences piled up.

THE CAPACITY FOR TRADITION.   The detailed conventions of an open communicative system cannot be transmitted wholly through genes. The young may emit some prelinguistic utterances instinctively. But they are also exposed to various composite utterances from their elders, and are obliged to infer the participating forms, the meanings of those forms, and the grammatical patterns, from the acoustic resemblances among the calls they hear and from the behavioral contexts in which they are uttered. (To this day, that is how human infants learn their native language.) Thus, the development of an open system puts a premium on any capacity for learning and teaching a species may have, and selects for an increase in the genetic basis of that capacity.

PLAY AND DISPLACEMENT.   If the conventions have largely to be learned before the system can be used efficiently, then eventually much of the learning will be carried on away from the contexts in which the utterances being practiced would be immediately relevant. Thus *verbal play* is added to the other categories of primate play (pp. 74–77). But this, in turn, means that situations are being discussed when they do not actually pertain—as, nowadays, we can talk about something not in sight or that happened yesterday or may happen tomorrow. This, of course, is *displacement* (p. 112). Communicating about things that are out of sight or in the past or future is much like carrying a weapon when there is no obvious need for it. Each of these habits can thus reinforce the other.

PRELANGUAGE AND TOOLS.   The *manufacturing* of tools, as over against the using and carrying of them, must have begun making great strides under the impetus of the consequences of openness we have just been describing, and in turn contributed to those consequences. If carrying a weapon looks like foresight, shaping a rough one into a better one looks like more of it. Moreover, tool-making became another activity at which the young could play, as they learned their communicative system and other adult ways by playing with them.

THE ERECTUS COMPLEX

✕ The transition from the Pliocene to the Pleistocene was signaled by the slow beginning of the Quaternary Ice Age (p. 412), roughly two million years ago.

Fossils show that hominids with a shuffling rather than a striding gait were still living in the southerly parts of Africa a million years later than that (the straggling remnants of *Australopithecus:* Figure 25-1, p. 363). They also show, however, that in eastern Africa a strain of hominids with a striding gait had appeared by some time nearer to two million years ago; in fact, one recent find in Kenya, attesting the more advanced form of bipedalism, has now been dated about 2,400,000 years ago. The earliest unarguable archaeological evidence for stone tools is from much the same horizon: we shall describe it shortly (p. 390).

We infer that, as of about 2,000,000 years ago, some hominid bands, in some part of the Old World not too far from eastern Africa, had achieved:

efficient stride bipedalism;

good prelanguage;

collective hunting, food-sharing, and individual carrying of various things in the interest of the whole band;

extensive transmission of ways of behavior via tradition rather than genetics (and the genetic makeup required for that).

We shall call this combination of features the *erectus complex*.

BY HIS BOOTSTRAPS

26

✖

THE EMERGENCE OF MAN: THE LIFE AND TIMES OF *Homo erectus*

Our term "erectus complex" derives from the fact that the hominids that achieved it became, in due time, the type of animal classed as *Homo erectus,* of which our own species, *H. sapiens,* is the successor.[1] The bearers of the erectus complex were premen, not true men. But they achieved so much on which true men later built that we shall use the adjective "human" of them as of ourselves.

The erectus complex was a key complex (p. 299). It gave rise to an adaptive radiation that we shall call *phase one* of *the human radiation.*

It had taken many millions of years of ground life for the constituent features of this key complex to evolve and to be brought together. There were still hominid bands that had only some of its features, or that had some of them in less developed form. The hominid communities, wherever they were (we do not know), that were first to achieve all the features of the complex had a survival advantage, particularly in that they had the wherewithal to migrate successfully into open country, away, at long last, from the fringes of the forest. But they were not, for a long while, precluded from exchanging genes with hominid communities that still lived in older ways. The innovations thus spread partly by population increase and migration, but partly also by continued gene flow.

Eventually there were no hominid groups left anywhere that were not heir to the whole complex. Some bands doubtless died out without ever having been touched by it, and some may have disappeared because they were unable to withstand the competition of the new sort of animal—that is what we can suspect of the slowly vanishing remnants of *Australopithecus* (p. 384). Other local types, however, as they were touched and transformed by genes from the erectus heartland, at the same time may have contributed some of their own genes to the total pool for ensuing generations. Thus, if a particular hominid population had achieved an effective genetic adaptation to the exigencies of some special sort of ecological niche, that benefit was not necessarily lost.

[1] The earliest fossils attesting to a striding gait are not necessarily *H. erectus;* this point is under debate amongst the experts.

The fossil evidence shows that the cranial capacity of the hominids of a couple of million years ago was hardly greater than that of gorillas (Figure 26-1). That would make the brain-body mass ratio greater for the hominids, of course, since gorillas are very big and the hominids were small. The ratio may have been increasing slowly from the time of the Stem Hominoids. It did increase steadily from the earliest fossils down almost, but apparently not quite, to the present (p. 416).

We know from Part One (p. 54) that a large brain is expensive—especially in an erect biped, in which the required blood supply must all be pumped uphill. The inference is immediate. The brain grew because, with the erectus complex, the hominids were relying more and more on learning and teaching. In general, individuals and bands with bigger brains had a survival advantage over those with smaller brains; the advantage was enough to outweigh the metabolic cost.

The growth of the brain pushed the top of the skull outwards, and the front of it forwards over the eyes to form a forehead. The appearance of the chin (p. 379), the recession of the jaw, and the development of the forehead ultimately yielded the essentially flat perpendicular physiognomy which, with only minor variations, now prevails.

PAEDOMORPHISM

Larger brains meant larger heads. At the same time, erect posture had reshaped the pelvis and was narrowing the birth canal (p. 378). Parturition was becoming painful and problematic.

The difficulty was combatted by *paedomorphism:* the fetus came to be expelled relatively earlier in its development. The newborn human being is not as "well done" as is the newborn ape. The length of the human period of gestation today is a sort of compromise. If it were shorter, delivery would be easier on the mother, but too many infants would die. If it were longer, too many females would die in childbirth.

LIFE CYCLE AND SOCIAL STRUCTURE

Earlier birth means a longer period of helpless infancy. But this is, at the same time, a period of maximum plasticity, during which the child can acquire the non-genetic heritage of its community.

The helplessness of infants demands longer and more elaborate child care, and it becomes useful for adult males to help the mothers; sooner or later, some of the skills that the young males must learn can be learned only from adult males. This, together with the habit of paying attention to past experiences and future contingencies (p. 383), promotes what we may call the "domestication of fathers." Perhaps it also contributes to the development of, or to an increase in, male jealousy, in that it now becomes reasonable for a male to reserve a female even when he is not sexually hungry, that she may be available when the need arises. Factors of this sort must have played a part in the earliest types of human family organization, but beyond this we have so distressingly little evidence that speculation is pointless (p. 160).

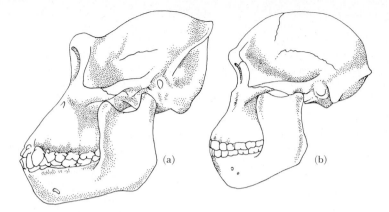

FIGURE 26-1. CRANIAL CAPACITY. Skulls of (a) an adult female gorilla and of (b) a specimen of *Australopithecus*. Here are ranges of cranial capacities (in cubic centimeters):

chimpanzees	320–420
gorillas	340–752
Australopithecus	435–700
Homo erectus	775–1225
Neanderthals	1200–1640
modern man	850–1700

(Figures after Clark 1960; data from Buettner-Janusch 1966 and Campbell 1966.)

The growth of the brain as a place to store learned information, coupled with the development of prelanguage, seems to have led not only to paedomorphism but also to a prolongation of life at and after maturity. Among the Stem Hominoids we may assume that the band leaders were the strongest adult males. In the hominid line this changes. The oldest members of the band, strong or feeble, are valued because they have had time to learn more. They are repositories of information on which the community can call as it is needed. This use of the elderly as encyclopaedias perhaps helped to select for a greater life span.

Certainly the increased social utility of the elderly promotes a protection of the old and feeble by the young and strong—and eventually also, by analogical transfer, of the sick or injured whether they are old or not (compare p. 44). Eventually it may contribute to doing something positive about the disposal of the dead (p. 408). No nonhuman primates do anything about this; all human communities do.

HAIRLESSNESS

The Stem Hominoids were presumably as hairy as most land mammals. In contrast, modern man, despite variations from one racial strain to another, is virtually hairless.

It is possible that the loss of hair in the hominid line was fortuitous (p. 283). A more realistic proposal is that two million or so years ago, when some hominids had achieved the erectus complex (with an efficient striding bipedal gait), they lost much of their hair as they moved from wooded savanna into more open country and came to engage in long, tiring pursuits of game. The tropical sun is merciless, and excess heat must be discarded. There is a survival advantage in less hair and in a more copious supply of sweat glands. Man has both. So does the tropical rhinoceros, which also faces the requirement of rapid motion under a hot sun.

Some of our residual patches of hair are located where hairlessness would be of little use: in the armpits and the crotch. But why we should retain long hair on the head and (in some males) on the lower part of the face, why the growth of hair follows the maturational pattern it does, and why we have sexual dimorphism in hirsuteness, are questions for which no convincing answers have yet been proposed.

VITAMIN D. Unlike most mammals (p. 359) we do not ingest the vitamin D we need by licking one another; instead, we absorb it directly from where it is synthesized in our skins. This could be the result of mutations that accompanied increasing hairlessness.

BATHING AND SWIMMING. Another innovation that may be tied in somehow with hairlessness is our extreme fondness for water. All apes and most monkeys avoid open water like the plague; gorillas will not cross even the narrowest running stream, and chimpanzees are miserably uncomfortable and bad-tempered if caught in the rain. Comparable water-avoidance has been observed for human communities in the ethnographic present only where the water is dangerously cold or where there is so little of it that people have no chance to get used to it. These are clearly secondary developments, and cultural rather than genetic.

INFANT CARE. A final consequence of loss of body hair is that an infant can no longer cling to his mother's hair as she moves about. The burden of the transport must be assumed entirely by the mother.

CLOTHING ✘ We have assumed above that our ancestors became hairless while still in the tropics. Later on, when some bearers of the erectus complex were slowly migrating out of the tropics (or were encountering cooler climates without migration, because of the temperature changes of the Quaternary Ice Age), hairlessness would have been fatal without some substitute for a pelage. Since they did in fact survive in cold places, we infer that such a substitute was available, in the form of clothing.

Today, clothing serves roughly three functions. Two of them are obvious: protection, as against the cold; and modesty and vanity. The third is easily overlooked: *carrying*! This was surely the function of earliest relevance. If one's way of life rests on hand-carrying, and if the number and variety of things to be carried is increasing to the point of awkwardness, then the invention of a device that helps one carry things, but leaves the hands free, is a great gain.

The single most widespread article of clothing in recent times, worn almost universally even if nothing else is, is a waist belt, supporting a breechclout and pouches, from which many sorts of weapons and tools can be hung, freeing the hands for other activities. The earliest clothing-as-harness could have been something no more elaborate than a piece of vine pulled from a tree and draped over the shoulder or around the waist—the shoulders and hips being the natural projections of the body that will hold something up. When the time came that the hominids were regularly killing small animals, the hides, worthless as food, may have been put to this use. A widely known technique for softening a hide is to chew it: the mechanical action of the teeth does part of the job, and the enzymes in the saliva do the rest. This practice could have arisen as hides were originally chewed for what little nourishment they contain. Furthermore, all these developments could take place in the earliest home of the erectus complex: although we do not know exactly where it was, we know it was in the tropics. The basic pattern for clothing would then already have been familiar when encounters with colder climates yielded a new used for it.

THE TOOLS THAT MADE MAN

× Before you can have a hide to chew you must kill an animal (or find one some predator has killed); and the original motivation for hunting was food, not hides or other byproducts.

Suppose you are a not very strong, not very large (perhaps 65 to 75 pounds for an adult male), and not really very bright, but definitely agile, striding biped, living in some stretch of Old World savanna in the early Pleistocene, and you want to kill a big, stupid herbivore in order to eat its flesh. There are a couple of things you can try. Both require cooperation with others of your band. If you must go it alone, stick to rabbits or other small game.

(1) Sneak up on your quarry and hit it as hard as you can with sticks and stones, if possible in vital spots such as the eyes or throat. Dash off before it tramples you. You will probably not have killed it, but if you have injured it seriously enough you can trail along behind it until, worn out from loss of blood, it falls and dies.

(2) Surround your quarry, and with loud shouts and menacing gestures drive it into the edge of a convenient swamp, where its feet will sink into the sticky muck and it will be unable to extricate itself. Since you are much lighter, the swamp won't catch you in the same way. Beat the animal to death.[2]

Either may require hours or days, during which you get little sleep and probably very little to eat. Neither is guaranteed to succeed. But suppose one of them has worked. You have your prey. What next?

Between you and the food there is a thick, tough hide. A rabbit's skin you could penetrate with your teeth and tear with your fingers and hands. Here that is impossible. To be sure, you have used tools of a sort in the earlier phases of the hunt. But any sufficiently large pebble will do as a projectile, and any reasonably stout piece of a fallen tree branch will serve as a club. It is just at this point, where the next requirement is to flay the carcass, that you are stymied unless you have a tool of a special sort: one with a rough, hard cutting edge. Without that, you might as well have skipped the hunt altogether.

[2]The first technique is surmised on the basis of procedures used by some hunters-and-gatherers today. The second is attested archaeologically: the foot bones of quadrupeds are found in standing position in deposits the geologists say were once mud, in association with signs of human activity. But even for the second we have had to extrapolate, since no such find dates as far back as the period we are talking about.

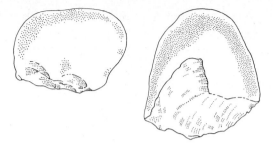

FIGURE 26-2. THE EARLIEST KNOWN HUMAN TOOLS. Left: from the Grotte du Vallonnet. Right: from Olduvai. (See the map in Figure 26-3.) (After Bordes 1968.)

We can thus be quite sure that our ancestors did not develop the practice of hunting big game until they had tools with cutting edges.

In some places the environment supplies such tools ready-made. The action of wind, water, and ice breaks large pieces of rock into smaller pieces, and it is not unusual for this process to yield pebbles with sharp edges. If you live where natural knives are available at the cost of a brief search, maybe you catch your quarry first and then go looking for one. When you are done with it, you throw it away. If rock outcroppings are scarce, or if streams have rubbed pebbles together and rounded off most of their fracture edges, you may go on special expeditions to collect suitable natural knives where they are more abundant, and then guard them with care, taking some along when you go on a hunt. In this case, too, the tools will eventually become unusable and will be discarded. Either way, your descendants, chancing upon a pebble you used as a knife, will probably have no way of knowing that you used it. It will bear no surviving testimony of your action—unless, as sometimes happens, it is one of a whole slew of pebbles found by archaeologists where there would be no stones at all except by virtue of human action.

How about ready-made flaying tools of other materials? One thinks of wood, bone, tooth, horn, antler. But pieces of wood do not come with ready-made edges, and the other materials we have just listed are part of the very carcass you are trying to dissect.

We shall never know for how long our ancestors made do with environmentally supplied cutting edges. We do know that eventually—and surely at various times and places independently, rather than in a unique breakthrough—they began giving the environment a hand, making a usable cutting edge by striking two pebbles together. When this is done clumsily the result cannot be distinguished from the result of stone fracture by other agents. But when it is done with sufficient care and skill it yields something that can only be achieved by the hand and brain of an animal very much like man.

PEBBLE CHOPPERS

Figure 26-2 displays two tools of this sort; the archaeologists call them *pebble choppers* (see also Figure 26-3). These or others much like them are on the order of two million

FIGURE 26-3. Lower Pleistocene archaeological sites. Those marked with black dots are older: two to one million years. Those in Europe shown as black squares date from between one million and seven hundred and fifty thousand years ago. (After Chard 1969.)

years old. At present that is as far back as the archaeological record goes. Nothing unambiguously identifiable as a tool is any older.

In the frame of reference of chapter 7 (pp. 86–89), pebble choppers are derivative tools—that is what makes them recognizable as human products. Their shapes show how they were made. You begin with a fist-sized pebble that is rounded at one end, so that it will fit comfortably in the hand. The other end may be rounded too, or may already have an edgelike narrowing. Holding it steady, you strike it with another pebble, as shown in Figure 26-4. The blow knocks off a *flake*. A series of blows removes a series of flakes, leaving an uneven but usable cutting edge. But sometimes one of the flakes has a sharp edge or point and is big enough to grasp; if so, you use it too.

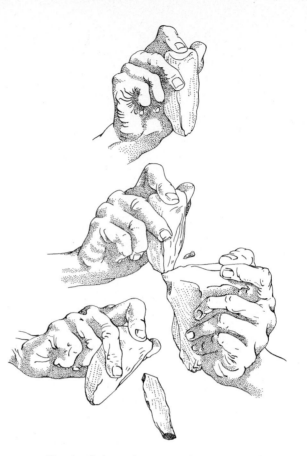

FIGURE 26-4. CHIPPING FLINT. The detail shows three successive positions of the hammer and the hand that holds it. (After Mewhinney 1957.)

If you are careless, the target pebble may shatter into worthless fragments. If the stone has a filamentous or laminal grain that just happens to run the wrong way, then even with care things may go awry. If the other pebble, the one you are using as a hammer, is too soft or brittle, a blow may break it instead of the target pebble. In any case you will surely nick and bruise your hands. The manufacture of "simple" stone tools is not really a simple task. But if you are hungry enough, or if you come to find pleasure in the operation, then you will persist, and in time you will acquire experience in the selection of pebbles to work on and with, and skill in delivering the crucial blows.

In fact, it did not take our ancestors long—only a few hundred thousand years—to learn what sorts of stone are the best. Whenever possible, they used obsidian, chert, or flint. Obsidian is volcanic glass: not a true solid (crystalline) but an extremely viscous liquid. It is therefore amorphous, with no favored direction of cleavage, and with care can be split in any desired direction. However, it is relatively rare. Cherts

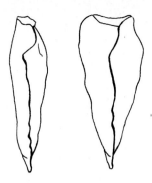

FIGURE 26-5. "Thin" and "fat" shanks.

and flints are more widely distributed. They are a family of rocks composed chiefly of microscopically small crystals of silica (SiO_2) pressed tightly together in such random orientation that, like obsidian, they are effectively amorphous. When a blow splits any of these, the fracture surface is bulbous: that of the flake is convex, that of the target pebble concave. These rocks are hard—the best flint is harder than steel—which renders the tools made from them effective, but brittle rather than tough, which helps make the rocks workable.[3] The early masons resorted to softer, tougher, or more cantankerously grained pieces of rock only when the preferred types were not to be had.

USES AND CONSEQUENCES

We do not know that flaying was the first use to which pebble choppers (and flakes) were put, but surely that use developed early. The cutting edge of either chopper or flake is a sort of compromise between the serrated edge of a modern steel saw blade and the sharp, straight edge of a modern knife; this is excellent for cutting through the hide of a herbivore. A flake is then much better for slicing the hide away from the flesh, since the chopper is too fat behind the edge (Figure 26-5). Once the hide is removed, either chopper or flake can cut off pieces of meat, or sever a haunch where a leg joins the trunk; hence a large carcass can be cut into pieces small enough to carry. The tools are also fine for small prey, such as rabbits. One does not suppose that our ancestors reserved their tools, once they had them, only for tasks that were otherwise beyond their powers.

The prey has been caught and killed, and the carcass has been skinned and cut up. Perhaps it has been carried back from the site of the kill to the band's home base. Next comes the eating—raw!

Our modern domesticated meat animals are bred and fed to yield tender flesh. Wild animals are not. Ask a butcher for a piece of the toughest stewing beef he has, and try to chew it. You will get some notion of how strong must have been the jaws

[3]Hardness means resistance to being scratched (see fn. 8, p. 493); toughness means resistance to being shattered.

of our ancestors before the invention of cooking (p. 405). For a jaw-relaxing dessert, they cracked open the bones and ate the marrow. We know this because at one site after another the cracked bones are found in association with pebbles that could have been used to split them open. Doubtless brains were another favorite dessert, whenever the skull could be broken open so as to get at them.[4]

The attainment of stone knives and of the cadavers of sizable animals constituted the foundation for a potential technological advance, because knives can cut things other than skin and flesh, and because a cadaver supplies more than food.

(1) STONE ON WOOD.   With patience, crude stone knives can cut wood, at least well enough to put some sort of point on the end of a stick. This yields hunting weapons better than stone projectiles and wooden clubs: long pointed poles with which to poke the cornered prey in the vitals or to spear him from a safe distance.

One of the earliest known specimens of a wooden spear is shown in Figure 26-6. It dates only from the middle Pleistocene (say, 750,000 to 150,000 years ago), well over a million years after the earliest pebble choppers. But discarded wood is not nearly so durable as stone, and so will be preserved only under unusual circumstances. We can probably infer that the first shaping of wood by stone was a lot earlier.

(2) THE CADAVER'S SOFT PARTS.   An animal cadaver is a mine of usable materials. A sheet of hide can be propped up on sticks as a windbreak, or can be draped directly on the body. A strip of hide can be used to tie things if you have anything to tie, and makes a better waist belt than does a length of vine. Rawhide stiffens as it dries, so that its uses must have been limited until the invention of some sort of tanning, but the simplest way to soften a hide is just to chew it (p. 389), and the next simplest way is to soak it in urine, which has rarely been in short supply. A stomach or bladder can be used as a pouch or water container. Sinew, split into thin strands, has all sorts of applications.

In the nature of the case, we cannot expect any very ancient archaeological attestation to the exploitation of these soft materials. The timetable therefore remains obscure. They may have been in use two million years ago, or may have been ignored as junk until only a few tens of thousands of years ago, but the latter extreme seems unlikely.

(3) THE CADAVER'S HARD PARTS.   Then there are these: always bones and teeth; sometimes horns or antlers; claws on the rare occasions when a carnivore is taken. The separation of a single bone or other hard piece from the rest of the cadaver presents no great problem. If its shape renders it usable as a tool with no reworking, fine. One can imagine a straight, hollow horn being squeezed onto one end of a stick, to supply a spear point tougher and sharper than one made by whittling the end of the stick with a stone knife.

Putting a point or edge on a bone is another matter. Percussion techniques, effective on stone, are useless. Accordingly, it is not surprising that derivative bone tools appear in the record only at a much later date (p. 399).

[4] Maybe this exploitation of marrow and brains began with scavenging hominids, and helped pave the way for hunting.

FIGURE 26-6. An early wooden spear. This, and the stone scraper shown to its left, are from Clacton-on-Sea, England. (After Oakley 1959.)

POPULATION SPREAD AND REGIONAL DIFFERENTIATION

✕ With the erectus complex and with only the crude technology described above for the early Pleistocene, our ancestors were able to spread out from the original erectus heartland (p. 385).

They continued, we suppose, to live in small bands, with headquarters on the shores of streams or lakes in open or wooded savanna or similar terrain. This gave them immediate access to water, and such habitats afford edible wild plant products, and edible insects and grubs and the like, as well as game. The variety of their hunting activities is attested by the diversity of species whose bones, found at one or another site, can be identified by palaeontologists: birds, rodents, snakes, frogs; pigs and boars; baboons; horses, antelope, camels, bison, water buffalo, sheep, deer, rhinoceros, and elephants (in some of these cases, species or varieties now extinct or altered by further evolution). They had to stay close to sources of usable stone. There is plenty of evidence that they went on quarrying expeditions when necessary, bringing back quantities of pebbles to headquarters. At one early site they seem to have piled stones in a ring, as though for protection.

The total geographic range of the tool-making hominids of the early Pleistocene is hinted at by the locations of the few known archaeological and fossil sites of the proper age, shown on Figure 26-3 (p. 391). The territory available to them expanded and contracted with the successive climatic alterations of the ice age through which Earth was passing. It is possible that some bands found their way to the seashore and were able to adapt to that environment, but there is as yet no positive evidence for this until much nearer the present. It seems clear that they were not yet able to survive in dry deserts, in rain forests and jungles, or in regions of extreme cold.

Thousands of generations passed, with no alteration in ways of life discernible in a single lifetime or in a hundred. The rate of change seems very slow to us, because we incline to take the pace of the last few millennia as the basis of comparison. That is the wrong basis. Remember that baboons may have been living much as they do now for twenty million years or more (p. 32). It is not changelessness but change that demands explanation, and not slow but rapid change that must be regarded as unusual.

In sweeping retrospect, of course, we can observe the changes. Brains were slowly getting bigger, and the techniques of working hard materials were slowly getting better.

What is more, as the archaeological record gets fuller we begin to observe what we would expect of a widespread tool-using species: increasing differences from one region to another. Technological innovations, like genetic changes, could occur any-

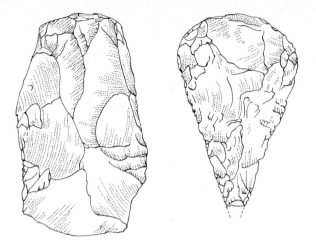

FIGURE 26-7. EARLY MIDDLE PLEISTOCENE STONE TOOLS. "Cleaver" on left; "hand ax" on right, both with heads down. (After Bordes 1968.)

where, and no natural law demanded that exactly the same ones occur in different places or that any of them diffuse to all hominid bands everywhere. For sufficiently recent eras the archaeologists are able to distinguish among first dozens, then hundreds, of local traditions, no two exactly identical, and are able to see some technological features spreading, others disappearing. The specialist's concern is with all the detail he can wrest from the evidence. Our concern is, first, with an example of early regional differentiation, thereafter only with those innovations that proved to be germinal in technological history.

CLEAVER AND HAND AX

The two sorts of stone tools shown in Figure 26-7 appear around 750,000 years ago, alongside the older types. The one on the left is a *cleaver;* that on the right has been dubbed a *hand ax.* Like the pebble chopper, both are "core" tools, made by removing unwanted parts from a pebble.

The cleaver is found first and chiefly in Africa, and shows an obvious similarity to the ancestral pebble chopper, except that typically flakes are removed from a larger area, perhaps in order to obtain a more efficient or more uniform overall shape, and except that the cutting edge is straighter.

The hand ax came in gradually, and almost exclusively in western Europe. It is quite different. It has a fairly fine point (broken off in the specimen that posed for our picture), and an edge to either side of the point. Side views (Figure 26-8) show that the edges are sinuous rather than straight. This contour was clearly intentional. Also, hand axes are surprisingly massive, some of them reaching three or more pounds. They were manufactured in large numbers at certain times and places, and must have been important. But we do not know just what they were used for.

Cleavers and hand axes show greater delicacy and accuracy of workmanship than

BY HIS BOOTSTRAPS

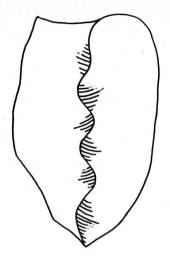

FIGURE 26-8. Side view of hand ax, showing sinuosities of edge.

had the earlier pebble choppers: in Figure 26-7, note that some of the hollows where flakes have been removed are very small, especially near the edge of the hand ax. (The same finer artisanry appears in the stone scraper shown to the left of the wooden spear in Figure 26-6, p. 395, also from the middle Pleistocene.) One might suspect that some essentially new technique of manufacture had been developed. The expert consensus says no: the difference was due only to more careful use of the classical percussion technique.

✖ Between about 200,000 and about 50,000 years ago, there is evidence for the following.

The Prepared Core

If you want a flake tool (that is, one made by removing the wanted piece from a larger hunk of stone) of a certain shape, there are two ways of proceeding. One is to knock flakes from a pebble until you get one of approximately the right size and shape, and then retouch it. That can be awkward if the raw flake is small. The other is to do most of the retouching *before* the flake is removed from the core. That is, one trims bits from the surface of the pebble until the shape of what remains is ideal for the production of just the kind of flake one wants, and then strikes the desired flake off. Figure 26-9 shows the sequence.

This *prepared core* procedure evolved about 200,000 years ago, independently in at least two different places. One was somewhere in the west. The new flake tools were superior to any available kind of core tool, and both hand ax and cleaver were slowly abandoned in the regions that had known them. The other was in eastern Asia, where

THE EMERGENCE OF MAN: THE LIFE AND TIMES OF *Homo erectus*   **397**

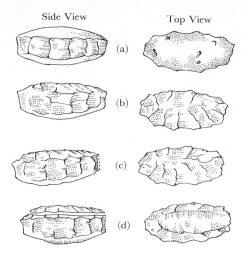

Side View   Top View

(a)

(b)

(c)

(d)

FIGURE 26-9. THE PREPARED-CORE TECHNIQUE. First (a) the edges of a pebble are trimmed. Then the top face is trimmed. Then a "striking platform" is prepared at one end (dotted line on the right end of the side view). Then a single blow (delivered right-to-left in terms of the orientation of the figures) removes a ready trimmed flake. (After Jean Zallinger in Jacques Bordaz, "First tools of mankind," *Natural History Magazine,* January 1959.)

the core tools that are eventually superseded were simply late forms of the pebble chopper.[5]

BIFACIAL WORKING OF FLAKE TOOLS

The earlier middle Pleistocene hand ax of Europe had been trimmed on both sides. But doing this to a flake tool, to get a more satisfactory cutting edge, seems to have come only in the era of which we are now speaking.

HAFTING

Hafting is the technique of fastening pieces of dissimilar materials together, so that a single tool can have (say) a handle made of the best material for handles and a head made of the best material for heads. The clear evidence is surviving projectile points: pointed bits of flint or the like too small to have been held directly in the hand for use. Presumably such a point was fastened securely to a wooden handle or shaft.

A pointed pebble hurled at a target can rotate during its flight, so that it is not the point that strikes the target. A long, thin, straight wooden shaft, properly balanced, has a kind of aerodynamic stability: if it is hurled point first, the point reaches the target first, with all the momentum of the whole piece of wood behind it. But a wooden point is at best not very effective. Hafting a flint point to a wooden shaft thus makes a more satisfactory throwing weapon.

[5]The replacement could not have been complete: pebble choppers much like those of the early Pleistocene were in use in Taiwan as late as 7000 years ago.

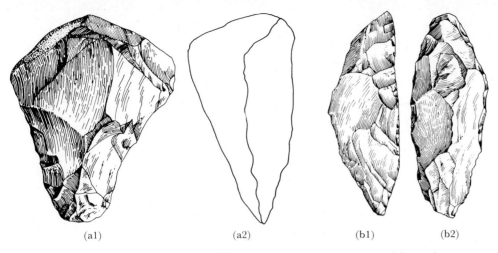

(a1)	(a2)	(b1)	(b2)

FIGURE 26-10. Massive stone tools from Africa. Two views each of two tools. (After various sources, via Chard 1969.)

Again, one can mount an edged pebble on a piece of wood so that the edge is parallel to the long axis of the wood; then, holding the other end of the wood, one can swing the edge at a target with much greater force than can be applied if one merely holds the pebble in one's hand. The principle is that of the lever. Such tools (true hafted axes) are attested only very late; it is clear that they could not have been devised until some technique of hafting had been invented.

Since it is only the stone points that have survived for our examination, not the wooden handles or shafts, we remain in the dark as to the exact method of hafting first used. But it must have involved either delicate shaping of the parts of the two pieces where they are to be fitted together, or else the use of adhesives (p. 528). The practice of squeezing the hollow end of a straight, pointed animal horn over one end of a wooden pole (p. 394) may have served as a model.

Massive Stone Tools

These, perhaps in time hafted, were for cutting and for the initial trimming of large pieces of wood—say, for the removal of a branch several inches in diameter from the trunk of a tree (Figure 26-10).

Bone-Carving

Such implements as those shown in Figure 26-11 testify that the difficulties of working bone (p. 394) were being overcome.

✴ The innovations we have just outlined did not all occur at the same place.

Bone-carving turns up first in the north, and was surely related to the invasion of the edge of the almost treeless taiga. There was plenty of game there, but you

FURTHER POPULATION SPREAD

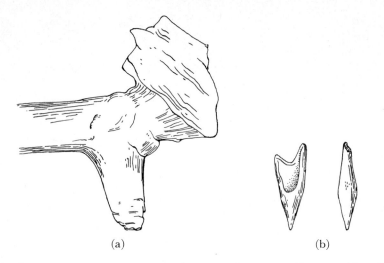

(a)   (b)

FIGURE 26-11. Early bone tools from a site at Salzgitter-Lebenstedt, Germany. (a) a pick or club of reindeer antler (handle to left). (b) is a projectile point (two views), requiring hafting for use. (After Hansjürgen Müller-Beck in *Science* 152.1197, 1966.)

can't exploit it if you are overly dependent on wood. The bands that succeeded were those that learned to make tools of bone, antler, horn, and tooth. Not only these new tools, but also the new technique of production, were important. Struck by a stone point or edge, of even the finest flint, a bone splinters, splits, or cracks. The effective working of bone requires specialized tools with which to abrade, scrape, and scratch (Table 7-1, p. 87), applying pressure delicately to a small area at a time. It may well have been the necessity of working bone that first gave rise to these manipulative techniques. Once available, however, they can with some adjustment be transferred to other materials, including wood and even stone itself; of this, more later.

The massive stone tools appear chiefly in Africa, where they made possible the invasion of the tropical rain forest, up to that time strictly off-limits. Here the raw material in short supply is stone itself. If you can take some with you (or import it), and can exploit wood more effectively, you are all right.

By some means, our ancestors during this period also managed to invade highland territory in various parts of the then inhabited world. Just what techniques turned this trick is obscure, though fire, as a source of warmth, may have helped (see below, p. 403). Figure 26-12 shows the extent of the human domain that resulted from these movements.

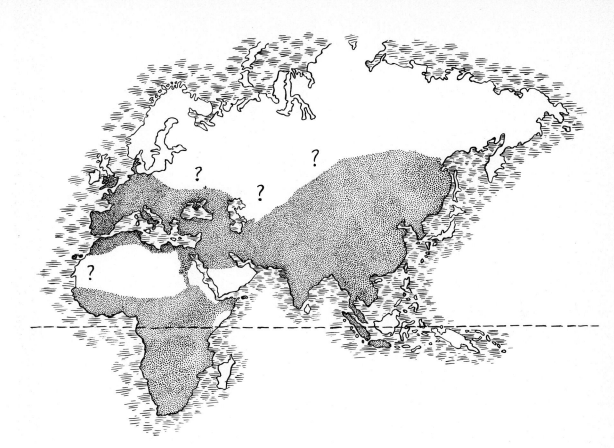

FIGURE 26-12 Man's distribution as of 100,000 years ago.

27

�֎

THE EMERGENCE OF MAN: FIRE AND TALKING

TO AN ANCIENT

Your claims to immortality were two.
The one you made, the other one you grew.
Sorry to have no name for you but You.

We never knew exactly where to look,
But found one in the delta of a brook,
One in a cavern where you used to cook.

Coming on such an ancient human trace
Seems as expressive of the human race
As meeting someone living face to face.

We date you by your depth in silt and dust
Your probable brute nature is discussed.
At which point we are totally nonplussed.

You made the eolith, you grew the bone,
The second more peculiarly your own,
And likely to have been enough alone.

You make me ask if I would go to time
Would I gain anything by using rhyme?
Or aren't the bones enough I live to lime?

Robert Frost[1]

We are getting closer to man. Have we reached him yet? How shall we recognize him when he appears? There are difficulties, but we will try not to be quite so nonplussed as the poet proposes. In the world today the difference between human and nonhuman is obvious. In the record of things past, we know the ravages of time

[1]From "Steeple Bush," in *The Poetry of Robert Frost,* edited by Edward Connery Lathem. Copyright 1947, © 1969 by Holt, Rinehart and Winston, Inc. Reprinted by permission of Holt, Rinehart and Winston, Inc.

have made gaps even thousands of generations can pass abreast. But we also know that in what actually happened there could be neither gaps nor leaps. The humanization of our ancestors was gradual. They vaulted over no sudden broad Rubicon, nonhuman one day or century, human the next.

They did, however, pass slowly through two major transitions. The first led to the achievement of the erectus complex (p. 384). It took those who inherited this complex two million years to reach the onset of the second major transition; it will take us only to the end of this chapter.

PROMETHEUS

⌘ The earliest known evidence of the controlled use of fire considerably predates the most recent epoch touched on in the preceding chapter: it is from a site near Nice on the Mediterranean coast of France, and the date may be as early as 1,000,000 years ago. After that there is a large gap until, about 450,000 years ago, there is testimony from two widely separated sites, Vertesszöllös in Hungary and Choukoutien in northeastern China. Even after that, direct archaeological evidence is hardly common until very close to the present.

It does not take the hand and brain of man—or his carelessness—to start a fire. Forest, brush, and swamp fires have been started, most often by lightning, from time to time for hundreds of millions of years, part of the natural order of the biosphere since the oxygenation of the atmosphere by photosynthesis and the emergence of land life. Fires have probably converted large areas of forest into grasslands. In some ecological zones, a periodic fire plays a part in maintaining botanical balance, in that it burns out underbrush and gives young trees of certain species a chance to mature.

Animals flee from a fire, and the early hominids were surely no exception. A campfire at night will ward off predators. Our ancestors of the Pleistocene were themselves predators, and until they came to terms with fire may have been as frightened by it as were their four-footed competitors.

On the other hand, a fire is a source of warmth, which under some conditions is exceedingly welcome. In eastern Africa today, chimpanzees run from a major forest fire as sensibly as anyone; yet if a farmer leaves a pile of burning trash to smolder overnight, he may, in the chilly dawn, find a ring of chimps warming themselves by it. Thus it may be that the hominoids, including ourselves, have for a long time been able to distinguish between a dangerous fire and a potentially useful one. The distinction is not always easy, so that this implies an ambivalence of attitude, maintained still: we use fire constantly, but are always a little afraid of it, and are repeatedly reminded of the legitimacy of our fear by reports of conflagrations that have claimed the lives of some of our fellows.

Steps in Fire Control

The first step in the control of fire must have been to stay close to a safe one of nonhuman origin, for warmth, instead of running away.

The second step was to keep such a fire going by feeding it fresh fuel (twigs and sticks of wood, dried ruminant dung) and to keep it safe by clearing flammable material away from its immediate vicinity. Bands may have established their headquarters where they happened to encounter a usable fire, paying for the privilege by being forced to scout in various directions, perhaps for considerable distances, for such necessities as water, food, stone, and fuel.

The third step was to borrow fire from a nonhuman source and carry it where it was wanted. This can be done by holding the cool end of a stick the other end of which is burning, and by igniting a new stick when the old one has burned down too close to the hand. Carrying fire around in this way made it possible to establish headquarters in terms of the locations of other needed things. However, fire-maintenance (when one does not know how to make fire to order) also requires protection against rain. This was probably the chief factor leading our ancestors, in some parts of the world, to move their camps into the mouths of caves.

The fourth step was probably not taken for hundreds of thousands of years after the first three: kindling a fresh fire when it was needed. People who can do this nevertheless nurture the fire they already have going, banking it when it is not in active use and carrying it from one place to another when that is indicated, because—until the invention of matches—that is less trouble than starting a new fire. One way to start a fire is to strike a siliceous pebble, such as flint, against a ferrous one, such as iron pyrites, letting the resulting sparks ignite some sort of tinder. Since the Pleistocene hominids were thoroughly familiar with stones of all sorts, made extensive use of flint, and were in the habit of striking stones together, this was probably the first fire-making technique to be discovered.

The Uses of Fire

The control of fire gave our ancestors their first way of channeling and using energy other than via the ingestion of food to power their own muscles. Of course, at first it could not be used in the same way: the conversion of heat into mechanical energy was hardly hinted at until Heron of Alexandria (around A.D. 50) designed a toy steam engine, and became practical only in England in the eighteenth century A.D. But fire was used in other ways: for warmth, for light, for protection, for waste-disposal, as a weapon in hunting and war, in a variety of manufacturing processes, and for cooking.

EARLIEST USES. Certainly the earliest use was for warmth, with night light, protection against nocturnal predators, and waste-disposal (of a limited and not very important sort) as immediate byproducts.

This does not mean that the mastery of fire had to begin in high latitudes. The tropics can be miserably cold in the early morning or where the elevation above sea level is significant. But the first hominids successfully to invade more northerly regions, or to stay put in such regions as glaciation lowered the ambient temperature, doubtless had fire, as well as clothing of a sort (p. 388), bone-working techniques (p. 399), and, before long, the beginnings of some kind of physiological adaptation to the cold (p. 411).

Old World monkeys and hominoids are not nocturnal and do not have night vision. Baboons, as we have seen (p. 36), settle in for the night before it gets dark, and stay put until dawn. Our ancestors before fire must have done much the same. With a campfire to see by after the sun has set, all this could change. Tasks not finished during the day could be completed by firelight. Social activities could go on into the evening. Also, the protection against dangerous quadrupeds afforded by the campfire meant that people could safely be noisier in their nighttime activities. Some investigators believe that this was an important factor in the development of pre-language towards genuine language, since now it was safe to indulge in evening chatter. Be that as it may, it is clear that with fire an animal whose ancestors for millions of years had spent nearly half of each twenty-four–hour period in sleep began to stay awake for fourteen, sixteen, or eighteen hours per day. Through selection, this must have had physiological consequences, but I do not know what they were, unless we register here the fact that most human beings today can do very well with about eight hours' sleep.

FIRE AS WEAPON.   A burning brand flourished in the face of an attacking carnivore (or enemy) will turn him aside or keep him at bay: a weapon of defense rather than of offense. Game can be driven into a snare or enclosure by setting a brush fire with proper care. War raiding parties regularly burn an enemy camp if they can. These practices may be very old.

FIRE FOR MANUFACTURING.   This use of fire depends on how hot the fire can be made and on how the heat can be applied. Pleistocene fires did not concentrate enough heat for the kilning of pottery or the smelting of metal ores. But they could be used in working wood. You char the outer surface of the end of a stick; then you can scrape the charred part away, working the end into a point. Also, the heat boils off some of the moisture; the sap then becomes gluelike and binds together the fibers, yielding a harder point. Some of the earliest wooden tools turned up by archaeologists show evidences of such fire-processing.

COOKING

Finally we come to the most consequential, though, in a sense, the most absurd application of all: cooking.

The most famous account of the origin of cooking is the fictional one by Charles Lamb in his "Dissertation on Roast Pig."[2] A straw house accidentally burns down, and the pigs that had shared the house with their owners are killed by and roasted in the flames. A boy, poking through the smoking ruins, burns his finger touching the hot carcass of a pig, "instinctively" puts his finger to his mouth, and forgets the pain in the glorious taste.

[2]One of his *Essays of Elia,* first published in *The London Magazine* in the 1820s. The setting is fake Chinese; Lamb may have been inspired by the fact that the Chinese written character for *jyā* 'home, house' shows a stereotyped pig under a roof.

The first part of Lamb's tale is realistic: surely the first cooking was accidental. The rest is ridiculous. There is nothing about which human beings in all known cultures are as picky as they are about their diet, and that trait can hardly be new. Food accidentally exposed to the flame of an early campfire would be spoiled food: its stench would be sickening. Why ruin good bloody meat or fine, tasty, freshly dug-up roots by sticking them in a fire? Those folks over in the next valley are crazy to do such things; they'll kill themselves with cramps. Raw food was good enough for my grandfather [who was lucky enough to survive to the magnificent old age of thirty-five before he lost his teeth and died a natural death from starvation], and it's good enough for me.

No; the first cooking was accidental, but the first eating of cooked food had to be an act of desperation, done only because there was nothing else available. The development of a positive *liking* for cooked food must have taken a very long time indeed.

KINDS OF COOKING.   There are, at bottom, only two kinds of cooking. In one, heat is applied via flame and hot gasses; this is *roasting*. It came first, because in its simplest form it requires nothing but the fire and the food; and even in recent times it remained the only kind of cooking known in Tasmania, Australia, Tierra del Fuego, and some other outlying regions. In the other method, heat is transmitted to the food through a liquid in which the food is wholly or partly immersed. When the liquid is water, we call this *boiling;* when it is some sort of oil, we call it *frying*. Both require a non-combustible container, or else some way of heating the contents of a combustible one without igniting the container; hence they were later developments. Archaeological evidence of nonflammable containers does not go back very far, but boiling itself may be much older. In modern times a widespread technique for boiling things in a combustible container has been to fill it with water, heat stones in a fire, and then drop the stones in.

In roasting, it is almost inevitable that some of the organic material will burn—that is, oxidize. What happens to the rest is very complicated. Organic tissue has a high water content (on the average, 65 to 70% by mass), and one thing that happens is that some of the water evaporates; in boiling, the water lost in this way is replaced from that in which the material to be cooked has been immersed. Chemical reactions take place that do not occur at all, or only slowly under the action of enzymes, at lower temperatures. The more complex organic molecules are broken down into simpler ones. Some fibrous tissues resist this heat-induced dissolution, but many do not, so that, by and large, cooked food is easier to bite and chew than is raw food.

CONSEQUENCES.   Cooking was the first major advance in alimentation in 200 million years or more in the line of genetic descent that led to man, the first essential change in digestive economy since the premammals stopped swallowing their prey whole and began to chew and predigest it in the mouth (p. 358). It was a new stage in the alimentary assembly line, inserted ahead of all the others. What the fire does, the jaws, teeth, and saliva do not have to do. Its consequences stem from that.

(1) LONGER LIVES. One consequence was that people could now outlive their

teeth. Boiling, when it came along, was especially valuable in this connection. The old man or woman whose jaws are too feeble to process something even as soft as thin mashed potatoes can still sip and swallow nourishing broth. It is possible that the first systematic use of cooked food was as pap for the aged, whilst younger folks stuck to their traditional diet of delicious raw victuals.

(2) DISEASE. Another consequence was a change in disease conditions, because cooking destroys all sorts of parasites that can otherwise transfer from the tissue that is ingested to the tissue of the ingester. Some types of parasites may have vanished forever. Some, of course, still hang on, transmitted by other channels or via food that is taken raw or not cooked long enough.

(3) FOOD-STORAGE. The germicidal effect of heat meant that heat-processed foods could be stored longer without spoiling. In time certain specialized techniques were devised for this, including smoking, drying, and sun drying;[3] but even the crudest roasting over the campfire has some preservative effect.

(4) NEW FOODS. Certain foodstuffs were rendered available for human consumption that otherwise could not be eaten at all. We have no knowledge of early instances. In recent times, however (the last few thousand years), the South American Indians obtained excellent nourishment from the root of the bitter cassava (*Manihot esculenta*) by heating it; this removes the hydrocyanic acid that renders the raw root poisonous.

(5) TEETH AND JAWS. Finally, a major consequence was that there was no longer constant selective pressure favoring strong jaws and teeth. The nonprotruding jaws of modern man, in contrast to the prognathism of his predecessors, would probably have been impossible but for the spread of the habit of cooking.

ANTIQUITY. The last point above is a clue to the antiquity of cooking. There is no direct archaeological evidence from even as early as forty or fifty thousand years ago. But by roughly that period typical modern small jaws turn up in fossils. So, unless the whole argument is wrong, cooking must have begun several tens of thousands of years before that.

✖ From the hundred-thousand-year period between 150,000 and 50,000 years ago, our evidence becomes rich enough (as compared to that for earlier intervals) to suggest certain social developments. The beginnings of these could have been earlier, but hardly much later.

SOCIAL INNOVATIONS

BAND EXOGAMY

Among tribal peoples of the recent past, band exogamy has been extremely widespread (p. 172). In contrast, bands of apes and monkeys are mainly inbreeding groups. The latter must be the archaic primate pattern. Hence human band exogamy had

[3] Freezing is good too, and has probably been used wherever and whenever man has encountered sufficiently low temperatures.

to be an innovation in our own lineage, coming about early enough to form part of our common heritage all over the world.

Next we note a seemingly unrelated fact. Archaeologists tell us that technical innovations during the period of which we are speaking tended to spread from their points of origins much faster than had comparable new things in earlier times.

It is inferred that the period witnessed increased trafficking between neighboring bands, that women came to be one of the commodities exchanged, and that in time the habit of seeking a wife in another band instead of in one's own became common.[4]

If this did happen, then the exchange of females, as well as that of artifacts, served to increase the rate of spread of technical innovations, since an incoming wife necessarily brought with her some stock of know-how acquired during her life with her ancestral band. Moreover, band exogamy of this sort produced a quickened pace of gene flow all over the inhabited world, with consequences we shall note later (p. 418).

The Sick and the Dead

From the latter part of our interval (nearer to 50,000 than to 150,000 years ago), there is evidence of systematic disposal of the dead and of care bestowed on the sick or incapacitated. Burial sites have been excavated (Figure 27-1), and the disposition of the bones, in some cases also of associated artifacts, is such as to bar absolutely the possibility of accidental interment. Furthermore, the condition of the bones tells us something of the physical state of their owners during life:

> In some cases, as at La Ferrassie in France, considerable care was expended. At Shanidar cave in Iraq, pollen analysis indicates that the body of one individual had been laid down on a bed of pine boughs and bright-colored flowers. Typical is the interment of the deceased in a flexed position: perhaps to save the labor of digging a larger grave than necessary. . . .
>
> That [our predecessor at this stage] . . . within his own group was living in a human type of social structure involving ethical considerations and humane sensibilities is indicated by the Shanidar cripple, who had been cared for from infancy until his accidental death at age forty. The arthritic old man from La Chapelle aux Saints is another case in point, though here we may suppose that the wisdom of age endowed him with a social value.[5]

The evidence does not mean they buried everybody, and there is plenty of equally direct evidence attesting to their ability to be as inhumane as their predecessors and successors in the treatment of aliens—despite the increase of negotiations and fruitful contact between bands. As for their reasons for burying at least some of their dead, rather than merely abandoning or discarding the corpses, we know nothing. Whatever the original motives, the results were meritorious, and systematic disposal of the dead eventually became a worldwide practice.

The earth-moving technology to which the graves attest was not very complicated. Most of the graves seem to have been dug in loose soil, and many of them required the special excavation of only eight or ten inches of dirt below the floor of a depression

---

[4]I don't know why it had to be wives rather than husbands that changed band affiliation. This part of the theory may have been read into the evidence by predominantly male investigators.

[5]From Chester S. Chard, *Man in Prehistory,* pp. 122–123. Copyright 1969 by McGraw-Hill Book Company. Used with permission of McGraw-Hill Book Company.

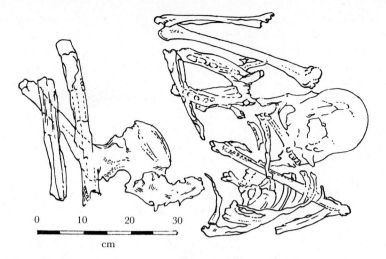

FIGURE 27-1. A BURIAL. Drawing of the bones, in situ, of one of ten burials found on the terrace of the Mugaret-es-Skhūl, Mount Carmel, Palestine. The bones would not be in this arrangement unless the limbs had been flexed at the time of interment. These graves show no signs of flowers or other materials buried with the corpse, but others do. (After Clark and Piggott 1967.)

already dug for some other purpose, perhaps for housing. The simplest sort of wooden digging stick, of the kind that had probably been in use for a million years or more for getting at edible roots, would suffice—plus some sort of container for carting away the dirt.

"Higher" Impulses

Some investigators see in the surviving mortal remains of our predecessors of this stage evidences of the faint beginnings of "art," of "ritual," of "religion."

Thus, why would the folks at Shanidar have put "a bed of pine boughs and bright-colored flowers" at the bottom of the grave before depositing the body, other than through some sort of aesthetic impulse? (Or do we suspect this merely because in our own Western culture we think flowers are nice?) Maybe a corpse was tied into flexed position not to save grave-digging labor, but to keep it from wandering around and bothering the living. (Or do we ascribe such a notion to them merely because we ourselves have only recently outgrown it?)

The impulses of modern man hinted at by the common-vocabulary terms "art," "ritual," and "religion" are not to be gainsaid, and, since we do not find them manifested very much in the behavior of nonhuman animals, we must assume that they arose largely during the separate history of the hominid line. The guesses we have cited are thus legitimate. But we must be realistic. A big impulse did not develop first, out of thin air, and then lead to practices that satisfied it. Both impulses and practices evolved in small increments, each conditioning the further development of the other.

✖ An important characteristic of modern man is his great racial variety. It has sometimes been thought that this variety is recent—a matter, say, of the last few thousands or tens of thousands of years. That cannot be so. Given the length of a human generation, such an interval is too brief for an initially uniform type to develop the degree of diversity we now manifest. The bulk of the differentiation, then, must have come about during the two million years of phase one of the human radiation.

THE PRESENT SITUATION

Racial differentiation (defined on p. 295) is the same sort of purely genetic phenomenon for our species as for any other. We tend to get confused about it partly because of inherited false theories (and, in some social settings, because of prejudice, fear, hate, and guilt), but also, in a peculiar way, because we are misled by experiences in small regions of the world.

Thus, let us take a ride in a New York City subway train and look about at our fellow passengers. A very high percentage of them fall clearly into one or another type—white, black, Puerto Rican, Oriental. The criteria by which we achieve these assignments are various. Obviously we cannot see the genes, and the clues on which we rely are not all genetically relevant. Some are matters of dress, or of hair style, or of features of body motion and facial gesture that depend mainly, perhaps wholly, on tradition. Nevertheless, we try to make airtight assignments—*and so do the other passengers.* An individual about whose assignment we are dubious is vaguely disturbing.

Extrapolating from such localized experiences, our ordinary inference is that the human population of the world must surely fall neatly into some small number of distinct "racial types" or "races": say, five or six, perhaps a few more if we allow for recent admixtures of earlier "purer" types.

But that is a mistake.

The point is, of course, that in the subway train we are viewing a small sample from a set of several populations which have been brought together in a single region (New York City) in the recent past, under conditions in which interbreeding has so far been somewhat limited—and in which, *socially,* most individuals tend to try to identify themselves towards one or another "norm."

If we now enlarge our view and consider human populations all over the world as they really are, we find that between any two of the seemingly distinct types we observe on the subway train there exists an exceedingly dense series of interconnecting gradations. Could we view them all in a single panorama, we should be totally at a loss in trying to draw boundaries segregating some groups of populations from the rest. Nor could we distinguish "purer" and "more mixed" types, since *any* type can be viewed as a "mixture" of those most similar to it. Any classification of human populations into some small number of "races" is doomed to arbitrariness.

The upshot is that in the discussion of human genetics the adjective "racial" is useful but the noun "race" is not. We can speak of "racial differentiation." We can legitimately say that one pair of populations is "racially similar" while another pair is "racially distant" (remembering that such judgments are relative). But the noun "races" cannot denote anything useful unless it is merely a synonym for "populations."

Origins

When the erectus complex was first consolidated (p. 384), there were still bands of shuffle-gaited hominids not heir to it. In a million years the latter had vanished, variously absorbed or extinguished by their striding cousins. The type classed officially as *Homo erectus* appears clearly only in the middle Pleistocene, but then from between 600,000 and 400,000 years ago this is the only type attested by the fossils.

Thereafter, particularly after about 150,000 years ago, the record grows more complicated as it grows fuller. There is good evidence from Europe and nearby for what used to be classed as a separate species, *"H. neanderthalensis."* We can still speak of the "Neanderthals" or "Neanderthaloids," and, in fact, the social innovations reported in the preceding section (pp. 407–409) are thought to have been Neanderthaloid achievements. But the type is now generally regarded either as a later variant of *H. erectus* or as an early regional form, now long gone, of our own species. Since *H. erectus* disappeared not by extinction but by evolving into *H. sapiens,* the choice of assignment does not matter much, but we will choose the former. This relatively recent part of the fossil record shows not only continued change in the direction of modern man but also, to some extent, regional differentiation. That the latter is not discernible from earlier periods is probably due only to the great paucity of earlier fossils.

Phase one of the human radiation was initiated by the consolidation of the erectus complex in some restricted region of the Old World tropics. In course of time the complex spread, as shown by Figures 26-3 (p. 391) and 26-12 (p. 401). This diffusion was obviously nothing like the steady radial motion of a wave when a pebble is tossed into still water. Rather, it was the result of multitudinous small movements of individual bands in many directions, away from a threat of danger or towards a promise of food and other resources, combined with population increase and band-splitting in unusually bountiful environments.

SELECTIVE FACTORS. Wherever bands wandered, their ways of life were such that selection favored more efficient central nervous systems, the more effective manufacture and manipulation of various sorts of artifacts, and more close-knit and better coordinated social structure. Everywhere, the brain got progressively larger, both in absolute terms and in terms of the ratio of brain mass to total body mass. Almost everywhere, body mass also increased, perhaps because larger and stronger hominids, though they needed more food, were sufficiently more effective as hunters to make up for that.

In other respects, however, the selective pressures differed with time, place, and circumstance. Cold climates select for one or another sort of physiological adaptation to the cold, and for a body shape that minimizes surface-to-volume ratio. Hot climates select for a lank body shape that can discard surplus heat more readily. High latitudes favor light skin that can maximize vitamin D production with limited sunlight. High altitudes require efficiency in the use of oxygen (p. 50). Life on the seashore, with a diet of shellfish and fish, high in iodine, may call for some modification of digestive chemistry. Different disease organisms are endemic to different regions. These are only the more obvious factors; there must be hundreds of more subtle ones.

CONTINUED UNITY.   In the typical adaptive radiation, environmental variety leads to speciation. That is: first there is accommodation to various ecological niches by racial differentiation, which becomes more extreme as time goes by; and then the bridges for gene flow are broken so that racially disparate types have become distinct species.

That is exactly what happened during phase one of the human radiation, except in one respect: as far as we can tell, none of the genetic bridges connecting different communities were ever completely severed.

Recall that the Quaternary Ice Age began just about when the radiation did (p. 384). That ice age has had—so far—at least five peaks of glaciation, as shown in Figure 27-2. At the peaks it was colder, but with water locked in glaciers there were land bridges over which migrations could take place. During the troughs the sea level was higher, migratory routes fewer and more circuitous, and hominid developments in different places consequently more independent of one another.

Thus, at certain intervals barriers of open water or of glacial ice may have isolated some populations from all others for thousands or tens of thousands of years, which means for hundreds or thousands of generations. For some life forms, that many generations of isolation would be enough to yield speciation. For our ancestors, it was not. Surely one important reason was that they were already able to adjust to environmental changes in part by altered culture (tradition), rather than only through slow genetic selection. When the barriers disappeared and fresh movements brought the temporarily segregated populations into contact with others, gene exchange was always still possible. Furthermore, the inclinations of our ancestors during this phase were enough like those of modern man that the exchange invariably took place.

OUTCOME.   The upshot was that, already at the end of the first phase of the human radiation (say, very roughly, 50,000 years ago), the genus *Homo* consisted of a racially highly diverse single species. All surviving hominids were heir to the full erectus complex. All had behind them two million years of the manufacturing and manipulating of artifacts. The brain had grown to its present size, with some variation of average mass from one group of populations to another; in fact, among the European Neanderthals the average was perhaps larger than it is for any population in the world today.

Differentiation and reintegration did not stop with the end of phase one. Yet our current racial diversity is largely a heritage from our varied predecessors of fifty thousand or so years ago, and of that heritage we should be proud. To be sure, without certain further developments (to be described shortly) the racial differentiation would be of no collective value. With them, however, the genetic and adaptive potential that racial diversity gives us has been of incalculable power. When the survival value of a particular genetic feature of some present-day population is not obvious (this is often the case), we can nevertheless know that it arose, directly or indirectly, in

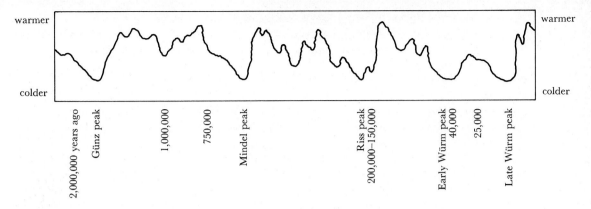

FIGURE 27-2. Temperature variations during the Quaternary Ice Age. (After Chard 1969.)

answer to the vicissitudes of existence of some earlier epoch, so that it stands as a monument to human success. If it is true that today any human being of any genetic constitution can live in reasonable physical comfort anywhere—even on Moon!—that is only because of very recent technological advances. In the vast sweep of hominid history, genetic accommodation has been as responsible as cultural adjustment in making us masters of the world.

✖ It is hard to see how the technology and social life of the period from 150,000 to 50,000 years ago, simple compared to our own and yet much more complex than those of any nonhuman animal, could have been achieved and maintained without extremely effective communication. I think this was the period during which prelanguage evolved into true language.

A strong reason for believing that true language must be at least that old is that the diversity of the world's languages today (four or five thousand of them: p. 100) could not have developed in less than about fifty thousand years. One reason for believing that it cannot be much older than that (other evidence will be touched on later) is that true language is such a powerful instrument for technological and social change: if our ancestors had it five hundred thousand or a million years ago, why did it take us so long to get where we are?

SHARED FEATURES

The prelanguage we have posited for our ancestors (pp. 381–382) was like true language in these respects: (1) free coinage of new messages to meet new circumstances, on the analogy of messages used successfully earlier in more or less similar circumstances (openness: p. 108); (2) use of the vocal-auditory channel;[6] (3) arbitrary

[6]Or (p. 380) of a complex channel involving both vocal sound and bodily gesture. If so, then the gradual relegation of gesture and of voice-quality effects (p. 99) to secondary status formed part of the transformations we are about to describe.

relationship between the sound of a form and its meaning (p. 105); (4) transmission of the conventions of the system via tradition rather than by genes; (5) displacement: the ability to discuss things that are not in evidence at the time and place of the discussion.

Until feature (1) appeared, the system was still closed (like a call system) and hence not yet prelanguage.

Features (3) through (5) imply something else shared by prelanguage and language: if a system has these characteristics, the nongenetic mechanisms of change described in chapter 23 are operative, and if a community splits into subcommunities that drift apart and cease to have much contact, the changes will be independent and the systems will diverge. Thus, though certainly all the hominid bands of, say, 200,000 years ago had prelanguage, we must surely assume diversity, comparable to the diversity of languages in the world today, by virtue of hundreds of thousands of years of divergence. Thus, if chance brought members of remote bands into contact, they would not be able to understand each other. In the light of hominid paedomorphism (p. 386), perhaps they could learn to when necessary. Certainly by the time of incipient band exogamy (p. 407) such learning by a young adult had to have been possible.

The Differences

The crucial feature shared by all languages in the ethnographic present, but which we asume was missing from prelanguage, is duality of patterning (pp. 105–107).

Closely allied with this is the use by all the world's languages today of essentially the same sound-producing articulatory motions (pp. 102–104). These motions are not used at all by contemporary nonhuman animals. If our diagnosis of the few surviving fossil jaws and skulls is correct, then *Homo erectus,* including even the relatively recent Neanderthals, did not have the anatomical structures to use them with any great efficiency.

The Changes

IN BEHAVIOR.   We envisage prelanguage becoming more and more complex and flexible because of its many advantages for survival. The constant rubbing-together of whole utterances (by blending: p. 381) generated an increasingly large stock of meaningful prelinguistic forms. Lacking duality, however, these prelinguistic forms had to be holistically different from one another in their acoustic contours. As the number increased, some prelinguistic forms became so similar to others that keeping them apart, in either production or reception, was too great a challenge for hominid mouths, ears, and brains.

Something had to happen, or the system would collapse of its own weight. Doubtless many overloaded systems did collapse, the bands that used them becoming extinct.

But in at least one case there was a brilliantly successful innovation. Prelinguistic forms began to be listened to and identified not in terms of their overall acoustic patterns but in terms of the smaller features of sound that occurred in them in varying arrangements. In pace with this shift in the technique of detection by a receiver,

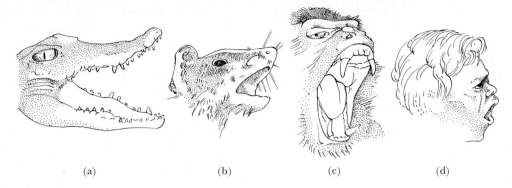

(a)   (b)   (c)   (d)

FIGURE 27-3. Mouth size. The relevant factor is the size of the external opening of the oral cavity relative to the volume of that cavity. (a) shows a crocodile, (b) the feather-tailed tree shrew (*Ptilocercus lowii*), (c) an adult male macaque monkey (*Macaca nemestrina*), and (d) a human being with an unusually large mouth.

articulatory motions came to be directed, by a transmitter, not towards the generation of a suitable acoustic contour, but towards the sufficiently precise production of the relevant smaller features of sound that distinguished one prelinguistic form from others.

In anatomy. It seems unlikely that the behavioral change just described could have been carried through if there had not also been some suitable anatomical changes, some of them in advance and paving the way, others concurrent and perhaps selected for because of the gain in communicative efficiency.

In monkeys and apes, and doubtless among the Stem Hominoids, the external opening of the oral cavity is quite large (Figure 27-3). In the hominid lineage it has grown smaller, perhaps in connection with successive reductions of tooth and jaw size. It is easy to verify, in any kitchen, the claim that a cavity with a narrow aperture (like a bottle) is a better resonator than one with a wide opening (like a glass). On top of this, the flexibility of the lips means that the size of the aperture can be varied, as can the size and shape of the resonating chamber because of the flexibility of jaw and tongue.

In monkeys and apes the glottis lies close to the velum. The development of upright posture by the hominids changed their location somewhat, but still for the Neanderthals the glottis is high in the throat, so that the pharynx (above the glottis, behind nose and mouth) is small. In *Homo sapiens* the glottis is high at birth, but with maturation it lowers and the pharynx elongates to serve as an additional crucial resonance chamber for the sounds of speech.[7]

[7] Our species shows sexual dimorphism in voice quality (men's and women's voices in general sound different, though the ranges of quality for the two sexes overlap). The origin of this may be tied up somehow with what is said above, or with hominid paedomorphism (p. 386), but I don't know how.

With these changes in behavior and anatomy, prelinguistic forms became true linguistic forms, the features of sound became the meaningless signaling units of a sound system, and prelanguage had become true language.

The earliest true language may have been very feeble compared with *all* languages in the ethnographic present. It may have lacked one or more features of detail that are now universal (p. 120). Yet it required no further adjustments of a basic sort, only time, to grow into language as we know it now. An acorn is not an oak tree, but if it grows at all it grows into nothing else.

A NEW BRAIN   ✘ Back on page 386 we mentioned that the hominid brain had achieved its present size by about 50,000 years ago. Its growth had been steady for two million years, but then seems to have leveled off (except perhaps among the Neanderthals).[8] The increase in size can be understood (p. 411). But why did it stop?

The best guess is that mutations produced some crucial reorganization of the workings of the brain, whereby greater efficiency was effected without continued metabolically expensive increase of size. The human brain is patently not a simple scale magnification of, say, the chimpanzee brain. There are differences of internal organization. We do not know exactly what they are, but one hypothesis is worth exploring.

HANDEDNESS.   We assume that the Stem Hominoids, like today's baboons and all other nonhuman primates, showed little signs of preference for one hand over the other. Now, in their increasing reliance on tools, the hominids were eventually confronted by situations in which the two hands had to act together, with careful coordination, though doing different things. Think (in modern terms) of holding a bow in one hand and drawing it with the other, or of steadying a nut between the jaws of a nutcracker with one hand while applying pressure with the other. With this differentiation of role, activities requiring only one hand would in time come to be done preferentially with one hand rather than with the other.

The first part of the hypothesis we are presenting is that this kind of experience led (via mutation and selection) to the sort of handedness that is now a human universal: almost everybody in the world is right-handed; a minority is left-handed; a negligible few seem to be ambidextrous.

LATERAL DIFFERENTIATION.   For the brain, handedness reflects "lateral dominance": one hemisphere of the brain governs the actions of one half of the body, the other hemisphere the other half, and the hemisphere that governs the dominant hand is usually dominant in other respects too. The second part of our hypothesis proposes

---

[8]These assertions have to rest on measurements of capacity of fossil crania. The growth is clear. Some specialists question its cessation, on the grounds that 50,000 years is not a long enough interval to be sure.

that the evolutionary importance of the rise of lateral dominance is better indicated by speaking of lateral differentiation.

Among monkeys, apes, and early hominids, we assume information was mostly stored in the brain in parallel: any information-carrying circuits (whatever their actual physical nature) in one hemisphere normally being matched by the same circuited in the other.

The inception of lateral differentiation would be a change of connecting circuits so that the two hemispheres could be used for storing *different* information, anything stored in either half being available for the behavior of either half of the body. To be sure, one need not assume that duplication was complete before the change and entirely missing thereafter. Even a partial change of the sort would be a valuable innovation, increasing efficiency without the need for a concomitant increase in expensive brain tissue.

EVIDENCE.   Evidence for lateral differentiation in the human brain includes the known presence of a region of cortex in the left hemisphere, known as "Broca's center," crucial for speech, but not matched by any functionally equivalent region in the right hemisphere. The two hemispheres are connected via a thick bundle of fibers, the "corpus callosum." In adults in which this has been accidentally severed, speech responses to stimuli presented to the left eye are approximately normal, but if the same stimuli are presented to the right eye there is no speech response at all. However, up to about the age of four this differentiation has not yet appeared.

Again: certain recent experiments suggest that we do not hear exactly the same way with the two ears. A person totally deaf in one ear can manage, but maybe he exploits emergency circuits not ordinarily used. Given normal hearing, one of the ears seems to work better for the detection and processing of musical sounds, the other for percussive noises involving irregular distributions of energy through broad bands of frequency. For language, that would mean (roughly) that the "musical" ear is used for intonation and for vowel sounds, the "percussion" ear for consonant sounds! Thus, the achievement of lateral differentiation might have accompanied the development of effective duality of patterning in language and the resort by speakers to the kinds of articulatory motions that are now universal.

Further study may show that the hypothesis of lateral differentiation is wrong. However, I think we must believe that *some* crucial change in cerebral economy took place at about the time we have mentioned.

✕ Towards the end of the first phase of the human radiation, features of what we **THE SAPIENS** shall call the *sapiens complex* began to crop up here and there in the form of various **COMPLEX** successful mutations. Eventually migration and gene flow had brought them together, so that some small set of populations somewhere had them all:

handedness;
smaller teeth and a less protruding jaw, a less sloping forehead, a reduced external opening of the oral cavity, and an elongated pharynx above the glottis;

a new and more efficient kind of brain;

true language, with duality of patterning, exploiting the kinds of articulatory motions still used today.

This emerged within the framework of the erectus complex and did not undo any of the advantageous features thereof. But it was a new key complex, and gave rise to a new adaptive radiation: *phase two* of the human radiation.

The sapiens complex spread just as had the erectus complex: by migration and gene flow. The tempo, however, was remarkable. If, as seems possible, the practice of band exogamy had already become widespread (p. 407), that would help explain the rapid rate. The complex bestowed on those who attained it an unprecedented capacity to cooperate, to move, to improve technology, to learn and adapt, and to absorb or eliminate less gifted competitors. With one exception, by not much later than 40,000 years ago there were no surviving groups of hominids anywhere which it had not touched and transformed.

The Neanderthals of western Europe were the exception: they persisted until the coming of the Late Würm glaciation (peak at about 16,000 B.C.; Figure 27-2). These latter-day Neanderthals retained the protruding jaw and receding forehead that had been modified elsewhere; their pharynxes remained short; and their brains averaged somewhat larger than either our own today or those of their contemporaries in other parts of the world. It looks as though they had to get along with prelanguage (or perhaps with true language that was very clumsy articulatorily), and it looks as though their only way of getting smarter was the old, slow process of growing bigger brains. If so, those old-fashioned ways proved inadequate. The Neanderthals were unable to overcome the double challenge they faced, the encroaching ice on the one hand, competition from more efficient cousins on the other. They died out. At least the type did; surely some of their genes passed to the earliest bearers of the sapiens complex to reach their habitat.

Meanwhile, as the sapiens complex had spread elsewhere, various other strains were effected by it, and each contributed whatever it had already attained that was of value for survival in the particular environment. It was in this fashion that the racial differentiation of *Homo erectus,* the product of two million years of varied experience and adaptation, was in some measure passed on to form part of our own heritage.

But the spread of the new complex also put a halt to certain trends—at least, to increasing brain size.

Today the smallest human brains (in terms of population averages) are found among the Australian aborigines and certain allied groups; the largest are in east Asia. All our brains today are fully human; the differences of size are irrelevant. Why, then, do the sizes differ? Because they differed fifty thousand years ago when size *was* important, and because since then there has been no selective reason anywhere for the size to change!

We don't know where the sapiens complex was first consolidated, but we can describe what happened thereafter. As the new pattern reached a small-brained population, the brains stopped growing; hence they are still small. As it reached a big-brained population, the brains did not proceed to shrink again, because full physiological accommodation to the size had already been achieved; hence they are still large.

Thus *Homo erectus* was swiftly transformed into *H. sapiens,* and true human history began. After the long, wandering, tangled trail from the first organic macromolecules of Earth's youth, finally nature had produced man. Earth had awakened and had acquired a voice.

28

✖

THE CONQUEST OF THE CONTINENTS

Earth had awakened and had acquired a voice: the voice of man, the talking tool-using efficient-brained hairless striding biped, close cousin to the apes, distant relative of every organism in the biosphere, part of the biosphere and hence of Earth itself—and at the same time something so new and different that the universe may never be the same.

Let us pause a moment and take stock.

The emergence of the erectus complex two million years ago produced a remarkably adaptable and variable animal. The sapiens complex piled Ossa on Pelion. As shown in Part One, our species has had the time, the patience, and the genius to work out tens of thousands of reasonably satisfying ways of life, each suited to the environment in which it emerged and each superimposing its own idiosyncratic numerator on the human common denominator. Many of these have disappeared, swamped by changing circumstances to which they could not adapt. But many endured with little change for untold generations, and thousands still survive. Man's contemporary culture is not monolithic. As jets stitch together the cities of the world they overfly an incredibly complex mosaic of human communities with differing practices, preferences, and protocols.

Our concern now is to outline human history, telling whatever it is possible to tell of man's career in every part of the world.

Our main instrument in chronicling the story of man, as in characterizing the lifeways of any contemporary human community, is compassion (p. 122). At the same time we have to be realistic. It would be great if we could achieve some feel for the inside views of our remote ancestors. We can't: the surviving evidence does not permit. There are vast chapters of human history known to us only in bare outline. Were there bards ten thousand years before Homer singing epics as glorious as the *Odyssey?* Were there moral leaders in aboriginal Australia who endorsed their beliefs by dying for them, as Jesus and Socrates did? Were there thinkers in aboriginal America whose genius matched Einstein's? As a matter of fact there probably were, because human lifeways tend from time to time to produce such unusual individuals. As a matter of the historical record, however, we cannot name them or locate them in time and

BY HIS BOOTSTRAPS

space, and their poems and teachings had become so diffused and diluted by the dawn of the ethnographic present as to be unidentifiable.

What most often—though rarely enough—survives as a trace of human action is man's hardware.

✖ In our initial discussion of tools and other artifacts (Part One, chapter 7) we described the game of "start over from scratch," the game played—not quite fairly—by the fictional Robinson Crusoe.

The ancestral hominids of two million years ago, with no tools except primary ones and with as yet no know-how for more drastic reshaping of the environment, were not playing the game of "start over from scratch" because it wasn't over and it wasn't a game. It was living. The only rules were those of selection: if you don't eat, you die; if you don't reproduce before you die, your strain becomes extinct; if you don't train your offspring in your ways of wresting a living from the environment, they are unable to cope and your strain becomes extinct.

Human history is not a novel. It has no plot, no climax, no dénouement. It is not the unfolding of some grandiose advance plan. There is no watchful referee on high, ready to award points when people do right and subtract them when they do wrong. *The universe doesn't care.* It is the brute physical and biological facts of the world that reward and punish; ethical principles are something worked out by human beings themselves, on the basis of their slowly accumulating experience.

But if human history has no plot it nevertheless has threads of continuity and causality that we must try to follow. The best way to do this is to highlight the technological base with which our ancestors began, and its manifold transformations in different parts of the world between then and now.

There are three reasons why this is the best way.

(1) EVIDENCE. The first reason is that for the bulk of human history our only evidence is "stones and bones"—the traces of human activity that have survived to be examined by archaeologists. Were it not for the willingness of a coterie of bright investigators to explore with diligence and minute care the cesspools, graveyards, garbage dumps, slag heaps, and trash piles of the world, our knowledge of the story of man would be confined to the ethnographic present. Nowhere in the world do surviving written records of our past carry us back more than a few thousand years, a temporal perspective so shallow as to be of little interest.

(2) IMPACT. It is true that our species is and has been enormously inventive (pp. 270–274). If the ancestral hominids before the emergence of *Homo sapiens* were less so, they were at any rate darned clever as compared with all other animals.

But innovations—new things, new ways of talking and thinking and organizing, new values—do not arise in a vacuum. They arise from experience, which means that at every step they are *conditioned* by the existing technological base. Not, to be sure, *determined* thereby—for if that were so then we should be able to infer everything about a human community from a knowledge of its technological base, and we know we can't. Yet you don't invent pencil sharpeners unless you already have pencils;

you don't speculate about the nature of wood or rock or ivory unless you have had occasion to handle and examine the substance.

Collectively, if not for the individual, our human imagination, however fanciful its flights, takes off from the concrete. Our hands teach our brains.

(3) LEISURE. Closely related to the second reason is that the technological base determines how much leisure the members of a community have to sit around and indulge in "idle" (that is, not immediately productive) chatter, speculation, and experimentation.

For a talking animal, philosophizing is good primate fun—when one can afford the time. The more advanced the technological base, the more free time. Surely from the very beginning of human speculation most of it has spun off in sterile directions. Profundity and stupidity are hard to distinguish. That is part of the price that must be paid for potential creativity. But some speculation has always turned back towards the primary data of collective experience, and towards the possibility of seeking new experiences exactly in order to learn from them, thus leading people to discover new facts about their world and to alter, in one way or another, their inherited technological base.

So, granting that there are many things in our past of which we shall never know, we need not be too regretful about the stringent limitations of the evidence. The limitations force us to focus our attention just where it should be focused: on the material and technological underpinnings of human life, on which all else rests.

The major benchmarks in human history are breakthroughs in the technological base: new ways of getting food, new styles of modifying the environment, new sources of energy for human use, new ways of channeling that energy, seemingly trivial new devices (such as the metal nail: p. 535) with ultimately large consequences, new ways of correlating information in the search for new ways of doing things.

TRUE MAN'S FIRST STEPS

✗ *Homo sapiens* began with the heritage of two million or more years of earlier hominid experiences, heir to a precious adaptive racial diversity (pp. 410–413) and to a considerable range of technological know-how. What is more, he was the *product* of earlier technology in this sense: were it not for the technologically supported ways of life of his immediate predecessors, the various genetic changes that formed the sapiens complex would have had no survival value. For the hominids of a million or so years ago, a suddenly better brain would have been useless, and a suddenly less massive jaw (with no cooking) would have been fatal. Pre-man made tools; tools made man.

Any teacher of manual training or "shop" in an American high school will tell you that, if you give two students identical raw materials, equipment, and instructions, one of them may nevertheless come out with a much better finished product than the other.

For quite a while after the sapiens complex had integrated and spread, this seems to have been the chief difference between the new technology and the old. That is, the earliest true humans did the same sorts of things their ancestors had done, but they did them better. Their bifacially retouched flakes were better; their hafting was better; their woodwork was better; their bone-carving was better; perhaps their fires were better; yet all the techniques involved were inherited.

Because their hardware was better and was used more skillfully, their hunting and gathering were more efficient, so that they ate and lived more abundantly. The population grew. The rate of increase may have been low, but in the course of centuries and millennia it led to population pressure. Stronger bands pushed weaker bands aside. Weaker bands adjusted as best they could to less desirable territory, or died out. At the fringes of the inhabited world, some bands moved into the unknown, surely in some instances because it held attractions (such as an obvious abundance of game) rather than invariably because of displacement by stronger competitors.

By 15,000 years ago, perhaps somewhat earlier, *Homo sapiens* had spread into almost all the territory he occupies today. The exceptions were remote islands, such as those of Micronesia and Polynesia, which could not be reached without seaworthy craft, and pieces of continental land still covered, and due to be covered for a few more thousand years, by glacial ice.

And by the time we have just named there had also been a host of new technological advances. Each developed at one or a few specific places and times, and then diffused more or less widely. But none became universal. The species was too far-flung for that, and each innovation left some human populations untouched until the ethnographic present.

THE SETTING

The consolidation of the sapiens complex took place during the warm interval between the Early and Late Würm glaciations, when the world's configuration of land and water must have been pretty much what it is now. The earliest true men were no more able than their predecessors to cross large stretches of open sea. We would thus assume that they were confined to the Eurasian-African land mass (but see p. 429 below). We find them, via reliably dated sites, in southern Africa and in Borneo as early as 40,000 years ago, but their ancestors had been living in or near those peripheral areas for a long time.

The Late Würm glaciation peaked perhaps 18,000 years ago. But for a long time before and after the peak, enough of the world's water was locked up in ice to expose a great deal of terrain which is now at the bottom of the sea, just as it had been exposed some 50,000 years earlier during the Early Würm. The British Isles were a peninsula, as (probably) was Ceylon. Where Bering Strait and the Bering Sea now are there was a broad isthmus, much of it low-lying and flat. Sakhalin Island was joined to the Asiatic mainland, Hokkaido to Sakhalin, and if Honshu was not joined to Hokkaido the intervening water was very narrow.

In southeastern Asia and beyond the situation was as shown in Figure 28-1. The continental land mass stretched out to include what are now Sumatra, Java, Bali, Borneo, and possibly Palawan; the Sulu Archipelago may have been a neck of land

FIGURE 28-1. Great Australia and adjacent territory, about thirty thousand years ago.

connecting Borneo to Mindanao. Beyond that, east and south of the "Wallace line,"[1] lay "Wallacea," an archipelago far more densely packed with islands large and small than it is today or than the sketchily drawn map indicates. For the most part, the

[1] Named (along with Wallacea) after the British naturalist Alfred Russel Wallace (1823–1913), who in 1860 surveyed the deep-water line and showed that it was a major biogeographical boundary.

islands of Wallacea were within sight of one another, and some of them may have been visible from the shore of the mainland. Beyond Wallacea lay the vast continent of Great Australia, including all of what are now New Guinea (and Salawati Island), Australia, and Tasmania. Wallacea and adjacent continental regions were as nearly tropical as any part of the world at the time. The southern tip of the Tasmanian Peninsula was covered by the antarctic glacier.

Geologists' estimates of the changing sea level in the Australian area will be relevant here. The dates are years before the present; the figures are feet below present sea level: 35,000: 430; 25,000: ?; 18,000-16,000: 270; 12,000-7000: oscillating between 210 and 140; 3000-present: 0.

THE MOVEMENTS

Tool-making pre-men in the Eurasian-African mainland had spread from the original savannas into wooded territory, into relatively treeless plains and the edges of the northern tundra, into tropical jungles, part way into the highlands, and perhaps onto seacoasts. Man went higher into the highlands, further north into the tundra, and definitely reached seacoasts all over the place.

Among the coastal regions reached must have been those of extreme southeastern Asia, by the Wallace line. There, about thirty-five thousand years ago, some people crossed the water and the islands and settled in Great Australia.

It is doubtful that they had boats fit for major traverses; at most, they may have floated on logs or have made crude rafts in order to fish and to gather shellfish from offshore reefs. It is likely that at no actual step in the crossing into Great Australia did they intend to abandon their homes. Perhaps at some times they were caught on rafts or on floating trees in storms and carried, terrified and half drowned, to a shore farther east. Perhaps at times they were being harassed by more powerful bands, and took to the sea as an act of desperation. We cannot know the circumstances. But we know that the movements took place, because there was no other route by which man could have reached Australia early enough to have left the remains found by archaeologists at various sites—the earliest so far known dates from approximately 30,000 years ago.

The first Great Australians surely made no effort to migrate back westwards. They stayed on in the land to which they had been carried. Their new environment must have seemed very strange. The vegetation was alien. As to animals, except for bats and a few rodents there were none of the familiar placental mammals that they had hunted (or been hunted by) back on the mainland or even in Wallacea. Instead, there were all manner of queer new beasts (marsupials and monotremes: p. 360). Luckily, this fauna included no large and dangerous carnivores to compete with and prey on man. By trial and error the invaders found out what they could eat and what they could not eat of the new plants and animals, and what sorts of trees and rocks made decent tools and what sorts did not. They prospered; their numbers increased; gradually they spread over the whole of their new continent.

Surely there were successive migratory waves. But when the world's climate finally got warmer and the oceans rose, turning the Torres and Bass Isthmuses into Torres

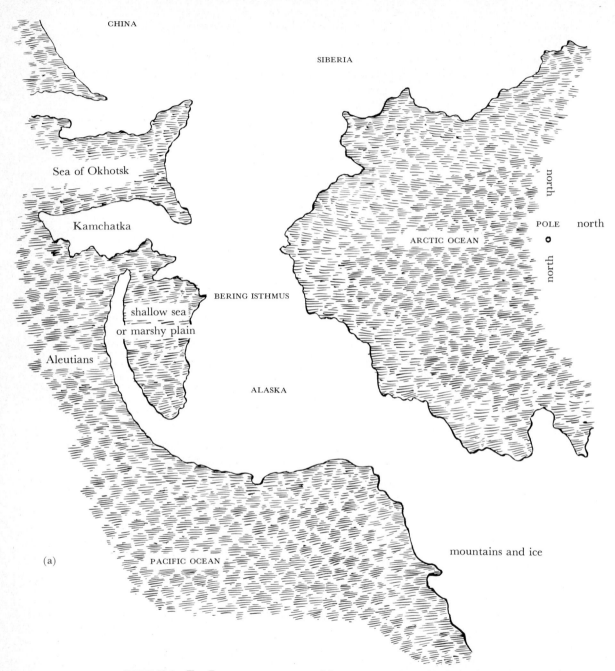

CHINA

SIBERIA

Sea of Okhotsk

north

POLE   north

ARCTIC OCEAN

Kamchatka

north

BERING ISTHMUS

shallow sea
or marshy plain

Aleutians

ALASKA

(a)

mountains and ice

PACIFIC OCEAN

FIGURE 28-2. THE BERING BRIDGE AND THE MACKENZIE CORRIDOR. (a) shows the conformation as it must
have been during the Late Würm glaciation. (b) shows the Mackenzie corridor and the location of ice
just before and just after the corridor was closed. The stippled areas in (b) show the probable distribution of man as the ice was receding and the corridor opening. [(b) after C. V. Haynes Jr., "Fluted
projectile points: Their age and dispersion," *Science* 145:3639.1408–1413,1964.]

(b)

and Bass Straits, there was no more commerce between Australia and Tasmania until the arrival of Europeans in the seventeenth and eighteenth centuries A.D., and not much between Australia and the rest of the world, though there was probably occasional interchange across Torres Strait, and eventually Melanesians may have landed on Australia's northeast coast. New Guinea lay on the paths of various later migrations, so that by the ethnographic present its peoples and cultures had become a melange in which its original quota of Great Australians played only a minor part. But the Australians were much more on their own, and the Tasmanians were the most isolated people in the world.

THE SETTING

Let us now go back again in time to the upward slopes of the Late Würm glaciation, and northwards in space to the Bering Isthmus. As Figure 28-2 shows, the conditions for hominid spread into the New World were totally different from those for the migration into Great Australia. There the barrier had been salt water; here the difficulties were cold and ice.

In the broad Bering Isthmus itself, and in a vast stretch of northeastern Siberia to the west, the climate was dry, so that no continuous ice sheets formed. In southern Alaska and western Canada matters were different. Then, as now, the prevailing winds coming inland from the Pacific dumped enormous quantities of water on the coastal mountains, which froze, century after century, into a great and totally impassable barrier. Another thick sheet of ice covered most of eastern Canada and parts of the northeastern United States. Between, say, 22,000 and 11,000 years ago these two ice sheets fused together in the Mackenzie Valley and precluded all movements of any land animals either northwards or southwards. But before the earlier of those dates, and after the later one, there was an ice-free corridor running north and south just east of the Canadian Rockies.

Conditions must have been pretty much the same 50,000 years earlier during the Early Würm. During the intervening warm period, they must have been more or less what they are now, with a strait instead of an isthmus between Alaska and Siberia and with no great ice sheets.

The Movements

Think of hominid bands moving north and east in Eurasia, farther and farther out into the tundra and taiga, exploiting the abundant game, and surviving the cold through the use of skin clothing, fire, and some sort of housing as well as by virtue of physiological adaptation. Band headquarters were always temporary, since the way of life required that one go where the game went, and the game wandered too. The movements of any single band might in time carry it towards every point of the compass. But since the land could support at most a thin population, the general drift was into virgin territory.

Thus, the "cutting edge" of expanding humanity in this northern region moved slowly all the way to what is now the Siberian shore between Kamchatka and East Cape, then out onto the flat plains of the Bering Isthmus, then on into Alaska—of course, without any of the participants having the faintest notion that they were passing from one major land mass to another.

For this to happen, the Bering Isthmus had to be there. In the same way, the subsequent movement of the frontier from Alaska to the east and south must have taken place when there was at least an ice-free corridor.

When

Someone has suggested that human beings living under late Pleistocene conditions will spread into new habitable territory at a long-term average rate of about 1 mile per year.

By the route through central Alaska and down the Mackenzie River Valley, East Cape in Siberia is about 4000 miles from the general area of Montana, which would have been just south of the ice when the corridor was closed. From there to the southern tip of South America is something over another 8000 miles.

Suppose that the Bering Isthmus was crossed as early as it was available for crossing during the Late Würm, say some 30,000 years ago. The Mackenzie route would have still been open when it was reached. The frontier could have reached Montana by 26,000 years ago, the Valley of Mexico by 24,000, the southern Peruvian highlands by 20,000, and could have been stopped temporarily well north of Tierra del Fuego until the antarctic ice sheet had shrunk away.

No one has yet dug up any particularly early hominid fossils in the Americas; the evidence of man's presence is relics of his action. Two of the earliest reliable dates fit the timetable just given. There is a site at Tlapacoya near Mexico City in which the earliest evidence of human habitation so far uncovered is just about 24,000 years ago. The oldest reliable testimony from South America is the earliest horizon at Flea Cave near Ayacucho in Peru, dated to about 20,000 years before the present.

A significantly later date for the initial Bering traverse is precluded by the evidence just cited (and at these time-depths it is futile to consider any other route from the Old World to the New).

Some experts have argued for an earlier date. Although a great deal of archaeological evidence is consonant with the schedule we have given, there is a scattering which may not be (Figures 28-3 and 28-4 show only the earliest of the reliable sites, a larger sample of the questionable ones). The problem about this additional evidence is whether it is reliably dated or, if it is, whether it really attests to the presence of hominids. For example, charcoal samples from two supposed fireplaces at Lewisville in northeastern Texas give radiocarbon dates not later than 38,000 years ago, but the fires may not have been man-made.

Of course, irrefutable evidence for an earlier date may yet be found. Now, we cannot suppose that the Bering traverse was made in boats. So, if the initial crossing was not made over the land bridge established by the Late Würm, it must have come several tens of thousands of years earlier during the Early Würm. But at that date the sapiens complex may well not yet have appeared! We should have to infer:

(1) that the domain of the hominids who carried only the erectus complex was not, after all, confined to the Eurasian-African land mass (p. 423) but reached also across the Bering bottleneck into the New World;

(2) that after the consolidation of the sapiens complex it diffused not only to all the hominids of the Old World but also, early in the Late Würm, across Bering, so that there were soon no surviving pre-sapiens strains.

Given the Bering route, there ought to be discernible similarities between archaeologically attested tool traditions in the Americas and those in relevant parts of Eurasia. They have been hard to find, partly because the amount of digging in the likely regions has so far been limited. Recently, however, some specialists think they have begun to turn them up.

SUBSEQUENT DEVELOPMENTS

When the Mackenzie corridor froze over, around 22,000 years ago, the people south of it were completely cut off from the rest of their species. Their fate was in their own hands, with neither help nor interference from others. Their sequestration was much like that of the Tasmanians (p. 427), even as to duration, but with two differences. The first is that the lengthy period of American independence came first. It was ending just as that of the Tasmanians began, because the very conversion of ice into water that reopened the Canadian corridor also created Bass Strait. The second is that the Tasmanians had access only to a bit over 26,000 square miles of land, with limited and relatively monotonous resources, whereas the Americans were un-

FIGURE 28-3. EVIDENCE FOR THE ANTIQUITY OF MAN IN NORTH AMERICA. On this map and the next, numerals in roman type are used for the earliest sites from which the evidence seems beyond serious dispute, numerals in italic type for the much larger number of sites from which the evidence, *if valid*, indicates a much earlier arrival of man in the New World.

1 Flint Creek, Alaska	4 Santa Rosa Island, California	8 Lewisville, Texas
2 Wilson Butte Cave, Idaho	5 Lake Manix, California	9 Lake Chapala Basin, Baja
3 Tlapacoya, Mexico	6 Tolchaco, Arizona	California
1 Farmington, California	7 Scripps Campus, La Jolla, and	10 Friesenhahn Cave, Texas
2 Tule Springs, Nevada	Texas Street, San Diego	11 Valsequillo, Mexico
3 Ellsworth Falls, Maine	California	

430

(Data from Willey 1966 and Jennings 1968.)

FIGURE 28-4. EVIDENCE FOR THE ANTIQUITY OF MAN IN SOUTH AMERICA. For numerals in roman type versus numerals in italic type, see the legend for Figure 28-3.

1	El Jobo, Venezuela	3	Viscachani, Bolivia
2	Ayacucho (Flea Cave), Peru	4	Ghatchi, Chile
3	Tagua, Chile	5	Ampajango, Argentina
1	Muaco, Venezuela	*6*	Tandilense, Argentina
2	El Manzanillo, Venezuela	*7*	Oliviense, Argentina

disputed claimants of some 13,000,000 square miles of incredibly varied and rich terrain.

As long as the corridor was closed, the Canadian ice sheet, rather than any serious obstructions in the vicinity of what is now Bering Strait, was the true boundary between the Old World and the New. The Bering Isthmus and the ice-free interior of Alaska were merely an extension of Siberia. People akin to the first American Indians occupied this part of extended Siberia from time to time; they could not move southwards in the New World, but their migrations took them all over the cold parts of Eurasia. There they traded fashions and genes with many other groups. Somewhere in this area, possibly in Alaska rather than in Siberia, a distinctive subtype eventually emerged, destined subsequently to spread along the Alaskan coasts, the Aleutian Islands, and all over the arctic littoral of North America as the Aleut and Eskimo.

Meanwhile, the American Indians were probably collectively heir to some type of physiological cold-adaptation, and this served them well as they approached the southern tip of South America, as they eventually doubled back into Canada behind the retreating glaciers (p. 10), and as they moved into the highlands of the Andes. Yet the adaptation seems to have constituted no serious barrier to their successful exploitation of either hot and wet territory, such as the basins of the Amazon and Orinoco, or hot and dry lands, as northwestern Mexico and the southwestern United States eventually became.

The isolation of the American Indians was reduced from absolute to merely extreme when the Canadian corridor opened again, and as the glaciers gradually melted and raised the sea level. As the ice barrier vanished, a water barrier formed, but the latter was not impenetrable. New trickles of migrants must have passed along the same old route, from Siberia through Alaska and south. Some may have moved in the opposite direction (in recent centuries there have been Eskimo settlements at several places on the Siberian coast fronting Alaska). Perhaps they had boats (the Eskimos did). Perhaps there was a stage during which they could walk across the ice between East Cape and the Seward Peninsula in winter though they could not cross the open water in summer. It was still a long, long way—now through populated rather than empty territory—from East Cape to Tierra del Fuego. Yet there must have been some new infusions of genes from the Old World, and it is clear that certain items of later technology were imported along this route (p. 438).

One more implication of the frigid port of entry to the Americas remains to be described. Both early and late comers had to spend many generations in the far north, before they could reach more equable climes. This served as a narrow funnel through which certain microbes and parasites could not pass. Some of the nastier diseases of the Old World did not make it, among them malaria, smallpox, plague, and (apparently) also measles, tuberculosis, and the common cold. The mechanism of exclusion need not have been the same for all. Certain genes afford protection from, or susceptibility to, certain diseases, and the immigrants to America may have had or lacked just the right genes for reasons unrelated to climate. Some exclusively Old World diseases may have evolved too late to be carried along by the immigrants. In their isolation, the American Indians seem to have developed no new diseases that

BY HIS BOOTSTRAPS

became pandemic, but they did come up with some new ones in specific localities—especially syphilis, which may have arisen in the Caribbean through a mutation of the microbe responsible for yaws.

LATER PRE-COLUMBIAN CONTACTS. Apart from the Bering route, the isolation of the New World continued until the emergence of true seafaring peoples.

The New World nurtured none; the closest approaches were the canoeing island-hoppers of the Aleutians and of the Caribbean. Yet we must not think of transoceanic contact as absolutely precluded until the first voyage of Columbus.

It is possible that a Faeroe Islander visited the West Indies in the fourteenth century A.D. Several hundred years before that, the Vikings who had settled Iceland (p. 483) also colonized Greenland, and touched the shores of Newfoundland and Nova Scotia. In the Pacific, the long voyages of the Polynesians carried them not only to the remote Easter Island, a good 2100 miles from central Polynesia, but 2300 miles beyond that to the coast of Chile or Peru; the evidence is botanical and pretty convincing (p. 485). It is possible that fishers or traders from Japan, moving clockwise along the northern and eastern perimeter of the ocean, got as far south as Colombia.

We cannot deny the reality of some of these pre-Columbian contacts nor the possibility of others, but we can pooh-pooh any proposal that their impact was important. The significance of Columbus's voyages was that they quickly opened the path for a great outpouring of Europeans and Africans into the New World, stirring together lifeways, artifacts, techniques, beliefs, genes, and diseases into a wild, wonderful, and often deadly mix.

✖ It is hard to imagine that *Homo sapiens,* when he appeared, was not everywhere heir to the basic tool kit of his predecessors. The sort of interband commerce required to spread the genes of the sapiens complex would surely also have carried every crucial technique to every group in a position to use it.

UPPER PLEISTOCENE HARDWARE

For example, every human community of the ethnographic present has had fire, and the inability to make fire is extremely rare (attested only for some of the mountain-dwelling Andaman Islanders and for the Bakango Pygmies of the northeastern Congo), and may represent the recent loss of an art formerly known.

Yet just a few centuries ago, at the time of their first observation by record-keeping Europeans, the Tasmanians knew nothing of hafting, which was otherwise universal and which we know had been a Neanderthaloid innovation (pre-sapiens: p. 398).

The answer is either that hafting had somehow not caught up with the invaders of Wallacea and Great Australia when they first moved out from the mainland, or that somewhere in transit they forgot how to do it. Much later, it was either independently reinvented in Australia or else diffused there from farther northwest, since sites in the lower Murray River valley attest to it as of about 3000 B.C. But that was too late for Tasmania, already cut off by Bass Strait.

That subsequent innovations should rarely have spread into universality, on the other hand, is not surprising, considering the enormous total territory occupied by the species, the long periods of isolation of some groups, and the wide variety of ecological circumstances to which different groups were adapting.

Chisel Flaking

In northern and western Eurasia, as early as 35,000 years ago, the prepared-core technique for the manufacture of flake tools (p. 397) was carried to a new high of efficiency. The raw pebble was shaped in advance in such a way that a whole series of suitably shaped flakes could be removed from it, almost like cutting slices from a loaf of bread (though, to be sure, considerably more strength and skill were required). The edged tools made from the flakes by bifacial retouching are called *blades* by the archaeologists.

The manufacture of blades attests to the mastery of the technique of *chisel flaking*, using two tools instead of a single direct tool. One, which we shall call a "chisel," is carefully placed against the target pebble; then the other end of the chisel is struck with some sort of hammer; the force of the blow is not only transmitted to the target via the chisel but also focused very precisely. The chisel needs to be fairly long and thin, and toughness is more important than hardness, so that wood and bone are both better than most stone.

Chisel flaking involves three objects (hammer, chisel, and target pebble), all of which must be manipulated with precision. Possibly the target pebble could be rested steadily enough on a convenient flat rock, or be held firmly enough between the knees. Otherwise the operation required three hands, implying the close coordination of at least one and one half people—perhaps the elderly master mason wielding the hammer and the chisel, his young apprentice holding the target pebble and sustaining the bloody knuckles if the tools slipped. It seems to me that the achievement of this sort of close technical coordination of the actions of two people would be difficult or impossible without language. That impression agrees with the other evidence that chisel flaking was done by *Homo sapiens,* not by his pre-sapiens predecessors.

The gain in efficiency was considerable. With the new technique, one could obtain from 10 to 40 feet of usable cutting edge from a single pound of raw stone, perhaps 10 times as much as the Neanderthaloids had been able to manage, 100 times as much as the earliest hominid makers of stone tools.

The Burin

The chisel technique for stonework may have suggested the specialized tool for bone-carving that appears in the record at about the same time and in the same region. Archaeologists call this new tool a *burin,* but it resembled the modern engraver's tool known by that name only in function, not in shape. In shape it was more like a modern screwdriver: a short, sharp edge at the head, at right angles to the long axis of the handle. In use it falls into category 12 of Table 7-1 (p. 87). With a set of good burins whose heads are of assorted widths, and with patience, one can carve bone, antler, horn, or ivory very delicately and accurately.

The Aurignacoid Tradition

With the new techniques and tools just described, there emerged, first in the plains of central and eastern Europe, a way of life that some call the *Aurignacoid,* though there are many special labels for its varied recognizable local manifestations. The source of the cover term is that the particular tradition later spread into France, where evidence for it was discovered long before its eastern source was known; the French version was called "Aurignacian" after a site in a cave near the town of Aurignac about 40 miles southwest of Toulouse.

Aurignacoid techniques spread very wide and persisted for a long time with only minor changes. In the west, they reached not only France but also southern Britain and much of Spain. They also moved in a broad band eastwards as far as Lake Baikal; by the latter part of the Late Würm some Aurignacoid features had moved southwards from there to Inner Mongolia, and eastwards through Sakhalin Island (or Peninsula: p. 423) into northern Japan; a site on Umnak Island in the Aleutians shows hardware much like the Aurignacoid dating from about 8000 B.C.

MEANS OF LIVELIHOOD. The geographical distribution of Aurignacoid success suggests that the peoples involved were exploiters of arctic and subarctic herd animals. Bones found in archaeological sites confirm this: reindeer, horses, mammoth (mainly young ones, easier to take), woolly rhinoceros, musk ox, glutton (a carnivore related to the wolverine of North America); and various others, some of them now extinct.

They also fished the streams and perhaps the shores, but we do not know how early that practice was; the clear evidence—fish remains at archaeological sites—is relatively late.

It was from the slaughtered herd animals that they obtained not only food and skins but also the bone, horn, antler, and ivory that were their most important raw materials for hardware. Their technology required some stone and wood, but at certain times and places both must have been in short supply and hard to get. As fuel for a fire, dried ruminant dung is a fair substitute for wood. A spear shaft must be of wood (unless one has metal, which they did not), but the point can be of bone or horn rather than of stone, and bone projectile points in fact abound in the sites that have been excavated.

HOUSING. We have scattered evidence on the housing of the bearers of Aurignacoid technology.

In some places in western Europe they lived at the mouths of caves—never deep inside, though for some unknown reason that is where the artists usually went to paint the cave-wall pictures we mentioned on page 274.

In the plains of central and eastern Europe and at sites near Lake Baikal they dug into the ground to obtain a sunken floor, and presumably covered the excavation with animal skins supported on sticks, though the evidence for the siding and roofing material is not very clear. Such partly sunken houses afford good protection against wind, rain, and snow. They may have used different housing in the summer, as did, in much more recent times, the Menomini and other Northeastern Woodlands American Indians (p. 16).

CLOTHING. We also have enough surviving material evidence of their clothing to assure us that they really were using what one would expect them to use: the hides of slaughtered animals.

ART. In addition to the cave-wall paintings, there is the fact that not all the objects carved from bone, ivory, and (occasionally) wood were strictly utilitarian. Some tools and utensils show stippled or streaked geometric designs, and there are also naturalistic carved figures such as animals or human heads; eventually human figurines appear.

THE SPEAR-THROWER

At some point during the Late Würm, the Aurignacoid hunters of the Eurasian plains made a signal step forward in weapons technology with the invention of the *spear-thrower* (Figure 28-5).

When a spear is held directly in the hand, the arm is stretched out from the body for the propelling swing, because in that way full use can be made of the principle of the lever. The fulcrum is at the shoulder, and the farther the hand is from the body the faster it can be moved. The spear-thrower carries this principle farther. It is in effect an extension of the arm, so that the initial momentum imparted to the spear can be even greater.

The combination of spear-thrower and spear is an *indirect* or *composite* tool, in contrast with the direct one-solid-piece tools we described and classified on page 87 (Table 7-1). As far as we know, this combination was almost the first indirect tool to be made and used; its sole predecessor was the hammer-and-chisel used in chisel flaking, very different in both design and purpose. A spear with a detachable point is not attested until later; it appears at about the same time as the harpoon, which is essentially the same thing except that a long cord is tied to the point and trails behind the weapon as it is hurled, enabling the hunter—if he is strong enough and if the point has caught securely enough in the prey—to prevent the quarry's escape.

The invention of these composite tools would be easier to understand if the spear with detachable point had come first. Perhaps it actually did, the record so far recovered being deceptive on this score. Anyway, let us pretend so for a moment, in order to offer an evolutionary explanation. A key feature of the composite tool could have arisen from observations of what sometimes happened when hafting was carelessly done. Suppose that as a hafted spear strikes its target the handle breaks loose and falls to the ground, leaving only the point embedded in the prey. The point is enough to do the job. In fact, from the hunter's point of view it is better than the whole spear, since if the shaft is still firmly attached the injured animal may be able to entangle it in brush, work the spear loose, and escape. And the detached shaft, unless trampled on and broken, can be recovered and used again—a great advantage if suitable wood happens to be in short supply. When this sort of thing has happened enough times by accident, people might start arranging for it to happen on purpose. That would lead immediately to an investigation of the art of careful loose attachment (as over against tight hafting), so that two pieces of a composite tool will hold together when they should and yet come apart at just the right moment.

TANGS

In the west, some Aurignacoid features eventually diffused southwards through Anatolia and the Levant and into the northeast corner of Africa. But that was late, and meanwhile something else had been happening.

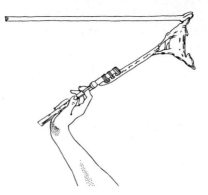

FIGURE 28-5. Spear-thrower. (After Chard 1969.)

As of about 30,000 years ago, the stone technology of northwestern Africa (now Morocco and Algeria) was akin to that of western Europe, showing none of the more northerly—and later—innovations we have just been describing. But a recognizably distinct variant had appeared, the *Aterian,* so called after a site near the Algerian city of Bir el Ater (the French call it "Constantine").

A special feature of Aterian technology was that its bearers developed the habit of making their blades and points with *tangs* to facilitate hafting. A tang is a thin pronglike projection at the end of the piece of stone away from its point or blades; this projection can be inserted securely—perhaps even glued—into a hole dug out of the end of the wooden shaft or handle. Most modern metal table knives are still made this way, even if the handle as well as the blade is of metal. If you find an old table knife that no one wants you may be able to pry the pieces apart and see how it works. Give the Aterians credit for the trick; it may have later been independently invented elsewhere, but they were first.

Bow and Arrow

As the Late Würm glaciation grew, the whole of northern Africa, now dry, sandy desert, developed into a vast, rich, well watered grassland, full of all sorts of grazing animals. The Aterian culture spread all over, bands developing a way of life that may have resembled that of the North American Plains Indians of a few hundred years ago. The resemblance extended even to their principal weapon, apparently an Aterian invention: the composite device known as the bow and arrow.

An arrow is just a spear, designed to be set into trajectory by a bow rather than by the hand and arm. A bow is therefore a kind of spear-thrower. But the principle involved is totally different from that of the northern spear-thrower we described earlier (p. 436): the principle of the spring.

To make a bow one must have some sort of strong, flexible wood and some sort of strong cordage. A pole of the wood is flexed, and its ends are tied to the ends of a piece of cord which is not as long as the unflexed pole. In doing this, one is storing energy in the wood, just as energy is stored in any spring if it is bent, compressed, or stretched from its rest position. Then the arrow is put in place and one hand holds the wood of the bow while the other draws the string back, bending the wood even more and putting still more energy into it. All this can be done relatively slowly. When the string and arrow are released, the stored energy expends itself very quickly, much of it transformed into the kinetic energy of the moving arrow and giving it much greater momentum than any human being could possibly impart to a hand-hurled spear.

There is, in this device, no new source of energy for human use, since all the energy involved is supplied by the archer; but it is processed and concentrated in a remarkable way. The bow and arrow, even in its most primitive form, was an awesome weapon, terribly useful in hunting, fearfully dangerous in war.

Unlike the other technological innovations we have been describing, the bow and arrow had no obvious antecedents. Good bows can be developed by experimentation from mediocre ones, and mediocre ones can be the result of tinkering with poor ones. But how about the first? What was there in either the environment or the earlier technological tradition of the Aterians that could have served as a suggestive clue? Well, if we stretch our imagination to the breaking point we can think of a length of vine caught at both ends to a flexible tree limb, of a spear getting caught in the vine, and of the spear accidentally being propelled into trajectory as someone tries to disentangle it. If something like this did happen, then the fact that someone caught the clue and made something practical of it is still remarkable: it was a sign of genius as great as our species has ever produced.

DIFFUSION. The bow and arrow spread far and wide. Very late upper Pleistocene cave-wall paintings in Spain show hunters shooting arrows at animals; this is our first pictorial evidence (Figure 28-6). The basic bow-and-arrow pattern is as versatile as is that of a stone cutting edge: it is subject to a great range of variations, some of them improvements of design, some of them adaptations to new or limited raw materials, some of them perhaps only a matter of taste in shape and decoration. One major advance in bow design seems to have been effected in northeastern Asia, where suitable wood was rare: strips of sinew were glued to the wood to strengthen it. We do not know where or when arrows were first feathered to improve their behavior in flight. The bow and arrow did not reach the major portion of the New World until the Canadian corridor opened up about 11,000 years ago. It then diffused everywhere except into the Caribbean Islands and possibly some of the jungle territory of northeastern South America. In the Old World it did not reach Australia (or, of course, Tasmania); otherwise at the dawn of the ethnographic present it was universal.

OTHER WEAPONS

In some parts of the world where the bow and arrow remained unknown, and in some places to which it spread, human ingenuity devised other improved weapons.

The *sling* appeared in southwest Asia in the sixth millennium B.C. and became so effective that it was preferred to the bow and arrow for a long time (remember

BY HIS BOOTSTRAPS

FIGURE 28-6. THE EARLIEST PICTORIAL EVIDENCE OF THE BOW AND ARROW. A painting on a Spanish cave wall, dating from the very late upper Pleistocene. (Reprinted from *Prehistoric Europe: The Economic Basis* by J. G. D. Clark, with the permission of the publishers, Stanford University Press. Copyright 1952 by J. G. D. Clark.)

David and Goliath). A sling is a flat pouch to which are attached two long cords. A pebble or pellet is placed in the pouch; the hand holds the far ends of the two cords and swings the pouch in a circle with increasing velocity; then the hand releases *one* of the cords and the pebble takes off.

Again: much of the territory occupied by the Australian aborigines is practically devoid of stone and contains few trees from which good wood can be obtained. The tribesmen preserved their stone and wooden implements with great care. And they invented the *boomerang,* a heavy curved throwing stick which, in the hands of an expert, can be hurled with enough force to kill large prey or a human enemy. Some boomerangs, thrown in just the right way, pursue a circular or figure-eight course and return to the vicinity of the thrower, but these were used principally for practice or for play.

In two jungle areas, eastern South America (and the Antilles) and southeastern Asia, two populations quite independently devised the *blowgun:* a long, hollow tube from which a dart can be propelled with considerable force by a sharp exhalation from the mouth.

In many places the efficacy of spears, arrows, or blowgun darts was increased by smearing poison on the tip. The ancient Chinese, the Gauls (predecessors of the Latin-speaking invaders of what is now France), and the hill peoples of southern India used or use aconite, a poison extracted from *Aconitum napellus* and allied plant species. The New World blowgunners had curare, a cover term for various substances extracted by a complicated process (including cooking) from a variety of tropical plants: species of *Strychnos, Chondodendron, Strophanthus,* and *Cocculus.* The Africans of the Congo used the juice of a *Strophanthus* species.[2] These are muscle poisons, painful and disabling, lethal if they prevent breathing or get to the heart. An interesting sidelight is that most of the plant substances first exploited in this way subsequently found important places in our modern medicinal pharmacopoeia.

THE PROGENY OF THE BOW AND ARROW

The derivatives of the prototypical bow and arrow include much more than weapons.

The *fire drill* is an ancient and honorable device, dating at least from the upper Pleistocene (Figure 28-7). A small pit is dug in a piece of dry softwood, with tinder lying near by; then a stick of hardwood is inserted into the pit and twirled between the hands until tiny fragments of the softwood, ignited by the friction, fly off as sparks and fall on the tinder. In this form the fire drill came to be known almost everywhere, even in parts of Australia. In ancient Egypt, among the Eskimo and the northern Siberians, and in a few other areas to which the bow and arrow spread, the drill is twirled not by hand but by looping the string of a short bow around it, pulling it taut, and moving the bow rapidly back and forth.

The progeny of the bow also includes all the stringed sound-makers. When the string of a bow is taut, plucking it sets it into vibration with a fundamental frequency dependent on the length and the tension. The tension, thus the pitch, can be varied by applying force to the ends of the bow. It is perfectly possible that the Aterians played with their bows in this way sometimes when not busy using them to hunt or fight. A later custom was to place one end of the string near the open mouth, and to vary the shape of the oral cavity in order to supply a resonating chamber to reinforce one or another of the harmonics of the vibrating string.

Reshaping the wooden part to supply a resonating chamber came much later, in recorded times or just before, yielding the whole gamut of stringed instruments of the Old World, from the samisen of Japan to the valiha of Madagascar to the violin of Cremona. The familiar "bowing"—no pun—of our Western stringed instruments, in origin the drawing of the string of one bow across that of another to set up and maintain the latter's vibration, seems to have originated in central Asia, whence it spread to Europe in early medieval times. Stringed instruments did not reach the New World or most of Oceania until transported there by Europeans. For example, the most famous instrument of Hawaii, despite its fine Polynesian name ('*uku-lele* 'leaping flea', probably in origin a person's nickname) is just a miniaturized Portuguese guitar, first imported in A.D. 1879.

[2]We have not given the full roster. The Maidu of California even used rattlesnake venom! (see Coon 1971, pp. 80 ff.).

FIGURE 28-7. Bow-operated fire drill. (After Lowie 1934.)

LATE UPPER PLEISTOCENE ACHIEVEMENTS

There remain to be mentioned several important developments during the later stages of the upper Pleistocene. The evidence is largely from Europe. It should be remembered that more digging has been done there than anywhere else, a fact which surely distorts the picture.

FISHING, possible though problematic at earlier times, was well established in many places by 10,000 years ago. The fish bones found by archaeologists include none of deep-water species, negative but persuasive testimony against any exploitation, as yet, of the open sea.

SEWING makes its appearance in the north, probably closer to 20,000 than to 10,000 years ago. The needles were of bone (you can't make them of stone). The thread was presumably sinew. The materials cut and sewn were animal skins. Some of the garments were decorated with shells or beads. This was the beginning of the tailored skin clothing whose essential style eventually spread around the whole world in the arctic and north temperate zones, the basic pattern to which our own Western clothing conforms to this day (p. 18).

FLUTES of a crude sort—perhaps better described as whistles and fifes—appear in various places in the north, their remote and refined descendants destined ultimately to be joined with the equally elaborated musical descendants of the Aterian bow to give us the modern symphony orchestra.

The sound-producing principle of a flute or fife is that a column of air, within a tube, is set into vibration by blowing across the edge of a hole in the tube. Almost any container with a small opening can be made to "speak" by blowing across the edge of the opening; the principle is so simple that people have probably been doing this wherever such containers were developed for any use, so that the northern location of the first archaeological evidence is surely fortuitous.

The use of a single reed (as in a clarinet) or of a double reed (as in an oboe or a bassoon) were refinements of just a millennium or so ago.

Finger holes, to vary the length of the air column and thus the pitch, may have been early; their precise placement was more recent. The fact that we have five fingers per hand has surely had an influence on the nature of the musical scales known in the ethnographic present; if the quota were six, the Western diatonic scale might have ten notes per "octave" instead of eight.

"Brass" instruments, for which the vibrating lips are the sound generator, probably began as large seashells with holes in them, and thus near the ocean in tropical or subtropical climates. Flutes and brass instruments were known aboriginally in the Americas; reeds, like stringed instruments, were not. Percussion instruments are older than man, and are found wherever he has wandered. If you have nothing else to strike or kick, you can beat your brow.

CERAMICS puts in its first timid appearance, in the form of (accidentally?) fired clay figurines found at two sites in eastern Europe. Clay containers are later.

FOOD-GRINDING equipment also appears in eastern European sites. This was important in two ways.

The first is that the kinds of tools and of tool-manipulations involved in grinding such materials as seeds are similar to those required for the polishing of stone; the one may have led to the other (p. 496).

The second has to do with food itself. We do not know why the first food-grinders treated their food in this way, but we can guess that the process and its results may have been something like those attested from recent aboriginal times in North America. A favorite method of food-processing in many parts of aboriginal North America was to dry it and grind it—wild seeds, berries, roots, meat, fish—into a powder and then add fat and work it into an almost solid paste. There were many variants on this. The Cree called their northern variant *pimihkān*, whence our English *pemmican*. Pemmican is concentrated, easy to carry along for nourishment en route when one sets out on a hunt or other expedition. Perhaps the early eastern European food-grinders did something similar.

It is clear that our ancestors were able to reduce plant products to paste or powder long before they learned to help the plants grow. Flour (finely ground seeds) has various culinary uses to which the whole grains cannot be put. So when agriculture did come along, one important food-processing technique was already at hand.

THE MAGLEMOSIANS. As the glaciers of the Late Würm receded (say, between 11,000 and 9000 years ago) a new variant on nonfarming ways of life arose in the boreal forests of northern Europe, and was flourishing even as the domestication of plants and animals was getting under way in more southerly climes. It is known to us from remains found in peat bogs, and our name for it, *Maglemosian,* from Danish *magle mose* 'great bog', reflects that.

The bearers of Maglemosian culture had bows and arrows, and made various other

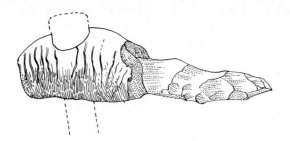

FIGURE 28-8. Three-part Maglemosian pick. (After Clark and Piggott 1965.)

tools of wood, bone, and antler, as well as of flint. Figure 28-8 shows a pick made by hafting three parts: the pointed head is of chipped flint, set into a hole in a wooden holder, and in this holder a hole has been drilled all the way through for the insertion of a wooden handle (not recovered). The implement was found while digging a canal to join the Elbe and Trave Rivers in Schleswig-Holstein.

The Maglemosians exploited the solitary game animals of the boreal forests; they killed and ate the migratory waterfowl that flocked around the numerous lakes the receding glaciers had left in their wake; they fished the lakes with traps, with bone fishhooks, and with "leisters," a kind of spear with three or more barbs.

This particular technological complex subsequently spread not only through all of arctic and subarctic Eurasia but also across into the New World, where it may have reached the earliest Eskimos before their own expansion across the North American arctic (p. 432). Many of its features survive to this day at various points on the perimeter of the Arctic Ocean. The spread of the Maglemosian tradition was as responsible as anything before or after it for the set of circumpolar traits we mentioned on page 22; and it was bearers of this tradition that contributed *sleds* and *skis* to the rest of the world.

29

✷

DOMESTICATION: WILD AND TAME

We are now ready for the story of how some of our ancestors took to farming. By "farming" we mean plant-raising, animal husbandry, or both. In this chapter we discuss the matter in a general way. In the next we present historical details.

LAND PLANTS ✷ The flowering plants (class Angiospermae of the subdivision Spermopsida, division Tracheophyta: Figure 24-29, p. 357) and the warm-blooded suckling vertebrates (class Mammalia) grew up together. Both got a good start only well after the close of the Permian Ice Age (p. 305). The Angiospermae proliferated and became the dominant land plants during the Cretaceous epoch, starting about 150,000,000 years ago, just as the mammals, along with birds and insects, were becoming the dominant land animals. Their evolutionary interplay has been intimate. All animals, as we know, are directly or indirectly parasitic on plants. In a world in which flowering plants prevail, it is not surprising that those mammals that eat plants instead of—or as well as—other animals should find some types of angiosperms both edible and appetizing. This applies to us today; it has applied to our ancestors for a hundred million years or more.

For most species of seed plants (Spermopsida) there is no sexual differentiation during the dominant stage of the life cycle—the multicellular stage represented by the trees, shrubs, grasses, and weeds that we see about us every day. The plant in this stage produces *spores* of two different kinds, which grow into small muticellular organs while still attached to the parent plant. It is from these that male and female gametes develop. The male gametes are typically released in light growths (called *pollen*). Fertilization takes place and the growth of the embryo goes through preliminary stages before the result, in the form of a *seed* with a tough protective coat made of specialized cells that grow no more, is released from the parent plant.

The early proliferation of the Angiospermae was an adaptive radiation (p. 299): the secret of angiosperm success is that the seed, after it develops within a *flower,* comes to be protected by a casing called a *fruit.* The seeds of other seed plants (for example, the Coniferales: fir, pine, etc.) have no such protective enclosures.

A chrysanthemum is a flower and a grapefruit is a fruit, but both are atypical:

many flowers are inconspicuous and most fruits are tiny and dry rather than large and succulent. A flower is a concentric ring of specialized leaves. The outermost layers are purely protective. Inside those layers there is a ring bearing the organs that produce the pollen, and inside that there is an organ in which the ova develop. The pollen that fertilizes an ovum may come from the same flower, from another flower on the same plant, or may be borne (by insects, birds, or breezes) from a flower on a plant of the same species many miles away. When the fertilized ovum has developed into a seed, it is surrounded by a shell of stuff that protects it and that it can use as food as it begins to grow. This shell is a fruit. Only after the fruit has developed does it either burst (as do peas), scattering the seeds, or fall from the parent plant (as do tomatoes, squash, cucumbers, apples, peaches, and acorns).

The seed-flower-fruit trick was a good one. Today Angiospermae are found everywhere on land except on glaciers and in very dry deserts, and the total number of species, about 250,000, makes up more than 95% of all the Tracheophyta and about 88% of all land plants (which include also some Bryophyta: p. 357).

PLANT PARTS AND TYPES

Every tracheophyte—meaning every such plant in its dominant stage—is composed of three distinct kinds of organs: *roots, stems,* and *leaves.* The roots are usually under-

TABLE 29-1. Plants raised or nurtured by man.

Although only a small sample, the list does include man's most important vegetable crops. The part of the plant used is specified; the use is as food unless otherwise indicated. Trees exploited only as sources of lumber and flowers raised only for decoration are excluded.

FUNGI
    Class BASIDIOMYCETES
        Order AGARICALES
           Family AGARICACEAE

1. *Agaricus campestris, A. bisporus,* and   mushroom   Fruiting body (above ground). Collection ancient; others (also some of family BOTELACEAE)   nurture recent.

    Class ASCOMYCETES
        Order ENDOMYCETALES
           Family SACCHAROMYCETACEAE

2. *Saccharomyces cerevisiae* and allied   yeast   For raising bread dough and fermenting wines and spp; also some of other families   beers. Ancient in southwest Asia.

        Order TUBERALES
           Family TUBERACEAE

3. *Tuber melanosporum* (France and nearby);   truffle   Fruiting body (underground). Mediterranean? *T. aestivum* (England)

    GREEN PLANTS; all listed are of Division TRACHEOPHYTA, Subdivision SPERMOPSIDA
        Class GYMNOSPERMAE
           Order CONIFERALES
               Family PINACEAE

4. *Pinus pinea* (Mediterranean); *P. cembra*   pine   Evergreen tree. Seeds. (central Europe, Siberia); *P. edulis, P. quadrifolia, P. monophylla, P. cembroides, P. sabiniana* (North America)

ground, where they draw raw materials from the soil, but some float in water or are suspended in the air. The stems are usually above ground, but occasionally partly below: for instance, in ordinary lawn grasses only the leaves are above ground. The leaves, growing in the air, provide for gas exchange with the atmosphere, and contain the chlorophyll which obtains from sunlight the energy for the plant's metabolism.

Within this basic pattern, the Tracheophyta have developed a number of distinct plans of organization that recur in ways that do not necessarily reflect phylogenetic connections.

(1) WOODY VERSUS HERBACEOUS.   Some plants are *woody*, in roots or stems or both (not in leaves). We know what this means because we know what wood is like.

Woodiness is achieved through a particular use of the polysaccharide cellulose (p. 330), a substance that all tracheophytes and many other organisms produce and use to strengthen their cell walls (but no animals do: animals do not have cell walls).

Since cellulose is built of glucose, it is fine food for any animal that can digest it. But no Metazoa have the means of breaking it down. Ruminants live on grass only by virtue of enormous clumps of specialized bacteria in their digestive tracts, which decompose the cellulose for them. For most mammals, including ourselves, cellulose is unusable.

TABLE 29-1.   Plants raised or nurtured by man (*continued*).

5.	*Pinus sylvestris, P. pinaster* (Europe); *P. palustris* (North America)	pine	Evergreen tree. Sap for turpentine and tar.
	Class ANGIOSPERMAE		
	Subclass DICOTYLEDONAE		
	Order CAMPANULALES		
	Family COMPOSITAE		
6.	*Cichorium intybus*	chicory	Herbaceous perennial. Root, leaf. Europe?
7.	*Cichorium endiva*	endive, escarole	Herbaceous annual/biennial. Leaf. Egypt?
8.	*Cynara scolymus*	artichoke	Herbaceous perennial. Fleshy bases of immature flower buds. Western Mediterranean.
9.	*Helianthus tuberosus*	Jerusalem artichoke	Herbaceous annual. Tuber. North America (recent).
10.	*Lactuca sativa*	lettuce	Herbaceous annual. Leaf. Southwest Asia.
	Order CENTROSPERMALES		
	Family BASELLACEAE		
11.	*Ullucus tuberosis*	ulluco	Tuber. Andes (aboriginal).
	Family CHENOPODIACEAE		
12.	*Beta vulgaris*	beet, chard	Herbaceous biennial. Taproot, leaf. Mediterranean, Europe.
13.	*Spaniacia oleracea*	spinach	Herbaceous annual. Leaf. Southwest Asia?
	Order CUCURBITALES		
	Family CUCURBITACEAE		
14.	*Colocynthus citrullus*	watermelon	Vine. Fruit. Sudan.
15.	*Cucumis sativus*	cucumber	Herbaceous annual vine. Fruit. Northern India or northeastern Africa?
16.	*Cucumis anguria*	gherkin	Herbaceous annual vine. Fruit. West Indies.
17.	*Cucumis melo*	muskmelon	Herbaceous annual vine. Fruit. Southwest Asia.

Now, in a woody plant, there is a lot of cellulose, and it is laid down in a special kind of tissue called "xylem" (Greek *xýlon* 'wood') which, in quantity, imparts great structural strength. One can perhaps think of xylem as the plant analog of the bony skeletal material of vertebrate animals. All really large tracheophytes are woody, because unless they had the strength that gives them they could not grow large.[1] If a woody plant is big enough we call it a "tree" and call its woody main stem a "trunk"; if it is smaller and branches out close to the ground we call it a "shrub." Almost all the Coniferales are woody, and many Angiospermae are.

A plant that is not woody is *herbaceous:* spinach. But the contrast is not sharp. Some plants are essentially herbaceous but develop woody lower stems if they live long enough: asparagus.

(2) TYPE BY SEASONAL CYCLE.   In adapting, over tens of millions of years, to a wide variety of climates, perhaps especially to the seasonal fluctuations of temperate zones, plants have worked out a number of different ways of adjusting their own cycles to those of the seasons. Some are *annuals,* some are *biennials,* and the rest are

[1]Strength is also imparted by columns of water held in the plant's capillaries. The maximum height a tree can attain—something less than 400 feet—is set by the height to which water can be carried by capillary action.

TABLE 29-1. Plants raised or nurtured by man (*continued*).

18.	*Cucurbita pepo*	summer squash	Herbaceous annual. Fruit. From Mexico south.
19.	*Cucurbita maxima*	winter squash	Herbaceous annual. Fruit. From Mexico south.
20.	*Cucurbita moschata*	pumpkin	Herbaceous annual vine. Fruit. From Mexico south.
21.	*Lagenaria siceraria*	bottle gourd	Fruit. Northern India?
	Order EBENALES		
	Family EBENACEAE		
22.	*Diospyros kaki*	Japanese persimmon	Deciduous perennial tree. Fruit. China, Japan.
23.	*Diospyros virginiana*	persimmon	Deciduous perennial tree. Fruit. North America.
	Order ERICALES		
	Family ERICACEAE		
24.	*Gaylussacia baccata* and allied spp	huckleberry	Deciduous perennial shrub. Fruit. North America.
25.	*Vaccinium myrtillus*	whortleberry	Deciduous perennial shrub. Fruit. North temperate zone.
26.	*Vaccinium oxycoccus, V. macrocarpon,* and allied spp	cranberry	Deciduous perennial shrub. Fruit. North temperate zone.
	Order FAGALES		
	Family FAGACEAE		
27.	*Quercus suber*	oak	Deciduous or evergreen perennial tree. Bark for cork. Mediterranean.
28.	*Quercus aegilops* (Mediterranean); *Q. infectoria* (Turkey)	oak	Deciduous or evergreen perennial tree. Bark for tannin.
29.	Other *Q* spp (over 300 in all)	oak	Deciduous or evergreen perennial tree. Seeds (acorns). Widespread.
	Order GENTIANALES		
	Family LOGANIACEAE		
30.	*Strychnos nux-vomica*		Tree. Seed, dried for nux vomica. South and southeast Asia, northern Australia. Origin?

lumped together as *perennials*. All three are represented among the Spermopsida, to which we confine our description and examples.

An annual plant (wheat, spinach) grows from seed to maturity within a single season, produces its own seeds, and dies.

A biennial plant (beets, carrots) takes twice as long. In the first year it grows from seed to complete plant, but produces no seeds. Instead, the leaves and the stems die, leaving only the root. From this, in the following season, a new complete plant grows, and this time seeds are produced. Then the whole plant dies.

Perennials live longer, some for a few years, some for a few thousand. Several seasons of initial growth may precede the first yield of seed, and after that some species produce flowers and seeds only every few years rather than annually.

Perennials are herbaceous or woody, and of the latter there are two subtypes.

A herbaceous perennial (asparagus, delphinium), unless it is growing in the tropics, is reduced to its root at the end of each season, just like a biennial at the end of its first. Woodiness, however, makes possible the survival of stems as well as roots through the winter.

Deciduous woody perennials (maple, elm, and so on), mainly angiosperms and mainly in mid and high latitudes, lose their leaves each fall and grow a new crop in the spring.

Evergreen woody perennials have leaves throughout the year. In cold climates most

TABLE 29-1. Plants raised or nurtured by man *(continued)*.

31. *Strychnos ignatii*		Tree. Source of strychnine. Philippines.
	Family OLEACEAE	
32. *Olea europaea* and allied spp	olive	Woody perennial. Fruit. Southwest Asia and eastern Mediterranean.
	Order GERANIALES	
	Family ERYTHROXYLACEAE	
33. *Erythroxylon coca, E. novagranatense*	coca	Woody perennial. Leaves dried for cocaine. Western South America.
	Family EUPHORBIACEAE	
34. *Aleurites moluccana*	candlenut	Woody perennial tree. Seeds for oil. Northern India.
35. *Hevea braziliensis*	para rubber tree	Woody perennial. Sap for rubber. Eastern South America.
36. *Manihot esculenta*	bitter cassava	Perennial herb. Root. Tropical South America.
37. *Manihot dulcis*	sweet cassava	Perennial herb. Root. Tropical South America.
38. *Ricinis communis*	castor oil plant	Herbaceous perennial/annual. Seed for oil. Tropical Africa.
	Family LINACEAE	
39. *Linum usitatissimum*	flax	Herbaceous annual. Seed for oil; stem bark for fiber. Southeast Asia.
	Family OXALIDACEAE	
40. *Oxalis crenata, O. tuberosa*	oca	Herb. Tuber. Andes.
	Family RUTACEAE	
41. *Citrus aurantium, C. sinensis, C. reticulata*	orange, tangerine	Perennial tree. Fruit. Southeast Asia; tangerine in south China.
42. *Citrus limon* (from *C. medica?*)	lemon	Perennial tree. Fruit. Southeast Asia.

evergreens are conifers (firs, pine, spruce, cedar, etc.), whose leaves are needle-shaped. Such leaves do die and fall, others replacing them, but they do not wither and drop all at once in an annual ritual as do the leaves of deciduous plants. In the tropics many evergreens are large-leaved angiosperms: for one example, the tree *Eugenia caryophyllata* whose unopened flower buds are gathered and dried as the spice cloves. But some evergreen angiosperms live in colder country: of the oaks (genus *Quercus*), the so-called "live oaks" (*Q. wislizenii, Q. chrysolepis, Q. agrifolia, Q. dumosa*), found in the New World as far north as California, keep their leaves the year round, while some of their close cousins of the same genus do not.

In some cases the style of a plant's adaptation to the yearly cycle is not wholly fixed by its genes. A number of herbaceous plants that are perennials in the tropics (including the tomato) have been removed by man to temperate zones, where they grow as annuals because their roots are killed by the frost.

(3) MONOCOT AND DICOT. When an angiosperm germinates and begins to grow, it soon puts out one or two tiny embryonic leaves called "cotyledons." One great subclass of the class Angiospermae is characterized (among other things) by the fact that the seed produces two cotyledons: these are the Dicotyledonae (lettuce, watermelon, olive, citrus fruits, and many others). A somewhat smaller subclass, the Monocotyledonae, have seeds that produce only a single embryonic leaf (grains and grasses, pineapple, onions).

TABLE 29-1. Plants raised or nurtured by man (*continued*).

43. *Citrus aurantifolia*	lime	Perennial tree. Fruit. Southeast Asia.
44. *Citrus medica*	citron	Perennial tree. Fruit. Southeast Asia.
45. *Citrus grandis*	shaddock	Perennial tree. Fruit. Southeast Asia.
46. *Citrus paradisi* (from *C. grandis*)	grapefruit	Perennial tree. Fruit. Probably Jamaica.
47. *Fortunella margarita, F. japonica,* and allied spp	kumquat	Perennial tree. Fruit. South China.
	Order JUGLANDALES	
	Family JUGLANDACEAE	
48. *Carya* spp	hickory, pecan	Deciduous tree. Seed. Eastern North America.
49. *Juglans cinerea*	butternut	Deciduous tree. Seed. North America.
50. Other *Juglans* spp	walnut	Deciduous tree. Seed. Central Eurasia?
	Order MALVALES	
	Family BOMBACACEAE	
51. *Adansonia digitata*	baobab	Woody perennial. Fruit; bark for paper. Africa, Sudan to Senegal.
	Family MALVACEAE	
52. *Althaea officinalis*	marshmallow	Herbaceous perennial. Juice from root. Eurasia, north Africa.
53. *Gossypium herbacium, G. arboreum, G. hirsutum, G. barbadense, G. tomentosum*	cotton	Herbaceous annual. Seed for oil; fibers on seeds for textiles. Worldwide in tropics; domesticated in Indus Valley, in Peru, perhaps in Sudan.
54. *Hibiscus cannabinus*	Guinea hemp	Fibers. Africa.
55. *Abelmoschus esculentus*	okra	Herbaceous annual. Unripe fruit. West African savannas.
	Family STERCULIACEAE	
56. *Cola acuminata, C. nitida*	kola	Woody perennial. Juice from nut. West Africa.

This classification, unlike the others we have mentioned, is supposedly of phylogenetic relevance: it is usually assumed that the Dicotyledonae appeared first.

ANIMAL USE OF PLANTS

PLANT FOOD-STORAGE.   Before a seed has sprouted its cotyledons, giving access to fresh energy through photosynthesis, it has to depend on its own inner resources. One thing, then, that every seed plant must do if its species is to survive is to store up a supply of rich food in the seed. This takes the form of proteins and of oils, sometimes of starch (p. 330). In some cases, angiosperms also put nourishment for the embryo into the fruit that encases the seed.

Another thing that almost every plant has to do is to store extra food somewhere within its own tissue, for use as a reserve when environmental conditions preclude access to fresh raw materials. Plants live through the night without sunlight; many of them live through the winter with no leaves and hence no chlorophyll. A biennial or a perennial in cold weather is dormant, not dead. There is little growth, but certain essential metabolism is maintained. The favorite spot for internal storage of food is in the root (sometimes in swollen segments called "tubers"), and the stored material is most commonly starch.

TABLE 29-1. Plants raised or nurtured by man (*continued*).

57. *Theobroma cacao* and allied spp	cacao, cocoa	Woody perennial. Seed ground, or oil extracted. Northwestern South America.
	Order MYRTALES	
	Family MYRTACEAE	
58. *Eugenia caryophyllata, Syzygium aromaticum*	cloves	Evergreen. Small unopened flower buds, dried. East Indies.
59. *Pimenta dioica*	allspice	Woody perennial. Nearly ripe berry (fruit), dried. West Indies and Central America.
60. *Psidium guajava*	guava	Woody perennial. Fruit. Eastern South America.
	Family PUNICACEAE	
61. *Punica granatum*	pomegranate	Tree. Fruit. Southwest Asia (Iran).
	Family TRAPACEAE	
62. *Trapa natans, T. bicornis*	water chestnut	Herbaceous. Fruit. China.
	Order PARIETALES	
	Family CARICACEAE	
63. *Carica papaya*	papaya	Woody perennial. Fruit. Northwestern South America.
	Family THEACEAE	
64. *Camellia sinensis*	tea	Woody perennial (shrub). Dried leaves. China (Szechwan?).
	Order PIPERALES	
	Family PIPERACEAE	
65. *Piper betle*	betel	Woody perennial climbing vine. Leaves dried, mixed with nuts and lime and chewed. Southeast Asia.
66. *Piper nigrum*	black pepper	Woody perennial climbing vine. Fruit, dried. Northern India.
67. *Piper methysticum*	kava	Woody perennial shrub. Root ground and mixed with water as beverage. Oceania.

Now, the basic metabolic processes of plants and of animals are enough alike that good plant food, ready to be used as a source of energy by the plant, is likely also to be good food for animals. We may therefore expect that—ruminants aside— mammals eating plant parts will chiefly eat buds, fruits, seeds, and roots. That is exactly the case. Young shoots and stalks (stems), not yet too woody, contain nourishment in process of internal shipment from one part of the plant to another, and leaves contain some, but these plant parts are rarely as satisfying to animals as are the parts where food is stored.[2]

PLANT VERSUS ANIMAL.   We may also reasonably expect that, faced with this sort of predation since their first appearance, the angiosperms will have evolved ways to fight back. Of course, we must think in terms of selection as the mechanism, not of any sort of purposive behavior. A plant may have burs or thorns that keep animals off. It may grow a hard shell around its seed or fruit, destined to decay in appropriate damp soil but too tough to be cracked open by any but a tool-using animal. Many plants produce, in seed, fruit, or root, not only stored food but also substances that

[2]Certain arboreal Old World monkeys have come to live exclusively on leaves. They have to consume enormous quantities of them. Nearly one fourth of the total body weight of such a monkey consists of the stomach and its contents.

TABLE 29-1.   Plants raised or nurtured by man (*continued*).

		Order POLYGONALES	
		Family POLYGONACEAE	
68.	*Fagopyrum esculentum, F. tataricum*	buckwheat	Herbaceous. Fruit. Central Eurasia.
69.	*Rheum rhaponticum, R. officinale, R. palmatum,* and allied spp	rhubarb	Herbaceous. Leafstalks; dried root as medicine. Asia.
		Order RANALES	
		Family LAURACEAE	
70.	*Cinnamomum camphora*	camphor	Evergreen tree. Oil extracted with heat from crushed wood; medicinal. Formosa and nearby.
71.	*Cinnamomum zeylanicum, C. cassia,* and allied spp	cinnamon	Evergreen tree. Inner bark of suckers, dried. Ceylon and nearby.
72.	*Persea americana*	avocado	Evergreen tree. Fruit. Mexico and Central American highlands.
73.	*Sassafras albidum*	sassafras	Deciduous tree. Root bark. North America.
		Family MYRISTICACEAE	
74.	*Myristica fragrans* and allied spp	nutmeg	Evergreen tree. Kernel of seed. Moluccas, New Guinea.
		Order RHAMNALES	
		Family RHAMNACEAE	
75.	*Ziziphus* spp	jujube	Fruit (probably the lotus of antiquity). North Africa.
		Family VITACEAE	
76.	*Vitis vitifera, V. labrusca, V. rotundifolia,* and allied spp	grapevine	Woody perennial vine. Fruit. Worldwide in north temperate zone; viticulture began near Caspian Sea?
		Order RHOEADALES	
		Family CAPPARIDACEAE	
77.	*Capparis spinosa* and allied spp	capers	Deciduous perennial shrub. Unexpanded flower buds. Southwestern Europe?

are repellent or poisonous to mammals and birds. Storage roots may lie deep; fruit and seeds may grow high where ground-walking mammals, at least, cannot get at them. Finally, plants fight back through nature's oldest trick: sheer quantity of seed production, so that however much is consumed by animals a little will escape to propagate the species.

OTHER ANIMAL USES OF PLANTS.   We have been speaking as though the only use animals had for plants was as food. This is not true, even of nonhuman animals. A snake can hide in the grass. A squirrel or fox can make his home in a hollow tree trunk. Birds and many primates live in trees, appropriating twigs and foliage for their nests. Our own ancestors used wood long before the beginnings of agriculture, as well, doubtless, as reeds, leaves, and other plant parts, for tools, utensils, housing, drugs, dyes, some items of clothing, and toys. We still do. Yet food, rather than any of these other things, was beyond dispute the original and principal reason for the development of agriculture.

STEPS IN DOMESTICATION ✘ Pleistocene man was a more dangerous predator on animals than were other carnivores, because his tools and his habit of hunting in efficiently cooperating groups made him powerful. There is evidence that Man the Hunter kept the members of

TABLE 29-1.   Plants raised or nurtured by man (*continued*).

	Family CRUCIFERAE	
78. *Armoracia rusticana, A. lapathifolia*	horseradish	Herb. Root. Mediterranean.
79. *Brassica oleracea*	cabbage, broccoli; cauliflower, brussels sprouts	Herb. Leaf, stem, flower bud. Probably both eastern Asia and southwestern Asia-Mediterranean.
80. *Brassica rapa*	turnip	Herb. Root. Central Eurasia.
81. *Brassica napabrassica*	rutabaga	Herb. Root. Central Eurasia.
82. *Brassica chinensis, B. pekinensis*	Chinese cabbage	Herb. Stalks, leaves. Central or eastern Asia.
83. *Brassica nigra, B. juncea, B. hirta*	mustards	Herbs. Leaves, pulverized seeds. Southwest Asia or Mediterranean.
84. *Nasturtium officinale*	watercress	Perennial herb. Leaf, leafstalk. Mediterranean? Eastern Asia?
85. *Raphanus sativus*	radish	Herb. Root. Mediterranean? Eastern Asia?
	Family PAPAVERACEAE	
86. *Papaver somniferum* and allied spp	poppy	Herb, usually perennial. Immature fruit ground to extract opium. Temperate Eurasia.
	Order ROSALES	
	Family LEGUMINOSAE	
87. *Arachis hypogaea*	peanut	Herbaceous annual. Seed (on underground stem). Eastern South America.
88. *Cicer arietinum*	chick-pea	Herb. Seed. South of Caucasus.
89. *Dolichos sphaerospermus*	black-eyed pea	Perennial herb (vine). Fruit. Tropics.
90. *Glycine max*	soya bean	Annual herb. Fruit. East Asia (northeastern China?)
91. *Lens culinaris*	lentil	Annual herb. Seed. Southeast Asia.
92. *Phaseolus vulgaris*	kidney bean, green bean, wax bean	Annual herb. Seedpod. South America.
93. *Phaseolus limensis*	lima bean	Perennial herb. Seed. South America.

certain animal species in check, and he may have brought about the extinction of some. One hypothesis about the peopling of the Americas from the Eurasian northlands (pp. 427–428) is that our ancestors repeatedly killed off a favorite local species of game and had to move into new territory looking for new sorts of prey.

Man the Hunter was also Man (or Woman!) the Gatherer of plant foods. But up until 10,000 or so years ago, the treatment plants received from man was pretty much the same as their treatment by other mammals. The depredations were slight, not likely to have much effect on the destiny of any one plant species. Then something strange started to happen, not like anything plants had ever before faced in their long, long history.

INCIPIENT CROP-RAISING

We can get some glimmering of these unprecedented developments from what certain essentially nonagricultural tribes have done to plants in the ethnographic present. We shall contrast the practices of four different sets of tribes in aboriginal North America.

(1) AND (2)   In central and northern California, and, across the Sierras, in the Great Basin (Nevada, Utah), the Indians used whatever plant products were available

TABLE 29-1.   Plants raised or nurtured by man (*continued*).

94.	*Phaseolus lunatis*	sieva bean	Annual herb. Seed. South America.
95.	*Pisum sativum*	garden pea, field pea	Annual herb. Seed, seedpod. Southwest Asia or central Eurasia.
96.	*Vicia faba*	broad bean	Herb. Seedpod. Central Asia.
97.	*Vicia sativa*	vetch	Herb. Seedpod. Southeast Asia.
98.	*Vigna sinensis*	cowpea	Herb. Seedpod, seed. India?
99.	*Vigna unguiculata*	cowpea	Herb. Seedpod, seed. Nigeria.
		Family ROSACEAE	
100.	*Fragaria vesca, F. virginiana, F. chloensis, F. moschata*	strawberry	Perennial herb. Fruit. Worldwide in north temperate zone, in Americas south to Patagonia.
101.	*Malus pumila*	apple	Deciduous tree. Fruit. South of Caucasus?
102.	*Prunus amygdalus*	almond	Deciduous tree. Seed. Southwest Asia.
103.	*Prunus armeniaca*	apricot	Deciduous tree. Fruit. China.
104.	*Prunus avium*	sweet cherry	Deciduous tree. Fruit. Southwest Asia or Aegean.
105.	*Prunus cerasus*	sour cherry	Deciduous tree. Fruit. Southwest Asia or Aegean.
106.	*Prunus insititia*	damson plum	Deciduous tree. Fruit. Caspian?
107.	*Prunus persica*	peach	Deciduous tree. Fruit. China.
108.	*Pyrus communis* and allied spp	pear	Deciduous tree. Fruit. Central Eurasia?
109.	*Rubus idaeus, R. strigosus,* and allied spp	raspberry, blackberry	Woody perennial shrub. Fruit. Eastern Asia, temperate North America.
		Family SAXIFRAGACEAE	
110.	*Ribes nigrum, R. sativum, R. rubrum*	currant (black, white, red)	Woody perennial shrub. Fruit. Worldwide in north temperate zone; western South America.
		Order RUBIALES	
		Family CAPRIFOLIACEAE	
111.	*Sambucus nigra, S. canadensis*	elderberry	Woody perennial. Fruit. Eurasia and northern Africa, North America and West Indies.

as food and for other purposes. It is dry in the Great Basin; vegetation is sparse, and hence both game animals and the human population were scant. People lived in small bands and had to wander over sizable territories to get enough to eat. In California, on the other hand, the population was dense, with settled villages. The Indians there relied heavily on acorns and pine nuts, the seeds of a number of species of trees that grew in great abundance. They were experts at gathering the seeds and had learned how to leach acorns to render them edible (without this, those of most species of oak are too bitter). They stored whole seeds for the winter, and they ground the leached acorns into a flour from which they prepared various baked and boiled dishes. The technology of food-processing was much like that used by agricultural peoples on some of their agricultural products. But neither the California Indians nor those of the Great Basin did anything to help the plants grow. The difference between the two was one of the bountifulness of the environment.

(3)   Our third set of tribes are those which lived along the shores of the lower Colorado River and its tributary the Gila River. They gathered all sorts of seeds and other foodstuffs from the plants that grew wild in the damp flats to either side of the watercourses. They did no planting or cultivating. But they built dams and ditches, directing the water onto the flats and thus securing the growth of the plants in larger areas than they would otherwise have occupied.

TABLE 29-1.   Plants raised or nurtured by man (*continued*).

		Family RUBIACEAE	
112.	*Caffea arabica, C. robusta, C. liberica, C. stenophylla*	coffee	Woody perennial. Seed. Ethiopia.
		Order SAPINDALES	
		Family ACERACEAE	
113.	*Acer saccharum* and allied spp	sugar maple	Deciduous tree. Sap for syrup and sugar. Eastern North America.
		Family ANACARDIACEAE	
114.	*Anacardium occidentale*	cashew	Woody perennial. Seed roasted. Tropical America.
115.	*Mangifera indica*	mango	Evergreen. Fruit. Southeast Asia, eastern India.
		Family CELASTRACEAE	
116.	*Catha edulis*	chat	Evergreen shrub. Seed. Ethiopia.
		Family SAPINDACEAE	
117.	*Blighia sapida*	akee	Evergreen tree. Fruit. Tropical western Africa.
118.	*Litchi chinensis*	litchee	Tree. Fruit. Southern China.
		Order TUBIFLORAE	
		Family BIGNONIACEAE	
119.	*Crescentia cujete*	calabash	Vine. Seedpod as container. Tropical America.
		Family CONVOLULACEAE	
120.	*Coleus* spp	Hausa potato	Herb. Tuber. West Africa.
121.	*Majorama* spp	marjoram	Herb. Leaves, dried. Eurasia.
122.	*Mentha* species	mint	Herb. Leaves, oil from leaves and stems. Northern Eurasia, Australia.
123.	*Origanum* spp	oregano, marjoram	Herb. Leaves, dried. Eurasia.
124.	*Salvia officinalis*	sage	Herb. Leaves, dried.

(4)   Finally we turn to the Menomini and other groups in the western Great Lakes region. These people sowed wild rice in a likely lake in which they found none growing (p. 20). Possibly this was a transfer from the bit of Iroquois-type agriculture that some of the groups practiced, but that is not necessarily so. They may have invented the procedure on their own. They did nothing else about the wild rice plants, except to reap the harvest when the time came.

KNOWLEDGE AND ACTION.   All these Indian groups unquestionably knew that plants produce seeds from which grow new plants of the same kind, and that some plants need ample water, others very little. Such practical botanical information, adapted to the flora of one's own region, is widespread and very old, certainly predating systematic agriculture by many thousands of years.

Knowing such things and putting the knowledge to work are two different matters. The California Indians did nothing with their knowledge because it was unnecessary. The trees they valued were all over the place and flourished with no intervention. The Indians of the Great Basin did nothing with their knowledge because it was impossible. There was no simple and obvious way to increase the plant yield, except to pray for rain (which they doubtless did). Even today, turning any sizable portion of the Great Basin into good farmland would require feats of agricultural engineering almost beyond our powers and certainly beyond our collective desire. But for the

TABLE 29-1.   Plants raised or nurtured by man (*continued*).

125.	*Thymus vulgaris* and allied spp	thyme	Herb. Leaves, dried. Eurasia.
		Family PEDALIACEAE	
126.	*Sesamum indicum*	sesame	Herbaceous annual. Seeds, oil from seed. Northeast Africa.
		Family SOLANACEAE	
127.	*Capsicum frutescens* and other *C.* spp	red pepper, sweet pepper, cayenne, chili, pimento	Perennial woody shrub. Fruit, fresh or dried and ground. Central and South America.
128.	*Lycopersicon esculentum, L. pimpinellifolium*	tomato	Shrub, perennial/annual. Fruit. Andes.
129.	*Nicotiana tabacum* and allied spp	tobacco	Herbaceous annual. Leaves, stems, dried for chewing, smoking, sniffing. Central or South America.
130.	*Solanum meiongena*	eggplant	Herbaceous perennial. Fruit. South and southeast Asia.
131.	*Solanum tuberosum* and allied spp	potato	Herb. Tuber. Andes and south.
132.	*Solanum commersonii*	Uruguay potato	Herb. Tuber. Andes and south.
		Order UMBELLALES	
		Family UMBELLIFERAE	
133.	*Anthriscus cerefolium*	chervil	Herbaceous annual. Dried leaves. Eurasia.
134.	*Apium graviolens*	celery	Herb. Immature fruit, stalk, root. Eastern Mediterranean or southwest Asia.
135.	*Daucus carota*	carrot	Biennial. Taproot and hypocotyl. Afghanistan or nearby.
136.	*Pastinaca sativa*	parsnip	Biennial. Root. Europe?
137.	*Petroselinum crispum*	parsley	Annual/biennial herb. Leaf, root. Southern Europe?

tribes on the Colorado and Gila Rivers, and for those in the small-glacial-lake region of the Northeastern Woodlands, certain techniques were both useful and feasible.

This is not to say that an invention of irrigation or of seed-planting is not a remarkable achievement. It is simply to underscore that human ingenuity manifests itself most effectively in the joint context of *need* and *opportunity*. All the Indians we have mentioned were intelligent, making the most of their heritages and their environments. Those in the Great Basin had need but no opportunity. Those in California had opportunity but no need. The other two groups had both.

INFERENCES. Now we can turn back to the state of affairs in the human world as of ten thousand or so years ago. People were living almost everywhere they live now (p. 423). The evidence, though indirect, is clear: all over the inhabited world, in many different localities where need, opportunity, and a modicum of ingenuity overlapped, people were devising ways to increase either the numbers of certain plants or else the amount of yield per plant.

From any one inside view, there may be many ways to try this. The Menomini, we remember, considered an appropriate power pack, appropriately manipulated, to be a vital ingredient of successful hunting (p. 21); in a similar way, a tribe may pray to or otherwise propitiate or implore a rain god, a maize goddess, or the spirit in charge of oak trees. Fertility ceremonies, evolving by cautious trial and error, take a myriad of forms, and some of them involve actions which in fact—that is, from

TABLE 29-1. Plants raised or nurtured by man (*continued*).

		Order URTICALES	
		Family MORACEAE	
138.	*Artocarpus altilis*	breadfruit	Tree. Fruit (cooked). Malay archipelago?
139.	*Broussonetia papyrifera*	paper mulberry	Tree. Bark for paper and tapa. Burma, China, Polynesia?
140.	*Cannabis sativa*	hemp	Herbaceous annual. Seed for oil; bast for fiber; source of hashish. North of Himalayas or central China.
141.	*Ficus carica* and allied spp	fig	Tree. Fruit. Mediterranean?
142.	*Morus rubra, M. alba, M. indica, M. negra*	mulberry	Perennial. Leaves fed to silkworms. China.
143.	*Treculia africana*	African breadfruit	Perennial. Seed ground for meal. Africa.
		Family URTICACEAE	
144.	*Pipturus albidus*		Tree. Bark for tapa. Polynesia.
		Subclass MONOCOTYLEDONAE	
		Order ARALES	
		Family ARACEAE	
145.	*Colocasia antiquorum*	taro	Herb. Tuber. Burma?
146.	*Colocasia esculenta*	elephant's ear	Herb. Tuber. Indonesia.
		Order FARINALES	
		Family BROMELIACEAE	
147.	*Ananas comosus*	pineapple	Herbaceous perennial. Fruit. Tropical and subtropical America.
		Order GRAMINALES	
		Family CYPERACEAE	
148.	*Eleocharis dulcis*	"water chestnut"	Tuber replaces number 62 in most Chinese restaurants outside of China.

the outside view—do promote the desired end, whether or not the people involved have an objectively correct theory about it. Those behavioral features which are objectively successful tend to be retained; others are discarded or altered. One objectively useful operation is to plant seed. One is to irrigate. One is to loosen the soil where the seeds are to be planted, rather than merely scattering them. One is to bury a bit of nourishment (perhaps by way of sacrifice) along with the seed. One is to save some of the seeds of a variety of plant one has found especially good or useful, and plant them in likely spots at a likely time of the year. One is to weed vegetable trash away from the plant one wants, giving it less competition in its search for minerals. Every one of these procedures must have been independently invented in many different places.

THE NATURE OF DOMESTICATION.   From the point of view of the plants (if we may speak in this fashion) what all this meant was that they were being conditioned to grow in ways that suited *human* convenience rather than their own needs. Exactly this is what is meant by *domestication*. And exactly this was the startling new development in plant evolution that we mentioned earlier, totally unprecedented in their long earlier history.

Some plants have changed very little under the impact of human use. This is true of wild rice, though possibly only because its exploitation by our species has not yet gone on for very long.

TABLE 29-1.   Plants raised or nurtured by man (*continued*).

	Family GRAMINEAE		
	Subfamily FESTUCOIDEAE		
	Tribe BAMBUSEAE		
149.	*Bambusa vulgaris, B. arundinacea, Melocanna baecifera, Dendrocalamus strictus*	bamboo	Woody perennial. Young shoots as food, stalks pulped for paper. Southeast Asia?
	Tribe AVENEAE		
150.	*Avena sativa* and allied spp	oats	Annual. Seed. From southeast Asia; separated from wheat (or barley) in Europe.
	Tribe HORDEAE		
151.	*Triticum vulgare*	wheat	Annual. Seed. Southwest Asia.
152.	*Hordeum vulgare* and allied spp	barley	Annual. Seed. Southwest Asia.
153.	*Secale cereale*	rye	Annual. Seed. From southeast Asia; separated from wheat (or barley) in Europe.
	Tribe ORYZEAE		
154.	*Oryza sativa*	rice	Annual. Seed. Central China, India(?).
155.	*Oryza glaberrima*	rice	Annual. Seed. West Africa.
	Tribe ZIZANIEAE		
156.	*Zizania aquatica*	wild rice	Perennial. Seed. Northeastern North America.
	Subfamily PANICOIDEAE		
	Tribe ANDROPOGONEAE		
157.	*Sorghum vulgare* and allied spp	sorghum	Annual. Seed; stalk for juice. China, India(?).
158.	*Sorghum bicolor*	sorghum	Annual. Seed; stalk for juice. Sudan and Chad.
159.	*Saccharum officinarum*	sugarcane	Annual. Stalks for juice. New Guinea.

For other plants, the consequences have been profound. For example: Wild grasses produce seeds that are attached very lightly to the stems, though the kernel is enclosed in a tight hull. When the seeds are mature, a slight breeze is enough to detach and scatter them. This is obviously to the advantage of the species. People gathering such seeds knock the grains off the stalks into a container. If they try to cut the stalks down for later threshing, most of the seeds are lost. Yet in archaeological sites we find sickles bearing clear evidence of their having been used on grasses (grass stems invariably contain silica, which polishes the flint blades used to cut them)—or on reeds (which also contain silica). If the supporting evidence points to grasses rather than to reeds, then they had to have been domesticated grasses in which, by selection, the seeds had come to adhere to the stems until forcibly removed by man. Without human intervention, mutated strains with tightly bound seeds would quickly have died out. We do not know how it happened that human intervention selected and promoted just those strains, but we know it did.[3] In time, human convenience also selected for looser hulls, from which the kernels could be removed more easily, and for larger numbers of grains per plant.

Today, a sudden withdrawal of domestication would mean that many species of

[3]Maybe this way: a gatherer tries to knock the seeds off into a container and finds it difficult; in exasperation, he cuts the whole stalk to work on later. Seeds saved from such a harvest for subsequent planting would propagate the modified plant.

TABLE 29-1. Plants raised or nurtured by man (*continued*).

		Tribe MAYDEAE	
160.	*Zea mays*	maize	Annual. Seed. Central Mexico.
		Tribe PANICEAE	
161.	*Panicum miliacem, Setaria italica*	millet	Annual. Seed. China.
162.	*Brachiaria deflexa*	millet	Annual. Seed. Guinea coast.
163.	*Eleusine coracana*	finger millet	Annual. Seed. Ethiopia to Uganda, highlands.
164.	*Pennisetum americanum*	pearl millet	Annual. Seed. Sudan to Senegal, dry savanna.
	Order LILIALES		
	Family AMARYLLIDACEAE		
165.	*Agave sisalana* and allied spp	agave	Perennial. Fibers from leaves (sisal). Mexico, Caribbean.
166.	*Agave atrovirens* and allied spp	maguey	Perennial. Sap fermented for pulque. Mexico.
167.	*Agave cantala*	cantala	Fiber from leaves. Philippines.
	Family DIOSCOREACEAE		
168.	*Dioscorea sativa, D. alata* and others	yam	Herb. Tuber (or rhizome). South and southeast Asia, western Africa from Sierra Leone to Congo.
169.	*Dioscorea rotundata*	yam	Herb. Tuber (or rhizome). Ivory Coast.
	Family LILIACEAE		
170.	*Allium cepa* and allied spp	onion	Herb. Thick part below stem, young shoot. Central Eurasia, Mediterranean.
171.	*Allium ascalonicum*	shallot	Herb. Thick part below stem, young shoot. Central Eurasia?
172.	*Allium sativum* and allied spp	garlic	Herb. Underground bud. Central Eurasia.
173.	*Allium porrum*	leek	Biennial. Underground bud. Southwest Asia, eastern Mediterranean.
174.	*Allium schoienoprasum*	chive	Herbaceous perennial. Leaf.

domesticated plants would become extinct, and that others would survive only if mutations reverted them to earlier more independent types. We have even developed some plants—perfectly good Spermopsida, such as the sweet potato—which in some of the climates in which we grow them can scarcely be persuaded to produce seed at all! Instead, a new plant is grown from a root sprout or from a stem cutting.

INCIPIENT ANIMAL HUSBANDRY

"Domestication" means the same thing for nonhuman animals as for plants: successful human efforts to make the species grow or breed in terms of human needs rather than in terms of their own.

Plants are sessile, specialists in adapting themselves to their environment. Land animals are motile, experts at adapting their environment (if necessary by moving to a new one) to themselves. Man has everywhere and always felt a sort of kinship for some of his fellow land animals quite different from any attitude of affinity for plants. This is shown by the literature of every known society, in which important characters are often half animal and half human, but seldom vegetable. And yet Pleistocene man's dealings with other animals were largely a matter of kill or be killed, whereas his treatment of plants was in general less drastic.

For these reasons, and perhaps for others, the gap between hunting and animal husbandry was bigger than that between gathering and cultivating. The domestication

TABLE 29-1. Plants raised or nurtured by man (*continued*).

175.	*Asparagus officinalis* and allied spp	asparagus	Herbaceous perennial. Young stalk. Eurasia.
176.	*Smilax officinalis, S. papyracea, S. aristochiaefolia*	sarsaparilla	Root, dried. Pacific coast, Mexico to Peru.
		Order ORCHIDALES Family ORCHIDACEAE	
177.	*Vanilla planifolia* and allied spp	vanilla	Herbaceous perennial with aerial roots. Fruit (pod), dried. Southeastern Mexico.
		Order PALMALES Family PALMAE	
178.	*Cocos nucifera*	coconut palm	Tree. Fruit, fiber from husk. Southeast Asia? or tropical America?
179.	*Elaeis guineensis*	African oil palm	Tree. Sierra Leone to Congo.
180.	*Hyphaene thebaica*	Doum palm.	Tree. Fruit. Africa.
181.	*Balanites aegyptici*	desert date	Tree. Fruit. Sudan to Senegal.
182.	*Phoenix dactylifera*	date palm	Tree. Fruit. Old World tropics.
		Order SCITAMINALES Family MUSACEAE	
183.	*Musa paradisiaca, M. acuminata, M. balbisiana, M. napa, M. cavendishii,* and others	plantain, banana	Herbaceous perennial. Fruit. Southeast Asia.
		Family ZINGIBERACEAE	
184.	*Zingiber melegeeta*	malaguetta pepper	Herbaceous perennial. Seeds, ground. Africa.
185.	*Zingiber officinale* and allied spp	ginger	Herbaceous perennial. Rhizome (underground stem). Southern or southeastern Asian tropics?

of animals[4] seems not to have begun quite so early as that of plants, and the initial moves were made, or at least were strikingly successful, in fewer places.

CURRENT EXAMPLE. Among the surviving hunters-and-gatherers of the ethnographic present, unusual exploitations of animals, of the sort that might in time lead to full-fledged domestication, are rare, but not completely unknown.

The aboriginal tribes of the Klamath River in northern California needed wooden tubes for various purposes, and there grew, along the river, a kind of reed that served well provided the rather tough pith could be removed. Instead of taking it out with tools, they put animals to work. They dug a slight pit in the pith at one end of a segment, inserted a certain kind of grub (species not identified), and then covered the opening with inedible material. The grub calmly ate its way to the other end of the segment, whereupon the reed was ready for use. The Indians did not breed the grubs or raise them in captivity. But they *harnessed* them. That is, they had learned to exploit, for their own purposes, a *source of energy* other than their own metabolism. If the example seems paltry, we should remind ourselves that appropriating cocoons

[4] In the present discussion it would be stylistically awkward always to have to use the logically correct expression "nonhuman animal." The reader will have no trouble knowing when the bare word "animal" is an abbreviation for the longer phrase and when it is not.

TABLE 29-2. Animals raised or nurtured by man.

	Phylum MOLLUSCA		
	Class GASTROPODA		
	Subclass PULMONATA		
	Order STYLOMMATOPHORA		
	Family HELICIDAE		
1.	*Helis pomatia, H. aspersa*	land snail	Food. Mediterranean(?); now raised in France and southern Europe.
	Class PELECYPODA		
	Order EULAMELLIBRANCHIA		
	Family OSTREIDAE		
2.	*Ostrea edulis* and allied spp	oyster	Food, shells (mother-of-pearl). China had oyster farms many centuries B.C., ancient Rome later.
3.	*Pinctada margaritifera, P. maxima, Avicula* spp	pearl oyster	Food, pearls, shells. Cultured pearls: China about thirteenth century A.D.
	Suborder SUBMYTILACEA		
	Family UNIONIDAE		
4.	*Unio margartifera*, other *U.* spp, *Anodonta* spp	mussel	Food, shells (fake mother-of-pearl). Sometimes cultured nowadays.
	Phylum ARTHROPODA		
	Subphylum MANDIBULATA		
	Class INSECTA		
	Order HYMENOPTERA		
	Family APIDAE		
5.	*Apis mellifera* (Europe); *A. dorsata, A. florea, A. indica* (India)	honeybee	Honey, beeswax. Apiculture presumably started somewhere in central Eurasia, several millennia B.C.

for silk began before, and led to, the special raising and breeding of silkworms, and we should note the vast extent of sericulture today.

POSSIBLE EARLY STEPS.   For larger animals, we have only scant clues about the first tentatives towards domestication. Three deserve mention.

(1)   Hunters with a (temporarily) settled home base sometimes adopt a young animal whom their hunting has orphaned, keeping it as a pet for a while before slaughtering or releasing it. The motive seems usually to be curiosity or fun—especially for children—rather than food. Yet the pet has to be fenced in or tethered in some fashion. So this practice could afford training in the care and constraint of animals.

(2)   People sometimes build fences or walls around their homes to keep ground-walking marauders away; early farmers did this also to protect their garden plots. A fence works both ways: it keeps things in as well as it keeps them out. Mild animals may occasionally have been enclosed by accident, conveniently ready for butchering when and if the need arose. The step to putting a separate fence around a more dangerous game animal was a small one.

(3)   Perhaps more important than either of the above is a way of hunting life that we think developed in various parts of more northerly Eurasia long ago: a

TABLE 29-2.   Animals raised or nurtured by man (*continued*).

	Order LEPIDOPTERA	
	Family BOMBYCIDAE	
6. *Bombyx mori* and allied spp	silkworm	Cocoon is source of silk. Sericulture known in China in middle of third millennium B.C.
	Phylum CHORDATA	
	Subphylum VERTEBRATA	
	Class OSTEICHTHYES	
	Subclass ACTINOPTERYGII	
	Superorder TELEOSTEI	
	Order HAPLOMI	
	Family ESOCIDAE	
7. *Esox lucius* and allied spp	pike	Food. Raised in farmyard ponds in many parts of Europe.
	Class MAMMALIA	
	Subclass THERIA	
	Infraclass EUTHERIA	
	Order LAGOMORPHA	
	Family LEPORIDAE	
8. *Oryctolagus cuniculus*	Belgian hare	Food, fur. Raised domestically for many centuries in Europe.
	Order RODENTIA	
	Suborder HYSTRICOMORPHA	
	Family CAVIIDAE	
9. *Cavia porcellus, C. cutleri*	guinea pig	Food. Aboriginal in Andes (Peru, Ecuador, Colombia).
	Family CHINCHILLIDAE	
10. *Chinchilla laniger*	chinchilla	Fur. Originally from Chile, Peru; raised in captivity in United States since 1920s.

wandering band trailed around behind a wandering herd of grazing animals, letting the latter search freely for the grass they needed, and killing a selected few from time to time for food and raw materials, but tempering their slaughter of the animals so that they would not destroy the source of supply.

What this could lead to in course of time would depend on the animal as well as on the people. Some species of grazers are too large and dangerous for much change. Some strains, however, may have been small and sufficiently mild-tempered that they became accustomed to the constant presence of men, and stupid enough that they remained individually unmoved by the occasional destruction of some of their follows. The men, in turn, learned to protect the animals against wolves and other predators, and eventually began to help them in their search for food, say by sending out scouts to find fresh grass and then driving the herd to it. Such people became herders, living in a sort of symbiosis with their herds (p. 158), and by a process of selection the animals became domesticated, no longer able to do for themselves what men had come to do for them.

Uses for animals. Domesticated animals and plants are both sources of food and both sources of raw materials of various other sorts. In addition, domesticated

TABLE 29-2. Animals raised or nurtured by man (*continued*).

	Order Carnivora	
	Family Canidae	
11. *Canis familiaris*	dog	Food, fur, hides, scavenging, burden, traction, hunting, corralling, companionship, show. Probably domesticated several places independently, between twenty and ten thousand years ago.
12. *Vulpes vulpes* (Eurasia); *V. fulva* (North America)	red, silver, and blue fox	Fur. Fox farms from nineteenth century, mainly in the United States.
	Family Mustelidae	
13. *Mustela lutreola, M. erminea* (Eurasia); *M. vison* (North America)	mink, ermine	Fur. Now raised on farms in the southern United States.
	Family Felidae	
14. *Felis catus*	house cat	Scavenging, companionship, show. Early Egypt; probably also independently elsewhere.
	Order Proboscidea	
	Family Elephantidae	
15. *Elephas maximus*	Indian elephant	Ivory, burden, traction. India and Burma from at latest first millennium B.C.
16. *Loxodonta africana*	African elephant	Ivory; burden 2000 years ago, then again beginning late in nineteenth century.
	Order Perissodactyla	
	Family Equidae	
17. *Equus caballus*	horse	Meat, milk, hides, burden, traction, riding, companionship, show. Central Eurasia by 3000 or 2500 B.C.
18. *Equus asinus*	ass	Hides, burden, traction, riding. Known in southeastern Egypt before 3000 B.C.
		Horses and asses have been interbred for at least 3000 years to produce mules and hinnies.

animals—even the Klamath River grubs—can be used in a way in which plants cannot: to do mechanical work that man would otherwise have to do himself, or even work that is beyond man's unaided capacities.

This use began early, and many animals have come to be so exploited; but we quite properly think first and foremost of the horse. It is no accident that Western physicists came to use the term *horsepower* to denote a certain rate of flow of energy. The Chinese word *mǎshang,* literally 'on horseback', is today simply a colorless adverb meaning 'fast, right away'; the metaphor makes sense when we remember that less than two hundred years ago riding a horse was far and away the fastest means of getting from one place to another.

✖ Both plant and animal domestication are vitally important to man's present ways of life. And they have affected each other. Some crops (clover, timothy) are raised mainly as fodder for domestic animals, and some animals (draft horses) are used chiefly for plowing and harrowing fields. Also, their manure serves to fertilize the soil.

ULTIMATE EXTENT OF DOMESTICATION

TABLE 29-2. Animals raised or nurtured by man (*continued*).

	Order ARTIODACTYLA		
	Suborder SUIFORMES		
	Family SUIDAE		
19.	*Sus scrofa*	pig	Meat, hides; trained for game-pointing in medieval England; still trained to root for truffles in France. Seventh or sixth millennium B.C. in southwest Asia; independently in central China and in southeast Asia.
	Suborder TYLOPODA		
	Family CAMELIDAE		
20.	*Lama glama*	llama	Burden, meat, hides, wool. Andes.
21.	*Lama pacos*	alpaca	Burden, meat, hides, wool. Andes.
22.	*Camelus bactrianus*	bactrian camel	Burden, meat, milk, hides, wool. Before 1000 B.C.; place unknown. Confined mainly to highlands of central Asia from Turkestan to Mongolia.
23.	*Camelus dromedarius*	camel, dromedary	Burden, meat, milk, hides, wool. Before 1000 B.C.; place unknown. Mainly in north Africa, Arabia and Near East, India.
	Suborder RUMINANTIA		
	Family CERVIDAE		
24.	*Rangifer turandus*	reindeer	Draft, burden, meat, milk, hides. Eurasian arctic and subarctic; time of domestication unknown.
	Family BOVIDAE		
	Subfamily BOVINAE		
25.	*Bubalus bubalis*	water buffalo	Draft, milk. South and southeast Asia, from "very early times"—at least first millennium B.C.

It remains true, however, that plants, on the whole, are more versatile than animals. Man eats, or has eaten, plants of perhaps 3000 different species, and has used many more in other ways; their original sites of exploitation are all over the world, and many are now grown widely. Thus, Table 29–1 presents only a small sample. We have only a few dozen species of domesticated animals: Table 29–2 is surely nearly complete. They come from a small number of places of origin, and a good proportion of them, such as the llama and alpaca of the Andes, are still confined almost wholly to their original homes.

FOCAL AREAS ✖ It is wrong to think of domestication as something that happened once, in a sudden wave, and then stopped. More domesticated species were in use five thousand years ago than ten thousand, and more are in use today than in the eighteenth century, though a few have declined (the training of birds of prey for falconry, for example, lost its importance upon the invention of firearms). We know of many unsuccessful efforts towards domestication in recent times. For instance, people have tried to raise beavers in captivity for their pelts, but so far it has not worked well. If the record were ampler, we should doubtless find such efforts being made in many parts of the

TABLE 29-2. Animals raised or nurtured by man (*continued*).

26.	*Bos taurus, B. indicus*	ox	Meat, milk, draft, burden, hides. In Anatolia by 7000 B.C.; domestication of *B. indicus* in India was much later and perhaps independent.
27.	*Bos grunniens*	yak	Meat, milk, draft, burden, hides. Tibet; time unknown.
28.	*Bibos gaurus*	gayal	Used much like ox. South and southeast Asia. Indochinese tribes in Assam and upper Burma use it for meat only.
29.	*Bibos sondaicus*	banteng	Burma, southeast Asia. Java. Used much like ox.
		Subfamily CAPRINAE	
30.	*Ovis* spp	sheep	Meat, milk, wool, fur. In Anatolia by 7000 B.C., but perhaps domesticated first in central Asia, where the number and variety of wild sheep are greatest.
31.	*Capra* spp	goat	Meat, milk, wool, occasionally traction, hides. Southwest Asia by 9000 or 8000 B.C.
	Class AVES		
	Order STRUTHIOFORMES		
	Family STRUTHIONIDAE		
32.	*Struthio camelus*	ostrich	Eggs, feathers, occasionally traction. Ostrich farms in East and South Africa since nineteenth century.
	Order ANSERIFORMES		
	Family ANATIDAE		
33.	*Anas platyhynchos*	duck	Meat, eggs. Perhaps first domesticated in southeast Asia; perhaps independently in China; date unknown.
34.	*Anser anser, A. cygnoides*	goose	Meat, eggs, feathers. Origins as for duck.
	Order FALCONIFORMES		
	Family FALCONIDAE		
35.	*Falco peregrinus* and allied spp; also birds of several other genera (eagles, goshawks)	falcon (and others)	Hunting. Caught wild and trained, or taken from nest as fledglings. Falconry known in Assyria around 700 B.C.; may be older.

world during the past ten millennia, some of them more and some less successful, some of them independent but many under the impetus of rumors or hints from elsewhere.

Moreover, if the record were fuller or better known, we should surely discover efforts towards domestication made hither and yon much earlier than ten thousand years ago—perhaps twice as long ago as that. *Homo sapiens* was just as intelligent then as he is now, just as able to respond to the combined factors of opportunity and need as were the relatively recent North American Indians we discussed earlier in this chapter.

The opportunities, to be sure, were somewhat limited geographically during the thousands of years of the Late Würm glaciation. People could and did live, as hunters-gatherers relying mainly on hunting, in regions where any sort of agriculture was precluded by the cold, as the Eskimo live with remarkable ingenuity today in such territory. Yet even at its climax the glaciation did not affect the whole land surface of Earth in that drastic way.

What would have been the need? One realistic theory is that in various localities an abundance of food led to population increase so that, although everyone preferred

TABLE 29-2. Animals raised or nurtured by man (*continued*).

	Order GALLIFORMES		
	Family PHASIANIDAE		
36.	*Phasianus colchicus*	pheasant	Meat, eggs. Raised in captivity for food; antiquity unknown.
37.	*Pavo cristatus*	peafowl	Meat, eggs, plumes. Ceylon and southern India, at latest in first millennium B.C.
38.	*Gallus gallus*	chicken	Meat, eggs. Probably southeast Asia, where it was known by 2500 B.C.; early also to China and India.
	Family NUMIDIDAE		
39.	*Numidia meleagris* and allied spp	guinea fowl	Meat, eggs. Africa; date unknown.
	Family MELEAGRIDIDAE		
40.	*Meleagris gallopravo*	turkey	Meat, eggs. New World; domesticated in Mexico and perhaps further south; date unknown (pre-Columbian).
	Order COLUMBIFORMES		
	Family COLUMBIDAE		
41.	*Columbia livia*	pigeon	Meat and eggs. Ancient Egypt. Use of pigeons as message-carriers is almost as old (about 3000 B.C.), and also started in Egypt.
	Order PSITTACIFORMES		
	Family PSITTACIDAE		
42.	*Psittacus erithacus,* *Amazona* spp, various allied genera	parrot	Household pets. Probably very old in Old World tropical and temperate zones. Some species can be trained to "talk."
	Order PASSERIFORMES		
	Family STURNIDAE		
43.	*Gracula religiosa*	mynah	Household pets; excellent "talkers." India and southeast Asia; antiquity unknown.

a diet high in animal protein, there wasn't enough to go around. The efficacy of hunting techniques may have contributed to this by sharply reducing the amount of game available. Migration into fresh territory could have been impossible because all adjacent regions were occupied. The effectiveness of food-getting had to be increased, or the human population would diminish through famine—as, no doubt, it often did. But where someone was clever enough, and the need was matched by opportunity, the effectiveness of food-getting *was* increased: by helping important plants to grow, or by rigid self-imposed constraints on the rate at which animals of certain species were slaughtered.

The reader must recognize the preceding paragraphs as speculative. The speculation is a kind we need, since archaeologists are not going to look for certain kinds of evidence unless they have some reason to believe that they may be found. But we should also acknowledge that the very earliest faint trials at domestication may well have left no physical evidence available for discovery. Thus, consider the casting of wild rice into glacial lakes in late aboriginal North America. It is obvious that we would know nothing of this if the practice had not been observed and recorded in writing.

The known archaeological evidence goes back, at most, only about ten thousand years, to the period during which the glaciers were melting away, raising the sea level but also exposing new land, and moving the winter frost line farther and farther from the equator. Maybe these radical climatic changes encouraged human efforts at domestication in one way or another, and perhaps the changes in the shape and nature of Earth's land surface erased some of the evidence of earlier efforts so effectively that we shall never find it.

The evidence we do have does not permit us to pinpoint the spots where individual creative efforts in domestication took place, not even with as blunt a pin as we used in speaking of the sowing of wild rice and of the irrigation of river flats. But, combined with the techniques of biogeography (which compares what is known of the history of domesticated species with the present and former distribution of kindred non-domesticated species), it indicates certain general regions as those within which the earliest *known* farming developed. We shall call these regions "focal areas":

(1) Southwest Asia: east and south of the Caspian Sea, south of the Caucasus Mountains, and south of the Black Sea, including Iran, Iraq, and the eastern shore of the Mediterranean (fairly early, also the Aegean area).

(2) Central Eurasia: from the Volga River eastwards through the Kirgiz Steppe and Kazakhstan to the Altai Mountains.

(3) The river valleys of central China.

(4) Peninsular and insular southeastern Asia.

(5) Some area of tropical or subtropical Africa.

(6) Mexico and Central America.

(7) The Andes and the coastal slopes west of them.

(8) Eastern South America.

30

❌

DOMESTICATION: THE OLDEST MACDONALDS

We proceed to survey the development of domestication in the focal areas listed at the end of chapter 29 and its early spread to other places.

❌ When, at the behest of Joshua and Jehovah, the walls of Jericho came tumbling down, they added to a pile of rubble that had been growing for well over seven thousand years.[1] Archaeologists have been reading this evidence with great care during the past few decades, and it tells part of the story we are after. **SOUTHWEST ASIA**

The earliest attested occupation of the site was about 9000 B.C., but with no signs of farming. However, the residents made some of their tools with obsidian (p. 392), a material not locally available. The nearest source of supply was the country near Lake Van, 400 miles to the northeast as the crow flies. This, and comparable evidence from many other sites, shows that there was already lively commerce and culture contact throughout the region, so that any useful innovation at one point might spread quite rapidly to others.

By shortly after 7000 B.C. the population of Jericho was an estimated 2000. There is still no direct testimony for agriculture or animal husbandry, but it is hard to see how that many people could have been fed without them. From a hundred years later (6800–6700 B.C.) we find actual grains of cereals, together with bones of goats of the "Pasang" type—a strain of the species to which all modern domesticated goats are assigned. At subsequent horizons the evidence increases, attesting to permanent village life, mixed farming, some use of dogs, sheep, pigs, and oxen[2] (none except the dog necessarily domesticated), and the making of pottery, which is absent at the earlier horizons we have mentioned.

The site of which we have just spoken is a mound in the valley of the Jordan River about one mile west of the modern town called "Jericho" by the Israelis and

[1] Modern scholarship puts Joshua toward the end of the thirteenth century B.C. However, the remark in the text assumes that the site of the Biblical battle reported in Joshua 6 was the same Jericho, which archaeological investigation now renders doubtful.

[2] *Oxen* (singular *ox*) is a more convenient term for what in the United States we usually call *cows, bulls,* and *cattle.* (The British restriction of the term *ox* to mean 'castrated male' is here ignored.)

in English, "Arihā" by the Jordanians. It is shown in Figure 30-1, together with the other major archaeological sites of the southwest Asia focal area. Our archaeological evidence for early Old World farming is confined almost entirely to this area. Nowadays much of the region is desiccated, unusable for agricultural purposes except with the aid of irrigation. Ten millennia ago that was not so. The climate and topography have changed, partly as the local manifestation of altering world weather (one imagines the great Arabian desert slowly creeping northwards as the glaciers of high latitudes melted and the amount of rainfall at low latitudes decreased), but in part exactly as a consequence of tillage, which exhausted the soil and promoted erosion.

OTHER SITES

(1)   At Qalat Jarmo (some 33 miles east of Kirkūk in northern Iraq), around 6750 B.C., there was a village of fifteen houses, say 150 people. They grew a variety of barley and two varieties of wheat (emmer and einkorn) that stand about halfway between the wild varieties and modern domesticated forms, and they kept goats. Their diet included certain plants and animals that were eventually domesticated but at the time may still have been obtained by gathering and hunting: lentils and peas, sheep, pigs, and occasionally an ox. They knew of the dog, because they carved—or imported—canine figurines.

The sickles with which they harvested their cereal crops were composite tools, made by inserting a row of small polished flint blades into a shaft of wood; the blades show signs of silica polishing (p. 458), clear evidence that the grains had been domesticated to the extent that the seeds clung to the stems rather than falling off at the slightest touch. On the other hand, the grains still required parching or roasting before they could be ground into flour, as modern cereal grains do not.

Before the site fades out, there is evidence that they had come to do this roasting in clay ovens. Their houses were built with mud walls, laid down in horizontal courses each of which was allowed to dry in the sun before the next was added. Such uses of mud and clay are akin to ceramics, but there is no sign of clay pots. The durable containers that have survived to be dug up are of polished stone, many of them of marble and very expertly made.

(2)   Slightly earlier evidence, though somewhat more disjointed, comes from other sites in or near the Zagros Mountains.

At Ali Kosh, near Dehlorān in Iran, there are not only signs of settled village life but also actual surviving grains of the three kinds found, from a somewhat later date, at Qalat Jarmo.

Zawi Chemi is a site in Iraq about 2.5 miles south-southwest of Shanidar Cave (p. 408); it attests to permanent village life and to various kinds of processing to which either wild or domesticated plant foods can be subjected; the important point here is the hint that sheep, still of a wild form, were being corralled instead of hunted, and that some of the younger and tenderer ones were being slaughtered for food, others kept as breeding stock. The date of these activities is estimated indirectly as almost 9000 B.C.

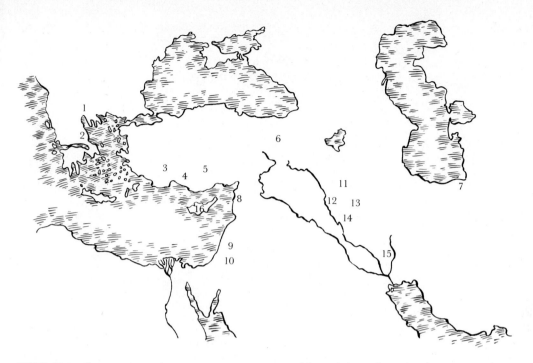

FIGURE 30-1. SOUTHWESTERN ASIAN ARCHAEOLOGICAL SITES. Most of those shown here attest to early agriculture or animal husbandry.

1	Nea Nikomedia	9	Eynan
2	Argissa	10	Jericho
3	Haçilar	11	Zawi Chemi and Shanidar Cave
4	Suberde	12	M'lefaat
5	Çatal Hüyük	13	Karim Shahir
6	Çayönü Tepesi	14	Qalat Jarmo
7	Belt and Hotu Caves	15	Ali Kosh
8	Ras Shamra	16	Khirokitia

(Data from Clark and Piggott 1965, Chard 1969.)

(3)   Most of the other sites so far investigated show the developments that concern us only at more recent dates.

Çatal Hüyük, about 31 miles southeast of Konya in Turkey, shows not only the domesticated grains we have spoken of but also, possibly, the earliest known use of sheep for their wool rather than just for meat and sheepskin. The date is about 6000 B.C. Wild sheep do not yield much wool, and its quality is poor. Our modern wool sheep are the end product of a long process of selective breeding, which may have been just beginning in Anatolia in the seventh millennium B.C. There is also the suspicion that the inhabitants of this site at the same horizon had oxen in process of domestication.

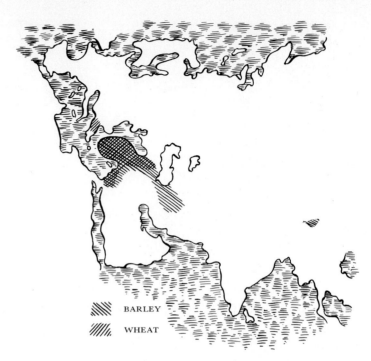

FIGURE 30-2. Distribution of wild wheat and barley. (After Clark and Piggott 1965.)

BARLEY

WHEAT

Our Figure 30-1 shows two sites on the Greek mainland: Argissa, near the present city of Vólos, and, due north of there, Nea Nikomedia, near Thessaloníki. The earliest date for Nea Nikomedia is something over 6200 B.C. Wheat, barley, lentils, peas, and (at Argissa) beans were being grown; goats and sheep were kept; pigs and oxen were eaten and possibly but not certainly penned. As at the other sites we have mentioned or listed, the earliest horizons show no pottery. In both of these Greek sites, a favorite tool material was obsidian. The nearest source was the island of Mílos, far to the south. As in the case of Jericho (p. 467), we have evidence of long-distance commerce, and here it shows that some of the people in this part of the world had mastered the art of transporting themselves and their wares over sizable stretches of water.

INFERENCES

To summarize: Farming arose in the southwest Asia focal area on the basis of two grains, wheat and barley, and then—probably somewhat later—with two ruminants, the goat and the sheep. The present-day distributions of wild (that is, nondomesticated) forms of these plants and animals are shown in Figures 30-2 and 30-3; their distributions when domestication was incipient, of course, may have been somewhat different, especially in that one or more of them may have thriven also further south, towards or into the Arabian peninsula. Wherever the earliest steps towards domesti-

BY HIS BOOTSTRAPS

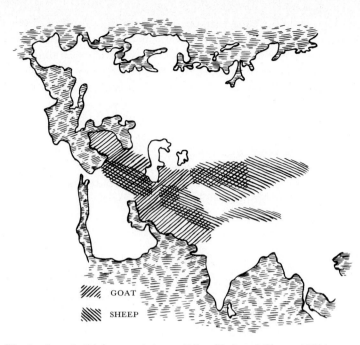

FIGURE 30-3. Distribution of wild goats and sheep. (After Clark and Piggott 1965.)

```
GOAT
SHEEP
```

cation were actually taken, by 7000 or 6000 B.C. all four species were being tended throughout the area.

By that date the dog had also appeared, but it may have come in from elsewhere already in partly domesticated form. We do not know what the earliest dogs in the region were used for, if anything, but eventually they were put to work at various tasks, such as helping in the care of sheep.

What had been successful with grains was tried with other familiar food plants, adding lentils, peas, and beans to the list of crops. These by no means exhaust southwest Asia's contribution to the modern world's vegetable diet, as a glance at Table 29-1 (p. 445) will show. But the dating of the others (lettuce, spinach, musk-melon, olive, pomegranate, grapevine, some cabbages and mustards, chick-peas, apples, plums, almonds, cherries, celery, carrot, rye, leek) is uncertain and in some cases probably much more recent.

Similarly, the techniques of handling goats and sheep were extended, with trial-and-error adaptation, to other familiar animals, bringing pigs into the barnyard and oxen into the pasture. The earliest domesticated animals (except perhaps the dog) were used only for meat and hides. By 4000 B.C. other uses had appeared. Sheep and some goats were sheared for wool; goats and oxen, sometimes also sheep, were milked; male oxen were castrated to render them docile and usable as draft animals. As indicated earlier (p. 469: Çatal Hüyük), some of these practices may have been developing as early as 6000 B.C. in Anatolia.

The taming of oxen must have been particularly difficult. All domestic oxen except those with humps presumably derive from the now extinct *Bos primigenius,* a fearsome giant with a bad temper and dangerous horns, which once ranged over much of Europe and central Asia. Perhaps a smaller strain lived in southwest Asia, but even that would have been a far cry from the sheep and goats to which the early farmers had become accustomed. An enraged domestic bull ox is still nothing to fool around with. Although the taming was eventually successful, bad experiences left their mark, in the form of the ritual bull-baiting ceremonies of ancient Minoa (Crete) and of parts of the Spanish-speaking world today, and in the sacred status of cows among the Hindus. Also tied up with this in some way are surviving habitual constraints on the uses of oxen: only for dairy products, not for meat, in a large region of east Africa; only for meat, not for milk, in China and nearby; for both, but not prepared with the same tools and utensils nor served at the same meals, among some of the later inhabitants of southwest Asia, including the Jews.

THE DOG ✗ We interrupt our sequential survey of focal areas because we don't know where the dog comes from.

The kinship of the dog and the wolf is unmistakable—as indicated on page 293, they belong to the same real species despite separate official labels. A northern origin for the dog has been suspected because the wolf is preeminently a cold-climate animal. But cold climates were closer to the equator ten to twenty millennia ago than they are now, so that this line of reasoning does not hold up.

Wolves and dogs are more alike than we usually realize. We think of wolves in terms of tales of predation on livestock and of hungry packs chasing lonely travelers over arctic wastes. The tales are true. But feral dogs do these things too.[3] Moreover, the very fact that wolves sometimes hunt in packs is indicative of their social nature and high intelligence. They are pretty much like primates. Their diet, like that of preagricultural man, is meat by preference, but in a pinch they can eat anything we do. They live in bands which include six or eight adults; mating is often for life; all members of the group share in caring for the young. Relations within the band are amicable. An interloper from another band is regarded with suspicion and usually driven off. They have nucleated territoriality, and indulge in extensive scent marking with urine of important places in their territory.

Whether two wolves are friends or enemies depends largely on whether or not they know each other. It appears that the same holds for a wolf and a human being. There are stories of abandoned human infants being adopted and cared for by wolves. A few of these stories are well documented. The mythical ones at least attest to some degree of ambivalence in human attitudes towards wolves, as does the widespread Old World belief in the werewolf, a creature that bears the guise of a man by day but sometimes assumes that of a wolf by night. This doctrine of lycanthropy is a veiled recognition of a dual nature shared by the two species: benign or malignant

[3]It is convenient to distinguish between *wild* 'not domesticated' and *feral* 'escaped from domestication'.

depending on circumstances and sometimes switching without notice from the one to the other.

Wherever wolves and hunting or livestock-keeping people have lived in proximity, they have been in competition for food. This competition, however, has been much like that between two wolf bands or between two human bands in comparable circumstances. Occasionally it has given way to cooperation. A band may adopt a young member of another band, who then grows up regarding those around him as friends, all outsiders—people or wolves—as aliens. The human infant raised by wolves does not long survive being weaned, through no fault of his foster family but because his anatomy and physiology cannot adapt to the wolf way of life (for example, it is pretty tough for *Homo sapiens,* with his miniaturized jaw and teeth, to eat raw flesh). The wolf cub raised by people does better. So the domestication of people by wolves never got off the ground, but the domestication of wolves by people was in time eminently successful.

The puzzle about dogs is where and when wolves were first domesticated. The solution is probably that they came under human care, in the way we have described, independently in many different places over a period of perhaps many thousands of years.

Dogs did not accompany Upper Pleistocene man in his earliest spread into Great Australia or the Americas, but they arrived in both places well before the dawn of the ethnographic present. Like hafted tools, they did not reach Tasmania. Otherwise they have lived wherever man has lived for at least the last 5000 years. The dingo of Australia is a feral dog that arrived about 6000 B.C. and was then partly redomesticated. Some experts think that certain other dog strains may stem, not from the gray wolf, but from more southerly lupine types: the jackal (*Canis aureus*) of Eurasia, the coyote (*C. latrans*) of North America. In any case, human intervention, planned or unplanned, has produced hundreds of different breeds, ranging in size from some larger than any extant wolf to some that can be held in the palm of the hand, of greatly varying shapes, colorations, and temperaments, and used in one place or another for everything, except milking, that any domestic animal can be used for: meat and hides, herding, hunting, retrieving, guarding, traction, burden, companionship, and show.

✘ When the folks in southwest Asia were first fooling around with barley and wheat, **CENTRAL EURASIA** it may still have been too cold a thousand miles farther north for similar experiments to meet with any success. As it grew warmer, crops and techniques moved northwards, forestalling any opportunity for independent invention, though, of course, permitting the transfer of methods to other plants and doubtless developing distinctive strains of some of the imported ones because of differences of soil and climate or through cross-pollination with local wild varieties. Some of the following surely originated in this second focal area, and all of them may have: certain peas and beans, buckwheat, pears, onions, garlic, shallots, turnips and rutabaga, Chinese cabbage, and perhaps hemp (but see p. 478).

However, when we speak of central Eurasia as a focal area the reference is primarily to animal husbandry. Wolves may have been domesticated here before the dog was known in southwest Asia, and this is probably the home of the horse and of the Bactrian (two-humped) camel.

THE HORSE

Wild horses ranged over much of more northerly Eurasia during the Pleistocene, and were one of the animals hunted by the Neanderthaloids and the earliest true humans. One variety, the tarpan, survived in desolate parts of Europe through the Middle Ages and finally disappeared only about A.D. 1900. The only wild horse extant today is Przhevalski's horse (assigned by taxonomists to *Equus przewalskii* instead of to *E. caballus,* but obviously the same real species). This animal lives now in the plains to either side of the Altai Mountains in Mongolia, but is fast disappearing as a separate type because humans are intentionally interbreeding it with local domesticated horses. A few thousand years ago it may have inhabited a much larger territory.

The preceding paragraph summarizes the biogeographical evidence. The archaeological testimony comes from much farther south, and is not decisive. About 3000 B.C. the Sumerians overran and took control of lower Mesopotamia (the valley between the Tigris and Euphrates Rivers in what is now Iraq). They had land sleds and wheeled carts, and for a while used as a draft animal an equine which may have been a domesticated form either of the tarpan or of the ass (*Equus asinus*). The identification is from carvings, and is uncertain. But the Sumerians came in from the north, and if they did not bring their equines with them they may anyway have arrived bearing the notion of exploiting horselike animals in this fashion. Before long, the horse (or ass) disappears from the Sumerian record, to reappear in southwest Asia only a thousand years later, this time in Anatolia.[4] While no exact locus of origin is indicated, it is significant that the subsequent evidence in southwest Asia shows the animal moving generally from north to south.

So central Eurasia is a good educated guess as the home of the domesticated horse.

The spread of the animal to other parts of the world postdated by many thousands of years that of the dog, and in the Old World was generally preceded by that of goats, sheep, pigs, and oxen. Through southwest Asia, the horse reached Africa, India, and parts of southern Europe. It moved directly from its original territory, rather than via southwest Asia, westwards into northern and western Europe, and eastwards into China. It reached the New World, Australia and Tasmania, and Oceania only a few centuries ago on European ships.

We should speak of the spread of horse culture rather than that of the domesticated horse itself. Whenever the notion of domestication reached a region where wild horses were still to be found, new wild stock was captured and interbred with imported domestic specimens to increase the supply. Conversely, at various times and places some animals have escaped and become feral. This happened early in the period of

---

[4]The disappearance is just as mystifying if the animal was an ass. Wild asses live in a broad belt from notheastern Africa to Tibet. Domesticated ones seem to derive from a northeastern African type. The time, place, and circumstances of first domestication are unknown.

Spanish exploration and exploitation both in the North American Plains and in the pampas of Argentina, and in both places the Indians redomesticated the feral animals, possibly but not certainly without any European model or guidance (p. 161).

The variety of types that the horse has by now developed in response to varied human demands is exceeded only by the diversity of dog breeds (p. 473). However, some of the uses we think of as basic actually developed late. For a long time—except in central Eurasia itself—the animal was the prerogative of kings and soldiers. First it pulled war chariots; later, when riding was invented, it carried warriors, official messengers, tax collectors, and aristocratic hunters. The peasant's animal of draft and burden was the ox. If he rode, it was on an ox or astride an ass. Just as the sons of kings often disported themselves with the daughters of peasants, so the horses of aristocrats from time to time got together with the asses of the lowly, resulting in mules and hinnies (p. 293). These halfbreeds were not fine enough animals to interest the rulers, but peasants found them stronger than asses and put them to work. The use of the horse as a farm animal, to pull a plow or to carry a cowboy, began only about a millennium ago with the invention of the horsecollar (p. 611), and has remained commonest in Europe and in Europeanized America and Australia.

None of these reasons for horse culture, however, played a part in the original domestication. In central Eurasia there were, until quite recently, pastoral nomads such as the Kazakhs who relied heavily on the horse as a source of meat, milk, and various nondietary products. They also used goats, sheep, and other domesticated animals of ultimate southwest Asiatic origin, but a few centuries ago some bands probably had a way of life totally dependent on the horse. In a similar way, there are tribes in eastern and southern Africa (the Nuer and other Nilotic tribes of the Sudan; the Zulu) which live intimately and single-mindedly with herds of oxen. Now, because of other evidence, we do not infer from the later fact that the domestication of oxen began in Africa or that the African way of using oxen was the pattern at the time of their first domestication. But in the case of the horse the available evidence converges towards such an inference. We believe that the horse was first domesticated in central Eurasia, very slowly over a long period of time, the process developing along the lines set forth earlier (p. 461): it began with hunters concentrating on an available and abundant game animal, and ended with the people caring for and breeding the same animal. Meat, milk, hides, bones for tools, and so on—uses of the horse alien to us in the Western world today—were the original motivations. Other uses developed later, mostly elsewhere, though some of them in time spread back into the original region. Anything like the original pattern of use has survived only in the area in which it began.

CAMELS

Some of the recent pastoral peoples of central Eurasia keep two-humped camels, which they treat much as they treat horses: for example, kumiss, an alcoholic drink, is made by fermenting milk from either a mare or a she-camel. The only Bactrian camels today that do not live with human beings are small herds in the Gobi Desert in Mongolia, and there is some question whether they are wild or feral. But that is all the evidence we have, and it points, however weakly, to central Eurasia as the site of original domestication. For the one-humped camel we have no clues at all other than its present distribution in domesticated form: Arabia and northern Africa. Original domestication in Arabia is as good a guess as any.

Camels do not have a stomach structure as complex as that of ruminants, but they do chew the cud. They can eat almost anything, and can imbibe a vast quantity of water at a single time. The humps consist of surplus food stored as fat. When fresh rations are unavailable, the stored fat is not only drawn on for energy but also oxidized to supply needed water. These arrangements explain the special merit of camels: that they can travel for a long time through either hot, dry territory (for this the one-humped species is better) or cold, dry lands (for which the Bactrian is preferable) with little fresh food and with no water at all.

The regions of exploitation of camels have remained those for which this merit qualifies them, and to which they could spread without traversing much territory of other sorts. There are fine deserts in southern Africa, Australia, and North America. If Columbus had been an Arab rather than a European, and if somehow he had landed in Lower California instead of in the Caribbean, perhaps caravans of majestic, smelly Ships of the Desert would now be crisscrossing Sonora and New Mexico. In actual history, one feeble effort was made in the 1850s to introduce camels into the American Southwest; its failure probably reflects not any inability of the camel to adapt but lack of adequate human motivation.

REINDEER

For many centuries there have been, in the Old World arctic from Lapland to Bering Strait, human communities living in complete interdependence with herds of reindeer. The domestication of reindeer may have been a late transfer to a new animal of the central Eurasian pattern of horse-use. However, there are authorities who believe that the reindeer was man's first domesticated animal (other than the dog), so that the transfer—if there was one—would have been much earlier and in the other direction.

CENTRAL CHINA ✗ The northwestern quadrant of China is a plateau composed largely of loess: fine particles torn from rocky surfaces by the wind and deposited in layers that can be hundreds of feet thick. There are scattered marshes, but in general the region is rather dry, and the soil is alkaline. Tree are rare. Most of the vegetation is herbaceous, with types similar to the sage brush of western North America. These conditions have pertained at least since the end of the Late Würm.

The Wei River flows from west to east through the southern part of the plateau. At 34°45′ N, 110°20′ E it meets the upper Yellow River, flowing from the north; from the confluence the (lower) Yellow River moves for a while due east before it turns, fans out into the vast alluvial plains of northeastern China, and empties into the Gulf of Chihli.

There is a cluster of archaeological sites in the region of the confluence, in northern

Honan, southern Shansi, and eastern Shensi (one outlying site is far to the northwest in Kansu). They attest to an early farming way of life the specialists call "Yang Shao."

The sites are on loess terraces or mounds, mostly near minor tributaries rather than along the major rivers. Farmers were living in settled villages, their houses built first over excavated pits but later completely above the ground. At one site (Pan P'o near the city Sian) there is evidence of a defensive ditch. The farming was intensive and probably involved fertilizing and crop (or field) rotation, but no irrigation. The staple was millet, a grain we have not mentioned before. We do not know how they turned the soil, but loess is easily worked with the simplest sort of wooden digging stick. They had dogs and pigs, doubtless eating both to supplement the venison obtained by hunting. They had pottery, much of it rough utilitarian ware but some with pictures of animals or with geometric designs. Pan P'o shows the ruins of six pottery kilns.

These finds have not yet been dated by modern direct methods, but indirect procedures give an interesting result. The Yang Shao pattern was succeeded in various parts of China by one called "Lung Shan," and a derivative of the latter is known from a Taiwan site with direct dating to about 2500 B.C. Working backwards, this puts mainland Lung Shan not later than 3000 B.C., and the origins of Yang Shao probably in the fifth millennium B.C. Maybe no known Yang Shao site retains relics that old, but the established way of life shown by the excavations must have a long period of earlier development behind it.

Independent or Derivative?

By the date we have just given, the early farming system of southwest Asia could have spread all the way to central China, by any of several routes. But the Yang Shao pattern is quite different. The typical early crops and animals of the southwest Asia focal area (wheat, barley, sheep, goats) do not appear in China until the Lung Shan period.

Another conceivable external source is India, which for a long time now has shared certain domesticated species with China. Close scrutiny of the evidence suggests that many of these passed from China to India rather than vice versa (though some may have been developed independently in both places). The evidence of written records is much later, yet it is perhaps significant that millet is mentioned in early Chinese written records considerably before it turns up in those of India. The Sanskrit word for 'millet' is *cīnaka*, a derivative of Sanskrit *cīna* 'China'. (The Persian word for 'millet', incidentally, is clearly a loan from the Chinese term.)

We conclude—of course, not with certainty—that the farming pattern of central China began there or nearby, in complete independence of comparable developments elsewhere. Millet grows well in relatively dry and alkaline soil and still grows wild (not feral) on the loess plateau. It was domesticated and became the staple. Both pigs and dogs may well have been domesticated locally. That each of these three species also passed into domestication elsewhere (millet in Africa: p. 480) has no particular bearing on the case.

It has also been argued, with considerable cogency, that this focal area was a locus of independent domestication of sorghum, rice, and hemp. There is possible evidence for all three in Yang Shao sites. Sorghum, like millet, prospers in dry, alkaline soil. Rice would have grown, rather, in the scattered marshes, gathered wild before the habit of planting it appeared. It became of major importance only as agriculture moved east and southeast into alluvial areas with monsoon seasons and as irrigation was added to the agricultural technology. A pottery vessel from a Yang Shao site shows the imprint of some sort of cordage, and hemp seems to be the only fiber plant indigenous to the region.

SUBSEQUENT DEVELOPMENTS

Other typical Chinese crops came considerably later: the mulberry and silk culture, tea (from Szechwan?), some types of cabbages, apricot, peach, litchee. The soya bean apparently emerged in northeastern China, and only shortly before the eleventh century B.C. Before its use, the diet of farmers in China had included no proteinaceous plant comparable to the beans, peas, and lentils exploited from very early times in the West. This, and the fact that there was relatively little meat in their diet, are reflected by the skeletal remains of pre-soya times, which show many early deaths and a prevalence of protein-deficiency diseases.

SOUTHEASTERN ASIA ✖ If this focal area be defined to include the parts of southeastern Asia characterized by monsoon seasons (which also typify peninsular and insular southeastern Asia in a more restricted sense), then recent archaeological discoveries in Taiwan are of potential relevance. They point to some raising of domesticated plants as early as 8000 B.C., 5000 years earlier than the spread of the Lung Shan farming pattern to the island from the Chinese mainland (p. 477). The details of the possible early plant domestication in Taiwan are not yet known.

It is also necessary to suspend judgment about the other excavated evidence in the area: from Spirit Cave, 35 miles north of Mae Hong Son in Thailand. If the claims of the excavators are verified, our views of the history of plant domestication may be in for surprising revision. But the issues have still to be resolved.

Biogeographical considerations, unsupported as yet by any particularly early archaeology, strongly point to southeastern Asia as the original home of a set of domesticates now of wide importance: the pig (independent of its domestication elsewhere); chickens, ducks, and geese; and the citrus fruits—orange, lemon, lime, citron, shaddock, kumquat. If the culture of these species started in lower southeastern Asia it spread early to the south China coast, which then served as a secondary center of dispersion. The kumquat belongs to a separate genus and may have started in south China. The tangerine is a specialized orange probably developed in south China: in the 1930s and 1940s growers of tangerines in Florida were importing pollen from southern China as the only way to make their fruit sweet. The grapefruit is probably a specialized offshoot of the shaddock, developed in Jamaica a few centuries ago. Another Jamaican derivative or hybrid is the ugli, not yet grown elsewhere but found distinctive and tasty by some people.

Southeastern Asia can put in a good claim for mango, taro, elephant's ear, yam (independently of Africa: p. 480), banana, betel, and coconut. India has solid grounds for disputing priority for some of these, and the coconut may have come originally, instead, from tropical America, halfway around the world.

That many "spices" have their origins in southeastern Asia or nearby is suggested by the early Western habit of referring to the East Indies as the "Spice Islands." However, the exploitation of particular plants for pungent parts need not imply selective breeding or cultivation. More important is sugarcane, which seems unquestionably to have evolved from some cereal predecessor only in New Guinea and to have been exploited and reduced to cultivation there before man carried it anywhere else. There are enthusiasts who believe sugarcane was part of a horticultural complex that arose in New Guinea with no prompting from outside, and of course they may be right.

An important reason for the proposal that domestication in southeastern Asia arose independently is that the pattern is so different from that elswhere. The cereal grains of southwest Asia led before long, not to the horizon-touching "amber waves of grain" now to be seen in the plains of Kansas and the Ukraine, which are a modern development dependent on sophisticated farm machinery, but at least to the clearing and plowing of sizable fields, or to the use of natural level areas along river bottoms; our word *agriculture* derives indirectly from Latin *ager* 'field'. The millet-planting of early central China also involved devoting an expanse of an acre or so to a single crop. The southeastern Asian custom must have been more like what we call "gardening" or *horticulture* (Latin *hortus* 'garden patch'), with rows or clumps of different crops close together, perhaps under trees or shrubs whose products were also used and which in due time were also planted.

✘ Several millennia after its origins, domestication of the southwest Asia type invaded three great river valleys and was differentially adapted to their diverse demands: the valley of the Tigris and Euphrates, northwest of the Persian Gulf; the valley and delta of the Nile in northeastern Africa; and the valley of the Indus, which empties into the Arabian Sea just southeast of Karachi. **AFRICA**

It is interesting to note that these obviously fertile places were not the *birthplaces* of agriculture—perhaps because they provided opportunity without need, just as frozen wastes and hot deserts provide need without opportunity. One can suspect that agriculture moved into them as other parts of the area were getting embarrassingly dry. At least, it is surely the case that agriculture survived in them after progressive desiccation had rendered it difficult or impossible elsewhere. All three river valleys can validly be regarded as integral parts of the southwest Asia focal area. At the same time, the Indus valley was a gateway to India, and the Nile had to be either crossed or followed to reach the rest of Africa.[5]

The latter concerns us here. The arrival of the southwest Asia farming complex

[5] Provided the migration routes were overland. By water, north Africa west of Egypt could have been reached through the Mediterranean, and northeastern Ethiopia is only a short hop from southwestern Arabia across the Bab el Mandeb.

in Egypt is heralded, in the archaeological record, by the appearance of wheat in 4600 B.C. in the Fayyum (a short tributary to the Nile Valley). Subsequently, some of the domesticates of Egypt are alien to the earlier southwest Asia pattern and are either local contributions or came in from other directions. Sesame is one of these; the cucumber is another (though for the latter, northern India also puts in a claim: p. 482). Our first record of the house cat is from ancient Egypt. It was used as a mouser and was worshiped. Its wild antecedent was perhaps the Lybian *Felis lybica* (but Persian and Siamese cats may have different ancestries, and the tailless Manx still another). The pigeon, used originally only for food, appears first in Egypt about 3000 B.C. If the evidence is reliable, Egypt was also the home of the notion, later carried far and wide by Jews and Muslims, that the pig is unclean and not to be eaten.

BEYOND EGYPT

For the enormous remainder of Africa, the big question is whether domestication started independently in one or more places or arose only under the impetus of influence from southwest Asia. This is currently under debate by the specialists, and one can find strong opinions in both directions.

A point to remember is that the Sahara, now a desert with crop-raising only possible in very limited and scattered spots, was more abundantly watered until as recently as three or four thousand years ago.[6] It is obvious that some domesticates, and some features of the technology of domestication, spread both westwards from Egypt along the Mediterranean shore and southwards up the Nile to parts of equatorial east Africa. For example, the date palm, apparently of Arabian origin, was widespread in the Sahara by 5000 B.C. The point at issue is only whether, in this expansion, southwest Asian domestication met and mingled with (and perhaps submerged) indigenous habits of a comparable sort.

Without resolving the question we can name the crops. Ethiopia (or some adjacent region) is believed to have developed millet and perhaps sorghum in parallel with central China, may have cultivated barley independently of southwest Asia, and is the home of coffee. The African lotus and the jujube are widespread; one variety of the latter was probably the "lotus" of antiquity, mentioned by the Greeks. When Asiatic yams were brought to tropical west Africa (by the Portuguese?) they were an addition to a number of African species, some of which had been under cultivation for a long time.

Also in west Africa, a rice is grown that belongs to a species different from that of all the other cultivated rice in the world (*Oryza glaberrima* instead of *O. sativa*). Okra was introduced into ancient Egypt from somewhere further south and west, and into the New World in early post-Columbian times from west Africa. Sesame, though first attested in Egypt, may not have started there. The watermelon, the castor plant (whence beans and oil), and the kola tree (from which nuts and a liquid extract) are today widely known, the akee (p. 263) somewhat less so.

Not generally known outside of Africa, but of importance there in various localities,

---

[6]Compare the situation during the much earlier Aterian period (p. 437). It is not clear whether there were earlier periods of dryness between Aterian times and the present.

are a number of others: the Hausa potato, malaguetta pepper, Guinea hemp, the shea-butter tree, an oil palm (*Elaeis guineensis*), the Doum palm, and the baobab.

Some of these species, such as yams, are confirmedly tropical, but others look like they might be refugees from a formerly damper Sahara. A few survive at oases and at favorable spots along the Mediterranean shore. The fig may be of Mediterranean rather than southwest Asian origin.

Africa's contributions to animal domestication include guinea fowl, ostriches, and elephants. Ostriches once lived wild in Arabia as well as Africa, but are now confined to Africa. Ostrich farming for plumes and eggs began in eastern and southern Africa only a century or so ago. African elephants served in the Carthaginian army under Hannibal around 200 B.C., but there are no traces of domestication thereafter until Belgians, following the pattern of India (p. 482), went to work in the Congo in the 1890s.

EUROPE

THE EARLY SPREAD OF OLD WORLD DOMESTICATION

The known archaeological record in Europe is relatively full. It shows, without much question, that as the extensive glaciers of the Late Würm receded in the north and from the flanks of the Alps, crops, domesticated animals, and the basic technologies of agriculture and animal husbandry moved in from elsewhere—largely from southwest Asia, partly from central Eurasia. Probably the Europeans of the time already had dogs. Of course, they added new plants to the agricultural roster: rye more in the south, oats more in the colder west and north, and (with many uncertainties as to exact place and date) artichokes, new types of onions, flax (probably Mediterranean), capers, horseradish, parsnips, parsley, beet and chard.

The matter of oats and rye is interesting. Let us distinguish between a crop and a weed. These are anthropological terms, not botanical: a crop is any plant you want; a weed is a naughty plant, one that gets in your way or may injure you. The domestication of plants by humans means human interference in the careers of both crops and weeds, though intendedly in opposite directions. Now, neither oats nor rye are indigenous to northern and western Europe. It is thought that they grew mixed in with wheat and barley in southwest Asia, where they were regarded as weeds and efforts were made to eradicate them. The efforts were not wholly successful, so that the seeds carried to and sown in new territory were also mixed. In time, fields were planted where wheat and barley would grow only poorly but the other two could prosper. The change from one climate to another sorted the grains out; farmers accepted the result because there was nothing else they could do; and the merits of oats and rye were then discovered. Wheat remained rare in Europe until the recent past. In the Middle Ages, wheat bread was beyond the means of any except aristocrats. Poorer folks used more "plebeian" grains.

SOUTH ASIA

Western Europe is a small peninsular projection from the main Eurasian land mass. The Indian subcontinent is another, actually of about the same size. There is no positive evidence for an independent origin of domestication in India, but there is also no positive evidence against it (as there is in the case of Europe). Thus, considering our uncertainty about Africa, it may have been unjust to mention the latter but exclude India in our listing of focal areas (p. 466).

It is clear that domestication of the southwest Asia type spread to the Indus Valley, in part (perhaps) along the seacoast, in part by moving east and south from the Caspian through Afghanistan. There are sites in the vicinity of Quetta, in the hills to the northwest of the valley, attesting to the raising of grain and the grazing of sheep and goats in the fourth millennium B.C., earlier by at least centuries than the oldest evidences of farming in the valley itself. These sites also show humped cattle. Humped cattle are *Bos indicus,* in contrast to the oxen (*B. taurus*) of further west, and may not be derivatives of the *B. primigenius* from which oxen are assumed to be derived. A separate line of domestication, perhaps partly independent, seems probable.

In the valley itself, archaeologists have excavated the sites of several dozen villages (there are evidences of many more) and of two large cities, Mohenjo-Daro and, 400 miles away to the northeast, Harappa. The earliest known spun cotton was found at Mohenjo-Daro, and dates from about 3000 B.C.

The Indus Valley agricultural complex was at its peak about 2500 B.C., by which time some of its ingredients seem to have spread considerably farther east and south. Meanwhile, one assumes, other domesticated species and practices were moving into the subcontinent through northern Burma, Assam, and Bengal, with both central China and southeastern Asia as their ultimate sources. If one assumes no independent indigenous contribution, which may be a mistake, nevertheless something distinctively Indian emerged as these diverse traditions came together and adjusted to one another and to local ecological conditions.

Typically Indian domesticated plants include not only cotton but also a pepper (from the north), cowpeas, cinnamon (nowadays mainly from Ceylon) and other spices, and possibly the cucumber. Rice may have been brought under cultivation here independently of events in early central China, and millet and sorghum independently of either China or Africa.

In addition to humped cattle, domesticated animals include water buffalo, elephants, peafowl, and the honeybee. The Indian way of using bovine animals may have diffused to yield the Tibetan exploitation of the yak, that of the gayal in northern Burma and Thailand, and that of the banteng in some parts of Burma but more widely far off in Java and Borneo. Peafowl are from southern India and from Ceylon; their fame spread westwards early enough for the peacock to be featured at sumptuous banquets of the aristocrats of ancient Rome.

HONEY

Human beings have gathered honey from time immemorial. Beekeeping, on the other hand, requires specialized techniques and probably emerged much more recently. Two places of origin are suggested by the fact that the bees of India and southeastern Asia (*Apis dorsata, A. florea,* and *A. indica*) are all of species different from the European *A. mellifera.*

We do not know where European beekeeping began. A number of the words of apiculture can be traced back to Proto Indo-European, and although we don't know exactly where this language was spoken we know it wasn't in western or southern Europe or in India (pp. 590–600). One of the words we can reconstruct is the ancestral form of modern English *mead*, the name of a formerly popular alcoholic beverage made by fermenting honey; but the original meaning of the word was 'honey'. The history of this word suggests how apiculture got to China and Japan, from farther west rather than from the south. An Indo-European language called Tokharian was spoken in Chinese Turkestan between A.D. 500 and 700, maybe also earlier. The word was borrowed from Tokharian into Chinese as something like *mīt*. You don't borrow such a word without reason: the inference is that the Chinese were getting features of apiculture from the Tokharians too. The Chinese word was then borrowed into Japanese, to yield eventually the modern Japanese *mitsu* 'honey'; within Chinese it came down as modern Mandarin *mì* with the same meaning.

The Old World Periphery

To complete this survey of the early spread of domestication in the Old World we shall begin in the northwest and proceed counterclockwise around the periphery, itemizing what is known of the movement of farming away from the Eurasian-African mainland to islands.

(1) THE BRITISH ISLES.   Though already separated from the mainland by the time agriculture and animal husbandry moved into western Europe, the short stretches of water constituted no barrier. Domesticators arrived in Great Britain by about 3000 B.C., in Ireland not later than 2500 B.C.

(2) ICELAND.   Northwestern European seafarers discovered this island as early as the fourth century A.D. In the early ninth century a few Irish holy men came in search of isolation, which they lost as serious settlement began from western Norway in 874. This constituted the earliest expansion of our species into Iceland, and the settlers were already not only fishermen, herders, and farmers, but also users of metals, including iron.

(3) THE CANARY ISLANDS lie in the eastern Atlantic; Fuerteventura, the one closest to Africa, is only about 60 miles from Cap Juby in Morocco. They were settled by Berbers, akin to the Berbers, Riffians, Shluh, and Kabyles of the western and northwestern Sahara. As in the case of Iceland, the first settlers were already farmers; unlike the first Icelanders, they had no metallurgy. This is our main clue as to the date. Metallurgy was reaching the farmers of the western Sahara in Roman times, around 2000 years ago. The migration to the islands cannot have been much more recent than that.

The islands could not have been reached without boats. But the art of boat-making subsequently disappeared both on the mainland and on the islands, in the latter case—if for no other reason—because the Canaries supply no stone of the sort needed for making polished stone axes for cutting and shaping timber. The marooned islanders made do with what they had brought along, which included wheat, barley, beans, figs, dogs, sheep, goats, and pigs, but no oxen. When the Spanish took over in the fifteenth century A.D., the dwellers on each of the seven islands had been isolated, perhaps for a millennium, not only from the rest of the human world but even from their kindred on the other six.

(4) MADAGASCAR. The early human history of this island is obscure. There is little question but that people from the African mainland have arrived from time to time, but we do not know when this began. There is no evidence that any such arriving group of Africans brought farming with them.

Nor is any language of Madagascar related to those of Africa. Instead, all dialects are of the Malagasy language, which belongs to the Malayo-Polynesian family and is most closely related to certain Malayo-Polynesian languages of western Indonesia, thousands of miles to the east across the Indian Ocean. This is absolutely indicative of an invasion from western Indonesia, and the farming pattern of Madagascar looks like a derivative of that of western Indonesia.

The only educated guess I have seen of this is that the invaders arrived early in the first millennium A.D. and that they came from Borneo. This is just the period when events in Indonesia were being strongly affected by the spread of Hindu culture (p. 605). The requirement of extensive ocean travel need give no pause, for (as we shall shortly see) an effective seafaring technology was by this date well established in insular southeastern Asia.

(5) CEYLON. Early events here are as hidden from us as are those on the adjacent mainland (p. 482). Maybe farming came in only with the Sinhalese, speakers of an Indo-European language who arrived, possibly from northeastern India, before 1000 B.C. But the Veddas, who preceded them, may have had some.

(6) OCEANIA. By this term we mean to exclude most of Indonesia, along with New Guinea, Australia, and Tasmania, and to subsume only Micronesia, Melanesia, Polynesia, and New Zealand. It may help in trying to grasp the nature of this territory to point out that Micronesia has a total land area only 1214 square miles, about that of Rhode Island, but that this is scattered in tiny bits over a watery expanse whose area is larger than that of the contiguous continental United States. Melanesia is about the same size, but with larger islands. Polynesia is much larger; its islands, except those of the Hawaii group, are small.

We do not know much of the settlement history. We do know that there were various secondary centers of dispersion: for example, it was from somewhere in central Polynesia (by tradition from Bora-Bora) that expeditions set forth in outrigger canoes and reached Hawaii in the north, New Zealand in the southwest, and such places as Tahiti and beyond in the east. This phase of scattering was late, taking place perhaps around one thousand years ago, but legends in both Hawaii and New Zealand hold that the new arrivals from central Polynesia encountered predecessors whom they proceeded to conquer.

Before people could spread out from Bora-Bora they had to get there, and linguistic evidence suggests that they arrived as one part of a much earlier series of dispersions that had its ultimate source somewhere in Melanesia. Melanesia, in its turn, seems to have received early settlers from two different places. The first, maybe quite ancient, was of "Papuans," people akin to the earliest invaders of Great Australia, who moved northeastwards from New Guinea. Later, speakers of Malayo-Polynesian languages arrived from some unidentified and perhaps unidentifiable part of insular southeastern Asia (Indonesia). All the attested languages of subsequent times in Polynesia and New Zealand, Micronesia, and Melanesia are Malayo-Polynesian, except for a few spoken in Melanesian islands close to New Guinea. A few of those in Micronesia, however, seem to have Philippine affinities (also Malayo-Polynesian, but a different branch), so that a separate wave of migrants may have come into Micronesia from the Philippines or perhaps from Borneo.

Thus, by working backwards, we have reached an indefinite place in insular southeastern Asia and an indefinite time almost certainly earlier than 2000 B.C. By then there was a well established pattern of horticulture and animal husbandry throughout southeastern Asia, combining indigenous features with imports from China and India.[7] The invaders of Oceania were good sailors to begin with and became better ones. The Polynesians, in particular, were remarkable preliterate masters of celestial navigation. They often set out in double canoes one hundred or more feet in length, heading for a known destination thousands of miles away. Probably many such an expedition ended at the bottom of the sea. Some were carried off course and took people to new islands. But there is reliable evidence that some of these voyages ended exactly according to plan.

Wherever they went, the invaders of Oceania carried their domesticates with them: pigs, dogs, and chickens; taro, yams, coconut, breadfruit, bananas. At the time of first European contact, the distribution of the three domesticated animals was spotty, one or two of the three missing from some of the islands. This attests the irregularity of interisland contact and the danger of the voyages: the animals sometimes died—or were eaten—en route even when the people made successful landfall. On the other hand, coconuts may have reached some of the islands before people did. That would be possible, since the nuts, in their protective husks, can be transported across great stretches of ocean by the currents and still germinate when washed ashore.

No such mechanism can account for the presence of wild cotton of the New World type (p. 486) in Hawaii, nor for that of the sweet potato in many parts of Oceania, grown as a staple at altitudes too high for the successful cultivating of yams, taro, and the like. These are clear evidence for Polynesian visits to the Pacific shores of South America (p. 433).

The Polynesian voyagers knew how to protect their plants while in transit. On cold journeys, women hunched over day after day, clasping yams between their breasts to keep them warm. Otherwise their power to grow would have been destroyed, and the life of the yams was the life of the people.

(7) HAINANDAO AND TAIWAN.   The first of these is biogeographically and anthropologically part of the south China coast (p. 478). For Taiwan see page 478.

[7]The linguistic evidence fits. Proto Malayo-Polynesian, the parent language of all the Malayo-Polynesian languages, would have been spoken not much earlier than 2000 B.C.; many words for seafaring technology and several for domesticated animals can be reconstructed. Quite possibly the migrations began when population pressure, built up by good farming, could be relieved because effective deep-water transport had become available.

(8) JAPAN AND THE RYUKYUS.   Japan has been inhabited for at least 10,000 years, and some of the earliest sites show pottery. There are no signs of tillage until between 2000 and 1000 B.C., and what then appears is akin to that nearby on the mainland. The Ryukyus were first settled from Taiwan; Japanese speakers, bearing agriculture, arrived perhaps a thousand years ago.

SUMMARY

When the movements we have just outlined were complete, the unconverted hunters-and-gatherers of the Old World had been crowded into the outlying spots shown in Figure 30-4.

That is not all. The conquest of Oceania was the first major expansion of our species into new territory since the spread into Great Australia and the New World. And, except for the subsequent settlement of Iceland (p. 483), it was the terminal phase of our radiation, since when it was over the only uninhabited habitable land remaining anywhere on Earth's surface was in the form of a scattering of remote specks, such as Tristan da Cunha in the south Atlantic. From then on, people in search of a new home have had to displace or double up with predecessors.

THE WESTERN HEMISPHERE   ✘ For a change of pace we shall begin here with a tabulation of the domesticated plants and animals known to be of New World origin.

NEW WORLD DOMESTICATES

Squashes and pumpkins, avocados, maize, and the maguey plant (a source of fiber and of a juice which is fermented to make pulque, then—nowadays—distilled to produce tequila) are Mexican. So is vanilla, which may not have been used aboriginally.

Squashes and pumpkins may have emanated rather from Central America and northwestern South America, and this is more likely to have been the place of origin of the cocoa plant, of papaya, of New World beans, and of various peppers, including the chili.

The pimento may be from Central America, the Caribbean, or both. The gherkin is from the Caribbean.

The Andes region is the home of coca, oca, ulluco, tomato, Uruguay potato, and potato. Wild varieties of cotton grew widely in the New World; its earliest known exploitation for fibers was in the Andes.

Agave, another source of fiber and of a fermentable juice, is widespread but concentrates in Mexico and the Caribbean.

The largest single list of plants is of those originally from eastern South America: the Para rubber tree, cassava, guava, peanut, cashew, pineapple, and sweet potato. Of the ones used for food, some require careful processing to render them edible: the cashew must be roasted; for bitter cassava see page 407.

The turkey was domesticated by the Aztecs (those given the Pilgrims by the Massachusetts Indians for the first Thanksgiving were wild). Other than the turkey

FIGURE 30-4. Residual Old World hunters-and-gatherers after man's spread into Oceania.

and the dog, domesticated animals were confined to the Andes region. Indigenous there are several high-altitude specializations akin to Old World camels, and two of these, the llama and the alpaca, were used for wool and hides, for meat (the Incas ate llama meat only ceremonially), and as beasts of burden. They were not ridden or used for traction. The dried dung served as fuel. Perhaps because of their adaptation to heights, their use never spread far from their original homes. The Incas kept, bred, and ate guinea pigs.

The extremes of our knowledge of place of origin are the cases of the potato and of tobacco. The former has been pinned down to Chiloé Island off the coast in southern Chile. Related strains and species are grown in various nearby regions, but the Chiloé

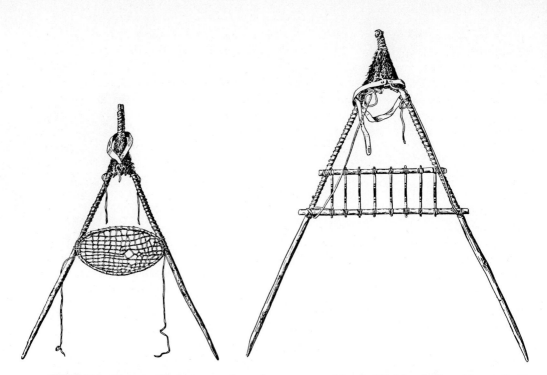

FIGURE 30-5. Travois. These are top views of two types used by the Blackfoot Indians. The smaller is a bit over 7 feet long, the larger more than 11 feet. A dog (or, in early European times, a horse) was harnessed at the point of the A; the burden was loaded on the webbed crossbar; the ends of the poles dragged on the ground. (From *Material Culture of the Blackfoot Indians,* by Clark Wissler, Anthropological Papers of the American Museum of Natural History, volume 5 part 1, 1910. Reproduced by permission of the American Museum of Natural History.)

Island type was the one carried to the rest of the world. For tobacco, we know only that its culture began in Central or South America rather than anywhere farther north than Mexico City.

The Spread of Agriculture

Agriculture moved northwards from central Mexico, in pre-Columbian times, in two prongs.

One prong, perhaps moving along the Gulf Coast of Mexico, reached the lower Mississippi Valley and the Southeast by about 1000 B.C., whence it fanned out to the northeast, north, and northwest in the form of the familiar maize-beans-squash-tobacco complex. We discussed this briefly in chapter 2 (p. 10). In most of the eastern United States agriculture remained strictly subordinate to hunting. There was no available draft animal except the dog, which was in fact used in certain regions of the northern Plains to pull lightly laden travois (Figure 30-5), but was never put to work at plowing or cultivating and perhaps could not have been.

The other prong was much earlier, and was simply an extension of agricultural practices in the highlands of western Mexico northwards into what is now the U.S. Southwest. This involved not only maize, beans, squash, and tobacco, but also chilis and other peppers and perhaps tomatoes.

In a similar way, by the time Columbus came along agricultural practices had spread in one form or another to almost all parts of Central America, some parts of the Caribbean, and through much of South America. At the dawn of the ethnographic present domestication remained unknown in northern North America, in a sizable part of southern South America, and probably among a scattering of isolated tribes in eastern and northeastern South America, the Caribbean, and Florida (see Figure 30–6).

Successful agriculture inevitably leads in time to major displacements of peoples. Some of the pre-Columbian movements that can be reconstructed from linguistic and archaeological evidence were probably instigated in this way. The great scattering of speakers of Arawakan languages in the Orinoco and Amazon basins and in the West Indies (p. 262) may have resulted from their being chased from one place after another by speakers of Cariban languages, and the movements of the Cariban speakers may well have been due to spreading agriculture—though by the ethnographic present some communities of both of these groups had themselves become agricultural.

ORIGINS

The question is whether New World domestication emanated from three original centers, from two, or even from just one.

Archaeology speaks for at least two: the highlands of central Mexico and somewhere in Peru. There are

> a group of sites in the Tehuacan Valley near Puebla . . . , representing over 9,000 years of human utilization of the area. The earlier inhabitants were hunters and gatherers of wild plant foods, but during the period roughly from 9,000 to 7,000 years ago they were growing a domesticated squash and avocados, and there are traces of other possible cultigens. However, such plants provided only an insignificant part of their diet. The people of the following stage (roughly 7,000 to 5,400 years ago) had ten kinds of domestic plants, including such future staples as maize and beans, but these are estimated to have supplied only 10 percent of their diet, which otherwise was obtained from hunting and from wild plants (available in great abundance), following a seasonal nomadic pattern of life. Only subsequently (approximately 5,400 to 4,300 years ago) did stable villages first appear and cultivated plants supply even 25 percent of the diet. Only two new species supplemented those previously known.[8]

Other Mexican sites have also been explored: in the Sierra de Tamaulipas to the north, the Sierra Madre to the northwest, and in Yucatán. What they reveal meshes well with the findings in the Tehuacán Valley.

Let the same voice now speak to us of Peru:

> The earliest known populations on the arid northern coast of Peru [in the Chicama Valley] no more than 6,000 years ago, already led a fairly stable existence based on the

[8] From Chester S. Chard, *Man in Prehistory*, p. 193. The second excerpt is from pages 193–194. Copyright 1969 by McGraw-Hill Book Company. Used with permission of McGraw-Hill Book Company.

FIGURE 30-6. New World hunters-and-gatherers at the dawn of the ethnographic present.

resources of the sea and wild plants, but grew lima beans and gourds, the latter apparently only as containers or net floats and not as food. After about 4,500 years ago they were growing, in addition, cotton, chile, and two kinds of squash but still living primarily off the sea, which made fairly large villages possible. Full time agriculture arose only during approximately the last 750 years before the time of Christ, and was marked by the arrival from outside of a number of important staple crops including maize, potatoes, and manioc.

In Mexico we have been remarkably lucky: it looks as though the archaeologists managed to dig exactly in a region where domestication arose with no outside help, and to uncover a set of horizons that reveal many successive steps in the slow process. In Peru, what the sites show seems rather to be people accepting certain domesticates from elsewhere and using them as supplements to an economic arrangement based mainly on fishing, hunting, and gathering. Maize reached these early Peruvians only three or four thousand years after its earliest known appearance in the Tehuacán Valley. Their potatoes, acquired about the same time, point south; their manioc (cassava) points east; their earlier lima beans and gourds probably were growing wild in the area as the notion of cultivating them either developed or came in from some closely adjacent region. In any case, the timing militates against any proposal that Peruvian cultivation was totally the result of influences spreading south from Mexico.

Evidence for a third focal area independent of the first two, one somewhere in the damp tropics, is less definite. Tropical river basins are not likely places for successful archaeology: things rot away too fast. Furthermore, such lush regions are often so full of food that efforts towards domestication are unnecessary. A third independent focal area in the Americas would have to have been some region marginal to the Amazon and Orinoco basins, where useful tropical plants, known to and wanted by the inhabitants, grew poorly unless helped along. We do not know the timing. It is thus possible that the habit of trying to help did not arise independently in such a region but reached it from the Andes or from Mexico.

31

✖

NEW ARTIFACTS FOR OLD

"The time has come," the Walrus[1] said,
"To talk[2] of many things:
Of shoes[3] and ships[4] and sealing-wax,[5]
Of cabbages[6] and kings.[7]"

C. L. Dodgson

The period of human history that saw the early rise and spread of domestication (say, roughly, 15,000 to 5000 years ago) also witnessed many technological developments of other sorts. Some were closely tied in with agriculture or animal husbandry. Others had their origins among unconverted hunters-and-gatherers and only subsequently, if at all, came to be associated with farming. We survey them in this chapter and the next, beginning with stone-polishing and ending with the first exploitation of metal. The arrangement is topical rather than strictly chronological, for in some instances we must leave the period named above, dipping deeply into man's early history or shallowly into the recent past in order to show the connectedness of things.

THE MASTER MASONS ✖ All early methods for the manufacture of stone tools (pp. 391 and 434) require that the target pebble receive sharp blows. Whether the core or a flake be wanted, it is percussion that breaks the one from the other. The force of the blow inevitably also produces incipient internal fracture surfaces running in various directions. The finished tool has been weakened by the very process of making it. Sooner or later it will split while being used. Smaller chips can be removed with less forceful taps; hence the finely worked flint knife blades of the late Upper Pleistocene retain more of the inherent strength of the raw pebble than had their cruder predecessors. But

---

[1] *Odobenus rosmarus* or *O. divergens*, suborder Pinnipedia, order Carnivora (Figure 24-23, p. 350). [2] Chapter 8. [3] Pp. 19 and 536. [4] Pp. 542 and 617–618. [5] P. 529. [6] *Brassica oleracea* (p. 471 and Table 29-1, p. 452). [7] Chapter 33 and pp. 587–589.

BY HIS BOOTSTRAPS

there is a limit to this. It would be hard to produce a chisel narrow and strong enough to take off chips of maximum linear dimension much less than, say, an eighth of an inch—unless, of course, one could make it of metal.

A radically new technique was invented somewhere in northern or middle Eurasia during the Late Würm, by people who were experts in the working of bone and ivory. We have seen (p. 442) that some people in this region were also food-grinders, which may have helped to set a technological climate appropriate for the innovation. The carving of bone (or ivory) begins with burins (p. 434), but the finishing touches involve rubbing with an abrasive: a piece of sandstone or emery, or powdered emery held in a patch of animal skin. The new technique was a transfer of this rubbing procedure from bone to stone. The flint tool continued to be roughed out by traditional percussion methods, but rubbing replaced chipping for the final stages.

This works if the abrasive is hard enough. Emery is easily reduced to powder by rubbing two pieces of it together. The individual grains (composed largely of corundum, Al_2O_3, but with an admixture of iron oxides and other minerals) have an effective hardness of about 8 on the Mohs scale.[8] Flints and cherts vary, but their principal ingredient, quartz in very tiny crystals, has a hardness of only 7. In one sense, rubbing flint with powdered emery is still a sort of chipping, for if we could watch through a microscope we would see the individual grains of the emery colliding with tiny protrusions from the surface of the flint and from time to time knocking one loose. To the artisan, however, chipping and polishing are very different, demanding distinct sorts of muscular control and diverse procedures for checking on how the work is progressing.

Polishing also requires considerable time and patience as compared with chipping. This means that the earliest polishers had to have the time to spare. Perhaps they did this work in off seasons when hunting and gathering were not possible. Perhaps the work was assigned to elderly people or cripples unable to make contributions of a more athletic sort to the collective welfare. Soon, though, the merits of the tools made in the new way turned out to represent a net saving of time. Let us suppose that the manufacture of a good polished stone tool of a certain sort took ten times as many man-hours (the figure is arbitrary) as that of the best chipped stone tool of the same sort. The investment was worth while if the polished tool lasted more than ten times as long as the chipped one, or if its greater strength and better design enabled one to do more than ten times as much work with it as with a chipped one.

New Materials and New Products

That is only the edge of the story. Stone can be polished and otherwise abraded into tools and utensils of kinds that cannot be produced by chipping, and abrasion will work on types of stone useless for chipping.

Let us illustrate the second point first. Soapstone, composed mainly of talc

[8]Established in 1812 by Friedrich Mohs (1773–1839) and still widely used. Mineral A is harder than mineral B if a point of A will scratch a smooth surface of B. The numbers run from 1 for talc to 10 for diamond. They *order* degrees of hardness but do not *quantify* them. That is, we can say that diamond is harder than any other mineral, but not that it is "twice as hard" as apatite with index 5.

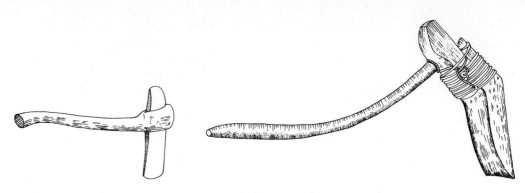

FIGURE 31-1. POLISHED STONE AX AND ADZE. Left: an early European stone ax. Right: a stone adze from pre-European Hawaii. (Ax after Chard 1969; adze after Coon 1955.)

$(Mg_3Si_4O_{10}(OH)_2)$ with hardness 1 on the Mohs scale, is so soft that a blow with a chisel merely dents it. But it is readily carved with a flint knife, and easy to polish. At the opposite extreme are stones like jadeite and nephrite, both known colloquially as jade. Jadeite is minute crystals of $NaAl(SiO_3)_2$ in a compact aggregate; its hardness is almost 7. Nephrite is long, fiberlike crystals of $Ca_2Mg_5Si_8O_{22}(OH)_2$ (sometimes iron, Fe, replaces some of the magnesium, Mg), tangled together in a tight mass; its hardness is 6.5. Both are extremely tough. If jade is struck with a chisel, it is more apt to be the chisel that breaks. Polishing jadeite or nephrite is tedious work, but the resulting artifact is very durable.

Polishing thus opened up for the mason a whole new world of raw materials, and in time this wealth was exploited. But some kinds of tools continued to be made of flints, cherts, and obsidian, not because of the dead hand of tradition but because they were the best materials available. You could make a knife blade of soapstone, but it would not cut anything. You can make superb blades of jade, and this was done, but the substance is too rare for extensive utilitarian exploitation. In several early civil societies, especially those of Mexico and of northeastern China, jade became the material wrought by specialized craftsmen into stunning objets d'art for the well-to-do, while poor folk made do with the more mundane flint.

Which is not to sneer at flint. One of the earliest attested types of polished flint tool was an ax designed very much like our modern steel-bladed axes. The similarity is because the early design was so effective that we have inherited it essentially without modification. Polishing made it possible to give the head a keen edge and yet keep the material strong, and also to resharpen the tool when it grew dull from use. Figure 31-1 shows an early polished stone ax from Europe and a polished stone adze from Hawaii (much more recent, but manufactured without any use of metal). The difference between an ax and an adze is that, although in both the head sits at right angles to the handle, the cutting edge of an ax is parallel to the hand while that of an adze is perpendicular thereto. Both are for use on wood. Note also the hafting, achieved by shaping the far end of the wooden handle rather than the more obdurate stone head. The perforation in the end of the handle of the European ax (as in the connect-

(a)

(b)

(c)

(d)

FIGURE 31-2. From digging stick to hoe . . .

ing piece of the Maglemosian pick shown in Figure 28-8, p. 443) looks like a direct transfer of the carving and rubbing techniques that had earlier been used to put an eye in an ivory or bone needle.

Polished Stone on Wood

The polished flint ax was almost as germinal an innovation as stone-polishing itself, for it revolutionized man's handling of wood. To be sure, heavy chipped stone tools had been used much earlier, in Africa and to some extent elsewhere, for cutting through thick pieces of wood (p. 399), but they were clumsy and the work was slow. The new tools were fast and accurate. In a recent experiment in Denmark, three woodsmen cleared about an eighth of an acre of silver birch (*Betula verrucosa*, a hardwood) in four hours, using axes with genuine ancient stone blades; one of them required rehoning only after it had felled more than 100 trees. The ax, the adze, and a few allied tools such as the gouge (a sort of burin: p. 434) also began to turn woodsmen into carpenters, for in skilled hands they can be used to trim logs into boards.

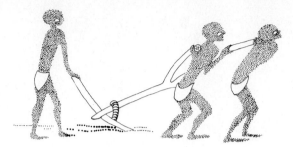

(a)

(b)

FIGURE 31-3. . . . to plow.

POLISHED STONE AND AGRICULTURE

Polished stone tools were a great aid to agriculturalists, and are attested by every archaeological site that bears witness to early crop-raising. The ax served, along with fire, to clear land when that was necessary. The earliest tool for working the soil in planting or cultivating was the wooden digging stick. In time this became the hoe, and then—in some places—the plow (Figure 31-2 and 31-3). Early hoes and plows were made *of* wood, but *with* polished stone tools. The early agriculturalists of southwest Asia had sickles for harvesting grain or reeds or both; we have already described them (p. 468). The stone parts of these sickles could not have been produced by percussion methods.

The grinding of grains into flour has everywhere traditionally been accomplished with paired implements of polished stone: a metate and mano or a quern and muller (Figure 31-4). A metate or quern is a shallow bowl—perhaps originally merely a flat piece of stone with no depression. A mano is a broad-faced tools that presses and abrades the grain against the bottom of the bowl. A muller has cylindrical shape and is rolled back and forth in the bowl, crushing the grain. Since food-grinding is older than agriculture (p. 442), equipment of this sort may have been among the first stone artifacts to be produced by abrasion techniques.

Finally, in both agricultural and nonagricultural communities foodstuffs and allied

BY HIS BOOTSTRAPS

(a)

(b)

FIGURE 31-4. Equipment for grinding grain. (a) is late pre-European or early European metates and manos from the Southwest. (b) is a figurine of an ancient Egyptian woman using a quern and muller. [(a) reproduced, with permission, from *The Artifacts of Pecos,* by A. V. Kidder, Yale University Press, New Haven, 1932. (b) courtesy of the Römer-Pelizäus Museum, Hildesheim.]

FIGURE 31-5. Big stone: The Easter Island statues. (Courtesy of Sergio Larrain, Magnum Photos Inc.)

substances may require storage, carrying, and sometimes heat processing. Our south-west Asia sites reveal polished stone bowls (p. 468) of workmanship so excellent that they must signal a long earlier tradition. Since stone is not flammable, stone pots can be used for cooking. In some parts of the world, containers of ground stone may have been the first truly nonflammable cooking vessels to appear. In others, ceramics first filled this need (pp. 519–520).

Origins

Although we spoke earlier of a (very vaguely defined) place of origin of stone-polishing, it is likely that the technique emerged independently more than one place in the Old World—perhaps even independently in Australia, where ground stone axes are attested as of 5000 B.C. Beyond any reasonable doubt it developed in the Americas with no hints from outside. As the glaciers of the Late Würm receded in North America, concomitant climatic changes—coupled, perhaps, with human depredation—reduced the sizes of the once enormous herds on which the Indians had been living. People turned, instead (especially in the eastern half of the continent), to the exploitation of more scattered game in forested country. One of their tools for this new way of life, well attested by the record, was the ax with a ground stone blade. They also had manos and metates, and bowls carved of soapstone. Similar ground and carved

BY HIS BOOTSTRAPS

FIGURE 31-6. Big stone: A Mayan pyramid. (Courtesy of Larry Keenan, Jr., Photofind.)

stoneware turns up also farther south, in the areas where aboriginal American agriculture had its origins (p. 488), and here, as civil society appeared, decorative stone-carving reached artistic heights.

BIG STONE

In various parts of the world, polishing techniques gave rise, in due time, to a great change in the way stone could be used in architecture and for other large constructions. The statues of Eastern Island (Figure 31-5) are 12 to 22 feet in height

FIGURE 31-7. Big stone: Stonehenge. (Courtesy of George Rodger, Magnum Photos Inc.)

and originally rested on areas paved with flat stones with a carefully built curb at the seaward side. All the work was done without metal and with only human power. The same is true of the pyramids and other large stone structures of Yucatán and the Valley of Mexico (Figure 31-6), and for a large number of "monuments" elsewhere. The ring of standing stones known as Stonehenge (north of Salisbury, in Wiltshire, England; Figure 31-7) dates from the middle of the second millennium B.C. Relics such as these attest to more than cutting, carving, and polishing; they show a mastery of methods for transporting extremely massive objects, and for placing them securely in precisely calculated positions.

Surely most impressive of all are the pyramids of Egypt, the largest of which were built during the third millennium B.C. However, in this case, though the structural material was stone, some of the tools were already of metal (e.g., bronze saws). The builders of the pyramids had stone rollers for use in transport, and a great store of technical know-how which properly fascinates modern students of the history of engineering, surveying, and mathematics. Approximately 2,300,000 stone blocks went into the Great Pyramid of Khufu (near Al-Jīzah, just south of the Nile Delta; Figure 31-8), with average mass over 2.5 tons. Many of these were brought from quarries 50 miles or more away, on barges along the Nile and then overland. The final dressing of the blocks was done so accurately that the seams where their faces touch are as narrow and tight as any ever achieved anywhere. The Greek historian Herodotos (fifth century B.C.) estimated that the whole task took thirty years and a labor force of 100,000 men.

FIGURE 31-8. Big stone: The Great Pyramid of Khufu. (Courtesy of Harrison Forman World Photos.)

ARCH AND DOME

While there is no denying that some of these early stone structures were very large, another factor contributes to the impression of massiveness: of the total volume occupied by the structure, a high percentage is taken up by solid stuff, only a small part by doors, passageways, and rooms.

The reason is that at first the builders knew no way of constructing a roof other than with horizontal beams supported by vertical columns, as shown in Figure 31-9a, or with successively overlapping horizontal beams, as in Figure 31-9b. Whatever the exact arrangement, the weight of the loftier stone exerts its force straight downwards, so that if one wants to put a lot of stone up high one is forced to put even more beneath to hold it up.

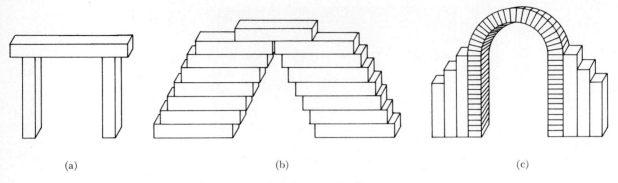

<table>
<tr><td>(a)</td><td>(b)</td><td>(c)</td></tr>
</table>

FIGURE 31-9. How to make a hole in a stone wall.

The Egyptians never escaped these limitations, nor did the Greeks, nor, until recent times, the builders of most of the rest of the world. But there was a breakthrough in Babylonia about 3000 B.C. (attested especially at Nippur), in the form of the so-called "true arch" and its three-dimensional analog the "true dome." This spread quickly to the Assyrians and then, bypassing Greece, to the Etruscans in Italy, from whom the Romans inherited it. The constituent pieces of a true arch (Figure 31-9c) are either wedge-shaped stones, or else rectangular parallelepipedal bricks with more mortar between them at one end than at the other. This arrangement converts some of the weight into a force acting horizontally, requiring staunch lateral supports in the form of buttresses. The process of construction requires a scaffolding, since the structure will hold itself up only when all the members are in place. But the technique allows the construction of fairy palaces in which a small amount of structural material encloses a large amount of empty space. The outer wall of the Colosseum in Rome (built late in the first century A.D.; Figure 31-10) is an example: rows of arches built one above another.

SUMMARY

The appearance of abrasion techniques in stone-working marked a major transition in human technology, the importance of which we can acknowledge by using the term "Palaeolithic" for earlier technological stages and "Neolithic" for ensuing ones. The transition, of course, occurred at different times in different places.

Also, the Neolithic lasted longer some places than others. The Neolithic came to a close in any one region as metallurgy came in. The master masons of the Neolithic worked stone with stone. Working stone with metal, which is what the Egyptian pyramid-builders did and what we do now, is very different. Our species uses more stone per capita per year today than ever before in man's history—one need only think of the untold millions of millions of tons of the stuff now supported by the bedrock of Manhattan Island. But that does not mean that we are living in a stone age.

Finally, we must note that there are a few corners of the world that never knew a Neolithic. At the dawn of the ethnographic present, abrasion techniques were very

FIGURE 31-10. Using the arch: The Colosseum in Rome. (Courtesy of Louis Goldman, Rapho Guillumette.)

widespread, but still unknown (or formerly known and then lost) in a few scattered areas.

✂ The biosphere supplies a wide variety of more or less flexible long, thin things: tree branches and saplings, grass stems and leaves, vines, canes, reeds, various vegetable fibers, strips of sinew, hair, animal intestines. It also affords a stock, somewhat less varied, of more or less flexible two-dimensional things: sheets of tree bark, broad leaves, the outer shells of some fruits and nuts, animal skins, the casings of certain internal organs.

Some of these are usable for some purposes just as they are plucked, stripped, pried, or excised from the organisms that have grown them. A length of vine can be tied around the waist (p. 388); an animal skin can be draped over the shoulders; boughs can be laid on a framework of sticks as a windbreak. But sometimes, for some uses, the available filaments are too short, thick, weak, or inflexible, or the sheets are too small, stiff, or porous, or have the wrong shapes.

For example, suppose you want a container in which to place berries as you gather them, or in which to store seeds. The half shell of a coconut will do. So will a calabash dried and then cut open and cleaned out. If there is nothing like a coconut or calabash around, what do you do?

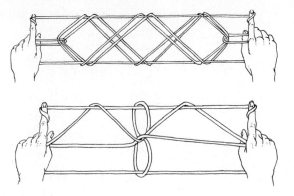

FIGURE 31-11. STRING FIGURES ("CAT'S CRADLES"). These specimens are from the Gilbert Islands in Micronesia, where dozens are known, each with its own name. Above: one version of Three Wells; below: Dragonfly. (From *String-Figures from the Gilbert Islands,* by H. C. and H. E. Maude; Memoir no. 13 of The Polynesian Society, Wellington, N.Z., 1958.)

Needs of these sorts led our ancestors to develop a number of interrelated arts: *tanning, knotting, braiding, spinning, sewing, weaving, coiling, knitting,* and *felting*.

All of these start with filaments or sheets, and all yield filaments or sheets with properties different from those of the raw materials. All but the first depend for their effectiveness on friction. Thus, tie the ends of two strings together. If the strings were completely frictionless, then no matter how complicated the knot it would not hold. No material is perfectly smooth, but there is great variation. A silk or nylon stocking "runs" more readily than a cotton one.

TANNING

This is the chemical and mechanical treatment of an animal skin. The beginnings of the art are older than man. The variants have exceeded all bounds. By 2000 years ago the skins of domestic animals were even being made into stuff to write on: *parchment* and *vellum,* the latter a high-quality material made from the skins of unborn or just born lambs or calves.

KNOTTING

This is also extremely old. That length of vine put around some hominid's waist a million or so years ago (p. 388) didn't grow in the form of a closed loop. The ends had to be twisted together to make them hold, or else had to be tied to each other with a separate piece of some sort of cord. Exactly the same procedures make it possible to fasten shorter cords together end-to-end to make a longer one, which is fine provided the bumps where the segments meet don't matter.

The antiquity of knotting is suggested also by the universality in the ethnographic present of games played with a loop of cord, in the form of "string figures" or "cat's cradles." The loop is held taut around the two hands, palms facing each other, and

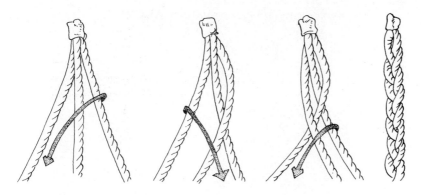

FIGURE 31-12. Braiding.

then the fingers grasp and pull the twine into some complicated symmetrical arrangement (Figure 31-11). Sometimes the hands of a second person must carefully lift the half-completed figure from the hands of the first. It is hard to find a community where this form of play is unknown, and certain designs are well-nigh universal.

The preceding paragraphs are a way of admitting that we know nothing of the origin of knotting from direct archaeological finds. The argument for great antiquity is based on indirect evidence, and on the essential simplicity of the process. But the latter part of the argument is weak, because, although tying knots is not obvious to a gorilla or a chimpanzee, *any* technological operation is "obvious" to us humans—once someone else has invented it and shown us how it is done.

Similar arguments, for whatever they are worth, speak for very early origins of the next two arts.

BRAIDING

This (Figure 31-12) uses three strands, and fastens them together not end-to-end but in parallel, making a stouter cord out of feebler ones. You can use three bunches of strands (as in braiding a girl's hair); or you can use more than three strands, by some sort of patterned handling of the extra ones; but you can't use fewer than three. Of course, cords made in this way can then be used as the component strands for a new operation of the same kind.

SPINNING

Spinning twists a number of strands together into a stouter, fatter thread. By starting with strands of different lengths, and by adding a new strand where one already used gives out, the spun thread can be made indefinitely long.

The tensile strength of a spun filament is reasonably uniform, since in any one short segment most of the participating strands do not have ends. For the same reason, a long piece can have a uniform diameter, rather than the periodic nodes that result when a long string is made by tying short ones end-to-end. In the finished thread,

FIGURE 31-13. Spinning without tools. This picture was taken by Kenneth Emory on the Polynesian Outlier island of Kapingamarangi in 1947. (Bernice P. Bishop Museum photo.)

each individual strand has the shape of a helix. If the participating strands are too springy to start with, they will tend to unwind. For that reason, some materials (such as sinew) do not lend themselves to the process. Usable fibers are those which, by being overtwisted in the manufacturing process, adjust their internal structure to a new rest position in the helical form, and which are helped to hold that position by their frictional contact with the other fibers.

Spinning can be done with no tools at all. One hand holds the strands; the other rolls them against the thigh (Figure 31-13). It helps, however, to have a special device called a *spindle* (Figure 31-14), which is rotated to twist the strands together and on which the thread is then wound. The earliest spindles were doubtless merely unshaped twigs (primary tools: p. 88). More carefully designed ones were developed in many parts of the world. A step taken only in the Old World was to put a balanced weight towards the bottom end. The spindle was held vertically, given a twist, and released. As it dropped, suspended by the forming thread above it, the weight served as a flywheel to keep it rotating. The completed length of thread was then wound up on it, and the operation repeated. This type of spindle is attested from early Neolithic horizons in southwest Asia, and was probably widespread by the time of the first serious moves towards farming as a way of life. Many New World spindles have a

BY HIS BOOTSTRAPS

FIGURE 31-14. A simple hand spindle, in use in Guatemala. (Photo by Esther Bubley for PepsiCo International.)

similar shape, but there is no evidence that they were used aboriginally with the twist, drop, and flywheel effect.

SEWING

Sewing is one of two arts crucial for the craft of *tailoring;* the other is cutting.

Sewing uses filaments to fasten separate sheets together into a larger one. Neither the constituents nor the resulting whole need be flat. Sewing requires one of two tools: an awl or a needle. An awl is simply a long, thin object with a sharp point at one end, used to pierce holes in the edges of the materials to be sewn together, and then to push the filament through the holes. A needle is an awl with a transverse perforation in its shaft, through which the filament is passed, so that as the needle is pulled through the holes in the material it pulls the thread through behind it.

Tailoring developed in northerly latitudes in the late Palaeolithic (that is, before the inception of stone-polishing): the first materials to be sewn were animal skins or cured hides; the first filaments used in sewing were of sinew; the first awls and needles were of bone (p. 441). In the Old World, tailoring techniques were in due

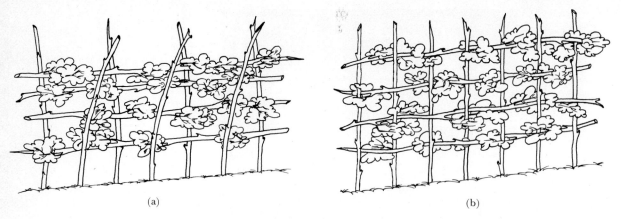

(a)   (b)

FIGURE 31-15. THE WRONG WAY (a) AND THE RIGHT WAY (b) TO WEAVE A WALL. The pictures are shown as "open" work to make the detail clearer; for an effective wall, the weft elements in (b) would be pushed down closer together, and leafier boughs would probably be used. (Drawings courtesy of Dennis Peacock.)

time transferred to woven fabrics, and after the development of metallurgy scissors were added to the sewing kit. In the Americas, tailoring and textiles did not effectively get together in pre-Columbian times.

NEEDLEWORK is related to sewing, but does not serve to fasten sheets together. Instead, it decorates a surface with attached threads of contrasting colors, or with shells or beads. Users of skin clothing decorate it in this way.

BUTTONS, together with the loops or buttonholes through which they pass, could be a derivative of needlework. They are attested from the third millennium B.C. from the Sumerian city Ur in Mesopotamia.

HAND WEAVING

Weaving starts with filaments and yields sheets. You can weave a fence or a house wall, and this may have been one of the earliest applications of the art. Suppose you have planted a row of poles in the ground, several inches apart, intending to add leafy boughs to the framework in order to ward off rain, snow, wind, or sun. One way is to have the poles slope in parallel, and just pile the boughs on; this is approximately what is meant by *thatching*. But the boughs may then be blown away. They need to be anchored. Thread a bough in front of the first pole, behind the second, and in front of the third: its springiness will then hold it in place. If you thread all the boughs in parallel (Figure 31-15a), you may put so much tension on the poles that they bend alternately away from you and towards you. If, on the other hand, you alternate the threading (Figure 31-15b), the tensions imposed by the successive boughs are in opposite directions. The structure is then flat and firm.

In this woven wall the poles, put in place first, are the *warp* and the boughs are the *weft*. Almost every type of weaving requires two sets of constituent filaments approximately orthogonal to each other; and in the process of weaving, if not in-

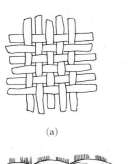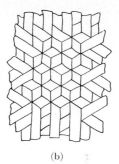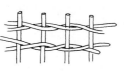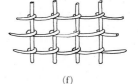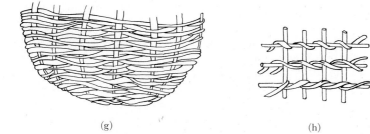

(a)   (b)   (c)

(d)   (e)   (f)

(g)   (h)

FIGURE 31-16. COMMON WEAVE PATTERNS. (a) checkerwork ("tabby" in textiles); (b) hexagonal; (c) twill; (d, e) twining; (f) wrapped; (g) wicker weave (checkerwork with warp and weft different); (h) lattice-work twined or wrapped, requiring, like (b), three sets of elements instead of two.

variably in the finished product, one set is clearly the warp, the other the weft. Weaving that does not involve two sets of filaments uses three: two wefts, forming angles of 60° with each other and with the warp (Figure 31-16b).

In our wall the filaments are large, and those of the warp are quite different in shape from those of the weft. There is no limit on the size of the filaments used in weaving as long as they are neither too big nor too small for human beings to handle, by hand or with suitable equipment. There are also no obvious limits to the extent to which warp and weft elements can differ in size or shape, and these variables yield virtually an endless variety of textures.

Another variable is the weave pattern. Our wall is *checkerwork* or *tabby* (the latter is the standard textile term), the simplest pattern possible. It is shown in Figure 31-16a;

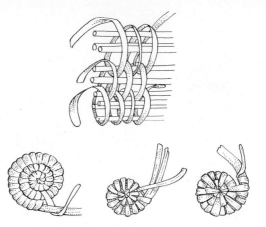

FIGURE 31-17. Coiling (basketry). Above: elements pulled apart to show their arrangement. Below: beginning of three variants, elements pulled tight.

other parts of the figure show some of the many other weave patterns that have been used.

When weaving is done completely by hand, the filaments must be large enough for the fingers to grasp and manipulate, and, though flexible, stiff enough that they do not flop around hopelessly when not being held. Hand weaving thus contrasts with *loom weaving,* to which we shall turn later.

Hand weaving produces baskets, mats, screens, furniture or parts thereof, house walls, clothing (straw hats!), toys, artistic and ceremonial figures, and many other sorts of objects. A loose weave, with flexible warp and weft elements tied together where they cross, produces nets. Hand weaving of one kind or another is universal in the ethnographic present, found, like knotting and spinning, even in Tasmania.

Sometimes the hand weaving merely yields a frame from which the completed artifact is made by pressing mud or clay into the interstices. The agricultural Swiss "Lake Dwellers"[9] of the fourth millennium B.C. thatched the roofs of their houses, but wove the walls, using thin, flexible wooden rods (as of willow) rather than boughs for the weft, and sealed the framework with mud. This style of construction, known as *wattle and daub,* was widespread in early agricultural Europe and is still found today in many places. The difference between a wattle-and-daub wall and one of dried mud or clay with no framework is like the difference between reinforced and unreinforced concrete. Again: when containers (baskets) are made by hand weaving, it is pretty hard to make them watertight. It is not impossible, because some of the basket-making experts of aboriginal California succeeded. But it is a great deal easier to render a woven container watertight by covering it with clay, and that procedure is attested from many parts of the world.

[9] So called from the location of the archaeological sites; the dwellings were not actually erected over water.

(a)   (b)   (c)

FIGURE 31-18. POMO BASKETS. (a) is a plain twined (woven) cooking basket; (b) is coiled; (c) is a carrying basket made by a type of weave known as diagonal twining. (Reproduced, with permission, from *Pomo Indian basketry* by S. A. Barrett, University of California Publications in American Archaeology and Ethnology 7:3, Berkeley, The University of California Press, 1907–1910.)

COILING

In the present context, this term denotes another way of making baskets (cf. p. 519). A bundle of flexible fibers is wrapped in a long, flat filament which is turned in a helix around the bundle (Figure 31-17). The bundle is curved around itself in a spiral, either flat or rising in a cone or cylinder. With each second or third turn of the wrapping filament, it is pushed through a hole in the adjacent coil of the bundle, fastening the new turn of the bundle to the part of the basket already completed. Something like an awl is needed to make the holes; otherwise the operation is completely manual.

Coiling is found in Australia, in Indonesia, in Africa, among the Labrador Eskimos, among the Indians of Tierra del Fuego, and in a large connected region running from the North American Southwest through southern California, the Great Basin, north through the Mackenzie-Yukon area into Alaska, and across into northeastern Asia. This suggests both that the technique was invented independently in several places, and also that it may be relatively recent—a matter of the last few thousand years at most.

In aboriginal California, baskets were made only by coiling in the south and only by hand weaving in the north, but by both techniques in the central valleys. Here, among such tribes as the Pomo and Maidu, basketry seems to have reached its utilitarian and artistic pinnacle. Pomo women wove baskets for seed-gathering and -storage (p. 454), seed-beaters in the form of stiff paddles, tight-weave baskets for stone boiling (p. 406), and many other objects, such as trays and ornaments. Most ornamental ware, though, was coiled, and this included baskets no larger than a thimble, with designs carefully added during the coiling process and executed with marvelous precision (Figure 31-18).

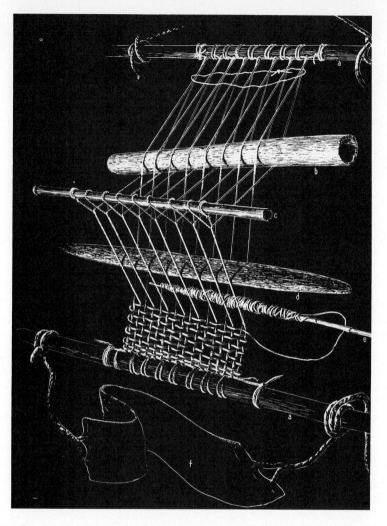

FIGURE 31-19. BELT LOOM. This is a diagram of the type used aboriginally (and still) in Peru. a, loom bars; b, shed rod; c, heddle; d, batten; e, shuttle (or "bobbin"); f, belt to go around operator's waist. (From *Andean culture history* by Wendell C. Bennett and Junius B. Bird, AMNH Handbook Series No. 15, New York, 1949. Copyright 1949 by The American Museum of Natural History and reprinted with their permission.)

LOOM WEAVING

Filaments too thin or flimsy to be woven by hand can be woven with suitable apparatus. Because the filaments need to be long, most loom weaving has used fibers produced by spinning, though this has been changed in the recent past by the invention of such man-made fibers as rayon and nylon. Sheets of material produced by loom weaving are called *textiles*.

BY HIS BOOTSTRAPS

FIGURE 31-20. SUSPENDED-WARP LOOM. The Menomini woman in the picture is weaving a blanket; behind her and the loom is the skeleton of a wigwam (see p. 14). This type of suspended-warp loom, weft elements inserted beginning at the top, was still widely used by the Indians of the Northeastern Woodlands early in the present century. (From Skinner 1921. Photograph courtesy of the Museum of the American Indian, Heye Foundation.)

The basic function of every loom is to hold the warp elements taut so that the hands are free for other things. One of the simplest types is the *belt loom:* one end of the warp is attached to a post, the other end to a belt around the weaver's waist (Figure 31-19). A strand of weft is threaded through the warp by hand, then pushed tight against the preceding weft strand with a comb or with a special tool called a *batten.*

One step beyond the belt loom is the *suspended-warp loom:* the warp hangs vertically between two horizontal poles, one high in the air and one close to the ground (Figure 31-20). The insertion of weft elements may begin at top or at bottom. The work can be rendered easier by using a *heddle.* This can be simply a fat stick which is threaded through the warp, separating the warp filaments into two sets, one on either side. The open space between the two sets of warp filaments is the *shed.* A strand of weft can be passed through the shed very quickly; when the heddle is removed, the shed disappears and the weft strand is in place.

In some simple looms, and in all more advanced ones, the warp runs horizontally. In advanced ones the heddle has become a complicated device that can quickly reverse the positions of the two sets of warp filaments, or even handle three or four sets for more complicated weave patterns. Also, one more device is added. A *shuttle* holds a supply of weft thread, and is passed through the shed leaving a trail of thread behind it like a spider (Figure 31-19e).

Textiles were known in the aboriginal New World everywhere except the extreme south of South America, California, the Great Plains, and the extreme north of North America. Spun cotton was the standard weaving fiber from Arizona and New Mexico on southwards. The Indians of the Northwest Coast of North America used shredded cedar bark. Andean archaeology reveals belt looms about 1400 years ago, followed before long by simple horizontal looms. These late dates indicate an independent New World origin of loom weaving, perhaps developed in response to the fact that spun cotton fibers do not lend themselves to being woven with the unaided hands. Aboriginal American looms never got terribly complicated, but some of the work done on them did. Peruvian textiles from about 800 years ago are as intricate in their designs and as precise in their workmanship as any ever made anywhere. The shapes are achieved without any cutting of the fabric, and intricate designs are produced in the process of weaving, not added afterwards by sewing or stitching. Some Peruvian textiles are double sheets, woven right through each other so that, as viewed from one face, one of the two sheets is nearer to you in some places, the other in others (Figure 31-21).

In the Old World, loom weaving began at least as early as the fifth millennium B.C., apparently in areas where domestication was starting to supply abundant suitable fibers (cotton, linen, hemp, silk, wool). Before the expansion of Europe, it did not reach the Old World arctic, but it met and mingled with tailoring in intermediate latitudes (p. 18). It did not spread far into the tropical forests of Africa, nor down to southern Africa. It did not reach Australia and Tasmania. If the invaders of Oceania (p. 484) had the art to start with, they mostly lost it, resorting to a type of felting for obtaining flexible sheets (p. 516).

KNITTING AND CROCHETING

These are other methods for starting with filaments and getting sheets. They differ from weaving in that one uses a single long filament instead of two sets at right angles to each other.

In essence, knitting and crocheting are systematic tangling. In the former, a row of partial knots is made—partial in that a loop of each must be held on some sort of stick to keep it from falling apart; then a second row is laid down by the first and fastened to it in such a way as to complete the knots of the first row (Figure 31-22a). Crocheting procedes knot by knot instead of row by row (Figure 31-22b). There are many variants. All require special implements (a crochet hook or two or more knitting "needles"—not really needles because they have no eyes). Nowadays knitting, like weaving, is done by machine. Women's hosiery is machine-knitted; a single stocking may involve as many as three million individual stitches.

Knitting and crocheting are at least several hundred years old, but possibly no older.

BY HIS BOOTSTRAPS

(a)

(b)

FIGURE 31-21. Peruvian textiles. (a) is a "gauze weave"; (b) is a double weave as described in the text. (From *Andean culture history* by Wendell C. Bennett and Junius B. Bird, AMNH Handbook Series No. 15, New York, 1949. Copyright 1949 by The American Museum of Natural History and reprinted with their permission.)

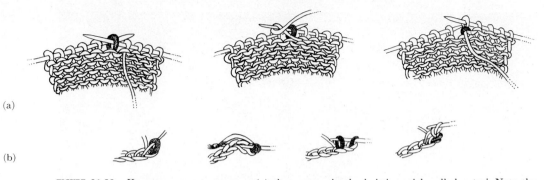

(a)

(b)

FIGURE 31-22. KNITTING AND CROCHETING. (a) shows steps in the knitting stick called a *purl*. Note the successive positions of the darkened loop as the right-hand "needle" adds another loop to those already on it. (b) shows steps in the simple crochet stitch. Between the third view and the fourth, the hook catches a loop of fresh yarn and draws it through both loops already on the shaft of the hook. (Taken, with permission, from *Learn to Knit,* Coats & Clark's Book No. 190, copyright 1968, and *Learn How Book,* Coats & Clark's Book No. 170-B, copyright 1959.)

FELTING

This is our last technique: it makes sheets out of filaments by tangling that is not orderly but intentionally random.

When the process is applied to animal hair (wool), the product is *felt*. Felt was invented only in Eurasia, later than loom weaving, and became of importance chiefly in southwest Asia, central Eurasia, and adjacent territory, where wild or domesticated wool-bearing animals abounded. When wool is to be spun into thread, it must first be "carded" (combed), to get all the fibers roughly parallel. But if it is to be felted there is no combing, because the more random the intertwinings of the fibers the better. A quantity of wool is repeatedly wetted, beaten, and squeezed, matting the hairs more and more intricately and closely, and finally formed into sheets, subjected to pressure, and dried. The exact shape of the finished product (say, nowadays, a hat) can be obtained by using a mold of the proper shape for the final pressing and drying; or flat sheets of finished felt can be cut and then sewn or glued together.

When the process is applied to bark fibers, the product is *bark cloth* (Figure 31-23). Bark cloth was invented, quite independently of felt, in Indonesia (whence it spread to Oceania), in central Africa, and in Central and South America: all of these are regions where certain tropical trees supply suitable sorts of bark. In Oceania the paper mulberry tree is cultivated for this use. The inner bark is stripped, scraped, beaten, sometimes wetted; bigger pieces are made from smaller ones by overlapping them and beating the overlap. The technical details differ from place to place, but the basic notion is the same everywhere and the same as that of wool-felting.

Bark cloth could just as well be called "bark paper": in the literate communities of Middle America it was used for writing, and in great quantity. One document pertaining to the emperor Moctezuma of the Aztecs specifies a yearly tribute of 24,000 reams.

FIGURE 31-23. Bark cloth. This piece of tapa (22″ x 27″) was made in Samoa about 1960; the design is in dark brown and light tan with a few spots of faint pink. Long before 1960 the Samoan tapa-makers were using imported cornstarch for sizing. Characteristic Polynesian tapa designs have been inherited in Hawaii for the textiles now used in making women's *muʔumuʔu* (loose gowns) and men's *aloha* shirts.

Certainly the most important felted product is (true) paper, invented shortly after A.D. 100 in China under the aegis of a court official named Ts'ai Lun who wanted something better to write on than the textile cloth which was at that time and place the most satisfactory material for the purpose. The first paper was made by felting a mixture of macerated tree bark, hemp waste, old rags, and pieces of fish net. If the rags and the net were of hemp, as they probably were, then only two kinds of fibers were actually involved. In any case, the chief ingredients were vegetable fibers composed largely of cellulose (p. 334), and that is still so today, when the immediate raw materials are pulped wood and cotton rags. Paper was an instant and continued success, and has come to be used for many things besides writing. As important as textiles are in the modern world, their production is easily outstripped by that of paper. The world yield of textiles in 1963 could have been sewn into a tent to cover South Carolina. The paper made that year, if finished in sheets of the thickness of the one I am now typing on, could have covered the whole of Dixie.

✘ Although only our own species can talk about it, any sizable land animal knows from experience that there are spots where the ground underfoot is soft and mushy when wet, hard as rock when dry. Man has been purposefully pushing dirt around **HARD THINGS FROM SOFT** at least since the middle Pleistocene, and he probably began exploiting this obvious wet-dry contrast earlier than that. If it doesn't rain, but you know how to haul water over short distances, then you can make mud out of dirt when you want to, and unless it is constantly cloudy and humid the sun will dry it out. Recall the dried-mud house walls made by the inhabitants of Qalat Jarmo in the seventh millennium B.C. (p. 468). The art was surely already ancient.

The stuff we walk on varies a lot from one part of the world to another (tundra, desert, beaches, grassland, forest floor), and there are small regions where there is a good deal of diversity from one acre to the next. Setting rock and sand apart, soils range from very loose to very clayey. Loose soils absorb water quickly, but the water also drains out readily if it has any place to go. Clayey soils resist seepage, and hold on more tightly to the water they already have.

All soils contain some clay. Soil is clayey if the percentage of clay is high, and there are randomly but widely scattered spots where the proportion is so high that we just speak of "clay" instead of "soil." Clay in the technical sense is any of a set of related minerals. All are hydrous aluminum silicates, with a sheetlike crystal structure. One type is $Al_2O_3(SiO_2)_2(H_2O)_2$; this includes kaolin and several others, which differ not as to chemical composition but as to details of crystal arrangement. The "montmorillonite" group is $Al_2Si_4O_{10}(OH)_2$, except that some magnesium (Mg), iron (Fe), or zinc (Zn) can replace some of the aluminum (Al); molecules of water (H_2O), plus ions of calcium (Ca), sodium (Na), potassium (K), or hydrogen (H), are held captive between the crystals. There are some further types whose structure is less well understood. The individual crystals, of course, are very small. In a lump of soft clay the included water and other impurities serve as a lubricant to enable the crystals to slide past each other, and as a glue to hold them together, giving the mass its familiar consistency.

Let us imagine that in the course of their manufacture of mud walls, wattle-and-daub walls (p. 510), mud pies, and other mud objects, our ancestors chanced to use some especially clayey soil. It would not have taken them long to discover several things. The first is that clay can often be worked without adding water to render it pliable. The second is that, when well dried in the sun, clay becomes very hard (though also brittle). Ordinary dried mud is not so hard: you can poke holes into it with a stick, or scrape layers off with a fingernail. The third is that, when so dried, clay resists erosion from wind and rain. Ordinary dried mud absorbs rainwater and wears away, so that a mud wall is apt to need repair after a storm. Sun-dried clay is, to be sure, slightly porous, but the rate at which a liquid will leak through it is so slow that a vessel of the substance is quite practical for short-term storage; in fact, the bit of leakage can be an advantage, since the moisture that has seeped through the walls of the vessel evaporates and keeps the contents cool. Eventually, sun-dried clay is resoftened by contact with water, but this takes a while.

ELEMENTARY CERAMIC TECHNIQUES

The properties of clay render it desirable for various uses. There are two simple ways of shaping soft clay into a vessel.

FIGURE 31-24. COILING (POTTERY). The potter is rolling a new strand of clay between her hands to narrow it down to the proper proportions. (After a drawing in *Ceramics for the potter,* by Ruth M. Home, The University of Toronto Press, 1952.)

One way, called *coiling,* is reminiscent of the building-up of a mud wall in successive horizontal courses, except that the drying is postponed until the vessel is finished. A long sausage of clay is coiled into a ring and the ends pressed together. Another ring is formed and put atop the first. This is repeated until the desired height has been reached. Then the joints between the rings are smoothed out and the vessel is pressed and patted into shape (Figure 31-24).

The other way imitates the construction of a wattle-and-daub wall, and was mentioned in connection with weaving (p. 510): first one weaves a basket, and then one stops up the interstices with clay and adds a clay layer inside or out or both.

A somewhat more elaborate method uses not a basketry framework but a mold of some hard material—perhaps itself of hardened clay. If a single mold is used there are obvious limitations on shape, since after the shaped clay has hardened part way it must be separated from the mold. But two molds can be used, building the vessel up in horizontal or vertical halves which are then pressed and worked together.

Whatever technique of shaping is used, exposure of the vessel to hot sunshine for a few days completes the manufacture—unless it is baked in a fire, the technique to which we turn next.

FIRING AND GLAZING

Clay, like stone, is incombustible. When clay vessels are used for holding and carrying foodstuffs, inevitably they are going to come close to fires. If a "wattle-and-daub" pot is left too close to a fire, of course the basketry will oxidize, but once the clay is hard the framework is no longer needed anyway. In fact, though at first the clay daubing may have been considered secondary, the basket the important thing, in time it became the custom in some parts of the world to view the basket merely as a device used in the manufacture of the pot, and special, artistically sloppy, disposable baskets were woven just for this purpose. Boiling can be done in a nonflammable container by suspending it directly over the fire, rather than by dropping hot stones in (p. 406). It was surely the availability of clay pots, more than anything else, that led to the widespread popularity of this more efficient boiling technique.

And, by accident or design, in various different parts of the world, the association of clay and fire led to the next great discovery. If the temperature of a piece of clay is raised sufficiently high, the exposed surface becomes vitreous or *glazed*. Physically, what happens (in addition to the boiling-out of water and other volatile inclusions) is that the individual crystals break up and fuse together into an extremely viscous liquid, in no way distinguishable from glass or obsidian. The glaze may be a very thin layer, and underneath it fades gradually into unconverted hard clay, but its practical effect is enormous. Fired clay is much harder than that which has merely been sun-baked, and not so brittle. It is completely nonporous and so will retain a liquid indefinitely without loss, and contact with water does not return it to the plastic state.

With any sort of clay, pure or impure, the lowest temperature that will produce these changes on a large enough scale for practical consequences is about 900°F, and for a good glaze temperatures as high as 2650°F may be needed. Achieving such temperatures is not altogether a matter of how hot a fire can be made to burn. Rather, it requires confining heat to a small volume and feeding it in faster than it can leak away. With an open campfire, 900°F is attainable if the fire is kept going long enough and the clay is close enough to it and is protected from air currents. If pots ready for firing are piled on a bed of rocks, and wood or dried dung is heaped over them and burned, temperatures from 1200° to 1700°F can be produced, and this method has been widely used. Even better is to heat the interior of a thick-walled closed chamber, a consideration that may have led to the invention of ovens (remember the clay ovens used at Qalat Jarmo: p. 468). An oven designed especially for the baking of clay is a *kiln*.

Fired pottery was a remarkably early human achievement. It is attested in Japan and in eastern Europe from at least 8000 B.C., at Çatal Hüyük in Turkey from about 7000 B.C. (p. 469), a thousand years before any evidence of domestication at that site, and in the central Andes from the second millennium B.C. Anyone who wants to defend a hypothesis of "monogenesis" (single place and time of origin) for fired pottery has got to postulate some bizarre migrations and diffusions. At least two separate origins, one in the Old World and one in the New, seems much more likely.

By the beginning of the ethnographic present, fired pottery was known in the parts of the world shown in Figure 31-25. Presumably it was known to the invaders of Polynesia, but abandoned because of the lack of adequate raw materials in their new homes. For cooking, the Polynesians made up for the loss by inventing a stone pit oven. In the New World, pottery was ignored in California and nearby because they had their superb baskets (p. 511), and in the Northwest because they liked their expertly made wooden boxes. The pottery in the late aboriginal Northeastern Woodlands of North America looks like it might represent a flowing-together of two separate traditions, one moving up from the south (ultimately from the Andes?), and one spreading from the west across Bering Strait, Alaska, and Canada, from somewhere in Asia.

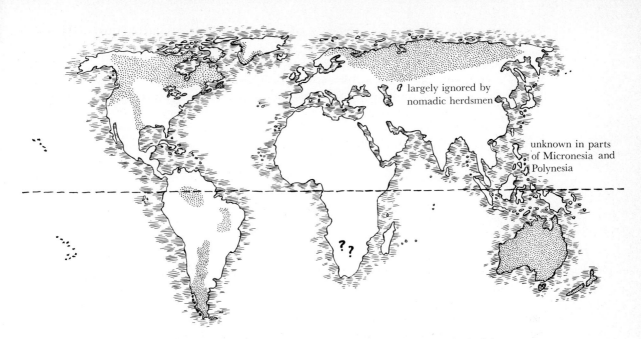

largely ignored by
nomadic herdsmen

unknown in parts
of Micronesia and
Polynesia

? ?

FIGURE 31-25. DISTRIBUTION OF POTTERY-FIRING. The blackened areas are the chief regions where the firing of pottery was *not* practiced at the eve of the ethnographic present, variously because the art had not been developed or had been lost, because suitable clay was not available, or because the fragility of pottery vessels was incompatible with nomadic ways of life.

THE WHEEL

None of the more complex developments in ceramic technology have spread as widely as the practice of firing. The chief of these, and the only one we need discuss, is the *potter's wheel.* This developed only in Eurasia, and it is hard to say just when it appeared because the appearance was gradual.

In shaping a pot, the potter must work all around it in a fairly uniform way, either by crawling around it or by turning the forming pot around on its vertical axis. It will not do to pick the pot up in order to turn it, since the clay adheres with some force to the surface on which it rests and lifting it would introduce unwanted deformations. But suppose the pot sits at the middle of a flat stone that has a slight projection from its bottom. The whole stone, if adequately balanced, can then be given a partial turn whenever required. Something like this was the beginning of the potter's wheel.

It was hardly the end. In time, the wheel became a mechanically operated vertical lathe, run by a foot pedal, whirling rapidly around its axis while the potter's hands and fingers pressed the clay up and down and changed its diameter at various elevations.[10] This technique can produce much more exact radial symmetry than any

[10] This sentence explains a less familiar thing in terms of a more familiar one; but, historically, the potter's wheel was the great granddaddy of all lathes of all types.

other. On the other hand, that is all it *can* do, so that spouts, handles, or feet have to be shaped separately and pressed into place, and noncircular ware has to be made in some other way. A pot made on a wheel is said to be *thrown* or *turned*.

The true potter's wheel is attested in Egypt and Mesopotamia as of about 3000 B.C.; in more primitive form it is doubtless much older. A modern one is shown in Figure 31-26.

PRODUCTS AND BYPRODUCTS

The word *pottery* is derived from *pot,* and may make us think of ceramics too narrowly in terms of basket-shaped vessels. That would be a mistake. Ceramic techniques have been used for manufacturing artifacts of a great many different shapes and uses.

There are certain constraints. No ceramic ware is sufficiently nonbrittle to be used for hammers, chisels, or other tools that must deliver or receive sharp blows, but it can be used for spoons, ladles, paddles, and beaters that will be applied to liquids or to soft substances (such as clay itself). The early Mesopotamians even used ceramic sickles. Good clay is too rare to be used in such massive constructions as walls, which would in any case be impossible to kiln. But one can make bricks and tiles of cheap clay bulked out with straw, and then build with them. Properly shaped tiles can also be used in place of bundles of straw or wooden shingles for roofing. Tiles in the form of circular or semicircular cylinders can be laid down as water conduits: the art of plumbing began with clay pipes and those of our bathroom fixtures of today which are not metal are still ceramic. Ceramic objects designed to hold or carry liquids or the like can be made in every shape from completely flat, like a plate, to narrow and tubular with a small neck, like a vase. Even fifes have been ceramic, and ocarinas still are.

Soft clay can be used as mortar to hold construction stones or bricks together, and, in fact, this was the first substance so used, other mortars being introduced as the results of experiments in search of something better. Clay mortar is thus the ancestor of the impure gypsum (calcium sulphate dihydrate, $CaSO_4(H_2O)_2$) used by the Egyptian pyramid-builders (p. 500), and of all the mortars developed since then. If instead of using big stones or bricks and mortar as a binder, you use more mortar and a lot of pebbles and sand, you can pour and mold the mixture; this is what we call "concrete." Hence soft clay, though never itself used in this way, is also the ancestor of the mixed lime and volcanic ash used as cement by the Romans and of the portland cement developed in the early nineteenth century A.D. in England, as well as of the various other binders we now use in building and highway construction, including tar (from certain pine trees) and asphalt (a mineral, probably, like petroleum, of ultimately organic origin).

Part of the foregoing has to do not with ceramics proper but with the strikingly germinal nature of early ceramic discoveries. Working with clay gave people ideas that they transferred to other substances. The search for good clays of various kinds, and for ways of removing impurities or of mixing clay with other materials to improve

FIGURE 31-26. MODERN POTTER'S WHEEL. Note the foot pedal. (Courtesy of William Rosenthal.)

its quality (or to make it cheaper) for certain uses, obviously promoted the discovery and exploitation of other sorts of substances available here and there in Earth's crust. The expert control of heat production and flow needed for kilning was transferred in time to the melting of metal and the smelting of metal ores, and the first melting of metal may have been an accident in a kiln intended for clay (p. 532). The first man-made glass may have come about in a similar way: the earliest artificed glass so far discovered is from the middle of the third millennium B.C., in Egypt and in Mesopotamia. In the same part of the world, the potter's wheel appears archaeologically at about the same time as do the first wheels used for transport, but the former was probably older and contributed to the development of the latter; in the New World, where pots were never aboriginally shaped by turning, wheeled vehicles also were absent—except in the Valley of Mexico, where they appear about A.D. 1000 but exclusively as children's toys.

All our discussion of pottery so far has been of its technical and utilitarian aspects. But from the very beginning, some people must have enjoyed the feel of clay in their hands and gotten a kick out of shaping it into something attractive to the eye. This is why I felt free to include, a few paragraphs back (p. 518), the allusion to mud pies: kids in our culture still make them if they live where they can and their parents are enlightened enough to allow it, and in many a kindergarten they are given plastic stuff to play with. The earliest ceramic objects yet dug up by archaeologists in Europe, mentioned on page 442, were figurines, not containers.

Primitive potters—meaning simply those who do not use a wheel—decorate their ware with incised lines or with designs painted on with some substance that will look different from the rest of the pot after baking. (Another method is mentioned below, p. 527.) Even when they don't do this, they try to achieve a shape that conforms to their own aesthetic preferences.

With or without a wheel, potters in most known societies, tribal or civil (there are scattered exceptions, such as Africa, where artists have preferred to work in other media), have conformed to the human universal for craftsmen, in that they have taken pride in doing well things that are extremely difficult to do at all (p. 272). In this way there have arisen a number of traditions, some of which are known to almost everyone in our own society. Everyone has heard of "Grecian urns" (ancient Greece, eighth century B.C. on) and of "Ming vases" (Ming is a Chinese dynasty, A.D. 1368–1644). In civil societies, wealthy people have become patrons of unusually gifted and dedicated potters and have made it possible for them to spend their lifetimes in the production of beautiful things.

BY HIS BOOTSTRAPS

32

✖

MORE NEW ARTIFACTS FOR OLD

✖ The way to protect a valued object *A* from a dangerous thing *C* is to put *B* between them, *B* being something that cannot hurt *A* and cannot be injured by *C*. This is the principle of *fencing* (p. 461) and of *wrapping*.

Most often *A* is inside and *C* outside. This is so when *B* is a cell wall, the bark of a tree, the integument of an animal, the clothing or housing of a human being, the detached animal hide in which the Menomini wrapped the important ingredients of a power pack, the fence around a garden plot, a slipcover drawn over upholstery. Less often, *C* is inside: radioactive isotopes are packed in thick lead-lined containers for shipment. In some cases there is disagreement. Visitors to a zoo think the cages are there to protect them. Zoo-keepers say they are at least equally intended to protect the animals.

Protective wrapping of things (as over against the clothing and shelter of people) is obviously a very old human practice. If a chipped flint knife is to be carried from one place to another, putting it into a skin sheath or pouch suspended from the owner's waist belt frees his hands, protects the blade from breakage, and protects the owner from getting cut. Wrapping thus gets mixed up with carrying. The confusion of the two is clearest in the case of liquids or granular substances, where a container at one and the same time keeps foreign substances out and makes storage and transportation possible. Therefore most of the manufacturing techniques discussed in the preceding chapter are of relevance here too.

But in the present connection another set of interrelated techniques comes up. We shall call them *surfacing*. This is done to solid things (artifacts or the human body); it either removes foreign matter from the surface or adds a continuous or discontinuous layer of some different substance to that surface. The aim can be protection, decoration, the imparting of desired properties such as slipperiness or roughness, or any combination of these. Note, however, that polishing a stone tool is not surfacing by our definition, since what it removes is part of the stone rather than extraneous adhering matter. In the same way, building out the wall of a clay vessel by adding more of the same kind of clay is not surfacing, since the material added is the stuff that is already there. But if the added clay is of a different kind or color, we had better count it in.

REMOVAL SURFACING

Removal surfacing is done often by brushing or washing.

A brush is a bundle of stiff fibers loose at one end but fastened together to form a handle, or into a separate handle, at the other. A big brush is a broom. Brushes or brooms are found all over the world, and their origin is unknown, since the substances used in making them are not likely to survive for archaeological recovery. But brushes are also used for additive surfacing (e.g., painting), and so we can suspect that they were available already to the cave-wall artists of the European late Pleistocene (p. 274). We are not certain of this, because those paintings may have been done without a brush.

For the treatment of hairy surfaces and for the care of human head hair, brushes are associated with combs, a derivative with a single row of very stiff projections ("teeth"). Combs are also widespread. Archaeologically they appear only at the time of the Swiss Lake Dwellers (p. 510) of the fourth millennium B.C. They are probably much older than that, for they are an excellent weapon against those perennial enemies of mankind, lice.

Washing in water will remove loose dirt from a surface that is not injured by the water; for example, from human skin. Hot water is better than cold, and hot sweat does nicely (p. 16). Washing is more effective if the water is infused with a saponifying agent that lowers its surface tension. Many tribes in the ethnographic present have found plants whose juices can be added to water for this purpose. The first mention of soap something like our own is by the Roman naturalist Plinius (about A.D. 23–79), who describes a type made by boiling goat tallow and causticized wood ashes and treating the resulting paste with salt.

If hair is to be removed from a hairy surface neither brushing nor washing will do. It can be cut off (*shaving*), singed off, plucked out, or removed chemically with a depilatory. Shaving and singeing must have begun very early, in connection with the dressing of animal skins, but the removal of beards, head hair, and even body hair is also widespread. Wealthy early Egyptians used razors of gold and silver. The sultans and merchant princes of Muslim times in southwest Asia and adjacent regions preferred their harem girls hairless from the neck down, and achieved this by having the body hair plucked out by the roots with tweezers. The problem with depilatories has always been that of finding a substance that will remove hair without injuring the skin. Despite this danger, people have been using them in some parts of the world for at least the last few centuries.

ADDITIVE SURFACING

Additive surfacing is sometimes done with a brush and sometimes without.

LUBRICATION. If the added substance is liquid and is supposed to stay liquid, rendering the surface slippery, it is a *lubricant*. (Some powders are lubricants too.) Many of the substances human beings have smeared on themselves have been lubricants, but the aim seems mainly to have been protection and decoration, not reduced friction. Lubricants are of course vital for the smooth working of a machine with moving parts. The first such machines are only about five thousand years old (in the river valleys of southwest Asia), and the archaeological evidence doesn't tell us whether animal fats were smeared at vital places from the beginning or this practice came later.

ROSINING.   The added substance may be intended to *increase* friction. Rosin is the opposite of wax. Rosin is obtained by processing the sap of certain pines and firs. It is rubbed on the hairs of a bow to make a stringed instrument speak; a baseball pitcher rosins his hand to get a firm grip on the ball (many a batter uses the dust near home plate for a comparable purpose). Workers in earlier ages may similarly have covered their hands with chalk dust or powdered emery so that their tools or the objects they were working on would not slip.

PAINTING AND ITS KIN.   Additive surfacing may apply a liquid which is then supposed to dry out and leave a solid (or supercooled liquid) film. Substances used in this way have no single name, but are variously known as paint, varnish, lacquer, dye, and ink, depending on the context.

Here, again, we have a category of great antiquity. The paints used by the late Pleistocene cave-wall artists (and found widely also in grave sites) were of a type known almost everywhere: *ochres* mixed with water or with some sort of animal fat. Ochres are either clayey or chalky soils that contain hydrated iron oxide; that ingredient gives them their colors, which range from pale yellow through red to brown and violet. Deposits of ochre are found in every part of the world, as pockets in stratified rocks or mixed up with rubble. Some types can be used virtually without processing. Colors can be modified, however, by a technique now available for tens of thousands of years: heating in a fire. For blacks and dark blues, the Palaeolithic artists had manganese oxides, which, like ochres, can be collected from Earth's crust. These substances are still used today as paint pigments, though often synthesized in exact proportions instead of being gathered.

Additive surfacing of this last type always involves a substance composed of two parts: the part that is supposed to evaporate (the *vehicle*) and the part that is supposed to stay.[1] If the latter supplies color, it is a *pigment,* but some residual films are intentionally colorless.

We can illustrate vehicle and residuum with a widespread potter's practice of finishing a pot, before baking, with a *slip* or *wash.* The shaped pot is dipped into a thin mixture of water and clay, the latter sometimes of the same type used for the body of the pot and sometimes different. Upon firing, the water disappears and the clay stays behind and becomes part of the glaze. This gives a smoother finish than can be obtained otherwise. Also, before the pot is dipped some parts of it can be covered by material (such as beeswax) that will shed the wash, so that a design is produced.

Wood fires yield an excellent black pigment in the form of *carbon black:* very small particles of amorphous carbon that result when almost any organic material is partly oxidized. The charred end of a stick will leave a trail of carbon black when drawn

[1] In certain very recent surfacing substances, the hardening is produced not by evaporation of a vehicle but by chemical changes.

across a rough surface, or it can be collected by letting smoke particles gather on something and then scraping them off. We do not know if the late Pleistocene painters used carbon black, but they could have. It is still the chief pigment for the special paints, called "inks," used in writing and printing.

Vegetable dyestuffs of various sorts have been discovered and used all over the world from time immemorial, for coloring animal skins, textiles, or basketry, for decorating the face and the body, or even for injection under the epidermis by tattooing. The dyeing of textiles was a complex and booming industry five thousand years ago in Egypt and Mesopotamia. Some of the dyes, such as indigo and madder, were still in use less than two centuries ago; so was woad, developed maybe a thousand years earlier than that in Europe. The history of the English word *purple* points to another source and attests to the avidity of the search for good pigments with interesting colors. It comes, via successive borrowings, from Ionic Greek *porphýra*, which named both the dye and the small mollusks (*Purpura haemastoma* and *Murex brandaris*) from which it was obtained by a process so complicated and costly that for many centuries only the very wealthy could afford it; hence the color purple as an emblem of royalty. Aboriginal Middle America made a comparable contribution in the form of *cochineal*, a red dyestuff obtained from the dried bodies of females of an insect (*Dactylopius coccus*) that feeds on cactus plants.

Vegetable oils as vehicles, rather than animal fat or water, perhaps did not begin in earnest until agriculture was increasing the available supply. Linseed oil (from flax) has been an important vehicle for 3000 years or more.

As recently as a century ago good-quality paints that would yield long-term protection as well as attractive appearance were expensive. Massive equipment that needed a coat of protection against weathering was covered often and cheaply with substances hardly more durable than whitewash (a mixture of calcium carbonate, water, and a little glue). Inexpensive paints and dyes of good quality were foreshadowed by the synthesis of the first coal-tar dye in England in 1856; sophisticated and productive investigations of paint chemistry began in earnest only after 1900.

PRINTING is a kind of surfacing, usually additive. Seals were used in early Mesopotamia to stamp distinctive marks into clay before it was hardened; perhaps sometimes they were inked and applied to surfaces that were already hard. Such seals appear in China in the fifth century B.C. By the third century A.D. the Chinese were printing words on paper, from wooden blocks on each of which the text of a whole page had been engraved. Since Chinese was written in a system that required thousands of different unit characters, there would have been little gain in efficiency in preparing separate blocks for the individual characters and assembling them into the proper arrangement for a page. This procedure (printing from "movable type") is efficient for alphabetical writing systems (p. 579), in which the number of different characters is relatively small; its development will come up later (p. 621).

GLUING

There is one further type of surfacing, akin to additive surfacing: the preparation of one surface so that it will adhere to another.

Machine shops use, as gauges, things called "Johansson blocks" (invented in 1896 by the Swede C. E. Johansson). A Johansson block is a cube of steel machined with such precision that its faces depart from absolute flatness, in some cases, by as little as one one-hundred-thousandth of an inch. If two blocks are put face-to-face it is difficult to pull, twist, or slide them apart. The two surfaces are so close together that electrons in each are actively attracted by positive ions in the other (p. 530). Astronauts trying to handle metal tools in the vacuum of outer space have found it difficult because the surfaces tend to "bind" together. These surfaces are not nearly so smooth as the faces of a Johansson block, but they are free of the layer of dust motes that inevitably forms on any surface in Earth's atmosphere and serves as a lubricant whether one wants it so or not; hence some chemical bonding can take place across the interface.

That tells us what gluing must do. Few solid materials can be machined as smooth as steel, and the force that holds two Johansson blocks together, though striking, is not all that strong. To make two solid surfaces adhere usefully, one inserts between them a layer of some substance that will penetrate the nooks and crannies of each surface and form scattered interface bonds with it. Additive surfacing of the kind we have called "painting" must adhere to a single surface in this way; gluing differs only in that it must adhere to two surfaces at once, and in that, as the glue dries, it must also develop strong internal bonding. We see immediately why different paints and glues are needed for different kinds of surfaces, and also why a layer of glue is stronger if it is thinner.

Early man had access to all sorts of sticky substances: mud and clay, vegetable saps, animal juices. Some of these can be rendered stickier by heating. The evidence is largely indirect, but it seems likely that gluing is about as old as hafting (p. 398). Dry hafting is possible if one of the pieces to be fastened is of wood and it is squeezed into or over the other piece in the process of joining. Yet the wood contains sap, and the squeezing may cause some to exude and, as it dries, to serve as a glue. Maybe something like this was what suggested the whole notion of gluing.

Fastening things together with cordage is improved if the string is first dipped into an adhesive; this is probably very early. The feathering of arrows is not so old as the bow and arrow (p. 437), but wherever and whenever it came along some sort of gluing was necessary. Making a sinew-backed bow also requires gluing. Seed-grinding in the early Neolithic yielded flour paste, still used. Milking domesticated animals gave casein glue, also still common today. By early Egyptian times casein glue and glues of animal gelatin were being used by artisans in the manufacture of wooden furniture. Sealing wax came into use in medieval Europe for marking or sealing official documents; it was first made with beeswax, turpentine, and some pigment, usually vermilion.

Gluing has also been used to make sheets out of filaments (pp. 503–517). The Egyptians cut stems of the papyrus reed (*Cyperus papyrus,* a sedge) into long strips, laid them down in a row with adjacent ones overlapping, put down a second row at right angles to the first, and then wet them with water and a glue. It is not clear what the glue was. It may have been produced by the reeds themselves, under the action of the water. After drying, the sheet was used for writing, not only in Egypt but eventually (by the fifth century B.C. at latest) all over the eastern Mediterranean and eastwards as far as Mesopotamia. Glued papyrus "paper" was the best portable writing material available in this region until the importation of true paper from China (p. 517).

METAL ✗ In our everyday life, a metal is any of a number of substances with rather shiny surfaces (unless they are tarnished), not easily described in an inclusive way but clearly distinguishable from rocks, soils, and clay. Like a mineral, a piece of metal has measurable hardness and toughness. In addition, metals are more or less *malleable* and more or less *ductile.* Malleability is the ease with which the material can be beaten into a thin sheet; ductility is the ease with which it can be drawn into a thread. As might be expected, both of these tend to increase with increasing temperature, except that both become meaningless at the point at which the substance melts.

Physically, a crystal is metallic if it consists of a regularly spaced three-dimensional lattice of positive ions and of a "cloud" of electrons (which would be the electrons of the valence shells if the atoms were separated) moving more or less freely through the spaces between the lattice points (Figure 32-1). Well over half the elements of the periodic table are metallic. Many metallic substances are *alloys:* the lattice points of the crystal are occupied by positive ions of two or more metallic elements rather than of just one. Most also contain "impurities": scattered bits of nonmetallic elements. The properties of alloys are often usefully different from those of any one-element metal, and even properly distributed impurities can be helpful (p. 537). A molar quantity of a metallic substance is never a single perfect crystal. Instead, there are planes of slight discontinuity where adjacent sets of lattice points are somewhat out of line with one another. This has something to do with rendering the material deformable and making for malleability and ductility. It also bears in some way on what is called "metal fatigue": subjected to repeated stresses and sudden changes of temperature over a long period of time, a piece of metal develops microscopic fracture surfaces and will eventually flake or break.

One of the commonest metallic elements is aluminum, which makes up about one sixth of Earth's crust. Its melting point is only 1220.3°F. Yet it took five or six thousand years of accumulating metallurgical know-how before aluminum could be extracted in quantity from the minerals in which it is so abundant and made available in bulk for human use. On the other hand, platinum, which is quite rare and whose melting point is a lofty 3216°F, was fashioned into decorative trinkets hundreds or thousands of years ago by the Indians of southern South America.

The reason for this is that metallic elements vary widely in their chemical behavior. Some, such as gold, silver, and platinum, enter into compounds only with great difficulty. Others, including aluminum and sodium, do so at the drop of a metaphorical hat. The hat in question was dropped thousands of millions of years ago when Earth's crust was still molten—if it ever was; if not, the compounds were formed during Earth's condensation (p. 319). The formation of the compounds released a lot of energy. To break the compounds and extract the metal, an equivalent amount of energy has to be supplied. But the chemically inactive metallic elements stayed

    BY HIS BOOTSTRAPS

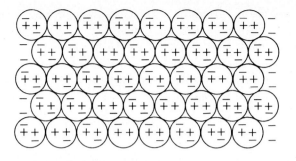

FIGURE 32-1. METAL STRUCTURE. The large circles represent the metallic ions, in a lattice. The isolated minus signs are electrons of the electron cloud, free to move through the lattice (as under the influence of a magnetic field), and, at the surface, giving the metal its sheen. (Modified, with permission, from *Chemistry: Principles and processes* by Michell J. Sienko and Robert A. Plane, 4th ed., McGraw-Hill, 1972.)

relatively aloof, and hence are to be found in Earth's crust in the "native" state, which means in the form of relatively pure nuggets.

Only fifteen metallic elements are known to occur natively, or in native alloys, on or near Earth's land surface: iron, cobalt, and nickel (all these of meteoric origin); copper, arsenic, ruthenium, rhodium, silver, antimony, tellurium, iridium, platinum, gold, mercury, and bismuth. Some of these are exceedingly rare. In addition, mercury is a liquid at ordinary biospheric temperatures, and arsenic is highly poisonous.

FIRST USE

The first metals used by man were those of the above list common enough in certain regions to be picked up and played with: copper, silver, platinum, and gold.

For someone whose tools are of stone, wood, bone, and clay, and who never heard of smelting, a nugget of gold or a lump of native copper is just another kind of pebble—until he tries to make something out of it. He then either gives up, because standard stone-or wood-working techniques are useless, or discovers by experiment that the lump can be hammered into a beautiful or useful shape and that polishing renders it interestingly bright and shiny. Silver, platinum, and gold are all malleable, but too soft to make into effective tools. That is why the Indians of southern South America (one of the few parts of the world where native platinum is—or formerly was—to be found) made only ornamental ware of their nuggets, and why the aborigines of the Andes and of Middle America used gold and silver only in the same way. This was equally the case of the earliest gold and silver artifacts of the Old World, and still holds to a remarkable extent today.

Native copper is another matter. It can be hammered; it can be abraded; it can be hardened by beating; it makes points and edges that compare favorably with those of polished flint; it is less brittle than flint. Coppercraft without smelting or casting, but possibly involving beating the substance while it is hot, may have arisen at various times and places where the stuff happened to be available. We know it was practiced aboriginally in the Great Lakes region of North America (though not by the Menomini and their nearest kin at the time of first European contact), and that it began in the Andes about 2000 B.C. A third place where we know it developed is southwest Asia. Recent excavations at Çayönü Tepesi (just southwest of Ergani in eastern Turkey) turned up an edged tool made by beating a lump of native copper, and three small copper pins, one of them bent and the other two represented only by broken-off ends, on which points had been produced by abrasion. They date from some time just before 7000 B.C.; these are the earliest metal artifacts so far known.

CASTING

The next step in metallurgy was taken in southwest Asia and in the Andes, perhaps nowhere else: *casting.* It was discovered that native copper can be melted. The liquid can then be poured into a mold to cool, yielding the desired shape more easily than it can be attained by beating. In southwest Asia casting seems to have begun between 6000 and 5000 B.C.; we don't know when it began in the Andes. The discovery may have been accidental, along the lines suggested on page 523. The melting point of pure copper—native copper lumps tend to be at least 99% pure—is 1981°F, hard to achieve with an open fire but in no way unrealistic for a pottery kiln. Or the first lumps to be melted may have been native alloys. If the lump contains some silver, zinc, or tin, the melting point is lower, ranging down to 1760°F for pure silver, 786°F for pure zinc, and a mere 450°F for pure tin.

Nevertheless, the casting of copper, pure or alloyed, calls for the establishment and maintenance of high temperatures, and either this or the southwest Asian ceramics of the same period led to two important innovations.

One was *charcoal,* made by piling sticks of wood (or bones) into a heap, covering with dirt to cut down on the oxygen supply, and firing. The wood is partly burned and partly baked. The more volatile ingredients are driven off. The hard residue is dry and porous. A piece of wood burns only at the surface, where oxygen from the air is available, and the moisture content tends constantly to quench the flames. The porousness of charcoal lets the air penetrate, greatly increasing the burning surface, and the dryness makes it burn hotter.[2]

The other innovation was the *bellows* (Figure 32-2), a springy bag-shaped contraption with two holes and a valve: when it is squeezed, air is forced out at one end; when the squeezing stops, air is drawn in at the other. Bellows let the metal-worker use his arms or legs instead of his lungs, which earlier on had been used to supply the fire with ample oxygen.

Gold has a melting point of 1945°F. It was melted and cast, as was silver, both in early southwest Asia and in the Andes. In addition, silver-copper alloy and electrum (silver-gold alloy) were used in the former region and gold-copper alloy in the latter. Andean gold was picked up in the form of nuggets or obtained by panning mountain streams. Copper, silver, and gold metallurgy, without smelting but with many sophisticated techniques of other sorts (including heat welding and soldering, p. 534), spread

[2]Charcoal remained the best fuel for metallurgical fires until the invention of *coke* in England in the sixteenth century. Coke is made from bituminous coal in essentially the same way that charcoal is made from wood.

FIGURE 32-2. "Drum bellows." Still in use recently in Rhodesia, where the photograph was taken. An Egyptian tomb painting of about 1500 B.C. shows a similar type, operated with the feet instead of with sticks (as in the picture) or with the hands. (From *Technology in the ancient world* by Henry Hodges, Allen Lane The Penguin Press, London, 1970. Copyright 1970 by Henry Hodges, and reprinted with his permission and that of the publisher.)

from the Andes southwards into northern Argentina and also north as far as Mexico, arriving in the latter region well before the coming of the Spanish.

Smelting and Fire Refining

The supply of surface native copper in southwest Asia was limited. Eventually it was all used up. Long before that, it had become too scarce to fill the demand. But the surface deposits tended to cluster about outcroppings of cupreous ores: that is, of minerals (copper sulfides and oxides) in which copper is a plentiful ingredient. Some of these ores, having been exposed at the surface to weathering for a long time, took the form of bright blue pebbles. Someone, in desperation because lumps of native copper were not to be found, must have tried various substitutes, and when he tried the blue stones it worked. Brought to red heat and then cooled, they had turned—presto!—into copper. Chemically, the compounds had broken up and the nonmetallic ingredients had boiled off.

This was how *smelting* began, around 4000 B.C. Smelting is the separation of metals from the ores that contain them by the application of heat. As soon as this process had worked with one kind of stuff, surely it was tried on other kinds. Thus various new metals became available, including tin, zinc, and lead (melting point 621.5°F).

The first smelted copper was about as pure as native copper, which means 99% or better. When the surface outcroppings had been used up and miners had to dig deeper, obtaining nonweathered ore, the percentage of copper went down and that of certain other metals, and of unwanted impurities, went up. A new technique developed: *fire refining*. After smelting, the crude product is melted under oxidizing conditions. The impurities oxidize first and rise to the top of the molten mass, where they can be skimmed off and discarded.

In Egypt during the third millennium B.C. the smelted alloy was 94 to 95% copper, the balance being principally either arsenic or tin. The copper-tin alloy, *bronze,* proved better for some uses than pure copper. The practice arose of smelting the two from their separate ores, fire-refining them, and then mixing them together, with 85 to 90 parts copper, 15 to 10 parts tin. Figure 32-3 shows the distribution in early southwest Asia of the sources of copper and tin ores, both in demand as bronze came more and more into use. Some of the man-made alloys actually contained zinc rather than tin, yielding what we now call *brass,* but the distinction seems not to have been fully recognized until Roman times.

Heat Welding and Soldering

At some point in the early history of metallurgy it became essential to have some way of fastening pieces of metal firmly together. Two techniques were devised, both still used.

One was *heat welding*. The surfaces or edges to be joined are heated until they begin to melt, and are then touched together so that they fuse as they cool.

The other was a special kind of gluing (p. 528) called *soldering*. The solder was a tin-lead(-zinc?) alloy with a low melting point. Dripped molten onto the joint, the solder wetted the metal surfaces and, in cooling and solidifying, held them tight.

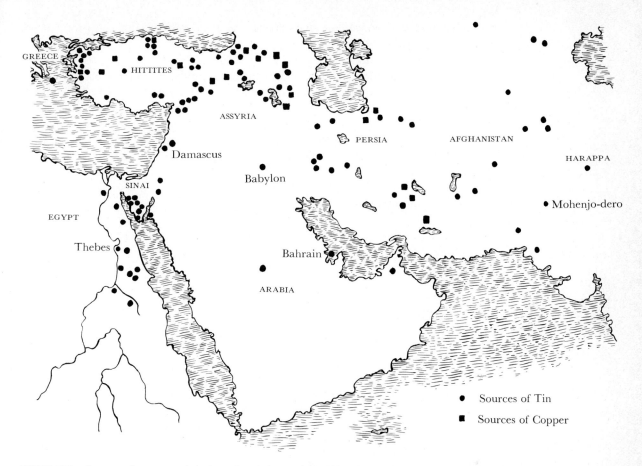

GREECE · HITTITES · ASSYRIA · Damascus · SINAI · EGYPT · Thebes · Babylon · Bahrain · ARABIA · PERSIA · AFGHANISTAN · HARAPPA · Mohenjo-dero

● Sources of Tin

■ Sources of Copper

FIGURE 32-3. Sources of copper and tin in early southwest Asia. (After Coon 1955.)

EARLY PRODUCTS AND EFFECTS

The first uses of copper and of bronze in the Old World were for decorative objects, and for tools of various sorts that had theretofore been made of diverse other materials, especially of polished stone.

With casting (probably no earlier), certain tools were invented that had no clear premetallic prototypes. One was scissors, for use on animal skins and on sheets of woven materials (p. 508). A second was the saw, for the cutting and trimming of wood or stone. If the metal saw had a forerunner, it could only have been some animal's jawbone with teeth in place, of little avail in carpentry.

A third was the metal nail, invented somewhere in southwest Asia or northeastern Africa not later than 2700 B.C. Ridiculously simple, it nevertheless afforded a new and more secure way to fasten together pieces of wood or of certain other materials, and led, in time, to a kind of architecture that otherwise could never have existed, as well as revolutionizing items as diverse as vehicles, cabinets and coffins, furniture and footwear.

Artisans got a fair supply of the metal tools they needed, but otherwise there was very early a specialization reminiscent of that which differentiated the uses of domesticated horses and domesticated asses in the same part of the world (p. 475). Metals were expensive materials and costly to work with. Decorative metal objects went to the wealthy. Metal hardware went chiefly to the military, while cheaper and less durable materials continued to be used for the hardware of household and farm. Soldiers were equipped with metal spears, javelins, and knives; they carried beaten copper or bronze shields in place of the earlier leather ones; when they took to chariots, the wheels were shod with metal to cut down on wear. The peasant's knife was of stone, his scythe of wood and flint or of clay, his cart—if he was lucky enough to have one at all—equipped with wheels of unprotected wood or stone. All this is a commentary on developing social structure, about which we shall say more in the next chapters.

Copper and then bronze spread rapidly from southwest Asia: Crete by 3000 B.C., Sicily and the region north of the Caucasus by 2500, mainland western Europe by 2000, Britain and Scandinavia by 1800. Copper is proposed in Chinese legend for 2500 B.C., which may be truth or myth, but by the second millennium B.C. archaeological evidence attests to a Chinese bronzeware tradition of great complexity.

Iron

Iron, so widely used today, is very different from the metals we have mentioned so far. Its melting point is 2795°F. Like aluminum (p. 530) it is highly reactive chemically, given especially to oxidation if there is any oxygen around. Hence, despite its abundance (the eighth commonest element in Earth's crust), virtually all of it is locked up in minerals. The exception is meteoric iron, and even that has an outer layer of rust.

The Aztecs managed to beat lumps of meteoric iron into decorative figures. The raw material was so rare and the working so difficult that they valued these objects more highly than any of their gold, silver, or copper work. The production of such "wrought iron" objects from meteoric iron, with no smelting or the like, probably arose in various other parts of the world, perhaps including southwest Asia as copper and bronze were first being exploited there.

Iron metallurgy beyond this cold-working stage developed late. The beginning seems to have been about 2000 B.C. The place may have been Anatolia, and the innovators may have been the Hittites (of whom more later: p. 593) or their vassals; but none of that is certain. Getting iron out of iron ore calls for more than mere heating. If you just heat it, then when the stuff cools off it is an unpromising mess of bits of iron mixed up with coagulations of the other substances present in the ore (the "slag"). In the far east (India and perhaps China), a way was worked out by which the ore could be taken to a much higher temperature, so that the slag also melted and could be dipped off. In southwest Asia that was not done. Instead, the half-molten mess was pulled hot from the furnace and beaten. This consolidated the iron and drove out some of the slag. Then it was reheated and beaten some more. This iterative procedure is costly of fuel and very hard work, but eventually one gets a lump of reasonably pure iron. However, iron obtained in this way is softer than well made bronze, and can only be worked by beating, whereas bronze can be cast. So iron at first offered very little competition for bronze and copper.

The next step eventually put iron in the forefront. About 1000 B.C. it was discovered that if a mass of iron is kept at red heat for a good long time in a charcoal fire it becomes much harder. It also helps if it is cooled suddenly, by being thrust into water or some other liquid, rather than slowly (the older iron permitted only slow cooling). The result of this treatment is *steel*. We now know—in a way—why the treatment works. Bits of carbon from the charcoal fire are absorbed by the iron, and affect its crystal structure (p. 530).

For a long time steel remained a curiosity. Its production was too slow and complicated for it to compete with the well established copper and bronze. But even low-quality steel is much harder than any bronze or copper, and finally it won. It usurped the honorable position of the earlier metals among rulers and soldiers, and spread outwards in a wave behind the expanding frontiers of the softer metals, reaching Italy well before Roman times and eventually affecting almost all parts of Europe and penetrating deep into Africa.

Heat Technology

Our ancestors used fire first for warmth, light, and protection, then for the preparation of food. Practical by-guess-and-by-God chemical engineering began the first time someone heated up something other than food and found a use for the resulting gunk, perhaps as glue or paint, perhaps as poison for the tip of a dart. The merit of fired pottery led to experiments in the hearthing and fueling of fires: hence the oven and the kiln, eventually the furnace used for the melting of metals and the smelting of ores, and hence, also, the invention of charcoal and of the bellows—all this, in a few parts of the world, before 3000 B.C.

Food-Handling

The first cooking of food was roasting and boiling. The latter was mainly stone boiling to begin with, eventually replaced in some parts of the world by pot boiling; but in the meantime the conveying of hot stones from a fire to a container required the development of tongs, scoops, or both.

The grinding of grains into flour led first to roasted and then to baked breads (baking is a closed-chamber variant of roasting: p. 406). Ovens for pottery and for foods perhaps developed together.

Somewhere in the Old World, the technique was invented, perhaps by accident, of raising dough with yeast. Yeast also led to beer; fermented fruit-juice wines may be older.

All these developments, also, predate 3000 B.C.

The oldest cooking implements were knives, spoons (including big ones: ladles and

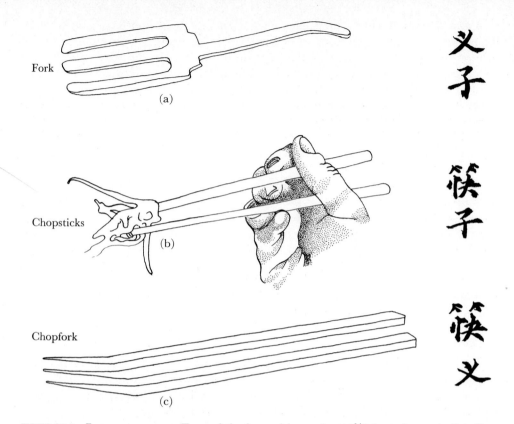

Fork

(a)

Chopsticks

(b)

Chopfork

(c)

义子

筷子

筷义

FIGURE 32-4. EATING IMPLEMENTS. Top: a fork of carved bone, about 4½″ long; dug up in Belt Cave, Iran, by Carleton S. Coon; about eight thousand years old, and presumably too small to be used as a cooking implement. Middle: modern chopsticks, about 10½″ long (chopsticks for cooking are usually longer). Bottom: a recently invented combination intended to promote understanding between East and West. (Top figure after Coon 1955.)

scoops), and tongs. The fork probably derived from a pointed stick; as an implement for eating, rather than for cooking, it was used aboriginally in Fiji for cannibal feasts but was not set on European tables until less than a millennium ago. Chopsticks look like an obvious development from tongs (Figure 32-4). Ivory ones were in use in China 3000 years ago, wooden and bamboo ones long before that.

SOURCES OF ENERGY

Fire was the first source of energy for man's use other than his own metabolism. By 3000 B.C. certain domesticated animals were being used as beasts of burden (at least oxen, in southwest Asia), and water power had long been used to move a laden raft or boat downstream, wind power to move such a vessel against the current (see below, p. 542). This roster of power sources—muscles, fire (heat), water, wind—remained unchanged until the first exploitation of nuclear power in the 1940s. Up

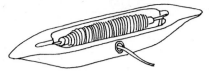

FIGURE 32-5. WEAVING SHUTTLE WITH SPOOL. The type shown is called a "boat shuttle," from its shape. Other modern types have the weft thread coming out through a hole at one end, instead of at the side. The earliest spool shuttles may have been much cruder, but involved the same principle and counted as moving-part artifacts. (After *Step-by-step weaving,* by Nell Znamierowski, Western Publishing Company, New York, 1967.)

to that time, developments in power technology consisted only of new fuels (coal, coke, petroleum), and of new and more sophisticated ways of applying the old sources (steam engines, turbines, internal combustion engine) or of shipping power from place to place (electricity).

MOVING PARTS; MACHINES

The earliest derived tools were made exclusively by *breaking things apart:* for example, flakes are removed from a pebble.

By the end of the middle Pleistocene some artifacts were being made by *fastening things together* (hafting).

In the upper Pleistocene there appeared techniques of *careful loose fastening*—as in a harpoon (p. 436).

The step to artifacts with *moving parts* was taken in the Neolithic. The parts do not separate, but one of them slides along or turns around another.

The only model for this in man's environment is in the bones, joints, muscles, and tendons of the animal body. Early man had plenty of direct experience with such physiological apparatus, in the animals he hunted or husbanded and in himself. It is therefore significant that this model was not followed. In fact, to this day it is very difficult to construct hardware apparatus that will move as arms and legs do. A piece of furniture may stand on legs; a vehicle does not walk on them.

The principle actually followed in moving-part artifacts may have been anticipated by a mat hung in a doorway. The mat can be swung up out of the way when one wishes to pass through, but will then swing back down into place. For it to have this particular freedom of action and yet not fall it must be fastened to the top of the door frame by *hingeing*, however crude. Better hingeing is required for the bellows (p. 532), and in scissors (p. 535). A weaving shuttle becomes a moving-part artifact when it is designed as shown in Figure 32-5: the hollowed-out part holds a shaft on which rotates a spool, so that weft thread can be payed out as needed. The potter's wheel becomes a moving-part artifact as soon as the wheel is mounted on a vertical shaft.

The great breakthrough in moving-part apparatus was something never devised by nature except through man, something as inappropriate for animal tissue as bones, joints, and muscles are for hardware: the *wheel* mounted on an *axle* that is free to rotate within a fixed *housing*.

Hauling things overland on a platform supported by cylindrical rollers (as in the building of the pyramids) is tedious, because as each roller is left behind it must be manhandled around and slipped under the leading edge of the platform. Wheels, axles, and housings produce much more efficient vehicles. In the Old World their development seems to have been taking place in southwest Asia at just about the target terminal date for the discussion of the last chapter and this one, 3000 B.C. In the New World, the wheeled children's toys of Mexico (p. 523) were never enlarged on for practical purposes.

The word *machine* is sometimes used to denote any apparatus with moving parts. I should like to use it in a slightly altered sense, to mean only a moving-part apparatus in which the supplying of power and the supplying of guidance and control are more or less separated. For example, consider the difference (in the modern world) between a piano and an organ. The performer controls either of these by deciding which keys and pedals to depress. The pianist's fingers also supply the necessary power—the harder he hits, the louder the sound. The organist does not do this. The air that blows the organ's pipes comes from a pump operated by electricity from some generating station; the organist merely channels this power properly. Thus, by our definition, though both piano and organ have moving parts only the organ is a machine.

The potter's wheel with a foot treadle was one of the earliest machines, if not the earliest. It is true that the same individual both powered and guided the apparatus, but he did the former with his feet and the latter with his hands. As soon as there is that much separation of the two functions, there can be more: and there was, since some potter's wheels were adapted so that an assistant could do the turning. More generally, as soon as the two functions begin to be separated then artisans can begin to *think* about them separately. On that fact rest all the developments in power technology of the last 5000 years.

Moving Wholes

The earliest carrying was by hand, supplemented by hanging things from the body with belts or in pockets.

For land transport, there were no known advances until the Neolithic, during which appeared land sleds (pulled at first by human beings) and domesticated beasts of burden. We have just mentioned the wooden platform on stone rollers, and the wheeled vehicles that slowly replaced it.

A single wheel at the center of one axle, with housings at either end of the axle, yields the *wheelbarrow,* possibly a Chinese invention. In Figure 32-6, note the similarity in overall design of the wheelbarrow and the plow (Figure 31-3, p. 496).

Two wheels, one axle, and two housings give the *cart* or its military opposite number, the *chariot* (Figure 32-7). As with a wheelbarrow, part of the weight of the load must be supported by the person or animal that supplies the motive force.

A front axle with two housings and two wheels, and a similar assemblage at the rear, make the *wagon* (Figure 32-8), which supports all the weight of the load.

There is a problem with carts and wagons, in that if the wheels are mounted solidly

FIGURE 32-6. Wheelbarrow. The picture is from *T'ien Kung K'ai Wu* (*'The exploitation of the works of nature'*), by Sung Ying-hsing, printed in China in 1637. Wheelbarrows of much this type were known in China as early as the fourth century A.D., probably even earlier. In Europe the wheelbarrow is not attested surely before about the twelfth century A.D., and from then to the present has been of an inefficient type with the load behind the wheel instead of over it, requiring more work from the operator. [Reprinted in Needham 1954, Vol. 4, Part 2 (1965); reproduced here with the permission of the Cambridge University Press.]

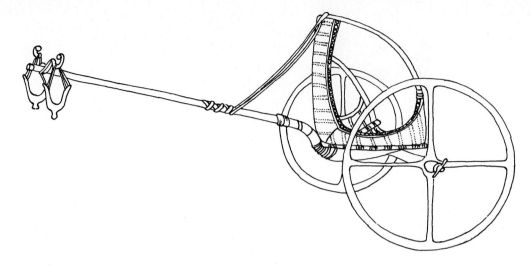

FIGURE 32-7. EARLY EGYPTIAN CHARIOT. (After a reconstruction by Judith Newcomer in *Technology in the ancient world,* by Henry Hodges, Allen Lane The Penguin Press, London, 1970.)

on the axles then those at one side have to drag on the ground when making a turn. This early defect was only slowly overcome.

The use of domesticated animals for draft instead of burden came about gradually, mostly after 3000 B.C.

Land transport requires trails, always marked and in some kinds of terrain requiring clearing or surfacing. As cross-country transportation became more complex, so did road engineering (p. 557). Meanwhile, however, rivers and streams were natural highways needing only very simple devices for their exploitation. Good methods of water transport developed much earlier than those for land transport.

When a solid object is placed in water it sinks until it has displaced a volume of water whose mass equals its own (this is just *isostasy:* p. 319). If the object is less dense than water, it will float, and if its density is low enough it will carry a load. This is the principle of the *raft.* But if the walls of an object are built up in a waterproof way, then even if the material used for the vessel is denser than water the displaced water may not rise high enough to get inside and cause the vessel to founder. This is the principle of the *boat.* Both principles were exploited many thousands of years ago, for travel and transport on inland waters or along shorelines (even the long-isolated Tasmanians could carry themselves and their goods across or along a river or to small offshore islands), and both have been adapted more recently for traversing the open sea.

There are several ways to propel a raft or a boat. One is to let the current carry it. That is fine if there is a current and it is moving in the right direction, not dangerously fast. A second is to pull or push it along from a nearby shore. A third requires that the water be not too deep: one pushes against the bottom with a long pole. A fourth is to push against the water itself, with the hand, a paddle, an oar,

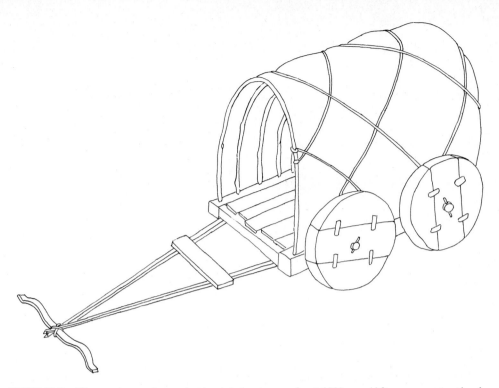

FIGURE 32-8. WAGON. A type in use in the Asiatic steppes about 2500 B.C. (After a reconstruction by Judith Newcomer in *Technology in the ancient world,* by Henry Hodges, Allen Lane The Penguin Press, London, 1970.)

a paddle wheel, or a propeller. An oar is a paddle hinged to the edge of the vessel, so that the combination constitutes a moving-part tool. Paddle wheels and propellers are modern. A fifth method is to arrange for the wind to move the vessel, by supplying a sufficiently large vertical expanse for it to blow against: some sort of sail.

Only the first and second of these five methods are so obvious that they required no special act of discovery. None of the other three is universal in the ethnographic present, but all three are very old. All were in use in southwest Asia by 3000 B.C. The record shows many improvements of technique; it does not show the origins.

33

✖

THE INCIPIENCE OF CIVIL SOCIETY

"The power to tax is the power to destroy" (Chief Justice John Marshall of the U.S. Supreme Court, in the decision on McCulloch *v.* Maryland, 1819).

By five thousand years ago some parts of man's world were becoming very thingy. In most places our ancestors still intimately lived with rain, with woods and streams, with deer and trout. But the noosphere was taking root:

> . . . a celestial observer, after scanning the face of the earth for tens of thousands of years and watching the movements of the glacial icecaps and the shifts in the edges of forests and deserts, could at length have seen, in certain mutilated places, numerous scars and bare spots on the planet's skin where the hand of man had been at work. A number of straight lines and crisscrosses, recalling the canals of Mars vaguely and in a minor way, indicated the presence of irrigation ditches and their dependent fields. Dots on the glassy surfaces of great rivers, moving independently of the direction and force of each stream, gave evidence of inland navigation, and rows of smaller dots crawling over the yellow hills revealed the continuation of this organized transport overland on the backs of animals. Here and there a protuberance, rising like an anthill, honeycombed like a wasp's nest, threw up streamers of smoke from the many fires of brick kilns and bakery ovens, smelteries and foundries, baths and altars, of a small city or large town. In a few parts of the world the Bronze Age had begun.
>
> During the Neolithic the material base of modern life was laid down. People had learned to till the soil and to herd animals. The foodstuffs that they grew are still the principal ones that we eat. Farmers with no better means of transport than the backs of oxen and small boats had found that living in villages is the easiest and most economical way to exist. In late Neolithic times large communities had arisen in the more favored parts of the world where transport was easiest, and where food could be accumulated and stored.
>
> It had already been found that quarrels between villages were unprofitable. Some central authority that kept the peace between villages more than earned its keep. Such authority, centered in the new large communities, must have arisen here and there before the end of Neolithic times because it was already functioning by the beginning of the Bronze Age.[1]

[1] From Carleton S. Coon, *The Story of Man,* pages 216–217. Copyright 1954 by Carleton S. Coon, and quoted with his permission and that of the publisher, Alfred A. Knopf.

The writer is speaking of the historical origins of civil society. The technological and social arrangements sketched in the passage were a key complex (p. 299). They were matters of tradition rather than of genetics. For any other species a nongenetic key complex would be impossible, but for *Homo sapiens* it is just what we should expect. Civil society developed in a number of places, and in each it led, as key complexes will, to an adaptive radiation. These have absorbed more and more of man's world and have enfolded an ever larger proportion of humanity. They have been the dominant determinant of human world history to the present moment.

How did civil societies arise from the once universal tribal background? What were the crucial ingredients of the new key complex, and how did they come together? Why did some people change their ways of living? In the first section below we deal with such questions—as best we can, remembering that the evidence is incomplete and that we therefore do not know all the answers. Once civil society existed, why did it spread? How did cities become city-states, states, empires? What was there about the new pattern that seems to have rendered it ineradicable? These issues, together with the actual history of civil society, will occupy us for the remainder of the book.

✘ Environmental variety promotes variety of ways of life. This principle applies to organisms in general in terms of genetic adaptation, and to our own species also in terms of cultural adjustment. To show its relevance in the present connection, we begin with a counterexample.

THE BEGINNINGS OF GOVERNMENT

Imagine a region 4000 square miles in extent occupied by twenty-five tribelets of about 150 people each. Each has 160 square miles of land in which to move around with little danger of unpleasant entanglements with its neighbors. We posit that the terrain is rich and varied in each 160-square-mile plot but monotonous from one plot to another. Each tribelet has a stretch of river bank or lake front for fishing. Each has woods for hunting and lumbering, well watered level land for raising a few crops, an ample supply of wild fruits and roots and nuts, of stone for tools, of clay for pots. A good variety of specialized activities is to be found within each community, but this variety is the same from one tribelet to another. The pattern of existence is approximately the same for all. So is the technological base, and so it is likely to remain, since no circumstance combining opportunity and need is apt to arise in one tribelet that does not appear in all the rest at the same time.

The state of affairs we have just described is unrealistically static. The biosphere is not ordered in such a way as to make it possible. To be sure, there have been approximations. But whenever a set of tribal communities lives spread through a fairly uniform territory, at the very least some dwell downriver or upwind from others, and those at the edges by definition have fewer neighbors than do those in the middle. Given enough time, these minor differences have led to change even in the absence of disruptive influences from outside. The most we can say realistically is that for people living in large and relatively homogeneous regions the rate of technological change has tended to be slow. A prime example is aboriginal Australia.

Imagine, now, a region similar in extent and in number of inhabitants to our first hypothetical case, but with great diversity. The region borders on the sea, and the coastal tribelets concentrate on offshore fishing and the collection of shellfish, though they do a little hunting and gathering and perhaps plant small kitchen gardens. A river flows through the region. The people along the river catch a few fish, but mainly they raise crops in the bordering alluvial flats. Upstream along tributaries there are pastures in which still other groups graze sheep. There are good clay deposits along the river and some of its tributaries, but not near the coast nor in the neighboring mountains. Flint, on the other hand, is available mainly in the foothills and mountains. The tribelets that have ready access to these materials use them.

This situation is unstable. The people in different parts of the region have differing ways of life and face diverse environmental challenges. Sooner or later, people are going to covet what their neighbors have and they do not. A drouth or a plague of insects may cause crop failure along the river and lead to famine unless the agriculturalists can get fish from the seacoast or flesh from the foothills. If the fish run is poor or a stormy season keeps the fishermen close to home, they will go hungry unless they can beg, borrow, or steal food from their inland neighbors. The farmers and fishers can do their work better if they can obtain good flint tools. Those who have no local sources of clay can perform their tasks more efficiently if they can get pottery utensils.

Intertribal Cooperation?

Clearly, life would be less uncertain for all if some system of cooperation could be worked out. Let the fishers fish, the farmers farm, the herders herd, the hunters hunt, the flintworkers polish their flint, and so on. Then let each group trade its surplus for what it needs but cannot produce or has not produced for itself. With a little good will, any group that finds itself temporarily embarrassed by some unkind turn of fate can be helped through its hard times by the rest, and will then gladly reciprocate when some other tribelet encounters difficulties. The arrangement carries with it also the great advantage that people get what they need without repeated destructive wars.

All this proposal amounts to is the notion of extending to the whole group of communities the habits of mutual aid that have been par for the course from time immemorial within each individual community.

Does this seem simple and obvious? Surely it does—when the total situation is scanned from celestial heights (as Coon does in his passage, p. 544), or with the perspective of the later historian. To the people primarily involved, living in their individual communities, doing the best they can with their heritage and their ingenuity, able to see only a bit beyond the physical horizon, wisely suspicious of strangers whose ways of life and systems of belief are mystifyingly different, it is not obvious at all. We must not forget primate conservatism, nor the age-old custom, dating back much farther than hominid beginnings, of living one's whole life in a *small* group in which everyone knows everyone else. It is no easy matter to enlarge the boundary between the friendly, familiar *we* and the alien, unpredictable *they*. Today some *we*-groups are very large, yet these remarks still apply. People in the modern world who try to promote collaboration and understanding among factions or nations find it a heartbreakingly frustrating enterprise. Cursèd is the peacemaker, because whatever side you are on he is on the other.

These impediments to intertribal collaboration should not be underestimated, but they shouldn't be overestimated either. Under external threat, groups of tribes have often been able to set aside their differences and enter into uneasy temporary alliances. Without such threat, the need for commodities not locally available has induced many a tribe to make more or less grudging concessions to the complementary need of some neighbor:

> Raw materials, such as Australian diorite, are limited to a few localities. The lucky residents, being monopolists, insist on getting skin bags in turn for allowing strangers to exploit their quarries. A ceremonial article, say, red ocher, is often regarded as a necessity, and Australians will go 300 miles to get it. The same holds for specialized manufactures. One West African village devotes itself to weaving, another to ironwork; and in Guiana one Indian group spins the cotton which a neighboring tribe weaves into hammocks. Throughout the Orinoco country manioc is grated, but two tribes supply the rest with the instrument used, every hut being a factory with piles of graters hanging from the roof ready for export.
>
> This is not a recent development. Even paleolithic Belgian cave-dwellers used flint peculiar to districts of France, whose residents surely exacted some compensation.[2]

We recall here also the use in Jericho, eleven thousand years ago, of obsidian from Lake Van (p. 467) and slightly less ancient evidences of lively commerce all over southwest Asia.

THE REQUIREMENTS

But temporary alliances, and extensive trade arrangements, were not enough. The steps from tribal to civil society were not taken easily. Like the inventions of plant or animal domestication, they required states of affairs combining opportunity and need. Like the invention of the bow and arrow, they called for true genius. Unlike any of these, they demanded one very unpleasant ingredient—the fourth of the factors we now list:

(1)   A relatively small densely populated region of environmental and technological diversity.

(2)   A predominance of settled villages, of the sort made possible by fishing or by agriculture.

(3)   A technology of food-production sufficiently efficient that about half the total number of man-days of the region are freed for other activities.

(4)   Some participating community whose leaders develop the desire and the ability to impose their will on the other communities without utterly destroying them.

(1)   As to the first of these, we already know why the diversity is necessary. The smallness of the region is dictated by the difficulty of transporting things over long distances.

[2] From Robert H. Lowie, *An Introduction to Cultural Anthropology,* Farrar & Rinehart, New York, 1934, p. 146.

(2)   The second is important because it puts an emphasis on *place* and *space*. For wanderers, headquarters are temporary and perimeters are vague; artifacts are light and portable or else hastily constructed and disposable. Fishing and farming render home bases more permanent, and promote an accumulation at fixed sites of a greater quantity and variety of nonportable capital goods: places to build, repair, and dock fishing vessels; pottery kilns, grain mills, handicraft factories, storage facilities for food and other commodities. Houses and buildings are more substantially constructed, huddled and walled for protection. Not only the people but also the stuff at headquarters requires to be defended, because it is the natural target for attack by jealous outsiders. Fishing and farming both make for the guarding of perimeters: fishers must have access to specific shoals and banks; farmers must delimit and protect their fields.

(3)   The third factor is essential because if the people of a diverse region are to participate in a unified economy then there are a lot of things that have to be done other than the mere production of food. Consider food itself. It is not produced everywhere in the region, nor at a constant rate (neither harvesting nor fishing goes on the year round). Both the direction and the rate of food flow must be monitored. Surplus must move from where it is produced to where it is not, and must be stored when production is high for distribution when it is low. The same is true for all other consumer commodities. Similar collective control may be necessary for the safe disposal of useless byproducts and of waste matter. All this requires man-days of labor, and specialized know-how, and the people engaged in distribution and its monitoring have to be fed and equipped.[3]

(4)   Without the fourth factor, the first three do not yield civil society. The communities of the region do some trading, even of personnel, but in an atmosphere of mutual suspicious hostility (p. 233) that may at any time break out into open combat, destructive alike of people and of resources. If you kill off the fishermen you will get no more fish, but you may be angry or frightened enough to forget that. If one group, or a coalition of two or three, manages to gain a sharp military advantage over the rest, it may be so anxious for revenge for earlier ill treatment that it simply lays waste the whole region. The first three factors therewith vanish, and can reappear only after a long interval of slow recovery. There must have been a lot of this before the new pattern finally took hold.

The first successful builders of civil society may have acted through pure self-interest (or may not!), but they were canny enough to temper their passions; this was their mark of genius. They discovered, or invented, a social principle of which Chief Justice John Marshall's aphorism, quoted at the beginning of this chapter (p. 544), was an unwitting paraphrase. The correct original form is: THE POWER TO DESTROY IS THE POWER TO TAX.

We don't know just how the first would-be governors put it, but what they said was equivalent to what a racketeer's agent in a modern city says to a shopkeeper

---

[3]Note that what we have outlined is an exact analog, on a larger and more complicated scale, of the problem of collective economic life in a band of hunters-gatherers, which is in turn an exact analog of the pattern of intake and internal distribution of nourishment and oxygen in a single multicellular animal.

in selling him "protection." I should not have put the word in quotes. The offer is genuine. Give us a part (that is the tax) and we will not take all (that is the destruction). Furthermore, we will help you get the things you need but cannot produce, and will keep other powerful predators off your backs. The Mafia, General Motors, the Roman Catholic Church, and the governments of the United States and of the Soviet Union, however greatly they differ, are all cultural cousins, all specialized descendants of the arrangements worked out by the earliest successful as-yet-undifferentiated racketeer-capitalist-bishop-laborboss-governors.

THE ROLE OF AGRICULTURE

Wherever the first three of our four requirements (p. 547) have been met and good agriculture has been one of the participating economic patterns, civil society has been born. This is not to belie the necessity of the fourth factor, only to imply that when the circumstances are ripe there is always someone clever enough to seize hold. Incipient government followed—not too closely—on the heels of domestication in southwest Asia (a population of 2000 for Jericho in 7000 B.C. certainly makes it look more like a city than a village), in northern China, in the Valley of Mexico, and in Peru; also elsewhere, but perhaps not independently. We can safely date the incipience of civil society to at least nine thousand years ago in the region (southwest Asia) where it seems to have arisen earliest.

Wherever good agriculture has spread, patterns of social organization suspiciously like those of civil society have followed or arisen. The tribes of the aboriginal North American Southeastern Woodlands, such as the Creek of Georgia and Alabama, had stable farm villages, a complex stratified society including some slaves, and powerful confederations. Hawaii, when first visited by Europeans (under Captain James Cook in A.D. 1778), was a rigidly organized metalless and potteryless kingdom with a bewildering system of castes and specializations and with a great concentration of prestige and prerogative in the ruling family. These are merely examples; there are dozens of others. Figure 33-1 shows part of the distribution of civil and incipiently civil societies in the world at the eve of the expansion of Europe.

Apparently we can also assert that wherever civil society has arisen independently, the required background was not only our four factors but also good agriculture—perhaps because only good agriculture can fulfil requirement number 3. Gathering, no matter how bountiful the environment, is not enough. The people of aboriginal California (p. 453) grew fat and sleek and numerous on acorns and pine nuts, had permanent villages, and gained the leisure for a wide variety of activities, but their social organization remained tribal.

There is, however, one attested instance in which good fishing might have sufficed had developments not been interrupted by a massive intrusion from elsewhere.

Consider the tribes of the North American Northwest Coast (say, northwards from the mouth of the Columbia River), whose staple was salmon. There was enough food to make some of the villages quite large, particularly in the area of Puget Sound and Vancouver Island. In the economy of some of the coastal tribes there was a dynamic factor in the form of the potlatch, which we mentioned on page 255. In

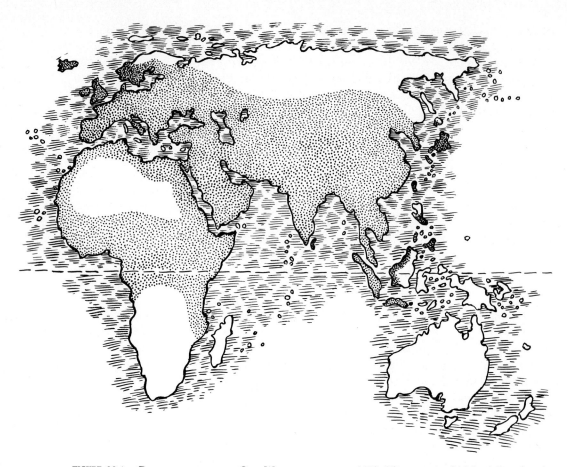

FIGURE 33-1. CIVIL SOCIETY IN THE OLD WORLD ABOUT A.D. 1450. The centers of high civil society in the Old World at this time were in the Near East, India, and China; Europe, sub-Saharan Africa, southeastern Asia, and central and northern Eurasia were marginal (see chapter 37). But remember that at the same time there were flourishing civil societies in Peru, Yucatán, and the Valley of Mexico, and incipient ones in other parts of the New World, as well as in Oceania (mainly Polynesia).

addition to food and ordinary consumer's commodities, the institution of the potlatch demanded the accumulation of valuables—both things and slaves—so that they could be destroyed in quest of prestige. The evidence suggests that in late aboriginal times the influence of the potlatch was indirectly spreading, in that commodities for destruction had to be gathered from an ever larger area. In 1750, tribes in the vicinity of the dalles of the Columbia River were engaging in local slave raids and selling the captives "down the river," destined for exploitation on the coast. By 1850 these raids were reaching a good 280 miles to the south, into northeastern California in the vicinity of Lower Klamath and Tule Lakes. If we consider the coast, the valley of the lower Columbia, and the rest of the territory that is now Oregon, Washington, and southern British Columbia, we have a (relatively) tight-knit region of great diversity of resources, inhabited at the time by tribes who made their living in many different ways, though nowhere with agriculture.

It is interesting to speculate what might have developed in this region if the expansion of Europe had been delayed, say, 500 years. I suppose the speculation is also futile, since things did not work out that way. We can hold to our generalization about agriculture and civil society. But it is weakened. It may be only a generalization of historical fact, not one of human ecological inevitability.

✖ Suppose you are one of the first Neolithic tribal leaders to try out the governing-racketeering scheme. Your territory is small, a half dozen villages or less. But it does not take you long to discover that you have a tiger by the tail. You have your bully-boys (the armed men of your own tribe) to enforce your decisions, but they are not really very strong. You have to keep your promises—and your threats—or the rabble will destroy them and you; they have no compassion, for you do not belong to the same tribe and they remember the bad things you have done, not the good ones. You have to keep your goons satisfied but under control: they must be neither too destructive nor too kindly. And in the next valley there is another boss, not at all averse, as far as you know, to taking over your territory if you can't handle it. He could use your unusually good source of clay (or copper or carrots); you wouldn't mind having access to his copper (or carrots or clay). It may therefore be wise to beat him to the punch. Your job is more complicated than you expected. But you can't retire. The only way out is to die.

THE CRAFT OF GOVERNANCE

We begin to see why the pattern of civil society, once well established, is ineradicable. There is a dynamic factor in it, a constant need for more resources, not for conspicuous consumption in a potlatch (though, to be sure, conspicuous consumption is not unknown, and every act of enforcement against your own people and every fracas with a neighbor destroys some stuff) but for supplying your people and arming your soldiers. However hateful some of the accoutrements of government may be for the governed, there are clear advantages to being part of a unified diversified economy, and the people who have experienced them rarely want to give them up. They may want a bigger slice, or more freedom of choice, but the basic gains are such that a successful revolt from within merely replaces one boss by another. Conquest from outside does the same. Thus it is that the history of civil society has from the outset been one of the "circulation of élites": periodically one set of rulers is replaced by another, but this is largely the assignment of new personnel to old posts. The social structure, while not completely inflexible, changes much more slowly.

To the constant need for more resources, mentioned in the preceding paragraph, must be added the constant tendency to exhaust the resources one already controls.

Hunters-gatherers sometimes deplete a region, but if they move out the recovery time for the abandoned territory is not very long. Agriculturalists can stay put for a longer time before they reach the point of diminishing returns, especially if they practice a bit of crop-rotation or allow each field to lie fallow every few years (when the immediate demand is high this is hard to do). But once land has been exhausted by crop-raising it can remain infertile for decades or centuries. The olive is particularly vicious in its demands on the soil: in three millennia it has rendered great stretches of Mediterranean shore virtually useless for anything. Intensive plowing can ruin land permanently, in that it removes the subterranean structure of interlocking roots that hold the topsoil, whereupon floods can carry it off. There are millions of acres of such wasteland in the river valleys of China, and parts of the North American Great Plains that were fertile a century ago are now dust bowl. Similar remarks apply to minerals, and even, as we are today beginning to learn, to the resources of the sea. Technological advancements can increase the effective yield of available resources, and the needs of civil societies for more yield have given technology great impetus. In the long run, though, even this is only a delaying action. It can postpone the fall of an empire; it cannot permanently save our species.

The destructiveness of political competition is as clear as its inevitability, and just as old. The archaeological record in southwest Asia attests to it wherever it has been examined with adequate care. Consider the site of Homer's Troy, in Turkey near the Aegean end of the Dardanelles. The site was occupied almost continuously from 3000 to 1000 B.C.; clearly the location was strategic. This was the period during which large empires were developing and succeeding one another in the great river valleys of southwest Asia. Troy was one of hundreds of small potatoes in the hinterland. The settlement never covered more than eight or ten acres, and even the king's quarters would strike us as cramped. Yet it was a genuine city (p. 163), the seat of government for some stretch of the surrounding countryside. The record shows that in the two millennia we have mentioned the city was destroyed no fewer than *forty times*—on the average, once every fifty years![4] Life in tribal society may have been "nasty, low, brutish—and *short*!" (as one nineteenth-century European anthropologist put it), but it was never like that.

To the present moment, states and empires have never been able to achieve anything more than an unstable equilibrium. That is ironic, because there is no question but that statecraft seeks stability. In the search, civil society has given rise to a whole series of technological and social innovations. Many of the developments described in chapters 31 and 32, especially those having to do with metallurgy, were mightily encouraged by the need and greed of rulers; otherwise we might yet be polishing flint. Certain key adaptations, in general still with us, emerged very early. They form the subject of the next two chapters.

[4]Sometimes the havoc was wrought by earthquakes rather than by human agency, but the point remains.

34

×

THE WHEELS OF EMPIRE: I

The crucial innovations of civil society to be dealt with in this chapter are *staples, cities, roads, stratified society,* and *soldiers.*

× A staple is the food you eat the most of, from year's end to year's end. Hunters-gatherers usually (though not invariably) have a diet that changes with the season. No food is produced constantly. A food for all seasons must be capable of storage without serious spoilage. Such a food for a civil society must be nourishing and must be produced easily enough to fulfill requirement number 3 (p. 547). The staples of civil societies have in fact been cereal grains that could be dried and stored, most of them then ground into flour and baked into bread. From chapter 30 we know that the crucial grains of southwest Asia were barley and wheat, while first millet and then rice served in China, and maize in the civil societies of the New World.

STAPLES

In early civil societies, and in many to this day, it is the masses of the people whose diet consists largely of the staple. The rulers may consume some of it, fancied up by fine chefs, but they get the lion's share of whatever variety foodstuffs are available. No Roman plebeian ever tasted the roasted peacocks featured at the banquets of the patricians.

In fact, any sort of flesh food has been a rare treat for the lower classes in most civil societies. The lack of meat and the prevalence of soft pap in the last few thousand years has changed our teeth. The classical arrangement, still kept by such recent hunters-gatherers as the Australian aborigines, was for the incisors to meet edge to edge. With soft foods instead of flesh we have less use for the incisors, and they have wandered. In the Far East both the upper and the lower incisors tend to slope forward. In the West everyone has "buck teeth," the upper incisors sliding down in front of the lower ones.

× We know what a city is (p. 163): an aggregate of the dwelling places of people who raise little or none of the food they eat.

CITIES

The earliest cities began as the villages of tribal leaders who had gone in for governing-racketeering and had found that they had to have administrative head-quarters for their operations: facilities for storing food and other commodities pending their redistribution, for receiving reports from agents and consulting with lieutenants, and for the keeping of essential records (even if, at first, there was no place to keep them except in the heads of people with good memories).

These administrative activities require a sizable staff. If the governor is successful, the new sorts of activities in time largely or wholly supersede the old ones (farming, fishing, or the like). The members of the administrative staff are busy, so that their mundane needs must be provided for by others: perhaps at first by their families, but later by servants or slaves. The servants or slaves require overseers. Skilled artisans must be at hand to convert imported raw materials into tools, weapons, utensils, and (eventually) objects of decorative art. Some of these artisans are entertainers to supply the rulers with needed relaxation. The accumulation of commodities stored in the city, and its strategic location, mean that it must be fortified and that the fortifications must be manned by armed guards. Before long there are far too many people around for each to know all the others personally (p. 162). Furthermore, virtually none of these people can produce their own food and equipment. All the stuff needed to maintain the life of the city must flow in from elsewhere. All the useless byproducts must flow out again. The motions of information, people, and things in and through the city become complicated and require control. The governor finds he must appoint one of his lieutenants to be city manager. Thus, urban government arises as something partly distinct from territorial government.

City Structure

The archetypical city layout is in concentric rings—not necessarily circular, for the contours depend on details of terrain. At the very center is the palace of the top dog, surrounded by fortifications and by the mansions of his cronies. Next outwards come the storehouses and the shops and homes of the artisans, then the hovels of the poor, and finally the outer bastions with barracks nearby for the guards who man them. In periods of quiet, some groups of "suburban" poor (woodcutters, truck-gardeners, or the like) may be allowed to settle just outside the city walls.

Fresh water flows into the city somehow. If it does not enter from below, through wells fed by underground springs, then the sources have to be guarded and an emergency supply must be stored. Food and raw materials enter through the gates in the walls. Sewage, garbage, trash, and corpses leave via sewers, are carried out, or are burned or buried. People are permitted to pass through the city gates, in either direction, only if they can show the proper credentials (sometimes in the form of a bribe for the guard).

What enters the city does not reach its heart without considerable screening. Dangerous things and people are turned back at the gates. Poor-quality materials stay in the outer ring. Raw materials for the artisans reach them, but only the finished products of their artistry move on inwards to the residences of the well-to-do. In the same way, the noxious byproducts of the metabolism of the wealthy are quickly whisked away, whereas the alleys and passageways that thread through the quarters of the poor are filthy. In mere ecological terms there is a polarization into mansion and slum. The Palace of Minos at Knossos (on Crete), a seat of empire between roughly 1800 and 1580 B.C., was equipped with running water and with flush toilets— among the earliest known. The hedging heap of hovels had, at most, honeybuckets and slit trenches.

The concentric layout is excellent for the rulers because it supplies them with several layers of protective padding against armed attack. But the strength of the city is at the same time its weakness. A powerful and patient enemy need not exhaust its resources in bloody invasion. It need only lay siege and wait. To invest a city is to plug up all its orifices. The city must then survive on its fat and encyst its wastes. This cannot continue indefinitely. Eventually the food and water are gone. Before that, rats, vermin, and disease have taken over at the edges and have begun to work their way inwards. Unless the rulers capitulate or the populace revolts and does it for them, the city dies.

VARIANTS

It is evident that few of the characteristic early urban features just itemized are universal in the modern world, though all still survive and some remain widespread. Every city today has some kind of urban government. A contemporary city which is not the center for the formal governing of some surrounding area is, at least, a commercial, financial, industrial, ecclesiastical, or educational focus—kinds of activities not originally distinct from those of government.

The concentric plan with key facilities at the center is still common: Washington, D.C., was laid out with the capitol building at its heart (though its subsequent growth has skewed that) and a thousand county seats in the United States are built around the courthouse square.

City walls, or their ruins, are rare in North America, Australia, and New Zealand, but common almost everywhere else. They are not always of stone. In some places, such as wet-tropical Africa, a wooden palisade serves. The nearest approach in North America was the military stockade of pioneer days, whither neighboring settlers fled for security in times of "Indian unrest." But in China, for example, only one city (Shanghai) lacks a wall. The Chinese word for 'city', *chéng,* also means 'wall', and the standard expression for "in the suburbs" is *chéngwài,* literally 'wall's exterior'.

Many larger cities have peculiarities of shape or of internal arrangement because they began as clusters of smaller cities that grew together. Thus both ancient Rome and modern Toronto were built on seven hills, and a few decades ago La Ciudad de Nuestra Señora de los Ángeles, in California, was aptly described as "six suburbs in search of a city."

SPECIAL POTENTIALS

As long as a city can be kept viable, the concentration of people makes possible certain kinds of developments that would be out of the question in tribal and village society. We give two modern examples.

(1)   In the nineteenth century many European cities became the proud possessors of symphony orchestras. Let us say that such an orchestra requires one hundred skilled instrumentalists (some are smaller, but some have been even larger). And let us estimate that one human being in every five hundred has the specialized abilities whereby, with the proper training, he can become a skilled instrumentalist. The players must come together frequently for rehearsals and performances, which means that, given the transportation facilities of the nineteenth century, none of them dare live more than a few miles from the concert hall. From just these factors (forgetting others that may be even more stringent, such as the source of economic support for such a crew of specialists), we see that a symphony orchestra was impossible except in an urban community of a minimum of about 50,000 people.

Instead of orchestras we could speak of opera companies, dramatic troupes, art museums, or professional athletic teams—all of these to be counted among the highly complex and varied recent descendants of the specialized artisans and entertainers of the earliest civil societies.

(2)   The period from 1850 to 1900 saw the founding of a number of medical schools in the United States. Each was placed in an urban center, each strategically at the edge of the slums. Medical students are perennially poor and the location gave them access to cheap living quarters. Furthermore, it guaranteed a supply of cadavers for dissection and of charity patients on whom they could learn their craft. Staff doctors could live nearby, in the direction opposite from that towards the slums. Wealthy patrons also came for expert hospital care, but for the carriage trade the location didn't matter.

Mansion, Slum, and Obsolescence

The most persistent feature of city design has been the contrast between mansion and slum. Technological and political developments of the last hundred years, especially innovations in transportation, have changed their relative locations in some parts of the world: people of means have been able to move to suburbia, leaving the decaying residential parts of the inner city for the poor. This reverses the arrangement of earlier cities (where, as we have seen, the slums encircled the mansions) without eliminating the contrast.

Slums, by definition, are the parts of a city in which the circulation of matter is most sluggish, so that poor-quality stuff arrives and noxious wastes clog up and accumulate. To put it bluntly but with absolute ecological validity, the typical city is chronically constipated and its slums are its ass-hole.

Two factors make for slums, and either suffices with no help from the other:

(1)   The first is the constant, age-old influx of poor country people destined to become poor city people. (We see this today; it was also how the earliest cities recruited new supplies of unskilled manpower.) The immigrants do not know that the difference of environment requires an altered set of habits of maintenance and disposal. Garbage can be cast out the back door of a farmhouse or over the outer wall of a village: the pigs and chickens, or a thin concentration of wild rodents, will dispose of it. In

the crowded city, where there are few open green areas, the same practice breeds rats and disease.

(2)   The second factor, whose pedigree is also as ancient as that of cities themselves, is the indifference or even the active hostility of people in positions of power, who have rarely been concerned with anything but their own welfare and have not often been very farsighted even about that. This can frustrate any efforts at self-help by the slum-dwellers, just as sporadic attempts at assistance by enlightened administrators are almost always brought to nought by the inertia of impoverishment and ignorance.

I am told that slums have been virtually eliminated in parts of Europe—and mansions too, everyone living at or near the level of lower-middle-class respectability. But there are still plenty of them everywhere else. There is constant talk of slum-clearance. Most of it does not dig deep enough. We may discover that the only permanent cure for slums is to abolish cities, which, in the twentieth century, six or eight thousand years after their origin, may be losing their last vestige of survival value. The question will then be whether our species is collectively clever enough to work out some new and more viable ecological pattern.

✕ A government, by definition, controls some territory within which produce and **ROADS** manufactures must be moved about. There must be well marked and travelable connecting routes, used not only for goods but also by the necessarily mobile enforcers of the ruler's will, by the defenders of his realm, and by his messengers.

Where waterways are good, land routes may not get much attention. This was largely the case in early Egypt, in which the multiple mouths of the Nile served the delta and the Nile itself sufficed for the long, skinny valley. It also tended to be true in Mesopotamia (which shows evidences of incipient civil society as early as 4700 B.C.), with its maze of minor tributaries of the Tigris and Euphrates. We do not know the early state of affairs in the Indus Valley, but it must be significant that most of the archaeological sites, of cities and villages alike, are not far from a river.

For land transport, there is a difference between a trail and a path, and between either of these and a road. A trail is just a route marked to keep travelers from going astray. When a trail is well traveled, feet or wheels wear away the vegetation and pack the dirt down, yielding a path. A road is like a path except that the clearing of obstructions and the surfacing are done in advance, rather than merely as a side effect of use. A road also requires maintenance, but this is worth the effort if it is then in good shape for important use when the occasion arises.

Roman Roads and Their Antecedents

The exigencies of extended empire require roads for military purposes if for nothing else, so that troops can readily reach the frontiers for defense or for further conquest and so that information, instructions, and reinforcements can travel quickly.

When the expansionist spirit first seized Rome, late in the fourth century B.C., the famous Appian Way was built, stretching off to the southeast for 160 miles. As Rome's hegemony spread, so did its network of highways. After 450 years, in the middle of the second century A.D., when the empire was at its acme, the main roads ran for a total of more than 50,000 miles (Figure 34-1), with a subsidiary feeder system of an additional 185,000 miles. The main roads had solid foundations; they were paved with concrete (p. 522); the surface cross section was slightly convex ("cambered") for drainage; their width was from 6 to 12 feet but averaged closer to the lower figure; they were as straight and as level as they could be made with piles and embankments over marshy ground and with cuts, occasionally tunnels, through hills. Rivers were spanned by concrete, masonry, or wooden bridges. There were mileposts,[1] stables for change of horses about every 15 miles (the military forerunner of our civilian gas stations), and facilities for rest approximately every 25 miles (the prototype of our motels). The system had been built, and was maintained, by prisoners of war and slaves working under the direction of soldiers.

Except for its magnitude and some technical details, this justly renowned Roman achievement in civil engineering was neither unprecedented nor unparalleled.

The Romans invented their road-surfacing material, and may have solved some of the tricky problems of bridge-construction. In all other respects their highway system was an imitation of that of the Persians, and in the eastern marches of the empire even incorporated what was left of the Persian system. The Persians, in the late sixth century B.C., with headquarters at Susa at the foot of the Zagros Mountains, had military roads running south to the Persian Gulf, southwest to Egypt, west to Anatolia and the Aegean, and southeast perhaps as far as the Indus River. This system was excellent. Royal messengers covered the distance between the Aegean shore and the capital, about 1500 miles, in nine days, one tenth the time it took travelers who could not use the road.

The Persians may have inherited some techniques of the road-building trade from their immediate predecessors the Assyrians, whose empire, enduring from about 2000 to about 615 B.C., had had its headquarters chiefly at Ashur, but which had never covered nearly so large a territory as did the Persian empire at its greatest extent. The evidence for this influence is uncertain. It appears possible that the Persians were innovative in road engineering, and likely that the Romans were not.

New World Roads

For a parallel to the Roman system we turn to the New World. Extended empire here required roads just as much as it did in the Old World, but with some differences of detail: chiefly, the fact that the aboriginal highways of the Americas were never trodden by draft animals pulling wheeled vehicles.

Mayan roads were well constructed, but mostly quite narrow, hardly more than walkways.

Little detailed information has survived about the Aztec road system, which centered at Tenochtitlán, the capital (in the Valley of Mexico where Mexico City now is). We do know that one road trailed eastwards, reaching altitudes as high as 8000 feet in the mountains, to touch the coast at Veracruz. Allowing for the rugged

---

[1] Literally, since English *mile* is from Latin *mīlia* 'thousands', in the phrase (——) *mīlia passuum* '(so-many) thousands of paces'.

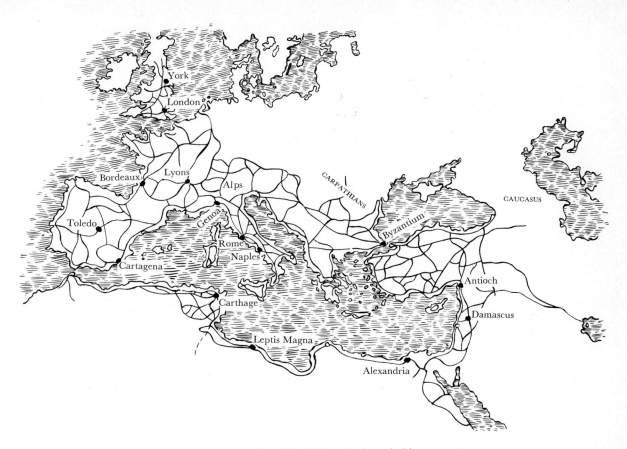

FIGURE 34-1. The Roman road system at its height. (After *Dictionnaire des antiquités grecques et romanes*, Vol. 5, by C. Darembers and E. Saglio, Librairie Hachette.)

land, this road must have been about 250 miles long. At Veracruz it connected with a coast road that ran from the Tropic of Cancer south, southeast, and east along the shore to the Laguna de Términos, for a total of perhaps 715 miles. These roads were narrow and rose and fell, turned and twisted, to fit the contours of the terrain, with little digging or filling. There is no evidence for bridges. When necessary, you forded or swam.

The aboriginal New World highway system that deserves comparison with those of Persia and Rome is that of the Inca empire. It is shown in Figure 34-2 as it was at the height of the empire, about A.D. 1500, with Cuzco at its administrative, if not geographical, heart. The standard road width was 24 feet, 3 to 4 times the average for Roman highways, and this was departed from only when the terrain absolutely required it. The total length of the system was about 10,000 miles. There was no deep roadbed, for that is unnecessary in the absence of vehicular traffic. Wherever the earth would not pack down tightly enough, the surface was paved with flat stones.

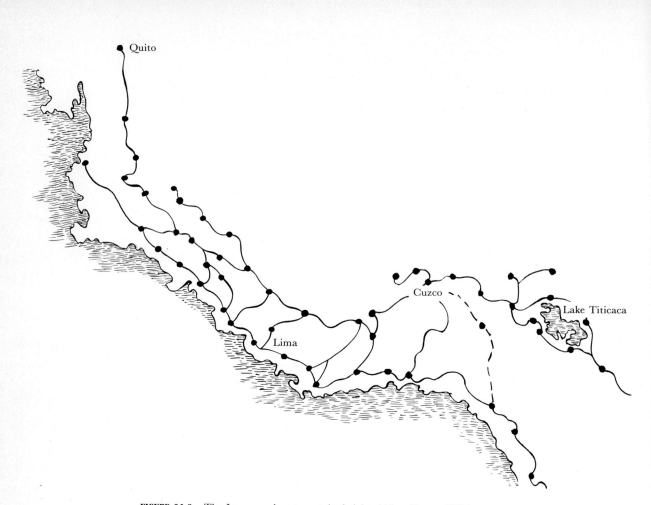

FIGURE 34-2. The Incan road system at its height. (After Hagen 1957.)

There were culverts for drainage, and sidewalls to prevent the drifting of sand or loose soil. One stretch in the mountains was constructed at an altitude of 17,150 feet, the highest highway known.

And there were bridges!—suspension spans over dizzyingly deep gorges, supported from fiber cables the thickness of a man's waist turned over a stanchion at each end and then buried deep in the ground. These, like the roads, required maintenance, a responsibility of the communities that lived nearby. The cables were replaced every two years. With that sort of care, the bridges were very durable. One of those over the Apurímac River northwest of Cuzco, fictionalized as *The Bridge of San Luís Rey* (Thornton Wilder, 1928), continued to be cared for by the local population when the Spanish replaced the Inca rulers, and had been in uninterrupted use for almost five and one half centuries when it was finally abandoned in A.D. 1890.

A Road Goes Both Ways

Just as a city wall can keep things in as well as out (p. 555), so a road can be traveled in either direction, by invaders as well as by defenders of an empire.

In A.D. 1519 Hernán Cortés landed briefly somewhere on the coast of Tabasco before sailing on west to Veracruz. The news of his coming preceded him, not only to Veracruz but all the way to Tenochtitlán, for the roads made fast messenger service possible. But Cortés and his party then followed exactly the same route to meet and defeat the emperor Moctezuma at his own imperial headquarters.

Twelve years later, Francisco Pizarro's two-year conquest of the Incas (1531–1533) made use of the preexisting highway system in just the same way.

Neither conqueror was doing anything new. The Persian road system served Alexander of Macedon in good stead in his takeover and enlargement of the Persian empire in 334–325 B.C., and this has been the standard practice of empire-invaders ever since. Every retreating army burns its bridges behind it, and every attacking army has a corps of engineers whose job it is to restore them.

✘ The Menomini were one of tens of thousands of tribal societies for whose members the notion of social stratification would have been completely incomprehensible. But it would be wrong to propose that tribal society is never stratified. Human beings untouched by civil ways have tried out all sorts of strategies of organization, including some at least superficially similar to those characteristic of all civil societies. Unless we want to redefine our terms drastically in order to make it not so, then the salmon-fishing tribes of the North American Northwest Coast (p. 549) were an example.

STRATIFIED SOCIETY

But a civil society *must* be stratified. It can arise, and can be maintained, in no other way.[2] We have said enough already to show why. Until at most the last few decades (still now in most of the world), productivity has been so low that civil society has absolutely demanded a vertical polarization with a pampered handful at the top and a sweating multitude at the bottom. Both the handful and the multitude have had to work, the former at administration and statecraft, the latter at the dull, repetitive, and often dangerous tasks of food-raising, mining, wall- and road-building, and transportation. But the rewards for their labors have been sharply different. The few have gotten the best food, the nicest housing, the prettiest women, the tastiest wine; the multitude have gotten little more than their lives, best characterized as "nasty, low, brutish—and *short*!" (p. 552).

The numerical ratio of the multitude to the handful has varied a good deal depending on technology and on environmental bounty. It took a constant labor force of 100,000 men thirty years to build the Great Pyramid of Khufu (p. 500). Apparently only the pharaoh himself was buried in it. That is quite a ratio. In 1965, of all the federal income-tax returns filed in the United States, 0.35% were for adjusted gross incomes of $50,000 or more, and only 1.15% for less than $1000. While these two sets of figures cannot be directly compared, they obviously signal a great difference.

Something else that has varied a lot is the number of people occupying various

[2]This is a generalization about the past; it pretends no prediction of the future.

strata between the top and the bottom. In the West in the last century there has been a totally unprecedented bulging in the middle, with a compensating reduction at the bottom (but little change at the top).

Atypical in another direction was the organization of the Inca empire. Under the Inca (the emperor) were four regional governors, answerable only to him. Each had a set of subregional lieutenants; each of these had two sublieutenants; and so on, in as many steps as necessary, down to the point where each ten ordinary male citizens were under the direct supervision of a straw boss. Each ordinary male citizen was in turn the head of his family if he happened to be married. Some female children were lifted from their families and inserted into a separate system, where they were trained for and devoted their lives to such specialized tasks as spinning and weaving, and remained virgins unless they caught the fancy of the Inca himself. A little over 8.5% of all the adult males were officials at some level of this smoothly conical administrative structure. The structure controlled *everything*—at least in avowed intent: there was no contrast between the political and the nonpolitical (p. 155) because in principle the Inca ran the whole show. The degree of responsibility, and the corresponding amount of privilege and wealth, increased from the bottom to the top. The Inca was responsible for everything (but only to himself); his privilege was unbounded.

FUNCTIONAL SPLITTING

Social stratification has been complicated in many civil societies (though not in those of the aboriginal New World nor in the earliest of those in the Old) by a development we may call "functional splitting."

Scholars investigating the evidences of the first civil societies of southwest Asia have tended to characterize them as "theocracies" or even to assert that they were not civil societies at all, but merely regional organizations run by religious leaders. But look: When the tax-collector comes around it does not matter whether he says "Pay or my soldiers will rape your wife and daughters" or "Be good or the goblins will get you"—provided you believe in the goblins. Either is, from the inside view, a power to destroy, which yields the power to tax. The fact that the evidences of early civil society in southwest Asia show what *we* interpret as religious trappings is irrelevant, unless it can be shown that, for the people actually involved, there was a functioning contrast between the religious and the nonreligious, or between the religious and the governmental, or the like (p. 129). The symbols of governing may be gods and devils, or spears and swords, or all of these at once from the same governor; this is a minor detail.

But it can come about that you have two governors at the same time, perhaps one with the threat of sword and spear, the other with the menace of eternal torment in the next world (or the promise of eternal bliss in a different compartment of the next world provided you behave yourself). A single multitude is then at the bottom of two different stratified hierarchies, with different bosses at the top—the social structure is a hydra-headed monster. This was true in the European Middle Ages, when a peasant was answerable to his lord on the one hand, to his parish priest on the other, and could escape neither. It is true in a different way today in any racket-ridden city, where a shopkeeper must manage to keep on the right side of both the law and the outlaw. And it is true of a workman who must satisfy both his employer and the leaders of his labor union.

In the presence of functional splitting, the heads of the monster may work in collusion (each offering an appropriate sort of symbolic fealty to the others), or may snap at one another, or one may suppress and supplant (or absorb) another. France in the eighteenth century, and Spain still in the nineteenth, were characterized by collaboration between the rulers of church and state, which meant that neither offered the common people any protection against the other. In the history of the United States there have been periods marked by thoroughgoing collusion between the government we call "the government" and the government we call "big business." Yet when the heads are at loggerheads, it is often—though not invariably—worse, since ordinary people are at one and the same time the bone of contention and the innocent bystanders.

Insecurity and Security

In most civil societies no social position has offered permanent security. This is not to deny that the rulers are better off than the peasants and the proletariat. Yet they have to work hard, and are liable to assassination.

All in all, the best thing to be (as though the average member of a civil society had any choice about it!) is an artisan. If you are competent, you are respected by the populace and protected by the ruler. If your city falls to a conqueror and you have survived the ordeal of the actual conquest, he may keep you at your work instead of impaling you at the city gate as an object lesson. You are given the chance to work creatively with your hands and head, and thus to earn the only sort of reward our species has ever found permanently meaningful (p. 272).

SOLDIERS

× There are no soldiers in a tribal society. Every able-bodied adult male is a warrior when he has to be, and not otherwise.

Professional soldiers arise in civil society as the enforcers of the governor's internal edicts, as protectors of the polity from outside interference, and as the machinery for extending control to new territories or communities. When Sir Robert Peel invented policemen in Britain in 1814, part of the original array of responsibilities of soldiers was turned over to a different crew, but it can be argued that a policeman is a kind of soldier (just as is a navy sailor). We are speaking here not of commanding officers, planners and administrators often high in the councils of the ruler, but of the privates and noncoms who do the bulk of the actual fighting and other dirty work.

No such corps of largely idle specialists can be collected except as farming increases the food supply and thus the population. Besides this, there is a natural process of selection about who becomes a soldier and who does not, partly suspended nowadays in times of national emergency when everyone gets drafted, otherwise still operative as at the beginning. The following characterization is in modern terms, but is too apt to permit paraphrase. The army is

> the last refuge for lazy men. It's a fact, however blasphemous it may seem, that ninety percent of the time, most members of any military organization have nothing to do. Floors, decks, and bulkheads don't have to be cleaned twice a day—not if that paragon of cleanliness, the housewife, does it only twice a week—but they are in the military, simply because there is nothing else to do. Labor and management both realize this and things proceed from there: if the bulkhead is cleaned, labor works off its resentment and occasionally the paint itself, thereby costing management money. Once there is no paint left, it is labor's job to repaint the bulkhead, which job is then done with the greatest waste of paint possible short of outright criminal negligence.
>
> Labor's other refuge, the one on which a thousand stories have been based, is that of gold-bricking, goofing off, call it what you will—the art, and it is an art, of doing nothing. No one has developed this skill to a higher degree than the military man. He thrives on inactivity, on putting something over on his hierarchy of bosses. He brags about how little he has done, and discusses the means of getting out of work with the passion of an artist discussing brush techniques.
>
> When the work comes, the real work, the thing he is paid his pittance for, he is ready and all the energy he has saved by avoiding busy work is used for whatever needs to be done. And if the job to be done entails danger, lack of sleep, excessive heat or cold so much the better: it is ammunition for his real war—that against the management. Two days without sleep furnish him with excuses for a week of sleeping through reveille and muster. A day without food entitles him to steal seconds, cadge from the galley, and lie about his privation to buddies who don't believe him but lie about their enforced diets. Too much heat entitles him to all the ice cubes he can hold. Too much cold to all the coffee he can drink during working hours.[3]

To which must be added that too extended a period of privation and continence justifies his participation in mass looting and round-robin screwing in the aftermath of victory, and sometimes when there has been no fighting, provided he respects the property and the women of his betters. On this aspect of the military there is no better source than Francisco José de Goya y Luciente's *The Disasters of the War* (*Los Desastres de la Guerra*), a gallery of etchings depicting his observations in Spain during the Napoleonic Wars of the early nineteenth century.

Soldiers are not chosen for cruelty. They are selected for stupidity and stolidity, and trained to be callous, which for the victims comes out all the same. The stupidity must be great enough to numb any reasonably intelligent man's realistic dread of being maimed or killed in battle, yet not so great as to preclude the mastery of the arts of combat through iterated drill.

Professional common soldiers stand outside the main hierarchy of the civil society that supports them. They are neither rulers nor peasants, nor do they occupy some stratum between the top and bottom extremes (as, for example, artisans do). Depending on the orders he receives from his immediate superior, a soldier may befriend or bedevil the peasants, defend or depose the king. He has no loyalty except to his

[3] From "Jump," by William Earls, *Analog Science Fiction – Science Fact* 84:2.134–135 (October 1969). Quoted with the permission of the author and of The Condé Nast Publications Inc.

source of food and entertainment, and that loyalty reflects also his awareness of the threat of extremely severe discipline. He fights not from patriotism but to stay alive. Military duty in early civil society was the first form of civil serfdom (p. 271).

Such is the human material with which most of the battles of history have been conducted. When kingdoms have clashed, the outcome has depended on factors of terrain and on which army was the larger or the better equipped and disciplined, sometimes on the skill and intelligence of the generals; it has rarely turned on any striking difference in the inherent capacities of the professional common soldiers on the two sides.

BARBARIANS AND CITIZEN SOLDIERS

A "people's army" of "citizen soldiers" is a horse of another color.

The average civil society has been able to use citizen soldiers only in limited numbers scattered among the professionals. The reason is that they may run instead of fighting, or, even more serious, may turn against their masters. Traditionally, then, the nonprofessionals in a military organization have been armed poorly or not at all, used mainly not for fighting but for ancillary tasks. When knighthood was in flower (as the fatuous saying goes), a lord's handful of professional men-at-arms carried metal weapons, were protected by metal armor, and rode horseback, while the yeomen, who were and remained peasants, used bows and arrows, wore leather or cloth, and walked. Partly, the reason was the shortage and high cost of metal and horses. Partly it was that yeomen so equipped could help in either attack or defense but could not effectively revolt. We have seen (p. 558) that most of the heavy work of Roman road-building, an army responsibility, was done not by the soldiers themselves but by prisoners of war or slaves, who also took care of the dirty chores around barracks and encampments. In eighteenth- and nineteenth-century Europe, impressed seamen manned the rigging, not weapons.

However, at the edges of expanding civil society empires have repeatedly had to contend with tribal or only incipiently civil peoples, usually referred to as "barbarians" or "savages." We shall call them "barbarians," and what we say will render that term an epithet of honor, not of scorn. The barbarians are dangerous because when they fight they do so as a people's army of citizen soldiers. Time and again it has been shown that a professional army cannot prevail against a barbarian horde unless it has a towering advantage of position, numbers, tactical organization, or weaponry. The barbarians do not know the rules of "civilized warfare"—in origin, a sort of unspoken arrangement among professional fighters, designed to make things look good to the bosses on both sides and yet minimize actual injury and death. The barbarians fight for moral principle, and are ready to die in order to win. Braddock's defeat near Ft. Duquesne (now Pittsburgh) on 9 July 1755 is one recent example. The slaughter of General Custer and his troops by the Sioux near the Little Bighorn on 25 July 1876 is another. Many of the engagements between American forces and the Vietcong in southeastern Asia in the 1960s illustrate the same principle. Written records show numberless comparable cases, some of the earlier ones hard to discern because it was the "civilized" side, not the barbarian, that wrote down the account.

When barbarians at the fringes of an empire manage to acquire the weapons and some of the tactics of the empire's military forces, and yet to retain their noncivil esprit de corps, the empire becomes a real sitting duck. Time and again in the early history of Old World civil society—in southwestern Asia, in southern Europe, in China, in India and southeastern Asia—a seat of empire was conquered by invading hordes, rather than by a competing empire. Interestingly, although the particular regime is thus destroyed, its civil framework is not. Conquest by barbarians turns out to be one of the mechanisms by which the pattern of civil society spreads. The invaders, having completed their ravishing, rarely retire. Instead, they stay on and establish their own dynasty. That forestalls possible recovery and retaliation by the vanquished. But they then slowly take on the ways of civil society, in imitation of their deposed predecessors, because that is the only obvious means by which they can maintain their newly established rule.

Western society in the last century has witnessed an increase in the role of the citizen soldier and an alteration, though no reduction, in that of the professional. The establishment of universal military training in many of the nations of Europe made for a ready supply of partly trained nonprofessionals in case of emergency. But it also did something else. It formalized the traditional selective process (p. 564), in that those of each year's inductees who were adequately lazy and stupid tended to stay on and become a part of the permanent professional cadre. The Morrill Land Grant Act of 1862, at first an emergency measure during the War of the Northern Revolution of 1861–1865, in time came to perform the same function in the United States.

Summary and Concession

In summary: civil society necessarily tended from the beginning to model its structure on that of a single organism, with soldiers as the teeth and claws.

But no such tendency can work itself out completely. For all the nasty things we have had to say about them, soldiers remain human beings, with human genes, human upbringing, human feelings, subject to all the "weaknesses" of sociality and compassion that are our heritage from a hundred million years of primate ancestry. Both privates and generals have performed acts of valor above and beyond the call of military necessity. Both have accepted torture and agonizing death as the price of not betraying those they love.

If a fighting man suffers only a temporary prick of conscience for some destructive deed, it can be because he assigns his victim to a *they,* not to any of his own *we*'s; for that there is hoary precedent. When this expedient fails, he can fall back on a standard feature of military dialectic by explaining to himself that he was only following orders. His topmost commander, also a human being, can sleep peacefully by telling himself that it was not he who actually did the deed. This mutual buck-passing is as old as civil society; without it the pattern could not have prevailed.

35

✖

THE WHEELS OF EMPIRE: II

Continuing the exposition of the preceding chapter, we here take up *law, criminals, record-keeping,* and *thought-police.*

✖ In tribal society there is (in general) no functioning contrast between law and custom.[1] The codified laws of civil societies derive from a consideration mentioned earlier (p. 551): the overly rapacious racketeer quickly fails and falls, because he ruins the resources on which his rule must rest.

LAW

No group participating in a civil society can function without reasonably reliable expectations as to the consequences of alternative courses of action. It is not enough for a villageful of farmers to know that if they don't turn over a quota of their harvest to the tax-collector they will be chastised. They need also the reassurance that if they *do* meet the obligation they will *not* be harmed. The threat of penalty and the promise of reward (if only in the form of the staying of punishment) must go hand in hand. Every ordinance of every legal code in the world has these two facets, implicitly if not overtly.

Viewed superficially, law seems to flow from the will of the governor (or government). Yet if the system is to work, the arrangements imposed on subjects must be binding also on administrators, enforcers, and the governor himself. Lawmaking cannot be completely whimsical. The governor must compromise with ecological and social realities, including the established customs of the participating communities. In this sense law flows *through* the governor but stems, at bottom, as much from these customs as from his own tribal or personal preference.[2]

These and related considerations yield a number of basic points about legal codes.

---

[1] This section is a general characterization of the law of civil societies as seen, so to speak, from the outside. Later (pp. 645–652) we shall have some much more specific remarks to make about the legal tradition of the West.

[2] Here we see, in passing, how the kinship patterns of face-to-face communities begin to impose themselves as models for the structures of civil societies (chapter 19). A shrewd ruler, approaching a father-son community, says "I will be as a father to you." To an uncle-nephew culture he says "I am the great mother's-brother of all your mothers'-brothers."

(1) *A law must be both violable and enforceable.* In extreme cases this is obvious. Legislation stipulating that when a person steps out of a second-storey window he must fall would not be violable. A decree fixing the value of pi at exactly 3 would not be enforceable. Lawmaking bodies have sometimes forgotten this principle, but when they do they enact in vain.

A law must deal with something about which people usually have a range of choice, and serve to alter the relative probabilities of their making one or another choice from the array of alternatives (this puts the matter in the terminology of chapter 18).

A law is also unenforceable, hence no law, if there is no way to detect violations, or if there is no adequate machinery for imposing punishment when a violation is detected. Many an act of many a legislature (and many a private contract) has been thrown out by the courts on just these grounds.

(2) *The severity of penalties tends to correlate with* (a) *the difficulty of conformance and* (b) *the moral heinousness of the crime.* Today in England the punishment for stealing a loaf of bread is trivial; two centuries ago the thief, if caught, was often hanged. In modern England people rarely have to steal to avoid starvation; in the eighteenth century it was quite otherwise, so that what strikes us as a peccadillo had to be held in check by drastic measures. On the other hand, the punishment for murder is extreme even though most of us are rarely even vaguely tempted to commit the crime: in our society, as in most, murder is the most heinous of crimes. In the same way, the stern Inca penalty for brother-sister incest (except by the emperor himself: p. 172) does not imply that most male commoners suffered an ineluctable lust for their sisters.

(3) *Laws must be known to those whose conduct they regulate.* At first this may sound absurd. No citizen of a modern civil society can know one tenth of one percent of the thousands of statutes on the books, to say nothing of the tens of thousands of case records that tell how the courts have interpreted them. But it is just in such recent law-ridden societies that there has come into existence a class of specialized artisans called "lawyers"—partly the cause of the prodigious proliferation of legal doctrine, but, more than that, the result of it, and a social device for trying to maintain the generalization we are talking about. Besides, most of the doctrine has little direct bearing on the average citizen's daily decisions. Much of it comes into play only for rare *slow* decisions—decisions of low urgency (p. 231), about which the person affected has time to consult an expert.

(4) *A law is an imperfect contingent prediction.* It is a prediction because it speaks of the future, not of the past. It is contingent because it says, in effect, *if* such-and-such *then* so-and-so. The such-and-such is the violation, the so-and-so the punishment. It is imperfect because it is never possible to detect and punish all violators.

A law is a "self-fulfilling prophecy," like a man's assertion in the evening "Tomorrow I shall wear my green necktie." But it is of a special sort, since the purpose is never to actualize the *then* but always to prevent, or minimize, occurrences of the *if.* Laws are an attempt to reorder people's schedulings, doing overtly what is done by genes and custom in communities of nonhuman animals and in human tribal societies.

(5) *Laws require interpretation.* Occasionally a lawmaker issues an "enabling act" that allows a unique event to take place legally, but there is some question whether such an act deserves to be called a law. In principle, a law is supposed to apply to a multitude of individual instances, spread over a certain amount of space and time. Just as a law is a prediction, so also it is a generalization. Since no two individual instances are ever absolutely identical, there has to be machinery for determining whether or not a law applies in a particular instance and, if so, how. Courts and judges are thus as old as law itself.

The earliest governor-racketeers may have been their own judges. But in Mesopotamia, where the record is relatively good, there is evidence for specialized judges as early as the third millennium B.C., and they are probably older than that. Note that barristers and juries were a later development. Early judges were obliged to plead both sides of a case, as well as passing on points of fact and of law.

(6) *The law must change slowly.* This is a corollary of points already made. If a particular law is altered, there needs to be some lead time to allow appropriate adjustment by those whom it will affect. To be sure, this principle has sometimes been honored in the breach. The result is always a period of general confusion, of benefit to nobody, before things settle down again.

Some events that look like sudden legal changes have in fact been reforms, intended to firm up fraying traditions. As early Sumerian ruler, Uru-ka-gina of Lagash (about 2370 B.C.), attempted such a recodification. Some five centuries later the sixth king of the first dynasty of Babylon effected a much more thorough updating; at least our record of it, famous as the "Code of Hammurabi," is fuller. In modern times the adoption of the Constitution of the United States in 1789 was, in part, the same sort of thing.

(7) *The laws of a civil society tend to preserve the structure of that society.* Like the collective decision-making process of any tribal community (p. 150), the legal machinery of a civil society is a homeostatic device. Conservatism, however, is not inevitable: in recent centuries Western law has become, in part, an instrument for carefully controlled reform (p. 645).

(8) *Laws need not be "just" or "fair."* The term "just" is properly applied not to a law but to its interpretation. A judge who rests his thumb on one pan of the goddess Dikē's scales, consistently edging his decisions in favor (say) of tenants and against landlords—or vice versa—is not being just. The most despotic of sultans have required their qadis to be impartial, on pain of boiling in oil.

As to "fairness"—this is simply not a legal term. What is fair depends on who you are. A white supremacist will call a law bad that promotes integration and equal opportunity. A believer in democracy will deem a legal code manifestly unfair if it prescribes narrow constraints and harsh punishments for peasants and slaves, broad freedoms and mild reprimands for the gentry. But if a civil society is organized that way, then that is how the laws will read.

Contemporary lay supporters of "law and order" do not know this. They use the phrase loosely for its rhetorical effect, intending to contrast it with "crime and destruction." The politician who delivers an impassioned address on the subject may then climb into his car and exceed the speed limit on his way to the next town, with no feeling of inconsistency.

The jurist who expresses deep faith in the law means something else entirely. He knows that many specific statutes and ordinances are out of date or immoral, and works to get them revised or repealed. His faith is in the modern legal process, not in that of a thousand or of five thousand years ago. The touchstone of his faith is a factor not in evidence in the earliest civil societies; we shall come to it later (p. 645).

(9) *Every legal code leaves some matters untouched.* This fact it is that yields the distinctive contrast, in civil societies, between law and custom. The earliest racketeer's regulations draped heavily, yet loosely, over the participating farm villages and other face-to-face communities. It did not matter to the central administration how a particular village managed to meet its tax quota or its levy of young men for military or other civic duty. The village worked out the details itself, as much as possible within the fabric of its own tradition, and it managed its parochial affairs the same way.

The Inca empire was an exception, or as close to one as we know. The accounts that have come down to us propose that practically everything was regulated (p. 562). The underlying principle was the Nazi totalitarian one: *Alles was nicht Pflicht ist, ist verboten* 'Anything not mandatory is prohibited'. This is the opposite extreme from the policy of "freedom under law" favored by many today, in which the government would impose on any one person only such legal constraints as were imperative to protect the welfare of others (but such a notion, of course, was alien to original law). When the Incas conquered a new tribe at the empire's borders, they required it to reorganize in conformity with the imperial scheme. If it was reluctant, whole villages were transplanted to some area nearer headquarters, whose former inhabitants, more schooled in imperial discipline, were sent in exchange to occupy the evacuated boundary region.

Some of the earlier empires of the Old World apparently came to be almost as rigorously regimented (at least in intent) as was that of the Incas. Clauses in the Code of Hammurabi (p. 569) prescribe uniformity throughout the realm for such things as marriage and divorce, the mutual obligations of fathers and sons, the conditions under which a newborn child was "slave" or "free" (dubious English renderings of the terms *wardum* and *mushkenum* of the original), the penalties to be imposed on a farmer if his ox gored a passing traveler, the limits within which two families could carry on a private feud. It is interesting, though not surprising (p. 146), the extent to which this and other early legal codes deal with *property* rather than people, and with people in terms of property.

Despite the partial exceptions we have mentioned, our generalization retains its validity. At any one place and time in the history of civil societies there are some matters on which the law is silent, so that it can be ignored as decisions are made.

This fact is concealed by the fondness of students of jurisprudence for inventing various additional kinds of "law" to fill the gaps in the sort we are talking about. To the theologist everything is religion; to the lawyer all is law—if only because that is his most comfortable vocabulary.

Aristotle, epitomizing the Greek tradition, gets the blame for distinguishing, not between the legal and the alegal, but between "man-made" and "natural" law, a bit of verbal legerdemain by which everything is law-dominated, since what is not subsumed by the former is covered by the latter. His blooper has had us in trouble ever since. On the one hand, rulers have found easy legal justification for the oppression of minorities or the slaughter of savages on the grounds that they are "naturally" inferior. On the other, it has been hard to come by the realization that "laws of nature" are not ordinances or edicts of any sort or source whatsoever, but simply *the way things are.* Historically, the notion of laws of nature was an analogical extension, and a very bad one, from the ways of civil society, yielding a prejudicial ethnocentric view of the universe which we have practically had to stand on its head in order to begin to glimpse things in proper perspective.

✂ Another thing law did was to create criminals—not the same (as we saw on p. 562) as mere social misfits, which can crop up in any sort of society.[3] The criminal class draws from every stratum: deposed kings, outlawed generals, artisans fleeing for having incurred royal displeasure, soldiers gone AWOL, disgruntled peasants and proletarians, escaping slaves.

CRIMINALS

Such force-outs and drop-outs, unless caught and executed, may haunt the alleyways of city slums as petty thieves and confidence men (what the Germans call the *Lumpenproletariat*). They may gather in rural fastnesses and prey, as brigands, on caravans and peasant villages, or on deserted shores and islands, as pirates and wreckers pillaging merchantmen. In such cases they become so many more unproductive mouths to be fed, like governors and soldiers, by the food-producers, without even the minimal quid pro quo of administration and protection.

Sometimes, however, they have been able to set up their own society, independent of the civil societies from which they stem but more or less imitative of the structure of the latter. We outlined such a case in chapter 21 (pp. 260–270).

Sometimes they have even been able to backtrack, depose the old rulers (who are by that act either destroyed or converted in their turn into criminals), and establish their own regime, thereby quickly shedding all taint of impropriety and becoming honorable leaders of men. This is another formula for the circulation of élites (p. 551). Parts of Latin America retain it to this day. It was pandemic in medieval Europe and, earlier on, had been out of fashion only during spells of domination of sizable territories by unusually mighty emperors. The rotation can be rapid. Many a baron is the grandson of a bandit, many a bank president of a bank robber.

✂ A golden horn found near Gallehus in southern Denmark and dating from about A.D. 400 bears one of the earliest known Germanic inscriptions. The form of speech in which it is written is, of course, different from any now used, since Germanic has

RECORD-KEEPING

[3]Law makes criminals, not vice versa; but they in turn are responsible for the now very widespread legal distinction between "criminal law" and "civil law," ignored here as too picayune for the scale of our treatment.

changed and differentiated a lot in the subsequent 1600 years. But we can read it. The writing is in runes, which when transliterated and translated say

ek hlewagastiz holtingaz horna tawido
'I, Fameguest of the Forest clan, made the horn.'

The earliest direct record of Latin which has survived is interestingly similar. It dates from a thousand years earlier (about 600 B.C.). It is an inscription on a large safety-pin-shaped clasp, also of gold, found near Palestrina in Italy. The writer modestly refers to himself in the third person and lets the clasp speak:

Manios med fhefhaked Numasioi
'Manius made me for Numerius.'

Fameguest and Manius were artisans, working skillfully with a rare and precious substance. They were literate, at a time when most members of their respective communities were not. To be sure, there must have been a fair amount of writing being done in each community, the bulk of it on perishable materials (parchment, vellum, or the like) and hence lost to us. But the artisans' *use* of writing is characteristic and far older than writing itself. They used it to identify their products with themselves and to boast of their pride of craftsmanship to all posterity. Artists are allergic to anonymity. When they produce something beautiful and durable, they want personal credit. Today a painter signs his name in the corner of his picture, and you will find a monogram or brand label of some sort on the shelf back or title page of any book, on the underside of many a plate or pot, on many a vase and jar, on many a screen and fan.

RECORDS BEFORE WRITING

We said that this attitude is older than writing. Upper Pleistocene artifacts of stone and bone have been found with incised designs, sometimes filled with colored paint, that were or may have been proprietary marks. Some of these have been spotted only recently, by investigators who decided it might be worth while to examine archaeological relics through a microscope rather than just with the naked eye. The point is not that the marks are minuscule, but that in the course of intervening millennia they have become obscured by cracks and ridges of other origin. Under the microscope one can begin to sort out the scratches made by the manufacturer from those that represent the ravages of time and weather. Obviously we cannot be sure of the interpretation, but it seems reasonable to suppose something of the following sort. Wib and Gug both make superb ax blades. When Wib makes one, he finishes it off by putting a few characteristic scratches on it which the members of his tribe recognize as meaning 'Wib made this'. Gug's mark is a scratch design clearly different from Wib's. The time could easily be thirty thousand years ago. Maybe thirty times that.

When civil societies were arising, the pride of governors soon equaled or surpassed that of craftsmen (if with less justification), and they, too, wanted to leave their mark. From various parts of southwest Asia we find *seals* of one sort or another (p. 528).

The seal of a governor or of his agent bore a cameo (raised) negative of an arbitrary but distinctive sort. It was pressed or rolled on soft clay, or perhaps sometimes inked and struck against a solid surface, to leave an intaglio (depressed) or superimposed (printed) positive, as an official acknowledgment that something had passed inspection as conforming to governmental specifications of quantity and quality, that the governor accepted responsibility for it, or that it now belonged to the government and could be disposed of only as commanded. Note that we still speak today of "inspection stamps" and of "seals of approval."

Such early trademarks and stamps were not writing, only one of its forerunners. There were others. We have already mentioned numerals consisting of notched sticks or scored stones (p. 138). There have been, and still are, many forms of record-keeping other than writing. Some involve no marking of a surface. Pebbles in a bowl can be a numeral. You can help yourself remember where a particular object came from, and what it is for, by storing it in one place rather than another: think of the in- and out-baskets on a secretary's desk. Mnemonic marks on a surface are not always writing. Consider a map. Erase the words from it and you still have an outline map, a sketchy scale picture, still of some use. Erase everything *but* the words and it becomes a meaningless jumble.

CIVIL RECORD-KEEPING

As early city-states grew into small kingdoms and then into large empires, the need for accurate administrative records became greater and greater, and it grew increasingly difficult to manage with just the kinds of devices we have so far mentioned. It is significant that all but one of the major empires of antiquity, in the Old World and the New World alike, used true writing systems. Were it not for the one exception, one would be inclined towards the proposition that extensive empire is *impossible* without writing. We cannot say that, but apparently we can assert that it is *almost* impossible.

The Incas seem to have managed without. The extremely tight-knit, beehive-like nature of their society, on which we have remarked before, may have been causally tied in with their illiteracy, in that without true writing it was imperative to distribute the total task of observing and remembering administratively important matters through a large number of officials, that each might not have more to keep track of than he could handle.

The most precise Peruvian mnemonic device was an assemblage of knotted colored cords called a *quipu* (Figure 35-1). One more use of cordage is hardly surprising among a people given to skillful spinning and weaving and to the construction and maintenance of unrivaled rope bridges. We know some quipus were numerals, working by a decimal system of notation with a special mark (a knot position with no knot) for zero. We do not know how the users of quipus managed to keep straight which numerical quipu recorded which numerical fact, and we do not know for sure that they were all numerals, since the whole tradition was destroyed early in Spanish days. Features of a quipu other than the arrangement of cords and knots (for instance, the colors and the exact types of knots) may have carried conventionalized meanings.

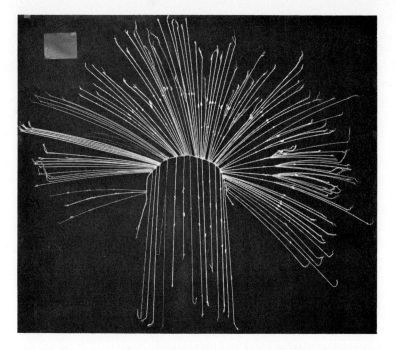

FIGURE 35-1. A quipu. (Courtesy of the Museum of the American Indian, Heye Foundation.)

The specialist class of quipu-interpreters may have had to supplement the information stored in the quipu by having excellent memories. Perhaps both.

Perhaps the quipu system was more like true writing than we realize. The details have vanished; we are left with the knowledge that the system worked well. When called for, demographic and economic statistics of the most varied sorts were gathered quickly and transmitted accurately to district, regional, or imperial headquarters, where they served as a reliable basis for administrative decisions.

All other empires have either invented true writing for themselves or inherited it from predecessors or neighbors.

In the Old World, writing developed first (1) among the Sumerians of Mesopotamia, late in the fourth millennium B.C. (2) Around 3000 B.C. it appears in Egypt; (3) slightly thereafter in the Indus Valley; (4) by 2500 in Elam (a district in southwestern Persia, approximately the present-day Khūzestān). (5) The earliest Cretan hieroglyphics date from a bit after 2000, (6) the earliest hieroglyphic Hittite (around Boğazköy, Turkey) from 1500, and (7) the earliest surviving Chinese inscriptions from some period in the second millennium B.C. that it has been impossible to date with much accuracy. We cannot yet read the Indus Valley script, the earliest Elamite inscriptions, hieroglyphic Hittite, or the earliest Cretan materials (p. 594). The writing systems we have listed are those first attested. Others may await discovery, or may have been used on materials or in climates such that they have been lost without hope of recovery. All the later writing systems of the Old World surely are derivatives of one or another of those mentioned. Whether the seven listed all derive by diffusion from a single origin (among the Sumerians?) or represent the results of three or four independent inventions is hotly debated. Opinions seem to rest less on the evidence, which is scant, than on the investigator's low or high opinion of human creativity. The reader already knows my stand on that issue.

In the New World, writing developed in or near Yucatán in the late second or early first millennium B.C., possibly among speakers of Mayan languages, possibly among their northern neighbors the Olmecs. It was carried to the Valley of Mexico by the Toltecs, from whom the Aztecs had it. The extent to which we can read any New World writing remains very limited. Believers in human creativity can take heart, in that the New World evidence means that writing was independently invented *at least* twice; any proposal of ancient culture-bearers from the Old World to the New is pure fantasy.

True Writing

Now, what is "true" writing?

Remember that those who developed writing systems were human beings with the full roster of human capacities and achievements; in particular, they all spoke a language. A system of graphic symbols becomes a writing system when the visual marks come under the influence of the (spoken) language. There are two successive steps to this process. Since we are concerned only with illustrating the principles involved, we can for convenience pretend that the (spoken) language involved is English.

(1) Suppose that your graphic shape for the number four is " $+\!\!+\!\!+$ " and that your linguistic form for the number (that is, the arrangement of distinctive speech sounds which carries that meaning) is *four*. You have three things: two symbols and one meaning. One symbol is visual; one is vocal-auditory; and both have the same meaning. The first step in the influence of language on the graphic system is for these three items to be realigned so that the graphic shape comes to mean the *spoken form*. Using an arrow to indicate that the thing at its tail means the thing at its point, the shift is from the arrangement shown at the top in Figure 35-2 to that shown at the bottom.

Again, suppose that your graphic shape for a bee is a conventionalized, easily drawn picture of a bee, and that your linguistic form for a bee is *bee*. Figure 35-3 shows the alignment of the three items (two symbols and one meaning) before and after the shift.

The shift of lines of connection we have described seems counterintuitive. Why should there be any advantage in having linguistic forms mediate between graphic marks and their meanings?

The answer is that the language already supplies linguistic forms to cover the whole universe of experience of its speakers, whereas a set of graphic shapes, as long as it remains free from the spell of language, probably does not. Early prewriting systems tend to use graphic shapes that are rough pictures of the things they mean. But some of the things one wishes to make a record about do not lend themselves to picture-

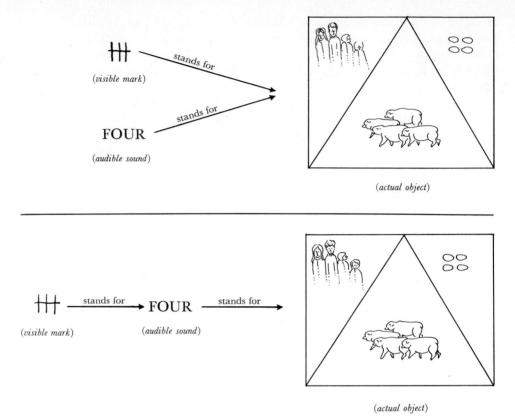

(visible mark)

(audible sound)

(actual object)

(visible mark)

(audible sound)

(actual object)

FIGURE 35-2.

drawing. If the connection between graphic shape and meaning can be indirect, mediated by the already well established linguistic form for that meaning, then the graphic shape for a particular meaning can be arbitrary (that is, does not need in any way to be a picture of what it means) and still not be too difficult to remember.

(2) The second step, not always taken, is for the graphic shape to cease to be associated with the linguistic form, and to come to represent only the *sound* of that form.

Remember (chapter 8) that a linguistic form is a phonetic shape *with a meaning*. But one and the same phonetic shape can be a family of "homonyms"; for example, English *bear* 'ursus', *bear* 'yield, carry', and (with different spelling but the same pronunciation) *bare* 'uncovered'. Before the second step is taken, a writing system would have to have three different graphic shapes for these three distinct linguistic forms. After the second step, a single graphic shape will do for all three.

Using the two examples given above for the first step, we note that after the new adjustment it would be possible for the form *before*, which resembles only in sound, not in meaning, the sequence of forms *bee four*, to be written as shown in Figure 35-4.

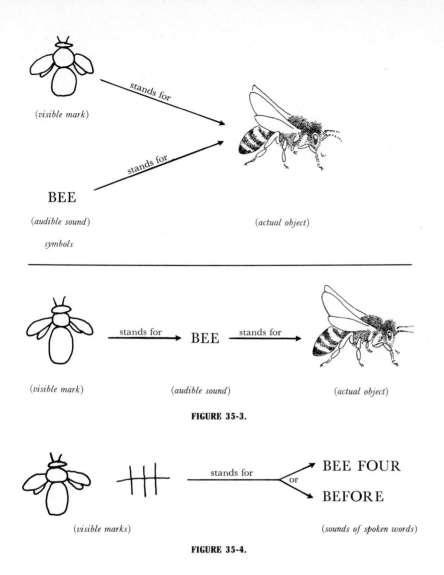

(visible mark)

stands for

stands for

BEE

(audible sound)

(actual object)

symbols

(visible mark)

stands for

BEE

stands for

(audible sound)

(actual object)

FIGURE 35-3.

(visible marks)

stands for

or

BEE FOUR

BEFORE

(sounds of spoken words)

FIGURE 35-4.

Every language has far more small lexical units than it has hunks of phonetic material that serve as the phonetic shapes of those forms; hence the second step is a great economy measure.

Some people think that these two steps would be extremely unobvious. I believe, on the contrary, that they were practically inevitable. Imagine clerks and accountants trying to keep track of complex commercial and administrative transactions, knowing that their lives may depend on their accuracy, resorting constantly to consultative prose, not only to pool their information but also to register the crucial facts indelibly in their own heads, and using some awkward set of graphic shapes—or some other type of information-storage—to label commodities and as an external aid to their memories. Associations between the graphic shapes and the spoken linguistic forms are bound to develop. The set of graphic symbols then gradually evolves into a writing system under the pressure of necessity, with no need for any single, sudden stroke of unusual acumen—just a thick scattering of little innovations, such as a helpful pun or a minor modification of an old character for a slightly different use.

The process *was* gradual. Early inscriptions typically show some graphic shapes that (probably) stand directly for meanings, some that represent linguistic forms, and some that stand for arrangements of speech sounds, mingled together in whatever way the literate folks of the moment found maximally convenient. At this distance we can't always be sure which marks are of which type, but that all types occurred is beyond doubt.

If all this is true, then the only way any budding empire can evade the devising of a writing system is by having one as part of its initial heritage. What, then, of the Peruvians? If the quipu was not a kind of writing, then it *prevented* the development of true writing. In expert hands, it got the practical job done well enough, and perhaps the physical medium (knotted cords) did not lend itself to gradual modification in the direction of a writing system as does the putting of marks on surfaces.

FURTHER STEPS

About 1500 B.C., inscriptions from ancient Ugarit (just north of Al-Ladhiqiyah in Syria) show speakers of a Semitic language taking another step in the simplification of writing and its subjugation to language. They were beginning to settle on a single written symbol for each consonant sound of the sound system of their language, and to leave the vowel sounds altogether unrepresented. Nglsh cn b wrttn ths wy wtht cmplt lss f ntllgblt, prvdd thr s ngh cntxt. The nonindication of vowel sounds made less trouble for the Semitic languages of the time than it would for English by virtue of a special feature of their structure that we need not dwell on. Learning to write was easier, since fewer characters were required; reading was probably a little harder, because the omission of vowels yielded ambiguities that had to be puzzled out from context. This style of writing became widespread among the speakers of Semitic languages in eastern Mediterranean lands and Arabia.

THE NAGARI PRINCIPLE.   In the east, a derivative of the Ugaritic system moved into India and became the script known as *nagari* (Sanskrit *nāgarī*), used for both Indo-Aryan and Dravidian languages (pp. 591–592). With further modification this script has served for most of the subsequent languages of India and for a number in adjacent regions, including Tibetan, Burmese, Thai, and Javanese.

For these languages, vowel sounds had to be indicated. The way in which nagari does this is not the alphabetical way we shall describe in a moment. As shown in Figure 35-5, a unit symbol stands for a fixed combination of a certain consonant sound followed by the vowel *a.* The basic symbol also appears with one or another of several "diacritics" (added strokes). The consonantal part of what the basic symbol represents remains unchanged by the diacritics; the vocalic part is altered. The absence of any following vowel sound can be indicated by a special diacritic, or by joining the basic symbol to the following one in a special ligatured form.

ka   ta   kta

ki   ti   kti

ku   tu   ktu

k   t   kt

FIGURE 35-5. THE NAGARI PRINCIPLE. This is "devanāgarī," as used for Sanskrit. The top symbols in the first two columns are single characters without diacritics; each stands for a consonant-vowel syllable. Added diacritics (the other symbols in the same columns) change the vowel or cancel it. The third column shows the ligatured forms which serve to suppress the vowel after the first of two successive consonants.

The nonalphabetical nature of this script is revealed by the fact that it takes two symbols to write a bare consonant, such as *k* or *s*, and only one to write a syllable such as *ka* or *sa*.

THE ALPHABETICAL PRINCIPLE. In the west, some North Semitic script was introduced into the Aegean area and was adapted to the writing of Greek. The earliest surviving Greek alphabetical inscriptions are from the ninth or eighth century B.C., but the record remains very thin until several centuries later.

As in India, so also for Greek the indication of vowels was imperative. The Greeks kept several of the borrowed North Semitic characters that they did not need for consonants, and assigned them to vowels. It was this that yielded *alphabetic writing*, in which, in principle, there is only one graphic symbol for each consonant or vowel phoneme (p. 103) of the language.

Apparently the alphabetical principle was hit upon only this once. Such a system, even if it has imperfections and discrepancies, is easier to learn and more efficient to use than any other kind. It shares with systems of the nagari type the fact that if you can *say* a word you can instantly *write* it.[4] Writing systems of other types do not guarantee this breadth of coverage. For instance, after years of experience with Chinese one may suddenly need to write a word for which one cannot recall the character, or even a new word for which perhaps no character has been devised. Of systems that possess the great merit of covering whatever the language itself covers, the alphabetical ones are the most efficient because they require the smallest stock of symbols. It is therefore not surprising that for the past 2500 years an increasing percentage of the world's writing systems have been of this type.

NUMERALS AND SPECIAL NOTATIONS

In the face of what has just been said, there is one range of vocabulary for which alphabetical writing is *not* the most efficient: numerals.

Every good alphabetical or nagari system is backed up by a set of "logographic" symbols standing for number words as wholes, not via their pronunciation. Our use of "1234567890" and the conventions of decimal notation make possible a rapid and accurate manipulation of figures that alphabetical writing of number words precludes. Try it: write down some figures in the spelled-out forms (such as "four thousand seven hundred eighty-two") and then attempt to multiply them.

For numerical notation, the great breakthrough was the invention of a mark for zero and of place notation. The Incas has such a mark for their quipus, and the Chinese for their abaci; in graphic symbolism, the Mayas invented a zero in the New World, and both the Chinese and the Hindus in the Old. Our "Arabic" numerals are Hindu in origin, spread to Europe via the Muslims.

Somewhat different from the foregoing is the fact that in many specialized enterprises it is helpful to have some succinct notation for use alongside ordinary writing. Sometimes the symbols are purely arbitrary logographs: thus the biologist's "♂" and "♀" for 'male' and 'female'. But often there is a mnemonic linkage via ordinary writing: for example, in the jargon of printed knitting instructions ("Row 1 — * P3, K3, repeat from * ending P3") or in the constitutional and structural formulas of chemistry.

LITERACY

Writing was in the beginning the prerogative of the clerks and accountants who invented it and improved it to help them with their jobs. Clerks and accountants have sometimes been "priests" and sometimes "slaves," but universally they have counted as artisans rather than as governors, peasants, proletarians, or soldiers. The lower classes have traditionally been illiterate, and still today are largely so in some civil societies. The ruling classes, to start with, scorned literacy as beneath their dignity, but it did not take them long to change their minds.

[4] This feature is disrupted when spellings get frozen and do not change to keep up with the inevitably changing language, as has happened in recent centuries especially in English, French, and Mongolian. Apperantly, tho, the concensis is that a mispelling will do in an emergensy to convay what you mean. Uniform spelling is hard on writers, easy on readers; beyond that, correct spelling is a sort of superimposed snob game, played by some authors and all publishers' copy editors, not really an essential part of a writing system.

Yet the artisans had a head start, and the association of literacy and creativity has been intimate ever since. The fact that the goldsmiths Manius and Fameguest could read and write was par for the course. Literacy deepened and strengthened the arts, and increased their variety. Apprentices could learn not only from their masters but from their masters' masters.

The chroniclers and jurists who did the detailed work of assembling the Code of Hammurabi were literate craftsmen; likewise the civil engineers who surveyed and designed irrigation systems, roads, and monumental buildings, with geometry as a byproduct; so the astronomers who accumulated their observations over the years and devised the calendars of early Mesopotamia, of Egypt, and of Yucatán and thus made both planning and chronicling more accurate; so the surgeons and physicians, the mathematicians, theologians, necromancers, and philosophers; so (sometimes only after great delay[5]) the poets, bards, and spinners of tales; and so, in modern times, the scientists.

MONEY

Money is another sort of machinery for keeping records: it is, in economics, what energy is for physicists. Energy is used to keep the accounts straight on the migrations and transformations of matter and radiation and to determine equivalences among them. Similarly, money is used to keep the accounts straight on the migrations and transformations of, and to establish equivalences among, commodities and services.

Trade in the earliest civil societies, as in tribal societies, was largely barter in kind. But as the variety of commodities increased, the need for some sort of standard became intense. It may not be too hard to figure out how many bushels of wheat should be equivalent in value to one yearling pig. But suppose there are 1000 different commodities sometimes available for exchange. That would mean establishing 999,000 pairwise equivalences in value. If we supply an arbitrary standard, then only 1000 pairwise equivalences are required: each is the standard "monetary" value of a single commodity, and equivalences between commodities can be computed arithmetically and indirectly when needed.

One way to achieve this—probably the first way tried—is to single out a specific type of commodity as the standard, in terms of which the values of all other types will be expressed. In late preliterate and early literate times in Europe the Germanic and Italic tribes were still doing this, with domestic animals as the standard. The practice is dimly reflected in our current English vocabulary: English *fee* is from Old English *feoh* 'head of cattle, wealth, money', cognate with German *Vieh* 'head of cattle'; English *pecuniary* is a borrowing from Latin *pecūniārius* 'pertaining to money', from *pecūnia* 'money', from *pecu(s)* 'cattle'.

The flaw in this sort of monetary material can be exposed very quickly.

A monetary unit, be it a printed piece of paper, a coin, or a cow, is a *numeral,*

[5]When writing came to India the Vedic scriptures were not transcribed because the new technique had connotations of crassness or was in some other way considered unfit for such elegant or holy use; the same held for the Druidic tradition when writing first reached the Celts in northwestern Europe. The Vedas were passed down orally for another 2000 years before they were finally written. The Druidic tradition passed away unrecorded.

though with one special feature not shared by other numerals. We pointed out earlier (p. 138) that for efficiency a numeral should be made of something useless for any other purpose, durable enough to last as long as the particular quantitative record is needed, and cheap to produce. But to serve as money, a numeral should be useless, durable, and *hard* to produce. If you can eat your money or make clothing out of it as winter comes, then in a pinch you will not hold on to it for buying things. If it disintegrates when stored (or can sicken and die), you may lose it and the value it represents. If you can manufacture as much as you want of it yourself, out of stuff you pick up in your back yard, then you will not accept it from anyone else as a record of value given.

In Old World antiquity these considerations, though unvoiced, slowly pointed away from cattle and the like and straight at silver, electrum (gold-silver alloy), and especially gold. There was limited use of standardized quantities of gold or silver in early Mesopotamia, and of uniform bars of precious metal in early Egypt. *Coins,* meaning pieces of metal of uniform mass and substance and bearing some sort of inscription as to their denomination, were invented by the Lydians of Asia Minor (capital city Sardis) in the seventh century B.C. and somewhere in China at approximately the same time. They were an instant success, and other kingdoms quickly began minting their own.

Gold, especially, was ideal for this use in antiquity: it was in short supply, hard to find more of, inedible and unwearable, and extremely durable. Moreover, it was almost entirely useless. It still is, which is why so large a portion of the world's reserves can lie in the vaults at Fort Knox without being missed. Gold jewelry has not really been an exception. The artistry that goes into its manufacture does not enhance its value for everyone.[6] It has been chiefly a way for the wealthy to store their excess assets compactly, attractively, and ostentatiously—really just another form of money.

So gold served this special function for a basically functionless substance from several thousand years ago until only yesterday. Even when other objects have been used as media of exchange (currency, instruments of credit, specialized receipts such as postage stamps), their stated value has typically been "backed," directly or indirectly, by gold. Only in the twentieth century has this arrangement begun seriously to falter.

THOUGHT-POLICE ✗ World views in tribal societies are shaped by heritage and modified by ongoing experience, and bear actively on the choices made among alternative courses of action.

The same is true in civil society, with two modifications. The first is that, since the society is complex, members of different strata or of different participating face-to-face subcommunities may hold strikingly different world views. The second is that the bosses take an active part in forcing a *Weltanschauung* on the lower classes that will help keep them suitably industrious and docile. If the particular civil society is big enough, this requires a corps of specialists on the ruler's administrative staff.

[6]Fameguest's golden horn (p. 571) was found in 1734 and its inscription was copied; in 1802 it was stolen from the museum where it rested, and melted down, by a thief for whom the artistry and inscription did not enhance its value one whit.

Whatever such specialists be called in specific societies, our term for them is "thought-police."

We said earlier in another connection (p. 562) that it does not matter whether the tax-collector says "Pay or my soldiers will rape your wife and daughters" or "Be good or the goblins will get you." Well, it does make this difference: The former remark is a threat of naked brutality and cannot but rouse hostility, even if the taxes are duly paid. The latter, if phrased properly, can bear the guise of friendly counsel for the peasant's own good. The source of menace is transferred from the government to malevolent forces of nature, whose evil intent can be thwarted by the tax-paying ritual or by a ritual that the taxes will help pay for. The government becomes a kindly protector instead of a vicious predator. That makes everybody feel better, and obviously cuts down on wastage.

Achieving this sort of understanding was probably not too hard as civil societies first arose. Tribal existence affords many opportunities for the ascription of anthropomorphized creatures, some good and some evil, to the natural environment, and many experiential reinforcements for the widespread belief that the souls of men live on after their bodies have died. What was necessary was only an appropriate realignment so that the government was on the side of the good gods and a bulwark against the bad ones.

The evidence suggests that this arrangement had been worked out even by the earliest city-states of the Sumerians in Mesopotamia, more than five thousand years ago. The archaeological remains look like those of temples, with statues and various ceremonial trappings as well as granaries and storerooms. The peasants could not have known that the ears of the gods were of stone. We are tempted nowadays to feel that the higher priests, at least, must have known this, but that may just be our own prejudice. The evidence does not tell us so. They may have been liars so artful that they came to swallow their own line, or they may have been sincere from the very beginning.

Either way, it is certain that in course of time a civilly useful world view became widespread in most strata of most civil societies, its details differing appropriately according to the stratum, so that the main task of thought-police became not that of inculcating proper beliefs but that of maintaining them against heresy. Peasants who were able to succumb to the proper doctrine and guide their miserable lives by it became the fellahin. Those who could not were destroyed or became slaves.

The distinctive contrast between the religious and the nonreligious entered civil society only upon the development of a special sort of functional splitting (p. 562), with political and religious edifices both erected on the same lowest social stratum. The religious organization was heir to that part of the earlier undivided civil tradition which had to do with gods and devils, good and evil, rewards and punishments in the afterlife. The political structure made do with the rest.

Karl Marx (1818–1883), assuming that church and state inevitably work together, proposed that the officials of the former have served as the thought-police (he did not use the term) monitoring the beliefs of the masses for the benefit of both sets of rulers. Hence he characterized religion as "the opium of the people." That is an oversimplification. In the first place, church and state have by no means invariably worked hand in glove. Sometimes they have contended mightily. In the second place, religious convictions have more than once roused people to revolt against political oppression. The Puritans and Quakers (p. 190) of seventeenth-century England illustrate this. Still in the second place, but contrariwise, political views have led people to try to throw off the yoke of a priesthood: the framers of the Constitution of the United States made specific provisions against church interference in state affairs. And in the third place, a political state can have its own thought-police. There is religion in the Soviet Union today, but the M.V.D. hardly serves its interest. Religious thought-police encourage piety. Political ones urge uncritical patriotism: "My country: may she always be right, but, right or wrong, my country!"

Madison Avenue is today the headquarters for a corps of thought-police with a most unusual assignment: that of making large numbers of people desire certain products and services whether or not they need them or can afford them. The ad-men are remarkably ingenious, but that should not conceal from us that their basic strategy is the soul of simplicity: they lie. It is only the wildly improbable technological success of capitalist society (pp. 624–634), in a few parts of the Western world in the last half century, that has made such an operation necessary. More goods can be, and are, produced than anyone needs! The excess cannot merely be distributed free to those who are unable to purchase them, because capitalist enterprises are such that they must show a profit in order to keep going.

But the affluent society is recent, geographically limited, and of doubtful durability. The fundamental fact about almost all civil societies, the brutal truth to which thought-police have had to try to make world views adjust, has been that *there is not enough to go around.* Rulers and ruled alike accept that as an unalterable basic law of nature, and those with the fellahin mentality bow to the corollary that one must always make do with less than enough. The range of rationalizations that have been offered—and accepted—for the consequent inequities is truly amazing, but bears testimony to the remarkable flexibility of our species.

BY HIS BOOTSTRAPS

36

✖

THE JUGGERNAUT: I

I met a traveller from an antique land
Who said: "Two vast and trunkless legs of stone
Stand in the desert. Near them, on the sand,
Half sunk, a shattered visage lies, whose frown,
And wrinkled lip, and sneer of cold command,
Tell that its sculptor well those passions read
Which yet survive, stamped on those lifeless things,
The hand that mocked them, and the heart that fed.
And on the pedestal these words appear—
'My name is Ozymandias, king of kings:
Look on my works, ye Mighty, and despair!'
Nothing beside remains. Round the decay
Of that colossal wreck, boundless and bare
The lone and level sands stretch far away."

P. B. Shelley

The wheels of empire turn not on fixed axles. They roll and grow as snowballs grow. A state cannot stay static (p. 551). Unless it develops it soon diminishes and disappears. This does not propose cessation of expansion as sufficient source of internal decay, or vice versa. Causalities are tangled and differ from case to case. No two regimes have ever toppled in identical ways. Nevertheless, no empire can just hold still.

But a government dare not expand too fast, or it outstrips its capacity and breaks up. The classical paradigm is the bloated empire won by Temujin (Genghis Khan, died A.D. 1227) and his successors. The twelfth-century Mongols were barbarians dwelling at the fuzzy geographical edge of the entrenched civil societies of Eurasia. In the manner outlined earlier (p. 566) they acquired the craft of conquest from "civilized" neighbors and put it to work. They added of their own, and Temujin capped it off with genuine genius. At its greatest extent, their realm stretched unbroken from Poland and the Arabian desert to the shores of the Pacific in China and Korea, a territory not noticeably smaller than that of the Soviet Union today. It is said of their reign that a virgin bearing gold could have traveled the length of the empire unmolested. Yet within a century and a half of Temujin's death it had fragmented, its chief legacy a broadcast seeding of Mongol genes and half a dozen regional Mongol dynasties.

We are struck by this because of the titanic territory. We think of states as occupying space: the more space, the more impressive.

We also think of states as having exact boundaries. From the Lake of the Woods to the Strait of Georgia, the United States and Canada impinge along 49°00′00″ north latitude. Stand an inch north of the boundary and you are in one country; one inch south of it you are in the other. That is how we want our borders—not always straight, but always vanishingly narrow. A disputed zone is distressing and the wrangle should be resolved.

This attitude is typically European and of recent vintage, though not wholly unknown elsewhere. In the fourth century B.C. the Chinese built cross-country walls, in imitation of those around their cities (p. 555), to set off kingdoms from one another. Whatever the motivation, the effect was like that of a boy drawing a line in the dust with his toe and daring his adversary to step across. The kings continued their quarrels, and in the span of a century one had triumphed, becoming the first emperor of the Ch'in dynasty. He then tried the same stunt on the largest scale the world has seen, erecting an overland wall from the Gulf of Chihli twisting inland for more than 1450 miles, partly for defense but also as the plainly marked northern rim of his dominion.

Most rulers have not worried about precise perimeters. Genghis Khan's generals may have used maps (cartography goes back at least to the fifth or sixth century B.C. in Greece and in China), but he sent forth no civil engineers to survey and delimit newly conquered territory. His concerns were those of the typical tyrant: vaguely bounded districts where food and other wealth had been and could be produced, people to supply the necessary labor, and routes tying the districts together and to headquarters. Barren land flanking a road or bordering a fertile valley was a nuisance. It yielded nothing, and yet had to be policed against bandits and aliens. In this way every empire has had its "marches": zones, not lines.

In other words, the classical dwelling pattern of civil societies was the same as that of most bands of hunters-gatherers or, indeed, of most land mammals: nucleated territoriality. To be sure, the nucleus—the capital city—was more permanent. Often there were subsidiary centers in the form of tributary towns, each with its own enclosing dependent terrain. Until 2000 years ago in China and until much more recently than that in Europe, boundaries remained as ill defined as ever.

Many monarchs, unlike Genghis Khan, have been wise or experienced enough to eschew what they could not securely bite off. For that matter, the aim of imperial expansion isn't inevitably increased acreage. Forget booty, which is always welcome but a one-shot deal with no future. In their more enduring aims, some regimes have been land-hungry, some labor-lorn, and some both. The Incas illustrate the last of these (p. 570). The British colonies in North America, and the young United States

BY HIS BOOTSTRAPS

they became, exemplify the first: the land was everything and its earlier occupants be damned.

Continental southeastern Asia shows us the second situation. Six or eight centuries ago there were kingdoms aplenty here, and they set their armies against one another as kingdoms always do. But when one king prevailed against a second, whose capital might be fifty or so miles away, he made no move to annex the defeated monarch's territory. That would have been pointless. The climate and the formidability of jungle transportation forbade exploiting a district so far from headquarters, and he knew it. He annexed some of the loser's *people* and herded them home. The land was fecund; good crops could be grown anywhere; only labor was in short supply.

The results of this form of statecraft endure today. Maps of southeastern Asia show neat lines purporting to separate Vietnam from Cambodia from Laos from Thailand. They are taken seriously by the foreign or foreign-trained politicians and generals who struggle to impose a totally outlandish political pattern on the whole region. They mean nothing to most of the populace. There are settlements of Cambodians and of Laotians (culturally and linguistically speaking) scattered all over. There are Vietnamese villagers in what the map says is Cambodia whose great grandfathers never saw what the map says is Vietnam. Loyalties are familial and local, not national—the very notion of a political entity called "Vietnam" is alien, and postdates the Second World War. Nobody would care much, except that Western culture, in both its "Western" and its "Russian" versions, proclaims that such arrangements are improper. Maybe contemporary Chinese culture says this too.

THE PATTERN AND THE RECORD

✕ The earliest states were wee, lost in a worldwide sea of tribal society. But they grew and touched and fought, and when the dust of combat settled some had vanished and the survivors were not so wee. The same happened again and again, and yet again, each time on a larger scale.

Except perhaps in Peru,[1] rulers soon hit on a trick that cut down on conflict, or at least postponed it. It was not a new strategy, just a transfer to interstate affairs of the technique used by the first governors-racketeers to force the submission of villages and tribes. A king of ten thousand people drew up his troops in battle array before the city of one who ruled but five thousand, and sent an expendable envoy to say "O Mighty One, bow down to my Master, who is Master of all the World, and accept Him as your liege lord; send Him each year a seemly gift as token of your loyalty and affection; and He will deign to turn his smile upon you." It was all very polite, but both sides understood, and diplomacy has been double-talk ever since. The lesser monarch took a hard look at the greater and decided whether he could lick him or should join him. There was enough joining—sometimes after an object lesson or so—to turn a few kings into emperors and the rest into vassals. It could happen at more than one level, setting up a triply or multiply layered hierarchy of bosses.

[1] Maybe there too at the beginning. The evidence does not tell us. By the time of the Spanish conquest the mature Inca empire had taken an idiosyncratic turn.

The common people were not consulted. Kings dealt with kings, governments with governments. Those at the edges of the total civil ecumene, fronting on tribal territory, were so schooled to the habit of speaking only with their peers that they unquestioningly expected tribal peoples, despite their obvious lack of refinement, to have the same kind of internal ordering (remember "King" Philip: p. 147). Sometimes wishing made it so. Tribes reorganized along civil lines as a last-ditch measure of self-defense. If they succeeded, the civil pattern had spread to them in one way. If they failed, it had reached them in another.

The common people were not consulted. For peasants, the spoliation often incident to a transfer of hegemony joined the roster of unpredictable and uncontrollable disasters: earthquake, volcanic eruption, storm, fire, flood, drouth, pestilence, famine, tax levies,—and armed invasion. Peasant culture everywhere adjusted to this atmosphere of perpetual uncertainty. When tragedy had struck, the survivors, if any, rebuilt. During intervals of calm one mustered one's dignity, sharing kindness and simple pleasures with one's fellows. The flow of human creativity can be reduced to a trickle by adversity, but can be shut off only by terminating life itself. Thus it is that many a face-to-face peasant community has been able to carry on (sometimes for decades without serious interruption) much in the traditional style of a band of hunters-gatherers. You hide your still deep in the wildwood, and are wary of revenuers and therefore, in typical fellahin fashion, of all strangers. But you are in a tight-knit *we*-group, the single most important requisite for any brand of hominoid happiness.

All the foregoing had been firmly established by the time the increasing intricacies of administration led to the invention of writing.

Here it is easy for us to trip over our keenness of hindsight. The dawn of literacy caused nary a ripple in the lives of most people. The earliest records were kept for immediate practical purposes, not for the edification of ensuing generations. Subsequently, indeed, overlords took to having the wonders of their reigns inscribed to awe posterity—part of the thought-police game. Most such pearls of wisdom from the lips of the kingpins tell us little except that they were paranoid braggarts. Percy Bysshe Shelley (1792–1822), not exactly noted as a historian, used hindsight well in his portrayal of this, cited at the beginning of the present chapter.

The slow rise of literacy left unaffected the majority of those alive at the time. Yet it properly alters our own perspective, notwithstanding the spreading blurs of hindsight, because, when the records can be read, they afford a new kind of evidence. The earliest decipherable written records show civil society as an ongoing enterprise already many cycles and several orders of magnitude beyond its beginnings. They help us understand the crumbled walls and broken tools that are the only direct testimony of those beginnings.

The interpretation is hard, for the Ozymandias effect is strong. Shelley's Ozymandias is, not Everyman, but Anyking. The most prominent early records speak tiresomely of megalomaniacal monarchs and too little of the stuff of daily life and the occasional technical advances. We do not know the names of the first civil bosses or of their realms; we know they were creative culture heroes, but our toasts to their memory must be drunk anonymously. With writing we begin to learn the names of kings, now become an institution rather than an innovation. Too many of them. In the summarizing codifications of modern historians they tumble one after another like the interminable sequences of *begats* in the Old Testament. The story of civil society bears the guise of the same plot repeated a thousand times: conqueror builds empire; empire flourishes; empire decays and is overrun by new conquerors. Only the names are changed to conceal the innocent who do the essential living and dying, the hard work that makes life possible and the creative work that makes it worth living. One Fameguest is worth a hundred farmers; one peasant is worth fivescore Khufus; but it is the appellations of the ten thousand tyrants of civil society that are dinned into our ears by the chronicle. This is not fit matter for memorizing nor for expository prose. It belongs not in heads or text, but in reference works and encyclopaedias, which is where we shall leave most of it.

I am saying that a ruler is nothing at all merely because he rules. Ozymandias was dust when his cadaver was rotted and his statue toppled; he was as dust during his lifetime. The hubris of the highborn blots and censors our inscribed record, both by preempting its points of prominence and by repeated burnings and bannings of the books of preceding epochs. Ch'in's first emperor (p. 586) in 213 B.C. sought to destroy all writings except those in his imperial collection; had he succeeded, the memory of Confucius and his disciples would have been erased forever. The main part of the great library at Alexandria, established by Alexander the Great's general Ptolemaios Soter early in the third century B.C., was burned in the late third century A.D. during the Roman Civil War under Aurelianus, and its surviving branch a century later by the Christians. The Academy of Athens, founded by Plato about 387 B.C., was closed—along with all other "pagan" schools—by the emperor Justinianus in A.D. 529. These are merely the most famous examples.

To be sure, such acts of administrative vandalism are also part of the record, also part of what has happened in history.

But we can read between the lines. We take the statue of an Ozymandias as a monument to its sculptor, not to the sculpted. We make all we can from the fortuitously surviving accounts of commercial transactions, of parochial administrative decisions, of the judgments or the prescribed criteria for judgment of provincial courts—mundane details at the time, but replete with implications as to what was really going on. We heed the physical context in which a scrap of writing has survived, paying as much attention to the shape and material of a potsherd as to the maker's trademark impressed on it.

In this way we learn that the true story of civil society is not the wearisome stamping out of one regime after another with the same old imperial cookie-cutter. That is merely the backdrop on a rotating stage. The real action is the slow changes and scattered innovations we have been talking about in the last few chapters.

The real action is also the gradual alteration in shape and increase in size of the cookie-cutter. In nine thousand years, the civil ferment that began so inconspicuously has totally altered the conditions of man's existence.

We shall outline the path of the juggernaut in four partly overlapping phases, two in this chapter, two in the next. We date them in terms of events in the Old World:

Phase One. From the beginnings to the river valleys (thus to about 3000 B.C.).
Phase Two. To the Persian empire of the Achaemenids, about 530 B.C.
Phase Three. To the fall of Constantinople, A.D. 1453.
Phase Four. The expansion of Europe.

PHASE ONE ✕ It took the first four of the nine millennia for the new key complex to become consolidated and, following agriculture, to spill into the great river valleys of southwest Asia, where it prospered and matured and began to leave traces of its passage in the form of written records.

PHASE TWO ✕ This phase opened with bronze and writing, but the former spread faster than the latter: barbarians acquire the military technology of their civil adversaries as fast as they can, and only subsequently develop any interest in new record-keeping techniques.

At the outset of Phase Two the largest states were those centering in Egypt, Mesopotamia, and the Indus Valley. With certain maritime exceptions (p. 594), individual states grew no larger than that throughout the phase. But the focal points moved and multiplied, and the total civil territory expanded greatly. Various peripheral groups of tribal peoples acquired animal husbandry or agriculture or both, increased in numbers, became barbarians, and started to wander, some of them moving towards the older centers of civil society and taking over.

We must convey the general flavor of events during Phase Two; but we want to avoid the deadly monotony of a recital of successive kings, dynasties, and empires. One way to attempt this is to combine what must be said about Phase Two with the history of the Indo-European languages—though the completion of the latter will force us to say a few things also about Phases Three and Four.

THE SPREAD OF INDO-EUROPEAN ✕ Between 3500 and 3000 B.C., as civil developments were proceeding apace in Mesopotamia but were barely starting in Egypt and the Indus Valley, the language we call "Proto Indo-European" (p. 300) was a small group of mutually intelligible dialects spoken by hunting, gathering, pastoral, fishing, and slightly agricultural peoples who lived—well, where?

The first clue to their location is the vocabulary that can be reconstructed for Proto Indo-European by comparing forms in its descendants. The recoverable vocabulary includes a number of names of animals and plants, and palaeontology and biogeography give us independent information about the earlier distributions of the species in question. Meanings, of course, can shift as life circumstances change. But with reasonable allowance for that we get two prime candidates for the home territory: (1) south of the Baltic in the valleys of the Vistula, Oder, and Elbe Rivers; (2) somewhere in an indefinite region north of the Caspian and Aral Seas in central Eurasia.

The second clue is archaeology. By the middle of the third millennium B.C., the

BY HIS BOOTSTRAPS

second of the two territories just listed had been reached by copper and bronze. As of the proper place and date, archaeologists find evidence for a way of life they dub the "Kurgan" pattern, with characteristic pottery, stone, and copper, plus evidence of sheep-raising, incipient farming, and the beginnings of horse culture. All this fits the linguistic evidence. Furthermore, there is clear archaeological testimony of the spread of the Kurgan pattern west, east, and south in the ensuing centuries, its typical artifacts tending to displace the types earlier attested in the invaded areas. The dates and directions of the earlier Kurgan migrations are congruent with the movements, as known through other evidence, of various groups of Indo-European speakers.

What happened to the Kurgans if they were not the Indo-Europeans? Where did the Indo-Europeans come from if they were not the Kurgans?

The evidence is persuasive. We conclude that the speakers of Proto Indo-European were indeed the bearers of the Kurgan pattern, living north of the Caspian and Aral Seas, and that they were set into expansion and migration around 2500 B.C. by a combination of two factors: (1) infiltration from the south of agriculture, cupreous metallurgy, and other civil features; (2) the domestication of the horse, achieved locally—possibly by the Indo-Europeans themselves.

By 2000 B.C. there were a number of differentiated branches of Indo-European, spoken over an area many times larger than that of the homeland. Figure 23-5 (p. 301) shows the differentiation *insofar as it is attested,* and its later consequences, but with no indication of chronology or geography. The italicized remark in the preceding sentence is meant to remind us, here once and for all, that at every early stage there were surely other dialects and languages, some related and some not, of which no trace has survived. The migrations of speakers of Indo-European that we can talk about did not take them through or into uninhabited territory (except only for the late move to Iceland: p. 483). All we know of these other people is that they were surely there, and that they lost their languages—or their lives—to the ones whose history we can trace.[2]

We proceed to deal with the *known* branches one by one. A dagger (†) means that the branch or subbranch is now extinct.

(1) †Tokharian

This (p. 483) is known only through documents from the vicinities of Tulufan and Kuche in Chinese Turkestan, dating from A.D. 500 to 700. We don't know when or by what route the language got there.

(2) Indo-Iranian

Proto Indo-Iranian must have been spoken not long after 2000 B.C., still close to the original Proto Indo-European homeland. Before any major migrations there was a three-way split.

[2]There is archaeological evidence of Kurgan culture in northern and northwestern Europe as early as 2000 B.C. This may mean that Indo-European speech had already reached the areas in question. But it is quite wrong to label any of these early forms "Germanic," "Baltic," "Slavic," or the like, since these terms apply to branches that differentiated much later—Proto Germanic, for example, surely no earlier than 500 B.C., Proto Slavic and Proto Baltic both even later than that.

(2a)   The speakers of *Indo-Aryan,* with their horses, moved southeast, and by 1500 B.C. were invading India on several fronts. The civil society and writing system of the Indus Valley were quickly destroyed at about that time, and the Indo-Aryans may have been directly or indirectly responsible. The Indo-Aryans became the ruling class in most parts of the subcontinent. Indo-Aryan languages spread northeast to the Himalayas, east into Assam, far into the south, and across the water to Ceylon.[3] The earlier languages (mainly *Dravidian*) were not totally wiped out; they survive and prosper today particularly in the south, also in the hills of Assam and a few pockets in the northeast and northwest.

Writing may have come into India as early as the eighth century B.C., but surviving written evidence is later: inscriptions (in Indo-Aryan and in Tamil, a Dravidian language) from the third century B.C., documents a century or so afterwards.

(2b)   Behind the Indo-Aryans came speakers of Indo-Iranian dialects that are neither clearly Indo-Aryan nor clearly Iranian. Their speech survives today as the *Nuristani* languages, spoken only in the northern part of Nangrahar Province in Afghanistan.

(2c)   The third subbranch of Indo-Iranian was *Iranian.* Some of its speakers stayed north of the Caspian, becoming the Scythians and Sarmatians who successively dominated southern Russia and parts of the Caucasus between the eighth century B.C. and the second A.D. Others migrated south, probably through the Caucasus.

About 1500 B.C. the Mitanni kingdom, centering in what is now northern Syria, had an Iranian-speaking ruling class whose soldiers rode in chariots drawn by horses. This is the earliest appearance of war chariots. It may have been the Iranians who first introduced the horse into southwest Asia, but more likely it was branch 3 (see below). Other Iranians established other kingdoms, such as that of the Medes in northwest Iran in the earlier part of the first millennium B.C. and that of the Parthians in Khorāsān in the latter part. In 615 B.C. one group, the Persians, overthrew the Semitic-speaking Assyrians and became the dominant power in Mesopotamia. The Iranians had caught on, and were actively playing the empire game, just as were their cousins the Indo-Aryans in India.

Today, despite the serious later inroads of Arabic (Semitic) and of Turkic, Iranian languages are spoken in Iran, in almost all of Afghanistan (*Pashto*), in the western part of West Pakistan (*Balochi*), in Tadzhikistan, and by scattered groups in Turkey. *Ossetic,* spoken on both slopes of the Greater Caucasus Mountains, is also Iranian, but may be a survival of the otherwise extinct speech of the Scythians and Sarmatians rather than the result of a later northward thrust from Iran.

The earliest written records of Iranian are Persian cuneiform inscriptions from the sixth through the fourth century B.C.

With help from branch 3, the Iranians did a pretty good job of wiping Asia Minor,

---

[3]The earliest attested form of Indo-Aryan is *Sanskrit,* already archaic and frozen for ceremonial and scholarly use when first written. Then came *Pali* and various *Prakrits,* later derivatives even though they were written before Sanskrit was. The modern vernaculars include thirty-odd languages in eight major groups.

Mesopotamia, and Persia clean of the languages they had found there upon their arrival. But in the extremely mountainous Caucasus, the repeated migrations of these various Indo-European speakers not surprisingly left untouched a dozen or so non-Indo-European languages, still spoken today.

(3) †Anatolian

Anatolian-speaking peoples had entered what is now Turkey, around one or the other end of the Black Sea, by about 2000 B.C., well ahead of Iranians.

The military use of the horse made the Anatolian speakers powerful (until their enemies got horses too). They established an empire centering in Asia Minor, whose rulers and some of whose peasants spoke Hittite, the Anatolian language about which we have the most information. The earlier Hittite empire sacked Babylon at a date given by some authorities as 1590 B.C. The Hittites made enough widespread fuss to be remembered in Hebrew tradition, and directly or indirectly may have instigated the movement of Semitic-speaking peoples into Egypt, an episode recorded in the Bible in one way, in Egyptian records in quite another (as the invasion and dynasties of the Hyksos, 1720–1567 B.C.). About 1500 the Hittites met with some reverses (from Iranians?) and had to retrench, but by 1450 they established the later empire, with headquarters at Hatusas, near the present village of Boğazköy. It was here, for the next few centuries, that they wrote the inscriptions some of which have been read (p. 574).

The later empire lasted until 1200 B.C. Then it was overrun by speakers of †*Phrygian*, who wrote enough of their language to tell us that it was Indo-European but not enough to identify its closer lines of affiliation, except that it was probably not Anatolian. The Phrygians took their brief turn at the empire business; their most famous product was the rich King Midas of the eighth century B.C. But about then along came the speakers of †*Cimmerian*, probably Iranians akin to the Scythians and Sarmatians (p. 592), and took *their* turn.

While Hittite was the chief language of the later empire in the north, a related language called *Luvian* had been spoken in the south and southwest. In the seventh through the fourth centuries B.C. later forms of this were spoken by the Lydians and Lycians. Lydia was one of the birthplaces of coins (p. 582); Lycia was a league of towns in the southwest.

We do not know when or under what circumstances the Anatolian languages finally disappeared, but they are now long gone.

(4) Armenian

Despite certain similarities to Anatolian, this forms a branch in its own right. Its speakers perhaps followed the Anatolians and Iranians south through the Caucasus, at a somewhat later date. The modern language is spoken in two divergent groups of dialects, in various parts of eastern Turkey and in a small area in southern Caucasia. The earliest written records date from the fifth century A.D., in an alphabet derived from that of Greek.

(5) Hellenic

When the Hellenic branch reached the Aegean from the north, its speakers came into contact with a flourishing Bronze Age civil society whose leading centers were on Crete. The development of writing was in its initial stages. Archaeology reveals various graphic experiments in the earlier part of the second millennium B.C., settling down about 1700 into a system called "Linear A." Two centuries later this was in part replaced by a derivative, "Linear B." Clay tablets bearing inscriptions in Linear B have been found in quantity from Knossos on Crete, and from Pílos and the ancient Mycenae in the Peloponnesus. Linear B has been deciphered, and the language is Greek. Linear A has not been deciphered, so that we don't know whether the language was Greek or a non-Indo-European predecessor, but the latter seems more likely. This evidence means that the Greeks had reached the southern part of the Aegean area by about 1500 B.C., the northern part correspondingly earlier, probably very close to 2000 B.C.

The pre-Hellenic Aegean had been commercial and maritime. We might note that numerous small harbors were usable then that have by now been rendered inaccessible by accumulations of silt. Even in classical times much of this silt was still ashore, in the form of soil supporting plants. It is crop-raising, especially olive culture continued over the millennia (p. 551), that has ruined the land and clogged the neighboring waters.

Give the Greeks about eight centuries (2000–1200) to absorb or destroy their Aegean predecessors and to acquire their technology. It was towards the end of this period that the historic prototype of Homer's romanticized Trojan War took place, and that iron began coming in to supplement bronze. Then there was a hiatus. The reasons are not known, but one of them may have been Thracian migrations (branch 6, below), pressing the Dorian Greeks at the north end of the Aegean into a southward movement. Maritime commerce was greatly reduced. People lived closer to home, in dozens or hundreds of small city-states. The Linear B script was forgotten. For several hundred years the Greeks were again illiterate.

New stimulus came from the eastern Mediterranean. Seafaring peoples such as the Phoenicians (Semitic) introduced other things besides the alphabetical writing that is attested as of the ninth or eighth century B.C. (p. 579). The Phoenicians were marvelous sailors: in their halcyon days they made regular trips for tin all the way to Cornwall in Britain, by sea except for the crossing of Gaul, and about 600 B.C., according to Herodotos, they circumnavigated Africa on behalf of the Egyptian Pharaoh Necho the Second (leaving from the Red Sea, coming back to Egypt's Mediterranean shore).

The Greeks caught the commercial contagion. Their cities quarreled and fought and formed various alliances, the smallest ones soon losing their independence. The victors began to plant colonies outside of the Aegean in competition with Phoenicia, Egypt, and Etruria (the home base of the Etruscans, In Italy). Each colonial city, to start with, was vassal to one or another of the cities of Aegean Greece, but in time some became independent. There were such Greek colonies in Italy and Sicily by the middle of the eighth century B.C. By 550 there were settlements scattered around

BY HIS BOOTSTRAPS

the whole rim of the Black Sea and throughout the Mediterranean except in the northern stretches of the Adriatic.

Greek language and culture were thus carried far and wide, and new things and ideas were imported from all over. The prosperity produced by the far-flung commerce formed the economic basis for Greek experiments in "democracy" (actually oligarchy, voting being the prerogative of the small minority of free citizens) and for the flowering, in the second half of the first millennium B.C., of Greek technology, philosophy, and literature, destined subsequently to play such a crucial part in the learnèd culture of Western society.

Macedon had a Greek-speaking ruling class when Alexander was born in 356, but he doubtless had to accommodate to a dialect quite different from that of his childhood when the Ionian philosopher Aristotle (born 384 at Stagira) became his tutor. His conquests spread Greek influence even more widely.

As a language of learning, classical Greek has not yet lost its importance. For everyday affairs, however, the vicissitudes of later history extinguished it almost everywhere. Today it survives only in the immediate vicinity of the Aegean.

(6)   (†)ILLYRIAN-THRACIAN

What little we know of this branch is based mainly on allusions and quoted names of places and people in the writings of classical (Latin and Greek) authors.

†*Thracian*-speaking people were in the Balkan Peninsula before 1300 B.C., north and perhaps west of the Greeks. At about that date they were destroyed or driven out by speakers of (†)*Illyrian.* One proposal is that the Thracians moved east, displacing the Dorian Greeks (p. 594) and crossing into Asia Minor, where they became the Phrygians (p. 593).

The Illyrians proceeded south to the Adriatic coast, but also southwest into northeastern Italy and across the Adriatic into east-central Italy. In the latter region their language was called †*Messapic,* and a few inscriptions survive from the time before it was extinguished by the spread of Latin.

Albanian, spoken now in and near Albania, may be a surviving descendant of Illyrian or may constitute a separate branch of Indo-European. If the latter is the case, then Illyrian is extinct.

(7)   ITALO-CELTIC

In 2000 B.C. the speakers of Proto Italo-Celtic could have been living almost anywhere west of the original Indo-European homeland. Wherever they were, by 1500 there had been a two-way split.

(7a)   *Italic* was carried into Italy in two successive migratory waves. The first crossed the eastern Alps into the valley of the Po not long after 1500, and had moved on through the Apennines to the west-central coastal plain by about 1200. This was the source of *Latin* and the closely related †*Faliscan;* a few inscriptions northeast of the Apennines bear testimony to the temporary survival of other dialects, such as †*Venetic.* A later wave yielded †*Oscan,* †*Umbrian,* and some allied dialects. Oscan moved all the way south to the toe of the peninsula and by 300 had crossed into Sicily.

All these people learned civil ways, including iron metallurgy, from the Etruscans and the Greek colonials. Alphabetical writing came from the latter, but via the Etruscans rather than directly. In the fourth century, Rome, home of Latin, was but one of many city-states. The others were inhabited by speakers of the other Italic languages, or of Etruscan, Messapic (p. 595), or Greek. The Ligurians, on the coast near the modern Genoa, also had a language of their own, but we know nothing about it. With the political success of Rome in subsequent centuries, Latin eventually submerged and replaced all these other languages. Still later, the Roman empire spread Latin far afield through western and southern Europe; it lives on today as the various *Romance* languages.[4]

(7b) *Celtic,* meanwhile, wherever it started, expanded and spread all over the place.

By 500 B.C. Celts covered Gaul, parts of Spain, most of Great Britain, and much of Ireland.[5] Within a hundred years some of them were in northern Italy. Others were harassing Macedon and Greece, and by early in the third century B.C. some of these had crossed over into Asia Minor and established themselves as rulers in Galatia, approximately where Phrygia had once been (p. 593). Off to the north, others reached southern Germany, and when they were later driven out by Germanic speakers the latter inherited a scattering of river names from them (*Rhein, Main, Neckar, Inn, Lech, Regen, Eisack*); in the first century B.C. there were Celts in what is now the Czech part of Czechoslovakia.

The reason for Celtic unrest and expansion was one we have seen in other cases, but with a different outcome. Civil patterns had been spread to all the shores of the Mediterranean by Egyptians, Phoenicians, Greeks, Etruscans, and Romans. The Celts were barbarians along the frontier. They took on civil ways, but (unlike the Greeks and Romans) did not become powerful enough to overthrow any major existing regimes. Instead, they slipped along the frontier, and away from it to the north and northwest. They had iron; they were most successful where their opponents had only bronze.

Celtic speech endured in Galatia for at least 500 years. In the west, it was largely submerged and extinguished by the spread of Romance (Latin) by the Roman empire and by an expansion, at about the same time, of the Germanic subbranch of branch 8 (see below). Continental Celtic is now completely extinct.

Insular Celtic had, at the outset, two forms: Brythonic in Great Britain and Goidelic in Ireland. The former was pushed into hinterland areas by the Anglo-Saxon invasions in the fifth century A.D., continuing as †*Cornish* in Cornwall, as *Welsh,* still kept alive in Wales although everybody there also speaks English, and as *Breton,* carried to

---

[4]In Iberia, from west to east, dialects of *Portuguese, Spanish, Catalan; French* and *Provençal* in France and Corsica (Provençal in the southeast towards Italy); *Rhaeto-Romance* in southern Switzerland; *Italian* dialects in Italy, Sicily, and Sardinia; †*Dalmatian* dialects surviving in Jugoslavia into the nineteenth century; *Rumanian* in and near Rumania.

[5]The Celtic expansion in the west began the sweeping-away of the pre-Indo-European languages of western Europe. The only traces are Pictish, attested by a few inscriptions in Scotland from the first millennium A.D., and Basque, spoken still in the Pyrenees.

BY HIS BOOTSTRAPS

northwestern France by fifth- and sixth-century refugees. Goidelic gave rise in the eleventh century to *Scotch Gaelic* and to †*Manx* (the latter on the Isle of Man), through migrations to escape invading Normans.

For the earliest written records of Celtic, see Box 38-1 (p. 620).

(8)   GERMANIC AND BALTO-SLAVIC

The eighth branch of Indo-European seems to have retained a unity of speech, with only dialectal variation, until some time between 1500 and 1000 B.C. Then minor migrations led to a split between *Germanic* and *Balto-Slavic;* about a half millennium later the second of these split in turn into *Slavic* and *Baltic.*

Germanic remained relatively homogeneous as late as 500 B.C., the approximate date of the Proto Germanic that can be reconstructed by comparing its descendants. During the fifth century its dialects were spoken in southern Sweden, in Jutland and the Danish islands, and in northern Germany as far south as the Harz Mountains and as far east as the Oder River. At this time the earliest Baltic and Slavic were way off to the southeast, towards the Carpathian Mountains.

(8a)   There were two important developments in the early Germanic region in the second half of the first millennium B.C. One is that iron reached the Germanic speakers, through the Celts or Illyrians living to their south (the Germanic words for 'iron' are early loans from Celtic or Illyrian, and originally meant the 'hard' metal in contrast with the softer bronze). The other is that the Scandinavian peninsula, which had been very cold, warmed up a bit. The communities in Sweden must have found life hard when they first got there, and doubtless stayed on only because routes to the south were blocked.

But in the last two centuries B.C., with the warming, the crops got better and the population increased. Some of the communities in the Danish islands and in southernmost Sweden managed to migrate to the southern Baltic coast between the Oder and Vistula Rivers. The dialects of these migrants, and the languages of their descendants, constitute †*East Germanic.* Those who stayed behind in Sweden and the islands fanned out into the warming Scandinavian Peninsula; their dialects became the *North Germanic* (or simply the *Scandinavian*) languages. Speakers of these also moved over into the northern part of the Danish Peninsula. The dialects originally in the Danish Peninsula, and those in northern Germany, gave rise to *West Germanic.*

EAST GERMANIC.   The East Germanic peoples known to us include the Vandals and the Goths.

The epithet *Vandal* seems originally to have meant 'wanderer'. That the word should now mean 'destroyer' (in English, French, and Spanish) is a sad and unfitting memorial: surely they were as callous towards strangers as anyone else, but their main purpose was to find somewhere to live in peace. They were routed from the Baltic shore by the Goths, and moved south, first to Silesia and then to northern Jugoslavia (fourth century A.D.). The Huns (p. 604) forced them to flee westwards: into Gaul, then south into the Iberian Peninsula, then across to Africa and east again to Carthage, which city they captured in A.D. 439. The (eastern) Roman empire put an end to their rule there in 534, and thereafter their language passed into oblivion, never having been recorded.

Meanwhile, by A.D. 200 the Goths had migrated to the plains north of the Black Sea, where they settled in two groups: the Ostrogoths lived east of the Dnieper river, the Visigoths west of it. In the early part of the fourth century a writing system was introduced. It subsequently went out of use again, but a sixth-century copy of a fourth-century translation of the Gospels survives, our earliest written evidence of any Germanic except for some runic inscriptions in northwestern Europe. The Ostrogoths established an empire, destroyed by the Huns about 370. Some of them moved westwards then, reaching Italy, participating in the seige of Rome that led to its downfall in 476, and then losing their separate identity and their language. A few stayed on in the east, moving into the Crimea as part of its peasant population and maintaining their language until the sixteenth century.

The Visigoths were forced westwards by the Huns in 376; they wandered through Greece and the Balkans and into Italy, sacking Rome in 410, and then moving on to establish a kingdom in southern Gaul and northern Spain which endured until it was destroyed in 711 by the Moors.

There were other East Germanic groups, less well attested. The trouble encountered by all of them is that they left the Germanic homeland in the wrong direction. Their migrations carried them towards strongly entrenched civil society, and like most of the Celts they were only powerful enough to slide along and nibble at its edges. Their migrations were bodily movements of whole communities, rather than expansions of small groups into larger ones.

WEST GERMANIC, on the other hand, expanded. By the time of Julius Caesar in the first century B.C., its speakers had spread west across the Rhine and south across the Danube, pushing Celts out of their way. By A.D. 500 Lombards were in the Alps (within a century they were to conquer northern Italy), Burgundians were in the Rhone Valley, Franks were in northeastern Gaul, and dwellers along the continental coast of the North Sea, having learned how to make excellent ships (p. 617), had invaded England as the Angles, Saxons, and Jutes. The only part of their original territory that they had abandoned was the northern part of the Danish Peninsula, taken over by Scandinavians.

Romance later replaced Germanic in northern Italy, the Rhone Valley, and much of the north of Gaul. Otherwise, continental West Germanic today has a virtually uninterrupted distribution in Holland, parts of Belgium, Germany, parts of Switzerland, and Austria. Dialect variation is continuous from village to village and slight between neighboring villages, although there are two sharply distinct "standard" languages, *German* and *Dutch-Flemish,* for literary and administrative use. The only holdout is the divergent *Frisian* of the coast and coastal islands of the North Sea.

The West Germanic of Great Britain is known as *English.* The original dialect variation of the diverse invaders has largely given way to a new range of dialects derived principally from the speech of London and the Midlands of a thousand years ago.

SCANDINAVIAN. This branch of Germanic spread continuously by expansion within

Scandinavia proper, and then also by the overseas migrations of some groups in ships as well built as those of the seafaring speakers of West Germanic.

For Iceland and *Icelandic,* see page 483; subsequent migrations carried kindred dialects to the Faeroe Islands. The standard languages of Scandinavia proper are reflected by the names of the current political units, with one complication: *Danish* in Denmark, *Swedish* in Sweden, but both *Dano-Norwegian* and *Norwegian Landsmaal* in Norway. In the eighth and ninth centuries "Northmen" invaded Ireland, England, and France. The Scandinavian of Ireland disappeared quickly. That in England survived in small pockets in the "Danelaw" of the northeast for many centuries, though the political power of the invaders was broken within a century and a half. In France, the language of the Scandinavian invaders was replaced by French before their descendants, now "Normans," crossed to England in 1066 and also embarked on various continental adventures which took some of them as far away as Sicily.

For the earliest written records of Germanic, see Box 38-1 (p. 620).

(8b)   The expansion of Slavic, starting from the region north of the Carpathian Mountains, began in the early centuries A.D., presumably because of disturbances from neighboring predatory Celts (and Illyrians?) and by East Germanic communities migrating southeast towards the Black Sea. But as late as the eighth century the various Slavic communities may have lived close enough together for their dialects still to be mutually intelligible.

The Slavs who moved to the east and northeast carried the dialects that became *Russian.* Some of them reached the area of Kiev in the ninth century, and that city became the principal seat of Russian political power, subordinate centers arising at Novgorod and Moscow. In the twelfth century, Kiev was weakened by attacks by Turkic-speaking nomads from the east, and then in 1240 the city was destroyed by Batu, grandson of Genghis Khan (p. 585). Only then did control switch definitively to Moscow.

The Slavs who moved to the west and northwest had to battle Illyrians, Celts, and Germanic speakers, but eventually they spread their dialects—ultimately *Czech, Slovak, Polish,* and some less prominent ones such as *Sorbian*—to approximately their present locations.

The ones who moved to the south, their migration accelerated by the arrival of the non-Indo-European Hungarians (p. 604), ended up as speakers of *Bulgarian, Serbo-Croatian* (a single group of dialects with two standard forms), and *Slovenian* (around the north end of the Adriatic).

(8c)   The northward movements of some of the Slavs apparently pushed Balts ahead of them. In contrast to all the other branches and major subbranches of Indo-European we have mentioned, the Balts experienced no real expansion, just a displacement.

One group ended up on the southeastern littoral of the Baltic Sea; their language, †*Old Prussian,* died out in the seventeenth century. The main body slid around to the east of the Baltic, where their descendants speak a number of fairly similar dialects from which the vicissitudes of political history have extracted two standard languages: *Lithuanian* in Lithuania and *Lettish* in what was once called Courland, later Latvia.

Both Russians and Balts were responsible for the narrowing of the earlier territory of the northern branch of the non-Indo-European Finno-Ugrian, now confined to Esthonia and Finland except for a scattering of small communities in the Scandinavian and Russian arctic.

For the earliest written records of Balto-Slavic, see Box 38-1 (p. 620).

37

※

THE JUGGERNAUT: II

We go back now to the latter part of the sixth century B.C., when Cyrus the Second, the first king of the Achaemenid dynasty, laid the foundations of the Persian empire.

The significance of this event was that the imperial cookie-cutter had rather suddenly gotten a lot bigger. As Figure 37-1 shows, by 450 B.C. the Persian empire was 20 or 30 times as extensive as the average single state during Phase Two. Innovations in military strategy seem to have been responsible for the initial Persian success, and new, more efficient, somewhat less ferocious administrative policies for the relatively greater durability.

PHASE THREE IN THE WEST

※ In the latter part of the fourth century B.C. an upstart yokel from the backwoods, Alexander of Macedon, took over the Persian empire and made it his own. From then until the fall of Constantinople to the Ottoman Turks in A.D. 1453, the westernmost spur of Old World high civil society was a succession of empires on the new large scale, sometimes temporarily fragmented, centering in the eastern Mediterranean or in southwest Asia. Regimes rose and fell, and Christianity and Islam were founded and promoted, but beneath all this there was an underlying cultural continuity.

It was during this period that Rome rose to prominence, seizing the reins for a time from the older centers and spreading its power around the whole rim of the Mediterranean and far to the north, as well as east to the borders of India. But Rome turned out to be too remote. In A.D. 350 the emperor Constantinus established an administrative headquarters half independent of Rome at Byzantium, that city then being renamed after him. In 476, after decades of strife in Italy, Rome fell to the Goths, and the center of civil gravity, already teetering, swung back eastwards.

Figure 37-2 shows the total distribution of civil society in Eurasia-Africa as of 1500 years ago, just before the takeover of Rome by the Goths; note the confirmation of our assertion that we are speaking only of the westernmost spur of Old World high civil society. Remember also that by the time of this map the entirely autochthonous empires of the New World had become vigorous and aggressive. Figure 33-1 shows a similar depiction of the state of civil affairs at the end of Phase Three, early in the 1400s.

FIGURE 37-1. The size of the Persian empire compared with the typical size of earlier political units.

In the sanitized and ethnocentric courses in the "History of Western Civilization" to which our youth are exposed in the schools, the second half of Phase Three, roughly 476 to 1453, is called the "Middle Ages" (or "medieval" period). The term is convenient and we shall use it, but we must dispel the misconception on which it was originally based.

Most students of European history have been Europeans. They have always heeded the evidence for the societies of classical antiquity, but have tended to shift their focus to Europe at the earliest possible date, which means with the northward spread of the Roman empire. In this perspective, the fall of Rome looks like a fall of darkness, the beginning of a hiatus in the otherwise steady stream of "progress" from primitive "savagery" towards modern enlightenment and "civilization." Accordingly, they divide "world history" (!) into three major periods: classical times; the Middle Ages; and modern times.

In fact, nothing of world-shaking significance happened in 476. Rome had itself been a marginal phenomenon, working out its own twists on the basic civil pattern and transmitting successful innovations back to the core area (a normal manifestation of the Turner effect: p. 298), but in the end not surviving as a separate entity. The unfolding of civil society did not grind to a halt; it merely shifted back east. Europe, for her part, experienced no sudden loss, no sudden plunging into cultural "darkness." She continued for another millennium to be just what she had been in Alexander's time and before: *frontier* territory. Her society was by no means purely tribal, but neither was it elaborately civil. The temporary dominance of Rome put no halt to the constant migrations and displacements of peoples; in fact, Rome's expansion in the west was an integral part of that unrest.

BY HIS BOOTSTRAPS

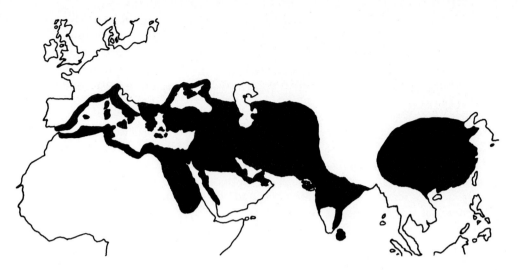

FIGURE 37-2. OLD WORLD CIVIL SOCIETY ON THE EVE OF THE FALL OF ROME. Middle of the fifth century A.D. The blackened portion includes all the major centers and the most important subsidiary centers of empire. The boundaries, however, are indefinite; some would choose to blacken a considerably greater part of northern and western Europe.

More and more, however, groups settled down, staying put even when their local rulers were replaced or were forced to change their allegiance.

The so-called feudal system developed, first in Gaul and then in slow waves spreading north, south, and east. Its aim, never fully achieved, was a static stability. Life was largely rural. The peasants were bound to the land and it is only because of a legal nicety that we refer to them as "serfs" rather than as "slaves." A "city" satisfying our definition in every way except as to size (p. 163) was in many instances merely the walled castle of a local baron, the residence of a few dozen people. The sway of overlords above the counts and barons was tenuous and ever shifting. The towns established by the predecessors of the Romans and by the Romans, at seaports and at the junctions of the Roman highway system, were largely deserted, people returning to the land and peasants even raising crops where there had been streets and other open spaces within the town walls.

Yet this desertion of the towns was by no means complete, some people—artisans, innkeepers, sometimes brigands—staying on. Nor did trade come to a standstill. Ships carried timber from Sweden to the coastal country of the Frisians, and cattle from there to Britain. In the seventh and eighth centuries wealthy Byzantines wanted, and got, furs from Scandinavia just as, a millennium later, wealthy Europeans wanted and got them from North America. Scandinavian archaeological sites of the right age reveal Byzantine coins and other metal objects received in exchange.

✘ Let us for the nonce set aside our knowledge of what happened later, and simply take a look at worldwide developments during the Middle Ages. We will see that

**PHASE THREE
OUTSIDE EUROPE**

frontier Europe held no obvious promise of the role it in fact played subsequently. There were other frontier regions, each holding expansionist seeds because of a combination of certain civil features with barbarian vigor: a belt of kingdoms just south of the Sahara (with agriculture and iron), a budget of them in southeastern Asia (with agriculture, iron, and writing), a bunch of them in the north-central parts of Eurasia (with agriculture, iron, some writing, and lots of horses). Nor were the empires of high civil society totally worn out or decadent.

Most of the empires and frontier populations of the Old World were at least vaguely aware of one another. No one, to be sure, knew of the Americas nor of the vastnesses of the Pacific. The educated minority who had learned that Earth is round (the Greeks had known this in the sixth century B.C. and had had an excellent notion of its size) badly underestimated its circumference, and thought that the same ocean bathed the shores of western Europe and of China.

Let us consider these various non-European regions one by one.

THE AMERICAS

Here we can give short shrift to the Americas. As far as can be determined, the civil societies of the New World were totally ignorant of world geography. With another millennium of independence, the Aztecs, Mayas, or Incas might have become strong enough successfully to resist attack from overseas. But as things actually were in the sixteenth century, they were a pushover for any Old World society able to cross the central Atlantic purposefully rather than by accident. The masses of people in New World civil societies were accustomed to being run by a hierarchy of bosses; the Spaniards merely shoved the old bosses aside and took over.

CENTRAL AND NORTHERN EURASIA

Nomads of this region repeatedly harassed China: the Great Wall (p. 589) would be sufficient evidence even if there were no other. Some of these peoples are known to us only by the epithets bestowed on them by the Chinese, and cannot be otherwise identified.

In the west, the Huns—whoever they were—crossed the Volga River late in the fourth century A.D. and quickly reached and passed the Danube. Within a century they had melted away.

In the ninth century a wave of immigrants from the area between the Volga and the Urals (speakers of a Finno-Ugrian language, thus linguistically akin to the Lapps, Finns, and Esthonians, but apparently not related to the Huns) settled in what thereby became Hungary.

About the same time, there was a great expansion of Turkic-speaking peoples, who took over Mongolia temporarily in the mid eighth century, made inroads into China, India, and eastern Europe, and by the end of the eleventh century, long since converted to Islam, were in eastern Anatolia; they reached the Aegean 200 years later.

We have already mentioned (p. 585) the moving-out of the Mongols in their immense but ephemeral burst of gory glory.

In the early seventeenth century the Manchus, speakers of languages related to

Mongolian, moved down from Manchuria and established a durable dynasty in China; their unrest may have been in part in response to pressure from the Russians (p. 609).

All the Asiatic peoples we have mentioned have gotten classed as "nomads," presumably because they were on the move when they came to the attention of record-keepers. In fact, they probably all practiced mixed farming when they could. It was probably agriculturally based population increase, complicated by recurrent periods of drouth, that set them forth on their conquests and migrations. The record is poor, but in a general way they were doing the same thing the "Kurgans" (Indo-Europeans, p. 591) had done before them, for the same ultimate reasons.

THE SOUTHEASTERN FRONTIER

Continental southeastern Asia, as we have seen (p. 587), did not lend itself to the formation of large empires. Even when its Pacific coastal strip was under the domination of the Chinese (third century B.C. to fifteenth A.D.), the sway of the foreign rulers was weak and frequently interrupted.

A bit over two thousand years ago Hindu culture became maritime and began to spread; in the west it reached the northeastern coast of Africa and inland as far as Ethiopia. Continental southeastern Asia and its flanking waters were the route by which Hindu influence moved southeastwards, greatly affecting many parts of Indonesia (where it probably triggered the migrations of Malayo-Polynesians to Madagascar: p. 484) and reaching the Philippines, to which it brought the torch of literacy, by the third or fourth century A.D. The famous ruins of Angkor Wat in Cambodia are of Hindu inspiration, and Bali remains Hindu to this day.

Back in northeastern India, Buddhism was founded around 500 B.C. by Gautama the Enlightened (Sanskrit *buddha* = 'enlightened one'). It did not endure in its homeland, but not only diffused northward to Tibet, China, Korea, and Japan but also, in the eleventh and twelfth centuries A.D., followed the same route to the southeast, prevailing in continental Indochina.

A century after that, Islam was carried to Malaya, Indonesia, and as far north in the Philippines as the southern tip of Luzon by Indian Muslim traders who largely bypassed the continent, though there came to be Arab quarters in seaport cities as far up the mainland coast as Amoy.

We are largely wrong in our tendency to class these diffusions as "religious." Surely they had an impact on the diverse inside views of the recipients; but they also spread and promoted the ways of civil society. When Europeans got to Indonesia in the sixteenth century they found little sultanates all over, very much like those in Muslim Iberia and north Africa.

SUB-SAHARAN AFRICA

The expansionist tendencies of the sub-Saharan frontier are not well attested, since writing arrived late.

When the Portuguese reached the Guinea Coast in 1470 they found small but flourishing kingdoms. In 1537, only two thirds of a century later, kindred African peoples speaking kindred languages invaded and took over half of Ethiopia; at the same time others were pressing southwards across the Limpopo River, partly pushing aside and partly destroying or absorbing the earlier inhabitants of southern Africa (peoples akin to the surviving Bushmen and Hottentots). While commerce with the Portuguese undeniably gave a boost to the Guinea Coast kingdoms, it could not have been wholly and so suddenly responsible for these events thousands of miles away.

One infers that agriculturally based civil society had been developing just south of the Sahara for a number of centuries, with some native ingredients, some imported via Arab traders, and some perhaps tracing back several thousand years to early contacts with the Egyptians of antiquity. Certain of the trappings of African kingship hint at this last, especially the common habit of executing a retinue of slaves and concubines to minister to the soul of a deceased monarch. It was, then, the unavoidable growth tendencies of these states, together with the increase of population caused by agriculture, that led, partly directly and partly indirectly, to the great expansion of peoples whose earlier homes had been (probably) in and near the Niger and Congo river basins, to almost the whole of sub-Saharan Africa.

The degree and type of civil organization achieved in Africa before the Portuguese arrived was of crucial significance for subsequent world history. Had Africa remained totally tribal, the Europeans could have taken few slaves and those few would not have submitted for long (note the futility of European efforts to enslave North American Indians). Had the kingdoms been larger and more powerful, they would have had no slaves to spare and would have been able to resist foreign efforts to capture them by force.[1] (For the actual story, see pp. 259–264.)

ISLAM

By the end of the European Middle Ages the greatest unifying force of Old World civil society was Islam. Its domain stretched from the westernmost tip of Africa, on the Atlantic, to Java and the Philippines in the Pacific (thus through more than 140 degrees of longitude), almost without a break, and far north into central Eurasia. For a while after the fall of Constantinople it completely surrounded the Black Sea.

To be sure, the Islamic world was not a political unity, not a single far-flung empire. But it showed a surprising degree of cultural uniformity, promoted by Muslim traders who carried goods and ideas from every part of the territory to every other part. The traders moved expertly by land and by water. For the latter they were heirs to the technology of ocean transport developed by such eastern Mediterranean peoples as the Phoenicians (p. 594) and the Greeks, and to that of the Hindus and perhaps the Indonesians. In their chief cities there were great centers of learning, preserving the intellectual heritage of Greece and Rome (largely lost in medieval Europe), and of the Persians and Hindus, and adding more of their own.

All this had been built—stably, not as a Mongol-type flash in the pan—in a mere eight centuries, since it was around A.D. 600 that the Prophet founded the faith (in

---

[1] It is even salubrious to consider the consequences of a minor interchange of technological achievements between the African and European frontiers. The Americas could then have been conquered by Africans importing European slaves to work the plantations and the mines.

and near Mecca in southwestern Arabia). Islam, like Christianity, is evangelistic, ready to seek converts by fire and sword as well as by talk (p. 250). But its adherents had labored patiently and carefully; furthermore, small enclaves of Jews, Christians, Magians, and other infidels were not only tolerated but permitted, within certain constraints, to thrive.

At the time of which we are speaking, an unprejudiced observer would surely have said that Islam was well on the way to unifying the whole (known) world. The Muslim doctrine served to moderate the desires and actions of the most despotically inclined rulers: it allowed them great latitude, yet precluded any of the earlier civil tendency, not altogether suppressed in Europe by Christianity, to confuse royalty and deity. A caliph knew he was mortal, at most a temporary vicar of Allah and a defender of the faith. The economic base, like that of any civil realm in the past, was everywhere a large number of fellahin (in the most literal sense, since this word is Arabic); the superstructure, however, achieved genuine elegance, with many of what we today regard as the indispensable amenities of civilized existence.

✄ In contrast, most of Europe in the Middle Ages—the Italian city-states were an exception—did not even have soap.

Soap had been invented in Roman times (p. 526), though probably not by Romans, since the Latin word for it, *sāpō, sāpōnis,* was a loan from some Germanic dialect (the native Latin cognate, *sēbum,* meant 'grease, tallow'). The Latin word 'soap', if untouched by anything but the wearing-away of its inflectional endings and by sound change (p. 291), would have come down into modern Spanish as *sabón.* But the Spanish is *jabón.* The explanation is that during the Muslim period in Iberia, in the eighth through the fifteenth centuries, the Moors used the stuff and the Spaniards didn't. The early Romance word was borrowed, together with the substance, into Moorish Arabic, became disused in Spanish, and was then borrowed back with its phonetic shape altered as Ferdinand and Isabella were successfully expelling the Arabs.

Yet it was this dirty, disorganized northwestern peninsular frontier of the high civil society of the Middle Ages that expanded its power and tied the whole world together.

From Land to Open Sea

In the eighth and ninth centuries overland travel and commerce were slowly increasing in western Europe and larger political units were putting in an appearance—even if the largest ones, such as the domain of the Frankish emperor Charlemagne about 800, tended to be either weak or short-lived. The Crusades, beginning in the eleventh century, and the Chinese expeditions of Marco Polo late in the thirteenth, awakened the rulers of Europe to the wealth of good things to be obtained from the Orient, and long-distance trade became lively. The Crusades had even put pieces of southwest Asia, including Palestine, into European hands. But the Turks soon threw the Europeans out again, and when, in 1453, the Turks took Constantinople and turned it into Istanbul, the established overland trails for European traffic with the Orient were blocked. The antagonism between Muslims and European Christians was too great.

The emerging powers of western Europe took to the deep sea in search of alternative routes. They found them, but they also found unexpected things.

AROUND AFRICA

The Portuguese sought to bypass Muslim north Africa by sailing south and east around the whole continent, though they did not know how long a trip this would be until, in 1487, Bartolomeu Dias de Novais succeeded in rounding the Cape of Good Hope. It was only in 1498 that his successor, Vasco da Gama, reached India.

The Portuguese proceeded to build a commercial empire for themselves in southern and southeastern Asia and in the East Indies, and before the end of the sixteenth century the Dutch were doing the same.

Meanwhile, the Portuguese had touched the Guinea Coast in 1470, opening up an African trade that soon became as important as any with more distant places. In the seventeenth century the Dutch began to colonize southern Africa. Otherwise, European concerns with sub-Saharan Africa remained coastal until the nineteenth century, during which the interior was explored and partitioned among various contending European nations.

WEST TO THE ORIENT

Similarly, when Ferdinand and Isabella of Spain, just completing their expulsion of the Moors, backed Columbus's attempts to reach the Indies by sailing west, the avowed aim was not achieved until 1520–1521, when Hernando de Magallanes (a Portuguese who changed his name from Fernão de Magalhães when he renounced his nationality to serve the Spanish crown) discovered and threaded through the strait named after him, crossed the Pacific, and reached the Philippines only to be killed in a fight with the natives on Mactán Island. His party continued west, the first human beings to circumnavigate the globe. Because of the prevailing winds, the return trip across the Pacific remained impracticable until 1565, when Andrés de Urdaneta hit on the great-circle course passing just south of the Aleutians. The Philippines then became actively Spanish; a century later so did Guam.

But all that was relatively trivial. It had long since become clear that Columbus, failing in his intended goal, had instead discovered for Old World civil society a thitherto unknown continental expanse. Its exploitation began forthwith. The Aztecs, Mayans, and Incas were no match for Spanish arms, deceit, and disease; their independent civil societies, so long in the building, vanished forever almost before the first European crossing of the Pacific. Other western European countries successfully sought their own slices of the new pie, Portugal in eastern South America, the British, French, and Dutch in the Caribbean and North America.

THE NORTHERN LAND BYPASS

Back in the fifteeenth century, in eastern Europe where there was no easy access to the open ocean, the Russians fought the Turks and sought overland routes to the Orient that would lie too far north for Muslim interference. Their aims were in part different from those in western Europe, but the net result was the same: European civil society expanded on another front.

In 1453 the Muscovites governed a region smaller than the Iberian Peninsula. As time went by they extended their control in all directions. Eastwards, by 1580 their domain stretched to the Urals, and by 1620 to the Yenisei River, with traders and trappers roving far beyond. Later in the seventeenth century the Russians reached the Pacific. By 1750, using ships constructed in Siberian ports, they were beginning to explore the northwestern shores of North America, from Bering Strait and the Aleutians down the coast as far as San Francisco Bay. The Russian empire was as far-flung as the Spanish, except that it was land close to headquarters and sea far away instead of the other way around. In the north Pacific the Russians and the Spanish came into minor conflict. The Russian efforts farther south were never very successful, but they held on to Alaska until its sale to the United States in 1868.

In passing, it is interesting to note that tobacco, which Columbus had taken from Cuba to Europe on his first return voyage and which was an immediate success in the Old World, was unknown to the aborigines of Alaska until the Russians brought it in. It had diffused almost all the way around the world to get there.

The Pacific

Australia, Tasmania, New Zealand, and the remoter islands of Oceania were variously sighted during European voyages of exploration in the sixteenth through the eighteenth centuries, but, like most of the interior of Africa, were not subject to extensive direct interference until the nineteenth. English missionaries led the way in Oceania, coming to Tahiti in 1797. British convicts initiated the settling of Australia and New Zealand in 1788 and of Tasmania in 1804. In another hundred years almost everything worth claiming had been claimed, almost everthing worth taking had been taken.

More Reasons for Expansion

Late medieval Europe had a degree of cultural homogeneity (for example, it was almost uniformly Christian), but was anything but unified politically. Its various states quarreled constantly. The expansion of Europe stepped up the pace, giving more to quarrel about and more places to fight in. The first "world war," in the sense of the first war fought between European powers not only in Europe but at scattered longitudes all around the world, was that between France and England in 1754–1763; its North American aspect is known to us as the French and Indian War.

European countries with far-flung overseas empires found it necessary to seize and control various odd islands and promontories of no inherent economic value, to serve as naval and military bases, and the protection of the bases one already possessed became one of the rationalizations for establishing even more of them. Think of the owner of a nested set of Chinese boxes who repeatedly finds the outermost precious enough to need sheltering in a still larger one. The world's politicians have not yet learned that this game is doomed to futility.

The Invasion of High Civil Society

As European might was reinforced by the manpower and resources of Africa and by the resources and manpower of colonial territory—above all, of the Americas—Europe grew impudent enough to venture inroads into the parts of the Old World that had been the domain of high civil society when Europe was still barbaric frontier.

All the maritime powers of western Europe were nibbling at India during the seventeenth century, but in 1717 Britain won out and began securing and extending her rule.

European activity in the rest of south, southeast, and east Asia continued to be largely coastal and insular. China, Thailand, and Japan remained independent, though during the nineteenth century the Chinese government was insultingly forced to grant many concessions along its Pacific shores, and had Russia to contend with to the north.

Britain led the way in subverting the control of the earlier governments of southwest Asia and northeastern Africa. During the nineteenth-century partitioning of Africa, the Muslim north was mostly split into Spanish, French, Italian, and British spheres of influence. The last step here was the elimination of Turkish power (which stretched along the southern Mediterranean shore through Libya), and that came only at the end of the First World War, when Turkey was also finally deprived of the sizable regions of southeastern Europe she had dominated for several centuries.

Last Steps

Of course, as European empires grew they developed instabilities. Starting late in the eighteenth century some of the edges broke loose.

By 1850 most of the New World had escaped from direct European political dominance. This changed the details of the political map, but did not halt the expansion of European civil society. The new nations were of, if not in, Europe; they were cut to the European pattern. Even the minor innovations in governmental structure, as in the United States (p. 650), while not to be belittled, stemmed from roots imported across the Atlantic. The United States joined its sister European-style nations instantly in the empire-building game. Similarly, when the Philippines were "granted" their independence during the Second World War—and after the Japanese had been expelled—their new political structure imitated the most recent Western models. There was little or nothing left of the old incipiently civil set-up the Spanish had encountered when they took over the islands in the sixteenth century.

In the interior of western New Guinea there are some peoples whose first direct contact with Europeans did not come until 1935. In the highlands of northeastern South America a straggling handful of hunters-gatherers were discovered (by Europeans, that is—they already knew about themselves) only in the late 1960s. Yet it is correct to assert that by the first decades of the twentieth century Europe's expansion was for all intents and purposes completed.

Moreover, that completion brought the expansion of civil society to a close, nine thousand years after its beginnings. Today, remaining tribal societies are wee, lost in a worldwise sea of civil society. The juggernaut finds no unbroken ground on which to roll.

BY HIS BOOTSTRAPS

38

✖

THE SECRET OF EUROPEAN SUCCESS

Not even hindsight answers all questions. We do not really know why it fell to the lot of Europe, rather than to that of some other civil region of medieval times, to tie the world of man together into a single big knot. Therefore the title of this chapter promises too much. What can be delivered is only a roster of technological devices and social arrangements that came together in Europe and that seem to have bestowed some advantage: *stirrup and horsecollar, windmill and waterwheel, clocks and spectacles, firearms, better ships, literacy and printing,* and *capitalism.*

✖ A mounted spearman using only bridle and saddle can obtain limited purchase as he hurls his weapon. Well secured stirrups for his feet allow him to impart to the spear's trajectory not only more of his own strength but also some of the horse's. Or he can rest the butt end of the spear against his upper arm, as a lance, and charge the target.

THE STIRRUP
AND
THE HORSECOLLAR

Stirrups for the big toes only were in use in India by the end of the second century B.C. They spread with Hindu culture east to the Philippines and west to Ethiopia. The Buddhists carried them to higher latitudes, where such people as the Chinese were for obvious reasons not in the habit of going barefoot, and they were there enlarged to accommodate the whole shod foot. The modified type diffused through central Asia to Iran, thence via Anatolia and Byzantium into Europe.

In the early eighth century A.D., Charles dubbed Martel ('the Hammer'), of the Germanic-speaking Frankish regime centered at Metz, discerned their military potential. Stirrups tipped the political balance in his favor, and he was able to wrest great tracts of land from the church and turn them over to retainers in exchange for their pledges of loyalty; this either started or greatly encouraged the development of the feudal system. They also helped him win a battle against the Moors fought in 732 or 733 south of the Loire River somewhere near Poitiers, after which the Moors never again ventured into the Frankish domain.

It is not known where the horsecollar was invented; possibly in Europe. The device makes all the difference in the use of horses as draft animals. There had been attempts since early in the Bronze Age to transfer the typical ox yoke to a horse, but it works badly for anatomical reasons, pressing on the windpipe to impair the animal's breathing and on the jugular vein to cut down on the blood circulation. The horse-collar is a padded ring fitted to the animal in just the right way to avoid these deleterious effects and still let him pull. Experiments have shown that a team of horses equipped with horsecollars and other matching modern harness can haul a load 4 or 5 times as great as they can manage with the earlier style of yoke.

Well harnessed horses were being used for plowing in the late ninth century in Norway, and within two or three hundred years the custom had spread all over Europe, from the Ukraine to Normandy.

Horseshoes, also of unknown origin, put in their appearance at about the same time.

For cartage, the more efficient utilization of horsepower in time encouraged the restoration of the old Roman roads (p. 557), long since in ruins from lack of maintenance, and the building of new ones.

WINDMILLS AND WATERWHEELS ✗ The Buddhists in India used windmills to turn prayer wheels. They may have been invented in the first place for that pious purpose. The mill was erected with the blades immovably oriented towards the prevailing wind, so that an ill wind blew nobody good. In this mechanical form, but with more worldly applications (such as the grinding of grain), the machine diffused to Persia and the eastern Mediterranean, and then was carried to western Europe by returnees from the earlier Crusades (the first started in 1095, the second in 1147). There were windmills in Normandy by 1180, in England a decade later.

The Buddhists of Tibet used the power of running water to turn their prayer wheels, but the immediate source of the waterwheel in Europe seems to have been Rome. Roman waterwheels were undershot: the bottom of the wheel was immersed in the flowing stream. The Arabs inherited them in this form. In the thirteenth century Europe got them back again. Somewhere along the line the overshot type was devised, the water guided along a millrace to fall on the blades at one side of the wheel and thus turn it. For obvious mechanical reasons this is much more efficient.

Windmills and waterwheels gave Europeans important sources of mechanical power, the chief ones until the harnessing of steam in the eighteenth century, and still widely exploited as recently as the middle of the twentieth. Tinkering with their design led to all sorts of improvements in axles, gears, belts, and levers for the transmission of the power and its application in the right form at the right place.

Waterwheels were harnessed in the thirteenth century to card wool, by 1300 to work the bellows of steel foundries along the Rhine (p. 617), by 1350 to draw wire, theretofore done entirely by human muscles. The direction of mechanical flow in the waterwheel was also reversed, so that by turning a crank one could lift water to start it on its way through irrigation ditches.

Efforts were made more than once to connect a waterwheel to a water lift so that the same water could be used over and over again. It took steam technology and the nineteenth-century theory of thermodynamics derived from it to explain why this was impossible.

Years, seasons, lunar months, and days can be counted with little trouble. The measurement of intervals of time smaller than a day is more difficult. Judging sun time by the eye is surely very old; the sundial, on the other hand, appears less than three thousand years ago, first in Egypt and then in Mesopotamia. The role of the number 12 in our modern time units is an Egyptian heritage, while that of 60 comes from the Babylonians. Early sundials were marked to give twelve approximately equal portions of daytime, and the comparable division of the diurnal period of darkness was an Egyptian notion. A sundial converts the sun's position into the angle of a shadow; hence we still divide both the hour and the degree of arc into sixty portions.

The Egyptian water clock or *clepsydra* is attested earlier than the sundial, from about 1400 B.C. The earliest form was simply a vessel from which water was allowed to escape very slowly; the sides were calibrated so that when the water level had dropped to a certain mark a certain amount of time was known to have passed. The hourglass (or "egg-timer"), with sand instead of water, was a derivative. To the Egyptian clepsydra the Romans added a float connected by levers and gears to a pointer on a dial, and they let the water drip into the vessel to raise the float, rather than leaking out to lower it.

Some unknown European inventor improved radically on these old methods in the thirteenth century, devising a clock run by a hanging weight (raised periodically by human muscles to store the necessary potential energy) that was permitted to drop only a bit at a time by a device called an *escapement*. This consists of a cogged wheel over which hangs a curved bar hinged in the middle with a toothlike projection downwards at each end. The teeth engage the cogs alternately, delaying the rotation of the wheel and forcing the motion to take the form of a series of short pulses. The precision with which the escapement is machined determines the accuracy of the timepiece. Since the mechanism ran at approximately the same rate all the time, hours of daylight and hours of darkness came (for the first time) to have the same standardized duration.

The first clocks, made chiefly of wood, were very large, placed in the towers of public buildings to serve everyone in sight, and they struck bells, or timed the striking of bells, to serve everyone within earshot (hence the English word *clock,* a loan via Dutch from the old French form which yields modern French *cloche* 'bell'). Smaller ones were built in the fourteenth and fifteenth centuries for use in private homes.

In 1500, Peter Henlein of Nürnberg devised a way of using the potential energy of a coiled metal spring (the *mainspring*) to drive a clock, and miniaturization in the direction of portability ensued, eventually yielding what we call watches (at one time *watch* meant also a clock face, and the connection with the verb *to watch* and with a military guard being *on watch* is patent). Eighty years later, when Galileo Galilei of Pisa and Florence discovered the principle of the pendulum—namely, that the period of the swing of a suspended weight depends only on the distance between the point of attachment and the bottom of the weight—he tried to use a pendulum as a new kind of clock-regulating device, replacing the escapement. It was Christiaan Huygens of The Hague who, in the 1650s, succeeded in this. Thereafter clocks and watches went their separate ways.

The Greeks had mirrors late in the fifth century B.C., and the Etruscans and Romans not long thereafter, used (as still today) by fine ladies and gentlemen as an aid in their toilets. They were made of metal—no glass—with a smoothly polished slightly convex reflecting surface. By the late fourteenth century A.D., glass mirrors with a metal backing were being made in Nürnberg. Half a century later, Johann Gutenberg of printing fame (p. 621) is reported to have devised an improvement. Whether or not his trick was of value, it is clear that a good deal of experimentation was going on. In 1564 in Venice, good mirrors of glass backed with an amalgam of tin and mercury were being manufactured on a commercial scale, and glassless metal mirrors, which had survived up to that time, quickly became obsolete.

Magnifying lenses mounted in frames were a common aid to reading in China in the tenth century. In the mid thirteenth, spectacles are supposed to have been described by the English friar Roger Bacon—who has also been given credit by some investigators, on shaky evidence, for a wide variety of other precocious technological notions, including gunpowder (p. 616). It is known that spectacles were introduced into Italy early in the fourteenth century by Alessandro di Spina of Florence. A portrait painted in 1352 at Treviso (north of Venice) shows the subject wearing eyeglasses. Concave lenses for the correction of myopia appear for sure only in 1517; before that glasses had only had convex lenses.

The derivatives of spectacles that chiefly concern us here are microscopes and telescopes, both of which underwent initial development in the neighborhood of 1600. The first compound microscope, with one convex and one concave lens, was made about 1590 by the Dutch spectacle-maker Zacharias Janssen. The first telescope was reputedly assembled by other Dutch spectacle-makers, about 1608. In 1611 a compound microscope with two convex lenses was proposed by the astronomer Johannes Kepler. He was too busy with other things—including the use of the telescope for astronomy—to execute his design, but this was done about 1628 by Christoph Scheiner of Nysa, a German Jesuit. It was only later in the seventeenth century that Anton van Leeuwenhoek of Delft fashioned an effective one-lens microscope, and began the exploitation of microscopy in the direction of what is now a great and endlessly varied range of biological and medical investigation. In another direction, the Englishman Isaac Newton, heir to mirrors, lenses, telescopes, and Kepler's astronomical findings, founded the scientific theory of optics, invented the calculus, and formulated his laws of motion and of universal gravitation—perhaps the richest technical bequest our species has ever received from a single man, despite the fact that the calculus was invented independently, at the same time, also by Gottfried Wilhelm von Leibniz.

Navigation

Clocks, mirrors, and lenses converged in the European answers to the problem of navigation.

This is the problem of knowing where you are when you are at sea with no familiar land in sight. You need to know which direction is which, and you need your location relative to known points of reference, such as your ports of origin and destination.

The most general frame of reference for location is given by latitude and longitude, a grid system known to, and perhaps invented or perfected by, the Greek astronomer Hipparchos in the middle of the second century B.C., using the units of angular measurement devised by the Babylonians (p. 613).

In the relatively small Mediterranean, the problem had been solved by dead reckoning, celestial observation with the naked eye, carefully made charts, and the magnetic compass, the latter either invented in Italy or imported from the Orient in the thirteenth century A.D. The Mediterranean charts made no allowance for Earth's curvature. When the Portuguese and Spanish ventured out into the open Atlantic, charting based on a flat Earth was misleading over long distances; in the face of this, flat-Earth charts were for some reason preferred by many mariners even after the Flemish geographer Gerhard Kremer (known as Mercator) in 1569 promoted the projection now known by his name. Also, the varying deviation between the true and magnetic poles was troublesome. This deviation was discovered by Columbus in mid Atlantic on 13 September 1492, and it may have been he who introduced the practice of using the fixed position of the star Polaris (the knowledge of which was no novelty) for correction.

LATITUDE is simple. A naked-eye survey of the night sky gives it approximately to one who knows the constellations. More precise determination requires more careful examination with an instrument.

The first device used for this by Europeans was the *astrolabe,* obtained from the Arabs who had in turn gotten it from one or another of the peoples of classical antiquity, possibly the Greeks. I think the astrolabe was the first computing machine. The raw data, fed in by adjusting its moving parts, are the line of sight to the horizon and that to Sun or to a known star at a specified time (usually noon or midnight). The output is the latitude, shown by the position of a marker.

In 1731 the astrolabe was so greatly improved by the Englishman John Hadley that its name was changed, first to "octant" and then, after a modification that rendered it even more efficient, to *sextant.* Hadley had clockmaker's or watchmaker's tools to work with, and good mirrors and lenses. The user of a sextant holds it horizontally and looks through a small telescope at Sun when it is at the zenith—that is, at high noon local time. The image of Sun is dulled by smoked glass to protect the eye. The device involves a set of mirrors whose positions are controlled by a handle or knob. The user turns the control until the images of Sun and of the horizon coincide. A pointer on a latitude dial has then been moved to the correct position.

Of course, one must know what day it is, to allow for the annual migration of Sun's apparent path through the sky.

LONGITUDE is harder. It was so difficult and so important that in 1714 British Parliament established a Board of Longitude to work on the problem, and the board offered a prize for a solution that would meet certain specifications as to accuracy.

The theoretical basis for a solution was clear. If, at the moment you make a celestial observation, you know exactly what time it is back home (say, in London), then you can compute your longitude. The practical problem, then, was that of designing an accurate clock. By about 1735 the improvement in seagoing clocks was noticeable, but it was not until 1759 that John Harrison, who had devoted virtually his whole life to the project, produced one that met the Board's prize specifications when it was tested on a run from England to Jamaica in 1761–1762. The terms "clock" and "watch" were too colloquial for such a precision instrument. It was called a *chronometer,* a term proposed back in 1714 by someone who thought the languages of classical antiquity were inherently more scholarly than English (Greek *chrónos* 'time', Latin *metrum* from Greek *métron* 'measure, rule').

Note the dates: Hadley's sextant in 1731, Harrison's chronometer in 1759. These were not medieval devices, though they were the true if tardy fruits of medieval seeds. By the time they became available, the maritime expansion of Europe was three centuries old and hundreds of European vessels were already plying the sea-lanes all over the world. Earlier generations of European seafarers had simply done without—and, as part of the price of European commercial success, the shores and seabottoms of the world were strewn with the wrecks of ships that had come to grief for lack of adequate navigational aids.

FIREARMS

✖ GUNPOWDER is a mixture of charcoal, sulphur, and saltpetre. Charcoal is mainly amorphous carbon; sulfur is sulphur; saltpetre (literally 'stone salt') is potassium nitrate, KNO_3, found, like sulfur, as a mineral. With a little heat, the potassium nitrate decomposes by the formula $2(KNO_3) \rightarrow 2(KNO_2) + O_2$. The oxygen combines with the other ingredients to form carbon and sulphur dioxides (CO_2 and SO_2), both gasses, and some of the KNO_2 may break down further to release gaseous nitrogen. The medieval alchemists who tinkered with the mixture were unaware of these intimate chemical details. But they knew that the properties of the mixture depended on the proportions and on the purity of the constituents: unconfined, some blends will fizzle while, confined, other types will explode violently.

The time and place of invention of gunpowder are hotly debated, which probably means that it was invented more than once. There is a dubious rumor of rockets and torpedos in military use in Arabia in the seventh century A.D. Gunpowder display fireworks were known in India and in China at about the same time. By the tenth century the Chinese were making bombs for combat by stuffing gunpowder into bamboo tubes. European experimenters with the stuff may have included Roger Bacon (p. 614), but historians have also filed claims on behalf of assorted Germans and Italians.

GUNS. The frightening and unarguably European invention was a way of harnessing the power of gunpowder to throw things. You pack some of it into the closed end of a stout and stoutly mounted metal tube, put a stone or a metal ball in on top of it, aim the tube in the proper direction, and then ignite the powder, hurling the ball into trajectory.[1]

[1]We don't know how the new device was invented, but it could have been an accident. Imagine someone trying to make a gunpowder bomb with a metal container. One part of the container, unintentionally weak, flies off, leaving the rest intact.

Such military devices, made of cast iron, were in use in Italy in the 1330s. The Italians called the thing a *cannone* 'large tube', from which the French, by 1339, had gotten their term *canon,* later borrowed into English and German (*cannon, Kanon*). A successful north European gunsmith of the same period is suggested by our English word *gun,* older form *gunne,* believed to be an abbreviation of the personal name *Gunhild* (compare our recent abbreviations *an Enfield, a Luger* from *an Enfield rifle, a Luger pistol*). In the absence of direct records, we can nevertheless infer a considerable period of experimentation with firearms before the 1330s, since, if the weapon is to do its job reliably rather than exploding amidst those who are using it, there are many technical details to be worked out. When the gremlins have been exorcised, then a gun can impart to a cannonball many times the momentum of any spear, arrow, slingstone, blowgun dart, arbalest bolt, or battering ram.

A crucial problem is to make the gun strong enough. Cast iron will do if you use enough of it, but then the weapon is very heavy. Steel is much better. Now, Toledo in Spain has been a justly famous steel-making center for 2000 years, and during its Moorish occupation the Arabs improved the quality of its products by importing techniques that had been developed far off in Asia by the Hindus (p. 536). These techniques were spreading northward into the rest of Europe during the thirteenth century. By 1300 there were steel mills along the Rhine (near sources of iron ore) using the Toledo methods, and using waterwheels to operate the bellows of their blast furnaces (p. 612). The exploitation of the better metal for firearms probably came quickly. The earliest guns were artillery pieces, but by the 1360s there were small arms that one man could carry, and these must surely have been of steel.

IMPACT.   Firearms gave Europe a clear military advantage vis-à-vis the rest of the world. They also stepped up the armaments race among European countries, encouraging the growth of heavy industry and forcing a certain amount of systematic attention to what we now call "research and development." By and large, the improvements in firearms worked by the intra-European competition kept Europe militarily ahead, as the basic notions spread beyond her frontiers. But not always. The Turks had cannon in their successful seige of Constantinople in 1452–1453, and the defenders of the invested city did not.

✘ Whilst the civil societies of the New World developed no maritime tradition at all, medieval Europe had two. One was that of the Mediterranean, shared with Muslims and, through them, influenced by the seafaring achievements of the Hindus. The other was that of the North and Baltic Seas, perhaps not independent in ultimate origin, but greatly modified by the ingenuity of northern Celts and of Germanic-speaking peoples. The northern tradition played its role in the various aquatic migrations of the insular Celts, the West Germanic peoples, and the Scandinavians (pp. 596–599). Then, in the twelfth and thirteenth centuries, it was a key stimulus for, and was greatly promoted by, the Hanseatic League, a commercial combine of north German cities which, in its heyday in the early fourteenth century, dominated trade from London in the west to the Gulf of Finland in the east.

BETTER SHIPS

Roughly speaking, one can say that around 1400 northern ships were inferior to southern ones in matters of rigging and other abovedeck features, but superior in hulls, keels, and rudders. But the two traditions were beginning to borrow from each other. The ships that explored and conquered the world for Europe, beginning late in the fifteenth century, combined the best features of both with some innovations known to neither.

This mingling of separate traditions was not left altogether to chance. In part, it was actively planned and promoted in the mid fifteenth century by Prince Henry the Navigator of Portugal, who had himself sailed—in Mediterranean-type vessels—on various military expeditions in nearby waters and who therefore knew what the problems were.

About 1440, Prince Henry built a residence, the Vila do Infante, at the south-westernmost tip of Portugal near Sagres. Thither, with the support of the Portuguese government, he invited navigators, geographers, and allied scholars and craftsmen, to constitute a sort of naval academy. The staff included Christians and Muslims. The first director was a Jew from Mallorca, chosen perhaps not only for his own technical competence but also as a way of avoiding the disruption of work that might have ensued had the head represented either of the majority religious groups. The academy revised charts, investigated techniques of navigation, trained marine officers, and designed and supervised the building of ships of new types.

It was probably here that the best of the north and the best of the south were put together. It was certainly here that the solution to one serious problem was found: that of how to mount guns on a ship so that, when fired, the recoil would not capsize the vessel. The answer lay in a hull design with the center of gravity not very far above the center of buoyancy and well below the epicenter (the fore-to-aft axis about which the center of buoyancy revolves when the ship heels), so that, after the ship is tilted by the recoil, it "tumbles home" to its normal position.

LITERACY AND PRINTING ✶

WRITING IN EUROPE

The art of writing spread into western and northern Europe first in a thin wave in the early centuries A.D., chiefly in alphabetical characters called "runes," unaccompanied by any special writing materials such as parchment or paper. From this there are surviving inscriptions from the second through the eighth centuries, some of them in languages that have since disappeared and some of them not decipherable (Pictish inscriptions from Scotland, not in runes but in the Ogham script invented in Ireland, illustrate both points: p. 596).

The growth of the Roman empire and the subsequent spread of Christianity largely extinguished this early literate tradition, though runes were occasionally used in remote parts of Sweden down to recent centuries. With the decline of the empire in the west, reading and writing became mainly the prerogative of the clergy, almost all of it in Latin.

To this there was from the outset one major exception.

Palestine had become part of the Roman empire in the middle of the first century

B.C., just when, in the other direction from Rome, Julius Caesar was reaching tentatively beyond Gaul into Britain. Small groups of Jewish families had migrated to Italy and beyond, in search of freer places to live, settling all around the Mediterranean and in most of the towns of western and central Europe. Under Roman rule they fared reasonably well. Their descendants stayed on as the empire collapsed. Some were forced by economic circumstances to become farmers, but even when the towns were at their nadir (p. 603) some managed to stay on in them. In the face of spreading Christianity most of them stuck stubbornly to their own beliefs—as had their ancestors for almost 2000 years, their determination being only forged the more firmly by repeated episodes of massacre, captivity, and slavery. Mostly, they took to the language of their immediate neighbors for everyday affairs. But they kept to Hebrew for their religion and for aspects of community life governed by it. What is more, they retained literacy in Hebrew through the darkest of the "dark ages," when no one else for many miles around could read any language at all; and as parts of a far-flung religious-cultural polity they maintained a thin network of intercommunication and travel among their scattered settlements when the vast bulk of the surrounding goyim were living out their lives within a stone's throw of their birthplaces. Their more scholarly rabbis learned Arabic, Greek, and Latin, and made contributions to learning so profound that Christian scholars had to heed them regardless of the attitude of their clerical superiors.

One thing the Jews did not do. They were not searching for converts, and so had no reason to try to supply writing systems for languages that had not been written. This enterprise was left to the Christians.

Even among Christians, writing was for a while mainly in Latin (in the west; Greek in the east). But as time passed people found reason to want to write the language they spoke. Though the internal affairs of the Church of Rome were conducted in Latin, as was the mass, priests where the everyday language was something else had to have ready access to religious matter written in the appropriate vernacular.

This need tended to come earliest where the language of everyday affairs was neither Latin nor one of its descendants. In the parts of Europe where Latin (carried by Roman soldiers and their slaves, turned farmers) had prevailed as the spoken language, it gradually changed to become what we now know as the Romance languages (p. 596). Until enough time had passed for the colloquial Latin of a region to differ in good measure from the increasingly archaic form used in reading and writing, there was no motivation for trying to write the vernacular.

In Box 38-1 we give the timetable of this (new) diffusion of writing to European languages (and to a few others) other than Latin and Greek.

NUMERALS. For some purposes, alphabetical writing is inefficient (p. 580). The special use of certain Latin letters to represent numbers ("Roman numerals") spread with the Latin alphabet. The more efficient Hindu-Arabic numeral notation made its way into Europe not later than the tenth century, for it is found in a manuscript from Spain dated 976. Before long, writers were using both systems, as we still do, but relying increasingly on the Hindu-Arabic system when computation, rather than a mere numbering of items, was at issue.

BOX 38-1. The post-Roman diffusion of writing in Europe.

The dating (by centuries A.D.) is that of the introduction of writing; the earliest surviving documents are typically somewhat later. All the writing is alphabetical. "G" means alphabet derived from that of Greek; "G-OB", such derivation via Old Bulgarian; no mark, derived from that of Latin. Basque survives in the Pyrenees; Georgian is in southern Caucasia; the other languages in the rightmost column are Finno-Ugrian. For Indo-European see pp. 590–600. Dagger: language now extinct. Question mark: date uncertain.

	ROMANCE	CELTIC	GERMANIC	SLAVIC	BALTIC	OTHER INDO-EUROPEAN	NON-INDO-EUROPEAN
4th:			†Gothic(G)				
5th:						Armenian(G)	Georgian(G)
6th:		Irish					
7th:			English				
8th:		Welsh	Continental West Germanic				
9th:	French, Provençal	Breton		Old Bulgarian(G), Bulgarian			
10th:	Italian, Spanish	†Cornish					
11th:			Norwegian, Icelandic				
12th:	Portuguese		Danish, Swedish	Russian (G-OB), Serbian(G-OB)*			
13th:	Catalan		Frisian	Czech, Slovak			Hungarian, Finnish
14th:				Polish			Lappish?
15th:				Croatian,* Sorbian	†Old Prussian	Albanian	Esthonian
16th:	Rumanian, Raeto-Romance, †Dalmatian?			Slovene	Lithuanian, Lettish		Basque
17th:		†Manx					

*The Serbo-Croatian dialects have two very similar literary standards; the Serbs use the G–OB alphabet, the Croats one from Latin.

SCHOOLS

Given the religious context of the invention of new writing systems, it is not surprising that for a long time a large proportion of the writing done in any language was religious in content.

But the church itself had secular interests as well as sacred ones. The books copied by medieval monks dealt with many topics. In the sixth, seventh, and eighth centuries, the lamp of literacy and learning was kept lit (other than by the Jews) especially in Ireland, where there seems to have been something of a school tradition in pre-Christian times.[2]

Beginning in the ninth and tenth centuries the church began to foster the establishment of centers of learning somewhat like those of the Muslim world (p. 606). As early as the ninth, there was a school of medicine at Salerno, famous from Ireland to Persia, and by 1000 there was an academy of law at Bologna. Other such establishments arose in the tenth and eleventh centuries in Italy, which was strategically located for intellectual interaction with Byzantium and with the Muslims. In the eleventh and twelfth centuries they were cropping up all over central and western Europe. These institutions began mainly for the training of priests and monks; they became what we now call universities. From the beginning, many of them had satellite preparatory schools for younger students, and other lower-level schools were sponsored by cathedrals and by synagogues.

BOOKS

The growth of the schools substantially increased the demand for books and for multiple copies of books.

In antiquity, books had mostly taken the physical form of scrolls, awkward to handle and bulky to store. By late Roman times the "codex" had appeared: this is the shape with which we are familiar today, consisting of sheets bound together at one edge, except that the early ones were very large, the page size approaching that of a modern newspaper (reduction to more modest proportions came well after printing). This new form was perfected especially in Ireland in the sixth and seventh centuries, and by the time of the incipient universities was standard.

The increased demand was too much for the monasteries. Part of the load was taken on by secular establishments of "stationers." But it was still hand work, and books were expensive. They were not likely to be found in private homes, except in those of the unusually wealthy and privileged.

PRINTING

Such was the nature of the literate scene when printing from movable type was invented in Germany in the middle of the fifteenth century.

[2]If there was it is worthy of note, because the school as a specialized institution is a cultural rarity. Apart from the Western tradition (begun by the Greeks, inherited by the Arabs and then by Europe), the school is known to have originated only in China, where it was instituted more than two thousand years ago to train middle-class youth in the classics and so equip them to take the civil-service examinations, and as the *whare wananga* among the (nonliterate) Maori of New Zealand.

No technical innovation ever met with such whirlwind success. Hand copying was a commercially viable enterprise for a few more decades (at least through 1486); but a letter dated 1467 reports books already selling for only one fifth their former price. The merchant William Caxton took the new art to England, and others carried it elsewhere. By the end of the century, presses were at work in every major European country except Russia. At least 35,000 titles had been printed (not counting ephemeral tracts and pamphlets); the total number of copies was close to 20,000,000.

The first books from Gutenberg's press included the Bible, in Latin. In 1482 Euclid's *Elements,* written in Alexandria early in the third century B.C., was printed for the first time, in Venice, in a Latin translation done by Johannes Campanus about 1260 from an Arabic version of the Greek original. These two deserve mention because the Bible has now been printed in more different editions than any other book, and Euclid's *Elements* has now been printed in more different editions than any other book except the Bible.

Most printing before 1500 was in Latin. Yet the proportion of books in other languages was respectable, and increased with the distance from Rome. Before 1500 there was even one in Breton! (p. 596). The long literate Jews, of course, did not delay. Several of the earliest families of printers in Italy were Jewish, and the first two printed Hebrew books appeared in 1474–1475.

Nearly three fourths of the works printed in this initial half century were written by contemporary authors. As to subject, the distribution of the 35,000-odd titles was 45% religion, 30% literature, 10% law, 10% technology, and 5% for everything else. During the sixteenth century this changed, at least in England; of all the books printed there or elsewhere for sale there, only 40% were religious and 20% literary, leaving 40% instead of the earlier 25% for other categories.

EFFECTS

It is obvious that printing was promoting literacy. Books ceased to be a luxury. The middle classes, if not the lowest, could afford them, so that there was increased motivation for learning to read.

It began to make sense for specialized artisans of all sorts to prepare and publish manuals, complete with illustrations (woodcuts: older by a couple of centuries in Europe than printing from movable type), for their own convenient reference and for the guidance of their successors. In this way, literacy and printing played a part in many of the other European technical developments we are talking about in this chapter. For example, it seems unlikely that John Hadley and John Harrison could have accomplished what they did without help from printed materials.

Again, the earliest marine charts, such as those prepared at Prince Henry the Navigator's academy, had to be copied by hand; but by shortly after 1500 they were being printed, first in Holland and then in England.

Even music got a boost. The first printing of music was done in Venice early in the sixteenth century. The process involved some sort of lithography rather than movable type (that is still largely true today), but otherwise made use of all the technical devices—presses, inks, and so on—developed by Gutenberg and his followers.

ORTHOGRAPHIES. Another quick effect of printing was to stabilize orthographies. Before Caxton, writers of English spelled as they pleased, influenced by the particular things they had read and by the sound systems of their own dialects. It was the requirement of wide distribution of printed materials, rather than any whim on Caxton's part, that put an end to this. Writing became harder because the writer had to conform to a standard spelling usage; reading, however, became easier because the reader had only to learn one usage rather than many. English spelling has changed very little since printing began; the only unfortunate result is that it now fits pronunciation (which has changed quite a bit) very awkwardly (*though, tough, cough, through, bough, hiccough*). For the other languages of Europe this particular effect has been somewhat less striking, but it is found to some extent everywhere.

PERIODICALS. Between 1600 and 1620, in the Netherlands, Germany, Austria, and Italy, the first newspapers appeared. Also at this time, publishers began issuing occasional "newsbooks," listing (and advertising!) their current and impending releases. These newsbooks seem to have been the immediate stimulus for the first periodicals. In Paris, Denys de Salla began a digest publication, the *Journal des sçavans* ('*Scholars' Journal*') on 5 January 1665. The *Philosophical Transactions* of the Royal Society of London (formed in the 1640s) made its debut in March 1665. The first periodical intended for entertainment was a little earlier: the *Mercuriosus Jocosus* ('*The Wingèd Messenger of Wit*'), started in 1654.

TECHNICAL DERIVATIVES. The technical progeny of the earliest printing presses includes flatbed and rotary presses (some of them extremely fast), type-setting machines, type-casting machines, and for the past century the increasingly ingenious use of photography at various stages. But it also includes the typewriter, first rendered reasonably practical in 1868, carbon paper, and in the twentieth century a whole slew of "office copying machines."

We need to remember the recency of the latter in order to understand the frequency with which certain kinds of earlier works were "privately printed." "Public" printing was done by businessmen ("publishers") for a profit, or by government- or institution-sponsored presses. Up to less than a hundred years ago, if a writer wanted a few dozen or a few hundred copies of something, contracting directly with a print shop was about as inexpensive as having them mimeographed would be today.

GROWTH. The catchphrase "information explosion" is, if anything, too weak to characterize what has happened in the 500 years since Gutenberg. Here are statistics in evidence.

In England in the first half of the eighteenth century the number of new works published in book form per year averaged slightly under 100. In a century the rate was up to 600; in the 1960s, it was 20,000. The rate in the United States in the 1960s was also about 20,000; the world total must thus have been close to 200,000. Two hundred thousand *new* books per year! Stocks are not depleted immediately; in the United States alone, in 1969, forgetting about cloth-bound books, there were over 70,000 *paperbacks* in print. In 1961, in the world as a whole, at least 8000 newspapers were published *daily,* others weekly; and at least 100,000 scientific and technical periodicals were being issued weekly, monthly, or quarterly. The world total of magazines of entertainment cannot be even vaguely estimated.

CAPITALISM ✕ Johann Gutenberg was neither a lay brother in the employ of a monastery nor a vassal artisan supported by some locally powerful baron or prince. He was a burgher, a "private citizen," born in Mainz, trained as a goldsmith, who developed his technical notions as a commercial venture, partly on his own and partly with financial backing from various other private citizens in Mainz and in Strassburg. In other words, he was an *entrepreneur,* attempting something potentially profitable at his own risk and that of his backers, neither helped nor hindered by the church, neither encouraged nor discouraged by the state.

Through most of the history of civil society no such arrangement would have been possible. There were artisans aplenty, but they worked under the close supervision of rulers, and any material gains from their technical innovations accrued to their sponsors, not to themselves.

Origins

The new social arrangement, whereby craftsmen—and merchants—were able to work for their own profit and at their own risk, emerged slowly during the Middle Ages in the seemingly unfavorable context of the feudal system.

The avowed aim of that system (as we remarked on p. 603) was a static stability. Lords and their knights, the clergy, and the serfs all had their clearly assigned roles. In theory, so did the artisans and merchants, who were supposed to be as subservient to the lords as were the peasants. In practice, the rulers could not treat them quite so cavalierly, because their skills produced and procured necessary things and because they had to have the wherewithal to transmit those skills to their sons and apprentices. Besides, only a few of the specialized artisans were directly in the employ of lords or clergy, living and working in the castles and monasteries where one could keep an eye on them. As decrepit as the towns had become after the withdrawal of Rome's imperial forces, that is where most of the artisans lived or had their headquarters. Significantly, some of the persistent town-dwellers were Jews (except in Britain, to which they moved only later, and Scandinavia, where there are few even today).

The rise of *capitalism* or "private enterprise" (where "private" means simply non-clerical and nongovernmental) was in many ways like the original rise of civil society.

Three of the four factors listed on page 547 were present: (1) the whole of frontier Europe could be regarded as a "relatively small densely populated region of environmental and technological diversity"; (2) as the migrations quieted down there came to be a "predominance of settled villages" based on farming—with the castles, the monasteries, and the towns superposed; (3) the technology of food production was more than adequate, and became better with horse-drawn plows and as new tracts of farm land were opened up, provided, as always in earlier epochs, that the food producers didn't themselves eat too well.

For the fourth requirement (a group able and willing to seize the reins of leadership) the situation was novel. The reins were already firmly grasped in two sets of hands. The artisans and traders did not hold the power to destroy which would give them the power to tax, and thus to rule. They took over, not suddenly and bloodily in the style of invading conquerors knowing exactly what they wanted, but subtly and slowly from within, never with any grandiose long-term plans.

INDUSTRY.   The towns built their capital through commerce and manufacturing of various kinds; the wool industry seems to have been the biggest single factor, important as early as the eighth century. By the beginning of the fourteenth the successful towns had grown into cities, concentrated especially in northern Italy, along the Rhine, in the Low Countries, and on the south shore of the Baltic. The wool industry was conducted principally in Venice and in Belgium. Many of the northern cities were bound together in the Hanseatic League (p. 617).

In theory, all these commercial cities belonged to one or another larger political unit. In practice, each was an independent city-state, its government run by its captains of industry and commerce. Some of them were limited "democracies," in that all people of means—not, to be sure, the unskilled laborers—had a voice in collective decision-making.

BANKING AND BOOKKEEPING.   In parallel with the rise of commerce and manufacturing, these cities had seen the development of *banking*.

At first the banks were mainly accounting institutions, striking balances for the mutual indebtednesses of merchants and manufacturers and thus minimizing the need for actual physical transfers of money. Before long, however, they were in a position to promote commercial developments by extending credit to entrepreneurs, running the risk that the entrepreneur would fail and not repay, and charging interest as payment for that risk.

The church strongly disapproved. The clergy saw (correctly in the first instance: p. 582) that money has no intrinsic value, and quoted scripture to the effect that one should lay up heavenly treasures, not earthly ones (Matthew 6:19–20). Insofar as they could, they prohibited the practice. Thus it was that the first financiering bankers were Jews, for whom a quotation from the New Testament carried no weight. But in the thirteenth and early fourteenth centuries various wealthy Christians were making loans for interest too, first in the Italian cities, shortly also in the Low Countries, then everywhere.

A technical device of great importance was invented in Italy in the fourteenth century, perhaps somewhat earlier: *double-entry bookkeeping*. It was adopted by businessmen and bankers all over Europe, and is still standard. Earlier on, people had kept track of their stocks and their finances in various ways, none entirely satisfactory. The new technique supplied a constant running account, with inbuilt cross-checks for accuracy, from which a balance could be struck on short notice whenever desired. From the beginning it used Hindu-Arabic numerals (p. 580); Roman numerals would have rendered the system impossibly cumbersome. Clearly it greatly promoted literacy. Also, its high reliability had a lot to do with the increasing willingness of people to accept an appropriate piece of paper, rather than "hard money" or goods, as full payment of a debt.

All that we have described in the foregoing paragraphs was the achievement of merchants and artisans, working on their own initiative as the strong but somewhat confused power of feudal state and church permitted. The townspeople changed and differentiated to fit changing demands. Some successful craftsmen stopped working with their hands to become managers and bankers manipulating symbols; some unsuccessful families of artisans and traders lost everything and became hired help. There were inbuilt weaknesses in the emerging system, and in the middle of the fourteenth century there was a major collapse.

The commercial cities had needed more than technical know-how and good management for success: they had also required abundant cheap labor. This had been supplied in part by the impoverishment of some of the long-time city-dwellers, but mainly by influxes of surplus peasants (p. 556). The proletariat lived very badly and were terribly exploited, especially in the wool towns. In effect they were still serfs, worse off in the cities than on the land, but able to plot revolt because they were concentrated together instead of scattered. They did revolt, and in the ensuing bloody suppression the wool industry of Venice and of the Low Countries was destroyed.

This gave England her big chance. Up to about 1300 she had exported all her raw wool to the continent, and even in the early 1300s she had done little of her own spinning and weaving. With the difficulties on the continent, she took over, capturing the markets, and avoiding comparable labor troubles by having most of the work done not in large urban establishments but by scattered villagers ("cottage industry").

PLAGUE.   Another factor contributing to the collapse was the great plagues that swept over Eurasia in the fourteenth century.

The Black Death (probably bubonic plague) came into Europe via the Italian seaports, from the Black Sea and beyond, in 1348. In a decade it had killed off a full third of Europe's population, and there were lesser, though certainly terrible, recurrences every five to ten years for another half century.

Although it was no respecter of persons, it hit hardest where people lived in the largest, densest clumps: thus, in the monasteries and in the city slums. Such minorities as the Jews and the Gypsies suffered doubly. They were as susceptible to infection as anyone else. In addition, others, in their ignorance and suspicion, were ready to blame the disease on the malevolent sorcery of the minorities, and in anger and fear mounted frightful pogroms.

In the absence of medical sophistication a plague seems like a fortuitous factor in history, but we should remember that the cities would not have been stuffed with tenements had it not been for the demands of commerce and industry. Five hundred years earlier, when the towns were tiny and fewer commercial caravans plodded from one to another, the effects of an equally dangerous disease would have been less ravaging. In fact, one suspects that the plague struck and raged just as soon as demographic conditions permitted. The epidemics died out when the disease had killed off everyone whose resistance was low enough; the survivors had an altered gene pool.

The recuperation of capitalism after the fourteenth-century disasters was marked by three themes: the enduring strength of the guilds; the rise of Protestantism; and the growth of capitalist-dominated "national states."

THE GUILDS were fraternal-economic-political organizations of people in a single craft: for example, shoemakers, tanners, dyers, bakers, painters, goldsmiths. They were somewhat like modern craft unions (which are descended from them), except that the masters were in business for themselves and owned their capital equipment. In many towns membership was obligatory for all but those in the permanent employ of a baron or bishop or other local bigwig. A shop's unskilled labor was supplied in part by a few hired hands with no future, more by apprentices who were supposed to learn the trade and who received nothing but their keep in exchange. Apprenticeship was the only road to full membership in the guild with master status. Most apprentices, to be sure, did not make it.

There had been craft organizations before, but they had not been so strong. A major reason for the new system was bad memories of the old days: work that should have been done only by experts had been turned over to ignorant peasants operating equipment they did not understand; this had led to the economic ruin of many a worthy artisan, and to all the troubles of the mid fourteenth century. Such catastrophe must not strike again. Of course, eventually it did, in the form of the factory system. Yet for a long time the guilds served to transmit specialized skills and high standards of workmanship, and to encourage innovations only when they were of genuine value. In some fields the small-workshop tradition is still vital. Mass-produced violins, for example, are utterly worthless.

PROTESTANTISM arose in the north. It would not be right to say that north European capitalism "produced" the German Martin Luther, the Swiss Huldreich Zwingli, King Henry the Eighth of England, or the Picard-turned-Swiss John Calvin, any more than it would be correct to claim that the revolts led by these men against the Church of Rome yielded capitalism as a social consequence. Luther, Zwingli, and Calvin were motivated by moral conviction, King Henry by patriotism or personal interest or both. But their views and their success were not unrelated to the climate of the time.

The resulting reduction in the influence of Rome made possible a splendid endorsement by the new churches of a life doctrine well calculated to promote capitalist enterprise. As the scriptures say, one must not be interested in earthly treasures. The way to lay up heavenly ones, however, is to work very hard to *produce* earthly wealth—and then to mortify the flesh in penance for one's inevitable sins by refusing to enjoy it. This applies to employees in that they must labor long hours for a pittance. It applies to employers in that they must be frugal, plowing most of their profits back into the business. So everyone lives in squalor, and capital assets mount like mad.

This view, that work is its own reward, is often called the "Protestant ethic." But it was adopted in parts of France, and in a particularly gloomy variant in Ireland, though those countries remained Catholic. It was exported in great gobs to South

Africa and to North America. In England it did not dominate until the Victorian era, by which time something similar had appeared (and still persists) in Russia. Catholic southern Europe fought back not only on the field of battle but by evolving (in the so-called Counter-Reformation) a modified world view that was considerably more sensible and happy-making yet did not preclude capital growth.

NATIONAL STATES.   The large national states grew first in the periphery of Europe: Portugal, Spain, France, and England in the west; Denmark and Sweden in the north; Poland, Austria, and Russia in the east. In central Europe, just where the city-states had formerly been strongest and where the guilds were now most powerful, the process was delayed. Central European military squabbles continued for a long time to resemble the conflicts of petty medieval princes, complicated by the religious antagonisms between Catholics and Protestants. Holland and Switzerland worked themselves free of this fairly early. Germany and Italy, on the other hand, did not emerge as unified national states until the nineteenth century, well after the militaristic idiot-savant Napoleon Bonaparte, an atavism if there ever was one, had throughly but temporarily mixed everything up.

In the periphery, on the other hand, especially in the west, wars increasingly became contests among competing groups of capitalists for the control of raw materials and markets. The national states were successful to the extent that their traditional rulers worked in cooperation with the rising class of bourgeois businessmen and bankers: Napoleon's contempt for the "nation of shopkeepers" (England) that eventually and inevitably defeated him was unrealistic. The rulers didn't always like the liaison, but they soon found that there was no viable alternative.

For one thing, the bankers repeatedly financed their military ventures, which in the earlier stages were often directed against upstart local nobles who did not want to accept their suzerainty. Most of the funds advanced by the bankers were passed on to the businessmen who could supply the needed military matériel. Sometimes the government's indebtedness was repudiated, but usually the bankers got their money back, with interest. Furthermore, the centralization of political authority and the maintenance of some degree of internal order enlarged the markets for the businessmen.

CHANGE OF PATTERN.   Clearly, the private-enterprise system was becoming something very different from what it had been to start with. Begun by medieval artisans and traders working as a more or less unified class within the fabric of feudalism, it had split that class three ways. A number of extremely successful families had become the capitalists, the owners of banks and of the ever more complicated machinery of production. A larger percentage were now the small independent shopkeepers in the cities and towns. By far the largest number had lost out entirely and had joined the ranks of the wage-earners.

The rest of the social system was being radically altered too. Industry competed with agriculture for the labor force, and imports from colonies undersold many domestic agricultural products. Landholding ceased to be a source of wealth. The landed gentry, who had once been the local lords in the feudal system, became impoverished. Serfs were freed—that is, were turned loose to make out on their own as best they could—in a wave that started in the west (just as had feudalism itself: p. 603) and reached Russia finally in the 1860s, at the same time that the slaves were being manumitted, ultimately for much the same economic reason, in the United States.

Meanwhile kings sat on their thrones, but they hobnobbed with the tycoons of banking and industry and in imperceptible steps became the servants of the latter instead of their masters or coequals.

By the end of the nineteenth century no government in the world controlled assets as massive as those in the hands of the most powerful bankers (that has since changed, especially in the United States and the Soviet Union). During the first decades of the twentieth the institution of royalty was almost everywhere dispensed with as superfluous. Political democracy had already been becoming widespread, suffrage being extended to an ever increasing percentage of the population; the economic order, however, remained oligarchic, and still is (even in the Soviet Union). Matters had swung full cycle: the élite had circulated, and the new rulers were more subtle and hidden than the old. Social stratification remained, as always in civil society.

To be sure, in a few countries the amount of accumulated wealth had become so prodigious that the proportion of really poor people was smaller than ever before in the history of civil society (p. 562); in most parts of the world, however, this was not the case.

Private enterprise, in the original sense of the free efforts of an independent artisan or trader to develop something, was becoming increasingly difficult just in the countries that were wealthiest. Before the birth of capitalism the artisan had had no choice but to work for a noble patron. Now his modern equivalent, the engineer, was helpless except as the salaried employee of an industrial establishment, since otherwise he could not have access to the complicated experimental facilities he needed.

Capitalism and European Expansion

But we have bypassed our immediate concern, which is the role of private enterprise in Europe's expansion.

In the first place, most of the technological developments that made the "age of discovery" possible were the achievements of private enterprise. With all its transformations, capitalism has never yet abandoned its role of promoting technical innovation. Capitalism produced the "industrial revolution," and the rate of technological change in the last 200 years has been greater than ever before in man's history. Table 38-2 bears ample witness.

It is a conceit of the apologists for capitalism to assume that all these changes represent unadulterated progress (they ignore or explain away the frightening wear and tear on the biosphere) and to claim that they have all come about through the "profit motive." The motives, in fact, have been human curiosity and the human drive towards creativity, the common heritage of all mankind for at least the past forty thousand years. Capitalism supplied no new incentive. It simply put a much larger number of clever people than ever before in a position to give free rein to those universal drives.

TABLE 38-2. Technical innovations in the past two centuries.

Of course this list is incomplete, particularly for recent decades. Some dates are approximate; place of origin is sometimes unknown or disputed.

1740s	crucible steel; lemon juice for prevention of scurvy	England
	roller skates (without springs or cushions)	Netherlands
1745	Leyden jar	Germany
1748	steel pen nib	England
1749	lightning rod	British North American Colonies
1758	achromatic lens	England
1764	spinning jenny	England
1765	Watt's condensing steam engine	Scotland
1768	hydrometer	France
1769	self-propelled steam vehicle	France
1770s	machinery for mass production	England
1770	"footed wheel" (predecessor of caterpillar tread)	England
1775	siphon water closet	England
1777	circular saw	England
1778	tumbler lock	England
1780	bifocal glasses	USA
1783	manned balloon flight	France
	puddling iron furnace; roller printing of textiles	England
1784	shrapnel shell	England
1785	power loom	England
	parachute	France
1787	steamboat	USA
1790	steam-powered ferry	USA
	sewing machine	England
1792	gas lighting	Scotland
1793	cotton gin	USA
1795	hydraulic press	England
1796	cowpox vaccination for smallpox	England
	lithography	Bohemia
1797	carding machine; cast-iron plow	USA
1798	bleaching powder	England
1800	electric battery	Italy
	engine-driven lathe; caterpillar tread	England
1804	glider	England
	marine torpedo	USA
1805	electroplating	Italy
	life-preserver	England
1806	extraction of morphine from opium	Germany
	food-canning	France
1808	band saw	England
1809	multiwire telegraphy	Germany
1810	gyroscope	Germany
	carbon arc light	England

	mowing machine	USA
1811	cylinder printing press	Germany
	breech-loading gun	USA
1812	Mohs hardness scale; storage battery	Germany
	practical steam locomotive	England
1813	public natural gas supply through pipes	England
1814	police	England
1815	valves for brass instruments (musical)	Germany
	miner's safety lamp (Davy lamp)	England
1816	stethoscope	France
	metronome	Austria
	percussion cap	USA
1817	kaleidoscope	England
1819	galvanometer	Germany
1820	cultivator	USA
1822	typesetting machine	USA or England
	electric motor	England
	accordion	Germany
	photographic camera	France
1823	passenger rail service; digital calculating machine	England
1824	portland cement; electromagnet	England
1826	screw propeller for ships	Bohemia
	reaper	Scotland
1827	water-driven reaction turbine	Switzerland
	friction matches	England
1828	safety razor	England
	blast furnace	Scotland
	first synthesis of an organic compound	Germany
1829	graham cracker	USA
	Braille printing	France
1830	lawnmower	England
1831	electric generator	England
	animated cartoon	Belgium
	commercial steam turbine; flanged railway rail	USA
1832	Boehm fingering system for flute	Germany
	home sewing machine; horse-drawn streetcar	USA
	stereoscope	England
1834	vapor-compression refrigerator	England
	electric traction	USA
1835–45	pedal timpani	Germany
1835	Colt revolver; single-wire telegraphy	USA

1836	type-casting machine	USA		linoleum	England
1839	pedal-operated steerable bicycle;			shoe-sewing machine; steam-powered	
	steam hammer	Scotland		warship	USA
	vulcanization of rubber; Babbitt			cocaine	Germany
	metal	USA	1861	machine gun	USA
	daguerreotype photography	France	1862	combination (Yale) lock	USA
	electrotype	Russia		dynamite	Sweden
1840	postage stamp	England	1863	underground railway for urban	
	binaural stethoscope	USA		transit	England
1842	ether as surgical general anesthetic	USA		military submarine	Confederate States
1843	mercerized textiles	England			of America
1844	nitrous oxide as surgical general			processed "breakfast foods";	
	anesthetic	USA		railway block signals	USA
	Boehm system of fingering adapted to			player piano	France
	clarinet	France		smokeless powder	Germany
1845	double-tube pneumatic tire	England	1865	antiseptic surgery (with carbolic	
	turret lathe	USA		acid spray)	England
	saxhorns	Belgium		celluloid; safe-deposit vault	USA
1846	saxophone	Belgium	1866	open-hearth steel furnace; undersea	
	guncotton	Germany		telegraph cable	USA
	nitroglycerin	Italy		clinical thermometer	England
	rotary printing press; steel		1867	reinforced concrete	France
	plowshare	USA	1868	typewriter; refrigerator freight car	USA
1847	chloroform as surgical general			dry-cell battery	France
	anesthetic	Scotland	1869	margarine	France
1849	safety pin	USA		railway air brake; cushioned truck	
	rifle bullet	France		for roller skates	USA
1850	anesthesia by hypnosis	England	1870	pedal-operated dental drill; stock	
	corn-picker	USA		ticker	England or USA
1851	powered flight (balloon with steam		1871	compressed-air rock drill	USA
	engine)	France	1873	vacuum bottle	England
	ophthalmoscope	Germany	1874	chain-driven bicycle	England
1852	passenger elevator	USA		barbed wire	USA
1853	condensed milk	USA		DDT	Germany
1854	skin-grafting; firearm magazine	USA	1876	telephone; microphone;	
1855	Bessemer-process steel; commercial			carpet-sweeper	USA
	dried milk	England		four-cycle gasoline engine;	
	safety matches	Sweden		carburetor	Germany
	Bunsen burner	Germany	1877	phonograph (cylindrical record);	
	rubber dental plate	USA		telephone switchboard	USA
1856	coal-tar-dye synthesis	England		cystoscope; analine-dye staining of	
1857	beginning of pasteurization			microscope slides	Germany
	(beer, wine, milk)	France		air-cushion vehicle	England
1858	erasers on pencils; sleeping car;		1878	disc harrow	USA
	mason jar; washing machine	USA		cathode ray tube	England
1859	internal-combustion engine;		1879	electric traction with third rail	Germany
	lead-acid battery	France		incandescent electric light;	
	spectroscope	Germany		screw-top for bottles; folding	
	oil-well drilling	USA		paperboard carton; saccharin;	
1860s	Boehm-type fingering adapted			cash register; benday process	
	for oboe	France		for engraving	USA
1860	continuous-current dynamo	Italy	1880	systematic use of fingerprints for	

(1880)	identification	Argentina/England
	cream separator	Sweden
	machine-manufacture of wide-mouthed glass bottles; evaporated milk	USA
	synthesis of indigo; high-speed internal combustion engine	Germany
1881	color photography	USA
	wirephoto	England
1882	commercial hydroelectric power plant; electric flatiron; electric fan	USA
1884	photographic roll film; fountain pen; punch-card accounting; electric trolley car; Linotype	USA
	rayon	France
	local anesthetic (cocaine, for eye surgery)	Austria
	iron-core transformer	Hungary
	motorcycle	England
1885	laryngoscope	Spain
	Monotype	USA
	Pasteur rabies treatment	France
	differential gear for automobiles	Germany
1886	commercial production of aluminum by electrolysis	France/USA
	halftone engraving	USA
1887	gasoline-powered automobile	Germany
	induction motor; disc record (gramophone)	USA
	cyanide process for gold extraction	England
1888	pneumatic tire improved	Ireland
	harvester-thresher; ball-point pen	USA
1889	interurban electric transit; steam-powered automobile	USA
	aspirin	Germany
1890	cheap formaldehyde	?
	tuberculin test	Germany
	pneumatic hammer; electric chair	USA
1891	telescopic gun sight	USA
	oil-cracking furnace	Russia
	diphtheria antitoxin	Germany
	basketball	Canada/USA
1892	diesel engine	Germany
	electric-powered automobile; AC electric motor; gasoline-powered tractor; acetylene	USA
1893	electrocardiograph	Netherlands
	measurement of basal metabolism rate	Germany
	zipper	England/USA
	motion pictures; commercial adding machine; addressing machine	USA
1894	card time-recorder	USA
1895	psychoanalysis	Austria
	photoelectric cell; X rays	Germany
	wireless telegraphy	Italy
1896	Johansson blocks	Sweden
	Strowger system automatic telephone exchange; electric range (stove)	USA
	beginning of discovery of vitamins	Netherlands
	synthetic camphor	France
1897	differential blood-count	Germany
1898	radiotherapy for cancer	France
	magnetic recording (on wire, then tape)	Denmark
	spinal anesthesia	Germany
1898–1905	hydrofoil	Italy
1899	automobile magneto	Germany
1900s	flame-thrower	Germany
1900	rigid airship	Germany
	Caterpillar tractor	USA
	cellophane	Switzerland
1901	vacuum cleaner	England
	mercury-vapor lamp	USA
	adrenalin	Japan
1902	disc brake	England
1903	airplane; bottle-making machine	USA
	barbital	Germany
1904	vacuum tube (diode)	England
	heckelphone (bass oboe)	Germany
1905	novocain for local anesthesia	Germany
1906	Wasserman test for syphilis	Germany
	animated cartoon on film; vacuum tube (triode); voice radio	USA
1907	Bakelite	Belgium/USA
	"radio" surgical knife	USA
	tissue culture	Germany
	man-carrying helicopter	France
1908	seaworthy gyrocompass	Germany
1909	Salvarsan for syphilis	Germany
	laminated glass; typhus vaccine	France
	gun silencer; portable typewriter	USA
1911	turbosupercharger	Switzerland
	automobile self-starter; seaplane; air-conditioning; Wilson cloud chamber	USA
1913	assembly-line production; radio receiver; multigrid vacuum tube; hot-filament X-ray tube; Schick test for susceptibility to diphtheria	USA
	multimotored airplane	Russia
	Geiger counter	Germany

TABLE 38-2. Technical innovations in the past two centuries (*continued*).

Year	Innovation	Country		Year	Innovation	Country
1913–15	watertight compartments for ships (whence compartmented tankers and slosh barriers for tank trucks)	Germany		1935	radar	Scotland
					parking meter	USA
1914	full-color photography	USA		1937	jet engine	England
	military tank	England		1938	xerography; first surgery for congenital heart disease	USA
1915	neon lamp; cure for pellagra	USA			nuclear fission of uranium; dive-bombing	Germany
1916	depth bomb	USA		1939	use of DDT as insecticide	?
	stainless steel	England			crease-resistant fabrics	England
1917	submarine detector	USA			commercial helicopter	Germany/USA
1918	aircraft carrier	England			jet engine in an airplane	Germany
	automatic toaster	USA			electron microscope; betatron	USA
	synthesis of quinine	Germany		1940	plutonium fission	USA
1920	isotope-separating mass spectrometer	England		1941	aerosol spray	USA
	autogiro	Spain			methadone	Germany
	condenser microphone (for telephone); electric typewriter	USA		1942	controlled uranium fission	USA
1920f	paratroops	USA		1943	streptomycin for tuberculosis	USA
1921	insulin for diabetes	Canada		1944	corrective heart surgery for "blue babies"	USA
1922	passenger bus with specially designed chassis	USA		1945	phototypesetting machine; first nuclear bomb	USA
1923	wind tunnel; bulldozer; television iconoscope scanner	USA		1946	holography	Hungary
1924	dynamic loudspeaker; bromine from seawater	USA			electronic computer; synthesis of cortisone	USA
1925	circuit-breaker	USA		1947	carbon-14 dating; Chloromycetin; tubeless tire	USA
1925–30	self-service grocery store	USA		1948	transistor; Polaroid Land camera; aureomycin; long-playing record	USA
	passenger air service	Europe		1949	ACTH; cortisone used medically	USA
1926	television	Scotland/USA			reserpine	India
	liquid-propellant rocket; vitamin B as treatment for anemia	USA		1950	kidney transplant	USA
1927	sound motion pictures	USA		1951	power-producing nuclear-fission reactor; first fusion (hydrogen) bomb	USA
1928	penicillin	England		1953	pump-oxygenator for open-heart surgery; cryosurgery (for dry-heart surgery)	USA
	teletype; iron lung; radio beacon; electric razor; differential analyzer (analog computer)	USA		1954	measles vaccine; hypodermic poliomyelitis vaccine; maser	USA
1929	commercial fast-freezing of foods; coaxial cable; airplane autopilot; insulin-shock treatment for schizophrenia	USA		1956	electric portable typewriter	USA
	electroencephalograph	Germany		1957	artificial satellite	USSR
1930	nylon and neoprene	USA			oral vaccine for polio	USA
	synthetic detergents	Germany			tunnel diode	Japan
1931	cyclotron	USA		1958	laser	USA
	synthetic resins	England		1963	artificial heart during heart surgery	USA
1932	polarizing glass	USA		1967	heart transplant	South Africa
1933	FM broadcasting	USA		1968	synthesis of ribonuclease molecule	USA
1934	launderette	USA		20 July 1969	Tranquility Base	the world
	sulfanilamide	Germany				

In the second place, the actual steps of discovery and conquest were more a matter of private enterprise than is sometimes realized.

Christopher Columbus was as much an entrepreneur as was Johann Gutenberg. His voyages were his idea, not that of his supporters. He turned to governmental sources for financial backing because the private banks and business establishments of southern Europe were not yet wealthy enough to launch such a large venture. But he tried some lesser nobles before approaching the court of Ferdinand and Isabella. What he got at the court was money and crucial moral support—he did not become a government employee. The ships he used were built in privately owned yards. The equipment and supplies came from other private establishments, and he hired his own crew.

The maritime explorers of the other countries of western Europe were also private citizens. Indeed, no European government mounted its own navy until the nineteenth century. For combat as for commerce, fleets were privately owned and operated. The commander of a fighting ship was a "privateer" if he sailed under government contract, a "pirate" otherwise, but the distinction was sometimes obscure. His profit was the booty he got, if any; thus he ran the risk and the operation cost the government very little.

The exploration and exploitation of overseas territory soon became too much for small private enterprises. So they banded together into larger ones, selling stock to obtain the necessary operating capital. (Of course they paid taxes; that kept the government happy.) This happened first in the north. The legal pattern used for it in England was inherited from the days when the old Hanseatic League had obtained certain royal concessions in London, and was later adopted for domestic manufacturing industries as well as overseas commercial companies. Eventually there were dozens of such companies, chartered variously by England, Scotland, Holland, France, Spain, Austria, Denmark, Sweden, and even Courland (Latvia).

It was British companies, not the government, that carried settlers to the east coast of North America. It was the British East India Company, not the government, that conquered India, and the Dutch East India Company that subjugated Indonesia. For varying lengths of time in different overseas regions these autocratic profit-seeking companies *were* the government, fighting wars against recalcitrant natives when necessary, shipping slaves where labor was needed, and holding the power of life and death over their employees. Only in the nineteenth century were some company functions (mainly those that had become too hot to handle) turned over to the respective governments.

Would the expansion of Europe have been possible without capitalism? Would bats have evolved into human beings if primates hadn't? Questions of this sort are tempting but futile. The important point is that the final phase of the adaptive radiation of civil society was, in fact, the expansion not merely of Europe but of a capitalist Europe.

39

✕

THE CHRYSALIS: ORIGINS

It all seems pretty grim. Not the whole story of man, but the nine-thousand-year journey of the juggernaut that has occupied us in the last three chapters, especially, because it is so close, the expansion of Europe.

There is a brighter side. The democratic surges of European society in the last few centuries may repeatedly have fallen short of their avowed goals, but they are not to be sneered at. Sparks of human creativity and compassion glimmer through the dark clouds of conflict and inhumanity that have so far been an ineradicable characteristic of civil society in all its varied manifestations. Some of them are tribal survivals, but many developed under civil conditions and could not have arisen otherwise, since they demanded leisure (p. 422) and a complex technological base. Optimists think the sparks are growing brighter, pessimists that they are winking out. Which are right may depend on what we ourselves do. In any case, for all its undeniable ferocity the West has something positive to contribute, certain values so profound and general that all surviving human cultural variants, Western and non-Western alike, can benefit from them.[1]

If this point could be demonstrated through a mere listing of recent technological developments, then the partial itemization of Table 38-2 would suffice. But that is not enough. We need to know what sort of cultural climate—what special "way of thinking," as some would say—has produced all these things. We need to learn how we can use our technological potential wisely rather than for destruction. That means pushing deeper, in an effort to perceive something of the evolving inside view of Western society.

✕ Whenever granted the necessary leisure, Western man is a *system-builder* (p. 332). We educated Westerners will not accept the bumbling discontinuity of daily experience at its face value. We seek hidden ties between superficially unrelated events; we are convinced that beneath the frothy mosaic there are deep underlying regularities. Sometimes this leads us astray (pp. 100 and 276), but mistakes of detail do not destroy

SYSTEM-BUILDING

---

[1] Of course I don't mean that we have already learned everything we can from non-Western cultures. Ethnography still has work to do. But here we concentrate on the West.

the general faith. The faith does not deny that the world is complicated; it proposes, though, that the complexities stem in a knowable (if only partly known) way from some set of simple (if only partly understood) "first principles."

We can imagine a universe in which this would not be so, but the notion panics us: such is the stuff of nightmares. The American mathematician-philosopher Norbert Wiener (1894–1964) gilds the terror with humor by his literary allusion in the following characterization:

> In a world ruled by a succession of miracles performed by an irrational God subject to sudden whims, we should be forced to await each new catastrophe in a state of perplexed passiveness. We have a picture of such a world in the croquet game in *Alice in Wonderland;* where the mallets are flamingoes; the balls, hedgehogs, which quietly unroll and go about their own business; the [wickets] . . ., playing-card soldiers, likewise subject to locomotor initiative of their own; and the rules are the decrees of the testy, unpredictable Queen of Hearts.[2]

Much of the preceding two paragraphs applies not only to the West but to every stable human culture, and even to nonhuman animal communities. For it could be argued that we have simply given a description of what it means to have a *world view.* More nearly unique to the West, though perhaps not enough to set it off definitively from all other cultures, is that our system-building tends to be *verbalized, inclusive,* and *consistent.*

The first means that, instead of just living on the basis of certain expectations, we talk about them and try to assemble our words into a coherent characterization. In our discussion of the Menomini world view (p. 27) we pointed out that they had not this particular habit, so that our act of pulling the various clues together into a nicely ordered description was a partial falsification. Compare, in the West, the powerful and poetic portrayal of the Christian conception of the cosmos in the *Divina Commedia* of Dante Alighieri (1265–1321).

The second means that we prefer to subsume everything under one systematic tent, and the third that we are unhappy when one feature of our world view seems to imply something that contradicts another. In our practical life we accept a certain amount of compartmentalization, but in our philosophizing we like to be sure the walls between the compartments are really there.

It is said that in earlier days in China many a man turned now to Confucianism and now to Taoism, depending on the situation, as a guide for his decisions, with no feeling of unease although the two doctrines are by no means obviously compatible. I was thinking of that when I wrote, on page 132, "It is perfectly possible to believe both that the world is round and that it is flat, as long as no crux arises in which one must base action on both beliefs at the same time." But the intellectual tradition of the West is opposed to this. No sort of drastic action need be in the offing. A sufficient crux is at hand merely when one realizes, perhaps with a start, that one has been holding mutually contradictory tenets, and one instantly feels a pressure to resolve the inconsistency in one fashion or another. As an elderly and devoutly

[2]From Norbert Wiener, *Cybernetics,* M.I.T. Press, Cambridge, Mass., 1948, pp. 62–63.

Christian acquaintance of mine put it forty years ago, "You can't compromise with the Devil." Einstein refused to compromise with the devil of inconsistency when he rejected the current notion that radiation and matter behave by arbitrarily unrelated rules, and it was this that led him to his theory of relativity.

Since I have alluded in the foregoing to both Dante and Einstein, it will be patent that by Western system-building I mean something much more inclusive than science. Science is part of it, but not all. The connection will be clarified in the sequel.

✵ In an earlier passage (pp. 138–140) we discussed the phenomenon of *favored numbers,* and saw that the favored numbers in the West have long been seven and three. A particularly pervasive and serendipitous instance of threeness appears in Western system-building in the form of the familiar triptych TRUTH, GOODNESS, and BEAUTY.

THE BASE VECTORS OF THE WEST

The order is not fixed, but the juxtaposition is extremely common, and for just that reason the phrase sounds hackneyed. It also tends to be embarrassing, because it strips social masks away and hits us where we live, and in our impersonal society we are choosy about the company in which we are prepared to wear our hearts on our sleeves. The good, the true, and the beautiful are the three Muses of the Western world. They form a normal orthogonal base which spans the three-dimensional vector space of everything contrastively distinctive in our Western way of living and thinking. We judge any event and any thing by measuring it on one or more of the three scales.

GREEK SOURCES

One can also refer to this triad with the philosophers' terms *logic, ethics,* and *aesthetics,* which denote the systematic investigation, respectively, of the true, the good, and the beautiful. The first two of these three words are the direct descendants in shape and meaning of terms used by the scholars of classical Greece: (*téchnē*) *logikḗ* 'verbal (craft)' = 'the art of reasoning', and *ēthikós* 'pertaining to morality or conduct'. The third does not have the same history. The Greeks had an adjective *aisthētikós* 'having to do with perception, feeling', but it played no special role in their philosophical discourse. Only in 1750 was the word introduced into the philosophical vocabulary (by the German scholar Alexander Gottlieb Baumgarten, 1714–1762), in the Latinized form *aesthetica.* The immediate and widespread acceptance of the term indicated that it filled a long-felt need.

The Greeks had lots of threeness: three was their favored number as it was that of the Romans (p. 140). For example, Greek tragedies came preferably in trilogies, and the classical syllogism of Aristotle is tripartite (two premises, one conclusion). The failure of *aisthētikós* or some equivalent to win a prominent place in their speculative discourse does not mean that they neglected beauty. No one who gazes on their sculpture, architecture, and ceramics, or reads their dramas, could think that. Yet in their scholarly discussions, as remnants of them have come down to us, they seem to have tried to get along with two base vectors (the true and the good), as though linear combinations of these two could span everything. There are rare exceptions. For example, in his *Laws* (2.653c–654a), Plato proposes three criteria, not two, for the judgment of art—by which, like other Greeks, he means primarily drama: its moral impact (ethics: the good), the pleasure it imparts (aesthetics: the beautiful), and the "correctness of its imitation" (logic: the true). Following Plato, Aristotle in his *Poetics* deals with drama and its derivatives at much greater length. He makes no overt listing of the three criteria. He alludes to all of them, but in a way which seems to imply that the pleasure factor is not independent. That is, proper art is pleasurable *because* it is true and good, and would otherwise necessarily be devoid of beauty. We shall see that this argument—about the independence or dependence of beauty, about two or three linearly independent base vectors—is not yet stilled.

Hebrew and Early Christian Sources

The Hebrew-Christian contribution to our Western triad is even stronger than the Greek, though partly cloaked in metaphor so that some exegesis is required.

The Jewish scriptures are in Hebrew. In Palestine in Jesus's time, Hebrew, already archaic, was the language of religion, but hardly to be written in the dust; for that, and in everyday affairs, people used another Semitic language, Aramaic. Roman political control meant that everyone knew a few scraps of Latin; the Roman administrators knew Greek, and that was the language in which one usually dealt with them. Presumably Jesus used Aramaic in his sermons and parables, inserting scriptural quotations in Hebrew. However, the earliest extant versions of the New Testament, in which—and only in which—the words and deeds of Jesus and his followers are reported, are in Greek.

In Deuteronomy 6:5 Moses expounds on the first of the Ten Commandments in words that have reverberated down through the corridors of time for more than three thousand years:

> And thou shalt love the Lord thy God with all thine heart, and with all thy soul, and with all thy might.

King James's translators, whose English version I have quoted, used *heart* for Hebrew *lebab,* which meant 'heart' in the concrete anatomical sense and also, metaphorically, something like 'mind, will'. *Soul* is for Hebrew *nefeš* 'self, vital being'; and *might* is *meʾod* 'strength, physical force'. The three *with*-phrases of the English faithfully reflect three syntactically parallel phrases of the Hebrew, except that *meʾod,* though used as a noun in this passage, was more often an adverb 'strongly'. Formally, then, the passage had a threeness, at least as powerful a rhetorical device in ancient Hebrew as in modern English (p. 140). Semantically the three are not parallel. The first two are instrumentals, specifying the device or object with which something is done, whereas the third is equivalent to a manner adverb expressing intensity. An English parallel, comic rather than solemn in its effect, would be "He operated the boat with the oars, with the rudder, and with great skill."

Three of the Gospels report Jesus quoting or paraphrasing Moses's words, variously to Pharisees (Matthew 22:37), to a scribe (Mark 12:30), and to a lawyer (Luke 10:27). The oral tradition that intervened between the events and the writing-down of the record had lost track of the exact identity of the addressees, perhaps because of excitement about what all three accounts say Jesus appended to the quotation. The Gospels also disagree about the exact form of the quotation. Luke has Jesus saying "with all thy heart, and with all thy soul, and with all thy strength," just as in Deuteronomy, and then tacking on "and with all thy mind." Mark has the same four, but with "mind" before "strength." *Strength* is Greek *ischýs* 'bodily strength, might, power', an accurate rendering of the Hebrew and, like Moses's original, an expression of intensity rather than of instrument. Luke's and Mark's versions lose formal threeness by adding a term to achieve genuine semantic threeness. Matthew omits "strength," thus achieving formal-semantic congruence.

The New Testament *heart, soul, mind* come very close to our Western base vectors. If they are not individually identical, at any rate they span exactly the same space.[3] *Heart* is Greek *kardía,* which meant 'heart' anatomically and, by extension, 'the heart as the seat of life, of feeling and passion', which means emotion and points to aesthetics and the beautiful. *Soul* is Greek *psyché,* concretely 'breath', then also 'life, spirit' and 'the organ of thought and judgment', thus bearing on intellect, logic, and truth. *Mind* is Greek *diánoia* 'a thought; intent, purpose', thus relating to planning, choosing, morality, ethics, and the good. No two of these three are exact matches for the Mosaic *lebab* and *nefeš,* which may be why the conversion from Hebrew into Greek required the expansion into three.

Today, when someone says "I love you with all my heart" or the like we assume—without even thinking about it—that he is indulging in metaphor. We know (because of the researches of William Harvey early in the seventeenth century) that the function of the heart is to circulate the blood. Would we be right to propose that the Hebrews and Greeks were using similar metaphors? Probably not. Certainly the Greeks were not intending to speak metaphorically when they asserted that the function of the brain is to cool the blood; they believed that this was so.

It would be better if we treated the Greek and Hebrew ways of speaking as based on perfectly serious anatomical-physiological theories that have since turned out to be inadequate. Their hypotheses had empirical roots. Various strong emotions involve a feeling at the "pit of the stomach"; what is more natural than to assume that one of the internal organs located there, the heart or the stomach, is in fact the "seat" of the emotion? The exact identification varies. The heart is widely associated with courage and cowardice, which is why that part of a brave slain enemy is often torn out and eaten (p. 250). The Fijians, however, assigned those attributes to the liver, reserving the heart for love and hate. Again, the identification of breath with life itself is realistic enough, since the two stop at the same time. Furthermore, though breathing is visible, breath usually is not—even when used in that most characteristically human activity, talking. That, plus the fact that we can think in words without uttering them aloud (p. 113), leads easily to the positing of invisible or even nonmaterial organs for certain functions for which the actual physiological ones, under ordinary observation, seem inappropriate. Western theologians, and many philoso-

[3]What I mean is that (for example) anything expressible as a linear combination of base vectors (1,0,0), (0,1,0), (0,0,1) can also be expressed as a linear combination of any number of alternative base vectors with the same origin; all that is required in a rotation of the axes.

phers and psychologists, still do this more or less systematically, as the Western man in the street does it casually, thus prolonging a physical-nonphysical dualism for which there is no longer any empirical justification.

For it is foolish to accept these various hypotheses of our predecessors. For us, if not for them, they must be metaphors. Their assignments of functions to real organs were oversimplified,[4] and their positing of nonmaterial entities has to be rejected out of hand. However, we would be compounding our foolishness manyfold if we refused to consider what our predecessors were trying to say in their terminology, merely because we have learned a little more than they had about physiology and physics.

In addition to the three crucial terms we have examined, our Biblical quotations contain two others requiring scrutiny: *love* and *God*.

Hebrew *ʾaheb* 'love' is like English in being ambiguous as between sexual passion and affection of a more general sort, but the ambiguity was surely eliminated by context. The ambiguity, if important, could have been retained in Greek with the verb *phileîn,* but it is not. In the New Testament one finds regularly *agápē* 'affection' and *agapân* 'to treat with affection', which contrast sharply with *erân* 'to desire sexually'.

God is harder. Man creates gods, not in his own image, but in terms of his social structure, with one or another sort of idealization. We recall that the Menomini, like the vast majority of tribal peoples, had no special political organization, no permanent "Biggest Man in Tribe"; in accord with this, they recognized various Higher Powers but did not assign supremacy to any one of them. The quite different nature of the earliest Hebrew deity is revealed by the words Moses claimed to be quoting from him, "Thou shalt have none other gods [*ʾelohim*] before me" (Deuteronomy 5:7). The Israelites did acknowledge one supreme being, alone entitled to be called 'God' (*Yhwh,* vowels unknown); all other unearthly entities, angels and such, were subordinate to him as a king's administrators and soldiers are subordinate to the king. And at this point in their history the Israelites, who had already been first rulers and then *personae non gratae* in Egypt, were living in a civil society with a single earthly chief. However, they thought of their God as exclusively *their* God. Other communities had their own kings—and their own deities. The commandment we have quoted is not only an assertion of supremacy within the local pantheon but also a demand for community loyalty.

By the time of Jesus this had changed. The Israelites had had further bitter experiences with various powerful empires and emperors. They had promoted their God to the status of Emperor of All Creation. But, as though in reaction to the oppression to which they had been subjected, this Emperor had a nature almost diametrically antithetical to that of the bestial, power-hungry rulers of this world.

In the kind of exegesis we are doing here we must bypass a conception such as that of an old man with a long beard sitting on a cloud, or any other version, no matter how attenuated, of an essentially anthropomorphic sort—without in any way denying that myriads of Jews, Muslims, and Christians, from the time of Moses to

---

[4] For that matter, who today could specify in any accurate fashion the physiological correlates of what we perceive and report holistically as "love" or "anger" or the like? I am not proposing that we know all the answers, but the very opposite: ignorance is grounds for humility and hard work, and cannot honorably be concealed by mystical double-talk.

the present, have held just such views. Our aim is not to poke fun at anyone's beliefs, but to try to interpret abstract and mystical notions in terms of the realities of everyday human social life from which, ultimately, they must derive—just as do the speculations of science (p. 652).

Fortunately, Jesus and his record-keeping followers give us excellent clues. Consider, first, Luke 17:21, "behold, the kingdom of God is within you"—and "among you," for here the Greek *entòs hymôn* felicitously means both at once. Add to this what Jesus appended to his quotation of the Mosaic commandment: "and thou shalt love thy neighbour as thyself." *Neighbour* is an accurate rendering of the Greek: a member of a nearby household rather than of one's own, and, by extension, any of one's fellow human beings. Finally, twice in 1 John (4:8 and 4:16) occurs a short clause best taken not as a characterization but as a simple, straightforward verbal definition: *ho theòs agápē estín* 'God is love'. If we know what the word *love* means, we know what the word *God* is intended to mean. It turns out that the commandment has a verb governing a cognate object: *love God = love love* (like *dream a dream* or *give gifts*); this is a rhetorical device for intensity and exclusiveness.

A mystery-free paraphrase of the whole commandment in Jesus's version is thus "Thou shalt love, in beauty, truth, and goodness, others as thyself." Whatever mystical overtones Jesus's words may have carried for his audience or for himself, whatever ethereal intervening parameters he and they may have reified and believed in, his words meant this, a clarion call to genuine democracy, a rejection of the depersonalization of civil society.

Love is compassion (pp. 122–124); love is affection (pp. 233–234). Not "man is" but "compassionate dealings *among* men are" the measure of all things. The role of love in connection with the Western triptych is not that of an additional—and superfluous—base vector. Rather, it applies to each of the three coordinate axes, to tell which direction is which. Only through love can one distinguish good from evil, beauty from ugliness, truth from falsehood.

THE CHURCH

It did not take the early church very long to conceal all the foregoing under a morass of mystical doctrine and of heated doctrinal dispute. The first members of the church, like Jesus himself, were Jews. But someone cooked up the notion that to be a Christian one had to accept Jesus as the Christ—that is, literally as the Messiah promised to the Jews by earlier prophets. That was more than most Jews could swallow. The church was soon making most of its converts elsewhere, and eventually the obstinacy of the unconverted Jews led to the completion of their diaspora. When Christianity achieved political success in the fourth century, even matters of doctrine became little more than rationalizations for naked power struggles in which whole populations were "converted"—from paganism to Christianity, or from one brand of Christianity to another—by fire and sword. The winning doctrines were not the most reasonable, but the militarily most powerful. As a paradoxical consequence, for a millennium or more the Jews were the most prominent segment of the population of Europe to practice, at least among themselves, a way of life that resembled the teachings of Jesus.

The official doctrine of the church, as it settled into reasonably permanent form, contained an unmistakable exemplar of threeness in the form of the *Holy Trinity* of Father (God), Son (Christ), and Holy Spirit. The last of these is Greek *pneûma hágion,* in which the second word means 'sacred, divine' and the first means 'wind, air; the air we breathe; breath', with the same extensions of coverage as *psyché* (p. 639); thus it is associated primarily with truth. The Son was the incarnation of the good. The Father, as we have seen, is love.

That was fine as far as it went, but something had been left out. The scholarly theologians who had elaborated the doctrine had goofed, and the heavenly assemblage was lopsided. They may not have noticed, but run-of-the-mill peasant Christians—who had mostly been forced into Christianity through no act of their own will—did, and in their everyday church-related behavior began to supply the missing factor. Fortunately, the tradition and doctrine of the church afforded an element that could be seized on for this purpose. Without rejecting the all-unifying God (though the priests must have made Him seem pretty remote and impersonal), nor the more directly accessible divine representations of the good and of the true, they rounded things out in proper Western fashion by adding an archetype of beauty: the Virgin.

It is significant that the addition was female. Most of the pre-Christian peoples of the Mediterranean had had female as well as male deities to look up to. For obvious reasons, femininity is associated especially with creativity, in turn linked easily to beauty.[5] The fact that the church's official heavenly roster had been all male must have been a source of discomfort. On this score, then, as well as in terms of our Western base vectors, the development of Mariolatry rendered Christianity much more satisfying.

The leaders of the Church of Rome did not devise Mariolatry. But they tolerated it as harmless (after all, one could freely pray to an appropriate saint to intercede on one's behalf with the celestial authorities) when they saw what a help it was in holding on to untutored adherents. Peasants, trained by civil society to be suspicious of intellectuality and to suppress their own creative urges (p. 271), and yet, as human beings, inevitably respectful of creativity, needed such a symbolic outlet. In slow steps, under popular pressure, the church authorities elevated the Virgin until she ranked almost, though not quite, with the Son and the Holy Spirit. A major step was taken as late as 1854, another in 1950, and Catholic theologians still wrestle with the problem.

The Protestant Reformation threw all this out. One cannot infer this from a superficial reading of Luther and Calvin and the other reform leaders, but it seems to have lurked underneath and to have motivated their complex theological disquisitions. That is, the Protestant ethic led to Protestantism, not vice versa. Adherents

[5] Something like this linkage seems to have been what Johann Wolfgang von Goethe (1749–1832) was getting at with his coined compound word *Ewig-weibliche,* which he introduces at the very end of *Faust* Part II: *Das Ewig-weibliche zieht uns hinan,* badly rendered into English as 'the Eternal Feminine draws us ever onward'.

Note also the abiding popularity of the cult of the early fifteenth-century Maid of Orléans.

of this ethic in its original form (p. 627) are two-dimensional. They believe in an austere good (and a frightening, prevalent evil), and in an ascetic truth which is hardly to be distinguished from the good; but they allow no place in life for beauty, taken as necessarily frivolous and lacking in seriosity; even its mildest manifestations, such as laughter, verge on the sinful. Nor is man creative (remember the close association of creativity and beauty), since to create one must have freedom of choice, and man has none: a man's salvation, thus, depends in no way on his works, but solely on the grace of God. Protestantism was a grim world view, and its history has been that of repeated dilutions to render it bearable and sporadic repurifications to render it "correct" again. Even today, small minorities cling to the original terrible version.

Meanwhile, the Protestant Reformation was the best thing that had ever happened to Catholicism. As soon as the Protestant leaders had raised the issues, the Catholic Church had a clear, if negative, guideline for its own counterreforms (p. 628), and took active steps to acknowledge and endorse the sorts of humane attitudes that Catholic laymen—and the Jews!—had clung to all along.

✘ The Reformation and Counter-Reformation are neither the only nor the last evidence for the continuing contention between twoness (or even oneness) and three-ness, between a flat or tubular world and a full one.

SEPARABILITY AND ABSTRACTION

The major philosophical traditions in Europe in the seventeenth and eighteenth centuries (about which more later: p. 645) placed primary emphasis on the role of the intellect, thus reversing the relative status ascribed to the good and the true by the Protestant reform leaders; but they continued to give short shrift to beauty and emotion.

Then came romanticism. We cannot discount the words of the English poet John Keats (1795–1821), "Beauty is truth, truth beauty," as an unpremeditated rhapsodic outburst. The romantics, whether poets or philosophers or, like Goethe, both, were out to refute and destroy not only the exclusive emphasis on intellect of the best known philosophers but also the still common north European Protestant claim that pleasure and beauty are mere hedonism. For ammunition they turned to a thoroughly though unintendedly anthropomorphized "nature" (among the English, especially William Wordsworth, 1770–1850, did this), and to classical Greece as rediscovered and inter-preted through rose-colored glasses during the European Renaissance. Thus it is no accident that Keats's line is in his *Ode on a Grecian Urn*. Because of his depth of feeling he went too far, since, if taken literally, the line yields a flat world perpendicular to that of the Protestant ethic. In fact, the most extreme of the romantics (such as the composer Robert Schumann, 1810–1856) did go that far, or farther. But the main burden of the ode is to avow the independent primacy and positive value of the aesthetic element in life; its climactic five words have been cited a thousand thousand times by successors whose aim was the same.

In the long run, three seems to have been winning.

The real proof of the independence of all three of our base vectors, however, has not come in the work of philosophers and poets, but in a quite different way. Three traditions have arisen in the West, have matured there, and have been carried to all parts of the world, receiving almost everywhere a warm welcome. The three developed largely out of touch with one another and with almost totally distinct personnel, each devoted passionately to just one of the three coordinate axes. Despite the dearth of direct mutual influence, the three show some remarkable parallelisms, especially in the degree of abstractness they have attained. We take them up one by one in the next chapter.

40

✖

THE CHRYSALIS: GROWTH

The good, the true, and the beautiful: we are still talking about these, and this is the order in which we now deal with them.

✖ In the seventeenth and eighteenth centuries it was fashionable in Europe to specu- ETHICS: LAW AND ABSTRACT CONTRACTUAL THEORY late about human affairs in terms of *the social contract.* The most naïve form of this speculation proposed that human society—by which was meant only what we have called civil society—rests on a set of legally binding agreements (the contract) freely and overtly entered into by its members. Before or without the agreements man is "primitive," while with them he becomes "civilized." The most prominent of the social-contract theorists[1] suggested nothing quite this simple. But lesser lights did, and although academicians have now long since abandoned the whole business one can still find educated laymen, and a few college sophomores, who think the simplistic theory is true.

It is false. We have seen in earlier chapters that social structure is older than law, older than civil society, older than language, older than man himself. Law is very recent indeed (pp. 567–571); anything resembling a formal contract overtly entered into is even younger.

The social-contract notion, in fact, was a late philosophical byproduct of a *legal* tradition that took shape in Rome in the late second and first centuries B.C. The mainstream of this tradition, transmitted through successive generations of technically trained specialists, has burgeoned into a systematic but open-ended doctrine much more far-reaching and elegant than armchair philosophers could ever have dreamed of. It has been able to do this because the pure and applied phases of the tradition have uninterruptedly influenced each other. Legal theory prevents decisions in individual cases from being totally whimsical (like the kaleidoscopic commands of the Queen of Hearts: p. 636), while the brute empirical facts—including, often, the human agonies—of individual cases constantly reshape the theory, update it, and, above all, prevent it from spinning futilely off into the empyrean. The dialectic connection

---

[1]The Englishmen Thomas Hobbes (1588–1679) and John Locke (1632–1704), the Scot David Hume (1711–1776), and the Swiss-French Jean Jacques Rousseau (1712–1778).

between practice and theory in law is exactly parallel to that between the two in science (p. 652), though the latter deals with truth and falsehood, the former with good and evil (redubbed "right" and "wrong" to render matters less emotional).

ROMAN LAW

Western law is law, so that the nine points of chapter 35 (pp. 565–571) all apply. Roman law before the second century B.C. was apparently very much like the law of other peoples just emerging from tribal ways into civil ones. A codification known as the "Twelve Tables" was made about 450 B.C. The tables have not survived, but extant allusions by subsequent writers suggest that the reasons for and the general nature of the codification were similar to those of the Code of Hammurabi (p. 569).

The legal innovations of the last two centuries B.C. came about through a combination of circumstances. Rome was a republic, not a kingdom, so that a good many people—not women, children, plebeians, slaves, or foreigners, but still a good many—were thought of as coequal in rights and duties except insofar as one of them was chosen by collective action for a temporary post of special power. The republic was prosperous and reasonably at peace (as such things went), affording time for leisurely meditation to those who were so inclined. A money economy established the habit of comparing diverse commodities along a single scale of value. Finally, the influence of Greek learning was making itself felt, especially as transmitted by the Stoics.

THE STOICS. The Stoics were moral logicians. They believed that ethical precepts lie at the bottom of everything, and they had evolved a narrowed derivative of the syllogistic logic of Aristotle to use in their ethical reasoning.

Aristotelian logic includes that of class-membership and class-inclusion: "All men are mortal; Socrates is a man; hence Socrates is mortal." Stoic logic was constrained to propositions: "If Socrates is a man he is mortal; Socrates is a man; hence he is mortal." In this pattern it is easy to make the first premiss an assertion of a moral or legal principle and the second the report of an ascertained fact, whereupon the conclusion becomes a judgment: "[the law says] if Gaius has not paid his debt to Marius he shall become Marius's slave; [the court determines] Gaius has not paid his debt to Marius; [the decision is] therefore Gaius herewith becomes Marius's slave."

The Roman Stoics Panaetius (about 180–109 B.C.), Poseidonius (about 135–50 B.C.), and especially Quintus Mucius Scaevola (died 88 B.C.) reworked the whole body of Roman legal theory and procedure into this and kindred syllogistic forms. To this day, though the original Latin legal vocabulary has been partly replaced by English in the English-speaking world, by French in France, by Turkish in Turkey, and so on, the syntax and logic of legal discourse retain the Stoic stamp.

CONTRACTS. A related innovation, supposed also to have been due at least in part to Stoic influence, was the contract, and the beginnings of the reinterpretation of all sorts of law in contractual terms.

Suppose Primus and Secundus enter into the following arrangement: Secundus will tutor Primus's son Primulus in Greek, in exchange for which Primus will supply

Secundus with quarters, clothing, and food. If this is just an informal agreement, there is little either can do if he feels the other is not living up to the plan. They can argue about it, and Secundus can leave in a huff or Primus can angrily send him packing; but that is about all.

Under contract law, Primus and Secundus can enter into a formalized arrangement in which penalties for default are spelled out and will be enforced, if the occasion arises, by a court as agent of the state. The agreement is still between Primus and Secundus, but is no longer entirely their private affair, since each has the state to deal with, as well as the other party, if he does not live up to the agreement, and the state to back him up if the other party does not.

A contract involves one or more explicitly defined *contractual relations*. Roman lawyers expressed the relations in words, but we can use symbols. Each relation is triadic, of the form $R(P_1, P_2, C)$; here P_1 and P_2 are each a *person* (an individual citizen or human being, or, in modern times, a corporation) and $P_1 \neq P_2$, while C is a *commodity*—a thing (which in some societies may be a slave), a prerogative, a service (pp. 145–146). In our example, P_1 is Primus and P_2 is Secundus. In one of the relations, say $R_1(P_1, P_2, C_1)$, C_1 is the quantity of tutoring in Greek that P_2 is to give P_1's son. In another, $R_2(P_1, P_2, C_2)$, C_2 is the clothing, food, and shelter P_2 is to receive from P_1. There will be at least two other relations: R_3 specifies the penalty (C_3) for default by P_1, and R_4 specifies that (C_4) for default by P_2. The contract might now state: If R_1 and R_2, then neither R_3 nor R_4; if neither R_1 nor R_2, then neither R_3 nor R_4; if R_1 and not R_2, then R_4; if R_2 and not R_1, then R_3.

Suppose, now, that Primus and Secundus quarrel and go to court. If all is in order, the contract supplies the judge with the first premisses of the Stoic syllogisms which will yield the decision. What remains is to ascertain the facts (p. 651), thus obtaining the proper second premisses.

LEGAL COMPUTATION.   However, the court must also determine whether the contract is valid—or, to express this better, whether the agreement between the litigants legally constituted a contract to start with. A written record helps, since memories are easily distorted by self-interest, but is not enough. Thus, imagine that two persons today drew up a carefully phrased written agreement in which one of the commodities was a theft or murder, or in which the penalty for default by one party was that he commit suicide. The judge would throw the case out and might see that other proceedings were instituted.

This is to say that an agreement between two persons cannot be a contract if it is inconsistent with various overriding legal privileges and obligations among people. Roman judges and attorneys had to deal with many cases in which such considerations arose, and as a result legal theorists began reformulating other sorts of laws (originally noncontractual ones) in contractual terminology. The reason was simply that uniformity of terms and format rendered legal "computation" a great deal easier.

We can illustrate with the law that asserts that no citizen may deprive another citizen of his life. If we set this up in the form $R(P_1, P_2, C)$, where C is P_1's life and R asserts that P_2 must respect it, then it is clear that we cannot merely take "P_1" as a synonym for Primus and "P_2" as one for Secundus. That would leave Secundus free to murder anyone except Primus, and Primus free to kill anyone at all. The formulation of a general obligation requires the use of variables. We could stick to the same symbols and redefine them, but let us change to $R(X, Y, C)$. Now X denotes *any citizen whatsoever*, and Y denotes *any citizen except X*. This reformulates the law prohibiting murder as a contractual relation—not one entered into by a specific pair of citizens, but one that automatically holds in both directions between *any* pair.

So when Primus and Secundus bring their case to court, the court's first task is to examine their agreement, with its presumed contractual relations R_1 through R_4, against the backdrop of "general" law. In any provision $R(X, Y, C)$ of the general law either Primus or Secundus is an instance of X and the other an instance of Y. If a contradiction is found, the specific agreement is thrown out as no contract. For that reason, it is of course the responsibility of the attorneys who advise Primus and Secundus to see to it at the outset that their agreement will be consonant with general law and hence valid.

OWNERSHIP. There is a third important difference between most early law and that inherited in the West from the Roman Stoics. It lies in the understanding of contractual relations as triadic (always with a C) instead of as dyadic, and in the concomitant legal acknowledgment of *ownership* as an abstract contractual relation $R(P, X, C)$ holding among any person P, any other person X, and P's property C.

In earlier law, generally speaking, a person's property was what he quite concretely and physically held or occupied (the latter in the case of land or housing). A case is reported in the English Book of Assizes from a time before Anglo-Saxon law had been partly reworked in Roman terms. The plaintiff accused the defendant of stealing and killing his horse. The case was thrown out because the horse, once in the defendant's physical possession, was his property rather than that of the plaintiff. (As a surviving trace of this we still say—wrongly—that "possession is nine points of the law.") The plaintiff might have been successful with a different charge, mentioning the horse incidentally but focusing on the personal injury the defendant had worked on the plaintiff through his action.

When ownership is recognized as an abstract contractual relation, all this changes. The mere physical removal of the horse does not change the ownership. If the plaintiff can prove that the defendant does not have clear "title" to the animal and that he (the plaintiff) does, he can recover the horse; or, if it has been destroyed, he can collect damages. It is in this last connection that a money economy looms important; without it there would be difficulty in fixing on damages equivalent in value to the lost property.

Post-Roman Developments

The Roman empire spread this new sort of law far and wide. When the empire declined in the west, Roman legal practices generally degenerated or disappeared, except that as the church became politically successful its canon law was derived from the Roman tradition.

In the Eastern empire, in the sixth century A.D., the emperor Justinianus set a group of legal consultants to work drawing up a careful compilation of extracts from the writings of earlier jurists. This became the *Digest* that largely guided legal matters for the ensuing centuries. It was a rediscovery of the *Digest* in the eleventh or early twelfth century in Italy that led to the founding of schools of law, as at Bologna (p. 621). The prestige of the schools drew students from all parts of Europe, and they took Roman law back home with them. The expansion of Europe then carried it to most of the rest of the world.

Law was born early in the history of civil society as a device for social control by the rulers over the ruled. Its origins hardly suggest that it could ever be transformed into a mechanism for the promotion of human dignity. Yet there are elements in the Roman legal tradition that actively militate against social injustice and promote democracy.

SLAVES.   When the system was spreading through Europe, jurists found it increasingly difficult to understand how, in a contractual relation $R(P_1, P_2, C)$, the third term, C, could be a *person*. Legal thinkers were among those who struggled against the feudal practice of serfdom, eventually with success. Slavery in colonial (and formerly colonial) territory was more persistent. It did not come to an official end until the nineteenth century, when changing economic circumstances joined forces with moral and legal arguments against it. While the economic factors were unquestionably the most important, it would be wrong completely to discount the legal tradition.

KINGS.   Again, jurists found it hard to reconcile the generality of a law in the contractual form $R(X, Y, C)$, where X and Y can each presumably be anyone at all, with the special privileges and immunities claimed by a king. A general law should always take precedence over a special contract between specific parties. But the jurists had to sacrifice this principle, pretending that everyone but the ruler had entered into a special contract with him and that the relations specified by that contract took precedence over those which were otherwise universally binding.

This issue came up in England in the time of Edward Coke (1552–1634), who inherited a Romanized legal tradition already made strong by such jurists as Henry de Bracton (died 1268) and Thomas Littleton (about 1407–1481). Coke and his colleagues refused the compromise. They insisted that a general law is just that, so that in $R(X, Y, C)$ either X or Y may be the king as well as anyone else. A new law binding on any one person was by definition binding on all. The king ruled *within* the law, not above it.

CONTRACTS AND "THE SOCIAL CONTRACT."   The deep influence of contractual theory on British law is attested also by the phrasing of such basic documents as Magna Carta (1215), the Petition of Right (1628), and the Bill of Rights (1689).

It was this sort of development that led philosophers to their notion of the social contract: here were people—or their representatives—assembling to revise the rules under which they would live together, and what is more reasonable than to assume that something of the same sort had gotten human society started in the first place?

The factual errors of the social-contract philosophers did not much disturb them or their contemporaries. Their writings were read less as history than as hope. What (according to the theory) man had done once he could do again, and what he had done badly could be redone better. Thus arose the notion of *amending* the groundrules. Partly through the philosophers and in part more directly, contractual theory shaped later political events. In colonial North America, for example, the Mayflower Compact (1620) led to the New England town meeting, in which all the adult males came together once a year to review and perhaps revise their rules. The Articles of Confederation of 1781 were an unsuccessful attempt at the same on a larger scale, and the Constitution of the United States of 1789, with its built-in provisions for amendment, was a remarkable improvement.

Abstract Contractual Theory

Meanwhile, in England in the eighteenth and nineteenth centuries, a group of attorneys (mostly Roman Catholics who were precluded by their religious affiliation, at that time, from practice at the bar) turned their talents to the unraveling of intricate cases of property settlement. In the process they elaborated contractual theory beyond anything known before, until it became a sort of calculus as powerful for its own purposes as the mathematical calculus of Newton and Leibniz is for application in physics.

The hallmark of this calculus is its abstractness and generality.

The first point of abstractness lies in that, in $R(X, Y, C)$, all it takes to be an X or Y is to be a *person*. One's size, shape, age, sex, or inclinations—anything that differentiates between one human being and another—are covered, when relevant, by the C's of various contractual relations. In fact, a particular X or Y may not have any such qualities at all, since in contractual theory a *corporation* is also a person—sexless, ageless, potentially immortal. This means also that, in principle, it is possible to *define* any specific person *entirely* in terms of the total network of contractual relations in which he is a term.

That looks like the very pinnacle of depersonalization of human relations. But it really is not, since it turns out that no two individuals, defined in this formal way, can be exactly identical.

Beyond this, the abstract theory, instead of dealing with a specific instance or even with open-ended sets of obviously similar instances, generalizes as much as possible. The following comparison may help:

	CONTRACT THEORY	ARITHMETIC
SPECIFIC INSTANCE	Smith owes 5 pounds to Jones	2 oranges and 3 oranges make 5 oranges
PARTIAL ABSTRACTION	A owes C to B	2 and 3 make 5
GREATER ABSTRACTION	A, B, and C stand in a relation of type T	if m and n are positive integers, then so is $m + n$

Abstraction for its own sake can lead to nonsense, but painstaking generalization yields power. One can first check to be sure one is using the proper general formulas for the case at hand, then operate on the formulas in abstract form, and then interpret the results for the particular case. This is what scientists do with mathematics, and it is what jurists do with abstract contractual theory.

The Second Premisses

For a specific case, laws supply the first premisses of the Stoic syllogisms to be used (p. 646); the second premisses require determination of the facts.

Legal procedures for determining the facts of a case, of course, reflect the world view of the particular culture. It has been believed in some societies—there is an allusion to it in one of Shakespeare's plays—that the wounds of a murdered man will reopen upon the approach of him who inflicted them. The guilt or innocence of a suspect can then be tested merely by confronting him with the corpse.

In incipient civil societies, and in the nearest approach to legal process in some tribal societies, the determination of crucial facts was often accomplished by *ordeal*. This has taken many forms, but all involve the participation of normally unseen Higher Powers. For example, a man accused of stealing may be required to plunge the possibly offending hand into a brazier of hot coals. There are then, in different societies, two contrary interpretations of the outcome. By the gentler theory, if the hand is burned the suspect is guilty, because only the intervention of a benign spirit who knows he is innocent could prevent it. According to the harsher belief, if the hand is burned the suspect is innocent, since he could escape injury only by being in league with some evil otherworldly protector.

We retain a trace of the ordeal in our ritual for swearing in a witness. Legally, being sworn in nowadays simply renders one liable to fine or imprisonment if caught in a lie; a falsehood told not under oath may be immoral but does not constitute perjury. But the trappings—hand on the Bible, the words "so help me God"—date from a day when the witness was literally acknowledging the certainty of heavenly punishment if he gave false testimony.

Otherwise the ordeal is long gone, and the determination of facts in law has come to be like that in science. For this change we owe most to the British tradition of the last eight centuries. The development was slow, and involved three points: (1) the emergence of a jury of disinterested fellow citizens as the arbiter of facts, guided by explicit instructions from the judge, who remains the arbiter of points of law; (2) the resort to "expert witnesses" whose special training equips them to pass on matters beyond the technical competence of judge, attorneys, or jurymen; (3) the evolution of "rules of evidence" designed to sort out the relevant from the irrelevant. The connection of the jury system with democracy is obvious. It is in the application of rules of evidence that the progress of a trial most resembles the procedure of a scientist, especially that of a historian (p. 653).[2]

Summary

Nowhere has the law become a perfect instrument for dealing with human good and evil. Its slow transformation from what it was originally remains incomplete, and doubtless always will.

[2] For a beautiful example see Bedford 1958.

In some areas, such as in dealings among nations, we still in effect have no law. Where laws do apply, some of them are hard on the poor and easy on the rich, some of them are not enforced equitably, and there are miscarriages of justice through human error or greed. The briefest glance through prison gates reveals that our penal practices are hardly less frightful than in the days when a thief was punished by having his hand chopped off. There are legally impeccable proceedings that yield egregious results. Despite much progress, legal "facts" are still often at variance with scientific facts, and whenever this is so the law is wrong.

Law has no source but man. Neither has any other human institution. For all its faults, law is the best we have for ethics, and the built-in machinery for its improvement, though dishearteningly ponderous, is our best hope. Only contractual theory, monitored by love, points our way towards the noblest ideal man has ever conceived, the ideal of a "government of laws, not of men" that would maximize the freedom of action of every individual.

LOGIC: SCIENCE AND MATHEMATICS ✖

What is this "Science"? Merely grown-up play?
An egghead sport? A pompous game whose rules
Can change by mere concurrency of fools
Jealous of that which other jesters say?
Or are there basic Laws of Thought, whose sway
Is now secured by Euclids, Gödels, Booles,
So that we really need no other tools
To find the Truth and put it on display?

Call it a game. But Nature deals the hands:
Hers, ours—and us. Nor are her dealings fair
Nor foul. Though we must play as she demands
Or else not play at all, it is our share
To keep the score. On this she simply stands
Unmoved. Except through us, she *does not care.*

Science is man's quest for information about his world, and about himself as part of that world, that will be both empirical and systematic.

Many a scientist is also an artisan or engineer, and often it is important that this be so—consider, for example, the intimate interplay of practical and theoretical considerations in the eighteenth and early nineteenth centuries without which we should have neither good steam engines nor thermodynamics. But science should not be confused with technology. The engineer seeks an immediate practical result. The scientist (even if he is merely the engineer in a different mood) seeks only information, whether or not any useful application awaits. In the same way, the scientist is—in principle—pledged not to refuse to investigate something merely because it seems evil rather than good, or ugly rather than beautiful. Thus is truth detached from goodness and beauty, logic from ethics and aesthetics.

METHOD.   It is rarely realized that the method of science, in its empirical aspect, is at bottom the same as the mechanism of organic evolution.

This is underscored in curiously inverted form by the common characterization of evolutionary events as "experiments of nature." The phrase anthropomorphizes nature, which is wrong. What should be meant is as follows.

A species invades a new environment. Genetic variation yields populations with slightly differing properties. Some of these variants may turn out to match the facts of the environment. If so, those strains survive and we say they have adapted. Insufficiently adapted strains die out. When, in evolution, selection had led to species for which learning, and then tradition, supplemented genes, the machinery for variation and adaptation had been enlarged, but the same survival paradigm applied as before. When, beyond that, our ancestors acquired language, it became easier for one organism or community to benefit from the experiences of another, and for alternative procedures to be mulled over verbally and tested out in small samples before a total go-for-broke commitment. But there was still no change in the paradigm.

Survival depends on successful adaptation to facts.

The method of science is a natural outgrowth of these forerunners. The major innovation is that in science it is in the first instance only a verbal formulation, a *hypothesis,* rather than an individual or a community, whose survival depends on adaptation to facts. Other factors remain unchanged. For example, just as there is never any guarantee that a particular population or species will be successful, so there is never any advance certainty that *any* twist on a hypothesis will work out or that *any* of a set of experiments will succeed.

We see from the preceding paragraph also that science is a peculiarly human phenomenon, since the formulation of hypotheses rests on a special use of *language* and of various symbolic systems that derive from and supplement language.

ASPECTS. *History* is one of the two basic aspects of science: it includes all efforts to find out about past events through the examination of present evidence (which is all the evidence we have: p. 97). This aspect thus subsumes not only the documentary collations of the academic historian but also the explorations of archaeologists, of palaeontologists, of historical geologists, and even of police detectives or of a chemist examining yesterday's laboratory notes before beginning today's experiments.

There is no customary cover term for the other basic aspect of science: its concern is general or (relatively) timeless facts. So-called physical scientists do a lot of work on this aspect; biologists do a good deal; students of human affairs at least try.[3]

The interconnections between the two aspects are obvious. Both must take off from current everyday reality, since that is where we always are. Our understanding of what *has* happened (history) is conditioned by our notions of how things *can* and *do* happen (the generalizing aspect); in turn, our generalizations are necessarily based on current observations of specific events and on reports of earlier observations.

ORIGINS

We can make science very old by making our definition of it sufficiently loose. Our ancestors have been gathering information for a long time; every branch and

---

[3] Thus, this book illustrates both aspects: in most of Part One and in the Intermezzo we sought generalizing aims, while in Part Two the approach has been historical.

twig of the human family has contributed something to our collective stock of empirically validated or validatable hypotheses (pp. 125–126).

But science as the search for information that is not only empirical but also *systematized* dates back just a few centuries. The English word *scientist,* in fact, appeared only in 1831, when it was coined by William Whewell (1794–1866); in the languages of continental Europe there is still no easy way to distinguish between a scientist and a scholar of some other sort.

Science in the narrow sense began when two theretofore largely separate traditions began to interpenetrate.

One was the age-old continuity of craftsmanship, which had made us human in the first place and which was greatly enlarged in the late Middle Ages by the rise of capitalism (pp. 624–634). The craftsmen had know-how, which was by necessity empirical, and those in any one craft had a measure of specialized ways of talking about their skills as they transmitted them to apprentices.

The other was the tradition of speculative armchair philosophy. The philosophers sought overarching systematized schemes, but believed in various avenues to the truth, of which empirical investigation, if valid at all, was markedly inferior to such sources as divine inspiration and "pure reason."

But then a few artisans began to explore the connection between their own crafts and other endeavors, and a few philosophers, in some investigations, began to rely on empirical evidence. As concrete instances we may mention Leonardo da Vinci (1452–1519) and Galileo Galilei (1564–1642).

Science began when craftsmen began to speculate and philosophers began to get their hands dirty.

DIFFICULTIES

There are two complementary reasons why the discipline of science is not easy.

(1) One is that the findings of scientific investigation are *always tentative.* To be sure, some propositions are backed by much more voluminous evidence than others, and our confidence is correspondingly greater. Thus, for history: the evidence for the date and place of signing of the American Declaration of Independence is precise; that for the origin of gunpowder is vague. And for generalizing (and predicting): in tropical and temperate zones we do not worry for fear the sun will not rise tomorrow, but we can find people who will give us odds as to whether its rays will pierce the clouds.

The most recent carefully checked results of objective investigation are invariably the best guide we have for practical action, but that does not mean they are absolute truth. New observations tomorrow may require a revision. Thus, acceptance of science as a frame of reference for living means abandoning any anchor to windward, any belief in some sort of ultimate absolute. That is difficult. Many a practicing scientist succeeds only within the confines of his own specialty.

(2) The other reason why the discipline is hard is that objective findings can be emotionally upsetting.

In principle, a scientific investigator is never supposed to reject or suppress results—his own or a colleague's—just because he finds them distasteful. But we know this principle is often honored in the breach. A scientist is conditioned by his specific cultural background; among other things, that includes the body of earlier scientific information which he has assimilated by very hard study and which, together with his own contributions, can tend to become ossified as absolute truth.

Thus Jules Henri Poincaré (1854–1912), having done brilliant work in mathematics and physics including a version of a theory of relativity, rejected, to his death, the similar but improved theory which Albert Einstein (1879–1955) published in 1905. In his turn, Einstein was never able fully to come to grips with the principle of quantum indeterminacy proposed by investigators like Niels Henrik David Bohr (1885–1962) and Werner Karl Heisenberg (1901–). If men of such stature can show this trait, we can hardly expect more run-of-the-mill participants in the scientific enterprise to be free of it.

SCIENCE AND DEMOCRACY.   But there is another side to this.

Caution about new findings is not inevitably a sign of pigheadedness or ossification. At the frontiers there are always great uncertainties, so that hesitancy about results that seem sharply at odds with expectations is the course of wisdom. Often a new proposal, upon careful pondering, proves inferior to an older and perhaps less glittering hypothesis.

We do not know what part this healthy conservatism played in the stances of Poincaré and Einstein. But in the long run it does not matter. Each did exactly what a scientist ought to do, exactly what, in the West, we claim to believe *every* human being should have the freedom and daring to do: he stood up for his own convictions, unswayed by arguments that seemed faulty and by experimental results that seemed inadequate. It is not this rugged independence that slows the development of science (or that of democracy in general). Rather, it is the all too prevalent tendency to jump on a bandwagon, new or old, for the sake of cheerful companionship.

LIMITATIONS?

Objective findings are hardest to accept when they run counter to our inherited notions about our own nature.

In Galileo's day even astronomy had this personal touch, for it was important for human dignity—or, perhaps, for the authority of those in power—that Earth be at the center of the universe. When Galileo rather diffidently supported the heliocentric theory of the Polish astronomer Nikolaj Kopernik ("Copernicus," 1473–1543), the educated public was outraged and the church forced him to recant.

Three centuries later the realm of the personal had contracted. Science was okay in its place, dealing with the "physical" world, but should leave life, or at least man, alone. So the outrage came when Charles Robert Darwin (1809–1882) and Thomas Henry Huxley (1825–1895) proposed that man was ascended from apes rather than descended from angels. This time there was no powerful church to force a retraction, but the uproar of protest could hardly have been greater if there had been.

This view on the limitations of science is still with us. Many an excellent physicist, chemist, astronomer, or biologist believes—or speaks as though he believed—that science is fine for everything else but must leave the "human mind" alone. They even defend this tenet by asserting, "after all, what is it that does all this science if it isn't the human mind?"

RATIONALISTS AND EMPIRICISTS.   It will suffice for us to trace this particular view back to the philosophers of the seventeenth and eighteenth centuries. They fell largely, though not neatly, into two contending camps, the "rationalists" and the "empiricists."[4]

All agreed, almost tacitly, on a basic dualism: that is, all assumed a "human mind" distinct from and in confrontation with the physical world. The "mind" of which they spoke was not the New Testament *mind* = Greek *diánoia*, but some conglomerate in which *soul* = *psychê* (p. 639) was uppermost; German *Geist* and French *esprit* are etymologically closer. It seems clear that they thought of this entity as nonmaterial, yielding a mind-matter dualism except for those in the lunatic fringe (like Bishop Berkeley) who denied the physical world altogether as merely the product of the imagination—usually of God's.

The disagreements between the rationalists and the empiricists had to do with the way or ways in which the human mind acquires knowledge.

The rationalists drew heavily on classical antecedents, especially on Plato's theory of "learning as remembering": that is, the information is already in the mind, and one merely has to recall it. Leibniz and Descartes made major contributions to mathematics, and we shall shortly see how this may have led them to their philosophical orientation. The extreme forms of rationalism even proposed that the mind, unaided by any observation whatsoever, could construct a correct picture of the whole world, including all its regularities and the totality of its history.

The empiricists agreed with part of this; at least, they were prepared to accept the proposition that the fundamental "power to reason" is resident in the mind at the outset. But they argued that this innate power can achieve no reliable knowledge of the surrounding world except with observational data to work with.

A shred of the rationalist view—the shred with which the empiricists had no quarrel—recurs today whenever one of us, in the heat of debate, says "But it *stands to reason!*" or the like. In the proposing of alternative hypotheses this is a valid rhetorical flourish, since here logic and analogy properly hold sway. As a *test* of a hypothesis it is invariably worthless. What stands to reason is merely what comfortably fits our inherited inside view; remember it once stood to reason that Earth is flat. More seriously, people sometimes assert "Man has to be logical [= reasonable] to understand a universe built by logic." This puts the cart before the horse. It is not logic that governs the structure of the universe, but the structure of the universe that should govern logic.

THE NINETEENTH CENTURY.   Throughout the nineteenth century dualism continued unchallenged in the saddle: witness the German pair *Naturwissenschaft* 'the science of nature' versus *Geisteswissenschaft* 'the science of mind', taken as coequal but requiring

[4]Among the rationalists, such giants as Leibniz (p. 614) and the Frenchman René Descartes (1596–1650); among the empiricists, Locke and Hume (p. 645) and the Anglo-Irish George Berkeley (1685–1753).

different investigative techniques because the fundamental regularities—the "laws" of nature and the "laws" of mind—were surely different.

What is more, in the nineteenth century an almost empirical justification was found for the dualistic view. Scientists in their more speculative moments had managed to transfer into their frame of reference a notion that had started as part of the Protestant ethic. There the term for it was "predestination"—the same as Muslim "kismet," the view that the world in its entire stretch through time is completely determined by God's will, so that man has no choice about his fate. In the scientific theory of the material world this became Laplacean determinism, named after the French astronomer and mathematician Pierre Simon de Laplace (1749–1827). The material world is determinate. If we could measure exactly the position and momentum of every particle in the universe at a given instant, we would be able to compute in exact detail everything that had happened before and everything that would happen subsequently. The limitations on accuracy and coverage of measurements were taken to be purely practical.

This view gave fine impetus to the development of better measuring techniques. But it presented the scientist with a dilemma. I do as I please: that is, I have, or seem to have, freedom of choice. If I am part of the material world, then in fact all my actions as a scientist are determinate, so that my sense of free will is a delusion (some settled for this answer). If, on the other hand, my free will is real, then it must be a manifestation of a nonmaterial essence, a mind, not subject to the causally deterministic laws of the physical world (others leaned this way).

Some scientists still hold to Laplacean determinism as a convenient working frame of reference. The dilemma, however, no longer exists. Grounds for it vanished with the development of relativity and of quantum mechanics early in the twentieth century. When these are taken into consideration, it turns out that while the *past* is always determinate, *the future never is*. In fact, we can *define* the past as the realm of the determinate, the future as that of the probabilistic. Thus the last trace of this presumably empirical argument for dualism evaporates.

MATHEMATICS

We mentioned above that Leibniz and Descartes may have been led to their rationalist orientation by their mathematical work. Here we are (they might have said) discovering mathematical truths without any empirical observations at all, merely by the exercise of our power to reason.

But that is wrong. Like the Greek geometers before them, they were unaware of how much of the world had registered on them as they grew up—motion, depth perception through sight and touch, and so on, yielding the empirically based phenomenon mathematicians call "spatial intuition." Even more important, they were unaware of what they had had to go through, in childhood, to learn a language. They did not understand the nature of language, reversing the truth about it to assume that speech is a mere outward manifestation of thought (it "stands to reason" that this is so!) rather than, as we have seen it to be (chapter 8), the major vehicle of human thinking.

Most practicing mathematicians are having too much fun to worry much about the position of mathematics in the universe. The few who have taken time for such considerations have tended to fall into inherited metaphysical traps or to speak in misleading metaphor. Beginning in the nineteenth century, a number of mathematical philosophers investigated the proposition that mathematics derives in its entirety from an absolute (nonempirical) logic—a thoroughly rationalist notion. In 1931 this bubble was burst by the Austrian logician Kurt Gödel (1906–). Meanwhile, scholars of a different background were investigating an alternative possibility, and in the third and fourth decades of this century it was shown by two investigators (both Americans, the psychologist Albert P. Weiss, 1879–1931, and the linguist Leonard Bloomfield, 1887–1949) that the alternative is in all likelihood correct:

Mathematics derives from language and from such ancillary communicative systems as writing. It arises in the human effort to communicate with precision about human experience. Its beginnings were the beginnings of counting, described on pages 137 and 138. Its ultimate foundations are thus empirical, just as are those of abstract contractual theory (pp. 650–651).

However, just as in the case of abstract contractual theory, the practitioners of mathematics become hypothetical, not constantly concerned with whether or not a particular bit of mathematical invention reflects empirical reality or will ever be useful in manipulating empirical data (they do worry about the tie between their new inventions and other parts of mathematics itself). This can be illustrated with anything from counting through Euclidean geometry to contemporary category theory, but the first of these is surely the best to use here. Early numerals were limited (p. 136), but our modern numerals have become a system characterized by *openness* (p. 108) so that we can make up new ones from old ones. It is thus now absurdly easy to produce a numeral that denotes no physically existent number: for example, "10^{650}" (if there is any residual doubt, then define $k = 10^{650}$ and consider 10^k). The abstract nature of mathematicizing is shown by the fact that the mathematician normally couldn't care less whether a particular numeral he exhibits does or does not name a physically existent number.

Mathematicians, thus, have become grammarians and inventors of new grammar. They go ahead on an "as if" basis and produce abstract symbolic machinery some of which then turns out to be enormously powerful when applied, with suitable interpretation, to the world. Mathematics stands to science as abstract contractual theory stands to law: there are many phases of modern science in which we would be utterly helpless without the appropriate mathematical machinery.

But there is no evidence in mathematical behavior for any "mind stuff" distinct from the ordinary stuff of which the (physical) universe is made. In Bloomfield's words, mathematics is "merely the best that *language* can do" (1933, p. 512).

SUMMARY

In recent decades there have been widespread antiscientific movements among well educated people who ought to know better; some of these have invaded and disrupted fields of investigation which, twenty years ago, were on the verge of becoming scientific.

The rigor of scientific discipline partly explains this, together with the inevitable tentativeness of all scientific results. The way in which the nature of science is distorted by Sunday-supplement journalists and by Madison Avenue contributes its bit. In addition, many twentieth-century technical developments—weapons designed for overkill, "truth" drugs used for political control, production procedures that work havoc on the environment—are genuinely frightening, and people transform their fear of the technology into animosity towards the science they unthinkingly hold responsible.

The error is patent. Moral responsibility is a function of decision-making, and science supplies, at most, the facts that can be called on in making a decision. We cannot shift the responsibility for our decisions to "science" any more than we can shrug them off and blame gods or devils or inanimate objects or nonhuman animals. But, in their panic, people have been turning to Zen, to astrology, to yoga, to LSD, to any of dozens of outmoded old mysticisms or half-baked new ones, in search of a sense of security. Temporarily they may find it; in the long haul it won't work.

For the truth, science remains the best we have, just as law is our best instrument for the good.

The comparison breaks down in one respect. The fundamental strategy of science is by definition *the best attainable;* in the case of law we have no such guarantee. Science, monitored by love, constantly nudges our inside view so that, insofar as it has to do with *facts* rather than with preferences, tastes, and choices, it comes ever more nearly in line with reality (p. 125). The survival value of this is obvious. We have no guarantee that the truth will make us free. We know merely that, if it doesn't, nothing can.

AESTHETICS: ART AND MUSIC

✖ No human community on record has been indifferent to beauty, and a number have achieved artistic heights recognizable despite all barriers of cross-cultural difference (p. 273). The West is distinctive in that its artistry has been able to draw on unusually elaborate technical resources, and in that it alone has witnessed the rise of an art form as generalized and abstract as are contractual theory and mathematics.

Background

The Greeks thought of art as involving "imitation" (p. 638). They meant, I think, that an artistic creation must in some fashion resemble, or remind one of, something else. A painting of a sunset resembles one or more actual sunsets; a statue of a man looks something like various men; the events in a drama are more or less like events in real life. To count as artistic, the creation must elicit some sort of emotional response in the audience, and the net effect must be pleasurable, though elements of ugliness or unpleasantness may contribute to this.

There are two paths by which imitative or "representative" art may affect the emotions. One is via the emotional content of that which is represented; the other is through the artist's choice and mastery of a particular representational technique. Despite our common humanness, there are wide variations in both of these from one culture to another, so that one may be almost as confused by an artistic achievement of some radically different culture as an untutored American is mystified by an English cricket game. That is, the audience has to "know the rules." As to subject matter: Western painters from Roman times to the present (with a few interruptions) have found beauty in a careful arrangement of commonplace objects on a kitchen table, or the like, and have pleased their audiences with such "still life" depictions; other traditions have lacked this. For technique: both Japanese and Western artists produce representations of landscapes and trees, but they are remarkably dissimilar.

The Greek theory does not seem to cover the nonrepresentational and yet clearly aesthetic aspects of the "practical" arts. It does not apply to architecture, except for the decoration of buildings with statuary and friezes. Some architectural structures are more pleasing than others, but this is hardly because they resemble or remind one of something else, such as mountains or caves or the vault of heaven. "Imitation" does not account for the emotional impact of the coloring and shape of a ceramic bowl, nor for that of purely geometric designs; it does not explain Fameguest's pride in his golden horn (p. 572), nor the fine feel of a well balanced flint tool, especially in the hand of its maker. I would venture that our primary source of aesthetic sensitivity lies in experiences of this sort, as in the taste of water when one is thirsty, of food after hunger, the welcome sight of the sun after a storm, the comforting touch of a mother, the appealing one of a child, the passionate one of a lover. The activities classed as art by the Greeks arose (very early: p. 272) through human efforts to capture these various moods, detach them from their original contexts, and work with them more directly. In intent, then, art is not so much imitation of environing nature as *improvement* over nature.

This means that art must be *ritualized* (p. 232 and Box 18-1). The unusually satisfying experience must be rendered durable or repeatable. The static arts (painting, sculpture, architecture, ceramics, and so on) do this by freezing the optimum moment to be contemplated subsequently at will. He who stands and gazes at the *Mona Lisa* of Leonardo da Vinci (p. 654) may experience a temporal sequence of emotional reactions, and these may change from one viewing to the next; but the stimulus, the painting itself, is immutable except for the slow deterioration of time and wear. This may not be the highpoint of ritualization and is not the pinnacle of art, but it is an acme of stability, characterized and praised by the poet Thomas Sterns Eliot (1888–1965) in the following passage:[5]

> Words move, music moves
> Only in time; but that which is only living
> Can only die. Words, after speech, reach
> Into the silence. Only by the form, the pattern
> Can words or music reach
> The stillness, as a Chinese jar still
> Moves perpetually in its stillness.

[5]From "Burnt Norton," in T. S. Eliot, *Collected Poems, 1909–1962*, Harcourt Jovanovich, Inc., New York, 1963.

ABSTRACTION

We may now ask: what sort of art would be as generalized and formal, relative to aesthetics, as mathematics is relative to logic and as abstract contractual theory is relative to ethics?

An answer is given in a brief incidental passage in a story by one of our most entertaining contemporary writers of science fiction, Robert Anson Heinlein (1907–). The setting is a utopian community of supermen who have surpassed the rest of mankind much as we once surpassed the ancestral hominids. A newcomer is introduced to a pleasant, elderly woman who is described to him as "possibly our most able and talented artist." When asked in what field, his host answers, "She composes moods—arranges emotional patterns in harmonic sequences. It's our most advanced and our most completely human form of art . . .."[6]

Heinlein probably did not realize that he was speaking of an art form that actually exists and that needed neither utopia nor supermen for its emergence. Perhaps for him it *doesn't* exist. For, just as very few of us are challenged by the intricacies of abstract contractual theory, and as no great number combine the special abilities and interest to come to grips with pure mathematics, so also only a minority are prepared to pay the price for a direct participation in the Western tradition of pure music.

Existing artistic media other than music are all precluded by one factor or another from attaining the degree of emotional abstraction characteristic of pure music. Representational art by definition must represent something: if the source of the emotion is that which is represented, it is too concrete, and is apt to have irrelevant connotations of good or evil, of true or false; if it is the manner of representation, then the constraint of representing militates against purity. Static arts (even if non-representational, as in geometric design) may elicit some sequence of emotional experience in the audience, but the changelessness of the stimulus prevents any delicacy of control by the artist of what that emotional sequence will be. The "practical" arts have the disadvantage of a necessary compromise with practicality. Finally, the unique central role of sound in human life, built into our genes by the development of language, as over against the general primate importance of sight, means, I think, that a truly powerful nonrepresentative art must use hearing, rather than vision, taste, smell, or touch, as its sensory channel. Heinlein, in his science-fiction context, was hinting at something like direct emotional "telepathy" with no physical channel at all. That is impossible, but in the real human world sound comes closest to it.

EMERGENCE

Pure music originated only in the West and is not very old there. Its antecedents, and its cousins in other cultural continua, are various more or less artistic uses of instrumental and nonlinguistic vocal sounds (unfortunately we have no term other than "music" for all of these), serving almost invariably as accompaniments for something else.

[6] From "Lost Legacy" (chapter 4) by Robert A. Heinlein. Copyright 1941 by Fictioneers, Inc.; copyright 1953, 1968 by Robert A. Heinlein, and quoted with his permission.

The Greek word (*téchnē*) *mousikē̃*, 'an art of the Muses', whence English *music*, meant not 'melody with or without words' but 'poetry whether spoken or sung'; thus the words were primary, the melody, when present, a contrapuntal commentary on them. A wordless song was a mother's lullaby or a workman's chant. A Menomini swain announced his presence to the girl he was courting by tooting a fife; bugles guided troops in battle or cleared the streets for a royal cavalcade; horns kept a hunting party together in the woods; and more elaborate instrumental music was background for dancing or for sung poetry.

In the Middle Ages a special kind of music evolved for use in the Christian liturgy, derived partly from a kind that had been used for centuries in synagogues; it was in this period that Western music became polyphonic (more than one pitch at a time: rare though not unknown in other musical traditions) and that musical notation evolved to almost what it is now. Johann Sebastian Bach (1685–1750), like many less well known contemporaries and predecessors, composed mainly church music, and made his living as a church organist and choir director. Franz Joseph Haydn (1732–1809) was typical of many who wrote music to serve as pleasant background for the genteel after-dinner chatter of aristocrats. Christoph Willibald Gluck (1714–1787) supplied instrumental accompaniment for vocal arias strung together to tell a story that was acted out, in a stylized way, by the singers.

All the foregoing may be called *applied music:* something other than the music is forefront in the audience's attention. Well into the eighteenth century the only "music for music's sake" was a certain amount of what the Germans call *Gebrauchsmusik* (we shall translate as 'utility music'), composed by musicians for other musicians to perform for the fun of it, or for instrumental learners to practice on, or for the entertainment of their families and friends.

But the skill of six or eight generations of musical craftsmen paved the way for a remarkable innovation about halfway through the brief but intensive career of Wolfgang Amadeus Mozart (1756–1791): people other than professional musicians discovered that it could be rewarding to sit quietly—without dancing or singing, without conversing or worshiping, almost without thinking—and concentrate wholly on instrumental music *for its own sake.* The emotional reactions originally attached to the nonmusical activities to which applied music had played second fiddle had been transferred to the music itself, and the nonmusical contexts had become superfluous.

It soon turned out that a lot of the older applied and utility music was fully worthy of the new use. Earlier musicians had overtly played the game of subordination demanded of them, but, like all true craftsmen, they had known the value of their art and had set standards for themselves far beyond the comprehension of the bishops and barons who employed them.

Also, of course, new music was composed for the new use. Mozart and Haydn got in on this before they died, but the great leader was Ludwig van Beethoven (1770–1827). The nineteenth century was filled by his followers and by followers of his followers. The same century saw a rise of virtuoso performers (some of whom were also composers of merit), and feverish activity by specialized artisans to improve old musical instruments, and to invent new ones, that could bear up under the demands composers and performers were putting on them and that would in turn stimulate the creators of music to try novel things. The violin, viola, and violoncello have not been improved since the days of Nicolò Amati (1596–1684) and Antonio Stradivari (about 1644–1737)—that would have been difficult. But almost all other instruments have been revolutionized.

Romanticism

The early nineteenth century also witnessed the spilling-over of romanticism (p. 643) from literature and philosophy into music, where it has had its most enduring success. Romanticism in music is not a special kind of music, but a theory of what music is for and of how it should be listened to: it is as rewarding and proper to listen "romantically" to Bach's organ fugues or to the contemporary compositions of Alberto Ginastera (1916–) as to the avowedly romantic tone poems of Richard Strauss (1864–1949). Extreme romanticism in words is doomed, because it simply is not the case that the true and the good can be inferred without residue from emotion. Romanticism in music has been successful because it fitted what music had already become: an art form dealing with pure emotion, free of any connotations of good or evil, of true or false.

Ritualization

The ritualization demanded of all art cannot be attained in music by change-lessness, since the very essence of music (a desirable property, despite Eliot's comment quoted on page 660) is a *becoming,* a planned development in time from a start to a finish. A single chord held steadily for five minutes would convey nothing. It is only the interplay of figure and ground, the recurrence of recognizable thematic elements in different contexts, that produces this sequential structure. The strongest "representational" element in music is the vague resemblance of sequential architecture to the seriatim experiences of real life; but the former is better, because it always comes out rounded and right, whereas often life does not. Ritualization is achieved not by changelessness but by *replicability:* one can listen more than once to the same composition. This is easier in the twentieth century, what with the invention of sound-recording devices, than it used to be, but from the very beginning of pure music it has been important.

Apotheosis

When we think of Heinlein's unintentional characterization of pure music we must avoid any easy one-to-one lineup of labeled moods against specific musical features. Only for the complete novice does major tonality elicit "happiness" and a minor key "sadness," or anything that simple. Our everyday emotional terms, like "joy," "long-ing," "sorrow," "fear," are, at best, rough labels for highly composite overlapping assemblages of elementary emotional ingredients. Music dissects these composites and operates directly with the constituents, without supplying us with any accurate way of talking about them—much to the distress of music critics, who have vainly been trying to do so for two hundred years. As a painter may observe a hundred sunsets and then put onto canvas a composite that draws features from each but blends them into something new, so the composer works with his materials to produce in the audience sequences of emotional states *unlike anything that can be evoked by nonmusical experience.*

So, once upon a time, Beethoven premiered a new piano sonata for a group of friends and patrons. One of them said "That's very fine, but what does it mean?" He replied "It means *this!*", turned around, and played it again.

Now

Many contemporary composers of pure music seem to have forgotten its artistic essence. This has always been the case, but the work of those who forget the essence is itself quickly forgotten. Perhaps it is true that a current composer would achieve little by writing a symphony that Beethoven could have turned out as his tenth or Johannes Brahms (1833–1897) as his fifth. But one cannot discard the factor that makes music music: sequential architecture and the thematic development and recurrence on which it rests. Without that, a temporal assemblage of instrumental sound has merely the choppiness of everyday life, thus parodying the worst of nature instead of improving on the best.

Music is technically the most complex of our arts (except, of course, for mixed media like moving pictures in which music is combined with various other ingredients). There are thousands of "Sunday painters." Art specialists may think they do very bad work, but at least they venture to try. The talent for musical composition is probably fairly widespread, but the technical requirements frighten most people off: there are very few "Sunday composers." While the performance of a piano sonata requires only a piano, a pianist, and the score, that of a symphony may demand a hundred highly skilled specialists, few of whom could trade places, no two doing quite the same thing, all using ingeniously designed delicate equipment, and all working in marvelously close coordination. As far as I know, this is unlike anything else in human history. This technical complexity marks music as an art form of a complex society.

It also renders music expensive, and there are signs that the expense is becoming too great. Unless we are willing to beat our swords into saxophones, music may die. That would be a pity.

There are pure mathematicians who sneer at all practical applications, and there are aficionados of pure music who consider any sort of dilution beneath contempt. This attitude is snobbish, unloving, and empirically unrealistic. The man who likes his whiskey neat can have it that way, but he has no grounds for complaint against him who finds the straight stuff too taxing but enjoys a shot in his after-dinner coffee. The role of pure music is only in small part to satisfy the minority who take direct enjoyment in it. Applied music did not die when pure music was born. It continued and proliferated, has repeatedly fed new ingredients into pure music, and has constantly been enriched by injections of the pure essence. The latter has happened to song, to opera, to musical comedy, to ballet, to music for social dancing, to every mixed medium in which applied music participates. The teen-ager who gets a kick from hard rock is under no moral obligation to try to dig Brahms, but he *is* ethically required to recognize that without people like Brahms there would be no rock worth his listening to. Thus, directly or indirectly, pure music has its benign impact on everybody.

41

CODA: WHAT HATH MAN WROUGHT?

We have met the enemy, and he is us.
Pogo (Walt Kelly)

Here we are, close to four thousand million of us, living in an era known laughingly as the twentieth century.

We have learned something in a general way of what we are and of how we have gotten where we are. That orientation should be of use to us in ordering our lives and in planning for the future.

We know that man's environment is inherently neither hostile nor friendly, but utterly indifferent. The universe does not care whether or not *Homo sapiens* survives. Only *we* care—if, indeed, we do. In the course of our career we have become exceedingly clever in shaping our environment to our immediate needs and whims. We have also become dangerously shortsighted. For a century or more, we have participated in a grand reproductive spree, and Western man in particular has been indulging in a colossal energy-binge, exhausting in decades resources that once would have lasted for millennia. As our numbers increase, as our supplies run short, as the biosphere is progressively poisoned by the growth of the inactive segment of the noosphere, we shall have no one but ourselves to blame for the inevitable hangover.

We know that man is neither ineradicably evil nor basically good. From the beginning, men have in general dealt compassionately with one another in their face-to-face communities, at the same time that they tended to confront strangers with suspicion and hostility. The incipience and spread of civil society required both of these social attitudes. Both remain with us today, though with changing circumstances the collective survival value of love is increasing and that of hate has been rapidly approaching zero.

Almost all of us, almost everywhere, almost all the time, live fairly quite lives, seeking good things for ourselves and our immediate neighbors and wishing no one ill. Obvious catastrophes normally strike elsewhere. If life is not constantly scintillating, nevertheless we don't want anyone to rock the boat and hence we have a hearty dislike for prophets of doom.

But the dangers are real, and wishful thinking does not banish them.

Many current problems bear a guise of similarity to issues our species has faced in the past. For example, some have compared the dissolution of the British empire to the decline of Rome. Such comparisons are superficial. The ramifications of present-day problems are different because twentieth-century conditions are unprecedented. Unless this uniqueness is acknowledged, diagnosis is faulty and treatment is at best an anodyne, not a cure.

Look:

The habitable world was full, though not crowded, as of about a millennium ago. Civil society completed its spread early in the twentieth century. The last phase of this diffusion was the expansion of capitalist Europe, during which mere fullness began everywhere to be converted into crowding and overcrowding.

As long as civil society retained a frontier, the Turner effect was operative and one or another empire could remain vigorous and creative. When the last acre of tribal land had been seized, the built-in machinery of imperialist expansion was not automatically turned off. What had been a competition in the scramble for colonial territory turned into head-on conflict.

The War of 1914–1918 marked the change—a change more deep-seated than anyone at the time was able to realize. One European power tried to alter the pattern by abandoning capitalism. The rapid conversion cost more than twenty million lives—that many in the Stalinist purge alone—but was not enough: the Soviet Union has become as expansionist as any other civil society. Two decades later other European countries, and a partly Europeanized one, tried abandoning any semblance of democracy. That worked even worse, and it took the War of 1939–1945 to suppress the viciousness of Nazi Germany (whose regime had cost, apart from battle casualties, another twenty million lives), the cruel inanities of Fascist Italy, and the belatedly acquired European-style ambitions of Japan. Various non-European territories broke loose from Europe, seeking self-determination but mostly following European models. China went about the way Russia had gone earlier, as did a number of east European countries; others tried to imitate the capitalist pattern of western Europe. In the course of all this, the world's few remaining tribal communities were wiped out or reduced to the status of moldering museum-pieces, and the technology of destruction was increased by many orders of magnitude.

Since 1945 the major world powers, properly fearful of the new weapons, have managed to conduct their squabbles in outlying regions, where the local population is too weak to resist and where some local issue could serve as the immediate excuse. This is a new form of European (or European-style) exploitation of non-European territory. Regions formerly subject mainly to economic domination by colonial powers now serve also as the theaters of "brush-fire" wars—except that the conflagration in southeastern Asia, though still localized, has continued so heavily and for so long that the epithet has become inappropriate. The localization of combat in far-off places serves the military purpose of protecting, at least temporarily, the military-industrial machinery of production back home, since that is not where the bombs fall. At first it also served to keep home populations complacent: of course the fighting was terrible, but it was remote and one could sleep at night. But that changed as the life of the man on the street was more and more deeply affected.

Not all our current troubles are international. Internecine quarrels, based on differences of economic status, age, political opinion, social practices, "race" (improperly defined), or religion, go on today as they have for centuries. Contrary to a widespread youthful opinion, they are not much more violent now than formerly, though the identity and location of the participants have changed. But they are given a new and more bitter flavor because of the complexities of the international situation.

And underlying that, as we have said, is the awful fact that empires still keep on trying to expand although there is no longer any place to expand into. Once upon a time dissident groups could escape to the frontier. Now there *is* no frontier. Not on this planet. Not on Moon—we have been there and know. Not in the Solar System. Further than that there is currently, probably permanently, no point in looking.

In one sense the juggernaut of civil society has unified the world: ten thousand years ago a locally important event could leave life untouched the next valley over, whereas now what happens in any one place may affect the lives of people at the antipodes. But the unification is superficial. Homogeneity, of course, would be undesirable. But with our remaining heterogeneity we have not learned how to live together in peace and mutual respect, and there is no reason to believe that any variant on the inherited pattern of civil society can achieve that aim.

Not only cities (p. 557) but most aspects of the civil pattern have ceased to have any survival value. Minor tinkering will get us nowhere. Obviously we cannot return to tribalism. We need something totally new—something at the moment unimaginable.

Man's task in the twentieth century is not to kid around with limited political, economic, or religious loyalties. No institution—no family, no city, no church, no nation, no international organization—deserves our respect and support except insofar as it functions to promote the welfare of the entire human species. Man's task in the twentieth century is to disassemble the juggernaut itself, before it shakes to pieces and in the process destroys the precious chrysalis within. That chrysalis is our only hope.

Can we do this?

Certainly we cannot if we continue to rely on the sorts of political leaders the nations of the world have chosen in recent decades—men with the breadth of perspective and imagination of a bunch of prunes. But it is not clear that other leaders could do any better. Despite our enormous collective ingenuity, it is possible that our problems now exceed our capacities.

However, that is not a prediction. The future cannot be predicted; it can only be worked for. Moses peered towards the promised land from afar, and died not knowing if it would be reached. That is the fate of every seeker after the good, the true, and the beautiful, for these are directions, not places. Yet there is nothing else worth seeking, with all due diligence balanced by a proper sense of humor and humility.

Maybe man is not alone. Maybe there is intelligent life on a planet of some other star, or perhaps, if we fail, chimpanzees or dogs will one day take up where we left off. Since our best efforts may be fruitless, so that man's place in nature will turn out to have been merely that of a fleeting episode of caring in the blind evolution of an uncaring universe, let us choose a mighty granite cliff and inscribe on its face, in letters graven high and deep, the following—

TENTATIVE EPITAPH

To read these lines we leave behind for you
We don't know if you'll ever find the clue—
There may not ever even be a you.

We learned to talk an age or so ago.
It changed our ways in ways we nearly know.
We're not the well-niched brutes of long ago.

We had a chance to live and die in love.
Some think this chance was giv'n from High Above,
Though "God" may just be synonym for "love."

In either case, the biogram for us
Demands that we grow wisely amorous.
If you read this, we failed. So say of us:

Man ran the specter of all passion spent
From infra-rend to ultra-violent.

POSTFACE, NOTES, AND REFERENCES

In the writing of this book, Carleton S. Coon has been a repeated source of stimulus and encouragement. His fount of wisdom is as bottomless as Útgarða-Loki's drinking horn, and he shares it without stint. Differing only in kind, not in degree, is the counsel I have received from Erwin A. Esper, an uncompromising behaviorist with a beautiful soul.

Beyond that, and in addition to the remarkably inspiring and supportive members of my immediate family, so many people have helped me that I am forced to resort to a bare alphabetical list. To all who have a piece of the action, my obeisance; to any whose names have inadvertently been omitted, my contrition:

Stuart A. Altmann, Robert Ascher, William W. Austin, Audrey S. Ball, Gregory Bateson, Leroy J. Benoit, Knight Biggerstaff, Ray L. Birdwhistell, Max Black, Ralph Bolgiano Jr., Sharon Bryan, the late John W. Campbell, Elizabeth Carr, Chester Chard, Irven DeVore, Mildred Dickeman, Thomas Eisner, Gordon H. Fairbanks, James W. Gair, James J. Gibson, Ward H. Goodenough, Charles R. Griffith, Robert A. Hall Jr., David Hays, the late Allan Holmberg, Francis L. K. Hsu, Iwao Ishino, Martin Joos, Gerald B. Kelley, Kenneth A. R. Kennedy, Ronald D. Kissack, Conrad P. Kottak, Bernd Lambert, Louis S. B. Leakey, Richard S. Leed, Alvin M. Liberman, Janice Litwin, Marilyn Martin, Gordon Messing, George B. Milner, Harry Nelson, F. S. C. Northrop, Morris Opler, Lita Fejos Osmundsen, Seymour Parker, Dianne Paynter, Dennis Peacock, Isaac Rabinowitz, John F. Roberts, Ben Russak, Carl Sagan, Lauriston Sharp, Henry L. Smith Jr., Robert J. Smith, Robert F. G. Spier, William A. Stini, W. Freeman Twaddell, Paul B. Weisz, John U. Wolff, Leroy K. Young, and David Zorc.*

To be sure, none of the above shares with me the responsibility for the organization, the approach, the styles of exposition, the choice of topics to emphasize or to underplay or omit, or the errors that have survived successive severe screenings.

NOTES

✕ The following notes tell where the information in this book came from and where to look for more if it is wanted. References are given in full beginning on page 682.

For locations and place names I have relied on *The International Atlas* (Rand McNally 1969). On many topics out of my own field of specialization, *Encyclopaedia*

---

*Of those named in these paragraphs I must now, in reading page proof, sadly report that an additional three can be spoken of only in memory: Louis S. B. Leakey died 3 October 1972, Henry L. Smith Jr. 13 December 1972, and Erwin A. Esper 15 December 1972.

Britannica (1968 edition) has been a useful source of general information and a good initial guide to more detailed treatments.

CHAPTER 2

The Menomini. General ethnography: Hoffman 1896; Skinner 1913, 1915, 1920, 1921. Ethnobotany: H. Smith 1923. Music: Densmore 1932. Native American Church: Slotkin 1952. Postcontact history: Keesing 1939. Tales: Skinner and Satterlee 1915; Bloomfield 1928a. Language: Bloomfield 1928a, 1962, Mss. Important asides in Bloomfield 1927, 1945.

Great Lakes and Northeastern Woodlands environment: Byers 1946. Algonquian personality characteristics: Hallowell 1946. Wild rice exploitation: Jenks 1900.

Proto Algonquian: Bloomfield 1946. Date and location of its speakers: Siebert 1967.

Our spelling of Menomini words follows Bloomfield (see above). For our purposes the details of pronunciation are unimportant, but those who want to make a stab at saying the words aloud can be guided by the following. Pronounce the consonants *h, k, m, n, p, s, t, w*, and *y* as in English (*h* as in *hay* even when it falls before another consonant or at the end of a word). Pronounce *c* like the *ch* in *chair*. The consonant represented by ʔ is made as a brief closure of the glottis, as in a slight cough or as in the middle of the English "grunt" of dissent, *uh-uh*. Pronounce the vowels *i, e, a, o*, and *u* as in Spanish, Italian, or German; when there is a line over them (*ī, ē, ā, ō, ū*) hold them longer. The vowels ε and ε̄ are more open than *e* and *ē*, the former about like the *e* of English *let*, the latter long and about like the *a* of English *cad*.

For the reader who wants to supplement our description of the classical Menomini by finding out about some other non-Western society, the literature is enormous. Readily available and of generally good quality are the successive paperback volumes of the series Case Studies in Cultural Anthropology, prepared under the editorship of George and Louise Spindler and published by Holt, Rinehart and Winston. The series began about 1960; new volumes appear each year, each on a single community and giving references to other literature on the same group. The most complete ethnographic bibliographies are doubtless those of the Human Relations Area Files; the bibliographies are in many libraries, and the files themselves are duplicated in some.

CHAPTER 3

Baboons. A digest of basic information, with extensive references: in the entry *Papio* in Napier and Napier 1967. Reports of field studies: Washburn and DeVore 1961, 1963; DeVore and Hall 1965; K. Hall and DeVore 1965; Kummer 1967; Altmann and Altmann 1971.

Possible avoidance of mother-son mating (based on observations not of baboons but of rhesus monkeys): Sade 1968.

CHAPTER 4

All general biology texts have sections on the topics of this chapter: for example, Keeton 1967, Weisz 1967. The terminology of scheduling: Hockett 1964. Genetics and closely allied matters: Anfinsen 1959; Lehninger 1965; with special emphasis on man, Lerner 1968. An introduction to multicellular animals: Griffin and Novick 1970. Nonhuman animal behavior, especially social and communicative: Scott 1958; Lanyon and Tavolga, eds., 1960 (focuses on communicative use of sound); Sebeok, ed., 1968. Learning: Hilgard 1956; Sluckin 1965. A popular but stimulating discussion of brains, primarily human: Pfeiffer 1955; if you want technical treatment, try: Penfield and Roberts 1959; John 1967; Eccles, Ito, and Szentágothai 1967. Confusion in the anthropological usage of the word *culture:* Kroeber and Kluckhohn 1952. Tradition in birds: Hochbaum 1955.

CHAPTER 5

Classification in general and of mammals: Simpson 1945. Of primates: Napier and Napier 1967; Buettner-Janusch 1966. On fossil hominids I follow Buettner-Janusch.

Primates. General information: Napier and Napier 1967. Anatomy: W. Clark 1959; Buettner-Janusch 1966; Campbell 1966. Behavior: Zuckerman 1932 (general); Carpenter 1940 (gibbon); Hooton 1942 (general); Bingham 1932, Schaller 1963 (gorilla); Nissen 1931 (chimpanzee); Bolwig 1959 (gorilla and chimpanzee); Harrisson 1960, Schaller 1961, Davenport 1967 (orangutan); also good articles and bibliography in a number of recent books: Southwick, ed., 1963; DeVore, ed., 1965; Schrier, Harlow, and Stollnitz, eds., 1965–1971; Altmann, ed., 1967; Morris, ed., 1967. For chimpanzees see also below, chapters 7 and 8.

The importance of touch: Montagu 1971. Copulatory experimentation of hominoids: Schultz 1954, 1964. Deprived young rhesus: W. Mason 1960.

Territoriality and its types: Hediger 1961; E. Hall 1968.

CHAPTER 6

Formal information theory: Shannon 1948; Wiener 1948 (more speculative); Hockett 1953 (a review).

Formal analysis of animal communication: Altmann 1967 brings together earlier work, especially his own (e.g., Altmann 1962) and mine (e.g., Hockett 1960a); Hockett and Altmann 1968 is a brief supplement.

CHAPTER 7

Chimpanzee tools: Goodall 1964, 1965a, 1965b, 1967.

The noosphere: Thomas, ed., 1956. The section title "The Biosphere and the Noosphere" is the title of an article (1945) by W. I. Vernadsky, who coined the term "noosphere" (Greek *nóos* 'mind', here reinterpreted nondualistically to refer simply to human action) to match Lamarck's "biosphere."

Estimates of masses mainly from Lotka 1925.

CHAPTER 8

Linguistics without anthropology is sterile; anthropology without linguistics is blind.

Bloomfield 1933 is the basic source; later works intended to supersede or revise it (e.g., Hockett 1958) correct some of its trivial mistakes but introduce worse ones. Two recent nontechnical books that do not try to cover the whole field are exceptions: Joos 1967 is profound, Chao 1968b delightful. Analogy and blending: Darmsteter 1877; B. Wheeler 1887; G. Middleton 1892; Thumb and Marbe 1901; Bergström 1906; Pound 1914; Esper 1925. Analogy, blending, and editing: Hockett 1960b, 1967. Editing and planning in general: Miller, Galanter, and Pribram 1960. Pivot grammar: several articles in F. Smith and Miller, eds., 1966.

The section title "Language in Action" is the title of a stimulating book (1941) by S. I. Hayakawa.

Washoe: Gardner and Gardner 1969, 1971. Footnote 7 (p. 117): Premack 1970, 1971.

Chapter 9

"Cultural relativism" is in some parts of the world (e.g., south Asia) such a trivial reality of everday life that it is taken for granted without talk. In the West it is the substance of most great literature, but had to be discovered slowly and painfully by scientists. Despite common opinion to the contrary, there are traces in Freud (e.g., 1920, lecture 22, paragraphs 23 and 24). More in Boas 1911. Bloomfield 1928b is a cogent example. Benedict 1934 is a classic.

The approach outlined here has been in the air at least since Edward Sapir: see Preston 1966, and Sapir's own essays (1949). The terms "inside" and "outside": Hockett 1964. The "ethnoscience" or "folk taxonomy" people use, instead, *emic* and *etic* (derived from the linguistic terms *phonemic* and *phonetic*): Frake 1961; Conklin 1962; Sturtevant 1964; Romney and D'Andrade, eds., 1964; Hammel, ed., 1965; Berreman 1966 and Burling 1970 are good correctives for any tendency towards faddism. M. E. Opler's "cultural themes" (1945, 1946, 1959, 1968) show an important kinship, with different preferred technical terms. There is some convergence with the "structural anthropology" of Lévi-Strauss (1963), which has quite distinct historical roots.

Chapter 10

Anthropological struggles with the word *religion:* Frazer 1890; Lowie 1924; Cohn 1967. Collections of good recent essays on world views: J. Middleton, ed., 1967a, b, and c.

World view and language: Whorf 1956; but anyone who reads Whorf's essays should also read Bloomfield 1942. Bororo counting: Lounsbury in Hoijer, ed., 1954, p. 129. Favored (or "holy" or "magic") numbers: Kroeber 1923; Jacobs 1964.

Chapter 11

Notions of ownership are obviously influenced by the nature of the environment of a community and by its economic technology. There are many studies of this: for example, Forde 1934; Dalton, ed., 1967.

CHAPTER 12

King Philip's War: Leach 1958. Ojibwa 'fake chief': Landes 1937, p. 3; exactly the same in Cree: Ellis 1960. Consultation, group size, and degree of formality: Joos 1967 and viva voce. Conformity and initiative: John F. Roberts viva voce.

Collective decision-making and its ramifications are dealt with in the essays in Bohannan, ed., 1967, and in Cohen and Middleton, eds., 1967.

"Tribal society" and "civil society" are essentially Morgan's *societas* and *civitas* (Morgan 1877). The terms "primitive" and "civilized" are barred from this book as ethnocentric and prejudicial. Also, it is quite improper to lump together all tribal societies as essentially the same—they have some features in common, yet show wide and fascinating variations in other respects. The debate about all this (for example, Engels 1884, Lowie 1927, White 1959, Fried 1960) has been obscured by irrelevancies. A good recent survey: Krader 1968.

CHAPTERS 13–15

Murdock's masterpiece (1949) is limited only by the unreliability of some of the reports on which he had to rely and because the distinction between inside and outside views had not clearly emerged (nor has it yet). More recent: Bohannan 1963; Fox 1967; Goodenough 1970. On hunters-gatherers: Lee and DeVore, eds., 1968; Coon 1971.

CHAPTER 13

Recognition of the significance of *we* dates back at least to Sumner 1906. Fijian language: Churchward 1941; Milner n.d. The horse in the North American Plains: Wissler 1914; Haines 1938. Land productivity, China versus North America: J. Buck 1937.

CHAPTER 15

Quaker pronouns: personal knowledge and Maxfield 1926. Language clues to social structure: Burling 1970. Tunica language: Haas n.d. Chinese language: Chao 1968a. Morgan's germinal study of kinship terminologies: 1870. Our examples are from diverse sources, mostly standard (and listed in Murdock 1949; e.g., Spier 1925); also Firth 1970. Kroeber's tabulation of criteria: 1909.

CHAPTERS 16–19

The approach stems from three "schools" of investigation:

(1) "Culture and personality": Linton 1945; Haring, ed., 1949; Kluckhohn, Murray, and Schneider, eds., 1953; Honigman 1954; M. K. Opler, ed., 1959; Wallace 1961; R. Hunt, ed., 1967. The earliest work in this field suggested that "cultural" and "psychological" facets of human life, though influencing each other, were fundamentally distinct and involved different lines of causality and continuity (Haring 1949 is a nice exception). Interest began to dissipate when the participants got their diverse

technical jargons calibrated and realized that ethnographers, psychologists, and psychiatrists were simply examining the same phenomena at different scales of magnification; the only *mechanisms* involved in making people what they are are just those outlined in our chapter 4.

(2) The intensive examination of subtleties in human communicative behavior that began in the 1950s: Birdwhistell 1952; Pittenger and Smith 1957; McQuown 1957; Trager 1958; E. Hall 1959; Pittenger, Hockett, and Danehy 1960; Hockett 1960b and 1964.

(3) Most of all, the insightful work on "kinship and culture" of Francis L. K. Hsu (1965 and, as editor, 1971). I have benefited greatly from interchange with Hsu, but have not accepted all his counsel.

Many of the examples are from Bohannan 1963. Asides (on Samoa, Japan, Hopi) rest less on printed sources than on personal observations and on consultations with knowledgeable colleagues.

CHAPTER 16

Guilt and shame: Benedict 1946. Ascribed and achieved status: Linton 1936.

CHAPTER 17

Age grading surveyed: Eisenstadt 1956. Haida: Murdock 1934. Gururumba: Newman 1965. Kapauku: Pospisil 1963. Manus: Mead 1930. Final paragraph (p. 228): apparently it was, in part, unease about the pronouncements on adolescence of culture-bound "authorities" that led to the South Seas field studies of Margaret Mead (1928, 1930, 1935).

CHAPTER 18

The chapter title is the title of a book by Wendell Johnson (1946). Windigo and amok: sources via Honigman 1954, pp. 378–381.

CHAPTER 20

Fiji: B. Thomson 1908; Roth 1954. Potlatch: Underhill 1953, chapter 13 and the bibliography on p. 354, note 14. The invention of the soul: Tylor 1871 (later theories are elaborations or variants, not alternatives).

CHAPTER 21

Slavery during the expansion of Europe: D. Davis 1966 (European view); Freyre 1933 (impact on Brazil); Herskovits and Herskovits 1934; Herskovits 1941.

Jamaica: Wiseman 1950; Roberts 1955; Carley 1963; M. Smith 1962 (family structure); *The Gleaner geography and history* 1967.

The Maroons: McMillan n.d.; Beckwith 1929; the ethnographically sophisticated visitor to Accompong mentioned on page 267 was the dancer Katherine Dunham (1946). I am indebted to Audrey S. Ball for letting me use her term report on the

Maroons (Department of Sociology and Anthropology, University of Georgia, May 1969) as an initial source of orientation (and, indeed, for many of the facts).

CHAPTER 22

Page 276: on the importance of extremes (not tabulated here): Kroeber 1955.

CHAPTER 23: INTERMEZZO

"Of Time and the River" is, of course, the name of the famous novel (1935) by Thomas Clayton Wolfe.

Genetics, variation and selection, organic evolution, speciation: Simpson 1949, 1953, 1958; Mayr 1963; Dobzhansky 1951, 1956, 1962. Innovation in tradition (other than language): Barnett 1953. Language change: Bloomfield 1933; Hockett 1958 (on sound change, few of the books written more recently are reliable). Parallels in genetic and language change, and the comparative method: Greenberg 1959; Stevick 1963; Diebold 1964. Holmes and Turner effects: Lief, ed., 1929; Turner 1920.

PART TWO

CHRONOLOGY. For the ethnographic present (p. 3), intercalibration of calendrical systems makes it possible to give the dates of many events with fair accuracy.

For the enormous stretch of Earth's history before human record-keeping and year-counting, dating requires other and more devious methods. The specialists in this are the palaeontologists, geologists, and astronomers. Because they keep cross-checking the results of old methods and occasionally discover new ones, their estimates of ages and durations keep changing—usually upwards. The early dates given in this book are thus not only rough but also tentative.

Oakley 1964 is a fine survey of the dating techniques of greatest relevance for late prehuman and early human times, but the book appeared too early to allow for two recent developments: (1) The dating of the Quaternary Ice Age is undergoing radical revision (Turekian, ed., 1971), so that some hominid fossils are two or perhaps three times as old as we formerly thought they were. (2) Wegener's theory of continental drift (Wegener 1920) has been revived on the basis of extensive new evidence, particularly from the sea bottoms, altering our notions of how Earth's structure changes and making geochronology a whole new ball game—hardly a month goes by without new articles on this (e.g., Dietz and Holden 1970; Dickinson 1971).

In the other direction, it is suspected that many radiocarbon datings achieved a decade or so ago erred on the high side: Renfrew 1971.

CHAPTER 24

Solar System: Whipple 1968. Universe and cosmology: Weizsäcker 1948; Sciama 1961; Bonnor 1964. Structure and (early) history of Earth: Gamow 1941; Hurley 1959; Emmons and others 1960; Shklovskii and Sagan 1966; Viorst 1967; Cloud 1968a; Drake, ed., 1968. Earliest fossils: Barghoorn 1971. Possibility of extraterrestial life: Jones 1940; Ovenden 1962; Shklovskii and Sagan 1966. Water: K. Davis and Day 1961; Furon 1963. Origins of life: Schrödinger 1945; Alexander 1948; Szent-Györgyi 1948; Blum 1955; Adler 1957; Rush 1957; Asimov 1961; Oparin 1961 and 1964; Wooldridge 1966; Shklovskii and Sagan 1966. From precells to cells via symbiosis: Margulis 1971. Metazoan origins: Cloud 1968b. Plants: Haupt 1956; Bold 1964. Invertebrates: Buchsbaum 1948. Animal history: Simpson 1949 and especially Romer 1959.

CHAPTERS 25–27

"The Emergence of Man" is the title of a fine popular book (1969) by J. E. Pfeiffer.

These chapters are a radical revision and enlargement of Hockett and Ascher 1964 (in a sense, the whole book is). Though there are many changes, a few passages have been lifted verbatim.[1] In that article we gave the following important references that have not yet been cited in this book: Bartholomew and Birdsell 1953; Chance 1961; Coon 1962; Count 1958; DuBrul 1958; Hewes 1961; Oakley 1961, 1962; Romer 1958; Schultz 1961; Sahlins 1959; E. Smith 1913; Spuhler 1959; Washburn 1959, 1960.

Added references. General, ecology, fossils, anatomy: Washburn, ed., 1963; Howell and Bourlière, eds., 1963; Hunt, Straus, and Wolman, eds., 1965; Buettner-Janusch 1966; Campbell 1966; Washburn and Jay, eds., 1968; Montagu, ed., 1968; Emiliani 1968; Livingstone 1969; Brace, Nelson, and Korn 1971. Handedness and lateral differentiation: Lenneberg 1967; Gazzaniga 1967; Alvin M. Liberman viva voce. Small mouth: Lenneberg 1967. Bipedalism: Napier 1967. Buttocks: Montagu 1966. Brain and skull: Weidenreich 1941; Holloway 1966. Hairlessness: LaBarre 1964; Montagu 1971. Glottis and velum: Lieberman, Klatt, and Wilson 1969; Lieberman and Crelin 1971. Vocal-auditory versus gestural communication: Hewes 1968. Fire: Oakley 1955; L. S. B. Leakey viva voce. Neanderthals: Jelinek 1969.

Archaeological evidence and interpretation: mainly Chard 1969; sometimes G. Clark and Piggott 1967; also Mewhinney 1957; Oakley 1959; Bordes 1968.

Human racial differentiation. Coon 1962, 1965; review of the former by Birdsell 1963; Kennedy 1971. Mainly I follow Coon—particularly as to the antiquity of human racial *differentiation* and on the point that (in my terms) the sapiens complex must have reached different groups of hominids at different times. I disagree as to the meaningfulness of classing human populations into any small number of *races,* as to the long-term stability of geographically distributed racial types (here I am persuaded by Kennedy 1971 supplemented by consultation with him), and as to the possibility that different sets of hominids passed from pre-sapiens to sapiens independently.

CHAPTERS 28–41

Coon 1955.

[1] For this self-plagiarism I have not only Robert Ascher's consent but also the kind permission of The University of Chicago Press, holders of the copyright on *Current Anthropology,* in which journal (5.135–147, June 1964) the article in question was first published.

CHAPTERS 28–32

Chard 1969; G. Clark and Piggott 1967.

CHAPTER 28

Australia: MacIntosh 1963; Mulvaney 1969. New World: Jennings and Norbeck, eds., 1964; Bryan 1965; Willey 1966; Jennings 1968; Bryan 1969; MacNeish 1971. Spread of knowledge of fire-making: Lowie 1934. Sinew-backed bow: Wissler 1923.

CHAPTER 29

Plants: Haupt 1956; Bold 1964; Keeton 1967; Weisz 1967.

Great Basin and California Indians: Underhill 1953, chapters 11 and 12 and references cited. Colorado River tribes: Spier 1933. Glacial lakes wild rice: Jenks 1900. Klamath River tribes: Kroeber, ed., 1925, under "Karok." For all these also Kroeber 1939; for western North America also Leslie Spier's seminars at Yale University, 1936–1938.

CHAPTER 30

Agricultural origins in general: Higgs and Jarman 1969; Harlan 1971. Southwest Asia: H. Wright 1970; G. Wright 1971. Central China: Ho 1969. Southeast Asia: Sharp 1962; Gorman 1969, 1971; Solheim 1971. New Guinea: J. Watson 1965. Africa: Davies, Hugot, and Seddon 1968. Ryukyus: Pearson 1969.

Horse: Hančar 1956. Reindeer: Laufer 1917. Cattle in Africa: Herskovits 1926. See also the regional references given below for chapters 33–37.

CHAPTERS 31 AND 32

The distribution of arts and crafts used to be a greater anthropological passion than it is now, so that systematic information is more abundant in older books: Tylor 1871 (e.g., string figures); Marett 1912; Wissler 1923; Kroeber 1923 (e.g., arch and dome); Dixon 1928; Sayce 1933; Lowie 1934. Singer, Holmyard, and Hall 1954–1958 is excellent for the Old World. Coon 1955 refers repeatedly to Forbes 1950.

Early copper at Çayönü Tepesi: Çamber and Braidwood 1970. Aboriginal North American cold-wrought copper: G. Phillips 1925.

CHAPTERS 33–37

For what is traditionally called the "ancient world," *The Cambridge Ancient History* (latest edition 1961–) is an outstanding source. Southeast Asia generally: Mellaart 1965. Egypt: Breasted 1909; Aldred 1965. Anatolia: Lloyd 1967. Mesopotamia and Iran: Braidwood 1952; Ghirshman 1954; Mallowar 1965. Phoenicians: Harden 1962. Greece: Hammond 1959. Hellenistic period: Rostovtzeff 1941. Rome: Cary 1954. Byzantium: Ostrogorski 1956.

Indus Valley and South Asia: M. Wheeler 1959, 1966. China: Needham 1954–; Goodrich 1959; Wm. Watson 1966. Central Eurasia: E. Phillips 1965.

High civil societies of the New World: von Hagen 1957; Bushnell 1968. Aztecs: Caso 1953. Maya: Tozzer, ed., 1940; J. Thompson 1954. Peru: J. Mason 1957. Their termination by the Spanish: Prescott 1843, 1847.

CHAPTER 33

The theory elaborated here derives from that of Adams 1966; see also Braidwood and Willey, eds., 1962.

CHAPTER 35

History of writing (in Old World): Diringer 1951; Gelb 1952. Quipus: Ascher and Ascher 1969. The golden horn: Gordon 1927, pp. 166 and 240; the golden safety pin: C. Buck 1933, p. 26.

CHAPTER 36

Indo-European. Introductory: Meillet 1937. Chronology: Trager and Smith 1950. Some data from Prokosch 1938. Inferences from vocabulary: Benveniste 1969. Correlations with biogeography and archaeological evidence: Thieme 1954, 1964; more convincingly, Gimbutas 1963.

CHAPTER 38

History of capitalism: Sombart 1916–1927; no English translation, but Nussbaum 1933 is based on it; Cox 1959. Capitalism and the Protestant ethic: Weber 1904–1905.

CHAPTERS 39 AND 40

The triggering inspiration for these chapters came at a conference in the summer of 1962 at Burg Wartenstein (Wenner-Gren Foundation for Anthropological Research), chiefly from F. S. C. Northrop.

Law: J. Smith 1964. Stoic logic: Mates 1961.

Science: Sarton 1927–1948 is the standard history; Reichenbach 1951. Interplay of practice and theory illustrated in thermodynamics: Cardwell 1971. Mathematics: Boyer 1968 (history); Barker 1964 (survey of "philosophies"); Gödel 1931; Bloomfield 1935, 1946; Aleksandrov 1956.

Music: Grout 1960; Austin 1966; Sachs 1940 (instruments).

REFERENCES ✕ In a reference to a serial publication, a period precedes page numbers, a colon precedes the number of a "number" or "part" of a volume. Thus "27.3–20" means volume 27, pages 3 through 20; "27:2" means volume 27, number 2.

ADAMS, R. McC. 1966: *The evolution of urban society,* Aldine, Chicago.
ADLER, I. 1957: *How life began,* John Day, New York.
ALDRED, C. 1965: *Egypt to the end of the Old Kingdom,* Thames and Hudson, London; McGraw-Hill, New York.

POSTFACE, NOTES, AND REFERENCES

ALEKSANDROV, A. D. 1956: "A general view of mathematics," in A. D. Aleksandrov, A. N. Kolmogorov, and M. A. Lavrent'ev (eds.) *Mathematics: Its content, methods, and meaning,* vol. 1 (in Russian). English translations, American Mathematical Society, Providence, R.I., 1962–1963, 3 vols.

ALEXANDER, J. 1948: *Life: Its nature and origin,* Reinhold, New York.

ALTMAN, P. L., AND D. S. DITTMER (eds.) 1972: *Biology data book,* 2d ed., vol. 1. Federation of American Societies for Experimental Biology, Bethesda, Md.

ALTMANN, S. A. 1962: "Social behavior of anthropoid primates: Analysis of recent concepts," in E. L. Bliss (ed.) *Roots of behavior,* Harper, New York.

———— 1967: "The structure of primate social communication," in Altmann (ed.) 1967.

ALTMANN, S. A. (ED.) 1967: *Social communication among primates,* The University of Chicago Press, Chicago.

ALTMANN, S. A., AND J. ALTMANN 1971: *Baboon ecology,* The University of Chicago Press, Chicago.

ANFINSEN, C. B. 1959: *The molecular basis of evolution,* Wiley, New York.

ASCHER, M., AND R. ASCHER 1969: "Code of ancient Peruvian knotted cords (quipus)," *Nature,* 222.529–533 (10 May).

ASIMOV, I. 1961: *The wellsprings of life,* New American Library, New York.

AUSTIN, W. W. 1966: *Music in the twentieth century,* Norton, New York.

BARGHOORN, E. S. 1971: "The oldest fossils," *Scientific American,* 224.30–42 (May).

BARKER, S. F. 1964: *Philosophy of mathematics,* Prentice-Hall, Englewood Cliffs, N.J.

BARNETT, H. G. 1953: *Innovation: The basis of cultural change,* McGraw-Hill, New York.

BARTHOLOMEW, G. A., JR., AND J. B. BIRDSELL 1953: "Ecology and the protohominids," *American Anthropologist,* 55.481–498.

BECKWITH, M. W. 1929: *Black roadways: A study of Jamaican folk life,* The University of North Carolina Press, Chapel Hill.

BEDFORD, S. 1958: *The best we can do,* Collins, London. Published the same year in the United States with the title, *The trial of Dr. Adams,* Simon & Schuster, New York.

BENEDICT, R. 1934: *Patterns of culture,* Houghton Mifflin, Boston.

———— 1946: *The chrysanthemum and the sword,* Houghton Mifflin, Boston.

BENVENISTE, É. 1969: *Le vocabulaire des institutions indo-européennes,* Editions de Minuit, Paris, 2 vols.

BERGSTRÖM, G. A. 1906: *On blendings of synonymous or cognate expressions in English,* H. Ohlsson, Lund.

BERREMAN, G. 1966: "Anemic and emetic analysis in social anthropology," *American Anthropologist,* 68.346–354.

BINGHAM, H. C. 1932: *Gorillas in a native habitat,* Carnegie Institute of Washington Publication 426.

BIRDSELL, J. B. 1963: Review of Coon 1962, *Quarterly Review of Biology,* 38.178–185.

BIRDWHISTELL, R. L. 1952: *Introduction to kinesics,* U.S. Department of State, Foreign Service Institute, Washington, D.C.

BLOOMFIELD, L. 1927: "Literate and illiterate speech," *American Speech*, 2.432–439 (July).

———— 1928a: *Menomini texts,* Publications of the American Ethnological Society, 12.

———— 1928b: "The story of Bad Owl," *Atti del XXII Congresso Internazionale degli Americanisti*, 2.23–34.

———— 1933: *Language,* Henry Holt, New York.

———— 1935: "Linguistic aspects of science," *Philosophy of Science*, 2.499–517.

———— 1936: "Language or ideas?" *Language*, 12.89–95.

———— 1942: "Philosophical aspects of language," in *Studies in the history of culture: The disciplines of the humanities (presented to Waldo Gifford Leland)*, Menasha, Wis.

———— 1943: "Meaning," *Monatshefte für deutschen Unterricht*, 35.101–106.

———— 1945: "About foreign language teaching," *The Yale Review*, 34.625–641.

———— 1946: "Algonquian," in Hoijer (ed.) 1946.

———— 1962: *The Menomini language,* Yale University Press, New Haven, Conn.

———— (mss.): Menomini-English lexicon.

BLUM, H. F. 1968: *Time's arrow and evolution,* 3d ed., Princeton University Press, Princeton, N.J.

BOAS, F. 1911: *The mind of primitive man,* Macmillan, New York.

BOHANNAN, P. 1963: *Social anthropology,* Holt, New York.

BOHANNAN, P. (ed.) 1967: *Law and warfare: Studies in the anthropology of conflict,* The Natural History Press, Garden City, N.Y.

BOLD, H. C. 1964: *The plant kingdom,* 2d ed., Prentice-Hall, Englewood Cliffs, N.J.

BOLWIG, N. A. 1959: "A study of nests built by mountain gorillas and chimpanzee," *South African Journal of Science*, 55.286–291.

BONNOR, W. 1964: *The mystery of the expanding universe,* Macmillan, New York.

BORDES, F. 1968: *The Old Stone Age,* George Weidenfeld and Nicolson, London; McGraw-Hill, New York.

BOYER, C. B. 1968: *A history of mathematics,* Wiley, New York.

BRACE, C. L., H. NELSON, AND N. KORN 1971: *Atlas of fossil man,* Holt, New York.

BRAIDWOOD, R. J. 1952: *The Near East and the foundations of civilization,* Oregon State System of Higher Education, Eugene.

BRAIDWOOD, R. J., AND G. P. WILLEY (EDS.) 1962: *Courses toward urban life: Archeological considerations of some cultural alternates,* Viking Fund Publications in Anthropology 32, Wenner-Gren Foundation for Anthropological Research, New York.

BREASTED, J. H. 1909: *A history of Egypt from the earliest times to the Persian conquest,* 2d rev. ed., Hodder and Stoughton, London; Scribner, New York, 1912.

BROCKELMAN, C. 1947: *History of the Islamic peoples* (in German). English translation, Putnam, New York, 1947.

BRYAN, A. L. 1965: *Paleo-American prehistory,* Occasional papers of the Museum, Idaho State University, no. 6, Pocatello.

———— 1969: "Early man in America and the late Pleistocene chronology of western Canada and Alaska," *Current Anthropology*, 10.339–365 (October). With comments and discussion by colleagues.

BUCHSBAUM, R. 1948: *Animals without backbones,* 2d ed., The University of Chicago Press, Chicago.

Buck, C. D. 1928: *A grammar of Oscan and Umbrian,* 2d ed., Ginn, Boston.

———— 1933: *A comparative grammar of Latin and Greek,* The University of Chicago Press, Chicago.

Buck, J. L. 1937: *Land utilization in China,* The University of Nanking, 3 vols. Reprinted by Paragon Book Reprint Corporation, New York, 1964.

Buettner-Janusch, L. 1966: *Origins of man: physical anthropology,* Wiley, New York.

Burling, R. 1970: *Man's many voices: Language in its cultural context,* Holt, New York.

Bushnell, G. H. S. 1968: *The first Americans,* Thames and Hudson, London; McGraw-Hill, New York.

Byers, D. S. 1946: "The environment of the northeast," in Johnson (ed.) 1946.

Çamber, H., and R. J. Braidwood 1970: "An early farming village in Turkey," *Scientific American,* 222.50–56 (March).

The Cambridge Ancient History, rev. ed. 1961–, Cambridge University Press, London.

Campbell, B. G. 1966: *Human evolution: An introduction to man's adaptations,* Aldine, Chicago.

Cardwell, D. S. L. 1971: *From Watt to Clausius,* Cornell University Press, Ithaca, N.Y.

Carley, M. M. 1963: *Jamaica: The old and the new,* G. Allen, London.

Carpenter, C. R. 1940: *A field study of the behavior and social relations of the gibbon,* Comparative Psychology Monographs, 16:5.

Cary, M. 1954: *A history of Rome down to the reign of Constantine,* 2d ed., Macmillan, London.

Caso, A. 1953: *El pueblo del sol,* Fondo de Cultura Económica, México. English translation, *The Aztecs: People of the sun,* University of Oklahoma Press, Norman, 1959.

Chance, M. R. A. 1961: "The nature and special features of the instinctive social bond of primates," in Washburn (ed.) 1961.

Chao, Y. R. 1968a: *A grammar of spoken Chinese,* University of California Press, Berkeley and Los Angeles.

———— 1968b: *Language and symbolic systems,* Cambridge University Press, London.

Chapple, E. D., and C. S. Coon 1942: *Principles of anthropology,* Holt, New York.

Chard, C. S. 1969: *Man in prehistory,* McGraw-Hill, New York.

Churchward, C. M. 1941: *A new Fijian grammar,* Australasian Medical Publishing Company, (Sydney?).

Clark, G., and S. Piggott 1967: *Prehistoric societies,* Knopf, New York.

Clark, W. E. LeGros 1959: *The antecedents of man: An introduction to the evolution of the primates,* Edinburgh University Press, Edinburgh; Quadrangle, Chicago, 1960.

Cleaver, E. 1968: *Soul on ice,* McGraw-Hill, New York.

Cloud, P. E. 1968a: "Atmospheric and hydrospheric evolution of the primitive Earth," *Science,* 160.729–735 (17 May).

———— 1968b: "Pre-Metazoan evolution and the origins of the Metazoa," in Drake (ed.) 1968.

Cohen, R., and J. Middleton (eds.) 1967: *Comparative political systems,* The Natural History Press, Garden City, N.Y.

Cohn, W. 1967: " 'Religion' in non-Western cultures," *American Anthropologist,* 69.73–76.

COLBY, B. N. 1966: "Ethnographic semantics: A preliminary survey," *Current Anthropology,* 7.3–32.

CONKLIN, H. 1962: "Lexicographical treatment of folk taxonomies," in Householder and Saporta (eds.) 1962.

COON, C. S. 1955: *The story of man,* Knopf, New York.

———— 1962: *The origin of races,* Knopf, New York.

———— 1965: *The living races of man,* Knopf, New York.

———— 1971: *The hunting peoples.* Little, Brown, Boston and Toronto.

COUNT, E. 1958: "The biological basis of human sociality," *American Anthropologist,* 60.1049–1085.

COX, O. C. 1959: *Foundations of capitalism,* Philosophical Library, New York.

DALTON, G. (ED.) 1967: *Tribal and peasant economies,* The Natural History Press, Garden City, N.Y.

DARMESTETER, A. 1877: *De la création actuelle de mots nouveaux dans la langue française,* F. Viewig, Paris.

DAVENPORT, R. K. 1967: "The orang-utan in Sabah," *Folia Primatologica,* 5.247–263.

DAVIES, O., H. J. HUGOT, AND D. SEDDON 1968: "The origins of African agriculture," *Current Anthropology,* 9.479–509. A symposium with discussion and comment by other specialists.

DAVIS, D. B. 1966: *The problem of slavery in Western culture,* Cornell University Press, Ithaca, N.Y.

DAVIS, K. S., AND J. A. DAY 1961: *Water: The mirror of science,* Doubleday, Garden City, N.Y.

DENSMORE, F. 1932: *Menominee music,* Bureau of American Ethnology Bulletin 102.

DEVORE, I. (ED.) 1965: *Primate behavior: Field studies of monkeys and apes,* Holt, New York.

DIAMOND, S. (ED.) 1960: *Culture in history,* Columbia University Press, New York.

DICKINSON. W. R. 1971: "Plate tectonics in geological history," *Science,* 174.107–113 (8 October).

DIEBOLD, A. R. 1964: Comments in Hockett and Ascher 1964.

DIETZ, R. S., AND J. C. HOLDEN 1970: "The breakup of Pangaea," *Scientific American,* 223.30–41 (October).

DIRINGER, D. 1951: *The alphabet,* Hutchinson, London. Third ed., 1968.

DIXON, R. B. 1928: *The building of cultures,* Scribner, New York.

DOBZHANSKY, T. 1951: *Genetics and the origin of species,* 3d ed., Columbia University Press, New York.

———— 1956: *The biological basis of human freedom,* Columbia University Press, New York.

———— 1962: *Mankind evolving,* Yale University Press, New Haven, Conn. and London.

DRAKE, E. T. (ED.) 1968: *Evolution and environment,* Yale University Press, New Haven, Conn. and London.

DuBRUL, E. L. 1958: *Evolution of the speech apparatus,* Charles C Thomas, Springfield, Ill.

DUNHAM, K. 1946: *Journey to Accompong,* Holt, New York.

ECCLES, J. C., M. ITO, AND J. SZENTÁGOTHAI 1967: *The cerebellum as a neuronal machine,* Springer-Verlag, Berlin and New York.

EISENSTADT, S. N. 1956: *From generation to generation: Age groups and social structure,* Free Press, Glencoe, Ill.

ELLIS, C. D. 1960: "A note on *okimāhkān,*" *Anthropological Linguistics,* 2:3.1.

EMILIANI, C. 1968: "The Pleistocene epoch and the evolution of man," *Current Anthropology,* 9.27–47 (February). With discussion by other specialists.

EMMONS, W. H., I. S. ALLISON, C. R. STAUFFER, AND G. A. THIEL 1960: *Geology: Principles and processes,* 5th ed., McGraw-Hill, New York.

Encyclopaedia Britannica, 1968 ed. (revision is now continuous), Chicago.

ENGELS, F. 1884: *Der Ursprung der Familie, des Privateigenthums und des Staats. Im Anschluss an Lewis H. Morgans Forschungen.* First English translation, *The origin of the family, private property, and the state,* C. H. Kerr, Chicago, 1902.

ESPER, E. A. 1925: *A technique for the experimental investigation of associative interference in artificial linguistic material,* Linguistic Society of America, Language Monograph 1, Philadelphia.

FIRTH, R. 1970: "Sibling terms in Polynesia," *Journal of the Polynesian Society,* 79:3.272–287.

FORBES, R. J. 1950: *Man the maker,* Schuman, New York.

FORDE, C. D. 1934: *Habitat, economy, and society,* Methuen, London; Harcourt Brace, New York.

FOX, R. 1967: *Kinship and marriage,* Penguin, Hammondsworth, Baltimore.

FRAKE, C. 1961: "The diagnosis of disease among the Subanun of Mindanao," *American Anthropologist,* 63.113–132.

FRAZER, J. G. 1890: *The golden bough,* Macmillan, London and New York. Condensed and edited to 1 vol. by T. H. Gaston, *The new golden bough.* Criterion Books, New York, 1959.

FREUD, S. 1920: *A general introduction to psychoanalysis,* Boni and Liveright, New York (first English edition of German original).

FREYRE, G. 1933: *Casa grande e senzala,* Schmidt, Rio de Janeiro. Fourth ed., 1942, translated into English, *The masters and the slaves,* Knopf, New York, 1946.

FRIED, M. H. 1960: "On the evolution of social stratification and the state," in S. Diamond (ed.) 1960.

FURON, R. 1963: *Le problème de l'eau dans le monde,* Payot, Paris. English translation, *The problem of water: a world study,* Faber, London; Elsevier, New York, 1967.

GAMOW, G. 1941: *Biography of the earth,* Viking, New York.

GARDNER, B. T., AND R. A. GARDNER 1971: In Schrier, Harlow, and Stollnitz (eds.) 1965–1971.

GARDNER, R. A., AND B. T. GARDNER 1969: "Teaching sign-language to a chimpanzee," *Science,* 165.664–672.

GAZZANIGA, M. S. 1967: "The split brain in man," *Scientific American,* 217.24–29 (August).

GELB, I. J. 1952: *A study of writing,* Routledge, London. Revised ed., The University of Chicago Press, Chicago, 1963.

GHIRSHMAN, R. 1954: *Iran: From the earliest times to the Islamic conquest,* Penguin, Hammondsworth.

GIMBUTAS, M. 1963: "The Indo-Europeans: Archaeological problems," *American Anthropologist,* 65.815–836.

The Gleaner geography and history of Jamaica 1967: 20th ed. Prepared and published by the staff of *The Gleaner* (newspaper), Kingston, Jamaica.

GÖDEL, K. 1931: *Über formal unentscheidbare Sätze der Principia Mathematica und verwandter Systeme, I.* English translation, *On formally undecidable propositions of Principia Mathematica and related systems,* Oliver & Boyd, Edinburgh, 1962.

GOODALL, J. 1964: "Tool-using and aimed throwing in a community of free-living chimpanzees," *Nature,* 201.1264–1266.

———— 1965a: "Chimpanzees of the Gombe stream reserve," in DeVore (ed.) 1965.

———— 1965b: "New discoveries among African chimpanzees," *National Geographic,* 128.802–831A.

———— 1967: "Mother-offspring relationships in free-ranging chimpanzees," in Morris (ed.) 1967.

GOODENOUGH, W. 1970: *Description and comparison in cultural anthropology,* Aldine, Chicago.

GOODRICH, L. C. 1959: *A short history of the Chinese people,* 3d ed., Harper, New York.

GORDON, E. V. 1927: *An introduction to Old Norse,* Clarenden Press, Oxford.

GORMAN, C. F. 1969: "Hoabinhian: A pebble-tool complex with early plant associations in southeast Asia," *Science* (14 February).

———— 1971: "The Hoabinhian and after: Subsistence patterns in southeast Asia during the late Pleistocene and early Recent periods," *World Archaeology,* 2.300–320.

GREENBERG, J. H. 1959: "Language and evolution," in Meggers (ed.) 1959.

GRIFFIN, D. R., AND A. NOVICK 1970: *Animal structure and function,* 2d ed., Holt, New York.

GROUT, D. J. 1960: *A history of Western music,* Norton, New York.

HAAS, M. R. n.d. (ca. 1940): *Tunica.* Extract from *Handbook of American Indian Languages* vol. 4 (never published). Augustin, New York.

HAGEN, V. W. VON 1957: *The ancient sun kingdoms of the Americas,* World Publishing, Cleveland and New York.

HAINES, F. 1938: "Where did the Plains Indians get their horses?," *American Anthropologist,* 40.112–117.

HALL, E. T. 1959: *The silent language,* Doubleday, Garden City, N.Y.

———— 1968: "Proxemics," *Current Anthropology,* 9.83–95.

HALL, K. R. L., AND I. DEVORE 1965: "Baboon social behavior," in DeVore (ed.) 1965.

HALLOWELL, A. I. 1946: "Some psychological characteristics of the northeastern Indians," in Johnson (ed.) 1946.

HAMMEL, E. A. (ED.) 1965: *Formal semantic analysis, American Anthropologist,* 67:5 part 2.

HAMMOND, N. G. L. 1959: *A history of Greece to 322 B.C.,* Clarenden Press, Oxford.

HANČAR, F. 1956: *Das Pferd in prähistorischer und früher historischer Zeit,* Herold, Wien.

HARDEN, D. B. 1962: *The Phoenicians,* Thames and Hudson, London; Praeger, New York.

HARING, D. G. 1949: "Cultural behavior," in Haring (ed.) 1949.

HARING, D. G. (ED.) 1949: *Personal character and cultural milieu,* rev. ed., Syracuse University Press, Syracuse, N.Y.

HARLAN, J. R. 1971: "Agricultural origins: Centers and noncenters," *Science,* 174.468–474 (28 October).

HARRISSON, B. 1960: "A study of orang-utan behaviour in semi-wild state," *Sarawak Museum Journal,* 9.300–309.

HAUPT, A. W. 1956: *An introduction to botany,* McGraw-Hill, New York.

HAYAKAWA, S. I. 1941: *Language in action,* Harcourt Brace, New York.

HEDIGER, H. 1961: "The evolution of territorial behavior," in Washburn (ed.) 1961.

HERSKOVITS, M. J. 1926: "The cattle complex in east Africa," *American Anthropologist,* 28.230–272.

——— 1941: *The myth of the Negro past,* Harper, New York.

HERSKOVITS, M. J., AND F. J. HERSKOVITS 1934: *Rebel destiny,* McGraw-Hill, New York.

HEWES, G. W. 1961: "Food transport and the origin of hominid bipedalism," *American Anthropologist,* 63.687–710.

——— 1968: "New light on the gestural origin of language," in Hewes (compiler) 1971.

HEWES, G. W. (COMPILER) 1971: *Language origins: A bibliography,* Department of Anthropology, University of Colorado, Boulder.

HIGGS, E. S., AND M. R. JARMAN 1969: "The origins of agriculture: A reconsideration," *Antiquity,* 43.31 ff (March).

HILGARD, E. R. 1956: *Theories of learning,* 2d ed., Appleton-Century-Crofts, New York.

HO, PING-TI 1969: "The loess and the origin of Chinese agriculture," *American Historical Review,* 75.1–36 (October).

HOCHBAUM, H. A. 1955: *Travels and traditions of waterfowl,* The University of Minnesota Press, Minneapolis.

HOCKETT, C. F. 1953: Review of Shannon 1948, *Language,* 29.69–92.

——— 1958: *A course in modern linguistics,* Macmillan, New York.

——— 1960a: "Logical considerations in the study of animal communication," in Lanyon and Tavolga (eds.) 1960.

——— 1960b: "Ethnolinguistic implications of studies in linguistics and psychiatry," Georgetown University Monograph Series in Languages and Linguistics, 11.175–193 (dated 1958).

——— 1964: "Scheduling," in Northrop and Livingstone (eds.) 1964.

——— 1967: "Where the tongue slips there slip I," in *To Honor Roman Jackobson,* Mouton, The Hague, pp. 910–936.

HOCKETT, C. F., AND S. A. ALTMANN 1968: "A note on design features," in Sebeok (ed.) 1968.

HOCKETT, C. F., AND R. ASCHER 1964: "The human revolution," *Current Anthropology,* 5.135–147 (June). With commentary and discussion by various specialists.

HOFFMAN, W. J. 1896: *The Menomini Indians,* Bureau of American Ethnology Annual Report for 1892–1893, part 1, 3–340.

HOIJER, H. (ED.) 1946: *Linguistic structures of native America,* Viking Fund Publications in Anthropology 6, Wenner-Gren Foundation for Anthropological Research, New York.

———— (ED.) 1954: *Language in culture,* American Anthropological Association Memoir 79.

HOLLOWAY, R. L., JR. 1966: "Cranial capacity and the evolution of the human brain," *American Anthropologist,* 68.103–121.

HONIGMANN, J. J. 1954: *Culture and personality,* Harper, New York.

HOOTON, E. 1942: *Man's poor relations,* Doubleday, Doran, Garden City, N.Y.

HOUSEHOLDER, F. W., AND S. SAPORTA (EDS.) 1962: "Problems in lexicography," *International Journal of American Linguistics,* 28:2, part 4.

HOWELL, F. C., AND F. BOURLIÈRE (EDS.) 1963: *African ecology and human evolution,* Viking Fund Publications in Anthropology 36, Wenner-Gren Foundation for Anthropological Research, New York.

HSU, F. L. K. 1965: "The effect of dominant kinship relationships on kin and non-kin behavior: A hypothesis," *American Anthropologist,* 67.638–661. Comments, same journal 68.997–999; reply 68.999–1004.

HSU, F. L. K. (ED.) 1971: *Kinship and culture,* Aldine, Chicago.

HUNT, C. B., W. L. STRAUS, JR., AND M. G. WOLMAN (EDS.) 1965: *Time and stratigraphy in the evolution of man,* The National Academy of Sciences Publication 1469, Washington, D.C.

HUNT, R. (ED.) 1967: *Personalities and cultures,* The Natural History Press, Garden City, N.Y.

HURLEY, P. M. 1959: *How old is the Earth?,* Anchor Books, Garden City, N.Y.

HUXLEY, T. H. 1863: *Evidence as to man's place in nature.* Williams & Norgate, London. Many reprintings, under the shortened title, *Man's place in nature.*

HYMES, D. (ED.) 1964: *Language in culture and society,* Harper & Row, New York.

The International Atlas 1969: Rand McNally, Chicago.

JACOBS, M. 1964: *Pattern in cultural anthropology,* Dorsey, Homewood, Ill.

JELINEK, J. 1969: "Neanderthal man and *Homo sapiens* in central and eastern Europe," *Current Anthropology,* 10.475–503. With discussion and commentary by various experts.

JENKS, A. E. 1900: *The wild rice gatherers of the upper lakes,* Bureau of American Ethnology Annual Report for 1900.

JENNINGS, J. D. 1968: *Prehistory of North America,* McGraw-Hill, New York.

JENNINGS, J. D., AND E. NORBECK (EDS.) 1964: *Prehistoric man in the New World,* Published for William Marsh Rice University by The University of Chicago Press, Chicago.

JOHN, E. R. 1967: *Mechanisms of memory,* Academic, New York and London.

JOHNSON, F. (ED.) 1946: *Man in northeastern North America,* Papers of the Robert S. Peabody Foundation for Archaeology, vol. 3.

JOHNSON, W. 1946: *People in Quandaries,* Harper, New York.

JONES, H. S. 1940: *Life on other worlds,* Macmillan, New York.

JOOS, M. 1967: *The five clocks,* Harcourt Brace and World, New York.

KEESING, F. M. 1939: *The Menomini Indians of Wisconsin: A study of three centuries of cultural contact and change,* The American Philosophical Society, Memoir 10.

KEETON, W. T. 1967: *Biological science.* Norton, New York.

KENNEDY, K. A. R. 1971: "The paleontology of human populations," *The Cornell Plantations,* 26:4.41–64.

KLUCKHOHN, C., H. A. MURRAY, AND D. M. SCHNEIDER (EDS.) 1953: *Personality in nature, society, and culture,* 2d ed., Knopf, New York.

KRADER, L. 1968: *Formation of the state,* Prentice-Hall, Englewood Cliffs, N.J.

KROEBER, A. L. 1909: "Classificatory systems of relationship," *Journal of the Royal Anthropological Society* 39.

————— 1923: *Anthropology,* Harcourt Brace, New York.

————— 1939: *Cultural and natural areas of native North America,* University of California Publications in American Archeology and Ethnology 38. Third printing, 1953.

————— 1955: "On human nature," *Southwestern Journal of Anthropology,* 2.195–204.

KROEBER, A. L. (ED.) 1925: *Handbook of the Indians of California,* Bureau of American Ethnology Bulletin 78.

KROEBER, A. L., AND C. KLUCKHOHN 1952: *Culture: A critical review of concepts and definitions,* Papers of the Peabody Museum of American Archeology and Ethnology, Harvard University, 47:1. Paperback reprint, Vintage Books, New York, n.d.

KUMMER, H. 1967: "Tripartite relations in Hamadryas baboons," in Altmann (ed.) 1967.

LaBARRE, W. 1964: Comments in Hockett and Ascher 1964.

LANDES, R. 1937: *Ojibwa Sociology,* Columbia University Contributions to Anthropology 29.

LANYON, W. E., AND W. N. TAVOLGA (EDS.) 1960: *Animal sounds and communication,* American Institute of Biological Science Publication 7, Washington, D.C.

LAUFER, B. 1917: *Reindeer domestication,* American Anthropological Association, Memoir, 4.

LEACH, D. E. 1958: *Flintlock and tomahawk: New England in King Philip's War,* Norton, New York.

LEE, I., AND I. DeVORE (EDS.) 1968: *Man the hunter,* Aldine, Chicago.

LEHNINGER, A. L. 1965: *Bioenergetics: The molecular basis of biological energy transformations,* W. A. Benjamin, New York.

LENNEBERG, E. 1967: *Biological foundations of language,* Wiley, New York.

LERNER, I. M. 1968: *Heredity, evolution, and society,* Freeman, San Francisco.

LÉVI-STRAUSS, C. 1963: *Structural anthropology,* Basic Books, New York. A collection of articles published earlier, here all in English though many of them appeared first in French. Paperback reprint, Anchor Books, Garden City, N.Y., 1967.

LIEBERMAN, P., AND E. S. CRELIN 1971: "On the speech of Neanderthal man," *Linguistic Inquiry,* 11.203–222.

LIEBERMAN, P., D. H. KLATT, AND W. H. WILSON 1969: "Vocal tract limitations on the vowel repertoires of rhesus monkeys and other non-human primates," *Science,* 164.1185–1187.

LIEF, A. (ED.) 1929: *The dissenting opinions of Mr. Justice Holmes,* Vanguard, New York.

LINTON, R. 1936: *The study of man,* Appleton-Century, New York.

————— 1945: *The cultural background of personality,* Appleton-Century, New York.

LINTON, R. (ED.) 1945: *The science of man in the world crisis,* Columbia University Press, New York.

LIVINGSTONE, F. B. 1969: "Genetics, ecology, and the origins of incest and exogamy," *Current Anthropology,* 10.45–61 (February). With discussion and comment by various specialists.

LLOYD, S. 1967: *Early highland peoples of Anatolia,* Thames and Hudson, London; McGraw-Hill, New York.

LOTKA, A. J. 1925: *Elements of physical biology.* Williams & Wilkins, Baltimore. Paperback reprint under the title, *Elements of mathematical biology,* Dover, New York, 1954.

LOWIE, R. 1924: *Primitive religion,* Boni and Liveright, New York.

——— 1927: *The origin of the state,* Harcourt Brace, New York.

——— 1934: *An introduction to cultural anthropology,* Farrar & Rinehart, New York.

MacINTOSH, N. W. G. 1963: "Origin and physical differentiation of the Australian aborigines," *Australian Natural History,* 14.248–252.

MacNEISH, R. S. 1971: "Early man in the Andes," *Scientific American,* 224.36–46 (April).

MALLOWAN, M. E. L. 1965: *Early Mesopotamia and Iran,* Thames and Hudson, London; McGraw-Hill, New York.

MARETT, R. R. 1912: *Anthropology,* Williams & Norgate, London; Henry Holt, New York.

MARGULIS, L. 1971: "Symbiosis and evolution," *Scientific American,* 225.48–57 (August).

MASON, J. A. 1957: *The ancient civilizations of Peru,* Penguin, Baltimore.

MASON, W. A. 1960: "The effects of social restriction on the behavior of rhesus monkeys: I. Free social behavior," *Journal of Comparative and Physiological Psychology,* 53.582–589.

MATES, B. 1961: *Stoic logic,* 2d ed., University of California Press, Berkeley and Los Angeles.

MAXFIELD, F. K. 1926: "Quaker 'thee' and its history," *American Speech,* 1.638–644.

MAYR, E. 1963: *Animal species and evolution,* Harvard University Press, Belknap Press, Cambridge, Mass.

McMILLAN, N. n.d.: *The land of look behind: A study of Jamaica.*

McQUOWN, N. A. 1957: "Linguistic transcription and specification of interview materials," *Psychiatry,* 20.79–86.

MEAD, M. 1928: *Coming of age in Samoa,* Morrow, New York.

——— 1930: *Growing up in New Guinea,* Morrow, New York.

——— 1935: *Sex and temperament in three primitive societies,* Morrow, New York.

MEGGERS. B. J. (ED.) 1959: *Evolution and anthropology: A centennial appraisal,* The Anthropological Society of Washington, Washington, D.C.

MEILLET, A. 1937: *Introduction à l'étude comparative des langues Indo-Européennes,* 8th ed., Hachette, Paris.

MELLAART, J. 1965: *Earliest civilizations of the near East,* Thames and Hudson, London; McGraw-Hill, New York.

MEWHINNEY, H. 1957: *A manual for Neanderthals,* University of Texas Press, Austin.

MIDDLETON, G. 1892: *An essay on analogy in syntax,* Longmans, Green, London and New York.

MIDDLETON, J. (ED.) 1967a: *Myth and cosmos: Readings in mythology and symbolism*, The Natural History Press, Garden City, N.Y.

———— (ED.) 1967b: *Gods and rituals: Readings in religious beliefs and practices*, The Natural History Press, Garden City, N.Y.

———— (ED.) 1967c: *Magic, witchcraft, and curing*, The Natural History Press, Garden City, N.Y.

MILLER, G. H., E. GALANTER, AND K. H. PRIBRAM 1960: *Plans and the structure of behavior*, Holt, New York.

MILNER, G. B. n.d. (ca. 1957): *Fijian grammar*, The Government Press, Suva, Fiji.

MONTAGU, A. 1966: "The buttocks and natural selection," *Journal of the American Medical Association*, 198.169.

———— 1971: *Touching: The human significance of the skin*, Columbia University Press, New York.

MONTAGU, A. (ED.) 1968: *Culture: Man's adaptive dimension*, Oxford University Press, New York.

MORGAN, L. H. 1870: *Systems of consanguinity and affinity of the human family*, Smithsonian Contributions to Knowledge, no. 17.

———— 1877: *Ancient society*, Henry Holt and Co., New York.

MORRIS, D. (ED.) 1967: *Primate ethology*, Aldine, Chicago.

MULVANEY, D. J. 1969: *The prehistory of Australia*, Thames and Hudson, London.

MURDOCK, G. P. 1934: *Our primitive contemporaries*, Macmillan, New York.

———— 1945: "The common denominator of cultures," in Linton (ed.) 1945.

———— 1949: *Social structure*, Macmillan, New York.

NAPIER, J. R. 1967: "The antiquity of human walking," *Scientific American* (April).

NAPIER, J. R., AND P. H. NAPIER 1967: *A handbook of living primates*, Academic, London and New York.

NEEDHAM, J. 1954–. *Science and civilization in China*, (Many vols.) Cambridge University Press, London.

NEWMAN, P. L. 1965: *Knowing the Gururumba*, Holt, New York.

NISSEN, H. W. 1931: *A field study of the chimpanzee*, Comparative Psychology Monographs, 8:1.

NORTHROP, F. S. C., AND H. H. LIVINGSTONE (EDS.) 1964: *Cross-cultural understanding: Epistemology in anthropology*, Harper & Row, New York.

NUSSBAUM, F. L. 1933: *A history of the economic institutions of modern Europe*, Crofts, New York.

OAKLEY, K. 1955: "Fire as paleolithic tool and weapon," *Proceedings of the Prehistoric Society*, 21.36–48.

———— 1959: *Man the toolmaker*, The University of Chicago Press, Chicago.

———— 1961: "On man's use of fire, with comments on tool-making and hunting," in Washburn (ed.) 1961.

———— 1962: "Dating the emergence of man," *The Advancement of Science*, 18.415–426.

———— 1964: *Frameworks for dating fossil man*, Wodenfeld and Nicolson, London.

OPARIN, A. J. 1961: *Life: Its nature, origin and development*, (translated from Russian original) Academic, New York.

——— 1964: *The chemical origin of life,* (translated from Russian original) Charles C Thomas, Springfield, Ill.

OPLER, M. E. 1945: "Themes as dynamic forces in culture," *American Journal of Sociology,* 51.198–208.

——— 1946: "An application of the theory of themes in culture," *Journal of the Washington Academy of Science,* 36.137–166.

———: "Components, assemblage, and theme in cultural integration and disintegration," *American Anthropologist,* 61.955–964.

——— 1968: "The themal approach in cultural anthropology and its application to north Indian data," *Southwestern Journal of Anthropology,* 24.215–227.

OPLER, M. K. (ED.) 1959: *Culture and mental health: Cross-cultural studies,* Macmillan, New York.

OSTROGORSKI, G. 1956: *History of the Byzantine state,* (translated from Russian original) Blackwell, Oxford.

OVENDEN, M. W. 1962: *Life in the universe,* Anchor Books, Garden City, N.Y.

PEARSON, R. J. 1969: *Archeology of the Ryukyu Islands: A regional chronology from 3000 B.C. to the historic period,* University of Hawaii Press, Honolulu.

PENFIELD, W., AND L. ROBERTS 1959: *Speech and brain-mechanisms,* Princeton University Press, Princeton, N.J.

PFEIFFER, J. 1955: *The human brain,* Harper, New York.

——— 1969: *The emergence of man,* Harper & Row, New York.

PHILLIPS, E. D. 1965: *The royal hordes: Nomad peoples of the steppes,* Thames and Hudson, London; McGraw-Hill, New York.

PHILLIPS, G. B. 1925: "The primitive copper industry of America," *American Anthropologist,* 27.284–289.

PITTENGER, R. E., C. F. HOCKETT, AND J. J. DANEHY 1960: *The first five minutes: An example of microscopic interview analysis,* Paul Martineau, Ithaca, N.Y.

PITTENGER, R. E., AND H. L. SMITH, JR. 1957: "A basis for some contributions of linguistics to psychiatry," *Psychiatry,* 20.61–78.

POSPISIL, L. 1963: *The Kapauku Papuans of west New Guinea,* Holt, New York.

POUND, L. 1914: *Blends: Their relation to English word formation,* C. Winter, Heidelberg.

PREMACK, D. 1970: "The education of Sarah: a chimp learns language," *Psychology Today,* 4.55–58.

——— 1971: "Language in chimpanzee?," *Science,* 172.808–822 (21 May).

PRESCOTT, W. H. 1843: *History of the conquest of Mexico,* Harper and Brothers, New York.

——— 1847: *History of the conquest of Peru,* Harper and Brothers, New York.

PRESTON, R. J. 1966: "Edward Sapir's anthropology: Style, structure, and method," *American Anthropologist,* 68.1105–1128.

PROKOSCH, E. 1938: *A comparative Germanic grammar,* Special Publications of the Linguistic Society of America, Philadelphia.

REICHENBACH, H. 1951: *The rise of scientific philosophy,* University of California Press, Berkeley.

RENFREW, C. 1971: "Carbon 14 and the prehistory of Europe," *Scientific American,* 225.63–72 (October).

ROBERTS, W. A. 1955: *Jamaica: The portrait of an island,* Coward-McCann, New York.

ROE, A., AND G. G. SIMPSON (EDS.) 1958: *Behavior and evolution,* Yale University Press, New Haven, Conn.

ROMER, A. S. 1958: "Phylogeny and behavior with special reference to vertebrate evolution," in Roe and Simpson (eds.) 1958.

———— 1959: *The vertebrate story,* The University of Chicago Press, Chicago.

ROMNEY, A. K., AND R. G. D'ANDRADE (EDS.) 1964: *Transcultural studies in cognition, American Anthropologist,* 66:3 part 2.

ROSTOVTZEFF, M. I. 1941: *The social and economic history of the Hellenistic world,* Clarenden Press, Oxford.

ROTH, G. K. 1954: *Fijian way of life,* Oxford University Press, London.

RUSH, J. H. 1957: *The dawn of life,* Hanover House, Garden City, N.Y.

SACHS, C. 1940: *The history of musical instruments,* Norton, New York.

SADE, D. S. 1968: "Inhibition of son-mother mating among free-ranging rhesus monkeys," *Science and Psychoanalysis,* 12.18–37.

SAHLINS, M. D. 1959: "The social life of monkeys, apes, and primitive man," in Spuhler (ed.) 1959.

SAPIR, E. 1949: *Selected writings in language, culture, and personality,* (ed. by D. G. Mandelbaum) University of California Press, Berkeley. The subsequent paperback reprint is cut.

SARTON, G. 1927–1948: *Introduction to the history of science,* Williams & Wilkins, Baltimore, 3 vols.

SAYCE, R. U. 1933: *Primitive arts and crafts,* Cambridge University Press, London.

SCHALLER, G. B. 1961: "The orang-utan in Sarawak," *Zoologica,* 46.73–82.

———— 1963: *The mountain gorilla: Ecology and behavior,* The University of Chicago Press, Chicago.

SCHRIER, A. M., H. F. HARLOW, AND F. STOLLNITZ (EDS.) 1965–1971: *Behavior of nonhuman primates,* Academic, New York, 4 vols.

SCHRÖDINGER, E. 1945: *What is life? The physical aspect of the living cell,* Cambridge University Press, London; Macmillan, New York.

SCHULTZ, A. H. 1954: "Bemerkungen zur Variabilität und Systematik der Schimpansen," *Säugetierkundliche Mitteilungen,* 2.159–163.

———— 1961: "Some factors influencing the social life of primates in general and early man in particular," in Washburn (ed.) 1961.

———— 1964: Comments in Hockett and Ascher 1964.

SCIAMA, D. W. 1959: *The unity of the universe,* Doubleday, Garden City, N.Y.

SCOTT, J. P. 1958: *Animal behavior,* The University of Chicago Press, Chicago.

SEBEOK, T. A. (ED.) 1968: *Animal communication: Techniques of study and results of research,* Indiana University Press, Bloomington.

SHANNON, C. 1948: "The mathematical theory of communication," *Bell System Technical Journal* (July and October). Reprinted 1949, with a paper by W. Weaver, under the same title, The University of Illinois Press, Urbana.

SHARP, R. L. 1962: "Cultural continuities and discontinuities in southeast Asia," *Journal of Asian Studies,* 22.3–11.

SHKLOVSKII, I. S., AND C. SAGAN 1966: *Intelligent life in the universe,* Holden-Day, San Francisco.

SIEBERT, F. T. 1967: "The original home of the Proto-Algonquian people," National Museum of Canada Bulletin 214, pp. 48–59.

SIMPSON, G. G. 1945: *The principles of classification and a classification of mammals,* American Museum of Natural History Bulletin 85.

———— 1949: *The meaning of evolution,* Yale University Press, New Haven, Conn. Paperback reprint (drastically abridged), New American Library, New York, 1951.

———— 1953: *The major features of evolution,* Columbia University Press, New York.

———— 1958: "The study of evolution: Methods and present status of theory," in Roe and Simpson (eds.) 1958.

SINGER, C., E. J. HOLMYARD, AND A. R. HALL 1954–1958: *A history of technology,* Clarenden Press, Oxford, 5 vols.

SKINNER, A. 1913: *Social life and ceremonial bundles of the Menomini Indians,* Anthropological Papers of The American Museum of Natural History, 13:1.

———— 1915: *Associations and ceremonies of the Menomini Indians,* Anthropological Papers of The American Museum of Natural History, 13:2.

———— 1920: *Medicine ceremony of the Menomini, Iowa, and Wahpeton Dakota, with notes on the ceremony of the Ponca, Bungi Ojibwa, and Potawatomi Indians,* Museum of the American Indian, Indian Notes and Monographs, no. 4.

———— 1921: *Material culture of the Menomini.* Museum of the American Indian, Indian Notes and Monographs (no number).

SKINNER, A., AND J. V. SATTERLEE 1915: *Folklore of the Menomini Indians,* Anthropological Papers of The American Museum of Natural History, 13:3.

SLOTKIN, J. S. 1952: *Menomini Peyotism,* American Philosophical Society, Transactions n.s., 42:4, Philadelphia.

SLUCKIN, W. 1965: *Imprinting and early learning,* Aldine, Chicago.

SMITH, E. 1913: "The evolution of man," *Smithsonian Report for 1912,* pp. 553–572.

SMITH, F., AND G. A. MILLER (EDS.) 1966: *The genesis of language [in the child],* M.I.T. Press, Cambridge, Mass.

SMITH, H. H. 1923: *Ethnobotany of the Menomini Indians,* Bulletin of the Public Museum of the City of Milwaukee, 4:1.

SMITH, J. C. 1964: "The theoretical constructs of Western contractual law," in Northrop and Livingstone (eds.) 1964.

SOLHEIM, W. G. 1971: "New light on a forgotten past," *National Geographic,* 139.330–339 (March).

SOMBART, W. 1916–1927: *Der moderne Kapitalismus,* 2d ed., München and Leipzig.

SOUTHWICK, C. H. (ED.) 1963: *Primate social behavior,* Van Nostrand, Princeton, N.J.

SPIER, L. 1925: *The distribution of kinship systems in North America,* University of Washington Publications in Anthropology, no. 1.

———— 1933: *Yuman tribes of the Gila River,* The University of Chicago Press, Chicago.

SPUHLER, J. N. 1959: "Somatic paths to culture," in Spuhler (ed.) 1959.

SPUHLER, J. N. (ED.) 1959: *The evolution of man's capacity for culture,* Wayne State University Press, Detroit, Mich.

STEVICK, R. D. 1963: "The biological model and historical linguistics," *Language,* 39.159–169.

STURTEVANT, W. 1964: "Studies in ethnoscience," *American Anthropologist,* 66:3 part 2, pp. 99–131.

SUMNER, W. G. 1906: *Folkways,* Ginn, Boston.

SZENT-GYÖRGYI, A. 1948: *The nature of life,* Academic, New York.

THIEME, P. 1954: *Die Heimat der indogermanischen Gemeinsprache,* F. Steiner, Wiesbaden.

——— 1964: "The comparative method for reconstruction in linguistics," in Hymes (ed.) 1964.

THOMAS, W. L., JR. (ED.) 1956: *Man's role in changing the face of the earth,* The University of Chicago Press, Chicago.

THOMPSON, J. E. S. 1954: *The rise and fall of Maya civilization,* University of Oklahoma Press, Norman.

THOMSON, B. 1908: *The Fijians,* Heinemann, London.

THUMB, A., AND K. MARBE 1901: *Experimentelle Untersuchungen über psychologische Grundlagen der sprachlichen Analogiebildung,* W. Englemann, Leipizig.

TOZZER, A. M. (ED.) 1940: *The Maya and their neighbors,* Appleton-Century, New York and London.

TRAGER, G. L. 1958: "Paralanguage: A first approximation," *Studies in Linguistics,* 13.1–12.

TRAGER, G. L., AND H. L. SMITH, JR. 1950: "A chronology of Indo-Hittite," *Studies in Linguistics,* 8.61–70.

TUREKIAN, K. K. (ED.) 1971: *The late Cenozoic glacial ages,* Yale University Press, New Haven, Conn.

TURNER, F. J. 1920: *The frontier in American history,* Henry Holt, New York. Includes the essay, "The significance of the frontier in American history," first read at a meeting in 1893.

TYLOR, E. N. 1871: *Primitive culture,* John Murray, London, 2 vols.

UNDERHILL, R. 1953: *Red man's America.* The University of Chicago Press, Chicago.

VERNADSKY, W. I. 1945: "The biosphere and the noösphere," *American Scientist,* 33.1–11 (January).

VIORST, J. 1967: *The changing Earth,* Bantam, New York.

WALLACE, A. F. C. 1961: *Culture and personality,* Random House, New York.

WASHBURN, S. L. 1959: "Speculation on the interrelations of the history of tools and biological evolution," in Spuhler (ed.) 1959.

——— 1960: "Tools and human evolution," *Scientific American,* 2–3.63–75.

WASHBURN, S. L. (ED.) 1961: *Social life of early man,* Viking Fund Publications in Anthropology 31, Wenner-Gren Foundation for Anthropological Research, New York.

———— (ED.) 1963: *Classification and human evolution,* Viking Fund Publications in Anthropology 37, Wenner-Gren Foundation for Anthropological Research, New York.

WASHBURN, S. L., AND I. DeVORE 1961: "The social life of baboons," *Scientific American,* June. Reprinted in Southwick (ed.) 1963.

———— 1963: "Baboon ecology and human evolution," in Howell and Bourlière (eds.) 1963.

WASHBURN, S. L., AND P. C. JAY (EDS.) 1968: *Perspectives on human evolution: 1,* Holt, New York.

WATSON, J. B. 1965: "From hunting to horticulture in the New Guinea highlands," *Ethnology,* 4.295 ff.

WATSON, W. 1966: *Early civilization in China,* Thames and Hudson, London; McGraw-Hill, New York.

WEBER, M. 1904–1905: "Die protestantische Ethik und der 'Geist' des Kapitalismus," *Archiv für Sozialwissenschaft und Statistik,* 20:1, 21:1. English translation, *The protestant ethic and the spirit of capitalism,* Scribner, New York, 1930.

WEGENER, A. L. 1920: *Die Entstehung der Kontinente und Ozeane,* F. Vieweg und Sohn, Braunschweig. English translation, *The origin of continents and oceans,* Dover, New York, 1966.

WEIDENREICH, F. 1941: "The brain and its rôle in the phylogenetic transformation of the human skull," *Transactions of the Philosophical Society,* n.s., 31.321–442.

WEISZ, P. B. 1967: *The science of biology,* 3d ed., McGraw-Hill, New York.

WEIZSÄCKER, C. F. VON 1948: *Die Geschichte der Natur,* S. Hirzel, Zürich. English translation, *The history of nature,* The University of Chicago Press, Chicago, 1949.

WHEELER, B. I. 1887: *Analogy and the scope of its application to language,* J. Wilson, University Press, Ithaca, N.Y.

WHEELER, M. 1959: *Early India and Pakistan,* Thames and Hudson, London; Praeger, New York.

———— 1966: *Civilizations of the Indus valley and beyond,* Thames and Hudson, London; McGraw-Hill, New York.

WHIPPLE, F. 1968: *Earth, moon, and planets,* 3d ed., Harvard University Press, Cambridge, Mass.

WHITE, L. 1959: *The evolution of culture,* McGraw-Hill, New York.

WHORF, B. L. *Language, thought, and reality,* (ed. by J. B. Carroll) Technology Press, Cambridge, Mass.; Wiley, New York.

WIENER, N. 1948: *Cybernetics,* Technology Press, Cambridge, Mass.; Wiley, New York.

WILLEY, G. R. 1966: *An introduction to American archaeology: Vol. 1: North and Middle America,* Prentice-Hall, Englewood Cliffs, N.J.

WISEMAN, H. V. 1950: *A short history of the British West Indies,* University of London Press, London.

WISSLER, C. 1914: "The influence of the horse on the development of Plains culture," *American Anthropologist,* 16:1 (March).

———— 1923: *Man and culture,* Thomas Y. Crowell, New York.

WOOLDRIDGE, D. E. 1966: *The machinery of life,* McGraw-Hill, New York.

WRIGHT, G. A. 1971: "Origins of food production in southwestern Asia: A survey of ideas," *Current Anthropology,* 12.447–477. With comment and discussion by various specialists.

WRIGHT, H. E., JR. 1970: "Environmental changes and the origin of agriculture in the Near East," *Biological Science,* 20.210 ff (15 February).

ZUCKERMAN, S. 1932: *The social life of monkeys and apes,* Kegan Paul, Trench, Trubner, London.

GLOSSARIAL INDEX

The index covers everything in the text and figures except the entries in the Running Calendar (pages 303–311) and the recent technological advances of Table 38-2 (pages 630–633). The formal taxonomic labels of plants and animals are not included as entries unless they have no familiar vernacular equivalents.

A reference to a figure (table, box, chart, or the like) is given by the figure number in parentheses, immediately preceded by the page number.

Supplementary information is enclosed in square brackets. A *location* is normally given by latitude and longitude (for a large region, or for a scattered or wandering group of people, this can be only suggestive). *Dates of individuals* are supplied if known and not given in the text; unless a date is marked "B.C." it is A.D.

Abbreviations: b. = born; c. = circa = approximately; d. = died; def = definition; fam. = family (taxonomic); fl. = flourished; mp = melting point given in text; site = archaeological site; spp = species (plural); subfam. = subfamily (taxonomic).

abacus, 580
Abbeville [site, 50°6′ N, 1°50′ E], 391(26-3)
Abenaki [Algonquian-speaking people, about 47° N, 68° W], 302(23-6)
aboriginal, aborigines [(pertaining to) the people already living in a region upon the arrival of the first record-keepers]
abrade, to, 87(7-1)
abrasives, 493
abstraction, 643–644
  in aesthetics, 661
  in ethics, 650–651
  in logic, 658
Academy of Athens, 589
Accompong [Maroon village, about 18°15′ N, 77°40′ W], 267
accounting, 625
Achaemenid dynasty, Persia, 590, 601
achieved versus ascribed status, 209, 214
aconite, 440
acorn, 445, 454
  (*See also* oak)
acquired characteristics, noninheritability of, 53, 56
active segment:
  of biosphere, 94
  of noosphere, 96
actor and state, 229–241
adaptation, genetic, 283
adaptive radiation, 299, 301, 444, 545
additive surfacing, 526–528
address:
  forms of, 185–204
  versus reference, kinship terms, 190, 196–197
adenosine diphosphate and triphosphate, 332–334, 340
Admiralty Islands [2°10′ S, 147° E], 226
adolescence, 227–228
  in male baboons, 41
adoption:
  Menomini, 25
  reasons for, 165
adornment of body, 19
  tattooing, 528
ADP = adenosine diphosphate
Adriatic Sea [42°30′ N, 16° E]
adventure, 233(18-1)
adze, 494(and 31-1)
Aegean Sea [38°30′ N, 25° E], 466, 558
Aegyptopithecus, 363(25-1a)

aesthetics, 637, 659–665
  (*See also* art; craftsmanship)
aestivation, 358
affection, 233–234, 641
  and sexuality, 220–221
affine kin, 193
affluent society, 584
Afghanistan [34° N, 66° E], 482, 592
Africa, 363(25-1b), 384, 396, 423, 466, 474, 479, 511, 537, 555, 610
  domestication in, 479–481
  east, 472, 475
  north, 437, 476
  northeast, 436, 474n.
  northwest, 437
  south, 495, 608
  sub-Saharan, 173–174, 180
    as frontier of civil society, 605–606
  west, 183–184
African breadfruit, 456(29-1)
African elephant, 462(29-2)
African survivals in Jamaica, 268
Africans in New World, 263–270, 433
afterlife, 253–254
  Menomini, 31
agave, 458(29-1)
age of discovery, 629
age grading, 151, 226
agnatic versus uterine kin, 199–200
agricultural dwelling patterns, 163
agricultural productivity, 163
agricultural tools, 496–497
agricultural village, 158
agriculture, 153, 260
  and civil society, 549–561
  destructiveness of, 551–552
  impact of, 146
  incipient, 453–459
  and migrations, 489
  New World, 10, 488–499
  and population increase, 162, 605
Ain Hanech [site in Algeria near Khenchela, 35°28′ N, 7°11′ E], 391(26-3)
akee, 263, 454(29-1)
Alaska [65° N, 153° W], 45, 426(28-2), 427–428, 432, 511, 609
Albanian language, 301(23-5), 595
  writing, 620(38-1)
alchemists, 616
Aleutian Islands [52° N, 178° W], 432–433, 435
Aleuts, 432

Alexander of Macedon ("the Great"), 561, 589, 595, 601
Alexandria [ancient city, the modern Al Iskandariyah, 31°12′ N, 29°54′ E, in Egypt], 622
  library at, 589
algae, 344(24-18)
  blue-green, 48n., 340
Algeria [28° N, 3° E]
Algonkin [Algonquian-speaking people; Ojibwa dialects], 602(23-6)
Algonquian language family, 11(2-1), 145, 157, 301–302, 302(23-6)
  Proto Algonquian, 10, 135, 302(23-6)
Ali Kosh [site near Dehlorān, 32°41′ N, 47°16′ E, in Iran], 468, 469(30-1)
aliens, 69, 72, 243
Alighieri, Dante, 636
allegory, 113
alligator [*Alligator* spp, order Crocodilia, subclass Archosauria, class Reptilia], 62(5-5)
allocation, inflection for, 143–144
alloys, 530
allspice, 450(29-1)
almond, 453(29-1)
alpaca, 463(29-2)
alphabetical writing, 579–580
Alps Mountains [46°25′ N, 10° E]
Altai Mountains [40° N, 90° E], 466, 474
altitude, selection, and racial differentiation, 50, 297–298, 411
aluminum, 90, 264, 530 (mp)
Amati, Nicolò, 663
Amazon River [mouth at 0°5′ S, 50° W], 262, 432, 489
amending the law, 650
America (*see* Middle America; New World; North America; South America)
American culture (*see* United States)
"American dream," 214
American Sign Language for the Deaf, 117, 156–157
amino acids, 328, 331(24-10)
Amoy [24°28′ N, 118°7′ E], 605
Ampajango [site, about 27°30′ S, 67°30′ W, in Argentina], 431(28-4)
Amphibia = amphibians, 349(24-22), 355–357
analogy, 382, 656
  in language, 107–110, 290
  in other behavior, 109, 270–271, 378
anarchism, 148

Anatolia = Asia Minor [the region south of the Black Sea which is now politically Turkey], 436, 469, 474, 558, 592

Anatolian languages, 301(23-5), 593

Andaman Islands [12° N, 93° E], 433

Andean culture (*see* Inca)

Andes Mountains [20° S, 68° W], 431–432, 466, 486–491, 532

  as human environment, 50, 298

Angiospermae = angiosperms, 357(and 24-29), 361, 444–450

Angkor Wat [13°25′ N, 103°52′ E], 605

Angles, 598

Anglo-Saxon law, 648

angular measure, 613

animal husbandry, 158, 474–476

  beginnings of, 459–463

animals, 344(24-18)

  classification of, 348(24-21)

  domesticated, 460–465(29-2), 538

  history of, 347–361

  human uses of, 462–463, 540

  origin of, 340

  response to fire, 403

annual plant, 447–448

ant [various genera of fam. Formicidae, order Hymenoptera], 284*n.*

antelope [various genera of subfam. Antilopinae, fam. Bovidae], 395

Anthropoidea = anthropoids [suborder], 57, 58(5-1), 351(24-24)

anthropology, 3 (def)

Antigone (Sophocles), 252

Antilles [islands, in Caribbean], 125, 260, 261(21-1), 433, 438–439, 486–491

  Greater and Lesser, 260

antimony, 531

antisocial individuals, 154

antler (for tools), 20, 394, 434–435, 443

anus, 349–350

anxiety, 231

Apache [various Athapaskan-speaking tribes and tribelets of the American Southwest], 424

  household pattern, 221

  kinship terms, 199(15-6), 200(15-7)

Apennine Mountains [43° N, 13° E]

apes [Hominoidea other than Hominidae] (*see* Hominoidea)

Apidium, 363(25-1a)

Appian Way, 557

apple, 445, 453(29–1)

applied music, 662, 664–665

apprenticeship, 272, 627

apricot, 453(29-1)

Apurímac River [mouth at 12°17′ S, 73°56′ W], 560

Arabia [= Arabian Peninsula, 25° N, 45° E], 476, 481

Arabian Nights' Entertainments, 174

Arabic language [Semitic], 592

Arabic numerals (*see* Hindu-Arabic numerals)

Arabs, 173, 263

  (*See also* Muslims)

Aral Sea [45° N, 60° E]

Aramaic language [Semitic], 638

Arapaho [Algonquian-speaking peoples, mid-central Plains], 302(23-6)

Arawakan language family, 262, 267, 489

arbalest [or crossbow: medieval weapon], 617

arbitrariness:

  in language, 105–106, 413–414

  in representative art, 660

arch and dome, 501–502(and 31-8c)

archaeology, 97, 421

arctic, 443, 476

  (*See also* circumpolar traits)

Argentina [34° S, 64° W], 163, 475, 534

Argissa [site, inland from city Vólos, 39°21′ N, 22°56′ E, in Greece], 469(30-1), 470

Ariḥā = Jericho, 468

Aristotle [384–322 B.C.], 148, 571, 595, 637–638, 646

armed invasion, 588

Armenian language, 301(23-5), 593

  writing, 620(38-1)

armor plates on early vertebrates, 353

arrow (*see* bow)

arsenic, 531, 534

art, 409, 494, 524, 659–665

  Aurignacoid cave-wall, 274, 435–436, 526–527

art museums and cities, 556

arthritis, 352

Arthropoda, 347, 348(24-21)

artichoke, 446(29-1)

Articles of Confederation, 650

articulation (in speech), 414

articulatory matching (in understanding speech), 102

artifact, 86–97

artifaction, 96

artisan, artisanry (*see* craftsman; craftsmanship)

artist, 571–572

ascribed versus achieved status, 209, 214

ash (tree) [spp of *Fraxinus,* fam. Oleaceae], 20

Ashanti [tribe or nation, 5°30′ N, 10°30′ W], 183–184, 201(15-8), 221, 263, 268

Ashur [ancient city, near modern Ash Sharqāt, 35°27′ N, 43°16′ E, in northern Iraq], 558

Asia, 397, 418

  central, 440

  northeast, 511

    (*See also* Siberia)

  south, 220–221, 256

    domestication in, 481–482

    household pattern in, 238

    (*See also* India)

  southeast, 423–425, 439, 466, 565, 587, 669

    domestication in, 478–479

    as frontier territory for civil society, 605

  southwest, 363(25-1b), 438, 526, 532, 534, 536, 549, 553, 562, 610

    defined, 466

    domestication in, 467–472

Asia Minor (*see* Anatolia)

asparagus, 447–448, 459(29-1)

asphalt, 522

ass, 293, 462(29-2), 474–475

  wild, 474*n.*

Assam [26° N, 92° E], 482, 592

Assizes, Book of, 648

Assyrians [speakers of a Semitic language], 502, 558

asteroids, 314, 315(24-1)

astrolabe, 615

astrology, 139, 659

astronauts, 529

astronomy, 139, 581

Aterian tradition [archaeological], 437

athletic teams and cities, 556

atmosphere, 322

  composition of, 321(24-6)

  early composition of, 322-323

  change of, 340

  mass of, 95(7-4)

ATP = adenosine triphosphate

attitudes, scheduling of, 234–235

aunt and uncle terminologies, 198–199

Aurelianus, Lucius Domitius, [d. 275], 589

Aurignac [site, about 43°15′ N, 0°50′ E], 435

Aurignacian, 435

Aurignacoid tradition (archaeological), 434–436
  art, 274, 435, 526–527

Australia, 360, 406, 425, 433, 438–440, 474, 511, 545, 553, 555, 609
  dog in, 473
  Europeanized, 475
  peopling of, 423–427
  stone-polishing in, 498

Australians [aborigines], 177, 418, 423–427

Australopithecus, 363(25-1b), 384–385
  cranial capacity, 387(26-1)

Austria [47°20′ N, 13°20′ E], 628, 634

autocatalyst, 330

autoeroticism, 68

autotroph [organism not dependent on other organisms for its source of energy], 286(23-3)

avocado, 451(29-1)

avunculate, 222, 225, 236n., 567n.

avunculocal residence, 170(14-2), 171, 176

awe, 132

awl, 507

ax, 399, 494(and 31-1), 498

axle, 539–540

Ayacucho [13°7′ S, 74°13′ W], 429

aye-aye, 58(5-1), 351(24-24)

Aztecs, 486, 516, 575, 608
  roads, 558

Bab el Mandeb [12°40′ N, 43°20′ E]

baboon, 32–44, 34(3-2), 51, 62(5-5), 142–143, 158–159, 375, 405
  as early human food, 395
  locomotion, 371(25-7)
  sleeping sites, 37(3-3)

Babylon [ancient city, 32°33′ N, 44°24′ E], 569, 593

Babylonia, Babylonians [speakers of a Semitic language], 139, 502

Bach, Johann Sebastian, 662

Bacon, Roger [c.1220–c. 1292], 614

bacteria, 48n., 285(23-2), 338, 340, 344(and 24-18), 446

bactrian camel, 463(29-2), 495

Baikal, Lake [53° N, 107°40′ E], 435

Bakango Pygmies [northeast Congo, according to Lowie 1934, p. 55], 433

baking, 537

Bakunin, Mikhail Aleksandrovich [1814–1876], 148

Bali [island; 8°25′ S, 115°15′ E], 423, 605

ball games, 14

Balochi language, 592

balsam [*Abies balsamea,* fam. Pinaceae], 15

Baltic Sea [57° N, 19° E], 597

Baltic languages, 301(23-5), 599–600

Balto-Slavic languages, 301(23-5), 597

bamboo, 457(29-1), 538, 616

banana, 459(29-1)

band, 71, 364
  baboon, 35–36
  hominoid, 365(25-2)
  human, 160
    and family, 158–160
    size of, 160–161
    and tribe, 160
    and village and city, 160–164
  merging, 161
  and multicellular organism, 158
  splitting, 161

band exogamy, 407–408, 414

bandit, 571

bankers, banking, 625, 628

banteng, 464(29-2)

baobab, 449(29-1)

barbarian, 565

bark cloth, 516, 517(31-23)

barley, 457(29-1), 468–471, 553
  wild, 470(30-2)

Barnard's star, 319

barrister, 569
  (*See also* law; lawyers)

basalt, 322

base line, human historical, 146, 153, 159, 276–279(22-1)

baseball, 527
  American versus Japanese, 480

Basin [culture area of aboriginal North America], 453–454, 511

baskets, 508–511

Bass Strait/Isthmus [39°20′ S, 145°30′ E], 425–426, 429, 433

bassoon, 442

basswood [*Tilia americana* and allied *T.* species, fam. Tiliaceae], 15

Basque language, 596n.
  writing, 620(38-1)

bat (animal), 62(5-5), 350(24-23), 361, 425

bathing and swimming, 388

battering ram, 617

Batu [d. 1255], 599

Baum, Lyman Frank [1856–1919], 211

Baumgarten, Alexander Gottlieb, 637

bauxite [rock high in hydrous aluminum oxides and low in silica], 264

beam and column, 501, 502(39-1a)

bean, 10, 452(29-1), 453(29-1), 470-471, 478

bear [*Ursus* spp, fam. Ursidae, order Carnivora], 15, 22, 350(24-23)

beauty, 659–665
  and goodness and truth, 637

Beaver [set of bands speaking northern Athapaskan language, around 56° N, 118° W], 199(15-6)

beaver [*Castor fiber, C. canadensis,* fam. Castoridae, order Rodentia], 88, 464

beckoning, 99(8-1)
  (*See also* gesture)

bee, 284
  honeybee, 460(29-2)
  Hoplitis producta, 294(23-4)

beekeeping, 482–483

beer, 537

beeswax, 460(29-2), 527, 529

beet, 446(29-1), 448

Beethoven, Ludwig van, 662, 664

behavior, social, 71

Belgian hare, 461(29-2)

Belgians, 481

belief, source of, 133

bellows, 532, 533(32-2), 612, 617

belt and breechclout, 18, 388

Belt and Hotu Caves [10 miles west of Behshahr, 36°43′ N, 53°34′ E, in Iran, near southeast corner of Caspian Sea; Hotu Cave is 100 yards east of Belt], 469(30-1), 538(32-4)

belt loom, 512(31-19), 513

Bengal [23° N, 90° E; later East Pakistan, then Bangladesh]

Berbers [in and inland from Atlas Mountains in northwest Africa], 483

Bering Sea [60° N, 175° W], 423

Bering Strait/Isthmus [65°30′ N, 169° W], 423, 426(28-2), 428, 432

Berkeley, George, 656

betel, 450(29-1)

betrothal, 171

GLOSSARIAL INDEX

Bible, 593, 622
biennial plant, 447–448
bifacial working of stone tools, 398, 423, 434
bifurcate collateral or merging kinship terminology, 200(15-7)
big toes, 370–372
big stone, 499–500
bilateral descent, 175(14-3), 179
bilateral symmetry, 349–350, 354(24-27)
Bill of Rights (English), 649
bilocal residence, 170(and 14-2)
biological units of organization, 158–159
biology:
    versus physics, 48
    scope of, 55n.
biosphere, 94–96
    mass of, 95(7-4)
bipedalism, 370–375, 378
Bir el Ater [= Constantine; 36°25′ N, 6°43′ E, site near city], 437
birch [Betula spp, fam. Betulaceae], 15
birds, 349(24-22), 357, 360, 444
    brains of, 54
    as early human food, 395
    life span of, 62(5-5)
    as tool-users, 88
birth, 132–133, 248, 373, 386
    Menomini, 29
    multiple, 63, 174n., 366
    origin of, 360
birth rate, primate, 61–62
bismuth, 531
bison [Bison bison, fam. Bovidae, order Artiodactyla], 158, 294
    as early human food, 395
    hunting of, 312
bitter cassava, 407, 448(29-1)
Black Death, 626
black-eyed pea, 452(29-1)
Black Sea [43° N, 35° E], 466, 593, 595
blackberry, 453(29-1)
Blackfoot [Algonquian-speaking tribe of the northern Plains, 50° N, 112° W], 302(23-6)
blade (type of Palaeolithic tool), 434
blast furnace, 617
blending in speech, 110, 381, 414
Bloomfield, Leonard, 658
blowgun, 439
Blue Mountains [18°6′ N, 76°40′ W, in Jamaica], 267
blueberry [Vaccinium spp, fam. Ericaceae], 12

blue-green algae, 48, 340n.
boar [= wild or feral pig, Sus scrofa]:
    as early human food, 395
    life span of, 62(5-5)
Board of Longitude, 615
boats and ships, 19, 425, 429, 432–433, 470, 483–485, 542–543, 617–618
    (See also maritime peoples and traditions)
body versus soul, 252–253
    (See also dualism)
body design, 349–351
    mammalian versus reptilian, 358, 359(24-30)
body mass, human, 411
body parts:
    as property, 142
    words for, 144
Bohr, Niels Henrik David, 655
boiling, 16, 20, 406
Bologna [city, 44°29′ N, 11°20′ E], 621, 649
bomb, 616
Bonaparte, Napoleon [1769–1821], 628
bone:
    origin of, 353
    as structural material, 447
    vertebrate, 345
bonework, 394, 423, 434–435, 441, 443, 507
    carving, 399, 400(26-11), 493
    polishing, 493
book, 621
bookkeeping, double-entry, 625
boomerang, 439
Bora-Bora [16°30′ S, 151°45′ W], 484
boredom, 233(18-1)
Borneo [0°30′ N, 114° E], 51, 423, 482, 484–485
Bororo [18° S, 57° W, in Mato Grosso of Brazil], 138
borrowing in language, 107, 290
boss-worker, 245–246
bottle gourd, 447(29-1)
boundaries, political, 586
    (See also territoriality)
bourgeois, 628
bow:
    and arrow, 20, 437–440, 439(28-6)
    musical, 527, 540
    sinew-backed, 438, 529
box, wooden, 520
Bracton, Henry de, 649
Braddock, Edward [1695–1755], 565

Braddock's defeat, 565
Brahmans [highest group of hereditary Indian castes], 182
Brahms, Johannes, 664
braiding, 505(and 31-12)
brain, 53–54, 351, 386, 411, 416–417
    as early human food, 394
    and language, 121
    mammalian and primate, 58–60
    mass of, 54
brass, 534
brass instruments (musical), 442
bread, 537
breadfruit, 456(29-1)
breath and life, 639
breathing, 356, 358
breechclout, 388
Breton language, 596–597, 622
    writing, 620(38-1)
bricks, 522
bride-price, 171
bridges, 558
    of rope, 560
Britain (see Great Britain)
British, 609
    colonies in North America, 586–587
    in Jamaica, 264–267
    law, 649
British Isles, 423
    domestication in, 483
broad bean, 453(29-1)
Broca's center, 417
broccoli, 452(29-1)
bronze, 534, 590
broom, 526
brothel, 174
brother-brother dominance, 218, 220–221
brother-sister dominance, 218, 220–221
brother-sister marriage, 172
Brown, John [1800–1859], 154
brush, brushing, 526
"brushfire" wars, 669
brussels sprouts, 452(29-1)
Bryophyta, 344(24-18), 357(24-29), 445
Bryozoa = bryozoans, 79, 348(24-21)
Brythonic language, 596
Buber, Martin [1878–1965], 215n.
bubonic plague, 432, 626
buck teeth, 553
buckwheat, 451(29-1)
Buddhism, 605
budding (in reproduction), 343(24-16)
buffalo, Asiatic or water, 294, 463(29-2)
    as early human food, 395

Bugiulesti [site, about 45° N, 23° E], 391(20-3)
Bulgarian language, 599
    writing, 620(38-1)
burden, animals used for, 540
Burgundians, 598
burial (of cadaver), 251, 408
burin, 434
Burma [22° N, 98° E], 482
Burmese writing, 578
burning (of cadavers), 251
bush baby, African, 58(5-1)
    brain size, 59
Bushmen [various parts of Kalahari Desert, 24° S, 21°30′ E], 606
butternut, 449(29-1)
buttocks, 373, 374(25-12)
    and copulation, 378
buttons and buttonholes, 19, 508
buttresses, 502
Byzantium [then Constantinople, then Istanbul], 601

cabbage, 452(29-1)
cacao, 264, 450(29-1)
cadaver, disposal of, 250–252
Caesar, Gaius Julius [100–44 B.C.], 598, 619
calabash, 454(29-1), 503
calcium, metabolism of, 359
calculus, 614
California [state; also aboriginal North American culture area], 453–454, 511, 520, 549
call system (closed), 368, 380, 414
Calvin, John [1509–1564], 627
cambering of road surface, 558
Cambodia [13° N, 105° E], 587
camel, 463(29-2)
    domestication of, 475–476
    as early human food, 395
    physiology of, 476
cameo, 573
Campanus, Johannes [13th century Italian], 622
camphor, 451(29-1)
Canada, 163, 426(28-2), 427–428, 432
canary, 62(5-5)
Canary Islands [28° N, 15°30′ W], 99(8-1), 483–484
candlenut, 448(29-1)
canine teeth, 358, 362, 365(25-2), 367(25-5), 378-379

cannibalism, 250–251
    ritual, 253
cannon, 617
canoe:
    double, 485
    outrigger, 484–485
    (See also boats)
canon law, 648
cantala, 458(29-1)
caoutchouc, 90, 448(29-1)
capers, 451(29-1)
capital goods [housing and equipment for the production and storage of commodities]
capitalism, 624–634, 654
    and European expansion, 629–634
    and royalty, 628
capuchin monkeys, 58(5-1)
carbohydrates, 328
carbon black, 527
carbon compounds, 328
carbon 14, 300
carbon paper, 623
carding (combing), 516
Cariban languages, 489
Caribbean Islands (see Antilles)
Caribbean Sea [15° N, 73° W]
caribou [North American spp of *Rangifer*, fam. Cervidae, order Artiodactyla], 158
Carnivora [≠ carnivores! see below] 350(24-23), 370
    in Pliocene, 368
carnivores [meat-eating animals; the Carnivora are an order of placental mammals, most of which are carnivorous, but some are not, and many Carnivores are not carnivora], 285(23-2), 357
carotenoids, 338, 340n.
carp [*Cyprinus carpio,* originally Asiatic, introduced to Europe and then to North America; also allied spp of fam. Cyprinidae], 12
Carpathian Mountains [48° N, 24° E]
carpenters, 495
carrier pigeon, 465(29-2)
carrot, 448, 455(29-1)
carrying by hand, 369–370
    and clothing, 388
    fire, 404
carrying angle, 378, 379(24-15)
cart, 474, 536, 540
Carthage [ancient city, 36°52′ N,

Carthage (*cont'd*):
    10°20′ E], 481, 597
cartilaginous fishes, 353
cartography, 586
    (*See also* chart for navigation)
casein glue, 529
cashew, 454(29-1), 486
Caspian Sea [42° N, 50°30′ E], 466, 482, 591
cassava, 448(29-1)
    bitter, 407
castle as city, 603
castor oil plant, 448(29-1)
castration of oxen, 471
cat, 62(5-5), 350(24-23), 462(29-2)
Çatal Hüyük [site, 37°38′ N, 33° E, 32 miles southeast of Konya in Turkey], 469(and 30-1), 520
Catalan language, 596n.
    writing, 620(38-1)
catalyst, 329
categories, taxonomic, labels for, 352(24-25) [for plants, the term *division* usually replaces *phylum*]
Catholic and Protestant, 628
Catholicism, 549, 643
catlinite = pipestone [a red indurated clay found in the upper Mississippi valley], 13
cat's cradles, 504
cattle:
    humped, 482
    as monetary standard, 581
    (*See also* goat; ox; sheep)
Caucasia, Caucasus, Caucasus Mountains [42°30′ N, 35° E], 466, 536, 592
    languages in, 593
cauliflower, 452(29-1)
cave as Aurignacoid dwelling, 435
cave-wall art, Aurignacoid, 274, 435, 526–527
Caxton, William [1422–1491], 622–623
cayenne, 455(29-1)
Çayönü Tepesi [site, 3 miles southwest of Ergani, 38°17′ N, 39°46′ E, in Turkey], 469(30-1), 532
cedar [*Cedrus* and other genera of fam. Pinaceae in Old World, *Juniperus* spp. of fam. Cupressaceae in New World, all conifers], 12, 15, 90, 449, 514
celery, 455(29-1)
celery-cabbage = Chinese cabbage 452(29-1)

consultation, consultative prose, 104, 149–150
  as information-processing, 113
containers, 525
contamination in household dyads, 227–228
context in understanding speech, 102
continents, history of, 324, 325(24-8), 354n.
continuity, household, 222–224
contract, 646–648
contractual relation, 647
contractual theory, abstract, 650
convention, communicative [a shared understanding in a community as to the meanings of communicative acts]
converse kin terms, 195
convex lens, 614
convolutions in brain, 54
cony (Jamaica), 262
Cook, James [1728–1779], 549
cooking, 405–407
  and dentition, 407
  and diet, 406
  kinds of, 406
  origins of, 407
cooperation:
  in early hunting, 375–376
  economic, 168
  intertribal, 546–547
Copernicus (see Kopernik, Nikolaj)
copper, 531–532(mp)
  arrowheads of, 20
  sources of, in southwest Asia, 535(32-3)
Copper Eskimo [around 36° N, 115° W], 201(15-8)
copperhead (snake), 62(5-5)
copulation, 356, 366–367, 378
  baboon, 40, 47–48
  mammalian positions for, 68
copying machines, office, 623
cordage, 529, 579
  (See also filaments and sheets)
core (of Earth), 322
core (tool), 396
  prepared, 397–398, 434
cork, 447(29-1)
Cornish language, 596
  writing, 620(38-1)
Cornwall [50°30′ N, 4°40′ W], 594, 596
corporation, 634, 650
  versus community, 246

corpus callosum, 417
corpus striatum, 53
correspondence, one-to-one, 137
Corsica [42° N, 9° E]
Cortés, Hernán [1485–1547], 561
corundum, 493
cotton, 449(29-1), 514
  spinning, 482
  wild, 485
cotyledon, 449
Counter-reformation, 628, 643
counting, origin of, 137–138
county seats, structure of, 555
Courland = Latvia, 599
court of law, 569, 647
cousin:
  kinds of, 171
  terminologies, 199–200, 201(15-8)
cowife-cowife, 218
cowpea, 453(29-1)
coyote, 473
cradle board, 29
craft union, 627
crafts, 492–543
  Maroon, 267
craftsman (= artisan), 536, 554, 563, 622, 624–634, 654
craftsmanship, pride of, 272–274, 524
cranberry, 447(29-1)
cranial capacity, 364(25-2), 387(26-1)
crease, to, 87(7-1)
creativity, 114, 270–274, 455–456, 635
  and beauty, 642
  factors in, 270–274
  and femininity, 642
  and literacy, 581
credit, instruments of, 582
Cree [Algonquian-speaking bands around Hudson Bay and west to central Alberta], 11(2-1), 118, 239, 302(23-6), 549
Cremona [45°7′ N, 10°2′ E], 440
creole language, 197n.
crests in hominoids, 364(25-2)
Cretaceous epoch [see Running Calendar, 306], 444
Crete [35°29′ N, 24°42′ E], 472, 536, 555, 594
  writing in, 574
Crimea [45° N, 34° E]
criminal, 154, 511
criminal versus civil law, 571n.
crisis, 248, 259
  in life cycle, 132–133

criterial features in kinship terminologies, 200–201
Croatian language (see Serbo-Croatian language)
  writing, 620(38-1)
crocheting, 514, 516(31-22)
crop versus weed, 481
crop rotation, 497
cross cousin, 22, 171
crossbreeding, 474
cross-pollination, 473
Crow [Siouan-speaking tribe, 46° N, 105° W], 201(15-8)
"Crow" cousin terms, 201(15-8)
Crusades, 607
crust of Earth, 322, 530
  composition of, 321(24-6)
cucumber, 445, 446(29-1)
cultivating soil, 457
culture = tradition, 55n.
culture hero, 273
cuneiform, 592
curare, 440
currant, 453(29-1)
currency, 582
Custer, George Armstrong [1839–1876], 565
custom, 567–571
  versus law, 570
Cuzco [ancient city, 13°31′ S, 71°59′ W], 559
cyclicities, 46, 282
  expected from inside view, 259
Cyprus [35° N, 33° E], 263
Cyrus the second ["the Great"; reigned 559–530 B.C.], 601
cytoplasm [the substance within a cell but outside the nucleus], 345
Czech language, 599
  writing, 620(38-1)
Czechoslovakia, [49°30′ N, 17° E], 596

Dactylopius coccus [insect of fam. Coccidae, order Homoptera], 528
dairy, 471–472
Dakota [Siouan-speaking peoples, large area west of Great Lakes, around 45° N, 95° W], 201(15-8)
Dalmatian language, 596n.
Danish language, 301(23-5), 599
  writing, 620(38-1)
Dano-Norwegian language, 599
Dante Alighieri, 636

Danube [mouth at 45°20′ N, 29°40′ E]
Darjeeling [city, 26°3′ N, 86°16′ E], 50
Darwin, Charles Robert, 92, 655
date palm, 459(29-1), 480
daughter-father, 218, 221, 238
day, changing length of, 319
dead:
   honoring, 254
   obligations to, 253
   treatment of, 366, 387, 408
dead versus extinct (species, languages), 299
dead reckoning [determination of location by keeping record of course and speed, without instruments], 615
death, 132–133
   baboon, 44
   Menomini, 31
   social handling of, 248–257
   sudden versus gradual, 248–249
death dues, 256
deciduous [disposable, sloughed off after use]:
   versus evergreen, of plants, 448–449
   hominoid dentition, 364(25-2)
   placenta, 360
decision-making, 26, 147–155
deer [*Odocoileus* and allied genera of order Artiodactyla], 19, 477
   as early human food, 395
Defoe, Daniel [c. 1661–1731], 93
Delaware [Algonquian-speaking peoples of southernmost strip of Northeastern Woodlands], 302(23-6)
delayed transmission of information, 79
Delft [city, 52° N, 4°21′ E], 614
delivery, order of (in speaking), 114
delphinium [*Delphinium* spp, fam. Ranunculaceae], 448
democracy, 148, 625, 629, 635, 641
   Greek, 595
   and law, 652
   and science, 655
demographic balance and marriage, 173–174
Denmark [56° N, 10° E], 628, 634
density [amount of mass per unit volume], 95(7-4)
dentition:
   and cereal diet, 553
   and cooking, 407
   history of human, 362–364, 366, 378–379, 407, 473, 553
   hominoid, 364(25-2), 367(25-5)

dentition (*cont'd*):
   mammalian, 358
   origin of, 353
deoxyribonucleic acid, 48–49, 332(24-11)
depersonalization, 641
   of decision-making, 153
   of property relations, 146
depilatory, 526
derivative versus primary tools, 88
Descartes, René, 656n., 657
descent groups, 174–178
descent and kinship terminologies, 201–202(and 15-9)
descent of man, 92
descent of tools, 92–93
descriptive versus classificatory (kinship terms), 194
designs:
   on body, 19, 525
   on early stone artifacts, 572
   on pottery, 524
destruction, funereal, 255–256
destructiveness of civil society, 551–552, 629, 668–669
dialect differentiation, 296
Dias de Novais, Bartolomeu [fl. 1478–1500], 608
dicot versus monocot, 449
diet, 365, 375, 377
   baboon, 38
   cooking and, 406
   lack of meat in, 553
   and racial differentiation, 411–412
   raw meat in, 393–394
dietary restrictions, 472, 480
differences among languages:
   in grammar and lexicon, 118–119
   in sound systems, 103–104
differentiation, divergence, 414
   and change, 100
   of dialects, 296
   of human lifeways, 395–396
   racial, 293–295
difficulties of science, 654–655
diffusion (cultural and general), 107, 408, 433
   of bow and arrow, 438
   of erectus complex, 411
   of man, 395, 486
   of sapiens complex, 418
   of tobacco, 609
   (*See also under specific item*)
Digest (Justinianus), 648–649
digestion, mammalian versus reptilian, 358

digging stick, 408–409, 477, 495(31-2), 496
dimorphism, sexual, 210, 378, 379(25-15)
   in hominoids, 364(25-2)
dingo, 473
Dinka [Nilotic peoples, about 8° N, 29° E], 201(15-8)
dinosaurs [extinct reptiles of orders Saurischia and Ornithischia, subclass Archosauria], 361
diplomacy, 149, 587
direct tool, 86–87
direct transmission of information, 79
disaster, 259
   sources of, 259, 588
discovery versus invention, 137
disease, 44, 478
   and fire, 407
   in New World, 432
displacement in language, 112–113, 383, 414
dissonance in household, 227–228
distinctions, ignoring of, 203
distinctive and nondistinctive, 46–47, 83, 127
   in counting, 137
   in features of social role, 206–207
distortion of science, 659
divergence (*see* differentiation)
diversified economy, 545–548, 551
Divina Commedia (Dante), 636
division, subdivision [used in plant taxonomy, equivalent to phylum and subphylum in animal taxonomy; 352(24-25)]
DNA = deoxyribonucleic acid
Dnieper River [mouth at 46°30′ N, 32°18′ E]
do-goodism, 123, 279
Dodgson, Charles Lutwidge [Lewis Carroll, 1832–1898], 492
dog, 62(5-5), 74, 293, 350(24-23), 462(29-2), 467–471, 477, 481
   breeds of, 473
   domestication of, 472–473
dogmatism, 134
dome, 501–502
domestication, 457, 467–491
   of animals, steps in, 459–463
   antiquity of, 463
   early needs promoting, 465–466
   of fathers, 386
   focal areas of, 464–466
   growth of, 464–465

domestication (*cont'd*):
    implications of for plants, 458–459
    of people by wolves, 473
    of plants, steps in, 452–459
dominant dyads, 215–228, 237
Dorian Greeks, 594–595
double descent, 177
double-entry bookkeeping, 625
Doum palm, 459(29-1)
draft animals, 463, 540–542
dramatic troupes and cities, 556
Dravidian languages, 578, 592
dreaming, 30, 113, 249
dromedary, 463(29-2)
Druidic tradition, 581*n*.
drum signals, west African, 99(8-1), 268
dry versus wet anxiety, 231–232
dry hafting [without use of an added
    adhesive; compare "dry wall," one
    made without mortar]
drying of foods, 20, 407
dryopithecines, 363(25-1b)
dualism, soul-body or mind-matter, 133,
    254, 639–640
    and science, 655–657
    Western, 133, 639–640
duality of patterning, 105–107, 414
    and sound change, 292
duck, 464(29-2), 478
ductility, 530
duel, 153
dung, dried, as fuel, 404, 435, 487
durability of dyads, 234ff.
durations, 318(24-4)
Dutch (people), 608
Dutch-Flemish language, 301(23-5), 598
dwelling pattern, 45–46
    agricultural, 163
    baboon, 35–36
    human, 158–159
dyads of people, 202, 215
    coexistent, 235–236
    durability of, 234–235
    in household, 218
    intimate, as prototypes, 242–247, 567*n*.
dye, 527–528

eagerness, 232
eagle [various spp of fam. Accipitridae,
    order Falconiformes], 464(29-2)
ear, 351, 355, 417
Early Würm glaciation, 413(27-2), 423,
    428

Earth, 315(24-1)
    age of, 314
    birth of, 314–322
    composition of, 321(24-6)
    current structure of, 322, 530
    history of, 314–361
    mass of, 95(7-4)
earth-moving, 408
    Aurignacoid, 435
earthquake, 259, 319*n*., 588
earthworm [*Lumbricus* spp, fam.
    Lumbricidae, order Oligochaeta,
    phylum Annelida], 52
East Cape [Siberia: 68°8′ N, 169°46′ W],
    428, 432
East Germanic languages, 597–598
East Indies (*see* Indonesia; Asia,
    southeast)
Easter Island [27°8′ S, 109°23′ W], 433
    statues, 498(31-5), 499
echidna [*Tachyglossus* and *Zaglossus,* fam.
    Tachyglossidae, order Monotremata
    subclass Prototheria], 350(24-23),
    360
ecological balance, 285–286
ecological niche, 285
ecological patterns, 158–159
ecological zone, 285
ecology, 160–161
    and selection, 285–287
    human, 158–159
        balance in, 97
        in early civil society, 548
economic cooperation, 168
economy of abundance, 584
Edentata, 350(24-23)
edge (of tool), 87(7-1) [sometimes the
    same word refers not to the cutting
    edge but to the narrower sides
    behind it]
editing in speech, 113–115
efficiency in stonework, 434
egg:
    as human food, 464–465(29-2)
    reptilian versus amphibian, 356
eggplant, 455(29-1)
ego (in description of kinship terms),
    190
Egypt, 172, 252–253, 363, 440, 522–523,
    526, 528–530, 533–534, 557–558,
    593–594
    pyramids, 500, 501(31-8)
    writing, 574
einkorn wheat, 468

Einstein, Albert, 637, 655
El Jobo [site, about 10°30′ N, 69°30′ W,
    in Venezuela], 431(28-4)
El Manzanillo [site, about 9°45′ N,
    72°15′ W, in Venezuela], 431(28-4)
Elamite writing, 574
Elbe River [mouth at 53°50′ N, 9° E],
    443
elderberry, 453(29-1)
elderly, social importance of, 151, 387
electricity, 539
electrum, 532, 582
elements, relative abundance of,
    321(24-6)
elephant, 63(5-5), 350(24-23), 402(29-2)
    as early human food, 395
elephant's ear, 456(29-1)
elimination:
    baboon, 37
    hominid and human, 376–377
Eliot, Thomas Stearns, 660
élites, circulation of, 551, 566, 571
Ellsworth Falls [about 44°33′ N,
    68°26′ W in Maine, site nearby],
    430(28-3)
elm [*Ulmus* spp, fam. Ulmaceae, order
    Urticales], 20, 448
embalming, 252
embankments, 558
embryo, 355
emergence of man, 362–419
emery, 493, 527
emic and etic, 676
emmer wheat, 468
emotion, 66, 132–133
    and internal organs, 239–240, 639–640
    and science, 121–123, 654–655
empire:
    growth of, 585–586
    machinery of, 553–584
    and writing, 573
empirical information, 134
empiricism, 113
    and science, 652–654
empiricists and rationalists, 656
enabling act, 569
endive, 446(29-1)
endogamy, 172, 236
    and gene flow, 172*n*.
Endothia parasitica [fungus, fam.
    Melogrammataceae, class
    Ascomycetes], 286
energy:
    compared with money, 581

energy (*cont'd*):
  Earth's sources of, 324
  history of, 91
  human sources of, 91, 404, 438,
    460–463, 538–539
energy molecules, 330
enforceability of law, 568
engineer and craftsman, 629
engineering:
  mechanical, 612
  and science, 652
engineers, corps of, 561
England [52°30′ N, 1°30′ W], 404, 532n.,
  599, 628
English language, 301(23-5), 598
  borrowings from French, 107, 119,
    192n.
  pronouns, recent history of, 190–191
  writing, 580n., 620(38-1)
English poetry, 140
entertainment, 554
  (*See also* fun)
entrepreneur, 624
entropy [the extent to which the
  distribution of energy in a physical
  system approaches completely even
  distribution], 81n., 91, 285(23-2)
environment:
  and genes, 49
  versus self, 145
environmental variety, implication of,
  545–546
enzymes, 49
ephemeral coincidence of dyads, 235–236
episode, 232, 233(18-1)
epochs and eras, geological [*see* Running
  Calendar, 304–311]
erectus complex, 384–385, 411, 420, 429
  spread of, 411
ermine, 462(29-2)
erosion, 468
escapement, 613
escarole, 446(29-1)
Eskimo [bands scattered over arctic
  littoral of North America, including
  southern and western coasts of
  Alaska, and parts of Greenland],
  99(8-1), 201(15-8), 432, 440, 443
"Eskimo" cousin terms, 201(15-8)
Esquivel, Juan de [fl. 1495–1515], 263
"establishment, the," 271
estate practices, 254–257
Esthonia, Estonia [59° N, 26° E], 600
Esthonian writing, 620(38-1)

"eternal triangle," 236–237
ethics, 421, 637, 645–652
  and science, 659
  source of human, 72
Ethiopia [9° N, 41° E], 479–480
ethnocentric history, 282n., 602
ethnographers, 147
ethnographic present, 3(def)
ethnography, 3, 635
etic and emic, 676
Etruria [central Italy, southwest of
  Rome, from 8th century B.C.],
  Etruscans, 502, 594, 596
Euclid [fl. 300 B.C.], 622
eunuch [castrated male human being],
  174
Euphrates River [mouth at 31° N,
  47°25′ E], 474, 557
Eurasia, 473
  central, 466, 590
    domestication in, 473–476
  central and northern, 493
    as frontier for civil society, 604–605
Europe, 396, 398, 435, 441, 474–475,
  494(31-1), 528, 537–538, 585–586
  domestication in, 481
  eastern, 434–435, 520
  expansion of, 93, 147, 160, 590,
    607–610
  medieval, 562, 571, 602
  northern, 163, 265n., 442
  southern, 474
  western, 536
European languages, pronouns, 187
euthanasia, 249n.
Eutheria [placental mammals],
  350(24-23), 360
evergreen versus deciduous, 448
eversion of city, 556
evidence:
  historical, 421
  legal, rules of, 651
evolution, organic, 287, 342
  and science, 653
excitement, 232
exclusiveness in dyads, 218–219
exile, 160–161
exogamy, 236
  of bands, 171–172
exoskeleton, 354(24-27)
expansion of Europe, 93, 147, 160, 590,
  607–610
expert, 151–152, 168
expert witness, 651

expulsion from band, 160–161
extended family, extended household,
  179ff.
external fertilization, 356
extinct versus dead (language), 297
extinction of animal species, 297,
  452–453
extremities, bodily, 353
  (*See also* limbs)
eye, 351
Eynan [site, about 32°30′ N, 35°28′ E],
  469(30-1)

face (of tool), 87(7-1)
facial gesture, 99(8-1), 368
  chimpanzee, 67(5-8)
facial muscles, 66, 362
fact at law, 652
  determination of, 651
  and in science, 651
factory system, 627
Faeroe Islands [62° N, 7° W], 433, 599
fairness, 569
faith, 132
falcon, falconry, 464(and 29-2)
Faliscan language, 595
Fameguest [4th century A.D.], 572, 582n.,
  660
family, 159–160, 165–184
  and band, 158–160
  Menomini, 22–23
  Maroon, 269–270
  origin of, 160, 386
  (*See also* household; marriage)
Fanti [west African people, about 7° N,
  1° E], 263
Far East [China, Japan, Korea, and
  adjacent territory], 553
Farmington [town, 37°56′ N, 121° W in
  California; site nearby], 430(28-3)
Faroese language, 301(23-5), 599
Fascist Italy, 609
fashion, spread of, 213
fat, 334
  animal, for human use, 527
  mammalian, 358
father, social, 166
father-daughter, 218, 221, 238
father-son, 216–218
Faust (Goethe), 642n.
favored numbers, 138–140, 637
Fayyum [valley or gorge; 29°19′ N,
  30°50′ E], 480

fresh versus salt water, 326
Friesenhahn Cave [site, about 30° N, 100° W, in Texas], 430(28-3)
Frisian language, 301(23-5), 598
  writing, 620(38-1)
frog [suborder Diplasiocoela, order Anura, class Amphibia], 355
  as early human food, 395
frontal approach in copulation, 378
fructose, 334(24-12)
fruit, 444–445
frying, 406
fuel, 539
  for fires, 404
Fuerteventura [easternmost of Canary Islands, 28°20′ N, 14° W], 483
fun, 73, 161, 272
functional interconnections, 276–277
functional splitting, 562–563, 583
fungus [pl. fungi], 343–344(and 24-18)
furniture, 15, 529
future versus past, 657

Galatia, 596
galaxies, 314, 316(24-2), 317(24-3)
Galileo Galilei, 554–555, 613
Gallehus [town, 54°57′ N, 8°48′ E]
gallstones, 352
Gama, Vasco da [c. 1460–1524], 608
game (entertainment), 233(18-1)
gamete, 345, 347(24-20), 444
garlic, 458(29-1)
garter snake, 62(5-5)
Gaul, 440, 597
Gautama Buddha [c. 563–483 B.C.], 605
gayal, 464(29-2)
gazelle [Gazella and related genera, fam. Bovidae, order Artiodactyla], 38
Gebrauchsmusik, 662
gel state, 337
gelatin, animal, 529
Gemeinschaft versus Gesellschaft, 246
gene, 48–49, 342
  and environment, 49
  and language, 121
gene flow, 408
  and endogamy, 172n.
gene pool, 49, 283
General Motors, 549
generation (in kinship terms), 193, 200–201
"generational" kinship terminology, 200(15-7)

genetic persistence, 50, 297–298
genetic selection, 283
genetics, 48–51
  and behavior, 50–51
  and language, 101–102
  and tradition, 55–56
Genghis Khan (see Temujin)
Genoa [44°25′ N, 8°57′ E], 596
genus name, conventions of, 352(24-25)
geological eras, periods, and epochs [see Running Calendar, 304–311]
Georgia, Strait of [49°20′ N, 124° W]
Georgian Bay [45°15′ N, 80°50′ W], 10
Georgian writing (Caucasus), 620(38-1)
German language, 301(23-5), 598
  pronouns, 190
  writing, 620(38-1)
Germanic languages, 301(23-5), 597–599
Germany [51° N, 11° E], 628
Gessellschaft versus Gemeinschaft, 246
gestation, 360
  hominoid, 364(25-2)
  primate, 61
gesture, 99(and 8-1), 413n.
  facial, 66, 67(5-8), 206
Ghatchi [site, about 23° S, 69° W, in Chile], 431(28-4)
gherkin, 446(29-1)
gibbon, 58(5-1), 351(24-24), 363(25-1a), 381
Gigantopithecus, 363(25-1b)
Gila River [confluence with Colorado River near Yuma, Arizona, 32°43′ N, 114°37′ W], 454
Gilbert Islands [0°30′ S, 174° E], 504
gills, 353
Ginastera, Alberto, 663
ginger, 459(29-1)
glass, 523, 614
  (See also glazing pottery; obsidian)
glazing pottery, 520
glottis, 415
Gluck, Christoph Willibald, 662
glucose, 334(and 24-12), 446
glue, gluing, 405, 528–530, 534
gluteus maximus, 373–374(and 25-12)
glutton [Gulo gulo, fam. Mustelidae, order Carnivora], 435
goal (of planning and choosing), 232
goal-directed behavior, 47, 83–85, 258
goat, 62(5-5), 463(29-2), 467–471
  wild, 471(30-3)
Gobi Desert [43° N, 106° E], 475
Gödel, Kurt, 658

gods and government, 153, 583
Goethe, Johann Wolfgang von, 642n., 643
Goidelic language, 596
gold, 262, 317, 530–531, 532(mp), 582
gold-bricking, 564
Gold Coast [now mostly Ghana, 8° N, 2° W], 263
gold-copper alloy, 532
golden plover [Pluvialis dominica, fam. Charadriidae], 45
goldsmith, 571–572
Good Hope, Cape of [34°24′ S, 18°30′ E], 608
goodness, 645–652
  and beauty and truth, 637ff.
goose, 464(29-2), 478
gorilla, 58(5-1), 351(24-24), 363(25-1), 368
  cranial capacity, 387(26-1)
  ground walking, 370–371(and 25-7)
goshawk [Accipiter spp, fam. Accipitridae, order Falconiformes], 464(29-2)
Gothic language, 301(23-5)
  writing, 598, 620(38-1)
Goths, 597–598, 601
gouge [woodworker's tool], 495
governance, craft of, 551–552
government, 147–155
  of a city, 554
  and gods, 153, 583
  origins of, 547–549
  and religion, 582–584
Goya y Lucientes, Francisco José de [1746–1828], 564
grains, 449, 458, 553
grammar and lexicon, 111–112
grandparent and grandchild, 218
granite, 322
grapefruit, 444–445, 449(29-1), 478
grapevine, 451(29-1)
graphite, 90
grasses, 449, 458, 553
Great Australia, 360, 424(28-1), 425, 484–485
Great Britain [53° N, 4° W], 435, 483, 536, 563, 596, 608
Great Lakes region (North America), 455, 531–532
Great Pyramid of Khufu [near al-Jīzah, 30°1′ N, 31°13′ E], 500–501(and 31-8), 561
Great Wall of China [touches Gulf of Chihli at 40°1′ N, 119°44′ E], 586

Grecian urns, 524
Greece [39° N, 22° E], 140, 208, 524, 586
Greek language, 638
  medieval, 619
  pronouns, 186(15-1), 187
  writing, 579, 594
Greeks, 480, 595–596, 637–639, 659–660
Green Bay [around 45° N, 87°30′ W], 8–10
green plants, 285(23-2), 340, 344(24-18), 444–450
Greenland [71° N, 40° W], 433
gregariousness, 68–69
grips, primate, 64, 65(5-6)
grooming, 19, 63, 143, 367
  baboon, 40
  and sex, 67
group marriage, 166(14-1), 173
group as pole of dyad, 239
Guam [island: 13°28′ N, 144°47′ E], 608
guava, 450(29-1)
guilds, 627
guilt and shame, 207–208
Guinea Coast (Africa), 605, 608
guinea fowl, 465(29-2)
Guinea hemp, 449(29-1)
guinea pig, 62(5-5), 461(29-2)
guitar, 440
Gulf Stream, 326
gun, 616–617
  on a ship, 618
gunpowder, 616
Günz glaciation, 413(27-2)
Gururumba [tribe in upper Asaro valley, about 6° N, 145° E, in eastern New Guinea], 226
Gutenberg, Johann [c. 1398–1468], 614, 621–622, 624
Gypsies [originally from India; their language, Romany, is Indo-Aryan], 626
gypsum, 522

habitats of hominoids, 365(25-2)
Haçilar [village, 37°44′ N, 30° E; site one mile west], 469(30-1)
Hadley, John [1682–1744], 615, 622
hafting, 394, 398–399, 423, 436, 529
Hague, The [city; 52°6′ N, 4°18′ E], 613
Haida [tribe on Queen Charlotte Islands, 51°30′ N, 129° W], 221–222, 226

Hainandao [island; 19° N, 110° E], 485
hair, mammalian, 358
hairlessness, 387–388
half sibling and half sibling, 218
Hamilton, Alexander [1755–1804], 266n.
hammer, 434
hammer, to, 87(7-1)
hammock, 267
Hammurabi [about 18th century B.C.], 569
hamster, 62(5-5), 68
hand ax (Pleistocene stone tool), 396(and 26-7)
hand carrying, 369–370
hand weaving, 508–510
handedness, 366, 416
  lacking in baboons, 35
handle (of tool), 87(and 7-1)
Hannibal [247–183 or 182 B.C.], 481
Hanseatic League, 617, 625, 634
Harappa [ancient city, about 31° N, 73° E], 482
harbors, silting of, 594
hardness, 530
hardware and history, 421–422
hare, 350(24-23), 461(29-2)
harem, 174, 526
harpoon, 436
Harrison, John [1693–1776], 616, 622
harrowing, 463
Harvey, William [1578–1657], 639
Harz Mountains [51°45′ N, 10°30′ E]
hashish, 456(29-1)
Hatusas [ancient city, near village of Boğazköy, 40°2′ N, 34°37′ E, in Turkey], 593
Hausa [west African people, around 12° N, 8° E], 219
Hausa potato, 454(29-1)
Hawaii, Hawaiians, [archipelago, 19°30′ N, 155°30′ W], 45, 172, 440, 484–485, 494(31-1), 549
  kinship terminology, 199(15-6), 200(15-7), 201(15-8)
"Hawaiian" cousin terms, 201(15-8)
Haydn, Franz Joseph, 662
head, hominid, 386
head (of tool), 87(and 7-1)
hearing, 351, 355, 417
heart, 639–640
heat technology, 523, 527
heat welding, 534
Hebraic tradition, 140, 593
  (See also Jews)

Hebrew language [Semitic], 619, 622, 638
heddle, 513
hedonism, 643
heights (bodily) of hominoids, 364(25-2)
Heinlein, Robert Anson, 661
Heisenberg, Werner Karl, 655
Hellenic languages, 301(23-5), 594–595
hemp, 456(29-1), 473, 477–478, 517
  Guinea hemp, 449(29-1)
Henlein, Peter H. [c. 1480–1542], 613
Henry the Eighth [1491–1547], 627
Henry the Navigator [1394–1460], 618, 622
Heraclitus of Ephesus [c. 540–c. 480 B.C.], 282
herbaceous versus woody, 446–447
herbivore [not a taxonomic label; any animal that eats only plants], 158, 285(23-2), 389
herd animals, 435
herding (see pastoral nomads)
hernia, 378
Herodotos [5th century B.C.], 500, 594
Heron of Alexandria [1st century], 404
heterotroph [organism dependent for its source of energy on other organisms], 286(23-3), 344(24-18)
hexagonal weave, 509(31-16)
hibernation, 358
hickory, 20, 449(29-1)
hide, animal, 389, 394, 435, 441, 507
  clothing of, 17–19, 428
high-altitude adaptation, 50
Higher Powers, 14, 22, 26, 135, 640, 651
  (See also gods and government)
highland, man's invasion of, 400
Himalaya Mountains [28°30′ N, 84° E]
Hindu-Arabic numerals, 580, 619, 625
Hindus, 472, 484, 580
  expansion, 605
hingeing, 539
hinny, 293, 462(29-2), 475
Hipparchos [fl. 146–127 B.C.], 615
hippopotamus, 62(5-5)
historians, documentary, 97
historical base line (see base line)
historical evidence, 96
  limitations of, 420–421
historical inference, 300
history:
  and hardware, 421–422
  laws of, 282
history, as science, 282, 653

India (*cont'd*):
   southern, 440
Indian elephant, 462(29-2)
Indians, American, 432, 475
   North American, 407
   South American, 139
   (*But see mainly by region or tribe*)
indigo, 264, 528
indirect tool, 436
Indo-Aryan languages, 301(23-5), 578, 592
Indo-European languages and peoples, 301(23-5), 590–600, 605
   Proto Indo-European, 300–301, 482–483
Indo-Iranian languages, 301(23-5), 591–593
Indochina [term used loosely for continental southeast Asia], 605
Indonesia [insular southeast Asia; 5° S, 120° E], 484–485, 511, 605, 608, 634
Indus River [mouth at 24°20′ N, 67°47′ E]
Indus Valley society, 482, 557–558, 574, 579, 592
industry, growth of, 625
infant care, 72–73, 365, 388
infanticide, 174
infidels, 607
information, 48, 78–85, 336
   quantification, 81–82
   rate of transmission, 79, 149
   redistribution, 104
   storage, 52–53, 416–417
inheritance practices, 254–255
inheritance taxes, 256
initiation, 150–151
ink, 527–528
inner circle (in social structure), 70
innovation, 270–274, 421–422
   in language, 108–111
   through play, 75–77
insanity, 239–241
   etiology of, 241
insects, 79, 347, 356–357, 444
inside view, 123, 132*n.*, 156–158, 420, 656, 659
   in ethnography, 129
   and outside view, 158
   self-validating features of, 139
intaglio, 573
interest (fiscal), 625
internal combustion engine, 539
internal fertilization, 356

internalization [learning an attitude or orientation so that it becomes habitual], 208
interpersonal transactions and kinship terminology, 202–204
interpretation of law, 569
intimate versus loose possession, 144
intonation, 116, 120, 417
invention versus discovery, 137
invertebrates [all Chordata except those of subphylum Vertebrata, and all animal phyla except the phylum Chordata], 79, 344(34-18)
ion [like an atom or molecule except with an excess or deficit of electrons], 327
ionosphere, 322
   origin of, 340
Iran [32° N, 53° E], 466
Iranian languages, 301(23-5), 592–593
   writing, 592
Iraq [33° N, 44° E], 408, 466, 474
Ireland [53° N, 8° W], 483, 596, 599, 621
iridium, 531
Irish language, 596
   writing, 620(38-1)
iron, 531, 536(mp), 537, 594, 596–597, 617
Iroquoian languages, 11(2-1)
Iroquoians [group of tribes in a league; all speakers of Iroquoian languages], 10, 455
"Iroquois" cousin terms, 201(15-8)
irreversibility, 551
   of language split, 296
   of results of sound change, 292
   significance of, 300
   of speciation, 295
irrigation, 454, 457
Isabella [1451–1504] and Ferdinand [1452–1516], 607–608
Islam, 250, 601, 605–607
isostasy, 319, 542
Istanbul [41°1′ N, 28°58′ E], 607
Italian city-states, 263
Italian language, 596*n.*
   writing, 620(38-1)
Italic languages, 301(23-5), 595–596
Italo-Celtic languages, 301(23-5), 595–597
Italy [42° N, 18° E], 537, 594, 628
ivory [= tooth, except that to be called "ivory" a single tooth must be big enough to supply material for one or more artifacts], 422, 434–435,

ivory (*cont'd*):
   462(29-2), 538

jackal, 38, 473
jade, jadeite, 494
Jamaica [island; 18°15′ N, 77°30′ W], 260–270, 262(21-2), 478
Janssen, Zacharias [late 16th century Dutchman], 614
Japan [36° N, 138° E], 433, 435, 440, 483, 520, 610, 669
   domestication in, 486
Japanese culture/society, 207–208, 247
   favored numbers in, 138
   household pattern, 236
   privacy in, 208
   pronouns, 189*n.*
   versus that of United States, 245–246
Japanese persimmon, 447(29-1)
Java [island; 7°30′ S, 110° E], 363(25-1b), 423, 482
Javanese writing, 578
javelin, 536
jaw, 362, 378–379, 415
   origin of bony, 353
jealousy of human males, 386
Jericho [city = Arīḥā, 31°52′ N, 35°27′ E, site about one mile west of city], 467–469(and 30-1), 549
Jerusalem artichoke, 446(29-1)
Jesuits, 9, 28
Jesus, 154, 638–641
jewelry, 582
Jews, 472, 480, 607, 618–622, 624–626, 636, 641–643, 662
   personal naming of, 256
   (*See also* Hebraic tradition; Judeo-Christian tradition)
Joan of Arc, 642*n.*
Johansson, Carl Edvard [1864–1943], 529
Johansson blocks, 529
jokes, 113
joking relationship, 24
Jordan River [flows into Dead Sea at 31°46′ N, 35°33′ E], 467
Juby, Cap(e) [27°58′ N, 12°55′ W], 483
Judeo-Christian tradition, 253
judge, legal, 569, 651
Jugoslavia [44° N, 19° E]
jujube, 451(29-1)
junk principle, 97, 342, 350, 668
Jupiter (planet), 315(24-1)
jury, 569, 651

Latin language (*cont'd*):
writing, 596
latitude:
determination of, 615
and longitude, 615
and racial differentiation, 411
latrine, 16, 243*n.*, 376–377, 555
lattice-work wrapped weave, 509(31-16)
Latvia [57° N, 25° E], 599, 634
law (man-made), 149, 153, 167, 567–571,
645–652
amending, 650
civil versus criminal, 571*n.*
versus custom, 570
and democracy, 652
early, 567–571
general versus contractual, 648
schools of, 621, 651
and science, 645–646, 651
source of, 652
law of history, 282
law of nature [or of physics], 282, 287,
571, 614
versus man-made law, 570–571
lawyers, 568–569
lead (metal), 534(mp)
leadership, 151–152, 547, 624–625
baboon, 42
in consultation, 152
leaf, 445–446
leaf-sponge, chimpanzee, 90(7-3)
learning, 51–52
to learn, 73
by play, 75
primate, 73–75
selection in, 288
Lee, Robert Edward [1807–1870], 154
leek, 458(29-1)
Leeuwenhoek, Anton van [1632–1723],
614
leg, origin of, 355
leg length, hominoid, 375
legal versus alegal, 570
legal computation, 647–648
Leibniz, Gottfried Wilhelm [1646–1716],
614, 656*n.*, 657
leister, 443
leisure, 422, 493
lemon, 448(29-1)
lens, 614
lentil, 452(29-1), 468
Lettish language, 599
writing, 620(38-1)
lettuce, 446(29-1), 449

Levant, the [= eastern Mediterranean
shore], 436
lever, principle of, 436
levirate, 169
Lewisville [town, 33°3′ N, 97° W; site
nearby], 429, 430(28-3)
lexicon, 108
and grammar, 111–112
Libya [27° N, 17° E], 480, 610
lice [*Pediculus humanus* and allied spp,
fam. Pediculidae, order Anoplura],
19, 44, 526
(*See also* grooming)
licking, 359
(*See also* grooming)
life, origin of, 328–337
life crises, 132–133
life cycle, 386
baboon, 40–44
life after death, 253–254
life span, 60, 62(5-5), 366
and fire, 406–407
light, fire for, 404–405
lightning, 327–328
Ligurian language, 596
lima bean, 452(29-1)
limbs, primate, 63–64
proportion of, 365(25-2), 372(25-9)
lime (fruit), 449(29-1)
limitations on science, 655–657
Limnopithecus, 363(25-1a)
Limpopo River [mouth at 25°15′ S,
33°30′ E], 606
lineage, 175(14-3), 196
lineal, collateral, and affine, 193, 200
"lineal" kinship terminology, 200(15-7)
Linear A and B writing, 594
linen [from flax], 448(29-1)
ling [fish: *Molva molva,* fam. Gadidae],
284(23-1)
linseed oil [from flax], 448(29-1), 528
lion, 294, 350(24-23)
and baboon, 36
litchee, 454(29-1)
literacy:
and creativity, 581
impact of, 588
spread of, 580–581
(*See also* printing; writing)
literature, 28–29, 113, 120, 225
lithography, 622
lithosphere, 322
Lithuanian language, 599
writing, 620(38-1)

litter size, 61–62
Little Bighorn River [45°54′ N,
107°34′ W], 565
Littleton, Thomas, 649
live oaks, 449
liver as seat of emotions, 639
llama, 463(29-2)
lobe-fin, 353–355
Locke, John, 645*n.*, 656
locking of knees, 372
locomotion:
arboreal, 64
of hominoids, 364–365(and 25-2)
water versus land, 353, 355(24-28)
loess, 476
logic, 109, 178, 637, 652–659
Lombards, 598
London [51°30′ N, 0°10′ W]
longevity, hominoid, 364(25-2)
Longfellow, Henry Wadsworth
[1807–1882], 106
longitude:
and latitude, 615
determination of, 615–616
loom weaving, 512–514
loose versus intimate possession, 144–145
loosely connected versus tightly
connected species, 295
Los Angeles [34°3′ N, 118°15′ W], 555
love, 170, 640–641
Lower Klamath Lake [41°55′ N,
121°42′ W], 550
loyalties, divided, 237
lubrication, 526–527
Lumpenproletariat, 571
lung, 353–354
Lung Shan tradition (archaeological),
477
lungfishes, 353–354
Luther, Martin [c. 1483–1546], 627
Luvian language, 593
Luzon Island [16° N, 121° E], 605
lycanthropy, 472–473
Lycia [36°–37°30′ N, 29°–30°30′ E], 593
Lydia [capital city Sardis, *which see*],
582, 593
lying, 112

macaque monkey, 58(5-1)
Macedon [centered in plain at head of
Thermaic gulf, about 40°40′ N,
22°40′ E], 561, 595
machine, 539–540

Mackenzie River [mouth at 69°15′ N, 134°8′ W], 428, 511
macromolecule, 329–335
Mactán Island [10°18′ N, 123°58′ E], 608
Madagascar [island; 20° S, 47° E], 266, 440, 605
  peopling of and domestication in, 484
madder [dye made from root of *Rubia tinctorum* and allied *R.* spp, fam. Rubiaceae], 528
Madison Avenue, 584, 659
Mafia, 549
Magallanes, Hernando de [1480–1521], 608
Magians [Persian religious group, probably followers of Zoroaster], 607
Maglemosians, 442–443
Magna Carta, 649
magnetic field, Earth's, 342
magnetism, 322
maguey, 458(29-1)
Maid of Orléans, 642*n.*
Maidu [bands centered around 38°30′ N, 121° W in California], 440, 511
mainspring, 613
Mainz [city, 50°1′ N, 8°16′ E], 624
maize, 10, 458(29-1), 553
Malabar [coastal region, 11° N, 75° E], 182–183
Malagasy language [Malayo-Polynesian], 484
malaguetta pepper, 459(29-1)
malaria, 432
Malay insanity, 239
Malayo-Polynesian language family, 484–485, 605
  proto, 485*n.*
male versus female (human), 131–132, 151, 166, 171, 237, 408*n.*
Malecite [Algonquian bands and dialects, in and near New Brunswick, 47° N, 66° W], 302(23-6)
malleability, 530
Mallorca [island; 39°30′ N, 3° E], 618
mammae = mammary glands, 359
Mammalia = mammals, 349(24-22), 350(24-23), 357–361, 444
  brains of, 54
  life-spans of, 62(5-5)
mammary apparatus, primate, 63
mammoth [extinct, *Mammuthus* spp, fam. Elephantidae, order Proboscidea], 435

Man, Isle of [54°15′ N, 4°30′ W], 597
man, emergence of, 302–419
Manchus, 604–605
mango, 454(29-1)
Manius [7th or 6th century B.C.], 572
Manix, Lake [site in Mojave desert, about 35°6′ N, 117° W], 430(28-3)
mano and metate, 496, 497(31-4)
mansion and slum, 554–557
mantle of Earth, 322
manure, 463
Manus [community in Admiralty Islands], 226–227
Manx cat, 480
Manx language, 597
  writing, 620(38-1)
Maori [Polynesian-speaking aborigines of New Zealand]: schools, 621*n.*
map, 586
  (*See also* chart)
maple, 454(29-1), 448
  sap, sugar, syrup, 12, 20
marble, 468
marches of an empire, 586
  (*See also* territoriality)
marginal kinship terms, 192
Mariolatry, 642
marital link in kinship terminologies, 200
maritime peoples and traditions, 433, 484, 594, 617
marjoram, 454(29-1)
market town, 164
marmoset [*Callithrix* spp, New World monkey]: brain size, 59
Maroons (Jamaica), 260–270
  origin of term, 266
marriage, 132–133, 166–167
  and demographic balance, 173–174
  kinds of, 166–167, 166(14-1)
  and kinship terminology, 201–202(and 15-9)
  Maroon, 269–270
  Menomini, 22, 31
  preferred, 22, 173
  and sex, 167
marrow as early human food, 394
Mars (planet), 315(24-1)
Marshall, John [1755–1835], 544
marshmallow, 449(29-1)
Marsupialia = marsupials, 350(24-23), 360, 425
Marx, Karl, 583
Mascouten [= Prairie Potawatomi], 11(2-1)

mass, 95(7-4)
  of hominoid bodies, 364(25-2)
Massachusett [Algonquian-speaking tribe or bands, centering aboriginally about 42° N, 71°30′ W], 302(23-6), 486
mastoid process in hominoids, 364(25-2)
masturbation, 68
mat, 15
  hanging in doorway, 539
material versus spiritual, 130
maternal care, 366
maternal effect, 55
maternity, 165
  social, 166
mathematics, 113, 657–658
  and language, 658
  origins of, 137–138
matrilineal descent, 175(14-3)
  versus patrilineal, 175–176
  sources of, 176
matrilocal residence, 170(and 14-2)
matri-patrilocal residence, 170(and 14-2)
Mattawa River [confluence with Ottawa River at 46°19′ N, 78°43′ W]
matter, history of, 90–91
Mauer [site west of Heidelberg, 49°25′ N, 8°43′ E, in Germany], 391(26-3)
Maya [Yucatán], 575, 580, 608
  roads, 558
Mayflower Compact, 650
Mazatecos [communities in Oaxaca and Puebla, Mexico, around 18° N, 97°30′ W], 99(8-1)
"mead" (the word), 483
meaning, 80(def), 105
  of kinship terms, 192
measles, 432
meat diet, 375, 377
  and feces, 377
Mecca [= Makkah, 21°27′ N, 39°49′ E], 607
mechanical engineering, 612
Medes [kingdom, about 35–37° N, 48–50° E], 592
medical schools and cities, 556
medieval period = Middle Ages (European), 602
Mediterranean Sea [35° N, 20° E]
Mediterranean shore, 481
medium, suspending, 336
megaliths (*see* big stone)

Melanesia [archipelago, 13° S, 164° E], Melanesians, 427, 484–485

Melanesian Pidgin English kinship terms, 197

memory, 383

men [see male versus female (human)]

Menominee River [mouth at 45°5′ N, 87°36′ W], 8, 10

Menomini [Algonquian tribe on and near shore of Green Bay], 8–31, 11(2-1), 125, 150, 160, 173, 435, 455, 561, 636, 640

and Europeans, 146

kinship terminology, 198, 199(15-6), 200(15-7), 201(15-8)

property talk, 143–144

technical know-how, 94

theory of communication, 135

world view, 27–29, 133–136

Menomini language:

affiliation of, 302(23-6)

noun classes, 134–136

personal pronouns, 157, 187

sound system, 126, 674

menstruation, 66–67, 366

Menomini handling of, 16

Mercator (see Kremer, Gerhard)

merchants, 624ff.

"merchant prince," 174

Mercury (planet), 315(24-1)

mercury, 531

merging of bands, 161

Mescalero Apache [band around 35° N, 105°30′ W], 199(15-6)

Mesopotamia [region above Persian Gulf between Euphrates and Tigris Rivers], 474, 479, 508, 522–523, 528, 557, 569

Messapic language, 595

Metacomet [fl. second half 17th century], 147

metal fatigue, 530

metal tools on stone, 500

metallurgy, 502, 523, 530–537

metals, properties of, 530

metamorphosis (biological), 355

metaphor, 108, 639–640

metaphorical uses of kinship terms, 196–197

metate and mano, 496, 497(31-4)

Metazoa [= multicellular animals], 347, 348(24-21), 446

meteoric metals, 531

method of science, 652–653

Metz [49°8′ N, 6°10′ E], 611

Mexico [23° N, 102° W], 432, 466, 486–491, 494, 533

wheeled toys in, 540

Mexico, Valley of [19°30′ N, 99° W], 428–429, 523, 549, 558, 575

stone structures in, 500

(See also Aztecs)

Mexico City [19°24′ N, 99°9′ W]

Miami [Algonquian-speaking tribe or bands, southeastern part of Northeastern Woodlands], 11(2-1), 302(23-6)

Micmac [Algonquian-speaking bands, New Brunswick and Nova Scotia], 302(23-6)

Micronesia [archipelago; 11° N, 159° E], 423, 484–485

microscope, 614

Midas, King [late 8th century B.C.], 593

Middle Ages (European), 602

Middle America [includes Mexico, Central America, and the Antilles, which see also], 528, 531

mileposts, 558n.

military dialectic, 566

military training, universal, 566

milk:

origin of, 359

from domesticated animals, 471

Mill, John Stuart [1806–1873], 214

millet, 458(29-1), 477, 553

Milne, Alan Alexander [1882–1956], 156

Mílos [island; 36°41′ N, 24°15′ E], 470

mimeograph, 623

mind, 655–657

mind-matter dualism, 254

Mindanao [island; 7°30′ N, 125° E], 424

Mindel glaciation, 413(27-2)

minerals, 327

Ming vases, 524

mink, 462(29-2)

Minoa (Crete), 472

mint (plant), 454(29-1)

Miocene [see Running Calendar, 306–307], 32, 362, 368

mirror, 614

mislearning, uncorrected, 111

missionaries, 147

Mississippi Valley, lower [mouth of Mississippi River at 29° N, 89°15′ W], 488

Mitanni kingdom [centered around 37° N, 39° E], 592

mitosis, 343(24-16)

mnemonic marks, 572–574

moccasins, 19

Moctezuma [1466–1520; "Montezuma" is a misspelling], 561

moderator, role of, 152–153

Mohenjo-Daro [ancient city, 27°40′ N, 68°70′ E], 482

Mohorovičić discontinuity, 323(24-7)

Mohs, Friedrich, 493n.

Mohs hardness scale, 493n.

moiety, 175(14-3)

molar motion, 324

molars, (teeth), 358

molded pottery, 519

mole (animal), 62(5-5), 350(24-23)

molecule, 327

Molière [Jean Baptiste Poquelin, 1622–1673], 149

Mollusca = mollusks, 348(24-21), 528

money, 581–582, 625

desirable properties of, 582

economy based on, 646

Mongolia [47°30′ N, 104° E], 474–475

Inner [= Neimenggu, 43° N, 115° E], 435

Mongolian writing, 580n.

Mongols, 585–586, 604

monkeys, 57, 58(5-1), 64, 66(5-3), 158

monocot versus dicot, 449

monogamy, 166(14-1), 173

reasons for, 168

Monotremata = monotremes, 350(24-23), 366n., 425

Montagnais [bands speaking eastern Cree dialects (Algonquian), east and southeast of Hudson Bay], 302(23-6)

Montana [state; 47° N, 110° W]

Montego Bay [town; 18°30′ N, 77°55′ W, in Jamaica], 266

month, lunar, 140, 613

Menomini names for, 12

montmorillonite clay, 518

mood, 232, 233(18-1)

Moon, 314, 315(24-1), 327

Moors, 263, 598, 607, 611

moose [Alces americana, fam. Cervidae, order Artiodactyla], 19

Morgan, Lewis Henry, 194n.

Mormons, 169n.

Morocco [32° N, 5°50′ W], 437, 483

Morrill Land Grant Act, 566

mortar, 522

Moscow [city, 55°45′ N, 37°35′ E], 599

Moses [13th century B.C.], 638, 640
mother, social, 165
mother-daughter, 218, 221
mother-in-law avoidance, 23, 236n.
mother-of-pearl, 460(29-2)
mother-son, 218, 220–221
mother's brother, 166
  and sister's son, 218
motility, 158, 349
mounting, 43, 68
mourning, color of, 136
mouse, 62(5-5)
mouth, 349–350, 415(and 27-3)
moving parts, 526–527
  tools with, 539–540
Mozart, Wolfgang Amadeus, 662
Muaco [site, about 11° N, 69° W in
    Venezuela], 431(28-4)
mud, 517–518, 529
  walls of dried, 466
Mugaret-es-Skhūl [site at Mt. Carmel,
    32°43′ N, 35°3′ E in Israel],
    409(27-1)
mulberry, 456(29-1)
mule, 293, 462(29-2), 475
muller and quern, 496, 497(31-4)
multicellularity, 342–347
  multicellular organism and band, 158
murder, 26, 153
Murex brandaris [mollusk of fam.
    Muricidae], 528
Murray River [mouth at 35°22′ S,
    139°22′ E], 433
museums and cities, 556
mushroom, 445(29-1)
music, 661–665
  criticism, 663–664
  equals emotion, 663–664
  printing of, 622
  Western musical scale, 442
musical instruments, 440–442
musk ox [Ovibos moschatus, fam. Bovidae,
    order Artiodactyla; now found only
    in North America], 435
muskmelon, 446(29-1)
Muslims, 480, 526, 657
  (See also Islam)
mussel, 460(29-2)
mustards, 452(29-1)
mutation, 49
Mycenae [ancient city, about 37°50′ N,
    22°50′ E], 594
mynah, 52, 103, 465(29-2)
Mystic Rite, 28

mysticism, sources of, 641
myth, 28–29, 282
  (See also literature)

nagari principle in writing, 578–579(and
    35-5)
nail versus claw, 64
nail (metal), 422, 535–536
name, personal, 23–24, 29, 143, 185, 256
  versus kinship term, 190
Nangrahar Province [34°30′ N, 70°30′ E,
    in Afghanistan], 592
Nash, Ogden [1902–1971], 112
national states, 628–629
Native American Church, 28
native state of metals, 531
Navajo [Athapaskan-speaking tribe,
    36°25′ N, 110° W; the Navajo
    themselves prefer this spelling to
    "Navaho"], 199(and 15-6)
navigation, 485, 614–616
navy, 634
Nayar of Malabar, 182–183, 201(15-8),
    220
Nazis, 570, 669
Nea Nikomedia [site, near Thessaloníki,
    40°48′ N, 22°56′ E, in Greece],
    469(30-1), 470
Neanderthals, Neanderthaloids, 411–412,
    414, 416, 418, 433
Near East [= southwest Asia], 180
  (See also Asia, southwest)
necessity and innovation, 76
Necho the Second [reigned 610–595
    B.C.], 594
need and opportunity, 456, 479
needle, 441, 507(def)
  knitting, 514
needle-shaped leaves, 449
needlework, 508
"Negros," "Negroes" (term), 265n.
Neolithic, 502–503(def)
neolocal residence, 170(14-2)
neoteny, 349
nephew-uncle, 218, 221–222
nephrite, 494
nepotism, 236
Neptune (planet), 315(24-1)
nest, 51, 63, 143, 364, 369
net, 510
neurosis, 239–241
New England town meeting, 650

New Guinea [island; 5° S, 140° E], 197,
    226–227, 360, 425, 427, 479, 485,
    610
New Testament, 625, 638–639
New World [= the Americas], 145, 438,
    440, 474, 553
  Africans in, 263ff., 433
  dog in, 473
  domestication in, 486–491
  Europeanized, 475, 610
  in medieval times, 604
  peopling of, 427–433, 453
  pre-Columbian contacts with, 433
  stone-polishing in, 498–499
  textiles, 514
New World monkeys, 57, 58(5-1),
    66(5-7), 351(24-24)
New Zealand [two islands, 41° S,
    174° E], 484–485, 555, 609
Newfoundland [island; 48°30′ N, 56° W],
    433
newspapers, 623–624
Newton, Isaac [1642–1727], 614
Nice [city; 43°42′ N, 7°15′ E; nearby site
    called by same name], 391(20-3),
    403
niche, ecological, 285
nickel, 531
Nicolet, Jean [1598–1642], 8
Niger River [mouth at 5°33′ N, 6°33′ E]
Nigeria [10° N, 8° E], 263
Nile River [mouth at 30°10′ N, 31°6′ E],
    479, 557
Nilotic tribes, 475
Nipissing, Lake [46°17′ N, 86° W], 10
Nippur [ancient city, about 32° N,
    45°36′ E], 502
nitrogenous wastes, 352
noise (versus signal), 82
  code noise, 82(6-1), 382
  cross-cultural, 126–127, 146–147, 157
noisiness of primates, 44
nomads (see pastoral nomads)
non- (see the term without the prefix)
noosphere, 96–97
Noquet, 11
Normans, 599
norms in the family, importance of,
    180ff.
north, invasion of, 399–400
North America, 360, 473, 498–499, 555,
    634
  (See also Indians, American)
North Germanic languages, 597–599

Northeast Woodlands [aboriginal North American culture area], 435, 520
Northmen, 599
Northwest Coast [aboriginal North American culture area], 162, 255, 520, 549–551, 561
Norway [62° N, 10° E], 483
Norwegian language, 301(23-5)
  writing, 620(38-1)
Norwegian Landsmaal (language), 599
notations, special, 580
nova, 317
Nova Scotia [45° N, 63° W], 433
Novgorod [city; 58°31′ N, 31°17′ E], 599
nuchal crest in hominoids, 364(25-2)
nuclear family/household, 179(and 14-6), 184
nuclear power, 538
nucleated territoriality, 69, 364, 369, 586
nucleic acid, 53, 330
nucleoside, 332(24-11)
nucleotide, 48–49, 328, 322(24-11)
nucleus of cell, 48
Nuer [tribe, about 9°30′ N, 31° E], 475
Nukuoro [Polynesian-speaking inhabitants of island, 3°51′ N, 154°58′ E], 199(15-6)
number (grammatical):
  in English, 203
  in pronouns, 187
number (mathematical):
  favored, 138–140, 288, 637
  versus numeral, 137–138
numeral, 288, 573, 581–582, 619
  definition, 137–138
  desirable properties of, 138
  large, 138
  versus number, 137–138
  spoken, 138
  written, 580
Nuristani languages, 301(23-5), 592
Nürnberg [city; 49°27′ N, 11°4′ E], 272, 613
nursery forms of kinship terms, 195
nutmeg, 451(29-1)
nux vomica, 447(29-1)

oak, 447(29-1), 449
  white [Quercus alba], 20
oar, 542–543
oats, 9n., 457(29-1), 481
objectivity and subjectivity, 123–124
obligations to the dead, 253

oboe, 442
obsidian, 392, 467, 470, 494
obsolescence:
  of city, 556–557
  of civil society, 670
  in language, 291
oca, 448(29-1)
ocarina, 522
Oceania, 440, 474, 609
  peopling of, 484–485
ochre, 527
Oder River [mouth at 53°33′ N, 14°38′ E]
odor, sexual, 68
Oedipus, 154
Ogham [or Ogam] script, 618
oil, 450, 528
oil palm, African, 459(29-1)
Ojibwa (= Chippewa) [Algonquian-speaking bands of Great Lakes area], 11(2-1), 148, 302(23-6)
  insanity among, 239
  sibling terms, 199(15-6)
okra, 449(29-1)
Old Bulgarian writing, 620(38-1)
Old Prussian language, 599
  writing, 620(38-1)
Old Testament, 174
Old World monkeys, 57, 58(5-1), 351(24-24), 451n.
Olduvai [site, 2°58′ S, 35°22′ E], 391(26-3)
Oligopithecus, 363(25-1a)
olive, 448(29-1), 449, 551–552, 594
Oliviense [site, about 47°30′ S, 66°30′ W, in Argentina], 431(28-4)
Olmecs [more or less contemporary with classical Mayas, in Isthmus of Tehuantépec, 17° N, 94°30′ W], 575
Omaha [Plains tribe, around 42° N, 97° W], 201(15-8)
"Omaha" cousin terms, 201(15-8)
Omo [site, about 4°30′ N, 36° E], 391(26-3)
one, 139
one-to-one correspondence, 137
onion, 449(29-1), 458
onomatopoeia, 106
openness = productivity (of communicative system), 108ff., 138, 413
opera company and city, 556
operational definition, 130

opium, 452(29-1)
opossum [Didelphis virginiana and other spp of D. or allied genera, fam. Didelphidae, order Marsupialia], 360
opportunity and need, 456, 479
orange, 448(29-1)
orangutan, 51, 58(5-1), 61(5-4), 62(5-5), 351(24-24), 363(25-1)
ordeal, trial by, 651
oregano, 454(29-1)
Oreopithecus, 363(25-1a)
organic evolution, 287(def), 342
organism, multicellular, 343
  and band, 158
Orinoco River [mouth at 8°37′ N, 62°15′ W], 262, 432, 489
orthographies and printing, 623
Oscan language, 595
Oshkosh [1795–1850], 24
Ossetic language, 592
ostracization, 160–161
ostrich, 464(29-2)
Ostrogoths, 598
Ottawa [bands speaking Ojibwa dialects, Algonquian], 11(2-1), 302(23-6)
otter [Lutra spp, fam. Mustelidae, order Carnivora], 19
outside view, 123
  and inside view, 158
  sources of, 125–126
oven, 468
  stone pit, 520
overcrowding, 69, 669
overlapping beams, 501, 502(31-9b)
overlapping dyads, 236–238
overshot waterwheel, 612
ovulation cycle, 66–67
owners, kinds of, 146
ownership and contracts, 648
ox, 62(5-5), 462(29-2), 467n.(def), 467–472, 475
oyster, 460(29-2)
ozone, 322, 328

paddle, 542–543
paddle wheel, 543
paedomorphism, 386, 414
  (see also neoteny)
paint, painting, 527–528
Palaeolithic, 502
palaeontology, 52n., 96
Palawan [island; 9°30′ N, 118°30′ E], 423

Palestine [32°30′ N, 35°15′ E], 607

Palestrina [region, 41°50′ N, 12°53′ E], 572

Pali, 592n.

pallium = cerebral cortex, 54

palm (tree), 459(29-1)

pampas of Argentina [35° S, 63° W], 475

Pan P'o [site near Sian, 34°15′ N, 108°52′ E], 477

Panaetius, 646

Pangaea, 324

panning gold, 532

Papago [tribe, around 32° N, 113° W], 199(15-6)

papaya, 450(29-1)

paper, 449(29-1), 456(29-1), 516–517, 530

paper mulberry, 456(29-1)

Papuans, 484–485

papyrus, 529

para rubber tree, 448(29-1)

parallel, metabolism in, 342

parallel cousins, 171

parallelism, 32

paramecium [*Paramecium* spp, class Ciliata, of Protozoa], 84–85, 159

parameters of state, 230–232

Parapithecus, 363(25-1a)

parasites, parasitism, 159, 285(23-2), 340

parchment, 504

parental dyad dominance, 223

parental relation in dyad, 218

parrot, 103, 465(29-2)

parsley, 455(29-1)

parsnip, 455(29-1)

Parthians, 592

parturition (*see* birth)

Pasang goat, 467

Pashto language, 592

Passamaquoddy [Algonquian-speaking bands akin to Malecites, northern Maine], 302(23-6)

past versus future, 657

pastoral nomads, 461–462, 475, 604–605

paternal attitudes, 367

paternal behavior, 159

paternalism, 246

paternity, 165–166
  knowledge of, 165
  social, 166

path, trail, road, 557

patrilineal descent, 143, 175
  versus matrilineal, 175–176
  sources of, 176

patrilocal residence, 170(14-2), 171

patriotism, 584, 587

patronymic, 256n.

patterned systems in language, 192

patterning, 45

Paul Revere's code, 106

paving, 558–559

pea, 445, 452(29-1), 453(29-1), 469

peach, 445, 453(29-1)

peafowl, 465(29-2)

peanut, 452(29-1)

pear, 453(29-1)

pearl, 460(29-2)

pearl millet, 458(29-1)

peasant culture (*see* fellahin)

pebble chopper, 390–393(and 26-2, 26-4)

pecan, 449(29-1)

Peel, Robert [1788–1850], 563

pelt, to, 87(7-1)

pelvis, 372, 373(25-10), 378, 386

pemmican, 442

penal practices, 652

penalties for law violation, 568

pencil, 86, 89–92

pendulum, 613

penis, 356

Penobscot [bands speaking Algonquian dialects, around 45° N, 69° W], 302(23-6)

people as property, 146, 649

people's army, 565

Peoria [Algonquian-speaking bands in southeastern part of Northeastern Woodlands], 302(23-6)

pepper, 455(29-1), 459(29-1)
  black, 450(29-1)

percussion instruments, 442

perennial plant, 448

perfume, 68

Pericles [c. 495–429 B.C.], 272

perimeter-marking territoriality, 69, 586

periodicals, 623–624

periods, geological [*see* Running Calendar, 304–311]

peripheral versus basic kinship terms, 192, 195–197

perjury, 651

permanent dentition, hominoid, 364(25-2)

Permian Ice Age [*see* Running Calendar, 305], 356–357, 361, 444

perpetuation of household pattern, 222–224

Perrot, Nicolas [1644–c. 1718], 9

Persian cat, 480

Persian Gulf [27° N, 51° E]

Persians, 592
  Achaemenid empire, 590, 601, 602(37-1)
  roads, 558

persimmon, 447(29-1)

persistence, genetic, 50, 297–298

person, legal, 647, 650

personal name (*see* name, personal)

personal pronoun (*see* pronouns, personal)

personality:
  concealment of, 208–209
  facets of, 206
  and role, 205–209
  and social structure, 157, 205–214

perturbation of transactions, 210

Peru [10° S, 76° W], 428–429, 433, 512(31-19), 549, 587
  (*See also* Inca empire)

Peruvian textiles, 514, 515(31-21)

"perversions," sexual, 68, 366–367

pet, 461

Petition of Right (English), 649

petroleum, 539

"Peyote Cult," 28, 30

pharmacopoeia, medicinal, 440

pharynx, 415

phase, suspended, 336

pheasant, 465(29-2)

pheromone, 79

Philippines [12° N, 123° E], 485, 605
  Europeanized, 610

philosophers, 136, 654

philosophizing, 422

philosophy, 113

Phoenicians, 594

phoneme, 103

phosphate, 332-334

phosphorylation, 338–340

photosensitivity, 351

photosynthesis, 95, 338–340, 344(24-18)

phratry, 175(14-3), 176
  Menomini, 23

Phrygian language, Phrygians, 593, 595

phylogenetic relatedness, 300

phylogeny versus taxonomy, 351(24-24)

phylum [*pl.* phyla: a major taxonomic category; *see* 352(24-25); for animal phyla *see* 348(24-21, middle column)]

pick, 443(and 28-8)

Pictish inscriptions and language, 596n., 618

pidgin (language), 197n., 263

pierce, to, 87(7-1)
pig, 463(29-2), 467–471, 477–478
  considered unfit as food, 480
  as early human food, 395
pigeon, 62(5-5), 465(29-2)
pigment, 527
pike (fish), 461(29-2)
Pílos [36°55′ N, 21°43′ E], 594
pimento, 455(29-1)
pine, 445(29-1), 446(29-1), 449, 527
  nuts, 454
pineapple, 449, 456(29-1)
pipestone (see catlinite)
pirates, 571, 634
Pisa [city, 43°43′ N, 10°23′ E], 613
pivot grammar, 116–117
Pizarro, Francisco [c. 1474–1541], 561
place notation (numerals), 580
placenta, 360–361
placental mammals, 425
plague, bubonic, 432, 626
Plains [aboriginal North American
    culture area], 161–162, 437, 475
planet, 314
planned coincidences of dyads, 236
plans and creativity, 114
plantain, 459(29-1)
plants:
  animal use of, 450–454
  flowering, 357(24-29)
  green, 340, 344(24-18)
  growth of, 48n.
  implications of domestication for, 458
  land, 357(24-29)
  origin of, 338–340
plasmagenes, 48n.
platinum, 530(mp), 531
Plato [428 or 427–348 or 347 B.C.], 589,
    637–638, 656
platypus, duck-billed [Ornithorhynchus,
    fam. Ornithorhynchidae, order
    Monotremata, subclass Prototheria],
    350(24-23), 359
play, 74–76, 153, 177–178
  and innovation, 75–76
  in language, 104
  as learning, 75
  and prelanguage, 383
  survival value of, 75
pleasantness of state, 231
Pleistocene [see Running Calendar,
    308–310, 369, 384
  middle, 411
  upper, 433–443, 572

Plinius [Gaius Plinius Secundus], 526
Pliocene [see Running Calendar, 307], 368
Pliopithecus, 363(25-1a)
plow, plowing, 463, 496(and 31-3)
plucking of hair, 526
plum, 453(29-1)
plumbing, 522
Pluto (planet), 315(24-1)
Po River [mouth at 44°57′ N, 12°4′ E],
    595
poetry, 114, 119, 140
Poincaré, Jules Henri, 655
point (of tool), 87(7-1)
poisoned arrows or darts, 439–440
Poitiers [town; 46°35′ N, 20° E], 611
poke, to, 87(7-1)
Poland [52° N, 19° E], 628
Polaris, 615
policeman, 208, 563
Polish language, 599
  writing, 620(38-1)
political versus nonpolitical, 147–148,
    154–155, 190
political competition, 551–552
"political science," 148
pollen, 444
Polo, Marco [1254–1324], 607
polyandry, 166(14-1), 174, 220
polygamy, 166(14-1)
polygyny, 166(14-1), 173–174, 219
  housing for, 169
  problems of, 169
  reasons for, 169–170
  sororal, 169, 236
  sporadic, 168–169
polymerization, 334(24-12)
Polynesia, Polynesians [scattered islands
    centering about 4° S, 156° W; but
    culturally and linguistically includes
    aboriginal New Zealand], 423, 433,
    440, 484–485, 520
polyphony in music, 662
polysaccharides, 330
pomegranate, 450(29-1)
Pomo [bands or tribe, about 39° N,
    123°30′ W, in California]: baskets,
    511
poppy, 452(29-1)
population, population growth, 49, 283,
    423
porcupine [fam. Hystricidae (old World),
    fam. Erethizontidae (New World),
    suborder Hystricomorpha, order
    Rodentia], 68

portland cement, 522
Portugal [39°30′ N, 8° W], 440, 628
Portuguese, 263, 480, 605, 608
Portuguese language, 596n.
  writing, 620(38-1)
Poseidonius, 646
positions, copulatory, 68
possession, loose versus intimate, 144–146
possessions versus nonpossessions, 145
postage stamp, 582
posture, 364, 377
  primate, 64–65
pot boiling, 519–520
potato, 455(29-1), 487–488
Potawatomi [Algonquian-speaking tribe
    or bands], 11(2-1), 173, 302(23-6)
potlatch, 255, 549–551
pottery (see ceramics)
pouched mammals, 360
power grip, 64
power pack, 21(and 2-5)
power technology, 538–540
Powhatan [tribe or bands speaking an
    Algonquian language, around
    37° N, 77° W], 302(23-6)
Prakrit, 592n.
precision grip, 64
predestination, 657
predictability, prediction, 230, 568
preferred marriages, 22, 173
pregnancy, 360
prehensile appendages, 63–64
prelanguage, 381–382, 413
  and tradition, 383
premolars, 358
prepared core, 397–398, 434
press, printing, 621–622
prestige and borrowing (language), 290
prestige and imitation, 218
pride of craftsmanship, 272–274, 524
primary versus derivative tools, 88
primary versus secondary kin, 194
primary versus secondary sexual
    characteristics, 210
Primates = primates [taxonomic term
    always capitalized and is a fixed
    plural; vernacular term not
    capitalized and has a singular],
    57–77, 158–159, 361
  brains of, 54
  classification of, 57, 58(5-1),
    350(24-23), 351(24-24)
  fears of, 36
  "primitives, primitive mentality," 125, 144

printing from movable type, 528, 621–624
impact of, 622–623
privacy, 169, 208
private enterprise, 624
privateer, 634
productivity of communicative system (*see* openness)
profane = secular, 130
pronouns, personal, 121, 156–158, 185–191
propeller, 543
proper names, 120
property, 141–146, 254–255, 570
ceremonial destruction of, 255–256
contractual, 648
incorporeal, 143
Menomini, 25
ways of talking about, 143–145
origin of human, 145–146
people as, 146, 649
rights, 142
prophecy, self-fulfilling, 568
Propliopithecus, 363(25-1a)
Prosimii = prosimians, 57, 58(5-1), 59(5-2), 351(24-24)
protection, fire for, 404–405
protein, 49, 330, 331(24-10), 450
protein-deficiency diseases, 478
Protestant and Catholic, 628
Protestant ethic, 627, 642–643, 657
Protestant Reformation, 627–628, 642–643
proto, 300(def)
Protozoa, 48*n.,* 344(24-18)
Provençal language, 596*n.*
writing, 620(38-1)
Przhevalski's horse, 474
Ptolemaios Soter [367–283 B.C.], 589
puberty, 132–133
baboon, 41
hominoid, 364(25-2)
Menomini ordeal at, 29–30
publisher, 623
Puget Sound [47°50′ N, 123°30′ W], 549
pulque, 458(29-1)
pumice [a fine-grained volcanic glass, easily powdered], 90
pumpkin, 447(29-1)
pun, 119, 577
punishment, 568
pure music, 661–665
Puritans, 584
purple, 528

purposes:
versus consequences, 289
learning new, 289
and selection, 288–289
purposive behavior, 83–85
Purpura haemastoma [mollusk of fam. Muricidae], 528

Qalat Jarmo [site, 35°30′ N, 45°30′ E, east of Kirkūk in Iraq], 468, 469(30-1), 518
Quakers, 190–191, 584
pronouns, 185–186, 190–191
quandary, 233(18-1), 232–241, 258–259
quantification of information, 81–82
quantum theory, 655, 657
quartz [silica, SiO_2, especially in crystals], 20, 493
Quaternary Ice Age [*see* Running Calendar, 308–310], 384, 388, 412, 413(27-2)
Quechuas [in Andes and on coastal territory to the west of them], 50
quern and muller, 496, 497(31-4)
Quetta [city; 30°12′ N, 67° E; sites in the region], 482
quipu, 573–574(and 35-1)
quiver, 20

rabbit [diverse genera of subfam. Leporinae, fam. Leporidae, order Lagomorpha; in North America mainly *Lepus*], 20, 24–23, 389
raccoon [*Procyon lotor,* fam. Procyonidae, order Carnivora], 19
races, 295
racial differentiation, 293–295, 410–413, 418
false theories of, 410
racial diversity, human, 385
value of, 412
racial prejudice, 265*n.*
racket, racketeer, 548–549, 563
radial symmetry, 349, 353(24-26)
Radiata, 348(24-21), 353(24-26)
radiation, hard [that is, very high frequency, very short wavelength], 342
radish, 452(29-1)
raft, 542
Ramapithecus, 363(25-1b)

Ras Shamra [site, 6 miles north of Al-Lādhiqīyah, 35°31′ N, 35°47′ E, in Syria], 469(30-1)
raspberry, 453(29-1)
rat, 62(5-5)
rationalists and empiricists, 656
rattlesnake venom [rattlesnakes are of genera *Sistrurus* and *Crotalus,* fam. Crotalidae, order Squamata], 440*n.*
raven, 62(5-5)
razor, 526
reason, 656–657
recalibration (of communicative system), 83, 104, 107
reciprocal kin terms, 195
reconstruction of common ancestor, 300
record-keeping, 571–582
records:
before writing, 572–573
written, 302
Red Sea [25° N, 35° E]
reduction division, 345, 347(24-20)
redundancy, 82(def)
reed, 458, 460
for musical instruments, 442
reference to people, forms of, 185–204
reference use of kinship term, 190
reincarnation, 254
reindeer, 158, 435, 463(29-2)
domestication of, 476
relativity, theory of, 655, 657
relief by contrast (in dyads), 245
religion, 28, 130–136, 409
definitions of, 130
and government, 582–584
versus the nonreligious, 133, 190
versus the political, 562
sample of, 131–134
removal surfacing, 526
Renaissance, 643
replicability of music, 663
replication of household, 222–224
representative art, 659–660
reproduction, 345–347
Reptilia = reptiles, 349(24-22), 356–357
life spans of, 62(5-5)
residence practices, 170–171
and kinship terminology, 201–202(and 15-9)
resignation (emotional attitude), 234
respiration, 356
resurrection of the body, 253
revelation, 134
reverence, 132

Rhaeto-Romance language, 596*n.*
    writing, 620(38-1)
rhesus monkey [*Macaca mulatta*], 58(5-1),
    75–76(and 5-9)
rhinarium, 64
Rhine River [mouth at 51°52′ N, 6°2′ E]
rhinoceros [*Rhinoceros, Ceratotherium,* and
    Diceros species in Africa, fam.
    Rhinocerotidae, order
    Perissodactyla], 388
    as early human food, 395
    wooly [*R. antiquitatis*], 435
Rhodesia [20° S, 30° E], 533(32-2)
rhodium, 531
Rhone River [mouth at 43°20′ N,
    4°50′ E]
rhubarb, 451(29-1)
ribonucleic acid, 48–49, 332(24-11)
rice, 9*n.*, 457(29-1), 477–478, 480, 553
riding horseback, 475
Riffians [northwest Africa, about 35° N,
    5° W], 483
rigging, 618
rights, animal and human, 142
Riss Glaciation, 413(27-2)
rite of passage, 226
ritual, 133, 233(18-1), 409
ritualization, 252
    of art, 660
    of music, 663
river valleys [of Nile, Tigris, and
    Euphrates (Mesopotamia), Indus,
    and Yellow River], 479, 559, 590
road, 542, 557–561, 557(def), 612
roasting, 20, 406(def)
Robert's Rules of Order, 149 [compiled
    by a U.S. army officer, Henry
    Martyn Robert, 1837–1923]
robin [American, *Turdus migratorius;*
    European, *Erithacus rubecola,* both
    fam. Turdidae], 46, 62(5-5)
rock music, 665
rockets, 616
Rodentia = rodents, 350(24-23), 370, 425
    as early human food, 395
role, 205
    and behavior, 206
    and communication, 206
    compatibility of, 237–238
    as control, 207–208
    and personality, 205–209
    and status, 209
    and subrole, 206
    vacated by death, 257

rollers with platform, 540
Roman numerals, 619, 625
Romans, 173, 502, 534
    aunt and uncle terms, 200(15-7)
    law, 646–648
    roads, 557–558, 559(34-1)
Romance languages, 596*n.*, 619
romanticism, 643
    in music, 663
Rome [city at 41°58′ N, 12°40′ E], 140,
    260, 482
    city structure, 555
    falls to Goths, 601
root (plant), 445–446
rope bridges, 560
rosining, 527
Rousseau, Jean Jacques, 645*n.*
Royal African Company, 264
Royal Society of London, 623
royal *we,* 189
rubber, 448(29-1)
rules of evidence, 651
Rumanian language, 596*n.*
    writing, 620(38-1)
ruminants [suborder Ruminantia of
    order Artiodactyla; complex
    stomach and cud-chewing], 446
runes, 572, 598, 618
Russia [40°14′ N, 84°24′ W], Russians,
    605, 608–609, 628
Russian language, 599
    writing, 620(38-1)
rutabaga, 452(29-1)
ruthenium, 531
rye, 457(29-1), 481
Ryukyus [archipelago; 26°30′ N, 128° E],
    486

Sabines [ancient Italic-speaking tribe,
    living near Rome; the story of the
    capture of Sabine women by
    Romans is probably legendary], 173
sacred versus secular, 131–133
sage, 454(29-1)
sagittal crest, 362, 366(25-4)
    in hominoids, 364(25-2)
Sagres [town; 37° N, 8°56′ W], 618
Sahara Desert [20° N, 13° E], 437, 480,
    483
sail, sailing vessels, 485, 543
sailor, 563, 565
Sakhalin Island [51° N, 143° E], 423, 435
Salawati Island [1°7′ S, 130°54′ E], 425

Salerno [town; 40°41′ N, 14°45′ E], 621
saliva, 358
Salla, Denys de, 623
salmon [*Salmo salar* in North Atlantic;
    Oncorhynchus spp in north Pacific,
    both fam. Salmonidae, order
    Isospondyli], 162
salt versus fresh water, 326
saltpetre, 616
Salzgitter-Lebenstedt [site near town,
    52°9′ N, 10°20′ E], 400(26-11)
samisen (Japanese 3-stringed musical
    instrument], 440
Samoa [archipelago, 14° S, 171° W;
    Polynesian-speaking inhabitants]:
    sibling terms, 199(15-6)
    privacy, 208
San Francisco Bay [37°43′ N, 122°17′ W]
sandstone, 493
Sanskrit, 592*n.*
    pronouns, 187
Santa Rosa Island [site; 33°58′ N,
    120°6′ W, in California], 430(28-3)
Santee Dakota [Siouan-speaking tribe,
    around 45° N, 93° W], 13
sap, vegetable, 529
sapiens complex, 417–420
saponification, 526
saprophytes, 285(23-2)
Sarci [or Sarsee; northern Athapaskan
    bands, around 49° N, 112° W],
    200(15-7)
Sardinia [island; 40° N, 9° E]
Sardis [ancient city, about 38°25′ N,
    28° E], 582
Sarmatians, 592
sarsaparilla, 459(29-1)
sassafras, 451(29-1)
satellite, 314
Saturn (planet), 315(24-1)
Sauk [bands speaking Algonquian
    dialects akin to Fox], 11(2-1),
    302(23-6)
Saulteaux [bands speaking Ojibwa
    dialects, around 46°30′ N,
    84°20′ W], 302(23-6)
savanna [tropical or subtropical
    grassland, with more or less
    scattered trees or shrubs]
saw (metal tool), 500, 535
Saxons, 598
Scaevola, Quintus Mucius [distinguish
    from a cousin of the same name
    who died 82 B.C.], 646

scaffolding, 502
scale, Western musical, 442
scales (fish), 353
Scandinavia [peninsula, 65° N, 16° E], 536
Scandinavian languages, 597–599
scavenged food, 370
scent marking, 79–80, 472
Schadenfreude, 234
scheduling, 45–48, 149, 568
Scheiner, Christoph [1579?–1650], 614
schools, 589, 621
  Muslim, 606
Schumann, Robert Alexander [1810–1856], 643
science, 113, 125, 134, 637, 652–659
  and democracy, 655
  and emotion, 121–122, 654–655
  and empiricism, 652–654
  and engineering, 652
    confused, 659
  and ethics, 659
  and language, 653
  and law, 645–646, 651
  and organic evolution, 653
  origins of, 653–654
  source of, 641
  revolt against, 658–659
  and technology, 652
scissors, 508, 535
Scotch Gaelic language, 597
Scotland [57° N, 4° W]
scorpion [order Scorpionida, class Arachnida, phylum Arthropoda], 38
scrape, to, 87(7-1)
scratch, to, 87(7-1)
Scripps Campus [site in La Jolla, 33°51′ N, 117°52′ W, in California], 430(28-3)
scrolls, 621
Scythians, 592
sea anemone, 353(24-26)
seacoasts, 425
seafaring (*see* maritime)
seal (stamp), 528, 572–573
sealing wax, 529
seamen, impressed, 565
seashells, 442
second law of thermodynamics, 81*n.,* 300
Second World War, 587, 669
secondary versus primary kin, 194
secondary versus primary sexual characteristics, 210

secular versus sacred, 130, 133
seed, 444
seed-planting, 455, 457
seed plants, 356, 357(24-29), 444
seed-selection, 457
selection, 342, 421, 451
  in learning, 288
  and purpose, 288–289
  in tradition, 288
  and variation, 283–289
selective factors in racial differentiation, 411
self versus environment, 145
self-image, 206, 208
self-validating features of inside view, 124–125, 139
Semitic languages, 578
  pronouns, 187
sense organs, special, 351
Serbian writing, 620(38-1)
Serbo-Croatian language, 599
serfdom, civil, 271, 564–565
serfs, 260, 603, 624
  freed, 628–629
series, metabolism in, 342
seriosity, 74, 153
  as state parameter, 231–232
servomechanism, 84
sesame, 455(29-1), 480
sessile versus motile, 158
seven, 139–140
Sewall Wright effect, 298
Seward Peninsula [65° N, 168° W], 432
sewing, 441, 507–508
sex, general:
  origin of, 345–347
  plant versus animal, 346
  in seed plants, 444
sex, human:
  in kinship terms, 192, 200–201
  and marriage, 167
  in personal pronouns, 187
  social regulation of, 167
  in social structure, 151
  temporary expedients for, 170
sextant, 615
sexual characteristics, primary, secondary, and tertiary, 210
sexual dimorphism, 210, 378, 415*n.*
  hominoid, 364(25-2)
sexual interest, primate, 67
sexual maturation, hominoid, 364(25-2)
sexual skin, 68

sexuality in dyads, 218
  and affection, 220–221
sexuality, primate, 66–68, 366
  implications of, 73
shaddock, 449(29-1)
Shakespeare, William [1564–1616], 2
shallot, 458(29-1)
shame and guilt, 207–208
Shanidar Cave [site, 36°50′ N, 44°13′ E, in Iraq], 408, 409, 468, 469(30-1)
Shansi Province [37° N, 112° E], 477
shape of linguistic forms, 105
shared features, explanations of, 32
shaving, 19, 526
Shawnee [Algonquian-speaking tribe, southern Ohio, Indiana, and Illinois], 302(23-6)
shed (weaving), 513
sheep, 463(29-2), 467–471
  as early human food, 395
  wild, 471(30-3)
sheets and filaments, 503–517
shell of turbulence (of Earth), 324
Shelley, Percy Bysshe, 585, 588
shellfish, 425
Shensi Province [35° N, 109° E], 476
Sherpas [Tibetan peoples on southern slopes of Himalayas], 50
shield, 536
Shilluk [tribe, around 10° N, 32° E], 201(15-8)
ship (*see* boats and ships)
shivering, 358
Shluh [people in southwestern Morocco, about 30° N, 8° W], 483
shoes, 19, 536
shopkeeper, 628
short-term forgetting, 110
shrub, 447
shuffle bipedalism, 370–371
shuttle (weaving), 512–513, 539(and 32-4)
siamang, 58(5-1), 351(24-24), 363(35-1a)
Siamese cat, 480
Siberia, 426(28-2), 427–428, 432
  northeastern, 249*n.*
  northern, 440
sibling [a brother or sister]
sibling terminologies, 197–198
  Chinese versus American, 203–204
Sicily [island; 37°30′ N, 14° E], 536, 594, 599
sick, care of, 249, 366, 387, 408
sickle, 458, 468

sickness in nonhuman primates, 44
siege, 555
sieva bean, 453(29-1)
Silesia [region, 51° N, 16°45′ E]
silica polishing, 455, 468
silk, silkworm, 456(29-1), 460–461(and 29-2)
silver, 530–531, 532(mp), 582
silver birch, 495
silver-copper alloy, 532
simian shelf, 362, 364(25-2), 366(25-3)
sinew [animal tendon], 394, 506–507
sinew-backed bow, 438
singeing, 526
Sinhalese language, 484
Siouan languages, 11(2-1)
Sioux [19th-century alliance of Siouan-speaking tribes of the northern Plains west of the Great Lakes, including the Dakota], 11(2-1), 565
sisal, 458(29-1)
sister-brother dominance, 218, 220–221
sister-brother marriage, 172
sister-sister, 218, 220–221
sister's son and mother's brother, 218
six, 139
sixty, 613
skepticism, 113
ski, 443
skins (see hide, animal)
slag, 536
slave trade, 608
slavery, slaves, 146, 246, 259–260, 554, 558, 565, 603, 606
  and law, 649
Slavic languages, 301(23-5), 599
  writing, 620(38-1)
sled, 443
  land [= travois], 474
sleep, 233(18-1), 249, 358, 364
  and fire, 405
sleeping sites:
  of baboons, 37(3-3)
  of hominoids, 365(25-2)
slice, to, 87(7-1)
slime molds, 343, 344(25-18)
sling (weapon), 438–439
slip (on ceramics), 527
slipped discs, 378
sloth, two-toed [Choloepus hoffmanni, fam. Bradypodidae, order Edentata], 68
Slovak language, 599
  writing, 620(38-1)

Slovene language, 599
  writing, 620(38-1)
slum, 554–557
smallpox, 432
smell, sense of, 351
smelting, 534
snail, land, 460(29-2)
snakes [order Squamata, class Reptilia], 360
  and baboons, 36, 38
  as early human food, 395
snowshoe, 12
soap, 526, 607
soapstone, 493–494
social behavior, 71
social change and pronouns, 187–190
social classes, 70–71
  in funereal practices, 253
  and personal pronouns, 187–190
social constraints on creativity, 271–273
social contract, 645–646, 649–650
social maternity and paternity, 165–166
social stratification, 561–563
social structure, 69–71, 148–149, 156–164, 367–368, 376, 386
  baboon, 38–39, 42
  and personality, 157, 205–214
sociality:
  primate, 68–73
  evolutionary sources, 72–73
society, mystical interpretation of, 205
Socrates [c. 470–399 B.C.], 154
sodium, 530
soils, 95
sol state, 337
Solar System, 314, 315(24-1)
  motion of, 342
solar wind, 319
soldering, 534
soldiers, 174, 558, 563–566
solid state (crystalline), 327
soliloquy, 113
solution, 336–337
son-father, son-mother, 218
Sophocles [497 or 495–406 B.C.], 252
Sorbian language, 599
  writing, 620(38-1)
sorghum, 457(29-1), 477–478
sororal polygyny, 169, 236
sororate, 169
soul, 27, 132–133, 249–250
  versus body, 133, 252–253
sound of linguistic form, 576–577

sound change, 291–292
sound systems of language, 102–104
  versus animal cries, 103–104
  origin of, 414
  patterning of, 106
  as a universal, 134
South America, 360, 428
  eastern, 439, 466, 486–491
  northeastern, 438, 610
  northwestern, 481–486
  southern, 530–531
  (See also Indians, American)
South American monkeys (see New World monkeys)
Southeastern Woodlands [aboriginal North American culture area], 488, 549
Southwest [aboriginal North American culture area], 432, 489, 511
Soviet Union, 584, 629, 669
  government, 549
soya bean, 452(29-1), 478
space occupied, as property, 142
Spain, 435, 438, 563, 628, 634
Spanish, 262–253, 534, 560–561, 608
  in Canary Islands, 483
  in New World, 161, 475
  world view, 265
Spanish language, 596n.
  pronouns, 189n., 190
  writing, 620(38-1)
Spanish-speaking world, 472
spatial intuition, 657
spear, 398, 436, 443
spear, to, 87(7-1)
spear-thrower, 436, 437(28-5)
specialist (see expert)
specialization for communication, 79–80
speciation, 293–295, 412
species [pl. identical with singular; but the abbreviation "spp" means the plural], 293
species name, conventions for, 352(24-25)
species-specific [characteristic of a single species]
spectacles, 614
speech tract, 414–415
speed of escape [the minimum velocity at which a particle will escape the gravitational field of a satellite, planet, or star; for Earth it is 6.95 miles per second], 319
spelling, conservatism of, 580n., 623

Spermopsida, 356, 357(24-29), 444
spices, 479, 482
spider monkeys, 58(5-1), 64
Spina, Alessandro di, 614
spinach, 446(29-1), 447–448
spindle, 506–507
spine, 372, 373(25-11)
spinning, 505–506(and 31-13), 507(31-14), 512
spirit (see soul)
Spirit Cave [site, 37 miles north of Mae Hong Son, 19°16′ N, 97°56′ E], 478
spiritual versus material, 130
splitting of bands, 161
spontaneous generation [the theory that organisms can and do continually arise from inorganic material], 92
spores, plant, 444
spread, spreading (see adaptive radiation; diffusion)
spring, principle of, 437
spruce [Picea spp, fam. Pinaceae, order Coniferales], 449
squash, 10, 445, 447(29-1)
squeeze, to, 87(7-1)
squirrel, 20, 62(5-5)
Stagira [ancient Greek city; inland from northwest Aegean coast but exact location unknown], 595
stamp, postal, 582
standard for exchange, 581
staples, 553
star, 314–319
starch, 334, 335(24-12), 450
state (of actor), 229, 258–259
parameters of, 230–232
state (political), 153, 647
and church, 583–584
stationers, 621
status, social, 209
ascribed and achieved, 214
and role, 209
steam engine, steam technology, 404, 539, 612
steel, 537, 617
stem (plant), 445–446
Stem Hominoids, 351(24-24), 362–368, 363(25-1b)
stereotypy of response, 72
Sterkfontein Extension [site, roughly 28°30′ S, 25°30′ E], 391(26-1)
stirrup, 611
stockade, military, 555
Stoics, 646

stone for building, 499–500
stone boiling, 406
stone bowls, 498
stone-carving, decorative, 499
stone pit oven, 520
stone-polishing, 442, 468, 492–499
and agriculture, 495
origins of, 498–499
and wood, 495
stone rollers for transport, 500
Stonehenge [north of Salisbury, 51°5′ N, 1°48′ W], 500(and 31-7)
stonework, 389–393, 396–399, 434, 436–437, 492–502
efficiency in, 434
Stradivari, Antonio, 663
Strassburg [city, 48°35′ N, 7°45′ E]
stratified society, 561–564
stratosphere, 322
strawberry, 12, 453(29-1)
stride bipedalism, 371–375, 376–377(25-13)
string figures, 504(31-11), 504–505
string instruments, 440
structural macromolecules, 330
structure of cities, 554–555
strychnine, 448(29-1)
sturgeon [spp of Acipenser and allied genera], 11, 20, 162
Suberde [site, about 37° N, 31°30′ E], 469(30-1)
subjectivity and objectivity, 123–124
sublimation [direct change from solid to gaseous state], 325
submissiveness, 233–234
subrole, 206
subspecies, 295
Subtainos [Arawakan-speaking aboriginal peoples of Jamaica], 262
sucker (fish) [fam. Catostomidae], 12
suckling, 143
sucrose, 334(24-12)
Sudan [10° N, 20° E], 475
"Sudanese" cousin terms, 201(15-8)
sugar, sugars, 264, 330–333, 334(24-12)
sugar cane, 457(29-1), 479
sugar maple, 454(29-1)
Sulu Archipelago [5°30′ N, 121°30′ E], 423–424
Sumatra [island; 0°5′ S, 102° E], 423
Sumer, Sumerians [lower Mesopotamia], 474, 508, 569, 583
writing, 574
Sun, 314–319, 315(24-1)

sun-drying:
of foods, 407
of pottery, 519
sundial, 613
supernatural versus natural, 130, 133
supernova, 262, 317(def), 342
superstition, 132, 134n.
surface of Earth, 322
surface tension, 526
surfacing, 525–530
surnames, 256
survival value, 283
Susa [ancient city, at foot of Zagros Mountains, about 32° N, 48°30′ E], 558
suspended-warp loom, 513(and 31-20)
suspension, 336
suspicious hostility, 233–234
suttee, 256
sweat baths, 16, 526
sweat glands, 359
sweating, 358, 388
Sweden [62° N, 15° E], 597, 599, 618, 628, 634
Swedish language, 301(24-5), 599
writing, 618, 620(38-1)
sweet pepper, 455(29-1)
sweet potato [Ipomoea batatas, fam. Convolvulaceae, order Tubiflorae; inadvertently omitted from Table 29-1, where it belongs on page 454], 459, 484–486
swimming and bathing, 368
swimming versus walking, 355(24-28)
swimming bladder (fish), 354
swipe, to, 87(7-1)
Swiss Lake Dwellers [many sites in the Alpine lake region in and near Switzerland], 510, 526
Switzerland [46° N, 30′ E], 628
syllogism, 637
symbols, 38, 142
symmetry in body shape, 349–350
symphony orchestra, 441
and cities, 556
syphilis, 433
system-building, verbal, 133, 635–637
Szechwan Province [31° N, 105° E], 478

Tabasco [state; 18°15′ N, 93° W]
tabby weave, 509(and 31-16)
tadpole, 355

Tadzhikistan [39° N, 71° E], 592

Tagua [site, about 38° S, 73° W, in Chile], 431(28-4)

Tahiti [archipelago, 17°37′ S, 149°27′ W], 484–485, 609

taiga [swampy arctic and subarctic terrain], 399

tail, 64, 358

tailoring, 507–508
  clothing, 17–19, 441

Taiwan [island; 23°30′ N, 121° E], 477–478, 485–486

talc, 494

Tamil language [Dravidian], 216, 592

Tandilense [site near Tandil, 37°20′ S, 59°5′ W, in Argentina], 431(28-4)

tang, 436–437

tangerine, 448(29-1), 478

tannin, 447(29-1)

tanning, 394, 504

Taoism, 636

Taos [pueblo and language, 36°24′ N, 105°34′ W, in New Mexico], 201(15-8)

tapa, 456(and 29-1)

tar, 446(29-1), 522

taro, 456(29-1)

tarpan, 474

tarsier, 58(5-1), 351(24-24)
  brain size, 59

Tasmania [island, 42° S, 147° E], Tasmanians, 360, 406, 425, 427, 429, 433, 438, 473–474, 510, 542, 609

taste, sense of, 351

tattooing, 528

tax, 548–549, 561–562, 567, 583

taxon [pl. taxa], 352(24-25)

taxonomy versus phylogeny, 351(24-24)
  (See also categories, taxonomic)

tea, 450(29-1)

teaching and learning, 55

technological advancements/innovations, 552, 629 (and Part Two passim)
  recent, 630–633(38-2)

technological base, 93, 160–161, 271, 421–422

technology and science, 652

tectonic movements, 319n.

teeth (see dentition)

Tehuacán Valley sites [near Puebla, 19°3′ N, 98°12′ W], 489

teleology, 47, 83–85, 421

telepathy, 661

telescope, 614

tellurium, 531

temperature of Earth's surface, 326

tempo effects in evolution, 298–299

Temujin [Genghis Khan, b. between 1155 and 1167, d. 1227], 585–586

tender emotions, 378

Tenochtitlán [where Mexico City now is], 558

tentativeness of science, 134, 654

tequila, 486

termite [various genera of order Isoptera], 88
  chimpanzee eating of, 88, 89(7-2)

territoriality, 143, 364, 369, 548
  kinds of, 69n.
  political, 586

tertiary sexual characteristics, 210

tethering, 461

Texas Street [site in San Diego, 32°43′ N, 117°9′ W, in California], 430(28-3)

textiles, 508, 512(def)
  Peruvian, 514, 515(31-21)

Thai writing, 578

Thailand [15° N, 100° E], 478, 482, 587, 610

thatching, 508

The Hague [city; 52°6′ N, 4°18′ E], 613

themes in world views, 136–137

theocracy, 562

Theria [all mammals except the egg-laying ones], 350(24-23), 360

thermodynamics, 329, 358, 612, 652
  second law of, 81n., 300

thermonuclear reactions, 314, 317

thief, 571

thinking, 113

thirteen, 139

thought-police, 582–584

Thracian language, Thracians, 301(23-5), 594–595

three, significance of, 139–140, 637

thyme, 455(29-1)

Tibet [32° N, 88° E], 174, 474n., 482
  writing in, 578

tidal forces, 319

Tierra del Fuego [island; 54° S, 69° W], 406, 428–429, 432, 511

tiger, 294

tightly connected versus loosely connected species, 295

Tigris River [mouth at 31° N, 47°25′ E], 474, 557

tiles, 522

time, measurement of, 613

timothy [Phleum pratense], 463

tin, 532(mp), 534, 535(32-3)

title (legal), 648

titles (for people), 185

Tlapacoya [site near Mexico City, which see], 429, 430(28-3)

tobacco, 13, 26, 455(29-1), 487–488, 609

toilet training, 376–377

Tokharian language, 301(23-5), 483, 591

Tolchaco [site near 36° N, 110° W, in Arizona], 430(28-3)

Toledo [city; 39°52′ N, 4°1′ W, in Spain], 617

Toltecs [predecessors, 10th to 12th centuries, of the Aztecs in central and southern Mexico], 575

tomato, 445, 449, 455(29-1)

tone language, 268n.

tongs, 537

tools, 86–93, 365, 416, 422
  chimpanzee, 88, 89(7-2), 90(7-3)
  composite or indirect, 436
  descent of, 92–93
  early, 389–399
  among hominoids, 365(25-2)
  human versus nonhuman, 88–89
  kinds of, 87–88
  and machines, 539–540
  Maroon, 267
  metal, 535–536
  and prelanguage, 383
  primary versus derivative, 88
  and property, 143

tooth for tools, 394, 422, 434–435, 462(29-2), 588

topic and comment, 116, 120

Toronto [city, 43°39′ N, 79°23′ W], structure of, 555

torpedo, 616

Torres Strait/Isthmus [10°25′ S, 142°10′ E], 425–426

tortoise, 62(5-5)

torture, 250

touch, sense of, 64, 351

toughness, 393n., 530

town, 159
  market town, 164
  medieval, 603, 624

town meeting, New England, 650

Tracheophyta = tracheophytes = vascular plants, 344(24-18), 357(24-29), 444

trade (commerce):
  intertribal, 547

velum, 415
Venetic language, 595
Venice [city; 45°27′ N, 12°21′ E], 614
venison (deer meat) (*see* deer)
Venus (planet), 315(24-1), 327
Veracruz [city; 32°25′ N, 115°5′ W, in Mexico], 558
vermilion, 529
Verne, Jules [1828–1905], 93
vertebrae in hominoids, 365(25-2)
Vertebrata = vertebrates, 344(24-18), 349(24-22)
Vertesszöllös [pronounced VER-tesh-söl-lösh; site, about 47°40′ N, 17°40′ E, in northwestern Hungary], 403
vetch, 453(29-1)
Vietcong, 565
Vietnam [17° N, 106°30′ E], 587
Vikings, 433
Vila do Infante, 618
village, 162–163, 547
  agricultural, 158
  and band and city, 160–164
  clustering of, 158–159
  fishing, 158
Vinci, Leonardo da, 654, 660
violability of law, 568
violin, 440, 627
Virgin, 642
virilocal, 170(14-2)
virus, 48*n.*, 337
Viscachani [site, about 17°30′ S, 68°30′ W, in Bolivia], 431(28-4)
Visigoths, 598
Vistula River [mouth at 54°22′ N, 18°55′ E], 597
vitamin D, 388, 411
vitamins, 359
vocal-auditory communicative channel, 379–380, 413
Volga River [mouth at 45°55′ N, 47°52′ E], 466
Volvox, 345–346
voodoo, 125, 268–269
vowel sounds, 417

"wage slaves," 246
wagon, 540, 543(32-8)
waist belt, 388
wall, 561
  city, 555
  woven, 508(and 31-15)
Wallace, Alfred Russel, 424*n.*

Wallace line, Wallacea, 424(and 28-1)
walnut, 449(29-1)
Wampanoag [an Algonquian-speaking tribelet of 17th-century New England], 147
war, 22*n.,* 151, 153
War of the Northern Revolution (United States, 1861–1865), 265, 566
warfare, rules of "civilized," 565
warm-bloodedness, 357–358
warmth, fire for, 404–405
warp (weaving), 508
wash (on ceramics), 527
washing, 526
Washington, George [1732–1799], 154
Washington, D.C. [city; 38°54′ N, 77°1′ W], structure, 555
Washoe [c. 1966–   ], 117, 156–157
waste:
  and artifaction, 96–97
  bodily, 143
  nitrogenous, 352
  (*See also* junk principle)
waste-disposal, fire for, 404
watch (timepiece), 613
water:
  geological role of, 324–328
  salt versus fresh, 326
  (*See also* bathing and swimming; washing)
water buffalo, 463(29-2)
  as early human food, 395
water chestnut, 450(29-1)
  false, 456(29-1)
water clock, 613
water closet, 555
water lift, 612
water power, 538
water transportation, 542–543
watercress, 452(29-1)
waterfowl, 56, 443
watermelon, 446(29-1), 449
waterwheel, 612
wattle and daub, 510
wax, 527
we, 156–157, 181, 186, 546, 588
weaning, 63
weapon, 375
  of defense, 368–370
  fire as, 405
  metal, 530
  (*See also* firearms)
weaving:
  frame for daubing, 510

weaving (*cont'd*):
  by hand, 508–510
  with loom, 512–514
  patterns, 509(31-16)
weed versus crop, 481
week, origin of, 140
weft, 508
Wei River, 476
Weiss, Albert Paul, 658
welding, heat, 534
Welsh language, 596
  writing, 620(38-1)
werewolf, 472–473
West Germanic languages, 597–598
  writing, 620(38-1)
West Indies (*see* Antilles)
Western culture/society, 125, 130, 136, 167, 179, 409, 587
  false expectations of, 277–278
  favored numbers in, 138–140
  world view, 635–665
wet versus dry anxiety, 231–232
whale, 62(5-5), 350(24-23), 361
wheat, 448, 457(29-1), 468–471, 481, 553
  wild, 470(30-2)
wheel (potter's), 521–522, 539–540
wheel (for transport), 474, 523, 539–540
  metal-shod, 536
  vehicles with, 539–540
wheelbarrow, 540, 541(32-6)
Whewell, William, 654
whitewash, 528
whortleberry, 447(29-1)
wicker weave, 509(31-16)
widows and widowers, 166, 168–169
Wiechert-Gutenberg discontinuity, 323(24-7)
Wiener, Norbert, 636
wife-husband, 218
wigwam, 14–15(and 2-2)
wild versus feral, 472*n.*
wild rice, 9, 12, 19–20, 455, 457(29-1)
Wilder, Thornton Niven [1897–   ], 560
will (last testament), 256
Wilson Butte Cave [site, 42°46′ N, 114°13′ W, in Idaho], 430(28-3)
wind power, 538, 543
windmill, 612
wine, 537
Winnebago [Siouan-speaking bands or tribe], 8, 11(and 2-1)
  cousin terms, 201(15-8)
wire, drawing, 612

witness, expert, 651
woad, 528
wolf, 293, 472–473
   and humans, 473
wolverine [*Gulo luscus,* fam. Mustelidae,
   order Carnivora], 435
women [*see* female versus male (human)]
wood, 443
   cutting of, 399
   as fuel, 404
woodcut, 622
wooded savanna, 371
woodwind musical instruments, 442
woodwork, 394, 423, 434, 495
   with stone tools, 495
woody versus herbaceous, 446–447
wool, 463(29-2), 464(29-2), 469, 516, 625
   carding, 612
wooly monkeys, 58(5-1), 64
wooly rhinoceros, 435
   (*See also* rhinoceros)
word, 118(def)
word games, 113
Wordsworth, William, 643
worker-boss, 245–246
world view, 133–134, 636
   controlling, 582–584
   as human universal, 133–134

world view (*cont'd*):
   inconsistencies in, 133
   Maroon, 268–269
   Menomini, 27–29
   themes in, 136–140
   Western, 635–665
world war, 609
wrapped weave, 509(31-16)
wrapping, 525
wreckers, 571
Wright, Sewall [1889–   ], 298–299
writing, 79, 99(8-1), 528, 590
   confused with language, 100
   in Europe, 618–619, 620(38-1)
   in India and nearby, 592
   nature of, 575–578
   origins of, 574–575
written records, 302, 421
wrought iron, 536

xylem, 447

yak, 464(29-2)
yam, 458(29-1)
Yang Shao pattern (archaeological),
   477–478

Yao [a people around 14° S, 36° E, in
   Nyasaland], 221
yaws, 433
yeast, 445(29-1), 537
Yellow River [mouth at 37°32′ N,
   118°19′ E], 496
Yenisei River [mouth at 71°50′ N,
   82°40′ E], 609
yeomen, 565
Yoruba [peoples around 7° N, 4° E], 263
Yucatan [peninsula, 19°30′ N, 89° W],
   575
   stone pyramids of, 499(31-6), 500

Zagros Mountains [33°30′ N, 47° E],
   468
Zawi Chemi [site, about 2.5 miles
   south-southwest of Shanidar Cave,
   which see], 468, 469(30-1)
zero, symbol for, 580
zinc, 532(mp), 534
zone, ecological, 285
Zulu [tribes or kingdom, around 27° S,
   31° E], 475
Zuni [pueblo, 35°15′ N, 106°40′ W], 139
Zwingli, Huldreich [1484–1531], 627
zygote, 345

ANALYTIC TABLE OF CONTENTS